# THE
# CATHOLIC
# ENCYCLOPEDIA

# THE CATHOLIC ENCYCLOPEDIA

ROBERT C. BRODERICK
*Virginia Broderick, Illustrator*

THOMAS NELSON INC., PUBLISHERS

Nashville

NIHIL OBSTAT

Reverend Richard J. Sklba, S.S.L., S.T.D.
*Censor Librorum*

IMPRIMATUR
✝ Most Reverend William E. Cousins
Archbishop of Milwaukee
November 14, 1975

All Scripture quotations are taken from the New American Bible.

Published in Nashville, Tennessee, by Thomas Nelson, Inc., Publishers and distributed in Canada by Lawson Falle, Ltd., Cambridge, Ontario.

Printed in the United States of America.

Library of Congress Cataloging in Publication Data

Broderick, Robert C          1913-
  The Catholic encyclopedia.

  1. Catholic Church—Dictionaries. I. Title.
BX841.B695               282'.03               76-10976

ISBN 0-8407-5096-X
ISBN 0-8407-5787-5 PB

# LIST OF ABBREVIATIONS

OT, Old Testament of the Bible

NT, New Testament of the Bible

Biblical abbreviations are given for the books of the Bible in the now accepted short form, e.g., Matthew, Mt.; Mark, Mk.; Luke, Lk.; John, Jn.; Genesis, Gn., etc.

c., a canon of Canon Law

cf., "confer" or compare with other entry

q.v., "which see" and refers to entry under preceding or following words

SS, plural of Saints

Documents of Vatican II

AA, Decree on the Apostolate of the Laity *(Apostolicam Actuositatem)*

AG, Decree on the Church's Missionary Activity *(Ad Gentes)*

CD, Decree on the Bishops' Pastoral Office in the Church *(Christus Dominus)*

DV, Dogmatic Constitution on Divine Revelation *(Dei Verbum)*

DH, Declaration on Religious Freedom *(Dignitatis Humanae)*

GE, Declaration on Christian Education *(Gravissimam Educationis)*

GS, Pastoral Constitution on the Church in the Modern World *(Gaudium et Spes)*

IM, Decree on the Instruments of Social Communication *(Inter Mirifica)*

LG, Dogmatic Constitution on the Church *(Lumen Gentium)*

NA, Declaration on the Relationship of the Church to the Non-Christian Religions *(Nostra Aetate)*

OE, Decree on the Eastern Catholic Churches *(Orientalium Ecclesiarum)*

OT, Decree on Priestly Formation *(Optatam Totius)*

PC, Decree on the Appropriate Renewal of the Religious Life *(Perfectae Caritatis)*

PO, Decree on the Ministry and Life of Priests *(Presbyterorum Ordinis)*

SC, Constitution on the Sacred Liturgy *(Sacrosanctam Concilium)*

UR, Decree on Ecumenism *(Unitatis Redintegratio)*

All scripture quotes are from *The New American Bible* except where otherwise indicated (cf. Abbreviations, Church).

# ACKNOWLEDGEMENTS

There are a multitude of sources, people, and institutions which contribute to the writing of any encyclopedia. This one differs in no manner from other basic research projects where a synthesis of thought and learning is gathered as in a granary where many may find food for their minds. But there are always instances where the writer finds a special indebtedness to the aids, helpers, and inspirers of such a work.

My personal gratitude goes first to my artist-wife who not only contributed her special talents but also sustained an equanimity of mind and disposition during the hours of my study and intensity of mind and nerves.

Also I wish especially to thank Father Mark Hegener, O.F.M. for encouragement and sources of unusual knowledge and insight.

I am also grateful to the members of the Milwaukee Archdiocesan chancery staff, notably its leader, Archbishop William E. Cousins, and to Reverends Robert Sampson, chancellor, and Raphael M. Fliss, vice-chancellor. And indeed a special thanks, not expressible in words, goes to Reverend Richard J. Sklba, the archdiocesan censor, for a painstaking and most thorough examination of the script, done in portions to accommodate my part-by-part submissions of the typed pages. Further I wish to express appreciation to Gerald M. Schaefer of the Milwaukee Office for the Laity, to Mrs. Ronald G. Laszewski who did the professional typing, and to Mrs. Lois Siegmund for duplicating the manuscript.

The people of Thomas Nelson, Inc., deserve a special mention in my appreciation, for they served to carry on the project in true publishing tradition. My gratitude goes to Mr. Sam Moore, the president; to his editor Mr. William Cannon, and to Ms. Jerie Jordan who was both editor and coordinator.

Before one can make a gathering of knowledge, ranging over many disciplines and areas of information, there are publications which uniquely serve. Notably the following are thanked and mentioned with honor:

To all, the author's sincere gratitude.

R.C.B.

# INTRODUCTION

Following the documentation and developments engendered by the Second Vatican Ecumenical Council, there have been introduced great changes in language and definition of church terms. These have affected not only the Roman Catholic Church but other Christian churches as well. It is advisable at this time to bring forward a broad compilation of new terms and a reassessment of the older, almost archaic, descriptive definitions of the past.

Thus in this first new *Catholic Encyclopedia* we have made every effort to be inclusive and enlightening. Of necessity, since this is a one volume reference work, there was a limit upon the length of explanation given to the entries. However, we have sought as far as possible to be inclusive and up to date. We have added pen-and-ink illustrations, photographs, and a section of pictures to give this book a rounded and complete new look.

The content embraces much that was selective; for example, notable persons of the Old and New Testaments are given a place so that the continuity of the Judaic-Christian history might be retained. Likewise the books of the Bible are briefly characterized. Further we have indicated the present usage of terms, especially those which still have a familiar sound but actually are historic. And we have made a special effort to give to this book of religious reference an ecumenical understanding by including terms of a broad spectrum of Christian experience.

Most essentially, this encyclopedia is modern, being adapted in language and inclusiveness to the ministries, both ordained and nonordained, so that there may be a singular sense of oneness in understanding. In a service and source book such as this, there is a synthesis of many areas of religious reference and related subjects. This makes for a readable condensation of knowledge which will be sufficient for the student, the lay minister, or the family, and also will lead the reader to seek further knowledge in the things of the Spirit.

Our hope is that this "sowing of seeds" will bring a rich reward in the harvest of truth which never changes but develops into new clarification and insights of lasting value.

R.C.B.

# THE
# CATHOLIC
# ENCYCLOPEDIA

A

B

C

D

E

F

G

H

## A-Ω

The first *(alpha)* and the last *(omega)* letters of the Greek alphabet are used in a monogram symbolically as the *beginning* and the *end* of all things in God, the Creator. In Rv. 22:13 the Evangelist John applies this title to Christ (cf. Is. 41:4): "I am the Alpha and the Omega, the First and the Last, the Beginning and the End!" These two letters are found as symbols in works of art, such as banners or stained glass, and historically they are a traditional *sign* of Christ in His divinity and are so used today in our churches. In its context the *sign* also means the resurrection of all who persevere in grace into the finality of peace and eternal joy in the Lord.

## Aaron

The meaning of this Hebrew name is not known. It is frequently used in the Bible as the name of the brother of Moses. According to tradition Aaron was appointed by God as the "Levite" (Ex. 4:14) when the Israelites were freed from Egyptian bondage. He also "spoke" for Moses and was called his "prophet" before Pharaoh. (Ex. 7:1-2). Also in accord with tradition, Aaron is used as the collective name for the entire priestly class, "the sons of Aaron" (Ex. 28:1), and this derives from the fact that Aaron was looked upon as the first high priest (Ex. 39:1–21; Lv. 8–10). His priesthood was confirmed by God through divine judgment (Nm. 16) as well as through the miracle of the flowering staff (Nm. 17:16–26; cf. Heb. 9:4). It is

from this that all members of the ancient priesthood were referred to as of "the house of Aaron" (Ps. 115; cf. Lk. 1:5), and this tradition also lends credence to women being of the priestly class though probably not of the priesthood itself. Although Aaron is sometimes thought of as a prefigure of the eternal priesthood of Christ, it can only be by contrast, for Aaron, like Moses, was barred from entering the Promised Land because of a lack of trust in the goodness of God.

## Abaddon

This is a Hebrew proper word meaning "place of destruction," and in poetic use a name for the place of the dead, as *sheol.* Through personification it is the word for "king of the abyss" (Rv. 9:11) or, in Greek, *Apollyon,* the "destroyer."

## Abandonment or Self-abandonment

This term is widely used in writings of mystical theology. It refers specifically to the first stage of the progression of the soul toward union with God whereby futility is found in all other than God. Abandonment is therefore achieved by conforming oneself to God's will, attaining a proper understanding of the use of worldly goods; it involves a passive purification of the soul through willingly undergoing trials and sufferings and leads to a surrender of natural consolations, which results in a feeling of desolation, or apartness, from God and His goodness. It also refers to the darkness of the soul in undergoing a period of purgation. (Cf. Union, Mystical.) It is this condition that many of the modern seekers of "possession of self" maintain that they are striving for through Yoga and prolonged meditation, but true abandonment is quite another matter, deriving from self-control and discipline.

## Abba

*Abba* is the emphatic form of the Hebrew noun for "father," and it was used in primitive Christianity for invoking God as the Father of us all (cf. Rom. 8:15). The word is a title of respect applied to Bishops of the Syrian, Coptic, and Abyssinian Churches. It is also a Hebrew title of honor and forms part of some Hebrew proper names.

## Abbacomites

This name was given to soldier-abbots or noble-abbots, who were lay intruders on whom the courts conferred abbacies for profit to the person or to themselves. In early medieval days it led to other abuses of lay investiture. The name is now obsolete except as an historical term.

## Abbe

The French title applied first to abbots, and later, corresponding to the English "Father," applied to all priests or clerics. It is sometimes applied to nonordained clerics who are engaged in teaching.

## Abbess

An abbess is the spiritual and temporal superior of a community of nuns in those religious orders in which monasteries of men of the same order are governed by abbots. The title is the feminine of abbot. Today it is a title of dignity and authority, limited by canon law. It is permissible for an abbess after election to wear a ring and use a staff or crosier as a mark of her rank and authority, but she does not have the jurisdiction of an abbot. The title goes back to the sixth century and was originally applied to Benedictine superiors, but later to the Poor Clares. An abbess cannot, or course, exercise any priestly function and today has a very limited role in the lives of women religious.

## Abbey

An independent and canonically erected monastery governed by an abbot; a convent that is governed by an abbess. An abbey must have a minimum of twelve religious, and it embraces all the principal parts of a monastery that are considered essential to the religious life carried on within. As such, the abbey is usually constructed around a quadrangle formed of those units.

## Abbey Nullius

Territory belonging to no diocese, or an area separated from any of the surrounding dioceses is termed an abbey nullius. It is governed under the active jurisdiction of a prelate, subject in most cases directly to the Holy See. In the U.S., Belmont Abbey, North Carolina, is an abbey nullius.

## Abbeylubber

This term of ridicule was used after the Reformation, implying that the residents of abbeys were idle and given over to soft living. It is now obsolete except in a jocular sense.

## Abbot

The superior of a religious community of men, elected by the professed members of the religious order is an abbot. His duties are quasi-episcopal and paternal, whereby he administers the property, maintains the rule and constitutions, and enjoins discipline. The position of abbot arose in the third century and continues to the present. At the installation of an abbot, the one elected is blessed; he may retire or resign, but if he resigns the title is lifted from him. At present, monasteries of the Benedictines, Cisterians, and Canons Regular of St. Augustine are governed by abbots. Other religious orders have given up the use of the title and supplant it with Guardian (head of a Franciscan priory), Prior (head of a Dominican convent), Rector (a Jesuit superior), or simply Brother Superior.

## Abbot of Unreason

This mock title was given to the leader of the Christmas revels in Scotland before the Reformation.

## Abbreviations

Catholic organizations, like other agencies with multiple purposes, have frequently used the simple initial letters to indicate their name and sometimes their activities. Currently used abbreviations are as follows:

A.A., Augustinians of the Assumption (Assumptionists)
A.A.S., Acts of the Apostolic See
A.B., Bachelor of Arts
Abb., Abbacy
Abp., Archbishop
ACTU, Association of Catholic Trade Unionists
A.D., Literally, "in the year of our Lord"
A.M., Master of Arts
A.M.D.G., To the greater glory of God (Jesuit motto)
Ap., Apostle
A.U.C., From the founding of the city
A.V., Authorized Version (of the Bible)

b., Born
B.A., Bachelor of Arts
B.C., Before Christ
B.C.L., Bachelor of Canon Law (or Civil)
B.C.S., Black Christian Students
Bl., Blessed
Bp., Bishop
Bro., Brother
B.S., Bachelor of Science
B.V.M., Blessed Virgin Mary

c., About (circa)
CARA, Center for Applied Research in the Apostolate
CAL, Catholic Aviation League
C.E., Common or Christian Era
CCC, Canadian Catholic Conference
CCD, Confraternity of Christian Doctrine
CEF, Citizens for Educational Freedom
C.F.A., Alexian Brother

CFM, Christian Family Movement
C.F.X., Xaverian Brothers
C.C., Code of Canon Law
C.I.C.M., Congregation of the Immaculate
Heart of Mary (Scheut Fathers)
C.J., Josephite Fathers (of Belgium)
C.M., Congregation of the Mission (Vincentians
or Lazarists)
C.M.F., Missionary Sons of the Immaculate
Heart of Mary
C.M.M., Missionaries of Marianhill
CMSM, Conference of Major Superiors of Men
C.O., Oratorian Fathers
COCU, Consultation on Church Union
C.P., Congregation of the Passion
CPA, Catholic Press Association
CPC, Association of Perfect Love
CPF, Catholic Press Features
C.P.M., Congregation of the Fathers of Mercy
C.P.P.S., Society of the Precious Blood
C.R., Congregation of the Resurrection
C.R.M., Clerics Regular Minor
CRS, Catholic Relief Services
C.R.S.P., Clerics Regular of St. Paul (Barnabite
Fathers)
C.S., Missionaries of St. Charles
C.S.B., Congregation of St. Basil (Basilians)
C.S.C., Congregation of Holy Cross
C.S.P., Paulist Fathers
C.S.S., Congregation of the Sacred Stigmata
(Stigmatine Fathers)
C.SS.R., Congregation of the Most Holy Re-
deemer (Redemptorists)
C.S.Sp., Congregation of the Holy Ghost
C.S.V., Clerks of St. Viator (Viatorians)
CTN, Catholic Television Network
CTN/C, Catholic Television Network, Chicago
CUM, Christians United in Mission
CYO, Catholic Youth Organization

D.C.L., Doctor of Canon Law (Civil)
D.D., Doctor of Divinity
D.N.J.C., Our Lord Jesus Christ
Doct., Doctor
D.O.M., To God, the Best and Greatest
D.V., God willing

E.g., For example
ER, Eastern Rite News Service
Er. Cam., Monk Hermits of Camaldoli
Et al., And others
Exc., Except

F.; ff., the following (singular and plural)
FDLC, Federation of Diocesan Liturgical Com-
missions
F.D.P., Sons of Divine Providence

F.M.S., Marist Brothers
F.M.S.I., Sons of Mary, Health of the Sick
Fr., Father
F.S.C., Brothers of the Christian Schools (Chris-
tian Brothers)
F.S.C.J., Sons of the Sacred Heart (Verona
Fathers)

I.C., Institute of Charity (Rosminians)
ICEL, International Committee on English in
the Liturgy
i.e., That is
IHS, Jesus, the Savior of Men
I.M.C., Consolata Society for Foreign Missions
I.N.R.I., Jesus of Nazareth, King of the Jews

J.C.D., Doctor of Canon Law
J.C.L., Licentiate in Canon Law
J.M.J., Jesus, Mary, Joseph
J.U.D., Doctor of both Civil and Canon Laws

K. of C., Knights of Columbus
K.H.S., Knight of the Holy Sepulchre
K.P., Knight of Pius IX
K.S.G., Knight of St. Gregory
K.S.S., Knight of St. Sylvester

LCWR, Leadership Conference of Women Reli-
gious
LL.B., Bachelor of Laws
LL.D., Doctor of Laws
LWF, Lutheran World Federation

M.E.P., Paris Foreign Missions Society
M.H.M., Mill Hill Missionaries
M.I.C., Marian Fathers
MM, Martyrs
M.M., Maryknoll Missioners
M.S., Missionaries of Our Lady of LaSalette
M.S.C., Missionaries of the Sacred Heart
M.S.F., Missionaries of the Holy Family
Msgr., Monsignor

NAB, New American Bible
NACC, National Association of Catholic Chap-
lains
NAWR, National Association of Women Reli-
gious
NBSC, National Black Sisters' Conference
NC, National Catholic News Service
NCC, National Council of Churches
NCCB, National Conference of Catholic Bishops
NCCL, National Catholic Council of the Laity
NCCM, National Council of Catholic Men
NCCRI, National Catholic Coalition for Respon-
sible Investment
NCCS, National Catholic Community Service

NCCW, National Council of Catholic Women

NCEA, National Catholic Educational Association

NCRLC, National Catholic Rural Life Conference

NCSAC, National Catholic Social Action Conference

NCSC, National Catholic Stewardship Council

NEB, New English Bible

NFPC, National Federation of Priests' Councils

NOBC, National Office for Black Catholics

NT, New Testament

O.A.R., Order of Augustinian Recollects

O.Carm., Order of Calced Carmelites (Carmelites)

O.Cart., Carthusian Order

O.C.D., Order of Discalced Carmelites

O.C.S.O., Order of Cistercians of the Strict Observance (Trappists)

O.de M., Order of Mercy (Mercedarians)

O.F.M., Order of Friars Minor (Franciscans)

O.F.M. Cap., Order of Friars Minor Capuchin (Capuchins)

O.F.M. Conv., Order of Friars Minor Conventual (Conventuals)

O.H., Hospitaller Order of St. John of God

O.M.I., Oblates of Mary Immaculate

O.P., Order of Preachers (Dominicans)

O.Praem, Order of Premonstratensians (Norbertines)

O.S.A., Order of Hermits of St. Augustine (Augustinians)

O.S.B., Order of St. Benedict (Benedictines)

O.S.B.M., Order of St. Basil the Great

O.S.C., Order of the Holy Cross (Crosier Fathers)

O.S.Cam., Order of St. Camillus (Camillians)

O.S.F., Order of St. Francis (various congregations of Brothers and Sisters)

O.S.F.S., Oblates of St. Francis de Sales

O.S.J., Oblates of St. Joseph

O.S.M., Order of Servants of Mary (Servites)

O.S.P., Order of St. Paul the First Hermit (Pauline Fathers)

O.SS.T., Order of the Most Holy Trinity (Trinitarians)

OT, Old Testament

P.A., Protonotary Apostolic

Ph.D., Doctor of Philosophy

P.I.M.E., Pontifical Institute for Foreign Missions (Missionaries of Sts. Peter and Paul)

Pont. Max., Supreme Pontiff

PP., Pp, Pope

P.C.S., Postal Church Service

R.C., Roman Catholic

R.I.P., May he (she) rest in peace

RNS, Religious News Service

R.P., Reverend Father

R.V., Revised Versions (of the Bible)

S.A., Franciscan Friars of the Atonement

S.A.C., Society of the Catholic Apostolate (Pallotines)

S.C.J., Congregations of Priests of the Sacred Heart

S.D.B., Salesians of Don Bosco

S.D.S., Society of the Divine Savior (Salvatorians)

S.D.V., Society of Divine Vocations

SEARCH, Teenage Youth Encounters

S.F., Sons of the Holy Family

S.J., Society of Jesus (Jesuits)

S.M., Society of Mary (Marists or Marianists)

S.M.A., Society of African Missions

S.M.B., Society of Bethlehem Missionaries

S.M.M., Company of Mary (Montfort Fathers)

S.O.Cist., Cistercians of the Common Observance

SODEPAX, Joint Commission for Society, Development and Peace

S.P., Servants of the Holy Paraclete (Piarist Fathers)

Sr., Sister

S.S., Society of St. Sulpice (Sulpicians)

SS.CC., Fathers of the Sacred Hearts

S.S.E., Society of St. Edmund

S.S.J., St. Joseph's Society of the Sacred Heart (Josephites)

S.S.L., Licentiate in Sacred Scripture

S.S.P., Society of St. Paul

S.S.S., Congregation of the Blessed Sacrament

S.; St.; SS.; Sts., Saint (singular); saints (plural)

S.T., Missionary Servants of the Most Holy Trinity

S.T.B., Bachelor of Sacred Theology

S.T.D., Doctor of Sacred Theology

S.T.L., Licentiate in Sacred Theology

S.T.M., Master of Sacred Theology

S.V.D., Society of the Divine Word

S.X., Xaverian Missionary Fathers

T.O.R., Third Order Regular of St. Francis

T.O.S.F., Tertiary of Third Order of St. Francis

UN, United Nations

UNCTAD, United Nations Conference on Trade and Development

UNESCO, United Nations Educational, Scientific and Cultural Organization

UNICEF, United Nations Children's Fund

USCC, United States Catholic Conference

V.A., Vicar Apostolic
V.B., Vulgate Bible
Ven., Venerable
V.F., Vicar Forane
V.G., Vicar General
V.T., Old Testament

WCC, World Council of Churches
W.F., White Fathers

Y.C.M., Young Christian Movement

## Abdication

In the ecclesiastical sense an abdication is the act of resigning or renouncing a benefice or clerical dignity. In each instance the resignation must be made to the proper authority; it must be freely made and apart from any simony or other consideration that would profit the one resigning or those who accept the resignation. When a pope resigns, the abdication is made to the College of Cardinals, but properly speaking the pope has no superior to whom he may resign his dignity, hence he alone has the power to dissolve his own tenure of the papacy.

## Abduction

Literally, abduction means "to lead away." In canon law and in moral theology the term applies broadly to rape and violence of a physical nature. It means the forcible carrying off or detention of a woman against her will, and it renders a marriage with her invalid as long as she remains in the power of the abductor. Thus, abduction is a diriment impediment to marriage. (Cf. Impediments of Marriage.)

## Abercius, Inscription of

The authentic Greek inscription of the second century was composed by Abercius, Bishop of Hieropolis in Phrygia, wherein he tells of his visit to Rome and the importance of the Church of Rome at that early time.

## Abjuration of Heresy

This term refers to the denial under oath whereby one renounces heresy, apostasy, or schism. It was at one time required as a preliminary to receiving the Sacrament of Baptism on the part of a convert before making his confession of faith, but now a baptized non-Catholic is received into full communion. More positively it may be considered a profession of faith. It must be made voluntarily and publicly and must be accompanied by some act of satisfaction or penance. It is an act of reconciliation of converts.

## Ablegate

An envoy of the pope who serves as a special representative is known as an ablegate. He is sent to carry the scarlet biretta in the pope's name to one whom the Holy Father has elevated to the Sacred College of Cardinals but who could not receive it directly. The conferring is reserved to the Holy Father alone, and the ablegate serves only in name and not as a delegate.

## Ablution

In the rubrics of the Mass both the act of washing and the wine and water used in the washing are called ablutions. However, the action is a purification, symbolic of the respect to be shown to the sacred elements. Formerly after the Communion of the Mass, the priest washed his thumbs and index fingers with wine and water, using the same to purify the chalice, and then consuming this water and wine. It is a ceremony whereby the Church shows the reverence held for the body and blood of Christ, permitting no least particle to remain after the celebration of Mass. In the New Order of the Mass this is not a washing but a simple cleaning of the paten and chalice. In the Greek Church the public washing of newly baptized persons is referred to as an ablution. In the OT the washings before Jewish worship are frequently referred to as ablutions.

## Abomination of Desolation

This term in the OT (1 Mc. 1:57) applied to false worship or idolatry. In speaking of the destruction of the Temple of Jerusalem (Mk. 13:14–18), Christ indicated a future profanation of the Temple, following the OT history when the temple in Jerusalem was profaned by Antiochus IV (cf. Dn. 11:31). When the Lord foretold the destruction of the Temple, He used these words, which could be read as "shameful abomination." Christ referred to the final destruction of the Temple as His "coming in judgment" or the parousia, as it was written of by St. Paul (see 2 Thes. 1–12).

## Abortion

In its direct, limited sense, abortion is the intentional expulsion or extraction of a fetus from the human womb before the expiration of the seventh month of pregnancy or before the embryo could live independently. This act resulting in the extinction of an unoffending life is never permitted directly or intentionally. Direct abortion is mortally sinful and may incur further penalty from the Church. "Those who procure abortion, the mother included, incur excommunication (c. 2350); those also are included who order the abortion, and those who are effectual or necessary co-operators in it." Grave fear and, of course, ignorance of the penalty excuse from the penalty. "It is to be observed that mere intention does not suffice for incurring the penalty; actual abortion must have taken place" (Davis).

Accident or disease may cause spontaneous abortion, more properly referred to as a miscarriage. Because this is not intentional, no moral guilt is involved.

Life forms and begins with the impregnation of the female ovum by the male sperm. Abortion causes this life to cease and may be followed by serious physical conditions affecting the mother such as infection, hemorrhage, sterility, blood clotting, psychological stress, or other complications.

Legal pronouncements or laws passed to permit or favor abortion are contrary to the right of the living being and are immoral by their end result and consequences.

### Abraham, also Abram

Abraham, because of his special calling by God and his response to this call, is named the father of the Jewish people, and, by extension, the father of all believers. His most distinguished characteristic was his faith, which was not one of response to teachings or dogmas but his justice and his assent to the will of God (Gn. 14:21–24; 15:6).

God's promise to Abraham was that he would have a numerous posterity, thus making him the father of the Chosen People and spiritually the ancestor of all true believers (Gn. 12:2–3; 18:18–19). In him were all peoples to be blessed (Acts 3:25), and it was because of his great faith that Abraham was recognized by the Apostles as a sign of the resurrection of mankind through the Savior, Jesus Christ (Heb. 11:17–19; cf. Gn. 12:3).

Abraham was called by God "my friend" (Is. 41:8) and the Apostle Paul considered this in a spiritual manner, teaching that all who follow in the deep faith and worship of the true God are most assuredly the friends and children of God (Rom. 4:16; 9:7–8). It was in the history of Abraham and the Hebrew people that the Chosen People later came to look upon Jerusalem as their "holy city" (Gn. 14:18–20), and that they claimed Palestine as their land because Abraham had purchased the burial ground of Machphela. The time of Abraham has been established as the nineteenth century before Christ.

### Abraham-Men, also Abram-Men

This name of contempt was given to those poor who, after the dissolution of the monasteries in Reformation days, could no longer appeal to the monks for alms but were forced to beg elsewhere.

### Abraham's Bosom

Used in Lk. 16:22, 23, this term refers to the place where the dead were to abide before admission to the beatific vision after the death of Christ. In the early writings of the fathers of the Church the term is often used as an expression for the "kingdom" or heaven.

### Abraxas

This Greek word was a magical symbol among Gnostic heretics, which referred to their concept of 365 heavens. Early Church writers mention the word in refuting the false teaching.

### Abrogation

This term in canon law refers to a law that is completely repealed, canceled, or revoked.

### Absolute

Absolute is a philosophical term that denotes: (1) pure actuality, i.e., existing without an efficient cause; (2) complete, perfect, unlimited; (3) that which exists by its own nature and therefore independent of everything else. In these three senses it may be referred to God. More broadly it denotes that which is related to no other being, or the sum total of all actual or possible being. Epistemology, the science of knowledge, declares that as absolute which is always and everywhere true, such as the principle of contradiction and the first moral principle, which are not derived from a process of reasoning but are known directly by man's reason once the elements for a right judgment are presented.

### Absolution

There are four types of absolution in Church usage.

1. *Absolution from sin.* This is the act whereby a priest, acting as a judge, passes on to the penitent from Christ the remission of sin. This follows from the power to forgive sin given to the Apostles by Christ and through them to their successors (Jn. 20:23). This power is exercised by the priest in administering the Sacrament of Penance. Two conditions are necessary without exception: (a) absolution can be given by none but priests and (b) since this is a judicial sentence, the priest must have authority or jurisdiction over the penitent. Author-

ity is had first by the bishop and arises from his office, and secondly is delegated to priests by one having jurisdiction. Since the bishop has the prerogative of conferring power to absolve, he may reserve such power or limit this power as exercised by others. All priests, however, have the power from the Church to absolve from reserved matter when the penitent is in danger of death. The expression of absolution is given in prescribed words: "I absolve you from your sins, in the name of the Father, and of the Son, and of the Holy Spirit." This form of absolution must also be spoken by the absolving priest in the presence of the person seeking absolution (cf. Penance, Sacrament of). Since publication of the *Ordo Paenitentiae* (Feb. 7, 1974) the essential words of absolution have not been changed but have been inserted into a new formula that expresses reconciliation of the penitent as a gift coming from the love of God the Father. A further expression of the forgiveness of sins is the *general absolution,* which is an exception granted for use when absolution is considered necessary and where, because of circumstances, confession is not possible, e.g., a group of soldiers about to go into battle. However, anyone so absolved is obliged to mention his sins when he makes his next private confession. *Conditional absolution* is sacramental absolving of sins given when the administering priest is doubtful of the disposition of the penitent. It may not be given without serious reason and great caution on the part of the priest.

2. *Absolution from censures.* This differs from the absolution of sins in the sacramental form in that it removes the penalties imposed by the Church and reconciles the penitent with the Church. The absolution from censures may be given either in the confessional or outside, as in a Church court, and may be given by anyone with the necessary jurisdiction.

3. *Absolution for the dead.* This is the short prayer, imploring eternal rest, said after a requiem Mass over the body of the deceased.

4. *Absolutions of the breviary.* These are certain short prayers petitioning the forgiveness of sin, which are recited before the lessons of Matins in the Prayer of the Hours.

## Abstinence

In its limited and special sense, abstinence is the depriving of oneself of certain kinds of food, in a reasonable manner, for the purpose of benefiting the soul. It differs from fasting in that a fast limits the quantity of food, whereas abstinence affects only the kind of food. The Church law

regarding abstinence does not forbid foods because they are impure; it considers abstaining a means of spiritual good; it is reasonable in demand and application. The law of abstinence is binding to all over 14 years of age; the obligation to abstain, to fast, i.e., limiting oneself to but one full meal and two lighter meals in a full day is binding on all Catholics from the age of 21 to 59 years. It forbids the eating of meat and soups of meat stock, gravy and sauces of meat. On days of complete abstinence, these foods may not be eaten at all. On days of partial abstinence, these foods may be eaten at the principal meal. Dispensation from the law extends to every member of the armed forces in active service and to his wife, children, parents, or servants if he resides with them habitually, whether on or off the post of his duty, except on Ash Wednesday, Good Friday, and the vigil of Christmas. Dispensations are also given to pregnant and nursing mothers, ill persons, and those traveling. This dispensation may be obtained from one's parish priest or confessor if reason for not following the law exists. Since Feb. 23, 1966, it has been authorized that a substitution of other works of penance may take the place of the observance of abstinence and fast on appointed days of the year. In the United States, the National Conference of Bishops has designated Ash Wednesday and Good Friday as days of fast and abstinence, and all Fridays of Lent as days of abstinence. The decision regarding Ember days as days of penance or abstinence rests with the Conference of Bishops.

## Abstinents

This name was applied in derision to certain dissenters who professed abstinence from lawful things such as wine and marriage.

## Abuse of Power

The Code of Canon Law applies this term to an evil and unlawful use of ecclesiastical power, office, or jurisdiction. Title XIX of the fifth book of the Code treats in details of such abuses.

## Abyssinian or Ethiopian Church

A group of Monophysite Christians in Abyssinia trace their origin back to the fourth century when the founding city of the Abyssinian Church was Axum. In the fifth century they rejected the Council of Chalcedon, and their heretical position continues to the present time. Their leader is the Abuna, a vicar of the Coptic patriarchate of Alexandria. The language of their liturgy is Geez, a mixture of Greek and Arabic. Their heresy consists in the teaching that Christ has only a divine nature; they reject all ecumenical councils since Ephesus.

## Acacianism

The schismatic teaching of the Acacian schism had its rise in the Monophysite heresy. As a teaching it was given impetus through an attempt of the imperial factions to control the Church by gaining the interpretative power of theological issues. Under the rule of Zeno (A.D. 474 to 491) of the Eastern Empire at Constantinople, in cooperation with Acacius, the patriarch of Constantinople, an attempt was made to achieve doctrinal unity, and political support, between the Catholics and Monophysites. This was done by demanding acceptance of a formula called the Henoticon, which in part maintained that the Son is "like to the Father," contrary to the doctrine of consubstantiality. Pope Felix III rejected the Henoticon and excommunicated Acacius. The East was separated from communion with Rome by this schism for 40 years. Members are called Acacians and also "Homoeans" since the difference was over the Greek words "like" or "unlike" in substance. (Cf. Monophysitism.)

## Academies, Pontifical

Societies have been founded at Rome under the auspices of the Holy See to encourage special studies in science, literature, art, archeology, diplomacy, and music. Some countries have also established like academies in Rome and support these independently of the Holy See, e.g., the North American College.

## Acathistus

Acathistus is the title of either a hymn or an office in the Greek liturgy, which is said in honor of the Mother of God. When it is sung, the people must stand. The day on which this hymn is used, the fifth Saturday of Lent, is also named Acathistus.

## Access

1. Access is the name of the preparatory prayers that are recommended to be said by a priest before celebrating Mass; these are no longer required in the New Order of Mass, but optional personal preparation of the celebrant remains.

2. In canon law, access refers to a reserved benefice to which one may accede when certain conditions have been fulfilled.

## Accident

This philosophical term means any reality that does not possess the power of subsisting alone but must have another reality to hold it in existence. It is thus that the taste of bread is an accident since it does not exist apart from the reality of bread. In a person happiness, anger, and love are accidents that may be present in the personality. That which is the support of accidents in a thing is called a substance. The accidents of a thing or person may change, but the substance does not. This is called accidental change, for example, a man who puts on weight or whose hair becomes gray. The classes of accidents are grouped under three categories: quantity, quality, and motion.

## Acclamation

Acclamation is the elevation of one to an ecclesiastical dignity by the unanimous voice vote of the electors. As such it is one of the three modes by which a pope may be elected by the College of Cardinals. The term is also applied to the "voice" responses, called *laudes,* which were shouted by the people following the coronation of a king. These responses are still recited in the Mass of coronation of a pope, after the Collects, when the senior cardinal-deacon chants the words, "Hear, O Christ," to which all present respond, "Long life to our lord, N . . . , who has been appointed Supreme Pontiff and universal Pope." This is repeated three times, and after each is added the invocation, "Do Thou help him!" Other meanings denote prayers and pious wishes found on tombs and short liturgical prayers or exclamations, as "Thanks be to God!" A similar acclamation is found in the ordination of a bishop. In the liturgy, the word *Amen* and the phrase "And with your spirit" are formal acclamations.

## Accolade

The act whereby knighthood is conferred either by a kiss or a light blow upon the upper shoulder is an accolade. The term is also applied to a form of salutation, such as the "kiss of peace" given during Mass, and sometimes to a greeting or farewell used in some countries by members of the clergy.

## Accommodation of Scripture, Biblical

In quoting Scripture to prove a point of doctrine, it is necessary to seek the precise meaning of the sacred writer and proceed to argue from the exact sense of the words. However, we may take the words of a text and make an application over and above that intended by the writer, thus "accommodating" the sense to our own words on some subject. This application is not intended by God and as such is not a sense of Scripture proper.

Accommodation may be made in several ways: by *extension,* as when the words of a description in the Bible are applied to a saint (e.g., using the phrase in quotes: he is "a man sent by God"—referring to someone other than St. John the Baptist), or to some current affair; by *allusion,* as when the words are suitable to the purpose of argument, but are not alike in their idea, e.g., referring to one as a "mustard seed" in Catholic work. There are certain cautions to be followed in making an accommodation of Scripture: (1) An accommodation should not be held as a genuine sense of Scripture. (2) There should be some likeness to or analogy with the original text, for the application or adaptation should never contradict the literal sense. (3) An accommodation should not be held as a proof of doctrine. (4) The texts of Scripture should not be applied loosely to secular or vain subjects. This latter does not limit the use of texts in teaching but merely indicates that they should be properly applied rather than used as vain illustrations of a point. (Cf. Literal Sense of Scripture.)

### Acephali

Literally the "headless," acephali was a term of derision applied in the fifth century to those heretics who did not go along with all the terms set forth by their leaders, notably the Acacians.

### Achiropoeta

Literally "not made by hand," achiropoeta is a plural term given to pictures or works of art that are alleged to have a miraculous origin. Examples are the painting of Christ in the *Sancta Sanctorum* of the Lateran, which is claimed to have been outlined by St. Luke and completed by angels; also the painting of Our Lady of Guadalupe in Mexico, miraculously imprinted on the mantle of Juan Diego at the instance of the Blessed Mother's declaration to him in 1531.

### Acoemeti

Literally "sleepless ones," this plural term applied to Eastern monks of the fifth and sixth centuries who constantly prayed in relays, day and night. In each monastery there were three choirs of monks who succeeded each other in their rounds of prayer. They fell into the Nestorian heresy and were condemned by the Fifth General Council.

### Acolouthia

Acolouthia is the arrangement of the prayers in the Divine Office in the Greek Church. The sequence begins with Little Vespers before sunset,

and Greater Vespers after it. The Orthros, in two parts, is recited at midnight, which corresponds to the Matins and Lauds of the hours of the Roman Breviary. Little Hours are recited during the day and the office closes with the *Apodeipnon.*

### Acolyte

Before the reexamination of the minor orders of the Church during the Second Vatican Council, the title acolyte was the first of these minor orders. With Vatican II there was a clarification of the role of the ordained and nonordained ministries of the Church. (Cf. Ordination; Laymen and Laywomen.) There was an examination of the role of the layman in the service of the Church, with provision that new dimensions of the ministerial nature of the Church's members be brought forward. It was declared from Scripture and tradition that such new roles of ministry were shared by every member of the Church: "The chosen people of God is *one:* 'one Lord, one faith, one baptism' (Eph. 4:5). As members, they share a common dignity from their rebirth in Christ. They have the same filial grace and the same vocation to perfection. They possess in common one salvation, one hope, and one undivided charity. Hence, there is in Christ and in the Church no inequality on the basis of race or nationality, social condition or sex, because 'there does not exist among you Jew or Greek; slave or freeman; male or female. All are one in Christ Jesus (Gal. 3:28, Greek text; cf. Col. 3:11). If therefore everyone in the Church does not proceed by the same path, nevertheless all are called to sanctity and have received an equal privilege of faith through the justice of God (cf. 2 Pt. 1:1). And if by the will of Christ some are made teachers, dispensers of mysteries, and shepherds on behalf of others, yet all share a true equality with regard to the dignity and to the activity common to all the faithful for the building up of the Body of Christ" (LG 32b–c; 58).

With this new recognition apostolic letters *(Ad Pascendam* and *Ministeria quaedam)* have focused on the ministry of all the people of God in carrying out the mission of the Church. This recognition has placed the roles of the laity in perspective. Thus, the acolyte is instituted and "appointed in order to aid the deacon and to minister to the priest." It is therefore his duty to attend to the service of the altar and to assist the deacon and the priest in liturgical celebrations, especially in the celebration of Mass; he is also to distribute holy communion as an extraordinary minister when the ministers spoken of in canon 845 of the Code of Canon Law are not available or are prevented by ill health, age, or another pastoral ministry from performing this function, or when the number of those approaching the sacred table is so great that the celebration of Mass would be unduly prolonged.

"In the same extraordinary circumstances he may be entrusted with publicly exposing the Blessed Sacrament for adoration by the faithful and afterwards replacing it, but not with blessing the people. He may also, to the extent needed, take care of instructing the faithful who by temporary appointment assist the priest or deacon in liturgical celebrations by carrying the missal, cross, candles, etc., or by performing other such duties. He will perform these functions the more worthily if he participates in the Holy Eucharist with increasingly fervent piety, receives nourishment from it and deepens his knowledge of it.

"Destined as he is in a special way for the service of the altar, the acolyte should learn all matters concerning public divine worship and strive to grasp their inner spiritual meaning: in that way he will be able each day to offer himself to God, be an example to all by his seriousness and reverence in the sacred building, and have a sincere love for the Mystical Body of Christ, the people of God, especially the weak and sick" (*Ministeria quaedam*, 1972). (See Ministries.)

### Acta Apostolicae Sedis

The official monthly publication was begun in Sept., 1908, as a journal of the Holy See. Canon Law (q.v.) names it as authoritative and official. Hence all decrees and decisions of the Roman Rota printed therein are officially promulgated and become effective after three months from the date of their promulgation. It is published as often as necessary to keep Church members informed of official actions.

### Acta Sanctae Sedis

The monthly publication issued in Rome, but not by the Holy See, presented important pronouncements of the Holy Father and Roman Congregations. For four years, 1904 to 1908, it enjoyed official status but was superseded by the *Acta Apostolicae Sedis*.

### Action Francaise

*Action Francaise* is the title of a monthly publication founded in France in 1897 by an avowed atheist, Charles Maurras. In 1908 Maurras and Leon Daudet founded a movement bearing the name of the publication, which became a daily newspaper. The movement grew into a nationalis-

tic political party, which sought the support of Catholic royalists. It was an attempt to use the Church for political and social purposes and won many Catholic followers. Its teaching led to an exalting of politics above religion and an identifying of the Church with a political movement opposed to established government and advocating a moral philosophy of hate and violence. As such it was condemned by Pope Pius XI in 1926. The pope insisted that Catholic Action or organized lay action for religious activities must be under the direction of the hierarchy. Pius XII lifted the ban on *Action Francaise* in 1939 when its directors expressed regret over past misconduct and promised to respect the wishes of the Holy See. It is now in permanent decline since the puppet government of Petain during World War II and because of its hostility to contemporary thought and the new political life of the French people.

### Act of God

Act of God is a legal term for an accident that occurs without the cause or foreknowledge of man. It is so attributed to God who is the author of the laws of nature.

### Act of Settlement

1. *English:* the law passed in 1701, and still in force, which requires that all future rulers of England be members of the Established Church of England.

2. *Irish:* the law passed by the Irish Parliament in 1662 whereby the confiscated lands of Leinster, Munster, and Connaught were to be restored, first to the Protestants and, second, to Catholics who could establish their innocence. It resulted in the Anglican Church regaining its estates and the reestablishment of its hierarchy in Ireland.

### Act of Toleration

Passed in England during the reign of William and Mary (1689), the Act of Toleration granted freedom of religious worship to all except Catholics and persons who deny the Trinity.

### Acts of the Apostles

This book of the NT follows in sequence the four Gospels of the evangelists; it is the writing of St. Luke, and with his Gospel forms a two-part presentation. The name "Acts" is derived from the Latin word *acta* and may be translated as the "proceedings" or "record" of happenings; the book in turn narrates the record of the early Church and the functions of the Apostles. Evidence from early canons of Scripture and writings of the fathers of the Church of the second and third centuries indicates that St. Luke is the author of the Acts. From internal evidence in the writings themselves and from early tradition, it appears that the book was written during or at the end of St. Paul's first imprisonment, i.e., in A.D. 63 or 64. The Acts were quite certainly set down in Rome in the years just prior to the persecution by Nero. The sources of these accounts were the eyewitness details of the author; the direct testimony of eyewitnesses, notably Sts. Paul and Mark; and written documents such as the writings on the early Church at Antioch. The book's historical value is attested by recent archeological findings, as well as by a comparison of the writings with other historical data such as the political functions of Roman authorities and governance of provinces at the time. The work narrates the activities of Sts. Peter and Paul, and to lesser extent those of Sts. John, James the Less, James the Greater, and Barnabas. Although historical, this work presents such basic theological truths as early conversions, the working of God the Father through the Holy Spirit, that Christ was the Messiah (2:16–36), the indwelling of the Holy Spirit, the sacraments and the liturgy and prayer of the early Church. Recorded in this book are also some eighteen speeches of apostles and early Christians.

The book proclaims the mission of the Church, the fufillment of Christ's prophesy that the Apostles and His disciples were to be "witnesses" of Christ. It enlarges on the promise made by Christ that "this good news of the kingdom will be proclaimed throughout the world as a witness to all the nations. Only after that will the end come" (Mt. 24:14).

### Acts, Canonical

These are actions that have a legal effect in ecclesiastical law, being either allowed or forbidden (c. 2256, n. 2). They include acts of official administrators of ecclesiastical property, the actions of personnel of ecclesiastical courts, those of sponsors at baptism and confirmation, the voting at ecclesiastical elections, and the actual exercise of advowson. Such actions are usually recorded and retained on Church records.

### Acts, Human

These are the acts of human beings, performed under control of the will and done knowingly and willingly. As such they are imputable to the one acting to the degree that the individual knows what is being done and the import or consequence of his

act. There arises from this the moral responsibility of the human act since it is freely performed with knowledge of its conformity or nonconformity to the law of rational nature or the moral law of man.

### Acts of the Martyrs

Acts of the Martyrs are the official and written accounts of a martyr's trial, sentence, and death. Originally these documents, of great edification to early Christians, were gathered to be used in the public testimony of the Church. Although many of these writings have been lost, there remain a considerable number that are outstanding sources of Church history. In the Western Church the most famous collection is the Golden Legend of Jacobus de Voragine (d. 1298). More recently the term "Acts of the Martyrs" has been broadly applied to writings of the lives and deaths of the saints without particular advertence to their historical position in the early record of the Church.

### Acts of the Saints ("Acta Sanctorum")

This famous collection of the lives of the Saints was gathered by the Bollandists. It is also called "Legend of the Saints" or "The Golden Legend."

### Actual Grace

The grace or supernatural gift from God, both operative and cooperative, acts upon the human will or intellect, perfecting both the will and intellect, and makes it possible for them to place acts directed toward eternal salvation. To clarify the twofold, operative and cooperative, divisions of actual grace, it may be pointed out that when the will is first appealed to by this gift of God, and before it responds, the grace is termed operative. When, however, the will accepts and responds to the gift and we find both God and the soul operating to perform the act, the grace is said to be cooperative. Thus man through his intellect (gift) being moved by God in the natural order might be said to have the first desire to happiness (operative motion) which then, through recognition and performance of the good necessary to attain such happiness (cooperative motion), ascends to the supernatural order where the supernatural end is sought (operative gift) and the virtues exercised to accomplish this end (cooperative gift). This sequence of desire, recognition, and action demonstrates in some manner the reception of the supernatural gift of actual grace.

This is the grace given for each particular act in one's life, but it is a manifestion, as are all graces (or gifts), of the presence within us of the Spirit of Christ. It is thus not only internal but also external and is a reality in that we may accept as gifts such spiritual aids as a good wife or husband, or good parents, talents, or others.

### Actual Sin

A personal act that is morally bad, or the omission of some obliged good, or an act against right reason or the law of God is an actual sin. It is a voluntary transgression of a moral law or a law obliging the will, resulting in sins of either commission or omission. According to the manner of their commission such sins may be interior or exterior; committed against God, one's neighbor, or one's self, according to their object; in gravity, either mortal or venial; from their cause, either committed in ignorance, weakness, or malice; and capital or noncapital with regard to whether they do or do not give rise to other sins.

### Acus

An acus is a small pin of gold or silver used to fasten the pallium to the chasuble.

### Ad Limina

The abbreviated form of the Latin phrase *ad limina Apostolorum* is translated "to the thresholds of the apostles." The word *limina* (thresholds) is not used in a restricted sense but refers broadly or inclusively to the "places" or "houses" themselves. It is a term descriptive of the quinquennial reports that all bishops and military vicars are required to make to the Holy See. Those bishops of dioceses on other continents may make this visit every 10 years, but their report must be submitted every five years. While in Rome, the bishop is expected to visit the tombs of Sts. Peter and Paul, and he receives a document attesting this fact. The cycle of visits of the bishops is a five-year span with bishops from various parts of the world assigned to a particular year. The report made by the bishop is a most detailed account of affairs concerning his diocese and other ecclesiastical jurisdictions and is made to the Sacred Congregation for Bishops of which the pope is prefect. When unable to go in person, the bishop may send a delegate.

### Adam

The word is Hebrew meaning "man." In the scriptural account in Genesis (1:26; 2:15 ff.) the name of Adam takes on a threefold meaning: it is that given to the first created man; by extension it included all mankind; and by interpretation the story of all men. But we also see that the name Adam is applied to Christ, the second Adam. Christ embodies all that previously existed: "But he

was incarnate and made man; and then he summed up (consummated) in himself the long line of the human race, procuring for us a comprehensive salvation, that we might recover in Christ Jesus what in Adam we lost, namely, the state of being in the image and likeness of God" (AG, 2). Thus Christ as the Incarnate Word of God sums up the race of Adam (all mankind), being Himself the second Adam. In Christ the human nature in its concrete and historical reality is substantially effected and in Him the Salvation of all, stretching from Adam to Himself, is completed. (Cf. Rom. 5 and 8; 1 Cor. 15:21.)

### Adamites

1. This obscure sect of the Gnostic heresy is said to have been founded in the second century by Prodicus. The Adamites observed pagan practices, met together without clothing, and were immoral.

2. A group of fanatics of the Middle Ages were supposedly founded by Picard, a Frenchman, who called himself Adam. They practiced sensuality and like their early predecessors went naked at their gatherings. They had their chief headquarters in Bohemia and were spread through France, Germany, and Holland. They were destroyed with great losses by the Hussite general, Jan Ziska, in 1421.

### Adjuration

Adjuration is an appeal or command to act, given in God's name or in the name of a saint or holy thing (Mt. 26:63). Such a command is not to be given lightly and should be given only when there is serious cause, when the request is not unjust, and when the person truly seeks a right answer or action. It is either solemn or private: the first is that used in the Church in an exorcism and by a set rite; the latter may be used by anyone.

### Administration Apostolic

This form of a diocesan organization is established by the Holy See where a new national boundary cuts off a portion of an existing diocese. This portion, made remote from the diocesan seat by the new boundary or for other reasons, is constituted an *administration apostolic* and usually placed under a titular bishop.

### Administration of the Sacraments

Administration of the Sacraments is the act of the authorized minister in conferring the sacraments on one of the faithful. Since all the sacraments are from Christ and take efficacy from Him, the minister acts in Christ's name and by His authority. Because the sacraments are for the faithful as means of sanctification, they are to be administered frequently, and the recipients are to be properly disposed to receive them. (See Sacraments, Seven; also under separate listings.)

## Administrator

An administrator is one responsible for the management of Church property; when a bishop dies, an administrator is appointed within eight days.

1. An "apostolic administrator" is a priest or bishop appointed by the Holy See to administer a diocese for an indefinite or specified time, because of the inability of the bishop to so administer, or during the vacancy of the diocese until another bishop is appointed.

2. The priest placed in charge of a cathedral parish by the bishop of the cathedral.

3. In the United States a priest appointed to administer a parish but having no canonical privileges concerning the parish.

4. One assigned to administer the affairs of an ecclesiastical institution. Usually this is a priest who has care of both the spiritual and material concerns of the institution.

A layman may be appointed an administrator of a Church institution but usually handles only the business affairs and is subordinate to the priest administrator.

## Admonitions, Canonical

Paternal admonitions, usually three in number, are given as quasi-severe warnings, in secret or in a confidential manner, by a prelate or ecclesiastical superior to a subordinate cleric who is suspected of or charged with misconduct of a scandalous nature. Following the third paternal admonition, a formal canonical or legal admonition is given, which amounts to a summons to judgment. In a religious order or congregation the admonitions are given by the superior before a judicial process of dismissal is begun.

## Adonai

The Hebrew plural word for "my Lords" is attributed to God out of reverence for the majesty and "unspeakably" great name, *Yahweh.* "My Lord Yahweh" was often shortened into *adonai* and came to be used as another name for God.

## Adoption, Canonical

Legally, adoption is the taking as one's own the child of another, with the consent and cooperation of the civil authorities. Traditionally, in law, this creates a legal relationship based on the natural relationship and does not permit marriage in the following instances: between the adoptive father and his adopted daughter, between the adopted children and the natural children of the same parents, between the adoptive father and the adopted son and their respective widows. Church law (c. 1059) provides that in those places where adoption constitutes an impediment to marriage in civil law, such a marriage is likewise canonically illicit. In the United States, adoption is regulated by statute of the various states and is usually undertaken only in the manner decreed by law. It is thus difficult or impossible to determine the precise manner in which legal relationship would be established. Hence, in the civil law of the United States, adoption is not a diriment impediment of marriage as considered by the Church and, thus, does not prevent marriage.

## Adoption, Supernatural

The act by which God takes us as His children and thereby makes us heirs of His kingdom—heaven is supernatural adoption. By sanctifying grace our souls are constituted in the likeness of Christ, the Son of the Father, and thus we are made co-heirs with Christ (Rom. 8:15–17; Eph. 1:5).

## Adoptionism

This eighth-century heresy derived from Nestorianism. It taught that Christ was only an adopted and not the "natural" Son of God. Over the years this early erroneous teaching changed to the extent that it was claimed Christ was by this adoption somehow "divinized," in short, that He was not truly God. The Nestorian adoptionism was condemned by a council of bishops of Asia Minor in A.D. 268 and the later heresy, which might be called neo-Nestorianism, was first condemned by Pope Adrian I in 785, then at the Second Council of Nice (A.D. 787), the Council of Frankfort (A.D. 794), and in the eleventh and twelfth centuries. In the early Church it was called "monarchianism," and after the eighth century it was sometimes called "the Spanish error."

## Adoratio

In the ceremony during the coronation of a new pope, the action called *adoratio* is performed when the Cardinals present signify their obedience to the new pontiff and acknowledge their acclaim of him. It is made in the Sistine Chapel before the public announcement of the new pope's name is made from the main balcony of the Vatican.

## Adoration

Adoration refers to the external act of worship or honor given to a thing or person of excellence.

1. As an act of religion it is the honor offered to God alone because of His divinity, infinite perfection, supreme dominion over creatures, and the dependence of all creatures upon Him. By this act man fulfills the first precept given by God to Moses (Ex. 20:2–7) and again affirmed by Christ when he declared, "You shall do homage to the Lord your God; him alone shall you adore" (Mt. 4:10). The form of worship is given only to God and is named *latria*. The greatest act of adoration is sacrifice that is most worthily offered in the Mass. Adoration is *internal* when we acknowledge God as possessing this divine excellence and our own subjection and intend this acknowledgment and subjection; it is *external* when we act to manifest our acknowledgment and subjection. It is an act of the intellect and will expressed by signs of humility in our bodies.

2. *Perpetual adoration* is the continuous exposition of the Blessed Sacrament and the day and night adoration by persons who take turns as adorers. The object of such worship is usually reparation to God for past or present offenses against Him. The Forty Hours' Devotion is a plan of such continual adoration. Adoration of the Blessed Sacrament is the highest form of worship, *latria* (cf. Latria).

3. *Adoration of the Cross* is an act of veneration that takes place in the ceremonies of Good Friday.

4. *Adoration of the Magi* is the Worship of the Three Wise Men in recognition of the divinity of the newborn Christ, commemorated on the Feast of Epiphany.

## Adultery

Adultery is sexual intercourse of a married man or woman with another than one's own wife or husband. It is a diriment impediment to marriage between the two who, while legitimately married to others, commit the act and pledge a later marriage; or who commit the act while one or the other is legitimately married and cause the death of one of the married parties. Adultery is always a mortal sin against the virtue of chastity. In the OT the act of adultery was not only condemned, but the penalty was death (Gn. 38:24; Lv. 21:9) or being pilloried (Jer. 13:26 f.; Ez. 16:38 f.). The prophets use adultery as a figure of speech, calling the breaking of God's covenant by seeking false gods adulterous (Jer. 2:2; 5:7; 13:22).

The NT condemned adultery (Mt. 5:27; Mk. 10:19; Jas. 2:11), but Christ placed even adulter-ous desires on the same plane of serious acts as adultery itself. And evildoers in general are labeled adulterous in a figurative sense (Rv. 2:22).

## Advent

This liturgical season begins the Church year. It includes the four weeks opening on the Sunday after the solemnity of Christ the King. It is a time of preparation for the Feast of the Nativity and is observed with some fasting, prayers, and meditation to dispose all to welcome Christ. The time was observed in the Church as early as the fourth century; it is mentioned in A.D. 380 at the Council of Saragossa. The season, although penitential, is not without a spirit of joy, hope, and anticipation. On the third Sunday, known as *Gaudete* Sunday, a special note of joy is introduced into the liturgy, indicating the assurance of everyone in the redemption of mankind by Christ. The Sundays of Advent take precedence over all solemnities and feasts of the Lord (as do those of Lent and the Easter season) in the modern liturgical calendar, which went into effect Dec. 1, 1974. Advent is a time when minds are directed to the second coming of Christ and is a season of joyful hope and spiritual expectation. It ends before the first evening prayer of Christmas.

## Advent of Christ

The Advent of Christ is the millennium. (Cf. Millennium; Parousia.)

## Adventists

These Christian groups believe that the second coming of Christ is near in point of time. These are members of fundamental Protestant sects who believe this because of their interpretation of the Bible, particularly of passages found in Rom. 13:12; 1 Pt. 1:20; Rv. 20:3. Among these groups are: members of the Church of God; the Seventh

Day Adventists; and Millerites; and some who deny the divinity of Christ such as Jehovah's Witnesses, and Mormons or Church of Christ of the Latter Day Saints.

### Advocate

An advocate is a defense lawyer, one who pleads a cause. Originally, this translation of the Greek word *parakletos* was applied to Christ as a title by St. John (1 Jn. 2:1). The evangelist points out that we have one who intercedes for us and all men by stating, "We have an advocate with the Father." (Cf. Paraclete.)

### Advocate of the Church

A layman in the Middle Ages or feudal times was appointed to defend the Church in civil courts when its holdings were challenged; he was literally a champion of the Church. Because of abuses it has long been discontinued as a title.

### Advocate of God

The person assigned to promote the cause of one whose life is being examined in the process of beatification or canonization is called the Advocate of God or the *advocatus Dei.* (Cf. Canonization; Devil's advocate.)

### Advocates of Roman Congregations

Lawyers, either laymen or clerics, trained in both civil and canon law and with a broad knowledge of dogmatic and moral theology and Church history, plead cases before Roman tribunals. They serve under a fixed salary, and no charge is made for handling cases of the poor. There are seven senior and five junior advocates in the consistorial college.

### Advowson

Advowson is the right of filling a vacant ecclesiastical benefice. Formerly this right belonged to the one who created, built, or endowed the benefice, but later it was attached to the place. The right may be exercised by nomination to the authority doing the appointing; where the property belongs to the bishop or diocese, a direct appointment is made. Since such patronage now is rare, it is chiefly of historic significance.

### Aeon

In Gnosticism, Aeon is a representation based upon the Greek concept of "elements," Platonic ideas, and mythology, which became to Gnostics descriptive of divine attributes, and sometimes referred even to Persons of the Trinity. It led to confusion even within the heresy.

### Aesthetics

This science of the fine arts is based on philosophical principles. It leads to the perception, the recognition, the execution, and the judgment of beauty as it conforms to the ideal of beauty existing in God. This is supernatural beauty, order, harmony, symmetry, and proportion not perceived by the senses but nevertheless a metaphysical reality. Since beauty consists of intuitive knowledge and delight, it is seen that the intellect is the proper perceiving power of the beautiful. In being presented to the intellect, beauty elicits delight, which is the excellence in proportion and balance of things in the highest faculty of human beings. With knowledge, these principles may be applied in perceiving through the senses, in recognizing the degree, in executing through creative urges, and determining the proportion in judgment. This in turn provides the critical estimate of a person, object, literary composition, poetry, painting, sculpture, architecture, or musical composition, which is an evaluation of the degree of beauty possessed by or the absence of beauty in the object. The aesthetic sense may be extended into the moral sphere where it judges the conformity of the conduct of human life with the idea in the mind of God as to how He wishes us to follow the life of Christ. (See Art, Christian; Architecture; Church.)

### Aetians

The followers of Aetiuss of Antioch ascribed to the heretical teaching that the Son was unlike the Father. Its founder and the heresy were condemned in A.D. 360. As such it was a form of Arianism.

### Affections

As used by spiritual writers, this term refers to the emotions and dispositions flowing from the intellectual recognition of the love, desire, and enjoyment of what is good, and the repulsion, disgust, and rejection of what is evil. The training of these "affections," the correct method of eliciting them, is basic to the training in virtue and asceticism and the understanding of mysticism in the spiritual life.

### Affective Prayer

Affective prayer is the kind of prayer in which devout affections predominate or wherein acts of the will are continually made to express love of God and the desire of glorifying Him. In such prayer there is more of an emotional than an intellectual motive, yet it follows the conviction of the mind as a habitual response on the part of the person praying without conscious effort. As prayer it leads to closer union with God, since it perfects the virtues arising from charity or love. It affords spiritual consolation and, because it concentrates by focusing the emotions to a more single purpose, it leads to the "prayer of simplicity," which is preliminary to contemplation. (Cf. Pentecostalism, Catholic.)

### Affinity

A diriment impediment to marriage arising from a valid marriage (c. 97) exists between the man and the blood relations of his previous wife and likewise between the woman and the blood relations of her previous husband. Affinity in the direct line annuls any such marriage, and no licit marriage can be contracted in the direct line in any degree (c. 1077). The direct line is of ancestors or descendants, and no dispensation can be given. Affinity in the collateral line annuls any such marriage, and no licit marriage can be contracted to the second degree inclusive. Dispensation may be given for either the first or second degrees of the collateral line for a just cause. (Cf. Consanguinity.)

### Africa, Christianity in

One must examine African Christianity in two major phases. The first is the natural "spread" of Christianity to the countries bordering the Mediterranean Sea, that is, Tripoli, Tunisia, Algeria, and Morocco. That this portion of the world was Christianized early in the history of the Church is known from the *Acta* of the Scillitan martyrs (A.D. 180), the *Passion* of St. Perpetua (A.D. 203), and the writings of Tertullian (197 to 220). All reveal a Church organized and widespread, so much so that the African Church was using a Latin Bible and liturgy while Christians in other areas were still using Greek as their liturgical language. Under the primacy of Carthage in Cyprian's time (the middle of the third century), there were more than one hundred bishops. The growth of the Church was disrupted by the persecutions of Decius (A.D. 250) and the rise of the Novatian schism over rebaptism. Africa, however, recovered under the leadership of Cyprian, Arnobius, and Lactantius. In the fourth century Donatism, which arose out of the Diocletian persecution, was combatted by the writings of Tyconius, Optatus, and St. Augustine, the Bishop of Hippo. Centuries of struggle and growth followed, during which the chief contribution made by the Christian Church was the rise of monasticism in the sixth century. By the end of the seventh century many of the developed churches and institutions were decimated with the fall of Carthage to the Arab conquerors in A.D. 698.

The second period of the Christian Church in Africa which came about chiefly through mission work among the many native tribes, is still gaining momentum. Some of this began in the fifteenth century in South Africa, by the Portuguese who explored the area. But this work was marred by the exploitation of the lands and people, which accompanied the missionary work. In the eighteenth century the Dutch, who ruled the Cape Colony, discouraged missionary efforts, and the Catholic missions were not permitted to restart their work until 1837. With settlement by white people and the opening up of communications in general, missionary work has continued on a lively and growing scale of endeavor. Agencies of Church groups, the input of economic aid, and the enduring work of missionary groups: the Jesuits, White Fathers, the Oblates of Mary Immaculate, and the Fathers of the Sacred Heart, along with many Christian enterprises, such as that of Albert Schweitzer, have brought the African Christian community to become one of the fastest growing in the history of mankind's response to the mandate of Christ (Mt. 24:14; Jn. 17:17–19). A strong native clergy and hierarchy have shown great leadership. There has arisen a devotion to the Blessed Virgin Mary expressed by the poet Ruby Berkley Goodwin in her poem "The Black Madonna," which concludes with the lines:

"Today I find you in this unmarked place
And in my heart I resurrect your shrine."

### African Church

The Church established by Christians of the second century in the Afro-Roman colonies comprises what is now Tripoli, Algeria, and Morocco. The chief see was that of Carthage, and in the time of its greatest son, St. Augustine (d. 430), the bishop of Hippo, there were 400 diocesan sees. The Church was bitterly persecuted by Decius in the third century. Many fell away and were termed "lapsi"; others who admitted some collaboration were called "traditores"; both caused much trouble to the Church. One of the effects was the rise of the Donatist and Arian heresies in the fourth century. When the Vandals of Spain conquered that portion of Africa, the orthodox Christians were again persecuted; after the defeat of the Vandals in the sixth century, Christianity was not strong enough to recover and the country fell to Mohammedanism. Only recently has there been achieved a return to Christianity by the mission work following the colonization by the French and Spanish.

After 1939 when the first Bishops from south of the Sahara were ordained by Pope Pius XII (Bishop Kiwanuka of Uganda and Bishop Ramarosandratana of Madagascar), missionary work, which had waned during the first World War, was accelerated greatly. But in some areas there are still restrictions on the Church. The Holy See has great interest in the evangelization of the African nations, as seen from the great number of documents concerning these missions and the extensive aid given to the peoples of this portion of the third world countries.

## African Councils

The seventeen councils of religious leaders, notably SS. Cyprian and Augustine, were held for the most part at Carthage, the last in A.D. 646. These councils contributed much to discussion of the doctrine and discipline that were the marks of Christianity in the world. In the main, the councils dealt with the Donatist and Arian heresies; the rebaptism of heretics, notably the "lapsi"; the Pelagian heresy; and matters of discipline as given by Rome for the African Church. After the last council the Caliph Othman brought about the ruin of both the Roman and Christian civilizations in Africa.

## African Rite

This development of the original Roman rite is no longer used.

## African Values

These seven noble ideals form a code of action. They have been ascribed to the black poet LeRoi Jones, now known as Imamu Baraka, but some say they are simply a gathering from various sources. In Swahili and English these values are: (1) Umoja (unity), which is a desired condition for the family, race, community, or nation. (2) Kujichagulia (self-determination), that which each is by him- or herself or as they are defined by themselves rather than by others. (3) Ujima (responsibility and united work), the building of a sense of community whereby the problems of each may be better resolved. (4) Ujamaa (cooperative economics), the direction toward a self-sufficiency in business and mutual profit programs. (5) Nia (purpose), the developing of community wherein the racial traditions are preserved. (6) Kuumba (creativity), action directed to the community to make it more beneficial and beautiful in fulfill-

ment. (7) Imani (faith), to believe in our people and our leaders so that the right may prevail.

This code is Christian, while at the same time racially oriented. The sense of community that is developing among the African and Black peoples is similar to that of the Christian sense of community.

## Agape

The agape, or love feast, was a memorial of the Last Supper. Its thought was somewhat analogous to the Jewish Passover dinner or the Greek custom of having a "brotherhood" meal before a solemn event. As practiced by the early Christians, it merely recalled the Last Supper. It did not, as has been charged, have a relationship to the Eucharist, since it was merely an eating before or after the celebration of the Eucharist. Abuses arose, and it was discontinued, even as a nonliturgical act, by the sixth century. In recent times there has been a revival of the concept through the emphasis upon the "sense of community" brought about by the ecumenical and liturgical movements, but it has more social overtones than association with the Holy Eucharist.

## Agde, Council of

Held in A.D. 506 at Agde (Agatha) in Languedoc, and presided over by St. Caesarius of Arles, this council published fifty canons, or rules, on Church discipline.

## Age, Canonical

Age, in canon law, is reckoned from the day of birth and not from the day of baptism. According to canon law this age fixes the time when members of the Church can receive obligations or enjoy special privileges. In canon law a person completes a year at midnight, the last hour of his or her birthday anniversary. Thus the age of reason is determined to be seven years for the reception of penance. Marriage contracted by males under 16 and by females under 14 is null and void. Fasting is of obligation for all over 21 years of age and under 59. Godparents at baptism must normally be at least 14 years of age. Those in religious life are likewise governed by a determined age as to when they may receive profession, make vows, receive Holy Orders, and be ordained a bishop.

## Age, Impediment of

In matrimony, this means that the person attempting to contract marriage is too young for valid reception of the sacrament, having not yet attained the canonical age. (Cf. Age, Canonical.)

## Age of Reason

1. Age of reason refers to the time when one, by legal definition of the Church, is capable of distinguishing right from wrong, begins to incur obligations such as abstinence, and takes on moral responsiblity.

2. In history, the Age of Reason was the period of the eighteenth century when the Encyclopedists and Deists were influential in France and England.

## Aggiornamento

This Italian word that means in general modernization, renewal, revitalization, has become, as a word, a focal point for the processes and procedures that Vatican Council II brought to the spiritual renewal and institutional reform in the Church through the implementation of the documents and decrees of the Council. (Cf. Vatican Council II.)

## Aglipay Schism

This movement was organized in 1902 by a priest of the native clergy as the Independent Philippine National Church with himself as archbishop. He nominated twenty assistant bishops and achieved quite a following among the native clergy and the baptized Catholics. The Church property seized by the Aglipayans was restored to the Catholic hierarchy by order of the United States Supreme Court in 1906. The movement had been supported by American money. Aglipay died, reconciled to the Church, in Sept. 1940. The movement is now minor and has but few followers in the Islands.

## Agnosticism

Agnosticism is a philosophical theory that holds that it is impossible to arrive at a knowledge of reality either because by its nature it is unknowable or because of limits of the human mind. In effect it denies that man by reason can come to knowledge of God and the truths of religion. Agnosticism in all its forms results in reducing man's knowledge to his own sense experience or to his subjective or emotional responses. The most general modern expression was set down by the English biologist Thomas Huxley in 1868, which can be said to hold that the human intellect is not able to come to a knowledge of anything immaterial, especially a knowledge of God and His nature, as well as the human soul. The correct doctrinal teaching was presented by Vatican Council I, reasserting the traditional claim of the Church as being in accord with reason.

Vatican Council II placed a more modern emphasis, directed toward our technological society: "No doubt today's progress in Science and technology can foster a certain exclusive emphasis on observable data, and an agnosticism about everything else. For the methods of investigation which these sciences use can be wrongly considered as the supreme rule for discovering the whole truth" (GS, 57).

## Agnus Dei

1. The Agnus Dei is a prayer of petition in the Mass just before the Communion, invoking Christ as the Lamb of God.

2. Oval disks of wax blessed by the pope on which the figure of a lamb is stamped are also called agnus dei. The wax is the remainder of paschal candles and solemnly blessed by the pope on the Thursday after Easter in the first and seventh years of his pontificate. On the reverse side is impressed the coat-of-arms of the pope. They are sacramentals and are not indulgenced and worn as medals around the neck in leather cases or may be carried in any suitable manner. They are intended as protection against Satan, sickness, sudden death, temptations or tempests, and as a medium of divine help for expectant mothers. They were used as early as the fourth century.

## Agony of Christ

These words manifest the anguish suffered by Christ in the Garden of Gethsemani prior to His apprehension by the Jews and Roman soldiers before His crucifixion. The word *agony* is used to describe the phenomenon of the bloody sweat, which is physiologically impossible. The suffering was most intense because of the two wills in Christ, His divine and His human. Instinctively, in His human will and nature, Christ shrank from suffering and death, yet in His divine, deliberate will He welcomed both death and suffering for the redemption of man as God willed it.

## Agrapha

Deeds or sayings of Christ, which find no mention in the Gospels, have been kept and handed down by tradition. The agrapha are found in writings of the fathers, in some biblical manuscripts, and papyri fragments, but few of them are considered authentic.

## Agrimissio

This service agency (the name literally means mission to or for the land) gives aid to religious institutes, the Food and Agriculture Organization of the United Nations, and other groups and their technicians who work in the rural development of mission territories throughout the world or wherever there is hunger caused by low harvest yields. It was founded in 1970 by the Union of Superiors General, the International Union of Superiors General, and the National Catholic Rural Life Conference. Its objectives are finding the best means to feed the hungry people of nations and to improve the means of production along with the quantity and quality of foodstuffs.

## Alais, Treaty of

Signed in 1629 between the royal forces of France and the Huguenots, the Treaty of Alais ended the religious wars, renewed the Edict of Nantes, and granted amnesty.

## Alb

1. The alb is the vestment of white linen, reaching from neck to feet, with full sleeves, which the priest puts on after the amice in vesting for Mass. The word comes from the Latin word *albus,* "white." The vestment is an adaptation of the tunic worn by early Romans and Greeks and is a full garment that is secured or "taken in" at the waist by a cincture. Dating from very early times, the alb symbolizes the purity of soul with which the sacrifice of the Mass should be offered. The surplice is a shortened alb, as is the rochet worn by prelates. The new Sacramentary states that the alb is a vestment common to all ministers. It may be made to fit without use of a cincture. If the alb does not completely cover the ordinary clothing at the neck, an amice should be worn under it. A surplice may replace the alb, except when a chasuble is worn, or when a stole is used alone instead of a chasuble or dalmatic with stole.

2. An alb is also a long white garment or robe, formerly worn by newly baptized persons from Holy Saturday until Low Sunday, from which the title *Dominica in albis* or "Sunday in white" is derived for this first Sunday after Easter.

## Albigenses

A sect of neo-Manichaean revolutionaries who held an extreme view on purity were also known as Catharists. They came into Europe by way of Bulgaria, became numerous in Languedoc, Southern France, Italy, and Spain. They borrowed from both paganism and Christianity. They repudiated the sacraments, especially marriage, promoted sexual promiscuity, and were vegetarians. They

also encouraged actions inimical to state authority and, because they were doubly dangerous, the barons of France, Germany, and Belgium waged a crusade against them. Albigensianism derived its name from a city in Southern France called Albi. It reflected the dualistic view of the world, the good God who created man in His image, and the evil one, Satan, who corrupts or defiles this image. It denied the Holy Trinity. The Albigensians directed a most virulent attack upon the Catholic Church. In the eleventh century they were condemned by Councils of the Church. The Albigenses disappeared by the fourteenth century. (Cf. Docetism.)

## Alexandria, Church of

Founded by St. Mark, the evangelist, at the port city of Egypt the Church of Alexandria became a great center of trade and learning. The church was administered by great bishops including Sts. Athanasius and Cyril. However, it also gave rise to serious defections from the Church and heresies such as Arianism in the fourth century and Monophysitism, widespread in the fifth and sixth centuries. Under this latter heresy, which held but one nature in Christ and rejected the Council of Chalcedon, the Church of Alexandria was severed from Rome.

## Alexandria, School of

From its contact with Christianity in apostolic times, this distinct school of theology flourished in the ancient city of Alexandria, already a center of Greek and Jewish learning. A famed catechetical school was founded, which attained distinction for its instruction of catechumens, its zeal in the study of Scripture, and its interest in apologetics. One of the first works coming from there was the Septuagint, the translation of the Hebrew Scriptures into Greek. It also contributed much to the allegorical interpretation of Scripture, and fostered such great writers as Clement, Sts. Athanasius and Cyril. While Christian philosophy was strong, it remained a leader among Christian thought, but the rise of the confusion of Arianism caused it to suffer and go into decline.

## Alexandrine Rite

The Alexandrine is one of the rites of the East used throughout the Patriarchate of Alexandria, Egypt. It has three forms: the Greek liturgy of St. Mark, which is no longer used; the three Coptic liturgies; and that used by the Abyssinian Church.

## Alimentation

Alimentation is the provision of whatever might be necessary to maintain life, such as food, clothing, and shelter. It sometimes referred to the support of members by religious orders and also to the maintenance offered to diocesan priests. (Cf. Benefice.)

## Aliturgical Days

Days on which the Sacrifice of the Mass is not permitted to be celebrated, e.g., Good Friday in the Latin rite and all Fridays of Lent in the Ambrosian rite, are termed aliturgical days.

## All Saints, Solemnity of

This feast instituted in the west by Pope Boniface IV (d. 615) is celebrated in the Church to honor all the saints, especially those who have not been assigned a day in the Church calendar. It has been celebrated on Nov. 1, since about A.D. 731 when Pope Gregory III consecrated a chapel in St. Peter's Basilica in honor of all saints and set the date of the feast. In the new calendar of the Church introduced with the official Sacramentary in 1974, All Saints Day is classed as a Solemnity, the highest dignity. It is a holy day of obligation in the United States.

All Souls' Day is a day of solemn prayer for all the departed souls, which the Church observes on Nov. 2. The day in the calendar is a solemnity (transferable to Nov. 3) and was initially instituted for celebration on the day after All Saints Day by St. Odilo in A.D. 998. By a decree of Aug. 10, 1915, issued by Pope Benedict XV, a priest is granted the privilege of saying three Masses on this day: one for all the faithful departed, one for the intention of the Holy Father, and one for his particular intention.

## Allegorical Interpretation, Biblical

This is a part of the spiritual or mystical sense of Scripture. It is the interpretation of words or portions of Scripture where persons, things, and events as described, signify other persons, things, or events. The former are called types, the latter antitypes. Hence there are antitypes in the OT that prefigure the Church on earth, and this sense is called the allegorical sense, which derives from the manner of expression as a sustained metaphor such as that exemplified in the Song of Songs.

As a method of exegesis allegorical interpretation attempts to find the meaning of a particular passage or word found in the Bible other than the literal sense. It does this by a transfer of the symbolic meaning, adding to the literal sense a deeper or more spiritual meaning. We are all aware that metaphoric writing is common in the Bible, but we should not attempt to give a symbolic or metaphoric meaning to a text that is evident, e.g., the words spoken by Christ. Nor can we by probing the psychology of the author come to understand something that he did not intend. There are only two genuine senses in Scripture: the literal (the text itself) and the typical (that about which the author speaks). (See Form Criticism.)

## Allegory

An allegory is a sustained metaphor. One sense of the allegory is really what the metaphor means literally, the other what is represents. Allegory as a literary device should not be confused with allegorical interpretation, which is a kind of sense found in Scripture by prefigurement or allusion.

## Alleluia

The liturgical call of praise in the Bible is taken from the Hebrew and means "praise God." In the liturgy of the Mass it is repeated as an expression of joy or thanksgiving. It is a word added to some of the Psalms but probably by a later writer. Only once is the word used in the NT (Rv. 19:1–6), where it is the cry of jubilation of the angels.

## Allocution

An allocution is a solemn speech or statement made by the pope to the cardinals in a secret consistory.

## Alma also Almah

This word refers to the Blessed Mother of God who was to fulfill the prophecy of the promised Messiah (Is. 7:14). Literally it means "gracious" or "loving," or maiden or virgin.

## Almoner

An almoner was originally the person named by a prince or lord to dispense alms or monies to indigent subjects. Now, it is the member of a religious institution whose duty it is to distribute alms, more rarely the chaplain of such an institution. The place where such alms are given out is referred to as an almonry.

### Alms

Alms are the material goods or monies that are given to the needy as a corporal work of mercy. An obligation to give alms arises out of the natural law and divine precept. It is a serious obligation of charity and not of justice, and hence the goods or monies are to be given out of one's surplus. It is not required that one give unless: his obligations to his family are first satisfied, his needs for reasonable comfort and social position are met, or the money is not otherwise owed in debt. Services of professional people are considered alms when extended to the poor without charge. However, alms are not to be confused with other works of charity such as fraternal correction or acts of a spiritual nature. Alms being the "fruits of your justice" were considered as both works and acts of charity (Acts 9:36; see also 24:17).

### Almuce

This ecclesiastical garment was formerly used to cover the head and worn in choir by chanters. Since the biretta has come into use, the almuce is more of a hood, hanging down in back of the head. Almuce also refers to the hood of a mozzetta.

### Alogi

Literally "against the word," this name was given by St. Epiphanius to all heretics who denied the doctrine of our Lord, the Word, and who rejected the biblical writings of St. John.

### Alpha and Omega

See A-Ω.

### Alphabetic Psalms

In the Hebrew text, these are the psalms whose successive verses begin with successive letters of the Hebrew alphabet, e.g. Ps. 25; 34; 145. They are a poetic form that was used by the Israelites, and in textual criticism they afford a basis for determining a break in the order that might indicate an omission or a mistranslation.

### Altar

This word comes from the Hebrew, meaning "place of sacrifice." The Christian altar is a table on which the sacrifice of the Mass is offered. It is the center of dignity and importance in the church building. In the early days of the Church, the Holy Eucharist was celebrated, in a home or any private place, on a table. Pictures in the catacombs show these tables to be of a variety of shapes, round, square, or semicircular, but now the essential feature is a stone slab (but it may be of other material considered worthy), and from this is derived the name "altar stone." It may or may not contain relics within it. This idea of a stone with relics follows from the early practice of celebrating Mass on or near the tombs of martyrs in the catacombs. There are two kinds of altars. The *fixed* altar, a table (the *mensa*) with a support or base (the *stipes*), is consecrated as a unit. The *portable* altar, a smaller stone, incised like the fixed with five crosses at the corners and center, is consecrated alone or apart from its support. Also permitted is a compromise between the two types, made up of a wood or stone permanent structure into the top of which a consecrated stone or portable altar is inserted in the sepulcher (*sepulchrum*), a small, square cavity in the top of the *mensa*.

In the new general instructions of the Sacramentary the following is most current: "The altar, where the sacrifice of the cross is made present under sacramental signs, is also the table of the Lord. The people of God are called together to share in this table. Thus the altar is the center of the thanksgiving accomplished in the Eucharist.

"In a sacred place the Eucharist should be celebrated on an altar, either fixed or movable. In other places, especially where the Eucharist is not regularly celebrated, a suitable table may be used, but always with a cloth and corporal.

"An altar is considered fixed if it is attached to the floor so that it cannot be moved. It is a movable altar if it can be transferred from place to place.

"The main altar should be freestanding so that the ministers can easily walk around it and Mass can be celebrated facing the people. It should be placed in a central position which draws the attention of the whole congregation. The main altar should ordinarily be a fixed, consecrated altar.

"According to the traditional practice of the Church and the meaning of an altar, the table of a fixed altar should be of natural stone, but any solid, becoming, and skillfully constructed material may be used with the approval of the conference of bishops.

"The support or base of the table may be of any solid, becoming material.

"A movable altar may be constructed of any solid, becoming material which is suited to liturgical use, according to the traditions and culture of different regions.

"Fixed altars are consecrated according to the rite of the Roman Pontifical; movable altars may be simply blessed. It is not necessary to have a consecrated stone in a movable altar or on the table where the Eucharist is celebrated outside a sacred place.

"It is fitting to maintain the practice of enclosing relics in the altar or of placing them under the altar. These relics need not be those of martyrs, but there must be proof that they are authentic.

"Minor altars should be few in number. In new churches they should be placed in chapels somewhat separated from the nave."

### Altar Boys

Boys or young men, privileged to serve the priest at Mass and other ceremonies, take the place of the acolyte. They are sometimes called "Mass servers." They are not considered as replacement for the instituted acolytes when such are available. Today they are used in religious processions and as candle bearers. (See Acolyte.)

### Altar Breads

Thin, round wafers of unleavened wheat bread are used as the Eucharistic elements in the Latin, Maronite, and Armenian rites. Altar breads are also the communion hosts. Bread is a natural "resurrection from the dead" symbol as described in Jn. 12:24–25. It is also a symbol of man's industry and the work of his hands (cf. Gn. 3:19; Offertory). And bread also is a symbol of unity that the Eucharist is intended to effect among men (cf. 1 Cor. 10:17), or as St. Augustine declared, "We are the very thing that we receive." When communion is to be received by intinction, the altar breads should not be too thin, but should be thicker and firmer, suitable to be dipped into the precious blood.

### Altar Cards

Formerly three printed cards or charts were placed in the center, under the crucifix, and at each side of the altar. Printed on the cards were fixed prayers said during Mass, and their purpose was to aid the memory of the priest.

### Altar Cloths

Strictly speaking, these were formerly the three cloths of linen or hemp that cover the altar. The top cloth must cover the entire surface of the *mensa* and its two ends must hang down to the ground, or floor, but not on it. The two undercloths or, permissibly, one large cloth folded in two, should cover only the actual surface of the *mensa*. An extra cloth should be placed on the altar if candles are placed on the altar surface during Benediction or exposition of the Blessed Sacrament. This does not mean the dustcover, which is nonliturgical and serves only a practical purpose.

With the new order of the Mass it has been declared that there should be at least one cloth covering the altar, and its shape, size, and decoration should be according to the structure of the altar itself.

### Altar Societies

Altar Societies are groups of devout persons, usually women, who give their service to the church in preparing vestments and altar cloths. Many also perform similar work for missions and poorer churches. They are semi–social service organizations of the parish and are considered "pious societies."

### Altar Stone

See Altar.

### Altar, Stripping of

This is the ceremony performed on Holy Thursday after the Blessed Sacrament is removed from the main altar to the place of reposition. It consists of removing the altar cloth, antependium, and tabernacle veil in memory of Christ being stripped of His garments before the crucifixion.

## Altarage

This seldom used term refers to the stipend offered to a priest for the intention of a Mass. It formerly meant the support of a chaplain as payment for his services.

## Alternation

Alternation refers to the response to alternate verses in singing, or alternate responses to prayers as in the recitation of the Rosary or litanies.

## Ama or Amma

This Hebrew word applies to deeply religious women in the Eastern Church. In the early Church, it was the name of the vessel in which wine was brought to be used in the sacrifice of the Mass.

## Ambo

An ambo is a raised platform, sometimes with steps leading up to it from both sides and surrounded by a low rail, placed in the nave of early Christian churches. From it the Scriptures were read, all announcements made, and sermons preached. It was later supplanted by the pulpit. In the Greek Catholic Church the ambo is a table in front of the iconostasis at which baptisms, confirmations, and marriages are celebrated. In more recent times this term has been applied to the lectern from which the lector proclaims the readings in the liturgy of the word, or from which the commentator leads the eucharistic community in responses.

## Ambrosian Chant

Hymns were written by St. Ambrose or his contemporaries in the fourth century in iambic dimeter verse form. They were syllabic in form (a single note to each syllable of text) and originally of a simple rhythm but underwent many changes leading to the later developments that were forerunners of the Gregorian chant.

## Ambrosian Hymnography, also Ambrosiani

This refers to all hymns having the metric and strophic measure found in the authentic hymns of St. Ambrose. More broadly, it is a poetical form or a liturgical use to which the hymns are applied. As introduced by St. Ambrose into Milan, it was of oriental origin and the first use of antiphonal psalmody or the singing of the psalms by two choirs.

## Ambrosian Rite

The liturgy of the Mass used in the churches of Milan, Italy, is so named because St. Ambrose (d.

397) introduced a revision of usage. Its origin is unknown although it is generally held to be an old Roman or Antiochene form. At present it is much like the Roman rite with these exceptions: a procession before the Offertory is made, presenting the oblations of wine and bread; a litany is chanted by the deacon; the Creed is read after the Offertory. It is used in the archdiocese of Milan today but not in every church.

The rite also includes other services such as the rite of baptism and the arrangement of parts of the Divine Office with the lighting of candles during the recitation of Vespers. It is considered a developmental stage toward the rich liturgy we have today.

## Ambry or Aumbry

An Ambry is a boxlike closet or cupboard attached to either the gospel or epistle side of the sanctuary wall. It may be built into or hang against the wall. In the ambry the holy oils are kept. The ambry should have a door that must be kept locked, and the words *Olea Sacra* (Holy Oils) should be inscribed on this door. The ambry may have a white or violet veil hung before it. If the sacristy adjoins the sanctuary physically, the ambry may be kept there.

## Ambulatory

A covered passage or walk around a cloister and open on the side toward the courtyard is known as an ambulatory. It is also the passage around the apse of a church building from which chapels radiate. By extension the term may be used for the route of a procession within the church.

## Amen

This Hebrew word means "truly," "certainly." According to Pope Benedict XIV, it indicates assent to a truth, as at the end of a Creed. It is used in its original meaning in both Scripture and the liturgy of the Church. When in the NT (Jn. 3:3) it is used double, as in some translations, it is considered more solemn. At the end of prayers, *Amen* signifies our desire to obtain our request and is commonly translated, "So be it."

In the OT the Israelites used the word *Amen* to show their willingness to accept and abide by the commandments of God. (cf. Dt. 27:15-26) In Ps. 72:19 the amen is repeated twice as an emphasis of praise for God. The NT continued the use of the word, even in the Greek translations, and so it is spoken at the end of the thanksgiving prayer, 1 Cor. 14:16, as also it was used by Christ as a guarantee of the truth of His words. In Rv. 3:14 Christ himself is called the "Amen," and St. Paul declares that we receive the promises of God through Christ who redeems us (2 Cor. 1:20).

## American Board of Catholic Missions

This organization was founded at Cincinnati, Ohio, in 1920, by a committee appointed by bishops of the United States. Its purpose is to distribute 40 percent of the annual collection of the Propagation of the Faith to archbishops and bishops of missionary dioceses of the United States and its dependencies. It consolidates missionary activities in the United States, coordinates them with Catholic missions of other countries under general jurisdiction of an international board chosen by the Vatican, and operates under the direction of the National Catholic Welfare Council.

Since 1970 this is known as the United States Catholic Mission Council and functions to "provide a forum and organ for the evaluation, coordination and fostering, in the United States, of the worldwide missionary effort of the Church."

## Americanism

In Catholic history, this refers to a controversy that attracted attention toward the end of the nineteenth century. It arose over French theologians who protested the missionary methods of Father Isaac Hecker, the American priest-convert, and the support given to American institutions. The charges included protests that methods of conversion used were heterodox, that American missionaries were placing the faith secondary and distorting Catholic doctrine, not following Church authorities, and belittling humility and obedience in regard to religious vows. In 1899, Pope Leo XIII in a letter, *Testem benevolentiae*, "Proof of affection," condemned the alleged practices that were included in the word "Americanism" and drew a clear distinction between the lawful and unlawful in the dispute. Notably the declaration made the following points clear: the necessity of spiritual direction, the subordinate position of the natural virtues to the supernatural, the relative place of the active and passive virtues. It also refuted the claim that liberty is limited in religious vows. It further set forth the methods of dealing with non-Catholics. The discussion continued for a few years, giving way to the issue of modernism, although the condemned teachings were never accepted by the bishops and clergy of the United States. It is now an historical anomaly.

## Amice

This is the vestment put on first by a priest in vesting for the celebration of Mass. It is an oblong linen cloth that is touched to the head before being placed over the shoulders. It is worn under the alb. The amice is required when the celebrant does not have on a cassock or clerical dress. Formerly a prayer was prescribed when putting on the amice, but now this is optional.

## Ammonian Sections

Ammonian sections are divisions of the four Gospels made in the margins of early Greek and Latin manuscripts of the Scriptures. These sections, named after Ammonius of Alexandria (c. 220), were an indication of the harmony of the four Gospels.

## Amos, Book of

The Book of Amos is an OT book of prophesy. Amos was a minor prophet who wrote about the eighth century before Christ. His writing has nine chapters and is directed to: the divine judgment and the sovereignty of God (Yahweh) both in nature and in history. It was written when Israel, because of its deliverance from Syrian domination, had become a wealthy nation with social injustices arising between the rich and the poor, and unjust treatment wreaked upon the farmers by the landowners. At the same time and because of their affluence, the Israelites had drifted away from their religious practices, and their worship of God was little more than formalism or external show. Against these social and religious abuses Amos raised his voice, calling for man to abandon his cultivation of material goods at the expense of the sovereign rights of God. It is in this book that the divine thrust for social justice finds origin and the fact that those having social position, materially and economically, bear the responsibility to correct the injustices. This applies to the judgment whereby nations and individuals also must come to seek a life according to the knowledge or gifts they have received and must likewise respond by living a morally upright life if their worship of God is to be of value and eventual reward. The book concludes, 9:8–15, with a Messianic promise of hope.

## Amovability

This canonical term describes the method and prerogative of a bishop of a diocese in moving a cleric from an office, which the bishop can do in prudent judgment, except in the instances of an irremovable office or a removable parish (c. 192, sec. 2, 3; c. 2147 to 2161).

## Ampulla

A bottle or small jar was used by early Christians to hold holy oils. Some were thought to contain the blood of a martyr. Later in the Middle Ages people making pilgrimages to holy wells carried water from the place of pilgrimage in small *ampullae* tied about their necks.

## Amra

An amra is an elegy written in prose or verse and recited to proclaim the virtues and life of a native saint of Ireland.

## Amula

See Cruet.

## Anabaptism

This religious sect began in Saxony in the early sixteenth century and spread throughout southern Germany. Its doctrine was derived from key Lutheran beliefs, but neither Luther, Calvin, nor Zwingli considered the Anabaptist position favorably. The main tenet of the Anabaptists was that baptism is for adults only and that infant baptism is invalid. They also rejected the teaching of the Church concerning the sacraments and the nature of the Church and held a belief that one who believes is directly and only influenced by the Holy Spirit. This is called the doctrine of Inner Light. Formulation of their eighteen chief teachings was made in 1632 in Holland. Mennonites are Anabaptists.

## Anagnostes

In the Greek Church the one who reads the Epistle is the anagnostes.

## Anagogical Sense, Biblical

In the interpretation of Scripture, this is a division of the spiritual or mystical sense. It derives from the "subject matter" and, as St. Thomas Aquinas points out, truth may be conveyed to us through Scriptures with (1) a view to right belief or (2) right conduct. When this is by "right conduct," it is moral or tropological sense of Scripture. When it is directed to right belief, then we have either the *allegorical* or *anagogical* senses. In the first, the allegorical, we have examples of types in the OT, which prefigure persons in the NT. In the second there are types in both the OT and NT, which foreshadow the Church triumphant in heaven, and this we term the anagogical sense, e.g., St. Paul (Gal. 4:26) using Jerusalem as a type of the city of heaven.

## Analecta

Literally "gatherings" or gleanings from the writings of authors, such as the fathers, analecta may appear as part of the title of the book.

## Analogy

An analogy is an argument from the lesser to the greater, the relation of one thing to another, a demonstrated form of reasoning. Analogy is used in the sense that by noting the degree of perfection in creatures we may come to know, however imperfectly, the infinite perfection of God (Wis. 13:5).

## Anamnesis

Something done in memory of someone or something, as stated after the consecration in the Mass, is an anamnesis.

## Anaphora

The word anaphora comes from the Greek, meaning an "offering." In the Latin rite the term refers to the Canon of the Mass, including the Preface, in the Liturgy of the Eucharist. The words, "Do this in memory of me," said in all the eucharistic prayers of consecration, are a recollection of the fact that Christ offered himself as a victim to God for our salvation.

In the liturgy of the Byzantine rite the anaphora is divided into seven parts: the *exhortation, eucharistic thanksgiving, consecration, anamnesis, epiklesis, the diptychs,* and the *conclusion.*

Traditionally the anaphora is an emphasis placed upon the acts of Christ in giving us the blessed Eucharist as our spiritual food.

## Anastasimatarion

This liturgical book of the Greek Church contains the text and notation sung during the Sunday office.

## Anathema

The ban as used in the OT meant that which is or must be set aside or separated, especially whatever would bring danger to the people because of inherent evil. In practice, the ban was the sacrifice of living creatures and offering them up to God. This was governed by the law of Moses. In some translations of the NT, St. Paul (Gal. 1:8) used the term "anathema" in the sense of utterly exluding a person from the kingdom of God (a curse). In this it is understood as an excommunication, a cutting off, or destruction. Later in the Church, the term was applied to one solemnly pronounced excommunicated or expelled from communion with the Church by the pope. Today anathema is used in Church declarations that state what the Church *does not* believe.

## Anchor

This mariner's aid in keeping a boat safe has been used from earliest times in the Church as a symbol of hope. It appears in the Epistle to the Hebrews (6:19) where hope is portrayed as the "anchor of the soul." Later, the symbol appeared frequently in the catacombs as an emblem of hope. In art the symbol has also been representative of several saints who were steadfast in hope. It is one of the most widely used Christian symbols representing "our salvation in Christ."

## Anchor-Cross

The symbol of the anchor represents hope, as used in the catacombs but, with its crosspiece, it is a veiled image of the cross. In this understanding it portrayed both faith and hope.

## Anchorhold

An anchorhold is a hut or cell built beside a church wall, having two openings one leading into the church and one through which food was passed to the hermit who lived within. Now seldom heard of except in a historical sense.

## Anchorite

A man who withdraws from the world to live as a hermit and in so doing devotes his life to penance and prayer is an anchorite. Women doing this are called anchoresses. Usually such persons are for some time a part of monastic life, spending preparatory years in monastic living or returning from time to time to a monastery.

## Ancren Riwle

This code of conduct, rather rigoristic, was drawn up in the thirteenth century for the direction of anchoresses. It is no longer considered except as a curio.

## Angel

The name "angel" is taken from the Greek translation of a Hebrew word meaning "messenger." The angels are spiritual beings, created by God, and superior in nature to man. They are immortal beings whose role is to minister to God and to do the will of God in obedience. They are bodiless, spiritual intelligences who have their knowledge, not as man who acquires knowledge through his senses, but by intuition. Thus they do not arrive at conclusions following upon principles by a process of reason but immediately know the principles as truth. Their intelligences are continually, eternally exercised, and while much is hidden from them, they understand and know much more than man. They have swiftness of movement, free will, and communication among themselves.

The number of angels is exceedingly great. Theologians and early writers, basing their reasoning upon an enumeration given in Scripture by Isaiah, Ezekiel, and St. Paul (Col. 1:16, Eph. 1:21), list three hierarchies, each containing three orders, making nine types of classifications. The first threesome are: Seraphim, Cherubim, Thrones; the second, Dominations, Principalities, Powers; the third, Virtues, Archangels, Angels. The classes or choirs of angels differ in the degree of perfection of their nature and of grace, and this in a descending order in the listing above. It should be pointed out that all are called "angels," yet it is also the name applied to the lower choir from which the "guardian angels" are usually chosen. Veneration is given angels because of their dignity, relation to God, and excellence of nature, and petition is made to them because they minister to God and may, if God so wills, minister to man. In the liturgy angels are memorialized on Oct. 2, the feast of the Guardian Angels. Only three angels are named: Michael, Raphael, and Gabriel.

The relationship of angels to God is multiple as

recorded in the Bible. They are of God's court, God's army, they assist God in the government of the world, and they are messengers to men.

### Angel, Guardian

The angelic representative and unseen companion of every person on earth (Mt. 18:10; also Acts 12:15) is the guardian angel. This teaching is held by the Church not as a defined article but as a proximate teaching of faith. As such, the angel assigned to the person represents him before God, watches over him, defends him, helps in prayer and in thought, and presents the soul of the just person to God after death. Devotion to one's guardian angel is encouraged, for we read in Ps. 91:11–12, "For to his angels he has given command about you, that they guard you in all your ways. Upon their hands they shall bear you up, lest you dash your foot against a stone."

### Angel-Lights

Angel-lights is an architectural term for the small windows separating the structural tracery of arches in church windows.

### Angelic Doctor

See Doctor Angelicus.

### Angelical Salutation

The Hail Mary prayer is the angelical salutation. More properly it is the greeting given to the Blessed Virgin by Archangel Gabriel at the annunciation, which is repeated in the first portion of the prayer (Lk. 1:26–38). (Cf. Ave Maria.)

### Angels of the Churches

As mentioned in the Book of Revelation (1:20), these were thought of by the Greek or Eastern Church fathers as referring to the guardian angels of seven cities (Ephesus, Smyrna, Pergamum, Thyatira, Sardis, Philadelphia, Laodicea) of the Asiatic Roman Empire. However, following the interpretation of the Western Church fathers, they usually are held to be the bishops of these cities to whom St. John addresses himself in writing.

### Angels, Evil

See Devil and Evil Spirits.

### Angelus

This devotion consists of praying three Hail Marys, versicles and responses, and a collect or prayer at morning, noon, and night in honor of the Incarnation and in veneration of the Blessed

Mother. Usually this is prayed at the ringing of the *Angelus* by the church bells at 6 A.M., 12 noon, and 6 P.M. The devotion began in 1318 when Pope John XXII called for the recitation of three Hail Marys in the evening for peace. Later, in France, it was used at noon and in the morning and by the sixteenth century was made universal with indulgences attached. During the season of Easter the verse "Regina caeli laetare" ("Queen of Heaven, rejoice") is said instead.

### Anger

Anger is a strong emotion that when aroused leads to other sins or the "inordinate inclination to take revenge." As such it is one of the seven capital sins. It may be considered inordinate by reason of the object that causes the anger or the extent to which it is aroused or expressed. The contrary virtue is meekness. (Cf. Jas. 1:19–20.)

### Anglican, Anglicanism

These are the names of the members and organization of the Established Church of England. Anglicanism is used more by the High Churchmen, but chiefly as an argument to identify the Established Church with that "Catholic Church" as named in the Magna Carta. It began with the break with Rome made by Henry VIII whose marriage problems were a scandal and against the law of the Catholic Church. The first step in this separation was not in the nature of reform but was taken in the publication by Henry of the Acts of Supremacy (1535), which declared the crown supreme in religious affairs. Having started thus, Henry drew up Ten Articles, which rejected the Catholic doctrine on the papacy, purgatory, relics, and images. The Catholic Church was persecuted and its properties seized, not always because of these teachings, however. Later, in the reign of Edward VI, the Book of Common Prayer was published. This first printing in 1549 was marred with many errors, and a later edition was strongly Calvinistic. Elizabeth, during her reign, adhered to this second edition but made certain amendments to appease and make the book useful to both the moderate members (Episcopalians) and the extremists (Calvinists). Parliament in 1563 set up the Church of England with the publication of the Thirty-nine Articles and established the heresy by the repudiation of many Catholic doctrines. Elizabeth then brought forth her Acts of Supremacy and Uniformity, which led to legalized persecution of Catholics for nearly 200 years under the nationalistic belief that the patrio-

tism of those outside the Established Church was questioned, and those recognizing papal authority were accused of committing treason. Elizabeth was excommunicated in 1570 by Pius V.

The desire for unity with the Roman Church has had great impact with the rise of ecumenism following Vatican II. The fathers of the Council recognized the position of Anglicans: "Among those in which some Catholic traditions and institutions continue to exist, the Anglican Communion occupies a special place" (UR 13). (See Ecumenism.)

## Anglican Orders

The validity of holy orders of the ministers of the Anglican Church is a disputed question. It follows that rejection of holy orders as a sacrament would put succeeding administrations in doubt because of faulty intent. Certainly the effects of ordination rest in authority from the Apostles, and the ordaining bishop intends to confer the right and duty to offer the sacrifice of the Mass in accord with that succession. Rejection of the sacrifice, the Eucharist, and the real presence make it impossible to intend the effects of ordination. The question for Catholics was settled by the publication of the papal bull, *Apostolicae Curae* (Sept. 13, 1896), which declared Anglican orders to be "absolutely null and utterly void," because of defect in (1) the form in the rite of ordaining and (2) the intention of the one ordaining.

In recent times the ordination of women has brought disruption and new controversy to the Episcopal churches. The ecumenical movement may also have been presented with a new obstacle that is both a block to unity and a serious consideration for intercommunion. (See Ecumenism.)

## Anglo-Catholics

Anglo-Catholics is the name of the Anglicans who are so-called High Church and who claim to celebrate Mass and use the Latin Missal. They favor union or identity with the Greek and Russian Orthodox Churches.

## Anima Christi

Literally translated "soul of Christ," Anima Christi is the title of an eucharistic prayer of devotion whose author is unknown. It dates back to 1370 where it was found stated in an English manuscript that Pope John XXII granted an indulgence of 3,000 days whenever the prayer was said following the consecration of Mass and the *Agnus Dei* prayer. The prayer unites one to the sacrifice of Christ and praising God. It reads:

Soul of Christ, sanctify me.
Body of Christ, save me.
Blood of Christ, inebriate me.
Water from the side of Christ, wash me.
Passion of Christ, strengthen me.
O good Jesus, hear me.
Within Thy wounds hide me.
Suffer me not to be separated from Thee.
From the malicious enemy defend me.
In the hour of my death call me,
And bid me come unto Thee
That with Thy saints I may praise Thee
For ever and ever, Amen.

## Animals in Church Art

From the earliest days of the Church, animals and birds were used as symbols representing animate and inanimate persons, e.g., the lamb as the soul, and the lion for the evangelist St. Mark. This use continued in Byzantine art and was carried into the later Gothic art, as can be seen in the Cathedral of Notre Dame in Paris. The use now has vanished with the exceptions of symbols of the older and classic representations.

## Annates

Annates are the revenue, in whole or part, paid to the papal Curia and derived from a benefice,

usually figured on a one-year basis. The revenue is now paid on appointments made to dioceses other than those subject to the Congregation of the Propaganda. Support thus given to the Holy See is small, and the chief source of revenue is the annual Peter's Pence collection.

### Anne de Beaupre, St., Shrine of

This shrine near Quebec, Canada, is a place of devotion to the Mother of the Blessed Virgin. It has come to be called the "Lourdes of the New World." Its history began with the reported cure of a cripple, Louis Grimont, on March 16, 1658, which occurred as work of construction started on a chapel honoring St. Anne. This building was enlarged and then replaced by a stone edifice that was classified as a minor basilica in 1888. Today the church is a magnificent Romanesque-Gothic basilica to which thousands of the faithful travel each year. The church features an eight-foot-high oaken statue of St. Anne and, a great relic, a portion of the forearm of the saint. (Cf. Oratory, St. Joseph's; Cap-de-la-Madeleine, Shrine of.)

### Anniversary

In the Church, days of commemoration known as anniversaries are celebrated in many instances. The anniversary of the consecration of a bishop is celebrated with a Mass in the liturgy. The anniversary of the consecration or dedication of a church is celebrated with a Mass and Office on the feast. More frequently the anniversary of a person's death is commemorated annually and may also be celebrated on the third, seventh, and thirtieth day after the day of death, and a special requiem Mass is designated for celebration of these anniversaries.

### Annual Pontifical

This annual statistical publication (*Annuaire Pontifical Catholique*) gives data on the personnel, the dioceses, the Holy See, and the Church throughout the world. Each volume is added to the first twenty volumes, begun in 1898 by Msgr. A. Battandier and published in Paris, which covered basic information of the Church, bishops, and properties.

### Annulment

The improper name often used for the Decree of Nullity, this is the declaration by authorities that a marriage is null and void because it was never valid, because of the presence of an invalidating impediment.

### Annunciation of Mary

The announcement made to the Virgin Mary by Archangel Gabriel (Lk. 1:26–38) that she was to become the Mother of Jesus and her acceptance of the will of God are known as the Annunciation. The act of declaring the Incarnation of the Son of God is celebrated by the feast of March 25 in the Church calendar. It is also, and more precisely called, Annunciation of the Lord.

### Anointing of the Sick, Sacrament of

This sacrament of the Church is an acknowledgment of the frailty of man who is to be redeemed through the mystery of Christ's own death and resurrection. "By the sacred anointing of the sick and the prayer of her priests, the whole Church commends those who are ill to the suffering and glorified Lord, asking that He may lighten their suffering and save them (cf. Jas. 5:14–16). She exhorts them moreover to contribute to the welfare of the whole People of God by associating themselves freely with the passion and death of Christ (cf. Rom. 8:17; Col. 1:24; 2 Tm. 2:11–12; 1 Pt. 4:13)" (LG, 11). Also Vatican II stated: "'Extreme Unction,' which may also and more fittingly be called 'anointing of the sick,' is not a sacrament for those only who are at the point of death. Hence, as soon as anyone of the faithful begins to be in danger of death from sickness or old age, the appropriate time for him to receive this sacrament has certainly already arrived" (SC. 73).

This sacrament of the living, when in the providence of God and expedient for the welfare of the soul, sometimes restores health through the aid given to natural or bodily forces or agents for the overcoming of dangerous illnesses. Therefore, it is of importance that the faithful seek to receive this anointing as often as they become ill and certainly whenever the threat to one's life is present because of sickness. Although it is not a necessary means of salvation, no one should for light reasons forego this sacrament. Some maintain that there is an obligation to receive it whenever possible and to fail to do so out of vanity or negligence would be seriously sinful.

The matter of the sacrament is olive oil or if necessary a vegetable oil, properly blessed for this ues by a bishop or a priest who has the faculty to do so. It is sufficient to make a single anointing on the forehead, or a single anointing of another part of the body suffices. The form is: "Through this holy anointing and His most loving mercy, may the Lord assist you by the grace of the Holy Spirit so that, when you have been freed from your sins, He may save you and in His goodness raise you up."

The anointing of the sick may be administered to more than one person during a communal celebration in some circumstances, e.g., a home for the aged, a convalescent home, or a pious association of the sick. When this is done, a brief instruction should precede the ceremony and usually the Sacrament of Penance is made available to the recipients.

### Anomean, also Anomoean

An Anomean was a member of the strict Arians who broke from the followers of Arianism. The name is derived from the Greek for "unlike" because of the heretical belief that God the Father and God the Son were "unlike." Anomeans rejected consubstantiality. Sometimes they are called Eunomians.

### Antediluvian

This term refers to people or events before the time of the flood (Gn. 6 to 8).

### Antependium

In early times this was a vertically hung cloth that went around the entire altar and was suspended from the four corners. It was called a "pallium" and was a vestment enveloping the altar. Later the antependium was a single piece of rich silk or brocade that hung down in front of the altar from the edge of the mensa to the floor, although some were metal or wood and appropriately ornamented. It is now more often called *frontal*. The rubrics now direct that a frontal is to be hung on the altar front below the *mensa* and is to be of the color of the feast or office of the day. It should be made of a suitable fabric, and have battens *(telaria)* or vertical lathes that strengthen and cause the material to hang without appearing tucked or folded. Since the introduction of the New Order of the Mass in 1970, the antependium is an optional visual decoration of the front of the altar and may vary according to the celebration. It should be worthy and truly decorative. (See Banner.)

### Athem

See Antiphon.

### Anthony's Fire, St.

This nonmedical term applies to a type of erysipelas, so named because of cures attributed to the saint, and to the Order of Canons Regular of St. Anthony that was founded partly to care for those afflicted with the disease.

### Anthropomorphism, Biblical

There are references in the Bible wherein God is spoken of, in metaphor, as being in human form or having human attributes. This use of an expression that ascribes to God terms of human qualifications is in keeping with human nature, for humans gain their knowledge from sensual objects. Thus, frequent mention is made in the scriptures of parts of humans and attributed to God, e.g., Gn. 33:23, lists "hand," "back," and "face."

### Antichrist

There is no specific one person or thing indicated by the term. Rather the title of Antichrist may be given to any person, idea, or group of persons who opposed, are opposing, or intend to oppose Christ and His Church. In particular this title is applicable only to the one enemy who will appear before the Last Judgment and draw many faithful away before being defeated by

Christ. St. Paul calls this enemy "the man of lawlessness" (2 Thes. 2:3); this is not to be considered literally but as apocalyptic language in keeping with Rv. (12:12). In brief, it is the one who will attempt to substitute himself for God.

The opinion of many scholars of Scripture is that the Antichrist is not the incarnation of antichristian hostility but rather an eschatological personage who will appear at the end of the world. The Church that Christ founded is of course guaranteed against any form of Antichrist until the end of time.

## Anticipate

To anticipate meant to read in private the Liturgy of the Hours before the hours assigned to them, e.g., reading Matins, which should be read before Mass in the morning, during the previous evening. Since Vatican II and with the approval of the conference of bishops the term has been applied to the fulfilling of a Sunday or holy day obligation by attendance at an anticipated Mass on the day preceding.

## Anticlericalism

The term applied to a movement or a personal reaction of hostility to the members of the clergy because of their alleged or real attempts to dominate the political, educational, or moral lives of those under their authority. This also extends to the Church as a whole and its social activities in many modern instances, but as a movement anticlericalism has been most prevalent in those countries where Catholicism was the religion of the state or was favored by the ruling group. It has been strongest in Europe, especially France since the revolution of 1830, and in certain Latin American countries, as in Mexico in the late 1920s. It has been fostered since the second World War by Communist parties in various countries throughout Europe and Latin America as a tool against any Church-directed program for the betterment of peoples. The entry of clergy representatives into the Congress of the United States has received anticlerical bias in some instances.

## Antidicomarianites

Literally, antidicomarianites are those opposed to Mary. Historically, it is the name given by Epiphanius (fourth century) to those who denied Mary's motherhood of God and her perpetual virginity.

## Antidoron

The fragments of bread remaining after the wafers have been cut from the baked mass are passed out, unconsecrated, to be consumed by the faithful before leaving the Church. This is still the practice in the Greek Church. Antidoron is also the *pain benit* of the French.

## Antilegomena

This collective name was given to the disputed writings of Scripture, as referred to by Eusebius of Caesarea.

## Antimension

An antimension is a substitute for an altar stone, used in Eastern churches. It is an oblong piece of silk, ten by fourteen inches, into which are sewn relics of saints and on which the instruments of the Passion are represented. It is spread on the altar top for the celebration of Mass. The antimension is consecrated by a bishop with a rite similar to that used for an altar. Because of its portability chaplains of World War II were given permission to use the antimension to celebrate the Eucharist. Bishops' conferences have, for similiar reasons, permitted its use for eucharistic celebrations in homes and other places. It is sometimes referred to as the "Greek corporal."

## Antinomians

Heretics who followed the false idea that Christians did not have to follow the commandments were called Antinomians. This idea broke out anew under the "justification by faith" teaching of Luther since some held that evil acts did not hinder one's salvation if good acts did not help one. Even Luther repudiated this. The teaching was condemned by the Council of Trent.

## Antioch

This ancient city of Asia Minor, located in Syria on the Orontes river, was held to be one of the three great episcopal cities of apostolic times. It was at Antioch that the name Christian arose (Acts 11:26), and there St. Peter was bishop for a time before going to Rome. In early times it was a center of theology and scriptural studies. It was called Antioch in Syria to distinguish it from the other ancient city of the same name in Phrygia.

## Antiochene Rite

In its original form this liturgy of the Mass differed chiefly because it omitted the Our Father and the saints' names. Later it was adapted to the Liturgy of St. James, a Greek form that was translated into the Syriac language. It is used in this form throughout the patriarchate, with the exception that twice a year the Greek form is used by the Orthodox Church. The rite is used by the *Malankarese* in India who returned to unity with the Roman Church in 1930, and the liturgical languages are Syrian and Malayalam. Also this rite is used by the *Maronites* and its liturgical languages are Syrian and Arabic, and by the *Syrians* who returned to unity in 1781 and their languages are Syrian and Arabic.

## Antiphon

Derived from the Greek, antiphon is a word meaning the alternate recitation or singing of verses as practiced by the ancient Greek dramatists. It was introduced into the Latin Church in the fourth century. The texts are usually from scripture. Later development brought it into its present form, namely, a phrase or verse immediately prefixed to and following a psalm or psalms, or a canticle that gives the key to the mystery the Church wishes to indicate in that particular portion of her liturgy. A double antiphon means that the antiphon is prayed both before and after the psalm. On minor feasts the antiphons are not doubled but are said to be "announced," which means the words are prayed only as far as the asterisk (or indicated break) at the beginning of the psalm, but recited entirely at the end. The term may also indicate any psalm or hymn sung in alternate responses by choir members or by the choir and congregation. (Cf. Liturgy of the Hours.)

## Antiphonary

The book containing all of the antiphons of the Divine Office together with the proper musical notation is the antiphonary.

## Antipopes

There were false claimants to the Holy See from the third through the fifteenth centuries. Over the years thirty-seven antipopes sought to seize the power of the papacy against the canonically elected pope. Usually these men were supported by (1) fractional or dissident groups of the faithful and clergy; (2) political, schismatic, or heretical groups; (3) the ruling barons or kings who demanded the right of investiture. The last antipope was Felix V (d. 1449), and the fact that the Church survived the disruptions and strife is evidence of her divine institution and mission.

## Anti-Semitism.

The psychological, social, and behavioral antagonism and hostility toward Jewish people and their organizations or businesses is anti-Semitism. It is a racist attitude, which like all racist attitudes is completely opposed to the Christian ideal of charity and the natural virtues of humanitarian relationships.

The Church has been historically accused of this attitude, but Pope Pius XI stated clearly the Catholic teaching: "Anti-Semitism is incompatible with the sublime ideas and truths expressed in this text. We Christians can take no part in anti-Semitism. We acknowledge that everyone has the right to defend himself, in other words to take necessary precautions for his protection against everything that threatens his legitimate interests. But anti-Semitism is inadmissible. We are spiritually Semites."

Vatican II was followed by several pronouncements that more specifically clarified the Catholic position. This was acknowledged by a statement of Rabbi M. H. Tanenbaum, National Director of Inter-religious Affairs in December, 1969: "The Vatican statement on Catholic-Jewish relations is undoubtedly one of the most perceptive, reconciling, and advanced pronouncements on Christian-Jewish relations that has been issued by any major worldwide Christian body in our lifetime.

"Building on the best elements contained in Vatican Council II's Declaration on Non-Christian Religions, and in the U.S. Catholic Bishops' Guidelines on Catholic-Jewish Relations, the latest policy position of the Catholic Church surpasses these earlier texts in that it overcomes some heretofore ambiguous and tentative formulations and takes clearcut and forthright positive stands on each of the critical issues on the agenda of Jewish-Christian Relations—namely, the permanent validity of Judaism as a source of ultimate truth and value; the exclusion of proselytization and conversion of Jews; the explicit condemnation of anti-Semitism and a call for the correction of those religious teachings which feed anti-Semitism; and the unprecedented public confession of responsibility for past persecutions of Jews by Christians for which the Church asks pardon of their Jewish brothers. . . ."

## Antistes

This Latin (from the Greek meaning "overseer") title is often applied in history or in prayers as a prefatory term of honor of a bishop or prelate.

## Antitrinitarians

Antitrinitarians is the name given to those who hold and promote the heretical teaching that denies the three Persons of the Trinity. The Arians were so named in the early history of the Church; more recently, the Socinians and Unitarians.

## Antitype

Through interpretation and a recognition of the economy of Scripture and the wish of God that both the OT and the NT together present a fullness of teaching, we find that persons, things, and events of the OT signify persons, things, or events in the NT. It is the typological or mystical sense of Scripture. Thus persons, things, or events as described in the early writing are the *types,* whereas the persons, things, or events they signify in the later writing are antitypes. Discovery of these continues through interpretation, but they were always present in Scripture, placed there by God through inspiration.

## Antwerp Bible

This six-volume polyglot Bible was published in Antwerp, Belgium, in 1573 by the Plantin Press.

## Apocalypse

The last book of the NT is entitled "The Apocalypse of St. John the Apostle." The word "apocalypse" means *an unveiling* and indicates that the writing is classed as prophetic. It is also declared that it is "of" St. John, i.e., written by St. John. There has been some dispute over whether St. John was the author, but internal evidence, the method of its outline, and other numerous factors indicate without doubt that he was the writer. The book itself is difficult to interpret since it contains teaching, instructions, direct and indirect prophecy, visions, and all are presented in symbolical language. It is divided into three parts: a prologue, the main book itself, and an epilogue. Its single theme is the final triumph of Christ in an antichrist world and the assurance of resurrection in Christ for those who are faithful. This book is now called "The Book of Revelation" in most Bibles including the most recent Catholic translations. (See Revelation, Book of.)

## Apocalyptic Number

A mystical number, especially 666 as stated in Revelation 13:18, is the "number of the beast." It was an ancient practice to have the letters of the Greek or Hebrew alphabets stand for a number (thus $A = 1$). Using this formula, a name could be stated as the sum of its letters, as the name of Jesus in Greek amounted to 888. The number 666 is explained thus: 777 being the perfect number and 888 meaning Christ or each unit of 7 augmented by 1, then 666, or each unit lessened by 1, was that of Antichrist. In the derived name then, it could be the sum of Nero. However, the number, apart from the many conjectures, might stand for any "Antichrist" or anyone who in time would stand

against Christ. This is a condemned form of numerology that has no place in the Christian understanding of the message of Christ.

## Apocatastasis

This term from the Greek means "reconciliation" or "restoration" of all things in Christ. It is applied to the false teaching that in the end all men will be saved or their state restored as though there were no consequence to the goodness or evil of their lives.

## Apocreos

In the Greek rite apocreos is that day when meat may be eaten for the last time before the Lenten season.

## Apocrisiarius

This title of a legate to the court of an emperor was used from the fourth to the ninth centuries.

## Apocrypha

The meaning of the word is "hidden" and thus *apocrypha* has been applied to a number of writings of spurious or at least doubtful relation to Christian thought. As applied by the Church, *apocrypha* means that body of writings on religious matters that are outside of the canon of Scripture and that are not inspired but at one time claimed the authority of Scripture. In Protestant circles the term is used to denote those books that Catholics hold to be canonical and inspired. The Catholic use of the word includes all uncanonical writings, of uncertain origin, which were written anonymously or under the assumed name of some Apostle or church leader. The Protestants call these writings *Pseudepigrapha.*

The term *apocrypha* was originally applied to writings of the first centuries, which held "secret" teachings for the initiate. Later, when the heretics were putting out their "secret" writings and claiming authorship by patriarchs, prophets, or apostles, the term became, among Christian writers, one of disdain. Finally, it was applied to Jewish and Christian writings that were written in the first centuries but were judged to be outside the canon. There are apocrypha of the OT that are broadly grouped under three headings: apocalyptic, historical, and didactic; these number more than twenty-eight, some of which are pre-Christian. The apocrypha of the NT are gospels, acts, epistles, apocalypses, and the *agrapha.* In all, these number more than forty. These writings though spurious still contain value: notably in the historical knowledge they offer, in the inducement they give to appreciation of the genuine Scriptures, and in the insight they afford into the early doctrinal disputes and the items the early followers found important. From a theological standpoint they are of slight value.

## Apodeipnon

The final daily part of the Greek Breviary is the apodeipnon.

## Apodosis

In the Greek Church apodosis is the final day of prayer commemorating a feast day.

## Apollinarianism

This heresy was advanced by Apollinarius the younger, bishop of Laodicea in the fourth century. It taught that Christ had a human body and a human sensitive soul but not a rational soul, thus that Christ's human nature was incomplete. The heresy was condemned by the first Council of Constantinople in A.D. 381, and disappeared in the early part of the fifth century. (See Monophysitism.)

## Apologetics

Originally this meant any apology (defense) of the reasonableness of any revealed religion. It is now that branch of the science of theology called "fundamental theology," which is a division of dogmatic theology whose special field is to prove religious truth has been revealed. Its object is that revelation has been made by God and that the Catholic faith is that revelation. More broadly, apologetics has been inclusive of all writings and investigations in science, history, and Scripture, which have defended or explained the truth of Catholic teaching. It has progressed as a study that seeks to prepare for a response to God through acceptance of the writings of revelation, the role of the Church in the work of salvation, the means of giving credibility to the facts which support faith, and the justification of belief through faith. (Cf. Church; Faith.)

## Apologist

This title of honor was given in the early days of the Church to writers among the fathers who defended the Church and its teachings. Now it is applied to one versed in fundamental theology, or one who teaches, speaks, or writes in defense or clarification of the teachings and practices of the Church.

## Apology or Apologia

Literally a writing in defense of a teaching, an apology is often also a "vindication" wherein one presents a reasoned viewpoint e.g. the "Apologia" of John Cardinal Newman.

## Apolusia

In Eastern rites the washing of those about to be baptized, the apolusia, is performed eight days before administration of the sacrament. During the eight days of preparation those so washed wear white garments as a mark of their catechumenate.

## Apolysis

The apolysis is the final blessing given in the Greek Church, either that at the end of Mass or after reciting certain parts of the Divine Office.

## Apolytikion

Apolytikion is the final prayer or hymn, spoken or sung at the conclusion of Mass, Matins, or Vespers, in the Greek Church.

## Apostasy

In the early Church this meant the going over permanently to paganism, the rejection, after an initial acceptance and baptism, of the graces of the faith (Heb. 6:1–8). Now apostasy is defined as the complete repudiation of the faith of the Church by one who has been baptized (c. 1325, 2). It is a grievous sin since it is a denial of the truth of God and the Church. One who so acts is called an apostate. Also this term is applied as apostasy from religious life, which is the unauthorized departure from his place of assignment by one in perpetual vows who does not intend to return (c. 644). (Cf. Secularism.)

## Apostle

An apostle is literally "one sent." In the Church the Apostles are the twelve men originally chosen by Christ to be the bearers of His teachings to the world. It was Christ who first called them "Apostles" (Lk. 6:13). The Hebrew word *"saliah,"* which is the translation for the word *apostle,* means "one who is entrusted to fulfill a task, acting in the name of the sender." Thus an Apostle is one who gives witness to the truth of Christ, His resurrection, and ascension. Before Pentecost the Apostles received the teaching, and thereafter they gave the teaching as from Him who sent them. They are referred to as twelve by our Lord. St. Peter defined an apostle as one who is "witness with us of His Resurrection" (Acts 1:21–22). They are listed as follows: Simon Peter, Andrew, James the greater (son of Zebedee), John the brother of James, Philip, Bartholomew, Matthew, Thomas, James the Less (son of Alpheus), Thaddeus (or Jude), Simon the Cananaan, and Matthias, elected to replace Judas Iscariot (Acts 1:23–26). The title is also given to St. Paul and to St. Barnabas. To the Apostles were entrusted the teachings of Christ, the jurisdiction and the authority to found and further the Church of Christ. They were the first bishops, and their successors, the bishops of the Church today, receive their fullness of authority to teach the faith directly from them. Also certain men who were the first missioners or founders of the true religion in certain countries or places are called apostles of that country or place. (Cf. Apostolic Succession; Apostolic Ministry.)

### Apostles' Creed

This prayer, in the form of a profession of faith, contains twelve articles or fundamental doctrines. It is true that even in apostolic times, a profession of faith was required of persons before receiving baptism (Acts 8:36–37). Its name is not because of the fact that it was written by the Apostles, but it is so called because it is a summary of apostolic teaching. Its present form is an extension of a form used in apostolic times. This is evident from similarities found in its expression by very early writers such as Irenaeus and Clement. (See Nicene Creed.)

The Apostles' Creed reads:

I believe in God, the Father almighty,
Creator of heaven and earth;
And in Jesus Christ, His only Son, Our Lord,
Who was conceived by the Holy Spirit,
Born of the Virgin Mary,
Suffered under Pontius Pilate,
Was crucified, died, and was buried.
He descended into hell;

The third day he rose again from the dead;
He ascended into heaven,
Sits at the right hand of God, the Father almighty;
From thence he shall come to judge
The living and the dead.
I believe in the Holy Spirit,
the holy Catholic Church;
the communion of saints,
the forgiveness of sins,
the resurrection of the body,
and life everlasting. Amen.

### Apostles of Places, Peoples

Nations, territories, and peoples have chosen or been assigned certain saints as their patrons, and such a listing is called in general *The Apostles of Places.* They are much like the patron saints who have been selected for countries. This list is as follows:

Alps: St. Bernard of Menthon
Andalusia (Spain): St. John of Avila
Antioch: St. Barnabas
Armenia: St. Gregory the Illuminator; St. Bartholomew
Austria: St. Severine
Bavaria: St. Killian
Brazil: Jose Anchieta
California: Junipero Serra
Carinthia (Yugoslavia): St. Virgil
Colombia: St. Louis Bertran
Corsica: St. Alexander Sauli
Crete: St. Titus
Cyprus: St. Barnabas
Denmark: St. Ansgar
England: St. Augustine of Canterbury, St. Gregory the Great
Ethiopia: St. Frumentius
Finland: St. Henry
Florence: St. Andrew Corsini
France: St. Remigius, St. Martin of Tours, St. Denis
Friesland (Germany): St. Suitbert, St. Willibrord
Gaul: St. Irenaeus
Gentiles: St. Paul
Georgia (Russia): St. Nino
Germany: St. Boniface, St. Peter Canisius
Gothland (Sweden): St. Sigfrid
Guelderland (Holland): St. Plechelm
Highlanders (Scotland): St. Columba
Hungarians (Magyars): St. Stephen, King, St. Gerard, Bl. Astricus
India: St. Thomas, Apostle
Indies: St. Francis Xavier

Ireland: St. Patrick
Iroquois: Francois Picquit
Italy: St. Bernardine of Siena
Japan: St. Francis Xavier
Malta: St. Paul
Mexico: The twelve Apostles of Mexico (Franciscans), headed by Fra. Martin de Valencia
Negro Slaves: St. Peter Claver
Netherlands: St. Willibrord
Northumbria (Britain): St. Aidan
Norway: St. Olaf
Ottawas (Indians): Fr. Claude Allouez
Persia: St. Maruthas
Poland: St. Hyacinth
Portugal: St. Christian
Prussia (Slavs): St. Adelbert, St. Bruno of Querfurt
Rome: St. Philip Neri
Rumania: St. Nicetas
Ruthenia: St. Bruno
Sardinia: St. Ephesus
Saxony: St. Willihad
Scandinavia (North): St. Ansgar
Scotland: St. Palladius
Slavs: Sts. Cyril and Methodius, St. Adalbert
Spain: St. James, Sts. Euphrasius and Felix
Sweden: St. Ansgar
Switzerland: St. Andeol
Tournai (Belgium): St. Eligius, St. Piaton

## Apostles, Teaching of the Twelve

See Didache.

## Apostleship of Prayer

The League of the Sacred Heart is a pious association founded at Vals, France, in 1844 by Francis Xavier Gautrelet, S.J. Its object is to promote prayer and devotion to the Sacred Heart and join the prayers of members in a single monthly intention. It serves in the United States to aid local centers of devotion in parishes, schools, and homes. Its publication is the *Messenger of the Sacred Heart* and *Monthly Leaflet,* which promote the daily offering.

## Apostolate

The broad area of service within the Church, known as the apostolate, extends to many undertakings. The term was generally applied to the pious works and participation of the laity in the ministerial, social, cultural, diocesan, parochial, evangelistic, and educational programs of the Church. However, the apostolate applies to everyone according to his talents, abilities, and the

activity by which that person seeks to carry out the mission of Christ and His Church in the world. The many aspects of apostolic activity are under the direction of the bishop. Vatican II stated: "In virtue of this power (as vicars of Christ), bishops have the sacred right and duty before the Lord to make laws for their subjects, to pass judgment on them, and to moderate everything pertaining to the ordering of worship and the apostolate" (LG 27).

Thus the apostolate is the work of both the individual as person and a member of the Mystical Body of Christ, and as a member of the organized Church and the wide community of the faithful. As Vatican II declared: "It is not enough for the Christian people to be present and organized in a given.nation. Nor is it enough for them to carry out an apostolate of good example. They are organized and present for the purpose of announcing Christ to their non-Christian fellow-citizens by word and deed, and of aiding them toward the full reception of Christ" (AG 15).

## Apostolate of Suffering

This pious association was founded in Milwaukee, Wisconsin, in 1926, to teach to the sick, invalids, and shut-ins the moral value of suffering, and to promote the offering of sufferings for the spiritual good of all.

## Apostolic Canons

The apostolic canons are teachings claimed to have been dictated by the Apostles to St. Clement of Rome. They are attached to the eight books of the Apostolic Constitutions and contain regulations pertaining to ecclesiastical persons. They cannot be ascribed to the Apostles and have no substantial doctrinal value.

## Apostolic Constitutions

1. Eight books, it was claimed, were written down by St. Clement of Rome at the dictation of the apostles. They are spurious in this claim and date from the fourth century. They were largely compiled from other writings of the time.

2. Apostolic or papal constitution is a document through which the Holy Father enacts or promulgates laws concerning the faithful.

3. Formal documents of doctrinal or pastoral teachings are binding on the entire Church and are issued by an Ecumenical Council. There were four issued by Vatican II: On the Church; liturgy; revelation; and the Church in the modern world.

## Apostolic Datary

The apostolic datary is now a lesser branch of the Roman Curia, though it formerly was the office for handling and countersigning all papal documents and granting favors such as benefices. Since Pope St. Pius X revised procedures, the Datary has the supervision of the conferring of nonconsistorial or minor benefices that are reserved to the Holy See. Its staff is a commission of three theologians presided over by the Cardinal Datary of the Pope.

## Apostolic Delegate

An apostolic delegate is a representative of the Vatican who has no diplomatic standing since he is not appointed to deal with the government of a country. Instead this delegate treats with the hierarchy of the country of his appointment in the supervision of ecclesiastical business and Church announcements of new bishops. Delegates are themselves usually bishops. The United States has an apostolic delegate residing in Washington, D.C.; this delegation was established in 1893. At present there are twenty-three countries with such delegates. (Cf. Nuncio.)

## Apostolic Fathers

The apostolic fathers are the Christian writers of the first and second centuries whose writings were at one time considered as possibly belonging to the canon of Scripture but were classed as apocrypha. These do, however, constitute a body of scholars and writers who were so named in the seventeenth century because of the accumulation of doctrinal matters that they recorded. Although several others might be included, six known by name are: Barnabas, a teacher of Alexandria who lived in the late first century and early second; St. Clement of Rome, first century; St. Ignatius of Antioch, first century; St. Polycarp of Smyrna, d. 156; Hermas, early second century; and St. Papias, early second century.

## Apostolic Indulgences

These are indulgences attached to religious articles when blessed by the Holy Father or by the person he so authorizes. The articles should, if possible, be carried on one's person or be kept in a suitable place and the prescribed prayers should be recited.

## Apostolic Ministry

Only the bishops have by ordination and office the role of apostle and the prime responsibility for the functions of teaching, sanctifying, and guiding the people of God. In Vatican II this was given exceptional study and emphasis. Pope Paul VI in the opening address (Sept. 4, 1964) noted that the Council ". . . is . . . particularly concerned to describe the prerogatives of the bishop and accord them full honor."

The bishops, the episcopacy, belong singularly and exclusively to the sphere of ministerial sharing in the action of Christ, for the bishop is the living, sensible, effective, and preeminent sign of Christ in His threefold function of teacher, sanctifier, and priest. The bishop is both a sign and an instrument: "Living instruments of Christ the eternal priest" (PO 12b/558). The Constitution on the Church teaches that "bishops in an eminent and visible way undertake Christ's own role as Teacher, Shepherd, and High Priest and that they act in His Person" (LG 21d/42).

Vatican II also declares: "In order that the mission assigned to them might continue after their death, they [the apostles] passed on to their immediate cooperators, as a kind of testament, the duty of perfecting and consolidating the work begun by themselves, charging them to attend to the whole flock in which the Holy Spirit placed them to shepherd the Church of God (cf. Acts 20:28). They therefore appointed such men, and authorized the arrangement that, when these men should have died, other approved men would take up their ministry" (LG 20). And: "Now Before freely giving His life for the world, the Lord Jesus so arranged the ministry of the apostles and so promised to send the Holy Spirit, that both they and the Spirit were to be associated in effecting the work of salvation always and everywhere" (AG 4). (See Ministries.)

## Apostolic See

1. Sometimes a see founded and ruled by one of the apostles was named an apostolic see, but now it refers to Rome, the see city of the pope, which he rules as bishop of the diocese of Rome. The name is also loosely applied to the Vatican.

2. This term is also applied to the pope himself together with the official governing bodies of the Church's central administration in the Vatican, the branches of the Roman Curia, which act only under the authority of the pope.

## Apostolic Signatura

Dating back to the thirteenth century, this was an important court and office handling papal affairs. Today, its full title is the "Supreme Tribunal of the Apostolic Signature," and it is a supreme court acting as a court of appeal from the decisions of the

Roman Rota, especially those cases appealed because of defective juridical procedures. It is made up of six cardinals under a cardinal prefect and minor officials. It is the supreme court of the State of Vatican City.

## Apostolic Succession

The sequence of apostolic succession follows from the apostles themselves down to the bishops of the present time. This is marked by (1) lawful, valid ordination conferred on bishops of the Church; (2) the giving over or delegating directly the powers entrusted to the Apostles of ordaining, ruling, and teaching, which were given by Christ to the Apostles; (3) the historic and scriptural truth that the Apostles did confer this power on others; (4) the intrinsic truth that the Church in all ages could not have preserved its identity and unity as intended by Christ ("I am with you all days, even to the consummation of the world") unless there were a giving over of such powers to others who would carry on the work of Christ's Church; (5) the pope, who is the successor of St. Peter in Rome.

"The apostles, handing on what they themselves had received warn the faithful to hold fast to the traditions which they have learned either by word of mouth or by letter (cf. 2 Thes. 2:15), and to fight in defence of the faith handed on once and for all (cf. Jude 3)" (DV 7).

## Apostolic Union

Apostolic union is an association of diocesan clergy who live a rule directed to their religious life, assist mutually in the duties and effectiveness of their ministry, and aid their work by conferences. It was begun in the seventeenth century in Bavaria by Venerable B. Holzhauser and was commended by Pope St. Pius X who became a member.

## Apostolicae Curae

Apostolicae Curae is the title of the papal bull of Pope Leo XIII, in 1896, on the validity of Anglican orders.

## Apostolici

This name was given to a group of followers of the Gnostic heresy who pretended to imitate the Apostles by absolutely renouncing the world; e.g., they rejected marriage as a sacrament. Other like groups with a similar name have arisen from time to time, most claiming all material goods to be evil and impure.

## Apostolicity

This mark of the Church sets the Church apart as that founded by Christ directly upon His Apostles. It is seen through the *mission* of the Church in being sent, through the Apostles and their successors, to teach and baptize all men in Christ's name; it further is recognized as a mark in the *doctrine*, which has been preserved throughout all time by the Church, and her infallible prerogative. (Cf. Apostolic Succession; Marks of the Church.)

## Apostolicus

This seldom used word originated in the eleventh century and applied to the Holy Father.

## Apostolos

The apostolos and the evangelion are two books in which the Gospels, Acts of the Apostles, and the Epistles are arranged according to the order of their reading in the liturgy and Divine Office of the religious calendar in the Byzantine rite.

## Apparel or Paratura

This piece of colored brocade or other rich material, usually the same color as the vestments, was attached to the neckband edge of the amice and could be removed when washing the amice. It served to form a collar on the vested cleric. The apparel is also the edging on an alb. Though still worn in some places, as Milan and Spain, it is not recognized for liturgical use.

## Apparition

An apparition is a vision or supernatural manifestation that God permits and that thus is seen by the person witnessing. It may be called corporeal; that is, it strikes the senses as reality, or it may be sensible, that is, appearing real because of luminous qualities. In both these senses it is not to be considered as a ghost or preternatural manifestation, but is rather of a mystical nature as arising from God.

These are not to be accepted as articles of faith, even though the Church has approved certain appearances and honors them with feasts or celebrations. The major approved apparitions of the Blessed Virgin Mary are as follows: (1) Banneux, Belgium in 1933; (2) Beauraing, Belgium, Nov. 29, 1932 to Jan. 3, 1933; (3) Fatima, Portugal, May 13, 1917 to Oct. 13, 1917, six appearances; (4) Guadalupe, Mexico, four appearances in 1531 to Juan Diego; (5) Knock, Ireland, Aug. 21, 1879; (6) La Salette, France, Sept. 19, 1846; (7) Lourdes, France, 18 appearances between Feb. 11, and July 16, 1858; (8) Paris, France, Our Lady of the Miraculous Medal, three appearances in 1830.

There are many apparitions, both corporeal and incorporeal, recorded in the Bible: e.g., Tb. 3:16–17; Lk. 1:11–26; Acts 8:26; Gn. 26:24; Ez. 1–3; Dn. 8:15–18; and Acts 9:10.

## Appeal

In canon law, an appeal is recourse to a superior court from an inferior court in a case of justice. It is judicial when the appeal is made from the sentence of a judge sitting in a court. It is extrajudicial when the appeal is from the injurious action of a superior in a question of rights. It does not imply injustice in the sentence rendered but rather a correction of the decision upon the entry of new facts into the testimony. There can be no appeal from a decision of the pope, because as Vicar of Christ he has no recognized superior.

## Appellant Controversy

A quarrel arose in England over the appointment of an archpriest by the crown after the death of Cardinal Allen in the late sixteenth century. The controversy was terminated in 1602 by a papal bull, but resentment followed for many years. There were thirty-one priests who made the initial appeal, and they were called "appellants." The final settlement in 1603 was made through the signing of a "Pledge of Allegiance."

## Appellants

This name was given to a group of French clergy who, under Cardinal deNoailles and four bishops, appealed to a future general council against a papal constitution condemning Jansenistic writings in 1713.

## Appetite

The inclination of a being to seek its proper end or perfection is an appetite. Used in a specific sense it means the inclination or seeking of any faculty or power of man of the proper object: thus, the eye is inclined to see. In spiritual language, it may mean the desire of the Good (God) taking precedence over the natural inclination to evil because of original sin.

There is also the sense appetite, the organic, which seeks the satisfaction of the senses and is called concupiscible and irascible. The emotions are such appetites. There is also the rational appetite that is really the judgment of reason in man over his sense appetites.

## Appropriation

In theology, appropriation is the attributing of one quality, name, or operation to a single Person of the Holy Trinity. This does not mean that the other Persons of the Trinity do not possess these qualities, names, or operations, since all three possess all in an infinite degree. It is a manner of human reference on our part, e.g., referring to Christ as the "God of Love." (Cf. Trinity, the Most Holy.)

## Apse

In church architecture the apse is the semicircular, vaulted end of the church building in the center of which the altar is placed. This was found in the tribunals of fourth-century Rome and was where the judges sat. Later when adapted to church use, it became the place where the bishop's chair was placed. Improperly the sanctuary is sometimes referred to as the apse, probably because an apse often contains the sanctuary, and today may be either square, polygonal, or semicircular and need not be vaulted.

In the architecture being developed for new Church structures there has been a change from the historical styles. Now the "apse" may be looked upon as no more than the space where the altar table is set up, together with the area where the actions of reading, preaching, and sacrifice take place. Thus, the architecture that looks to the area called the sanctuary in building design designates this "space" as useful and as satisfying the needs of the worship area as separate from the community area. (Cf. Synaxis; Community.)

## Apsidiole, also Apsidiale

An apsidiole is a small apse or a lesser apse on either side of the main apse of a church, sometimes forming small chapels or places for side altars. It is now considered only in the newer churches that might have a chapel of reposition.

## Aquamanile

Rarely used today, aquamanile was an early name for the basin in which the water is poured when the priest washes his hands in the celebration of Mass.

## Aquarians

Aquarians were a sect of the second-century Gnostics who held that the use of wine in the Mass was sinful.

## Aquileian Rite

An early liturgy of the fourth century was

developed in the province of Aquileia but abandoned in the thirteenth century in preference for the Roman or Latin liturgy.

## Aramaic

The earliest liturgical language of the Church was Aramaic. It was the language spoken in Palestine, the northwest Semitic language; Hebrew and biblical Aramaic are dialects of Canaanite and true Aramaic; it was in use from the Babylonian captivity until apostolic times. Christ spoke Aramaic. Along with Hebrew and Greek, it is one of the three languages of the Bible.

## Arca

An arca was a box in which the early Christians kept the Eucharist in their homes, thus an early tabernacle. Now sometimes referred to as a place where special offerings are kept.

## Arcani, Discipline

See Discipline of the Secret.

## Archaeology, Christian

This branch of the science of archaeology studies, investigates, explores, and judges the remains of early Christian monuments, including literature, objects of art, and inscriptions. It is interested not only in the discovery of early records and their classification but also in the scientific cataloging and the integration of such Christian records into the entire historic record of the science of archaeology.

A special part of this science is the study of monuments of the past that contribute to knowledge of the Bible. This in particular examines sites and artifacts, such as pottery and weapons, by which the dates of biblical happenings may be determined. Also of great advantage to scholars has been the discovery of the Dead Sea Scrolls, the most valuable of which is the complete text of the

Book of Isaiah. This biblical archaeology continues and much work has yet to be completed. (See Scrolls of the Dead Sea.)

## Archaeology, Commission of Sacred

The Commission of Sacred Archaeology, one of the papal commissions of study, was founded in 1852 by Pope Pius IX. Its purpose is to promote the exploration and study of the Roman catacombs, the excavations of the Vatican, and to care for the museums of Vatican State. It was this commission that supervised the excavations beneath St. Peter's Basilica to unearth the tomb of the first pope.

## Archangel

The angels of a high order, the archangels, are specially mentioned in the Bible. Tradition lists four: Michael, Raphael, Gabriel, and some include Uriel. (See Angel.)

## Archbishop

This title, used in the Western Church from the ninth century, is given to a bishop who governs one or more dioceses that form an ecclesiastical province. As such he presides over the metropolitan see, which is usually that of the principal city of the territory. Bishops of other dioceses within the province are called suffragan bishops; their dioceses are suffragan sees. The title archbishop may be *titular,* and then the archbishop is not known as a metropolitan. An archbishop has a wider jurisdiction, having the right to summon provincial councils (of the suffragans), and serving as an appeal court to the suffragan sees. The office of archbishop is marked by the *pallium* with which he is invested by the Holy See, and by the "cross with double bar" or archiepiscopal cross. Archbishop is the title of a bishop who has jurisdiction over an archdiocese. There are also *archbishops ad personam,* which is the title of honor and distinction given to some although they do not have jurisdiction over an archdiocese.

## Archconfraternity

An archconfraternity is an association of confraternities or sodalities established in many places. Enjoying certain privileges over and above those of the confraternity or sodality, it is a special affiliation of confraternities sanctioned by the Church. Most prominent among the archconfraternities are those of: the Blessed Sacrament, the Holy Name Society, and the Christian Mothers. (Cf. Confraternity.)

## Archdeacon

In the early Church an archdeacon was a deacon appointed by the bishop to assist him in certain jurisdictional details. Some abuses arose, and the office was abolished upon the demand that the deacon take the order of priesthood. Today it does not exist as a rank in the Church, and the work of aiding the bishop is done by the vicar-general and vicars-forane of the diocese.

## Archdiocese

The territory, ecclesiastical province of jurisdiction, governed by an archbishop is an archdiocese. (Cf. Jurisdiction; Province.)

## Archiepiscopal Cross, also Patriarchal Cross

An archiepiscopal cross has two cross-bars. Its upper bar is shorter and is part of the coat-of-arms of an archbishop. Mounted on a long staff, it is carried before the archbishop in processions. (See Cross.)

## Archimandrite

The superior of a monastery in the Oriental Churches is an Archimandrite. This is also an honorary title of a chancery official of certain oriental Churches.

## Architecture

The ecclesiastical design and erection of Catholic and Christian buildings received its greatest impetus in the eleventh century, although it dates back to the fourth century. The first phase followed the edict of Constantine (A.D. 313) and was adapted from Roman and Greek building. It is known as the Latin or Basilican. The progress then was through the Byzantine, the Romanesque, Gothic, Renaissance, which followed the styles of the several countries, thence to the Baroque or Rococo, and finally to the modern revival, which is chiefly Gothic but with various adaptations. In the

twentieth century there is an emphasis upon a departure from the traditional to a more functional design, centering on liturgical simplicity and marked by the uses of new materials, such as concrete. In the eleventh century, architecture broadened to include the allied religious arts, as mosaics, bronze work, enamel work, stained glass, and woodwork. Ecclesiastical architecture extends to churches, monasteries, convents, chapels, bell towers and, less properly, schools and some hospitals.

Since Vatican II a great emphasis has been placed on the Church as a place where the liturgy is celebrated. "When churches are to be built, let great care be taken that they be suitable for the celebration of liturgical services and for the active participation of the faithful" (SC 124). The present thinking is to make the place of the liturgy reflect the nature of the event taking place within and to show concern for the assembly of people and for the best manner of accommodating them for hearing the Word and the mystery of the eucharistic celebration. Thus, the architecture of the present and future will differ greatly from that of the past styles and the rigid forms of eclectic selection. Rather the modern church will concentrate on "sacred space" adaptable to the liturgy and the convenient participation of the assembly. It will have an emphasis on creating an environment both beautiful and dignified but also expressive of the coming together of the eucharistic community. (Cf. Community.)

## Archives

The term archives is used for both the place and the contents. The contents are records pertaining to the spiritual and temporal affairs of the Church; as place, it means where such records are kept. The archives may be *diocesan* or *papal*. They are maintained under lock because of the nature of the documents; the chancellor of the diocese has the key, and permission of the bishop or of both the vicar-general and the chancellor is needed for admission. Canon law requires that a catalogue or index be kept of all documents.

## Archivist

The chancellor of a diocese, or the one who has care of the archives of a diocese, is the archivist.

## Archpriest

1. Formerly archpriest was a title conferred on one who took the place of the bishop in civil affairs or public worship. Now it is applied to a *dean*.

2. The priest who assists the newly ordained

priest at his first Mass or who assists at the Solemn Mass of major prelates is an archpriest. As such he is vested in a cope.

### Arcosolium

An arcosolium is an arched recess over the sepulcher of one buried in the catacombs. Within this arched area, Mass was celebrated on the stone slab above the tomb.

### Arculae

The small boxes used for carrying the Blessed Sacrament in the early persecutions of the Church were arculae. They were also a primitive form of the pyx. (Cf. Arca.)

### Areopagite

This name was applied to one who practiced or spoke in the outdoor court of Areopagus, located on a hill near Athens. It is sometimes applied to St. Paul because of his speaking in Athens as recorded in Acts 17:16–31, which is called his "areopagus speech."

### Argia

Literally inactivity, but argia in Church usage applied to the refraining from servile work on Sundays and holy days and to other practices of a spiritual nature.

### Arianism

This heresy was condemned at the Council of Nicaea in 325. It took its name from Arius, a priest of Alexandria who was trained at Antioch. The heresy was probably based in part on Judaism, Eclecticism, and Sophism. It taught that the Son of God is not of one nature or substance with God the Father, nor equal to Him in dignity and not co-eternal. Historically this caused a number of disputes over the teachings of the Church and set a precedent for civil authorities to interfere in church affairs.

### Ariel

This name was given to a part of the city of Jerusalem (Is. 29:1), meaning "hearth of God." Ariel is also a group of the tribe of Gad (Gn. 46:16).

### Ark

1. The boat built by Noah at the time of the flood (Gn. 6), was later cited as a type of the Church (1 Pt. 3:20-21).
2. Sometimes ark referred to the basket in

which Moses was placed after being born, which was found by Pharaoh's daughter (Ex. 2:1–22).

3. The "Ark of the Covenant" (Ex. 37:1–9) was a chest of acacia wood overlaid with gold within and without. Its cover was of pure gold and was the place of propitiation on which the blood of the sacrificial victims was sprinkled on the Feast of Atonement. The ark contained the Decalogue, a lasting testimony of the Sinaitic covenant; it was also to serve as the throne of Yahweh. Ark of the Covenant is a title given to the Blessed Virgin to signify her divine motherhood.

### Arles, Councils of

The first of these councils of the Church assembled in this city of southern France in 314 to settle the Donatist dispute. Later there were seventeen more councils convened there, the last in 1273. (See Donatism.)

### Armageddon

Mentioned in Rv. 16:13–16 Armageddon is the place where the beast and the false prophet will meet in final combat with Christ. The location is identified as the "mountain of Mageddo," which was in the plain of Esdraelon; the plain was vulnerable to attack in Jewish history, especially with the forces descending from Mageddo.

### Armagh, Book of

Named after the Irish legendary Queen, this book is on vellum dating from the eighth or ninth century. It is a collection of documents and writings, among which are two lives of St. Patrick, a text on the life of St. Martin of Tours written by Sulpicius Severus, and a complete non-Vulgate text of the Latin NT books in this order: Matthew, Mark, John, and Luke. Also contained in Latin are the Pauline "Catholic" epistles, the Acts of the Apostles, and the Book of Revelation. The entire Book of Armagh is a work attributed to the scribe Ferdomnach of Armagh (d. 846). It is now at Trinity College in Dublin, and textual critics refer to it as the *"Codex Dublinensis."* (Cf. Codex.)

### Armenian Church

In Armenia, in northern Asia Minor, the Church was outstanding until the Council of Constantinople (381). After the defeat of the Armenians by the Persians in the seventh century, the people gave way to heresies. At the time of Chalcedon (593), the Church was split; some followed Rome but the majority set up a separate church. Efforts for reconciliation have failed, so the Armenian Church as a separate group has cut itself off from communion with the Roman Church and has ever since been reputed monophysite. (See Armenian Rite.)

### Armenian Rite

The rite of the Armenian Church was originally in the Syriac language but is now in ancient Armenian. It is used by the Uniat and Gregorian churches, both separated from Rome. There are some 150,000 Armenians who are in communion with Rome, chiefly in West Germany and the United States. Where they are located, they are under the jurisdiction of the local bishop. Their celebration of the Eucharist is called a liturgy and is a single fixed ceremony that is very simple, but much of it follows the Byzantine rite. The Armenian Liturgy has five parts: (1) preparation prayers recited in the sacristy, (2) preparation prayers in the choir (there are many sung melodies), (3) preparation of the gifts at the altar of preparation, (4) the Mass of the Catechumens, (5) the Mass of the Faithful. The Catholic Armenian rite receives only under one species, bread, but the Uniat and Gregorian give communion under two species. (Cf. Byzantine Rite.)

### Art, Christian

The fine arts were used by the Church from earliest times. Their Christian character is found in their expression and in the use to which they are put in service of the Church. Many examples of primitive Christian art are found in the catacombs. From here more than any other place came the use of symbols that were both a religious and a "guarded" method of expression. Once the Christians were given freedom of worship, art became an expression in the decoration of churches and a method of teaching, since reading was enjoyed only by the scholars. It became the means of expressing Christian ideas and doctrines, in mosaics, paintings, stained glass, calligraphy, illumination of manuscripts, metalwork for vessels of the Mass, woodcarving, and textiles. It became a part of church architecture and centered around the doctrine and teaching of the Church. Later it allied with the whole of the fine arts, influencing writing, music, and sculpture as well as painting. It remains a part of the life of the Church, depicting the truths of faith. Art as such must be theologically sound in expression, because of its tradition, while at the same time it must be governed by dignity in approach. Esoteric forms have consistently been discouraged.

Vatican II stated: "Holy Mother Church has always been the friend of the fine arts and has continuously sought their noble ministry, with the special aim that all things set apart for use in divine worship should be truly worthy, becoming, and beautiful, signs and symbols of heavenly realities. For this purpose, too, she has trained artists. In fact, the Church has with good reason, always reserved to herself the right to pass judgment upon the arts, deciding which of the works of artists are in accordance with faith, piety, and cherished traditional laws, and thereby suited to sacred purposes" (SC 122).

Pope Pius XII in his encyclical *Mediator Dei* (1947) declared: "Modern art should be given free scope in the due and reverent service of the Church and the sacred rites." And Josef Jungman writes, "Church art is a profession of faith, just as public worship is a profession and proclamation" *(Pastoral Liturgy)*.

In keeping with the insights of Vatican II each diocese in the world is to establish a Commission on the Liturgy, including a committee to supervise the art and architecture as it affects the local church and the community of the faithful.

### Articles of Faith

See Dogma; also, Basic Teachings for Catholic Religious Education.

### Artoklasia

Artoklasia is the final service of Vespers in the Greek Church at which five loaves of bread and measures of wine and oil are blessed and incensed.

### Ascension of Christ

The Ascension was the "going up" into heaven of Christ by His own power, in the presence of the Apostles, the Blessed Mother, and His disciples, 40 days after His Resurrection (Acts 1:6–12). St. Thomas Aquinas asserts that He ascended, not indeed by the power proper to a natural body, but by the virtue proper to Him as God and by that which belongs to a blessed spirit. The feast commemorating the event was celebrated in the Church from earliest times. It is a holy day of obligation occurring 40 days after Easter.

The eight days, from the solemnity of the Ascension to the eve of Pentecost, are called Ascensiontide. The solemnity was not celebrated in the Church until the fourth century because traditionally it was a part of the paschal mystery, associated with the Resurrection. (Cf. Eph. 1:19–20.)

### Ascetae

Ascetae was the false teaching that through bodily exercise, discipline of the senses, and moral faculties of man, one could rise to spiritual heights; a form of Christian stoicism. It is paralleled today in the beliefs of Yoga and some tenets of Christian Science. The term also applies to followers of the practice, who held themselves to be

a group between the laity and the clergy, or semireligious. (Cf. Transcendental Meditation; Charismatic Renewal, Catholic.)

### Asceterion, also Ascetery

This name was given to a monastery or home for religious where they could retire for the practice of spiritual exercises, in some respects a retreat-house.

### Ascetical Theology

This branch of theology is strictly a part of moral theology, or an intermediate study between moral theology (the study of God's laws, and right and wrong acts) and mystical theology (the study of the extraordinary ways of perfection). Thus ascetical theology rises a step above moral theology and considers the methods by which we may make progress in the pursuit of perfection by study and practice of the ordinary means of self-discipline, prayer, and the sacraments, by which we bring ourselves gradually more in harmony with the will of God and progress to our end—personal salvation. It has been variously named: the science of the saints, the spiritual science, and the science of perfection. (Cf. Theology.)

### Asceticism

This term from the Greek means exercise or effort. It is the name given to the "science that deals with the efforts necessary to the acquisition of Christian perfection." It is the practice of principles learned through a study of ascetical theology.

It points to the practice, both moral and psychological, of spirituality or the performance of spiritual exercises through which one can acquire habits of virtue. The purpose of asceticism is the attaining of Christian perfection. It should not be confused with austerity, or the practice of denial as found in fasting. Rather it is a positive approach whereby the ideal of self-perfection, as found in Mt. 5:48, is sought through the application of natural means and virtues, such as chastity, charity, meekness, together with a desire to fulfill the will of God through reason raises one to a higher aspiration. As such asceticism may be cultivated by all persons.

### Aseity

Aseity is the characteristic of a being that exists by virtue of its own nature, independent of all else. It affirms absolute existence; it excludes any external causality. Aseity means a being whose existence proceeds from a nature that is in itself its own existence—thus, only God is such a being. It is the prime attribute of God from which we infer all other attributes, and it expresses the very essence of God.

## Ash Wednesday

In the present Church calendar Ash Wednesday is the first day of the observance of the 40 days of Lent. It takes its name from the solemn ceremony of the liturgy of the day wherein the ashes of palms or other suitable substances are blessed and then marked on the foreheads of the faithful in the form of a cross with the accompanying words, "Remember, man, you are dust and to dust you shall return." Or: "Repent, and believe the Good News." It is thus a solemn call to penance so that one may enjoy eternal life.

It was established as the first day of Lent by St. Gregory the Great (590 to 604). Pope Paul VI declared this moveable observance in the Church calendar to be a day of universal fasting and abstinence.

## Ashes

In the Church, ashes have been used according to the ancient symbolism of the scriptures where ashes were used to signify "worthlessness" (Jb. 30:19; Sir. 40:3), "sorrow" (Jb. 2:8; Jon. 3:6), grief and penance (Mt. 11:21), or a sign of affliction (Ps. 102:10). Today, however, ashes form a continuity from the mystery of Easter to the following Ash Wednesday when the palm branches blessed on Palm Sunday one year are burned, blessed, and signed on the foreheads of the faithful on the next Ash Wednesday. (Where palm branches are not available, another suitable material, such as dried branches or leaves, may be substituted.) Ashes are also used in the Catholic liturgy in the ceremonies for the dedication of a church and the consecration of altars. In the days of early Christians the practice of public penance was often performed in biblical imitation with the putting on of "sackcloth and ashes."

## Asperges

This term is applied to the blessing and sprinkling with holy water of the celebrant, clergy, and people by the celebrant before Mass. Its name is taken from the first words of Psalm 50. The sprinkling is done with an aspergillum while an antiphon or other appropriate song is sung. During the Easter season the antiphon *Vidi aquam* replaces the Psalm.

## Aspergillum

This instrument, with handle and hollow container for holy water, is used to sprinkle holy water during liturgical ceremonies, blessings, or consecrations. The aspergillum may be both sprinkler and water-containing instrument, or it may be a simple sprinkler carried, together with the holy water, in a bucket called an aspersory.

## Aspirations

Aspirations are short prayers expressing sentiments of charity or petition. Many aspirations are indulgenced, e.g., "My Jesus, mercy." (Cf. Ejaculation.)

## Assessor

A consultor to a judge in an ecclesiastical court is an assessor.

## Assistant Priest

1. This term is applied to any cleric who aids another priest in carrying out his ecclesiastical duties. Also it formerly applied to the curate, now the associate pastor, who was assigned to a parish to aid in the service of the faithful.
2. In liturgical functions the title is given to the chief clerical attendant of the bishop whenever the bishop presides at a liturgical function.
3. Prelates with pontifical privileges may also use an assistant priest.

## Associate Pastor

The title associate pastor is given to the priest assigned to a parish to assist the pastor. The title came into use following Vatican II as a mark of recognition of the dignity of the priesthood and to indicate that the "pastoral" or shepherd role of the pastor is shared equally in the care of souls. It replaces the title of curate or assistant priest. There may be one or more associate pastors in large urban parishes.

## Associations Law

Enacted in 1901 by the French government, the Associations Law forbade the forming of religious groups of men or women without an act of legislation by the civil government. As such it limited the Church and deprived it of rights. It became inoperative in 1928.

## Assumption of the Blessed Virgin Mary

The doctrine of the taking up of the body and soul of the Mother of God into heaven after her death was an early teaching of the fathers and of special interest to all Christians. Tradition and theological reasoning show that the privilege of the Assumption was revealed implicitly. On Nov. 1, 1950, Pope Pius XII declared the Assumption of the Blessed Mother of God a doctrine of faith. The solemnity is celebrated on Aug. 15 and is a holy day of obligation.

The feast was celebrated by the Christians of the seventh century, based on the Scriptures. In the OT, the singularity of the Blessed Mother as the "woman" was declared (cf. Gn. 3:15) as a being through whom the redemption would become fulfilled. The NT declares that redemption (Lk. 1; 1 Jn. 3:9) and the Blessed Virgin Mary was "full of grace" and could not be perfect as God foretold unless she remained incorruptible (cf. 1 Cor. 15:54–57). Pope Alexander III (1159 to 1181) wrote: "Mary conceived without detriment to her virginal modesty, brought forth her Son without pain, passed hence without decay, according to the word of the angel, or rather God speaking by the angel, that she might be shown to be full, not half-full, of grace."

## Asteriskos

In the Byzantine liturgy the support of the veil placed over the consecrated bread is made of two curved half-circles of gold and silver that form a double arch when spread. From the center of the crossed arches a gold star is suspened, thus the name asteriskos.

## Astrology

Astrology, the practice of attempting to determine actions by the influence of the stars on the bodies of men, is based on probabilities. But in no way can such prediction of the future be made, since the will of man is free. It was condemned in 1586 by Pope Sixtus V and by Urban VIII in 1631. Astrology is a pseudoscience, which attempts to assess as a fact the presumed influence of the stars and planets upon the lives of people. Predictions based upon such zodiac interpretations and the confluence of moons, stars, and planets are a form of fortune-telling that denies the free will of humans and preempts the providence of God, who alone knows the future.

## Asylum

Historically, an asylum was a place one could enter to escape harm or avoid pursuit from the law, also called *sanctuary*. Now it refers to an institution where dependents or orphans may be given the best of care and enjoy the benefits of social supervision until such time as placement may be made in a normal environment.

## Athanasian Creed

This approved expression of the beliefs of faith is said to have been written by St. Athanasius but was probably written by St. Ambrose, or revised by him. It is a summary of the Church's teachings concerning the Trinity, the Incarnation, and the Redemption. The Athanasian Creed is a part of the Liturgy of the Hours for the Solemnity of the Holy Trinity, and is also used in some other Christian Churches.

## Atheism

Atheism is the opinion that God does not exist. It can be a denial of God as a first cause, or the substitution of some lesser object in the place of God. Moral atheism holds that human acts have no morality with reference to a divine lawgiver; this is sometimes called practical atheism. Vatican II stated: "In her loyal devotion to God and men, the Church has already repudiated and cannot cease repudiating, sorrowfully but as firmly as possible, those poisonous doctrines and actions which contradict reason and the common experience of humanity, and dethrone man from his native excellence.

"Still she strives to detect in the atheistic mind the hidden causes for the denial of God" (GS 21).

And: "Undeniably, those who willfully shut out God from their hearts and try to dodge religious questions are not following the dictates of their consciences. Hence they are not free of blame" (GS 19).

## Atonement

Through His Incarnation, suffering, and death on the cross, Christ reconciled sinners to God. Atonement was the essential element of the redemption of mankind by Christ. This was the promise of God the Father who reconciled humanity to Himself through His divine Son, and Christ by His perfect obedience gave back to His Father the worship that was violated by sin. Christ is thus the Mediator of men because He won for Himself the glory to which He was destined by the Father, and also pardon for men. Through Christ we have remission of sins, reconciliation with God, the graces of salvation and justification (2 Cor. 5:18f). Also we are all loved in Christ from all eternity by God who has chosen us (Cf. Eph. 1:4).

### Atonement, Day of
The highest of the Jewish holy days called *Yom Kippur*, or Day of Atonement, is held on the tenth day after Rosh Hashana. The prescriptions of the strict fast and its observance are found in Lv. 16, but it was only later in the history of the Israelites that the day came to be observed on the one day, combining many of the sacred observances. It is called the "autumn fast" in Acts 27:9.

### Attention
Attention is the directing of our mind and senses to the accomplishment of some task that is undertaken. In a spiritual sense, it is the care we have in prayer, the receiving and administering of the sacraments. Thus in vocal prayer, we should say the prayers with correct pronunciation so that we may be led to think of what the words mean; in mental prayer we should concentrate on the subject of our meditation without distraction so that the most beneficial affections or response may be aroused; and in the reception or administering of the sacraments we should be aware without distraction so that there may be no mistake and that our intention may be of the highest order.

### Attributes of God
Everything that distinguishes God from His creatures may be called an attribute of God. The Jews placed emphasis on three attributes of God, majesty, spirituality, and holiness. However, we mean more basic concepts that arise out of the understanding of God's nature by reason when we speak of His attributes. God's essence is one with His existence (cf. Aseity). His attributes also are identical with His nature and are infinite and perfect because nothing can be less in one whose nature is in itself infinite and perfect. In speaking of the attributes of Christ we recognize three classes of properties: (1) those that are His because of His divine nature, e.g., omnipotence; (2) those that are His because of His human nature, e.g., His

capacity for suffering; (3) those that are His because of the union of His two natures in one divine Person, e.g., His Mediatorship. (Cf. God.)

### Attrition
As used by spiritual writers, this means an imperfect sorrow for sin; an imperfect contrition because it is wanting in motive. Thus the sorrow, hatred of sin committed, and the resolve of not sinning again and sorrow for having offended God, are not because of pure love of God (which would be perfect contrition) but because of a lesser reason such as the fear of hell. This is nevertheless good, and results from the grace of God.

### Audiences, Papal
Papal audiences are the visits or conferences with major and minor officials of the Roman Curia or an official of the Holy See or of the diplomatic corps whereby the Holy Father carries on the work of the Church. These are arranged in a regular schedule. Besides these the pope receives in private conference the great majority of bishops of the world. There are also interviews with the press, dignitaries, or individuals, which are granted, whether in public (many people at one time) or private (one person), in a reception parlor of the Vatican palace. Such visits and interviews for lay persons are granted upon letters of recommendation of their bishop or upon appeal to the Vatican master of the chamber.

General audiences are scheduled once a week, at noon on Wednesday. These are held in the Audience Hall on the south side of St. Peter's Basilica, which was opened in 1971. When the Pope is in residence at his vacation home, Castel Gondolfo, they are held in a small hall reserved for that purpose. These audiences are 60 to 90 minutes in length, and the Pope usually speaks. Arrangements for these are made through the office of the Prefecture of the Apostolic Household.

### Augsburg, Diet of
See Diet of Augsburg.

### Augustinism
This term is sometimes applied to the philosophical and theological teachings of St. Augustine (354 to 430), especially his theories on grace.

### Aumbry
See Ambry.

## Aureole

The golden blaze often seen around the sun, was borrowed by artists of the Middle Ages to portray the heavenly glory of the saints. It is usually represented by a gold-colored haze or shafts of gold surrounding the figure of the saint in an oval shape. However, it is also depicted by a halo or nimbus. The aureole of the saints in theology is defined as a certain accidental reward of happiness and merit over and above the usual that is given to saints in heaven to distinguish them because of their special degree of sanctity in overcoming the world. St. Thomas Aquinas says that this mark of excellence is given to virgins, martyrs, doctors of the Church, and preachers. It is also mentioned as the golden and colored aura around the entire figure of the Madonna of Our Lady of Guadalupe.

## Auricular Confession

The declaration by voice of one's sins to the priest in receiving the Sacrament of Penance is an auricular confession. It is so called because it is spoken "to the ear" and, thus, distinguished from public confession. In the early days of the Church, public confession and public penance were frequent, but since the fourth century auricular confession has been the accepted method. (See Penance, Sacrament of.)

## Austerities

Austerities are the rigorous practices of self-mortification imposed on oneself in the attaining of perfection. Many of the saints practiced various austerities, such as unusual fasts, abstaining from sleep, use of flagellation and wearing a hairshirt. Such practices, though commendable, should not be lightly undertaken, and usually only on the advice of a spiritual director or confessor.

## Australia, Christianity in

In 1788 Australia was first settled by whites, almost all of British origin; the predominant religion was and remains Anglican in this "down under" continent. The Church of England carried on missionary work; its most effective activities were called "Bush Brotherhoods." Founded in 1903, these consisted of groups of evangelists who served for a period of five years among the natives.

Now about a quarter of the population is Roman Catholic. The first titular diocese was created in 1834 with jurisdiction over all of Australia. This was divided into other dioceses in 1841. The Irish Catholics who entered Australia during the gold rush of 1851 swelled the Catholic population to its present proportion.

Methodists, Presbyterians, and Congregationalists also have small followings in Australia with limited missionary work, directed chiefly to the natives and the people living far from any religious center.

## Authenticity, Biblical

Though often referred to the inerrancy of the Bible, it is directed primarily at the trustworthiness of the text, its official recognition by authorities, and the exactness with which it expresses the known thought of the Scriptures. The Scriptures derive their authenticity first from the authors of the books and second from the studied declaration of the Church. Continual study of the Bible goes on through the Pontifical Biblical Commission, which was founded on Oct. 30, 1902, by Pope Leo XIII. The Commission was reorganized in 1971 by Pope Paul VI in the light of declarations of Vatican II, and it works closely with the Congregation of the Doctrine of the Faith. Its main objectives are: (1) to receive questions and subjects from referral groups, such as the Pope, Catholic universities, and biblical associations; (2) to meet in a plenary session at least once a year; (3) to promote joint undertakings and studies with non-Catholic and Catholic institutes of biblical studies; (4) to be consulted before any new rules or norms are issued on biblical subjects; (5) to have the authority to confer academic degrees in biblical studies. (See Bible.)

## Author of Life

This title (Acts 3:15) acknowledges Christ as the Savior of mankind and as the one in whom we all have existence. (Cf. Mystical Body of Christ.)

## Authority

The power of self-government in the Church derives from its foundation by Christ and from His teachings. In action, it means the cooperation of all members toward their ultimate sanctification in Christ. Inasmuch as the Church is a society, its authority has a corresponding subordination, that is, the ministers and those ministered to, or as St. Paul expresses it, a "blending of authority and humility," as interpreted from his Epistles. This authority of the Church, possessed by the Church as a society, may not be usurped by others, for example, the state, since it is the purpose of the Church to sanctify all. The authority of the Church in her accredited officials, her ministers, is to be exercised within the "body of its followers," the faithful. Hence, those that have a ministering role exercise that also in a humble cooperation, realizing that theirs is the responsibility of proclaiming the Word, Christ, to all people. It is through this *authority* that organic harmony is had within the Church not only in the spiritual mission of the Church but also in maintaining the firmness of the human structure that derives first from Christ and second from the Apostles.

Vatican II stated clearly concerning the authority within the Church: "There is only one Spirit who, according to His own richness and the needs of the ministries, distributes His different gifts for the welfare of the Church (cf. 1 Cor. 12:1–11). Among these gifts stands out the grace given to the Apostles. To their authority, the Spirit Himself subjected even those who were endowed with charisms (cf. 1 Cor. 14)" (LG 7).

Also, "Bishops govern the particular churches entrusted to them as the vicars and ambassadors of Christ. This they do by their counsel, exhortations, and example, as well, indeed, as by their authority and sacred power. This power they use only for the edification of their flock in truth and holiness, remembering that he who is greater should become as the lesser and he who is the more distinguished, as the servant (cf. Lk. 22:26–27)" (GS 27).

"Within his diocese, then, the bishop is and must be, regularly and in the full sense, teacher, priest, and shepherd. There as vicar of Christ and in the name of Christ, he has the *proper* (not vicarial), *ordinary* (not delegated), and *immediate* (without an intermediary) power that is needed for the exercise of his pastoral office. There he can and must make laws, judge, and see to the ordering of all that has to do with worship and the apostolate" (Eccl. of Vat. II, Kloppenburg, p. 251). (See also Bishop; Magisterium of the Church.)

### Autocephali

This name is given in the Greek Church to archbishops or metropolitans who are not subject to a patriarch but instead are responsible to a provincial synod or the Holy See.

### Auto-Da-Fe

Literally "edict of faith," the Auto-da-fe was the public ceremony of the sixteenth century, especially in Spain wherein the decision of a court of the Inquisition was proclaimed. This gradually evolved into a semireligious and official action of the Church and State authorities. It consisted of a procession, condemnation of the guilty, reconciliation of the penitent, and the pardoning of those previously sentenced or "paroled." After the ceremony the guilty were turned over to authorities of the state for the carrying out of the sentences.

### Autos Sacramentales

These religious plays, like the earlier miracle and morality plays, were put on during the season of Corpus Christi in Spain in the late seventeenth and early eighteenth centuries. They were intended to instruct the people in the doctrine of the Eucharist but were suppressed because they departed from their purpose.

### Auxiliary Bishop

An auxiliary bishop is a titular bishop appointed by the Holy See, who does not have jurisdiction but a fullness of holy orders, and who assists a ruling bishop of a diocese in carrying out the work of that diocese. Because they are not appointed to a diocese in a jurisdictional capacity, they are named titular bishops and, unless by special privilege, do not have the right to succeed to the governance of the diocese should it become vacant.

### Avarice or Covetousness

One of the capital sins, avarice is the inordinate love of temporal or earthly things, particularly riches. It need not be the direct possession of money or wealth, but it is inordinate when one is not guided by reason, or by suitableness or need, or when one goes to unusual lengths for attainment or is selfish or miserly in giving. This vice leads to failures of charity through hardness of heart, a worried state of mind over possible loss or failure to obtain, and dishonesty and unjust practices in acquiring wealth. Its opposite virtue is liberality, a balanced attitude toward wealth, and the control or moderation of one's desires. (Cf. Alms.)

### Ave Maria

Literally "Hail Mary," Ave Maria is the title of the familiar two part prayer: "Hail Mary full of grace, the Lord is with thee, blessed art thou among all women, and blessed is the fruit of thy womb, Jesus. Holy Mary, Mother of God, pray for us sinners now and at the hour of our death. Amen." (Cf. Angelical Salutation.)

### Aversion

Aversion is the opposite of desire. Theologically, it is said to be directed against the good, the useful, or the pleasurable. (Cf. Detachment.)

### Avignon Popes

For 68 years, from 1309 to 1377, seven popes led the Church while exiled from Rome to the city of Avignon in France. The first, Clement V (1305 to 1316), fled to Avignon to seek asylum from the attacks of the Colonna family who sought to control all of Rome. Although the papacy was in virtual restriction, its succession was intact. This period is sometimes named the Babylonian captivity. During this time the popes were very much under the influence and domination of the French Kings. The popes were: Clement V, John XXII (1316 to 1334), Benedict XII (1334 to 1342), Clement VI (1342 to 1352), Innocent VI (1352 to 1362), Urban V (1362 to 1370), and Gregory XI (1370 to 1378). The last of the Avignon popes was greatly urged by the Dominican mystic, St. Catherine of Sienna, to return to Rome.

### Azymites

This name, not always derogatory, was applied by Greek schismatics to members of the Roman Church because the latter use unleavened bread in the Eucharist.

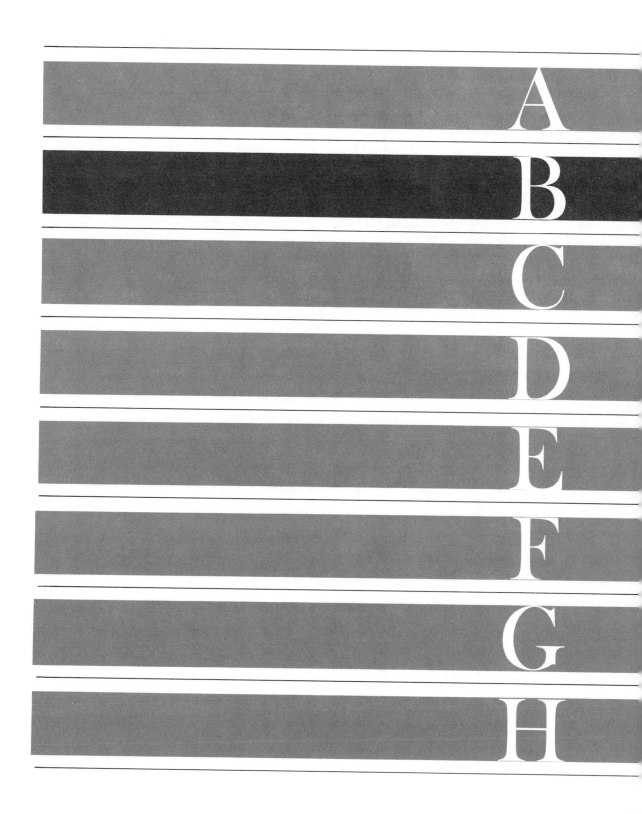

## Baal

A divinity in the Canaanite religion, Baal was variously called "the god of the mountaintops," "god of the clouds," "the god of storms" (cf. Ps. 68:5). In Israel the cult of Baal as "lord of the city" was opposed and denounced by the prophets (cf. Jer. 2:23; Hos. 13:1–3). At Accaron Baal was given the title of Beelzebub, but not as the lord of the underworld. The worship of Baal continued despite the importunings and denunciations of the prophets declaring this false god to be an unworthy idol.

## Babel, Tower of

This structure was near the site of ancient Babylon, probably at what is today Bias-Nimrud. The inhabitants started to build this great stage-tower or ziggurat but could not complete it (Gn. 11:1–9). The popular story misinterprets the Hebrew word *babel*, which means "confusion." In this version, by miraculous intervention God introduced different languages among the population (Hebrew word *balel*) and thus effected the stopping of the work, which was one of pride and arrogance together with a will to intimidate enemies. The tower had arisen to a height of 60 feet. It is more accurately accepted that because of discord and lack of harmony in settling on a policy, the work was halted and a migration started. As early as the fourth century, St. Gregory of Nyssa was emphatic in declaring that God did not impose a variety of languages upon mankind. Etymologically, the name *babel* means "gate of God."

## Babylonian Captivity

This was a period of enforced exile of 70 years, which began in 605 B.C. with the first deportation of the Jews and continued until 537 B.C. when the 42,360 Jews and 7,337 slaves were led back to Judah by Zorobabel after a decree by Cyrus the Great permitting their return. The Jews had been induced, under Zedekiah, against the inspired counsels of the prophet, Jeremiah, to revolt against Nabuchodonosor in 587 B.C. after having suffered two defeats and the partial deportation and enslavement of their people. This was the final blow and upon defeat the temple was destroyed, Jerusalem laid waste, and all but a few taken into captivity (2 Chr. 36).

## Baldachino, also Baldaquin and Baldachin

1. This lesser civory or *ciborium* is a smaller, lighter structure of metal, wood, or cloth-covered framework that is projected over the altar and its footpace. It consists of the canopy that is a roof-like projection supported by chains from above or from brackets or by two posts; with this, descending from the canopy behind the altar is a dossal. This baldachino has a symbolic meaning since it is representative of the *arcosolium;* it also has a practical purpose since it protects the Eucharist from falling dirt. However, this latter use in modern construction might be said to be symbolic also (cf. Civory). The modern altar and its requirements preclude the structure of the baldachino.

2. A baldachino is also the canopy supported on four poles, which is carried above the priest who carries the Blessed Sacrament in procession.

3. The canopy projected above an episcopal throne is a baldachino.

## Balm or Balsam

This aromatic resin derived from the terebinth tree or certain West Indies trees is mixed with olive oil and then blessed as Holy Chrism. Balm grew abundantly in Palestine and was one of its principal exports (Sir. 24:15–16). It was considered to have some medicinal qualities.

## Baltimore, Councils of

A series of provincial and plenary councils held at Baltimore, Maryland, by the bishops of the United States. The first provincial council was convoked in 1829 by Bishop England to settle problems confronting the Church in America and published decrees to promote religious life among the twenty-eight states and territories. Some of the problems were: providing Catholic literature, dispelling Protestant prejudice, and amendment of the trustee system. Six other provincial councils followed the first. It was at the sixth provincial council, in 1846, that the Blessed Virgin Mary, under title of the Immaculate Conception, was chosen as Patroness of the United States. Then there was convoked the first plenary council in 1852 whose main objectives, following rapid growth of the Church, were to unify the Catholics, to check the trend toward mixed marriages, and to promote Catholic education. It was here that the bishops decreed that parochial schools should be started wherever possible, that catechism instruction be given to children, and seminaries created in each diocese or province. After the Civil War, in 1866, the second plenary council convened. It was one of consolidation. In 1884 the third plenary council was called. It is designated the great educational council, for at this parents were commanded to see that their children receive a Christian education, parochial schools were to be erected near churches, a uniform catechism was prepared, annual collections for Negroes and Indians were prescribed, a wide distribution of Catholic literature was called for, secret societies were censured, and the choice of six holy days of obligation was made for observance by Catholics of the United States. These councils laid the groundwork for the Church and its missionary work in the growing United States. Now the work of the N.C.C.B., the administrative boards of the hierarchy, and the bishops' annual meetings in Washington, D.C., carry the Church's program to its expanding membership.

The rulings of the three plenary councils have had the force of law for the Church in the United States, and their deliberations have set a standard for the synods and annual meetings of the bishops ever since.

### Bangor Antiphonary

This old Latin manuscript codex was at the library of Bobbio and later sent to the Ambrosian library at Milan.

### Banner

1. A banner is the ornamental cloth supported on a crossbeam above a single upright, which during a sermon is placed before the exposed Blessed Sacrament.

2. Any such mounted cloth, carried in procession as an emblem of a society or an order of knighthood in the Church, is a banner.

In the liturgy developed since Vatican II, there has been a widespread use of banners as church decorations. This was inspired not only by practical advantages, but also by the statement of Vatican II. "Elevated from within by the grace of Christ, let them vigorously contribute their effort, so that created goods may be perfected by human labor, technical skill and civic culture for the benefit of all men according to the design of the Creator and the light of His Word" (LG 4/36).

Banners are communication between God and person, between person and person, in a place of worship, school, home, or hospital. They have an uplifting psychological effect because they appeal to the senses in a noble manner by using symbols and words to inspire.

### Banneux, Apparitions of

These are a series of eight appearances of the Blessed Virgin Mary, occurring between Jan. 15 and Mar. 2, 1933, to an eleven-year-old girl, Mariette Beco. These took place in a garden area behind the family home in the village of Banneux, near Liege in Belgium. Here the Blessed Mother gave herself the title "Virgin of the Poor" and since the approval of the apparitions was given in 1949 by Bishop Louis J. Kerkhofs of Liege, the Blessed Virgin has been venerated under the title: Our Lady of the Poor, the Sick, and the Indifferent.

The devotion to the Blessed Virgin Mary under this title has been widespread with more than two million members belonging to the *International Union of Prayer* throughout the world.

### Banns

The public proclamation of an intended marriage is given on three successive Sundays or holy days of obligation during Mass or at a service where the attendance is large. The banns are for the purpose of helping to determine if any impediments exist to the proposed marriage and should be published by the pastor of the two parties or where they have legal residence or a domicile. If the marriage does not take place before the expiration of six months, the banns must be repeated. This question of banns is governed by canon law, which permits exceptions and dispensations according to the decision of the ordinary (c. 1023–1030).

### Baptism, Sacrament of

Christ gave His command to baptize universally to the Apostles: "Full authority has been given to me both in heaven and on earth; go therefore, and make disciples of all the nations. Baptize them in the name 'of the Father and of the Son, and of the Holy Spirit.' Teach them to carry out everything I have commanded you. And know that I am with you always, until the end of the world!" (Mt. 28:18–20.) And baptism was the normal conclusion of the apostolic preaching and teaching (Acts 2:37–41). The effects of this sacrament are: (1) it cleanses us from original sin; (2) it makes us Christians through grace by sharing in Christ's death and resurrection and setting up an initial program of living (1 Cor. 6:9–11); (3) it makes us children of God as the life of Christ is brought forth within us (Rom. 8:15–17); (4) it makes us heirs of heaven for through baptism we "walk by the Spirit" whereby we will possess the kingdom of God (Gal. 5:21–25). The ordinary minister of baptism is the priest, but in cases of necessity any person may baptize by pouring ordinary water on the forehead, saying while pouring: "I baptize you in the name of the Father, and of the Son, and of the Holy Spirit." Infants should be baptized as soon as possible (c. 770), and whoever would defer it without reason for more than three weeks to a month would sin. Baptism is the sacrament of mystical union with Christ, which creates a new society, the "glorious Church."

Vatican II declared: "through baptism we are formed in the likeness of Christ: 'It was in one Spirit that all of us, whether Jew or Greek, slave or free, were baptized into one body' (1 Cor. 12:13). In this sacred rite, a union with Christ's death and resurrection is both symbolized and brought about" (LG 7).

And also: "Baptism constitutes a sacramental bond of unity linking all who have been reborn by means of it. But baptism, of itself, is only a beginning, a point of departure, for it is wholly directed toward the acquiring of fullness of life in Christ. Baptism is thus oriented toward a complete profession of faith, a complete incorporation into the system of salvation such as Christ Himself willed it to be, and finally, toward a complete participation in Eucharistic communion" (UR 22).

Vatican II also called for a revision of both the rite of baptism for infants and for adults. A revised rite for infants was introduced June 1, 1970, and the revised rite for "Christian Initiation of Adults" was issued Jan. 6, 1972.

The Church recognizes three forms of giving valid baptism: *immersion,* the lowering of the body into the water; *aspersion,* the sprinkling of the water; and *infusion,* the pouring of the water. In the Roman Rite the method of infusion is prescribed. All adapations in the liturgy of baptism belong to the authority of the Conference of Bishops or the local Ordinaries. However, the minister of the celebration of baptism may introduce those accommodations that are permitted to him in the liturgical rite. "(1) Regulation of the Sacred Liturgy depends solely upon the authority of the Church, that is, on the Apostolic See, and, as laws may determine, on the bishops. (2) In virtue of power conceded by the law, the regulation of the liturgy within certain defined limits belongs to various kinds of competent territorial bodies of Bishops legitimately established. (3) Therefore, absolutely no other person, not even a priest, may add, remove, or change anything in the liturgy on his own authority" (*Sacrosanctum Concilium,* 22).

The Church recognizes as valid baptisms properly performed by non-Catholic ministers. Baptism is conferred *conditionally* when there is doubt concerning a previous baptism or the dispositions of the person to be baptized. Because baptism is necessary for salvation, anyone may baptize an infant in danger of death, and an aborted fetus, if alive, should be baptized, or if no sign of life is present, then the fetus should be baptized conditionally. A sponsor or godparent is required for the person being baptized (see Sponsors). Baptism may be administered to an infant during the Liturgy of the Word at a eucharistic celebration.

". . . all the baptized are called to be gathered into one flock, and thus to be able to bear unanimous witness before the nations to Christ their Lord. And if they are not yet capable of bearing witness to the same faith, they should at least be animated by mutual esteem and love" (AG 6).

## Baptismal Font

The permanent or semipermanent basin where baptism is administered is the baptismal font. Recent building of churches has placed this font near the entrance to the church so that upon entering, people may dip their fingers into the font to bless themselves, "to recall their baptism." Other norms of church construction place the font near the sacred area so that it will have a "useful" place in the participated liturgy.

## Baptismal Name

This is the name given to the one baptized. It is taken from the list of the saints of the Church. The saint then is the person's patron, whose virtues it is hoped the person will imitate, and this symbolizes a renewal of Life in Christ.

## Baptismal Robe

See Chrismal.

## Baptismal Vows

Three renunciations are required of all adults before the Sacrament of Baptism is conferred and are spoken in behalf of infants by the sponsors. They are given in the form of three questions addressed to the one to be baptized; they ask for the renunciation of Satan, all his works, and all his pomps. In the reception of baptized Christians into the Church, the person is asked to state: "I believe and profess all that the holy Catholic Church believes, teaches, and proclaims as revealed by God." This is followed by the priest placing his hand on the head of the person, saying the words of admission to full communion, and, in the absence of a bishop, confirming the person, and giving the sign of peace. If this has taken place during a eucharistic liturgy, holy communion is given.

## Baptismal Water

This water, blessed in the baptismal font on Holy Saturday, must be used in solemn baptism.

## Baptistery

The Baptistery is the portion of the church set apart for the administering of baptism, wherein the baptismal font is located. It should be near the main entrance of the church whenever possible, but where no special area has been set aside for such construction, the font may be located in any useful or available place. Liturgical reform has broken with tradition in having a formal structured place for the administering of baptism.

## Baptists

This group of American Protestant Christians is the largest denomination in the United States, numbering more than 29 million among the thirty Baptist bodies. The first Baptist church in America was founded by Roger Williams at Providence, Rhode Island, in 1639. The largest in membership of these churches in the United States are: the Southern Baptist Convention; the National Baptist Convention, U. S. A., Inc.; the National Baptist Convention of America; and the American Baptist Churches in the U. S. A. Central to the teaching of the Baptists is their doctrine on baptism, which is called an "ordinance" rather than a sacrament. Baptism is given to adults only, by immersion. Thus, baptism is the sole criterion of salvation and requires that the recipient accept and pursue a life of virtue.

There is no formal creed but the Baptists in general subscribe to two professions of faith formulated in 1689 and 1832 and thus regard Scripture as the sole rule of faith, recognize original sin, and personal justification through faith in Christ and the nature of the Church. There is a variety in the worship services from church to church, with the Lord's Supper, which is also called an "ordinance," celebrated at varying intervals. There are several factions among the Baptists ascribing to changed teachings. Among these are: Arminianism, a rejection of the Calvinist teachings on grace and predestination; Fundamentalism, which is a belief in a strict, literal interpretation of Scriptures; Millenarianism, which espouses a literal interpretation of Chapter 20 of the Book of Revelation; Modernism, a swing toward the individual's interpretation of Scripture; and Predestinationists, who teach that man's salvation is determined by God's will alone and cannot be changed by virtue or grace.

## Barefoot Friars

The name barefoot friars is given to any discalced monks.

## Barnabas, St.

The man named Barnabas by the Apostles because of his work with the Apostle Paul. Originally called Joseph, the given name of Barnabas, from the original Aramaic, means "son of prophecy," or "son of encouragement" (cf. Acts 4:36). He was a cousin of the evangelist Mark and became a pioneer in missionary work outside Jerusalem and Palestine and travelled to cities in southern Asia Minor. It is believed he was martyred during the reign of Nero.

## Baroque Art

This style of architecture and art expression is characterized by sweeping imagination, picturesqueness, immensity, and harmony between the building and environment by the suggestion of movement. Baroque arose in the sixteenth century and is generally considered as an expression of the Counter-reformation. It was flamboyantly aristocratic, international, and unified; although it produced some excellent architecture, it often degenerated into showiness and a straining after effect merely for effect's sake. For this reason it is said to be the end of the Christian content of art and was generally condemned without always receiving recognition for its merits.

Baroque art applies not only to architecture but also to sculpture and painting. In both these it is characterized not by the orderly, clear, and independent arrangement of figures, but by an assembly of the parts so that no part or figure stands alone. It thus adapted to several nations and developed its own characteristics; for example, in Spain the style became extreme in ornate expression, as in the Plateresque style.

## Bartholomew, St.

St. Bartholomew was one of the twelve Apostles (Nathaniel) whose name in Aramaic means "son of Tolmai" (cf. Acts 1:13). According to tradition, he preached in Ethiopia, India, Persia, and Armenia, and he is honored with a feast, Aug. 24, in the Roman Rite calendar, and Aug. 25 in the Byzantine Rite.

## Baruch, Book of

The name Baruch is of Hebrew derivation meaning "blessed." This deuterocanonical book of the OT was probably not written by one having this name, but by an unknown author, or authors. It was written in Babylonia following the destruction of Jerusalem, probably during the second century before Christ. In its six chapters it points to a religious reform made by the prophet Jeremiah several centuries earlier, calling for penance and justice, as well as an appeal to courage and hope for the exiles. Its final prose chapter repeats Jeremiah's denunciation of idolatry and the disgrace that befalls even the just man who worships idols.

## Basel, Council of

Under the title of Basel-Ferrara-Florence, from the three cities of Switzerland and Italy where it was held, this Ecumenical Council was convened July 23, 1431, at Basel, Switzerland, by Pope Martin V. Its purpose was to effect reforms within the Church, but it was not entirely successful because of factionalism that developed. The Council became involved over the question of papal supremacy, and there was a serious dispute with Pope Eugenius IV. It was then dissolved by the Pope and reconvened in Ferrara, Italy, although this brought about a split among the attending bishops, some of whom continued on at Basel with no definitive result. The work was finally resolved by the final session at Florence, Italy. Among its reform acts were: legislation against concubinage of the clergy, the move to call more frequent local synods, and the establishment of standards for papal candidates and election procedures. (See Ecumenical Councils.)

## Basic Teachings for Catholic Religious Education

The National Conference of Catholic Bishops in consultation with the Catechetical Office of the Holy See prepared a statement of what is considered essential and basic to the doctrinal instruction of Catholics. This was promulgated in 1973 and forms the basis of all instruction and communication in the faith-living of the people of God. It is thought that religious instruction is "formation in Christ," and thus it follows the enunciation set forth in Vatican II where: "Catechetical training is intended to make men's faith become living, conscious, and active, through the light of instruction. Bishops should see to it that such training be painstakingly given to children, adolescents, young adults, and even grownups. In this instruction a proper sequence should be observed as well as a method appropriate to the matter that is being treated and to the natural disposition, ability, age, and circumstances of life of the listener. Finally, they should see to it that this instruction is based on sacred Scripture, tradition, the liturgy, and teaching authority, and life of the Church.

"Moreover, they should take care that catechists be properly trained for their task, so that they will be thoroughly acquainted with the doctrine of the Church and will have both a theoretical and a practical knowledge of the laws of psychology and of pedagogical methods" (CD 14).

Thus the Bishops formulated this objective of religious instruction, not as a minimum, but as essential elements to attain the objective of an informed laity as well as one that is able to transform and make real the Gospel message for themselves and others. There are hence, three main themes, among the many possible ones, through which religious education is brought to people:

1. *The importance of prayer.* Without prayer and its conscious pursuit, formally or informally, the person is faced with difficulties that preclude the formation of a reasonable response to instruction. Among these prayers are: Sign of the Cross, the Our Father, the Hail Mary, the Apostles Creed, an Act of Contrition, and the recitation of the Rosary.

2. *Participation in the Liturgy.* The deeper involvement of the members of the Christian community in the prayers of worship of God, the eucharistic celebration, and the example of sharing in these prayers.

3. *Familiarity with the Holy Bible.* The reading of the word of God, the help it affords in learning the mind of God and the knowledge and love of Christ. Together with the Scripture there is the combination of tradition, which is the descending embodiment of the Church's teaching from earliest times.

In seeking the salvation promised by Christ through His Church there are twenty-five basic teachings that are supportive of an active faith. These are briefly: (1) the mystery of the one God, Father, Son and Holy Spirit; (2) the true worship of God in a world that ignores Him; (3) knowledge of God and the witness of Christian love; (4) Jesus Christ, Son of God, the Firstborn of all creation, and Savior; (5) creation, the beginning of the history of salvation; (6) Jesus Christ, the center of all God's saving works; (7) Jesus Christ, true man and true God in the unity of the Divine Person; (8) Jesus Christ, Savior and Redeemer of the world; (9) the Holy Spirit in the Church and in the life of the Christian; (10) the Sacraments, actions of Christ in the Church, which is the universal sacrament; (11) religious instruction on the sacraments; (12) the Eucharist, center of all sacramental life; (13) the Sacrament of Matrimony; (14) the new person in the Spirit; (15) human and Christian freedom; (16) the sins of man; (17) the moral life of Christians; (18) the perfection of Christian love; (19) specifics in the teaching of morality; (20) the Church, people of God, and institution for salvation; (21) the Church as a community (cf. Community); (22) the quest for unity; (23) the Church as the institution for salvation; (24) Mary, Mother of God, Mother and model of the Church; (25) final reunion with God.

Aids to the redemptive understanding of these basic teachings are the Ten Commandments, the Beatitudes, and the precepts of the Church.

**Basilian Rule**

This method of religious life was propounded by St. Basil the Great (d. 379) who was a founder of the religious life and the first to insert the obligation of a vow. His rule prescribed poverty and chastity and placed great emphasis on obedience, required fasting five days a week, set hours of meditation, study, work, and community prayers. It was the basis of many religious rules that were to follow. The monks were called Basilians.

**Basilica**

Formerly a basilica was a place of justice or civic hall, which consisted of a long hall with an apse at one end. Later Christian churches built over the tombs of martyrs were so named. Today it is merely a title of honor given to various kinds of churches. There are two classes of basilicas, *major* and *minor*. There are four *major* basilicas, all in Rome: St. John Lateran—the Cathedral of Rome, St. Peter's of the Vatican, St. Paul's outside the Walls, and St. Mary Major. The Basilica of St. Lawrence outside the Walls at one time held the title and privileges of these four but is now a minor basilica. The title of *minor* basilica is granted to certain churches by the pope: their clergy have precedence in rank and certain decorative insignia that indicate their dependence on the pope; the papal arms may be displayed on the churches' exteriors.

In the United States the churches designated as basilicas are: Cathedral of the Immaculate Conception, Mobile, Alabama; Mission Dolores and Mission of San Carlos, San Francisco, California; Our Lady of Sorrows and Queen of All Saints, Chicago, Illinois; Old Cathedral, Vincennes, Indiana; St.

Francis Xavier, Dyersville, Iowa; Our Lady of Gethsemani (Trappist), Kentucky; Cathedral of Assumption, Covington, Kentucky; Cathedral of St. Louis, King of France, New Orleans, Louisiana; Assumption of the Blessed Virgin Mary, Baltimore, Maryland; Perpetual Help, Roxbury, Massachusetts; St. Mary, Minneapolis, Minnesota; Basilica of Immaculate Conception, Conception, Missouri; Cathedral of St. Louis, King of France, St. Louis, Missouri; Our Lady of Perpetual Help, Brooklyn, New York; St. Adalberts, Buffalo, New York; Our Lady of Victory, Lackawanna, New York; Shrine of Our Lady of Consolation, Carey, Ohio; St. Vincent Basilica, Latrobe, Pennsylvania; Basilica of the Sacred Heart, Conewago, Pennsylvania; St. Josephat, Milwaukee, Wisconsin.

In Canada the basilicas are Cathedral Basilica of St. Boniface, St. Boniface, Manitoba; Cathedral Basilica of St. John the Baptist, St. John's, Newfoundland; St. Mary's Basilica, Halifax, Nova Scotia; Basilica of Notre Dame, Ottawa, Ontario; St. Peter's Cathedral, London, Ontario; Basilica of St. Dunstan, Charlottetown, Prince Edward Island; Cathedral Basilica of St. Michael, Sherbrooke, Quebec; Cathedral Basilica of St. James the Greater; St. Joseph of Mount Royal, Montreal. Basilica of Our Lady of the Cape, Cap-de-la-Madeleine, Basilica of Notre Dame; St. Anne de Beaupre, Basilica of St. Anne, Quebec.

### Basilidians

Followers of the Gnostic heresy who practiced magic were known as Basilidians.

### Bay Psalm Book

This is not a book of the scripture, but by its full title: *The Whole Book of Psalms Faithfully Translated Into English Metre*, which was shortened to the "Bay Psalm Book." It followed closely the Book of Psalms and was the first book to be published in the English Colonies of America, appearing in 1640, and printed by Stephen Day on the press owned by Harvard College. The popular name is derived from its publication in the Massachusetts Bay Colony. Because of the emphasis on singing in Congregational churches, this translation of the Book of Psalms into English verse was done to make them more singable. Music notation was later added to editions of the books. (See Psalms, Book of.)

### Beads

This is a popular, descriptive name given to the rosary. (Cf. Rosary.)

### Beatific Vision

By definition of Pope Benedict XII, this is an act of the intellect of the blessed in heaven, which is the clear, intuitive, immediate sight of the divine essence that is God. Its clarity is the dispelling of the knowledge we have of God either as reflected in created things, by reason or by faith. Its intuitive and immediate character is found in its immeasurably superior knowledge to any knowledge we might have otherwise, and it is the supreme reality of the living God giving intrinsic evidence of the Trinity. The blessed "see" because they are elevated by the "light of glory" of the higher faculties of intellect and will arising from the consummation of sanctifying grace, which being fully developed makes the blessed able to see God as He sees Himself. It is the fulfillment of human happiness, seeing all in the light of supreme Truth.

It follows from the errorless teaching of the scriptures: "Now we see indistinctly, as in a mirror; then we shall see face to face. My knowledge is imperfect now; then I shall know even as I am known. There are in the end three things that last: faith, hope, and love, and the greatest of these is love" (1 Cor. 13:12–13). And: "Dearly beloved, we are God's children now; what we shall later be has not yet come to light. We know that when it comes to light we shall be like him, for we shall see him as he is" (1 Jn. 3:2).

### Beatification

Beatification is the declaration made by the pope that one of the faithful because of a life of virtue or the heroic death of martyrdom is entitled *blessed*, i.e., is living in the happiness of heaven. This permits veneration of the person, not throughout the Church, but only in those places where the beatified lived or in the houses of the religious community that he or she founded. Beatification is formally the final phase in the cause of one who is being considered for ultimate canonization. The pope's declaration states that the cause may proceed and fixes the date for the ceremony in St. Peter's, which is the reading of the decree of beatification, the unveiling of the picture of the "Blessed" above the chair of St. Peter, the singing of the *Te Deum*, and celebration of the newly beatified. The pope does not take a personal part in this ceremony, only assisting at Benediction in the evening and veneration of the relics of the beatified. (Cf. Cause; Canonization.)

### Beatitude of Heaven

Beatitude of Heaven is the good that satisfies

perfectly and completely the desire of created things. It is (1) essential, consisting of the vision of God and is consummated in the love that follows the vision; (2) accidental, which is the aggregate of the things we possess in possessing God, such as glorified bodies and society of the blessed. One's beatitude in heaven will be the eternal preservation in souls of all they have by nature and grace, and the degree of beatitude will be according to merit; hence each shall not have the same degree of beatitude in heaven. Each person will be unique in glory because of the merit and will of God as Creator.

### Beatitudes, The Eight

These are the blessings spoken by our Lord at the Sermon on the Mount (Mt. 5:1–12). The place where our Lord spoke was probably a hill near Capharnaum, above the plain of Genesar. The qualities meriting the blessings as given in the pronouncements of Christ outline a single, consistent spiritual outlook. They assure entry, or possession of the kingdom of God (heaven), and are guarantees that the basic teachings of the Church are especially important in teaching the specifics of morality. They are: (1) Blest are the poor in spirit; the reign of God is theirs. (2) Blest are the sorrowing; they shall be consoled. (3) Blest are the lowly; they shall inherit the land. (4) Blest are they who hunger and thirst for holiness; they shall have their fill. (5) Blest are they who show mercy; mercy shall be theirs. (6) Blest are the single-hearted; for they shall see God. (7) Blest are the peacemakers; they shall be called sons of God. (8) Blest are those persecuted for holiness' sake; the reign of God is theirs.

### Beauraing, Our Lady of

This title of our Blessed Mother derived from the village of Beauraing in Belgium where the

Blessed Virgin appeared thirty times during a period from Nov. 29, 1932, to Jan. 3, 1933, to five children: Fernande, Gilberte, and Albert Voisin; Andree and Gilberte Degeimbre. Final approbation of the apparitions was given July 2, 1949. The message given was a promise to convert sinners. It was, next to the apparitions of Fatima, the most significant mystical occurrence of the twentieth century.

The Marian Union of Beauraing was formed (in America the Pro Maria Committee is the organizing group). It is composed of members throughout the world who seek the conversion of sinners through prayer. (Cf. Apparition.)

### Beautiful Gate

This is the name of one of the entries of Herod's temple (Acts, 3), which is not identified clearly by archaeology but is believed to be the same as the Corinthian Gate of Josephus located on the east side of the inner enclosure leading from the outer court to the Women's Court.

### Beauty

Philosophically, beauty consists of intuitive knowledge and delight. It is received through the intellect as its power or sense and has three integral elements: integrity, proportion or consonance, and radiance or clarity (cf. Aesthetics). Beauty is essential to both truth and goodness. Philosophically the three: truth, beauty, and goodness are referred to as transcendentals, meaning they transcend all attributes and apply to all being. The higher the order of being, the greater degree of all three the being possesses, e.g., angels over men, and God the infinite possessor of all three to an infinite degree. Spiritual beauty, however, is the shining forth in the soul of a person of the reflected virtues of Christ.

### Beelzebub

This is the name of the OT god of Accaron (2 Kgs. 1:2), which is spelled Baalzebub, and which in the usual translation of the Hebrew word means "the lord of the flies." In the NT this name is given to "the prince of devils" (cf. Mt. 10:25), but this does not follow the course of language when referring to *Satan* or the *Devil*, for the name Satan is derived from the Hebrew word meaning "accuser, enemy" (cf. Mt. 12:25–32).

### Befana

Befana is a fair or carnival held at Rome during the season of Epiphany.

## Beguines and Beghards

These were associations of laymen of the thirteenth century who followed the religious rule of St. Francis or St. Dominic but who did not take vows. They were suppressed because of heresy. The females were called "beguines" and were widows or unmarried women who practiced a communal life of prayer. The name is probably derived from the Flemish word *beghen,* meaning "to pray." The male members were called "beghards," and the places where the lives of both men and women were seeking their self-sufficient ways of prayer were called "beguinages."

## Being

Everything that actually exists is a being and also that which can exist. This includes every created object in the entire universe, and also a thought, for while the thought does not have an actual existence, still that to which it refers may have reality. There are three kinds of being: the *real* being, which exists in himself; the *imaginary* being, whose existence is in another; and *possible* being, or something that could become real. It is only the first that should be called true beings for they have real actuality and are substantive—or have substance. Thus, only in a real being can there be accidents such as size, shape, weight, and these are said to be *of* a thing rather than *in* the thing. And essence is that which distinguishes the kind of being a thing is in reality, for essence tells what a being is, e.g., each human being has his own essence that is received from another, namely, the Creator-God. In this sense we can say in natural theological terms that God is both creator and sustainer of the human creature, as we read in scripture: "In him we live and move and have our being" (Acts 17:28).

## Belfry

A belfry is an extended structure above a church, as a steeple, where church bells are housed. It also applies to the frame supporting the bells. When such a tower stands independent of the church proper, it is called a *campanile* (q.v.).

## Belief

See Basic Teachings for Catholic Religious Education; Creed.

## Bell, Book, and Candle

This was a symbolic act of medieval times. At the reading of a sentence of major excommunication the book was being closed, the lighted candle thrown to the ground, while the bell tolled.

## Bells

When blessed (incorrectly called a "baptism") or consecrated, bells are sacramentals of the Church and used in the service of religion. Thus, there may be a large church bell, a carillon of many bells, or the small sanctuary bell used during Mass, called a "sacring bell." They have been used since the sixth century.

## Bema

Literally, a bema is a step. In the Greek Orthodox Church it is the space surrounding the Holy Table behind the iconostasis.

## Benedicite

This is the Latin title of the Canticle of the Three Children (Dn. 3:51–90). It is a hymn of praise in the form of a litany psalm.

## Benedictines

Followers of the rule established by St. Benedict shortly before his death in 543 are Benedictines. St. Benedict is called the "Father of Western Monasticism." His rule cultivated the family spirit of the community, established moderation as an ideal, and exacted no unusual austerities. The monks were to be self-supporting and spend their lives under an abbot with full authority. The rule began in Monte Cassino in 529, and the movement spread and became a great force in the development of Europe. The rule has been adapted to groups of women religious; many of these have communities in countries and have been distinguished because of these nations, e.g., Benedictine Sisters of Bavaria; of France. Others follow a diocesan structure with each having one priory with autonomous government.

### Benediction of the Blessed Sacrament

This devotion to the Eucharistic Christ in the Roman rite consists of exposition of the Blessed Sacrament in the monstrance, or a pyx, adoration of the faithful, hymns, the blessing where the priest makes the sign of the cross with the Blessed Sacrament over the people, and the recitation of Divine Praises.

This is a paraliturgical service of worship that has as its center the eucharistic presence of Christ in the reserved bread. Since Oct. 18, 1973, the Congregation for Divine Worship has made it permissible for the Blessed Sacrament to be exposed for worship by men or women religious or by members of the laity when no priest is present, but only the priest may give the blessing. (See Divine Praises.)

### Benediction with Ciborium

A less solemn form of Benediction of the Blessed Sacrament, Benediction with Ciborium consists of opening the tabernacle door so that the ciborium containing the Blessed Sacrament can be seen, hymns, and the blessing of the people in the form of the cross with the ciborium containing the Blessed Sacrament. It is now seldom used.

### Benedictionale

A benedictionale is a nonliturgical book containing a collection of blessings from the Ritual, Missal, and Pontifical.

### Benedictus

Benedictus is the Latin title of the canticle of Zachary as recorded in Lk. 1:68–79. It marks the recovery of Zachary's speech and is in the form of a prayer for the people. Its chief feature is that the Messiah, born of the house of David, is hailed as a divine being.

The Benedictus is always a part of the Liturgy of the Hours, and it is spoken or sung at the graveside ceremonies in the burial of the dead.

It also is referred to as the title of that part of the eucharistic celebration with the words "Blessed is he who comes in the name of the Lord" (cf. Ps. 118).

### Benefice

Benefice is the juridical right established by competent Church authority in favor of an ecclesiastical person, for the life of the person, whereby the revenue from some Church property is received by the person for the discharge of his spiritual office. These are now controlled by canon law with certain exceptions permitted because of concordats between governments and the Vatican.

The benefice is both the *office,* which is the spiritual obligation implicit in the discharge of the attendant duties, and *material,* which is the income or salary through which the person in office is compensated. In the United States the commonest example is the pastor of a church who is entitled to a regular salary derived from the contributions of the faithful (cf. 1 Cor. 9:13). In other countries a benefice may be from the government, from investments, or from land holdings. All benefices are regulated by canon law as to who may be appointed to a benefice, who may establish one, and who may do away with a benefice.

### Benefit of Clergy

Benefit of clergy is the privilege granted to persons in holy orders to be tried in the diocesan court rather than the civil court, except in cases of treason or arson, in accord with c. 120 of the Code of Canon Law. The benefit was denied by Congress in 1790 in the United States and in other countries is controlled by custom or concordats with the government.

### Benemerenti Medals

These pontifical decorations were originated by Gregory XVI. They are awarded for exceptional military or civic service and are worn suspended from the neck by ribbons of the papal colors. The medal means by name "to a well-deserving person." They may be conferred on men and women, are made of gold, silver, or bronze, and bear the likeness of the pope who is reigning at the time they are conferred.

### Berretta

See Biretta.

## Bestiaries

Books of the Middle Ages, called Bestiaries, had descriptions and pictures of animals, both real and fabled. They served to instruct, were often the basis of animal symbols, and were sources for the use of animals in decoration, such as the gargoyles in Gothic architecture. (See Animals in Church Art.)

## Bethlehem

A town of Palestine five miles south of Jerusalem is called the Bethlehem of Juda; its name is taken from the Hebrew, meaning "house of bread." It was in this place according to the prophet Micah (5:1ff) that Jesus Christ was to be born (cf. Mt. 2:1–20). Over the cave that was the site of our Lord's birth, as written by Justin the Martyr in A.D. 160, the emperor Constantine erected a basilica that is standing to this day and visited by pilgrims travelling to the place of the Nativity.

## Betrothal also Espousal

This is the formal mutual promise of future valid and lawful marriage. Made in due canonical form, a betrothal must (1) be in writing; (2) the date and year must be given with the day and month indicated; (3) it must be attested by the signatures of the persons bethrothed, by the parish priest, the ordinary, or two witnesses.

## Bible

Holy Scripture, the Scriptures, or the Bible are the names given to the collection of the sacred books of the Jews and Christians. The Bible is the inspired word of God written under inspiration of the Holy Spirit and gathered in the order of the providence of God, which destined man to a supernatural end. In keeping with that divine decree, it follows that it is necessary that God's purpose be supernaturally revealed, that God be known, and His counsels and goodness be made manifest. This heavenly knowledge is the written portions of the divine tradition that is formed of Scripture and historic tradition and makes up the font of doctrine and teaching in the Church. The Bible has been called the Book of Spiritual Perfection, for to be ignorant of the Bible is to be wanting in the knowledge of Christ. Pope St. Pius X lists three rewards to be gained in the reading of the Bible: spiritual delight, love of Christ, and zeal for His cause.

The Bible is divided into two chief parts: the forty-six books of the Old Testament, and the twenty-seven books of the New Testament. In turn these seventy-three books are classified as:

The Old Testament

*The Pentateuch*
(The *Torah*—"law," or "instruction.")

The Book of Genesis (Gn.)
The Book of Exodus (Ex.)
The Book of Leviticus (Lv.)
The Book of Numbers (Nm.)
The Book of Deuteronomy (Dt.)
The Book of Joshua (Jos.)
The Book of Judges (Ju.)
The Book of Ruth (Ru.)

*The Historical Books*

The First Book of Samuel (1 Sm.)
The Second Book of Samuel (2 Sm.)
The First Book of Kings (1 Kgs.)
The Second Book of Kings (2 Kgs.)
The First Book of Chronicles (1 Chr.)
The Second Book of Chronicles (2 Chr.)
The Book of Ezra (Ezr.)
The Book of Nehemiah (Neh.)
The Book of Tobit (Tb.)
The Book of Judith (Jdt.)
The Book of Esther (Est.)
The First Book of Maccabees (1 Mc.)
The Second Book of Maccabees (2 Mc.)

*The Wisdom Books*

The Book of Job (Jb.)
The Book of Psalms (Ps.)
The Book of Proverbs (Prv.)
The Book of Ecclesiastes (Eccl.)
The Song of Songs (Sg.)

The Book of Wisdom (Wis.)
The Book of Sirach (Sir.) (Ecclesiasticus)

*The Prophetic Books*

The Book of Isaiah (Is.)
The Book of Jeremiah (Jer.)
The Book of Lamentations (Lam.)
The Book of Baruch (Bar.)
The Book of Ezekiel (Ez.)
The Book of Daniel (Dn.)
The Book of Hosea (Hos.)
The Book of Joel (Jl.)
The Book of Amos (Am.)
The Book of Obadiah (Ob.)
The Book of Jonah (Jon.)
The Book of Micah (Mi.)
The Book of Nahum (Na.)
The Book of Habakkuk (Hb.)
The Book of Zephaniah (Zep.)
The Book of Haggai (Hg.)
The Book of Zechariah (Zec.)
The Book of Malachi (Mal.)

The New Testament

*The Gospels and Acts*

The Gospel according to Matthew (Mt.)
The Gospel according to Mark (Mk.)
The Gospel according to Luke (Lk.)
The Gospel according to John (Jn.)
The Acts of the Apostles (Acts)

*The Epistles and Revelation*

The Epistle of Paul to the Romans (Rom.)
The First Epistle of Paul to the Corinthians (1 Cor.)
The Second Epistle of Paul to the Corinthians (2 Cor.)
The Epistle of Paul to the Galatians (Gal.)
The Epistle of Paul to the Ephesians (Eph.)
The Epistle of Paul to the Philippians (Phil.)
The Epistle of Paul to the Colossians (Col.)
The First Epistle of Paul to the Thessalonians (1 Thes.)
The Second Epistle of Paul to the Thessalonians (2 Thes.)
The First Epistle of Paul to Timothy (1 Tm.)
The Second Epistle of Paul to Timothy (2 Tm.)
The Epistle of Paul to Titus (Ti.)
The Epistle of Paul to Philemon (Phlm.)
The Epistle to the Hebrews (Heb.)
The Epistle of James (Jas.)

The First Epistle of Peter (1 Pt.)
The Second Epistle of Peter (2 Pt.)
The First Epistle of John (1 Jn.)
The Second Epistle of John (2 Jn.)
The Third Epistle of John (3 Jn.)
The Epistle of Jude (Jude)
The Book of Revelation (Rv.) (Apocalypse)

The Book of Revelation is considered the one prophetical book of the New Testament. (Cf. Canon of the Scripture; Inspiration of Scripture.)

Spiritual favors or indulgences may be gained, by decree of Leo XIII, Dec. 13, 1898, as follows: "The faithful who spend at least a quarter of an hour in reading Holy Scripture with the great reverence due to the Word of God and after the manner of spiritual reading may gain an indulgence of 300 days, and a plenary indulgence may be gained monthly by those who make this reading a daily practice."

The Church's teaching concerning the Bible is that this written word of God comes to us within the enlivening atmosphere of the Church as the Body of Christ, and that the members must therefore be guided by the judgment of the Church who can speak and teach with the authority of Christ and who has the right to preach, interpret, and teach the Bible. (See under separate listings of each Book and Epistle.)

### Bible Service

This devotion, also called Bible Vigil is centered around prayers, reading of several passages of the Scriptures, and a homily on the texts read. It is intended to give a greater appreciation and understanding of the Word of God. It is considered a paraliturgical devotion wherein the Scriptures speak to us as Christ, the Teacher among us.

### Bible Societies

Biblical associations have been founded to spread the reading, study, and meditation of the Scriptures. The encyclical *Divino afflante Spiritu* treats of this modern biblical study. Such groups should be under the direction of competent religious authorities. (See Basic Teachings for Catholic Religious Education.)

### Biblia Pauperum

Literally "Bibles of the Poor," these were popular picture books of the Bible of about forty pages, each with short explanatory texts used in the fifteenth century.

## Biblical Commission

The official title of this group is *Pontificia Commissio de Re Biblica.* It was established as a commission under the Holy Father by Pope Leo XIII when he issued his apostolic letter *Vigilantiae* on Oct. 30, 1902. Its stated purpose is to procure "that Holy Writ should everywhere among us receive that more elaborate treatment which the times require and be preserved intact not only from any breath of error but also from all rash opinions."

There are many official groups and learned societies that study and continuously work toward a greater understanding and appreciation of the Word of God. Among these are: *World Catholic Federation for the Biblical Apostolate,* established in 1969; the *U. S. Center for the Catholic Biblical Apostolate,* Washington, D.C.; *The Catholic Bible Society,* Dallas, Texas; *The Catholic Biblical Association of America,* Washington, D.C. (See Biblical Institute, Pontifical.)

## Biblical Institute of Jerusalem

A biblical school was founded at Jerusalem by the Dominicans, especially Lagrange, in 1889. It publishes a quarterly, *Revue Biblique.*

## Biblical Institute, Pontifical

Established by apostolic letter, *Vinea Electa,* of May 7, 1909, the Institute is directed to the promotion of the reading and understanding of the Bible. It publishes a biblical quarterly, *Biblica,* which is a scientific treatise, and a less technical bimonthly called *Bulletin of Biblical Theology,* and a special quarterly *Orientalia.*

This Institute is "a center of higher Scripture studies that promotes Biblical and related sciences in the spirit of the Church." Its purposes are to train professors for the teaching of the Scriptures in seminaries and other institutions, do special work in archaeology, and study in oriental fields. The Institute may confer a Doctorate in Sacred Scripture after an intensive period of study over a span of five years. Located in Rome, the Institute not only has the resources of the Vatican Library but has a specialized library of more than 100,000 volumes. A daughter institute was recently established in Jerusalem, and through this, annual tours are organized and firsthand knowledge is available to all its students.

## Bill of Rights

In the United States, the first ten amendments of the Constitution are known as the Bill of Rights.

The bishops of the United States declared at Washington, D.C., Nov. 16, 1952: "The concept of man which they set forth in the Declaration of Independence and on which they based the Constitution and our Bill of Rights, is essentially a religious concept—a concept inherited from Christian tradition." The first amendment guarantees religious freedom to all citizens and noncitizens, and this freedom of belief and thought is considered by all to be the basic absolute that human beings require for the seeking of personal salvation.

## Bilocation

Bilocation is the actual presence of one finite person in two places at the same time. This is not impossible according to reason, since it does not mean the extension of the body or increase of its substance but rather the multiplication of the person's bodily relations to other bodies. It may be said concerning the real presence of Christ in the Holy Eucharist, but this is not because the presence is in place by quantity but by means of its substance, hence not limited by place as are material bodies.

## Bination

Also called "duplicating," this is the permission given to a priest to celebrate more than one Mass on a single day, granted by the ordinary and limited to two Masses, except by apostolic indult. Its purpose is to provide a sufficient number of Masses to give all the faithful a chance to fulfill their obligations. Thus, in a time when priests are fewer in number, trination, or the three times celebration of the Eucharist, has become a common practice.

## Biretta

A biretta is a stiff square cap having three or four projecting "leaves" or prominences rising from the ridges of its top, and usually having a pompom at the top center. It is worn by the clergy; a cardinal's is red, a bishop's purple, and black is for other clerics. The pope does not wear a biretta but instead wears a more loose headpiece called *camauro*. The use of the biretta, since Vatican II, has become a sometime occurrence.

## Birth Control

Birth control is the willful perversion of the natural gifts of God for the engendering of children, whereby conception is prevented: by interrupted or arrested coition, by contraceptive instrument, or by surgery that prohibits the functioning of otherwise healthy organs, or by medical or chemical means. The effects of such actions are to limit the number of offspring, to prevent births, and often to escape the responsibilities of parenthood. It is essentially wrong because: to employ the sexual function for self-gratification in a manner to prohibit the natural purpose of that function is to pervert the function; to defeat the primary purpose of the marriage relation without serious reason is to oppose the divine will. The committee of the bishops of the United States stated the position of the Church in a statement of Jan. 30, 1922: "The Church condemns all positive devices and methods of birth control as necessarily immoral because they are perversions of nature and violations of the moral law. Moreover, they lead inevitably to weakening of character, degradation of conjugal relations, decline of population, and degeneracy of national life. As a remedy for social and economic ills, birth control is not only mistaken and futile, but tends to divert attention from genuine methods of social betterment."

Vatican II declared: "When there is question of harmonizing conjugal love with the responsible transmission of life, the moral aspect of any procedure does not depend solely on sincere intentions or on an evaluation of motives. It must be determined by objective standards. These, based on the nature of the human person and his acts, preserve the full sense of mutual self-giving and human procreation in the context of true love. Such a goal cannot be achieved unless the virtue of conjugal chastity is sincerely practiced. Relying on these principles, sons of the Church may not undertake methods of regulating procreation which are found blameworthy by the teaching authority of the Church in its unfolding of the divine law" (GS 51f.). (See Marriage, Sacrament of.)

## Bishop

From the Greek word meaning "overseer," a bishop is a supreme, divinely instituted member of the Church hierarchy. He has received the highest of the holy orders, is invested with the authority to govern a diocese, and is a successor of the Apostles. Bishops are responsible directly to the Holy Father for the affairs of their diocese (cf. Hierarchy; Jurisdiction). The sacrament of holy orders confers on a bishop spiritual power in its fullness, and he may administer confirmation and holy orders, and ordain other bishops. Besides administration of the temporal and spiritual affairs of a diocese, it is the bishop's duty (1) to teach, that is to guard the purity of doctrine and see that it is given to others; (2) to guard the morals of the faithful under his care, to maintain discipline, and to provide that the faithful receive the sacraments, and ensure divine worship; (3) to reside in his jurisdiction; (4) to visit the parishes of his diocese regularly.

The Second Vatican Council devoted an entire decree on the Bishop's Pastoral Office in the Church *(Chistus Dominus)*. Among its many statements concerning the apostolate of bishops it declared: "As successors of the apostles, bishops automatically enjoy in the dioceses entrusted to them all the ordinary, proper, and immediate authority required for the exercise of their pastoral office. But this authority never in any instance infringes upon the power which the Roman Pontiff has, by virtue of his office, of reserving cases to himself or to some other authority.

"Except when it is a question of matters reserved to the supreme authority of the Church, the general law of the Church gives each diocesan bishop the faculty to grant dispensations in particular cases to the faithful over whom he exercises authority according to the norm of law, provided he judges it helpful for their spiritual welfare" (CD 8). (See Authority; Collegiality; Diocese.)

## Bishop, Auxiliary

See Bishop, Coadjutor.

## Bishop, Coadjutor

Vatican II stated: "Coadjutor and auxiliary bishops should be granted those faculties necessary for rendering their work more effective and for safeguarding the dignity proper to bishops. These purposes should always be accomplished without detriment to the unity of the diocesan administration and the authority of the diocesan bishop" (CD 25). (See Auxiliary Bishop; Coadjutor.)

## Bishop in Partibus Infidelium

A bishop *in partibus infidelium* is ordained to a diocese that existed at one time in the Church but which, because of the loss of faith in that part of the world, no longer exists as a distinct diocese. He is thus a "titular" bishop, and because his diocese as such does not exist he need not make an *ad limina* visit.

## Bishop of Rome

His Holiness the pope is the bishop of Rome, with the Eternal City as his diocese. He is also: Vicar of Jesus Christ, Successor of St. Peter, Supreme Pontiff, having primacy of honor and supreme power of jurisdiction over the Universal Church, Patriarch of the West, Primate of Italy, Archbishop and Metropolitan of the Province of Rome, and Sovereign of the State of Vatican City (cf. Papacy).

## Bishop, Suffragan

See Suffragan Bishop.

## Bishop, Titular

See Bishop; Bishop in Partibus Infidelium.

## Black Fast

The strict abstaining from meat, eggs, butter, cheese, and milk is a black fast.

## Black Friars

1. This name is applied to members of the Dominican order, because of the black mantle they wear over their habits.
2. Black friars are also places, notably in England and Scotland, where the Dominicans had monasteries.

## Black Monks

This is the name given to members of the Benedictine order because of their black habits.

## Blasphemy

Although in English this originally meant any injurious words or statements, it has come to mean explicitly words or actions dishonoring God or words or actions of irreverence against God. Primarily it means verbal attacks on God, but it includes also thoughts, writings and actions, and is divided into two categories: (1) heretical blasphemy, which is a denial of God's providence, etc., and is more grave because it is also a sin against faith; (2) imprecatory blasphemy, which is an imprecation against God that evil may follow. Blasphemy may be indirect in that it is directed against God's attributes, His angels, saints, etc. All blasphemy against God is a grievous sin, the most serious against religion, and transgresses the second commandment (Ex. 20:7).

Blasphemy comes from the Hebrew word meaning "pierced," but as it appears in the NT it comes from the Greek word meaning "reviling." Christ called the accusation of his enemies that his miracles were performed by the power of Satan blasphemous (Mt. 12:25–37). Christians consider blasphemy those actions or words that revile God or Christ. (Cf. 1 Tm. 1:13.)

## Blessed

This official Church title is conferred on one at the pronouncement of the judgment of beatification. (See Beatification; Canonization.)

## Blessed Sacrament

See Eucharist, Sacrament of.

## Blessing

In a scriptural sense, blessing is always opposed to *cursing* and means placing a thing or person under the favor of God, dedicating or giving something or someone to God. In its liturgical meaning it is the ceremony and prayer by which an authorized cleric sanctifies persons or things or invokes God's favor upon them. The ceremony includes the naming of the object and the signing of the cross over it. This latter may be accompanied with a sprinkling of holy water or anointing with holy oils.

In the OT God alone blesses (Gn. 49:25–26), or His blessing is given through His representatives (Dt. 33). In the NT Jesus blesses the children (Mk. 10:16), and blessing is contrasted with the curse by which the damned are deprived of eternal happiness (cf. Mt. 25:34–41).

## Blessing, Apostolic

This benediction or blessing is given by the pope at the close of liturgical functions at which he presides and sometimes at the close of papal audiences. To this blessing a plenary indulgence is attached. This blessing may also be delegated by the pope to be given by others; priests attending the sick at the moment of death may give the apostolic blessing. Also this is referred to the blessing or solemn benediction *Urbi et orbi* given by the pope from the balcony of St. Peter's after his election and on other solemn occasions.

## Boat

1. A symbol in art, the boat represents the Church, or the boat of St. Peter as a fisherman.
2. The container in which incense is kept and used during liturgical ceremonies is called a boat. It is usually accompanied by a small ladle.

## Body, Relation of Soul and

The substantial union of body and soul is a human person. Body and soul are incomplete substances that complete and perfect one another, forming a union of one complete substance. Thus it is the human composite united in one substance and nature, which constitutes the human person and to which all actions of humans are ascribed. (See Being.)

## Body, Resurrection of the

Resurrection of the body is the conversion whereby the body of a person, separated from the soul by death, is reunited with the soul and restored to its complete condition. The resurrection is a dogma of faith. This teaching, first revealed and found in numerous scriptural texts, and defined by the Church, is that the body will live again, will be a part of the accidental beatitude of heaven, and will be glorified (1 Cor. 15:53). It is

a restoration of human nature, since body and soul are incomplete without each other and should not be separated from each other (Mt. 5:29; Jn. 5:29; Acts 17:31). (Cf. Body, Relation of Soul and.)

## Bollandists

This name was given to the writers and editors who, led by John Bolland (d. 1665), a Jesuit of Antwerp, following the plan of the Flemish Jesuit Rosweyde, undertook to compile a complete lives of the saints. Their work goes on and is recorded in the *Analecta Bollandiana*.

## Bolshevism

Bolshevism was the historic forerunner of atheistic communism. The term was applied in 1903 to the movement of the radical leftists in the Social Democratic Party in Russia. They were revolutionaries who moved into power on Nov. 6, 1917, when Nicolai Lenin became dictator of Russia. The aims of bolshevism were: (1) a so-called liberation of the people, (2) the overthrow of capitalism and substitution of communism under the dictatorship of the proletariat, (3) nationalization of all resources and industries. (Cf. Communism.)

## Bona Mors

Bona mors is the name of the Happy Death Confraternity, founded in the church of the Gesu in Rome by Fr. V. Caraffa in 1648. It was later raised to an archconfraternity and has for its objective the preparing of its members for a good death in grace, through a well-regulated life, and meditation on the Passion of Christ and the suffering of Mary.

## Book of Common Prayer

The primary book of public worship, ritual, and prayers used by Anglicans and Episcopalians is the Book of Common Prayer. The first edition was published in 1549 under the auspices of Edward VI of England and was based on the Latin texts of the missals of the time together with other manuals and the breviary. Subsequent editions were issued with strong leanings toward the Reformed churches, as the revisions of 1559, 1604, 1662. The Episcopal Church in America adopted the Book of Common Prayer in 1789 and has revised it twice, with the present use being the edition of 1928. There is at present a trend toward a book more in keeping with the liturgical tradition and the widespread ecumenical exchange between the Episcopal Church and the Roman Catholic Church. (See Ecumenism.)

## Book of Hours

This book was used in the Middle Ages, containing prayers, Psalms, and antiphons, to be recited at the canonical hours. It was a form of breviary for common use in a monastery and a contributing source for the later breviary and the modern Liturgy of the Hours.

## Books

See Index of Forbidden Books.

## Boys Town

This unique establishment for homeless and underprivileged boys is an incorporated, self-governed city located ten miles west of Omaha, Nebraska. It was founded on Dec. 10, 1917, by Father Edward J. Flanagan and was first known as Father Flanagan's Boys' Home. Beginning with five boys and less than one hundred dollars, the Town now has more than fifty buildings with complete educational and housing facilities for 900 boys from the fifth grade through the high school. The teachers are lay men and women, providing fully accredited training not only in the academic courses but also excellent vocational training in the manual arts including ceramics, woodworking, printing, machinery, auto mechanics, baking, tailoring, electronics, and agriculture along with many others. It has a social program including a band, a sixty voice choir, which tours the United States and Canada, livestock exhibitions, 4H club activities, and athletics. Religious training is stressed as the foundation of good personal and civic growth, and every boy is required to attend the service of his faith each week. The Town is supported by voluntary contributions, and no religious agency or government funds have been sought to maintain the many boys and their projects and education. Recently girls have been admitted to the educational facilities.

## Brahmanism

Brahmanism, a system of religious response originated in India, became the forerunner of Hinduism. There is still an elitist group that call themselves Brahmans in the Hindu complex. The religion was started a thousand years before Christ, deriving its original thinking from the Aryans whose work, the *Rig-Veda,* was basic. In its worship Brahmanism and its development center around a complex deity group including the Prajapati (lord of creation), Vishnu (the preserver), and Siva (the destroyer). These gods represented the higher existence under whose guidance the world was ruled. There are elaborate ceremonies, sacrificial rites, offerings, and an involved system of ritual that has a priestly form of worship, family religious rites, and rigid training in the literature and cult of renouncement.

## Branch Theory

This is the misconception, advanced chiefly by Anglicans, that the one, true Church is composed of the Anglican, Catholic, and Orthodox Churches. It is opposed to the "oneness" of the Church as a mark of its authority.

## Brasses

Brasses are engravings on incised sheets of heavy brass, called latten. They were used as memorials of the dead and placed over sepulchers or as ends of sepulchral niches used from the thirteenth to the eighteenth century. They were often inscribed with pertinent details or carved with figures of the person buried and so became valuable records.

## Bread for the World

This new organization has as its purpose to enlist the aid of Christian Churches to overcome the poverty and hunger of the Third World and underdeveloped nations. In May, 1974, this ecumenical group made an appeal to United States' citizens (and those in other countries) to abstain from meat three days a week as a means of aiding those nations with serious food shortages. Through this tactic it was estimated that there would be an increase in the grain reserves. The broader aspect calls for a Christian effort to conserve food supplies so that they may be distributed to nations unable to provide adequate food for themselves because of population, crop failure, or drought.

## Bread of Life

Bread of Life is the name given to the eucharistic

Christ, the sacrament of the body and blood of Christ under the appearances of bread (Jn. 6:35–40). The name was given to Himself by Christ: "I am the bread of life" (Jn. 6:48).

### Breaking of Bread

In Latin called the *Fractio panis,* this famous fresco in the catacomb of St. Priscilla depicts the early (second century) celebration of the Eucharist. It is also the sign of recognition wherein the Apostles at Emmaus knew it was the Lord who spoke with them (Lk. 24:30).

This became a technical term applied to the Eucharist (cf. 1 Cor. 10:16) and was so used in the postapostolic Church according to the writings of Ignatius of Antioch, as also in the *Didache* (14:1). It is not, however, a description of the manner of celebrating the Eucharist in its liturgical form in the early Church.

### Brethren of the Lord

Reference is made in several instances in the Bible to "the brethren" of our Lord (Mt. 12:46; Mk. 3:3–35). These were not full brothers of our Lord, that is, sons of Joseph and Mary, nor were they half-brothers, that is, sons of Joseph by a former marriage. They were at most cousins of Jesus. Only four of the "brethren" are named in the Gospels: James, Joseph, Simon, and Jude. This is evident from the passages of scripture (Mt. 13:55; Mk. 6:3) where the "brothers" are shown to be of a mother other than the Blessed Mother. Likewise the "brothers" (or sisters) appear in the Gospel accounts only in the public life of Christ, and since Christ at his death commends his mother to John, his disciple, it is further apparent that Mary and Joseph had no other offspring.

### Breviary

This is the liturgical book containing the Divine Office assigned to the canonical hours, which must be recited by all persons in holy orders and by men and women religious who have professed solemn vows.

The breviary is now referred to as the *Liturgy of the Hours.* It is the public prayer of the Church, used by the laity, ministers, deacons, clergy, and religious, for the praise of God and the sanctifying of each day. Vatican II stated: "By tradition going back to early Christian times, the divine Office is arranged so that the whole course of the day and night is made holy by the praises of God. Therefore, when this wonderful song of praise is worthily rendered by priests and others who are deputed for this purpose by Church ordinance, or by the faithful praying together with the priest in

an approved form, then it is truly the voice of the bride addressing her bridegroom; it is the very prayer which Christ Himself, together with His body, addresses to the Father.

"Hence all who perform this service are not only fulfilling a duty of the Church, but also are sharing in the greatest honor accorded to Christ's spouse, for by offering these praises to God they are standing before God's throne in the name of the Church their Mother.

"Priests engaged in the sacred pastoral ministry will offer the praises of the hours with fervor to the extent that they vividly realize that they must heed St. Paul's exhortations 'Never cease praying' (1 Thes. 5:17). For only the Lord can give fruitfulness and increase to the works in which they are engaged. 'Apart from me,' He said, 'you can do nothing' (Jn. 15:5). That is why the apostles, appointing deacons, said: 'This will permit us to concentrate on the ministry of the word' (Acts 6:4)" (SC 84–86).

Revision of the Liturgy of the Hours was set forth by Pope Paul VI in the apostolic constitution *Canticum Laudis* of Nov. 1, 1970. This Office now consists of: Lauds and Vespers, the morning and evening prayers called "the hinges" of the Office. Matins is to be said at any time of the day and retains the form of a nocturnal vigil service and is called the Office of Readings. Terce, Sext, None are the prayers that may be said at any appropriate hour or time of the day, as 9 A.M., 12 noon, 3 P.M. Compline is the night prayer. Thus, the only hour of the previous breviary that is no longer included is that of Prime.

The new Liturgy of the Hours has the following characteristics distinguishing it from the former breviary: the hours are shorter, with greater variations in the readings, meditation aids, provision for intervals of silence and meditation; the Psalms are distributed in arrangement over a four-week period, while some Psalms are entirely or in part not included; additional scriptural readings have been added, and canticles from the Old and New Testaments are assigned respectively for Lauds and Vespers; and greater unity and closer conjunction with the liturgical year has been achieved through corresponding the readings to those of the Mass; and readings from the fathers of the Church have been made more selectively, together with the lives of the saints to keep all in relevance to the major themes of salvation history.

An interim book called the "Prayer of Christians" has been substituted since 1971 after approval of the Federation of Diocesan Liturgical Commissions, because the Latin text had not been translated into English or published. The new

Breviary, under the title of *Liturgy of the Hours* has been published by Catholic Book Publishing Company in 1975, and will be universal. (See Calendar, Church.)

## Bride of Christ

This term is applied in a figurative sense to (1) the Church (2 Cor. 11:2), (2) a woman who dedicates her virginity by vow to God, (3) a state of mystical union enjoyed by certain saints.

## Brief, Apostolic, also Breve

An apostolic brief is a letter issuing from the chancery of the pope, less solemn and formal than a bull, to which has been affixed a seal marked with the Fisherman's Ring. Such apostolic letters are issued when a beatification is announced and when public statements arising from the Secretariat of State are given for general communication.

## Brothers

Generally, those members of a religious community or society of men who are not priests are called "brother." It may be that some of these are preparing for the priesthood and prior to ordination are so called. Others who have no intention to receive ordination are, properly speaking, brothers who live according to the rule of the religious order, dedicate their lives to service of religion within the purpose of the order, and are frequently referred to as "lay brothers." There are also religious communities of men whose members do not intend to enter the priesthood, but who serve a special purpose of religion in particular fields such as education or hospital work, e.g., Christian Brothers; Brothers of Mary.

The National Assembly of Religious Brothers was founded in 1972, representing the twenty-four brotherhoods in the United States, and as a service organization for the purpose of making more effective their apostolate. Mixed institutes of priests and brothers may also belong to this Assembly. Its primary objectives are: "to encourage actively the development of the religious life of its members and of all brothers, to be concerned and involved with the needs of the Church and society, to establish realistic and effective means of communication and cooperation."

## Buddhism

The religion that centers around Buddha, who was called the Sage of India and the Enlightened or Awakened One and who is recognized as its founder. He was born in what is now Nepal in about 563 B.C. and was named Siddhartha Gautama. In His early life Buddha spent much time in severe penance and abnegation, but this was too harsh a self-inflicted life of no meaning and he became a holy beggar. One night about 531 B.C. he was meditating when he experienced an "enlightenment" wherein he saw the visible world was empty and that nothing earthly was permanent. This spiritual insight was the foundation of the prime spiritual influence of the Asiatic world for the past two and a half thousand years. The basic teachings are fourfold: (1) Suffering is universal in a constantly changing world. (2) Suffering comes from desire. (3) The extinction of desire is to follow an eightfold path: right understanding, right purpose, right speech, right conduct, right work, right effort, right mindfulness, and right contemplation. This path is called the Buddhist Way of Perfection. Buddha died about 483 B.C. There were developments over the years, but in the twentieth century the religion lost much of its spiritual and cultural force, though a contemplative form called Zen Buddhism is being studied as contributory to the intellectual life of the present time.

## Bull, Apostolic

An apostolic bull is a major decree from the Apostolic Chancery. These bulls take their name from the lead seal affixed to them by the official known as the *Plombator*. Formerly all such documents were known as "bulls," but now they are chiefly the Apostolic Bulls for the appointment of bishops, erection of dioceses, and decrees of the Sacred Congregations or the pope. The bulls are signed by the Cardinal Chancellor and by two of the Prothonotaries Apostolic of the College of Notaries of the Roman Curia. They are the most solemn of communications originating in the Vatican.

## Bulla Cruciata

This is a collection of papal bulls, documents, letters, and briefs, which conferred certain privileges upon the people of Spain for their service and support during the Crusades against the Moslems. Beginning in 1063, these privileges were made permanent after the defeat of the Moslems by Spain in 1492. These grants of favor were: a plenary indulgence for all Spanish subjects during the reconquest of Spain, similar to that granted the Crusaders to the Holy Land and the jubilee indulgence for pilgrims to Rome; dispensation from fasting and abstinence on all but a few days of the year. Although these were made to coincide with the Code of Canon Law in 1928, the privileges are still in force for the benefit of everyone on

Spanish territory, regardless of their nationality or place of residence, and this extends to other countries that were once under the domination of Spain, e.g., Portugal.

## Bullarium

This term is applied to any collection of papal bulls.

### Bureau of Information

See National Catholic Welfare Conference; United States Catholic Conference.

### Burial, Ecclesiastical

The interment of the body of a deceased person in consecrated ground after the funeral rites of the Church is ecclesiastical burial. This honor is conferred by the Church and can be withheld because of grave reasons, such as: public life of sin and dying unrepentant; deliberate suicide; membership in forbidden societies; apostasy; heresy or schism; excommunication; interdiction; or dueling. Final determination of such cases is referred to the bishop (c. 1204; 1239–1240). A person who is a non-Catholic partner of a mixed marriage may be buried in a Catholic cemetery. (See, Funeral; Cremation.)

### Burse, also Bursary, Bursa, Pera

1. Known in medieval times as the "corporal case," this is a square (9 inches by 9 inches) case, usually made of two stiff pieces of cardboard, bound at three sides, covered with silk to match the vestments, ornamented with a cross, and lined with linen into which the corporal used at Mass or Benediction is placed. It is carried to the altar above the veiled chalice.

2. The leather, silk-lined purse in which the pyx is carried when the Blessed Sacrament is brought to the sick is also a burse. To this there are usually attached two tie-bands with which the priest may secure the burse to his person while carrying the host.

### Burse, Financial

This fund or endowment, in whole or in part, is invested to provide for the expense of educating one or more aspirants to the priesthood. Such funds may vary according to need and are of no fixed amount as a rule.

### Buskins

Buskins, ceremonial stockings, reaching to the knees, are worn over the ordinary violet stockings by a bishop when celebrating a pontifical Mass. Buskins are ornamented with embroidery and are usually of silk, matching the color of the vestments, but they are not worn when black vestments are used, or for a requiem Mass.

### Byzantine Art

This form of art, developed in Constantinople in the fourth century, was a combination of early Greek and Christian art, centered on lavish color and somewhat florid decoration. It was protected by the Church and followed the norms laid down by the Church for art to be used in the expression of religious truths. In architecture, it is characterized by rejection of wood in construction, the use of vaulting, and a balance of thrust and counterthrust; in sculpture, it did not carve in the round but used flat surface and incised design; in painting, it was expressed by painting on wood, in miniatures, and reached its greatest expression in mosaic work.

### Byzantine Rite

A development of the Antiochene rite, this is the liturgy followed in the celebration of the Mass, administration of the sacraments and other Church functions, by the Greek Church of the Patriarchate of Constantinople, the Orthodox Churches of Greece and Russia, and the Eastern Churches in union with Rome. Next to the Roman, it is the second most used rite. As of now it is a combination of the modifications introduced by St. Basil the Great and St. John Chrysostom after whom the two Greek Mass books are named. Baptism is administered by immersion, and confirmation is conferred immediately after. In the calendar of the Byzantine rite the liturgical year begins on Sept. 1, called the Day of Indiction, and the calendar itself is called the Menologion. The dating of feasts follows the Gregorian Calendar.

## Caeremoniale Episcoporum

This liturgical book contains the rites and ceremonies to be observed by bishops and certain lesser prelates in performing episcopal acts. It also contains the order of rank to be followed in determining precedence of clergy and lay persons.

## Caeremoniarius

A caeromoniarius is an officially appointed master of ceremonies.

## Caesaropapism

This term applied to the interference of rulers of states or civil authorities with the authority and control of Church affairs exercised by Church officials. Originally this arose at the time of the Roman Empire in the fourth century and as a policy was first called Byzantinism, later Caesaropapism. It began when the emperors assumed religious jurisdiction, deciding theological questions by order of the throne, appointed bishops and treated them as officials of the court. It meant a divided authority in the handling of heretics, erroneous teachings, and the control of internal affairs of the Church. It led to a division into spheres of influence between the East and the West. Since that time various other leaders of countries have attempted to seize the spiritual rule of the Church, and only by vigilance and strong diplomatic policies has the authority of the Church in executive and doctrinal matters been maintained.

## Cagots

Cagots was the name given to a group of Christians, of a presumed lower class of people, of the tenth century in Southern France. They were limited to country living and could only be trained as butchers or carpenters and were not welcome in the main part of the churches. This attempt at establishing a caste system in Christian circles failed and does not exist today.

## Calatrava, Order of

This is one of the three military orders of Spain founded in the twelfth century, which were under the direction of the Cistercians and espoused a rigorous rule of life in carrying out the pledge of knighthood. All were done away with by Isabella and Ferdinand in the fifteenth century when they attached all such orders to the crown. However, the title now exists as an honorary distinction.

## Calced

This descriptive word is applied to those persons in some branches of religious orders who wear shoes. This is in contrast to those members of religious orders who do not and who are designated as "discalced." The term is less in use today because of the travel and greater mobility of members of these religious orders.

## Calefactory

1. Calefactory referred to a heated room in early monasteries.
2. A form of hot-water bottle, a hollow metal globe, filled with warm water, the calefactory was used in early medieval times by the priest to warm his fingers so he could distribute communion more securely in cold churches.

## Calendar, Church

The Church calendar is also called the "Liturgical Calendar." It has been the traditional practice of civilized peoples to have the cycle of the times of the year associated with their religious practices. This has been true of the Jewish Calendar, the calendars of the Moslems, which begin with the year *1* corresponding to the year A.D. 622, as well as the Chinese and Japanese calendars.

The early Church calendar followed the time cycles of twelve lunar months, amounting to 364 days in the year, but this was incorrect and could not be brought into proper reckoning with the Julian Calendar. There arose severe differences in the Church over the timing of feasts. Then in A.D. 325 at the Council of Nicaea, it was decided that Easter was to be determined as on the first Sunday following the first full moon of the spring equinox.

There were inaccuracies in the Julian Calendar in calculating the length of the year and this error, amounting to ten days by 1582, was corrected by the Gregorian Calendar under the urging of Pope Gregory the XIII. The accumulated error of ten days was eliminated, and the slight astronomical difference was corrected by the new reckoning of leap-year. Even today this is not entirely corrected since according to the true astronomical year the twelve month cycle is off by 26 seconds annually.

With this brief background we turn to the Church calendar, which for the Roman Church is an arrangement of a series of liturgical seasons throughout the year and a daily assignment of feasts of the saints or commemorations. There is unity and harmony in this procedural course of integrating each day of the year into a continuing, interrelated cycle of divine worship that takes into account both the daily celebration of the Eucharist and the Liturgy of the Hours.

Vatican II stressed the importance of the Church calendar and pointed to a new assessment of feasts and complete reorganization.

"Holy Mother Church is conscious that she must celebrate the saving work of her divine Spouse by devoutly recalling it on certain days throughout the course of the year. Every week, on the day which she has called the Lord's day, she keeps the memory of His resurrection. In the supreme solemnity of Easter she also makes an annual commemoration of the resurrection, along with the Lord's blessed passion.

"Within the cycle of a year, moreover, she unfolds the whole mystery of Christ, not only from His incarnation and birth until His ascension, but also as reflected in the day of Pentecost, and the expectation of a blessed, hoped-for return of the Lord.

"Recalling thus the mysteries of redemption, the Church opens to the faithful the riches of her Lord's powers and merits, so that these are in some way made present at all times, and the faithful are enabled to lay hold of them and become filled with saving grace.

"In celebrating this annual cycle of Christ's mysteries, holy Church honors with special love the Blessed Mary, Mother of God, who is joined by an inseparable bond to the saving work of her Son. In her the Church holds up and admires the most excellent fruit of the redemption, and joyfully contemplates, as in a faultless model, that which she herself wholly desires and hopes to be.

"The Church has also included in the annual cycle, days devoted to the memory of the martyrs and the other saints. Raised up to perfection by the manifold grace of God, and already in possession of eternal salvation, they sing God's perfect praise in heaven and offer prayers for us. By celebrating the passage of these saints from earth to heaven the Church proclaims the paschal mystery as achieved in the saints who have suffered and been glorified with Christ; she proposes them to the faithful as examples who draw all to the Father through Christ, and through their merits she pleads for God's favors.

"Finally, in the various seasons of the year and according to her traditional discipline, the Church completes the formation of the faithful by means of pious practices for soul and body, by instruction, prayer, and works of penance and of mercy.

"Accordingly, this most sacred Council has seen fit to decree as follows:

"By an apostolic tradition which took its origin from the very day of Christ's resurrection, the Church celebrates the paschal mystery every eighth day; with good reason this, then, bears the name of the Lord's day or the day of the Lord. For on this day Christ's faithful should come together into one place so that, by hearing the word of God and taking part in the Eucharist, they may call to mind the passion, the resurrection, and the glorification of the Lord Jesus, and may thank God who 'gave us new birth; a birth unto hope which draws its life from the resurrection of Jesus Christ from the dead' (1 Pt. 1:3). Hence the Lord's day is the original feast day, and it should be proposed to the piety of the faithful and taught to them in such a way that it may become in fact a day of joy and of freedom from work. Other celebrations, unless they be truly of overriding importance, must not have precedence over this day, which is the foundation and nucleus of the whole liturgical year.

"The liturgical year is to be revised so that the traditional customs and discipline of the sacred seasons can be preserved or restored to meet the conditions of modern times; their specific character is to be retained so that they duly nourish the piety of the faithful who celebrate the mysteries of Christian redemption, and above all the paschal mystery" (SC 102–107).

Thus on May 9, 1969, Pope Paul VI gave his approval for a complete reorganization of the Church Calendar declaring the purpose to be that "the faithful (may) communicate in a more intense way, through faith, hope and love in the 'whole mystery of Christ which . . . unfolds within the cycle of the year.'"

The new calendar was promulgated and went into effect Jan. 1, 1970, with the full implementation made after the work on the liturgical texts was completed. In 1972 the Bishops of the U. S. and many other countries ordered the new calendar into effect, and usage was complete with the introduction of the Sacramentary in 1974. The general norms listed for the Liturgical Calendar are: "The Church celebrates the memory of Christ's saving work on appointed days in the course of the year. Every week the Church celebrates the memorial of the resurrection on

Sundays, which is called the Lord's Day. This is also celebrated, together with the passion of Jesus, on the great feast of Easter once a year. Throughout the year the entire mystery of Christ is unfolded, and the birthdays (days of death) of the saints are commemorated." (Exceptions are the Feast of St. John the Baptist who is honored on the day of his birth and Sts. Basil the Great and Gregory Nazianzen, and Sts. Cyril and Methodius who have shared feasts.)

"A liturgical day runs from midnight to midnight, but the observance of Sunday and of solemnities begins with the evening of the preceding day," and thus the celebration of the Eucharist, with fulfillment of the Sunday or holy day obligation, may be on the evening before. (See Feasts of the Church; Breviary and Readings, Cycle of.)

## California Missions

Missionary work was carried on in the territory of California by Franciscans from the middle of the eighteenth century till 1834. It included the conversion and instruction of the native Indians, and the building of religious institutions. When the far southwestern portion of continental United States became a part of Mexico in 1822, the missions were exploited and plundered by the state-appointed commissioners. This led to a great loss of faith among the Indians. Many of the sites and the mission buildings remain as memorials of the missionary activity of the time and are examples of skillful architecture and adaptation to a difficult terrain by Church missioners. These missions and the dates of their founding are:

San Diego   July 16, 1769
San Carlos Borromeo   June 3, 1770
San Antonia   July 14, 1771
Sun Luis Obispo   September 1, 1771
San Gabriel   September 8, 1771
San Francisco   October 9, 1776
San Juan Capistrano   November 1, 1776
Santa Clara   January 12, 1777
San Buenaventura   March 31, 1781
Santa Barbara   December 16, 1786
La Purisima Concepción   December 8, 1787
Santa Cruz   August 28, 1791
Nuestra Señora de la Soledad   October 9, 1791
San José   June 11, 1797
San Juan Bautista   June 24, 1797
San Miguel   July 25, 1797
San Fernando   September 8, 1797
San Luis Rey   June 13, 1798
Santa Inés   September 17, 1804

San Raphael Arcángel   December 14, 1817
San Francisco Solano   July 4, 1823

## Calixtines, also Hussites

This name was given to those who demanded Holy Communion under both species.

## Calling

Often referred to one's vocation to service in the ordained or nonordained ministries of the Church, the word calling is descriptive of service in the religious sphere. This has foundation in Scriptures as a term meaning God's invitation to share in His work (Prv. 1:24; 2:1–5). In the NT frequent use of the term as directed to men is found, e.g., Mt. 22:14; Rv. 19:9, and even to sinners (Mt. 9:13). The calling of God indicates His love for the chosen one (1 Cor. 1:2; Jude 1), and it can mean the calling of one to special endeavors as in 2 Tm. 1:9–10: "God has saved us and has called us to a holy life, not because of any merit of ours but according to his own design—the grace held out to us in Christ Jesus before the world began but now made manifest through the appearance of our Savior." The word also refers strongly to the calling God gives to the Christian's work of salvation as in 2 Thes. 2:14, "He called you through our preaching of the good news so that you might achieve the glory of our Lord Jesus Christ."

## Calumny

This is a more serious form of detraction, in that it is lying as well as an injustice against another. Thus, calumny is the uttering or publishing or otherwise relating to others of statements which are known to be false, which harm the character or reputation of another. It is a grave sin depending on the nature of the statements and the damage that may follow to the good name of the person. It demands retraction and repair of the damage insofar as the resulting damage was foreseen. An oath disclaiming calumny is given, under canon law, by both sides in a litigation. (Cf. Detraction.)

## Calvary

In Aramaic, *Gulgulta,* in Greek, literally, "the place of the skull," and translated into the Latin equivalent *calvarium,* this was originally the name given to a place of execution that was customarily located on a rocky site or a small rise. Calvary was the place near Jerusalem where Christ was crucified. It is also called Golgotha (Mt. 27:

33–38). In the plural "calvaries," this refers to the wayside shrines in which the crucifix is shown. This is also applied to outdoor stations of the Cross, as that at the Shrine of Our Lady of Lourdes.

### Calvinism

The theological system developed by the French Reformer, John Calvin (1509 to 1564) has had the greatest influence, outside the work of Martin Luther, in the Reformed Churches of Protestantism. Calvin's most important work was contained in a writing, *Institutes of the Christian Religion.* In its theological concepts it shows Calvin to have been most concerned with the knowledge of God, and this is reflected in the very beginning of the *Institutes* where it is affirmed by the author that all human wisdom consists in the knowledge of God and ourselves. The knowledge of God is twofold: God as Creator and Sustainer of man, and of all the world.

Calvin had already founded his church by the time of the Council of Trent (1545 to 1563) and in its development of doctrine the following are the principal teachings: (1) God's plan in regard to man and creation is one of predestination; thus, man cannot through his own merits change his ultimate salvation or damnation. (2) Faith in Christ is alone the saving factor that justifies man's actions, leading to a conclusion that man must perform good works and lead a life of probity not to attain salvation but as a sign that he is already saved. (3) Man is completely corrupt, because of original sin and cannot choose between good and evil; thus, he cannot resist sin. As a consequence man's assurance of salvation comes from the belief that once God has given grace to man, the person cannot resist this grace. (4) Man, enlightened by the Holy Spirit, interprets the written word of God in his own mind and the Bible is the sole fountain of faith. (5) The sacraments do not have a saving efficacy, but are merely signs of one's salvation. Thus, only two sacraments, Baptism and the Lord's Supper, are recorded in the Bible, and the first only is a sign of one's membership in the Church with all remission of sin being a sign, since sin is remitted by faith in Christ. The second is only a sign or signification of the body and blood of Christ and this has now been interpreted as a memorialization of Christ's action. (6) Those who profess faith in Christ make up the visible Church, which was founded by Christ and thus commands obedience and can exact laws. (7) Moderation of all worldly goods is encouraged but man need not forego possessions since these are signs of God's

favor to men. (8) The Church and the State must work together, but the Church is dominate in the control of the State.

The leading groups of the Calvinist extraction are the United Presbyterian Church and the United Church of Christ. The leading modern theologian is Karl Barth whose *Church Dogmatics* rejects many of the rigid positions of his predecessors in the Reformation theology as it progressed to the twentieth century. (See Edict of Nantes.)

### Camauro

This is the headpiece worn by the pope instead of the biretta, and which is a loose, full cap of red velvet trimmed with white fur. It has no brim. Permitted only on extraliturgical occasions, it is seldom used today but is frequently seen in paintings of the popes.

### Camera

Literally, a camera is a room. (See Curia, Roman.)

### Camerlengo, also Camerarius

A camerlengo is an official of the Holy See who is always a cardinal. The office is largely honorary today, although previously it called for wide financial dealings. However, with the death of a pope, the interim administration of the Holy See is carried on by the cardinal camerlengo. His duties are limited to the temporal affairs of the Church. He issues the official notice of the pope's death, closes the papal apartments, and places the documents and effects of the dead pope under seal. His authority ceases with the election of a new pope.

### Camisia

This name is infrequently applied to the alb. Originally it referred to the place where the book of Gospels was kept in the early Church. (See Alb.)

### Campaign for Human Development

This social action was begun by the United States Catholic Conference, Nov. 1969, to overcome poverty in the United States in a threefold program: (1) by making all people, but Catholics in particular, through the media of news and education aware of poverty existing among the many millions of people throughout the country; (2) through the annual solicitation of funds, which were gathered to fight the basic causes of poverty rather than as a means of overcoming the blight of poverty itself; (3) through the funding of self-help programs begun by the poor and implemented by them for the overcoming of the sources of poverty and the self-inflicted degradation that such poverty causes.

The first collection was taken up in all parishes of the country on Nov. 22, 1970. The National Office of the Campaign is in Washington, D.C., where the screening of fund requests and the allocation of funds are made each year.

### Campanile

A campanile is a tall, slender structure erected adjoining a church building or standing apart from it, in which bells are kept. This bell tower differs from the steeple. The leaning tower of Pisa is a campanile.

### Campus Ministry

According to the guidelines drawn up by an eight member commission of the National Catholic Educational Association, the general purpose of the ministry is to make the Church present and take an active role in the academic and social environment of the college and university communities. "Campus ministry is a pastoral apostolate of service to the members of the entire college community through concern and care for persons, the proclamation of the Gospel, and the celebration of the liturgy."

The program is to provide greater participation in the religious aspects of the college communities with emphasis upon liturgical leadership, pastoral counseling, Christian witness regarding the social and moral issues, and an ecumenical effort among various groups on the campus. (See Ministries.)

### Cana

A place name from the Hebrew meaning "place of reeds," it was an important Canaanite city (Jos. 19:28). In the NT it is a city of Galilee where Jesus was present at a wedding and changed water into wine (Jn. 2:1), and it is the hometown of Nathanael (Jn. 21:2).

### Cana Conferences

This is a twofold program: preparation for the reception of the Sacrament of Marriage is classed as pre-Cana, and programs for married couples are Cana Conferences. This movement of special purpose has the long-range intent of deepening the religious experience of persons, overcoming through counseling, discussion, and practical preparation, the problems confronting those who wish to contract marriage and those who have already done so. Conference groups are open to persons of all religions and have as leaders priests, physicians, psychiatrists, marriage experts, and special lecturers. The movement named after Cana (cf. Cana) had its origin in New York city as the Family Renewal Days begun in 1943 under its founder, Father John P. Delaney, S. J. The Bishops of the United States in their statement of 1949 urged the promotion of the Cana Conferences throughout the country.

The movement operates through conferences that offer instruction and discussion under the leadership of the priest-director. There are two divisions, but both have a single purpose: First, the pre-Cana Conference, which is to instruct those who are preparing for receiving the sacrament of marriage; second, the Cana Conference, which aims at instruction in the true, dignified and happy conduct of life in the married state. Its program of instruction is directed primarily at the married state as a spiritual state of mutual work toward the salvation of the married parties and the responsible execution of obligations to promote the salvation of their children. It is also directed to the physical, moral, economic, and psychological relationships of the married state or any subjects that are salutary to this state. Its chief aim is the formation of family life in Christ, and to this end it seeks to promote retreats for the family, understanding through reading and instruction, Holy Hours for the family, and frequent reception of the sacraments (cf. Marriage, Sacrament of; Christian Family Movement.)

### Canada

The largest country of the North American continent, on the northern boundary of the United States, is a bilingual nation. Its religious population is predominantly Catholic. The Canadian Catholic Conference of Bishops has four major departments with twenty-five offices. These are: *Doctrine and Faith Department* with six offices; theology (French and English); religious education; liturgy. *Social Life Department* with five offices: social action (French); social action and family life (English); social communications (French and English); health and welfare (French). *Internal Relations Department* with six offices: clergy (French); clergy, seminaries, education, vocations (English), religious orders (French and English), lay apostolate (French and English). *Missions and Ecumenism Department* with eight offices: apostolic and missionary assistance (French and English), ecumenism (French and English), nonbelievers (French). (See Canadian Shrines.)

### Canadian Shrines

Many of the shrines that have become known to travelers and tourists came about through French devotion in the settling of much of Canada after 1600, with a temporary setback by Wolfe's victory on the Plains of Abraham in 1759 resulting in English supremacy. All the shrines mentioned here are of historic and artistic importance. They are: Sainte Anne-de-Micmacs, Restigouche, Quebec; Sainte Anne-de-Beaupre, Quebec; Our Lady of the Holy Rosary, Cap-de-la-Madeleine, Quebec; Hermitage of Saint Anthony, La Bouchette, Quebec; Saint Joseph's Oratory, Montreal, Quebec; Chapel of Atonement, Pointe-aux-Trembles, Quebec; Our Lady of Lourdes, Rigaud, Quebec; Saint Benoit-du-Lac, near Magog, Quebec; and the Martyrs' Shrine, near Midland, Ontario. (See under separate entries.)

### Cancelli

Literally, these are the communion railings separating the sanctuary from the nave of the church. In the new emphasis on community since Vatican II, the communion railing has been replaced by communion stations. Hence, the sacred space about the altar is no longer closed off by a railing except where this was architecturally impossible to accomplish without serious damage. (Cf. Chancel.)

### Candle

Blessed candles are sacramentals used in the liturgy of the Church. They were used from very early times and according to St. Jerome were symbols of joy. There are no strict rules concerning the size or shape of candles. However, those used during liturgical functions and exposition of the Blessed Sacrament contain more than 50% of pure beeswax, but the general rule is that as requisites for liturgical use, candles should be of "a worthy material and suited to their purpose." So-called vigil or votive lights are not blessed as a rule.

### Candle, Paschal

This is a large, i.e., tall, candle that is blessed and lighted on the Vigil of Easter and is symbolic of the risen Christ. It is lighted from Easter to the Reading of the Gospel on the Solemnity of Ascension. It is placed and remains on the Gospel side of the altar (*sic*) until Ascension Day, but current liturgy permits its presence, unlighted,

through the Easter and Pentecostal seasons. The candle itself is generally highly ornamented with colored wax forms or symbols, but it must have, in

the form of a cross, five imbedded or mounted grains of incense representing the wounds of Christ. The paschal candle is used at the ceremony of blessing baptismal water at which time a part of the candle is immersed into the water.

### Candlemas

This name is sometimes applied to the feast of the purification of the B.V.M. celebrated on Feb. 2, now called in the new Church Calendar "The Presentation of the Lord." It is so called because candles are blessed on this day. (See Presentation of the Blessed Virgin Mary.)

### Candlesticks

These belong to the furnishings of any altar and, as the word indicates, they should be single, that is, on one base and not a part of a branch. They may be made of wood or metal but should not stand higher than the base of the crucifix at the altar's center.

### Canon

1. A canon is either the rule or law of guidance, or standard or norm that follows reason; or it may be the sum total (Kant) of all such principles in the correct application of our knowledge. In art, it means an established rule directive to a reasoned standard. (Cf. Canon of the Scripture; Canon of the Mass.)

2. Canon is the title of members of a cathedral chapter. These clerics are appointed by the bishop to assist in divine services and Church government. They are governed by special legislation since the office grants the spiritual right of a voice in the chapter and a share of the revenue of the chapter. As a title it is seldom used in the United States.

## Canon Law

The official body of ecclesiastical law for the Latin Church is gathered in a single volume known as the Code of Canon Law (in Latin: *Codex Juris Canonici*). There always existed in the Church groups of laws, collections of canons that were formally recognized. In 1234 Pope Gregory IX issued five books of "Decretals" and later additions were made. However, there was great necessity for a codification of laws that would contain the regulating decrees and application of legal thought to the administration of the Church. Under Pope St. Pius X the monumental task of codification was begun late in 1903. In a little less than 14 years the work was completed, examined by the bishops throughout the world, and promulgated on Pentecost Sunday, 1917, by Pope Benedict XV. After one year of study, it was decreed that this code would have the force of law beginning on Pentecost, May 19, 1918. In the Code the whole of canon law is reduced to 2,414 canons, divided into five sections or books. There are 86 canons on the general principles under which the Code is applied; 639 canons on categories of persons in the Church; 826 canons on the means employed by the Church to achieve its purpose; 643 canons on procedures and rules governing Church tribunals; and 220 canons on the penal code of the Church. It is this body of law that is exercised in behalf of the faithful by the Roman Curia and all Church courts and regulates the functioning of all Church affairs. At the time of promulgation, a special Pontifical Commission was set up to interpret, clarify, and pronounce on the meaning of any disputed part of the law.

There is, since Vatican II, a complete revision of Canon Law. Not only is this true for the Roman Rite but also for the Code of Oriental Canon Law. Progress on this latter, since its beginning in July 1935, has reached 1,950 canons concerning marriage; processes; religious, church property, and terminology; Eastern Rites and persons. In those portions completed but not yet published, the number of canons reaches a total of 2,666.

The code for the Roman Rite is undergoing extensive revision and was given new impetus in Dec. 1973, when Pope Paul VI declared that the updating "is a valid way of giving new vitality to Christian life." All the Canon Law Societies of the countries of the Roman Rite are contributing to the revision, but no final date for completion is foreseen at the present time.

## Canon of the Mass

The Canon of the Mass is also called "Action" of the Mass, the main part, the "heart" of the sacrifice of the Mass. The Canon begins immediately after the "Holy, Holy, Holy," the divine praises that are sung or recited by the priest and people, and ends at the Lord's Prayer. This was followed by the lesser canon or "action," the canon of the Communion. The Canon of the Mass is the portion of the Mass where the liturgy of the Mass, by representation and repetition, reenacts the Last Supper and the sacrifice of Calvary.

Under the new liturgy the canon is a part of the eucharistic prayer where the central portion is the act of consecration, the solemn and essential act of sacrifice in which the changing of the species of bread and wine into the Body and Blood of Christ takes place. The prayers of the canon are: one of the four Eucharistic Prayers; petitions for the Church, the living, and the dead; remembrance of the Virgin Mary and the saints. These prayers are said by the celebrant only, with the conclusion being the holding up of the hosts and the chalice while he says: "Through Him, with Him, in Him, in the unity of the Holy Spirit, all glory and honor is yours, almighty Father, for ever and ever. *Amen.*" The Amen is referred to as the "Great Amen" and is the word of fulfillment and acquiesence made by all the people. (See Liturgy)

## Canon of Muratori

This is also known as the "Muratorian Fragment." It is the oldest and perhaps the most important listing of the books of the Old and New Testaments. It is now kept in the Ambrosian Library in Milan, Italy. The original writings upon which L. A. Muratori (1672 to 1750) based his compilation date back to about A.D. 180 to 190. (See Canon of the Scripture; Scrolls of the Dead Sea.)

## Canon Penitentiary

This is the title of that member of a chapter of a cathedral or collegiate church who is appointed according to canon law by the bishop to hear confessions. He is the confessor extraordinary who is delegated to absolve, in the internal forum, censures and sins reserved to the bishop.

## Canon, Privilege of

See Immunity.

## Canon Regular

A cleric who lives in a community under the

governance of one of his own order is a canon regular. Most follow the rule established by St. Augustine.

## Canon of the Scripture

The word "canon" comes from the Greek and means "a measuring rod." It later came to mean a rule or standard. In adaptation the term came to be used in the Church for the decrees, pronouncements, and decisions, enacted as to a "standard" doctrine, and the Canon of Scripture began to be spoken of as the "standard" source of faith. However, the term as commonly used and understood today means the collection or list of books acknowledged and accepted by the Church as inspired. Thus, they conform to the "rule" or "standard" required for classification as inspired. (See Bible for list of books so accepted.) Likewise a "canonical" book of the Scriptures is any book that forms a part of the Canon. (cf. Inspiration of Scripture). Extensive study and research have confirmed the list of books of the Bible as contained in the Canon.

## Canon Theologian

A member of a cathedral or collegiate chapter, versed in theology, the canon theologian serves as a consultant to the others of the chapter. It may also be applied to a priest-theologian who is trained in canon law, usually having a doctorate of canon law, J.C.D. Also one appointed in a diocese to serve as an authority on matters of theology or morals.

## Canoness

A canoness is a woman following the religious rule comparable to that of a Canon Regular. Originally they were women following a religious life in common who were permitted to hold private property.

## Canonical Hours

The division of the prayer of the Church into several hours or periods (cf. Breviary; Divine Office) was probably derived from Ps. 118:164, "Seven times a day I give praise to thee."

## Canonicals

Canonicals are vestments required by Church law to be worn by a priest officiating at a liturgical ceremony. (See Vestments.)

## Canonist

A person trained in canon law, usually holding a doctorate in canon law, a J.C.D. is a canonist. The term is sometimes applied to the ranking canon lawyer of a diocese.

## Canonization

This is the final declaration, the seal of approval, whereby the soul of a person is declared to be in heaven. It follows the process of beatification. Through this declaration, veneration of the person as a saint is not only permitted but ordered for the entire Church. The title of "saint" is given to the person. The process of beatification and canonization is conducted by the Sacred Congregation of Rites, but the declaration of canonization is made only by the Supreme Pontiff, and he acts and is protected under his prerogative of infallibility. The initial step of the process is a formal inquiry, called the Ordinary Processes, instituted by the bishop of the diocese wherein the person lived. This inquiry is accomplished by a tribunal of three judges, a notary, and the "promoter of the faith," more commonly called the "devil's advocate." This is then reported to Rome and the examination is made as to whether or not a "cult" has been begun before the pronouncement of the Church. Following these reports, the Sacred Congregation opens the process, enlarging on the previous inquiries, with a promoter of the faith again presenting the flaws or weak points in the evidence. Only thereafter is the apostolic process authorized by commission directly to the Sacred Congregation, and investigation is made of the "reality and nature of the virtues and miracles ascribed to the person to be beatified." Extensive precautions are taken, and the "cause" once introduced proceeds slowly. Two fully authentic miracles are required before beatification and two distinctly different miracles must be attested to and proved before canonization. (Cf. Beatification; Martyrology.)

## Canons of the Apostles, also Apostolic Canons

Canons of the apostles are a collection of early decrees of the Church, eighty-five in number, on matters of discipline. These are attributed to the Apostles, but were written no earlier than the end of the fourth century.

## Canons, Chapters of

These are groups of clerics assigned to a cathedral church who live a community life of religion, recite the Divine Office in choir, and live off the revenue of the church, each being allotted a share called a prebend. They serve the church in the dignity and solemnity of the divine services, and the bishop in his duties of governing. The Council of Trent calls the chapter an "ecclesiastical senate" and recognizes their services in maintaining the dignity of the cathedral, setting examples of pious lives, and giving assistance to the bishop. This is a seldom experienced custom in the United States, and in no way is to be considered as the "Priest's Senate," or the Presbytery of a diocese.

## Canopy

There are two forms of shelter or covering: the first is portable, that is, carried on four poles, and called a processional canopy; the second is a fixed covering arising on four pillars or suspended from the sanctuary ceiling or back wall, usually placed above an altar. In the present time, the canopy is seldom constructed, for its functional purpose of protection is no longer necessary. (See Baldachino; Ombrelino.)

## Cantate Sunday

This name was given to the fourth Sunday after Easter from the Introit of the Mass, dating back to the twelfth century.

## Canticle

A canticle is a sacred prayer or song of praise or love directed to God as found in Scripture, excluding the Psalms, which many consider canticles. Canticles have been incorporated into the Divine Office of the Church. There are fourteen from the OT and three from the NT. Those from the NT are also known as the "evangelical canticles." The canticle is a sacred chant or hymn of praise in poetic form, e.g., the *Magnificat* (Lk. 1:46–55), the *Benedictus* (Lk. 1:68–79), and the *Nunc Dimittis* (Lk. 2:29–32).

## Canticle of Canticles

Formerly the title, canticle of canticles is sometimes still used for the twenty-fourth book of the OT in the Catholic Bible. Its authorship has always been popularly attributed to Solomon, but it was most likely written much later. It is a love poem whose interpretation is that God's love of Israel was a parallel figure of Christ's love for His Church. (See Song of Songs.)

## Cantor, also Precentor

Cantor is the title of a seldom named semiofficial who is the chief singer and often director of a church choir. Under the new understanding of the ministries attendant to the Eucharistic Liturgy, the term *cantor* or "psalmist" is one who leads the psalm between the first two readings in the Liturgy of the Word, the person who leads the liturgical assembly in processional psalms or other songs, the leader of hymns and songs sung by the liturgical assembly, the leader of the choir or parochial director of music. Sometimes this role is filled by the organist. (See Ministries; Music, Church.)

## Cantoral Staff

This ornate staff was carried by the cantor of a choir as a mark of dignity and authority in the Middle Ages.

## Cap-de-la-Madeleine, Shrine of

This shrine is known as the Shrine of Our Lady of the Rosary but takes its name from the first chapel built at the place where it is located and is one of the most famous in Canada. The first church was built in 1659 on the little cape that juts out into the St. Lawrence River, east of the city of Three Rivers in the province of Quebec. It was served by Jesuit missioners until 1680 when it became a church served by diocesan clergy. In 1694 a Confraternity of the Rosary was established, the first in Canada. The present stone shrine was completed in 1720 and is the oldest building of its kind in Canada, perhaps in all of North America. It was rededicated in 1888 as the Shrine of the Queen of the Most Holy Rosary and became a place of pilgrimage for all, especially the Canadian and American people. In 1909 the church was declared a shrine of national pilgrimage, and in 1964 it was titled a minor basilica. The center of the shrine is the little fieldstone chapel of the Holy Rosary, and here the miraculous statue Our Lady of the Cape is enthroned. The statue is reputed to have been observed with the closed eyes opened, and the cure of a sick man, Pierre Lacroix, has been attributed to Our Lady of the Cape through this statue. Testimony to this remains, and in the years since, many cures have been recorded and it continues a center of devotion for pilgrims.

## Capital Sins, also Capital Vices, or Deadly Sins

Properly, these are vices in the sense that each has many facets, any of which may be a sin. Seven in number, the capital vices are the sources of other sins, but the chief or first is the origin of all the others and is found in all sin to some degree. The seven are: pride, covetousness, lust, anger, gluttony, envy, sloth. (See listings under individual titles.) They are considered as deadly because they lead to mortal sin, and vices because in themselves they are passions or habits that dispose one to sin and even prompt the occasions for sin rather than being distinct acts of sin themselves. (Cf. Sin; Basic Teachings for Catholic Religious Education.)

### Capitulary
A collection of rules or laws, a capitulary is sometimes used in the ecclesiastical sense as a collection of canons passed by a provincial council.

### Cappa Magna
The cappa magna is a full long cape with a train, made of purple wool (for bishops) or red (for cardinals). It has a full cowl that is lined with silk for summer use or fur for winter use. The cowl portion that fits over the neck and shoulders in front and back may be detached. It is worn by bishops, cardinals, and certain prelates, but less in the new liturgy since Vatican II.

### Cappa Pluvialis, or Pluviale
See Cope.

### Captivity Epistles
The four epistles written by St. Paul while he was imprisoned in Rome in the years 61 to 63 are called Captivity Epistles. Recent biblical studies place the location of their writing in Ephesus, but there is scant evidence for this except the reference in 1 Cor. 15:32 where Paul wrote: "I fought those beasts at Ephesus." They are: to the Ephesians, to the Philippians, to the Colossians, and to Philemon. All are concerned with the union of Christ and the Church.

### Cara
The initial letters of Cara form the popular name for the *Center for Applied Research in the Apostolate,* an agency for the research and development of the worldwide mission of the Church from both the religious and social aspects. Its purpose is to gain information to aid in the decision making process of the Church in a wide spectrum of enterprises and for development of effective programs in the ministries of the future. Cara was incorporated as a nonprofit corporation in the District of Columbia, Aug. 5, 1964, with headquarters at 1312 Massachusetts Ave. N.W.,

Washington, D.C., 20005. At present its work is focused on: Church personnel (seminaries, vocational counseling, recruitment, selection, training, utilization of facilities, effectiveness, due process, retirement, health); the town and country environments as they affect religion and religious life; overseas areas of Latin America, Africa, Oceania, and Asia; the campus ministry; urban affairs; social theology; diocesan planning; and religious life. It cooperates with many other agencies of the Church in an ongoing pursuit of the best means of relating the Church to the world in which we live.

### Cardinal
A prince of the Church is appointed solely by the pope. In the Code of Canon Law (c. 230), the place of the cardinals in the Church is stated: "The cardinals of Holy Roman Church constitute the senate of the Roman Pontiff and aid him as his chief counselors and collaborators in the government of the Church." There are three orders or categories of cardinals: (1) Cardinal bishops, the six cardinals living in Rome, are bishops over seven small dioceses adjoining that of Rome and serve as major officials of the Roman Curia. (2) Cardinal priests, who are usually bishops or archbishops, and who are given title to one of the major churches of Rome. In these churches the cardinal titular exercises the authority that he has in his own diocese. (3) Cardinal deacons, who act as deacons when the Holy Father pontificates solemnly and serve in a special way in the Roman Curia. These were assigned to a church of Rome, called their "deaconry," by title, but are now titular bishops who are assigned special duties in the Roman Curia. Today according to canon law only ordained priests may be elevated to the cardinalate. All cardinals are members of the College of Cardinals and enjoy a wide variety of privileges. (See College of Cardinals; In Petto.)

### Cardinal Legate
See Legate.

### Cardinal Protector
A Cardinal Protector is a member of the College of Cardinals who represents at the Holy See the people of a nation, a religious institution, or a pious association by solicitude and interest in their affairs.

### Cardinal Vicar
The Cardinal Vicar is a cardinal appointed to assist the pope, who is the bishop of the diocese of Rome, in the spiritual and temporal administration of that diocese. (Cf. Bishop of Rome.)

## Cardinal Virtues

The cardinal virtues, the four chief moral virtues are: prudence, justice, fortitude, and temperance. (See listings under individual titles.) All other moral virtues may be considered under aspects of these four. Moral virtues are those, in the exercise of which, our moral life or conduct is brought to conform with right reason and the Commandments of God and the Church and the duties of our vocation in life. (See Basic Teachings for Catholic Religious Education.)

## Care of Souls

The cura animarum, properly "the care of souls," is entrusted by authority to a priest whose obligations are: instruction, the administration of the sacraments, the celebration of the "Mass for the People," preaching, and the care of the poor and sick. It is actually a delegated authority, descending from the pope who has the universal care of souls. In practice it is the assumption of pastoral duties and properly does not include the administration of physical or temporal affairs.

## Caritas Internationalis

The international federation of national Catholic charities organizations operates as the overall unit to provide funds and goods for emergency relief and ongoing charity to nations of the Third World and undernourished peoples. The Catholic Relief Services of the American Bishops are an affiliate, and to this Catholics of the United States contribute annually.

## Carlsruhe Fragments

Two portions of early manuscripts, four pages each, known as the Carlsruhe Fragments, contain portions of Masses. They date back to the early ninth century and are retained in the Carlsruhe library in Germany.

## Carmel, Mount

This mountain, or high hill, frequently mentioned in the Scriptures, is to the east of the plain of Esdraelon on the Mediteranean Sea, and to the south of Acre. The name Carmel in Hebrew means "orchard." It was there in a cavern that the prophet Eliah took up his abode, and later a community of men must have established an early monastery or hermitage because ruins were found in the twelfth century. Thus, it was and is one of the earliest places where religious life was followed according to any kind of a regimen.

It is now usually called "Mount St. Eliah," and is the entire promontory running from southeast to northwest in the northeast of Samaria. It is likened to a place of desolation (Is. 33:9) and a place of verdant beauty (S. of S. 7:6).

## Carnival

A carnival is a time of celebration before a religious feast day, but usually the three days preceding the lenten season. In the United States this time is referred to as *Mardi Gras.*

## Carolingian Schools

This system of education, in the nature of a reform, followed the issuance of the capitulary of Charlemagne in the late eighth century. It was the first establishment of free Church schools. The Carolingian Schools influenced the spread of Christian doctrine and gave a broader scope to the training in monastic and cathedral schools. Alcuin of York was named head of the Palace School at Aachen and served later as the minister of education for Emperor Charlemagne. This development of education is often given credit for the Renaissance, for among its attainments were: an authentic edition of the Vulgate Bible, a revision of Church liturgy, and a new style of cursive writing.

## Carthage, Councils of

The first of these councils of bishops at Carthage in North Africa was held in 220. Of importance was the council of 397 because it published a list of "canonical" Scriptures; the one in 404 condemned the Donatist heresy, and the council of 411 was notable because St. Augustine there refuted the Pelagians. (See Council.)

## Cases of Conscience

This term applied to real or imaginary instances or examples in canon law or moral theology that are gathered to exemplify and teach practical application of principles to problems. Usually each such case is discussed in detail and is a basis of pedagogy or learning such as in study clubs. The applications are sometimes given in a question and answer pattern and in some instances have been applied to catechetical instructions.

## Cassock, also Soutane

A cassock is an ankle-length gown worn by clerics, usually of black cloth. The sleeves generally have a deep cuff. There are two styles in use: one buttoning down the full front length from the collar to the hem, called "Roman style;" the other is open and fastened by hooks and eyes at the collar and waist, usually worn with a black bandbelt of cloth, called "Jesuit style." Cassocks are worn by acolytes serving Mass or assisting at other services.

The Holy Father wears a white cassock; bishops wear purple, cardinals red; and other prelates are entitled to wear purple. Where purple is permitted, it is often replaced with a black cassock trimmed with red and referred to as a "house cassock." (See Habit, Religious.)

### Castel Gandolfo

Castel Gandolfo is the place in the Alban Hills where the summer residence of the Holy Father is located. It is about 18 miles southeast of Rome and is held as extraterritory of Vatican State by concordat with the Italian government. Since 1934 it has been the place where summer audiences with the Pope are held.

### Casuistry

This is the method of studying causes of conscience or solving questions of obligation by application of general principles in ethics or moral theology in regard to concrete problems of human conduct. This form of inquiry requires an extensive knowledge of law, precepts, interpretation of like cases, and skill in analyzing conditions affecting motive and consent. (Cf. Cases of Conscience.)

### Casus

Literally, case, a casus is an example used to point out a problem, whether the case is a real or imaginary one.

### Catacombs

These were subterranean cemeteries that served a double purpose: that of burial for Christians who had died or been martyred, and a place to which Christians could resort to conduct devotions, administer sacraments, and celebrate the Eucharist in secrecy. There are some twenty-five catacombs that have been excavated, the majority located along the Via Appia and the Via Ardeatina, all within two and a half miles of the old Roman walls of Aurelius. The catacombs were dug into hill areas by burrowing into a midstratum called *tufa*

*granolare,* a soft stone. The practice was to excavate a stairway and then open a narrow gallery. Off this gallery there were *loculi* cut into the wall, capable of holding from one to three bodies. These were sealed with a slab of stone when the bodies had been placed within. Also leading from the gallery there were a number of *cubicula,* chambers or vaults. Along the walls, there were occasionally cut into the wall above a single tomb *(loculus)* an *arcosolium,* a vault above a tomb. In these *arcosolia* it was customary to celebrate the mystery of the Eucharist, the Mass, using the top of the tomb for an altar surface. When a gallery became full, it was the usual practice to cut lateral galleries and continue on with each. In the fourth century, after the end of the persecutions, the catacombs became places of pilgrimage and have remained so until the present. The catacombs, however, are most notable because of the testimony of art and practice that they supply to modern ages. Chief of these testimonies are: that of the sacramental religion observed by these early Christians and the purity of the spiritual truth that is manifest. These facts are deduced from the art, the carvings, artifacts, and inscriptions with which the catacombs are replete. (Cf. Symbol.)

### Catafalque

From the Latin word for "scaffold," a catafalque is a bier on which rests a mock coffin. Covered with a black cloth called the pall or hearsecloth, it is used at requiem Masses when the corpse is not present. Catafalque is also a name for the *castrumdoloris,* which is an elaborate structure placed over the coffin in some Latin countries and used in St. Peter's in Rome at requiem Masses when the pontiff dies.

### Catechesis

This is the oral instruction, which may also be accompanied with written, printed, or visual aids, whereby the faithful are informed of the truths of Christ's teaching and the Church's. In scripture it is called "the new way of the Lord" (Acts 18:25), which means the entire body of Christian doctrine as offered by the Church and her representatives. It was certainly a part of the teaching given to new converts to Christianity and was given by one who already knew or had been instructed (Gal. 6:6). In more recent times this has come to be the pertinent instruction that accompanies the reception of the sacraments, the new liturgy, and the general preparation one is to receive so that each may participate more fully in the everyday worship of the Church. In the statement prepared by the Sacred Congregation for the Clergy (March 18,

1971), it was stated that catechesis is that form of the ministry of the word which "is intended to make men's faith become living, conscious and active, through the light of instruction." (Cf. Preaching; Basic Teachings of Catholic Religious Education.)

## Catechetics

From the Greek word meaning "to sound forth," catechetics is the procedure for the teaching of religion, particularly those basic doctrines that instill a deeper faith and a greater understanding of the Gospel message of Christ. This formal presentation may use all the modern techniques of teaching and communication, such as visual aids, television, recordings, readings, instruction manuals, and pictorial representations or graphs. (See Catechesis.)

## Catechism

Among early Christian writers this meant both the subject matter and the method of instruction. However, today it is more frequently applied to the text or manual that is a summary of Catholic doctrine presented in question and answer form. The word comes from the Greek word *catechesis,* which means oral instruction. Today the word catechism is applied to a wide variety of booklets, texts, question and answer forms, and study notes relating to various aspects of Christian doctrine. The basic work, however, in the United States is the Baltimore Catechism, the compilation of instructions authorized by the Third Plenary Council of Baltimore and first published in 1885 and variously presented since that time. Revisions are undertaken, not with the purpose of changing teaching, but solely for clarification and improvements in the teaching method.

At present the NCCB is preparing what is tentatively titled "National Catechetical Directory" (which will remain as a subtitle). This is an official document, intended to be a pastoral and practical document containing norms and guidelines for teaching religion to Catholics of all ages and circumstances in the United States. This publication, under the approval of the bishops, will be for parents, religious educators and catechists, priests and deacons, publishers, and authors of catechetical materials. Although this will not supplant the catechism, it will serve as a guide to *what* is to be taught and to the *method* of communication to be used. This meets the new developments in the changing world, directed toward reconciliation within the Catholic Church in the United States, and a restoration of hope and Christian joy among Catholics and all Christians.

## Catechist

Originally catechist was the title given to the one who instructed those about to receive baptism. Now it is loosely applied to any instructor versed in Christian doctrine who teaches others, especially in missionary schools.

Vatican II stressed the role of the catechist in the modern world: "In our time, when there are few clerics to preach the gospel to such great numbers and to exercise the pastoral ministry, the role of catechists is of maximum importance."

And: "Their training must be so thorough and so well adapted to cultural advances that, as powerful co-workers of the priestly order, they can perform their task as superbly as can be even though it is weighed down with new and expanding burdens."

And: "Worthy of praise are the ranks of men and women catechists, to whom missionary work among the nations owes so very much. Animated with an apostolic spirit, they by their immense efforts make an outstanding and altogether necessary contribution to the spread of the faith and of the Church" (AG 17). (See Ministries.)

## Catechumens

In the early Church when a pagan sought to become a Christian, he was basically instructed and became an "inquirer" and was permitted to be present only during the first part of the Mass. Thereafter, having been given additional instruction and having become versed in doctrine, he was called a *catechumen* and allowed to remain at Mass until the beginning of the Mass of the Faithful. After more instruction, the catechumens were baptized and became "competents" and were received into the "body of the faithful." Now the term refers to anyone who desires to become a convert.

As stated by Vatican II, "Catechumens should be properly instructed in the mystery of salvation and in the practice of gospel morality. By sacred rites which are to be held at successive intervals, they should be introduced into the life of faith, liturgy, and love, which God's People live" (AG 14).

And: "Catechumens who, moved by the Holy Spirit, seek with explicit intention to be incorporated into the Church are by that very intention joined to her. With love and solicitude Mother Church already embraces them as her own" (LG 14). (See Baptism, Sacrament of; Liturgy.)

## Categorical Imperative

Categorical imperative is a term introduced by the philosopher Immanuel Kant (d. 1804). He stated: "Act on maxims which can at the same time have for their object themselves as universal laws of nature." It is an absolute moral law of reason, acting for the sake of law itself, making man a law unto himself. However, it must be recognized in contradistinction that reason does not manufacture moral law but only recognizes it and interprets application, and that only God is the supreme lawgiver and is Himself the end of morality, being the supreme good.

## Cathari, or Catharists

Cathari were a sect of Neo-Manichaeans. (See Albigenses.)

## Cathedra

The chair-throne of a bishop is always located in the sanctuary against the left wall on the gospel side in the cathedral church of the diocese. *Cathedra* is the Greek word for chair or throne, from which is derived the word cathedral. (Cf. Ex Cathedra).

## Cathedral

The official church of a bishop who has jurisdiction over a diocese is the cathedral. It is located within the diocese, generally in the see city in which the bishop exercises his authority and conducts worship for all under his jurisdiction. As the principal church of a diocese it need not be the largest or the most beautiful. However, those traditional cathedrals of Europe and America have become the focal points of tourists and artists. Some of the great Cathedrals of the world are: Notre Dame in Paris; Amiens, Chartres, Tournai, Rheims in France; St. Peter's in Rome; those of Milan, Assisi, Venice, Siena, Orvieto in Italy; Cologne in Germany; Wells, Salisbury, Exeter, Ely, Canterbury in England; Leon, Gerona in Spain; St. Mary's, Trenton, N.J., St. Louis, St. Louis, Mo., St. Helena, Helena, Mont., Mary Our Queen, Baltimore, Md., St. Paul's, Pittsburg, Pa., in the United States; Our Lady of Guadalupe, Mexico.

## Cathedraticum

Cathedraticum is a small dues or tax exacted of all churches and benefices under a bishop's jurisdiction as a symbol of their subordination to the bishop and for his financial support, stated as a right of the bishop under canon 1504.

## Catholic

The term meaning "universal" was first applied to the Church by St. Ignatius of Antioch (d. 107) writing to the Church at Smyrna: "Wheresoever the bishop shall appear, there let the people be, even as where Jesus is, there is the Catholic Church" (Smyr. VIII, 2). It was later used by many writers referring both to the Church and to individual members of the Church, the most famous being perhaps that of St. Pacianus, a bishop of Barcelona in the fourth century, "Christian is my name; Catholic is my surname." The term as used by the fathers of the Church means the true Church as distinct from all other religious groups. It is thus used today and applies to the body of the faithful, the creeds, churches, institutions, clergy, and hierarchy who follow the same teachings of Christ as given to the apostles. (Cf. Marks of the Church; Church.)

## Catholic Action

Catholic Action as defined by Pius XI is, "The participation of the Catholic laity in the apostolate of the hierarchy." Catholic Action has four essentials that help to explain it more fully: (1) it is an apostolate, working toward the conversion and salvation of souls; (2) it is formed by the laity, who are called by the bishops to work for the salvation of souls; (3) it is organized, that while an individual may be engaged in Catholic Action, it is in organized lay associations that the work will be most successful since the work is social in nature; (4) it is under the direction and control of the bishops who have the direct responsibility of teaching and ruling the Church. Such Catholic Action may be effected through a variety of means, cultural, physical, or spiritual. It calls particularly for informed leaders of personal ideals of sanctity who can clearly state the position of the Church on essential questions of doctrine, moral, or practice.

In practice, for the majority, Catholic Action may be no more than the cooperation with the bishop in the enterprises he sets forth. It is not a political activity; its work is in the religious circle, the moral, and those border areas where religion or morals are directly or indirectly related to the good of the individual or the community, or the universal good of the Church. The Sacrament of Confirmation is sometimes called the "sacrament of Catholic Action," meaning that all the faithful through the Holy Spirit are made cooperators in the work of the bishops, teachers, and leaders of the community.

However, in its popular use, it must be distinguished from "Catholic Activity." The bishops of the United States, in Nov. 1935, issued the qualifying statement: "The bishops remind all groups according to the instruction of our Holy Father, Pope Pius XI, that there is no such thing as Catholic Action until there is an episcopal commission. For a diocese there must be a commission from the bishop of a diocese, for a province from the bishops of a province, and for the country from the bishops of the United States. The Holy Father only can give a commission for the universal Church on Catholic Action. When His Holiness does so, he communicates with the bishops."

Vatican II, clarified this concept saying, "All associations of the apostolate must be given due appreciation. Those, however, which the hierarchy has praised or recommended as responsive to the needs of time and place, or has directed to be established as particularly urgent, must be held in highest esteem by priests, religious, and laity and promoted according to each one's ability. Among these associations, moreover, international associations or groups of Catholics must be especially prized today" (AA 21). (Cf. Apostolate; Ministries; Laity.)

## Catholic Church

The Church founded by Jesus Christ, which was first taught and governed by the Apostles, is taught infallibly by the successor of St. Peter, the pope, the vicar of Christ on earth, and by the bishops, and is formed by the society of the faithful. This divinely founded society extends to every nation and race, is neither national nor ethnic, but truly universal. Those members composing this society are of one faith, profess one doctrine found in the Creed, participate in the same seven sacraments, and are governed by the pope. St. Paul writing to the Ephesians spoke clearly of the Church from which we derive the distinct marks of this Church: It is *one*, having one body to the single head that is Christ; it is *holy*, since its members are in Christ and through Him are made holy and are saved; it is *universal*, extending to the Gentiles and Jews, all in the household of God (2:19); it is *apostolic*, its doctrine being direct from Christ through the apostles (2:20). (See Church.)

## Catholic Eastern Rites

See Eastern Churches.

## Catholic Epistles

This collective name is given to those seven Epistles of the NT that were directed by certain Apostles to the Church as a whole rather than to particular areas or groups. They are: the Epistle of St. James; Epistles 1 and 2 of St. Peter; 1, 2, and 3 letters of John; and that of St. Jude. They receive their title because they were addressed to the "universal" Church rather than to individuals or singular groups of churches in particular places, as were the Pauline Epistles.

## Catholic Foreign Mission Society of America

This society of the Maryknoll Fathers was founded in 1911 and incorporated under the laws of the State of New York in 1912. Its aim is to train priests to conduct foreign missions.

## Catholic Truth Society

A group organized first in England in 1872, reorganized in 1884, its purpose is the spreading of the means of wider information of their faith among Catholics and true information of the Church among Protestants. It aids and promotes the writing, printing, and distribution of inexpensive printed matter. In the United States its official title is International Catholic Truth Society.

## Catholic University of America

The foremost Catholic school of higher education in the United States was founded in Washington, D.C., in 1889 by the bishops of the United States and is maintained as an institution by them. It has canonical value, conferring degrees by apostolic faculty (c. 1378). The University is both undergraduate and graduate and consists of the Schools of Sacred Theology, Canon Law, Philosophy, Law, the college and graduate schools of Art and Sciences, schools of Social Service, Nursing Education, and Social Services. Its student body is both male and female, religious and lay. In conjunction with the University, many religious orders have houses of study for the training of their members or which serve as residences for their members while studying at the university.

## Catholicos

This name of distinction is given to certain patriarchs of the churches of Mesopotamia, Armenia, and Persia, signifying their wide jurisdiction.

## Catholics in Statuary Hall

The twelve notable Catholics, missioners, pioneers, and statesmen, who are honored by nomination of their states to be represented in the National Statuary Hall or the National Capitol building in Washington, D.C. Those states and their nominations are: Arizona: Rev. Eusebio Kino, S.J.; California: Rev. Junipero Serra, O.F.M.; Hawaii: Father Damien of Molokai; Illinois: Gen. James Shields; Louisiana: Edward D. White, Justice of the Supreme Court; Maryland: Charles Carroll, signer of the Declaration of Independence; Nevada: Patrick A. McCarran; New Mexico: Denis Chavez and Archbishop Jean B. Lamy; North Dakota: John Burke; Oregon: Dr. John McLoughlin; West Virginia: John E. Kenna; Wisconsin: Rev. Jacques Marquette, S.J.

## Cause

As used in its religious, nonphilosophic sense, this is the process or procedure of investigation and justification. (Cf. Beatification; Canonization.) The Sacred Congregation for the Causes of Saints now handles all research and procedures for the processes of beatification and canonization, and also for the preservation of relics. These matters were formerly the responsibility of the Congregation of Rites.

## Celam

Celam is the popular title of the Latin American Bishops' Conference (Consejo Episcopal Latino Americano). It was first established in 1956, and its statutes were approved experimentally in 1969. The Conference represents twenty-two Latin American national Bishops' conferences and seeks to unify and coordinate the work of the Church in these countries.

## Celebrant

This term is applied to either the priest who celebrates Mass or the bishop pontificating. Because he presides at the celebration of the Eucharist, he sits in the celebrant's chair, which is sometimes called "president's chair" but is not so named in the new Sacramentary of 1974.

## Celebret

Celebret is the name given to the "grant of privilege" whereby a priest of one diocese is declared to be in good standing. It is used chiefly for travel outside of the country or within the country. The document, no more than a formal letter of commendation, is issued by one bishop or religious superior to testify that the bearer should be permitted and given the opportunity to celebrate the Eucharist or perform other priestly functions. The celebret is carried by the priest and presented as evidence to bishop, pastor, priest, or religious superior of another diocese or religious institution.

## Celestial Hierarchy

Although there is no degree of authority in heaven excepting that of God, this term is applied to the three categories of angels according to rank. (Cf. Angel.)

## Celibacy

Celibacy is the ecclesiastical law in the Western Church imposed on clerics forbidding those in the married state from being ordained and those in holy orders from marrying. It includes the obligation of observing perfect chastity under vow. The reasons for this are: that those being ordained may serve God with a greater singleness of purpose (1 Cor. 7:32), and that so living a life of continence they observe the state of virginity, which is holier and higher than that of marriage. In the NT the celibate or virginal state is raised to a higher calling than that of the married. However, this must be voluntary for as Christ said: "Not everyone can accept this teaching, only those to whom it is given to do so. Some men are incapable of sexual activity from birth; some have been deliberately made so; and some there are who have freely renounced sex for the sake of God's reign. Let him accept this teaching who can" (Mt. 19:11–12). Although celibacy was practiced by the majority of clergy in the first three centuries of the Church's history, it was after the Council of Elvira in 305 that the law became more definite. A council held at Rome in 386 and two later councils at Carthage imposed continence on all bishops, priests, and deacons.

Vatican II states: "Through virginity or celibacy observed for the sake of the kingdom of heaven, priests are consecrated to Christ in a new and distinguished way. They more easily hold fast to Him with undivided heart. They more freely devote themselves in Him and through Him to the service of God and men. They more readily minister to His Kingdom and to the work of heavenly regeneration, and thus become more apt to exercise paternity in Christ, and do so to a greater extent" (PO 16).

## Cell

1. A numerically small group of monks who formed a colony apart from some large monastery.

2. The individual room or living quarters of a monk, friar, nun, or hermit.

3. A small, effective group set up for work or study as a part of a Catholic Action program.

4. In early ages, the name of a small chapel usually erected over a tomb.

5. The apartment in the Vatican assigned to each Cardinal during the election time of a new pope.

### Cellarer

In early monastic life cellarer was the title of the one who saw to the provision of food, drink, and clothing for all members of the community. Today the title is procurator.

### Celtic Cross

This ancient cross of Irish origin has a circle about the juncture of the Cross arms, usually with the continuous weaving line, which symbolizes eternity.

### Celtic Rite

The term Celtic Rite applied to a variety of liturgical features that were used by the early British, Scottish, and Irish churches, based on French and Roman forms. It was used until the thirteenth century but no longer.

### Cemetery

Derived from the Greek meaning "place of rest," a cemetery is the place set apart for burial of the bodies of Christians and consecrated for this purpose. Solemn blessing or consecration can only be performed by the ordinary of the diocese, while simple blessing may be either by the bishop or a delegated priest. It is not necessary to bless the individual graves, but rather the area as a whole is consecrated. However, it is permitted to bless the individual graves in those places where no Catholic cemetery exists, or because of other regulations of the State or government.

The Church laws governing cemeteries are contained in the Code of Canon Law, canons 1205 to 1214 inclusive. Today there is great emphasis upon mausoleums where multiple burials are possible through individual vaults in the wall structure. Such mausoleums are to be well maintained, of suitable construction, and may have a chapel within the building or complex, which in turn must conform to the norms of church building regulations.

### Cenacle

The cenacle was the upper room where Christ and His apostles ate the Last Supper at which the Eucharist was instituted (Lk. 22:12). It was here also that Christ appeared to the assembled Apostles eight days after His death (Lk. 24:36), and where the Holy Spirit descended upon the Apostles (Acts 2:1–36, 1:13–14). Metaphorically this has been called the first Christian church. Although it is not known where this room was located, tradition places it in the house of St. Mark's mother in the southwest quarter of Jerusalem; it was also the meeting place of the faithful at the time of St. Peter's imprisonment (Acts 12:12).

### Cenobite

The equivalent of our word monk, cenobite means one who lives a religious community life rather than as a hermit or anchorite. This was the name given to the individual member in the first centuries of the Church, derived from the *Cenobium* or group. The earliest rule for cenobites was written by St. Pachomius (d. 346), who is commonly called the "Founder of Monasticism."

### Censer

The censer is a cup or bowl, usually of metal, having a perforated cover, the whole suspended on chains, in which lighted charcoal is placed. Onto this charcoal, grains of incense are sprinkled to provide the scented smoke used in liturgical functions. It is also called a thurible. In biblical times the form of the censer was that of a fire pan (Rv. 8:3–5), and it was not swung. This fire pan (Ex. 27:3) was carried to the altar and served as a censer (cf. Nm. 16:6).

## Censor

The censor is the cleric, appointed according to canon law by the bishop of a diocese, whose duty it is to examine, read, and judge a writing before publication to assure that there is nothing contained in the writing contrary to the teaching of the Church regarding faith or morals. When a book has been censored and approval given in writing by the censor, this is signified by the term *Nihil Obstat*. The writing and *Nihil obstat* are then submitted to the bishop who attaches his Imprimatur, or permission to publish. Together these assure that the writing can be read without harm to faith or morals but are not an approval of the contents otherwise. The Church requires censorship of the following writings: (1) Those books of holy Scripture as well as commentaries or annotations on any part of Scripture; (2) those books treating of Scripture, theology, Church history, canon law, natural theology, and ethics; (3) all prayer books, devotional, catechetical, moral, ascetical, and mystical books or pamphlets; (4) all books that treat particularly of religion, faith, or morals; (5) all sacred images or pictures when printed, whether or not a prayer is printed with them (c. 1384 to 1405). "Censorship of books" is that process whereby approval is given. (Cf. Index of Forbidden Books.)

## Censure

A Church censure is a spiritual penalty by which a baptized person, being delinquent and contumacious, that is, conscious and obstinate, is deprived of certain spiritual benefits until that individual has ceased being obstinate or is absolved from the censure. The state of being delinquent is defined (c. 2195) as one who has committed an external and morally imputable violation of a canonically sanctioned law. It must thus be a seriously sinful act, both from the internal and external aspects. Such Church penalties are primarily corrective and secondarily seek to punish the crime. Excommunication, suspension, and interdict are three types of censure. A censure may be inflicted by law (*a jure*), i.e., when it is contained in the law or precept as written or promulgated, or inflicted by an individual having jurisdiction (*ab homine*) when it is expressed as part of the penalty

or imposed by a judicial sentence. A censure that is incurred by the very fact of being deliberately delinquent is said to be *latae sententiae,* or incurred *ipso facto,* i.e., without a pronounced sentence. A censure that must be imposed by a judge or competent superior is said to be *ferendae sententiae.* The following can inflict censures because of their office: the pope, an ecumenical council, congregations and courts of the Roman Curia, bishops in their dioceses, a plenary or provincial council, cathedral chapters before election of a vicar capitular, the vicar capitular, apostolic administrators, abbots and prelates with episcopal jurisdiction, vicars and prefects apostolic, higher superiors in clerical exempt religious orders and their chapters. Absolution from a censure may be reserved to the bishop or to the Holy See, but in danger of death any priest may absolve from all censures.

All censures given by the Church are intended to be corrective or remedial, for the intent of the one imposing the censure is to bring the offender into harmony with the Church so that graces may again enliven his or her soul.

## Center for Applied Research in the Apostolate

See Cara.

## Cerecloth

A linen cloth, the cerecloth is more properly called *chrismale.* It is waxed on one side and should be spread upon the entire top, the *mensa,* of an altar before the altar cloths are spread as long as any traces of the holy oils may remain on the surface of the altar after its consecration. It is not, as formerly, a part of the altar covering. (Cf. Altar.)

## Ceremonial

The ceremonial is the book that contains the procedure to be followed in religious ceremonies and solemn worship as prescribed for church functions. There are two such official publications: the *Roman Ceremonial (Caeremoniale Romanum),* and the *Ceremonial of Bishops (Caeremoniale Episcoporum).* In the United States the *Ceremonial for use of Catholic Churches* as approved by Cardinal Gibbons is in general use. Since Vatican II the *Roman Ceremonial* has been replaced largely by the *New Order of the Mass,* which is contained basically in the front of the *Sacramentary.*

## Ceremony

In the wide sense ceremony is any external act, gesture, or movement made in the worship of God. Such actions may be of two classes: (1) essential, such as the ceremonies that are part of the matter and form of the sacraments; (2) accidental, when they are not a part of worship as such. (See Holy Week, Liturgy of.)

## Certitude

The firm assent and adherence of the mind to any proposition without possible fear of being mistaken are termed certitude. There is implied a quietness or satisfaction of the intellect in the thing known, either because of evident truth or because a sufficient reason is seen to exist. (See Faith.)

## Chains of St. Peter

Bonds forged to keep St. Peter a prisoner in Jerusalem, as recorded in Acts 12. The feast, formerly celebrated on Aug. 1, is no longer on the calendar of the Church.

## Chair

In the church, besides the throne of the bishop, chairs are used in one form or another. (Cf. Cathedra; Faldstool; Sedilia.) Now the central chair of the sacred area about the altar, called the Celebrant's Chair, is behind the altar facing the Congregation.

"The Celebrant's Chair should express his office of presiding over the assembly and of directing prayer. Thus the proper place for the chair is in the center of the Sanctuary facing the people, unless the structure or other circumstances are an obstacle, for example, if there is too great a distance between the priest and people. Every appearance of a throne should be avoided. The seats for the ministers should be located in the sanctuary in places convenient for their functions" (Gen. Inst.).

## Chair of St. Peter

A portable chair preserved in the Vatican, this chair is believed to be that used by St. Peter in Rome. Evidence for this dates back to the second century. The feast, celebrated on Feb. 22, commemorates the first service held by St. Peter in Rome and the establishment of the see of Antioch by St. Peter. It is also a liturgical emphasis on the apostolic succession and the episcopacy within the Church.

## Chair of Unity Octave

This term refers to the eight days of prayer, from Jan. 18 to the feast of St. Paul's Conversion (Jan. 25). This devotion was begun by Father Paul James Francis, S.A., while still an Episcopalian, at Graymoor, N.Y., in petition that all Christians may be united in the true faith. A plenary indulgence is granted, under the usual

conditions, on the first or last day of the octave. It places emphasis upon the gospel plea "that all may be one" (Jn 17:21) and is a rallying term for the ecumenical movement given urgency by Vatican II. (See Ecumenism.)

## Chalcedon, Council of

See Ecumenical Councils.

## Chaldean Rite

Also called the East Syrian, Assyrian, or Persian rite, this is a liturgy of the Uniat East Syrians written in old Syriac. Communion is given by dipping a bit of consecrated bread into the chalice of consecrated wine. The Rite is listed as separate and distinct by the Sacred Congregation for the Oriental Churches. The Chaldeans are the oriental Christians of the East Syrian Rite. Their liturgy is adopted from the Antiochene Rite and structured uniquely. The sanctuary is a chapel, enclosed by high walls, with a door with a curtain that is closed at all times other than those of the Holy Sacrifice. The Mass begins with a prayer at the foot of the altar, a thanksgiving, an offering of bread and wine, and the Trisagion. There follow a reading from the Epistles, the Gospel, a prayer for the catechumens, and the prayer of the laying on of hands. Mass of the Faithful begins with a washing of hands; a second offertory; a memento to the Lord, His Blessed Mother, the saints, and departed souls. An Entry prayer and Creed are said, followed by the great Entry, a solemn approach to the altar, then the kiss of peace and the Canon, Preface, Consecration, and adoration after the consecration, intercessions and invocations of the Holy Spirit. The Communion begins after the elevation of the Sacred Host, the Our Father, the Thanksgiving, and blessing.

## Chalice

1. The most important of the sacred vessels, the chalice is the type of cup used in the Mass to hold the wine to be consecrated. Formerly it was a cup

on a low base, but it has now come to be a cup supported on a stem and base, usually eight inches in overall height. The chalice cup may be of gold or silver, and if the latter, then the inside must be surfaced with gold. The base and stem may be of any metal. The base should be sufficiently heavy to provide firmness to avoid upsetting; the stem has a knob or node beneath the cup to provide a more secure grip in handling. Chalices are consecrated with chrism by a bishop or one delegated by him. "Chalices and other vessels which are intended to hold the blood of the Lord should have a cup of non-absorbent material. The base may be of any other solid or worthy material." And, "The artist may give a form to the vessels which is in keeping with the culture of the area and their purpose in the liturgy" (Gen. Inst.). The chalice is an object of great dignity because of its unique use in the celebration of the Eucharist.

2. The "chalice" or cup spoken of by Christ in the agony in the garden (Mt. 26:42) and after His arrest (Jn. 18:11) is interpreted as the "portion" accepted by one voluntarily.

### Chalice Veil, also Peplum and Sudarium

This is the cloth, made of the same material and color as the vestments of the Mass, which is used to cover the chalice when it is carried to or from the altar and before the unveiling after the Creed in the celebration of Mass.

### Chamberlain

Chamberlain is the title of several classes of officials serving at the papal court and also the title, usually honorary, of those who serve in the apartments of the pope.

1. Chamberlain of the Holy Roman Church is the Cardinal who, upon the death of the Pope, convenes the College of Cardinals and summons its members and directs the conclave for the election of a new pope. His ordinary duties are the administration and care of the revenues of the Holy See.

2. Chamberlain of the Sacred College of Cardinals oversees the revenues of the College and records the business of the consistories.

3. Chamberlain of the Roman Clergy is the president of the secular clergy of the city of Rome.

### Chambre Ardente

Literally "burning room," the chambre ardente was a court or commission established by the French government in the sixteenth century, which put heretics on trial. It was so named because the court was lighted by burning torches.

### Chancel

The chancel is that part of the sanctuary which specifically is the area between the high altar and the nave of the church. It was formerly marked by a screen but derives its name from the *cancelli,* the railings that came to separate the area from the body of the church. It is also that part of the church building set aside for the priest and other ministers, but today this is more frequently referred to simply as the sacred area about the altar.

### Chancellor

In the Church, the chancellor is the priest appointed in accord with canon law by the bishop of a diocese. His title is "diocesan chancellor," and he serves as an ecclesiastical notary. His duties include the supervision of the diocesan archives, the authentication of documents, and the drawing up of written reports on the official government of the diocese.

### Chancery

The chancery is the diocesan office where the administration of a diocese is carried on and where records, documents, and proceedings of diocesan courts, are kept. Today this has often become a part of the administration complex where the business, secular and religious, of a diocese is done.

### Chancery, Papal, also Apostolic Chancery

The Papal Chancery is the oldest of all official groups of the Church administration. At present its task is to prepare and send all apostolic bulls for appointment of bishops or the erection of a diocese and any others that might be required by the Sacred Congregations or the Pope. (Cf. Bull, Apostolic.) Today under the reorganization of the Roman Curia, this is the office of the Secretariat of State who provides the Pope with assistance in carrying on the affairs of the Universal Church. This post, usually assigned to a Cardinal, is the office wherein the operations of the Curia are coordinated.

### Chant

The official music used in the liturgy of the Roman rite, made up of Ambrosian chant, plain chant, and Gregorian chant is largely referred to today as Gregorian chant or music. It was formerly official in the sense that ecclesiastical authority prescribed that those parts of the liturgy that were to be sung required the officiating clergy to sing according to this chant. It is distinguished from other musical notation or composition permitted in hymns. In make-up, chant is monodic, usually diatonic, and ranges from simple recitation of a text in a slightly variated tone to the more elaborate melodies. The chant uses a four line staff and a concise form of notation printed in square or diamond shapes with a variety of combinations and elisions. Gregorian chant was derived from several sources going back to the earliest days of the Church—the Hebrew, represented in the Psalm tones; the Oriental, with its singular rhythm; the Greek and Latin in its choral makeup; and the Frankish, which was chiefly syllabic. The part that St. Gregory the Great (d. 604) played in the founding of the chant bearing his name has been disputed, but a collection of chants called the Antiphonal was prepared by him or caused to be published by him in the late sixth century. He also introduced a school of Church music and fostered its development toward use in the divine services. In the ninth century when this "Gregorian" type was introduced among the Franks, they found the compositions somewhat elaborate and wrought a modification that led to the adaptation called "plain chant." More recently, the monks of Solesmes, in a work begun under Dom Andre Mocquereau, have done much to authenticate the early versions and to provide editions of restored texts of the Church's chant.

While this form of chant is still in use and is considered the more solemn, the church has encouraged the use of other hymns in keeping with the new developments in the liturgy. (See Music, Church.)

## Chantry

An endowment, the chantry is set up to provide: (1) the upkeep of one or more priests; (2) the place for saying Mass; or (3) both priest and place, with the provision that the priest offer Masses for a deceased person in that place. Chantries were common in England in the Middle Ages but were done away with entirely under the Acts of 1545 to 1547.

## Chapel

A chapel may be either a small church other than the parish church or a small area or part of a larger church set apart for special devotions. It was customary to call the small churches erected on palace grounds by the name chapel. Today it is more frequently applied to the small rooms where the Blessed Sacrament is kept and established for convenience such as in convents or schools. These may be designated as public or semipublic oratories. (Cf. Oratory.)

The category of chapels ranges according to their use: (1) *public chapels*, usually in large religious communities, which are open to the public and where the Sunday obligation may be satisfied; (2) *winter chapel* is that accommodation in a larger church where, because of heating problems, the weekday liturgies are celebrated; (3) *semipublic chapels* are those serving a specific religious community or institution, such as at a retreat house, where the precept of attending Mass on Sunday and holy days may be fulfilled; (4) *private chapels* are those in a private home. Specific rules govern their use.

## Chapel of Atonement

This Canadian National Shrine of the Sacred Heart at Pointe-aux-Trembles, Quebec, in the outskirts of Montreal, was founded in 1886. The original chapel burned in 1905 but was replaced by a splendid edifice in 1910. The Shrine is under the direction of the Capuchin Fathers. In 1927 pilgrimages of men and women from many places in Canada and the United States began, directing their intentions to penance for the sins of mankind. Today, at the fieldstone shrine, Sunday Mass is celebrated and draws great crowds. The Archconfraternity of Prayer and Penance has its headquarters here, and the Shrine is affiliated with the Shrine of the Sacred Heart, on Montmartre in Paris. The singular appeal of the chapel and shrine is evident through the response that continues and the indulgences granted to those who come to the Shrine.

## Chapel of Ease

A chapel of ease is a chapel or small church built in a remote part of a parish territory to accommodate parishioners living a considerable distance from the parish church. Today this would most likely be referred to as a "mission" of a parent parish, served by the clergy of the parish.

## Chapelle Ardente

The name Chapelle Ardente applies to the chapel or room in which the body of a deceased person lies in state, derived from the candles burning around the bier. Such are found chiefly in the residences of royalty.

## Chaplain

1. A chaplain is the priest appointed to conduct liturgical functions for a lay association or group, a religious or public institution such as a hospital or prison. The appointment is made by the ordinary or a religious superior of exempt religious orders. The chaplain does not have

parochial rights over the community unless by special privilege, and he serves to accommodate those in the place of his assignment.

2. A military chaplain is a priest permitted by his diocesan or religious superior to enter military service, in the army, navy, or air force, to have charge of religious services in the place of his assignment. As such he is subject to either the ordinary of the place wherein he serves or the bishop-ordinary of the armed forces.

In 1965 the National Association of Catholic Chaplains was founded and operates under the Department of Social Development and World Peace of the United States Catholic Conference. The Association conducts seminars for hospital chaplains in pastoral work twice each year.

### Chaplet

1. Originally, a wreath worn about the head as at religious professions.

2. Name applied to the rosary of five decades.

3. More commonly today a string of beads, varying in number, upon which prayers or ejaculations of special devotions are said.

### Chapter, Cathedral

In the Middle Ages, it was the practice to join the priests serving a cathedral into administrative groups who were to assist the bishop. These groups became autonomous and usurped the authority of the bishop in some areas of his jurisdiction, and as a consequence, special rules were made to curtail their activities. Today in England every diocese has a chapter, usually numbering ten canons (cf. Canon, 2) and presided over by a provost. These serve under rules prescribed by the Council of Trent, as aids to the bishop in the performance of divine services and in the execution of the temporal affairs of the diocese. In the United States this practice is not followed.

### Chapter, Conventual

It was the custom in certain religious houses for the members of the community to gather each morning to hear the reading of a part of their religious rule. Both the place of meeting and the practice came to be known as the "chapter." Today any formal meetings of monks or religious, whether of a province or an entire religious order, are commonly called "chapters," and it is the practice to hold such meetings at regular intervals. The chapter may be called to assemble to elect superiors, to discuss business pertaining to the community's institute, or to expand its mission in the Church.

### Chapter, General

See General Chapter.

### Chapter House

The meeting place of a conventual chapter or the members of a cathedral chapter is a chapter house.

### Character

1. Character includes the collective qualities, emotional, intellectual, and volitional, which distinguish the mind and personality of an individual.

2. In a religious sense, character is the indelible, invisible, seal or mark impressed upon the soul of a person through reception of the Sacraments of Baptism, Confirmation, and Holy Orders. It is a spiritual mark that consecrates and dedicates the person to Christ in a singular manner, and thus these sacraments can be received but once. (See Baptism, Sacrament of; Confirmation, Sacrament of; Orders, Holy, Sacrament of.)

### Chardinism

See Teilhardism.

### Charismata, also Charisms

Charismata, the gifts or graces of an extraordinary type, called *gratis datae*, are given to individual Christians for the benefit of others. They may be defined as functions that are present continuously and exercised at a particular time and which, whether or not they are extraordinary, by their very nature tend to aid the faithful either locally or universally. St. Paul (1 Cor. 12:4–11; 14, 15) lists nine of these graces *gratis datae*, including prophecy, the working of miracles, and others, and declares them to be given by the Holy Spirit. Also in Rom. 12:6–8, he includes other gifts that are not so extraordinary in themselves, as "he that exhorteth" and "he that showeth mercy." St. Thomas Aquinas groups these graces as: those pertaining to knowledge, those pertaining to speech, and those pertaining to miracles.

The word comes from the Greek and means in a broad sense any favor or gift. In its technical sense as used by St. Paul and applied by Christians, it means these extraordinary gifts granted to early Christian communities for the benefit of others and for the more rapid spread of Christianity. In Mk. 16:17–18. they are called "signs" and are interpreted by scholars as "services of help," and the "powers of administration," especially for the community. Such charisms do not belong to the essence of the Church, which is an hierarchical institution, founded on apostolic authority. St. Paul places the virtue of charity above all charisms (cf. 1 Cor. 13), as do such modern theologians as R. Poulain, S.J., and Karl Rahner.

### Charismatic Renewal, Catholic

This is also called the Catholic Pentecostal Movement. This new movement, which has acquired a large and devoted following in the United States and Canada, began in Feb. 1967 with a group of about twenty students and faculty members at Duquesne University. This event was marked by charismatic activity like the apostolic intensity recorded in Acts 1:8: "You shall receive power when the Holy Spirit comes down upon you; then you are to be my witnesses . . ." Many present testified to receiving gifts such as that of tongues (glossolalia), prophecy, discernment of spirits, and the power of exorcism. The movement then spread rapidly to the campuses of Notre Dame, Michigan State, and Michigan Universities, as well as to other campuses and to some groups centered around religious institutes.

The claims of these people are that there is a new outpouring of the Holy Spirit in the Roman Catholic Church, that there is need to draw the attention of the world to a spiritual reawakening through charismatic gifts, and that this movement makes the world conscious of the Catholic Church.

Fully cognizant of the Pentecostal sects, such as the Assembly of God churches, the neo-Pentecostals among whom Baptists, Lutherans, Presbyterians, and Episcopalians may be numbered, there is a revival of the conviction that the Catholics are also called to a life in the Holy Spirit with the accompanying gifts.

The procedure for the various assemblies, composed of people from all walks of life, begins with the prayer meeting, where there is communication with God through private meditation in a community atmosphere. There may be during this silent exercise, vocal attestations of public edification, thanksgiving, or praise of God. There is usually also a reading from Scripture and extemporaneous prayer based upon the text read. There follow formula prayers, doctrinal presentations, revelation of personal experiences, and interpretation. Guitar and drum music may accompany these procedures. Each person simply permits himself to be guided by the Holy Spirit. As a part of the prayer meeting, but distinct from it, is the "baptism of the Spirit," which as a means of initiation is intended to create a sense of community among the individual members of the group. The term is not a dogmatic phrasing, but rather a symbolic term that may be a dangerous confusion

with the traditional wording for a sacred event. This baptism is received by anyone who, emotionally or rationally, decides to dedicate himself or herself to Christ (cf. calling), and any charism or gift manifested thereafter may be a confirmation of this baptism. In the group such baptisms *(sic)* are received through the physical action of imposing hands upon the head of the recipient, and the action may be repeated upon request of any member. This action is in turn symbolic of the dedication or rededication of someone to God, and this in turn may be considered a sacramental, like the Sign of the Cross.

The central cause, the rationale of Catholic Pentacostalism, is the exercise of the gifts of the Holy Spirit in an openness to His influence and a response to His spiritual urgings and graces. Thus there are two results: the charismatic responses, like those listed by St. Paul in his first epistle to the Corinthians (12:4–11), such as speaking with wisdom, discernment of spirits, prophecy, and speaking with tongues. The other, and the more significant, is the contemplative, which is a deepening of faith and its power through God (cf. Mk. 11:23).

Not all group meetings result in the phenomenon of speaking in tongues, the charismatic gift of glossolalia. This can be a rhythmic, sing-song making of sound or the phrasing of language-like utterances. The languages are said to be historic, that is, no longer understood by man, but nevertheless a speaking to God directly. But without an area of proper reference and some understanding, this wants further proof. Psychologists and psychiatrists for the most part do not put much stock in such glossolalia, but to dismiss the speakers as psychosomatic is not entirely an explanation. Upon this charism alone the movement does not rest its claims.

The Bishops of the United States are keeping a watchful eye on the movement, aware as most Christians are, that "The natural man does not accept what is taught by the Spirit of God. For him that is absurdity. He cannot come to know such teaching because it must be appraised in a spiritual way. The spiritual man, on the other hand, can appraise everything, though he himself can be appraised by no one. For, 'Who has known the mind of the Lord so as to instruct him?' But we have the mind of Christ" (1 Cor. 2:14–16). The movement has been called ecumenical by Cardinal Suenens of Belgium and is perhaps better referred to as "renewal in the Spirit." (See Charismata.)

Vatican II in the *Dogmatic Constitution on the Church* (n. 12) stated: "It is not only through the sacraments and Church ministries that the same Holy Spirit sanctifies and leads the People of God and enriches it with virtues. Allotting His gifts 'to each as he wills' (1 Cor. 12:11), He distributes special graces among the faithful of every rank. By these gifts He makes them fit and ready to undertake the various tasks or offices advantageous for the renewal and upbuilding of the Church, according to the words of the Apostle: 'To each person the manifestation of the Spirit is given for the common good' (1 Cor. 12:7). These charismatic gifts, whether the most outstanding or the more simple and widely diffused, are to be received with thanksgiving and consolation, for they are exceedingly suitable and useful for the needs of the Church.

"Still, extraordinary gifts are not to be rashly sought after, nor are the fruits of apostolic labor to be presumptuously expected from them. In any case, judgment as to their genuineness and proper use belongs to those who preside over the Church, and to whose special competence it belongs, not indeed to extinguish the Spirit, but to test all things and hold fast to that which is good (cf. 1 Thes. 5:12, 19–21)."

### Charity

Charity is a supernatural virtue infused with sanctifying grace, by which we love God above all as the greatest good and for His own sake, and ourselves and our neighbors for the love of God. It is the greatest of the three theological virtues and of all virtues. The object of the virtue is our union with God through love; the act itself is the giving of ourselves to God. Charity is given as the greatest commandment (Mt. 22:34–40), and it is joined inseparably by the command to love one's neighbor (cf. 1 Cor. 13:8–13). St. Bonaventure points to charity as "a life which unites the lover with the beloved." Although charity may be manifested in many ways, it is not to be confused with almsgiving as such, nor is it only good deeds that may arise out of natural virtue and the emotion of good will or compassion. Rather charity is the very basis, the foundation that prompts and is the motivating force by which all acts of good directed toward ourselves or our neighbors are performed for love of God. St. Thomas Aquinas states: "Essentially the perfection of the Christian life consists in charity, first and foremost in the love of God, then in the love of neighbor" (S.T. IIa IIae, q. 184, a3). (Cf. Love of God.)

### Charity, Heroic Act of

This act includes the offering to God for the souls suffering in purgatory all the merits of good deeds performed during life and the benefits or suffrages gained after death in one's behalf. It is advisable to consult one's confessor or spiritual guide before making the act; however, it is revocable at any time. This act is based on the teaching of Christ: "Anyone who loves me will be true to my word, and my Father will love him; we will come to him and make our dwelling place with him" (Jn. 14:23).

### Charity, Works of

These are the actions of a social nature, which are resultant from the love of God, and are more than emotions, feelings, or sentiment. They are directed primarily toward our neighbors. Thus, social justice is a work of charity. (Cf. Corporal Works of Mercy.)

Vatican II speaks of charity, stating: "Let them (Christ's followers) all see that they guide their affections rightly. Otherwise, they will be thwarted in the search for perfect charity by the way they use earthly possessions and by a fondness for riches which goes against the gospel spirit of poverty. The Apostle has sounded the warning: let those who make use of this world not get bogged down in it, for the structure of this world is passing away" (cf. 1 Cor. 7:31, Gr. Text) (LG 42). And: "These charitable enterprises can and should reach out to absolutely every person and every need" (AC 8).

### Chartophylax

This title in the Eastern Church, corresponds to Chancellor in the Western Church.

### Chartres, Our Lady of

This title was given to the famous Gothic cathedral consecrated in 1260 at Chartres, the capital city of Ense-et-Loir in France. The church is famed for its beauty and the blue color in its stained glass windows. It was erected as a singular devotion to the Blessed Mother and to foster veneration to her through (1) the statue of Our Lady under the Earth, from an ancient Druid figure; (2) the "Black Virgin" in the upper church; (3) and the "Veil of the Virgin" enshrined there.

### Chartreuse, the Great

The original founding house of the Carthusians was set up by St. Bruno 14 miles northeast of Grenoble, France, in 1084.

### Chastity

The exercise of this moral virtue checks, controls, moderates, or excludes the desire and pleasure of carnal or sexual thoughts or actions. It is called the "angelic" virtue because the angels are pure by nature. There are two kinds of chastity: *conjugal* chastity, which is exercised in the control and moderation of legitimate acts of the sexual relations of married persons; and *continence* or *purity*, which is chastity exercised by youths and the unmarried, and includes more essentially the control and exclusion of sexual or voluptuous desires, thoughts, and acts. Chastity differs from celibacy and virginity while being an essential virtue of both. Chastity is the virtue contrary to lust and is exercised by (1) refraining from thoughts, fancies, daydreams, and imaginings of sexual matters; (2) by restraining the temptations of lust by practical, energetic means; (3) by directing one's thoughts by prayer and reason to a love of God who made the senses for His own glory. (Cf. Modesty.)

Vatican II urged: "Especially in the heart of their own families, young people should be aptly and seasonably instructed about the dignity, duty, and expression of married love. Trained thus in this cultivation of chastity, they will be able at a suitable age to enter a marriage of their own after an honorable courtship" (GS 51).

### Chasuble

The chasuble is the vestment worn by priests or bishops over all other garments or vestures when they celebrate Mass. Originally the chasuble was a full, semicircular cloak and is so mentioned by St. Paul (2 Tm. 4:13). Through gradual development the chasuble evolved into two forms that are common today, though no particular shape is prescribed. The first and more common is the "Italian" or "Roman" style, which is rectangular at the back extending to either side beyond the shoulders and cut away in front in a fiddle-shape with a square-shaped opening for the neck. It is decorated with a T-shaped cross in front and a broad orphrey in back. The second style is called "Gothic" or "Gothic revival." This type is more like

a cloak; it is cone-shaped with a semicircular cut, causing it to rest more loosely on the shoulders. Recent liturgical studies have brought about a trend toward use of the Gothic style. Among many symbolisms attributed to the chasuble, the most popular is that it is a figure of the love of God, charity being the greatest of all virtues.

In the general instructions on the vestments for Mass, it is simply stated: "The chasuble, worn over the alb and stole, is the proper vestment of the priest who celebrates Mass or other services connected with Mass, unless otherwise indicated." Design and materials, such as patterned cloth, variegated color, and a practical looseness in the cut, have been freely accepted and approved by many liturgical commissions. Liturgical colors have been retained, with borderline adaptations permitted, but black has been replaced by white or purple for Masses for the dead.

### Cherubim

The angels of the second highest of the nine hierarchies or choirs are called the Cherubim. The word from the Assyrian means "great, powerful," and St. Gregory says the name signifies "the fullness of knowledge." They were revealed as the angels who guarded the gate of the garden of Eden (Gn. 3:24) and formed the throne of God in heaven. (Cf. Angel.)

### Chester Plays

A series of miracle plays were performed at Chester, England, during the early fifteenth century during the Pentecostal season. They were particularly intended to teach the Scriptures and took their themes from biblical events.

### Chevet

Chevet is the French architectural term for that part of a church which is at the easternmost end of the building where the apse is closed over by a screen. Behind the screen there is an aisle leading to an area opening into three or more smaller chapels.

### Child of Mary

A member of a confraternity of the Blessed Virgin Mary is referred to as a child of Mary. Originally begun by the Jesuits in the sixteenth century for the instruction of children, the movement was taken up again in 1847 by the Sisters of Charity to promote the devotion of the miraculous medal. Since then various sodalities have been founded to promote devotion to the Blessed Mother among youth.

## Childermas

The medieval name for "Children's Mass," Childermass is the Feast of the Holy Innocents, celebrated on December 28.

## Children, Duties of

Obligations are required of children by the fourth commandment. The obligation to honor one's parents includes the giving of respect, love, and obedience. The same duties are to be extended by children to authorities, superiors, and teachers. In its *Declaration on Christian Education,* Vatican II specifically states: "It is particularly in the Christian family, enriched by the grace and the office of the sacrament of matrimony, that from their earliest years children should be taught, according to the faith received in baptism, to have a knowledge of God, to worship Him, and to love their neighbor" (GE 3).

## Children, Mass for

After the General Instruction of the revised Roman Missal (see Sacramentary) in 1969, a special directory was prepared concerning children and the eucharistic celebration. "In bringing up children in the Church a special difficulty arises from the fact that liturgical celebrations, especially the eucharist, cannot fully exercise their inherent pedagogical force upon children. Although the mother tongue may now be used at Mass, still the words and signs have not been sufficiently adapted to the capacity of Children" (Int. *Directory for Masses with Children,* 1974). In recognition of participation, it was thus decided to encourage special liturgies for children, to intensify their participation and to involve as many as possible in the celebration. The mystery and the parts of the Mass remain the same, but the effort on the part of the celebrant should be to make the Mass "festive, fraternal, and meditative." To ensure the instruction of the children, the use of visual aids, processions, and simple songs are encouraged. (See Eucharist, Celebration of.)

## Children's Communion

By his decree of Aug. 8, 1910, Pope St. Pius X granted that children who have reached the "age of discretion" (declared to be seven years) may receive first Holy Communion.

## Children's Crusade

Under the erroneous belief that the Holy Land would be captured by the pure of heart, 40,000 children were gathered in 1212 for this purpose. Following the Fourth Crusade, the children were marched as far as Brindisi, but many died on the way, some were sent home, and others were sold into slavery by treacherous Christian traders. There were two groups, one from France, the other from Germany. Very few reached Palestine, and it was a frightful use of children in a cause that could only fail because of lack of any genuine leadership. (See Crusades.)

## Chiliasm

Chiliasm was the belief of early Christians in the reign of a thousand years, as recorded in the twentieth chapter of the Book of Revelation. (Cf. Millenium.)

## Chinese Rites

Early missionaries permitted the Chinese converts to retain various religious practices of a superstitious character, in ceremonies, particularly Confucianism and veneration of ancestors. Known as the Chinese Rites, these were forbidden by an apostolic constitution of Pope Clement XI in 1715.

## Chi-Rho

This monogram or christogram is formed of the Greek letters *Ch* and *R,* which are an abbreviation of the Greek word for Christ. They resemble the Roman letters *X* and *P* and are usually represented as one imposed upon the other. (See Symbol.)

## Chirograph

A personal papal letter, usually addressed to a church dignitary on a serious current problem is called a chirograph. It is also referred to as an "autograph letter."

## Chirotony

The sacrament of orders in the Byzantine rite is known as chirotony. The term is derived from the Greek and means "stretching forth of the hands."

## Chivalry

The system of ideas that formed the ideals of conduct of the medieval knight is called chivalry. It was the basis of his conduct in both civil and church society and at peace and war. At the core were honor and devotion under a discipline that governed his personal life and developed a spirit of Christian service for others. As such it arose in the ninth century as a means of saving the Christian West. The knight was invested and dedicated himself to a life of valor in protecting the weak and upholding the cause of Christ. Chivalry has made a notable contribution to romantic literature of an inspiring nature.

## Choir

1. A degree in the hierarchy of the angels.

2. The place in cathedral or collegiate churches set aside for the recitation of the Divine Office by canons, monks, priests, or religious. Each place occupied by these is called a stall.

3. A group of singers who sing the portions of the liturgy in response to the celebrant and represent the people; also the place in the church occupied by such singers, usually where the organ is erected. (Cf. Music, Church.)

## Choral Vicar

The choral vicar is the choir director of a group of canons of a cathedral chapter.

## Chrism

Chrism, a mixture of pure olive oil and balm, or balsam, is blessed by the bishop on Holy Thursday and used in the administration of baptism, confirmation, holy orders, and at the consecration of bishops. It is also used in the consecration of churches, altar stones, chalices, patens, the solemn blessing of bells, and the blessing of baptismal water. The two elements together signify a "fullness of grace."

In 1971 The Congregation for Divine Worship sent a directive permitting the use of other oils, such as vegetable, seed, or coconut oils, in place of the traditional olive oil. Grant was also given that oils could be blessed at other times than at the Mass of Holy Thursday, and conferences of bishops were authorized to extend to priests the right to bless oils in cases of necessity. (See Holy Oils; Oil Stock.)

## Chrismal, also Chrismatory

These words have been applied to a variety of objects in the history of the Church and are now seldom used. Most commonly is meant a jar or vessel, usually larger than an oil stock, for holding a holy oil. Formerly the words were used for: a small container for the Holy Eucharist similar to a pyx, a corporal, a reliquary, the head-covering of a newly baptized child, the first cloth covering a consecrated altar.

## Chrismarium

A chrismarium was an area once set aside in a cathedral where the sacrament of confirmation was customarily administered. It is sometimes used for the name of a container of chrism.

## Chrismation

The term chrismation is sometimes applied to an anointing where holy oils are used.

## Chrismons

The word Chrismons is formed from two words, *Christ* and *Monograms*. These are decorative monograms or symbols of Christ, which are made in white and gold colors. The white symbolizes the purity of Christ the God-Man; the gold symbolizes the majesty of Christ as the Son of God. The design of the chrismons is that of any symbol, with the size usually limited to less than a foot in diameter, although they may be of a size suitable to their purpose. Groupings of chrismons are used as decorations during liturgical seasons, especially Christmas and Epiphany, and are constructed of braiding, beads, cordings, or wire. (See Symbol.)

## Chrisom

Chrisom is an old English word for a baptismal garment.

## Christ

The use of "Christ" (not "the Christ"), meaning "the anointed," the "Messiah," as a proper name became common after the death of our Lord, particularly in the writings of St. Paul (Phil. 1:1–2). It might be used either before or after the name "Jesus" (cf. Acts 24:24). Its use by St. Paul declared the Apostle's belief and affirmation of the divinity of Jesus, explicit in Phil. 2:5–11. However, the word *Kyrios* in Greek is a translation of the Aramaic equivalent of "the prophesied king." Thus, Jesus fulfilled in His Incarnation the promise made to Abraham, as given in the genealogy found in the first chapter of St. Matthew's Gospel.

Vatican II spoke of Christ: "He who is 'the image of the invisible God' (Col. 1:15), is Himself the perfect man. To the sons of Adam He restores the divine likeness which had been disfigured from the first sin onward. Since human nature as He assumed it was not annulled, by that very fact it has been raised up to a divine dignity in our respect too. For by His incarnation the Son of God has united Himself in some fashion with every man. He worked with human hands. He thought with a human mind, acted by human choice, and loved with a human heart. Born of the Virgin Mary, He has truly been made one of us, like us in all things except sin" (GS 22).

## Christ of the Andes

This heroic statue of Christ was erected to commemorate the friendly settlement through arbitration of a boundary dispute between Chile and Argentina in South America in the last years of the nineteenth century. It was cast from the metal of guns intended for the possible war and placed on the border between the two countries on a mountain 14,000 feet above sea level. An inscription on its pedestal reads: "He is our peace who hath made both one."

## Christ, Supreme Order of

A papal decoration, with one class of knights, the Supreme Order of Christ was founded in the fourteenth century by Pope John XXII in Portugal. It is now called Militia of Our Lord Jesus Christ.

## Christening

See Baptism, Sacrament of.

## Christian Brothers

This religious order, properly called "Brothers of the Christian Schools," was founded by St. Jean Baptiste de la Salle (d. 1719). The order is devoted to the Christian education of youth. It is abbreviated F.C.S.

## Christian Democrats

Christian Democrats are followers of the political philosophy of Christian Democracy, which adheres to the inalienable rights of individuals and society in regard to the civil authority of the state, whereby individuals may act in accordance with Christian principles. Christian Democracy, established as a party in France, Belgium, Holland, Germany, and Italy, opposes socialism but seeks no political objective in the governance of property. It is composed of two groups: the radical seeks its purpose through republican government; the mild or less radical permits monarchial government but with representation of the people in executing government. Its limitations as a political party are inherent in its makeup. It attracts Christians but few other adherents; it tends to be identified as a Catholic party; its members are cautious in social matters; it has an ill-defined idea of political freedom in practice.

## Christian Doctrine

Christian doctrine includes the teachings and instructions that are applicable to all Christians. In the Catholic Church this is a broad term embracing primary instruction as well as the most advanced theology. It is progressively systematic and may be applied to the entire course of learning from the child's first learning of simple prayers to catechism, religion courses, and theology, sometimes including Church history and allied subjects. In its basic meaning it is the developed form of the early teachings given by the apostles to the Christians of the first century of the Church.

## Christian Doctrine, Confraternity of

In 1905, Pope St. Pius X decreed the canonical establishment of the Confraternity of Christian Doctrine (CCD) in every diocese and parish of the Catholic Church. This was incorporated in the New Code of Canon Law in 1917. Its purpose is to extend and improve education in the faith for converts, youth, and those unable to attain knowledge through the Catholic school system. In 1934 a committee of the Catholic hierarchy of the United States was set up to organize the work of the Confraternity. This work of spreading knowledge and practice of the faith is accomplished in the following manner: religious training of Catholic children attending non-Catholic grade schools through classes of instruction either during the school term or vacation times, the instruction of Catholic high school students who are attending public high schools or vocational schools through study clubs or other means, aiding parents in the religious instruction of their children at home, the provision of instruction for non-Catholics. The discussion club has been the most commonly used means of instruction of the Catholic laity. Through a publications department the Confraternity provides books, texts, manuals, graded courses of study, discussion club aids, catechetical aids, pamphlets, and leaflets.

The CCD is a parish-based organization operating through the education commission or the education committee of the parish council. In the diocese the program works through a director appointed by the bishop, and in some instances this is through an office of religious education. Nationally the Division of Religious Education, CCD, since 1969 has been under the Department of Education, U. S. Catholic Conference, with offices at 1312 Massachusetts Ave., N.W., Washington, D.C. 20005. Internationally it participates in programs of the Congregation of the Clergy.

## Christian Family Movement

This organization of the laity for married couples began in Chicago in 1947; its aim is to restore family life in Christ and to promote an entire community that emphasizes Christian living. It follows a program of religious formation through practical discussions and organized action to meet the family and community needs as well as a genuine concern for the problems that arise in families; parishes, both urban and rural; and the broader aspects of life in civil society.

In the United States in 1960, the CFM joined Young Christian Students and Young Christian Workers to form the Specialized Lay Apostolate. Thereafter it was affiliated with the Lay Organization Department of the National Conference of Catholic Bishops. (Cf. Apostolate.)

## Christian Mothers, Archconfraternity of

Societies of Catholic women are established in many parishes whose purposes are: spiritual advancement for each member, particularly through the introduction of Christian ideals into their homes, and the works of Christian leadership in their parishes and communities. Their patronesses are Our Lady of the Seven Sorrows and St. Monica.

## Christian Name

See Baptismal Name.

## Christian Science

Christian Science is the title of the religious system introduced by Mary Baker Eddy in 1879. Its basic beliefs are that all physical objects and experiences are imaginary and that disease is only an error of the mind that disappears when one comes to the realization that the body does not exist. It follows a pseudoscientific system of divine healing. Thus, mind has a superior control over disease and illness. Mrs. Eddy's best known and basic book is *Science and Health, with Key to the Scriptures.* At first her ideas, which she considered divinely inspired, were not accepted by other Christian groups to the degree that she had anticipated. It was thereafter that a distinctly new Church was founded in 1879 to propagate her teachings, and the *Church of Christ, Scientist* was begun. Others were built in cities outside Boston. The Church as an organization is now under the direction of a national board of directors who are appointed for life and name their successors. However, the governance of church related matters is according to Mrs. Eddy's official *Church Manual.*

The Church is considered one of the forms of Protestantism, a divergence from the Congregationalist concepts. Its doctrinal background is: belief in God is taken for granted, and there follow Six Tenets that are expressed in Christian terms but are at variance with the traditional Christian expressions. These tenets are: the Bible is the word of God, but only as interpreted by Mrs. Eddy; belief in the Trinity is in terms of God as the Father-Mother, Christ as the spiritual embodiment of sonship, and the "Holy Comforter" as divine science. Forgiveness of sins is through a grasp of the unreality of sin. Christ is not the savior, but the one who shows the way to union with God. The crucifixion and resurrection of Christ are parables that demonstrate the "allness" of God. And, prayer's only purpose is to bring the mind to be

like that of Christ and the mercifulness, justice, and purity that follow, together with the golden rule of doing to others as you wish them to do to you.

## Christian Socialism

Christian Socialism is the political and economic system that espouses the objectives of socialism concerning social reorganization but seeks to bring them into effect through the application of Christian principles. Thus, it stresses private ownership and social duties. In organizations, Christian socialism operates in England, Austria, and Germany.

## Christianity

The establishment of the Christian faith is essentially a part of history. It has been a rejuvenation of the human race, influencing government, social living, the arts and sciences for two millenia. However, it had its origin in the religion and the Church established by Jesus Christ and cannot be understood apart from knowledge of the history and development of the Catholic Church. As such Christianity is the embodiment of the teachings of Jesus Christ, the founding of His Church, and the inspiration and authority found in Scripture. The teachings were continued through the Apostles, expanded, and disseminated throughout the world, and many obstacles to their introduction were overcome. After the founding and the introduction of this teaching came the organization and the erection of the hierarchical order, the bishops as successors of the Apostles, and the continuing administration of the seven sacraments that Christ instituted. With organization and growth there followed the great consequences of that teaching, notably its effect on the family and society, especially the overcoming of slavery, the dignifying of the human personality, new concepts of property rights and duties and the understanding of poverty, and influence on the thinking, actions, and expression of authority by civil authorities. It is the whole of revealed religion in content and execution.

Vatican II stated: "Christians, on pilgrimage toward the heavenly city, should seek and savor the things which are above. This duty in no way decreases, but rather increases, the weight of their obligations to work with all men in constructing a more human world" (GS 57). (See Community.)

## Christians

The name of those who follow the faith of Christ is Christian. They are of no particular nationality but very early were recognized as a distinct group

(Acts 11:26). St. Luke's names for Christians are "holy people" (Acts 9:13), "disciples," "brethren," "those of the way," "those who invoke the name" (Acts 9:14), and "believers." King Agrippa used the term as a taunt: "A little more, Paul, and you will make a Christian out of me!" (Acts 26:28.) In later days the name has been more widely applied to those who imitate Christ in their lives, to Catholics as a single group; to all baptized persons who believe in Christ, and to all who were baptized whatever their belief might be. (See Christianity.)

## Christmas

The day on which is celebrated the Nativity of Jesus Christ is called Christmas. Its story is narrated in Lk. 1:26–80, and 2:1–18. In the Church calendar the solemnity is commemorated on Dec. 25. Following the celebration of the Church, the world as a whole honors this day as the anniversary of the birth of Christ. On Christmas, by special privilege, priests are permitted to celebrate three Masses. (Cf. Incarnation.)

## Christology

Christology is the name of the body of theology dealing especially with the nature and personality of Jesus Christ, the Scripture concerning Him and His life and teachings. It is the theology centered on Jesus simply rather than on Christ as the Second Person of the Trinity. (See Theology.)

## Christophers

This name is given to the followers of the Christopher movement, founded in the United States in 1946 by the Rev. James Keller, M.M. The purposes and ideals of the Christophers are attained by no closelyknit, dues-paying membership, but by allying oneself with the movement to bring Christian principles to American public and private life. This program is one of positive thought and action in the fields of government, education, trade-unions, and the fields of drama and writing, or any walk of life. Although the membership is largely Catholic, it is not limited to those of a particular religious affiliation. The work is done on a purely individual basis, by an individual becoming first an exemplar and second a responsible leader, willing to take the initiative in Christian action. It is supported entirely by voluntary contributions. It has radio and TV programs on some 4,000 broadcasting facilities and distributes a million and a quarter leaflet publications called *Christopher Notes* seven times a year. A syndicated column, *What One Person Can Do*, is carried by more than four hundred newspapers, and twenty-eight daily papers carry a column

entitled "It's Your Life." Annual awards are given to authors, directors, and writers of motion pictures and TV network specials. The organization motto is: "It is better to light one candle than to curse the darkness." Present headquarters are at: 12 E. 48 St., New York, N.Y. 10017.

## Chronicler

This is the name or title given to the unknown author of the First and Second Books of Chronicles. From the evidence of style, vocabulary, and the identical nature of some passages, he was also the author of the Books of Ezra and Nehemiah. It is not certain when the chronicler lived, but it is evident from some of the events of which he wrote that it was the latter part of the fifth century before Christ.

## Chronicles, Books 1 and 2 of

The Books of Chronicles are the two historical books called 1 and 2 Paralipomenon in many versions of the Bible. The name Chronicles is a translation of the Hebrew meaning "the annals." St. Jerome in writing of the Vulgate described these works as a "Chronicle of all divine history," but he retained the title "Paralipomenon" from the old Latin term that is a transliteration of words from the Greek meaning "of the things omitted." The author planned these books as one continuous account and also wrote the Books of Ezra and Nehemiah as a part of the historical continuity.

The writing of these books embraces the Israelitic history from Genesis through the Books of Kings, giving a special interpretation of these times and demonstrating the religious community that they were under through the divine guidance of God. It also serves to demonstrate how the people worshipped God, their response to the formal cult of worship, and their governance by kings who received their authority from God and acted in His behalf. These books recount chronologically the establishment of the kingdom under David, its downfall, and the efforts to reestablish it and properly reform it as a preparation for the model reign of David, whose house was given the promise of an everlasting reign. The final faith that was a trust in God's promise of what was to come to His Chosen People is evidenced in the Books of Chronicles. (See Ezra, Book of; Nehemiah, Book of.)

## Chronista

The name, chronista from the Latin meaning narrator, is given to the deacon or cantor who sings the narration portions of the scriptural passions during Holy Week. There is usually a three-part division of these readings, consisting of the narrator (*Chronista*), the one who speaks the words of Christ *(Christus)*, and the speech of others *(Synagoga)*. The words of our Lord are reserved for the priest or celebrant as a rule in these readings. (See Holy Week, Liturgy of.)

## Chronology, Biblical

Biblical chronology refers to the record by years of the history of Israel, but more particularly that record of the reigns of the Hebrew kings under the divided monarchy. This history is briefly divided into three periods; that of hostility (931 to 885 B.C.), that of alliance (885 to 841 B.C.), and that of independent development (841 to 721 B.C.). There is general historical agreement on these dates, but the accord between dates in the Jewish history and that of secular history is attained only after extensive research.

## Church

1. When *the* Church is spoken of, it means that visible religious society, founded by Jesus Christ, under one head, St. Peter, and continuing under the governance of his successors, the popes. In its founding, Christ promised protection of the Church until the end of time (Mt. 28:20) and commissioned the preservation and extension of His teachings in His name. It is thus the role of the Church to present the means of salvation given by Christ, i.e. the sacraments and sacrifice (cf. Marks of the Church).

2. The Church is the mystical body of Christ. Pope Pius XII describes it in his encyclical, "The Mystical Body of Christ," thus: "If we would define and describe this true Church of Jesus Christ—which is the one, holy, Catholic, apostolic, Roman Church—we shall find no expression more noble, more sublime or more divine than the phrase which calls it 'the mystical body of Jesus Christ'" (cf. Mystical Body of Christ).

3. In a limited sense, the word Church may mean a particular Church of a country, nation, or city, usually stated as such, for example, the American Church. This is not to be confused with "national Churches," which are those circumscribed by the country and governed by a separate jurisdiction, such as the Armenian Church.

4. In its most limited sense, a church is a building set apart and dedicated to the public worship of God, the celebration of Mass, the singing of the Holy Office, the administration of the sacraments, and for the use of all the faithful.

Vatican Council II addressed itself especially to the first two meanings of the Church. In two Constitutions, *Pastoral Constitution on the Church in the Modern World* (GS), and the *Dogmatic Constitution on the Church* (LG), the Council fathers made many distinctions that provide us with a greater insight into the Church as it is understood in our time.

*The Church by its nature is a saving force.* Its members are a covenanted people: "Rather, the man of any nation who fears God and acts uprightly is acceptable to him.'" (cf. Acts 10:35). It has pleased God, however, to make men holy and save them not merely as individuals without any mutual bonds, but by making them into a single people, a people who acknowledge Him in truth and serve Him in holiness. He therefore chose the race of Israel as a people unto Himself. With them He set up a covenant; step by step He taught this people by manifesting in their history both Himself and the decree of His will, and by making them holy unto Himself. All these things, however, were done by way of preparation as a figure of that new and perfect covenant that was to be ratified in Christ, and of that more luminous revelation that was to be given through God's very Word made flesh.

"The days are coming, says the Lord, when I will make a new covenant with the house of Israel and the house of Judah . . . I will place my law within them, and write it upon their hearts; I will be their God, and they shall be my people . . . All, from least to the greatest, shall know me, says the Lord" (Jer. 31:31, 33–34). Christ instituted this new covenant, that is to say, the new testament, in His blood (cf. 1 Cor. 11:25), by calling together a people made up of Jew and Gentile, making them one, not according to the flesh but in the Spirit.

"This was to be the new People of God, for, those who believe in Christ, who are reborn not from a perishable but from an imperishable seed through the Word of the Living God (cf. 1 Pt. 1:23), not from the flesh but from water and the Holy Spirit (cf. Jn. 3:5–6), are finally established as 'a chosen race, a royal priesthood, a holy nation, . . . . Once you were no people, but now you are God's people . . . (1 Pt. 2:9–10).

"That messianic people has for its head Christ, who was delivered up for our sins, and rose again for our justification (Rom. 4:25), and who now, having won a name which is above all names, reigns in glory in heaven. The heritage of this people is the dignity and freedom of the sons of God, in whose hearts the Holy Spirit dwells as in His temple. Its law is the new commandment to love as Christ loved us (cf. Jn. 13:34). Its goal is the kingdom of God, which has been begun by God Himself on earth, and which is to be further extended until it is brought to perfection by Him at the end of time. Then Christ our life (cf. Col. 3:4) will appear, and 'the world itself will be freed from its slavery to corruption and share the glorious freedom of the children of God' (Rom. 8:21).

"So it is that this messianic people, although it does not actually include all men, and may more than once look like a small flock, is nonetheless a lasting and sure seed of unity, hope and salvation for the whole human race. Established by Christ as a fellowship of life, charity and truth, it is also used by Him as an instrument for the redemption of all, and is sent forth into the whole world as the light of the world and the salt of the earth (cf. Mt. 5:13–16)" (LG).

*The Church is a mystery.* The Council meant by this term that the Church is a divine, transcendant, and salvific reality that is visibly present among men. Pope Paul VI in opening the second session of the Council (Sept. 29, 1963) declared: "The Church is a mystery, a mystic reality, steeped in the presence of God." Further: "It is of the essence of the Church that she is both human and divine, visible yet invisibly endowed, eager to act and yet devoted to contemplation, present in this world and yet not at home in it. She is all these things in such a way that in her the human is directed and subordinated to the divine, the visible likewise to the invisible, action to contemplation, and this present world to that city yet to come, which we seek" (SC 2). The Church is "a sign of God's presence in the world" (AG 15), "a sign which points out Christ to others" (AG 20), and "it is the function of the Church . . . to make God the Father and His Incarnate Son present and in a sense visible" (GS 21).

*The Church is a Sacrament.* "By her relationship with Christ, the Church is a kind of sacrament or sign of intimate union with God, and of the unity of all mankind" (LG 1). It is likewise a "sacrament of unity," as St. Cyprian wrote in his book, *Concerning the Unity of the Catholic Church.*

*The Church is a Communion.* The Church embracing the People of God continues to grow, for the Church is a Eucharistic people, "truly partaking of the body of the Lord in the breaking of the Eucharistic Bread, we are taken up into communion with Him and one another" (LG 7). Realizing that Eucharist means communion, fellowship, the very Church itself, we see this as a singular unity and the very fount of Christian life. The Church is thus built up into the Body of Christ for we learn, "The other sacraments, as well as every ministry of the Church and every work of the apostolate, are linked with the holy Eucharist and are directed toward it. For the most blessed Eucharist contains the Church's entire spiritual wealth, that is, Christ Himself, our Passover and living bread. Through his very flesh, made vital and vitalizing through the Holy Spirit, He offers life to men. They are thereby invited and led to offer themselves, their labors, and all created things together with Him. Hence the Eucharist shows itself to be the source and apex of the whole work of preaching the gospel. . . . The faithful . . . are through the reception of the Eucharist fully joined to the Body of Christ" (PO 5f).

*The Church is a Mission.* The Council's teaching on the mission of the Church states that the Church and its mission are so closely one as to be identical. The mission of the Church must be sought in the mission of Christ Himself. "Inspired by no earthly ambition, the Church seeks but a solitary goal: to carry forward the work of Christ Himself under the lead of the befriending Spirit" (GS 3). This role stems from "unity in communion," for as the Apostle John wrote: "What we have seen and heard we proclaim in turn to you so that you may share life with us. This fellowship of ours is with the Father and with his Son, Jesus Christ" (1 Jn. 1:3–4).

*The Church is a community.* "As the first-born of many brethren and through the gift of His spirit, He founded after His death and resurrection a new brotherly community composed of all those who receive Him in faith and in love. This He did through His Body, which is the Church. There everyone, as members one of the other, would render mutual service according to the different gifts bestowed on each.

"This solidarity must be constantly increased until that day on which it will be brought to perfection. Then, saved by grace, men will offer flawless glory to God as a family beloved of God and of Christ their Brother" (GS 32). (Cf. Ministries; Infallibility.)

## Church History

The record of the activity of the Church since its founding by Christ is usually presented in the concurrent setting of secular events that are the accounts of mankind's course since Christianity became the major influence on that course. The history of the Church is a recounting of the events that mark the progress of an imperishable society. This society has unusual features, namely, a divine Founder, supernatural powers, the promise of enduring, the inspired word of Scripture, and infallibility in doctrinal matters of faith and morals. Together with these there is the completeness of revelation, to which nothing is or can be added, but which from the apostolic deposit of faith may be presented in its development and unfolding. Moreover, the Church's history spans more than 1900 years and reaches into every nation and race and is included in every known language of those years. Because of the complex nature of this history, there are many approaches made to encompass the record. This may be accomplished by making an arbitrary division of the time into centuries or periods. This latter system is usually followed thus: (1) First period: from apostolic times to the time of Charlemagne, crowned emperor in A.D. 800; (2) second period: from Charlemagne through the Middle Ages to the rise of the Protestant religion; (3) third period: from the sixteenth century to the present day. Strictly speaking, since the Church is universal, its history cannot be considered nation by nation, except in special studies. The study of Church history is unique in that there is a necessary distinction to be made between the divine and human factors.

### Church Militant, Suffering, Triumphant

This division of the Church into three distinct groups has a pedagogical value rather than an estimated numerical division. The Church Militant is made up of living members of the Body of Christ (cf. Apostolate) who are actively working out their salvation within faith, love, and hope—virtues given by the sacraments and the teachings of the Church. The Church Suffering is that group who have died in grace and whose souls are being purged in purgatory. No numerical estimate of course is intended by this classification. The Church Triumphant consists of known souls in heaven, the Blessed Virgin Mary, the saints, and all who are united with Christ and enjoy the beatific vision. Again no specific numerical amount can be given other than the listings of canonized saints and the martyrologies. This division is primarily a tripartite expression of the totality of souls making up the Church under the salvific mission that is hers from Christ Himself.

### Church Property

Church property is legally the movable and immovable possessions of the Church, which she has by right. The Church as a society has the right of purchasing and possessing property, personal or real, in order to carry on the work she is commissioned to do. Just as the state may tax its citizens, so the Church has the right to assess its members for the means of functioning. Each

diocese is structured by civil law either as a multicorporation, i.e., each parish and institution is a separate corporate entity, or as a corporation-sole, i.e., all properties are the corporate assets of the one diocese and are so governed in their functions.

### Church and State

Although the relationship between Church and State is customarily presented as a problem, it need not be if proper understanding of the two entities is pursued. Both the Church and the State are complete societies in themselves, each with a purpose and so endowed with rights and powers to attain that purpose. However, each, while operating in its own sphere, must also overlap the activity of the other since both exercise authority over the same individuals as subjects. Stated as principles we see: the Church is supreme in spiritual affairs, the State in temporal and material affairs. Each is separate and distinct judicially and legislatively, but the State must foster and preserve in a positive manner the purposes of the Church, since the spiritual sphere is greater than the temporal, and the Church must teach the recognition and acceptance of the authority of the State and the practices that further the qualities of good citizenship. The Church likewise has a right to the temporal things that are necessary for her to carry out her mission, such as church property and schools. Lastly the Church's rights must have precedence over those of the State in affairs where the two spheres of activity are in conflict.

The bishops of the United States have stated: "Authoritative Catholic teaching on the relations between Church and state, as set forth in papal encyclicals and in the treatises of recognized writers in ecclesiastical law, not only states clearly what these relations should normally be under ideal conditions, but also indicates to what extent the Catholic Church can adapt herself to the particular conditions that may obtain in different countries. Examining, in the full perspective of that teaching, the position which those who founded our nation and framed its basic law took on the problem of Church-state relations in our own country, we find that the First Amendment to our Constitution solved the problem in a way that was typically American in its practical recognition of existing conditions and its evident desire to be fair to all citizens of whatever religious faith. To one who knows something of history and law, the meaning of the First Amendment is clear enough from its own words: 'Congress shall make no laws respecting an establishment of religion or forbidding the free exercise thereof.' The meaning is even clearer in the records of the congress that enacted it" (Letter of Nov. 21, 1948).

### Church Unity Octave
See Chair of Unity Octave.

### Church Year
See Calendar, Church.

### Churches Orthodox
See Eastern Churches.

### Churching of Women
Churching of women refers to the blessing given to a woman after childbirth. It is not mandatory that women receive this blessing or make the act of thanksgiving accompanying this, since there is no taint attached to childbearing; it is simply recommended. The blessing is not given when the child is illegitimate. The thanksgiving rite is reminiscent of the OT ceremony found recorded in Lv. 12:2–8. There is also a blessing given to expectant mothers, which is a prelude to the future reception of the child into the Church at baptism.

### Churchyard
The property or land surrounding a church building is called the churchyard. It may or may not be enclosed, but it often specifically refers to a cemetery when this adjoins church property. The term is almost obsolete today except where a rural church has distinct confines, and the total has an exemption from taxes under the law.

### Ciborium
1. A ciborium is the metal vessel similar to a chalice but having a cover in which small hosts or particles of the Blessed Sacrament are reserved in the tabernacle for distribution in Holy Commu-

nion to the faithful. When containing the Blessed Sacrament, it is covered with a silk veil. Under the new rulings of the Church "vessels which are intended to hold hosts, such as a paten, ciborium, pyx, monstrance, etc., may be made of other materials which are locally considered valuable and appropriate for sacred use, such as ebony or hardwoods."

2. A ciborium is also a baldaquin. (Cf. Civory.)

### Cilicium
Literally cloth of hair, a cilicium is a penitential garment, a hairshirt, sometimes worn next to the skin, as an act of penance or abnegation.

### Cincture or Girdle
A cord 12 to 14 feet in length, with tassels at each end, is used to bind the alb at the waist when the priest is vesting for Mass. The cincture is usually white but, properly, should be the same color as the vestments. It may be of any material, but that of prelates is of silk.

### Circumcelliones
A wandering group of fanatic Donatist heretics of the early fourth century were known as circumcelliones. (Cf. Donatism.)

### Circumcision, Feast of
This was the title of a feast that has been supplanted in the New Church Calendar by the "Solemnity of Mary, Mother of God," celebrated on Jan. 1. The readings pay tribute to the maternity of the Blessed Mother and also the submission of Christ to the surgical rite of the removal of the prepuce or foreskin from the penis as prescribed in OT law (cf. Lk. 2:21–24). The Solemnity of Mary, Mother of God is a holy day of obligation in the United States.

### Circumincession
Circumincession refers to the indwelling of the three distinct Persons of the Blessed Trinity, the Father being whole and entire in the Son and in the Holy Spirit, and each one in the other as well as in the Father. (Cf. Trinity, the Most Holy.)

### Citation
In canon law (cc. 1711 to 1725), a citation is the summons of a defendant to an ecclesiastical court.

### City of God
The book *De Civitate Dei* was written by St. Augustine between A.D. 412 and 427. An apologetic work defending the Church against

paganism, it portrays a "city" or group of men ruled by the love of God, free of self-love and self-interests and, perhaps more important, it presents a philosophy of history for universal man.

### Civil Allegiance

This is the Christian's duty to the State to which he is bound by loyalty and, as a citizen, by obedience to its laws. It is the acceptance of the civic obligations, as secondary and necessary since they follow the higher obligation to God, in recognition of the fact that the state has its authority from God. (Cf. Church and State.)

### Civil Law

Broadly, civil law includes the body of laws and governing legislation of the State, as distinct from the canon law of the Church. An example of this is the divorce laws of the several states, which the Church considers unjust because the State has no authority over the sacramental bond of matrimony.

### Civil Marriage

Civil marriage refers to the pronouncement of the marriage vows and the execution of the contract by which a man and woman are declared to be husband and wife by a representative of the State, such as a justice of the peace, a judge, or other official. The State does not have the juridical right in the case of baptized persons, nor has it the power to dissolve the bond of any marriage. The Church alone is competent in all matters pertaining to the bond of baptized persons (c. 1960). A Catholic who goes through a ceremony of marriage before a minister or official of the state contracts no marriage. Further, a Catholic marrying before a Protestant minister must seek a dispensation from form under conditions established in each diocese. Non-Catholics are exempt from this law, and their marriages before ministers and state officials are valid unless otherwise null. Questions concerning the civil effects of matrimony, such as registration and legal residence, are the province of the State, and the marriages of Catholics must be registered with the civil authorities. In countries where civil marriage is demanded by the state, Catholics are allowed to fulfill this requirement but with the understanding that no act of marriage is intended. (Cf. Marriage, Sacrament of.)

### Civory, also Ciborium

A civory is a solid structure of stone, metal, or wood, erected over the altar and its *predella* or footpace, and supported by columns or posts, usually at the corners. (Cf. Baldachino.) In the new architecture of church buildings such structures are no longer recommended since they interfere with the liturgical actions taking place in the sacred area about the altar. Historically such a structure was considered as a protection over the altar and as a device that set the altar apart from the other areas of the sanctuary.

### Clandestinity

An impediment to marriage, clandestinity is illegal secrecy or an agreement affecting the form of marriage. Thus for a marriage to be valid, it must be contracted before the pastor of the parish, or the ordinary of the diocese (or before a priest delegated by either) and at least two witnesses (c. 1094). Clandestine marriages may be made valid by a remarriage under the proper form.

### Clapper, also Clepper or Crotalum

A clapper is a wooden device, with a handle and swinging hammer, which strikes two surfaces, making a clapping noise. It is used in place of bells in ceremonies from Holy Thursday till the Gloria of the Mass on Holy Saturday, chiefly in processions.

### Clausura

See Enclosure.

### Clementine Instruction

This is the title of the regulations governing Forty Hours' devotion, so called because they were first set down by Clement XII in 1731. The regulations were revised by Pope St. Pius X in 1914.

### Clergy

This collective term refers to male persons who administer the rites of the Church through holy orders and jurisdiction. It includes all bishops and priests, and more broadly the deacons and permanent deacons. Formerly, all who had received tonsure were considered members of the clergy.

The *diocesan* or *secular clergy* are those who exercise their apostolate in parishes of a diocese and serve in other appointed capacities under the direction of their bishop, to whom they are bound by a promise of obedience unless this is transferred to another bishop by the process of excardination.

The *religious clergy,* those called *Regular clergy,* are those members of religious orders, congregations, or societies. They serve their apostolate in accord with their rule of life. When they are assigned to pastoral duties, they are under the direction of the bishop of the diocese in which they serve.

The primary function of all ordained ministers of the Church is to "join the faithful together in one body," as the documents of Vatican II declare. Presbyters by their ordination "are consecrated to preach the gospel, shepherd the faithful, and celebrate divine worship as true priests of the New Testament" (LG. 21).

## Clergy, Byzantine

In the Byzantine Rite there are both married and celibate members of the clergy. Men already married may be accepted for ordination and are permitted to continue in the married state, except in the United States where such candidates have not been accepted since 1929. Those deacons and priests who are celibate cannot marry after ordination, and all bishops must be unmarried. One who is a married priest may not remarry following the death of his wife.

## Cleric

1. A member of the diocesan clergy.
2. Anyone who has received tonsure.
3. Anyone who may incur clerical penalties, bishops excepted.

This title is also given to members of the Regular clergy or to some Brothers. In a religious community clerics are bound to pray the Breviary each day. In England and some other countries a cleric is called "clerk."

## Clerical Privilege

Besides having certain obligations arising from their state, the clergy have privileges that are set forth in canons 118 to 123. More specifically this means that (1) clerics are not under the jurisdiction of the lay courts and are not to be tried before a lay judge, but before an ecclesiastical court, unless by specific exception set forth in the law; (2) clerics have freedom from military service or the bearing of arms and freedom from the imposition of secular occupations or duties.

## Clericalism

Clericalism refers to the claim on the part of the clergy, or the charge by others, that priests or bishops exercise jurisdiction pertinent to the State. It is usually a derogatory term for any attempt to apply religious principles to questions of society, morals, economics, or political life. Historically, certain movements begun by churchmen were branded as clericalism in order to defeat their good purposes. The opposite claim is anticlericalism, which is a certain hostility and opposition to the actions of the clergy. This may arise out of real or imagined faults of the clergy as individuals or because the nonordained ministers, the laity, want to usurp the role and service areas proper to the clergy. (See Ministries.)

## Clerks Regular

This is a term for those groups of men in religious life who live under community rule but are engaged primarily in the activities of the diocesan clergy, such as the care of parishes or teaching, rather than the monastic life. Jesuits and Redemptorists are examples.

## Clinical Baptism

A term no longer used, clinical baptism in early times referred to baptism given to one who was ill.

## Cloister, also Close

1. A covered passageway around the quadrangle (or garth), usually open on the quadrangle side, with the opposite side formed by the walls of the buildings of a monastery.
2. A term signifying the restrictions from egress of members of a monastic order of religious and the prohibition of outsiders from entry.
3. The enclosure itself.
4. This term sometimes referred to the life led by members of an encloistered convent or monastery.

## Clothing

This name is given to the formal admission of a candidate to a religious order at which he or she is solemnly clothed in the habit of the order.

## Coadjutor

1. A coadjutor is one who assists another; in church use it refers to the one appointed to assist a bishop or a priest.

2. A coadjutor bishop is one appointed by the Holy See as an assistant to a bishop governing a diocese. As such he may be given either to the person of the bishop governing or to the diocese. If he is given to the bishop, he may have or not have the right of succession to the diocese upon the death of the governing bishop. If he is given to the diocese, he continues in office after the death of the incumbent bishop until the diocese is again filled. A coadjutor given to a bishop who is incapacitated usually has the rights and duties of a residential bishop. (Cf. Auxiliary Bishop.)

## Coat-of-Arms

In Church heraldry an arms insignia may be that of religious corporations, schools, or religious rank or dignity, sometimes the emblems or devices of saints, and the orders of knighthood. Most frequently seen are the coats-of-arms of dioceses or bishops. Those used by bishops are marked by the use of the miter, the crosier, and the ecclesiastical hat. The hat is low-crowned, flat, wide-brimmed and has cords and tassels hanging from either side. For example, a cardinal's coat-of-arms is shown surmounted by a scarlet hat with fifteen tassels on each side. The hats of a patriarch, an archbishop, or a bishop are green as depicted above the coat-of-arms; the patriarch's has fifteen tassels with gold interwoven in the cord and tassels; an archbishop's has ten tassels, and a bishop's six. The hat above a priest's coat-of-arms is black and has two tassels. The papal coat-of-arms consists of the tiara above the crossed keys of St. Peter, one key gold, the other silver.

## Coat, the Holy

See Holy Coat; also, Shroud, Holy.

## Co-Consecrators

Co-consecrators are the two bishops who assist the presiding bishop at the consecration of a newly appointed bishop.

## Code of Canon Law

Code of Canon Law refers to the compilation and codification of the law of the Church. (See Canon Law.)

## Codex

In biblical use, a codex is a manuscript of the Sacred Scriptures. In the absence of original manuscripts and the first copies of the NT, the text is dependent upon manuscript codices of a later date. Codices are grouped according to their contents as either pure or mixed. Pure codices provide only original Greek texts, whereas the mixed give, in addition to the original text, commentaries or versions in Latin, Greek, or Syriac. Some codices are named according to their past or present place of storage or their former owners. The oldest and most important codices are: *Vaticanus,* of the fourth century, probably of Egyptian origin, containing the entire Bible from Gn. 46:28 to Heb. 9:14; *Sinaiticus,* probably of the fourth century, discovered in the monastery of Mt. Sinai and now in the British Museum; *Alexandrinus,* fifth century; *Codex Ephraemi Rescriptus,* fifth century, now in the Paris National Library; *Codex Bezae,* sixth century, in the possession of Cambridge University; *Claromantanus,* sixth century, now in the Paris National Library. (See Bible; Canon of the Scripture.)

Codex is also used as a collective title of rules or laws, for example, *Codex Iuris Canonici,* the code of canon law.

## Coenobite

An early term, equivalent to monk, coenobite was used by St. Jerome to distinguish one of a religious life from an anchorite or hermit. Later listed by St. Benedict as one type of monk who lives in a community under an abbot.

## Coenobium

The Latin name for a monastery or convent refers to the place where monks or coenobites live in community life. Sometimes it means the church building of a monastery as distinct from the other buildings.

## Collateral

Collateral is the term for the blood relationship in the indirect line, as brother or sister, uncle or aunt, nephew or niece, first or second cousins. Such relationship is an impediment to marriage, rendering it invalid to the third degree inclusive (c. 1076) Collateral may also be called cognate line.

## Collation

1. The name collation is applied to the light meal taken on a day of fast, other than breakfast and the main meal. The amount of food is not specified but must be less than a full meal. The name derives from the *collationes*, the spiritual reading from the Fathers, which was customarily read aloud in monasteries at meal time.

2. Collation is also the act of appointment of a new incumbent to an ecclesiastical benefice.

## Collect

The *Collect* of the Mass consists of a short prayer, said just before the Epistle is read; both are now referred to as Opening Prayer spoken by the celebrant of a Eucharistic celebration. The name is derived from "assembly" and was the prayer said in the early Church while the people gathered for the celebration of the Eucharist. Today this is a prayer of petition said on behalf of the community gathered for the liturgy. (See Liturgy.)

## Collection, Offertory

The offeratory collection is the custom of accepting voluntary contributions from the faithful. The practice now is to accept money donations, frequently in envelopes of the parish, which are used for various church expenses. Formerly, such collections were of food or coin and were to support the priest. Custom keeps this collection, but today there is frequently the giving of food, which is intended for the poor and brought to the altar by parish members along with the bread and wine for the celebration of the Eucharist. The envelope offering may be a separate gathering of gifts, made upon entering the church, and later brought to the altar. The convenience of such envelopes, like those offered by Postal Church Service, is the ready handling and computing of the monetary collections.

The Scriptural basis for collections for the Church and the poor are evident in many passages of the Bible, e.g., Acts 11:29–30; Gal. 2:10; Rom. 15:15–31; 1 Cor. 16:1–4; 2 Cor. 8:15.

## Collectivism

This social theory maintains the goods and services that are the work of mankind are better distributed and exploited through a central authority having all political and economic power. As a theory this is diametrically opposed to the free enterprise system and private ownership, which are the democratic practices in a free society. This theory of collectivism is the basic formula behind communism, socialism, and fascism; the differences between the three governmental formulations involve only the exercise of the authoritarian control.

Pope John XXIII, writing in his encyclical *Mater et Magister*, notes the trend of nations toward collectivism and warns against the depersonalization of the individual in this system: "One of the principal characteristics of our time is the multiplication of social relationships, that is, a daily more complex interdependence of citizens, introducing into their lives and activities many and varied forms of association, recognized for the most part in private and even in public law. This tendency seemingly stems from a number of factors operative in the present era, among which are technical and scientific progress, greater productive efficiency, and a higher standard of living among citizens. . . .

"But as these various forms of association are multiplied and daily extended, it also happens that in many areas of activity, rules and laws controlling and determining relationships of citizens are multiplied. As a consequence, opportunity for free action by individuals is restricted within narrower limits. Methods are often used, procedures are adopted, and such an atmosphere develops wherein it becomes difficult for one to make decisions independently of outside influences, to do anything on his own initiative, to carry out in a fitting way his rights and duties, and to fully develop and perfect his personality."

Thus, the danger of collectivism is a denial of fundamental rights and the free exercise of one's mind in making the judgments that are necessary for the free pursuit of his salvation in accord with free will. (See Communism.)

## College

1. A college is an association, corporation, or organized society or group of persons with a common purpose, forming a moral body. Such are the College of Cardinals and the colleges of collegiate churches. Every Church college must be canonically erected.

2. A *pontifical college* is a seminary, directly subject to the Holy See, for the training of priests and missionaries.

3. *Apostolic college* designates the group of the Apostles under St. Peter as their head (Lk. 22).

4. *A national college* is a seminary established at

Rome for the education of priests of a particular country, e.g., North American College for the United States.

5. An institution of higher learning, a college is distinguished from a university.

## College of Cardinals

The collective body of all cardinals is chosen by the pope; cardinals individually serve as advisers and assistants in the administration of the Church. The first college as we know it today was organized in the twelfth century. The number of cardinals varies, and the distinction as "Prince of the Church" is not a degree of holy orders but an honor conferred by the pope. The college members serve in the curial offices and as the heads of papal commissions; they have privileges of distinction in their own national conferences. Since Jan. 1, 1971, cardinals are to retire at 80 years of age and cease to be heads of curial departments, but they retain their membership in the college and the related rights and privileges of their rank.

There are three categories of cardinals in the college: *Cardinal bishops,* the six titular bishops of the suburban sees of Rome, Italy, together with the two Eastern Patriarchs; *Cardinal priests,* or bishops with dioceses outside Rome; and *Cardinal deacons* who are titular bishops serving in the Roman Curia. (See Curia, Roman.)

## Collegiality

A term arising out of Vatican II and its deliberations, collegiality is no more than a recognition of the fact that the episcopate is a single organism instituted by Christ and operating through the members of the bishops as an aiding body in the saving of souls, working together with the successor of Peter, the Pope.

As one of the Council Fathers, Archbishop Emile Guerry of Cambrai remarked in 1963 in a pastoral letter: "What does episcopal collegiality mean? It means directly the common responsibility which the whole episcopal body, under the pope, has for the evangelization of the world and the establishment of the Church throughout the whole world. This collegiality therefore involves for each bishop, in addition to his role as special shepherd of his particular Church in the diocese which the pope entrusts to him and in which he exercises jurisdiction, a universal responsibility for the apostolic mission of the Church, in union with the episcopal body, under the direction of the pope as head. This shared responsibility even takes priority for each bishop; it is dominant and ought to inspire him in his special mission as head of a diocese. As

soon as he becomes a bishop, he becomes a member of the episcopal body and thereby shares in the body's all-embracing responsibility."

In the *Dogmatic Constitution on the Church* Vatican II declared: "Just as, by the Lord's will, St. Peter and the other apostles constituted one apostolic college, so in a similar way the Roman Pontiff as the successor of Peter, and the bishops as the successors of the apostles are joined together. The collegial nature and meaning of the episcopal order found expression in the very ancient practice by which bishops appointed the world over were linked with one another and with the Bishop of Rome by the bonds of unity, charity, and peace; also, in the conciliar assemblies which made common judgments about more profound matters in decisions reflecting the views of many. The ecumenical councils held through the centuries clearly attest this collegial aspect" (LG 22). (See Subsidiarity.)

## Collegiate Church

A collegiate church is one served by a group of secular priests, called a chapter. The members of the chapter are called canons. (Cf. Chapter, Cathedral.)

## Collegium Cultorum Martyrum

Collegium Cultorum Martyrum is the Latin title of the "Association for Venerating for Martyrs in the Catacombs." It was founded in 1897 by the Commission of Sacred Archaeology to further devotion to the martyrs, to aid in excavation work, and to extend learning of the early Church.

## Colors, Liturgical

The use of color in the Church as an aspect of its symbolism in the liturgy is of early origin, although in the days of the Roman Empire white was most commonly used. Color as such became a mark of distinction in dress, and in the Middle Ages there was added the sequence of colors in vestments to be used for various feasts. The modern sequence of colors are five: white, red, green, violet and rose. Any shade of these colors is permitted, while cloth of gold may be used in place of white, red, or green on major feast days. Cloth of silver may replace white. Rose vestments may be worn on the fourth Sunday of Lent and the third Sunday of Advent.

The colors and their use are: *green* for the Pentecostal season of the liturgical year; *purple* for Advent and Lent (it may also be used for Masses for the dead or funeral Masses, but white is used in the Resurrection Masses of funerals by choice); *red* for

Passion Sunday, Wednesday of Holy Week, Good Friday, Pentecost, feasts of the Passion of our Lord, feasts of the Apostles, Evangelists, and martyrs. *Rose* is used by privilege on the third Sunday of Advent (*Gaudete* Sunday) and the fourth Sunday of Lent (*Laetare* Sunday); white is for the Christmas Season, Easter season, feasts commemorating Our Lord (except those noted previously), the feasts and solemnities of the Blessed Virgin Mary, angels, saints other than martyrs, All Saints Day, the feasts of St. John the Baptist, St. John the Evangelist, Chair of St. Peter, Conversion of St. Paul. (*Black* is a permitted color for funeral services but is rapidly being abandoned.) (See Vestments.)

### Colossians, Epistle to the

One of the "captivity epistles" written by St. Paul, this letter was intended for the people of the Lycus valley to correct certain errors in their teaching; it is thus a polemical treatise. The epistle lays great emphasis on the divinity and manhood of Christ, stating that Christ is supreme over all creation. He rules the world because of this fact of creation; He is the Redeemer of the world; and He is the Head of the Church, His mystical body.

It contains two special doctrinal references: that against false teachers who distort the true Christian teaching; and one on the conclusions to be drawn by the faithful from their mystical union with Christ through the Church (See Church.)

### Columbus, Knights of

See Knights of Columbus.

### Comes

Comes is the name of the compiled book containing the lessons of the Breviary, the Epistles, and Gospels. (See Lectionary.)

### Commandments of the Church

Usually called precepts, the commandments of the Church might be taken to include all the legislation of the Church as a teaching and governing body. However, the term more generally applies to the six precepts of a moral and ecclesiastic nature, which are directed to the observance of religion in practice. In the United States the following precepts were presented by the Third Plenary Council of Baltimore:

1. Keep the Sundays and holy days of obligation by assisting at Mass and desisting from servile work.

2. Fast and abstain on the days appointed by the Church.

3. Go to confession at least once a year if serious sin is involved.

4. Receive the Blessed Sacrament during the season of Easter.

5. Contribute to the support of the Church and its pastors.

6. Do not marry within certain degrees of kindred nor solemnize marriage during a forbidden time.

The bishops of the United States stress also as duties worthy of all Catholic Christians that they "join in the missionary spirit and apostolate of the Church."

### Commandments of God, also Decalogue, or Ten Commandments

The moral commands or laws were given by God to Moses (Ex. 20:1-21) on Mount Sinai. It is certain that the Decalogue was made up of ten distinct commandments (Dt. 5:2-33), no matter how they may be grouped. These commands are interpreted by Christ in the NT (Mt. 5:17-48). The first three are concerned with the love and true worship of God, and the other seven are directed to the love and justice due our neighbor. The wording varies in either the original or translation, but the substance of the law remains. The order traditional in the Church is that found in the New American Bible translation:

1. I, the Lord, am your God. You shall not have other gods besides me.

2. You shall not take the name of the Lord, your God, in vain.

3. Remember to keep holy the Sabbath day.

4. Honor your father and mother.

5. You shall not kill.

6. You shall not commit adultery.

7. You shall not steal.

8. You shall not bear false witness against your neighbor.

9. You shall not covet your neighbor's wife.

10. You shall not covet anything that belongs to your neighbor. (See Basic Teachings for Catholic Religious Education.)

### Commemoration of Feasts

In the celebration of feast days in the Church, some feasts are movable (i.e., vary in date because of the time of Easter changing), and thus two feasts may fall on the same day. In these occurrences, the Church directs: "If several celebrations fall on the same day, the one that holds the higher rank (according to the Sacramentary listing) is observed." (See Calendar, Church.)

## Commemoration of the Living and the Dead in the Mass

At the Prayer of the Mass, formerly the *Memento, Domine,* the priest silently commends to God benefactors, friends, and others, who are living. At the Canon the priest mentions by name the one or many who are dead for whom he is to pray. Such commemorations may be made by any of those attending Mass at the reading of these prayers and may include anyone of their choice for whom they wish to pray.

## Commenda

Formerly commenda referred to the custody of a church or institution exercised by one not the regular incumbent.

## Commendation of the Soul

Commendation of the Soul is the prayer for the dying said by a priest or other, as contained in the Roman Ritual. It includes the last blessing, the plenary indulgence, a short form of the Litany of the Saints, three prayers of farewell asking the forgiveness of sins and commending the soul of the dying person to God and the saints, a prayer in the form of a litany beseeching deliverance, followed by three more prayers of forgiveness and commendation. It is often called "final commendation" or simply "commendation." The prayers may vary according to custom or by request.

## Commentaries, Biblical

Commentaries are explanatory writings on the books of the Bible. Strictly speaking these are not works of biblical criticism but are for the study and understanding of the texts of Scripture. They are grouped as: Jewish, patristic, medieval, and modern. (See Bible.)

## Commentator

This title is given to the lay assistant at a Eucharistic celebration, or a sacramental or paraliturgical service, who reads the scriptures, or serves as a leader of prayer or devotion, or comments upon or describes the liturgical service taking place. It usually refers to the person, man or woman, who reads or "proclaims" the first and/or second readings in the Liturgy of the Word. The role of the commentator may be distinct from that of the Lector or Reader. Sometimes the title of "Proclaimer" is used interchangeably, but less euphoniously. (See Lector; Ministries.)

## Commissary

1. *Apostolic commissary* is one delegated by the pope to take evidence and pronounce judgment in an important case, or to serve as an administrator.

2. *Provincial Commissary* is the superior of a province of Friars Minor and Conventuals where there are insufficient members to form a real province, and hence it is dependent on another established province.

3. *Simple Commissary* is any ecclesiastic with delegated jurisdiction from a bishop.

4. *Commissary of the Holy Land* is the Friar Minor who receives and collects alms for the upkeep of the Holy Places of Palestine. It may also refer to the place where this friar resides.

## Commissions, Ecclesiastical

1. An ecclesiastical commission is a group of persons, lay or cleric, legally appointed to perform some duty or special work.

2. *Pontifical commissions* are those set up to aid the Holy Father. Principally, these commissions are for study of the Scriptures, for interpretation of the Code of Canon Law, for the revision of the Vulgate, for sacred archaeology, for the protection of historical and artistic monuments, and for the heraldry of the papal court.

Pope Paul VI in meeting the needs of the present time has established several special commissions. These are: *Commission on Justice and Peace* instituted Jan. 6, 1967, to promote international social justice, to aid underdeveloped nations, and to seek ways of encouraging peace among all peoples; *Theological Commission,* instituted Apr. 11, 1969, as an advisory group of specialists to aid the Congregation for the Doctrine of the Faith; *Commission on the Role of Women,* an ad hoc commission established in 1973, to study the roles of women in society and the Church.

## Commixture, Liturgical

In the celebration of Mass the priest breaks the host in two halves, and from one half breaks a smaller fragment. After making the Sign of the Cross three times over the chalice with this particle, he drops it into the chalice. This is a symbol of Christ's union with the Church, His mystical body.

## Common

1. *Common life* is the community or group living of members of a religious order.

2. *Common teaching* of theologians is a doctrine that all theologians hold is true, is taught as true doctrine; and is binding in the doctrine of the faith.

3. *Common of the Mass* is the collective name for the ceremonies and prayers of the Mass that remain the same, the ordinary.

4. *Common of the Saints* is the division of prayers into groups, e.g., Apostles, martyrs, which are found in the Missal and Breviary and said where no Proper is assigned to these saints.

## Communicatio Idiomatum

This term refers to the "interchange of properties," whereby the divine attributes of Christ as God may be affirmed of Christ as Man and *vice-versa.* The reason for this is that, for example, in speaking of the God-Man, or God the Son incarnate, we imply not only the human nature of Christ but also the divine Person united with it. Care must be exercised that no detraction or distortion is wrought in this interchange. Thus it is wrong to say, "Divinity suffered," but correct to say, "God suffered."

## Communications Foundation, Catholic

Abbreviated, the CCF, this organization was founded in 1968 in New York by the Catholic Fraternal Benefit Societies to give support and assistance to all phases of the development of the broadcasting, radio, and television apostolate of the Church. Its headquarters are: Suite 1224, 500 Fifth Ave., New York, N.Y., 10036.

## Communion

1. *Holy Communion* is the body, blood, soul, and divinity of Christ, which is received whole and entire under the form of bread alone and/or wine and consumed by the recipient. All persons who are baptized, have the right intention, are free of mortal sin (in the state of sanctifying grace), and observe the proper fast from food may receive the sacrament of the Eucharist. Exceptions are infants and children who have not reached the age of reason, those who are notorious public sinners, those who have been legally separated from the Church by censure, and those who because of mental or bodily illness cannot receive with reverence. The rules for the Eucharistic fast are: (a) Water may be taken up to any time before receiving Communion, but it must be plain, with no other food element added. (b) The sick, with the permission of a confessor, even though not confined to bed may take liquids and medicine, in addition to water, before receiving Holy Communion. (c) Persons who are not sick may take liquid and solid nourishment up to one hour before receiving. (Cf. Fast, Eucharistic.)

2. Manner of receiving Holy Communion in the Roman rite is under the species of bread; the priest places a Eucharistic host (or particle) on the tongue of the one receiving. In the Byzantine rite, the consecrated bread is given by spoon after the bread has been dipped into the consecrated wine (known as intinction). Those of the Ethiopian rite receive under both species. These methods are now extended to the Roman Rite within the rules of the diocese.

3. *Spiritual Communion* is the desire to receive Communion when one is not able to do so, and the expression of this desire by acts of love and thanksgiving when one is not able to receive in actuality.

4. *Communion in the Mass* is the title of the antiphon that varies with the feast, which is read directly after the Communion of the Mass. (See Eucharist, Celebration of.)

## Communion of the Mass

After saying a preparatory prayer, the priest (or other designated ministers) gives communion to himself and then to all the other recipients of the congregation at a "communion station." This consumption of the sacred species is the conclusion of the Eucharistic banquet. When the Eucharist is given to the people, the priest or minister says, "Body of Christ" (or if the Eucharist is administered under both species, "The Body and Blood of Christ"), and the recipient replies, "Amen." During this time of distribution to the faithful, a communion song is sung by the choir, congregation, or cantor. After the Eucharist is distributed, there is a period of silent meditation or thanksgiving. This is followed by the Prayer after Communion, called the Communion prayer, which is a presidential prayer spoken by the celebrant.

Vatican II declared: "Truly partaking of the body of the Lord in the breaking of the Eucharistic bread, we are taken up into communion with Him and with one another. 'Because the loaf of bread is one, we many though we are, are one body, for we all partake of the one loaf.' (1 Cor. 10:17)" (LG 7). (See Eucharist, Celebration of.)

## Communion of Saints

The ninth article of the Apostles' Creed declares the spiritual union that exists between the saints in heaven, the souls in purgatory, and the faithful living on earth. This union is one of grace and good works, and in recognition of this the faithful imitate, venerate, and pray for the intercession of the saints in heaven and for the souls in purgatory. (See Church Militant, Suffering, Triumphant.)

## Communion Station

This name is given to the designated place or the fixed stand where Holy Communion is given to the faithful. In the new architecture of the church building, the communion station replaces the communion railing that formerly was between the sanctuary and the nave of the church. The station is merely a convenient term, for the recipient stands before the one who ministers the Eucharist. (See Eucharist, Celebration of.)

## Communism

This extreme form of socialism is based on the theory of state absolutism as propounded by Karl Marx (1818 to 1883). Communism seeks to set up a worldwide collectivism under the dictatorship of the proletariat. It is a doctrine of totalitarianism whereby the state becomes the supreme authority, answering to no other. As a system its aims are world control and the elimination of private property and rights, production for profit, the rights of the individual, and belief in God. As a political and economic system, the Communist party repudiates Christianity and belief in God and advocates a policy of violence—even toward its own members and allies.

In 1935 at the Seventh Congress of the Third International, there was begun a new program aimed at world domination: (1) party affiliates in other countries were freed from the strict practices of the Russian party except in adherence and recognition of the Russian leadership; (2) local groups were to oppose fascism even by the means of joining other Socialist, Laborite, or even Christian parties. This was a method of strategy and propaganda. The Church has been opposed to communism because of its atheistic materialism, promotion of class war, and denial of human rights. Pope Pius XI in his encyclical *Divini Redemptoris,* published in March, 1937, condemned communism and instructed Catholics of the world not to cooperate with communists in either social or political activities. In 1949 the Church issued a decree by which the sacraments are denied to nominal communists or their supporters, and this applies even to those who, *without authorization,* read communist literature or who freely and knowingly perform actions aiding the communists. A further more dire penalty of excommunication may be applied "by the very fact" to Catholics "who profess, defend and spread the materialistic and anti-Christian doctrine of the communists." Today not only the Church but all peoples of freedom-loving nations oppose communism.

## Community

This term as used in the modern Church does not mean, as is commonly understood, those persons living in one locality. Rather this means those people with a common interest and bond of faith and love through which they individually and collectively strive for salvation. There are several distinct divisions of this in active application within the Church.

1. *Community of the Faithful.* Pope Paul VI formulated the principle of community as follows: "God does not save us apart from this purpose for the collectivity, but within a plan in which each individual is part of a community which God chooses and helps" *(Osservatore Romano,* Feb. 10, 1966). And Vatican II expressed this by stating: "God did not create man for life in isolation, but, for the formation of social unity. So also 'it has pleased God to make men holy and save them not merely as individuals, without any mutual bonds, but by making them into a single people, a people which acknowledges Him in truth and serves Him in holiness' (LG 9). So from the beginning of salvation history He has chosen men not just as individuals but as members of a certain community. Revealing His mind to them, God called these chosen ones 'His people' (Ex. 3:7–12), and, furthermore, made a covenant with them on Sinai.

"This communitarian character is developed and consummated in the work of Jesus Christ. For the very Word made flesh willed to share in the human fellowship. He was present at the wedding of Cana, visited the house of Zacchaeus, ate with publicans and sinners. He revealed the love of the Father and the sublime vocation of man in terms of the most common of social realities and by making use of the speech and the imagery of plain everyday life, He sanctified those human ties, especially family ones, from which social relationships arise. He chose to lead the life proper to an artisan of His time and place.

"In His preaching He clearly taught the sons of God to treat one another as brothers. In His prayers He pleaded that all His disciples might be 'one.' Indeed, as the Redeemer of all, He offered Himself for all even to the point of death. . . . He commanded His apostles to preach to all peoples the gospel message so that the human race might become the Family of God, in which the fullness of the Law would be love" (GS 32).

2. *Community of the Bishops.* There is further a "hierarchical communion," which is expressed in the teaching, ministering, and directing actions that belong to the bishops and through which they as one speak the truths of faith, minister to the faithful, and direct them in the way of salvation. Each particular church (cf. LG 23) in the body of churches is where "the one, holy, Catholic, and apostolic Church of Christ is truly present and operative" (CD 11). (See Church.)

3. *Community of Christians.* Christ did not come to save an elite or a special group. He came that "all may be one as He is one with the Father." This Vatican II saw in its truly "catholic" or universal sense: "In the exercise of their teaching office it is the duties of pastors to preach God's word to all the Christian people, so that, rooted in faith, hope, and charity, they may grow in Christ, and that the Christian community may bear witness to that charity which the Lord commended. Pastors should bring the faithful to a full knowledge of the mystery of salvation through a catechetical instruction which is adapted to each one's age" (CD 30).

4. *Community of all humans.* There is a broad recognition that all mankind is to be gained for Christ. The Church is only an instrument that seeks through the fulfillment of her mission to bring all people into the peace and harmony that will encourage and foster those human relations in which men may best seek their salvation. Vatican II was aware of this and declared: "Brotherly dialogue among men does not reach its perfection on the level of technical progress, but on the deeper level of interpersonal relationships. These demand a mutual respect for the full spiritual dignity of the person" (GS 23).

5. *Community of the parish.* Although it is true that the parish is a locality and a specifically placed entity, yet it has a special place in the role of the mission of the Church. It brings into a commonality of ends the most practical means of fulfilling the religious desires of all its members. Vatican II placed emphasis on the parochial role, declaring: "In exercising this care of souls, pastors and their assistants should so fulfill their duty of teaching, sanctifying, and governing that the individual parishioners and the parish communities will really feel that they are members of the diocese and of the universal Church" (CD 30). (See Church.)

## Comparative Religion

Comparative religion is the science or study of the teachings, founding, practices, and development of the known religions, their history and evolution. In all religions there are common factors that either set them apart or bring them together. For example, the divinity may be only a vague concept in some religious groupings, such as those of magic and mythology, yet there is a recognition of the "sacred" or "other worldliness."

This is an historical analysis that is valuable in the surge of the ecumenical movement. The psychology of religion and its relationship to the culture and social patterns make it possible to estimate its impact on the social structures under which people live.

## Compline

The compline is the final hour of the Divine Office, following Vespers. (See Breviary.)

## Compostela, Pilgrimage of

The practice of making a penitential visit to the shrine of St. James the Greater, at Compostela, Spain, began in the eighth century.

## Concelebration

Concelebration refers to the simultaneous celebration of Mass by more than one priest, consecrating the same bread and wine. This is done at the Mass of Ordination of priests and bishops in the Roman rite and at other permitted times.

In the history of the early Church, concelebrating was practiced frequently. Vatican II decreed that this be returned as a controlled procedure. Concelebration takes place with the concelebrants speaking with the principal celebrant the words of consecration while holding their right hand and arm out before them, and they all speak the prayers in unison from the Offertory onward. The new norms set by Vatican II are: "Concelebration, by which the unity of the priesthood is appropriately manifested, has remained in use to this day in the Church both in the East and in the West. For this reason it has seemed good to the Council to extend permission for concelebration to the following cases: 1. (a) on the Thursday of the Lord's Supper, not only at the Mass of the Chrism, but also at the evening Mass; (b) at Masses during Councils, Bishops' conferences, and synods; (c) at the Mass for the blessing of an abbot. 2. Also, with permission of the ordinary, to whom it belongs to decide whether concelebration is opportune: (a) at conventual Mass, and at the Principal Mass in churches when the needs of the faithful do not require that all the priests available should celebrate individually; (b) at Masses celebrated at any kind of priests' meetings, whether the priests be secular clergy or religious.

"I. Rules concerning concelebration within a diocese are under the control of the bishop . . ." (SC 57).

## Conception, Immaculate
See Immaculate Conception.

## Conciliar Theory, also Conciliar Movement
This movement, which arose in the fourteenth century, sought to make the pope subordinate to a general council. It lost force when the danger to unity was seen and it was finally condemned in 1870 at the First Vatican Council. Known as Conciliarism, this was a threat to the papacy, based on a loose interpretation of the gospel verses of St. Matthew 16:18–19.

## Conclave
Conclave refers both to the assembly of the cardinals and the place where they gather to elect a new pope. In the conclave an area or small cell is constructed and allotted to each cardinal with accommodations for two of his companions. The strictest enclosure separates this area from the rest of the Vatican, allowing no communication between the cardinals and the outside world. Extreme caution and special rules govern the conclave.

## Concomitance
In philosophy, concomitance is the act or state of being associated. In theology, by natural concomitance, the whole Christ is present in the Eucharist under each species of bread and wine, meaning that both *body* and *blood* are present together with His soul, or by virtue of the fact that soul, body, and blood of a living being cannot be separated. Thus by supernatural concomitance the divinity of Christ is also present under each species of the Eucharist as understood by the hypostatic union.

## Concord Formula
In 1577 the basic formulation of the Lutheran faith was issued as a statement that was in great part both a reply and a parallel pronouncement to the canons set forth by the Council of Trent. This was expanded by the addition of other doctrinal teachings of the Lutherans and the several formulas were published in 1580 in the *Book of Concord*. (See Lutheranism.)

## Concordance
A concordance is the tool for biblical study, which consists of an alphabetical index of all the major, or substantive, words in the books of the Bible. Together with the title of the book, the chapter and verse, each reference is given so that ready location of any passage of the Bible may be made. A concordance is a utility book for all scholars and readers of the Bible. Because of the difference in language and translations, each concordance in most instances is useful with one of the translated versions, e.g., the New American Bible (NAB). The term has also been applied to those reference works that list all happenings, persons, or parables of the Bible, but these are not concordances in the accepted sense and useful purpose.

## Concordat
A concordat is a special agreement, compromise, or treaty drawn up between the Holy See and the civil government of a country, nation, or dominion. Its sole objective concerns spiritual matters, in particular the spiritual welfare of Catholics residing as nationals of the country. These concordats usually arise in the Sacred Congregation for Extraordinary Ecclesiastical Affairs, but the Supreme Tribunal of the Apostolic Signature has special competence regarding certain of these agreements, especially the Council for the Public Affairs of the Church. Concordats are means of better regulation of religious life in certain countries and in no way are a capitulation to dominance by the State. There have been to date some one-hundred fifty concordats negotiated since that of Worms in 1122.

Notable Concordats of recent years are that with Nazi Germany in 1933, which was often broken by the Nazi officials, and the Lateran Treaty with the Italian State, which set up the property rights of Vatican State.

## Concordat of Worms
This agreement made in 1122 between Pope Callistus II and Emperor Henry V ended lay investiture; it is also called the *Pactum Calixtinum*.

## Concupiscence
The word has two meanings: (1) the passionate desire of a person, inclining the sense appetite toward sensible good or away from sensible evil; (2) the inclination toward evil, particularly the inclination toward impurity. In both instances concupiscence arises in the imagination and arouses the sensual appetite. In the second meaning it is an inclination against right reason and a giving way to the propensity of human nature toward sin.

We learn from Scripture that the object is what makes desire evil. For example, St. Paul speaks of the flesh and lusts as the "degradation" of man's body (Rom. 1:24–32). Concupiscence is not of itself a sin but serves as a force leading to sin, as St. James writes: "Rather, the tug and lure of his own passion tempt every man. Once passion has conceived, it gives birth to sin, and when sin reaches maturity it begets death" (Jas. 1:14–15). St. John calls concupiscence both the "world" and the "flesh" (1 Jn. 2:15–17).

### Concursus

1. A concursus is a competitive examination by which candidates to ecclesiastical offices are chosen.

2. The divine concursus is the act by which God as the First Cause operates through secondary or created causes.

### Condign Merit

A deserved merit or grace, a condign merit is the right of a human person in justice to receive from God the supernatural reward for the performance of a supernatural act. The act and the reward are presumed to be equal or proportionate. Only Christ as the God-man could claim all merit for His every act. However, a human may receive graces if he fulfills the necessary conditions, namely: being alive, being in the state of sanctifying grace, acting freely, the action being morally good and directed to God, and the reward promised by God the Creator and in keeping with His will. The graces merited for mankind by Christ are thus justly man's if he cooperates with Christ and His Church and fulfills the necessary conditions. (See Grace.)

### Conditional Administration of the Sacraments

Under certain circumstances, the Sacraments of Baptism, Penance, and Holy Orders may be administered on condition as stated, e.g., in the words of the form, "If you are not baptized, I baptize . . . (See individual sacraments.)

### Conferences, Clergy

Meetings of the diocesan clergy are usually held monthly in the principal city of the diocese or in each deanery. Their purpose is to discuss pastoral problems, cases of conscience, particularly questions of liturgy or moral theology. These meetings are also called pastoral conferences. (See Priests' Councils.)

### Conferences, Episcopal

Episcopal conferences are meetings, gatherings, synods, or councils wherein bishops counsel together for the better devotional, educational, and efficient carrying out of their individual responsibilities and the collective good of the Church. Vatican II addressed itself to such gatherings: "An episcopal conference is a kind of council in which the bishops of a given nation or territory jointly exercise their pastoral office by way of promoting that greater good which the Church offers mankind, especially through forms and programs of the apostolate which are fittingly adapted to the circumstances of the age.

"Members of the episcopal conference are all local Ordinaries of every rite, coadjutors, auxiliaries, and other titular bishops who perform a special work entrusted to them by the Apostolic See or the episcopal conferences. Vicars general are not members. *De jure* membership belongs neither to other titular bishops nor, in view of their particular assignment in the area, to legates of the Roman Pontiff . . ."

Each episcopal conference is to draft its own statutes, to be reviewed by the Apostolic See. In these statutes, among other agencies, offices should be established to aid in achieving the conference's purpose more efficaciously; for example, a permanent board of bishops, episcopal commissions, and a general secretariat . . .

"Contacts between episcopal conferences of different nations should be encouraged in order to promote and safeguard their higher welfare" (CD 38). (See National Conference of Catholic Bishops.)

### Confession

1. Sacramental Confession (see Auricular Confession; Penance, Sacrament of).

2. Annual confession is the obligation to confess at least once a year; it is imposed on all who have reached the age of reason (c. 916). This may be done at any time or place and to any authorized priest. Properly, the obligation does not extend to those who have not committed mortal sin, but it is recommended to them.

Sacrilegious confession is that made by a penitent who willfully withholds the confession of a known mortal sin, willfully fails in sorrow for sin or purpose of amendment, or does not intend to make satisfaction or restitution if required. In such cases the Sacrament of Penance is made void, absolution is not effective, and the confession must be repeated, and the fact of the sacrilegious confession confessed.

### Confession of a Martyr, also Confessio

This originally was the tomb of a martyr, particularly those in the catacombs where Mass was celebrated. Now it refers to the crypt where the remains of a martyr are kept beneath the main altar of a church, e.g., the crypt beneath St. Peter's in Rome containing the body of the first pope. (See Catacombs.)

## Confessional

The confessional is the enclosed place where the priest behind a screen hears the confession of a penitent and administers the Sacrament of Penance. It may be single or double; that is, in the single the priest sits in one side of the enclosure while the penitent kneels on the other side with the screen between them; in the double, the priest sits in a compartment between two screens with the penitents on either side. The priest then alternates, hearing the confession first from one side and then from the other, alternately sliding soundproof panels across the screens.

The term is sometimes used, but erroneously, for that room where spiritual counseling is given, even though auricular confession accompanies the counseling. (See Reconciliation Room.)

## Confessor

1. Confessor is the title of a canonized male saint, one whose life gave testimony to the faith. There are two groups, those who were bishops and those who were not.

2. A confessor is a priest, having the required faculties or jurisdiction from the bishop of the diocese, who hears the confession of penitents and administers the Sacrament of Penance. His role is not only to act in the place of Christ as judge and impart sacramental absolution but also to serve as counselor and spiritual guide.

3. An extraordinary confessor is the priest appointed to hear the confession of men or women religious over and above their regular confessor. (See Penance, Sacrament of.)

## Confirmation Name

The name of a saint is chosen by the one confirmed and imposed by the bishop, and added to the Christian name. It is recommended that the person confirmed imitate the virtues of the saint whose name is chosen. Whether one wishes to use the name is optional since it is not a legal name as such.

## Confirmation, Sacrament of

Confirmation is a sacrament of the New Law by which grace of the Holy Spirit is given to one baptized by anointing with chrism in the form of a cross on the forehead, the imposition of hands and saying the words: "N . . . receive the seal of the Holy Spirit, the Gift of the Father." The effects of the Sacrament are an increase of sanctifying grace and the gifts of the Holy Spirit; a seal or character imparted on the soul (so this sacrament may not be repeated), and a strengthening of actual grace so that the recipient is enabled to fearlessly profess the faith and fight against temptation. The bishop is the ordinary minister of confirmation, while the extraordinary minister is a priest to whom the power has been granted by office or by apostolic indult. It is the custom of the Church to have each one confirmed presented by a sponsor. We learn much about the Sacrament of Confirmation in the Acts of the Apostles (1:5; 11:16; 2:38). It was early called "the baptism of the Spirit," and the Council of Trent declared confirmation a "true and proper sacrament."

Pope Paul VI in his *Apostolic Constitution on the Sacrament of Confirmation* (Aug. 15, 1971) emphasizes that the Sacraments of Baptism, Confirmation, and the Eucharist have a threefold effect and are constituted as Sacraments of Initiation. These make for a real embodiment into the Mystical Body of Christ: "The faithful, already marked with the sacred seal of baptism and confirmation, are through the reception of the Eucharist fully joined to the Body of Christ" (PO 5).

The Apostolic Constitution states: "In baptism, neophytes receive forgiveness of sins, adoption as sons of God, and the character of Christ, by which they are made members of the Church and for the first time become sharers in the priesthood of their Savior (cf. 1 Pt. 2:5, 9). Through the sacrament of confirmation, those who have been born anew in baptism receive the inexpressible Gift, the Holy Spirit himself, by which 'they are endowed . . . with special strength.' Moreover, having received the character of this sacrament, they are 'bound more intimately to the Church' and 'they are more strictly obliged to spread and defend the faith both by word and by deed as true witnesses of Christ.' Finally, confirmation is so closely linked with the holy eucharist that the faithful, after being signed by holy baptism and confirmation are incorporated fully into the body of Christ by participation in the eucharist."

Confirmation, wherever possible should be proceeded by a catechesis for not only the recipients but also those of the parish community. And the sacrament should be conferred during a Eucharistic celebration, following directly after the Liturgy of the Word. With total involvement of the parish community in this "initiation," there is recognition of new fellowship with Christ among all members of the parish community.

The promise of the Spirit was given by Christ (cf. Jn. 14:9–21), and the apostles carried this into the community life (cf. Acts 2:44–47). Confirmation is the Sacrament of Christian maturity—"You yourselves will not be the speakers; the Spirit of your Father will be speaking in you" (Mt. 10:19–20).

### Confiteor
Literally, "I confess," Confiteor is the title and the first Latin word of a prayer. A form of confiteor is sometimes recited in unison by the parish members and the celebrant during the penitential rite at the beginning of a Eucharistic celebration, saying:

> I confess to almighty God, and to you, my brothers and sisters, that I have sinned through my own fault in my thoughts and in my words, in what I have done, and in what I have failed to do; and I ask blessed Mary, ever virgin, all the angels and saints, and you, my brothers and sisters, to pray for me to the Lord our God.

The celebrant then says the absolution, with the words: "May almighty God have mercy on us, forgive us our sins, and bring us to everlasting life." And the people respond: "Amen."

In wording it is an open confession and petition for prayer and forgiveness. It is recommended that it be said in preparation for receiving the Sacrament of Penance.

### Confraternity
In canon law a confraternity is a voluntary association, generally of the laity, established under Church authority, for the promotion of some work of devotion, charity, or instruction undertaken for the love of God. Confraternities are not free-acting groups but subject to the assent of the bishop, and their statutes are subject to his approval. The Confraternities of the Blessed Sacrament and of Christian Doctrine should be established in every parish.

### Confraternity of Christian Doctrine
See Christian Doctrine, Confraternity of.

### Confraternity Edition of the Bible
This revision of the Challoner-Rheims Version of the NT was produced in 1941. It is a new version that retains the "thou" of the original, but the wording and grammar have been modernized and all archaic forms have been eliminated. Basic sources were the Vulgate and Greek editions. The Confraternity edition of the OT, translated from the Hebrew into modern English, was begun in 1948 and published shortly thereafter.

In 1970 the *New American Bible,* sponsored by the Bishops' Committee of the Confraternity of Christian Doctrine, was translated from the original languages and ancient sources, such as the Dead Sea Scrolls, and was introduced in several editions.

### Congregation
1. *Religious congregation* is a community of religious whose members are bound together by a common rule and take only simple vows.

2. A monastic *congregation* is one or more monasteries under a single superior.

3. A congregation is a group of Catholics who are members of a parish, usually living within the territory designated as the parish by the bishop. This also refers to members of a parish assembled in the parish church for divine worship.

4. *Sacred Congregations* are departments of the Roman Curia and are the highest ranking bodies serving the pope in the administration and government of the Church. They include: Sacred Congregation for the Doctrine of the Faith, Sacred Congregation for the Oriental Churches, Sacred Congregation for Bishops, Sacred Congregaton for the Discipline of the Sacraments, Sacred Congregation for Divine Worship, Sacred Congregation for the Causes of Saints, Sacred Congregation for the Clergy, Sacred Congregation for the Affairs of Religious, Sacred Congregation for Catholic Education, and the Sacred Congregation for the Evangelization of Peoples and the Propagation of the Faith. These are headquartered in the Vatican and collectively called the Curial Congregations. (See Tribunals, Roman.)

5. Congregations are appointed at general councils and are made up of bishops appointed or approved by the pope for the carrying out of the program.

### Congregationalism
The name given to two lines of Protestant formation: the first embracing Puritanism and Presbyterianism; the second, besides those called Congregationalists, are Baptists, Churches of Christ, and Disciples. There have been numerous changes and adaptations in these since the inception of the first bible groups, which at first bore the name "independency" religions, in the years between 1570 and 1620.

The principal tenets of congregationalism are: that the New Testament places as foremost the principle of a "gathered church" rather than a geographical, national, or parochial church. One of their early writers (Robert Browne) declared

(1583): "The church is a company or number of Christians or believers, which by a willing covenant made with their God are under the government of God and Christ, and keep His laws in one holy communion." Each church is thus distinct and is said to have a direct covenant with Christ as the head of the universal church. Thus each church has autonomy under the guidance of the Holy Spirit. Congregationalism also proposes an interdenominational ecumenism and missionary effort. Its chief teaching today is the free sovereignty and Lordship of Christ, and this leads the churches readily to seek association with others who favor an ecumenical renewal.

### Congresses, Eucharistic

Eucharistic congresses are gatherings of the clergy and faithful for the purpose of giving glory to God in the Holy Eucharist by public adoration and general reception of Holy Communion. They also serve to promote the spiritual, social, and intellectual welfare of the faithful, especially through discussion and means of furthering devotion to our Lord in the Blessed Sacrament. They may be (1) international when all countries of the world participate or (2) national when they are held for one country. There have been forty international congresses held from 1881 through 1974.

### Congruism

This theory of grace was originated by Molina and developed by Suarez and others. It maintains that efficacious grace is adapted to suit *(congruus)* the person receiving the grace and in proportion to the person's future cooperation once the grace is given. This degree of cooperation, they maintain, is known by God because of His *scientia media,* mediate knowledge. St. Thomas Aquinas' teaching is that the good use of grace by free consent is itself an effect of grace and it would be contradictory to say that the grace of God is only efficacious by the consent of the recipient, since this would detract from the divine causality in giving the grace.

### Consanguinity

Blood relationship in either the direct or collateral line is a diriment impediment to marriage. Consanguinity renders marriage invalid in the direct line in all degrees (i.e., parents-children-grandchildren), and no dispensation can be granted (Lv. 18:6–18). In the collateral line it extends to the third degree inclusive. In the first degree of the collateral (side) line, that of brother and sister, no dispensation can be granted because of the prohibition of natural law; the second degree (first cousins) and third degree (second cousins) may be dispensed. (Cf. Diriment Impediment.)

### Conscience

Conscience is the judgment of our reason with regard to the morality, goodness, or badness of an act. This judgment is called the "dictate" of conscience. Conscience is the proximate rule of moral action; that is, it resides in the mind and proposes to the will the morality of a given course of action. Hence, conscience binds and must be followed. However, one must strive to form a right conscience (Rom. 14:22).

In their *Statement on the Formation of Conscience,* the Canadian Bishops declared (Dec. 1, 1973): "It [conscience] has always been a somewhat ambiguous term and has frequently been presented with more poetry than clarity. Conscience is not simply some 'still small voice' which is evoked by some mysterious mechanism within us when we are faced with a practical decision as to whether a given course of action is acceptable or not. Conscience is that ultimate judgment that every man is called to make as to whether this or that action is acceptable to him without violating the principles which he is prepared to admit as governing his life. If he goes against those principles, he is said to be acting 'against his conscience.'" Vatican II stated: "In the depth of his conscience, man detects a law which he does not impose upon himself, but which holds him to obedience . . . Conscience is the most secret core and sanctuary of a man. There he is alone with God, whose voice echoes in his depths" (GS 16).

### Consecration

1. Consecration is the act and ceremony by which a person or thing is dedicated to sacred service or set apart for sacred use. The ceremony is more solemn than a blessing; once consecrated the object cannot be consecrated again, and any profanation is a sin of sacrilege.

2. Consecration at Mass is the solemn portion of the Canon at which time the celebrating priest, in commemoration of the act of our Lord at the Last Supper, changes bread and wine into the body and blood of Jesus Christ. By this, the bread and wine lose their substance, retaining only their appearances (cf. Transubstantiation).

3. The consecration of a bishop is the act and ceremony conferring the fullness of holy orders on the one consecrated and imprinting on his soul the episcopal character. Three bishops, the one con-

secrator and two co-consecrators perform the ceremony, imposing hands, anointing, blessing, giving the insignia of a bishop (crosier, ring, miter and gloves), and enthroning the one appointed by the pope.

### Consecration Cross

The Consecration Cross is one of the twelve small crosses that are painted or sculptured directly on the inside walls of a church when it is consecrated. These mark the twelve places where the chrism was signed in the form of a cross during the consecration, and they may never be removed. On the anniversary day of consecration each year a lighted candle is burned before each of the twelve crosses.

### Consistorial Congregation

See Congregation; Sacred Roman Congregations.

### Consistory

A consistory is an ecclesiastical court. Formerly the consistories were governing bodies of the Church, meeting regularly three times a week to weigh questions of faith, discipline, and policy. Today these have been replaced by the Sacred Congregations of the Roman Curia. However, the pope may call an assembly of the cardinals, which would be a consistory, with its function chiefly that of promulgation of an official decision or announcement.

### Constance, Council of

The sixteenth ecumenical council was held at Constance (Baden) in Germany from November, 1414, to April, 1418. In its forty-five sessions it effected: repair of the schism of rival popes and rival emperors, reform of the Church, legislation on Holy Communion, pronouncements on the forty-five errors of Wyclif and the thirty errors of Huss. (Cf. Ecumenical Councils.)

### Constancy

Constancy is a moral virtue by which one learns to persist in the struggle and suffering of life to the end without giving in to weariness, discouragement, or indolence. It is attained by prayer, with the understanding that perseverance is a gift of God; by concentrating on the everlasting reward awaiting us; and by courage supported by God's grace and our love of God. (See Final Perseverance.)

### Constantinople, Councils of

There were four ecumenical councils held at Constantinople situated in the Bosporus, the seat of the Byzantine Empire. The first (second ecumenical) was held in 381 and endorsed the Nicene Creed, condemned the Arian and Macedonian heresies, and formulated the Catholic doctrine concerning the divinity of the Holy Spirit. The second, in 553, condemned the "Three Chapters" (writings of three anti-Monophysites) and the Nestorian heresy. The third, in 681, confirmed the doctrine set forth at Chalcedon, namely, that Christ possesses both a divine and human will; this council also condemned the Monothelite heresy. The fourth, in 869, condemned Photius and his followers and denounced iconoclasm and affirmed the unity of the human soul. (Cf. Ecumenical Councils.)

### Constantinople, Patriarchate of

Formerly a great jurisdictional power in the Church, claimed to be "second to Rome," the patriarchate of Constantinople fell into definite schism in the Middle Ages and formed the Orthodox Eastern Church. There have been since that time fractions falling away from its power and the patriarchate today is minor, embracing only a few thousands of faithful. The patriarch of the Orthodox Church resides there, but there is no Catholic patriarch with jurisdiction in Constantinople, present-day Istanbul, Turkey. It was not represented at the first or second Vatican Councils, but Pope Paul VI has met with the spiritual leader in recognition of the ecumenical roles that Orthodoxy and the Church of Rome may play in the future in uniting Christians. (See Ecumenism.)

### Constantinople, Rite of

This liturgy was developed from the ancient Antiochene. It used the Greek, Arabic, Old Slovenian, and Rumanian languages and followed the old style (Julian) Calendar (the liturgical year beginning on Sept. 1). Today it is commonly referred to as the Byzantine rite. (See Byzantine Rite.)

### Constitutional Clergy

Constitutional clergy were those clerics who took the oath to uphold the civil constitution set up for the Church by the National Assembly of France in 1790. It was a political scheme proposed by "liberal" Catholics in the interest of "liberty" as set up by the Revolution. It served to suppress many dioceses and brought persecution on priests who did not sign. The constitution was condemned by

Pius VI. It ended with the Concordat of 1801. However, one salutary effect was that emigrant priests, rather than be forced to uphold false legislation, fled France and thus helped to carry the faith to the New World.

## Constitutions

1. A *papal constitution* is a decree or pronouncement in the form of a bull usually issued in the pope's name. It is also called "Apostolic letter *sub plumbo*" or apostolic constitution.

2. The applications of the general rule of a religious order developed as principles to govern a particular society.

3. The most solemn and profound of the doctrinal documents issued by an ecumenical council, with binding force on the entire Church. (See Vatican Council II.)

## Consubstantial

Consubstantial means being of one and the same substance, as the three Divine Persons of the Trinity are of but one substance, as set forth by the first ecumenical council of Nicaea in 325.

## Consubstantiation

This heretical teaching of the Lutherans maintains that the substance of bread and wine exist *together with* the substance of the body and blood of Christ after consecration. This was condemned by the Fourth Lateran Council and the Council of Trent. As a theory, also called impanation, this is in direct opposition to the doctrinal teaching of transubstantiation.

## Consuetudinary

Consuetudinary is the title of a book setting forth the liturgical customs of a monastic order. (See Liturgy.)

## Consultors

1. Technicians or specialists who serve the Roman Curia, consultors supply the initial study of a problem and formulate possible solutions. They are prelates, priests, or religious versed in theology and canon law and serve the various sacred congregations at the request of the prefect or secretary of a particular congregation.

2. In the United States, in place of cathedral chapters, four to six diocesan consultors must be appointed by the bishop of a diocese to assist and advise him in administrative affairs. This group is not to be confused with the diocesan advisers who are generally a number of laity who advise in practical affairs.

## Contemplation

A form of affective prayer higher than meditation, in which the mind and will are engrossed in viewing truth above reason and joined with profound admiration. It is accomplished not by reasoning or vocal expression but by a deep, sincere concentration on God, a loving knowledge of Him and His works, which aided by grace is a simple, wordless act of love of God. It is the perfection of prayer, a real, vibrant, and personal awareness of God, more intimate than other prayer experiences. It is the prayer proper to the contemplative life but may be practiced by anyone. St. John of the Cross states: "Contemplation is the science of love, which is an infused loving knowledge of God." Generally, authors distinguish two types of contemplation: acquired and infused. However, while acquired contemplation may attain to a degree of mystical union with God, which is the height of "infused and loving knowledge of God," it is more a prayer of simplicity or developed meditation. Acquired contemplation is, according to St. Teresa, "acquired prayer of recollection." In contradistinction, infused contemplation is a simple and loving knowledge of God and His works, which results not from human activity aided by grace but only through inspiration of the Holy Spirit. It is always passive and if this infused contemplation persists and becomes frequent, the result is mystical union, or the mystical state.

## Contemplative Life

Contemplative life is an austere religious life adapted to foster contemplation such as that in a contemplative order. In the religious life it is the highest form, for not only does it encourage the members to seek union with God through love, but by seclusion and freedom from the worldly spirit, the objective worship of God is perfected. In purpose it is a continuous life of prayer to God "that His kingdom may flourish," and of mortification or atonement for sinners. This life calls for a generous vocation of a special degree of love of God and should not be considered lightly.

Vatican II stated: "Members of those communities which are totally dedicated to contemplation give themselves to God alone in solitude and silence and through constant prayer and ready penance. No matter how urgent may be the needs of the active apostolate, such communities will always have a distinguished part to play in Christ's Mystical Body, where 'not all members have the same function' (Rom. 12:4)" (PC 7).

## Continence

1. Continence is the virtue, derived from that more profound virtue of chastity, which in practice preserves the mind from impure thoughts and desires and restrains the will from actions following aroused sexual desire.

2. In marriage continence is voluntary abstinence from marital intercourse, for any period of time by the mutual consent of husband and wife (cf. Chastity).

There are two degrees of continence, and everyone is obliged by natural and divine law to practice one of these degrees: (1) *Partial* or relative continence is that restraint or abstention from an excess of indulgence, e.g. in the married state. (2) *Absolute* is that continence obliging all outside the married state. This may be strengthened by a vow of chastity, which then becomes perpetual, or perfect, to distinguish this from the temporary.

Both psychological and physiological studies have demonstrated that partial continence is salutary for the human body and also that absolute continence may be practiced without physical harm to or impairment of the human body.

## Contract

In the Church, the civil laws and contracts are adopted (c. 1529), except when they are in opposition to the divine law or to special prescriptions of canon law.

## Contrition

Contrition is the sorrow that arises in the soul, making one's mind repent past sins and resolve not to sin again. There are two divisions: (1) Perfect contrition takes place when the motive of one's sorrow is the love of God as God, the highest Good. With this are all the elements of contrition including the desire to confess. (2) Imperfect contrition occurs when the motive is other than God but is supernatural in that it refers to God, e.g., through fear of God's punishment. In the reception of the Sacrament of Penance, contrition must be genuinely present, that is, at least implicitly in preparation for receiving the sacrament and virtually during the time of receiving absolution.

True contrition for sin must be interior (from the mind and heart), supernatural (motivated by faith and love), supreme (a strong dislike for sin as offensive to God), and universal (encompassing every mortal sin). (See Attrition.)

An Act of Contrition is a prayer expressing sorrow and repentance:

My God, I am sorry for having offended You, and I detest all my sins, because of Your love for me, but most of all because they offend you, my God, who is all good and deserving of all my love. I firmly resolve, with Your helping grace, to sin no more and to shun sin in the future.

## Contumacy

In Church law, contumacy is contempt of court. It is the failure to appear in an ecclesiastical court when summoned, or failure to carry out an order of this court. This presupposes that the transgression is with knowledge of the law and its attached punishment. Censure follows the fact of one being contumacious, and contumacy is presumed in censures *latae sententiae* (q.v.). One is "purged of contumacy" when it is proved in court that one was lawfully hindered from answering the summons or order.

## Contumely

Contumelious acts are those against justice and charity whereby one treats another person to ridicule and a loss of dignity through insults of language or gesture, thereby bringing that person into contempt by others. They are not detraction or lies whereby one is derided, but a lesser evil than derision. They are malicious damage done to one's honor, character, and dignity, causing that person to suffer. St. Paul called for such actions to be met with patience and even silence (Rom. 12:19). (Cf. Calumny.)

## Convent

The word comes from the Latin, meaning a "gathering."

1. When the term convent means the entire corporate capacity of a religious community, that is, its director and effects, it is used for both male and female communities of monks or nuns.

2. Popularly, convent is the establishment, similar to a monastery, where sisters or nuns live in community life.

3. Less precisely, the word convent is referred to the parochial residence of the teaching sisters of the parish school.

## Conventual Mass

The daily Mass celebrated publicly in churches where professed religious live in a community is the Conventual Mass. It is also that Mass celebrated in churches of religious who daily recite the Divine Office publicly.

## Conventuals

Conventuals are those members of the Franciscan Order who, by approval granted in 1322, possess and use property in common. They are called: Friars Minor Conventual, Conventual Franciscans, or Black Franciscans.

## Conversion

The word conversion is used in several different ways, philosophically and theologically, by Church writers. It is from the Latin, meaning "to turn toward."

1. Total physical conversion is the passage or "turning into," the transmutation of the matter and form of one entire substance into another substance already existing, without any change in this latter substance. This is transubstantiation (q.v.).

2. Conversion is also taken to mean a turning toward God on the part of a sinner. It also refers to a turning toward the Church of God, that is, accepting its doctrine and discipline as true and of faith; this is called becoming a convert. According to St. Thomas there are three phases of this conversion: preparation, merit, and glory. To each of these there is a corresponding grace: first, the operation of divine grace through God; second, the habitual state of grace; and third, the consummation or fulfillment of these graces and all other graces.

3. In philosophy, logical conversion is the transposition of the terms of a proposition without the loss of the truth of the proposition.

4. The "conversion of manners," spoken of in the religious life, is both the process and the accomplishment of doing away with vices that afflict one and the acquiring of virtues.

There is also that conversion called for by the approach of "the reign of God" (Mt. 3:2; 4:17). Vatican II spoke of this, saying: "The Sacred liturgy does not exhaust the entire activity of the Church. Before men can come to the liturgy they must be called to faith and to conversion: 'But how shall they call on him in whom they have not believed? And can they believe unless they have heard of him? And how can they hear unless there is someone to preach? And how can men preach unless they are sent?' (Rom. 10:14–15)" (SC 9).

And: "All must be converted to Him as He is made known by the Church's preaching. All must be incorporated into Him by baptism, and into the Church which is His body" (AG 7).

## Convert

A convert is anyone who has made a conversion to God, precisely, a person who has not been baptized, is of the age of reason, is instructed, and receives baptism. This also means one who having been baptized, but brought up as a non-Catholic, abjures his error, submits to the Church and by conditional baptism, profession of faith, and confession and absolution, becomes a Catholic.

## Cope

In Latin *pluviale,* literally a "raincoat," the cope was used in the early Church for a practical purpose. It is now a vestment, used for other ceremonies than the Mass itself, made in a semicircular shape, worn draped around the shoulders full length, and fastened in front across the upper chest by a clasp called the morse. On the back it is necessary that the cope have a flat hood or shield that may be round or pointed, falling almost to the waist. The orphreys, or embroidery, usually of a markedly different color from that of the vestment, are customarily not too broad. The morse may be of cloth or metal. A jeweled morse may be worn only by prelates.

## Copt

An Egyptian Christian, a Copt is a member of either the Catholic or dissident Coptic Church. The Copts returned to Catholic unity in 1741; the Ethiopians who also follow the Coptic Rite returned to Catholic unity in 1846.

## Coptic Rite

The administration of the sacraments and liturgy of the Coptic Rite are followed by both Catholic and dissident members of the Coptic Church. The liturgical language is the early Egyptian (Coptic) along with Greek and Arabic. The dissident church followed the Monophysite heresy after the Council of Chalcedon (A.D. 451). The dissidents deny the supremacy of the pope, and although their orders are valid, they administer the sacraments in a different manner, for example, baptism by immersion. This Church is governed by the Patriarch of Alexandria. The Catholic Coptic Church was reconciled in the eighteenth century and under Pope Leo XIII was given a patriarch who is located at Alexandria and appointed by the Holy See. (See Alexandrian Rite.)

## Cor Unum

Literally from the Latin "one heart," this is the title of a group instituted by Pope Paul VI, July 15, 1971, as a service organization to supply information and coordinate services of Catholic aid and human development organizations and their many worldwide projects. (See Campaign for Human Development.)

### Coram Cardinale (Episcopo)

Literally, *coram cardinale* means "in the presence of a cardinal" (or bishop). A Mass celebrated *coram cardinale* is one at which a cardinal, not being the celebrant, assists from either the throne or faldstool.

### Cordeliers

In France in the Middle Ages Cordeliers was the name given to the Franciscan Recollects because of the knotted cord worn about their waists. The name is also sometimes applied to those who assist the sick at the Shrine of Our Lady of Lourdes in France.

### Corinthians, Epistles 1 and 2 to the

The letters that St. Paul wrote to the Christians of Corinth, the ancient capital city of the Greek province of Achaia, form two books of Scripture. St. Paul arrived at Corinth in A.D. 49 or 50 and remained perhaps a year and a half. In the First Epistle the apostle answers certain questions that had arisen because of the erroneous doctrines of the "false apostles or false teachers." Its doctrinal message is St. Paul's fullest teaching on the makeup of Christ's Church as His mystical body, on the Resurrection, on the Eucharist, and on Christian chastity. It is a writing of spiritual counsel and probably the most valuable historical document of all the Epistles of the NT. The Second Epistle was written about A.D. 57 to confirm those who had remained loyal but also to set forth in plain language the issues by which the true doctrine was to be recognized. Its doctrinal content again speaks of the unity of Christ with His Church and also of the authority of the Christian minister. Its spiritual message is: the good of suffering with Christ and the hope of immortality.

Because of references to other writings contained in these two epistles (1 Cor. 1:16 and 2 Cor. 1:1–6), it is quite certain that St. Paul addressed two other letters to the Church at Corinth. Little is known about these except that one dealt with Paul's anguish at the failure of the people's response and the other spoke of the Apostle's joy (cf. 2 Cor. 7:2–9).

### Cornette

The large, spreading white linen headdress worn by the Sisters of Charity had its origin in a French type of head-covering of the fourteenth century. This has been abandoned in all but a few convents since the modernization of the religious habits that followed Vatican II.

### Corona

1. The band of hair about the head of a religious whose crown is shaved after receiving tonsure.

2. A circle of candles or vigil lights used in the church; also the circular candlestick holding the lights.

3. A seldom used word for any five mysteries of the Rosary.

### Coronation of Our Lady

1. The name of the fifth glorious mystery of the fifteen meditations that are the subjects of mental prayer during the recitation of the Rosary.

2. The representation in art or literature of the arrival and reception of the body of the Blessed Mother assumed into heaven; also called the Coronation of Mary as Queen of Heaven. (See Mary, Virgin Mother of God.)

### Coronation of the Pope

This ceremony takes place after the newly elected pope celebrates Mass, shortly after his election. It is the official act of his becoming pope but not of receiving the jurisdiction over the Church, which is received immediately after his election. During the coronation, the new pope is solemnly blessed by three cardinals and the tiara is placed on his head by the senior cardinal-deacon.

### Corporal

The corporal is the small linen cloth, about 20 inches square, upon which the sacramental species rests during the Mass. Upon it both the chalice and sacred host are placed. It is pleated in three folds, overlapping inwardly so that no fragment of the consecrated host may be dropped. It is carried to and from the altar in the burse. The corporal is also placed on the altar before the tabernacle when the Blessed Sacrament is placed in the monstrance at Benediction, or when the tabernacle is opened to transfer consecrated hosts from the ciborium to the pyx. Corporals are also used as the cloth liners of small baskets or flat containers that hold the consecrated hosts when several ministers of Holy Communion serve the people. Prudence dictates that care in the laundering of the corporals be exercised out of respect for the elements of the hosts that might still adhere to the fabric. (See Greek Corporal.)

### Corporal Works of Mercy

The seven acts of charity, in practice directed toward relief of the physical needs of our fellow human beings are: to feed the hungry, clothe the naked, give drink to the thirsty, shelter the homeless, tend the sick, visit those in prison, and bury the dead. (Cf. Mercy, Spiritual and Corporal Works of; also 1 Jn. 3:17.)

## Corpus Christi

Literally, from the Latin, Corpus Christi means "the Body of Christ." The Solemnity of *Corpus Christi,* celebrated on the Thursday following Trinity Sunday, is in honor of Christ in the Blessed Sacrament and to recall the institution of the Blessed Sacrament; it was ordered celebrated by Pope Urban IV in 1264 at the request of St. Thomas Aquinas. It is customary to carry the Blessed Sacrament in procession about the church, often stopping at temporary altars to give benediction, with final benediction at the main altar of the church. The original office of this feast was written largely by St. Thomas Aquinas and is considered one of the most beautiful of the Roman Breviary.

## Cosmology

This division of formal philosophy studies in particular the characteristics and basic principles of the material universe with special emphasis on time, place, and motion. Based on the findings of the physical sciences, it examines chiefly the causes of material bodies. Cosmology is called special or applied metaphysics, embracing psychology, the study of the soul, and theodicy, the study of God.

## Costume, Clerical

According to canon law, the ordinary dress (that is suits, hats, and other articles) of those in holy orders is black (c. 136, 2379). By special permission white may be used in certain missionary countries. Clerical attire also includes the Roman collar and the cassock.

## Cotta

This white vestment with full sleeves reaches just below the elbow, with its hem descending just below the hip line. This short kind of surplice is worn by priests over their cassocks and by acolytes and altar boys. The cotta is commonly worn by the priest for blessings, administration of the sacraments, and sometimes, but improperly, instead of the alb. (Cf. Surplice.)

## Council

A council is a group of church officials, scholars, hierarchy, or clergy, called together in assembly to discuss, deliberate, or study doctrinal or disciplinary matters pertaining to the Church.

1. A *diocesan council,* referred to as a synod, is a

gathering of the chief clergy of a diocese called together by the bishop, at least every 10 years, at which the position of the faith and matters of government in the diocese are examined. As a group, this is only advisory.

2. A *national council* is an assembly, either plenary or provincial, called by the bishops and representing an entire country. The last in the United States was the Third Plenary Council of Baltimore in 1884.

3. An *ecumenical council* (q.v.) is one to which all the bishops of the Catholic world and all other prelates or dignitaries entitled to vote are invited to gather under the presidency of the pope or his representative. The decrees of an ecumenical council, when ratified by the pope, are binding in conscience upon all Christians. It is now sometimes called "general" council. There have been twenty-one ecumenical councils to date.

4. A *plenary council* is the hierarchy having jurisdiction of a nation.

5. A *provincial council* is the meeting of the suffragan bishops of a province called by the metropolitan. (See Ecumenical Councils; Vatican Councils; Diocesan Pastoral Council; National Pastoral Council; Priests' Senate.)

## Council of Jerusalem

See Jerusalem, Council of.

## Council, Sacred Congregation of the

See Congregation.

## Counseling, Pastoral

In effectively carrying out his role as priest and thus teacher and director of souls, it is often necessary for a pastor to give advice, propose aids, and supervise the spiritual good of individual souls entrusted to his care. This is usually done when instructing persons who are to receive a sacrament or who seek special guidance in spiritual matters. However, such counseling may extend to the social, psychological, or even physiological spheres, e.g., in the instance of one suffering from the illness of alcoholism. If the priest is especially trained, his counseling may be extended to other areas of human activity, but without training the pastor would advise the pursuit of proper guidance from a professional, even though this may be in the realm of the sacramental duty of the applicant, such as in the cases of marriage where special guidance is called for because of the nature of the problem. Where special skills or competencies are required, such as in mental illness, the priest counselor best serves by making a referral to competent agencies.

The areas of counseling might include the following diverse subjects: educational, vocational, youth, and personal.

### Counsels of Perfection
See Evangelical Counsels.

### Counter-Reformation
This movement, more correctly called "The Catholic Reform," and recently termed by historians the "Catholic Reaction" or "Catholic Restoration," began as a reaction to the defection from the Church, the Protestant revolt at discipline and authority, and the political and social upheaval that stemmed from the new type of religion based on individual interpretation of the Bible. It lasted not much longer than 100 years, but the effects are still present. The reform for the Church began with the Council of Trent (1545 to 1563) which, in twenty-five sessions, gave a definite statement on Catholic doctrines denied by Protestants. It was a revitalizing period for the Church when her great leadership was expressed in the Baroque in art, in great national and missionary endeavors, as at Lepanto, and in great development in expression and mystical devotion, as evidenced in the writings of St. Robert Bellarmine and Sts. Teresa of Avila and John of the Cross.

### Courts, Ecclesiastical
The Church, because it has the power to make laws to govern its members in their seeking after fulfillment of the mission of Christ and His Church, also has the right and power to establish courts.

A court is a place for the administration of justice. The Church's procedure through its courts is to seek by way of the judicial process, legal discussion and settlement; the prosecution or vindication of the personal rights of individuals; the application of the law to specific cases; and where the offense warrants, the imposing of a penalty.

The ecclesiastical law is the passing of judgment in spiritual matters or those temporal matters attached to spiritual concerns. Also the law of the Church when violated calls for correction in justice and the exactions of penalties. Since the pope alone is the highest legislator or maker of laws in the Church, certain cases are reserved to him alone for adjudication. Thus Cardinals and legates of the Holy See can only be tried by a special court appointed by the Holy See.

The trials are conducted in courts of the diocese where the defendant resides; in the case of a contract the trial may be held in the diocese where the contract was made; a person accused of an offense has the right to be tried in the diocese where the offense was committed.

The hierarchy of the courts ranges from the diocesan court through the diocesan court of appeal to the highest tribunals of the Church, called the *Sacred Roman Rota* (the ordinary court of appeals to the Holy See), or to the *Apostolic Signatura* (the supreme court of the Church, which handles all cases of laws and rights). There is another court of the Holy See, called the *Sacred Apostolic Penitentiary,* which is a tribunal with jurisdiction over sacramental or nonsacramental questions of the internal forum, such as, dispensations, decisions of conscience, grants of absolution and commutation of censures, and all nondoctrinal questions pertaining to indulgences.

The process of an ecclesiastical court is a legal procedure, with testimony, witnesses, depositions, and decisions. All cases are ordinarily tried in the order of the court's calendar, but effort to avoid unnecessary delays is always a foremost consideration.

In many dioceses since Vatican II a provisional court called "Due Process" has been instituted. The juridical decisions of this court are arrived at more through discussion and beneficial settlement, or arbitration. This process rather than a court procedure is directed at the misapprehensions, abuses, and conflicts of rights or interests that arise in a diocese where corporate bodies such as parishes, lay organizations, or clergy come into conflict. The decisions of this court are subject to review by the ordinary in most instances. (Cf. Authority; Process, Due.)

### Covenant
A covenant is a contractual agreement between two persons, or between a person and his superior, or between distinct groups. Its religious meaning is that of "testament," and in the OT the covenant establishes a new relationship, a promise of an exchange of powers, and the attendant rights and duties that follow the contract. The first of such covenants was that made by God with Abraham wherein possession of the land of Canaan was to belong to Abraham and his numerous offspring (Gn. 15; 17:3–8). The most famous of the OT covenants is that made by God with the Israelites through Moses. The conditions were the ten words or commandments, and if they followed this covenant, God would be their God and they would

be His people (Ex. 19). This covenant was renewed (Dt. 28). Other covenants followed, such as that with David (2 Sm. 23:5), as well as the promise of a new covenant that would reform and renew the people (Jer. 31:31–34). This new covenant was the disposition of God whereby His will was to bring about the promise of redemption of all mankind and the salvation of all through Christ, His divine Son.

In the NT the new covenant is a refined concept of both contract and conditions from that of the OT. It is spoken of twenty-six times in the NT. This covenant of the New Law is with us yet as the means of our attaining salvation (Mt. 26:28; Lk. 22:20; 1 Cor. 11:25). This new covenant surpasses the older covenants because of the priesthood of Christ being superior to that of the old, and because the blood of Christ is the most pure of any possible victim, and the "testament" of Christ's death is the greatest pledge possible since His resurrection is the surest "testament" to confirm our faith in Him and our hope of salvation. (See Salvation History.)

## Covetousness

See Avarice.

## Cowl

Cowl is the name commonly given to the hood of a religious habit. More properly, a cowl is the sleeveless garment worn by religious, covering their head and shoulders. The confusion, resulting from translation difficulties, was recognized early, and the Council of Vienna defined cowl as "a habit long and full, but without sleeves." In the years immediately following Vatican II, a "mini-cowl" or "shadow-cowl" was a part of the rear neckband of some chasuble designs, but it was both too small and too shallow to serve as a head covering.

## Creation

An act of God, creation means bringing something into existence, or causing something to exist, which had no previous existence either in itself or in a subject. This means the production of something from nothing. The beginning of the world is related in the first two chapters of Genesis; that God created out of nothing is declared in 2 Mc. 7:28. Creation in this sense does not imply a theory of evolution or transformism. The act of creation is proper to God alone. It is also a part of the creative act to sustain a thing, once created, in its created state. This is also the work of God, and is described as being linked to the role of the Son of

God in His work of Redemption. Since "all power in heaven and earth" belongs to "Christ enthroned," Christ's divinity is reflected, so to speak, in His Sonship and in the fact that He is the conserver of creation (Heb. 2:8, 10) and exercises power over it (Mt. 26:64).

There is constant study going on concerning the time element involved in the "period" of creation. (Cf. Evolution.)

The teachings of Vatican II state: "Sacred Scripture teaches that man was created 'to the image of God,' is capable of knowing and loving his Creator, and was appointed by Him as master of all earthly creatures that he might subdue them and use them to God's glory" (GS 12).

And: "He [God] planned to assemble in the holy Church all those who would believe in Christ. Already from the beginning of the world the foreshadowing of the Church took place. She was prepared for in a remarkable way throughout the history of the people of Israel and by means of the Old Covenant. Established in the present era of time, the Church was made manifest by the outpouring of the Spirit. At the end of time she will achieve her glorious fulfillment" (LG 2). So we see the Church as an extension of the creation by God and its end as the fulfillment of creation.

## Creator

This title is proper to God alone (Ps. 102:26–29) who creates, sustains, and commands the universe by His will, exercised through laws He develops.

## Credence

This piece of sanctuary furniture is a simple table large enough to hold whatever is needed for liturgical functions. On it also rests the chalice covered with the humeral veil at a solemn high Mass. The table should be to the right of the altar, as usually viewed from the celebrant's place, and covered with a white linen cloth.

## Creed

A creed is a summary of the principal truths of the Church written as a profession of faith. Quite literally creeds are prayers of belief. In the Church there are four "creeds," each an expression of the same truths that were developed historically: (1) The *Apostles' Creed* is a development of the Apostles' practice (Acts 8:37) of having persons who desired baptism profess their faith. (2) The *Nicene Creed* was put forth by the fathers of the Church at Nicaea in A.D. 325 and recorded by Eusebius of Caesarea in a letter to his people. It is popularly known as the "Creed of the Trinity." (3)

The *Athanasian Creed* is attributed to St. Athanasius in a writing of the seventh century Council of Autun where the reference states it as "the faith of the holy prelate Athanasius." However, the earliest known copy is contained in the Utrecht Psalter, a manuscript of the sixth century. (d) The *Creed of Pius IV* was published first in 1564 in the papal bull *Iniunctum nobis* and restates the truths of the Nicene Creed and the doctrines defined by the Council of Trent. Pius IX, in 1877, added a declaration of the Decrees of the Vatican Council, especially affirming the primacy of St. Peter and the infallibility of the pope. In 1910, Pope St. Pius X appended a solemn repudiation of the error of modernism, to be taken as an oath by all ecclesiastics when Church law obliges.

The Creed of the Mass is the Nicene Creed, which the people speak as a profession of faith just prior to the Prayer of the Faithful. (Cf. Liturgy.) This Creed is:

We believe in one God the Father, the Almighty, maker of heaven and earth, of all that is seen and unseen.

We believe in one Lord, Jesus Christ, the only Son of God,

Eternally begotten of the Father, God from God, Light from Light, true God from true God, begotten, not made, one in being with the Father. Through him all things were made. For us men and for our salvation he came down from heaven: by the power of the Holy Spirit he was born of the Virgin Mary, and became man.

For our sake he was crucified under Pontius Pilate; he suffered, died, and was buried. On the third day he rose again in fulfillment of the Scriptures; he ascended into heaven and is seated at the right hand of the Father.

He will come again in glory to judge the living and the dead.

And his kingdom will have no end.

We believe in the Holy Spirit, the Lord, the giver of life,

Who proceeds from the Father and the Son.

With the Father and the Son he is worshiped and glorified.

He has spoken through the prophets.

We believe in one holy catholic and apostolic Church.

We acknowledge one baptism for the forgiveness of sins.

We look for the resurrection of the dead, and the life of the world to come. Amen.

(See Liturgy.)

## Cremation

The Church generally forbids ecclesiastical burial to those who order that their bodies after death are to be burned, even if the act is not executed by the relatives. The Church opposes cremation because the practice was historically an act of disbelief in immortality by members of certain societies and others and because cremation does not show reverence to the human body, the temple of the Holy Spirit. For a grave reason, such as plague, the Church permits the destruction of bodies by fire.

The Congregation for the Doctrine of the Faith, May 8, 1963, gave to all bishops an instruction that upheld the Church's traditional teaching but modified the previous legislation. Thus, for serious reasons of a private or a public nature, provided the cremation does not show any contempt of the Church or religion or deny, question, or belittle the teachings concerning the resurrection of the body, cremation may take place. The person may receive the last rites and ecclesiastical burial; a priest may say prayers for the deceased at the crematorium; but full liturgical ceremonies may not take place at the crematorium or during the act of cremation.

## Crib

1. The name crib is given to the manger where Christ was born. The term includes the immediate area of the stable, especially as applied in the following definition.

2. This fabricated representation of the manger contains statues of the Christ Child, the Blessed Mother, and St. Joseph. Tradition and custom also include figures of the Magi, shepherds, animals, and sometimes angels. The crib is erected in churches during the Christmas season, from Christmas Eve until Epiphany. The practice arose in 1223 as a devotion founded by St. Francis of Assisi. Cribs may be erected in the home or elsewhere. In French, the term is *creche,* which is often used in English also.

## Criticism, Biblical

Criticism in general, and as applied to the Bible, may be defined as the art and science of distinguishing in a literary work, what is genuine, true, authentic, from what is added or false, and evaluating and assessing the whole work in literary terms and according to other standards. Biblical criticism is divided into three types: (1) *Textual* or *literary,* called "higher" criticism, is the fundamental type. It is study directed to the material given through a manuscript tradition, and it seeks to eliminate accidental corruptions of the text, such as errors in copying, and determine the exact wording in the original. From this point textual criticism goes on examining the text as established, determining its origin, method or style of composition, the authors, their plan, and other factors. (2) *Historical criticism* is directed to a variety of questions, examining each after the basic findings of the textual criticism, and may be concerned with the history recorded, the theology propounded, the legal or moral context. (3) The third type, *evaluative,* which is commonly grouped with the "higher," judges the value and significance of the books of the Bible, the Bible's place and importance in history, and it arrives at a synthesis of the general and particular information contained within. This third type is not only concerned with historical importance or sociological significance, but also is directed to formulating a biblical theology, a systematic analysis of the doctrine or teaching of Scripture concerning God and religion. (See Form Criticism.)

All of these types of criticism are fundamental and basic aids to exegesis, which is the exposition of the text of Scripture (cf. Exegesis; Inspiration of Scripture). In the twentieth century there has been great growth in Catholic critical work. A most important step was the publication, on Sept. 30, 1943, of the encyclical, *Divino afflante Spiritu,* which ended the era of modernism's attack upon inspiration and the history of Israel, pointed out what was dangerous doctrine, restored a "true freedom" to Catholic exegetes, and gave tribute to textual criticism. It emphasized the importance of biblical theology and encouraged a continuing study of the Bible.

Vatican II in its *Constitution on Divine Revelation* instructs: "Those who search out the intention of the sacred writers must, among other things, have regard for 'literary form.' For truth is proposed and expressed in a variety of ways, depending on whether a text is history of one kind or another, or whether its form is that of prophecy, poetry, or some other type of speech. The interpreter must investigate what meaning the sacred writer intended to express and actually expressed in particular circumstances as he used contemporary literary forms in accordance with the situation of his own time and culture. For the correct understanding of what the sacred author wanted to assert, due attention must be paid to the customary and characteristic styles of perceiving, speaking, and narrating which prevailed at the time of the

sacred writer, and to the customs men normally followed at that period in their everyday dealings with one another" (DV 12). (See Bible; Scrolls of the Dead Sea.)

**Crosier, also Crozier**

The "pastoral staff" is a symbol of office carried by the ordinary of a diocese. It is an ornamental staff, shaped like a shepherd's crook, pointed at the lower end, of varying heights, usually a little taller than the crown of the head. It is usually made of metal tubing, and the crook portion is carved (of wood, ivory, gold, or silver) or ornamented. The shaft may be separated at the middle for convenience in handling. The crook itself is symbolic of the bishop's role in keeping the members of his flock, while the pointed end is a symbol of the possible prodding needed by the spiritually lax. The bishop in his diocese always carries the crosier with the crook pointing outward. Others entitled to the crosier carry it with the crook turned inward. The popes have not used the crosier since the eleventh century.

**Cross**

The most widespread and important of the Christian symbols, the cross is for the Catholic the sign of our redemption, since it is the instrument upon which Christ sacrificed Himself (cf. Crucifix) and is also a symbol of faith. When blessed, the cross or crucifix is a sacramental. There is a wide variation of crosses derived from four basic types, the T (tau)-form, the Y-form, the X-St. Andrew's form (the cross saltire), and the Greek cross of four equal extensions, e.g., the Red Cross symbol. The shape of the cross upon which Christ died is not known for certain, but it is determined that probably it was the T-form with the upright beam *(crux immissa)* extending slightly above with room for an inscription (St. Irenaeus). The transverse beam was called the *patibulum,* and in Roman practice the one condemned carried this beam. This was probably true in the case of Christ (Jn. 19:17). It was also the practice to have a small block or seat in the middle of the upright, but in Christian art this has become a foot support. Our Lord's feet were probably not nailed together, an observation derived from the fact that all representations of the Crucifixion until the twelfth century show them nailed separately.

In the Church a variety of crosses are used: (1) the archiepiscopal cross, with two lateral beams, the top slightly shorter; (2) the hand cross, used by bishops of all Eastern rites; (3) the processional cross, a crucifix mounted on a long staff, carried at the head of a procession; (4) the pectoral cross, a small cross, jeweled and ornamented, often containing relics, worn on the chest by bishops and abbots, suspended from the neck by a chain or cord; (5) the cross *pro Ecclesia et Pontifice,* a papal decoration instituted by Leo XIII.

### Cross, Relics of the True

The wood of the cross upon which Christ was crucified was found by the Empress St. Helena about 318. It was of pine, and portions have been sent throughout the world.

### Cross, Veneration of the

1. Veneration of the Cross is the honor paid to a relic of the true cross. As a relic it may be carried under a canopy in procession, is genuflected to when on exposition, and is kissed as a mark of respect.
2. The liturgical action of the Good Friday celebration of the Lord's Passion is known as Veneration of the cross. This is the beginning of the second part of the celebration, following the general intercessions, at which time the priest, clergy, and faithful approach in a procession to where the unveiled cross is presented, and make a

simple genuflection or give some other appropriate sign of reverence, e.g., kissing the cross or corpus. During this time an antiphon is sung. (See Holy Week, Liturgy of.)

### Crown, Episcopal

The episcopal crown is a tall rounded headdress, worn as a miter by Byzantine and other Eastern bishops.

### Crown, Franciscan

Also called the *Seraphic Rosary,* the Franciscan Crown is a rosary of seven decades recited in honor of the seven joys of the Blessed Mother. It was introduced in 1422.

### Crown, Papal
See Tiara.

### Crown of Thorns

Plaited, thorny branches were impressed upon the head of Christ as a mark of ridicule before the crucifixion (Mt. 27:29–30). In all probability it was fashioned of the *Poterium spinosum,* which is found around Jerusalem and used as firewood. It has a slender spike. The form of the crown is disputed; it may have been made as a headdress (helmet), covering the entire top of the head as it is shown in the Catacomb of Proetextatus dating from the second century, or as a fillet, a rounded wreath form.

### Crowned Shrine

A shrine is a place of pilgrimage that has been approved by the Holy See. Such Church approval permits devotion at the shrine and usually indicates that a miracle has taken place there as a result of devotion by the faithful, for example, Lourdes, in France; and Fatima, in Portugal. (See Canadian Shrines.)

## Crucifix

Properly speaking, a crucifix is a cross to which there is attached, in relief, an image of the body of Christ. However, if the figure is painted, impressed, or otherwise represented, it is classed as a crucifix. A crucifix should be placed over an altar where Mass is celebrated; it is recommended that there be a crucifix in each home; and a crucifix is attached to the pendant portion of all rosaries. The skull seen upon some crucifixes is not essential to the crucifix; it is simply a symbol of Calvary ("the place of the skull"). More proper is the tablet or banner, called the "title," attached near the top of the upright beam, bearing the letters: *I N R I,* the initials of the Latin words for "Jesus of Nazareth, King of the Jews." Special indulgences are attached to the crucifix and to certain prayers recited before it. In the liturgy a crucifix upon a standard called a "processional cross," is carried into the sacred area at the time of the entrance procession.

## Crucifixion

Crucifixion is the manner of execution by which Christ suffered, died, and effected our redemption. It was a method used by Egyptians, Romans, and others and embodied a degree of ridicule and mockery in the procedure besides being a mark of degradation. The condemned was either nailed or bound to the cross, remaining there until dead. In the case of Christ, He was nailed to the cross, both feet and hands. (Cf. Calvary; Cross.)

## Cruet

A cruet is a small vessel or jug. The cruets used during the celebration of Mass to carry water and wine are usually made of glass or crystal and should have a loose-fitting stopper to keep out dust. A glass saucer should be provided for the cruets to stand in. The shallow dish into which

water is poured at the washing of the celebrant's hands may also be placed in the saucer or may be any other basin. Sometimes one cruet is marked with the letter A, the other with V, to indicate their contents (*aqua*—water; *vinum*—wine). Today, in times of concelebration, the cruets are larger, in the form of a jug or pitcher. Several cruets may be used during a celebration of the Eucharist if needed.

## Crusades

In Christian history, a crusade was a major military expedition undertaken for an exalted purpose. They were promoted and partly financed for nearly 200 years by the popes and as such were internationally organized movements. The name is derived from the cross of cloth worn on the garments and inscribed on the pennants of those who participated. Once proclaimed, they were preached as a holy undertaking. All classes of people took part: kings, knights, soldiers, religious, and peasants. As individuals they were inspired by a variety of motives: religious idealism, politics, economic reasons, adventure, or a hope of spoils.

While crusades have been undertaken for many purposes, we include here only the eight major movements. The numbering is arbitrary, for they were an almost continuous series of expeditions directed primarily at regaining the Holy Land from the Turks and Moslems. The *First Crusade* (1095 to 1101) was announced by Pope Urban II at the Council of Clermont. It set out in four units, with the Christian army entering Jerusalem in 1099. The *Second Crusade* (1145 to 1148), began with the commissioning of St. Bernard by Eugene III to preach the expedition to recapture Edessa from the Moslems. It ended in disaster with the crusaders reaching Damascus in 1148 but never getting to Edessa. The *Third Crusade* (1188 to 1192), begun by Gregory VIII and Emperor Frederick Barbarossa, Philip Augustus of France, and Richard the Lion-Hearted, effected a truce with Saladin in 1192. The *Fourth Crusade* (1202 to 1204) was undertaken at the plea of Innocent III. It ended with the leaders abandoning their purpose and being excommunicated. The *Fifth Crusade* (1212) was the so-called Children's Crusade (See Children's Crusade). The *Sixth Crusade* (1228 to 1229) undertaken by Emperor Frederick II secured possession of Jerusalem by treaty with the sultan. The *Seventh Crusade* (1248 to 1254), led by St. Louis of France and proclaimed by Innocent IV, was unsuccessful, ending with the imprisonment of Louis and his being sent home. The *Eighth*

*Crusade* (1267 to 1270), also led by St. Louis and by Charles of Anjou, ended disastrously with the death of St. Louis and the loss of the last Christian towns.

The crusades failed to save Palestine. However, they had great effects on history. They encouraged travel and commerce, broadened the outlook of Europe, fostered religion, established the conception of the papacy as the center of Christendom, developed a sense of freedom among peoples, and played a part in the development of capitalism because of expanded financial activities. The bad effects were also numerous as far as the Church was concerned. It widened the gap in the Eastern schism and permitted the entrance of heretical teachings into the West.

### Crypt

The lower, excavated portion of a church, similar to a cellar, was used for divine worship in early times. Originally it was intended for the burial of martyrs. (Cf. Confession of a Martyr.)

### Cubiculum

A cubiculum is a hewn-out burial chamber in the Roman catacombs. (Cf. Catacombs.)

### Culdees

Culdees was the name of religious men who lived a community life in Ireland and Scotland from the eighth to the eleventh centuries but were never established as a religious order.

### Cult, also Cultus

Broadly, honor to a thing or person, cult thus includes worship and veneration. As such it is usually divided into: *latria,* worship that is accorded to God alone; *hyperdulia,* which is the esteem and veneration given to the Blessed Mother; and *dulia,* which is the veneration given the saints. It also refers to the liturgy in a loose sense and is controlled strictly in the Church by the Sacred Congregation of Doctrine of the Faith. Canon law "On Divine Cultus" sets up specific laws concerning worship and veneration (cc. 1255 to 1277).

### Cult, Disparity of

A diriment impediment to marriage, disparity of cult means that a person baptized in the Catholic Church or converted to it from schism or heresy cannot validly marry a nonbaptized individual (c. 1070).

### Cura Animarum

See Care of Souls.

### Curate

A curate is one ordained to the care of souls. In French, he is the *curé* or parish priest. More commonly in the United States it refers to a member of the diocesan clergy assigned as an assistant to the pator of a parish. Now the term is supplanted by the title "Associate Pastor."

### Curia, Diocesan

Diocesan curia is the broad term for the chancery offices and the administrative offices of a diocese together with the personnel. The personnel of the curia includes: the vicar-general, the chancellor and vice-chancellor, the administrative secretary, the officials of the diocesan courts or tribunals, as, examiners, consultors (lawyers), auditors, and notaries. Vatican II states: "Priests and lay people who belong to the diocesan curia should realize that they are making a helpful contribution to the pastoral ministry of the Bishop.

"The diocesan curia should be so organized that it is an appropriate instrument for the bishop, not only for administering the diocese but also for carrying out the works of the apostolate" (CD 27).

### Curia, Roman

The term *curia* is translated from the Latin as "court," but is broader in meaning. The Roman Curia, *Curia Romana,* is not to be taken in the sense of a "legal court" or as the "court" of a king. As used in the Church it means the center of government and includes all administrative groups together with the personnel. The present function and the makeup of the Roman Curia were established by Pope St. Pius X in 1908 and were a revamping of procedures in government that are embodied in the Code of Canon Law. The Roman Curia is thus the entire body of officially organized agencies who assist the pope in the government and administration of the Church, that is, the Sacred Congregations, the Tribunals, the Offices, and Commissions. They make up in large part the "Holy See" in its popular usage (cf. Congregation). Under offices are included: the Apostolic Chancery, Apostolic Datary, Apostolic Chamber (*camera*), and the Secretariat of State. All units of the Curia exercise only delegated authority and are subject to the pope (c. 243), and they can initiate no action of importance without consulting the pope (c. 244). Vatican II declared: "In exercising supreme, full, and immediate power over the universal Church, the Roman Pontiff makes use of the departments of the Roman Curia. These, therefore, perform their duties in his name and with his authority for the good of the churches and in the service of the sacred pastors." (See Courts, Ecclesiastical.)

### Cursillo

A Christocentric movement originated in the monastery of San Honorato on the Island of Majorca, Spain, Jan. 7, 1949. Literally the term from the Spanish means "little course." As one manual points out, "The Cursillo Movement was not an accident. It began when a group of men dedicated themselves to bringing the men of their city to know Christ. It grew as they talked together, prayed together and worked together. It is the story of how God taught a group of men to work for him in an effective way that bears fruit" (Desarollo).

The objective of the movement is to change the world by remaking it according to the mind of Christ and thereby restoring to Christ the entire Christian life through a restructuring of the Christian environment. It is a unity movement, for "an isolated Christian is a paralyzed Christian." The strength of the movement lies in its cooperation with others in concerted action after a complete spiritual readying through prayer, thought, and discussion toward the implemented means of mutual salvation.

The manner in which the movement is structured and the procedure conducted are called the *method.* It is a progressive course of three-day exercises called *cursillistas* (also the name of those making the three days). Through these exercises those attending are encouraged to cooperate and work in other Church organizations and the parish. The ongoing process begins with pre–three days *(precursillo),* the three days *(cursillo),* and the post–three days *(postcursillo).*

"The manner in which the movement is conducted, is referred to as the method.. The method is the way in which the leaders go about implementing the various phases of the movement. It should be stated that method and form are only as important and valid as the quality of truth and love that go into carrying them out. Cursillistas must always be careful that they do not become worshippers of the method. To lose sight of what the Cursillo Movement is attempting to accomplish is a form of nearsightedness that is self-destructive. Therefore, it is always imperative that method is treated as a means to achieve the end result" (Blatnik).

Following upon the postcursillo is the active, intense sharing of learned leadership and the Christ-centered objective, which is making Christ relevant in the daily lives of the cursillistas.

Thus there are periodic, weekly if possible, gatherings of cursillistas in a given area. These gatherings, called *ultreyas,* are the "fourth day" when witness is given to the extent of Christ working among them. Each ultreya may consist of a theological lecture, responses by cursillistas, a discussion on some part of the Scripture, and a visit to the Eucharistic Christ with prayers.

There are thus social and spiritual recognition given to the relationship of man and God. The thought among cursillistas is that there is a God-to-man and a man-to-God relationship that brings about both the horizontal and vertical action. This is founded upon the statement of Christ: "You shall love the Lord your God with all your heart, with all your soul, with all your strength, and with all your mind; and your neighbor as yourself . . . Do this and you shall live" (Lk. 10:27–28). The active application of this to each life together with spiritual direction places the relationship with God on a one-to-one basis. An entire vocabulary has evolved and been applied to this movement, with some Spanish words, others English, but all descriptive of the details of the movement. "The Cursillo Movement can be defined as a method of linking Christians together into an apostolic Christian community to enable them to live what is fundamental to being a Christian in order to penetrate and Christianize environments" (A. Blatnik, *Your Fourth Day*). Many dioceses have appointed directors of the Cursillo Movement.

### Cursing

Cursing is the calling down of evil, either spiritual or temporal, upon one's neighbor, oneself, or any other of God's creatures. It is a sin against charity. But if the evil is seriously wished, cursing can be against religion (irreverence) or against justice, and thus it becomes more serious. It may also include scandal, e.g., if done in the presence of children. Cursing and swearing are often popularly understood as profanity, blasphemy, or abusive language.

### Cursing Psalms

Those prayers of the Psalmist in which a curse is invoked over the enemies of Israel appear in Psalms: 79:6–12; 83:10–19; 129:5–8. Also included are those like prayers directed at personal enemies who the Psalmist considered his opponents or oppressors. They are: Psalms 5:11; 6:11; 7:10; 10:15; 28:4; 31:19; 35:4; 40:15–16; 54:7; 58:7–11; 69:23–29; 139:19; 140:9–12; 141:10; 143:12.

It must be noted that these imprecations are to be considered in the context of their writing, with an awareness that the "tool of the curse" was a legitimate means of defense for the Israelites and was used in the manner of impassioned speech. (See Psalms, Book of.)

### Custodia

The name custodia is given to any temporary receptacle wherein the Blessed Sacrament is kept.

### Custom

Custom is a term meaning legalized usage that creates a right; this is also understood as unwritten law. If custom is invoked in law, it must be proved, reasonable, and continued without interruption. Forty years of regular uncontradicted usage establishes that usage as custom. In Church law, established usage gives custom the force of law only with the consent of competent ecclesiastical authority (c. 25).

### Custos

Literally a custodian, a custos is one having restricted authority, as in a religious community or a cathedral chapter.

### Cycle

A series of numbers, or letters standing for numbers, are recounted again in the same order when the cycle is completed. The solar or cycle of Dominical Letters is a series of 28 years, after which Sundays and weekdays again fall on the same days of the month. By calculation, the church calendar can be computed. (See Calendar, Church.)

### Cycle of Readings

See Readings, Cycle of.

A

B

C

D

E

F

G

H

## Dalmatic

A dalmatic is an outer liturgical vestment with short open sleeves, an opening for the head, and open at the sides from the hem to the shoulders. It reaches to or below the knees and is worn by the deacon at solemn Mass and processions. It is so named because originally it was made from Dalmatian wool. This garment has become an auxiliary or optional vestment worn by the deacon or assistants at a pontifical function.

## Dancing

This art form has come to be used in some liturgical functions as an expression of joyous or somber emotions connected to the celebration of the Eucharist. Although this has not been widely approved, there is a basis in the scriptures for such practices; for example, David danced before the Ark of the Covenant after its recovery from pagans; he "came dancing before the Lord with abandon" (2 Sm. 6:14). Also the children of Israel are reported to have danced out of joy (Ex. 15:20–21).

However, it should be pointed out that this is not yet considered a liturgical action, and when introduced the dance should be done with expertise, dignity, and solemn restraint. (See Liturgy).

## Daniel

The name Daniel is from an older form of Hebrew that means "God is my judge." Daniel was of a noble family of Juda; he was deported to Babylon where he and three of his Jewish companions received special training in the Chaldean language. Because Daniel strictly followed the dietary laws of the Hebrews, God favored him with gifts of wisdom and the ability to interpret dreams and visions. It was through this last gift that Daniel was able to interpret the dream of Nebuchadnezzar, the Babylonian King. Later when he was out of favor with the King, he was cast into a den of lions where he was miraculously saved. While in the king's favor, Daniel had been given the name of the king's god, Belteshazzar, who was considered to have the spirit of God. Daniel lived in the sixth century B.C. (See Daniel, Book of.)

## Daniel, Book of

This prophetical book of the OT is named after its traditional author, Daniel, but the actual author is not known. It was written about 165 B.C. in Palestine. The book treats of the "almighty, all-knowing God" and His rule. Its prophetic content speaks of the extension of the Messianic kingdom over all the earth, that it will be a spiritual kingdom not gained by the sword, and that it will derive from God (4:14). It also has an eschatological aspect, in that it speaks of this kingdom of God that is the Church of Christ as being a prelude to the heavenly kingdom.

The protocanonical Daniel has two parts: the first, chapters 1 to 6, relates the story of Daniel's relations with the Kings of Babylon. The second part, chapters 7 to 12, tells of Daniel's visions, which are more apocalyptic than prophetic, and tell of the coming Messianic kingdom.

In the book, the literary quality is high, showing that the writer was of the educated class. This is apparent in the notable "Song on the three youths in the fiery furnace," which begins: "Blessed are you, O Lord, the God of our fathers, praiseworthy and exalted above all forever; And blessed is your holy and glorious name, praiseworthy and exalted above all for all ages . . ." (Dn. 3:52–90). It is one of the great songs of praise of God in the Bible.

The book has been adjudged to be, especially in the second part, more apocalyptic than prophetic because in its writing the author used the characteristic form of apocalyptic writing; namely, writing with the use of a pseudonym, the author attributes the revelations to someone in the past, that is, Daniel.

## Dark Ages

The term Dark Ages is applied variously to the period from the fifth to the fifteenth century, but scholarship has repudiated this as inaccurate and nondescriptive. In Catholic circles this period is more appropriately called the "Age of Faith," for it was a time of such great men as Pope St. Gregory the Great, St. Boniface, Pope Nicholas the Great, St. Bernard, St. Francis of Assisi, and a host of others. Although this was a time when the first fervor of religious life went into decline and the barbarians upset the progress of the Church, it was also the time when the world saw the rise of monasticism, the great schools, and the richness of Gothic architecture. (See Middle Ages.)

## Dark Night of the Senses

This is a period of transition spoken of by St. John of the Cross wherein one passes from meditation to contemplation (cf. Contemplation). It is a time when the soul seeks God by pure faith and is given no assistance from the senses, when it may be difficult to make acts of prayer, when nature rebels against self-scrutiny and the effort demanded to draw closer to God. This period may be accompanied by actual suffering of the spirit, as through scruples and temptations against faith, or physical suffering in the form of sickness, permitted by God as a trial.

**Dark Night of the Soul**

This term was applied by St. John of the Cross to that period of passive purification that the soul undergoes after having attained the grace of contemplation. It is a purification, a purging before being brought into the full joy of mystical union with God. St. John of the Cross says: "For this night is drawing the spirit away from its ordinary and common sense of things, that it may draw it toward the divine sense, which is a stranger and an alien to all human ways; so much so that the soul seems to be carried out of itself." It is a final purging, since no one can stand before or penetrate the "deep things of God" (1 Cor. 2:10), effected while one merits and grows in charity. (The alternative is purgatory, which is purification without merit, and the way of sanctity is to be purified in this passive manner before death instead of after.) St. John of the Cross further defines it: "The dark night is a certain inflowing of God into the soul which cleanses it of its ignorances and imperfections, habitual, natural and spiritual" (Bk. II, ch. 5). It is called a suffering of the soul in the sense that there is intense yearning for God while experiencing a desolation or feeling of being abandoned by God. It is a transitory state during contemplation, but once undergone it may return.

**Datary, Apostolic**

See Apostolic Datary; Commissions, Ecclesiastical.

**David**

The name from the Hebrew means "beloved," and is that of the second and greatest King of the Israelites. His ancestry places him as an Ephrathite of Bethlehem in Juda, the youngest son of Jesse (cf. 1 Sm. 16:10–13). He ascended to the throne of Israel by becoming the armor bearer of King Saul. His call to such a station was attributed to his being both an excellent harpist (1 Sm. 16:14–23) and the young boy who slew the giant Goliath (1 Sm.

17:1–51). He was praised in song: "Saul has slain his thousands, and David his ten thousands" (1 Sm. 18:7).

After the death of Saul in the battle with the Philistines at Mount Gilboa, David, who had won a large following among the many tribes, had himself proclaimed King. He went on to capture Jerusalem (2 Sm. 5, 6) and transformed the tribes into a nation with unity and an organized state. The city of Jerusalem became "David's City."

King David was the founder of the independent kingdom of Israel, and his reign was the measure of excellence of the later kings of the Israelite nation. He also was brought into the Messianic tradition, as the prophecies were to proclaim (Is. 11:1–10; Jer. 23:5; Mt. 9:27). He was also to be rightly declared a great poet (cf. 2 Sm. 1:19–27) and the author of a great number of the Psalms, but probably much fewer than the seventy-three usually attributed to him. He died about the year 973 B.C., saddened by the revolt begun by his sons, although he died repentant of his sins and knew he had served God through obedience to His law. The Star of David, the six-pointed star formed by two triangles superimposed, became the symbol of the Hebrew people and appears on the national flag of Israel today. (See Psalms, Book of.)

**Day of Atonement**

This is the Hebrew feast called Yom Kippur. It is the highest holy day in the Jewish calendar and occurs 10 days after Rosh Hashana. It is observed with a fast from the evening of the ninth of Tishri to the evening of the tenth. This is a feast of expiation, of solemn rest during which time all work is forbidden under the threat of being cut off from the chosen people of God. The solemnity is mentioned and explained in Lv. 23:27–32. In general this feast stresses repentance and reconciliation with God.

**Day Hours**

Day Hours are the times, or parts, arranged in sequence in the Divine Office, except the morning hours or matins. (Cf. Divine Office; Breviary.)

**Day of Indiction**

Day of Indiction is the title of that day on which the liturgical year begins in the Byzantine calendar, Sept. 1. This contrasts with the Roman Calendar, which starts on the first Sunday of Advent, while the Byzantine season of Advent begins on Dec. 10. (See Menology.)

## Day of the Lord

Also called Day of Yahweh, Day of the Lord is an oft-repeated term in the Bible and is referred to as "that day" (*dies illa*) (Is. 2:11; Mt. 7:22; Lk. 10:12), and "the day of the Lord" (Acts 2:20). It is that day when the judgment of God will come upon all men and the ungodly will meet with their destruction in justice. It is the day of the parousia, the second coming of Christ (1 Thes. 4:13–17; 1 Cor. 1:8), the culmination of all living when the Lord will claim those of His own (Rv. 20:11–15), and when the sin of men will end (1 Thes. 4:14–18). This day is in reality many years hence; its exact date is unknown; it transcends time and becomes the historic supratemporal period of God's rule in the salvation history of mankind (Cf. 2 Pt. 3:8). (See Salvation History.)

## Days of Prayer

These are specially designated days when prayers for particular needs are to be celebrated with assigned readings for the Celebration of the Eucharist. The Conference of Bishops in November, 1971 decreed "that there be observed in the dioceses of the United States, at times to be designated by the local Ordinary in consultation with the diocesan liturgical commission, days or periods of prayer for the fruits of the earth, prayer for human rights and equality, prayer for world justice and peace, and penitential observance outside Lent. This is in addition to observances customary on certain civic occasions such as Independence Day, Labor Day, and Thanksgiving Day, for which either proper text or texts of the *Sacramentary* and *Lectionary* for Mass are provided.

"The Bishops' Committee on the Liturgy presented the above decision in these terms: the expression of such days or periods of prayer should be left as general as possible, so that the time, length, occasion, and more specific intentions of prayer should be determined locally rather than nationally. In this way no arbitrary rule is imposed until it becomes evident that a pattern of such supplications is emerging from practice."

## De Condigno

From the Latin, meaning "out of worthiness" de condigno may refer to merit where the reward is in justice, or the action is equal to the reward; or the reward may be in fidelity, beyond what the action deserves.

## De Congruo

From the Latin, meaning "out of suitability," de congruo is a term used for merit where no reward is due, but where a reward would be appropriate.

## De Profundis

The Latin words that translate the opening of Psalm 129 have long been the title of this Psalm, which begins:

Out of the depths I cry to you O Lord,
Lord hear my voice!
Let your ears be attentive to my voice in supplication.

It is in reality a prayer for mercy and pardon and is one of the songs of Ascent. (See Songs of Ascents.)

## Deacon

Literally, a "servant," the diaconate is the first of the major orders of holy orders, but the lowest in the hierarchical order of the Church. In the Sacrament of Holy Orders the diaconate is received prior to ordination to the priesthood; the bishop confers the stole and dalmatic and says the words, "Receive the power of reading the gospel in the Church of God, both for the living and the dead, in the name of the Lord." The duties of the deacon are: assisting the celebrant of Mass, preaching, administering Holy Communion, and baptism with permission.

From apostolic times the diaconate has had a clearly outstanding position among the ministries of the Church. St. Paul included the deacons in his greetings (Phil. 1:1), and he states the qualities that a good deacon should possess: "In the same way, deacons must be serious, straightforward, and truthful. They may not overindulge in drink or give in to greed. They must hold fast to the divinely revealed faith with a clear conscience. They should be put on probation first; then, if there is nothing against them, they may serve as deacons" (1 Tm. 3:8–11). Their role, as we read in Acts 6:1, was to serve the needs of the community, and they also assisted in the preaching of the word and instructing and baptizing converts (Acts 6:1–7; 8:40).

"Later, when the early writers of the Church acclaim the dignity of deacons, they do not fail to extol also the spiritual qualities and virtues that are required for the performance of that ministry, namely, fidelity to Christ, moral integrity, and obedience to the bishop" (Study Text 3).

Vatican II declares: "It is the duty of the deacon, to the extent that he has been authorized by competent authority, to administer baptism solemnly, to be custodian and dispenser of the

Eucharist, to assist at and bless marriages in the name of the Church, to bring Viaticum to the dying, to read the sacred Scripture to people, to instruct and exhort the people, to preside at the worship and prayer of the faithful, to administer sacramentals, and to officiate at funeral and burial services" (LG 29). (See Permanent Deacon; Ministries.)

### Deaconess

The title deaconess was given to women in the first centuries, who were appointed to assist the minister and perform other worthy duties, such as caring for the sick. The practice of having women deacons was discontinued after the Council of Nicaea (325). St. Paul, however, did not exclude women from serving as deacons (1 Tm. 3:12), but the Church in this time does not propose the service of women in holy orders.

### Deacons, First Seven

In the earliest days of the Church the Apostles needed special assistants. They asked that men be selected from the community of the disciples. "Following this they selected Stephen, a man filled with faith and the Holy Spirit; Philip, Prochoros, Nicanor, Timon, Parmenas, and Nicholaus of Antioch, who had been a convert to Judaism. They presented these men to the apostles, who first prayed over them and then imposed hands on them" (Acts 6:4–6). Thus, the seven became the first deacons and served both the Apostles and the community, and Stephen became the first martyr (Acts 6:8–15; 7:1–60).

### Dead, Mass For

See Requiem; Mass, Funeral.

### Dead Sea, Scrolls of the

See Scrolls of the Dead Sea.

### Dean

The dean is a minor official who presides over a deanery, called a *vicar forane*. He is appointed by the bishop and may be removed by him. His office includes these activities: to see that the clergy observe canonical and liturgical laws and follow instructions of the bishop, to summon deanery conferences and preside over them, and to make a yearly report to the bishop. However, he may have other duties. Within the deanery he has precedence over the other priests. In today's Church, the title and office of the dean have been largely

replaced by the vicariate or district divisions that are represented on the Priests' Council of the diocese.

### Deanery

A district of a diocese, usually a territorial division, is a deanery. A diocese must be divided into deaneries by canon law (c. 217).

### Death

In the OT the death of a person was the going out of his "vital force," hence the word for death in Hebrew meant "weak" (cf. 1 Kgs. 17:21). As the ideas of Plato entered the Hebrew thought and literature, the concept of body and soul became more evident (cf. Wis. 3:1). In the NT, which borrowed heavily from the OT, there was still the traditional thought that death was a weakening whereby no one could follow the religious requirements (cf. Ps. 30:10–13; Is. 38:18–20).

However, in the NT there was a definite establishment of the idea that the principle of life is the spirit, the soul. Death is the giving up of the spirit (Mt. 27:50; Acts 7:59). The full realization of this principle is spoken of by St. James (Jas. 2:26) and by Matthew (10:28).

Also in the NT death is spoken of as "spiritual death," probably resulting from the ancient Jewish concept that death was evil and a punishment for personal sins (cf. Prv. 1:12). Death is also spoken of as a result of disbelief and sin or as St. James says, "Once passion has conceived, it gives birth to sin, and when sin reaches maturity it begets death" (1:15).

And while we believe that in baptism we pass from a state of sin to one of grace, and the one who believes dies to sin (Rom. 6:2–11), we are consoled by the many biblical assurances that we will rise with Christ to a new life in God the Father who prepared our reward from all ages (Col. 2:20; 3:1–11).

### Deborah, Song of

The first woman named Deborah mentioned in the Bible was the servant of Rebecca, the wife of Isaac and mother of Esau and Jacob (Gn. 24:59; 35:8). But the Song of Deborah was that of a prophetess of the Israelite tribes who lived about 1125 B.C. Because of her noble work she is called "Mother of Israel" (Jgs. 5:7). She inspired the armies of the Israelites to victory over the army of Sisera and the Canaanite king, Jabin. This inspiration is recorded in the poem or song, which is one of the earliest preserved pieces of Jewish literature, sometimes called the Canticle of Deborah. It makes up the entire fifth chapter of the Book of Judges, and begins: "On that day Deborah [and Barak, son of Abinoam] sang this song: Of chiefs who took the lead in Israel, of noble deeds by the people who bless the Lord, hear, O kings! Give ear, O princes! I to the Lord will sing my song, my hymn to the Lord, the God of Israel . . ." (5:1–3). (See Judges, Book of.)

## Decade

A decade is a section of the Rosary, which consists of one Our Father, ten Hail Marys, and one Glory be to the Father. These prayers are recited while meditating on one mystery. The ten corresponding beads of the section are also called a decade. (See Rosary.)

## Decalogue

A Greek word meaning generally "ten words," decalogue is sometimes applied as a title to the Ten Commandments of God. (See Commandments of God.)

## Declaration

A formal and solemn statement that presents a new teaching or a new interpretation of an earlier policy is called a declaration, e.g., the Declaration of Independence by the American colonies.

In Church procedure a declaration is that document which offers a new interpretation of an existing law, or presents a stand upon a specific subject whereby in-depth understanding and additional clarification are given. Thus, the documents of Vatican II contain three declarations, those on religious freedom, non-Christian religions, and Christian education. (See Vatican II.)

## Decorations, Pontifical

Pontifical decorations are honors conferred by the Holy See, usually on laymen, because of outstanding service to the Church, the Holy See, or the welfare of society. They are titles of nobility, varying from prince to baron inclusive, six orders of knighthood, and medals (*Benemerenti* and others), and crosses (*Pro Ecclesia et Pontifice*). (See Knights, Papal.)

## Decree

A decree is a decision or a regulation for a community or place issued by Church authority. Decrees are documents issued by a Sacred Congregation for a specific purpose. They are: (1) *general*, if applicable to the entire Church; (2) *particular*, if directed to only a part of the Church. The decrees are generally on questions of faith and morals, and those of the pope or a general council are binding on all the Church, whereas particular decrees bind those to whom they are directed. (cf. Rescript). Of the documents of the Second Vatican Council there were nine decrees: on the instruments of social communication, on ecumenism, on Eastern Catholic Churches, on the bishops' pastoral office in the Church, on priestly formation, on the appropriate renewal of the religious life, on the apostolate of the laity, on the ministry and life of priests, and on the Church's missionary activity. (See Vatican Council II.)

## Decretals

Decretals were decisions handed down by the popes, generally on questions of discipline, which preceded the Code of Canon Law. These were frequently in the form of letters and were also called "constitutions." (See Canon Law.)

## Decretals, False

A collection of papal letters and conciliar canons gathered in the ninth century in Gaul are known as the false decretals. The majority were forged and, while they were for a time considered genuine, they were chiefly issued as an attack on the authority of the pope. They were also called "Decretals of Pseudo-Isidore" (see Pseudo-Isidore). They were attributed to popes from St. Clement (88 to 97) to Gregory II (715 to 731) and supported the autonomy and rights of bishops over the Holy See and Councils. All were repudiated in 1628.

## Decretist

The name decretist was formerly given to one versed in canon law.

## Decretum Gratiani

This writing by Gratian (d. 1160), a professor of law in Bologna, was published in 1140. These

*Decrees of Gratian,* which mark the end of the first period in the history of canonical legislation, became the common text upon which canonists based their commentaries.

### Dedication of a Church

The setting apart of a Church building for divine worship is the dedication. This is often confused with the more solemn consecration. However, each public and semipublic oratory is to be dedicated by the blessing of the bishop or a priest. The church may be dedicated by consecration, but this must be performed by a bishop, and the anniversary of consecration is observed by a feast of the Church calendar if the church is especially dedicated.

### Defect, Irregularity of

No one may be ordained a priest unless the state of irregularity is done away with or dispensed (c. 984). This refers to: illegitimates; those with bodily defects; bigamists; the infamous; judges who have pronounced a death sentence; executioners and all who are voluntary and immediate assistants in carrying out a death penalty. Epileptics, the insane, and the diabolically possessed may not be ordained even if cured or exorcised. (Cf. Irregularity, Ecclesiastical.)

### Defender of the Bond

The bishop of every diocese appoints a priest (in Latin, *Defensor vinculi*) to serve as defender of the marriage bond (tie) and of sacred ordination. The one appointed must be a priest of good standing, learned in canon law, and prudent and just. His duties are to act in all cases of solemn trial or simple process where the bond or contract of marriage is challenged or parties to a marriage seek a dispensation. He sees to it that the law is properly applied, offers reasonable objections, and when a court makes a declaration of nullity in the first instance he must appeal to a higher court (c. 1968 to 1969).

### Defender of the Faith

This title was conferred on King Henry VIII of England by Pope Leo X in 1521 for the king's writing in defense of the sacraments and the Sacrifice of the Mass against Luther. It is still carried as an official title by the sovereigns of England and appears on British coins. A similar title was given to James V of Scotland by Pope Paul III.

### Defensor Ecclesiae

This was the Latin title of one appointed by a ruler in the early days of the Church to take care of the temporal affairs of the Church.

### Defensor Matrimonii

See Defender of the Bond.

### Definition, Papal

Papal definition is a solemn and irrevocable decision, from which there is no appeal (c. 1880), rendered by the pope as the supreme head of the Church. When this directly concerns faith or morals and is made by the pope as universal teacher of the Church *(ex cathedra)* or by an ecumenical council acting with the pope's consent and sanction, it is infallible and binds all the faithful. As such this is not a definition, or decision as a sentence of law, but a statement of truth that always existed in the deposit of faith. For example, when Pope Pius XII declared the Assumption of the Blessed Virgin as a dogma of the Church in 1950, he proclaimed: "By the authority of Our Lord Jesus Christ, of the Blessed Apostles Peter and Paul, and by Our own authority, we declare and define as a truth revealed by God: that when the course of her mortal life was completed, Mary, the Immaculate Mother of God, ever a Virgin, was taken up, body and soul, into heavenly glory" (cf. Infallibility).

### Definitors

Definitors are those who form the governing council of a religious order, each having a vote equal to that of the general or provincial superior.

### Degradation

The most serious canonically vindictive penalty (c. 2305) that the Church can inflict on a cleric is degradation. It directs that the cleric: (1) be deposed (see Deposition); (2) suffer the loss of the right to wear ecclesiastical garb; (3) be reduced to the lay state; however, he is bound by celibacy and the obligation to recite the Divine Office. Its infliction is governed most rigidly by canon law.

### Degrees, Academic

According to canon law, no degree conferred by a school of higher learning has canonical value unless by apostolic faculty. Examples of such schools are the Catholic University of America and the Gregorian University of Rome, (c. 1377 to 1378). Persons with a doctorate or licentiate are preferred when ecclesiastical appointments are made.

## Deipara

This Latin translation of the Greek word *Theotokos,* which means "God bearing," was conferred as a title on the Blessed Mother by decision of the council of Ephesus in A.D. 431.

## Deisis

1. A prayer of petition in the Byzantine liturgy.
2. A representation in art of our Lord as judge, accompanied by the Blessed Mother and St. John the Baptist.

## Deism

This philosophical system, developed in the seventeenth and eighteenth centuries, was both naturalistic and rationalistic. It is popularly called "freethinking." It denies essentially the providence of God and destroys the personal relationship between God the Creator and man as creature, between Christ as Redeemer and man redeemed.

The tenets of deism are primarily four, and they are representative of the four major groupings of freethinkers: (1) Deists deny revelation, for they maintain, since God is known through created works, there is therefore no need for a revealing of God to man. (2) A denial of a future life or hereafter is asserted since God made only the material world and set in motion its forces, and thereafter abandoned it. (3) The denial of God's providence is implicit, for it is maintained that God does not care about or manifest any concern over man's duties, free moral acts, or his rights as a human person. (4) The deists also deny the immanence of God, thus declaring that God has no further concern for the universe and its creatures.

Deism is further divided into two broad groupings, the "critical" deists attack the foundations and principles of Christianity; the "constructive" deists make an effort to theorize about how God operates and how He appears in the universe.

Deism is essentially a self-destructive philosophy for it can go nowhere in the Christian context. We know that the Church is immanent in the society of man, that historically and by tradition God has exercised a deep concern for His creatures, and that Christ entered into human history and through the Church becomes identified with the history of salvation. As Vatican II declares: "In order to be able to offer all of them (the people of God) the mystery of salvation and the life brought by God, the Church must become part of all these groups for the same motive which led Christ to bind' Himself, in virtue of His Incarnation, to the definite social and cultural conditions of those human beings among whom He dwelt" (AG 10).

## Delator

A delator was one who denounced early Christians to the pagan authorities, thereby causing their seizure and possible martyrdom.

## Delegate, Apostolic

See Apostolic Delegate.

## Delegation

That grant by one who has ordinary power or jurisdiction, that is, the jurisdiction conferred by reason of his appointment to an office, (bishop, etc.) is known as delegation. This power can be delegated, totally or in part, to others unless restricted by law (c. 199). One delegated by the Holy See to an office of jurisdiction can subdelegate another person, either for a simple act or habitual performance, unless restricted by law. That authority delegated by an office inferior to the Holy See may be subdelegated, but one having subdelegated power may not subdelegate again except when this is expressly granted by law.

## Deluge

The flood, the rain of waters for 40 days visited upon the earth by act of God, is narrated in Genesis (6:5 to 8:14). The idea of a worldwide flood covering the entire earth has been abandoned by all scholars. The reasons for this are that a series of unheard-of miracles would have been required, e.g., bringing animals from all over the earth, housing them, and getting them accustomed to a change of climate. A new and accepted theory is that the flood was of mixed or relative universality. Thus, only a limited portion of the earth's surface was inundated, but all mankind perished except those in the ark of Noah since the race of humans had not spread beyond this region. The purpose of the flood was twofold: (1) it was a punishment of the wicked after they had failed to repent; (2) it was a means of freeing the "sons of God" from the corruption surrounding them and providing them the opportunity to bring up a new generation, the ancestors of the Chosen People, in virtue, which was the covenant of God with Noah. The ark was commonly held by early fathers of the Church, from apostolic times (1 Pt. 3:20), to be a type, a figure of the Church. As the ark saved Noah and his family by divine providence, so the Church is the divinely appointed means of mankind's salvation. In the deluge God showed an interest in and a direct action for the development of the religious concerns of mankind (cf. 1 Pt. 3:18–21) and their salvation through baptism and the Church Christ founded.

## Demiurge

This term was first introduced by Plato in the *Timaeus* to signify the intermediate creator of the material universe. It was borrowed by several heresies, notably Gnosticism, to refer to an imperfect God or an emanation from God, and by others as the personification of evil.

## Demon

Demon is a term for devil, used in the NT (cf. Devil and the Evil Spirits).

## Demoniac

Demoniac is the term for a person possessed by a demon, a devil, or evil spirit. Instances are narrated in the Gospels (Mk. 5:1–20; 9:14–32; Lk. 8:26–39) and demonstrate the power of Christ over the demons. (Cf. Exorcism.)

## Denunciation

In canonical usage, denunciation is the report made of wrongdoing on the part of another. This is only for serious cause, such as when the crime is in self-defense or for the public welfare. It should be made in writing, signed, and sent or read to the ordinary, chancellor, or dean.

## Deposing Power, Papal

Papal deposing power is the right by which the pontiff, out of spiritual necessity, releases from allegiance the subjects of a ruler who is flagrantly in opposition to religion, morality, and the pursuit of Christian life. Although the right exists, it has not been exercised since the seventeenth century.

## Deposit of the Faith

This comprises the body of teachings and commands given to the Apostles and to their successors, the bishops, which are to be retained, taught, and offered to all mankind. The deposit is the sum of revelation and tradition and is entrusted to the Church that Christ founded and its *magisterium,* or teaching and defining role. It is

attested to in Scripture (Jn. 16:13) that through the illuminating action of the Holy Spirit the Church will grow and is recognized by the Apostles (1 Tm. 6:20) as having been "committed" to them.

Vatican Council I declares: "Faith's doctrines which God has revealed are not put before us as some philosophical discovery to be developed by human ingenuity but as a divine trust (*depositum*) handed over to the Spouse of Christ for her faithful safeguarding and infallible exposition (Vat. Sess. III, cap. 4, Dz. 1800). (Cf. Magisterium of the Church.)

Vatican II states: "The Roman Pontiff and the bishops, in view of their office and of the importance of the matter, strive painstakingly and by appropriate means to inquire properly into that revelation and to give apt expression to its contents. But they do not allow that there could be any new public revelation pertaining to the divine deposit of faith" (LG 25). (See Basic Teachings for Catholic Religious Education.)

## Deposition

Deposition is a vindictive penalty of the Church. By it (c. 2303) a cleric is suspended from office, deprived of all offices, benefices, dignities, and functions in the Church, and forbidden to acquire these in the future. The cleric is not reduced to the lay state but retains his clerical privileges and by the law is bound to celibacy and the recitation of the Breviary. The reasons for imposing deposition must be serious and are governed by canon law.

## Deposition, Bull of

This is the name of the bull of St. Pius V, issued Apr. 27, 1570, wherein Queen Elizabeth of England was named a tyrant and heretic and declared anathema. The proper title, taken from its opening words, is *Regnans in excelsis.*

## Deposition, Day of

The anniversary day of the burial of a saint is often named the day of deposition.

## Desecration of Churches

Desecration is the defilement, also called violation, of a blessed or consecrated church by which the blessing or consecration is lost, not totally as in execration, but partially. The church must be reconciled according to the Roman Ritual before it can be again used for divine services. The church is defiled by homicide committed within, the sinful and serious shedding of blood, use of the church for sinful purposes, burial within the church of one excommunicated by sentence.

## Desire, Baptism of

In its proper meaning, this consists of an act of perfect contrition or perfect love, and the simultaneous desire for baptism. It does not imprint an indelible character on the soul, and the obligation to receive baptism by water remains. (Cf. Baptism, Sacrament of.)

While the tradition of the Church has acknowledged that there is a "kind of anticipation" of sacramental grace, this arises primarily from the action of God to save all people even those outside of the boundaries of Church membership as we understand them. Vatican II speaks of this action of God toward all: "Finally, those who have not yet received the gospel are related in various ways to the People of God. In the first place there is the people to whom the covenants and the promises were given and from whom Christ was born according to the flesh (cf. Rom. 9:4–5). On account of their fathers, this people remains most dear to God, for God does not repent of the gifts He makes nor of the calls He issues (cf. Rom. 11:28–29).

"But the plan of salvation also includes those who acknowledge the Creator. In the first place among these there are the Moslems, who, professing to hold the faith of Abraham, along with us adore the one and merciful God, who on the last day will judge mankind. Nor is God Himself far distant from those who in shadows and images seek the unknown God, for it is He who gives to all men life and breath and every other gift (cf. Acts 17:25–28), and who as Savior wills that all men be saved (cf. 1 Tm. 2:4).

"Those also can attain to everlasting salvation who through no fault of their own do not know the gospel of Christ or His Church, yet sincerely seek God and, moved by grace, strive by their deeds to do His will as it is known to them through the dictates of conscience" (LG 16).

## Despair

Despair is the deliberate, willful distrust of God's goodness, fidelity, and power, or the abandoning of all hope of salvation and the means necessary to obtain it. As such it is a grave sin against hope. It is not to be confused with anxiety, fear, or defection, which arise often from bodily ills and are not sins against hope even though they cause a temporary abandonment of "seeking after God."

Vatican II declares: "But rather often men, deceived by the Evil One, have become caught up in futile reasoning and have exchanged the truth of God for a lie, serving the creature rather than the Creator (cf. Rom. 1:21–25). Or some there are who, living and dying in a world without God, are subject to utter hopelessness" (LG 16). Despair is a sin against the mercy of God, against the Holy Spirit, and the love that Christ manifests to all through His Church. (See Hope.)

## Detachment

As a practice of the ascetical life of any Christian, detachment means a balance and proportion of attitude, in actual possession and desire for, the natural goods of the world, including honors, fame, wealth, and degrees of success. It is an exercise toward perfection arising from the three theological virtues of faith, hope, and charity and the three counsels of poverty, chastity, and obedience. It is a recognition that the things of the material world are not bad in themselves but are "lesser goods" of relative unimportance in the light of perfection or salvation. Spiritual goods are of primary importance, involved in the love of God for Himself and in the abandonment to Him and His will in regard to us. Through detachment we overcome cupidity, the concupiscence of the eyes, the desire for riches, and forgetfulness of the poor, which distract us from God. We learn to follow Christ "in spirit" even when having possessions. The basis for detachment can be found in Matthew 5:3 (cf. Mt. 6:19–33), and in the words of St. Paul we read of the spirit required: "Those who weep should live as though they were not weeping, and those who rejoice as though they were not rejoicing; buyers should conduct themselves as though they owned nothing, and those who make use of the world as though they were not using it, for the world as we know it is passing away" (1 Cor. 7:30–31). Through the practice of detachment we are able to give alms ungrudgingly and be humble in acceptance of honors. More essentially it enables us to desire God, the goods of heaven, and to rely upon God as our means of attaining salvation. Through this we can concentrate on our destiny and be recollected in God (cf. Recollection).

## Determinism

Determinism is the doctrine that every fact or effect in the universe is guided or caused entirely by law or necessity. The name was applied to the doctrine of Hobbes (d. 1679), which stated that the physical universe and human history are dependent on and conditioned by their causes. It excludes free will. Leibnitz (d. 1716), a later determinist, denied the "liberty of indifference," maintaining that the mind is compelled by the motive not realized through any deliberation.

In the denial of both man's will and all moral responsibility, determinism makes the human person a robot, or one who is good only through acquired knowledge, or evil only because of ignorance.

### Detraction

Usually associated with calumny, both detraction and calumny are unjust injuries to the good name of another. Detraction is committed by revealing the true faults of our neighbor, calumny by imputing false defects. Both include the sinful judging and censuring of one's neighbor and arise in resentment and envy. A detractor assumes that which belongs to God alone as judge (cf. Jb. 4:17). Detraction and calumny are serious sins against justice. Also listening to detraction and calumny is sinful if in so listening one is induced to commit either, if the one listening takes joy or satisfaction from the revealed defect, and if the one listening does not stop the defamation when he can do so. The sins of detraction and calumny demand restitution or repair to the neighbor's reputation and reparation of material loss suffered therefrom in so far as this was foreseen. (See Calumny; Contumely.)

### Deuterocanonical Books

These books, some of the OT and some of the NT, are all genuine and inspired, but their full canonical status was not universally acknowledged for some time. This hesitancy in acknowledgment resulted from many circumstances such as the correlating of tradition regarding them, the difficulty in communication and transmission, and the necessity of eliminating possible errors from copying the originals. Those of the OT are: Books of Tobias, Judith, Wisdom, Ecclesiasticus, Baruch, 1 and 2 Maccabees, parts of Esther, parts of Daniel (3:24–90 and 13, 14). Those of the NT are: Hebrews, James, Jude, 2 Peter, 2 and 3 John, and the Book of Revelation. Protestants do not accept the OT books or portions as scriptural (cf. Canon of the Scripture; Bible).

### Deuteronomy, Book of

This fifth book of the Bible is the last of the five books of which the Jewish *Torah*, the Law, is made up; the last book of the Pentateuch. The name means literally "a second law." In content it is "a homiletic exposition of law in an historical setting," given with the persuasion of oratory. Christian tradition holds that Moses is the author. Doctrinally, Deuteronomy stresses practical theology, a firm fidelity to God, His love for the Chosen People, and the gratitude to be given to God.

In the early Church this book was called "repetition of the law" or "Second legislation," not because it offered a new law, but because it contained most of what was treated in earlier books of the Pentateuch. It was authored by several members of the levitical school and was written probably within the years 740 to 530 B.C. In composition the book closely recalls the spirit of Moses himself, and thus many thought that he had written the text.

Its purpose was to teach the Israelites how to live in the Promised Land after the reform of Josiah. Thus, there is an appeal for a more pure worship of God and the exhortation to return to the love of God (Dt. 6:5; 11:1; 19:9). It might be said that the appeal to the love of God was the center of its teaching along with the blessing of Moses (Dt. 33), and the recording of the death of the great prophet. (See Bible; Pentateuch.)

### Development of Doctrine

Since the death of the last Apostle, revealed truth is complete and is not added to or increased. However, revealed truth is unfolded gradually, in a sense becoming more fully and explicitly understood. Only by stages is it penetrated to the full depth of its meaning. The truth made known by our Lord and the Apostles was received by the Church, made clearer in the following centuries, and, if demanded because of some obscurity, the truth was made explicit by definition. This continues, not as different doctrine or new revelation, but as an enlargement toward deeper understanding of what is known. There is also a developing tradition that goes on throughout the Church, for while the message and mission of Christ are clear and complete for salvation, there is the constant adaptation of teachings to the needs of people within their culture. Thus, we have the social doctrine of the Church, the means of presentation of doctrine in keeping with new developments and procedures, and the integral life of Church members in the community through service and new ministries. (See Tradition.)

### Development, Human

See Campaign for Human Development.

## Development of Peoples

In the social teachings of the Church and particularly as exemplified by the great encyclicals *(Rerum Novarum,* 1891; *Quadregesimo Anno,* 1931; *Mater et Magistra,* 1961; *Pacem in Terris,* 1963; and *Populorum Progressio,* 1967), there has been special emphasis on the free society necessary for people and the social structure of that society for man to attain his salvation. This concerns the human rights of individuals, the needs of the poor, and the conditions of peace and justice that are required for the full reception of and the full response to the gospel message.

Vatican II in its *Pastoral Constitution on the Church in the Modern World (Gaudium et Spes),* devoted much thought to this area of teaching regarding the development of peoples. Excerpts point this out:

"Since there are so many people in this world afflicted with hunger, this sacred Council urges all, both individuals and governments to remember the saying of the Fathers: 'Feed the man dying of hunger, because if you have not fed him you have killed him.' According to their ability, let all individuals and governments undertake a genuine sharing of their goods. Let them use these goods especially to provide individuals and nations with the means for helping and developing themselves" (GS 69).

"The Development of any nation depends on human and financial assistance. Through education and professional formation, the citizens of each nation should be prepared to shoulder the various offices of economic and social life. Such preparation needs the help of foreign experts. When they render assistance, these experts should do so not in lordly fashion, but as helpers and co-workers.

"The developing nations will be unable to procure the necessary material assistance unless the practices of the modern business world undergo a profound change. Additional help should be offered by advanced nations, in the form of either grants or investments. These offers should be made generously and without avarice. They should be accepted honorably" (GS 85).

## Devil and the Evil Spirits

Christ opposes the devil, Satan, and the evil spirits, with the Spirit of God. The name is applied to the chief of the fallen angels, Beelzebub (also Lucifer) (Mt. 12:24), and to those other angels who followed his leadership in rebellion against God. Christ has power over the devil and evil spirits and can free souls and bodies from their domination (Mk. 5:1-20), and He empowered the Apostles to drive out devils. The devils, like the angels, are pure spiritual beings who have lost none of their powers except supernatural grace. It is an article of faith that the fall of man came about because of Satan and that the devils continue to tempt and persecute mankind (1 Pt. 5:8). Vatican II states: "Although he was made by God in a state of holiness, from the very dawn of history man abused his liberty, at the urging of personified Evil. Man set himself against God and sought to find fulfillment apart from God. Although he knew God, he did not glorify Him as God, but his senseless mind was darkened and he served the creature rather than the Creator" (GS 13).

The name *devil* comes from the Latin through the Greek language, and means "one who throws something against." But the devil is one who "acuses falsely" or "judges" (Lk. 10:19). (Cf. Angel; Diabolical Possession.)

## Devil's Advocate

Devil's Advocate is the traditional name of the "Promoter of the Faith" whose duty it is, in the cause of canonization, to raise objections and possible difficulties against approval of the cause. The office was instituted early in the eleventh century and is attached to the Congregation of Rites. The task is much like that of a prosecuting attorney, examining the evidence in favor of canonization for adverse arguments, and in so doing helping the Church to arrive at final certainty. (Cf. Canonization.)

## Devolution

1. In canon law devolution is an appeal or recourse for judgment to a higher authority when a previous appeal does not suspend or alter the effect of a decision by a superior.

2. This may also refer to the filling of a vacant benefice by devolution on the part of the Holy See when the ordinary has not acted to fill it by appointment after six months (c. 1432).

## Devotion

1. Devotion is prayer or a formula of pious practices devoted to the veneration of a particular saint, or in honor of the Trinity, the Sacred Heart, or to the Blessed Mother under one of her titles, made in common or in private.

2. Spiritual devotion is the sensible response or consolation felt in the service of God. While such feelings of joy have advantages, such as making it

easier to pray or be recollected, they have certain dangers that prompt one to be proud of accomplishment in spiritual things, to expect to be rewarded for every prayer, and to be presumptuous. The opposite of this spiritual devotion is aridity.

3. Devotion is the voluntary giving of oneself to the service of God; assuming freely a life of devotion.

(See Paraliturgical Actions.)

## Diabolic Possession

The possession of a human person by the spirit of a devil is called diabolic possession. Such possession by an evil spirit is the preternatural control of the imagination, the sensibilities, and the physical abilities of the human person. This possession cannot affect the soul of the human person because there is not a personal union nor a taking over of the soul of the person. The reasons for such possessions are not explained by the parapsychological sciences or by rationalistic approaches to some form of "spiritism."

In the OT it is recorded that an evil spirit tormented King Saul (1 Sm. 16:14), but this was permitted by God. The demon Asmodeus also influenced Sarah in the Book of Tobit (3:8). In the NT there are many references to demonic possession, some instances recording more than one demon in a single person (Lk. 8:2; 8:30). There were exorcisms, or expulsions, of such demons by our Lord (Mk. 1:23–28; 9:13–29), and this action by Christ is through the "Spirit of God" (Mt. 12:28). Exorcisms also were performed in Jerusalem (Acts 5:16; 8:7) and by St. Paul at Philippi (Acts 16:16–18) who acted "in the name of Jesus Christ."

Before an exorcism is permitted or ordered by Church authority, there must be three evident conditions; namely, speaking or understanding a previously unknown language, revealing hidden knowledge or happenings of the future, and performing feats beyond the physical capabilities of the person. It is further required that such actions be not a one-time occurrence but be repeated. Today modern studies in psychology have demonstrated actions that are not logically explained by prior reference to reality or by mental diseases that sometimes give rise to a masquerade of unusual phenomena or neuroses.

Provision is made in the Church for the rite of exorcism, but this is performed only after the most thorough investigation by authorities considered competent by the ordinary of the diocese and with his permission. (See Exorcism.)

## Diaconate

See, Deacon; Permanent Deacon.

## Diakonikon

1. In the Byzantine church a diakonikon is an annex or part of the sanctuary where the priest and deacon rest and where the necessary supplies for the altar are kept.

2. A diakonikon is a book of the liturgy containing the deacon's functions.

3. A book of prayers to be recited by the deacon before the people is a diakonikon. (See Byzantine Rite.)

## Dial-a-Saint

This is a program whereby people may telephone a special number (usually listed in the telephone directory) and receive (1) a brief life of the saint of the day, or (2) a one-minute spiritual message that has been previously recorded. The value of such programs is dependent on the competency of those preparing the messages, which are not to be considered as "special revelations" or spiritual gimmickry.

## Dialogue Mass

Dialogue (also dialog) is a form of communication wherein there is an exchange of ideas and an interpersonal relationship through actions that are verbal, sung, or spoken. This term was more widely used as an expression for a liturgy in which people of the congregation responded to the words of the celebrant. However, today all celebrations of the Eucharist include participation by the laity and the clergy through responses, recited prayers, and the singing of antiphons and hymns. (See Eucharist, Celebration of.)

## Diaspora

The dispersion; diaspora is the name given to those Jewish communities that settled outside Palestine. These groupings of Jews were occasioned by deportations of the conquering Assyrian and Babylonian rulers in the eighth to the sixth centuries B.C., and during the next centuries by migrations of Jews to foreign countries for trade. The most important Jewish community outside Palestine was at Alexandria, a successful group who spoke Greek and carried on cultural activities. In the Roman Empire under the rule of Julius Caesar (d. A.D. 44) Roman citizenship was permitted to be conferred on Jews of the diaspora, e.g., St. Paul. Also, these Jews contributed large sums to the support of the temple in Jerusalem. It came to mean, even in biblical times, the Jewish minorities all over the world. Certainly because of these migrations, and the impact of a people who believe in the one God, the spread of Christianity was more rapid and widely accepted. (See Anti-Semitism.)

## Diatessaron

The Diatessaron, the first Syriac version of the four Gospels in a harmonized form, was written by Tatian probably in the years 160 to 180. It was written in narrative form ostensibly to provide a popular life of Christ. Also, the name is applied to any harmony of the Gospels.

The term applies primarily to that consecutive narrative of the Gospels prepared by Tatian and used by the Syriac Church as the only Gospels until the fifth century A.D. (See Peschitto.)

## Didache

This short treatise in two parts called "Doctrine of the Twelve Apostles" was written about A.D 65 to 80, but attributed to the second century. The first part of it is moral and the second disciplinary, especially on the administration and ministry of the Sacraments of Baptism and Holy Eucharist. It was highly regarded by the early fathers of the Church and provides interesting insights into the early practices of the Church and its governance.

## Didascalia Apostolorum

A third century writing in Greek concerning doctrine and discipline, the Didascalia Apostolorum is sometimes attributed to the Apostles, but probably was written by a bishop of Syria.

## Dies Irae

Dies Irae are the opening words of the Latin version (meaning literally, "day of wrath") of a dirge-like prayer-poem written by a thirteenth century Franciscan, Thomas of Celano. It was a part of the Roman Requiem Mass but is no longer a part of the funeral Masses in the new Sacramentary. It is found in the music for the Mass composed by Mozart, Berlioz, and Verdi. But the English translation is not melodic because of the triple rhyme of the Latin text.

## Diet of Augsburg or Peace of Augsburg

This is the compromise reached with the Protestant states of Europe in 1555 under Emperor Charles V of Spain who signed. It established religious toleration by international law, cleared

the title of German Lutheran rulers to church lands, and gave them equal status with Catholic rulers.

## Dimissorials

Letters of authorization and testimonial, called Dimissorials, are issued by a bishop or religious superior regarding candidates for ordination under their jurisdiction to another bishop who is to ordain the candidates. This authorization testifies to the qualifications of the one to be ordained and requests such ordination. It may be given validly by word of mouth rather than by letter (c. 958 to 967).

## Diocesan Clergy

Diocesan clergy are those in holy orders, not members of a religious order, society, or congregation, who administer the temporal and spiritual affairs of a diocese by delegation of the ordinary and are attached to the particular diocese. They are often loosely called "secular" clergy. (See Priests' Councils.)

## Diocesan Pastoral Council, also Archdiocesan Pastoral Council

The concept of a Pastoral Council to assist the bishop is still evolving into full participation by all dioceses. The reasons for the existence of such councils, and their role and makeup, are more or less fixed. By definition, the Diocesan Pastoral Council is a collegial action wherein members of the laity, clergy, and religious of a diocese serve in a consultative capacity to the ordinary in the administration of the diocese. It is in the area of consultation that both the benefits and the problems of a pastoral council exist. Although there is a sharing of responsibilities in such councils, this in no way is a usurpation of the magisterial role of the bishop, by virtue of his office, which is all-inclusive of the teaching, shepherding, and priestly leadership of his diocese. "In the bishops, therefore, . . . our Lord Jesus Christ, the supreme High Priest, is present in the midst of those who believe" and through them teaches, sanctifies, directs, and guides the People of the New Covenant (LG 21).

Within his diocese, the bishop is and must be, in the true and full sense, teacher, priest, and shepherd. However, the bishops "also know that they themselves were not meant by Christ to shoulder alone the entire saving mission of the Church toward the world" (LG 30). And it follows according to the principles of Vatican II that: (1) The laity share in the mission of the whole Christian people in the Church and in the world. "They are in their own way made sharers in the priestly, prophetic, and kingly functions of Christ. They carry out their own part in the mission of the whole Christian people with respect to the Church and the world" (LG 31). (2) Without the active, apostolic presence of the laity the Church could not be the perfect sign of Christ among men: "The Church has not been truly established, and is not yet fully alive, nor is it a perfect sign of Christ among men, unless there exists a laity worthy of the name working along with the hierarchy" (AG 21). (3) All are called to the apostolate: "The lay apostolate . . . is a participation in the saving mission of the Church itself" (LG 33). (4) The laity receive a deputation to the apostolate from the Lord himself: "Through their baptism and confirmation, all are commissioned to that apostolate by the Lord Himself" (LG 33). (5) There can be an apostolate that arises from the free initiative of the laity. "In the Church there are many apostolic undertakings which are established by the free choice of the laity and regulated by their prudent judgment. The mission of the Church can be better accomplished in certain circumstances by undertakings of this kind" (AA 24). (6) There can also be a group or team apostolate that springs from the spontaneous initiative of the laity: "As long as the proper relationship is kept to Church authorities, the laity have the right to found and run such associations and to join those already existing" (AA 19). Thus, in cooperation with the clergy and the religious, whose duties are indicated and directed by their office, lay members may participate in a more informed and sophisticated form of consultation with the bishop. (7) "It is not only through the sacraments and Church ministries that the same Holy Spirit sanctifies and leads the People of God and enriches it with virtues" (LG 12). (8) "An individual layman, by reason of the knowledge, competence, or outstanding ability which he may enjoy, is permitted and sometimes even obliged to express his opinion on things which concern the good of the Church" (LG 37). "Let it be recognized that all the faithful, clerical and lay, possess a lawful freedom of inquiry and of thought, and the freedom to express their minds humbly and courageously about those matters in which they enjoy competence" (GS 62). (Kloppenburg.)

In this understanding, a circular letter was sent by the Vatican Congregation for the Clergy to bishops throughout the world (Jan. 25, 1973). Among its most salient points are the following excerpts:

"As far as the composition of the pastoral council

is concerned, although the members of the council cannot in a juridical sense be called representatives of the total diocesan community, nevertheless, as far as possible, they should present a witness or sign of the entire diocese, and, therefore, it seems extremely proper for priests, religious and laity who offer various experiences and needs to take part in the council. The persons, then, appointed to the pastoral council ought to be selected in such a way that the entire composition of the People of God within the diocese is truly represented, taking into consideration the different regions, social conditions and professions, as well as the parts which individuals and associations have in the apostolate, especially those which possess noteworthy excellence and prudence. Among these it is appropriate to appoint laymen and priests who have been chosen for offices exercised throughout the diocese. However, all the members of the council should be in full communion with the Catholic Church and able to accept and properly exercise this function in the Church.

"Whatever form the bishop freely chooses for determining the composition of his pastoral council, *most of the members should be laymen* since the greatest part of the diocesan community is made up of the laity.

"Besides the priests, permanent deacons, where they exist, should also be chosen for this council. Religious men and women should be named by the bishop with the permission of their own superior or mother-general.

"Finally, the number of members of the pastoral council should not be too great so that it is able to carry out effectively the work that is committed to it. . . .

"The pastoral council 'enjoys only a consultive voice.' The counsels and suggestions of the faithful which they propose within the confines of their ecclesiastical communion and in the spirit of true unity are of great value for the formation of decisions. The actual obedience and reverence which the faithful must show their sacred pastors does not prevent but rather fosters an open and sincere manifestation of those things demanded for the good of the Church.

"Therefore the bishop should greatly esteem its propositions and suggestions and seriously consider the judgments on which they agree, preserving the freedom and authority which are his by divine law for his pastoral service to that portion of the People of God committed to his care.

"It is the function of the pastoral council 'to investigate and to weigh matters which bear on pastoral activity, and to formulate practical conclusions regarding them so as to promote conformity of the life and actions of the People of God with the gospel.'

"Accordingly those questions may be committed to its study which, whether indicated by the diocesan bishop or proposed by the council members and accepted by him, refer to pastoral care exercised within the diocese. It is however, beyond the competence of this council to decide on general questions bearing on faith, orthodoxy, moral principles or laws of the universal Church; for the teacher of the faith in the diocese is always and obviously the bishop alone, with his bond of communion with the head of the episcopal college and its members."

The basic structure of the Diocesan Pastoral Council is made up of members who are nominated, elected, and appointed. Thereafter, the council members draw up a constitution and by-laws, whereby the group can carry out its objectives in a procedural manner that will provide interest and action and limit debate.

The Diocesan Pastoral Council, besides being consultative, can (1) provide communication between Church groups for more effective action; (2) make recommendations to the State Catholic Conferences; (3) promote action of the apostolate in the areas of legislation, judicial procedure, and individual rights; (4) consider programs of human development, social action, and work toward the proper informed action through educative means; and (5) take part in the National and International aspects of the Church's mission and worldwide evangelization. (See Parish Council; National Pastoral Council; International Council of the Laity.)

## Diocese

A diocese is the territory under the jurisdiction of a bishop, decided canonically only by the Holy See, which comprises the institutions and properties of the Church and the people within the area. The diocese in turn is divided into deaneries each with several parishes, and each having its own proper pastor or administrator appointed by the Ordinary.

Diocese is spoken of by Vatican II as a "particular church." (LG 23), and by this is meant a group of communities that form a local church. It is defined as that "entrusted to a bishop to be shepherded by him with the cooperation of the ministry" (CD 11).

Also Vatican II states: "They [the laity] should constantly foster a feeling for their own diocese, of

which the parish is a kind of cell, and be ever ready at their bishop's invitation to participate in diocesan projects" (AC 10).

The purpose of a diocese as a unit is expressed by Vatican II thus: "For a diocese to fulfill its purpose, the nature of the Church must be clearly evident to the People of God who belong to that diocese. Likewise, bishops must be able to carry out their pastoral duties effectively among their people. Finally, the welfare of the People of God must be served as perfectly as possible" (CD 22).

## Diptychs

This term is from the Greek meaning "folded double"; diptych came to mean two leaves or tablets bound together by a hinge or thong along one edge. Diptychs were made of metal, ivory, wood, or leather, and the inner surfaces were coated with wax so that they could be inscribed with a stylus. In Christian usage they contained lists of names, particularly those of benefactors or the newly baptized, and were considered "lists of approval." These were used in the liturgy; the deacon read them during the Mass. This practice was a forerunner of what is now a "memento" of the living or dead. Diptychs can also be considered the original of the Church calendar of feasts, preceding the "Martyrologies." They are still represented in Church art (cf. Triptych).

## Direct Line

In matrimonial legislation, direct line includes all ancestors and descendants, legitimate or natural. Marriage between any such is invalid (c. 1076). (Cf. Consanguinity.)

## Direction, Spiritual

The guidance of souls to perfection, spiritual direction, although not absolutely necessary for sanctification, is a normal means taken to assure progress since one's own judgment may be doubtful or erroneous regarding spiritual procedures. The spiritual direction of souls is neither easy nor to be taken lightly. St. Francis de Sales said of the spiritual director, "He must be full of charity, of knowledge and of prudence: if he lacks one of these, there is danger." Such a person must have knowledge of the spiritual way even before being a person of holiness himself. He must have insight and understanding, firmness in counsel, and detachment from emotion. For the one receiving spiritual direction, there are certain basic requirements, such as respect for the one giving counsel, and docility in accepting advice. This spiritual direction is not to be confused with advice or admonitions that are customarily given in the confessional. Rather this is a program set up by the director, including the practices and counsel, which one undertakes as a more than ordinary means of arriving at a high state of virtue and the higher forms of prayer. (See Asceticism.)

### Directorium

Directorium was an early term for the "Ordo" (q.v.).

### Diriment Impediment

An impediment is an external fact or circumstance that prohibits marriage or makes it invalid or unlawful. These impediments arise from the natural and positive divine law or the general and particular laws of the Church, or they may be established by civil law. Impediments may be: (1) prohibitive or diriment, rendering marriage unlawful or unlawful and invalid; (2) absolute or relative, according to whether they affect the person with or without regard to certain other persons; (3) public or occult, depending on whether they can be proved in an external court; (4) temporary or perpetual, according to their time; (5) major or minor, depending chiefly on the relative difficulty of dispensation; and (6) of divine or human right.

Diriment impediments that render a marriage invalid and unlawful are: age, i.e., a boy who has not completed his sixteenth year and a girl who has not completed her fourteenth year cannot validly marry; impotency (antecedent and perpetual); a previous and existing marriage (cf. Pauline Privilege); disparity of cult, i.e., between an unbaptized person and one baptized in, or converted to, the Catholic faith; holy orders; solemn vows of religion; abduction (holding a person in one's power with intent to marry the person);

crime (certain cases of adultery combined with murder or a promise of subsequent marriage); consanguinity; affinity; public decency; spiritual relationship (between the person baptizing and the one baptized or between the baptized person and the sponsors); legal relationship. Inculpable ignorance of a diriment impediment does not make a marriage valid. Under certain circumstances and conditions governed by canon law dispensations may be had for some impediments.

### Discalced

Literally, "barefoot" or "without shoes," the term discalced is applied to certain religious orders of both men and women, who by their rule wear sandals instead of shoes. It also serves as a term of distinction between two divisions of the Carmelite Order.

### Discernment of Spirits

1. Discernment of spirits is the grace, mentioned by St. Paul (1 Cor. 12:10), by which the saints and others can see and judge correctly if one is speaking or acting out of charity or only simulating the virtue.

2. The particular grace of prudence infused by God and acquired through the practice of the gift of counsel, granted to one, or to a spiritual director, enables the receiver to judge whether a spiritual activity is genuinely prompted by God or by the devil as a temptation to perplex the faithful (1 Jn. 4:1–6; Gal. 5:19–23).

### Disciple

1. Broadly, this may apply to the Apostles and the seventy-two "students" who received instructions from Christ (Lk. 10:1–24) and were in turn sent out by Him to instruct others. They have thus been likened to the hierarchy (the Apostles) and the priests (the disciples). There were others added to the body of disciples by the Apostles after the Ascension of Christ, for one hundred twenty are mentioned as gathered at Jerusalem in Acts 1:15. The mission of the disciples differed from that of the Apostles, however, in that they were sent out "two by two" by Christ and were specifically to prepare for the coming of Jesus Himself (Mk. 6:7).

2. The term "Beloved Disciple" is applied to St. John since he was called "the disciple whom Jesus loved" in the account of the Last Supper (Jn. 13:23).

### Discipline

1. Name of the small whip or scourge used by some austere religious orders in penitential prac-

tice as a means of bodily mortification. The prescribed use is called "taking the discipline." Voluntary use by individuals should only be undertaken on advice of a competent spiritual director.

2. An instruction, or system of teaching.

3. The teaching authority of the Church. (See Authority.)

### Discipline of the Sacraments, Congregation of

See Congregation.

### Discipline of the Secret, or Disciplina Arcani

In the early days, it was the custom of the Church to withhold certain doctrines and aspects of worship from those seeking eventual membership in the Church, out of fear that there would be blasphemy, persecution, or interruptions in divine service. Actually full instruction was given before one was baptized, but in the liturgy the Mass of the Catechumens was open only to those receiving instructions. Likewise, there were various symbols employed as a "secret" representation of truths, e.g., the fish meaning Christ, as a means of communicating without interference. This withholding at the beginning of certain teachings is still in practice among some missionary groups.

### Discrimination

The various forms of action, from the subtle to the cruel, which are brought against minority groups are called discrimination. Fundamentally, such action is contrary to the Constitution of the United States, but more basically it is against charity and justice, and sometimes against the virtue and rights of religion.

Such discriminatory actions are often brought against black people, those of Mexican birth or Puerto Ricans, Jews, the foreign-born, and Catholics. The Church has taught against discrimination from the beginning, and Vatican II stressed this again: "A man's relationship with God the Father and his relationship with his brother men are so linked together that Scripture says: 'The man without love has known nothing of God' (1 Jn. 4:8).

"The ground is therefore removed from every theory or practice which leads to a distinction between men or peoples in the matter of human dignity and the rights which flow from it" (NA 5). (See National Catholic Conference for Interracial Justice.)

### Diskos

The diskos is the paten used in the Byzantine rite. It is larger, dish-like, with a raised rim, differing from the paten used in the Roman rite. But the Byzantine form of paten, or dish, has been adopted by many parishes of the Roman Rite because of its greater capacity.

### Disparity of Worship

Disparity of worship, also called disparity of cult, is a diriment impediment to marriage (c. 1070). Marriage is null and void if contracted between an unbaptized person and one baptized in or converted to the Church. (Cf. Impediments of Marriage.)

### Dispensation

The relaxation of the obligation of a law because of special circumstances of a case can only be granted by the proper and competent authority (c. 80). Dispensations are given only by one having jurisdiction and only for Church laws. They are applied to particular laws of fasting, abstaining, vows, or certain marriage laws, as well as other laws. A dispensation can be recalled and thereby ceases. It is not granted except for just and proportionate reasons. Many officials of the Church are granted the power of dispensing, by delegation or office. The grant of a dispensation never requires the petitioner to pay for such action, unless there is clerical expense involved, which then may be defrayed by the one receiving the dispensation.

### Dissident Eastern Churches

See Eastern Churches.

### Dissolution of a Marriage

This question, covered completely in canon law, can only be briefly treated here.

1. A person who is already married validly cannot enter into a second marriage validly until

the bond of the first marriage is legitimately dissolved. This is divine law, binding all persons.

2. In the event of desertion by one of the parties, most serious investigations must be made in accord with instructions laid down by the Holy See, should the party remaining wish to enter into contract of a new marriage.

3. The marriage bond between two baptized persons can only be dissolved if the marriage has not been consummated.

4. The Pauline privilege can dissolve the marriage bond of unbaptized persons even though the marriage has been consummated. The bond of a nonsacramental marriage can be dissolved by the Pauline privilege or by the vicarious power of the pope in favor of the faith (cf. Pauline Privilege; Montana Case).

5. A nonconsummated marriage between two baptized persons is dissolved by the solemn religious profession of one or both of the parties or by dispensation of the Holy See (c. 1119). It is to be understood that this is not divorce in a legal sense ("divorce" as such has no effect before God).

The dissolution of the bond of marriage in the Church is an examination of the contract itself from the primary and secondary ends of marriage, its essential properties, its validity, and the spiritual welfare of the parties. Although the civil law may claim to dissolve the bond of marriage, a Catholic can go through the civil legal procedure of dissolving the bond (divorce) only when one of the parties or both cannot otherwise obtain the civil effects. The parties in this case must obtain ecclesiastical permission, must promise in writing that only the civil effects are sought, and must intend not to remarry.

**Distraction**

In its religious sense, distraction is a lack of advertence or attention when praying. Distractions are: voluntary, when one willfully sets the mind to thinking about vain things or deliberately ceases to pray because of preoccupation (this may be gravely sinful); involuntary, when fleeting thoughts, caused by objects seen or mental fancies, turn one away from the prayer. Distractions are obstacles to prayer and should be overcome by directing the attention. This may be done by: (1) making an effort to pronounce the words of prayer correctly, called *verbal attention;* (2) attempting to understand the meaning of the words of the prayer, called *intellectual attention;* (3) the mental sweeping upward of our thoughts to God in worship and love, called *spiritual attention.* This latter is recommended mostly for one who has achieved the first two. (See Meditation.)

**Divination**

Divination is a form of occultism wherein the person uses objects such as tea leaves, a crystal ball, Tarot cards, Ouija boards, or any superstitiously interpreted object as the means of attempting to gain or elicit knowledge or information that is beyond ordinary human intelligence. The attempts to contact the dead through a seance, for example, are spiritistic divinations that have been contested by parapsychological testings and proved false. Likewise astrology, witchcraft, zodiac readings, or horoscopes are forms of divination. Although it is natural for human beings to attempt to "lift the curtain" and see beyond the present, the tendency should be controlled lest it distract from the unfolded and true vision of God contained in His revelation to mankind. (See Spiritism.)

**Divine Comedy**

*Divine Comedy* is the title of a three-part allegory, written in a verse form called *terza rima,* by Dante Alighieri in 1321. It is composed of the *Inferno,* treating of hell; the *Purgatorio,* treating of purgatory; and *Paradiso,* treating of heaven. Each division is written in an imaginative manner but shows great insight into the theology of the fathers of the Church and the philosophy of the fourteenth century.

**Divine Office**

The public, official, and common prayer of the Church is called the Divine Office. It is offered daily in public or liturgically in union with Christ in adoration and supplication of God. It is the prayer of the mystical body. The Divine Office derives from the authority of the Church, and its content is formulated by the Church. Thus by direction of the Church it is prescribed to members of the priesthood, deacons, and all religious, under solemn obligation, to be prayed in the name of the Church and all the faithful who also pray in this recitation. (Cf. Breviary; Liturgy of the Hours).

**Divine Praises**

A litany of praises, called the Divine Offices, are said after Benediction of the Blessed Sacrament. Each is said by the celebrant and repeated by the faithful. They are:

Blessed be God
Blessed be His Holy Name
Blessed be Jesus Christ, true God and true Man
Blessed be the name of Jesus
Blessed be His most Sacred Heart
Blessed be His most Precious Blood
Blessed be Jesus in the most holy Sacrament of the Altar

Blessed be the Holy Spirit, the Paraclete
Blessed be the great Mother of God, Mary most
  holy
Blessed be her holy and Immaculate Conception
Blessed be her glorious Assumption
Blessed be the name of Mary, virgin and mother
Blessed be St. Joseph, her most chaste spouse
Blessed be God in His angels and in His saints
(Cf. Benediction of the Blessed Sacrament.)

## Divinity of Christ

This is the answer to the question of Scripture:
"Who do people say the Son of Man is?" (Mt.
16:13). The answer is found in a twofold examination concerning first, the Messiahship of Christ;
second, the Sonship of God. Subordinate but
supporting these two is a synthesis of Christ's
works, miracles, teachings, and associations.

Concerning the first, Christ as Messiah: In the
Gospel of St. John we recognize Jesus as the
Messiah, "the one Moses spoke of in the law—the
prophets too" (Jn. 1:45). We further find it
recorded that others recognized Christ in His role
as Messiah: ". . . because they knew that he was the
Messiah" (Lk. 4:41). Although Jesus did not
proclaim Himself the Messiah in words, it is
revealed that He permitted others to ascribe to
Him the most popular of all Messianic titles, "the
Son of David" (Mt. 12:23), and that Christ knew
Himself to be the Messianic Son of David in
propounding the meaning of Ps. 110 (Mt. 22:41–
46). Finally, Jesus explicitly affirmed the role of
Messiah when the high priest asked: "Are you the
Messiah, the Son of the Blessed One?" He replied:
"I am" (Mk. 14:61).

Concerning the second, Christ as the Son of
God, this term "Son of God" is applied to Jesus
frequently in the synoptic Gospels. For example,
the confession of Peter, "You are Messiah the Son
of the living God" (Mt. 16:16), and in the
confession of the centurion (Mk. 15:39). More
profoundly we find in the prologue of St. John's
Gospel, attestation of the "Word of God," His
preexistence, the action of the Word in the
creation of the world, and the fact that the Word
has become incarnate in Jesus Christ. Christ's
becoming incarnate, "being made flesh," is no
longer a matter of prophecy only, but actually is
the fulfillment of the OT prophecies. And most
conclusively, Christ is presented by St. John as the
one who reveals the secrets of the Godhead, which
is only possible to the "only-begotten Son." This is
summarized in the protestation of faith by
Thomas, "My Lord and my God" (Jn. 20:28), and
in the confession of Catholic Christianity in the
divinity of Jesus Christ. Relative to and supporting

these scriptural texts are further distinctions of
Christ in the Gospels: His works were to be done
according to "the will of Him who sent Me" (Jn.
4:34); also His many miracles show His power over
demons (Mt. 9:32–34), over nature (Mk. 8:22f),
over cosmic forces (Mt. 8:26), and finally over
death in His Resurrection (Lk. 24); His teaching
identifies Himself as "the way" (Jn. 14:6); and His
associations or His knowledge were exclusively His,
such as that of heaven and intimacy with God the
Father (Jn. 1:18). All of these together present the
personality of Christ and from this we know Him
as the divine Christ (Jn. 7:17) who speaks with
authority. Christ in virtue of the hypostatic union is
a divine Person, the second Person of the Blessed
Trinity. (See Christ.)

## Divino Afflante Spiritu

The first three Latin words are also the title of
the encyclical issued by Pope Pius XII, Sept. 30,
1943, in favor of a scientific, researched interpretation of the Bible rather than an intuitive and freer
explanation of the word of God. It was published
to commemorate the fiftieth year of the publishing
of Pope Leo XIII's encyclical *Providentissimus Deus*
which marked a charter course for biblical studies.

The Divino document stressed a study of the
scripture texts in the languages in which they were
originally written, and thus a fundamental goal for
biblical studies became the literal sense through the
science of textual criticism. Pope Pius XII wrote:
"What the literal sense of a passage is, is not always
as obvious in the speeches and writings of ancient
authors of the East as it is in the works of our own
time. For what they wished to express is not to be
determined by the rules of grammar and philology
alone nor solely by the context; the interpreter
must, as it were, go back wholly in spirit to those
remote centuries of the East and with the aid of
history, archeology, ethnology, and other sciences
accurately determine what modes of writing, so to
speak, the authors of that ancient period would be
likely to use and in fact did use." (See Bible; Scrolls
of the Dead Sea.)

## Divorce

The OT took divorce for granted; a "bill of
divorce" is mentioned as a tool of procedure (Is.
50:1; Jer. 3:8). However, in the NT Christ
condemned divorce most decisively (Mk. 10:2–12;
Lk. 16:18). And St. Paul taught that divorce was
wrong and states it as the Lord's teaching (1 Cor.
7:10–11). (See Dissolution of a Marriage.)

## Divorce From Bed and Board

In canon law, this compares to the civil judicial
action called a "separation" (c. 1128 to 1132).

## Docetism

Docetism is a heresy of the second century. It is not truly a Christian heresy, i.e., arising from a denial of a dogma by the faithful, but it arose from another heresy, Gnosticism. The Docetae taught that Jesus was not real but only a phantom.

Docetism had a strong spiritualist leaning and denied the reality of Christ's material body and hence, the Incarnation of the Word, the hard earthly life, the passion and death of Christ. The modern docetist is still in evidence in that he denies the human, earthly, visible, social, and juridical part of the Church and its organization and external rites.

## Doctor

1. A doctor is one who has received the highest of the university degrees (cf. Degrees, Academic).

2. Doctor of the Church is a title conferred on eminent ecclesiastical writers because of their learning and holiness of life; they are always canonized. These persons of special title who have been recognized as "reliable" teachers are: Ambrose, Jerome, Augustine, Gregory of the Great, Athanasius, Basil, Gregory of Nazianzus, John Chrysostom, Thomas Aquinas (1568), Bonaventure (1588), Anselm of Canterbury (1720), Isidore of Seville (1722), Peter Chrysologus (1729), Leo the Great (1754), Peter Damian (1828), Bernard of Clairvaux (1830), Hilary of Poitiers (1851), Alphonsus Liguori (1871), Francis de Sales (1877), Cyril of Alexandria (1882), Cyril of Jerusalem (1882), John of Damascus (1890), Venerable Bede (1899), Ephraem of Syria (1920), Peter Canisius (1925), John of the Cross (1926), Robert Bellarmine (1931), Albert the Great (1931), Anthony of Padua (1946), Lawrence of Brindisi (1959), Catherine of Siena (1970), Teresa of Avila (1970). The dates are those of their official recognition by the Church; all others were before A.D. 750.

## Doctor Angelicus

From the Latin, the Angelic Doctor, Doctor Angelicus is a title of St. Thomas Aquinas (1225 to 1274), the great scholastic theologian of the Dominican Order.

## Doctrine of the Catholic Church

In its most broad sense the doctrine of the Church embraces all those beliefs and teachings that are contained in and reflect the message of Jesus Christ. To this must be added those refinements of teachings that the Church has taught and continues to teach through the unfolding tradition that is hers from apostolic times and which she teaches infallibly as the one Church founded by Christ.

In its limited sense the doctrine of the Church, considered apart from its body of dogmatic teachings, is directed to the application of those teachings in the moral, social, and missionary or communicative areas.

In the *Dogmatic Constitution on the Church,* Vatican II promulgated the relationship of the Church to the kingdom of God, the People of God, and the salvation history that is the mission of the Church and its members. "We have, then, the firm teaching that the one Church, as Christ has intended exists in historical form and is knowable as such, and that its concrete existential form is the Church as this has been directed by the successor of Peter" (Kloppenburg).

"It is through Christ's Catholic Church alone, which is the all-embracing means of salvation, that the fullness of the means of salvation can be obtained. It was to the apostolic college alone, of which Peter is the head, that we believe Our Lord entrusted all the blessings of the New Covenant, in order to establish on earth the one Body of Christ into which all those should be fully incorporated who already belong in any way to God's People" (UR 3).

"By her relationship with Christ, the Church is a kind of sacrament or sign of intimate union with God, and of the unity of all mankind. She is also an instrument for the achievement of such union and unity. For this reason, following in the path laid out by its predecessors, this Council wishes to set forth more precisely to the faithful and to the entire world the nature and encompassing mission of the Church. The conditions of this age lend special urgency to the Church's task of bringing all men to full union with Christ, since mankind today is joined together more closely than ever before by social, technical, and cultural bonds. . . .

"When the work which the Father had given the Son to do on earth (cf. Jn. 17:4) was accomplished, the Holy Spirit was sent on the day of Pentecost in order that He might forever sanctify the Church, and thus all believers would have access to the Father through Christ in the one Spirit (cf. Eph. 2:18). He is the Spirit of life, a fountain of water springing up to life eternal (cf. Jn. 4:14; 7:38–39). Through Him the Father gives life to men who are dead from sin, till at last He revives in Christ even their mortal bodies (cf. Rom. 8:10–11).

"The Spirit dwells in the Church and in the

hearts of the faithful as in a temple (cf. 1 Cor. 3:16; 6:19). In them he prays and bears witness to the fact that they are adopted sons (cf. Gal. 4:6; Rom. 8:15–16, 26). The Spirit guides the Church into the fullness of truth (cf. Jn. 16:13) and gives her a unity of fellowship and service. He furnishes and directs her with various gifts, both hierarchical and charismatic, and adorns her with the fruits of His grace (cf. Eph. 4:11–12; 1 Cor. 12:4; Gal. 5:22). By the power of the gospel He makes the Church grow, perpetually renews her, and leads her to perfect union with her Spouse. The Spirit and the Bride both say to the Lord Jesus, 'Come!' (cf. Rv. 22:17).

"Thus, the Church shines forth as 'a people made one with the unity of the Father, the Son, and the Holy Spirit" (LG 1 and 4). (See Marks of the Church; Basic Teachings for Catholic Religious Education.)

## Documents of Vatican Council II
See Vatican Council II.

## Dogma
Dogma refers to a teaching, a firm principle. In the Church, the word today in its strictest sense as "dogma of the faith" or "Catholic dogma" means a truth revealed by Scripture or contained in tradition, and for belief proposed by the Church through solemn definition or arising from the magisterium of the Church as a teaching of divine revelation (c. 1323). The fathers of the Church used the term to designate revealed teachings of our Lord, and later a distinction was made between dogma and moral teaching.

In human life there is a transcendental necessity for man, both mind and spirit, to hold certain truths absolutely. This is addressed to man's freedom, whereby knowledge in action enables man to attain his own salvation through a commitment to truth and spiritual beliefs.

Dogmas of the Church are derived directly from revelation and from the self-communication of God through grace, which in its basic analysis is faith. Through this the individual comes to the unity of the Spirit, and sacramentally through baptism and the spiritual growth, comes to that oneness of mind wherein his whole mental and spiritual life are taken up into the reality of God. Man's knowledge becomes thus the imperative of his nature and his relationship with his Creator through love and obedience now and hereafter. (See Church.)

## Dogmatic Fact
Certain truths which, while not revealed by God, are proclaimed by the teaching authority of the Church. By infallible authority the Church judges and proposes these facts for belief. These facts come to us through revelation (cf. Heb. 1), which is progressive through the Church and the unfolding of tradition. (See Doctrine of the Catholic Church.)

## Dogmatic Theology
This division of theology has as its object to demonstrate the existence of dogmas, to show that they are contained in the deposit of faith, and to further show the causes, the connections, and logical conclusions of these dogmas. It is the "science of the Church's dogma." Thus, it differs from fundamental theology that demonstrates that these truths are revealed. Dogmatic theology receives the dogmas from the Church from whom the deposit of faith is received. Thus, it takes the definitions of the Church, accepting the authority of the Church as infallible. Dogmatic theology then proves the existence of each dogma from scripture and tradition, showing the Church's teaching to be in agreement with the sources of revelation. It further proves that the Church's teaching does not change, that there are no new dogmas handed down, and that these truths were taught from the very beginning. Dogmatic theology is also called "special dogma."

## Dolors of the Blessed Virgin
See Sorrows of the Blessed Virgin Mary.

## Dom
1. This title, an abbreviation of the Latin word *dominus,* master, is given to professed religious of the Benedictine, Carthusian, and Cistercian Orders. In Italy the term is "Don" and is applied to all clerics except mendicant friars and regular clerks.

2. Dom is the formal title of a cathedral in Germany.

## Domestic Prelate
Domestic Prelate is a title now classed as "honorary prelate," along with Apostolic Prothonotaries, Honorary Prelates of His Holiness, and Chaplains of His Holiness. This honorary title of rank and distinction conferred on priests by the Holy See designates the recipient as a member of the pope's court and household. With the title go certain privileges; recipients are addressed Reverend Monsignor; they use a black biretta with a purple pompom; they have a cassock of violet with

a rochet and mantellettum; they never let down the train of the cassock, and at solemn Masses they may use the bugia, or special candlestick.

## Domicile

Domicile refers to one's fixed residence. In canon law one has a domicile if he resides or dwells in a place with the intention of remaining there unless some unforeseen event occurs, or he has spent ten years in that place. A wife's domicile is that of her husband. The location of the domicile determines the bishop who has jurisdiction over the person in the domicile, making him subject to that bishop and the laws established for that diocese.

## Dominations

Dominations is the name of one of the choirs of the hierarchy of angels. (Cf. Angel.)

## Dominical Letters

In the early method of reckoning the Church calendar, the first seven letters of the alphabet were used to indicate the days of the week and were called dominical letters. (Cf. Cycle; Calendar, Church.)

## Donation of Constantine

The Donation of Constantine was a forged letter falsely attributed to Constantine the Great, written probably as early as the eighth century, allegedly conferring supremacy of the pope over all bishops and temporal rulers.

## Donatism

A schism known as Donatism was caused by Donatus in A.D. 311 at Carthage over the election of Caecilian as successor to Bishop Mensurius by appeal to the Emperor Constantine. It brought about the breakdown of the African Church since it lasted for 300 years or until the conquest by the Saracens. Donatists also affirmed the heretical belief that the validity of a sacrament depends on the spiritual condition of the minister. The schism and heretical teachings were answered and condemned by a council held in Carthage in 404.

## Doorkeeper

Doorkeeper, or porter, was formerly the first of the four minor orders in the Roman rite. It was conferred after tonsure, and while the office it entails is now more symbolical than actual, it literally entrusts the "entry" of the church to the recipient, granting the "ringing of bells, opening the church and sanctuary, and opening the preacher's book."

Since Vatican II, the term is no longer used, and the role is given to one of the lesser ministries and might be likened to that of an installed usher, lector, or commentator. (See Ministries.)

## Dormition of the B.V.M.

Dormition refers to the falling into sleep, rather than death, of the Blessed Mother. Also, this term is sometimes applied to the Assumption.

## Dossal, also Dorsal

A dossal is a suspended curtain of rich cloth, tapestry, or brocade, behind the altar, extending the length of the altar or beyond. It may serve to form the background of a large hanging crucifix. Now, dossal refers to any banner-like hanging used as a backdrop. (Cf. Banners.)

## Douay, also Douai, or Doway Bible

The standard translation of the Bible into English has been in use for three and a half centuries. It is called the Douay-Rheims Bible because the OT volumes were published in Douay (France) in 1609 to 1610, and the NT books published in Rheims in 1582. Both testaments were translated by Gregory Martin at Rheims where the English college of Douay was temporarily removed for fifteen years (1578 to 1593) and where he was professor of theology and scripture. However, the text as we know it now has had several revisions, the first by Dr. Witham in 1730, which was superseded by five revisions by Dr. Richard Challoner (1691 to 1781). Our present version is based upon these, so more precisely it should be referred to as the "Douay-Challoner," or "Rheims-Challoner." Since this work notably had some literary flaws in style, including many Latinisms, perhaps because of translation difficulties in rendering from the Latin, revisions were necessary. It must be remembered that Catholics are bound to use a text approved by Church authority (see Leo XIII's encyclical, *Officiorum ac munerum*) and may not print a text without authorization (cc. 1391, 2318), and hence any text so authorized may be considered a Catholic text. In recent years many authorized texts have been published in the United States. They are texts of the entire Bible or of Old or New Testaments, e.g., the Baltimore Bible (1899); Herder's Cardinal Farley's Bible of 1911; Benziger's *Red Letter Bible* of 1943; Sheed and Ward's New Testament of Dr. Arendzen—all of which are revisions and improvements of the Douay-Challoner. More sweeping changes have appeared in the Confraternity Edition of 1941 and that of Father Carey in 1935. In 1945 and 1949, an entirely new translation was made from the Vulgate by Msgr. Ronald Knox, and a rendition from the Greek by J. A. Kleist, S. J., and J. L. Lilly, C.M., of the NT was published in 1954. The revised Standard Version (1885, 1901, 1952, 1957, 1966) and currently the New American Bible (NAB) sponsored by the Bishop's Committee of the Confraternity of Christian Doctrine are new translations. The Jerusalem Bible was translated into English from the French version in 1966, and many other versions have been introduced.

## Double

Double was formerly the highest rank of feast in the liturgical order. They were thus: doubles of the first class, e.g., Christmas; doubles of the second class, the major doubles and ordinary doubles (cf. Feasts of the Church). The term arose in the fourth and fifth centuries as a result of the then current practice of saying two, or "doubling," the offices on certain days, saying one for the fixed feast and one as a special office in honor of a saint.

## Dove

1. A Catholic symbol of the Holy Spirit, the dove is used because of the form assumed at the baptism of Christ (Jn. 1:32) and recognized and associated with the Pentecostal baptism of fire. Thus it also became a symbol of baptism for early Christians.

2. A medieval pyx was shaped like a dove, and sometimes the tabernacle that was suspended from the ceiling of the sanctuary was formed in the dove shape.

## Dowry of Mary

This fourteenth century title of the "land of England" included the islands of the realm.

## Doxology

A doxology is a prayer or tribute of praise offered to God or the Trinity. There are two classes: the greater, e.g., the *Gloria in excelsis* of the

Mass; and the lesser, e.g., the prayer "Glory be to the Father, . . ." There are frequent doxologies in the Scriptures (2 Pt. 3:18; Rom. 11:36), and the reason may be found for such prayers in the words of St. Paul (Col. 3:17).

The lesser doxology is most common and is a familiar prayer to the Blessed Trinity:

Glory be to the Father, the Son, and the Holy Spirit; as it was in the beginning, is now and ever shall be, world without end. Amen.

The doxology of the Mass is that prayer of praise said or sung by the celebrant at the conclusion of the Eucharistic rite when he holds aloft the chalice and paten of the consecrated species and with the words:

Through Him, with Him, in Him, in the unity of the Holy Spirit, all glory and honor is yours, almighty Father, forever and ever.

And the people respond: "Amen."

## Dreams

Dreams are activity of the subconscious mind during sleep. They have been used by God as means of revealing courses of action and truths otherwise unknown (Gn. 37:1–11; Dn. 2:19; 7:1; Mt. 1:20; 2:13). However, it is gravely sinful to attempt to use dreams as a means of reading the future out of superstition or attempted diabolical aid.

## Dress, Clerical

See Costume, Clerical.

## Drug Education, Catholic Office of

This is the established center where the Church's activities toward the control of drug abuse, the rehabilitation and education regarding drugs is carried on. The United States Catholic Conference established the Catholic Office of Drug Education (CODE) in 1972. Its headquarters are at 1312 Massachusetts Ave., N.W., Washington, D.C., 20005. There have been rehabilitation centers established in many dioceses of the country, which work with the CODE directors.

## Dualism

That philosophical theory, which is in opposition to monism and holds that two equally primordial and mutually opposed principles of life and reality exist, is called dualism. It is a contradiction that rests in opposites such as good versus evil, material and immaterial, reality and nonreality. In its religious context dualism places a contradiction between what is and what ought to be, between man as a sinner and man striving to be God-like through his free-will effort toward salvation.

### Duel

A duel is a fight between persons conducted by previous agreement on time, place, and weapons, with death or maiming of one of the parties as its outcome. It is forbidden by the Church under grave penalties, excommunication reserved simply to the Holy See (c. 2351), together with infamy of law incurred by the action itself. Ecclesiastical burial is denied to those who die in a duel (c. 1240).

### Dulia or Cultus Duliae

Dulia is the special worship, generally called veneration, given to the angels and saints because as friends of God they share in His excellence (Cf. Cultus; Hyperdulia; Latria.)

### Duplication

See Bination.

### Duties

The Church recognizes many areas of human action that have attached to the office or person a duty or obligation exacted by law or responsible response of the individual. The Easter duty is that moral obligation whereby Catholics are by precept to receive Holy Communion at least once during the Easter season, or from the first Sunday of Lent to Trinity Sunday.

There are also parental duties, which are those obligations and responsibilities whereby parents are morally bound to attend to the welfare of their children, especially their education, succor, health, and religious training.

Also there are social or earthly duties of which Vatican II speaks thus: "This Council exhorts Christians, as citizens of two cities, to strive to discharge their earthly duties conscientiously and in response to the gospel spirit. They are mistaken who, knowing that we have here no abiding city but seek one which is to come, think that they may therefore shirk their earthly responsibilities. For they are forgetting that by the faith itself they are more than ever obliged to measure up to these duties, each according to his proper vocation.

"Nor, on the contrary, are they any less wide of the mark who think that religion consists in acts of worship alone and in the discharge of certain moral obligations, and who imagine they can plunge themselves into earthly affairs in such a way as to imply that these are altogether divorced from the religious life" (GS 43).

### Dying, Prayers for

Any prayers suitable to the serious condition and recognized by Church authorities are prayers for the dying. Also those prayers that may be said at the time when the Sacrament of the Anointing of the Sick is administered to one seriously in danger of dying or at the giving of holy communion to such a person. (See Commendation of the Soul.)

# Ee

## Early Church

The historic period spanning the time from A.D. 30 to the declaration of the Peace of Milan between the Emperor Constantine and Licinius (A.D. 313) is referred to as the early Church era. It is in the continuity of world history that this almost three hundred years was a period of formation, identity, and cultural evolvement. There are two periods that make up the time of the early Church, namely, the *apostolic* age, during which the "primitive Church" gathered the recording of revelation and the apostolic testimony of Christ and formed the canon and the basic structure of the Church makeup together with a drafting of its creeds against heresy. The Church itself took on a structure as Church or ecclesial entity. This period lasted until about A.D. 180. The second period is the *subapostolic* age when the image of the Church became fixed and identified with the universal mission it was to fulfill. This was a period of numerical growth, theological activity, and in spite of the persecutions, there was an opening up of the Church to the empire and a turning toward the world and its problems. It was also during this period that schools of theology at Antioch and Alexandria brought forth scholars of unusual insight whose writings were to be instrumental in solidifying the early traditional action of the developing Church.

From the primitive community at Jerusalem, the missionary work among the Greeks, Romans, Africans, and others began. The Church developed a culture that was an amalgam of the Jewish, Hellenistic, and the Roman. This was manifest in the writings, the liturgy, and the sociological makeup of the Church.

The missionary effort and its attendant dangers were expressed by St. Paul: "Keep watch over yourselves, and over the whole flock the Holy Spirit has given you to guard. Shepherd the church of God, which he has acquired at the price of his own blood. I know that when I am gone, savage wolves will come among you who will not spare the flock. From your own number, men will present themselves distorting the truth and leading astray any who follow them" (Acts 20:28–30). But even in the face of this known danger, the Church took on

a hierarchical structure with a collegial makeup that was ready to meet the challenge of heresies when they arose, and the purity of the gospels was preserved together with a unity (cf. Koinonia) centered around the Eucharist.

The early Church is characterized by the continuity of the redemptive act and its application, together with its development and the basis for Christianity as expressed later in all its splendor of art, architecture, and social teachings. (See Church.)

## Easter

The solemnity of the resurrection of Jesus Christ is celebrated in the Church calendar on the first Sunday after the vernal equinox. Easter is thus a movable feast, falling on a different Sunday in about a twelve-year cycle. Vatican II, however, left open the probable and possible determination whereby Easter would fall on the same day: "Until such time as all Christians desirably concur on a fixed day for the celebration of Easter, and with a view meantime to promoting unity among the Christians of a given area or nation, it is left to the Patriarchs or supreme authorities of a place to reach a unanimous agreement, after ascertaining the views of all concerned, on a single Sunday for the observance of Easter" (OE 20).

The word Easter, which comes from the Anglo-Saxon, is a term derived from the pagan goddess of the dawn. The Latin variation, *Pascha,* is from Hebrew antecedents; it is derived from the Passover, or their freedom from the Egyptians, which is celebrated in the Jewish calendar of feasts. Easter is the greatest feast of the Christian Church.

The liturgy of the Church celebrates Easter with an Easter Triduum as set forth in the *Sacramentary:* "Christ redeemed mankind and gave perfect glory to God principally through the paschal mystery: by dying he destroyed our death and by rising he restored our life. The Easter triduum of the passion and resurrection of Christ is thus the culmination of the entire liturgical year. What Sunday is to the week, the solemnity of Easter is to the liturgical year.

"The Easter triduum begins with the evening Mass of the Lord's Supper, reaches its high point in the Easter vigil, and closes with evening prayer on Easter Sunday.

"On Good Friday and if possible, also on Holy Saturday until the Easter vigil, the Easter fast is observed everywhere.

"The celebration of the Lord's passion takes place on Friday during the afternoon hours.

"The Easter vigil, in the night when Christ rose from the dead, is considered the 'mother of all vigils.' During it the Church keeps watch, awaiting the resurrection of Christ and celebrating it in the sacraments. The entire celebration of this vigil should take place at night beginning after nightfall and ending with dawn."

The resurrection of Christ is recorded in the Bible in the following citations: Mt. 28:1–15; Mk. 16:1–14; Lk. 24:1–12; Jn. 20:1–21. (See Calendar, Church.)

### Easter Controversy

This was the dispute between the East and the West in the second century (circa 155) wherein the Asiatic bishops protested against the Roman custom of celebrating Easter on Sunday, instead of on whatever day of the week the fourteenth Nisan might fall according to the old Jewish calendar. The dispute arose again in 325. The controversy points to the historic relationship of the bishops and the pope. It was settled finally with the 95-year cycle that was followed everywhere after the ninth century.

### Easter Duty

The obligation of all the faithful who have attained the use of reason to receive Holy Communion at least once during the season of Easter is called the Easter Duty. It is recommended that each fulfill this duty in his own parish church, or if he does so elsewhere, he should inform the pastor of his parish (c. 859). The season in the United States extends from the first Sunday of Lent to Trinity Sunday inclusive. It is also recommended that the faithful fulfill their obligation of annual confession (c. 906) at this time out of practical considerations. (Cf. Commandments of the Church.)

### Easter Season

Following the great solemnity of Easter there is in the Church calendar a period of time when the celebration of the Eucharist and the cycle of readings recall the event of Christ's resurrection. The *Sacramentary* notes this time: "The fifty days from Easter Sunday to Pentecost are celebrated as one feast day, sometimes called "the great Sunday."

"The singing of the *alleluia* is a characteristic of these days.

"The Sundays of this season are counted as the Sundays of Easter. Following the Sunday of the Resurrection, they are called the Second, Third, Fourth, Fifth, Sixth, and Seventh Sundays of Easter or of the Easter season. The period of fifty days ends on Pentecost Sunday.

"The first eight days of the Easter season form the octave of Easter and are celebrated as solemnities of the Lord.

"The Ascension is celebrated on the fortieth day after Easter. In places where it is not a holyday of obligation, it is assigned to the Seventh Sunday of Easter.

"The weekdays after the Ascension to Saturday before Pentecost inclusive are a preparation for the coming of the Holy Spirit." (See Calendar, Church.)

### Easter Water

Holy water is blessed on Holy Saturday in special ceremonies, and distributed then. It is used in the liturgy of the Easter octave for blessing the faithful, homes, and objects. (Cf. Easter.)

### Eastern Churches

These are groups of Christians, Uniate (returned to Catholic unity from the corresponding non-Catholic church of their rite), dissident, or schismatic. To the *Catholic* belong those of the Byzantine rite including Catholic Armenians, Chaldeans, Catholic Copts and Ethiopians, Maronites, Catholic Syrians, and those of the Malabar rite. These are classified as Uniates (except the Italo-Greeks) and returned to Catholic unity. Each is as fully and completely Catholic as the Western Church. They retain their own liturgies, canon law, and customs by right, differing among themselves and from the Western Church but teach the same faith and morals and are obedient to the Holy See like the Western Church. The *dissident churches* are made up of two categories: (1) those national churches that collectively form the Orthodox Eastern Church, and (2) the Nestorian, Armenian, Coptic, Ethiopic, and Syrian Jacobite Churches. Although these were at one time parts of the

Catholic Church, they now deny the authority of the Holy See and variously teach erroneous or heretical doctrines. Each does teach the Real Presence, the Eucharistic Sacrifice, confession, veneration of the Blessed Mother and the saints, and other doctrines and, except for the Copts and Ethiopians, have valid orders and sacraments.

The Second Vatican Council issued the *Decree on Eastern Catholic Churches*, which declares: "Such individual churches, whether of the East or of the West, although they differ somewhat among themselves in what are called rites (that is, in liturgy, ecclesiastical discipline, and spiritual heritage) are, nevertheless, equally entrusted to the pastoral guidance of the Roman Pontiff, the divinely appointed successor of St. Peter in supreme governance over the universal Church" (OE 3).

"All Eastern rite members should know and be convinced that they can and should always preserve their lawful liturgical rites and their established way of life, and that these should not be altered except by way of an appropriate and organic development" (OE 6).

"This sacred Ecumenical Synod endorses and lauds the ancient discipline of the sacraments existing in the Eastern Churches, as also the practices connected with their celebration and administration, and ardently wishes that they be restored where circumstances warrant" (OE 12). (See Ecumenism.) Eastern Catholic groups in the United States are Armenians, Chaldeans, Italo-Greeks, Maronites, Melkites, Romanians, Russians, Ruthenians, and Syrians.

## Eastern Monasticism

In the earliest centuries of Christianity, in Egypt and Syria, monasticism had its beginnings. This was caused by two predominant factors: (1) Christians wanted to flee from the pagan society, and (2) they wished to seek a closer bond with God in solitude and a life of prayer. Thus was established the eremitic life of the hermits, the anchoritic life of communes, and the ascetic life, all of which gave rise to the earliest monastic endeavors.

The first of these was St. Anthony (251 to 356) who is acclaimed to be the founder of monasticism. There followed specific rules or formulas that began with that of St. Pachominus (292 to 348), recognized as the founder of the cenobitic life. Thereafter St. Basil (329 to 379) and St. Benedict (d. 547), each borrowing upon the thought of the earlier writers, brought out rules.

This was the beginning of the life of Christian perfection sought through the austere living and submission of the will to obedience through the love of God and the cultivation of virtues. (See Monasticism.)

## Eastern Mysticism

This is the all-encompassing term for all the religious theories and practices of the orient from the occult to the more modern, such as the devotees of Hare Krishna. It also includes some of the monastic practices of the Orient and the Tibetan countries. The Hare Krishna has as its aims the liberation of one from matter, desire, care, and worry and the identification of the person with a variety of absolutes ranging from complete passive surrender to one or more reincarnations, culminating in the final impersonal fulfillment of the individual. There are many strange adaptations of eastern mysticism, which include divination, theosophic illuminism, and borrowings from ancient religious and Christian practices. One aspect that seems paramount is the absence of charity or love as understood by Christians, for there is a self-seeking incompatible with the message of Christ. Some rites of meditation practiced by the eastern mystics are largely self-hypnotic in nature and sometimes drug induced, which are not compatible with the findings of modern psychology. (Cf. Guru.)

## Eastern Studies, Pontifical Institute of

Also called the Oriental Institute, this house of study for oriental clergy, Catholic or dissident, is under the direction of the Jesuits. It was founded by Benedict XV in 1917 and is part of the Gregorian University in Rome.

## Ebionites

This heretical sect arose in the first centuries around Jerusalem (Acts 15:1–3). The Ebionites taught that the Jewish law still bound Christians, that Christ was a mere man, and St. Paul an apostate. The sect, its remainder having been absorbed into the Gnostic heresy, had disappeared by the fourth century. The name *Ebionite* comes from the Hebrew word for "poor."

## Ecce Homo

These Latin words meaning "behold the Man" (cf. Jn. 19:5) were the presentation or introduction of Christ to the Jews and the chief priests by Pontius Pilate after He had been scourged and crowned with thorns during His passion. It has become a much used title in art for pictures depicting Christ at the beginning of His passion. Also there has been a resurrection representation called the "Eucharistic Ecce Homo," which is the picturing of the figure of Christ after the resurrection.

### Ecclesia

This Greek word was translated into Latin, meaning "church." Originally it meant "assembly." It applies to both a building and a group of religious believers. Today this word has become the root-word of Church-related activities and structure. It also is applicable to the "assembly" or the particular community of Christians in the Church. (See Church; Community.)

### Ecclesiam Suam

The Latin title of the first encyclical of Pope Paul VI, translated "His Church," was published Aug. 6, 1964, and was widely acclaimed because it was a statement of the intentions and principles under which this successor of Pope John XXIII would carry on the work of the Second Vatican Council. It proclaimed especially the "full liberty of ideas and discussion" granted to the Council Fathers in their deliberations. In content it dealt with (1) the nature of the Church, or what did Christ intend through the mission He gave it; (2) what reforms, changes, and adaptations are necessary to make the Church what Christ intended; and (3) what direction must be taken and what role played by the Church in fulfilling its mission for modern man. (See Vatican Council II)

### Ecclesiastes, Book of

This book of the OT is claimed to have been written by Solomon under a pseudonym, but critics today agree that this was a literary artifice. It was written probably toward the close of the third century before Christ. Its theme is retribution; the theory of earthly rewards is weighed and found wanting, but the infinitely just God has a purpose that man finds unsearchable. It is asserted that God will intervene and right apparent injustices (3:17).

Ecclesiastes is classed as one of the books of wisdom in the bible because it measures the purpose and value of human existence. In the flow of salvation history it marks the progress of God's revelation to mankind between the thought of the Book of Job and the New Testament. The title is the Greek translation of the Hebrew name

*Qoheleth,* meaning "one who speaks to the assembly." The final verse bespeaks the course of persons until the end that is attained through Christ and his Church, declaring, "The last word, when all is heard: Fear God and keep his commandments, for this is man's all; because God will bring to judgment every work, with all its hidden qualities, whether good or bad" (12:13–14) (cf. Mt. 16:26).

### Ecclesiastic

This term is applied to a cleric in major orders, but most frequently to a church dignitary. It is seldom used today.

### Ecclesiastical

This adjective means simply "of or pertaining to the Church." Thus we have ecclesiastical courts, calendar, honors, law (cf. canon law), jurisdiction, studies, and others. It is derived from the Greek word *ecclesia.*

### Ecclesiastical Reservation

This term was given to that legal principle and process that was drawn up in Germany during the sixteenth century and that made provision that a church would retain its property when one of its clergy, of benefice or not, would convert to another religion. There had been a long standing dispute during the time of the Protestant Reformation, chiefly between the Catholics and Lutherans, over the ownership of property. Priests and religious converting to Protestantism would take their position, titles, and stipends or benefice privileges with them. This resulted in a loss for the Catholic Church, and there were recriminations and bitterness. The matter was finally settled at the close of the Thirty Years' War with the signing of the Peace of Westphalia, Oct. 24, 1648.

### Ecclesiasticus

In recent translations of the Bible this is called the "Book of Sirach." In the prologue to this OT book we learn that the author is one, in the Hebrew idiom, named "Jesus, son of Sirach." He lived in Jerusalem, was probably a scribe, and was versed in the Scriptures. The book was written according to historical data referred to in the text between 190 to 180 B.C. The theme of the book centers upon moral teaching in relation to human life and man's relationship to God; it teaches that sin is evil, but that God draws good out of evil, and that God judges and punishes evil (17:13–19). (See Sirach, Book of.)

## Ecclesiology

The study of the nature, powers, the place of the hierarchy, structure, mission, functions and members of the Church is known as ecclesiology. The *Dogmatic Constitution on the Church* of Vatican II gave new emphasis and clarity to the Church as a mystery or the invisible instrument that the Lord uses. There is need for such study because churchmen and members should meditate on the Lord and on the mission and nature of the Church. Today emphasis is placed upon accepting the Church as mystery, sacrament, communion, brotherhood, and people of God. (See Church; Vatican Council II.)

## Economic Affairs, Prefecture of

This office and department, established by Pope Paul VI, Aug. 15, 1967, coordinates and supervises the administration of the temporal affairs of the Holy See such as finance, investment, and properties.

## Economics

This branch of social science is concerned with the exchange, production, and distribution of goods and services in human society. It also investigates and studies the general laws that apply in any given society to the use and consumption of goods. In its strict moral sense, in the direction and application of general laws of both goods (production) and skills (means of production), economics is the science of justice in social life. The natural law among Christians applies to economics as a supplemental or supportive code deduced from the changing circumstances and development of a society. There is an ethical order that is interrelated to the entire order and culture of economics.

## Economy, Divine

The providence, orderly plan, employed by God in the exercise of His divine will, is the best possible since it arises from an omniscient being.

## Ecstasy

Ecstasy is an enraptured condition of the soul and body. In the mystical understanding of this condition, it follows the affective state and entails a suspension of the activity of one's exterior senses. It attains to that state where the interior, intuitive senses are active within one. It is thus the highest form of spiritual union or direct transmission of divine mysteries and must be, beyond the sense suspension, an absorption of the soul in God. It has

two phases; the first is a fading away from the normal perception through the senses and can be deliberately or involuntarily induced. The second is the intense state that cannot be induced. The end results of ecstasy are positive: holiness of life, deepened joy and love, patience, sorrow for sins, confirmation of one's belief, and the pursuit of perfection in one's state of life and in spiritual insight. (Cf. Contemplation.)

## Ecthesis

This general term used in the early Church meant an exposition of doctrine. It was also one of the two titles *(Ecthesis* and *Type)* given by a Lateran Council in A.D. 649 to two erroneous formulas issued by the Emperors Heraclius and Constans II as means of reconciling the members of the Monophysite heresy with the Church; the formulas were also condemned.

## Ecumenical Councils

The Church has held twenty worldwide councils. With dates and primary actions, they include:

1. Nicaea I, 325, condemned Arianism and declared the Son "consubstantial" with the Father.

2. Constantinople I, 381, condemned Macedonians and declared the Holy Spirit consubstantial with Father and Son.

3. Ephesus, 431, condemned Nestorians and Pelagians and declared the divine maternity of the Blessed Mother.

4. Chalcedon, 451, condemned Monophysitism.

5. Constantinople II, 553, condemned the Three Chapters.

6. Constantinople III, 680, condemned Monothelitism and censured Honorius.

7. Nicaea II, 787, condemned Iconoclasm.

8. Constantinople IV, 869, ended the Greek schism and deposed Photius.

9. Lateran I, 1123, issued decrees on simony, celibacy, lay investiture and confirmed the Concordat of Worms.

10. Lateran II, 1139, ended the papal schism and enacted reforms.

11. Lateran III, 1179, condemned Albigenses and Waldenses and regulated papal elections.

12. Lateran IV, 1215, planned a crusade, issued decrees on annual communion, repeated the condemnation of Albigenses, and enacted reforms.

13. Lyons, I, 1245, deposed Frederick II and planned a crusade.

14. Lyons II, 1274, reunited the Church with the Greeks and enacted disciplinary reforms.

15. Vienne, 1311 to 1312, abolished the Knights Templars and enacted reforms.

16. Constance, 1414 to 1418, ended Great Schism and condemned Huss.

17. Basle, Ferrara, Florence, 1431 to 1445, effected union of Greeks and enacted reforms.

18. Lateran V, 1512 to 1517, treated of the Neo-Aristotelians and enacted reforms.

19. Trent, 1545 to 1563, condemned Protestantism and enacted reforms.

20. Vatican I, 1869 to 1870 (not yet officially closed), condemned errors and defined papal infallibility.

21. Vatican II, opened by Pope John XXIII, Sept. 11, 1962, until the close of the first session on Dec. 8, 1962. After Pope John's death it was reconvened by Pope Paul VI in three additional sessions: Sept. 29 to Dec. 4, 1963; Sept. 14 to Nov. 21, 1964; Sept. 14 to its solemn closing Dec. 8, 1965. It promulgated 16 documents.

See Vatican Council II.

## Ecumenical Theology

Although theological considerations have been addressed to unity "of all in Christ" for some time, it has only recently, within the past 20 years, taken on new alertness to the shared theological thought of diverse churches in general. As stated by the document "Catholicity and Apostolicity" prepared by the Joint Working Group, with members from the Catholic Church and the World Council of Churches, the fact is recognized that "the Gospel promises the full achievement of the unity of all in Christ for the time of his return in glory. Then the universal communion of men will be realized, the final gathering of Israel and the nations (Rom. 11). For, Christ prayed to the Father for the unity of all those who should believe in him (Jn. 17:20–26); this unity remains a goal that is never reached on earth, but one toward which we must always be moving, in order that the world might believe that God sent him."

It is thus the theological impulse to preach the one gospel of Christ through dialogue with the world, and salvation through Christ, which presupposes a unity of the entire Church in love and faith. Hence such dialogue demands that churches understand themselves and others and also know the world so that faith can be voiced, learned, and transmitted to all men. (See Theology.)

## Ecumenism

This question was treated by Vatican II in its *Decree on Ecumenism* and *Decree on Eastern Catholic Churches.* It explained ecumenism as "promoting

the restoration of unity among all Christians" (UR 1) and spoke of the activity, giving impulse to the effort, meetings, spirit, and training for carrying on a dialogue and cooperation with Christian Churches and ecclesial communities.

The Church is now and always was the Church founded by Christ as the instrument of His mission. This understanding of its own nature it neither concedes to other churches or ecclesial communities nor offers compromise. However, the Church does not consider these ecclesial groups as entities that should not or do not exist, nor that they should be abolished or anathematized. Rather it holds these church groups as partners in a dialogue and collaborative effort to assess what they share in common and what they may do cooperatively to overcome the obstacles the world places in the way of fulfilling the universal mission of Christ.

Vatican Council II referred to these Christians and ecclesial communities as "separated brethren," and thus opened a new expanse of shared love and charity to all peoples. It stated: "Insofar as religious conditions allow, ecumenical activity should be furthered in such a way that without any appearance of indifference or of unwarranted intermingling on the one hand, or of unhealthy rivalry on the other, Catholics can cooperate in a brotherly spirit with their separated brethren, according to the norms of the Decree on Ecumenism" (AG 15).

It is for the bishops of the Church to initiate and direct the efforts of ecumenism. As directors they "should deal lovingly with the separated brethren, urging the faithful also to conduct themselves with great kindness and charity in their regard, and fostering ecumenism as it is understood by the Church" (CD 16).

And the Council urged Catholics themselves to approach ecumenism with a desire for unity. "In ecumenical work, Catholics must assuredly be concerned for their separated brethren, praying for them, keeping them informed about the Church, making the first approaches toward them. But their primary duty is to make an honest and careful appraisal of whatever needs to be renewed and achieved in the Catholic household itself, in order that its life may bear witness more loyally and luminously to the teachings and ordinances which have been handed down from Christ through the apostles" (UR 4).

To attain the ends of ecumenism, the Church has made provisions and entered into dialogue and deliberations at every level in the world community. The *Vatican Secretariat for Promoting Christian*

*Unity* was first begun in 1960 as a preparation for Vatican II and has continued working relations with representatives of the Eastern Churches, the World Council of Churches, the Lutheran World Federation, the Anglican Communion, and the World Alliance of Reformed Churches.

Two notable documents have been formulated: "The Canterbury Statement" by the Anglican–Roman Catholic International Commission of theologians, concerns certain points of agreement regarding ministry and ordination (Dec. 13, 1973). And the National Lutheran-Catholic Dialogue group of theologians issued the joint statement entitled: "Papal Primacy/Converging Viewpoints" (March 4, 1974). Other studies will follow these preliminaries.

The Bishops' Conferences have established Committees for Ecumenical and Inter-religious Affairs. The American Committee was established in 1964 and sponsors several national consultations annually. It has Secretariats for Non-Christians and for Catholic-Jewish Relations. All are head-quartered at 1312 Massachusetts Ave. N.W., Washington, D.C. 20005.

In all dioceses there have been set up offices with appointed directors to carry on the local aspects of ecumenism. Among a variety of other activities, they foster the Week of Prayer for Christian Unity (Jan. 18 to 25) on an interfaith basis.

### Eden, Garden of

Eden is the metaphorical name for the happiness and the place of primeval man as recorded in the first two chapters of Genesis. No one knows where this might have been located, but it is placed somewhere along the middle Euphrates River. Eden is mentioned in the Book of Ezekiel to designate a particularly fertile place, and in the Book of Joel it denotes the promised land of the Lord's coming. By interpretation it is likened to paradise (cf. Sir. 40:27) where all is glorious once again in God's love.

### Edict of Milan

Also called Edict of Toleration, this announce-ment in 313 was a political compromise between two emperors, Licinus of the East, a pagan, and Constantine of the West, soon to be a professed Christian, which made Christianity one of the recognized religions.

### Edict of Nantes

Henry IV of France (d. 1610) signed the Edict of Nantes in 1598, ending the seventh of the religious wars. It restored the rights and privileges of the Catholic clergy and gave to the Huguenots civil rights, freedom of worship in many parts of France, and possession of 100 fortified cities. In 1685 Louis XIV (d. 1715), thinking he could bring about religious unity but chiefly for political reasons, revoked the Edict of Nantes, seized or destroyed the property of the Huguenots, and forced many to flee, thus actually aiding the spread of Protestantism. When Pope Innocent XI (d. 1689) expressed disapproval, relations between France and the papacy were strained and almost led to a French schism, which was not settled until after the pope's death.

### Edict of Restitution

This document issued at the close of the Thirty Years' War in 1629 by Emperor Ferdinand II (d. 1637), gave an official interpretation of the Peace of Augsburg. It nullified privileges that Protestants had enjoyed for years and restored Catholic properties. However, the Holy See remained indifferent to this edict, perhaps foreseeing the resultant disturbance in this hazardous legislation.

### Edification, Christian

This metaphoric term is applied to the "building up" of the body of Christ, i.e., effecting the completion of the mystical body, the Church (Jude 1:20). This can only be done through the Holy Spirit. St. Paul uses it similarly in the sense that Christians rebuilding the sanctuary of Christ's body are like the resurrection by their influence of good on one another (Rom. 4:25; Eph. 4:11–13). From this we arrive at the term "edifying" in regard to proper conduct, which is a great departure from the scriptural sense.

### Education

Properly, education is the formal and general quest of wisdom. It is thus mentioned in the Bible (Sir. 6:18–37). However, we also learn that it is in vain if it does not prepare for a deeper spiritual life and for the happiness of the next world. This has been the centuries-long struggle of the Church, to instruct all toward their eternal salvation. For this the Church has developed systems of study such as the Jesuit Code and that of the Christian Brothers. She has established schools from the first century at Antioch and Jerusalem to today's parochial and university institutes spread over the world. Likewise the Church has fostered the arts of drama, rhetoric, and oratory as well as developing entire philosophies such as Scholasti-cism. Among many pronouncements, the Church's attitude toward education may be restated in the words of the bishops of the United States on April 25, 1933: ". . . the unchangeable elements of education and its real purpose—to fit men for life in eternity as well as in time; to teach men to think rightly and to live rightly; to instill sound principles in our youth, principles not only of civic righteousness, but of Catholic faith and morality; to educate groups, according to their capacity, so as to make them the best men and the best women of our country—and all this with a thorough training in the secular branches of knowledge." To this end there continues to the present the use of means to instruct Christ's people to truth through parochial schools, high schools, universities, through the Confraternity of Christian Doctrine, through study clubs, through the radio, television, and Catholic press.

Education in its present and traditional Christian concepts has stressed the importance of values—it is a learning to be oneself and a response to act for others. Vatican II declares: "For a true education aims at the formation of the human person with respect to his ultimate goal, and simultaneously with respect to the good of those societies of which, as a man, he is a member, and in whose responsibilities, as an adult, he will share" (GE 1). (See Basic Teachings for Catholic Religious Education; Christian Doctrine, Confraternity of.)

### Efficacious Grace

This is the actual, effective grace, for the Church affirms *de fide* (of faith) that no act conducive to salvation can be performed without grace, which causes us to act for our salvation. As said in Ezekiel (36:27): "I will put my spirit within you and make you live by my statutes, careful to observe my decrees." And the Council of Orange states: "It is God who works in us both to will and to do." The grace that causes us to act is efficacious, effective not only for supernatural power, but also effective in operation, producing the good action through our will concurring with the grace. Although efficacious grace is conferred, it is not the only kind of grace, nor is the liberty of the will taken away by it. It is the grace by which the hard heart is overcome and we yield to act, aided in our will by the efficacious forces of the grace. (Cf. Grace.)

### Eikon

See Icon.

### Ejaculation

This is the name for short affective prayers of a few words, e.g., "Jesus, I love You." Many of these prayers are indulgenced, and they need not be said aloud to gain the indulgences. They are sometimes called "aspirations," perhaps because they can be uttered in one breath; they are also called "invocations."

### Elcesaites

This sect arose in the beginning of the second century; it was a mixture of pagan, Jewish, and Christian thoughts, which followed the teachings of a man named Elcesai. However, its origin may have been a hundred years later and based upon a book named the "Book of Elcesai," which was called "Sacred Power." This book was considered as sufficient for salvation through its teaching; hence, revelation as recorded in the Bible was not necessary. In practice the sect had elements of pagan and oriental practices and emphasized healing powers and abstention from meat; marriage was obligatory. The sect continued for several centuries and in the tenth century was identified with the Sabaeans of the Koran.

### Elect

In St. Paul's letter to the Romans these are the "chosen ones" who by favor of God's grace merit heaven and are united eternally with Christ. It is also the title of an individual Christian. It is through the entire Christian life that we understand our own "election," which occurs in Christ (cf. 1 Thes. 1:4; Eph. 1:4). It is the Christian community that, in a special way, forms "a chosen race, a royal priesthood, a holy nation, a people he claims for his own to proclaim the glorious works of the One who called you from darkness into his marvelous light. Once you were no people, but now you are God's people; once there was no mercy for you, but now you have found mercy" (1 Pt. 2:9–10). (See Community.)

### Election, Papal

One of those methods of selecting a pope, recognized as valid by the Constitution of Pope Pius XII, is the papal election. Two-thirds plus one of the votes of the electing cardinals are necessary for a valid election.

### Eleemosynary Office

This branch of the Roman curial offices is in charge of distributing alms and aid to the hungry, aged, sick, and handicapped persons who are in need. It was first established as an office of charitable works by Pope Gregory X who reigned from 1271 to 1276.

### Elevation of the Mass

In this ceremony, which was introduced by Eudes de Sully, bishop of Paris (d. 1208), in the Mass of the Roman rite, after the consecration of the host the celebrant raises it briefly above his head for the adoration of the faithful. Likewise, immediately after the wine has been consecrated, the chalice is raised. In the Middle Ages the people considered it most important that those attending Mass should look upon the Blessed Sacrament, and for this reason, so that no one would fail to see, the practice of ringing a handbell at the elevation was begun.

However, in the New Order of the Mass this is a simple raising of the consecrated host and chalice to show them to the people. The bell is no longer rung. A more profound elevation now takes place at the conclusion of the Eucharistic prayer, just before the start of the communion rite, when the celebrant raises both the paten with the consecrated hosts and the chalice with the consecrated wine while saying: "Through him, with him, in him, in the unity of the Holy Spirit, all glory and honor is yours, Almighty Father, for ever and ever." And the people respond: "Amen." (See Eucharist, Celebration of.)

### Elizabethan Settlement

In 1559 the authority, liturgy, and creed of the Church of England were placed in law, and this became known as the Elizabethan Settlement. This established that the ruling monarch, Elizabeth, and her successors were the supreme heads of the Church of England and that belief and liturgy were to be determined by the government. This was based on a series of legal precedents and statutes enacted during the reigns of Kings Henry VIII and Edward VI. It was a comprehensive approach to the official religion of England combining the Act of Supremacy, declaring the civil ruler to have ecclesiastical jurisdiction, and the Act of Uniformity, which declared the book of

Common Prayer as the only legal form of worship. The Settlement was promulgated June 24, 1559.

### Elne, Council of

This minor council held in 1027 was notable for introducing the "Truce of God," which prohibited armed hostilities from the Saturday night *Angelus* to the Monday morning *Angelus*.

### Elohim

Elohim is the plural of the Hebrew word that in its many usages is equivalent to the adjective "divine" but as a plural form is used with a singular meaning. It is the *general* name for the God of Israel, whereas Yahweh is the *personal* name by which God was known to the Israelites. The Vulgate renders Elohim as "God," while Yahweh is translated "Dominus," i.e., "Lord" in Latin. The two together, "Yahweh Elohim," appear twenty one times in the OT. (See Yahweh.)

### Elvira, Council of

This first Spanish council of record was held about the year 300 at Elliberis, near the modern city of Granada. It published the oldest known positive law concerning clerical celibacy, stated the Catholic rule concerning the indissolubility of marriage, and enacted eighty one disciplinary canons. It also defined the office and authority of bishops, and empowered the bishop to direct the duties and works of priests and deacons, to be the sole minister of the sacrament of Confirmation, and to have the authority to impose excommunication. It is significant that the leading bishop at Elvira was to preside at the Ecumenical Council of Nicaea in 325.

### Ember Days

Ember days originated in Rome about the fifth century and were days of special penance intended to prepare the faithful for entry into each of the four seasons of the year. They were observed on the Wednesday, Friday, and Saturday that follow Dec. 13, the first Sunday of Lent, Pentecost, and Sept. 14. Since the calendar reform of 1969 the observance of ember days is at the option of the National Conference of Bishops. (Cf. Abstinence; Fasting.)

### Emblems of Saints

A symbol, object, or sign is usually associated with particular saints according to the tradition of the Church, and is most used in art or illustration of the saint. Emblems are not replacements for the saints' representations, but since few pictures of saints are extant, they serve as reminders. Following is a list of some saints and their emblems.

St. Agatha: Tongs, veil
St. Agnes: Lamb
St. Ambrose: Bees, dove, ox, pen
St. Andrew: Transverse cross
St. Anne, Mother of the Blessed Virgin: Door
St. Anthony, Abbot: Bell, hog
St. Anthony of Padua: Infant Jesus, bread, book, lily
St. Augustine of Hippo: Dove, child, shell, pen
St. Barnabas: Stones, ax, lance
St. Bartholomew: Knife, flayed and holding his skin
St. Benedict: Broken cup, raven, bell, crosier, bush
St. Bernard of Clairvaux: Pen, bees, instruments of Passion
St. Bernardine of Siena: Tablet or sun inscribed with IHS
St. Blaise: Wax, taper, iron comb
St. Bonaventure: Communion, ciborium, cardinal's hat
St. Boniface: Oak, ax, book, fox, scourge, fountain, raven, sword
St. Bridget of Kildare: Cross, flame over her head, candle
St. Bridget of Sweden: Book, pilgrim's staff
St. Catherine of Ricci: Ring, crown, crucifix
St. Catherine of Siena: Stigmata, cross, ring, lily
St. Cecilia: Organ
St. Charles Borromeo: Communion, coat of arms with word *Humilitas*
St. Christopher: Giant, torrent, tree, Child Jesus on his shoulders
St. Clare of Assisi: Monstrance
Sts. Cosmas and Damian: A phial, box of ointment
St. Cyril of Alexandria: Blessed Virgin holding the Child Jesus, pen
St. Cyril of Jerusalem: Purse, book
St. Dominic: Rosary, star
St. Edmund the Martyr: Arrow, sword
St. Elizabeth of Hungary: Alms, flowers, bread, the poor, a pitcher
St. Francis of Assisi: Deer, wolf, birds, fish, skull, the stigmata
St. Francis Xavier: Crucifix, bell, vessel, Negro
St. Genevieve: Bread, keys, herd, candle
St. George: Dragon
St. Gertrude: Crown, taper, lily
Sts. Gervase and Protase: Scourge, club, sword
St. Gregory I (the Great): Tiara, crosier, dove

St. Helena: Cross
St. Hilary: Stick, pen, child
St. Ignatius Loyola: Communion, chasuable, book, apparition of Our Lord
St. Isidore: Bees, pen
St. James the Greater: Pilgrim's staff, shell, key, sword
St. James the Less: Square rule, halberd, club
St. Jerome: Lion
St. John Berchmans: Rule of St. Ignatius, cross, rosary
St. John Chrysostom: Bees, dove, pen
St. John of God: Alms, heart, crown of thorns
St. John the Baptist: Lamb, head on platter, skin of an animal
St. John the Evangelist: Eagle, chalice, kettle, armor
St. Josaphat Kuncevyc: Chalice, crown, winged deacon
St. Joseph, Spouse of the Blessed Virgin: Infant Jesus, lily, rod, plane, carpenter's square
St. Jude: Sword, square rule, club
St. Justin Martyr: Ax, sword
St. Lawrence: Cross, book of the Gospels, gridiron
St. Leander of Seville: Pen
St. Liborius: Pebbles, peacock
St. Longinus: In arms at foot of the cross
St. Louis IX of France: Crown of thorns, nails
St. Lucy: Cord, eyes
St. Luke: Ox, book, brush, palette
St. Mark: Lion, book
St. Martha: Holy water sprinkler, dragon
St. Mary Magdalene: Alabaster box of ointment
St. Matilda: Purse, alms
St. Matthew: Winged man, purse, lance
St. Matthias: Lance
St. Maurus: Scales, spade, crutch
St. Meinrad: Two ravens
St. Michael: Scales, banner, sword, dragon
St. Monica: Girdle, tears
St. Nicholas: Three purses or balls, anchor or boat, child
St. Patrick: Cross, harp, serpent, baptismal font, demons, shamrock
St. Paul: Sword, book or scroll
St. Peter: Keys, boat, cock
St. Philip, Apostle: Column
St. Philip Neri: Altar, chasuble, vial
St. Roch: Angel, dog, bread
St. Rose of Lima: Crown of thorns, anchor, city
St. Sebastian: Arrows, crown
Sts. Sergius and Bacchus: Military garb, palm
St. Simon: Saw, cross

St. Simon Stock: Scapula
St. Teresa of Avila: Heart, arrow, book
St. Therese of Lisieux: Roses entwining a
   crucifix
St. Thomas, Apostle: Lance, ax
St. Thomas Aquinas: Chalice, monstrance, dove,
   ox, person trampled under foot
St. Vincent: Gridiron, boat
St. Vincent de Paul: Children
St. Vincent Ferrer: Pulpit, cardinal's hat, trum-
   pet, captives

## Embolism

An embolism is an added or inserted prayer,
e.g., the prayer said immediately after the "Our
Father" in the Mass, which is an extension of the
last part of the Our Father and expands the
petition beyond the prescribed wording of the
prayer. It is said by the priest and the people
respond: "For the Kingdom, the power, and the
glory are yours, now and forever."

## Eminence

This term is addressed to cardinals only, by
decree of the former Congregation of Rites, thus,
"most eminent"; "his eminence"; "your eminence."
The sole exception is that "eminence" may be given
in titles of address to the Grand Master of the
Knights of St. John of Jerusalem.

## Emmanuel, also Immanuel

The symbolic name of the child born to the
virgin (*alma*) in the Hebrew language means "God
is with us." Emmanuel was the name spoken to
Ahaz the King of Judah as recorded by Isaiah:
"Again the Lord spoke to Ahaz: Ask for a sign
from the Lord, your God; let it be deep as the
nether world, or high as the sky! But Ahaz
answered, 'I will not ask! I will not tempt the Lord!'
Then he said: Listen, O house of David! Is it not
enough for you to weary men, must you also
weary my God? Therefore the Lord himself will
give you this sign: the virgin shall be with child,
and bear a son, and shall name him Immanuel'"
(Is. 7:10–14).

Whether or not this is a Messianic prophecy has
been debated by the editors of the Jerusalem Bible,
for example, and the scholar J. J. Steinmann.
However, because of the use of the word "sign" in a
miraculous sense, it is more reasonable to consider
this to be Messianic as recorded in Mt. 1:23: "The
virgin shall be with child and give birth to a son,
and they shall call him Emmanuel, a name which
means 'God is with us.'"

## Empire, Holy Roman

The empire of single rule was founded by
Charlemagne with the aid of the Roman Pontiffs.
It collapsed for a time through dissension but was
revived in 962 with the coronation of Otho (Otto) I
as king of Germany by Pope John XII. It lasted for
more than eight centuries. The addition of the
adjective "Holy" appeared for the first time in the
reign of Frederick I (d. 1190) and became
customary after Charles IV (d. 1378). For the states
involved, chiefly Germany and Italy, it became an
extension of an aristocratic system, feudalizing the
old Roman Empire. It held advantages for both the
states and the Church but actually brought the
Church into sharp contrast with the temporalities
and created a number of problems, such as lay
investiture. The Holy Roman Empire dissolved in
1806 when the Hapsburg Emperor Francis II was
defeated in the war with Napoleon. Succeeding
attempts at confederation failed, but the Church
was not party to their make-up or failure, because
the times had changed the political aspect of the
world and democratic principles had altered the
protective necessity of the empire as it once
existed.

## Enchiridion

The title of the best known writing of H.J.D.
Denzinger (d. 1883) is *Enchiridion*. It is a compilation of the chief conciliar decrees together with a
list of propositions they condemned and is frequently quoted as a source book. (See Trent,
Council of.)

## Enclosure, also Coister

This is the enclosed place reserved to religious,
including the physical barriers that surround it,
together with the special laws governing admission
to it or exit of religious from it. This enclosure is
either papal or by the bishop of the diocese in
which the monastery or convent is erected: (1) in
regard to male religious (regulars) with solemn
vows, the enclosure is papal and must be observed
strictly. The area of the enclosure must be clearly
indicated; e.g., certain public rooms or visiting
parlors and the nave of the monastery church are
excluded generally. Laymen may enter a monastery of men, but women are strictly prohibited
under penalty of excommunication for the woman
and the one who permits her to enter, reserved to
the Holy See; (2) in monasteries of nuns taking
solemn vows, the law of enclosure is equally strict,
though exceptions of diocesan sisters and episcopal
enclosure are made. It is not understood that nuns

who wish to return to the world permanently may not do so. Laws governing the enclosure, entrance and egress, dismissal and voluntary leaving are contained in canon law with full provisions (cs. 597-606; 2342).

## Encratism

A rigid moral and ascetic doctrine practiced by certain Christians of the second century, Encratism was based on the misconception that matter is evil. Those practicing this were called Encratites, a sect of the Gnostic heresy.

## Encyclical

The term comes from the Latin description of these letters, *literae encyclicae*, literally "circular letters." An encyclical is a profound letter addressed by the pope to all the patriarchs, primates, archbishops, bishops, and prelates nullius of the worldwide Church. An encyclical may also be addressed to the hierarchy of a single country or confederation of nations. Each is written in Latin. The purpose of an encyclical is not personal but to condemn certain current errors; to inform the faithful, through the hierarchy, of adverse government legislation interfering with the mission of the Church; or to explain conduct that should be followed by Christians. They are intended for all the faithful, and in turn the faithful are to give the message of these letters assent, obedience, and respect because of the weight and truth they contain. The authority of encyclicals was stated by Pius XII in *Humani Generis* (1950): "Nor must it be thought that what is contained in encyclical letters does not of itself demand assent, on the pretext that the popes do not exercise in them the supreme power of their teaching authority. Rather, such teachings belong to the ordinary magisterium, of which it is true to say: 'He who hears you, hears me' (Lk. 10:16); for the most part, too, what is expounded and inculcated in encyclical letters already appertains to Catholic doctrine for other reasons." (See Authority.) Each is titled usually by the first words in Latin. Recent notable encyclicals are: Pius X, 1904, on the Blessed Virgin Mary, Mediatrix of Graces (*Ad Diem Illum Laetissimum*); Pius X, 1907, on Modernism *(Pascendi)*; Pius XI, 1922, on Church and State *(Ubi Arcano Dei);* Pius XI, 1929, on Catholic Education *(Divini illius Magistri)*; Pius XI, 1930, on Christian marriage *(Casti Connubi)*; Pius XI, 1931, on the social and industrial order *(Quadragesimo Anno);* Pius XI, 1937, on atheistic communism *(Divini Redemptoris)*; Pius XII, 1943, on the mystical body *(Mystici*

*Corporis)*; Pius XII, 1954, on the state and merit of virginity *(Sacra Virginitas)*; John XXIII, 1961, on Christianity and Social Progress *(Master et Magistra)*; John XXIII, 1963, Peace on Earth, *(Pacem in Terris)*; Paul VI, 1965, The Eucharist *(Mysterium Fidei)*; Paul VI, 1967, Development of Peoples *(Populorum Progressio)*; Paul VI, 1968, Birth Control*(Humanae Vitae)*. (See under separate listings.)

## Encyclical Epistle

An encyclical epistle differs only slightly from an encyclical letter. It is primarily directed to instruct concerning some devotion or special need of the Holy See, e.g., a worldwide charity or some special event such as a Holy Year.

## Encyclopaedists

A group of rationalists and free thinkers wrote articles for the French *Encyclopedie* (published 1751 to 1765), notably Voltaire (d. 1778), Rousseau (d. 1778), and Diderot (d. 1784). They attempted to inject a trend toward infidelilty to the Church, prepared the thinking on irreligion preceding the French Revolution, and opposed the pontificate of Pope Clement XIII (d. 1769). In general they denied the divinity of Christ and maintained that all religion was only a highly individualistic concern between the person and God. They denied the teaching concerning original sin and praised material progress and scientific methods. The *Encyclopedie* was placed on the Index of Forbidden Books in 1758 by decree of the Church. (See Enlightenment, the Age of.)

## End

In scholastic philosophy, end means "that object for the attainment of which the agent moves and acts." It is divided into: (1) the "end which" *(finis qui),* the good intended to be attained; (2) the "end for whom" *(finis cui),* the person or subject for whom the "end which" is obtained; (3) the formal end (the end by which or *finis quo),* the actual attainment of the thing intended. Further, the end of the work *(finis operis)* is that to which an act is ordered, or tends, by its own nature, e.g., study is to enlighten the mind; and the *end of the one working (finis operantis),* that toward which one directs an action, e.g., study of a science because it is useful. Ends may be proximate, intermediate, or ultimate; also, *primary end* is that which is sufficient for prompting one to act, and *secondary end,* one not sufficient but auxiliary in prompting the act.

## End of Man

The End of Man is the final, ultimate goal to the attainment of which all other actions are subordinate, which can only be God, or beatitude in God. (Cf. Heaven; Eschatology.)

## End of the World

At no place in Scripture, the teaching of the Church, mystical revelations, or elsewhere is the time of the world's end set forth. The only certainty refers more precisely to the final or last judgment (Mt. 25:31–46) described by Christ. The judgment at which the kingdom of the Son, all the individuals of the faithful, is purified before coming into the kingdom of the Father is settled ultimately on religious grounds: Christ is to be the judge. Human history will be at an end, and humans will continue in eternal life of happiness or loss.

That the end of the world is certain is a truth revealed in Scripture and taught as a dogma by the Church. Christ foretold the end of the world (Mt. 25:31–46; Mk. 13:1–37; Lk. 21:5–28). Christ also compared the end to a harvest, saying, "Just as weeds are collected and burned, so will it be at the end of the world" (Mt. 13:40). The Apostles also frequently spoke of the end of the world; St. Peter declared: "What we await are new heavens and a new earth where, according to his promise, the justice of God will reside" (2 Pt. 3:13). (Cf. Eschatology.)

## Endowment

An endowment is a fund set apart for the support of an institution of the Church, either a church building, school, or hospital. Sometimes the term is applied to a house or fund for the education of candidates for the priesthood, or the general support of education in any institution of higher learning.

## Ends of the Mass

There are four solemn intentions for which every Mass is offered: (1) adoration, the worship of God, (2) thanksgiving, (3) reparation for the sins of the world, (4) petition for the needs of all people. (See Eucharist, Celebration of.)

## Energumen

Energumen is a term applied to one possessed by evil spirits, a demoniac. (Cf. Demonic.)

## English Martyrs

Those who were put to death for the faith in England between the schism of Henry VIII and 1681 are known as the English Martyrs. There are records of 602; some of these have been canonized, and petitions for others started with the Holy See, but this does not include all who suffered death in persecution during this time. The feast is celebrated in England on May 4.

The first recognition of martyrdom was given by Pope Gregory XIII in 1583 when he allowed depicting some of the martyrs in the painting on the wall of the church of the English College in Rome; sixty-three were recognized as beatified. Archbishop Plunkett was beatified in 1920, and one hundred thirty-six others on Dec. 15, 1929. Sts. John Fischer and Thomas More were canonized by Pope Pius XI in 1935.

## Enkolpion

This medallion is worn suspended from the neck and resting on the breast by bishops of the Byzantine rite. It bears either a representation of our Lord or the Blessed Mother and sometimes contains relics.

## Enlightenment, The Age of

This broad title was given to the eighteenth century because of the prevalent intellectual atmosphere of the time. Throughout the Western world this time was heralded as the Age of Reason, because all aspects of learning were given a status that challenged the teachings of Christianity.

It was most notable that the entire intellectual world placed new emphasis upon humanism, attributing to the social and moral sciences the same exactness found in the natural laws of the physical sciences. This led writers, philosophers, and scientists to rationalize concerning religion, ethics, and the natural law. This in turn gave rise to secularism and subjective thought that placed the teachings of revealed religion in an outmoded grouping. The most secure guide to human knowledge and behavior came to be scientific inquiry. Human reason became the arbiter of the nature of religion, social sciences, political and economic life. Deism and atheism became the "natural" course replacing in the minds of intellectuals revelation and Christian concepts.

In the political sphere Thomas Hobbes and John Locke advanced an absolutist concept; the "social contract" theory of Hobbes and the individual's natural right to revolt as conceived by Locke were dominant and dangerous arguments against all existing authority. The rejection of the Christian's basic teachings caused some clashes, but the question of civil and human rights were for the first time focused on man and society. The outcome was a series of ideological errors that we still are molested with and that only the firm social teachings of the Church can combat effectively. (See Humanism.)

## Entelechy

The philosophical theory that maintains that all physical bodies are directed toward or predisposed toward a final goal as the perfection of the individual of any species. The Catholic teaching is that human acts cannot be determined by physical laws, whereas finality in the organic processes may exist. Thus the finality of the soul is only perfected in the mystical union of the person with God through Christ and by conformity of human actions to the will of God. Teilhard de Chardin held that the physical world is in its totality oriented toward a single divine plan and that inorganic matter, of its nature, tends toward the production and all-embrasive fulfillment in keeping with a divine plan. (Cf. Teilhardism.)

## Enthronement of the Sacred Heart

A devotion centered around the Sacred Heart of Jesus was first developed by Father Mateo C. Boevey, SS.CC. in the early twentieth century. Father Mateo was born about 1876 and after ordination was working in Valparaiso, Chile. It was here that he introduced the enthronement idea whereby a picture of the Sacred Heart or an image is solemnly enthroned or installed. This is done to recognize the Kingship of the Sacred Heart of Jesus in the family and home. The installation can be made in schools, hospitals, retirement homes, factories, or religious communities, but the chief emphasis is upon the home. Pope Pius X gave his approval to the devotion in 1907 and urged that it be preached throughout the world, and six years later when it was first introduced into the United

States (1913), indulgences were granted to Chile and two years later extended to the entire world.

The ceremony of enthronement is the installation, with a priest blessing the image, and the head of the house placing this in a proper and honored place while a hymn is sung. Together those present recite the Creed; the priest explains the meaning and character of this action; an Act of Consecration to the Sacred Heart of Jesus is made; the Our Father and Hail Mary are recited for the absent members of the family; an Act of Thanksgiving and a prayer honoring the Immaculate Heart of the Blessed Mother is followed by a general blessing for all by the priest. (See Sacred Heart of Jesus.)

## Enthusiasm, Catholic

Every person has, what the Greek word declares, a "rapture," a joyous eagerness, something to be caught up in and which impells him onward. It is in the Christian and Catholic sense seeking to become more than human; it is the redemptive pursuit that comes from membership in the Mystical Body of Christ and through the Holy Spirit. Pope Paul VI spoke (June 2, 1974) of the members of the Church "who live the joyful and generous enthusiasm" of professing their Christianity. He said: "We would like Pentecost to bring its spirit of truth, charity, and unity into the hearts of those many who are still Catholics and still call themselves Catholics but who are drooping and sad. They vegetate in doubt and silly criticism. They have acquired the unhappy taste of contradicting Mother Church. They delude themselves that they live the Church's charisms while isolating themselves from her indispensable organism, her hierarchy, and her community." Enthusiasm for the Catholic is a willing acceptance of what is ever in the mind of Christ, namely, salvation even though it means bearing the cross of suffering everyday. It is hope applied in ordinary living through love. Vatican II stated: "They are mistaken who, knowing that we have here no abiding city but seek one which is to come, think that they may therefore shirk their earthly responsibilities. For they are forgetting that by the faith itself they are more than ever obliged to measure up to these duties, each according to his proper vocation" (GS 43). (See Hope.)

## Envy

One of the capital sins, envy is the willful grieving or sadness because of another's spiritual or temporal good, looked upon or considered as a lessening of one's own goods, e.g., if he didn't have that, I could have it; or an honor paid to another is considered a disgrace reflected upon oneself. It is begrudging of what one's neighbor has and wishing seriously that he did not have it so that the envious person would not feel at a disadvantage.

## Eparchy

This term corresponds to diocese in Eastern churches, notably the Russian. The residing bishop is called an Eparch or Exarch.

## Ephesians, Epistle to the

One of the four captivity Epistles, the letter to the Ephesians was written by St. Paul about A.D. 63. It was not addressed exclusively to the Ephesians, for while Paul was there for about three years, critics agree it was intended for a broader group, e.g., the Church in Laodicea. The Epistle is a noncontroversial exposition on mankind being one with Christ and God's purpose in the world through His Church (1:15–23). It is also directed at the development of a Christian life, particularly of the Christian family (5:22–28; 6:1–4), but its chief doctrine is that of the Mystical Body of Christ as it exists in the Church.

## Ephesus, Council of

An ecumenical council held in 431 was summoned by Theodosius II. It condemned Pelagian and Nestorian heresies. This council is most notable for having defined the Catholic dogma that the Blessed Virgin Mary is the Mother of God. It also defined the hypostatic union of the two natures, divine and human, in the one divine person, Jesus Christ. Although the Council had been intended to bring harmony to the schools of Christian thought, it failed to do so but did establish the Nicene Creed as the true statement of faith. (Cf. Deipara.)

## Ephesus, Robber Synod of

Also called *Latrocinium,* this was a meeting in 449 presided over by the heretical Dioscurus of Alexandria. The synod advanced Nestorian doctrines, ignoring the pope and his rights. All of its decrees were revoked by the Council of Chalcedon in A.D. 451.

## Epieikeia, also Epikeia

This Greek term, meaning equity, is applied to the interpretation of a law. It is reasonably taken for granted that the lawgiver does not wish to bind in some particularly difficult case because the exercise of the law would work an unforeseen hardship; thus, there is an examination of the law and a judgment of the intent of the lawgiver in the spirit of the law but against its rigor in application. Epieikeia may not be used in the following cases: when the lawgiver may be approached directly for an interpretation or dispensation; in the case of laws that make an act invalid; in the case of one being incapable of undertaking legal action; divine law, positive or natural; or where the lawgiver could not oblige, e.g., where one in following the law would commit sin.

## Epigonation

This eucharistic vestment of all Eastern Church bishops, archimandrites, and other dignitaries consists of an oblong of embroidered silk, stiffened with cardboard, which is worn suspended at one corner, attached to the cincture (girdle) or hung from one shoulder, falling to the right knee. In the West, it is called the subcinctorium and worn only by the pope. It symbolizes the spiritual sword of justice.

## Epiklesis, also Epiclesis

From the Greek meaning "invocation," epiklesis is a prayer found in all the liturgies of the East and West. It is said immediately after the words of institution by the celebrant and is addressed to God the Father and God the Son, asking that the Holy Spirit be sent down upon the sacred species to change the bread and wine into Christ's body and blood so that the recipients can be thereby filled with grace. It has four essential elements: (1) an invocation of God the Father, (2) a plea to send the Holy Spirit, (3) a prayer that the Holy Spirit may change the gifts into the body and blood of Christ, and (4) the prayer that these gifts may then be productive of grace in the faithful. Thus the theological significance is that God the Father shows his love, that this love is manifest through the Son of God, and that the Holy Spirit sanctifies all by working out God's divine plan among men. It thus holds that the Eucharist is central in God's plan of redemption and that the Trinity, three divine Persons, accomplishes the salvation of people.

## Epimanikia

From the Greek word meaning "upon the sleeves," this is a liturgical vestment of all Eastern rites. It consists of an over-sleeve that binds the fuller sleeve of the *sticharion* or alb at the wrist.

## Epiphany

The solemnity celebrated on Jan. 6 commemorates (especially in the West) the visitation of the Magi and Christ's manifestation of His glory to them. The feast arose in the Eastern Church and remains there one of more broad significance, celebrating also Christ's glory manifested to the Gentiles through the Magi and His divinity manifested at His baptism in the Jordan, as well as at the miracle of the marriage at Cana. It is sometimes called Twelfth Night, since it is 12 days after Christmas. The word from the Greek means "manifestation," making Christ known to the world as the Messiah, the divine Son of God (Jn. 2:11). Where the solemnity is not observed as a day of obligation, it is assigned in the calendar of the Church to the Sunday between Jan 2 and 8.

## Episcopacy

1. The full group of the hierarchy known as bishops, who acting collegially are the government of Christ's Church.

2. The completion to fullness of the Sacrament of Holy Orders conferred through consecration. By this completion the recipient is consecrated bishop, is given the power to ordain and consecrate others, to confirm, to consecrate objects for divine worship, and to wield jurisdiction under delegation from the pope. This fullness of the Sacrament of Holy Orders is an article of faith defined at the Council of Trent (sess. 23, c. 7). The existence of bishops was confirmed in apostolic times (1 Tm. 5:19–22), but at first the right of jurisdiction was not fully theirs. However, from the beginning of the second century the title *episcopos* was reserved to the superior now known as bishop. Vatican II teaches that "episcopal consecration, together with the office of sanctifying, also confers the offices of teaching and of governing" (LG 21).

## Episcopalians

The general name for all members of the Protestant Episcopal Church in the United States is Episcopalians. The Episcopal Church is one of fourteen self-governing churches arising from the Anglican Communion and is the oldest outside Britain. When the Anglican Church was first introduced into North America in the mid–sixteenth century, it quickly became the established church of colonies in Virginia and other southern states. But in most colonies of New England it was outlawed until late in the seventeenth century. Where established, it thus had ties with the British Anglican Church and acted under the jurisdiction of the Bishop of London. This led to a greater increase in lay control throughout North America, and following the American Revolution, the first convention of the Protestant Episcopal Church met in Philadelphia in 1789 where it adopted a separate name, laws, constitution, and a revised version of the Book of Common Prayer. The name Protestant Episcopal meant only that it was (1) non-Catholic, and (2) had bishops in authority. It remains a church whose structure is largely centered in the laity, with each General Convention held every three years having a tri-partite make-up, namely, bishops, clergy, and elected lay representatives.

In 1919 the National Council of the Episcopal Church was established, which puts into practice the programs developed and approved by the General Convention, namely those concerning missions, education, and more recently, the ecumenical movement. The Church has three orders of clergy: bishops, priests, and deacons. In each diocese the bishop is elected by the clergy and lay representatives, and the diocese also has its own constitution and rules that are supplemental to those of the National Church. The pastor of a parish, called a rector, is chosen by the parish vestry, which is an elected group of laity from the parish. Church members consider themselves as belonging to one of three groups: Protestant, a third branch of the Catholic Church (the other two being Roman Catholic and Eastern Orthodox), or a mixture of Protestant and Catholic.

## Episcopalism

This doctrine teaches and declares that the supreme authority in the Church rests not alone in the Supreme Pontiff but in the collective body of bishops, whether throughout the world or assembled in Council. Over the years this has come to have some unacceptable aspects, e.g., the Ultramontanists. The Church is built upon this teaching (cf. Eph. 2:20; Rv. 21:14), with Peter the leader, not because he was other than an Apostle, but because he was given special promises (the "rock" upon which the Church was to be built), special powers ("filled with the Holy Spirit," Acts

4:8), and privileges from Christ Himself and not from the other Apostles as a group. Vatican II has spoken of authority exercised by the collegial body of bishops or by the pope alone serving as the head of the collegial body even when performing some noncollegial act. (See Collegiality; Authority.)

### Epistle

1. A letter; in a broad sense a letter of instruction, information, or command from a superior addressed to subordinates.

2. Biblical Epistles are the books of the NT named either by reference to the people to whom they are addressed or by the name of the writer. The authenticity of these writings is guaranteed by the fact that all Councils of the Church that treated of the Canon of the Scripture included these. The form of these letters, and undoubtedly there were many others written but now lost, follows that of ordinary secular letters of the times. As a rule, they consist of three parts: an introduction giving the name of the writer, the name of the party to whom it is addressed and a greeting; the middle portion or main message; and a concluding paragraph of farewell. In those of St. Paul the greeting is characteristically Christian, "grace and peace" instead of the pagan "health." Often all of these Epistles have been called "Catholic" in the sense that rather than being directed to a particular group they were addressed to the universal Church. This can be determined from their wide doctrinal content and internal evidence. This term also appears in this sense in a portion of the Muratorian Canon, as well as in the writings of Eusebius (d. 340). It is from the Epistles that the second scriptural lesson read in the Mass is taken, in the liturgy of the Word. (See Readings, Cycle of.)

### Epistolae Ecclesiasticae

Literally, Church letters, each letter written by Church dignitaries has taken on special classifications that are included under this title. They are: (1) apostolic letters, written by authority of the pope; (2) commendatory letters; (3) letters of communion, or those authenticating one's affiliation with the Church; (4) confessorial letters, those asking that one be reunited with the Church; (5) decretals; (6) dimissorials; (7) encyclicals; (8) letters of enthronement, or orthodoxy addressed from a bishop to other bishops; (9) paschal letters, issued at Easter (formerly those that declared the date of Easter as a feast); and (10) pastoral letters, those of instruction sent by a bishop. (Cf. Encyclical.)

### Epistolary

This book contains authentic texts of the biblical Epistles. Written in Latin, sometimes with tonal notation, it is the book from which was chanted the first lesson in solemn Masses of the Roman rite. (See Lectionary.)

### Epitrakhelion, also Epitrachelion

The word means in Greek: "upon the neck," which in Eastern Churches of the Byzantine Rite, is the priestly stole. This is usually highly embroidered or ornamented, and the two descending ends are joined from below the neck to the fringed bottom so that the stole remains in place. It is symbolic of purity.

### Equality

Each person has by right through creation by God a unique and singular equality, i.e., a dignity, equal rights under the law, freedom both of mind and will, and a possession of access to the graces God provides for one's salvation. The abuse of this equality exists in any form of denial of these rights.

Vatican II taught this equality for all, not just the Christians or privileged. It declared regarding equality before the Law: "Government is to see to it that the equality of citizens before the law, which is itself an element of the common welfare, is never violated for religious reasons whether openly or covertly. Nor is there to be discrimination among citizens" (DH 6).

And regarding the equality of all men, it declared: "Since all men possess a rational soul and are created in God's likeness, since they have the same nature and origin, have been redeemed by Christ, and enjoy the same divine calling and destiny, the basic equality of all must receive increasingly greater recognition" (GS 29).

And within the Church there exists a pervading equality possessed by all men: "The chosen People of God is one: 'one Lord, one faith, one baptism' (Eph. 4:5). As members, they share a common dignity from their rebirth in Christ. They have the same filial grace and the same vocation to perfection. They possess in common one salvation, one hope, and one undivided charity. Hence, there is in Christ and in the Church no inequality on the basis of race or nationality, social condition, or sex, because 'there does not exist among you Jew or Greek, slave or freeman, male or female. All are one in Christ Jesus' (Gal. 3:28, Greek text; cf. Col. 3:11).

"If therefore, everyone in the Church does not proceed by the same path, nevertheless all are called to sanctity and have received an equal privilege of faith through the justice of God (cf. 2 Pt. 1:1). And if by the will of Christ some are made teachers, dispensers of mysteries, and shepherds on behalf of others, yet all share a true equality with regard to the dignity and to the activity common to all the faithful for the building up of the Body of Christ" (LG 32). (See Freedom.)

## Erastianism

This term has become the adopted title of the theory which states that the State has supremacy over the Church in ecclesiastical affairs. It is derived from the Swiss writer, Thomas Erastus (1524 to 1583) who first proposed the theory in Church-State relationships. Because it is contrary to the traditional teaching of the Catholic Church, this became an influence upon those rulers who sought to control the Church. Erastus had written, however, that state officials should consult with Church scholars and men in authority, but this aspect was merely a sop, for the writer held the Church to be ungodly.

## Eremite

See Hermit, Eastern Monasticism.

## Eschatology

Eschatology is the part of theology that treats of the final things: death, the Day of Yahweh, the second coming of Christ (Parousia), judgment, heaven, and hell. The word, from the Greek, means "teaching of the last things." More specifically this is concerned with a study of the Resurrection of Christ and His teaching to the disciples concerning His second coming, the establishment of the Kingdom of God. The time of Christ's coming is known only to the Father (Mt. 24:36–39); we do not know the hour of His coming (Mt. 24:42–51); but we are assured of a last or final judgment that will reward or condemn eternally the faithful (Mt. 24:31–46). The summation of this study is that mankind must prepare for the second coming of Christ (Phil. 1:6) at the end of time when Christ will judge the living and the dead.

"He planned to assemble in the holy Church all those who would believe in Christ. Already from the beginning of the world the foreshadowing of the Church took place. She was prepared for in a remarkable way throughout the history of the people of Israel and by means of the Old Covenant. Established in the present era of time, the Church was made manifest by the outpouring of the Spirit. At the end of time she will achieve her glorious fulfillment. Then, as may be read in the holy Fathers, all just men from the time of Adam, 'from Abel, the just one, to the last of the elect,' will be gathered together with the Father in the universal Church" (LG 2).

And: "When the Lord comes in His majesty, and all the angels with Him (cf. Mt. 25:31), death will be destroyed and all things will be subject to Him (cf. 1 Cor. 15:16–27). Meanwhile some of His disciples are exiles on earth. Some have finished with this life and are being purified. Others are in glory, beholding 'clearly God Himself triune and one, as He is'" (LG 49). (See Heaven; Parousia.)

## Esdras

See Ezra, Book of.

## Espousal, also Betrothal

An espousal was an engagement of marriage, or a promise of marriage. In early times this was equivalent to a binding contract of marriage, but the engagement should in no way be confused with the essential contract that is the sacramental sign and source of sacramental grace. Thus the actual indulgence in sexual intercourse or the use of the rights of marriage are not permitted or granted by the espousal or engagement. (See Marriage, Sacrament of.)

## Espousals of the Blessed Virgin

This feast was celebrated in previous times and is still observed in some countries on Jan. 23. Its observance was never extended to the universal Church and is not listed in the English edition of the *Sacramentary*.

## Essence

Essence is that which tells us what a thing is, answers the question: What is it? It tells strictly the nature of reality and indicates its genus and species. Like being, essence defines the nature of the thing, or that which makes it something. This must be extended to the things that are but also to the innumerable possible things or realities that could be brought into existence.

There are two aspects of essence: (1) We observe in every existing thing of our experience that it continuously changes, yet it retains its identity; it remains the same in its character as a static and dynamic being, and without its essence, it would not be what it is. (2) Each existent in the world of our experience both *becomes* and *changes,* and this demonstrates what it is as a being, and what it becomes apart from other beings or existents.

## Essenes

The Essenes were a rigoristic Jewish sect. They were known by four early writers of the first century A.D., namely, Pliny the Elder, Josephus the historian, Solinus, and Philo. The members were said to reside on the western shore of the Dead Sea; they were a solitary people and lived a quasi-monastic life without women. The Essenes renounced all commerce with the goddess Venus and all money, and only those who were chaste and innocent could be admitted to the order. They were concerned with purity of food and pursued an intense intellectual life according to their standards. Near them there stood the town of Engadda (Engedi), now destroyed, and beyond this the Masada fortress on a rock not far from the Dead Sea.

According to Josephus there were three principal sects of the Jews: the Pharisees, Sadducees, and the Essenes. Since Josephus was at one time a member, we learn that the Essenes were more closely bound together in a brotherhood like that of the Pythagoreans. There was an emphasis on temperance and self-control, together with the renunciation of all pleasures, particularly marriage, which they did not condemn for others but "they wished to protect themselves against women's wantonness, being persuaded that none of the sex keeps her plighted troth to one man" (Josephus). They were hailed as surpassing the Greeks and barbarians in virtue because of their emphasis upon discipline.

The Essenes were called "holy ones." Josephus declares they were very courageous and happy: "They make light of danger, and triumph over pain by their resolute will; death, if it comes with honor, they consider better than immortality. The war with the Romans tried their souls through and through by every variety of test. Racked and twisted, broken and burnt, and made to pass through every instrument of torture, in order to induce them to blaspheme their Lawgiver or to eat some forbidden thing, they refused to yield to either demand, nor ever once did they cringe to their persecutors or ever shed a tear. Smiling in their agonies and mildly deriding their tormentors, they cheerfully resigned their souls, confident that they would receive them back again."

The Essenes have been likened to early Christians because of their brotherhood, their teaching of baptism, and communal life. Among the Dead Sea Scrolls was found the "Manual of Discipline" of the Essenes telling much of their practices, hierarchical structure, and the disciplinary actions. From this writing we also learn many of the practices that illuminate the ritual and liturgy of the Last Supper, such as, wherever as many as ten shall gather together for a banquet, they shall take their seats in order of precedence and the company may not touch the bread and the wine till the priest has blessed them and taken some. This has led to some insight into the evangelist Luke's description of an incident in the Last Supper of Our Lord: "A dispute arose among them about who should be regarded as the greatest. He said: 'Earthly kings lord it over their people. Those who exercise authority over them are called their benefactors. Yet it cannot be that way with you. Let the greater among you be as the junior, the leader as the servant'" (Lk. 22:25–26). This also gives rise to the speculation that Christ not only knew of the Essenes but was setting up a new order of procedure for his Church and its leaders while repudiating the Essenes. (See Scrolls of the Dead Sea.)

## Established Church

The religion recognized, established, and/or fostered by a civil state as the official religion is known as the Established Church. It places other religions on a "tolerated" basis. The most notable example is the Church of England, but exclusivity of any one religion over another in modern states is becoming more rare as the world grows in communication.

## Esther, Book of

This book of the OT by an unknown author was probably written a short time after the events narrated (fifth century B.C.). It is an historical book telling of God's providential care of Israel in protecting the nation from peril while it was in exile during the reign of Ahasuerus (Xerxes), King of Persia. It is also a teaching book, since it tells of faith in God and repentance. The book is named after Esther who was made queen by Ahasuerus in the seventh year of his reign, after he deposed Queen Vashti. It also records the beginning of the Hebrew feast of Purim. One of the prayers of the OT was spoken by Esther (4C: 14–30) as an acknowledgement of God's oneness and as a plea for protection.

## Eternity

We understand eternity only from the standpoint of time, and thus it is an infinite extent of time in which every event is considered as simultaneously past, present, and future. In a more profound sense we may understand this as an instant *now* with neither beginning nor end. It is in this sense that we may say God's essential Being is an eternal *now*. Putting this in accord with our understanding, we find St. John speaking of Christ as He "who is and who was and who is to come" (Rv. 1:4). On the other hand, we speak of a thing as eternal or without end when it is not subject to change or founded in time and will continue forever, for example, the laws of nature. Eternity is limitless, without boundaries on its extension from "now." (Cf. Immortality of the Soul.)

## Ethics

Ethics is that branch of philosophy which is practical in its application, religious in its orientation, and studies and draws conclusions of the degree of goodness or badness of human actions and conduct in relation to the purposes of human living. It recognizes that humans are moral beings. They are responsible in life for choices of what to do and what not to do, both good and bad.

Throughout one's personal life and throughout the evolving of oneself as a responsible human being in the historical context of life, one is acting as an individual and a social being. The person assumes human obligations and duties that are steps to self-realization. It becomes for the individual a basic morality in determining the "moral" values that must be chosen or rejected. Thus ethics is a practical moral philosophy of action, not based upon revealed rules of conduct, such as the ten commandments, but rather on what is best in the scale of values in regard to oneself and one's neighbor. Because human beings are free agents, they have to form their lives as individuals and as members of society.

It is in the area of the human freedom to act that ethics has its structure, for some people may bow down to "imposed" actions, such as those by the State, or they may leave the choice to others. Human beings thus may act according to a structured existence, tolerating the good along with the oppressive, or they may choose according to the material good, the concrete content of a natural imperative to act.

It is in this latter instance, where the content of the good to be gained or dispensed is considered, that ethics as a moral imperative has its weakness. It is here that ethics should open itself to religion if it is to raise human beings above a mere formality of conduct. The attaining of good order in time, transcending the material experience, is the only way that ethics can be made a genuine morality or take on a fixed order rather than remain purely philosophical. And so in each age there is the moral necessity to bring to the natural moral law that ethics articulates, a revelation that is found only in the concrete imperatives of religion, for ethics itself is too arbitrary and cannot give the concrete individual directives that are required in

true salvation history. In short, ethics is historical, anthropological, and insufficient for establishing true norms for human conduct. (See Ethics, Situation.)

## Ethics, Situation

Since ethics treats of the goodness or badness of human conduct in an atmosphere of freedom, there arises a subjective, individualistic approach to moral conduct. One, acting ethically and by free choice, and with no regard for revealed morality, merely does what is expedient and in keeping with what the situation dictates (cf. Conscience). These actions without principles that are universal and in accord with the norms of moral conduct are arbitrary and not in keeping with objective morality, that is, what is good for the common welfare.

In May, 1956, the Congregation for the Holy Office spoke out against situation ethics: "The authors who follow this system state that the ultimate determining norm for activity is not the objective order as determined by the natural law and known with certainty from this law. It is instead some internal judgment and illumination of the mind of every individual by which the mind comes to know what is to be done in a concrete situation.

"This ultimate decision of man is, therefore, not the application of the objective law to a particular case after the particular circumstances of a 'situation' have been considered and weighed according to the rules of prudence, as the more important authors of objective ethics teach; but it is, according to them, immediate, internal illumination and judgment. . . .

"Much that is stated in this system of 'Situation Ethics' is contrary to the truth of reality and to the dictates of sound reason. It gives evidence of relativism and modernism, and deviates far from the Catholic teaching handed down through the ages."

## Ethiopian Church

The members of this Church and rite are the four to five million Christian Ethiopians, descendants of those who migrated to Africa from southern Arabia. Their centers are the ancient cities of Aksum and Gondar. The Church was founded from the school and Church around Alexandria, probably about the mid–fourth century, when St. Athanasius consecrated Frumentius, as bishop of Aksum, then the capitol city of Ethiopia. When the Alexandrian Church fell into

Monophysitism and formed the Coptic Church, Ethiopia fell into the same error.

The head of the Church, since 1941, has been the Abuna (Father) who is in Negus and is also the Abbot General of all monasteries. After missionary work of the nineteenth and twentieth centuries about an eighth of the Ethiopian Church has returned to Roman Catholic union. The rite of the Ethiopian Church has many similarities to the Roman Rite, and with progress in ecumenism a greater percentage will return to union with Rome and the Holy See. (See Abyssinian or Ethiopian Church.)

### Eucharist, Celebration of

The Holy Sacrifice of the Mass has in recent times been frequently referred to as the celebration of the Eucharist. The Mass is indeed the celebration of the Eucharist in the various forms or liturgies prescribed by the Church. We make a distinction in regard to the Eucharist, namely between sacramental sacrifice and the permanent sacrament. Briefly these are: (1) The Eucharist as *sacramental sacrifice* is the Mass, wherein the body and blood of Christ, the same offering that took place on the cross at the crucifixion of Christ, becomes the sacrifice of the Church because Christ unites the Church's offering to His own. Through this offering and sacrifice, the efficacious sign of the consecration of the bread and wine, the sacrifice of the cross becomes present in a sacramental manner. (2) The consecrated bread and wine are the *permanent sacrament,* the Real Presence of Christ among us, and the efficacious sign of Christ's presence, the food that satisfies our spiritual needs in a superabundant manner. It also is an efficacious sign of sanctifying grace and of the union of Christians through and in Christ.

"Every legitimate celebration of the Eucharist is regulated by the bishop" (LG 26). In the sacramental sacrifice there is an established order of the Mass consisting of Introductory Rite, Liturgy of the Word, Liturgy of the Eucharist, Communion Rite, and Concluding Rite. This has been introduced in a permanent form through the Sacramentary. The parts of the Mass have this sequence in the New Order:

1. *Introductory Rite.* This includes all those actions that precede the Liturgy of the Word: the vesting of the priest; the entrance procession with the ministers who may carry the cross, the gospel book, or lectionary; the entrance song, which is sung during the procession; the greeting by the priest; the penitential act; the *Kyrie*

and *Gloria* as prescribed; the opening or invitational prayer spoken by the priest.

2. The *Liturgy of the Word* is an essential part of the Order of the Mass. It includes the first reading in the cycle of readings, taken from the OT, during which the people are seated; a recited or sung response called the responsorial psalm; the second reading, which is from the Epistles; the sung or recited response, which is the psalm of the lectionary, the gradual in the Roman Gradual, or the responsorial or alleluia psalm in the simple Gradual; the reading of the assigned Gospel by the priest-celebrant with the congregation standing; the homily with the people seated, which is given on all Sundays and holy days of obligation at Masses celebrated with a congregation; the profession of faith, which is an assent to the Word of God; the general intercessions or prayer of the faithful with a response by the community; the concluding prayer by the celebrant.

3. The *Liturgy of the Eucharist,* the essential part of the sacrifice, includes: the preparation of the altar; the preparation of the gifts: bread, wine, and water are brought to the altar (and the money offerings or offerings for the poor), the offertory song is sung during this preparation; the priest washes his hands; an invitation to prayer is prayed by the priest (cf. Presidential prayers). There follows the Eucharistic prayer, which is a prayer of thanksgiving and sanctification and the center of the Eucharistic celebration. It contains: the preface, expressing thanksgiving in the name of the entire people of God; the acclamation or *sanctus* (holy, holy, holy), which is recited by the priest and people or sung; the Eucharistic prayer; the invocations for the Church, the epiclesis; narration of the institution and consecration of the bread and wine in the words of Christ; the fulfillment of the command given by Christ to the Church to carry on this mystery of the sacrifice, called the anamnesis; the offering of the victim to God the Father in the Holy Spirit; the intercessions for the living and the dead and for the faithful present; the final doxology, and concluding Amen.

4. The *Communion Rite* is the consuming of the paschal meal in the Eucharistic celebration. It begins with the Lord's Prayer and doxology; the rite of peace, which is an expression of charity by the members of the community present (the form of this ritual action is left to the conference of bishops to decide.) (cf. Com-

munity); the breaking of bread (cf. 1 Cor. 10:17); the commingling wherein the celebrant drops a part of the consecrated host into the consecrated wine; the *Agnus Dei,* the three-part invocation said during the commingling; the preparation to receive the Eucharistic bread and the reciting of the act of humility; the distribution of Holy Communion (a song is sung or an antiphon recited during this time); an optional moment of silent thanksgiving; the prayer after communion by the priest.

5. The *Concluding Rite* includes: the prayer and blessing over the people; the dismissal; the recessional, during which a song is sung by the congregation.

This New Order of the Mass permits the greater association of the priest-celebrant with the faithful, and according to practices prescribed or arising by custom, opportunity for an ongoing instruction by the celebrant. Although the Mass, considered as the Eucharistic sacramental sacrifice, is a mystery presided over by the priest, the people share in its every moment, and in the evolving tradition of the Church the Mass has been restored to the people. Vatican II teaches: "For all their (the laity's) works, prayers, and apostolic endeavors, their ordinary married and family life, their daily labor, their mental and physical relaxation, if carried out in the Spirit, and even the hardships of life, if patiently borne—all of these become spiritual sacrifices acceptable through Jesus Christ (cf. 1 Pt. 2:5). During the celebration of the Eucharist, these sacrifices are most lovingly offered to the Father along with the Lord's body" (LG 34).

And: "Taking part in the Eucharistic sacrifice, which is the fount and apex of the whole Christian life, they (the faithful) offer the divine Victim to God and offer themselves along with it" (LG 11). (See Mass; Sacramentary.)

**Eucharist, Sacrament of**

The word Eucharist is derived from the Greek and means "good grace." The term is applied to the sacrament and sacrifice of the New Law in which Christ Himself is present, is offered and received under the species of bread and wine. The Church teaches and believes that in the Holy Eucharist the body, blood, soul, and divinity of Christ, the God-Man, are truly and substantially present under the appearances of bread and wine. This presence of the entire Christ is by reason of the transubstantiation of the bread and wine into the body and blood of Christ, which is accomplished in the unbloody sacrifice of the Mass. Jesus Himself instituted the Eucharist and requested its repetition (Lk. 22:19–20). That this was accomplished and continued we know from the many references in the Epistles. (Cf. Transubstantiation.) The Sacrament of the Eucharist is a true sacrifice, a representation of the sacrifice of Christ on the cross, for the ritual elements of the sacrifice are identical with the body and blood of Christ (Heb. 9:12, 14). As a sacrament the Eucharist is most excellent first, in *dignity;* second, *in the grace it contains,* for it is Christ Himself, the source of all grace; third, *in its permanency,* because it is a perfect sacrament when we receive it and also when it is retained in our churches. The Holy Eucharist is known by many titles of truth and esteem; it is called the Bread of Life, the Most Blessed Sacrament, Holy Communion, the Sacrament of Life (Jn. 6:58), the Sacrament of Love, and the Sacrament of Unity.

The Basic Teachings document of the National Conference of Catholic Bishops declares: "The Eucharist has primacy among the sacraments. It is of the greatest importance for uniting and strengthening the Church. The Eucharistic celebration is carried out in obedience to the words of Jesus at the Last Supper: 'Do this in memory of me.'

"When a priest pronounces the words of Eucharistic consecration, the underlying reality of bread and wine is changed into the body and blood of Christ, given for us in sacrifice. That change has been given the name 'transubstantiation.' This means that Christ himself, true God and true Man, is really and substantially present, in a mysterious way, under the appearances of bread and wine.

"This sacrifice (of the Mass) is not merely a ritual which commemorates a past sacrifice. In it, through the ministry of priests, Christ perpetuates the sacrifice of the cross in an unbloody manner. At the same time, the Eucharist is a meal which recalls the Last Supper, celebrates our unity together in Christ, and anticipates the messianic banquet of the kingdom. In the Eucharist Jesus nourishes Christians with His own self, the Bread of Life, so that they may become a people more acceptable to God and filled with greater love of God and neighbor.

"To receive the Eucharist worthily the Christian must be in the state of grace (cf. 1 Cor. 11:27–28).

"Having been nourished by the Lord himself, the Christian should with active love eliminate all prejudices and all barriers to brotherly cooperation with others. The Eucharist is a sacrament of unity. It is meant to unite the faithful more closely each day with God and with one another.

"The Eucharist, reserved in our churches, is a powerful help to prayer and service of others. Religious instruction should stress the gratitude, adoration and devotion due to the real presence of Christ in the Blessed Sacrament reserved." (Cf. Communion.)

## Eucharistic Congresses

See Congresses, Eucharistic.

## Eucharistic Devotions

The presence of Christ in the permanent sacrament of the Eucharist has provided and continues to provide one of the most inspiring means of devotion. Formerly, the Sacrament was reserved primarily for the sake of the sick, but there arose an expansion of the worship of Christ in His real presence, which continues to the present.

On May 25, 1967, the Sacred Congregation of Rites gave an instruction on Eucharistic worship declaring: "When the faithful adore Christ present in the Sacrament, they should remember that his presence derives from the sacrifice and is directed toward both sacramental and spiritual Communion. In consequence, the devotion which leads the faithful to visit the Blessed Sacrament draws them into an ever deeper participation in the Paschal Mystery. . . . They offer their entire lives with Christ to the Father in the Holy Spirit and receive in this wonderful exchange an increase of faith, hope, and love. Thus they nourish those right dispositions which enable them with all due devotion to celebrate the memorial of the Lord and receive frequently the bread given us by the Father" (n. 50).

Thus Eucharistic devotion is "a subjective prolongation of Mass and a beginning of one's next communion" (K. Rahner).

These devotions may be personal, that is, by visitation to the church or chapel where the Blessed Sacrament is reserved; or they may be personal and private, that is by advertence in prayer to Christ present among us. These devotions may also be by exposition, that is, through the solemn annual exposition, the Forty Hours Devo-

tion; or by a solemn exposition on a designated Sunday called "Eucharistic Sunday." The devotion may also be most efficacious through the Benediction of the Blessed Sacrament, whether or not this is associated with the more solemn expositions or a holy hour devotion.

There are also Eucharistic Societies of which the Confraternity of the Most Blessed Sacrament (founded in 1539) is the oldest. There is also the Nocturnal Adoration Society begun in 1810, whose purpose is adoration of Christ in the Blessed Sacrament in reparation for sins against the Holy Eucharist. Also, the society known as the Catholic Youth Adoration (CYA) was organized in 1948 by Father Joseph Bernier, S.S.S., at St. Jean Baptiste Church in New York City, and this consists of a monthly Holy Hour for young people.

## Eucharistic Prayers

The new Sacramentary provides four prayers of commemoration and consecration that may be used by the celebrant in the liturgy of the Eucharist. In their essential parts they are identical; in wording they differ only on length of expression; they are the same in all their chief elements such as thanksgiving, acclamation, epiclesis, consecration words, anamnesis, offering, intercessions and final doxology. There are additional Eucharistic prayers that are used at special liturgies, such as children's liturgies, but all have the essential elements and sacramental language. (See Eucharist, Celebration of; Sacramentary.)

## Euchites

This heretical group of the fourth century was also called Messalians. They rejected all religious practices except prayer and were the forerunners, in a sense, of the Quietists.

## Euchologion

This liturgical book of the Byzantine rite contains the prayers of the eucharistic liturgies, the prayers of the Divine Office, and the ceremonies of blessings. Also called the Euchology, it is a combination of the missal, ritual, and breviary of the Roman rite.

## Eulogia

This unconsecrated bread was given to those who could not communicate but wished to join in early Church rites. The practice is now obsolete.

## Eunomianism

Begun in the last half of the fourth century by Eunomius of Cappadocia, this branch heresy was an offshoot of Arianism. It denied the divinity of the nature and will of Christ.

## Eusebians

Followers of the Arian heresy among the West Goths were converted from paganism to Arianism by Eusebius of Nicomedia in the latter part of the fourth century.

## Euthanasia

Active euthanasia, the termination of life of a living person, is a decisive act against the life of that person. The word is derived from the Greek, meaning "euphoric" or pleasant death. Euthanasia is an act of murder when the victim is put to death or allowed to die by neglect. Vatican II teaches: "Whatever is opposed to life itself, such as any type of murder, genocide, abortion, euthanasia, or willful self-destruction . . . whatever insults human dignity . . . all these things and others of their like are infamies indeed. They poison human society, but they do more harm to those who practice them than those who suffer from the injury. Moreover, they are a supreme dishonor to the Creator" (LG 27).

The denial of life through abortion, by passage of laws making abortion on demand legal, has created an atmosphere wherein the acceptance and practice of euthanasia become a social menace. Mercy killing, the direct action by drugs or other means whereby a person is caused to die, is murder and morally illicit.

## Eutychianism or Monophysitism

This heresy was developed by Eutyches, an influential monk at the court of Constantinople, in opposition to Nestorianism. It is most confused in its early writings, but it maintained that there was only one nature in Christ following the Incarnation. Eutychianism was condemned by the Council of Chalcedon (451).

## Evangeliarium

An evangeliarium is a book containing the Gospels to be sung at solemn Mass by the deacon; also a lectionary.

## Evangelical Counsels

These are voluntary poverty, chastity, and obedience. St. Thomas Aquinas teaches that there are two essential procedures to the attainment of perfection: first, the keeping of the commandments and, second, the observance of certain counsels. The commandments are absolute and rest upon all. The counsels are not absolutely necessary for salvation, but essential for perfection. Such counsels may be undertaken by anyone, and every counsel, because it is rooted in charity, helps remove the obstacles to the practice of charity and makes possible the perfection of love of God and neighbor. The counsels are specifically related to one's facility and exercise of carrying out the requirements of a particular state of life. Thus the evangelical counsels are willfully assumed as vows by priests and religious, either as vows or promises, in order to enable themselves more readily to attain sanctification. By *poverty*, religious free themselves of worldly wealth and attachments in order to concentrate more fully upon God; by *chastity*, they renounce the pleasures of the flesh, even those legitimate to the marriage state, that they may be even naturally centered on God; by *obedience*, the pride of will is overcome and subjection to the will of God is attained. Besides the commandments and precepts taught by Christ, there are also certain principles that are recommended for one to attain salvation with greater assurance. The three called "evangelical counsels" are not obligatory or absolutely necessary for salvation, but they are a means of attaining with greater certainty that salvation. Even when reduced to a minimum of response on the part of the individual, they are choices one makes to take a short-cut to perfection.

It was always understood by the Christian community that they were to "follow Christ," not always, as they knew, ideally, but with a strong adherence to the good news of Jesus as it was preached (cf. Acts 5:42). In the fourth century a fervid group called the "Apostolics" were rebuked because they made a law out of the counsels. The following of Christ in the early Church was voluntary (cf. Koinonia) and recognized as a "better way" of perfection to "follow the way of love" (Eph. 5:2).

Today the Church urges and teaches that all the faithful are to practice in so far as possible the counsels, for each Christian is to "breathe out Christ," as St. Anthony said. Vatican II brings this teaching into greater focus within the Church, declaring: "Faith teaches that the Church, whose mystery is being set forth by this sacred Synod, is holy in a way which can never fail. For Christ, the Son of God, who with the Father and the Spirit is praised as being 'alone holy,' loved the Church as His Bride, delivering Himself up for her. This He did that He might sanctify her (cf. Eph. 5:25–26). He united her to Himself as His own body and crowned her with the gift of the Holy Spirit, for God's glory. Therefore in the Church everyone belonging to the hierarchy, or being cared for by it, is called to holiness, according to the saying of the Apostle: 'It is God's will that you grow in holiness' (1 Thes. 4:3; cf. Eph. 1:4).

"Now, this holiness of the Church is unceasingly manifested, as it ought to be, through those fruits of grace that the Spirit produces in the faithful. It is expressed in multiple ways by those individuals who, in their walk of life, strive for the perfection of charity, and thereby help others to grow. In a particularly appropriate way this holiness shines out in the practice of the counsels customarily called 'evangelical.' Under the influence of the Holy Spirit, the practice of these counsels is undertaken by many Christians, either privately or in some Church-approved situation or state, and produces in the world, as produce it should, a shining witness and model of holiness" (LG 39).

### Evangelical United Brethren

In 1946 two groups of Protestant Christians were joined to form one church called the Evangelical United Brethren. The two groups were the United Brethren in Christ and the Evangelical Church. The United Brethren had originated in the early nineteenth century through the preacher, Philip William Otterbein, who had a Calvinist background. The Evangelical Church was founded by Jacob Albright, who was a Methodist preacher and, after forming the evangelistic association, became its bishop in 1807. Their first meeting was held in 1816, but later a schism developed, and the Evangelical Church was begun in 1922. Although both groups of the Evangelical United Brethren have strong Methodist ties as far as doctrine is concerned, they teach individual conversion and sanctification with a present-day trend toward altars, liturgical ritual, and the ceremony of the Lord's Supper. Current negotiations are under way for the Evangelical United Brethren to be merged with the larger Protestant group, the Methodist Church.

### Evangelion

This book, together with the *Apostolos*, is the gathering of the Gospels, Acts of the Apostles, and the Epistles arranged in the cycle of their reading in the Divine Liturgy and Divine Office. The two books are the principal lectionaries used by the Byzantine Rite according to their calendar, the menologion.

### Evangelists

An Evangelist is a "bringer of the Good News." Originally this term was applied only to the one who

preached. Since the third century it has been referred to the four writers of the Gospels: SS. Matthew, Mark, Luke, and John. Traditionally these four have been distinguished in symbols derived from the vision of Ezekiel and the creatures spoken of in the Apocalypse; thus St. Matthew is symbolized by the human head, St. Mark by the lion, St. Luke by the ox, and St. John by the eagle. (Cf. Gospel.)

### Evangelization

The fulfillment of our supernatural vocation is to make the message and mission of Christ known to the world. Evangelization originally meant preaching the Gospel to those who had never heard of Jesus or His teachings. But following Vatican II the term has come to mean, more broadly and rightly, "the whole mission of the Church and the activities of the apostolate through which she announces, implants and brings to maturity the Kingdom of God."

Evangelization, in the proper understanding of the word, will always mean proclaiming the good news of Christ concerning the Kingdom of God, but it is also "to promote God's glory through the spread of His kingdom and to obtain for all men that eternal life which consists in knowing the only true God and Him whom He sent, Jesus Christ" (AA 3). By evangelization is meant that strictly religious activity aimed at preaching God's kingdom, showing the Gospel as a revelation of the plan of salvation in Christ through the action of the Holy Spirit, and carrying on this activity through the ministry as the instrument for the building up of the Church itself for the glory of God.

Because the life of the Church is apostolic, there should be missionary action on the part of all from their earliest membership in the Church. Vatican II teaches: "Every disciple of Christ has the obligation to do his part in spreading the faith. Yet Christ the Lord always calls whomever He chooses from among the number of His disciples, to be with Him and to be sent by Him to preach to the nations (cf. Mk. 3:13–19). Therefore, through the Holy Spirit, who distributes His charismatic gifts as He wills for the common good (1 Cor. 12:11), Christ inspires the missionary vocation in the hearts of individuals. At the same time He raises up in the Church certain groups which take as their own special task that duty of preaching the gospel which weighs upon the whole Church" (AG 23).

And: "All sons of the Church should have a lively awareness of their responsibility to the world. They should foster in themselves a truly catholic spirit. They should spend their energies in the work of evangelization.

"Yet, let all realize that their first and most important obligation toward the spread of the faith is this: to lead a profoundly Christian life" (AG 36).

### Evangelization of Peoples, Congregation of

The direction of the activities of missionary work throughout the world is entrusted to this congregation. This is still popularly known as the Propagation of the Faith Commission. Its works include fostering missionary vocations, training missionaries, assigning the areas of missionary apostolate, encouraging native vocations, and soliciting and mobilizing the spiritual and financial support of missionary activities. The Congregation has in its makeup a Supreme Council for the Direction of Pontifical Missionary Works; subject to this council are: the Missionary Union of the Clergy, the Society for the Propagation of the Faith, the Society of St. Peter the Apostle for Native Clergy, the Society of the Holy Childhood, and the *Fides* news agency. Ex officio members of this congregation are the Secretariat for Promoting Christian Unity, the Secretariat for Non-Christians, and the Secretariat for Non-Believers. It was first founded in 1622 by Gregory XV. (See Ecumenism.)

### Eve

The name that the first man conferred upon the first woman, derived from the Hebrew word meaning "living" (Gn. 3:20), declares her to be "the mother of all the living."

Vatican II states: "In their preaching not a few of the early Fathers gladly assert with him (St. Irenaeus): 'The knot of Eve's disobedience was untied by Mary's obedience. What the virgin Eve bound through her unbelief, Mary loosened by her faith.' Comparing Mary with Eve, they call her 'the mother of the living,' and still more often they say: 'death through Eve, life through Mary'" (LG 56).

Eve was created equal to Adam in all things, sharing his life, but she merited first the pain of loss through the first sin. The Virgin Mary is called the "Second Eve," because through her the Incarnate Son of God became man and redeemed all. Early writers in the Church played upon the word Eve (in Latin *Eva*) saying that it was the first word of the archangel Gabriel spoken in reverse in addressing the Blessed Mother, namely, "Ave." Eve and Mary are type and antitype in biblical interpretation.

### Eve of a Feast

See Vigil.

### Evil

There is not a "principle" of evil by which it can be defined. Evil can best be observed and realized in its effect. Evil is not to be identified in the moral order only. According to St. Thomas Aquinas who based his argument on St. Augustine (who in turn derived much from Plotinus), evil is not a reality. Rather, evil is the lack of perfection that should be present in a person, action, or thing as a part of its reality; for example, it is evil for one to be blind since sight is an integral part of the natural sense of seeing. Thus this lack may be present in the physical order as in the previous example, or the moral order, or may be extended to both at the same time.

Evil creates a conflict of good with good in the exercise of the will. St. Paul said: "Detest what is evil, cling to what is good" (Rm. 12:9). And Vatican II declared: "All of human life, whether individual or collective, shows itself to be a dramatic struggle between good and evil, between light and darkness. Indeed, man finds that by himself he is incapable of battling the assaults of evil successfully, so that everyone feels as though he is bound by chains" (GS 13).

Thus we see that evil is a discord within the good; it is disharmony with God and man. Through love and reconciliation gained for us by Christ, we are linked with God once again and through the Spirit can turn to God as our heavenly Father.

### Evolution

In the Catholic understanding, the theory of evolution, or transformism from lower forms of life through a sequence to human beings, remains a theory. However, should proof be eventually produced, the teaching of Genesis and its inspired narrative would remain, for it tells that the world was created for human beings and that human beings themselves came from God no matter what course was followed by divine wisdom in forming the human frame. More essentially, humans have a spiritual rational soul and as a spiritual substance could not have an origin in a material source. It is in the spiritual part of man that he differs from brute beasts. Apart from the field of natural science, we are cautioned by revelation. Pius XII, in *Humani generis* (1950), speaks on one current aspect of the theory, namely, polygenism, and warns that the faithful may not believe that after Adam there were true men who were not generated from Adam "since it is not at all clear how such an opinion can be reconciled with what the sources of revelation and the acts of the Church's teaching authority put forward concerning original sin."

Evolution regarded here only in its religious or Catholic sense implies that there is a quality leap from the brute, and this in no way takes away the causal act of God in creating human beings. Thus the creation of the spirit of man is a dogma of faith because the spirit (soul) could not emerge from material potential.

That in the biosphere we might still arise to even greater exemplars can only mean that this would take place in the physiological and not in the spiritual sphere, for revelation is complete for salvation.

## Ex Cathedra

Literally, *ex cathedra* means "from the chair." (Cf. Infallibility.)

## Ex Opere Operantis

This term from the Latin means "from the work of the one working" or more loosely "from the action performed," (cf. Ex Opere Operato). This term is used concerning grace to indicate that grace flows in reception of the sacraments because the one administering the sacrament has the power and authority to do so (See Grace.)

## Ex Opere Operato

This technical phrase was first used in 1205; it was then defined by the fathers at the Council of Trent and thereafter by theologians to declare that the grace of the sacraments is caused by the sacramental rite *validly performed*. Translated, it means, "from the work of the work itself," or more loosely, "from the act itself"; this means that grace is the result of the objective act. It is thus opposed to the subjective *ex opere operantis*.

## Exaltation of the Cross

The feast celebrated in the Roman rite on Sept. 14, is called in the new calendar the Triumph of the Cross. It originated in commemoration of the recovery of a portion of the true cross of Christ from the Persians by Emperor Heraclius in 629.

## Examen

An examination of conscience made daily or at special intervals as a devotional practice (not by necessity as before confession) is called an examen. It enables one to eliminate faults and imperfections by recognizing them as well as their causes and helps to develop practicing the opposing virtues. It is *particular* when directed against a single fault,

*general* when it is concerned with a complex or variety of similar faults or all faults.

## Examination of Bishops

Examination of Bishops includes questions put to a bishop-elect before his ordination concerning obedience to the authority of the Church, the episcopal life, the faith, and the rejection of errors.

## Examination of Conscience

The act of recalling, in so far as possible, the number and seriousness of sins made by one in preparation for reception of the Sacrament of Penance is known as the examination of conscience. This is in reality an examination of oneself as a spiritual exercise wherein one remembers what sins are to be mentioned in the confession. It also serves the following spiritual purposes: it elicits the necessary sorrow for sins and offenses against God and affords one the occasion of thanking God by recognizing the ingratitude expressed by one's sins; it enables one to make a resolve not to sin again, a necessary requirement in the reception of the sacrament. (Cf. Examen; Confession; Penance, Sacrament of.)

## Examiners, Synodal

When a vacancy arises between synods (c. 385), at least four members of the clergy, proposed and approved by the clergy in the diocesan synod or appointed by the bishop, are to carry out the following functions: examine the fitness of the clergy for the care of souls and advise the bishop on the subject.

## Exarch

Historically, exarch was the title of a ruler of a province of the Roman empire. In Church use, it is a title of limited jurisdiction, usually appointed temporarily, to carry out some mission. In the Western Church, the title has been supplanted with that of "vicar apostolic" or "primate." In the Eastern Church, the title is conferred on the head of a Church whose position is neither that of a patriarch nor a metropolitan. Bishops of the Ukrainian rite in North America are called exarchs, or eparchs, as are other bishops of Eastern Rite Churches.

## Excardination

It is required that a cleric belong to a diocese, vicariate, or other jurisdiction, or be a member of a religious community. Excardination is the formal transfer of a cleric from one diocese to another or from the jurisdiction of one bishop to that of another. A cleric can be excardinated by formal letters of perpetual and unconditional excardination, signed by the cleric's bishop and followed, necessarily, by letters of incardination (cs. 111-118). (Cf. Incardination.)

## Excellency

The polite and official term of address is used in the Roman Church for all archbishops, bishops, and prelates nullius; thus, "Your Excellency," "His Excellency."

## Exclusion

No longer recognized by the Church, exclusion was a claim whereby nations, such as France, Austria, Spain, and Germany, vetoed the election of a·cardinal elected as pope.

## Excommunication

This is the most serious censure of the Church. By excommunication a person is excluded from the communion of the faithful; loses the right of attending divine services, except at preaching; is forbidden the reception of the sacraments (c. 2260); loses the suffrages of the Church and public prayers and all participation in indulgences; may not act as sponsor, or perform other ecclesiastical acts; loses the right of plaintiff in Church trials except according to canon 1654; may not fill ecclesiastical offices, such as trustee or organist; may not receive Christian burial. In the case of clerics, in addition to the censures already mentioned, they may not administer the sacraments except under specified circumstances (c. 2261) or be appointed to ecclesiastical offices.

Excommunication may be imposed: *ipso facto,* that is, as a consequence of the commission of an act calling for the imposition of the censure, if that consequence is known, or by a condemnatory or declaratory sentence, that is, by imposition of the censure by authority. There are two degrees of excommunication: (1) Excommunicates *vitandi* are those so named by sentence and with whom members of the faithful are forbidden to associate. (2) Excommunicates *tolerati* are those with whom the faithful may associate. Absolution may be received by an excommunicate from any priest, even from a priest who himself is under censure, if in danger of death. Absolution otherwise depends upon the authority to whom the censure is reserved. Excommunication may be reserved to the Holy See in a very special manner, reserved to the Holy See in a special manner, simply reserved

to Rome, reserved to the ordinary, or nonreserved (cs. 2347; 2352). (Cf. Censure.)

Excommunication is imposed according to the reservation as follows: (1) Acts reserved to the Holy See in a very special manner are: throwing away, taking, or retaining for evil purposes the consecrated species; striking the Roman Pontiff; absolving or pretending to absolve one's accomplice in sin; violating the seal of sacramental confession. (2) Reserved in a special manner to Rome: heretics, apostates, and schismatics; publication of books of formal heretics, apostates, or schismatics wherein these sins are defended; reading or retaining such books or other books condemned in apostolic letters; forcing cardinals or one's ordinary to appear as defendants in civil courts without permission of the Holy See; pretending to say Mass or hear confessions when not a priest; falsely accusing a confessor of solicitation, either personally or through others in a solemn manner. (3) Simply reserved to Rome; fighting, accepting, or aiding a duel; joining the Masons or societies that plot against the Church or state; practicing simony in regard to ecclesiastical offices, dignities, or benefices; presuming to absolve from excommunication cases reserved very specially or specially to the Holy See, except in urgent necessity; bringing suit in civil courts against bishops other than their own ordinaries; clerics who attempt marriage and those who contract marriage with them even by civil action; anyone who steals, destroys, conceals, or vitiates a document of a diocesan curia, or causes another to do so. (4) Reserved to the ordinary: all who procure an abortion, including the mother and all cooperators; marrying before an heretical minister acting as a religious agent; all who strike clerics, sisters, or others who enjoy the privilege of the Canon; commission of certain crimes in the education of children, e.g., agreeing to bring up the children outside the Church (c. 2319); selling, making, or distributing false relics. (5) Nonreserved: unlawful alienation of property without apostolic indult; using force to induce a person to become a cleric or religious; writing or publishing books of Scripture or commentaries on it without due permission.

The censure of excommunication may be lifted by anyone having the necessary faculties. Church censures in general are under review and will be placed in a new perspective by the present revision of Canon Law.

## Exeat

The formal letter of excardination is called the exeat.

## Execration

See Desecration of Churches.

## Exegesis

Exegesis is the study whereby the investigation and exposition of Sacred Scripture is presented. In general it seeks through tradition, archaeology, history, and criticism to expound the true meaning of the Scriptures. In particular it concerns itself with the various senses of Scripture, the literal, spiritual senses, and the accommodation of Scripture. The Church sets forth no restriction upon the extent of investigation regarding the Scriptures, teaching only the absolute truth of inspired Scriptures and disallowing any restriction of inspiration to certain parts of the Bible such as doctrinal parts, and the Church forbids the concession that the sacred writer may have erred. (Cf. Inspiration of Scripture; Interpretation, Scriptural.)

Vatican II teaches: "Since God speaks in Sacred Scripture through men in human fashion, the interpreter of sacred Scripture, in order to see clearly what God wanted to communicate to us, should carefully investigate what meaning the sacred writers really intended, and what God wanted to manifest by means of their words.

"Those who search out the intention of the sacred writers must, among other things, have regard for 'literary forms.' For truth is proposed and expressed in a variety of ways, depending on whether a text is history of one kind or another, or whether its form is that of prophecy, poetry, or some other type of speech. The interpreter must investigate what meaning the sacred writer intended to express and actually expressed in particular circumstances as he used contemporary literary forms in accordance with the situation of his own time and culture. For the correct understanding of what the sacred author wanted to assert, due attention must be paid to the customary and characteristic styles of perceiving, speaking, and narrating which prevailed at the time of the sacred writer, and to the customs men normally followed at that period in their everyday dealings with one another.

"But, since Holy Scripture must be read and interpreted according to the same Spirit by whom it was written, no less serious attention must be given to the content and unity of the whole of Scripture, if the meaning of the sacred texts is to be correctly brought to light. The living tradition of the whole Church must be taken into account along with the harmony which exists between elements of the faith. It is the task of exegetes to work according to these rules toward a better understanding and explanation of the meaning of sacred Scripture, so that through preparatory study the judgment of the Church may mature. For all of what has been said about the way of interpreting Scripture is subject finally to the judgment of the Church, which carries out the divine commission and ministry of guarding and interpreting the word of God" (DV 17). (See Form Criticism.)

And: "Catholic exegetes then and other students of sacred theology, working diligently together and using appropriate means, should devote their energies, under the watchful care of the sacred teaching office of the Church, to an exploration and exposition of the divine writings. This task should be done in such a way that as many ministers of the divine word as possible will be able effectively to provide the nourishment of the Scriptures for the People of God, thereby enlightening their minds, strengthening their wills, and setting men's hearts on fire with the love of God. The sacred Synod encourages the sons of the Church who are biblical scholars to continue energetically with the work they have so well begun, with a constant renewal of vigor and with loyalty to the mind of the Church" (DV 23).

## Exegete

A biblical scholar, versed in exegesis, is called an exegete.

## Exemption

This term is used in canon law to denote the position of a subject or thing in relation to the jurisdiction or law of a superior. An exempt religious, for example, is one not under the jurisdiction of the bishop of the diocese wherein he resides, except in certain specified laws (c. 615). An exempt diocese is one not subject to a metropolitan but directly under the authority of the Holy See.

## Exequator

Exequator was the right claimed by rulers to examine and judge papal bulls and constitutions before the regulations contained within them would go into effect in the territories they governed.

## Exequial Mass

This is the requiem Mass said at a funeral where the body of the deceased is present and the absolution is given. (See Funeral.)

## Exercises, Spiritual

Spiritual Exercises is the name given by St. Ignatius of Loyola (d. 1556) to the meditations, counsels, and exhortations that form a spiritual guide. Broadly, any course of spiritual precepts or counsels that are presented to be practiced by religious or laymen are spiritual exercises. Basically these constitute a system whereby one may seek a deeper sense of perfection and spiritual maturity.

## Existence

The first or prime act of essence in being, existence is the perfection of being whereby what was possible becomes actual through the operation of an efficient cause outside the being. Since God has no efficient cause, existence and essence, or pure actuality, are identical in Him.

Existence has taken on a different meaning from the scholastic concept. Today existence means the actuality of human existence; this understanding has come about through the trend in the philosophy that emerges from the Existentialists, even though they differ somewhat among themselves in the meaning of the term. For example, Heidegger holds that "being" becomes known as an actual event through the medium of self-understanding, whereas Sartre poses the immanent but systematized or categorized.

Present day theology views humans not in the categories of finite beings but as from creation under God's saving care and grace.

## Existence of God

The demonstration of God's existence in Church teaching is not based solely upon revelation. It is and has been declared, following St. Paul's statement: "God's eternal power and divinity, have become visible, recognized through the things he has made" (Rom. 1:20), that human beings can by use of reason deduce the certitude of God's existence. As stated by St. Pius X in his moto proprio *Sacrarum antistitum* (Those in Charge of Holy Things) of 1910, this is a kind of proof called demonstration.

One knows through faith of God's existence, but humans should always seek the amplitude of knowledge or the highest truth that is knowable. Thus apart from faith, God can best be known from material things or things existing within human experience, by reasoning from something secondary in being to something prior or first, a prime or first cause, God.

In Catholic thought the first formally presented proofs for God's existence were the five most valid proofs offered by St. Thomas Aquinas (1225 to 1274). The first argument reasons from motion to a prime or first mover, which means that some-

thing progresses from a state of potentiality to actuality, with a cause bringing about such movement without the movement acting independently. The second argument reasons from an order of efficient causes to a first efficient cause, or things happening in a reasonable manner, which could not happen without being subordinate to a prior cause. The third indicates the necessity of a being or one who brings material being, because matter cannot of itself generate into existence and then go on to corruption or dissolution. The fourth argument goes from the degrees of goodness, truth, nobility, or beauty, which are observed in things and could not be present unless they had their origin in a cause that has these qualities to their highest perfection. The fifth argument arises from the purposefulness of things, which is observed in nonknowing things, for this demands an intelligent agent or cause, because man of himself cannot order things to intelligent, effective ends, so there must be a supreme source from which purposefulness arises.

In all of these arguments the cause is God, manifest in the observed truths that man's reason declares to him. The metaphysical truth is attained, not without effort, by seeing the entire universe in its dependence upon God as the prime mover, the efficient cause, and the perfect being worthy of our faith. (See Faith; God.)

## Existentialism

Existential philosophy, as propounded by the Danish scholar, Soren Kierkegaard (d. 1855) and developed by others, notably Heidegger, Jaspers, and Marcel, declares that the source and elements of knowledge are not in relation to truth as demonstrated but are parts conditioned by the *concrete existence* of the individual or by his consciousness of them. Kierkegaard stated: "I can only legitimately speak of my *feelings,* I cannot speak of my *existence.*" As a philosophy it is a cross between realism and idealism, confusing the internal and external realities. Existentialism posits an agnostic attitude toward God, a denial, for the most part, of the supernatural; it accepts the problematical as a quasi-absolute. Thus it tends toward pessimism since no definite solution to life's problems seems possible. In the area of psychology, existential philosophy treats experiences of the mind as separate *existences,* which become unified in the individual; hence it must deny imageless thought.

The Catholic theologian, Karl Rahner, in his *Being and Time,* gives the concept of the *supernatural existential:* "The question of existence can only be clarified by existing. The self-understanding which leads to this we call existentiell. . . . The interconnection of the structures (which constitutes existence) we call existentiality. Their analysis is in the nature of an existential understanding, not an existentiell one."

## Exodus, Book of

This second book of the OT is one of religious history. Its authorship is attributed to Moses, but most probably it was compiled by later writers for it contains, besides the account of the liberation of the Hebrews from Egyptian captivity, stories, poems, liturgical rules, moral laws, and folk tales. The time of its writing is not known; two dates are usually given, both uncertain according to interpretation, either in the fifteenth century before Christ or in the twelfth to eleventh centuries before Christ; more probably the sixth century before Christ. The narrative tells the oppression of the Israelites under their Egyptian masters, the call of Moses, and the deliverance of the Israelites, their march through the desert to Sinai, God's miraculous care of them, the Sinaitic Covenant, and the giving of the Decalogue. The teaching of the book is that God chose the Hebrew people in the execution of His plan of redemption. There are also many teachings and a variety of parallels to the NT, for example, the release from bondage is a type of the redemption; the manna of the desert is a type of the Eucharist.

In meaning this book shows us the "God who acts," in the course of human history. It also informs all that God is one who demands the attention of mankind (20:3) and who made the Hebrews His own people (19:4–6). The book instructs that faith in God is essentially moral and that He is compassionate and ever present to fulfill His promises.

## Exorcism

Exorcism is the rite whereby devils are expelled from possessed persons or *energumeni*. This rite is now administered properly by a priest and may be exercised only with permission of the bishop and in accord with formulas of the Roman Ritual. The authority over evil spirits was given by Christ to the Apostles, and Christ manifested His own power over devils by driving them from a possessed person (Mk. 6:7). Lesser exorcisms are frequent in Church liturgy, for example, in the baptismal ceremonies and the blessing of holy water. However, these lesser exorcisms are directed at placing the objects beyond the use of evil spirits and preserving their use for holy purposes. (See Possession, Demonic; Devil and Evil Spirits.)

## Exorcist

One who performs an exorcism is called exorcist. Formerly the third of the minor orders, also called *exorcistate*, it conferred on the one receiving, the power to impose hands on the possessed and to recite prayers to expel devils. This office as a minor order dates back to the third century but in present-day discipline is exercised only by a priest. The only instance of the use of the term in the Bible is in Acts 19:13, but the use of the power to exorcise is granted only to priests who act with the bishop's permission and only through Jesus Christ, as St. Paul declares in Acts 19:13–16. (Cf. Exorcism; Possession, Demonic.)

## Experimental Parish

An experimental parish is one with an assigned priest-pastor or director but no specified territorial boundaries. Such parishes in the modern Church have arisen only since Vatican II and claim a freedom of their membership and the method of their administration. They usually do not have a church building but celebrate the Eucharist in homes or places of their choice. The members also do not erect or maintain schools but follow a self-imposed manner of instruction for their children and members. The first of these experimental nonterritorial parishes, that of the Community of John XXIII of Oklahoma City, has withdrawn from the jurisdiction of the archdiocese. Others have returned to the territorial parish or have disbanded, but there are still some of these parishes.

Why the title experimental was adopted remains a question, but it follows from an attempt at a different method of establishing a community adherence. The word experimental has been mistakenly applied to those parishes where innovations in liturgy, music, decoration, and procedure were introduced. Such innovations have been discouraged since the introduction of the New Order of the Mass and the Sacramentary, but there remains a certain degree of freedom for the discovery of new means of using childrens' liturgies, decoration, and music together with the ad lib comments that may be made by the celebrant at a Eucharistic Celebration. (See Community; Parish.)

## Experts

Experts are those persons of exceptional training or education who are able to give in-depth counsel or advice on matters of great importance. (See Periti.)

## Expiation

See Atonement.

## Exposition of the Blessed Sacrament

This is the ceremony, either private or solemn, whereby the Blessed Sacrament is removed from the altar tabernacle by a priest for the adoration of the faithful. Private exposition, that is, without the use of the ostensorium, may be merely an opening of the tabernacle so that the faithful can see the Blessed Sacrament in the ciborium or lunette, and this can take place any time for a sufficient reason and without the permission of the bishop. Solemn Exposition with the monstrance (c. 1274) is permitted on the feast of Corpus Christi and within its octave by all churches where the Blessed Sacrament is reserved. However, other public and solemn Exposition requires a just cause and permission of the ordinary. Solemn Exposition is governed by laws of the liturgy to preserve the dignity of the occasion and show reverence; the "O Salutaris" is sung, the host is incensed, and the "Tantum Ergo" is sung in English. Today such solemn Exposition is usually followed with Benediction. (See Eucharistic Devotions; Divine Praises.)

## External Forum

A forum is the word for that place or circumstance where ecclesiastical jurisdiction or authority is exercised. Such authority is exercised in the *external forum* when it has to do with the public welfare of the Church or its members. Bishops of dioceses, called "ordinaries," have such authority because of their office. They may delegate such authority. When spiritual counseling is required because of the circumstances arising from a condition or problem of auricular confession, the confessor may ask the penitent to address the matter in a counseling manner or in the external forum, but this is rarely the occasion unless there is a most grave matter involving others or a physical handicap involved.

Authority is also exercised in the *internal forum* where the spiritual good of a member of the Church is concerned. This is the sacramental forum, that of auricular confession when the Sacrament of Penance is administered by one who has the faculty to do so. The nonsacramental forum may also be the internal forum where jurisdiction is exercised, for example general absolution given to troops before a battle. (See Authority; Confession; Counseling, Pastoral).

## External Grace

External grace is the name applied to those facts or events that aid individuals because of moral influence. It is a type of sufficient grace and may include the Scriptures, preaching of the gospel, miracles, the examples of Christ and the saints. (Cf. Grace.)

## Extreme Unction, Sacrament of

Now called Sacrament of the Anointing of the Sick, this sacrament is conferred on baptized Catholics who are ill, or "suffering" from old age, or in danger of death. As a sacrament of the New Law, we learn all its elements in the text: "Is there anyone sick among you? He should ask for the presbyters of the church. They in turn are to pray over him, anointing him with oil in the Name of the Lord. This prayer uttered in faith will reclaim the one who is ill, and the Lord will restore him to health. If he has committed any sins, forgiveness will be his" (Jas. 5:14–15). The sacrament may be conferred by a priest or bishop. The purposes of receiving this sacrament are found in its effects: its reception completes the effects of the Sacrament of Penance, removes the remnants of sin, brings grace to the soul, disposes the recipient to undergo his sufferings with the conscious joining of these with the sufferings of Christ, and sometimes brings health to the body. The sacrament is conferred in a brief ceremony consisting of the recitation of the Asperges, three prayers for health, safety, and peace, and beseeching the care of the angels, followed by the Confiteor and a brief exorcism. The priest then touches his thumb to the Holy Oil (oil of the sick) and anoints the recipient saying a prayer asking forgiveness to the person for any sins that may have been committed. There follow three prayers for the health of the soul and body of the sick person. The form of the sacrament is the prayer, and its matter the Holy Oil. (See Anointing of the Sick, Sacrament of.)

## Ezekiel, Book of

This prophetical book of the OT was written by Ezekiel, the son of Buzi and priest of the line of Sadoc. The name Ezekiel (also spelled Ezechiel) is from the Hebrew, meaning "may God make strong." In the text he refers to himself as merely "son of man" (2:1). The authorship is attributed to Ezekiel but also to some later scribe. He became a prophet in 597 B.C. We learn of him only from his own writings and do not have the dates of his birth and death. His book is concerned with the period between the death of Josiah (609) and the destruction of Jerusalem (587 B.C.).

In content the book has five parts: (1) the call of the prophet by the Lord, (2) the prophecies of judgment before the seige of Jerusalem, (3) the prophesies against the seven foreign nations, (4) the prophecies made after the fall of Jerusalem and of the salvation of Israel, and (5) the concluding prophecies that tell of the new Jerusalem and the new Temple there.

The theology of this book is that of the transcendence of God, His holiness, and the manifestation of this holiness toward the individual and the nation. Although the prophecies refer to God's dealings with His people, there is a nonmessianic reference to "one shepherd," which Christ used to characterize Himself (Jn. 10:14–16).

### Ezra, Book of, also Esdras

This historical book of the OT is one of the last four of the Hebrew Canon, which includes Ezra, Nehemiah, and Books I and II of Chronicles. In more recent translations of the Bible the Book of Ezra has been separate from the Book of Nehemiah, whereas they were formerly known as Books I and II of Esdras.

The author is an unknown writer of chronicles, but the book is generally ascribed to one named Ezra, a scribe and leader of the restoration of the Jews at the end of the fifth century before Christ. The book records the history of the Chosen People after the Babylonian exile beginning with the decree of Cyrus, the Persian King (538 to 529 B.C.), telling of the restoration of the altar and the efforts to rebuild the Temple as well as the opposition of the foreign nations. Together with the Book of Nehemiah, it is a history of the development of the Israelites into a national community and a people whose worship of God was centered around the Temple.

## Fabric, also Fabrica

This term applied to the church building and its fittings, but it also means the funds for repair, reconstruction, or maintenance as distinct from the funds of the benefice or those for the living of the priest and curates. However, the term is sometimes applied to one who has charge of maintenance, usually a layman; it is seldom used.

## Faculties, Canonical

Canonical faculties are explicit powers, granted as authorization to enable a person to act validly or at least licitly. Such powers are granted by the Holy See or by a bishop or prelate and must be authenticated. Faculties are understood to include all the necessary power or authority for their use and may be granted for varying lengths of time or may be designated to cover a single or numerous cases. Most commonly we hear "faculties" referred to the permission given to priests to administer the Sacrament of Penance. The word means "the ability to act" and varies according to the practical application of such ability. In canon law such faculties may be *particular*, that is given for a specific case, or *habitual*, that is, to be used perpetually or for a specified period of time.

## Faculties, Ecclesiastical

Ecclesiastical faculties are the teaching groups in schools of theology, seminaries, and universities, which have been canonically erected and authorized by the Sacred Congregation for Catholic Education. These may award degrees in prescribed fields of study. They may be established in State universities and in houses of study of certain religious orders. At present such faculties have been authorized in Australia, Canada, Germany, Great Britain, India, Italy, Madagascar, Peru, Poland, Spain, the United States, and South Vietnam.

Vatican II declared: "The Church looks for rich results from the painstaking work of faculties of the sacred sciences. For to them she confides the most serious task of preparing her own students not only for the priestly ministry, but especially for teaching in seats of higher Church studies, for advancing branches of knowledge of their own efforts, and for undertaking the more arduous challenges of the intellectual apostolate" (GE 11).

## Faith

1. The assent given to a truth.

2. An entire body of dogmas or truths to which one gives assent; for example, one is of the Catholic faith.

3. The first of the three theological virtues; the virtue by which one, through grace, adheres in intellect to a truth revealed by God because of the authority of God rather than the evidence given.

4. The faith called "justifying," that is, the belief necessary for personal justification (Mk. 16:15–16).

In its Catholic interpretation, faith is a *habit* and an *act*, and so is in the mind and will. It is described as divine or supernatural. It is habitual when it is an infused habit, assisted by grace, wherein the mind assents to a truth revealed by God, making the assent because God is Himself the essential truth, who cannot be deceived in His divine knowledge and cannot deceive when He reveals a truth. When such habitual faith is informed by charity or the love of God, it becomes a "living" faith. Faith is actual when, again aided by grace, the mind assents and together with the will prompts one to both the internal and external expression of faith, for example, when we recite the Creed. Divine faith and Catholic faith demand that we believe all those points of doctrine that are contained in the Scriptures, in the unwritten word of God and all those proposed to our belief as revealed by God or by the solemn definition of the Church acting as the ordinary and universal teaching authority of Christ on earth. According to the Council of Trent, faith is necessary for sanctification and salvation.

Faith is the primary approach to man's confrontation with himself in his nature as a free and responsible being. It is not automatically renewed but must be continuously re-awakened so that it may be more than mere formulations.

Having the courage of the faith is manifested through the actions of the individual, one's response to the teachings that only the Catholic Church claims from all time to have had directly from Christ, in constitution and teaching. Faith and knowledge are one in the Gospel of St. John: 8:24–28; 14:12–20; 17:21–23. To be a Christian is to profess and to accept the mystery of Christ, His death, resurrection, and His mission through the Church (cf. Acts 11:26; 16:31).

Vatican II teaches: "The body of the faithful as a whole, anointed as they are by the Holy One (cf. Jn. 2:20), cannot err in matters of belief. Thanks to a supernatural sense of the faith which characterizes the People as a whole, it manifests this unerring quality when, 'from the bishops down to the last member of the laity,' it shows universal agreement in matters of faith and morals.

"For, by this sense of faith which is aroused and sustained by the Spirit of truth, God's People accepts not the word of men but the very Word of God (cf. 1 Thes. 2:13). It clings without fail to the faith once delivered to the saints (cf. Jude 3), penetrates it more deeply by accurate insights, and applies it more thoroughly to life. All this it does under the lead of a sacred teaching authority to which it loyally defers" (LG 12).

And: "The Roman Pontiff and the bishops, in view of their office and of the importance of the matter, strive painstakingly and by appropriate means to inquire properly into that revelation and to give apt expression to its contents. But they do not allow that there could be any new public revelation pertaining to the divine deposit of faith" (LG 25).

And: They are fully incorporated into the society of the Church who, possessing the Spirit of Christ, accept her entire system and all the means of salvation given to her, and through union with her visible structure are joined to Christ, who rules her through the Supreme Pontiff and the bishops. This joining is effected by the bonds of professed faith, of the sacraments, of ecclesiastical government, and of communion" (LG 14). (See Church; Authority; Theological Virtues.)

### Faith, Congregation for Doctrine of the
See Congregation.

### Faith Healing
The direct healing or cure of the sick through divine power is called a miracle. This is effected through the intervention of God in the order of nature and human life. In faith healing there is an attempt on the part of individuals to use this divine power as though it were of itself a natural and curative agent, which is impeded or brought about by the degree or lack of faith on the part of the suffering one.

That there were miracles of healing is evident from the Scriptures where Christ performed many acts of a supernatural nature. In the earliest days of the Church: "The people carried the sick into the streets and laid them on cots and mattresses, so that when Peter passed by at least his shadow might fall on one or another of them. Crowds from the towns around Jerusalem would gather, too, bringing their sick and those who were troubled by

unclean spirits, all of whom were cured" (Acts 5:15–16). This exercise of the charism of healing was and has been found throughout the history of the Church (for example, some saints were able to effect cures), but it was always dependent on the will of God and beyond the human capacity.

In modern religions the ritual of healing has been introduced into several religious cults. But these are always marked by the indispensible factor of faith or belief of the one to be cured, and failure is always based upon an insufficient degree of faith. The Church does not deny that in certain instances healing effects have been known to take place, but these are in scientific terms psychosomatic rather than supernatural. The healings that take place are not of organic disease such as cancer and are never to be sought out of superstitious practice nor at the expense of neglecting the regaining of one's health through good medical treatment.

### Faith, Mysteries of
There are supernatural truths that cannot be known without the revelation of God. Among these are the Trinity, the Incarnation, and the Eucharist. Although these are not contrary to nor beyond reason, they are not understood fully even through revelation, and the human person is dependent upon the Church to attain the greatest appreciation of these mysteries. Revelation and faith are supernatural because of their formal structure, for divine revelation is the communication of God's self-knowledge in such a way that we may rely on the absolute truth of God as it communicates itself through His word. Faith is that supernatural participation of human beings in God and through Him, that is, in God's very life. Even though one cannot through reason comprehend the intrinsic truth of God's word, man's free act of faith is not unreasonable because in his natural quest for truth he comes to a recognition of the credibility of God's word and the credibility of the Christian faith.

### Faithful
In early days of the Church those who were baptized and instructed and who were admitted to communion were known as the faithful. Today this includes all those who are members of the Church, addressed as such by the pope, and who have not been excluded by declaration or by their own acts.

Vatican II teaches: "The Spirit dwells in the Church and in the hearts of the faithful as in a temple (cf. 1 Cor. 3:16; 6:19). In them He prays and bears witness to the fact that they are adopted sons (cf. Gal. 4:6, Rom. 8:15–16, 26)" (LG 4).

And: "Incorporated into the Church through baptism, the faithful are consecrated by the baptismal character to the exercise of the cult of the Christian religion. Reborn as sons of God, they must confess before men the faith which they have received from God through the Church" (LG 11). (See Apostolate; People of God.)

## Faithful, Communion of

See Communion of Saints.

## Faithful, Prayer of

See Eucharist, Celebration of.

## Falda

This garment of white silk with a train is worn by the pope over his cassock on solemn occasions.

## Faldstool

A faldstool is a movable folding chair of wood or metal, with arms at the side but no back. It is used at pontifical functions by a bishop outside his cathedral or when he is not at his throne. The seat of the chair is made of cloth or leather and may have a cushion corresponding in color to that used in the liturgy of the day.

## Fall of Man

In the third chapter of the Book of Genesis we read of how the first woman, acting contrary to God's command, was induced to eat of the forbidden fruit of the tree of knowledge. She then persuaded the first man to do as she had done. The account is the recording of a symbolic act rather than the eating of a specific fruit of a designated tree. Thus it is the presentation of the experience of the human persons in a psychological or moral order that presents the human failure.

The consequences of this free action of failure to obey a positive command of God were, by interpretation: (1) death, which was the result of being shut off from that condition of God's care that would preserve him from death; (2) the change of man's relationship to God from one of intimacy and joy to one of fear and trembling in all encounters with God; (3) the rise of inordinate desires, concupiscence; hence human persons would have to fight against such to attain any degree of goodness; (4) a worsening of man's condition by his actions; he would experience in his social and material life pain, sorrow, and struggle; and (5) the most devastating consequence, the "darkening of man's mental capacities and his will" or the ignorance that man must strive to overcome but cannot fully even with the graces of revelation and the teachings of the Church.

The doctrine of original sin has been one of the prime teachings of the Church, and it has taught that sin blocks man on his path to fulfillment (cf. GS 13).

## False Decretals

See Decretals, False.

## Familiar

This name is given to a lay attendant who lives in and works for a monastery; also the title of the priests in the household of a bishop. Seldom used.

## Family

In the Bible, the people of Israel were divided into tribes and clans, and the clans were made up of "ancestral houses" or families. It was thus that families followed the descent from a famous ancestor, such as, the "house of David." The family was also a unit in worship (cf. Jb. 1:5), and the books of wisdom speak of the goodness of a family, its blessing, and the rearing of children (Prv. 17:1; 20:20; 31:10–31; 4:1–5; Sir. 7:18–36).

The family in modern social and religious thinking is an institution that consists of parents and children, with the children not a necessity, but which may also include others of relationship. In the societal structure of humans in both the State and the Church, the family is a prime entity because through the family the care and education of all members continues, and the future of maturity and development are best secured.

Vatican II teaches: "It has always been the duty of Christian couples, but today it is the supreme task of their apostolate, to manifest and prove by their own way of life the unbreakable and sacred character of the marriage bond . . . and to defend the dignity and lawful independence of the family" (AA 11).

And: "The spouses help each other to attain to holiness in their married life and by the rearing and education of their children. And so, in their state and way of life, they have their own special gift among the People of God (cf. 1 Cor. 7:7).

"For from the wedlock of Christians there comes the family, in which new citizens of human society are born. By the grace of the Holy Spirit received in baptism these are made children of God, thus perpetuating the People of God through the centuries" (LG 11).

And: At all times and places but particularly in areas where the first seeds of the gospel are being sown, or where the Church is still in her infancy or is involved in some serious difficulty, Christian families give priceless testimony to Christ before the world by remaining faithful to the gospel and by providing a model of Christian marriage throughout their lives" (AA 11). (See Christian Family Movement.)

And concerning the family apostolate: "Among the multiple activities of the family apostolate may be enumerated the following: the adoption of abandoned infants, hospitality to strangers, assistance in the operation of schools, helpful advice and material assistance for adolescents, help to engaged couples in preparing themselves better for marriage, catechetical work, support of married couples and families involved in materials and moral crises, help for the aged not only by providing them with the necessities of life but also by obtaining for them a fair share of the benefits of economic progress" (AA 11).

### Family Life Division of the United States Catholic Conference

This agency established in 1931 by the Bishops of the United States is a service organization for assisting, developing and coordinating family life; it was instituted after the publication of Pope Pius XII's encyclical *Casti connubi* (*Of Chaste Marriage,* 1930). Its purpose is to improve the Christian family, using the cooperation of some members from agencies related to family life. Its program was expanded in 1969 to embrace the entire social mission of the Church. In particular it focuses attention on the education of children, the cultural needs of the family, the preparation for marriage, sex education, prenatal instruction, and the promotion of marriage courses. Its modern concern has been the exertion on the social structures and political activities of pressure to improve the atmosphere and circumstances that would aid

family life in general. Family life directors are assigned in most dioceses, and many of the Division's activities are carried on through these affiliates. The headquarters are located at 1312 Massachusetts Ave. N.W., Washington, D.C. 20005.

### Fan

See Flabellum.

### Fanon

A vestment worn over the alb at pontifical ceremonies by the pope only, a fanon is circular or cape-like in shape, made of two pieces of white silk, with an opening at the center where it slips over the head. It is ornamented with two stripes of gold and red and an embroidered cross on the center front.

### Fascism

A form of state absolutism, fascism professes a philosophy of economic and social practicality, but in reality it is a political theory that seeks to establish the dictatorship of a single political party to the exclusion of all others and with distinct limitations of personal freedom. In this sense it is totalitarian. In application, fascism is national or racial and seeks to gain its ends by party means while keeping the party in power. It may differ from country to country. In June, 1931, Pope Pius XI denounced the fascist ideology in his encyclical, *Non abbianno bisogno,* calling it a "pagan worship of the state" and declaring it destructive of the natural rights of the family. He condemned it, saying: ". . . to monopolize completely the young, from their tenderest years up to manhood and womanhood, for the exclusive advantage of a party and of a regime based on the ideology which clearly resolves itself into a true, pagan worship of the state—the 'Statolatory' which is no less in contrast with the natural rights of the family than it is in contradiction with the supernatural rights of the Church."

### Fast

A fast is an ascetic practice, limited in duration, undertaken as a means of mortification or penance for one's spiritual welfare; the act of fasting. This was accepted by the primitive Church as a principle (cf. Acts 13:2–3; 14:23). (See Abstinence.)

### Fast, Eucharistic

There has been much change in what was previously the rule concerning abstaining from food or drink before the reception of the Holy

Eucharist. In the present discipline, and for reasons of reverence, the eating or drinking of any liquid or solid foods is forbidden for one hour before the reception of Holy Communion. One's fast is never broken by drinking water. When one is sick, whether or not confined to bed, or when taking medicine by mouth, the period is limited to fifteen minutes of fasting, and this is extended to those caring for the sick when it would be inconvenient to fast longer. When medicine is required, there is no length of time of the fast. This grant was made through the instruction *Immensae Caritatis* by the Congregation for the Discipline of the Sacraments, Jan. 29, 1973.

### Fasting

Fasting is a limitation of the quantity of food eaten, as distinguished from abstaining from foods (cf. Abstinence). The Church, both in its traditional practices and its present legislation on fasting, asks its members to fast, not because she considers certain foods as evil, but because she wishes her members to mortify their appetites, to progress spiritually, and to overcome self-indulgence. The essence of fasting consists of taking only one full meal each day. By custom, and since the Church does not require that the faithful injure their health or be wanting in the necessary strength for daily work, two other meatless meals each day are permitted. No specific amount is prescribed for these two meals except that together they should not equal one full meal in amount. In practice, breakfast is the lighter with a consideration that the normal amount would be about two ounces. Meat may be taken at the principal (full) meal on a day of fast, except on Fridays and Ash Wednesday. No eating between meals is permitted, but liquids including milk and fruit juices are allowed. The term meat includes the flesh of mammals (whale meat excepted by interpretation) and birds, broth or bouillon made from these, marrow, blood, brains, meat extracts, mince pie, beef tea, mutton soup. The law of fasting binds everyone over 21 years of age and under 59 years. The law may be revoked because of personal needs by permission of one's confessor. The present canonical discipline of penance for the United States, in addition to the general character of the Lenten season may thus be summed up: (1) Ash Wednesday and Good Friday are days of abstinence from meat and also of fast, that is, limited to a single full meal. With regard to Good Friday, the teaching of the second Vatican council should be recalled: "Let the paschal fast be kept sacred. Let it be celebrated everywhere on Good Friday and, where possible, prolonged throughout Holy Saturday, so that the joys of the Sunday of the Resurrection may be attained with uplifted and clear mind" (SC 110). (2) The other Fridays of the season of Lent are days of abstinence from meat. (3) The Fridays of the year outside Lent remain days of penance, but each individual may substitute for the traditional abstinence from meat some other practice of voluntary or personal penance; this may be physical mortification or temperance or acts of religion, charity, or Christian witness. The determination of these days of obligatory penance—which may even be reduced in number because of the occurrence of a holy day of obligation or diocesan regulations—should not be understood as limiting the occasions for Christian penance. The tradition of vigils and ember days, periods of special need and supplication, and above all the season of Lent as a whole should be maintained and respected.

### Father

This title is extended to all priests of the English-speaking world, because they are regarded as spiritual fathers. Holy Father is a title of the pope alone. God the Father is the First Person of the Blessed Trinity.

### Fathers of the Church, also Apostolic Fathers

As a title of excellence this refers to the writers and bishops of the early Christian centuries who either had direct contact with the Apostles or were sufficiently close to them and the influence of the Apostles' teaching to have expressed their teaching most clearly. Sometimes they are referred to as *Latin* or *Greek* Fathers because of their locations and areas of operation, but Christendom, while divided into two great parts, was one in thought. At first the title was conferred only on the heads of churches, that is, the bishops who were responsible for both discipline and doctrine. Later, it was conferred on those who were defenders of the faith and notable for the purity of their doctrinal teachings. Thus the title of father of the Church connotes orthodoxy and is extended to include many early writers of the Church. In order to be considered a father of the Church, an author must have lived during the first ages of the Church, his doctrine must be true, he must be known for holiness of life, and he must have merited the approval of the Church.

The period of time of the Patristic Church may be divided into four stages: (1) the time of the Apostolic Fathers, from the earliest writings down to the last half of the second century; (2) the time of the School of Alexandria, from the end of the second century to A.D. 315; (3) the so-called golden age, from the Council of Nicaea (325) to A.D. 444; (4) the decline, from A.D. 450 to A.D. 750.

The Apostolic Fathers are chiefly: St. Clement of Rome (d. 97); St. Ignatius of Antioch (50 to 107); St. Polycarp (69 to 155); and the authors of the *Didache, Shepherd of Hermas,* and the *Epistle of Barnabas.*

The greatest of the Fathers in the succeeding eras were: St. Ambrose of Milan (d. 397); St. Augustine (d. 430); St. Jerome (d. 420); St. Gregory of Nazianzen (d. 390); St. Basil the Great (d. 379); Basil's brother, Gregory of Nyssa (d. 394); St. John Chrysostom (d. 407); and St. Athanasius (d. 373).

Vatican II states: "Students should be shown what the Fathers of the Eastern and Western Church contributed to the fruitful transmission and illumination of the individual truths of revelation" (O.T. 16).

### Fatima, Apparitions of

Named after the city of Fatima in Portugal, these are perhaps the most well-known appearances of the Blessed Mother during the twentieth century. Following three preliminary visitations by a being who identified himself as the Angel of Portugal, the Blessed Mother appeared first on May 13, 1917, to three children, Lucia dos Santos, aged ten, and her two cousins Jacinta and Francisco Marto, who were seven and nine years old. With the exception of that of August, the apparitions took place at the Cova da Iria, a grazing ground near the village of Aljustrel, within the parish of Fatima, north of Lisbon, Portugal. In this series there were six monthly apparitions, May through October 13. (A seventh took place June 18, 1921 to Lucia.) On the October occasion an attested miracle of confirmation took place, called the miracle of the sun, wherein the sun appeared to plummet to the earth, spin, and give a multicolored light. The message of Fatima as declared by the Blessed Mother of God is that there is need for: the performance of penance, the frequent recitation of the Rosary, the practice of prayer and mortification for the conversion of sinners, prayers for priests, devotion of all peoples of the world to the Immaculate Heart of the Blessed Mother, and the offering of Holy Communion of reparation on the first Saturday of each month. The promised results of following these requests would be: the saving of many souls, the avoidance of a more terrible world war, the conversion of Russia, and world peace. In Oct. 1942, Pius XII consecrated the world, with special reference to Russia, to the Immaculate Heart of

Mary. The site at Fatima has become a world-famous place of pilgrimage; a church, a chapel of the apparitions, hospitals, hospices, and religious institutions have been erected there. (See Apparition.)

### Fear of God

This embraces two forms: (1) *servile,* which is the mental anxiety and emotion arising from the knowledge of the punishment that God may inflict; (2) *filial,* which is the dread of offending God who is all-good, and the fear of being separated from God by offenses that incur the loss of sanctifying grace. Filial, also called reverential, fear is a particular means of sanctification, a gift of the Holy Spirit, since it enables one to acknowledge God's greatness, have sorrow at any offense against God, and avoid occasions of possible offense, yet avoid familiarity with God and presumption. The fear of God permeates all religion, for it is called "the beginning of wisdom" (Prv. 1:7; Sir. 1:14; Ps. 115:11). It is one of the perfections, namely wisdom, which is prophesied of Christ (Is. 11:2). In the NT the term "fear" is used more in the sense of being afraid to offend the all-good God (Heb. 10:31), and that fear is supplanted with confidence and love through Christ—"Love has no fear; rather, perfect love casts out all fear. And since fear has to do with punishment, love is not yet perfect in one who is afraid" (1 Jn. 4:18).

### Feasts of the Church

In the calendar of the liturgical year feasts are the sequence of festivals to commemorate a teaching or event of religious importance, or saints' days.

In the course of the new calendar of the Church year, as the Church celebrates the mystery of Christ, Mary the Mother of God is especially honored, and the martyrs and other saints are proposed as examples for the faithful.

The celebration of the days of saints who have universal significance is required throughout the entire Church. The days of other saints are listed in the calendar as optional or are left to the veneration of particular churches, countries, or religious communities.

The different types of celebrations are distinguished from each other by their importance and are accordingly called *solemnities, feasts,* and *memorials.*

Solemnities are the days of greatest importance and begin with first vespers of the preceding day. Several solemnities have their own vigil Mass, to be used when Mass is celebrated in the evening of the preceding day.

The celebration of Easter and Christmas continues for eight days. Each octave is governed by its own rules.

Feasts are celebrated within the limits of a natural day. They do not have first vespers, with the exception of feasts of the Lord that fall on Sundays in ordinary time, Sundays of the Christmas season, and feasts that are substituted for the Sunday office.

Memorials are either obligatory or optional. Their observance is combined with the celebration of the occurring weekday according to norms included in the general instructions for the Mass and divine office. Obligatory memorials that occur on Lenten weekdays may be celebrated only as optional memorials. Should more than one optional memorial fall on the same day, only one is celebrated; the others are omitted.

On Saturdays in ordinary time when there is no obligatory memorial, an optional memorial of the Blessed Virgin Mary may be observed. (General norms; Sacramentary.) (See Calendar, Church.)

## Febronianism

This theory first appeared in a book published in 1763 by Bishop John von Hontheim who wrote under the pen name "Febronius." It primarily expressed opposition to the jurisdiction of Rome in ruling the affairs of the Church, in favor of the state or secular ruler, and it favored ecumenical councils as the courts of last appeal. These teachings were condemned by Popes Clement XIII and Pius VI. The movement was paralleled by Josephism, which was named after Emperor Joseph II and was an attempt to make the Church in Austria independent of the pope. Both of these exaggerated forms of Gallicanism were strains on Church and state relations. Their chief influence was in some ecclesiastical reforms begun in the last half of the eighteenth century. Their problems were chiefly the creation of opposition of bishops to the Pope. The matter was settled by Vatican Council I when the primacy of the Holy See of St. Peter was established.

## Federated Churches

In the United States there has developed a consolidating of church groups among many Protestant churches. In such federations one or more denominations conduct their activities as single religious bodies, but the members retain their own affiliation within their own denomination. Through this practice there is usually one minister, a common community service, and a joint program of social action with the added benefit in some instances of having only one church building.

They have been called interdenominational, undenominational, or community churches, but these are often misleading characterizations because members sometimes claim allegiance to only one congregation. The federated churches usually operate with a joint committee, directing the activities, and made up of an equal number of members from each denomination. Those churches that most frequently federate are the local church groups of the Methodists, Baptists, and Presbyterians, with but two church groups participating and with a practice of alternating ministers over a multi-year schedule.

## Federation of Diocesan Liturgical Commissions (FDLC)

This is the national organization made up of the delegated members of the diocesan or archdiocesan Liturgical Commissions. Its role is to coordinate the liturgical activities of the dioceses, disseminate printed instructions and guidelines, and to propose educational procedures as well as serve as an overseeing body. Its actions are subject to episcopal direction and do not have official sanction unless approved. The federation publishes "Federation Notes," a newsletter and organization publication.

## Ferendae Sententiae

This term is used to describe the punishment of censure that is added to a law or precept by the sentence of a judge or a proper ecclesiastical superior. The penalty is thus not automatic (cf. Latae Sententiae) but is yet to be inflicted following the crime. (See Censure.)

## Feria

A weekday of the Church calendar on which no feast or vigil is observed is called a feria. The Mass said on a ferial day is normally that of the previous Sunday. (See Calendar, Church; Feasts of the Church.) The ferial days of Advent and Lent are in special categories and vary with the seasonal sequence.

## Ferraiola

A ferraiola is a short cape, attached to a cassock and reaching halfway down the upper arm.

## Ferraiolone

Literally, "big cape," a ferraiolone is a cape of black cloth worn over the cassock, reaching to mid-calf or floor length. It must be worn by diocesan priests attending papal audiences.

## Ferrara

See Florence, Council of.

## Ferula

1. A small rod with which a penitent, usually in a religious community, is lightly struck to signify acceptance of a penance.

2. In former times, before sitting was permitted at Church functions, a T-shaped staff used to support one as a crutch during lengthy ceremonies. It is still used in choir by Maronite, dissident Ethiopian, and Coptic monks.

## Festival of Lights

The feastday of Judaism called Hanukkah (a threefold festival including the Feast of Lights, the Feast of Consecration, and the Feast of the Maccabees) is the eight day festival during which candles in an eight-branch candleholder, the Menorah, are lighted in succession, one for each day. It occurs close to the winter solstice.

## Fetishism

Derived from the Portuguese word for "magic," fetishism is magic or a form of spiritism centered around an object called a fetish. If such an object is precious, a gem or coin, it is called a talisman; if it is to control good or evil spirits, it is called a charm; and if it is worn on one's person, it is called an amulet. Undue or unreasonable powers are ascribed to fetishes, and their superstitious value becomes sacrosanct to the persons possessing them. Fetish dolls or representations of people are used in the voodoo practice of piercing the doll in the place where an evil is to befall the person. A psychological fetish is an inordinate affection or sexual emphasis attached to an object such as shoes, underclothing, or pillows.

## Feudalism

The political, social, and economic system of class distinctions of the Middle Ages, known as feudalism, seriously affected the Church. As a system it was essentially the organization of the land-owning aristocracy into a sort of hierarchy with lesser lords serving overlords in a mutual agreement. Beneath these were the masses of people, soldiers, farmers, craftsmen, and others. The aristocrats and freemen fought battles and offered protection to the serfs and villeins. The clergy also fell into classes, higher and lower, with higher Church offices going to members of noble families. From the standpoint of the Church, one of the evils of the feudal system was the lord's claimed right of appointment to Church offices, thus placing ecclesiastics under secular control. This practice gave rise to "lay investiture" with its attendant evils, wherein the temporal ruler could place upon one of his choice the symbols of spiritual jurisdiction: the crosier, the episcopal ring, and miter.

## Fides

The international Fides Service is a news agency of the Congregation for the Evangelization of Peoples. Its main function is to issue periodic news releases, comments, and background information on all phases of missionary activity and the many missions themselves throughout the world. Its office is located at Via di Propaganda, 1 C. 00187, Rome, Italy.

## Filioque

This Latin word, translated "and from the Son," is used in the Nicene Creed to declare the twofold procession of God the Holy Spirit from the Father "and from the Son." It was first added to the Nicene Creed at the Council of Toledo, held in A.D. 589. It was a word of controversy, not because of the question of its doctrine, but because ever since its first use in the sixth century and acceptance by the Western Church it had become a source of contention with the Greeks who objected to its insertion in the Creed. It was settled, with the Greeks accepting the dual procession, at the Council of Florence (1438 to 1445), where it was agreed that the single principle of progression, namely, that the Greek "through the Son" did not differ essentially from the Latin "from the Son." After the signing of the documents, political factors were introduced, the Greeks reverted to schism, and even at the present time the Greek Orthodox Church and other schismatic Eastern Churches condemn the "filioque" wording.

## Film and Broadcasting, Division for (DFB)

This division is one of the Department of Communications of the National Conference of Catholic Bishops and of the United States Catholic Conference. It was founded in Jan. 1972 as a reorganized unit of the former National Catholic Office for Motion Pictures and the National Catholic Office for Radio and Television.

The division provides a national information service, training and cooperation for all diocesan communications offices throughout the United States. Through the use of workshops, seminars, and institutes in film and broadcasting it serves to bring cooperation and information to the media people. It also publishes *Share*, a packet of film and broadcasting information, and *Catholic Film Newsletter* for the motion picture medium; both are published twice monthly. The film newsletter carries reviews of all current nationally released motion pictures of 35 mm films and provides information concerning resources for film use in education, including books, magazines, or festivals. The central office maintains a library of 16 mm films for use by Catholic programs as well as a consultative service for educational and religious films.

In the area of broadcasting, liaison is maintained with all the major networks, both radio and television. The division is an affiliate member of the international Catholic organizations for films and broadcasting, and both consultation and information services are provided for the Pontifical Commission for Social Communications as well as the communications offices of national episcopal conferences throughout the world. The headquarters for the United States are at 1011 First Ave., New York, N.Y. 10022.

### Final Perseverance

Final perseverance is the gift from God whereby one may remain in the state of sanctifying grace until death. The grace to persevere can come from God alone; it implies that sufficient grace will be given to aid one not to fall in seeking salvation.

### Finding of the Cross

This feast is celebrated on Sept. 14 under the title "Triumph of the Cross" in commemoration of the finding of the true cross of Christ by St. Helena in the year 326. (Cf. Cross, Relics of the True.)

### Fire, Blessing of

Stemming from an early Celtic practice, the blessing of fire has been adapted to the preliminary ritual in celebration of the Resurrection of Christ.

At the beginning of the Easter vigil, on Holy Saturday before daybreak of Easter Sunday, a fire is lighted outside the church (if this is not possible an adaptation is made to suit the circumstances). The priest then instructs the Congregation about the vigil, the Service of Light. He then blesses the fire saying: "Let us pray. Father, we share in the light of your glory through your Son, the light of the world. Make this new fire holy, and inflame us with new hope. Purify our minds by this Easter celebration and bring us one day to the feast of eternal light. We ask this through Christ our Lord. Amen."

The Easter candle is then lighted from the new fire. (See Holy Week, Liturgy of.)

### Fire of Hell

See Hell.

### First Born

In the Mosaic Law the first male child in a family had certain rights and obligations. This was carried over to the firstlings of the animal kingdom who were to be sacrificed as offerings, the "unblemished" (Ex. 13:2; 22:28–29; 34:19–20). In a figurative and much broader sense God called Israel, His chosen people, "my first born" (Ex. 4:22; Sir. 36:11).

In the NT Christ is called the "first born of many brothers" (Rom. 8:29), "the first born of the dead" (Col. 1:18), and the "first born of all creatures" (Col. 1:15). Because of His resurrection He is given a comparable title as the most honored, "the first fruits of those who have fallen asleep" (1 Cor. 15:20).

### First Communion

The reception of the consecrated host for the first time is called the first communion. This traditional event takes place after a child has been suitably instructed and has reached the age of reason. Sometimes by custom, the recipients carry a candle, and the event is often solemnized in various ways.

The Eucharist should not be administered to children who are not old enough by an arbitrary reckoning or do not have the knowledge or intention required for the reception of the sacrament. However, children in danger of death are to be given the Eucharist if they are able to distinguish between the Blessed Sacrament and ordinary bread and there is no irreverence to be shown. The obligation of the precept of children under the age of puberty receiving the Eucharist is primarily the charge of those who have the care and rearing of these children, namely, their parents, guardians, confessors, teachers, and pastors (c. 860).

The Holy See judges that the practice of receiving Confession before first Communion should still be observed (Directorium Catechisticum Generale, n. 5).

### First Friday

First Friday is the devotion of receiving Holy Communion on consecutive first Fridays for nine months in honor of the Sacred Heart. This practice arose following one of the promises made by Christ to St. Margaret Mary Alacoque (1647 to 1690), by which one gains the grace of repentance, an assurance of receiving the last sacraments, and the consolation of the love of Christ's Sacred Heart at the time of death. This is often referred to as the Communion of Reparation, following the twelfth promise made to St. Margaret Mary.

There has also been the custom of observing a Holy Hour in the evening of the first Friday, and this is a devotion of reparation, indulgenced by the Church. Such paraliturgical devotions have been especially promoted by the members of the Apostleship of Prayer. The holy hours may be public with Exposition and Benediction of the Blessed Sacrament, but although recommended, this is not necessary for the fulfilling of the requirement for private or limited devotion. (See Sacred Heart of Jesus.)

### First Friday Clubs

These groups are part social, religious, and instructional in nature. Organized in 1936, they have as their objectives: encouragement of the devotion to the Sacred Heart of Jesus, the practice of the First Fridays, and a meeting together for breakfast, lunch, or dinner to discuss and be informed concerning Catholic matters. There are about ninety such clubs in the United States and additional clubs in Canada that have basically the same objectives.

### First Fruits

According to the law of Moses, the first produce of man, animals, and "whatsoever was sown in the field," was to be given to the Lord (Ex. 23:16). This OT law has been ascribed to the physical support to be given to the Church and her priests in present times. However, it no longer refers to the substance given but rather to the monetary contribution made by the faithful. (See Tithing; Stewardship.)

### First Saturday Devotion

This devotion began after the apparitions of the Blessed Virgin Mary at Fatima, Portugal, in 1917. Those who practice this devotion are to receive Holy Communion on the first Saturday of each month, to receive the Sacrament of Penance within eight days before or after this day, recite five decades of the rosary, and make a fifteen minute meditation on one of the mysteries of the rosary.

Although this devotion gained momentum after Fatima, its source may also be traced to St. John Eudes (1601 to 1680) who is considered the apostle of devotion to the Sacred Hearts of Jesus and Mary, and to Venerable John J. Olier (1608 to 1657), the founder of the Sulpician Fathers. The essential character of the devotion is reparation for the blasphemies and acts against the divine Son of the Blessed Mother. Pope Benedict XV (1914 to 1922) granted a plenary indulgence at the hour of

death to all who make acts of reparation on eight consecutive Saturdays.

It is reported that the Blessed Virgin Mary promised her intercession at the hour of death to obtain the necessary graces for all who make the First Saturday devotions on five Saturdays of successive months and who in so doing offer reparation to her Divine Son through her Immaculate Heart.

Saturday has been the traditional day of devotion to the Blessed Virgin Mary, and on Saturdays of the season of the year on which optional memorials are permitted, there can be celebrated the optional memorial of the Virgin Mary with its own proper reading in both the Sacramentary and the Liturgy of the Hours. (See Fatima, Apparitions of.)

### Fiscal Procurator

A fiscal procurator is an official appointed to a diocese whose duty it is to start proceedings against criminal offenders and bring them to trial in Church courts.

### Fish

In Christian art, a fish is a symbol of Christ, our Savior. The use of this symbol is derived from the Greek word for fish (phonetically *ichthus*); its letters are the initials of the phrase, "Jesus Christ, Son of God, Savior." Fishes are used as a symbol of the faithful, referring to the miraculous catch of fish narrated in Lk. 5; and as a symbol of the Apostles who by their missionary work were designated as "fishers of men" (Lk. 5:10).

### Fisherman, Ring of

This is the official ring of the reigning pontiff, upon which is incised a semblance of St. Peter sitting in a boat, fishing, with the pope's name around it. The ring is emblematic of the pontiff's succession to the Chair of St. Peter. It is used only for the sealing of official documents, as an impression on wax. Upon the death of the reigning pontiff, the Fisherman's ring is solemnly destroyed

by the papal chamberlain, and a new ring is made for the newly elected successor to the Holy See. It was first used by Pope Clement IV (d. 1268).

### Fistula

This term is applied to the small gold pipette by means of which the pope receives the consecrated wine during a solemn papal Mass.

### Five Wounds

The devotion that arose during the Middle Ages gave rise to veneration of the five wounds inflicted upon the body of Jesus Christ at the crucifixion, namely, those in His hands (*sic*), His feet and the lance cut in His side. A representation of these wounds was incorporated into a shield or heraldic device and adopted as a badge of pilgrimages of grace, and this device became a part of the coat-of-arms of the nation of Portugal. (See Shroud, Holy.)

### Flabellum

A flabellum is a large fan, usually with a leather haft supporting a spread of feathers, and mounted on a long staff. It is chiefly used in pontifical liturgical functions, serving only an ornamental purpose. Originally it was used to keep insects from the sacred species. Two large *flabella* are carried behind the portable throne (*sedia gestatoria*) when the Pope is carried into St. Peter's Basilica on solemn occasions.

### Flagellants

Self-flagellation was a common penitential practice among religious orders, but in the middle of the thirteenth century an Umbrian hermit organized a brotherhood that became known as the Flagellants. It gained strength because of the feeling among devout people that the plague of 1259, the famine, and the almost continuous warfare were all caused by the sinfulness of men. This group of fanatics made a custom of marching through the streets scourging themselves and exhorting the people to repentance for their sins. The group became heretical and had political leanings. They were prohibited by papal order in 1261, but after the Black Death (1346 to 1350) they were again active. The movement spread widely, and north of the Alps the Flagellants developed an organized religious ceremony and their own set of heretical doctrines. They were condemned by Pope Clement VI in 1349.

Today any group who fanatically or excessively inflict scourging by rod or whip on themselves or others are referred to as "flagellants." However, the practices have been done away with, except for occasional instances among primitive peoples, but in modern times such practices are in disfavor and seldom witnessed in public or done in private.

### Flectamus Genua

These Latin words were formerly a prefatory bidding, meaning "Let us bend the knee," given in chant to the people by the deacon during Mass. To each bidding the response was "levate" (arise!).

### Flock

An adapted synonym for the Church used by early writers for the concept of the shepherd, referring both to Christ and His representative, the bishop. In Latin this was *parvulus grex,* the "little flock." Vatican II often used the term to apply to the Church and its ministry: "She (the Church) is a flock of which God Himself foretold that He would be the Shepherd (cf. Is. 40:11; Ez. 34:11–31). Although guided by human shepherds, her sheep are nevertheless ceaselessly led and nourished by Christ Himself, the Good Shepherd and the Prince of Shepherds (cf. Jn. 10:11; 1 Pt.

5:4), who gave His life for the sheep (cf. Jn. 10:11–15)" (1G 6).

## Flood
See Deluge.

## Florence, Council of
This Council is commonly known as the Council of Ferrara-Florence. As a continuation of the Council of Basle (1431), it first reconvened at Ferrara in 1438, but because of the ravages of the plague, Pope Eugene IV transferred it to Florence. The Council discussed the reunion of the Latins and the Greeks and the insertion of the word *Filioque* in the Creed. A degree of union was agreed upon in 1439, but rejected later in 1472 by Gennadius, the patriarch of Constantinople, who had been appointed by the sultan of the Turks. The Council was finally adjourned in 1445 at Rome. (Cf. Ecumenical Councils; Filioque.)

## Florida Pascua
The Spanish name for Palm Sunday is Florida Pascua.

## Focolare Movement
This movement was begun in Trent, Italy, in 1943 by Chiara Lubich and a group of her companions. It is an association of men and women, which is officially approved by the Church, but it is not a secular institute, although vows are taken by many of the unmarried persons among its totally dedicated membership. Centers of Movement have been established in thirty countries throughout the world. United States' centers are located in New York City, Chicago, and Boston. The purposes of this association are broad, but chiefly they are for personal spiritual benefit, the influence of a greater prayer life among the members, and the bringing about of spiritual good through the everyday conditions of work and service for the social welfare of many.

## Font
See Baptismal Font; Baptistry.

## Footpace
See Predella.

## Forbidden Books
See Index of Forbidden Books.

## Foreign Missions
See Mission.

## Forgiveness of Sins
See Penance, Sacrament of.

## Form
1. In scholastic philosophy, form is (a) *substantial,* that is, the principle of reality that determines a being into what it is. Together with prime matter, form is the first act or potentiality determining a being in existence through the operation of an efficient cause. In a being, form determines the nature or cause. In a substance, it determines the nature or essence in existence. Form, however, may be designated as apart from matter, for example, pure spirits; or by its nature, form may be made to inform matter, for example, the human soul; or form may be constituted in the potentiality of matter (passive), for example, animals; (b) *accidental* form is what is added to that which is substantially complete, for example, roundness or firmness; in this sense, form has an aesthetic significance.

2. Sacramental form, or the form of a sacrament, is that designated in theology as the words and signs that accompany the matter being used. These words are an established and authentic sign determining the sacrament and cannot be substantially changed without invalidating the sacrament. The matter of the sacrament, the physical element, is determined or signified only by what the words clearly express. (See Sacraments, Seven.)

## Form Criticism
The Church has continuously encouraged the study and investigation of the Scriptures. In form criticism there is the most modern approach to (1) the literal sense of the Bible and the meaning intended by the writers; and (2) the scientific examination of the literature of the Old and New Testaments with the aid of history, archeology, ethnology, and other sciences by which new and accurate means may be used to determine the precise expression of the writers and in interpretation of the biblical writings.

In past pronouncements the Church has charged scholars with the burden of scientifically investigating and interpreting the Scriptures in order "that as many ministers of the word as possible may be equipped to impart the nourishment of Scripture to the people of God in a truly beneficial manner." (See Vatican Council II.)

The method of form criticism attempts to carry on this mandate. In order to come to the most exact interpretation, the scholar examines the conditions of the author, the literary style, the milieu in which the writing was done, the cultural and ethnic surroundings, the influences of the time and place, the linguistic aspects of biblical writing, and the tradition and oral transmission of the texts, together with the distinctive marks that these made upon the writings. Such studies reveal the nature of the gospels as compilations of oral and written traditions. Thus form criticism examines the literary and traditional laws that give shape to these writings. "To trace these laws back, to make the emergence of those small units comprehensible, to work out and explain their characteristics, and in these and similar ways to arrive at an understanding of the tradition—this is what it means to investigate the gospel form—critically" (M. Dibelius).

The understanding of biblical literature in the light of the process by which it came into being, together with its content and subsequent transmission, means to examine and know the smallest units (the *formulae*), the larger literary forms (parables, poetry, narration), and the overall forms that embrace all the literary types.

Form criticism provides the insights into the social and historical settings or the reality of life as it existed in the primitive Church and the earliest communities. It provides a knowledge of the tradition that makes it possible to better understand Jesus Himself in the apostolic and primitive Church. It makes for an historical reconstruction of the times as well as a biographical testimony through the transition from early times to the present.

Thus it may be concluded that form criticism, which began only in the very late nineteenth century and has come to fruition in the past 20 years, has shown the documentation of the preaching and teaching Church from earliest times. It contributes to our understanding of the Scriptures and the Church in this our day. As Vatican II teaches: "The Church has always venerated the divine Scriptures just as she venerates the body of the Lord, since from the table of both the word of God and of the body of Christ she unceasingly receives and offers to the faithful the bread of life, especially in the sacred liturgy. She has always regarded the Scriptures together with sacred tradition as the supreme rule of faith, and will ever do so. For, inspired by God and committed once and for all to writing, they impart the word of God Himself without change, and make the voice of the Holy Spirit resound in the words of the prophets and apostles. Therefore, like the Christian religion itself, all the preaching of the Church must be nourished and ruled by sacred Scripture. For in the sacred books, the Father who is in heaven meets His children with great love and speaks with them; and the force and power in the word of God are so great that it remains the support and energy of the Church, the strength of faith for her sons, the food of the soul, the pure and perennial source of spiritual life. Consequently, these words are perfectly applicable to sacred Scripture: 'God's word is living and effective' (Heb. 4:12) and 'can enlarge you, and give you a share among all who are consecrated to him' (Acts 20:32; cf. 1 Thes. 2:13)" (DV 21). (See Interpretation, Scriptural.)

**Fortitude**

Fortitude is a cardinal virtue and a gift of the Holy Spirit. Considered as a virtue, it is the strength of soul, or the firm and assured practice of all other virtues exercised in the pursuit of good and the love of God. Thus it is a strength that overcomes the fear of not doing right and is manifest in the character of an individual who acts rightly and does not succumb to temptation. It thus aids in the effort demanded by a good act, helps to eliminate the fear of criticism, and provides the will to continue to perform good acts.

As a gift of the Holy Spirit, it is the action of the Holy Spirit within us, granting the impulse to act rightly, the will to do so, and the joy in so acting, and so it perfects the virtue of fortitude and serves to gain other virtues. It aids us in living the Christian life fully and seeking the self-control necessary to face death with courage.

**Fortune-Telling**

Fortune-telling is that form of superstition or divination as practiced by an individual, which attempts to foretell the future or to predict events by inadequate and spurious means. The most common tools of the fortune teller are the crystal ball, ouija board, playing cards, tarot cards, stars, the palm of the hand, and the lumps or conformation of the head. However, it is impossible to predict the future except through grace granted by God who alone knows the events that will take place in the future. Since fortune-telling is a form of superstition, it is seriously sinful, prohibited by the First Commandment for both the practitioner and the one consulting the fortune-teller.

**Forty Hours' Devotion**

This is the solemn Exposition of the Blessed Sacrament held for the duration of forty hours. This devotion, which began in the sixteenth century, is held each year (c. 1275) in parochial and other churches that have the right to reserve the Blessed Sacrament on days determined by and consented to by the local ordinary. Usually there is continual progression, an Exposition of the Blessed Sacrament each day throughout the year at some church of the diocese. Appropriate prayers and ceremonies accompany this devotion. By special grant of the Holy See, the United States is permitted a modified form of this traditional devotion, known as the "Thirteen Hours' Devotion." (See Liturgy; Paraliturgical Actions; Eucharistic Devotions.)

## Forum

This term (plural: *fora*) has a wide variety of meanings that have been adapted to the canonical language of the Church. Originally the word *forum* meant a public market place or a court of justice. It also came to mean the bench or tribunal and then the judge who exercised authority within the court. By wider application it came to include the entire territory wherein a judge had authority, and then it finally applied to judicial power as such.

In Church use it may refer to any one of these meanings, but the word is always qualified, for example, *competent forum* is the court or the judge who has authority to try and determine a case. Forum of the Church means the sphere in which jurisdiction is exercised, in courts or the sacramental tribunal of the confessional. This is further classified as internal or external. *Internal forum* is the exercise of judicial acts in regard to matters of sacramental confession or those of a secret nature. *External forum* refers to the social and juridical effects of jurisdiction, for example, a dispensation granted and recorded. A juridical act, such as the lifting of a censure, given in the external forum is valid in the internal forum, but the reverse is not; that is, a power of jurisdiction exercised in the internal forum has no acceptance in the external forum. A priest may receive power for both fora. The *Privilege of the Forum* refers to the right of clerics and religious, including sisters, to be tried before ecclesiastical courts in civil or criminal causes. (See Courts, Ecclesiastical; Process, Due.)

## Fossor

A fossor was one who served officially as a gravedigger in the catacombs, sometimes he was considered to be of minor clerical rank.

## Foundation Masses

The Masses that are requested to be celebrated as a part of a bequest given to a diocese, church, or religious order are known as foundation Masses; a specified number of Masses are to be celebrated for a particular purpose over a specified period of time. Canon Law regulates these (c. 1513 to 1577),

and while the Church wishes to carry out the intent of the donor and always has done so, it is practical in many dioceses to limit these foundation Masses to a maximum of 25 years or some similar period of time.

## Fraction

The "breaking," from the Latin, *fractio,* this is the act of breaking the bread of the species consecrated in the Mass. In the Latin Mass this takes place just prior to the Agnus Dei, but in the New Order this is the third action of the communion rite: "The breaking of the bread: this gesture of Christ at the Last Supper gave the entire eucharistic action its name in apostolic times. In addition to its practical aspect, it signifies that in communion we who are many are made one body in the one bread that is Christ (1 Cor. 10:17)." It is thus a sign of unity and community. (See Eucharist, Celebration of.)

## Franciscan Controversy

There arose a dispute over the interpretation of the original rule of St. Francis of Assisi (1182 to 1226) concerning especially the adherence to the rule of poverty first set down in 1221 and revised in 1223. The members were concerned about two camps of thought: those who were in favor of no relaxation of the rule, called the Spirituals or *Zelanti* (Zealots), and their opponents who favored a modification of the rule, the *Relaxati* (the Lax).

This difficulty went on for more than 200 years. Arising primarily because of the great response to the Franciscan way of life, with great growth in members, and to their special activities, this dispute had some basis in the practicality of their life. First, it was felt that they could not carry on their work without having some workable use of monies. Second, the application of the rule was applied by the Spirituals to both the individual members and the corporate makeup of the monasteries. Pope Gregory IX (1227 to 1241) attempted to alleviate the dispute by authorizing the Friars to use agents to handle the donations to the communities of monks and to permit them to exercise the purchasing of necessities and carry on business for the monks. This was not satisfactory to the Spirituals, and when St. Bonaventure became general of the Order (1257 to 1274), he sought to bring harmony, teaching that the rule forbade the ownership but not the use of worldly goods. This was supported by Popes Alexander IV (1254 to 1261), Nicholas III (1277 to 1280), and John XXII (1316 to 1334). The latter lost patience with the Spirituals and brought restrictive measures against them. This led to a break of a more serious nature, which was not resolved until the rule of Pope Martin V (1417 to 1431), but final settlement was made only with the approved reform among the Friars of Strict Observance in the fifteenth century. (See Franciscans.)

## Franciscan Missions of California

The Spanish march northward along the western side of North America faced many setbacks, but Father Junipero Serra came to what is now the city of San Diego, California and built the first of the California missions in 1769. These mission churches, with enclosures, gardens, and towers in the Spanish style stretched along the Camino Reál to the northernmost part of the state of California. A chain of twenty-one missions was erected over the next 54 years, and these have been landmarks and points of historic interest since that time. The missions and their dates of founding are:

1. San Diego de Alcala, July 16, 1769
2. San Carlos Borromeo, June 3, 1770
3. San Antonio de Padua, July 14, 1771
4. San Gabriel Arcángel, Sept. 8, 1771
5. San Luis Obispo de Tolosa, Sept. 1, 1772
6. San Francisco de Asís, Oct. 9, 1776
7. San Juan Capistrano, Nov. 1, 1776
8. Santa Clara de Asís, Jan. 12, 1777
9. San Buenaventura, March 31, 1782
10. Santa Bárbara, Dec. 4, 1786
11. La Purísima Concepción, Dec. 8, 1787
12. Santa Cruz, Sept. 25, 1791
13. Nuestra Señora de la Soledad, Oct. 9, 1791
14. San José de la Guadalupe, June 1, 1797
15. San Juan Bautista, June 24, 1797
16. San Miguel Arcángel, July 25, 1797
17. San Fernando Rey de España, Sept. 8, 1797
18. San Luis Rey de Francia, June 13, 1798
19. Santa Inés, Sept. 17, 1804
20. San Rafael Arcángel, Dec. 14, 1817
21. San Francisco de Solano, July 4, 1823

Many of these early missions have been restored and have become places of tourist attraction while also serving as churches.

## Franciscans

Franciscans are members of the Order of Friars Minor that was founded by St. Francis of Assisi (d. 1226) in 1209. The rule written by St. Francis, like that of St. Dominic, was later to apply to three orders: one for men, one for women, and one for men and women living in the world. The rule was revised in 1221 and again in 1223 but basically was adapted to the changing social and religious structure of society at that time. The rule is now observed by three separate bodies of religious men: the Friars Minor, Friars Minor Conventuals, and Friars Minor Capuchins. The Second Order of Franciscans, the Poor Clares, used the basic rule as first written for them by the future Gregory IX in 1219, which was later adapted by St. Clare. The Third Order was not entirely a new application, since the Benedictine Rule had been adopted to lay participation in religious life (tertians) as early as the ninth century. However, the Franciscan application was made in 1221 under the name of the Brothers and Sisters of Penance. From this developed the Third Order Secular and the tertiary order for lay persons. Later, other tertiary groups sprang from this application of the rule. (See Tertiaries.)

The core of the rule and life as given by St. Francis is *poverty*. "It was love for Christ that impelled Francis to put aside everything that could keep him from perfect union with Christ and to embrace complete and unrestricted poverty" (*Franciscan Omnibus*).

## Frankfort, Council of

A local council was called by the Frankish bishops in 794 to protest the Council of Nicaea. Because of incorrect translations, it was thought that Nicaea had approved "image adoration." Hence, the Franks sent a refutation of the error and condemned such practices. At the same time, besides confirming the Church's true teaching on the questions of images (actually set forth correctly at Nicaea), the Council of Frankfort attacked and condemned Adoptionism.

## Frankincense

Frankincense is the white resin from various trees of the genus *Boswellia*, which are native to southern Arabia, Somaliland, and Abyssinia. When this resin is burned, it gives a pleasant aroma. The resin is clear as it comes from the first cutting of the bark, and it whitens upon exposure to the air. The word "frank" means "pure," and the resin from later cuttings is discolored or mixed with impurities. It was thus the "pure white" incense that was given by the Magi to the Infant Jesus with offerings of gold and myrrh (Cf. Mt. 2:11).

## Fraternal Correction

Fraternal correction is the practical application of the virtue of charity in which love of neighbor is extended to another to aid him to avoid sin and its occasion or to refrain from further sin. By application it need not be given only in instances of sin but may be given in instances where faults or imperfections exist. The method or manner of giving such correction may be by words, glances, or by refusing to support one by financial means in order to correct the error. Chiefly it is a matter of counsel. However, fraternal correction is not to be lightly indulged. Before one assumes the corrector's obligation, the following conditions should be present: the one to be corrected must be in serious spiritual distress; there should be a reasonable hope that the correction will be profitably received, and it must be possible to bring about the correction without great personal detriment.

Prudence should be exercised in judging the time, the degree, and the manner of giving correction, for no spiritual benefit is likely to follow if this is done in haste, pride, or anger. In the practical sphere, such correction has often been practiced by those who witness another becoming addicted to alcohol or drugs and thereby opening themselves to the attendant diseases. (See Counseling, Pastoral.)

## Freedom

There are three aspects of freedom of beings, all having negative and positive concepts: (1) the "freedom from" something, as opposed to enslavement; (2) moral freedom, the freedom of the will, or not being forced to act in a certain way; (3) the transcendental freedom that is the fundamental propriety of man, or his faculty to alone say he "*is*," "over and beyond" every other individual being. This third aspect of freedom is often called the "perfect act of freedom," because of its spiritual significance for man, as stated in the Epistle of James: "There is, on the other hand, the man who peers into freedom's ideal law and abides by it. He is no forgetful listener, but one who carries out the law in practice. Blest will this man be in whatever he does" (1:25).

The freedom of man is never a simple state; it has a political and social dependency, for out of the possibilities of life, through free actions, man produces fellowship, the contract of marriage, the responsibility of family, society, and the state. With the freedom of being one before God and one in God, man becomes an entity of the Church and a viable part of the Mystical Body, through the sacraments and the liturgy of the Church.

There are five principles that underlie the Christian concept of social freedom. (1) Freedom has a transcendental aspect, whereby it is indivisible, both spontaneous and actuated by decision; it follows the voice of conscience determined by nature, culture, education, and other factors. (2) Freedom is not a simple state or a pure act (like divine freedom), but it uses the technical, acquired, and environmental conditions to transform man's actions into art or works of beauty, for example. (3) Freedom has a principle of sociality, meaning that the individual does not act alone in most works but unites with other free persons to achieve a division of labor and integrated achievements. (4) Freedom acts through the person who freely disposes himself to come into full self-possession. (5) All of these culminate in the principle of subsidiarity—freedom to act is essential to the person's personality, his very mode of being. All other works toward the realization of self are only modes referred back to the person. Thus he can be nothing else but an end in himself, a person with inviolable dignity.

In the Christian view of freedom, freedom lacking a religious dimension, freedom that does not have grace and make use of it, is fallen freedom. Man must be free if he is to rise again in glory, to take up God's offer obtained through Christ and continuously proffered by the Church, for we are healed through Christ and are called to be the "children of God."

Vatican II teaches: "The values of human dignity, brotherhood and freedom, and indeed all the good fruits of our nature and enterprise, we will find them again, but freed of stain, burnished and transfigured. This will be so when Christ hands over to the Father a kingdom eternal and universal: 'A kingdom of truth and life of holiness and grace, of justice, love and peace'" (GS 39).

"Let all Christians appreciate their special and personal vocation in the political community. This vocation requires that they give conspicuous example of devotion to the sense of duty and of service to the advancement of the common good. Thus they can also show in practice how authority is to be harmonized with freedom, personal initiative with consideration for the bonds uniting the whole social body, and necessary unity with beneficial diversity" (GS 75).

"As educators in the faith, priests must see to it, either by themselves or through others, that the faithful are led individually in the Holy Spirit to a development of their own vocation as required by the gospel, to a sincere and active charity, and to that freedom with which Christ has made us free" (PO 6).

## Freedom, Religious

Religious freedom is the right inherent in the lives of human persons whereby they freely exercise and pursue religious practices and teachings in civil society. Concerning this, Vatican II declares with emphatic words: "Among the things which concern the good of the Church and indeed the welfare of society here on earth—things therefore which are always and everywhere to be kept secure and defended against all injury—this certainly is pre-eminent, namely, that the Church should enjoy that full measure of freedom which her care for the salvation of men requires. This freedom is sacred, because the only-begotten Son endowed with it the Church which He purchased with His blood. It is so much the property of the Church that to act against it, is to act against the will of God. The freedom of the Church is the fundamental principle in what concerns the relations between the Church and governments and the whole civil order.

"In human society and in the face of government, the Church claims freedom for herself in her character as a spiritual authority, established by Christ the Lord. Upon this authority there rests, by divine mandate, the duty of going out into the whole world and preaching the gospel to every creature. The Church also claims freedom for herself in her character as a society of men who have the right to live in society in accordance with the precepts of Christian faith" (DH 13).

## Freedom of the Will

Freedom of the will is the exercise of the spiritual faculty or power of the soul (the will) in making a choice. Through will, an individual seeks to perform an act or to attain an object proposed by the intellect. The will always has for its object the good, and even the choice of evil must be suggested under the appearance of good. Freedom of the will has this essential: a freedom of contradiction, that is, to act or not to act on something proposed by the intellect. It likewise possesses, but not essentially, the freedom of contraries, that is, the choice of doing one thing or another. It also has spiritual significance in the choice of the individual vocation in service of the good. As St. Paul declares: "My brothers, remember that you have been called to live in freedom—but not a freedom that gives free rein to the flesh. Out of love, place yourselves at one another's service" (Gal. 5:13).

## Freemasonry

This fraternal society arose in 1717 from Masonry, the international fraternity called the Free and Accepted Masons. Membership in Freemasonry is forbidden to Catholics under provision of c. 2335 with penalty of excommunication reserved simply to the Holy See. Eight popes

in seventeen different pronouncements and six separate councils have condemned freemasonry. Today the Church and the Order of Freemasons have a greater understanding and often work together on charitable and civic enterprises, but the prohibition of Catholic membership is still in force. On Sept. 18, 1974, the Congregation of the Doctrine of the Faith stated an exception, saying that Catholic lay persons may join Masonic lodges that do not plot against the Church: "In considering particular cases, it must be remembered that penal law is always subject to strict interpretation. Therefore, one may safely teach and apply the opinion of those authors who hold that c. 2335 refers only to those Catholics who join associations which plot against the Church." Excluded were members of the clergy, religious, and secular institutes who are still denied any Masonic membership.

## Friar

Originally a term of address among Christians, after the thirteenth century friar was applied as a title to any member of a mendicant order. The friar differs from the monk in that he does not remain within a monastery following a religious life in allegiance to an abbot and an individual monastery but exercises his ministry to the world in a variety of ways. He is a professed religious working under a central director. Friars are considered under two divisions: (1) mendicant orders of the common law, the Dominicans, Franciscans, Carmelites, and Augustinians; (2) the "lesser" orders, the Servites, Minims, Trinitarians, Mercedarians, Order of Penance, and the Brothers of St. John of God. (Cf. Monasticism.)

## Friary

This term is applied to any residence of a group of members of the orders of friars but usually refers to Franciscan houses.

## Friday

See Abstinence

## Friends of God

Friends of God was the title of those loosely knit groups of ecclesiastical and lay persons in the fourteenth century who wished to cultivate a religious life and who took their name from the designation of Christ: "Instead, I call you friends, since I have made known to you all that I heard from my Father" (Jn. 15:15). This "call of love" as disciples accepted in a literal sense led the Friends of God to seek an interior life of spiritual fervor. They produced many writings of a devotional nature and were influential until the religious crisis in Germany at the time of Martin Luther. The Friends of God should not be confused with the Society of Friends, known as the Quakers.

## Friendship

The bond of intimacy and love between two persons wherein the expression of charity is founded upon the love of God is friendship. It has a basic, classical order founded upon trust, confidence, appreciation of the other persons's individuality, and deep honesty.

The Christian concept of friendship, although it parallels that described by Cicero in his work on friendship *(De Amicitia)*, rises more profoundly from the Scriptures. As Christians we are to seek the "friendship of God" (Wis. 7:14), and there is a permanence to this friendship because God is the best of friends (Prv. 27:10). In the NT Christ spoke of the greatest form of friendship, the laying down of one's life for another (cf. Jn. 15:13–17). We see also the examples of the friendship of Christ for Lazarus (Jn. 11:17–43) and St. John (Jn. 13:23).

Friendship is urged upon all of us because it gives an aid to a sense of Christian community, as Vatican II stated: "By giving spiritual help to one another through friendship and the sharing of experiences, they (the laity) gain strength to overcome the disadvantages of an excessively isolated life and activity, and to make their apostolate more productive" (AA 17).

## Frontal

See Antependium

## Frontier Apostles

In the diocese of Prince George, British Columbia, Canada, the name Frontier Apostles is given to those volunteers who offer their services for a minimum of two years in their professional vocations, including priests, sisters, seminarians, and lay persons. Since the start of this special corps, more than 1300 have served in various ministries, but their work is primarily in the area of education.

## Fruits of the Holy Spirit

Fruits of the Holy Spirit is the collective name for the resultant acts that follow the practice of those supernatural graces infused into the soul by the Holy Spirit. St. Paul (Gal. 5:22–23) lists them as: charity, joy, peace, patience, kindness, good-

ness, faith, modesty, and continency. The Church includes: benignity, longanimity, and chastity. These are in general the result of virtue in action and the attendant consolation and delight that come from being attentive to the inspirations of the Holy Spirit. (See Gifts of the Holy Spirit, the Seven.)

## Fruits of the Mass

The Mass is in and of itself infinite in value. However, there are *general* fruits because the Mass is the sacrifice of the whole Church and a public act of worship; the benefits of grace are gained by everyone who is a member of the Church including the Church Suffering. There are also *special* fruits, those that are ministerial and apply to those persons whose intentions the celebrant specifies and to the faithful assisting at Mass; such intentions may be personal. Finally there are *most special* fruits, which are for the celebrant himself or his personal intention unless he has accepted a stipend for a particular celebration. (See Eucharist, Celebration of.)

## Fundamental Articles

Fundamental Articles is an inclusive term for those teachings of Christianity that Protestant theologians accepted from among the truths of faith and considered essential. Dispute and differences in acceptance of these doctrines have marked the sectarian approach of Protestants to all true doctrines. The Catholic position is an acceptance of all truths or doctrines revealed by God, some essential for salvation, others centristic in relation to truth, without consideration of their degree of importance in relation to each other, since all form a special unity in the overall plan of salvation history.

## Fundamental Theology

Fundamental theology is that branch of theology that progressively follows the study of philosophy, which culminates in natural theology. The term is now applied particularly to what was formerly apologetics. It does not supplant this but makes apologetics a part of a more complete and comprehensive theological reflection. Fundamental theology is the foundation of the thought and practice that faith demands. As St. Peter said: "Should anyone ask you the reason for this hope of yours, be ever ready to reply" (1 Pt. 3:15). It is thus the study that prepares one to be confident in faith.

Strictly speaking, fundamental theology is basic

to dogmatic theology, perhaps to such an extent that it may be termed a first subdivision of dogmatic theology. The object of fundamental theology is to establish the fact that a revelation has been made by God and that the Catholic faith is that revelation. It first establishes the possibility of revelation, examines the evidence underlying the fact of a revelation, and traces through the OT and the prophets this revelation and its culmination in the revelation of Christ and the Apostles. It then proceeds to prove that this revelation was committed to a teaching body, that this body is the Catholic Church, that this Church is the authorized teacher and that this Church is assured of divine assistance and infallibility. (Cf. Dogmatic Theology; Theology; Kerygma.)

**Funeral**

The rites and ceremonies accompanying the burial of a deceased person are referred to as the funeral. In the Catholic Church this consists of the preliminary ceremony in which the priest sprinkles holy water upon the coffin containing the body and recites the De Profundis and Miserere. Then the Office of the Dead or the requiem Mass, is said or both. This is followed by prayers, the sprinkling of the body with holy water, the incensing, and the final prayers. When the body is committed into the grave, the ceremony consists of a blessing of the grave, the recitation of the Benedictus, the Kyrie Eleison, the Our Father, and additional prayers for the deceased and those present. (See Mass, Funeral.)

## Gabbatha

Gabbatha was the paved space occupying the highest point of the court at the eastern side of Jerusalem where Pilate tried Christ (Jn. 19:13).

## Gabriel

Gabriel is the name of one of the three archangels mentioned in the Bible; the others are Raphael and Michael. There are four instances when Gabriel is spoken of in the Bible, and each has to do with the prophecies of or the Incarnation of Jesus Christ. (1) Gabriel twice explained dreams to Daniel, the vision of the ram and the goat (Dn. 8:16–26) and (2) the meaning of the 70 weeks (Dn. 9:21–27) (cf. also Jer. 25:11; 29:10). (3) In the NT Gabriel appears to Zechariah to announce the birth of John the Baptist (Lk. 1:11–20). (4) It is Gabriel who tells the Blessed Virgin Mary that she is to become the mother of the Messiah, saying to her: "Rejoice, O highly favored daughter! The Lord is with you. Blessed are you among women" (Lk. 1:28). From these accounts we learn three facts concerning archangels: they "stand before the throne of God"; they have direct knowledge of God's intention; and they are sent as messengers to proclaim special events and give unusual information.

In the new calendar of the Church the feast of Michael, Gabriel, and Raphael, Archangels, is celebrated on Sept. 29. (See Angelic Salutation; Angel.)

## Galatians, Epistle to the

This letter of St. Paul, addressed to the converts of his first missionary journey, was probably sent while the apostle was on his way to Jerusalem for the Council in A.D. 49. It is considered to be the earliest of St. Paul's Epistles (Acts 15:3). The writing was occasioned by the knowledge that the Galatians, mostly Gentiles (Acts 13, 14), were espousing the false teaching that circumcision and the Mosaic Law were necessary to salvation, leading to the conclusion that the redemption by Christ was insufficient. This Epistle sets forth many dogmatic teachings, notably the authority of the Apostles (1:9), the doctrine of the Blessed Trinity (4:6), and especially the salvation for all according to faith in God's promises (1:4; 4:5). A few final words speak of the freedom of the Gospel (5:11–18).

The Galatians were descendants of the Celts and Gaels who had come out of Asia and went into northern Europe. In the third century before Christ some of these people had invaded the Balkans, Macedonia, Thrace, and Greece. Later three tribes settled in Asia Minor. It was during his first missionary journey that St. Paul founded Christian communities among the people of the province of Galatia north of Antioch and in Iconium, in modern Turkey.

## Galilee

The northernmost portion of ancient Palestine extends east from the Mediterranean sea to the upper valley of the Jordan River and south of the Plain of Esraelon. From the Hebrew name we know this to be a "district of various peoples." It was here in the centrally located city of Nazareth, 20 kilometers from the Mediterranean, that Christ spent his early years; as a province it was ruled at that time by Herod Antipas (4 B.C. to A.D. 39). Here also Jesus began and continued the early years of his ministry (cf. Mt. 4:23; Mk. 1:39; Lk. 4:14; Jn. 7:9). It is a land productive of olives and grapes, grain and fruits. In NT times the languages spoken there were Aramaic, Greek, and Hebrew.

## Gallican Liturgies

Gallican liturgies were rites developed in Gaul (France) in the eighth century, followed by a version of the Roman rite. These historic rites were full liturgies in many respects, but they were abandoned except for certain vestiges that still remained in use in certain dioceses, such as that of Bayeux, until the new liturgy following Vatican II.

## Gallican Psalter

A revision of the Vulgate psalter done by St. Jerome in 346, was called the Gallican Psalter because it was introduced in the churches of Gaul by St. Gregory of Tours and established by Charlemagne as an official book.

## Gallicanism

This term refers to the false teachings set forth in a writing called "The Gallican Liberties" (1682). Primarily, Gallicanism was an attack on the temporal power of the papacy. It demanded supremacy of ecumenical councils over the pope's authority, an independent position for the Gallican churches, and restriction of the pope's authority on matters of faith, even subject to the consent of the Church. The teachings were condemned by a constitution of Pope Alexander VIII (d. 1691) in 1690. The term Gallicanism has come to be applied to any instance where a national Church claims authority at the expense of the authority of the Holy See.

## Gambling

Gambling is the risk of loss of some material or physical good with the hope or intent of gaining more at some future time. It may be the wager that some event will take place in the future. This leaves to chance the outcome of both the gain and the occurrence, but it cannot be determined otherwise unless by fraud or deceit.

Gambling may be allowed by civil law and is not directly contrary to divine law. However, because of the excesses, abuses, and deceit that may be involved, acts of gambling have been forbidden in many instances by both civil and religious or moral law. Frequently gambling also encourages or is accompanied by other evils. Local interpretation of the law and reasonable limitation or control may be such that gambling is no more than an act of recreation, but prudence should be employed and scandal avoided.

## Garden of Eden

The Garden of Eden is that place considered the epitome of happiness. It was both the condition and the place where Adam and Eve lived before the fall through the commission of original sin. Early translators, such as St. Jerome, referred to Eden as a place of "delight" or ideal peace and happiness. Only once in the Bible is the place mentioned as Eden (Gn. 4:16). It has no known location, but following the thought of early biblical writers the requisites for a "garden of pleasure" (often places of abomination to God, as in Is. 1:29–31; 63:3) were several: it must have water; it must produce good food, and it must be protected. Only in the NT is the word "paradise" used (Lk. 23:43; 2 Cor. 12:4), not as a reverting to the place narrated in the Book of Genesis but as the place of God's reward for the faithful.

## Gaudete Sunday

The name for the third Sunday of Advent is Gaudete Sunday; it derived from the first Latin word of the Introit, meaning "rejoice." The liturgy permits rose colored vestments for this day, which is one of rejoicing over the closeness of the Redemption.

## Gaudium et Spes

This is the Latin title of one of the most important of the documents of Vatican II. (See Vatican Council II.)

## Geez

This classical Ethiopian language is the liturgical language of the Ethiopian Rite. It is a dialect form of the Semitic language used in ancient Ethiopia or Abyssinia. There was an extensive Christian literature written in Geez, and only recently studies have been made of some of the more obscure writings.

## Gehenna

Derived from the Greek short form of the Hebrew *Ge-Hinnom,* this name was originally applied to a public place south of Jerusalem where trash was burned. It has been associated with hell (Mt. 5:22). (Cf. Hell.)

In the NT the word is mentioned in all the Gospels (Mt. 5:22–29; Mk. 9:43; Lk. 12:5) and in the Epistle of St. James (3:6) where it is spoken of as "hell." In each instance the place mentioned is associated with fire. From this it is deduced that Gehenna refers to the eschatological place of final punishment.

## Genealogy of Christ

The record of Christ's descent, tracing the fact that He was of Israelite stock and from the line of David, is recorded in Mt. 1:1–17, giving the ancestry of Joseph and evidence of his legal fatherhood. Since Jewish usage ignored descent from the female line, the descent of Jesus from David is established juridically through Joseph. The descent is also recorded in Lk. 3:23–38. Luke traces the descent of Christ back to Adam, thus presenting Him as the universal Savior of mankind. In the genealogy recorded in Matthew's account there are fourteen generations given, divided into three periods: from Abraham to David, from Solomon to the captivity, and from the captivity to Jesus. In its conclusion Joseph is given only as the legal husband of Mary, and so in the text the fact of Mary's perpetual virginity is maintained. Christ is the seed of Abraham, who is the "father of peoples," and He is the fulfillment of the promise of salvation made to all (cf. Gn. 12).

## General

The shortened version of superior general, the title General is given to the chief in spiritual authority over members of a religious order or congregation of men. The title is conferred by election in a general chapter of the order and may be for a limited number of years or for life, as are the generals of the Dominicans and Jesuits.

## General Absolution

1. The form of sacramental absolution that is given without auricular confession of sin, when confession by the individual is not possible. This type of absolution requires that the persons will confess their sins at the next reception of auricular confession, including all grave or mortal sins from which they were absolved at the time of the general absolution.

2. A blessing that is given at the hour of death (and at designated times to members of religious orders and tertiaries) and to which the Church has granted a plenary indulgence. (See Penance, Sacrament of.)

## General Chapter

This is an assembly of all members or delegates of an entire religious order or congregation. It derives its name from the place where members of a religious community were accustomed to gather daily for a reading of a chapter of the rule of the order; this place was called the chapter-house, and later any assembly was called the chapter. A general chapter is gathered to deal with serious problems of policy and matters that affect the religious order as a whole.

## General Confession

General confession is that sacramental confession in which, despite previous confessions, sins and particularly grave sins, committed in one's life or over a lengthy period of time are again confessed. It may be required where serious doubt exists concerning previous confessions or where willful omissions made previous confessions incomplete. Such confessions are not to be made unless by counsel of one's confessor.

## Genesis, Book of

The first book of the Bible, Genesis, consists of fifty chapters, written between 950 and 550 B.C. In Greek, its title is translated "beginning," but in most languages it means "the origin." It was written largely by Moses and traces the descent of the ancestors of the people of Israel from the beginning of the world to the twelve sons of Jacob and his family's residence in Egypt (ch. 46), closing with the death of his son Joseph. The doctrine of Genesis presents (1) a noble concept of God as Creator and Master of the world, (2) God's omnipotence (18:14), (3) the fact that God gave a law and that man's obedience to God's law must be free (2:17), (4) the fact that transgression of God's law brings punishment. In this first writing, the Messianic promise is originally given (3:15), and the promises are made to Abraham.

In general Genesis shows that divine Providence guided the history of man as created by God from the beginning. It shows God's purposes and the meaning of that purpose. Oral tradition certainly was important in the composition of this book, which has two major parts: (1) the origins of man and the peoples of the earth (cf. Ziggurat; Babel, Tower of) are described (1–11); (2) the patriarchal history and the early ancestors of the chosen people are recorded (12–50). As history it is the first synthesis of the narrative of man up to the tenth century before Christ and presents the spiritual descent of man from the fall. It demonstrates the transcendence of God, the divine reality, the God of the universe.

## Genocide

The planned, wholesale, unrestricted killing of a race of people, a nation, a tribe, or large numbers of people is genocide. There have been and still are many instances in history where the abuse of power on the part of governments was directed to the slaughter of great numbers of innocent people: the slaughter of the innocents by Herod as prophesied by Jeremiah (Mt. 2:16–18); the Roman decimation of the Carthaginians; the Mandan Indians in the nineteenth century; the Jews under the ruthless and amoral Adolph Hitler during World War II; and the legally adopted but morally corrupt practice of abortion in the twentieth century.

Vatican II spoke out against genocide, teaching: "Furthermore, whatever is opposed to life itself, such as any type of murder, genocide, abortion, euthanasia, or willful self-destruction, whatever violates the integrity of the human person . . . whatever insults human dignity . . . all these things and others of their like are infamies indeed" (GS 27).

"Among such (actions against universal principles) must first be counted those actions designed for the methodical extermination of an entire people, nation, or ethnic minority. These actions must be vehemently condemned as horrendous crimes. The courage of those who openly and fearlessly resist men who issue such commands merits supreme commendation" (GS 79).

## Gentiles

From the Latin word meaning "peoples," this is the term used in the Vulgate to refer to those people who were non-Jews. The OT word "nations" was distinct from the people of Israel (Cf. Is. 10:22; Ez. 35:10). The Jews at the time of Christ considered the Temple desecrated if a Gentile entered it (Acts 21:28).

The status of the non-Israelite nations in the NT was always as people other than Jews, or people of another "nation," but the term Gentile came to mean all those people who have not received divine revelation (Mt. 10:18; Acts 21:21; Rom. 3:29; 9:24), and in practice referred to the Greek-speaking Gentiles (Rom. 10:12; 1 Cor. 10:32; Gal. 3:28). Christ sent His apostles to instruct "all nations" (Mt. 28:19), and following the baptism of Cornelius (Acts 10) and the decrees of the Council of Jerusalem (Acts 15) the principle was established that the Gentile could be received into the Church without having to observe the Jewish law and could become a sharer in salvation without Judaism. The first great conversion of Gentiles took place at Antioch in Syria (Acts 11:20f), and St. Paul not only accepted the commission to convert the Gentiles (Gal. 2:8) but was pleased to call himself the "teacher of the Gentiles" (1 Tm. 2:7; 2 Tm. 1:11).

Today we do not speak of "Gentile-Christians" or "non–Gentile Christians," but we use the term chiefly in its scriptural or historic sense.

## Genuflection, also Genuflexion

Genuflection is an act of reverence made either singly, by touching the right knee to the ground, or doubly, by kneeling on both knees and bowing the head slightly. A single or simple genuflection is the proper act of veneration accorded Christ in the Blessed Sacrament within the tabernacle; a double or solemn genuflection is the proper act of reverence before the Blessed Sacrament when it is exposed. This act of reverence may be made during ceremonies, for example, after the Eleva-

tion of the host during Mass. The simple genuflection is also an act of homage made to certain dignitaries of the Church, for example, the pope, cardinal, or a bishop in his diocese, although more recently this is seldom performed. It is also customary to make a simple genuflection when one kisses a bishop's ring, but again this is not the present practice, and bishops do not care for the awkwardness this presents.

## Georgian Byzantine Rite

The territory of Georgia is located in the southern part of the Soviet Union, south of the Caucasus Mountains. A small number of the population are Christians who returned to Catholic unity in 1861. There are also members of the Georgian Church in France. Their liturgical language is Latin or Georgian, and some worship in the Latin Rite and some in the Byzantine Rite. Because of poor communications with the Soviet Union concerning these matters, there are no specific figures regarding membership. Since Vatican II, the Church has appointed an apostolic administrator for all the membership.

## Gethsemani

In the time of our Lord, this was a garden area situated at the foot of the western slope of the Mount of Olives (Lk. 22:39). The name means "olive press," a device for extracting the oil of olives. It is the place chosen by Christ for His meditation prior to His apprehension by the Jews and Roman soldiers and thus, the scene of the agony in the garden, Christ's betrayal by Judas, and His arrest (Mt. 26:36–46).

A church was erected at Gethsemani as early as the fourth century, and above the ruin of this church the modern Catholic "Church of All Nations" has been built. In front of the sanctuary the rock, which was the traditional place where Christ prayed, has been left exposed.

## Gifts of the Holy Spirit, the Seven

Wisdom, understanding, knowledge, counsel, piety, fortitude, and fear of the Lord are the special graces granted by the Holy Spirit which, together with habitual grace, make us docile to the influence of the Holy Spirit. They are conferred with the virtues of the Holy Spirit but are distinct from them, chiefly because of the mode of their action within us; their function is to perfect the exercise of the virtues.

The gifts are habits by which the soul responds to the inspiration of the Holy Spirit. They are superior to the intellectual and moral virtues but less perfect than the three theological virtues, which have God as their object. St. Thomas Aquinas taught that the gifts of the Holy Spirit were necessary to salvation but not as absolutes in their fullness of expression, and he likened them to the beatitudes Christ taught (cf. Mt. 5:3–11).

## Gifts, Preternatural

Preternatural gifts are those abilities and endowments that are beyond the need and powers of human nature, such as those gifts enjoyed by Adam and Eve in the state of original justice. These include freedom from suffering and death, superior knowledge, and total or perfect control of the passions. They were lost through original sin, and this does imply that the human dignity or the nature of mankind was impaired by such loss. Man remains an entire human being with dignity and the ability to seek higher gifts through prayer, meditation, contemplation, and control of his will and passions.

## Gifts, Supernatural

Supernatural gifts are those that the individual cannot merit or achieve by nature. They are God's endowments bestowed on the souls of human beings.

## Gift of Tongues

The gift of tongues is one of the charismata, whereby one is given the miraculous gift to speak one language and be heard and understood by many individuals who ordinarily speak and understand a different language. This is called the "miracle of Pentecost" because the first recorded instance is its use by the Apostles after the descent of the Holy Spirit (Acts 2:4–13). The miracle had a twofold purpose: that Christ's teaching was to go to all peoples, and that many would be able to hear and understand from the beginning of the Apostles' teaching. The miracle was one of speaking, not of hearing. The gift of tongues is called glossolalia, and in the modern charismatic movement attested instances of some oral outpourings have been reported, but the lack of understanding on the part of the listeners makes it evident that these were not effective, that is, for the benefit of others. To be understood, such sounds require another charism, that of hearing and interpreting, which is a patent complication. The propriety of such gifts is placed in perspective by St. Paul who declared: "The gift of tongues is a sign, not for those who believe but for those who do not believe, while prophecy is not for those who are without faith but for those who have faith" (1 Cor. 14:22). The more perfect way, according to St. Paul, is not in tongues or fine speech, but in charity (1 Cor. 13:1–2). (See Charismatic Renewal, Catholic.)

## Gilds

See Guilds.

## Girdle

See Cincture.

## Girovagi

See Gyrovagi.

## Glagolitic Alphabet

The Glagolitic alphabet was an early version of the Cyrillic alphabet probably composed also by St. Cyril (827 to 869). Ancient documents found through paleographic research indicate that the Glagolitic alphabet was derived from the cursive Greek; both had round or flowing characteristics. The Cyrillic has more of the block letter formation found in many early inscriptions. The Glagolitic letters are used by Catholics who celebrate the Roman Rite in the ancient Slavic language.

## Gloria in Excelsis Deo

The Greater Doxology of the Mass, translated "Glory to God in the highest," is the beginning of the hymn sung by the angels at the birth of Christ. The Greater Doxology is omitted from the Mass during Lent and Advent when the priest wears purple or black vestments. The first part is found in the Gospel of St. Luke (2:13–14). The second part was taken from the fathers of the Church. It is recited in the Mass after the Kyrie in the Latin Mass.

In the New Order of the Mass, the Gloria, an ancient hymn of the Church through which the assembly of the faithful speaks through the Holy Spirit, praises and prays to the Father and Christ, the Lamb. It is said or sung on Sundays except in Advent and Lent, on solemnities and feasts, and in solemn local celebrations. It precedes the presidential prayer, the collect, which the celebrant prays for all the faithful just before the Liturgy of the Word. It is:

"Glory to God in the highest,
  and peace to his people on earth.

Lord God, heavenly King,
  almighty God and Father,
    we worship you, we give you thanks,
    we praise you for your glory.

Lord Jesus Christ, only Son of the Father,

Lord God, Lamb of God,
  you take away the sin of the world:
    have mercy on us;
  you are seated at the right hand of the Father:
    receive our prayer.

For you alone are the Holy One,
You alone are the Lord,
You alone are the Most High,
  Jesus Christ,
  With the Holy Spirit,
  in the glory of God the Father.

  Amen.

### Gloria Patri

Translated "Glory be to the Father," the Gloria Patri is the first words and the title of the lesser doxology. It is a prayer of praise, recited frequently, for example, after the Psalms of the Divine Office, except during the last three days of Holy Week and the Office of the Dead. It is also the concluding prayer of each decade of the rosary. The Gloria Patri is:

Glory be to the Father, to the Son,
  And to the Holy Spirit.
As it was in the beginning, is now,
  And ever shall be,
  World without end. Amen.

### Glorified Body

It is Catholic doctrine that all persons shall arise from the dead and that their bodies will be "glorified" or spiritualized in some humanly unknown manner. Resurrected bodies will have four essential qualities: (1) impassibility, or the inability to suffer pain and the absence of defects; (2) clarity, meaning the brightness of glory, the beauty and splendor that overflows from the beatific vision and transforms all bodies, as St. Thomas Aquinas teaches; (3) subtlety, by which is meant that all bodies will be in their true nature but will be entirely docile in a spiritual manner; (4) and agility, which is that the body, as a perfect instrument of the soul, will be in accord with and have access to

the wonders of the universe by being able to understand the mysteries of creation. (See Resurrection of the Body; Heaven.)

### Glorious Mysteries

See Mysteries of the Rosary.

### Glory

1. Praise, splendor, honor attributed to one because of excellence.

2. In Scripture the term "glory" is (a) the physical phenomenon resulting from a manifestation of God (Ex. 24:16); (b) the revelation of God found in His creation (Ps. 18:1); (c) the external manifestation of the Incarnation, the Only-Begotten of the Father (Jn. 1:14).

3. The glory of the blessed is the eternal reward, the participation in divine glory, the beatific vision and love of God. In this sense it is called the "light of glory."

4. Perfect glory is an attribute of God, because of the perfect knowledge of His own goodness. Any glory of man or nature is imperfect and only a reflection of God's glory.

God's glory is that which makes Him esteemed and honored by men. It is thus that this attribute of God is most in evidence with His power and holiness (cf. Ps. 29:1-2). And in the NT the transfiguration of Christ was a manifestation of the glory of the God-man (Mt. 17:1-4). St. John in Rv. 15:8 refers to God's glory as light and power.

Vatican II spoke of future glory, teaching: "Let all religious spread throughout the whole world the good news of Christ by the integrity of their faith, their love for God and neighbor, their devotion to the Cross, and their hope of future glory. Thus will their witness be seen by all, and our Father in heaven will be glorified (cf. Mt. 5:16)" (PC 25).

### Glossator

A glossator is the writer of a "gloss." The first glossator was Walafrid Strabo (d. 849).

### Glosses, Scriptural

Scriptural glosses are the inserted words, marginal notes, expansions, and alternative readings made by the scribe or translator on an original text of Scripture. Usually glosses are only a few words not in the original texts. The word "gloss" may also describe an entire commentary composed of interpretations of passages from the Scripture given in sequence. Technically, today, the term glosses may be likened to "footnotes."

## Gloves, Episcopal

Made of silk in the color corresponding to the liturgical color of the vestment, and ornamented with embroidery, these gloves are worn by a bishop in celebrating a pontifical Mass, before the Offertory. A bishop, at his consecration, is invested with gloves but they are ceremonial rather than essential vesture of his office.

## Gluttony

A capital sin of a twofold nature, gluttony is the inordinate longing for or indulgence in food and drink. In the first instance, since hunger is a natural reaction that prompts one to eat, this longing is directed to the desire for food over and above the necessity of bodily requirement. In the second instance, gluttony results from the use of food or drink in such quantity as to be unnatural or unreasonable. This also extends to the quality of food or drink, the overindulging in special dishes or drinks, simply because they are so tasty. Immoderation in eating or drinking is only venially sinful unless there are other reasons that make it more serious, for example giving scandal or injuring one's health. Thus the excess in drinking of alcoholic beverages may be: (1) venially sinful when it results in a partial loss of reason, becoming more seriously sinful because of scandal or injury to one's health; (2) mortally sinful when it results in complete loss of reason brought on without sufficient cause. Such loss of reason means the failure to be able to distinguish between good and bad acts or, where memory is impaired, the failure to remember what occurred during the time of intoxication. The taking of narcotics, such as morphine, opium, barbiturates, and others is venially sinful if taken without a sufficient reason, for example, by prescription of a doctor; the taking of drugs is mortally sinful when loss of reason results. All of the abuses of the appetite for food or drink, or the unwarranted taking of drugs, have attendant ills such as mental illness, moral lassitude, or immodest or indecent actions. (See Intellect.)

## Gnosis

Gnosis is the philosophical concept that does not flow from grace or faith but is that knowledge derived from man's being itself. It is "self-consciousness" and not the hearing of the word of God, or faith, but a meeting or fusion of the soul with the godhead. This form of self-knowledge that took on the divine was one of the foremost ideas of Greek mysticism in the first centuries of the Christian era.

Gnosis has three basic forms: (1) Hermetism, of the first to fourth centuries after Christ, which was a philosophical concept of a mythological, esoteric nature. (2) Christian gnosis, which is presented by St. Paul as an understanding of the incomprehensible love of God (cf. 1 Cor. 8:1–3; Gal. 4:8–11), through faith, a philosophical, theological concept. (3) Popular gnosis, which was chiefly oriented to magic, esoteric language, and formulae.

In each of these three there are specific characteristics: (1) Knowledge in its human aspect is acquired by prophecy, vision, divination, or revelation. (2) God is the object of knowledge, together with the relations of man and the world to God, and here is introduced the myth (cosmogonic myth especially) that the distance of man's relationship to God is abbreviated through knowledge and likewise man's recognition of good from evil. (3) The knowledge of God once gained causes a deliverance from evil, thus from pain and death, and grants immortality.

We are here concerned only with Christian gnosis in which there is an existential intensification of man's knowledge through faith (1 Cor. 13:12), of "knowing and being known." It should come about through instruction, prayer, the liturgy, and a total understanding of the entire unifying force of faith illumined by knowledge viewed in the light of the grace of faith. This can be clarified by considering gnosis in an existential light: religious knowledge comes from a special capacity in a few individuals but is present in all by previous potentialities; knowledge is obedience to faith especially through hearing the word of God, perhaps through myth (story) or concept, individually or in community, or the celebration of mysteries; knowledge is in itself redemptive in being directed by grace toward a lasting unity with a transcendent God. (See Mysticism; Hermetic science.)

## Gnosticism

Gnosticism is the collective name for a group of vague and false religious philosophies that took many forms. They arose in the first century of the Church, and St. John in writing Revelation was aware of this pseudoreligious philosophy. Gnosticism was a syncretistic religion that competed with Christianity for ascendency in the first four centuries. The errors common to this system, which arose in Samaria and Syria, were based upon "personal revelations" and lacked the universality of revealed truth. In general these were: that our Lord's body was unreal, being something like a phantom (Docetism); attendant to this was the belief that divine Power merely took hold of a "human body" and used it as a tool instead of Christ being a true Person. Also there was the false teaching that all "matter" was bad, and that there was an antagonism between soul and body. This latter led to immoralities and fanatical "purgings." For example, one form of Gnosticism, the Aphite, included serpent worship. The Gnostics, the "Know-ers," were refuted by many early writers but claimed special revelations. Each form was condemned by early councils of the Church, and the many early forms of Gnosticism were refuted by the First Council of Nicaea (c. 325). (Cf. Docetism.)

## God

God is the sovereign, Supreme Being, who alone is simply "self-dependent," who exists of Himself, and who is infinitely perfect (cf. Trinity the Most Holy). In speaking of God as "a spirit infinitely perfect," we are describing the physical essence of God; when we consider that God "exists of Himself," we indicate the metaphysical essence of God. From the metaphysical essence we deduce the attributes of God, His pure perfections. According to St. Thomas Aquinas, these attributes are entitative: simplicity, omniperfection, goodness, infinity, immensity, unchangeableness, eternity and unicity, invisibility, and ineffability. The other perfections of God are called "operative." To name God, the best we can do properly is to take a name from the perfection that distinguishes Him from His creatures, that is, His *aseity,* of which God himself spoke when addressing Moses (Ex. 3:14) saying, *"I am who am."* Describing Him otherwise, we are guided by God's effects, for "He is that infinite reality which is the exemplary and efficient cause of every reality that exists or is possible to exist."

Philosophers and theologians, notably St. Thomas Aquinas (a. 3, I, 13), have presented arguments of reason that prove the existence and attributes of God. Briefly, these arguments are: (1) *Causality:* Since every effect must have an adequate or efficient cause, and since the universe is itself an effect and could not produce itself, and since the adequate cause of the universe must itself be uncaused and eternal, it follows that the prime cause (efficient and adequate) is God. (2) *Motion:* Passage from power to act, as potentiality to existence, implies a first mover who is both unmoved and unchanged, and such alone is God. (3) *Contingency:* Beings cannot exist of themselves; the universe does not exist of itself, independently. Beings must be produced ultimately by a being, independent and existing of itself. Such a being is

God. (4) *Order:* The universe could not exist without order or design, and such order and design demand a plan and a Lawgiver, which in turn demands an intelligence. Such a supreme intelligence is God. (5) *Perfection:* Existing in the universe are many perfections; these cannot produce themselves nor exist, nor be understood unless they are produced by a being who possesses all of them in Himself and in whom such perfections can be understood by comparison. This perfect being is God. (6) *Conscience:* Man is aware of moral obligation; moral obligation presupposes a law, and law presupposes a lawgiver. That sovereign lawgiver is God who created nature and implanted His law. (7) *Consent of Mankind:* Universally, in all times and places, both anthropologically and historically, men testify to God's existence.

When we speak of the attributes of God, we must first consider His love. This reveals to us the fatherhood that can be considered the ultimate definition of God. As St. John writes: "The man without love has known nothing of God, for God is love. God's love was revealed in our midst in this way: he sent his only Son to the world that we might have life through him. Love, then, consists in this: not that we have loved God but that he has loved us and has sent his Son as an offering for our sins. Beloved, if God has loved us so, we must have the same love for one another. No one has ever seen God. Yet if we love one another God dwells in us, and his love is brought to perfection in us. The way we know we remain in him and he in us is that he has given us of his Spirit" (1 Jn. 4:8–13). (See Adoration; Liturgy; Latria.)

## Godparents

See Sponsors.

## God-spell

The word Gospel is derived from the Anglo-Saxon word "god-spell," and this was taken from the Greek word meaning "good news" (evangelion). (See Gospel.)

## Golden Bull

The name Golden Bull is sometimes attached to exceptionally important papal bulls. Specifically, the bull of 1356 regulating the election of the Holy Roman emperors is so named.

## Golden Legend

The Golden Legend was a widely read book of the Middle Ages, originally titled *The Legends of the Saints.* This outstanding book of the Italian language was written by Jacopo de Voragine, O.P. (1228 to 1298), about 1270 and first printed in 1470. It is a collection of stories about the saints and a contribution to the devotional writings on the saints. (See Hagiography.)

## Golden Mass

Golden Mass is the popular name given to certain Masses that were celebrated as votive or special Masses on occasions when it was customary to wear "golden" vestments—those so colored, or at least partly woven of golden threads. They were usually reserved for feasts of the Blessed Virgin Mary, notably those recalling or celebrating the Annunciation. This is still the custom in some countries, for example, the feast day of Our Lady of Guadalupe in Mexico City.

## Golden Militia

The Order of the Golden Spur, one of the oldest of the papal orders of knighthood, is under the patronage of the Blessed Mother and its membership is limited to 100. The order is conferred for distinguished service in propagating the faith, or for service in writing or other acts giving glory to the Church, but it is now more restricted, usually conferred only on those of aristocratic status. (See Knights, Papal.)

## Golden Rose

A golden rose is an ornament in the form of a spray of roses, stem, and leaves, and decorated with gems. Blessed by the pope and solemnly conferred on Laetare Sunday, it has been given to cities, countries, or sovereigns as a token of appreciation for services of loyalty. In recent times it has been reserved to Catholic queens and sovereigns; it was given in 1925 to Queen Elizabeth of Belgium and most recently, in 1956, to the Grand Duchess of Luxemburg.

## Golgotha

See Calvary.

## Goliath

Goliath was the name of the Philistine giant (who was over six feet tall) from the land of Gath who challenged the Israelite army under the command of King Saul. He was engaged in solitary combat by the boy David and slain with a stone from the boy's leather sling. (1 Sm. 17.) The fight is poetically described:

> The man from Gath
>     a haunt of wrath
>         challenging death
>             a taunt to breath.
>
> The dare was heard,
>     the thundering word
>
> Then David's shout—
>     arm girt about
>         with God's own might—
>             his stone took flight.
>
> The Philistine, a smitten ox,
>     his shield a waterfall of sound
>         in ten thousand ears across the plain—
>             the giant thundered to the ground.
>
> With swiftness of the Godly bold
> David raised the fallen sword
>     and struck the mountain's crest.
>
> Hail! Hail! was heard the hero's call
> When David knelt before King Saul.
>
> (By Robert C. Broderick.)

## Good Friday

The Friday of Holy Week on which the anniversary of the passion and death of Christ is commemorated, Good Friday, is the only day of the year on which Mass is not said. In accordance with the New Order of the Mass, the liturgy of Good Friday consists of the following: The altar is bare, with no candles, cross, or cloths. The passion of our Lord is celebrated (*sic*) in the afternoon, beginning about three o'clock. (This may be later by pastoral option.) It consists of: liturgy of the Word, veneration of the Cross, and Holy Communion. The vestments are red. After the entrance and introductory prayers, all sit during the three prescribed readings. (A homily may be given.) This is followed by general intercessions, with each prayer said or sung and a silent prayer observed by all. After these general intercessions, the veneration of the cross takes place: (1) by unveiling the cross, each part separately, elevating the cross and singing, "this is the wood of the Cross," to which all respond: "Come, let us worship." This is repeated for each part unveiled. Then the cross is carried to a suitable place and veneration follows, with the priest and people approaching the cross in some form of procession, each genuflecting or making some sign of reverence. (2) Or the priest or deacon, carrying two lighted candles, goes to the church entrance and while approaching the altar in procession, unveils the cross and prays as in the previously mentioned ceremony. Then songs are sung, with antiphons, and the Improperia.

The Holy Communion service begins, following the Veneration of the Cross, with the altar being covered, the corporal and altar book (Sacramentary) placed upon it, and the ciborium containing the Blessed Sacrament brought from the place of reposition to the altar. Two ministers with lighted candles accompany the Blessed Sacrament, and the candles are placed on or near the altar. The celebrant prays, inviting the people, and all say the Our Father together. Then the priest (celebrant) says the Communion Prayers, and Holy Communion is distributed. There follows a time of silent prayer; the priest says the Postcommunion prayer, prays over the people, and all then depart. The altar is then stripped of its cloth at a convenient time. (See Holy Week, Liturgy of.)

**Good Shepherd**

1. A title and symbol of our Lord based upon the Gospel account of the shepherd found in John 10:1–16. In representation the symbol usually shows Christ bearing a lamb upon His shoulders. Under this traditional title, Christ was portrayed by early Christians as the master of the flock (cf. Flock; also Jn. 21:15–17).

2. The Parable of the Good Shepherd.

3. Good Shepherd Sunday is celebrated during the Easter season.

**Goodness**

The physical quality that resides in a thing simply because it exists is called goodness. All created things are said to be good insofar as they exist, but not all things are completely good because some are lacking perfection in some degree and are called bad. Thus evil is not a thing in itself but only the lack of something.

Goodness is found in human nature, but the individual becomes morally good only by the exercise of his will in avoiding evil and choosing the good, that is, in keeping the divine commands and the precepts of nature. Of all God's creatures it is only humans who can make this free choice; hence, only humans can know and love God and pursue a course of salvation.

Goodness for human beings is a societal undertaking as well as an individual enterprise. Humans act for the good in conjunction with others (community) and individually (in conscience), and failure to fulfill both of these does harm to the individual's own striving for salvation and hinders that of others. Vatican II teaches: "Wisdom gently attracts the mind of man to a quest and a love for what is true and good. Steeped in wisdom, man passes through visible realities to those which are unseen" (GS 15).

"In the depths of his conscience, man detects a law which he does not impose upon himself, but which holds him to obedience. Always summoning him to love good and avoid evil, the voice of conscience can when necessary speak to his heart more specifically: do this, shun that" (GS 16).

"While human progress is a great advantage to man, it brings with it a strong temptation. For when the order of values is jumbled, and bad is mixed with the good, individuals and groups pay heed solely to their own interests, and not to those of others" (GS 37).

**Gospel**

The word gospel is taken from the Old English and means literally, "good tidings," or "good news" (cf. God-spell). The Gospels of the New Testament are the first century writings of the four evangelists, SS. Matthew, Mark, Luke, and John. In them we are told of the life, person, and teachings of the Son of God, Jesus Christ, and we learn of the founding of His Church. These four Gospels are the only "gospels" accepted by the Church for inclusion in the canon of the Scriptures. The Gospels of Mark, Matthew, and Luke are called the "Synoptic Gospels" (q.v.). The word gospel has also been applied to the entirety of Christian teaching, for example, preaching the gospel and, because of this, it has become an expression of designating the truth, for example, the gospel truth. (See Matthew, Gospel of St., and other separate headings; also, Readings, Cycle of.)

Vatican II teaches: "It is common knowledge that among all the Scriptures, even those of the New Testament, the Gospels have a special pre-eminence, and rightly so, for they are the principal witness of the life and teaching of the incarnate Word, our Savior.

"The Church has always and everywhere held and continues to hold that the four Gospels are of apostolic origin. For what the apostles preached in fulfillment of the commission of Christ, after-ward they themselves and apostolic men, under the inspiration of the divine Spirit, handed on to us in writing: the foundation of faith, namely, the fourfold Gospel, according to Matthew, Mark, Luke, and John" (DV 18).

### Gospel, The Fifth

This literary title is applied to the Holy Land where the very "stones" speak of Christ in history. The term is popularly derived from the writing of Gino Concetti in the March 21, 1974 edition of *L'Osservatore Romano:* "The geographical and his-torical setting of Palestine bears a quite special witness (to Christ). It has been said that the Holy Land is itself a gospel, the fifth gospel. The judgment is not an exaggerated one. Everything in Palestine speaks of Christ, his announcement by the prophets, his birth, his life, his miracles, his passion, his death and his resurrection. Those places that Christians have venerated, since the beginning, as sacred because sanctified by the Savior, are still able today, 2000 years later, to re-echo his voice and his message . . ."

### Gospel, The Last

The prologue of the Gospel of St. John (1:1–14) was prescribed by Pope Pius V in 1570 for all those who followed the Roman Rite, and thus it was the "last" gospel read in the Mass.

### Gospel, The Liturgical

The portion or selection from the writings of the evangelists which is read in the Liturgy of the Word of the Mass is called the Liturgical Gospel. (See Readings, Cycle of.)

### Gospel of Thomas

The discovery in 1945 of the Coptic version of a writing called the Gospel of Thomas indicates that this is new. However, it was probably written about A.D. 140, and it is doubtful if the actual work was

that of the Apostle Thomas. The writing seems to have been a basic book of the Gnostics insofar as it supported their erroneous beliefs, but it was known by Hippolytus, Origen, and Ambrose and was never considered a serious work of the stature of the Gospels in the approved canon of the Scriptures. The book contains 114 sayings of Jesus, but their primary theme is that Christ is only some heavenly messenger, one who has a special mes-sage for those who were of an elect sect, such as the Gnostics. The sayings are limited, alien to the universal thought of Christ's message, and they lack the humanity characteristic of Christ, the God-man. They thus are no more than novel sayings of doubtful value. (Cf. Essenes.)

### Gospel, Preaching of

In the command of Christ to His Apostles, it was essential that they preach and teach His message. In every homily, properly speaking, the gospel message should be elucidated to the faithful that they might have a greater understanding of the teaching and life of Christ. It is not the role of the one preaching to do other than explain and exhort his listeners to follow Christ's teachings. Vatican II states: "God, who 'wants all men to be saved and come to know the truth' (1 Tm. 2:4), 'spoke in fragmentary and varied ways to our fathers through the prophets' (Heb. 1:1). When the fullness of time had come He sent His son, the Word made flesh, anointed by the Holy Spirit, to preach the gospel to the poor, to heal the contrite of heart (cf. Is. 61:1; Lk. 4:18), to be a 'bodily and spiritual medicine,' the Mediator between God and man (cf. 1 Tm. 2:5)" (SC 5).

And: "The task of proclaiming the gospel everywhere on earth devolves on the body of pastors, to all of whom in common Christ gave His command, thereby imposing upon them a com-mon duty, as Pope Celestine in his time reminded the Fathers of the Council of Ephesus" (LG 23).

### Gothic Architecture

This style of building design, introduced at the end of the twelfth century, has been distinguished by the pointed arch and the system of stone vaulting. It was not limited to use in church building but is considered to have been distinctly Christian. In addition to architecture, the word Gothic was applied to sculpture, painting, stained glass, tapestry, and other minor arts in the Christian countries of Europe. Beginning in France about 1230, the Gothic style spread to other countries (England, Germany, the Netherlands, Spain, and Italy), with each country giving a distinct contribution of its own to the basic style. Its characteristics were its organic structure, its use of space, and its light and symbolism. Gothic art is perhaps the highest point in artistic and architectural achievement. In varieties it has been classified as "decorated," "perpendicular," and "early English," but its name has been applied broadly to other arts where its principles were adapted, for example, Gothic vestments.

There was an application of the title "Gothic" to a literary form in the eighteenth and nineteenth centuries and still extant, which emphasized the mysterious and desolate, especially in the novel.

### Gothic Rite

See Mozarabic Rite.

### Grace

There are three common acceptances of the word *grace*.

1. It refers to something freely bestowed, which is not due. In this sense it is used classically and in biblical writings.

2. Grace also means the very gift itself, for example, the grace granted as a favor at court.

3. Grace means gratitude for the thing received.

In understanding the theological meaning of grace, that is, in the supernatural significance of the term, we find three acceptances. First, the love of God through which supernatural life is conferred is uncreated grace. Second, grace is the supernatural, free gift of God. Directing toward and ordained to eternal life, this is created grace. It is either *exterior* or *interior*. Third, grace is in turn our gratitude to God. This parallel is not exact, but the three aspects of grace must be considered to reasonably understand this mystery. The word grace is not found in the Gospels of Matthew, Mark, nor John except in the Prologue to John's Gospel (1:14). However, in the entire NT the idea of "gift" or that something "will be given" is of constant recurrence (Mt. 21:43; Rom. 8:32). Indeed Christ's love is the *gift* of His life (Mt. 20:28) and of His body in the Eucharist (Mt. 26:26; Lk. 22:19). Further, while this idea of a gift is present, there is also the idea of "merit," arising from grace itself and "demerit" or the loss of grace (Mt. 6:4). We see then that the entire order of grace is found in the "giving" by God and the "receiving" on the part of man.

By definition, grace is "a gratuitous gift infused by God into the rational creature with reference to the end: eternal life." By this we mean specifically created grace. We may further speak of this as *external* or *internal*. External grace, for instance, would be the example of Christ; internal grace is that received in the interior of the soul, enabling us to act supernaturally. This internal grace may be: (1) *gratum faciens,* or that which makes one pleasing or that which is given for the recipient himself and which establishes a "divine friendship"; such would be actual, habitual, sanctifying grace, or charisms; (2) *gratis datae,* or "freely given," graces are bestowed on one to be used for the benefit of others, for example, the gift of prophecy and for ourselves the vitality to act. Grace is of many kinds, defined according to its creation and effects. It may be studied briefly under its separate listings: sanctifying, actual, habitual, sacramental, efficacious, and sufficient.

Vatican II declares: "Allotting His gifts 'to each as he wills' (1 Cor. 12:11), He distributes special graces among the faithful of every rank. By these gifts he makes them fit and ready to undertake the various tasks or offices advantageous for the renewal and upbuilding of the Church, according to the words of the Apostle: 'To each person the manifestation of the Spirit is given for the common good,' (1 Cor. 12:7). These charismatic gifts, whether they be the most outstanding or the more simple and widely diffused, are to be received with thanksgiving and consolation, for they are exceedingly suitable and useful for the needs of the Church" (LG 12).

And: "All the sons of the Church should remember that their exalted status is to be attributed not to their own merits but to the special grace of Christ" (LG 14).

### Grace at Meals

Brief prayers asking a blessing on the food to be eaten at a meal, and offering a thanksgiving after the meal are known as grace. This was an early custom in the Church (Acts 27:35) and certainly a part of the *agape* (q.v.) practices of early Christians. The prayers may either be spontaneous or follow prescribed forms.

### Gradine

Gradine are shelves or steps erected in back of an altar, customarily used for storing candlesticks, flowers, and the like. However, this is not a liturgical part of the altar and should be clear of the tabernacle and apart from the altar proper. In the modern understanding of the "sacred space" about the altar, there is no place or requirement for a gradine.

## Gradual

The Gradual is a short song or antiphon consisting of a brief text taken from the Scriptures, frequently from the Psalms. The Gradual is sometimes referred to as the Responsory. (See Liturgy; Antiphon.)

## Gradual Psalms,

The Psalms from 119 through 133 are called the gradual Psalms. They were also called pilgrimage Psalms, or "songs of ascent," because they were sung by the pilgrims going up to Jerusalem for the major festivals.

## Graduale Romanum

Graduale Romanum is the Latin title of a book containing the liturgical chants of the Mass, both the Proper and Ordinary, throughout the year.

## Graffito

The plural form of this term, graffiti, has been applied to the many crude inscriptions and pictures scratched or drawn upon ancient monuments, the walls of tombs, or catacombs. Although they were frequently erroneous and in no manner official, graffiti offer to archaeologists and historians valuable records of early customs or practices. For example, the early graffito of the Palatine depicting the use of a loincloth in the crucifixion of Christ, contrary to the pagan custom of nakedness in executions, has served as a guide to artists in all ages.

## Grail, the Holy

The legendary vessel, either a chalice or shallow dish, used by Christ at the Last Supper was called the Holy Grail. Although the Holy Grail has figured in story and verse from medieval times to the present, no such authentic relic has been found among the objects of Christian antiquity. In romantic literature, the story concerning the Holy Grail began in the twelfth century in the epic poem *Perceval* in France, later in Germany as *Parzifal*, and then in England as *Sir Percyvelle*. The story was tied to the legends of King Arthur.

## Grail Movement

An international organization of Catholic laywomen is banded together to help create a more Christian world. Called The Grail, the movement is active in seeking the full development of all peoples through teaching, social work, and the expanding of all cultural areas of human activity.

The movement began in 1921 in Holland when the Jesuit professor, Jacques Van Ginneken, presented to his students the idea and formula for a worldwide women's undertaking to achieve spiritual renewal. The salient points of the plan are: the Church is a continuation entrusted to all of Christ's mission to the entire world; the laity as the People of God and called to union with Christ are to share in the upbuilding of His kingdom; and women are eminently suited for a God-centered renewal through love, extension of peace, and establishing the dignity and worth of the human individual among all people. It places emphasis upon the formation in modern life of spiritual values, the apostolic work of spreading the good news of Christ, and the structure wherein the individual woman can exert influence to attain greater spiritual good for individuals and society. Its work is centered around social, professional, cultural, educational, ecumenical, and international activities in twenty-two countries. The International Secretariat is located at: 5 rue Sayed Sokkar, Matareya, Cairo, Egypt. Headquarters in the United States are: Grailville, Loveland, Ohio, 45140.

## Greater Double

Greater Double is the former designation of the highest rank of feasts in the Church calendar of which there were two classes. (See Calendar, Church.)

## Greca

The name greca is given to the black overcoat frequently worn as semi-official dress by the clergy of Rome.

## Greek Church

Greek Church is the church of the Greek people, subject to the Archbishop of Athens and All Greece. The term has been erroneously applied to the entire Orthodox Eastern Church. (Cf. Eastern Churches.)

## Greek Church, United

The term United Greek Church is often applied erroneously to all Catholics of the Byzantine rite. (Cf. Eastern Churches.)

## Greek Corporal

The Greek Corporal is the *eileton* used in the Byzantine Rite. This is the name of the square, two-piece, highly decorated linen cloth, which is used in place of an altarstone. It has relics stitched between the two cloths at the corners and center, and the two square cloths are bound or sewn together. The Greek Corporal is used by privilege by priests of the Roman Rite to celebrate the Eucharist in places apart from a church altar, chiefly because of the portability of this corporal.

## Greek Fathers

The collective term Greek Fathers is used for all those patristic writers of the early Eastern Church who wrote or taught in Greek. (Cf. Fathers of the Church.)

## Gregorian Calendar

The calendar initiated and named after Pope Gregory XIII in 1582 became the official time-keeping record of twelve months and 365 (366 every fourth year) days. It was adopted by countries throughout the world and is still is use. (See Calendar, Church.)

## Gregorian Masses

Gregorian Masses is the name given to a series of thirty Masses celebrated on thirty consecutive days for a deceased person. The Mass offering is optional in amount but should not be less than the customary sum given for thirty individual Masses. It is often difficult to have such a series celebrated in one's parish; consequently such a request is fulfilled by religious order priests. The pastor or parochial priest will assist in placing a request for Gregorian Masses if they are unable to fulfill them at the parish. Bequests that are made and include an amount to satisfy the request may be placed wherever the executor wishes unless otherwise stated in the wording of the bequest.

KÝ- RI- E  E-ILÉ-I-SON

## Gregorian Music

The plain chant, which is the liturgical music of the Church, derives its name from Pope Gregory the Great (d. 604), who gave impulse to chant in church singing (cf. Chant). Pope St. Pius X, by his *Motu Proprio* (1903), restored the Gregorian as the official chant of the Roman Church, and it is referred to as Vatican chant.

Gregorian chant is for vocal music only, and its best renditions are a cappela. It uses the conventional diatonic scale of eight tones, or notes, to an octave. It is written in the ancient ecclesiastical modes, and hence is said to be modal. The melody rises and falls to accent the stressed syllable of the word and hence it was very adaptable to the Latin language.

The music is written on a four-line staff and employes square, diamond-shaped, and elided notes. The singing, called plainsong, unless performed with vigor and great attention to the rhythm, becomes sluggish and dreary, even monotonous. However, when the singing is warm, virile, and graceful, it is one of the most melodic of sounds, as attested by the singing of the Solesmes monks. As Father Joseph Jungmann, S. J., writes: "Music spread its gorgeous mantle over the whole Mass, so that the other details of the rite had scarcely any significance." It was thus that new music was introduced into the liturgy following Vatican II. (See Music, Church.)

## Gregorian Sacramentary

Originally issued in the eighth century, the Gregorian Sacramentary was a book containing the Ordinaries and Propers of the Mass and the prayers for ordination. It has undergone many revisions and changes, but when first introduced it was a basic source of the Roman rite. The name *Sacramentary* has been given to the official altar book in modern times. (See Sacramentary.)

## Gregorian Water

Sometimes called the "water of consecration," this is the holy water blessed and used by the bishop at the consecration of a church. In the blessing, small amounts of wine, salt, and ashes are mingled with the water.

## Gremial, also Gremiale

An oblong veil, usually of silk and decorated with embroidery, called the gremial is laid on the bishop's knees when he sits during various episcopal ceremonies. Its purpose is to serve as an apron to keep ashes, drops of oils, and candle wax from falling on the vestments. It corresponds in color to that of the vestments. A linen gremial is used when Holy Orders are conferred. It is not strictly a pontifical vestment, since it was used at all high Masses at one time; a similar lap-cloth, the *mappula,* is still used by the Dominicans and the celebrant in Carthusian and calced Carmelite orders.

## Grille

1. A wooden or metal grating separating the enclosure of cloistered nuns from the visiting rooms of the public. Frequently the grille has an opening where offerings are passed to the members of the community. It also may be covered by a thin veil.

2. The partition, usually a grating, which, though separating a penitent from the confessor, does not obstruct the sound of the voice; it also is covered by a cloth.

### Guadalupe, Our Lady of

This title has been given to our Blessed Mother because of her apparitions to the Mexican convert, Juan Diego, in 1531. At the time, to confirm the apparitions, an image of the Immaculate Conception was imprinted on the *tilma* or mantle of Juan. The cloth was an *ayate,* a coarse fabric made of cactus fiber. It showed the Virgin Mary with the sun, moon, and stars, and with an angel beneath the crescent. Under this title the Blessed Mother is the declared patroness of Mexico. The feast, celebrated on Dec. 12, is a holy day of obligation in Mexico.

The five apparitions are well attested to in ancient documents, especially the Codex of Seville, which was started before 1454. In keeping with the request of the Virgin Mary, a shrine-church was erected, which is a place of pilgrimage because the original miraculous painting is still exhibited there. The heart of her message is in these words: "You must know, and be very certain in your heart, my son, that I am truly the eternal Virgin, holy Mother of the True God, through Whose favor we live, the Creator, Lord of Heaven, and the Lord of the Earth" (First apparition).

A prayer to her is as follows:

Our Lady of Guadalupe

Hear and let it penetrate your heart, my dear little son.
Let nothing discourage you, nothing depress you, let nothing alter your heart or your countenance.
Do not fear any illness or vexation, anxiety or pain.
Am I not here, your Mother?
Are you not under my shadow and protection?
Am I not your fountain of life?
Are you not in the folds of my mantle, in the crossing of my arms?
Is there anything else that you need?"

### Guardian

Guardian is the title of an elected superior of a Franciscan friary, usually referred to as "Father Guardian."

### Guardian Angel

See Angel, Guardian.

### Guilds

In Europe guilds (formerly spelled "gilds") were voluntary associations or societies of the Middle Ages, organized for the promotion of individual initiative, special skills, social standing, and the religious life of their members. Chiefly these were of three classes: the merchant guilds, formed by the tradesmen; the craft guilds, incorporating three groups, namely, the learners or apprentices, the more proficient journeymen, and the masters or employers; the religious guilds, made up of all classes of people who directed themselves to social work, collective alms-giving, and instruction. The guilds had patron saints and chaplains, and their members celebrated religious feasts by attending Mass and receiving Holy Communion in a body. In a distinct manner the guilds were the forerunners of labor unions and groups later organized for Catholic Action.

### Guilt

Guilt is that state of the mind and soul which results from and follows a deliberate, known act against a law that one knows himself to be obliged in conscience to follow, or the omission of an act recognized as obligating.

In the NT sin and guilt are closely related: Jn. 9:41; 15:22; Rom. 3:9. There is recognized responsibility of sinners and exhortation to repent because sin can be forgiven through Christ (Mt. 9:6; Lk. 7:47–50). Also there is recognition of the disobedience that is culpable action against the all-good God (Rom. 2:8; Eph. 2:2; Ti. 3:2–7).

### Guru

The title guru is assumed or conferred on a teacher or spiritual guide in the religion of Hinduism. In some instances where a belief in reincarnation is held, he has been regarded as the incarnation of some past deity, and hence salvation is only possible through adherence to such a guru. It is a superstitious manner of attaining undeserved allegiance.

The principal function of the guru is to lead formalized meditation, requiring physical posturing, the overcoming of bodily action often through rigid self-control such as diet or abstention from meat or alcohol, and the establishment of a system to be followed in other prescribed meditations. Often unusual charisms are claimed by a guru, but it is difficult to document such allegations.

In the Sikh faith of India, which arose in the early sixteenth century as a result of syncretism with the faith of Islam, the successive leaders of the movement were called gurus until the tenth who then decreed that the Granth, the sacred book, should be considered the guru.

There have been many followers of one or another guru in the modern religious cultic emphasis, especially by those seeking after some tangential relationship to the fount of truth. Basically only the abiding faith in God and the revelation by Him are satisfying, and hence many are disillusioned by the claims of gurus.

### Gynaeceum

The gynaeceum is a portion of the church set apart for women in the Byzantine and other Eastern Churches.

### Gyrovagi

This name was given by St. Benedict (d. 543) to the so-called "tramp monks" who wandered about the various countries but were never attached to any monasteries. They became laws to themselves, and their behavior brought about Church regulation to do away with such "aimless" religious life.

## Habakkuk, Book of, also Habacuc

The Book of Habakkuk is the writing of the eighth of the minor prophets; it is a prophetical book of the Bible written by an unknown prophet of the same name. It was written before the invasion of Palestine by the Chaldaeans (Babylonians) sometime probably between the years 605 and 602 B.C. The book is divided into three distinct parts: the first, a dramatic dialogue between the prophet and God; the second, the "Woes of the Wicked"; and the third, a canticle (ch. 3). The message takes up the problem of injustice on earth, God's reassurance that man's faithfulness will be rewarded, and the petition that God come and bring consolation.

Its doctrine is the foretelling of salvation, with the central theme expressed in the words: "The just man, because of his faith, shall live" (Hab. 2:4; cf. Rom. 1:17).

## Habit

That acquired or infused quality or disposition which influences a person's action is called a habit. Those habits that are infused are given by God accompanying sanctifying grace and are always good, such as the supernatural virtues. When cooperated with, habits dispose a human person to act rightly. The acquired habits are the result of repeated acts; they may be good or bad and thus are either natural virtues or vices.

The facility of action, the cultivated method of doing some act so that it becomes easy or is done with little effort, is a modification of action, which marks it as habitual. These are the results of good or bad actions repeated often, but there are habits that are present without acting, such as good health or memory.

Habits are of two kinds: (1) entitative, those that modify the substance itself, such as beauty, strength, health; (2) operative, those habits that limit or augment human acts or operations, such as the ability to write or swim. Thus virtues that give man a more certain and assured sense in the performance of good acts are operative.

Both forms of habits are basic to human activity; they are necessary for successful living. (See Virtue.)

## Habit, Religious

The official and distinctive external garment worn by members of a religious order is called the habit. These are generally variations of black, brown, or white, but grey and blue are also used. In general, except for some societies who use a variation of the cassock, the habit of male religious is comprised of a tunic, belt or girdle, a scapular, and a hood. Among women's orders, the garments are generally a veil, guimpe, full dress, and a scapular. The ceremony marking the reception into the religious life is called the "clothing" and sets a member apart as a prospective or professed member of the religious order.

In modern times a freedom of choice regarding the dress of religious has been introduced. In some instances the habit or dress of tradition has been supplanted with the ordinary garments of our time, with some identifying adjunct such as a cross, a veil, or bonnet as the only distinctive feature. Thus traditional identity has been sacrificed to utility in keeping with the directives of Vatican II: "Since they are signs of a consecrated life, religious habits should be simple and modest, at once poor and becoming. They should meet the requirements of health and be suited to the circumstances of time and place as well as to the services required by those who wear them. Habits of men and women which do not correspond to these norms are to be changed" (PC 17). (See Religious Life.)

## Habitual Grace

The supernatural gift of God infused into the very essence of the soul as a habit is habitual grace. This grace is also called *sanctifying* or *justifying* grace, because it is included in both. Habitual grace also includes the virtues and gifts of the Holy Spirit. This grace is spoken of by St. Paul as the essential and constant possession of the soul of man, the created, internal gift of God (Rom 5:5; 1 Tim. 4:14). The Council of Trent (Sess. VI, c. 11) declares the teaching: "If anyone should say that men are justified either by the imputation of Christ's justice alone or by the remission of sins alone, exclusive of grace and charity, which are diffused in their hearts by the Holy Spirit and that it inheres in them, or even that grace, by which we are justified, is only a favor from God: let him be anathema." Habitual grace is both operative and cooperative. (Cf. Grace; Sanctifying Grace.)

## Haceldama

The name meaning in Aramaic "field of blood" was given to that potter's field near Jerusalem, used first as a dumping grounds for broken pieces of pottery and later as a burial site. It is mentioned as the place purchased with the thirty pieces of silver Judas Iscariot flung back to the priests after his betrayal of Jesus Christ. "The chief priests picked up the silver, observing, 'It is not right to deposit this in the temple treasury since it is blood money.' After consultation, they used it to buy the potter's field as a cemetery for foreigners. That is why that field, even today, is called Blood Field. On that occasion, what was said through Jeremiah the prophet was fulfilled: 'They took the thirty pieces of silver, the value of a man with a price on his head, a price set by the Israelites, and they paid it out for the potter's field just as the Lord had commanded me'" (Mt. 27:6–10).

The place is also mentioned in Acts 1:18–20 as the place where Judas committed suicide. The exact location is doubtful, but according to the tradition of the Jews, it was on the southern side of the Valley of Hennon as found in Jer. 19:1–11.

### Hades
See Hell.

### Haggai, Book of, also Aggai, or Aggeus
This is a postexilic prophetic book of the OT whose name is derived from the Hebrew word meaning "festal," which is the name of the author and one of the minor prophets. Probably written about 520 B.C., it consists of five brief pronouncements sometimes called oracles. It appears more as an account of the activities of Haggai, since it is written in the third person. Its chief message is the prophesy concerning the building of the second Temple, with greater glory and greater wealth flowing into Jerusalem. It follows this with a warning of the threats to the Temple and its sacrifices. The book concludes with the pronouncement that from the Davidic line will come the promised Messiah.

### Hagia
From the Greek word for "holy things," Hagia is the name of the consecrated elements in the Byzantine rite.

### Hagiography
Hagiography includes writings not only on the lives and works, but also on the sanctity of saints; thus it is more than biography. Whereas biography narrates the life of a person in a chronological or topical manner, hagiography includes an evaluation of a saint in the light of the principles of ascetical and mystical theology. It also includes, at least implicitly, the spiritual lessons to be learned from the saint whereby the reader may be directed toward emulation of the virtues exemplified by the saint's life. As a literary form, hagiography requires research into the life of the saint, knowledge of theology, and a critical sense in regard to spiritual happenings. In Scripture, the term "Hagiographa" is used to refer to those OT writings that treat of neither law nor the prophets.

It is apparent that the writing of the life of a saint is not a simple undertaking. The results for the reader and the benefits to be gained are in direct ratio to the ability of the writer.

There are many brief accounts of the Saints gathered, for example, the multi-volume set of *Butlers Lives of the Saints,* as well as the martyrologies. Strictly speaking these compilations are not hagiography but listings with biographical data given.

### Haikal
From the Arabic word for "temple," this is the name of the sanctuary of a Coptic Church.

### Hail Mary
Translated from the Latin *Ave Maria,* these are the first words and the title of the prayer, the Angelical Salutation. The prayer is composed of the words of annunciation addressed to the Blessed Virgin by the angel and by Elizabeth (Lk. 1:28–42) with a supplication added by the Church. Its present form dates back to 1568. Although the prayer is not used in the liturgy, it is said in reciting the Divine Office, the Little Office of the B.V.M., and in numerous devotions, notably the Rosary.

It reads:

Hail Mary, full of grace!
The Lord is with thee,
blessed art thou among women, and blessed
is the fruit of thy womb, Jesus.
Holy Mary, Mother of God,
pray for us sinners, now and at the
hour of our death. Amen.

### Hair Shirt
The name hair shirt is given to that penitential undergarment worn by many of the saints and those who seek to do continuous acts of penance. It was woven of coarse hair of animals and its abrasive effect was a constant irritation to the wearer, since it was worn next to the skin. Although prescribed in some religious rules, its use should not be undertaken, even in a lesser form of abrasiveness, without the consent of a spiritual director. In modern times its use has been

supplanted by other forms of penance and mortification more in keeping with the condition of our cultural and social living habits.

## Halo

The representation in Christian art of a circle of gold or light surrounding the head of a saint is called a halo. It is a device of portraying holiness or the "light of grace" in a saint. The halo is distinct from the aureole or nimbus. Its origin was not Christian, for it was used by pagan artists and sculptors to represent in symbol the great dignity and power of the various deities. In the fourth century it was adopted by Christians and applied chiefly to Christ as King and Lamb of God. The adaptations have evolved to where the circle of light takes on other forms, as in Byzantine art, and is sometimes joined with other symbols.

## Hampton Court Conference

The name Hampton Court Conference was given to that gathering of church leaders at Hampton Court Palace, in 1604, near London, England. Its purpose was to settle the differences in practice and religious thought between the Puritans and the Anglican Church. The Conference was presided over by King James I (1603 to 1625) as the head of the Church of England. The reforms presented by the Puritans, a more strict group than the Anglicans, were rejected by King James, who proposed a new guideline: "One doctrine and one discipline; one religion in substance and ceremony."

Although this meeting led to new antagonisms between the two religious groups, it had several beneficial consequences: (1) A resolution was advanced and put into effect whereby a new translation of the Bible was undertaken by some fifty scholars and produced in 1611 as the Authorized or King James Version; this has long been hailed for its beauty of phrasing and literary makeup as well as its excellent rendering of the original texts. (2) The disputes and antagonisms caused many of the Puritans to set out for America where the colonies were to grow and religious patterns were set for the new settlements and their later revolution against England, which resulted in the founding of the United States of America.

## Hanukkah

The Hebrew word meaning "dedication" is the title of the Jewish feast celebrating the victory of the armies of Judas Maccabaeus over the Syrian King Antiochus IV and the rededication of the Temple of Jerusalem in the year 165 B.C. This is recorded in the first and second Books of Maccabees, the last of the historical books of the OT.

The feast is celebrated on the twenty-fifth day of the month of Kislev in the Jewish calendar, corresponding to November-December in the Gregorian calendar. In the NT the feast is mentioned by John: "It was winter, and the time came for the feast of the Dedication in Jerusalem. Jesus was walking in the Temple area, in Solomon's Portico" (Jn. 10:22–23).

## Happiness

The euphoric state of the human spirit, which occurs when the wants and needs, both physical and spiritual, of the human person are satisfied, is known as happiness. Obviously complete happiness cannot be attained in our human existence on this earth. The Christian can best approach this state when he is moved by faith, encouraged by supernatural hope, and through grace and love seeks his salvation, putting emphasis on spiritual good rather than material possessions.

In many instances, the Bible speaks of happiness as spiritual joy: Tob. 13:10; Ps. 20:6. Isaiah proclaims: "I rejoice heartily in the Lord, in my God is the joy of my soul" (Is. 61:10). The early Christians found their happiness in the praise of God (Acts 2:46–47; 13:52). The ultimate of happiness is the belief in everlasting life, the reward of infinite love promised by God, and the enjoyment for eternity of the beatific vision. (See Heaven.)

## Harmony, Biblical

Biblical harmony is the study of the four Gospels wherein (1) differences in text are explained, (2) the Gospels are integrated into a single narrative, or (3) an arrangement of verses of the Gospels is made according to the historical order. (Cf. Synoptic Gospels.)

## Hasmoneans

Hasmoneans is the name of the ruling dynasty of the Jews from 142 to 63 B.C., the period between the Greek and Roman domination of the Israelites. It was founded by Judas Maccabaeus (cf. Books 1 and 2 of the Maccabees), and gave the people a time of unity and strength that was a preparation for the future coming of the Messiah.

## Hatred

Hatred is a human emotion of the mind and will and is the negative of the proper appetite of the human person. It is in direct opposition to charity and is based on pride, envy, and the desire to do ill to another. In and of itself hatred is not sinful, for there must be in the Christian's makeup and his love of God a hatred of sin. However, hatred is sinful when it is misdirected, excessive, or leads to direct action against another, because it destroys fellowship and love of neighbor: "The modern world shows itself at once powerful and weak, capable of the noblest deeds or the foulest. Before it lies the path to freedom or to slavery, to progress or retreat, to brotherhood or hatred" (GS 9).

### Hearse

A candleholder in the form of a triangle with 15 candlesticks, one placed at its apex and seven on each side, is known as a hearse. It is made of wood or iron and usually mounted on a standard. The hearse is also called the Tenebrae candleholder since it is used during Holy Week when the office of Tenebrae is sung. (Cf. Tenebrae.)

### Heart of Jesus

See Sacred Heart of Jesus.

### Heart of Mary Immaculate

Specifically, this is the devotion to the Blessed Mother of God and to the person of Mary as God's Mother. The word "heart" in Hebrew, and as used in the Scriptures, often stands for the higher part of the soul, the intellect and will. In portraying the heart of Mary and in directing our devotion thereto, we honor her interior fullness of grace, the perfections of her soul. When the heart of Mary is shown pierced by swords, we are directed to the sorrows she experienced in her motherhood of God; when it is represented surrounded with roses, we recall her virtues; when it is shown surrounded with thorns, we are reminded of her sorrow at man's ingratitude toward her divine Son. The devotion has been greatly increased since the Immaculate Heart of Mary was a prominent

feature of the apparitions at Fatima in 1917. August 22 was designated by Pope Pius XII in 1945 as the date for the celebration of this feast, but the modern calendar lists this date as the memorial of the Queenship of Mary. (Cf. Fatima, Apparitions of.)

### Heaven

The state of perfect happiness that exists in no restricted place is heaven. It is where God's special manifestation will be made to all. Heaven is mentioned frequently in Scripture under a wide variety of names: "Reign of God" (Mt. 5:3), the "Father's house" (Jn. 14:2), and the "crown of glory" (1 Pt. 5:4). St. Paul speaks quite fully of heaven, the requisite justification for attainment (Rom. 8), and he speaks of the judgment that will declare the reward (1 Cor. 4:1–5). Heaven is the reward and the manifestation of God, through Christ, and is the result of the love of God for mankind and man's love of God in return (1 Cor. 2:9). The happiness of heaven will consist primarily of an infusion or submersion in God's love or the participation through love of the beatific vision, the knowledge of God as He is in His being. The degree to which each one will participate will depend on his merit. Joined to this essential and fundamental supernatural beatitude will be the enjoyment of contemplating Christ's humanity, companionship of the angels and saints, the perfection of natural endowments, and the satisfactions of peace without struggle, and the continued enjoyment without end, or for all eternity.

Pope Benedict XII, in his constitution, "The Blessed God" (1336), set forth the Church's teaching concerning heaven, giving the scriptural tradition and stating that the blessed "see God's essence directly, and face to face, and thus the souls of the departed enjoy the divine nature, and are thereby rendered truly happy in the possession of eternal life and peace."

Apart from the tradition of the Church, we can arrive at a knowledge, having faith, whereby we reason through the "law of contradictions," for example, one cannot be perfect and imperfect at the same time; or because each one is created unique, there cannot be a duplication of being without contradicting the Creator, since duplication is a limitation. (Cf. Beatific Vision; Glory.)

### Hebdomadarius

In monasteries, this is the title of the one appointed each week to be the leader in chanting the canonical hours and other services.

### Hebrew Feasts

Days of religious observance and festivals of the Hebrew people are traced from the books of the OT. The ceremonies, the customs associated with them, and their meaning and significance we know from scriptural tradition. The origin of these feasts is often known in less detail.

Those feasts that are most frequent are the *Sabbath* and *Rosh Hodesh* (the Feast of the New Moon Day). The most ancient and related to the agriculture of the Israelites are: *Passover*, a seven-day festival commemorating the liberation of the Israelites from Egypt, which is celebrated beginning on the fourteenth day of Nisan in the Hebrew calendar (March-April), and called the Feast of the Unleavened Bread; *Shabuoth*, the Feast of Weeks, observed 50 days after Passover, and regarded by some Jews as commemorating the anniversary of the revelation of the Law of Moses, and sometimes called Pentecost; *Sukkoth*, the Feast of Tabernacles or Booths, a seven to nine day festival celebrated in the month of Tishri (September-October), taking its name from the temporary shelters of the harvest workers in the field and commemorating the reading of The Law.

There are also two special feasts, *Purim* and *Hanukkah*. Purim is a joyful festival on the fourteenth day of Adar (February-March), which commemorates the rescue of the Israelites from the Persians. This feast is preceded by a day of fasting, and it has been customary from medieval times to give gifts or alms on this feastday. *Hanukkah*, called the Festival of Lights or the Feast of Consecration and of the Maccabees, is observed for eight days; on each day a succession of candles is lit on an eight-branched candle-holder; this takes place near the time of winter solstice. The Feast of the Trumpets, *Rosh Hashana*, celebrated on the first day of Tishri (September-October) of the old Hebrew calendar, thus New Year's Day, is marked by meditation on death and

the day of judgment; Rosh Hashana takes place ten days before the highest holy day. The highest of holy days in the calendar of Hebrew Feasts is *Yom Kippur*, the Day of Atonement. It is observed with strict fasting and penance.

In Hebrew practice observance of the Sabbath and all festivals begins at sundown and continues until the following sundown. (See under separate entries.)

### Hebrew Language

A variety of the West Semitic language, rather than a dialect, Hebrew is the language spoken and written by the Israelites in Canaan. In the Bible the name Hebrew is first used in speaking of Abraham (Gn. 14:13) and in the prologue of the Book of Sirach, although the people were called Hebrews by the Egyptians (Gn. 39:14). Hebrew is called "the language of Canaan" (Is. 19:18). It was a so-called dead language from the time of the Mishnaic form, the oldest Hebrew preserved in the oldest part of the Talmud, to modern times. The present-day Hebrew, or Neo-Hebrew, is different from the ancient form in pronunciation and syntax. The ancient form is a reconstructed language, preserved in documents and inscriptions, such as the Scrolls of the Dead Sea and the Qumran manuscripts. The study of the Hebrew grammar began in the tenth century with the first book by Saadia in about A.D. 942.

### Hebrew Poetry

Although the translation does not always indicate this, about half of the OT was written in verse form. Characteristics of Hebrew poetry are: imagery, rhythm or meter, parallelism, alliteration (the repetition of consonants), assonance (the repetition of vowel sounds), and rhyme. (See Parallelism.)

### Hebrews, Epistle to the

This richly doctrinal writing of the NT is by an

unknown author (though often attributed to St. Paul) and was written between A.D. 80 and 90. It was not addressed, as the title indicates, to the Hebrew people but to Christians of pagan background and strong Hellenistic cultural ties. This, and the fact that it was written by someone other than St. Paul, is based upon internal evidence of the writing itself, the structure of the composition, and the nature of the work, which is not a letter but more of a discourse on doctrinal matters. The writer refers to it as "a word of encouragement" (13:22).

In substance the Epistle to the Hebrews stresses: the high-priesthood of Christ, through His sacrificial death; the harmony between the OT and the NT while making the distinction between the old law and the new law of Christ to the People of God; the mediatorship of Christ between God and man; the pilgrimage of the people of God to the heavenly reward; and especially the Christological interpretation whereby divine revelation is shown as a progression from the beginning, through the history of Israel, and now through the Church founded by Christ and the worship that the People of God must carry on. We are encouraged by the words: "Wherefore, we who are receiving the unshakable kingdom should hold fast to God's grace, through which we may offer worship acceptable to him in reverence and awe. For our God is a consuming fire" (12:28–29). But we know this epistle emphasizes the "fire" as the love of God for His people if we but follow the leadership given to us and the graces gained through Christ: "all that is good, that you may do his will" (13:21).

## Hedge Schools

When the ordinary means of giving Catholic primary education were suppressed by the Irish Parliament of King William III in 1695, the so-called hedge schools came into existence in rural Ireland. Because the laws made both buildings and teaching on an organized basis impossible and because even homeowners were forbidden to use their premises for Catholic education, the hedge schools were an ingenious, flaunting manner of rebellion against the laws and a means of carrying on some Catholic instruction.

These schools were no more than secluded places in remote areas where qualified teachers would gather the young people and instruct them. The name "hedge schools" derives from the practical fact that the sunny side of a hedge or bank was suitable, since it was warmer and partly protected from the winds as well as from the minions of the law. Fees for attendance were high;

the number paying indicated the quality of the teacher hired, and consequently there was a great loss of religious education for many students. It was not until relaxation of the laws after 1760 that the schools moved into buildings.

## Hedonism

The system of ethics based upon the erroneous conclusion that all natural goods are only a means of pleasure and that the only and highest good is pleasure itself is called hedonism. As a system it places pleasure, the feeling of goodness in all choices of life, above happiness as understood in the Christian sense. There are varieties of hedonism, some centered on one or the other sense, such as the pleasure given by the eating of food or on a human activity such as the sex instinct. In modern times hedonism is much concerned with material things; hence it is classified in the limited sense as materialism. In general all forms of hedonism tend to place emphasis upon the quantity rather than the quality in value judgments.

## Hegumenos

From the Greek word meaning leader, this is the title of an abbot in the monasteries of the Eastern Churches, particularly those of the Basilian rule. He is elected by the monks of the monastery, then appointed, blessed, and installed by the bishop or patriarch. He rules for life, is assisted by a council of seniors, and is deposed only for misconduct. He does not have the rights comparable to those of a Western church mitred abbot.

## Hell

Hell is the place and state of everlasting punishment prepared for Satan and the rebellious angels and to which the souls and bodies of those who die with grave and unrepented sins will be consigned after the last judgment (Mt. 25:31–46). The English name is derived from Teutonic mythology as the place of the dead. It corresponds to the OT idea of "Sheol," the state of the dead. The nature of this supernatural suffering is not known. However, theologians declare that essentially it consists of two facts: first, the pain of loss because of being deprived of the sight and love of God in the beatific vision; second, the actual physical suffering that will result from an outside agent, notably fire, which will be supernatural in character and nonconsuming. The suffering will be in degree according to the guilt of each and will last forever. The reasonable deductions concerning the nature of hell are not the result of speculation but are derived from recognition of the goodness, justice, and glory of God.

In the NT the concept of hell is not a clear revelation. It is "the realm of death" (Mt. 11:23), and "abode of the dead" (Lk. 16:23), a "sheol" concept. In the direct discourse of Christ the word "Gehenna" is used (Lk. 12:5; Mk. 9:43), and the word "hell" appears only in the Epistle of James (3:6).

Descriptions of hell often mention a condition of fire: Mt. 3:12; 5:22; Mk. 9:43–47; Lk. 3:17; Jude 7; Rv. 19:20. It is also told that a condition of hell is darkness (Mt. 8:12; 25:30), and this is understood as the absence of light or the contrast with the light "outside." The recurrent theme of punishment in hell is exclusion from the kingdom of God as recorded in the epistles (1 Cor. 6:9). Thus although in the "judgment discourses" of Christ no clear revelation is given of hell as a place or its nature, it is evident that the pain of loss or the separation from God will be the most intense of all the punishments suffered by the unloving and sinful. (See Heaven.)

### Hellenism

This embrasive term in Church usage means the culture, language, and intellectual attitudes that influenced the Church in its earliest development. Hellenistic ideas were a great influence on the philosophical and theological concepts of the early Christian communities, and Scripture was recorded and translated in the language of the influential and educated Greek people.

After the colonization by Alexander the Great (356 to 323 B.C.) Greek had become the most widely used language of the educated; thus there were many among the early Christian communities who spoke Greek (cf. Acts 6:1). St. Paul addressed the Greek-speaking people but was not well received (Acts 9:29–30). The Catechetical School of Alexandria, one of the first and greatest schools of Christian theology, became the forerunner in synthesizing the teachings of the OT and Jewish religious thought with the Christian philosophical understanding of the message of the NT. The third century Greek translation of the OT, the *Septuagint,* gives evidence of this activity. Further, the central teachings and conclusions of the first four ecumenical councils were expressed in language and philosophical thought influenced by Hellenism.

### Henoticon

Henoticon was a formula of unity of doctrine proposed by the Acacians to effect a compromise between the Catholics and the heretical Monophysites in 482. It was rejected by Pope Felix III in 484.

### Heortology

The study of the origin, meaning, and development of the Church's feasts is known as heortology. (See Calendar, Church.)

### Heptateuch

Heptateuch is the word from the Greek meaning "seven" and "container" and is thus ascribed to a tube that would hold seven scrolls. The name is given to the first seven books of the OT, the Pentateuch plus the Books of Joshua and Judges, which some scripture scholars claim should be considered as a unit because they were composed from the same literary source. (See Bible.)

### Heresies

In the history of the doctrinal Church, its dogmas have come face to face with a wide variety of heresies. The oldest known in the history of the Church was that of the *Judaizers,* who rejected the dogma that the Church was truly Catholic, that is, intended for all human persons. Hence the Judaizers were for closing membership in the Church to all but those who observed the Mosaic as well as the Christian law. The Judaeo-Christians formed different sects, among which were the *Ebionites* or Poor Ones. The views of the Judaizers were condemned by the Council of Jerusalem in A.D. 51 when James spoke out concerning the Church founded by Christ, saying that it was intended to be built up "so that all the rest of mankind and all the nations that hear my name may seek out the Lord" (Acts 15:17). Yet, the Ebionites persisted until the fifth century.

Next came the *Gnostics* who were attempting to be both pagan and Christian, and their spawn was a variety of heresies centered around the question of creation and evil, asking in a variety of ways, "If God is Creator of all, then why evil?" They believed that there was a kingdom of darkness, in opposition to the kingdom of light, which would persist through many centuries. For them Christ took on the role of a leader of the true gnosis. They claimed that all matter will one day return to the fullness of God, once the gospel has performed its work on earth, and the fullness of God will return and remain a kingdom of darkness. Strangely, Gnosticism continues even in our times in the *Theosophists* or the *Spiritualists.* (Cf. Gnosticism.)

Branches of the tree of Gnosticism include the

*Ophites,* the worshippers of the serpent, or Satan. Another was *Montanism,* the branch begun in an Asiatic village by Montanus who proclaimed himself the Advocate, the spirit promised by Christ; he and his followers went into ecstacies and followed the teaching of the *Millinarianists,* or that of the thousand years of the kingdom foretold in the Book of Revelation. They were rigorists in all moral matters, preparing themselves for the Second Coming so that they would surely be ready. They were finally condemned but lurk in the wings for a possible uprising again in a modern setting.

In the second and early third centuries there arose a series of anti-trinitarian heresies. *Adoptionism* was twofold since it denied the Trinity and the divinity of Christ by proclaiming that Christ was only the "adopted" son of God the Father. Then came *Sabellianism,* which claimed that there was no distinction in persons in the Trinity; hence all were three aspects of the same person. These Sabellianists were called *Patripassians,* believers in the Father. There were also the *Modalists* who looked on the three Persons as only modes of expression.

Following the third century condemnation and refutation of the anti-trinitarian heresies there came *Subordinationism,* which in brief taught that the soul of Christ in His man's body was replaced by the Word and only thus is called God. This placing of Christ in an inferior role gave rise to the *Arian* heresy. For a time this gave way to *Photinianism,* which was a throwback to Sabellianism. After Constantine's death in A.D. 337 *Semi-Arianism* arose, and this was an attack upon the consubstantiality of the Word. Varieties of Semi-Arianism came along, carrying different terminology like banners: The Son was "similar in substance," "dissimilar," "similar to" with regard to the Father, all without coming to grips with the similarity of substance. Around these the battle raged for a true formulation of teaching, and there arose the *Macedonians,* who added to the confusion by declaring against the Holy Spirit. This merited for them the title of *Pneumatomachi,* which is a long word for "opponents of the Spirit."

Then in the Western Church *Donatism* arose, which professed two heretical ideas: it claimed that public sinners could no longer belong to the Church because of their known sins and that all sacraments administered outside the true Church were invalid. These were refuted by the doctrinal affirmations that sin does not exclude one from the Church, but only apostasy from the faith does this, and that the state of grace of the minister was not necessary for the recipient of the sacrament to receive its graces.

There followed *Priscillianism,* which is summarized in the words of Gregory the Great's condemnation: "The Priscillian heretics think that all men are born under a conjunction of stars, and they claim in support of their error that a new star' appeared when our Lord showed himself in the flesh."

*Pelagianism* arose in the late fourth century, taking its name from the English-born Pelagius, a severe moralist who denied original sin, declaring that a soul created by God could not be tainted by sin that it has not committed. Hence, baptism was only for adults who had sinned, not infants. And this in turn gave rise to *Semi-Pelagianism,* which scanned the scene and declared that without original sin there need not be a redeemer, and since humans were sufficient unto themselves, they did not need prayer.

From the fourth to the seventh centuries there arose *Apollinarianism,* a throw-back to Arian error, which attacked the soul of Christ, saying that since Christ was whole, man and God, the completion of such a being could only be made where there was sin. It was rejected by several councils, chiefly the Council of Constantinople in A.D. 381.

Next came *Nestorianism,* which disputed the right of Christians to call the Virgin Mary the Mother of God; the confusion was between "God-bearing" as opposed to "man-bearing." This was settled by the Council of Ephesus in A.D. 431.

There was a reaction against Nestorianism, called *Eutychianism,* itself a plague of errors, which claimed that the humanity of Christ was absorbed by the divinity, thus making only a man-God rather than a God-man. This was refuted by the Council of Chalcedon in A.D. 451, which gave the true teaching that the sole person of the Word possessed all the human and divine attributes; this teaching is called the *communication of idioms,* that is, the exchange of properties of each nature, the divine and the human. Those who did not submit to this doctrine became *Monophysites,* claiming only one nature in Christ; this persists to the present day where there are still Monophysite Churches in Syria, Mesopotamia, and Egypt.

At the beginning of the seventh century there leaped up *Monothelitism,* the theory of only one will in Christ and a single activity. This was solemnly condemned at the sixth Ecumenical Council in A.D. 681.

A departure from the doctrinal concerns was brought about with the *Iconoclast* heresy. This was the wholesale condemnation of saints, angels, martyrs, along with representations of them, together with the proscription of all images or representations of Christ and the Blessed Virgin.

Social conditions and changes brought about by the ferment of the Middle Ages caused new heresies. Berengarius *(Berengarians)* became an opponent of the Real Presence by maintaining that the consecration of bread and wine gave only a certain sanctifying power. Along with other rationalist heretical thought, such as that of Amalric of Bena, Berengarianism gave rise to false mysticism, pantheism, and free love movements.

There sprang up in the twelfth century the *Petrobrusians* who were against infant baptism, the use of prayer in church, prayers for the dead, belief in the Real Presence, and obedience to the clergy. Then came the *Vaudois,* following Peter Valdo of Valdes; they gave everything to the poor, encouraged others to do so, and preached the Gospel although they all were untrained and adopted a teaching like that of the Donatists, making the sacraments dependent upon the sanctity of those administering them. This grew and in 1533 the Vaudois adopted the teachings of the Protestant reformation and became an appendage of Calvinism. (Cf. Calvinism.)

More dangerous, but of shorter duration, was the *Albigensian* heresy, whose name is derived from the town of Albi. Its adherents were also called *Cathari,* the "pure ones." This was a strong followup on *Manicheism* from which they derived anticlericalism, anarchism, and communism, with a distinction made between the simple adherents and the elect. However, their rigorous asceticism made a strong impression on the common people even though it forbade marriage or sexual relations. Both the Vaudois and the Cathari were anarchic attempts to reform the Church by creating excessive abuses themselves.

Forerunners of Luther, taking their cue from the anarchists, were the *Wyclif* heresy and that of John Huss. Wyclif, a Yorkshireman, born about 1326, became a well-educated reformer who maintained among other teachings that God is sovereign but man in the state of grace becomes sovereign over the entire universe through God; hence the Papacy lost its power. The *Hussites* following John Huss who was born in 1369, came forward with a strange collection of teachings such as: the scriptures alone are the source of truth, the papacy is only an institution in which Christ has no part, all superiors of religious orders lose their authority if they fell into sin, and that the Church is made up of only the predestined, and that predestination is infallible. Some of these ideas were to recur later when Luther took up his reform.

The greatest break in unity, of course, came with the Protestant Reformation, more serious than the great schism of the Greek and Latin Churches in 1054. The errors of the Protestant reform were that a rediscovery of faith could take place with recourse to scripture alone, that is by exegesis, and that this recourse to scripture could effect an absolute principle of reform, which only led to a constant redivision because of the recourse of others to this principle.

Following the urge to "reform" there was a succession of heresies that were attempts from within the Church. Such were *Baianism* and *Jansenism,* the former against grace and freedom on the part of man, and the latter a confusion of grace and predestination, which was semi-Pelagian in character but also eluded condemnation by the Church for many years.

Between the seventeenth and twentieth centuries there came a succession of diffused ideas that border on heretical thoughts, all having to do with the extremes of being "lost in God" or being lost in naturalism. The first was *Quietism,* which is defined as "the quest for an extreme spiritual passibility tending to the destruction of the human self through absorption in God." Since it has very early traces, it is thus the root of Buddhism whose ideal is a "lost-in-God" state of nirvana. The opposite of Quietism and neo-Quietism is *Naturalism,* which is the "denial of the supernatural, of divine revelation, of all positive religion, such as Christianity, of the miraculous, even of its possibility, of all binding and infallible dogmas." Thus man becomes his own religion through his own conscience, and this has been characteristic of much of the modern society in which the lack of a guide for spiritual matters is prevalent, as in *Humanism.* Such are the *Free-Thought* movements, along with *Americanism,* which is not a formal heresy but a naturalistic growth; and *Modernism,* an attempt to change or compromise the truth of the Church with modern changes or advances, and as such was condemned in the encyclicals of St. Pius X, Sept. 8, 1907 *(Pascendi)* and of Pius XII, Aug. 12, 1950· *(Humani generis).*

It must be concluded that over the ages the attempts to disrupt the unity of the Church have a certain similarity of obdurate ignorance. Both those of the past and present can best be offset by the efforts of ecumenism as presented in the *Decree on Ecumenism (Unitatis Redintegratio)* of the Second Vatican Council.

## Heresy

Heresy is the denial or doubt by error of judgment, publicly or privately, by a baptized, professed person of any truth revealed by God and proposed for belief by the Catholic Church (cf. Apostasy; Schism). It differs from apostasy and schism and incurs excommunication (c. 2314); censure is reserved to the Holy See in the inner forum, and to the Ordinary in the outward forum (c. 2314 par. 2). Heresy must be: deliberate, that is, with a sufficient knowledge of the true teaching; and obstinate, that is, the person continues in the error of judgment without seeking further to learn the truth. Heresy is of two kinds: *formal*, which is the deliberate and obstinate denial of a truth and the neglect of inquiry into the truth; *material*, when the denial is the result of ignorance and is not accompanied by obstinacy. This latter does not incur canonical censures. Certain persons, because of their political extremism, are heretics according to the extent to which they ascribe to principles of their party in opposition to the revealed truth and defined teachings.

All heresies are against the unity of the Church, for which Christ prayed when He asked the Father: "O Father most holy, protect them with your name which you have given me that they may be one, even as we are one." (Jn. 17:11; cf. 17:20) Heresy comes from the exercise of freedom of thought and the personality and the temperamental adverse attitudes of people to the acceptance of that mark of the Church which is unity. (See Heresies.)

## Heretic

A baptized and professed person who denies or doubts a truth revealed by God or proposed for belief by the Catholic Church is a heretic. The term is usually reserved for one who is guilty of formal heresy. (See Apostasy.)

## Hermeneutics

Hermeneutics is the science of interpreting the meaning and true sense of the books and texts of Scripture in accord with the principles of exegesis. It is an aid to understanding something that is not external to the mind but is intersubjectively agreed to by individuals. (Cf. Exegesis; Interpretation, Scriptural; Form Criticism.)

## Hermesianism

The title Hermesianism is applied to the erroneous teachings concerning reason and faith propounded by Rev. G. Hermes (d. 1831). These teachings were condemned by the Holy See in 1835 and by Vatican Council I.

## Hermetic Science

Hermetic Science includes esoteric or occult teachings that urge man to control nature by will, concentration, and higher consciousness. It had its origin in Egypt and was named after Hermes Trismegistus of Greece. The terms and theories are borrowed from physics, parapsychology, and psychology, and concern vibrations, attraction, mental suggestion, laying on of hands, subconscious activity, glossolalia, and in general, ceremonial magic. (Cf. Charismatic Renewal, Catholic; Gnosis.)

## Hermit

A hermit is one who lives alone and apart from the society of others for the purpose of devoting himself to prayer and the cultivation of a personal spiritual life. The practice arose early in the Church, following the persecution of the third and fourth centuries. Hermits were the pioneer monks and gave rise to the religious life. (Cf. Stylite; Monk; Anchorite.)

## Hermitage of St. Anthony

This Canadian shrine was founded in 1907 by Father Elzear de Lamarre on the north shore of Lake Bouchette in the province of Quebec. At first a chalet was built, then a chapel dedicated to St. Anthony of Padua was added. Later there was discovered a natural niche in a ridge of rock, and here a statue of Our Lady of Lourdes was set, and this new shrine dedicated to the Blessed Virgin Mary is now called Our Lady of Saguenay.

Since the death of Father Lamarre in 1925, the Hermitage has been under the direction of the Capuchin Fathers. A monastery has been built, and a large church for pilgrims, which is an outstanding example of modern architecture. Catholic Action groups from the cities of Canada come to the Hermitage and Shrine, and the place has become a great place of pilgrimage for thousands who honor the Blessed Mother and St. Anthony. (See Canadian Shrines.)

## Heroic Act of Charity

See Charity, Heroic Act of.

## Heroic Virtue

Heroic virtue is the practice of the cardinal and theological virtues in such manner and degree as to be extraordinary both in motive and perseverance.

It is essential to prove heroic virtue on the part of one who is to be beatified and canonized. (Cf. Virtue.)

## Hesperinos

Hesperinos is the Vesper service in the Byzantine rite.

## Hesychasm

This Eastern Church system of mysticism was first practiced by the monks of Athos in the fourteenth century. Drawn from Platonist philosophy and borrowing from Asiatic Yoga practices, it is a form of rationalist asceticism that does not interrelate with contemplation in its true sense. (Cf. Quietism.)

## Hesychasts

The name Hesychasts is sometimes applied to monks of the Orthodox Eastern Church who lead a life of contemplation.

## Hexaemeron, also Hexahemeron

Taken from the Greek, Hexaemeron is the title for the narration of the six days or periods of creation of the physical world as recorded in the first chapter of Genesis. (Cf. Creation.)

## Hexapla

This monumental compilation by Origen, giving the text of the Scriptures, was made about A.D. 240. Origen's aim was to give what was actually contained in the Hebrew text and to provide the Church with a uniform text by eliminating the variations found in the codices. The book, about 12,000 pages, is named from the six corresponding columns into which it was divided. It contained both Hebrew and Greek texts. An edition containing only the four Greek versions was called *Tetrapla*.

## Hexateuch

Hexateuch is the collective name for the first six books of the Bible considered as a unit because of their literary similarity. They are: Genesis, Exodus, Leviticus, Numbers, Deuteronomy, Joshua. However, the inclusion of Joshua is being questioned among critical scholars because it is considered to have a markedly different literary style of its own. (See Heptateuch.)

## Hierarch

From the Greek word meaning "sacred ruler" or "holy ruler," this is any member of a hierarchy, but especially an archbishop or patriarch.

## Hierarchy

1. Celestial hierarchy includes the nine choirs of angels (cf. Angel).

2. The hierarchy of the Church has two distinctions. First, by reason of holy orders, the hierarchy is composed of bishops, priests, and deacons. Second, by reason of jurisdiction, the hierarchy is made up of the pope and the bishops under his authority. The jurisdiction of the second group may, by delegation, be shared in part by clerics of the first group (cc. 108 to 144). Thus the hierarchy of the Church includes all grades or ranks of the clergy. It is the institutional order representing the invisible Lord in the structure of the Church. In summary of the teachings of Vatican II "one could say that the Church is the new people of God living in hierarchical order in the service of the kingdom of God." (Cf. Bishop; Jurisdiction.)

As Vatican II teaches: "The hierarchy should promote the apostolate of the laity, provide it with spiritual principles and support, direct the exercise of this apostolate to the common good of the Church, and attend to the preservation of doctrine and order" (AA 24).

And: "Certain forms of the apostolate of the laity are given explicit recognition by the hierarchy, though in various ways.

"Because of the demands of the common good of the Church, moreover, ecclesiastical authority can select and promote in a particular way some of the apostolic associations and projects which have an immediately spiritual purpose, thereby assuming in them a special responsibility. Thus, making various dispositions of the apostolate according to circumstances, the hierarchy joins some particular form of it more closely with its own apostolic function. Yet the proper nature and individuality of each apostolate must be preserved, and the laity must not be deprived of the possibility of acting on their own accord. In various Church documents, this procedure of the hierarchy is called a mandate.

"Finally, the hierarchy entrusts to the laity some functions which are more closely connected with pastoral duties, such as the teaching of Christian doctrine, certain liturgical actions, and the care of souls. By virtue of this mission, the laity are fully subject to higher ecclesiastical direction in the performance of such work" (AA 24). (See Authority; Episcopacy.)

## Hierarchy of the United States

See United States Catholic Conference.

## Hieratikon

In the Eastern Churches of the Byzantine Rite,

the Hieratikon is a compilation or book containing the prayers most used by a priest; these may vary according to feasts. This is also called the *Leitourgikon* or Little Eukhologion.

## Hierodeacon

In the Byzantine Rite this is the title of a monk who has been ordained a deacon.

## Hieromonk

A monk of the Eastern Church who has been ordained a priest is called a Hieromonk.

## Hierurgia

A liturgical rite, such as the Mass, is known as Hierurgia.

## High Mass

The term High Mass was applied variously to the principal Sunday Mass; a Mass celebrated with solemnity above the ordinary, such as one with a choir; or a solemn Mass read in Latin. With the introduction of the new liturgy this term has been abandoned. (See Eucharist, Celebration of.)

## High Priest

This refers to both the name and the office of the principal head of the Temple officials of the Israelites. In the NT the High Priest exercised supreme authority over the Temple, the worship therein, and the entire group of servants of the Temple of Yahweh in Jerusalem. The plural "Chief Priests" is also used in the NT, but these were subordinate to the High Priest, although some maintain that the usage is actually a loose translation. Because of his place in the liturgical functions of the Temple, the High Priest had a greater ritual purity demanded of him (Lv. 21), and he was accorded a residence in the Temple area (Mk. 14:53–54) because he was expected to remain close to the Temple at all times. The position of High Priest was for life.

## Hindering Impediments

Hindering impediments are conditions that make it unlawful to contract marriage but do not affect the validity of the contract. (Cf. Impediments of Marriage; Validation of Marriage.)

## Hinduism

The religion of the greatest number of people of India, this is the third stage in the development of the religion that has been a dominant factor in the cultic life of that country for the past 2500 years. The first stage was the Vedic religion, brought into the country from the Nordic races about 1500 B.C. The result of a meshing of the Vedic with the native religious traditions of India resulted in Brahmanism (cf. Brahmanism). Hinduism then evolved somewhat independently in about the fifth century before Christ; it places its chief belief in a supreme personal deity and demands an intense personal devotion to that deity. As a result there is a great variety of beliefs in Hinduism, ranging from polytheism to belief in one god.

The god most worshipped is Vishnu, the supreme deity, who was an early sky god, but later regarded as the one under whose providential care the people exist. The Vishnu doctrine developed from the ancient tales, a kind of traditional record, called the *Puranas,* but their scripture of the worship of Vishnu is found in the Bhagavad-Gita, the "Song of God," a sacred poem composed about the third century before Christ. It stresses that man's highest religious life is found in union with God through love and devotion, but the greatest expression of this teaching came about after the recordings of appearances of Vishnu in bodily forms called the avatars. This then developed into two distinct incarnations, one called Rama and the other Krishna. These were elevated by writings, with large groups of adherents gathering to follow each incarnation.

There are also a wide variety of lesser dieties, such as Indra, the storm god; Surya, the sun god; Varuna, the cosmic god; and Yama, the god who rules the world of the dead. Distinctively Hinduism erected a great number of temples of worship with images of many varieties suited to the likes and devotion of a wide number of people.

Hinduism was not overlooked by Vatican II, not as an endorsement but as an estimate of this as a religion of personal attainment: "In Hinduism men contemplate the divine mystery and express it through an unspent fruitfulness of myths and through searching philosophical inquiry. They seek release from the anguish of our condition through ascetical practices or deep meditation or a loving, trusting flight toward God" (NA 2).

Many branches of Hinduism do not have a specific creed; they are individualized by personal response to a particular deity, and as such these are prone to amalgamation with other beliefs through adaptation. Many of these come to strange idolatrous practices, and while their ritual and ceremonies are elaborate, they become allied with superstitions and demon worship.

## Historical Books of the Bible

See Bible.

## Historical Sciences Commission

The Historical Sciences Commisson is one of the scholarly commissions of the Vatican, originally established in 1883 and instituted as an ongoing commission by Pius XII, April 7, 1954. It calls upon all leaders of historical groups in national bodies, coordinates special studies, and prepares the findings for publication. It is headquartered in Vatican City.

## History, Church

The study and account of the story, facts, and personages from its beginning to the present of the imperishable society known as the Church is called Church history. It shows this society at work throughout time, giving the record of Christ's revelation and its extension among human beings during succeeding ages. It thus narrates the spread of the Church and its efforts to teach divine truths, and gives an account of the persons who aided or obstructed that spread of truth. Church history is always presented together with secular history since the Church as a society lives and exercises her authority and official organization among the nations of men.

As a recording of both events and knowledge, Church history extends itself into many disciplines of knowledge within the Church such as history and theology. Vatican II points out: "Other theological disciplines should also be renewed by livelier contact with the mystery of Christ and the history of salvation. Special attention needs to be given to the development of moral theology. Its scientific exposition should be more thoroughly nourished by scriptural teaching. It should show the nobility of the Christian vocation of the faithful, and their obligation to bring forth fruit in charity for the life of the world. Again, in the explanation of Canon law and Church history, the mystery of the Church should be kept in mind, as it was set forth in the Dogmatic Constitution on the Church (LG), promulgated by this holy synod" (OT 16). (See Salvation History.)

## Hogan Schism

This movement of short duration began in Philadelphia, in 1820 under the assumed leadership of William Hogan. It was an aspect of trusteeism, which attempted to form an independent American Catholic Church along parochial lines. Hogan, born in Ireland about 1788, was an ordained priest of the diocese of Limerick, Ireland. He came to the United States in 1819 and intended to become active in the Archdiocese of New York, but without the permission of his bishop, moved to Philadelphia and took up residence there. Because of his preaching ability, distinguished appearance, and personal bluster he won over the trustees of St. Mary's Parish, and with the cooperation of the trustees administered the parish, since there was no bishop in the city. When the new bishop, Henry Conwell, arrived in December, 1820, Hogan remained at St. Mary's.

Bishop Conwell soon became aware of the unpriestly actions of Father Hogan and gave him several admonitions. But the popular Hogan would not change and began to publicly speak against the bishop. Finally the Bishop placed him under suspension.

Gaining support, Father Hogan was proposed by the trustees as bishop; the petition was refused by Rome; and the clash was openly carried on between the two supporting groups, those favoring Bishop Conwell and those supporting the unrecognized claim of Father Hogan. It was during this time that Father Hogan began preaching against the authority of the Church and proposed the founding of an independent Church, a movement that was soon given the name of Hoganism and that was the worst form of trusteeism, the arrogant control of both church property and the clergy. It was short-lived because of the personal failings of Father Hogan who ceased to serve as a priest, married, and later married a second time. He then became a lawyer, a supporter of nativist movements, an anti-Catholic pamphleteer, and died in 1848. The result of this foray of domination by trustees led Bishop Conwell to make concessions to the trustees; he was censured by Rome and removed as bishop of Philadelphia.

## Holiness

1. In regard to material things, holiness means their dedication or consecration to God's service. In regard to persons, holiness means a degree of union with God through sanctifying grace and the performance of morally good acts.

2. A title of honor conferred on the pope and used in addressing him, for example, His Holiness, Pope_____.

The word holiness means separateness, that is, freedom from defilement and therefore fit to be made holy. In its highest sense in the philosophy of religion it is *numinous* as exists in the Godhead, and this coincides with God's glory as His absolute attribute. In its cultic sense holiness means separated from the profane and directed toward God. In the OT God called Himself holy because His essence was holiness itself (Is. 40:25; Prv. 9:10). God directs men to holiness by the moral mandate of His commandments and by direction of their lives: "Be holy for I, the Lord, your God, am holy" (Lv. 19:2). The NT shows the holiness of Jesus: "the Holy and Just One" (Acts 3:14), and Christians are to be the anointed holy ones because they are "consecrated in Christ Jesus and called to be a holy people" (1 Cor. 1:2). Likewise Christians are "a chosen race, a royal priesthood, a holy nation, a people he claims for his own to proclaim the glorious works of the One who called you from darkness into his marvelous light" (1 Pt. 2:9). And so we are called to the numiosity, which is glory and salvation.

As Vatican II declares: "Faith teaches that the Church, whose mystery is being set forth by this sacred Synod, is holy in a way which can never fail. For Christ, the Son of God, who with the Father and the Spirit is praised as being 'alone holy,' loved the Church as His Bride, delivering Himself up for her. This He did that He might sanctify her (cf. Eph. 5:25–26). He united her to Himself as His own body and crowned her with the gift of the Holy Spirit, for God's glory. Therefore in the Church, everyone belonging to the hierarchy, or being cared for by it, is called to holiness, according to the saying of the Apostle: 'It is God's will that you grow in holiness' (1 Thes. 4:3; cf. Eph. 1:4).

"Now, this holiness of the Church is unceasingly manifested, as it ought to be, through those fruits of grace that the Spirit produces in the faithful. It is expressed in multiple ways by those individuals who, in their walk of life, strive for the perfection of charity, and thereby help others to grow. In a particularly appropriate way this holiness shines out in the practice of the counsels customarily called 'evangelical'" (LG 39).

### Holiness Churches

In a revival by some Protestant groups following the Civil War in the United States, an adherence to the "entire sanctification" theory as preached by John Wesley (the founder of Methodism) arose, and the several sects called themselves the Holiness Churches. These maintain that man by conversion and baptism becomes free from sin, but it is through the "second blessing" that the sense of being close to God comes after prayerful preparation. They teach a fundamentalist approach to the scriptures, a strict moral code, total abstinence from alcoholic drinks, and the imminent Second Coming of Christ.

There are two branches of the Holiness Churches: the left-wing, which are the Pentecostal Churches; and the right-wing groups, called Perfectionists, who tend more to Methodism. Of these

latter there are six sects in the United States: the Church of the Nazarene, the Church of God, the Pilgrim Holiness Church, the Wesleyan Methodist Church, the International Christian Church, and the Free Methodist Church.

In their worship the Holiness Churches have a Sunday morning service, a Sunday evening service, midweek prayer meetings, and revivals. They are also most generous toward missionary activity, more so than other Protestant Churches, and have been very successful in South America.

### Holiness, Mark of the Church

The visible community of the faithful gives testimony to the entire work of salvation: the Father's love in sending His only Son as Redeemer, the Redemption by the Son, and the sending of the Holy Spirit. Likewise this community gives example to all men of the goodness of God and His many divine gifts, which St. Paul declares are "a certain wisdom which we express among the spiritually mature. It is not a wisdom of this age, however, not of the rulers of this age, who are men headed for destruction. No, what we utter is God's wisdom: a mysterious, a hidden wisdom. God planned it before all ages for our glory" (1 Cor. 2:6–8).

### Holocaust

Holocaust is the first kind of sacrifice, the whole burnt-offering as used in the Hebrew law (Lev. 1, 3). According to the Old Law, the offering was consumed with none of it remaining to be eaten. When we speak of Christ as an offering or sacrifice, it is as a memory of His own sacrifice, done as He directed, and eaten as He wished, that we might share Himself as spiritual food.

### Holy Alliance

The treaty between Russia, Prussia, and Austria signed in 1815 was called the Holy Alliance. It was a nonaggression pact but religious in character since it introduced Christian morality into politics after years of political pragmatism. Unfortunately, it was later replaced by expedient alliances but served to point the way for future democratic negotiations.

### Holy Coat

Holy Coat is the name of the seamless tunic worn by Christ (Jn. 19:23) just prior to His crucifixion. There are claims to two such garments, one held at the Cathedral of Trier, Germany, and the other at Argenteuil, France. No determination of authenticity has been made by the Church. Both relics have been honored. That of Trier is alleged to have been given by St. Helena, based on the testimony of a sixth century tablet; the coat of Argenteuil is recorded in a document of the eleventh century. Claims are made that the coat at Trier is the outer garment and not the seamless one.

## Holy Communion

Holy Communion is the reception of the Body and Blood of Christ at the Communion of the Mass. (See Eucharist, Celebration of.) There are four ways of receiving Holy Communion: (1) under the one species of consecrated bread, usually in the form of a wafer; (2) by intinction, that is, by the dipping of the consecrated bread into the consecrated wine; (3) by receiving the consecrated bread and taking a drink (sip or mouthful) of the consecrated wine; (4) by taking a drink of the consecrated wine alone. The most usual method in the Roman Rite is the eating of the consecrated bread. (See Immensae Caritatis; Communion.)

## Holy Days

Known as holy days of obligation, these are the days on which it is required that members of the Catholic faith who have attained the age of reason rest from servile work and attend Holy Mass. The Apostolic See alone can declare, transfer, or abolish holy days of obligation for the universal Church (cc. 1244, 1247). Those established now are: all Sundays; the Solemnity of Christmas; the Solemnity of Mary, Mother of God (Jan. 1); Epiphany; Ascension; Corpus Christi; the Immaculate Conception; Assumption of the B.V.M.; St. Joseph; SS. Peter and Paul; and All Saints. By a special decree of the Sacred Congregation of Propaganda, Nov. 25, 1885, the feasts observed as holy days of obligation in the United States, besides Sundays are: the Solemnity of the Immaculate Conception (Dec. 8); Christmas (Dec. 25); Solemnity of Mary, Mother of God (Jan. 1); Solemnity of the Ascension; the Assumption of the Blessed Virgin Mary (Aug. 15); All Saints (Nov. 1).

In the Byzantine Rite there are five holy days of obligation: Feasts of Epiphany, the Ascension; SS. Peter and Paul; the Assumption of the Blessed Virgin Mary; and Christmas.

## Holy Family

The Holy Family includes Jesus, the Son of God, the Blessed Virgin Mary, His Mother, and St. Joseph, His foster father. The feast is celebrated on the Sunday after Christmas, or if there is no Sunday within the octave, it is celebrated on Dec. 30. In art it is customary to portray the Holy Family with Jesus as a baby or child, based upon the fact that St. Joseph died while Jesus was young.

## Holy Father

This title of reverence is accorded the pope as spiritual father of the universal Church. (See Pope.)

## Holy Ghost

See Holy Spirit; Trinity, the most Holy.

## Holy of Holies

This is the name, a fairly literal translation from the Hebrew word meaning "most holy," which is given to the innermost room of the Temple of Yahweh. It was the inner shrine or sanctuary of the Temple: "At the rear of the temple a space of twenty cubits was set off by cedar partitions from the floor to the rafters enclosing the sanctuary, the holy of holies" (1 Kg. 6:16). It was built in a square because this was considered the most pleasing form. Here the Ark of the Covenant was enthroned, resting on two carved cherubim. No one except the high priest was permitted to enter the Holy of Holies, and he could do so only on the Day of Atonement. (Cf. Hebrew Feasts.)

## Holy Hour

A holy hour is a devotion for one hour's duration consisting of exposition of the Blessed Sacrament, meditation, and vocal prayers, followed by Benediction. Custom and purpose determine the prayers to be recited as well as whether or not a sermon is to be preached. In March, 1933, the pope, by decree of the Sacred Penitentiary, granted a plenary indulgence to all who assist at the Holy Hour, with the usual requirements of confession, reception of Holy Communion, and prayer for the intention of the Holy Father (S.P., Mar. 21, 1933). A partial indulgence of ten years is granted to those who attend the Holy Hour with contrite hearts. (See Paraliturgical Actions.)

## Holy Name of Jesus

1. The name "Jesus" is the Latin spelling of the Greek, which derives from the Hebrew *Yesua*, the word meaning "Yahweh is Salvation." The name was given by God and declares the redemptive act of love, the salvation of man from sin through Jesus (Lk. 1:31).

2. The name of Jesus has been honored from apostolic times (Phil. 2:9–10). Celebration of a Feast of the Holy Name arose in the fifteenth

century and was extended to the universal Church in 1721. With the introduction of the new calendar of the Church, the feast of the Holy Name has been dropped from the list of the traditional feasts of our Lord.

### Holy Name Society

This association of Catholic laymen was founded by the Dominican preacher, Blessed John of Vercelli (d. 1283) at the command of Pope Gregory X, to combat the blasphemies and profanities rampant at the time. The society remains under the direction of the Dominicans. It is an archconfraternity of the Church, richly endowed with spiritual benefits. It is widely established in dioceses and parishes throughout the United States, for the purpose of promoting reverence for the name of Jesus and the spiritual progress of laymen by encouraging frequent reception of communion, the attendance at retreats, and other devotions. Its headquarters in the United States are located at 141 E. 65th St., New York, N.Y. 10021, and here also is the central office of the National Association of Holy Name Societies.

### Holy Office, Congregation of the

The most eminent of the Roman Congregations, this is now called Doctrine of the Faith Congregation and is entrusted with complete competence (c. 247) regarding all matters of faith and morals, the Pauline privilege, mixed marriages, the examination and condemnation of books or teachings contrary to faith or morals. It is also the tribunal for crimes brought to it for judgment, such as apostasy, heresy, schism, profanation of the Holy Eucharist, and certain cases of immorality. It functions under the greatest degree of secrecy because of the nature of its proceedings. The members of this Congregation are: a cardinal secretary assisted by five other cardinals, an assessor, a Dominican serving under the title of commissary who is assisted by two others. It is likewise assisted by twenty consultors, besides numerous specialists in theology and canon law, notaries, and secretaries. (See Congregation.)

### Holy Oils

Holy oils are sacramentals blessed by a bishop. The three types are: oil of catechumens, holy chrism, and oil of the sick. The first and last are pure olive oil, while chrism is olive oil mixed with a small quantity of balsam. The blessing takes place on Holy Thursday in the cathedral of the diocese. (Cf. Oil Stock.)

### Holy Orders

See Orders, Holy, Sacrament of.

### Holy Places

Holy Places are sites in Palestine (Israel) that are connected with the life of Christ, notably the Holy Sepulcher, Calvary, the Upper Room, the Way to Calvary, Gethsemani, the Church of the Assumption, the Sanctuary of the Ascension, and the place where the Temple of Jerusalem stood. Since the thirteenth century these were all in the care of the Friars Minor of the Franciscan Order; the Sanctuary and Temple sites are now Moslem shrines.

### Holy Roman Empire

Begun by the German ruler Otto I (d. 973), the Holy Roman Empire was a union to bring imperialism and feudalism together. It did not succeed in this intent but later effected a tie between Church and state. At its founding it was not called "Holy Roman Empire"; the word "holy" was used for the first time during the reign of Frederick I (d. 1190). Substantially an extension of the empire established earlier by Charlemagne in the West, it was an intended bond between rulers whereby the states involved through concerted action could serve as temporal protectors of the Church. As such it failed, bringing frequent clashes between the Church and sovereigns. The imperial crown was conferred on one of the member rulers by election, thus making the emperor nominal head of the others. Dante, the Italian poet, in the fourteenth century called for the restoration of the Empire, thinking this would solve the ills besetting Italy and Europe, but his writing "Concerning Monarchy" was the last voice to support the idea and the concept faded. The Holy Roman Empire was abolished by Napoleon I in 1806.

### Holy Saturday

The Saturday of Holy Week is called Holy Saturday. (See Holy Week, Liturgy of.)

### Holy See

The Holy See is the composite of authority, jurisdiction, and sovereignty vested in and exercised by the pope and his governing groups in the spiritual and temporal governance and guidance of the universal Church. It is located in Rome, chiefly in the Vatican State. The pope as the sovereign pontiff is the visible head of the Church, the mystical body of Christ. He is the infallible guide of the spiritual welfare of the Church, and in him is recognized, by the clergy and faithful, the fullness of jurisdiction in governing the body of the Church. He governs with the authority and power of Peter, the leader of the Apostles. The nature and extent of the governmental functions of the Church demand that the pope have aides and assisting groups. Thus under the direction of the pope the various functions are carried out by the Sacred Congregations, three tribunals, five offices, six commissions (cc. 242-244). From the pope and these varied groups there is a transmission of either jurisdiction or orders to the bishops, vicars, and prefects apostolic, mission superiors, and superiors of religious communities, and through these to diocesan synods and provincial and plenary councils, and then to the clergy and faithful. Also serving, not as intermediaries but as convenient representatives, are a number of nuncios and apostolic delegates. The Holy See is also called the Apostolic See. (Cf. Papacy; Vatican State, City of; Congregation.)

### Holy Sepulcher

This was the burial place of the body of Jesus after His crucifixion. It belonged to Joseph of Arimathea, and tradition locates it in a garden very near the place of crucifixion (cf. Jn. 19:41). The Church of the Holy Sepulcher is now located on what is probably the exact spot of the death and burial of Christ.

The sepulcher was a new tomb and was fronted or sealed with a heavy circular stone (Mk. 16:4) that could be moved to the side along a trackway. The entry was low (Lk. 24:12) and led into a small vestibule that opened into the burial chamber. There was most likely a rock ledge or *arcosolium* cut into the side of this inner chamber, and here the body was placed parallel with the inner wall.

### Holy Sepulcher, Knights of the

This papal order of knights was first approved in 1113. There are three classes of the order with varying insignia: Grand Cross Knights, Commanders, and Knights. The insignia may be conferred on women, who wear it on the left side and whose titles are Dames or Matrons of the Holy Sepulcher. (See Honors and Awards.)

### Holy Souls

Holy Souls is the name for the souls of the dead who died in the grace of God but are detained in purgatory to make satisfaction for temporal punishment resulting from sins. Their release into heaven may be obtained by prayer and works of suffrage on the part of the living faithful, and such prayers are a work of charity. The feast of All Souls is celebrated on Nov. 2, except when that date falls on a Sunday, in which event it is Nov. 3. (Cf. Purgatory; Church Militant, Suffering, Triumphant.)

### Holy Spirit

The Holy Spirit is the Paraclete, the third Person of the Blessed Trinity. In the OT the Holy Spirit means a divine active power through whom God Himself is active in man, the universe, history, and nature (Jb. 12:9–10; Ps. 104:30; Ez. 37:9–14). And in the NT the Holy Spirit leads and guides all: Acts 2:1–11; 13:2. He is called the "Spirit of Grace" (Heb. 10:29). He is the Holy Spirit and the Eternal Spirit (Heb. 2:4) and is referred to as the "Love of God personified." He is consubstantial with the Father and the Son from both of whom He proceeds as from a co-principle. The redemption of men through Christ is completed by Christ's sending of the Holy Spirit from the Father (Acts 1:8). As a Person, the Holy Spirit is distinct from Divine Essence or the other Persons of the Blessed Trinity (1 Cor. 2:10; 12:4). Through the Holy Spirit, Christian life flows to men from the Trinity; through Him the love of God enters our hearts (Gal. 4:6); in Him all are baptized to make one body in Christ (1 Cor. 12:13); He dwells in us as in a temple, giving us life in Christ (1 Cor. 3:16); through Him we know the deep things of God (Jn. 16:3; 1 Cor. 2:4–5). The Holy Spirit, by His work, gives life to the Church. He was sent as the necessary condition for the founding of the Church, the One who is the Spirit of Truth and the One leading toward truth (Jn. 16:5–15). Opposition to the Holy Spirit on the part of men is called the unforgiveable sin: Mt. 12:31–32; Lk. 12:10; Mk. 3:29–30. (Cf. Trinity, the Most Holy.)

Vatican II teaches widely concerning the Holy Spirit in the Church, the gifts of the Spirit, and the operations of the Spirit through members of the Church. "Now, the gifts of the Spirit are diverse. He calls some to give clear witness to the desire for a heavenly home and to keep that desire green among the human family. He summons others to dedicate themselves to the earthly service of men and to make ready the material of the celestial realm by this ministry of theirs. Yet He frees all of them so that by putting aside love of self and bringing all earthly resources into the service of human life they can devote themselves to that future when humanity itself will become an offering accepted by God" (GS 38).

And: "For the exercise of this apostolate, the Holy Spirit who sanctifies the People of God through the ministry and the sacraments gives to the faithful special gifts as well (cf. 1 Cor. 12:7), 'distributing them to each as he wills' (1 Cor. 12:11). Thus may the individual, 'according to the gift that each has received, administer it to one another' and become 'generous distributors of God's manifold grace' (1 Pt. 4:10), and build up thereby the whole body in charity (cf. Eph. 4:16). From the reception of these charismata or gifts, including those which are less dramatic, there arise for each believer the right and duty to use them in the Church and in the world for the good of mankind and for the upbuilding of the Church. In so doing, believers need to enjoy the freedom of the Holy Spirit who breathes 'where He will' (Jn. 3:8). At the same time, they must act in communion with their brothers in Christ, especially with their pastors. The latter must make a judgment about the true nature and proper use of these gifts, not in order to extinguish the Spirit, but to test all things and hold fast to what is good (cf. 1 Thes. 5:19–21)" (AA 3). (See Stewardship.)

And: "The Holy Spirit, who calls all men to Christ by the seeds of the word and by the preaching of the gospel, stirs up in their hearts the obedience of faith. When in the womb of the baptismal font He begets to a new life those who believe in Christ, He gathers them into the one People of God which is 'a chosen race, a royal priesthood, a holy nation, a people he claims for his own' (1 Pt. 2:9)" (AG 15).

And the Holy Spirit is active in the very sources of faith and the Church: "Sacred Scripture is the word of God inasmuch as it is consigned to writing under the inspiration of the divine spirit. To the successors of the apostles, sacred tradition hands on in its full purity God's word, which was entrusted to the apostles by Christ the Lord and the Holy Spirit. Thus, led by the light of the Spirit of truth, these successors can in their preaching preserve this word of God faithfully, explain it, and make it more widely known. Consequently, it is not from sacred Scripture alone that the Church draws her certainty about everything which has been revealed. Therefore both sacred tradition and sacred scripture are to be accepted and venerated with the same sense of devotion and reverence.

"Sacred tradition and sacred Scripture form one sacred deposit of the word of God, which is committed to the Church. Holding fast to this deposit, the entire holy people united with their shepherds remain always steadfast in the teaching of the apostles, in the common life, in the breaking of the bread, and in prayers (cf. Acts 2:42), so that

in holding to, practicing, and professing the heritage of the faith, there results on the part of the bishops and the faithful a remarkable common effort" (DV 9, 10). (See Gifts of the Holy Spirit, the Seven.)

## Holy Spirit, Sins Against

Because of the dignity and honor due the person of the Holy Spirit and because of the esteem in which all Christians must hold the Holy Spirit as the One sent by God to be our special aid, there are grave sins that should be avoided if one is to come to salvation. Among these are: (1) the loss of hope or despair of salvation; (2) presumption upon the mercy of God or the belief that one is saved without effort; (3) the denial or impugning of the truths of faith; (4) envy of another's spiritual progress or good; (5) the obstinacy in sin that follows from a complete lack of penitence; (6) final impenitence, which is the persistence to the close of one's life without sorrow or penitential advertence to the goodness of God. All of these sins demonstrate a personal resistance to grace and the forgiveness of sins.

## Holy Thursday

Holy Thursday is the Thursday of Holy Week, also called Maundy Thursday. (See Holy Week, Liturgy of.)

## Holy Water

Water, blessed by a priest, thereby becomes a sacramental, used by the faithful to invoke God's blessing. There are four kinds of holy water, distinguished chiefly by their use: (1) ordinary holy water, blessed with a small mixture of salt as a preservative, and used at the Asperges, blessings, and in fonts other than baptismal; (2) baptismal water, blessed with a slight mixture of chrism and oil of catechumens and used in the administration of baptism; (3) water of consecration, sometimes called Gregorian water; and (4) Easter water.

## Holy Water Font

This font is an open container for holy water. When placed at the entrance of a church, it is sometimes called a stoup. (cf. Baptismal Font.)

## Holy Week, Liturgy of

Holy Week precedes the feast of Easter, beginning with Passion (Palm) Sunday and ending with Holy Saturday. The liturgy of the week commemorates the apprehension, suffering, and death of Christ.

On Passion Sunday the Church celebrates

Christ's entrance into Jerusalem to accomplish his pascal mystery. Accordingly, the memorial of this event is included in every Mass, with the procession or the solemn entrance before the principal Mass, and the simple entrance before the other Masses. The solemn entrance (but not the procession) may be repeated before a Mass that is usually well attended.

On Holy Thursday (Maundy Thursday), the liturgy calls for a Chrism Mass. This Mass, which the bishop concelebrates with his presbyterium and at which the oils are blessed, manifests the communion of the priests with their bishop. It is thus desirable that, if possible, all the priests take part in it and receive communion under both species. To show the unity of the presbyterium, the priests who concelebrate with the bishop should come from different parts of the diocese.

In his homily the bishop should urge the priests to be faithful in fulfilling their office in the Church and should invite them to renew publicly their priestly promises. The profession of faith and general intercessions are omitted.

Holy Thursday is also the beginning of the Easter triduum. According to the Church's ancient tradition, all Masses without a congregation are prohibited on this day. The Mass of the Lord's Supper is celebrated in the evening, at a convenient hour, with the full participation of the whole local community and with all the priests and clergy exercising their ministry. Priests who have already celebrated the chrism Mass or a Mass for the convenience of the faithful may concelebrate again at the evening Mass. Holy Communion may be given to the faithful only during Mass but may be brought to the sick at any hour of the day. The tabernacle should be entirely empty; a sufficient amount of bread should be consecrated at this Mass for the communion of the clergy and laity for both Holy Thursday and Good Friday. After the homily, depending upon pastoral circumstances, the washing of the feet follows. Following the postcommunion prayer, the Holy Eucharist is transferred in procession to a place of reposition, a side chapel, or a place suitably decorated for the occasion; here the priest puts incense into the thurible and kneeling, incenses the Blessed Sacrament, while the Tantum Ergo is sung. The tabernacle of reposition is then closed. After a period of silent adoration, the priest and ministers genuflect and return to the sacristy. Then the altar is stripped and, if possible, the crosses are removed from the church. It is desirable to cover any crosses that remain in the church. Vespers are not said by those who participate in the evening Mass. The faithful should be encouraged to continue adoration before the Blessed Sacrament for a suitable period of time during the night, according to local circumstances, but there should be no solemn adoration after midnight.

For the Good Friday celebration of the Lord's Passion, see Friday, Good, Liturgy of; Easter Season Liturgy.

**Holy Year**

Also called Jubilee Year, a Holy Year is one proclaimed by the Holy See. A plenary indulgence is granted to all who during this time visit Rome, the tombs of the Apostles and the See of Peter, or who fulfill special requirements. It has been the custom to declare a Holy Year every 25 years since 1475. The background of the custom is found in the Jewish Law (Lv. 25:8–19). (Cf. Jubilee.)

**Homiletics**

The study whereby one learns the composition of sermons and the effective means of preaching them is called homilectics.

**Homily**

A homily is a more or less brief, instructive discourse on a passage of Scripture wherein the spiritual lesson of the scriptural text is made clear, especially the readings assigned to the Sundays or days of obligation. It is generally to be instructive, informal, and intelligent, since it is a basic form of the preaching art.

Concerning this form of teaching procedures, Vatican II teaches: "By means of the homily the mysteries of the faith and the guiding principles of the Christian life are expounded from the sacred text during the course of the liturgical year. The homily, therefore, is to be highly esteemed as part of the liturgy itself; in fact, at those Masses which are celebrated with the assistance of the people on Sundays and feasts of obligation, it should not be omitted except for a serious reason" (SC 52).

**Homoeans**

See Acacianism.

**Homoousian**

Homoousian is a term derived from the Greek, accepted by the Council of Nicaea in 325 and incorporated into the Nicene creed. Literally "consubstantial," it expresses the substantial unity of the Son and the Father. The term was given as the definitive answer to the Arian and semi-Arian heresies by the teaching authority of the Church based on the tradition of essential unity. (Cf. Consubstantial.)

## Honors and Awards

Because of its interest in personal attainment in all fields of endeavor and because of its extensive organizational and institutional structure the Church gives a series of honors and awards to many worthy recipients, some for life, and others annually. The outstanding honors and awards are listed here with the realization that many are given by other countries and institutions for similar attainments.

*Pontifical Orders.* The Papal Orders of Knighthood are secular orders of merit; membership depends entirely upon the Pope and is granted upon request of a bishop or religious superior through the Secretariat of Briefs, a branch of the Papal Secretariat of State.

These are: (1) Supreme Order of Christ (Militia of Our Lord Jesus Christ), (2) Order of the Golden Spur (Golden Militia), (3) Order of Pius IX, (4) Order of St. Gregory the Great, (5) Order of St. Sylvester.

*Ecclesiastical Orders.* (1) Order of the Holy Sepulcher, (2) Knights of Malta.

*Papal Medals.* (1) Pro Ecclesia et Pontifice (For the Church and the Pontiff); (2) Benemerenti (several medals) "To a well-deserving person."

*American Catholic Awards:* Listed alphabetically these are:

1. *Aquinas Medal,* by the American Catholic Philosophical Association for outstanding contributions to the field of Catholic Philosophy.

2. *Bellarmine Medal,* by Bellarmine College, Louisville, Kentucky, for service in national and international affairs to those who exemplify characteristics of St. Robert Bellarmine in charity, justice, and temperateness.

3. *Borromeo Award,* by Carroll College, Helena, Montana, for zeal, courage, and devotion in the spirit of St. Charles Borromeo.

4. *Campion Award,* by the Catholic Book Club for distinguished service in Catholic letters.

5. *Cardinal Gibbons Medal,* by the Alumni Association of the Catholic University of America for distinguished and meritorious service to the Church, the United States, or the Catholic University.

6. *Cardinal Spellman Award,* by the Catholic Theological Society for outstanding achievement in the field of theology.

7. *Catholic Action Award,* by St. Bonaventure University, Allegheny, New York.

8. *Catholic Press Association Award,* by the

Catholic Press Association for distinguished contribution to Catholic journalism.

9. *Cecilia Medal,* by the Music Department of Boys Town, Nebraska, for outstanding work in liturgical music.

10. *Christian Culture Award,* by Assumption University of Canada, to outstanding exponents of Christian ideals.

11. *Christian Wisdom Award,* by Loyola University of Chicago, to outstanding American or European theologians.

12. *CIP Award,* by the Catholic Alliance for Communications for service in the communications media.

13. *Collegian Award,* by *The Collegian,* a weekly student newspaper of La Salle College, Philadelphia, for public service in the field of communications.

14. *Damien-Dutton Award,* by the Damien-Dutton Society for service toward conquering leprosy or for the promotion of better understanding of social problems connected with the disease.

15. *Dinneen Award,* by the National Theatre Arts Conference.

16. *Edith Stein Award,* by the Edith Stein Guild for service toward better understanding between Christians and Jews.

17. *Emmanuel D'Alzon Medal,* by Assumptionists to persons exemplifying the ideals of their founder.

18. *Father McKenna Award,* by the national headquarters of the Holy Name Society for outstanding service to the society's ideals.

19. *Franciscan International Award,* by the Conventual Franciscans of Prior Lake, Minnesota, for outstanding contributions to the American way of life.

20. *Good Samaritan Award,* by the National Catholic Development Conference to recognize the concern for one's fellowman exemplified by the Good Samaritan.

21. *Hoey Awards,* by the Catholic Interracial Council of New York for the promotion of interracial justice.

22. *Honor et Veritas Award,* by the Catholic War Veterans to outstanding Americans.

23. *Insignis Medal,* by Fordham University of New York City for extraordinary distinction in the service of God through excellence in professional performance.

24. *John Courtney Murray Award,* by the Catholic Theological Society for distinguished achievement in theology.

25. *John Gilmary Shea Prize,* by the American Catholic Historical Association for scholarly works

on the history of the Catholic Church, broadly considered.

26. *John La Farge Memorial Award for Interracial Justice,* by the Catholic Interracial Council of New York City.

27. *Laetare Medal,* by the University of Notre Dame for distinguished accomplishment for Church or nation by an American Catholic.

28. *Magnificat Medal* by Mundelein College, Chicago, to Catholic college alumnae for leadership in social action.

29. *Marian Library Medal,* by the Marian Library of the University of Dayton for books in English on the Blessed Virgin Mary; beginning in 1971, the medal is awarded every four years at the time of the International Mariological Congress to a scholar for Mariological studies.

30. *Marianist Award,* by the University of Dayton, Ohio, for outstanding contributions to Mariology, until 1966, and for outstanding contributions to mankind since 1967.

31. *Mater et Magistra Award,* by the College of Mt. St. Joseph on the Ohio River, to women for social action in the pattern and spirit of the encyclical *Mater et Magistra.*

32. *Mendel Medal* by Villanova University for scientists.

33. *Msgr. John P. Monaghan Social Action Award,* by the Association of Catholic Trade Unionists.

34. *Peace Award,* by the Third Order Secular of St. Francis.

35. *Peter Guilday Prize,* by the American Catholic Historical Association.

36. *Pius XII Marian Award,* by the Montfort Fathers for promotion of the devotion of consecration to the Immaculate Heart of Mary.

37. *Poverello Medal,* by the College of Steubenville, Ohio, in recognition of great benefactions to humanity, exemplifying in our age the Christlike spirit of charity that filled the life of St. Francis of Assisi.

38. *Regina Medal,* by the Catholic Library Association for outstanding contributions to children's literature.

39. *Rerum Novarum Award,* by St. Peter's College, Jersey City, New Jersey, for outstanding work in the interests of industrial peace.

40. *Richard Reid Memorial Award,* by the Catholic Institute of the Press (the Catholic Alliance for Communications) in memory of its founder.

41. *The Saint De La Salle Medal,* by Manhattan College for significant contribution to the moral, cultural, or educational life of the nation.

42. *St. Francis Xavier Medal,* by Xavier University of Cincinnati, to persons exemplifying the spirit of St. Francis Xavier.

43. *St. Vincent de Paul Medal,* by St. John's University of Jamaica, New York, for outstanding service to Catholic charities.

44. *Serra Award of the Americas,* by the Academy of American Franciscan History for service to Inter-American good will.

45. *Signum Fidei Medal,* by the Alumni Association of La Salle College, Philadelphia, for contribution to the advancement of Christian principles.

46. *Soteriological Award,* by the Confraternity of the Passion, Union City, New Jersey, for outstanding exemplification of sharing in the Passion of Christ in contemporary society.

47. *Stella Maris Medal,* by Mary Manse College of Toledo, Ohio, for service.

48. *Thomas More Association Medal,* by the Thomas More Association, Chicago, for distinguished contributions to Catholic literature during the year.

49. *Vercelli Medal,* by the Holy Name Society for distinguished service to ideals of the society.

*CPA Awards* are given annually to outstanding magazine, newspaper, and books during a given year.

*Christopher Awards* are presented annually for outstanding books for adults and for young people, for motion pictures, and for television specials.

*Gabriel Awards* are presented annually for excellence in radio, television, broadcasting by UNDA-USA, the Catholic fraternal association for broadcasters and allied communicators.

## Hood

The hood is a cone-shaped headdress attached to a religious habit at the back of the neck. A remnant of the hood as a liturgical and clerical headdress is found in that small cowl-shaped cloth attached to the mozzetta of a bishop; it is now sometimes used in the design of modern vestments as a vestigial of the cowl, symbol of humility.

## Hope

One of the three theological virtues, hope is a supernatural, infused virtue that moves the will to trust in eternal happiness and the all-good God and gives the assurance that the necessary graces to merit eternal life will be ours. Hope is necessary for salvation since, joined to faith, our knowledge and belief in God, and charity, our love of God, it supplies the inducement to exercise our faith and love. It is a positive exercise toward salvation and a negative one in the sense that we fear the loss of heaven. Hope is infused in the soul with sanctifying grace and is a longing given by the Spirit of Grace, the Holy Spirit, for His indwelling within us. From the Holy Spirit comes the encouragement to prevent even the thought of possible loss from weakening us in our exercise of hope (Rom. 8:1–39). (Cf. Theological Virtues; Holy Spirit, Sins Against.)

Vatican II teaches: "Only by the light of faith and by meditation on the word of God can one always and everywhere recognize God in whom 'we live and move and have our being' (Acts 17:28), seek His will in every event, see Christ in all men whether they be close to us or strangers, and make correct judgments about the true meaning and value of temporal things, both in themselves and in their relation to man's final goal.

"They who have this faith live in the hope of what will be revealed to the sons of God and bear in mind the cross and resurrection of the Lord" (AA 4).

And: The Christian man, conformed to the likeness of that Son who is the firstborn of many brothers, receives 'the first-fruits' of the Spirit (Rom. 8:23) by which he becomes capable of discharging the new law of love. Through this Spirit, who is 'the pledge of our inheritance' (Eph. 1:14), the whole man is renewed from within, even the achievement of 'the redemption of our bodies' (Rom. 8:23). 'If the Spirit of him who raised Jesus from the dead dwells in you, then he who raised Christ from the dead will bring your mortal bodies to life also, through his Spirit dwelling in you' (Rom. 8:11).

"Pressing upon the Christian, to be sure, is the need and the duty to battle against evil through manifold tribulations and even to suffer death. But, linked with the paschal mystery and patterned on the dying Christ, he will hasten forward to resurrection in the strength which comes from hope" (GS 22).

In the theological virtues we have a threefold strength: faith and hope are the two inseparable moments of one action, with love the joining force at the center. Without hope faith is weakened or disappears, and love (charity) is blocked from seeking God in the eschatological sense of being "one with Him" who is all Love. (See Salvation History.)

## Horologion

This liturgical book contains the divine office, hymns and prayers, and ecclesiastical calendar of the Byzantine rite.

## Hosanna

Hosanna is a word from the Hebrew, meaning "Do save!" (Ps. 118:25). The expression came to mean a cry of acclamation and it was used in the salutation given Christ when He entered Jerusalem in triumph (Mk. 11:10).

## Hosea, Book of

In some translations the name of this book is Osee. The name of the author, Hosea, comes from the Hebrew, a variant word meaning "Yahweh is salvation." Hosea belonged to the Northern Kingdom of the Israelites. He lived in the eighth century before Christ, and he is one of the minor prophets. There are two major themes in the Book of Hosea: (1) the marriage of the prophet and its lesson and meaning; (2) the guilt of Israel because of its idolatrous ways.

In examining these themes we find emphasized the use of the biblical "marriage" image between God and His people. This is basically the manner of expressing the covenant God made with His people—God offered His love to a bride—humanity, a daring image that broke the previous tradition (Hos. 1 and 2) (cf. Song of Songs; Ps. 45). This image is carried on throughout the Scriptures (cf. Jn. 3:29), and through Christ the Church becomes the bride (1 Cor. 11:1–3), and Christ has prepared an everlasting marriage (Rv. 19:6–8).

And the punishment that was to be Israel's for breaking the covenant of God was spoken of by the prophets many times (Is. 51:17–23; Jer. 25:15–29) as well as by the prophet Hosea in chapter 13 of his book.

## Hospitallers

1. Name given to religious of either sex who follow the rule of St. Augustine and are devoted to service of the sick.

2. Women of the Middle Ages who formed an auxiliary group to aid the military orders in caring for the sick.

3. Hospitallers of St. John of Jerusalem, members of a powerful military order founded in 1092 to care for the poor and strangers in the Holy Land, notably Jerusalem. They fell into decadence in the sixteenth century.

## Host

The host is unleavened bread, the consecrated species of bread used in the Mass, Benediction of the Blessed Sacrament, and Holy Communion. It is made of white or whole wheat flour. For practical use the hosts are round thin wafers rather than fragments of a larger loaf of baked bread. (Cf. Altar Breads.)

## Hours, Canonical

See Canonical Hours; Liturgy of the Hours.

## House of Prayer Experience

The purpose of this movement (HOPE) is to aid active members of religious communities, priests, and lay persons to acquire a modern style of contemplative prayer life for personal renewal, inner spiritual growth, and a more joyful personal and communal life in the light of the Gospel. The starting point of one's participation in the movement is an individual commitment over an extended period of time, lasting several weeks or years, during which time concentration on intensive prayer with a community is carried on—hence the title, "House of Prayer Experience."

The desired result is the development of a style of prayer and contemplation that will be taken by the individual and continued until it becomes integrated with one's style of life and action and thus permeates religion and life.

HOPE is essentially a movement of the Spirit. It was first carried out by a group of apostolic religious women who were forced by ever increasing apostolic demands to seek a deeper prayer life. In meeting this need Bernard Haring, C.SS.R. recommended that at least one house of an active congregation have prayer as its essential service, adopting a life-style determined by the needs of prayer rather than the demands of apostolic work. He took the name from the words of Isaiah: "Them I will bring to my holy mountain and make joyful in my house of prayer" (Is. 56:7). This concept was first proposed at the annual meeting of the Conference of Major Superiors of Women Religious in 1965. It was offered as an instrument for renewal in depth.

In 1968, the Immaculate Heart of Mary Sisters, Monroe, Michigan organized a center to clear ideas, and a planning conference was scheduled. At this four-day meeting 96 congregations of Sisters from the United States and Canada formulated the first rationale of a House of Prayer.

The spread of the movement to other communities and congregations has taken place with emphasis upon the following objectives: (1) Prayer is basic to integrating religion with life; (2) long-standing prayer forms and practices were not adequate to achieve a prayer-life among religious, priests, and laity in the mobile, fast-paced life of modern living, hence; (3) new forms of prayer, in

particular a contemplative approach that would fit into modern living, were sought; (4) programs are flexible rather than rigid and include the liturgy, meditation, reading of the scriptures, exposition and discussion, shared prayer in the life of the community, silence and solitude, and new forms of prayer and adaptations of the traditional or older forms of prayer—all to achieve an interpersonal relationship and experience. (See Charismatic Renewal, Catholic; Pentecostalism, Catholic; Mysticism.)

## Huguenots

This term, derived from the German word for "confederates," became the title for the French Protestants of the sixteenth and seventeenth centuries who followed Calvin. This broad title for French Protestants, who until the French Revolution were officially referred to as "the so-called Reformed Church," is now reduced to simply "Reformed."

The road of the Huguenots has not been an easy one. Their religious ideas, patterned after Luther and developed by Calvin and Lefevre d'Etaples, were attacked by the theologians of the University of Paris, and this brought about pressure from the State. Under Kings Francis I and his son Henry II, from 1539 to 1559, courts had inquisitorial power and trials were vigorously prosecuted in the court called *chambre ardente* ("burning chamber").

In their reforms, forty articles based on Calvin's *Institutes,* the Bible was declared the sole rule of faith necessary for salvation, a doctrine of predestination was affirmed, and only Baptism and the Lord's Supper were retained, but these were not recognized as sacraments giving grace to the recipient.

Having finally gained recognition, the Huguenots were not content with toleration but meted out suppression to Catholics wherever they could gain political power. More adversity followed for the Reformed Church under Catherine de Medici, and the national solution was gained at the Edict of Nantes in 1598, only to have Louis XIV wage open war on French Protestants; since 1685 Protestants have been a minority in France.

## Human Acts

That act which is performed with free knowledge and consent is empirically called human. Since man is a rational creature, having intellect and will, his actions proceed from these as moral responses to personal needs (autonomous) and as those that he directs to society (heteronomous).

Not all of man's actions are human, since those over which his faculties exercise no control (such as digestion, respiration, or reflexes) are instinctive or spontaneous. Those acts not done purposefully are not called human acts but acts of man.

Through human acts man progresses toward his destiny, and the prerequisite is that these actions be recognized as good or bad. Although the human act is a complex operation involving the intellect, the will, and the physical ability to perform the act, there is a transcendental quality to human acts whereby man acknowledges the norm of morality (moral law) and relates his act to the norm. It thus has a goal or purpose conforming to the will of God, whether it is erroneous because of limitation, or imperfect because it is abstract, the process of human activity draws man toward his eternal goal of perfect happiness with God.

Vatican II speaks of the value of human activity: "For man, created to God's image, received a mandate to subject to himself the earth and all that it contains, and to govern the world with justice and holiness; a mandate to relate himself and the totality of things to Him who was to be acknowledged as the Lord and Creator of all. Thus, by the subjection of all things to man, the name of God would be wonderful in all the earth.

"This mandate concerns even the most ordinary everyday activities. For while providing the substance of life for themselves and their families, men and women are performing their activities in a way which appropriately benefits society. They can justly consider that by their labor they are unfolding the Creator's work, consulting the advantages of their brother men, and contributing by their personal industry to the realization in history of the divine plan" (GS 34). (See Social Encyclicals.)

## Human Development Campaign

See Campaign for Human Development.

## Human Dignity

This dignity means the worth inherent in man, a value that man has, granting him special consideration and treatment because he is different from the irrational creatures. While this concept is based upon the ideas about man from Jewish, Greek, and Roman thought and the natural law, for the Catholic there is a special character derived from the teachings of Jesus Christ. This is manifest through the continual application of Christ's teachings to the changing conditions of human history and society.

Vatican II declares regarding an awareness of

this dignity in social action: "The freedom and dignity of the person being helped should be respected with the utmost delicacy, and the purity of one's charitable intentions should not be stained by a quest for personal advantage or by any thirst for domination. The demands of justice should first be satisfied, lest the giving of what is due in justice be represented as the offering of a charitable gift. Not only the effects but also the causes of various ills must be removed. Help should be given in such a way that the recipients may gradually be freed from dependence on others and become self-sufficient" (AA 8).

And: "In the depths of his conscience, man detects a law which he does not impose upon himself, but which holds him to obedience. Always summoning him to love good and avoid evil, the voice of conscience can when necessary speak to his heart more specifically: do this, shun that. For man has in his heart a law written by God. To obey it is the very dignity of man; according to it he will be judged" (GS 16).

And: "The possibility now exists of liberating most men from the misery of ignorance. Hence it is a duty most befitting our times that men, especially Christians, should work strenuously on behalf of certain decisions which must be made in the economic and political fields, both nationally and internationally. By these decisions universal recognition and implementation should be given to the right of all men to a human and civic culture favorable to personal dignity and free from any discrimination on the grounds of race, sex, nationality, religious or social conditions" (GS 60).

## Human Life Foundation

In 1968, in response to Pope Paul VI's appeal for some organized insight into the scientific research to improve methods of child spacing in keeping with the teachings of his encyclical *Humanae Vitae,* the Bishops of the United States established the Human Life Foundation. They provided an initial grant of $800,000 as a source to meet the organizational needs, and the foundation was put into operation in 1969. It is nonprofit, tax-exempt, independent, and self-governing, operating with a board of twelve directors, all of whom are secular scientists.

The foundation's sponsored research is performed in the strictest manner, aided by many independent scientists and research institutions, and they have verified the validity and reliability of natural methods of birth regulation as opposed to chemical or mechanical methods and devices. The present headquarters are at 1776 K Street, N.W., Washington, D.C. 20006.

## Humane Vitae

The Latin words "of Human Life" form the title of the encyclical of Pope Paul VI, issued July 29, 1968, concerning the Church's teaching on marriage and issues related to marriage. In substance the encyclical follows the traditional teachings formulated by Vatican Council II.

There were reactions against the encyclical offered by theologians of Belgium, France, and Austria on the grounds that it impeded the free exercise of personal conscience, that the natural law concepts were rigorously interpreted, the thesis of totality was too evident, and they offered the presentation of the contrary concept that contraception may in some cases be the lesser of two evils. However, all agreed that conscientious objection could not be taken without grave reasons and reflection on all conditions and future consequences. The Bishops of Australia stated their support of the encyclical in 1974 but urged that priests show understanding toward all those Catholics who find the teachings difficult to accept. They further said that a Catholic, who in good conscience, finds himself at variance with the encyclical's teaching "would certainly not have cut himself off from the Church."

Pope Paul VI did not alter the teaching nor lessen its binding force.

## Humani Generis

The Latin words that form the title of the encyclical of Pope Pius XII issued Aug. 12, 1950, mean "the Human Race." Its full English title is: *Warnings against Attempts to Distort Catholic Truths.* It is a basic document presenting the integrity of Catholic teachings and declaring the role of the Church in presenting those teachings. It declares among other statements: "Nor must it be thought that what is contained in encyclical letters does not of itself demand assent, on the pretext that the popes do not exercise in them the supreme power of their teaching authority. Rather, such teachings belong to the ordinary magisterium, of which it is true to say: 'He who hears you, hears me' (Lk. 10:16); for the most part, too, what is expounded and inculcated in encyclical letters already appertains to Catholic doctrine for other reasons." (See Magisterium of the Church.)

## Humanism

1. Any theory or movement in which interest in human welfare is central.

2. Historically, the term applies to that movement of the fourteenth to the sixteenth centuries, which sprang from the Renaissance and aimed at placing all learning, literary and scientific, on a basis of classical antiquity as opposed to learning based on both classical and Christian principles.

3. Humanism has taken several forms: as an ethical movement beginning with Auguste Comte's work, which developed into "humanitarianism"; as a philosophical movement, which developed into pragmatism; as a literary cult, which rebelled against vocational education; as a sociological endeavor, which attempted to make abstract ideals the basis of social action; as a religious movement of the twentieth century, which sought to subordinate "faith in God" to a social consciousness. This latter was the product of left-wing Unitarians who in 1933 published "The Humanist Manifesto."

Marxist humanism, developed under the radical followers of Hegel, is the complete realization of man's possibilities fused with the political economy. Karl Marx believed that man is his own creator because objective reality is actually the product of human labor. This has developed into social policy governing production, political thought, society, and religion. In modern times it has further come to a "second enlightenment," which rejects any social goals through a planned self-alienation in society.

The error of humanism, amid its many philosophical aspects, is that it neglects Christian revelation, ignores the necessity for Christ's Second coming, and makes man serve only his own purposes. It denies God in the areas of life where God is most needed, as Vatican II states: "Unlike former days, the denial of God or of religion, or the abandonment of them, is no longer an unusual and individual occurrence. For today it is not rare for such decisions to be presented as requirements of scientific progress or of a certain new humanism" (GS 7). Thus humanism has become a possessor of man's efforts and the goal of his attainments.

## Humanitarianism

1. A social philosophy that mistakenly places the natural good of the human race above the revealed will of God. It may be idealistic, altruistic, or moral and may center on the lesser animals of God's creation.

2. The so-called positivism of Auguste Comte's philosophy of humanism. (Cf. Humanism.)

## Humeral Veil

A scarf, about 8 to 9 feet long and 21 to 36 inches wide, the humeral veil is worn over the shoulders of the priest at Benediction of the Blessed Sacrament, in Eucharistic processions, and by the deacon at liturgical ceremonies. The humeral veil is usually made of silk, and white or golden in color, and may be highly decorated.

## Humiliati

Literally, "the humble ones," the Humiliati were members of a pious association who espoused a penitential way of life. The group was wealthy and suffered pride and consequent suppression by Pope Pius V in 1571.

## Humility

Humility is a supernatural virtue whereby one is enabled to make a true and just estimate of himself and is inclined to hold himself and his accomplishments in contempt in recognition that all good arises from God alone. It is said that "dependence on God gives wings to prayer" (cf. Sir. 35:16–18). St. Ignatius terms it a relinquishment of "self-will, self-love, and self-interest." It is positive in not seeking honors and the esteem of others, and self-condemning because man knows evil is his own doing. Humility is exercised toward God and neighbors: toward God who as the Creator gives man whatever he possesses, and toward one's neighbors by recognizing their worth in the eyes of God. This virtue is the opposite of pride, which is the root of all evil; hence humility is basic to the practice of all the virtues. It is the fundamental of prayer, notably the prayer of simplicity, for Christ rewarded the Syro-phoenician woman for her humility (Mk. 7:26–30); it is likewise to be found in Christ's example (Phil. 2:1–11). (Cf. Pride; Virtue.)

Vatican II teaches: "We should pray to the divine Spirit for the grace to be genuinely self-denying, humble, gentle in the service of others, and to have an attitude of brotherly generosity toward them" (CD 7).

## Hussites

See Heresies.

## Hylics

Hylics were an offshoot of the Gnostic heresy; the adherents claimed that material things were superior to the spiritual. Also called Materials, they differed from the Gnostic Spirituals in whose doctrinal system there was almost a balance between good and evil. (See Heresies.)

## Hymn

A hymn is a poetic composition set to music, generally having a religious theme. By derivation, hymns are usually songs honoring God and sung in praise of Him. They are a part of the liturgy of the Celebration of the Eucharist, sung during the processional entrance, the Offertory, the distribution of Holy Communion, and the recessional. (See Eucharist, Celebration of; Liturgy.)

Hymns are ritualistic in nature, but they are also an expression of personal devotion and piety.

## Hymnal

A book containing a collection of hymns together with the musical notation for each hymn is referred to as a hymnal. It may include a variety of hymns suitable for various occasions, such as those for paraliturgical services, for the congregation during the celebration of the Eucharist, for children's liturgies, and for choir members. Some hymnals have been gathered by national groups and sponsored by Conferences of Bishops who recognize these as semi-official and appropriate for liturgical services.

## Hymnody

1. All hymns.
2. Religious lyric poems. Hymnody in the Church is of two kinds: liturgical or nonliturgical. The former are those hymns that form parts of the Mass, for example, the Dies Irae sung at requiem Masses, or that form portions of the Divine Office. Of these there are some 175, for example, Veni Creator and Stabat Mater. The nonliturgical are those hymns sung at devotions or recited in private prayer.

## Hyperdulia

Hyperdulia is the veneration proper to the Blessed Mother alone; it is the highest form of veneration short of adoration. (Cf. Dulia; Latria.)

## Hypostasis

A philosophical term from the Greek, meaning "stand under," hypostasis denotes a complete essence, subsistent in itself and not communicable to another being. When this essence is endowed with intelligence, it is called a person, and this personality is referred to as an hypostasis.

## Hypostatic Union

This theological term introduced at the Council of Ephesus (431) expresses the union of the human and the divine natures in Christ. An hypostatic union is the personal union by which the Incarnation was brought about; that is, in Christ there are two complete and distinct natures joined in the one Person of Christ, the Word, who pre-existed from all time. The result of the union is the one Person who is perfect God and perfect Man. Although this is a mystery, we can reasonably know that Christ because of His Sonship (Heb. 1:1–14) is heir of all things (Gal. 4:7) and is given all power "in heaven and on earth" (Mt. 28:18). Being God and Man in the Incarnation, Christ effected our redemption.

### Hyssop

Hyssop is a caper plant that grows in the Holy Land. Its sprigs were bound into a bunch and used for sprinkling liquids (Ex. 12:22). (Cf. Asperges.)

## Icon, also Eikon

The Greek word for "image," icon is the name of a religious image, painted or glazed on flat surfaces and used in Eastern Churches instead of statues. Icons may be large or small and may be representations on wood or metal. Some of the smaller have a

hinged metal cover, usually ornate, which serves as a shield and thus enshrines the icon. The icons play a part in the liturgy of the Eastern Churches, more so than the statues of the Roman rite. An icon representing the saint whose feast is celebrated is hung on the analogion of the church during the

celebration. The Iconostasis, or chancel screen, is decorated with rows of revered icons. Icons are given to a child at birth, usually of his or her patron saint, and also to newly married couples, along with those enshrined in the home.

The tenth and eleventh centuries were to bring forth the best of the Byzantine style of art, which was governed and directed by the rules set down at Mount Athos, one of the greatest monastic art centers of the Byzantine Empire and Church. Excellent color, design, technique, and rhythm, as well as composition, mark the schools of art that developed following these rules such as those at Novgorod, Stroganov, and Moscow.

## Iconoclasm

From the Greek, meaning "image-breaking," Iconoclasm is the name of a heresy that declared religious veneration of pictures and images unlawful. This heresy, fostered by the Paulicians, Jews, and Moslems, arose in the eighth century and, aided by Eastern emperors, developed into a major struggle between Church and state. In 787, at the seventh ecumenical council, the second of Nicaea, the Church defined the distinction between adoration given to God and the veneration paid to saints and declared that such veneration is an act of homage not to the image but to the person depicted. (See Heresies.)

## Iconoclasts

Followers of the heresy of Iconoclasm were called Iconoclasts.

## Ideology

In history this term first appeared after the French Enlightenment during the reign of Napoleon Bonaparte. The "Ideologues" were considered unwordly doctrinaries, but the application may have preceded this period as far back as the seventeenth century. The term is now used in many ways, ranging from that of programmed lying to constricted thought patterns, to the Marxist class-determined consciousness, and some Christian ideologues. The nonempirical speculation, the free-minded thinking of various groups espousing strange and difficult philosophies that are almost beyond reasonable assessment has led to conflicts and extremes of conduct in many areas of living.

Vatican II declares concerning the propaganda and indoctrination of these ideologies: "If an economic order is to be created which is genuine and universal, there must be an abolition of excessive desire for profit, nationalistic pretensions, the lust for political domination, militaristic thinking, and intrigues designed to spread and impose ideologies" (GS 85).

## Idioms, Communication of

Derived from the Latin, *Communicatio idiomatum,* the "interchange of divine and human predicates," this theological term means that because of the hypostatic union of the two natures, divine and human, in Christ, the properties or attributes that can be declared of Christ as God may also be affirmed of Christ as man. The reverse of this is consequently true also, that is, what is Christ's through His human nature is also possessed by Christ as God. Thus we may say, "God suffered and died." However, there is a limitation in the manner of expressing this communication, for example, it cannot be said "the Divinity suffered and died." (Cf. Hypostatic Union.)

## Idol

Idols are representations of animals, objects, false loves, or persons, which are set up for the purpose of worshipping them as gods or magic sources of power. In the Bible it is often recorded that the people of God made crude representations like the pagans, the false gods set against the true God. Man thus sought to discover in creatures what could only be discovered in God Himself. (Wis. 13:1–10; Rom. 1:18–32). This debasing of the true idea of the hidden God was an act of man's refusal to admit the greatness and grandeur of God (Is. 40:18–26; Hos. 13:1–8; Jer. 2:26–37).

The idols of the OT were overthrown by the coming of Jesus Christ and the establishment of the new covenant (Mt. 4:8–10; Gal. 4:1–11; Jn. 14:6–11; 1 Jn. 5:18–21). However, modern man has often made idols of material things or the greed for such things themselves, but Christ will finally triumph (cf. 1 Cor. 10:14–22; Eph. 5:1–20; Rv. 13:11–17). (Cf. Images.)

## Idolatry

Idolatry is the giving to another person or object that worship which is due to God alone. Idolatry, always a grave sin, is committed: (1) by intending and actually worshiping a creature as God, called formal idolatry; (2) by worshiping God only externally, called material idolatry. Worship is owed to God alone not only because of the positive, direct law given in the first commandment, but also because God alone is worthy of worship. No act of worship, however great, could satisfy the worthiness found in God (Is. 42:5–12).

## Ignorance

The absence of knowledge in one in whom such knowledge could be present is ignorance. In moral and Church law, ignorance affects the imputability of actions, the validity, or the censures to be incurred. Ignorance can be invincible, that is, irremovable. Invincible ignorance does not incur responsibility and does not alter the validity of an otherwise valid act. Vincible ignorance may be: (1) affected or assumed, that is, one wills not to learn in order that he may sin; it never excuses from the responsibility to or the penalty of the law; (2) crass or supine ignorance; existing in one because he has done nothing to dispel his ignorance, it does not excuse from the penalties of the law that are incurred by the very fact, unless otherwise qualified in the statement of the law; (3) simply grave ignorance, present in one who tried to free himself of it but did not go far enough in his efforts; it excuses from penalties that arise from the law itself, for example, if one learned that there was a law, but did not make himself aware of the conditions or penalties (cc. 16, 2202, 2229). (See Conscience.)

## IHS, or sometimes IHG

The letters IHS form the monogram of His holy name; they are derived from the Greek six-letter word for Jesus, thus the first three letters are: Iota, Eta, Sigma, so the monogram should not be used with periods after the letters. Other interpretations of the characters are only pious fancies.

## Illuminative Way

The term illuminative way is given to the second degree or stage in the progress of the spiritual life toward perfection. The first is the purgative; the second, illuminative; the third, unitive. It is a secondary step in the sense that one, after having gained by mortification and meditation, a facility in the practice of virtue, proceeds to the more difficult task of overcoming faults. In the illuminative way the aim is to perceive Christ and follow Him through the infused gifts of the Holy Spirit. As expressed in Jn. 8:12, "I am the light of the world. No follower of mine shall ever walk in darkness; nor he shall possess the light of life." There is both invitation and assurance declared in the words of our Lord. (Cf. Contemplation; Union, Mystical.)

## Image of God

Man is created in the likeness of God (Gn. 1:26), and since man is composed of body and soul, this likeness is not of one part only but of man as a whole. However, likeness is in the spiritual faculties of man. This likeness is also to be found in man's lordship over created things, which are finite and subordinate to man as they are to their Creator. This superiority over other created things exists in man because of man's exclusive possession of intellect and will and, therefore, it is in these faculties of the soul that man's likeness to God rests. In receiving his life directly from God, man received that which is Godlike, as the Psalmist declares: "You have made him little less than the angels, and crowned him with glory and honor. You have given him rule over the works of your hands, putting all things under his feet" (Ps. 8:6–7). Man further improves this image of God he possesses by the practice of supernatural virtues (Col. 1:15; Heb. 1:3).

## Images

Images are representations of sacred things or persons so constructed that something is really present in a conceptual manner. Thus image and a work of art are not one and the same in a philosophical sense because image is a more comprehensive term. But image may be considered a created reality or simply a work of art.

Vatican II clarified the use of images further and urged their limitation: "The practice of placing sacred images in churches so that they may be venerated by the faithful is to be firmly maintained. Nevertheless, their number should be moderate and their relative location should reflect right order. Otherwise they may create confusion among the Christian people and promote a faulty sense of devotion" (SC 125).

It follows that there is a reappraisal of Christian art, thus making all such art a matter of conceptual content, using what best may serve to demonstrate that the entire world is a vehicle of communication of the creator to his creatures. In Christian art every concept reflecting God should add to man's understanding of God, both in execution and in what is presented. (See Banners.)

## Imitation of Christ

This is the title of a devotional book of personal directions for the practice of the virtues found so eminently in the life of Christ; it is a collection of maxims and prayers urging one to pattern his or her life after that of Christ. It was first published early in the fourteenth century and has been attributed to Thomas à Kempis but it is now held to be the work of Gerard Groote (d. 1384), a native of Deventer in Holland. This book is also titled *The Following of Christ.* Its directives are arranged in such a manner that they seem to be communicated by Christ Himself as teacher and guide.

## Immaculate Conception

This is the privilege and the singular grace that divine omnipotence bestowed upon the Blessed Virgin Mary to preserve her from original sin by infusing into her soul sanctifying grace from the very instant of conception in the womb of her mother, St. Anne. Through this, Mary, who was to be the Blessed Mother of the Son of God, was conceived in the state of holiness and justice. This effect, caused by the act of God, resulted in her being free of the consequences of original sin, such as the slavery to the devil, subjection to concupiscence, and darkness of intellect. Further, Mary was not subject to the law of suffering and death, which are penalties of the sin of human nature, even though she knew these, experienced them, and endured them for our salvation. The dogma of the Immaculate Conception was defined for the Universal Church's belief by Piux IX, Dec. 8, 1854, as follows: "We declare, announce, and define that the doctrine which states that the Blessed Virgin Mary was preserved, in the first instant of her conception, by a singular grace and privilege of God Omnipotent and because of the merits of Jesus Christ the Savior of the human race, free from all stain of original sin, is revealed by God and must be believed firmly and with constancy by all the faithful." This state proclaimed for Mary is found in Gn. 3:15 where the Blessed Mother is referred to typically, and more directly as "virgin" in the prophetic statement in Is. 7:14, as well as in the angelic salutation recorded in Lk. 1:28. It is significant that the declaration of the Church through the Holy Father was made four years before the apparitions to St. Bernadette at Lourdes, France, in 1858, in which the Blessed Mother declared herself to be the Immaculate Conception. Under the Blessed Mother's title of the Immaculate Conception, the United States is dedicated to her patronage. The feast of the Immaculate Conception is celebrated on Dec. 8 and is a holy day of obligation for the universal Church (c. 1244). (Cf. Mary, Virgin Mother of God; Virgin Birth of Christ.)

## Immaculate Conception, Shrine of the

The Bishops of the United States of America in 1847 petitioned Pope Pius IX that the Blessed Virgin Mary be declared patroness of the United States under the title of the Immaculate Conception. This was not unreasonable because the Blessed Virgin had proclaimed herself the Protectress of the Americas at her appearance to Juan Diego in Mexico as celebrated in the apparition of Guadalupe. Also this title was one that had been made vivid to the Americans following the report of an unverified apparition to a Selish Indian girl at what is now St. Mary, Montana, reported by Fathers de Smet and Ravalli.

Upon the granting of the petition, plans were

made to erect a Cathedral-Shrine to be called the National Shrine of the Immaculate Conception in the country's capitol city, Washington, D.C., at Fourth St. and Michigan Ave., N.E. The cornerstone was laid in 1920, and the shrine-church, eclectic in design, a more or less contemporary design of both neo-Byzantine and Romanesque extraction, covering 77,500 square feet, was dedicated formally November 20, 1959. Although some work continued on the decoration and interior of both the upper church and the crypt, at the present time the church may be said to be completed.

There are many outstanding features of this edifice; among them the marble pillars supporting the baldachin over the chief altar, which are decorated with bas-relief carvings of the Greek and Roman fathers of the Church; the seven-foot statue of Mary Immaculate by sculptor George Snowden, which surmounts the baldachin; and the huge mosaic on the north wall of the apse entitled "Christ in Majesty," designed by John de Rosen.

This monumental church, the gift of the American Catholic people, has become a place of devotion and pilgrimage for visitors to the capitol city. It is the largest Catholic church in the nation, and while it has architectural limitations, it is a fitting tribute to the Immaculate Virgin. (See Canadian Shrines.)

### Immanence

1. In scholastic philosophy, a cause is immanent whose effects begin and end in the same agent.

2. Theologically, divine immanence is that we are in God and God in us. We are in God in that He made us and constantly aids us through grace, and God is in us through the presence of sanctifying grace in our souls. A confusion of this gave rise to modernist ideas that we are emanations from the divine, which is contrary to the teaching of the first Vatican Council. The Christian teaching of immanence rests upon transcendence, that is, that there is a self-existent "other" and it remains this "other" even when it subsists in another. Were it not that God is in us and we in God, the Christian teaching would become a metaphysical immanentism.

### Immensae Caritatis

The Latin title (Boundless Charity) of the "Instruction on Facilitating Communion in Particular Circumstances" was approved by Pope Paul VI, January 20, 1973 and thence published for the world by the Congregation for Divine Worship on March 29, 1973. The instruction grants the reception of Holy Communion at a celebration of the Eucharist a second time on the same day.

The provisions granted this favor on the following occasions: (1) Sunday Mass on Saturday evening or a holy day Mass the previous evening when one has received at a celebration of the Eucharist the morning of that day; (2) at a second Mass on Christmas or Easter, following reception at midnight Mass or the Mass celebrating the Easter Vigil; (3) the evening Mass of Holy Thursday, following reception at the earlier Mass of Holy Chrism; (4) Masses during which the Sacraments of Baptism, Confirmation, Holy Orders, Matrimony, Anointing of the Sick, First Communion, or Viaticum are administered; (5) some Masses for the dead, such as the first anniversary of Christian burial; (6) Masses celebrated on special occasions, such as the consecration of a church or altar, religious profession, conferring of an ecclesiastical assignment (for example, that given to lay missionaries); (7) the solemnity of Corpus Christi; (8) parochial visitation, canonical visitation or special meetings of religious; (9) Masses celebrated at Eucharistic or other religious congresses; (10) pilgrimages and preaching missions; (11) other occasions designated by the local bishop. (Cf. Fast.)

### Immensity

By this attribute of God we understand that He is not limited to any one place but that He is everywhere, in heaven and on earth and in every place.

### Immersion, Baptism by

The Church recognizes baptisms conferred by immersion as valid. Since no one can baptize himself, in the case of immersion it is not sufficient that the one to be baptized immerse himself in the water, walking or jumping into it, but the minister must lead him into the water or out of it while the prescribed words of baptism are pronounced. (See Baptism, Sacrament of.)

### Immortality of the Soul

Immortality of the soul is the attribute by which man's spiritual substance, the soul, is immune from death. That the soul (here we do not consider the body; cf. Resurrection of the Body) will continue to exist forever is known by both faith and reason. In Scripture, we read of man being created of body and soul (Gn. 2:7); that a part of this creation, man, continues after death (Eccl. 12:7); and, more specifically that this creature returns to God, for "the souls of the just are in the hand of God, and no torment shall touch them" (Wis. 3:1–3.)

The teaching of Christ confirms the OT truth, and He fulfilled in Himself and for man the hope of an existence outside of time and satisfied the longing of man for security and purpose in life.

This truth we learn not only in the Beatitudes (Mt. 5:1–12) but in the "formula" of eternal life as presented by St. John (Jn. 16:33; 17:3; 10:10; 12:32) in a sequence that culminates in the necessity of Christ's death on the cross.

Everlasting life is given by Jesus (Jn. 1:4; 5:21); our faith and the Eucharist are pledges of the resurrection (Jn. 6:34–36); our resurrection will be truly corporeal (body and soul), cf. 2 Tm. 2:16–18. There are also ample arguments from reason that demonstrate this truth of the immortality of the soul. To present only a few: (1) man universally believes in a future life and this belief, arising from his rational nature, cannot be in error; (2) man can know truth that is eternal, but he could not know truth unless in him there was a part capable of such knowledge, a receiver for that which is received, and this must be the soul; (3) man, in doing good and avoiding evil, does so for a sanction or reward, and as God's justice demands such a reward for obeying His law, yet there is no such reward in this life, it must, therefore, be reserved for the soul. (Cf. Judgment, General.)

### Immovable Feasts

Feasts given fixed days in the calendar, which are not determined by the date of Easter, are known as immovable. Such a feast may be supplanted by a feast of higher designation falling on the same day. (See Calendar, Church.)

### Immunity

1. An exemption from military service, civil office, etc., extended to the clergy (c. 121).

2. Diplomatic immunity is the protection from physical harm granted to both persons and properties outside their own nation.

### Immutability

Immutability is the state of being unchangeable; an attribute of God alone, since He alone is unchangeable not only in His essence but in the perfection of all His attributes. Since change implies an imperfection in the sense that something new could be added to the principal, there can be no change in God who is infinitely perfect. Created things do not have existence of themselves but receive it from God the Creator. They are dependent upon God's creative will. Created beings are thus of parts, those of nature and those of existence. God alone in His existence, simple, not made up of parts, is absolutely perfect and immutable.

### Impanation

See Consubstantiation.

### Impeccability

The state of being incapable of committing sin is called impeccability. Man's freedom of will, is both the fountainhead of his "willing" to sin and his "willing" to do good. It is the part of the human person's nature that through reason and free will one is able to respond to the grace that God freely gives.

The ability to respond to grace, actual and habitual, is a reflex to the exercise of the virtue of love of God or charity. Because of love of God fully exercised by the individual, the probability of sinning becomes more remote. Also because of this love a human person responds to the grace of repentance should he fall into sin. And it is because of love of God that the human person will overcome sinfulness and persevere to the end in the grace of God, and thus ultimately attain salvation.

Only Christ was perfectly impeccable; even in His human nature assumed by the Second Person of the Holy Trinity, Christ could not sin although He could be tempted. "For we do not have a high priest who is unable to sympathize with our weakness, but one who was tempted in every way that we are, yet never sinned. So let us confidently approach the throne of grace to receive mercy and favor and to find help in time of need" (Heb. 4:15–16).

The Blessed Virgin Mary was incapable of committing sin since she was free from original and personal sin because of the divine favor of God in choosing her to be the mother of His Son, which favor is called the Immaculate Conception.

### Impediments of Marriage

An impediment of marriage is either an external fact or circumstance that forbids marriage, sacramental or legal, and makes it invalid or unlawful. Impediments arise from the natural or divine law, from ecclesiastical law, and from civil law. As such they may be divided according to their effect into: (1) prohibitive or diriment, these making marriage either unlawful, or unlawful and invalid; (2) absolute or relative, these forbidding marriage absolutely or between certain persons; (3) public or occult, known or proved by legal action or not; (4) temporary or perpetual, that is, they may cease or continue; (5) of degree, or according to the defect of testimony; (6) of divine or human right. Canon law treats all of these, but makes a division into two chief groups. The first is prohibitory, making marriage unlawful but not invalid: (1) a simple vow of virginity, a vow of perfect chastity, a vow not to marry, a vow to receive holy orders or enter religious life (c. 1058); (2) legal relationship, for example, adoption, if it is an impediment in civil law (c. 1059); (3) mixed religion, the law forbidding a marriage between a Catholic and a baptized non-Catholic or a member of an heretical sect (c. 1060). The second group are known as diriment impediments. The third may be set aside by dispensation or the fulfilling of the prescriptions of the local ordinary. (Cf. Diriment Impediment.)

## Imperfections

Any deficiency or lack of a necessary or natural quality is called an imperfection. In the ascetical teachings of the Church imperfections are those faults, tendencies, or proclivities that are less serious in the order of morality and are considered less than venial sins, but are acts of moral significance because they impede one's spiritual progress. And when such tendencies are not overcome, they may develop into serious sin.

Here we do not speak in a psychological or parapsychological sense but in the practical order of the Christian fulfilling his call to spiritual perfection. It is through fraternal correction, spiritual guidance, and counseling that one is enabled to overcome imperfections rather than through the Sacrament of Penance, for these imperfections are not a matter of confession. In the natural and spiritual order it is to one's benefit to overcome imperfections so that nothing may impede the progress toward right living and fulfillment of the counsels of Christ that one be perfect as He and the Father are perfect.

## Imposition of Hands

At the administration of the Sacraments of Baptism, Confirmation, and Holy Orders, imposition of hands is the act whereby the priest, religious, or bishop places his hands on the head or touches in a solemn manner the body of the recipient. (Cf. Orders, Holy, Sacrament of.)

The Apostles were conscious of the power given to them whereby they could transmit to others the Holy Spirit through whom they became preachers of the word and leaders of the community (cf. Acts 5:29–32; 13:1–2; 9:17–19; 11:15–18; 1 Cor. 15:3–7).

## Imprecatory Psalms

This collective term indicates those Psalms in which there are passages that seem to invoke curses or revengeful punishment on an enemy: Psalms 17, 34, 51, 68, 108, 136.

## Imprimatur

This Latin word, literally "Let it be printed," is used by Church authorities to extend permission for the printing of writings, prayers, pictures, and other material. The word is generally followed by the name of the ordinary of the diocese in which the printing or publishing was done or where the author lives.

The precensorship of written material is based on the (1) natural law, or the Church's right to protect itself from harm; (2) this right is based on the supernatural mission of the Church, instructing the faithful in its doctrine and its code of morals.

Canon 1394 requires that when a work is printed, notice of the grant of the permission be printed in that work. The reason for this law is apparent. By this means the reader is furnished with an assurance that the work conforms to ecclesiastical standards. It is the simplest and most efficient way to acquaint the public with the fact that the permission was granted.

It is usual in writings that are not under special regulation, such as works by religious (c. 1385), to print an explanation of the Imprimatur and Nihil obstat in wording similar to the following: "The *Nihil obstat* and *Imprimatur* are a declaration that a book or pamphlet is considered to be free from doctrinal or moral error. It is not implied that those who have granted the *Nihil obstat* and *Imprimatur* agree with the contents, opinions, or statements expressed." This applies only after precensorship; it is not specifically applied to the permission of a major religious superior.

## Improperia

That portion of the office of Good Friday recited or sung during the veneration of the cross is called the Improperia. It consists of the "reproach" addressed to all by Christ, speaking to the Jews, notably from Micah 6. The term sometimes is applied to the musical notation for singing this portion. The practice dates back to the seventh century.

## Impurity

Impurity is the unlawful indulgence in sexual pleasure. This abuse of the human person's appetite for sensual pleasure through the sexual responses arises from many aspects of sexual abuse as it is naturally, morally, and psychologically understood. Undue excitation, immodesty, masturbation, fornication, adultery, and incest are all manifest transgressions of the virtues of purity, chastity, or modesty. The proper use of the sexual appetite should be understood. Ascetical writers have all spoken out against the occasions of sins of impurity, citing those that come from one or several of the following: touches that are self-excitatory; reading that beclouds the mind and arouses lustful responses; pictures, photos, or motion pictures that arouse prurient or lustful stimuli; immodest language or dress; and the association with others of lower moral standards or moral practices that distract and arouse unduly.

It must be cautioned that too great an emphasis on the virtue of purity sometimes creates scruples that are psychologically and religiously difficult to overcome. The proper approach to a right understanding of the virtue of purity is through education in the home and school, the cultivating of a prayer-life, and the avoidance of the modern inducements that a secular society presents to all. Prudence and caution are the courses to be followed in all events that challenge one's conscience regarding impurity. (See Chastity; Modesty.)

## In Articulo Mortis

Literally from the Latin, this means "in a moment of death." Now a seldom used expression, except in pastoral handbooks. (See Anointing of the Sick, Sacrament of.)

## In Petto

Literally "in the breast," this term is applied to the procedure whereby the Holy Father sometimes decides to elevate one or more to the rank of cardinal but, for various reasons, wishes to withhold the publication of his decision for a period of time. Thus the cardinal is created "in petto."

## Incardination

Incardination is the formal, canonical act whereby a cleric is subordinated to a superior of a diocese, a vicariate, or becomes a member in some religious community (cc. 111-118). Incardination is a necessity, for without it one cannot be ordained. Incardination may take place in several ways: (1) by reception of first tonsure, that is, a bishop can confer tonsure on a layman who is his subject, who resides in the diocese of the bishop's jurisdiction; (2) by formal letters of excardination followed immediately by formal letters of incardination (c. 112); (3) rarely, by reception, with written permission of his superior, of a residential benefice on the part of a cleric in a diocese other than his own.

In the teaching of Vatican II, incardination was encouraged so that a more proportionate distribution of priests according to demographic areas would result. "The norms of incardination and excardination should be so revised that while this ancient practice remains intact it will better correspond to today's pastoral needs. Where an apostolic consideration truly requires it, easier procedures should be devised, not only for the appropriate distribution of priests, but for special pastoral objectives on behalf of diverse social groups, whether these goals are to be achieved in a given area, a nation, or anywhere on earth" (PO 10). (Cf. Excardination.)

## Incarnation

Incarnation is the assumption of human nature, including human body, human soul and will, and all human characteristics except sin, by God the Son. Jesus Christ as the incarnate Word of God is the supreme manifestation of God's self-communication, which, by this very fact, also manifests God's will, which is identical to God Himself. Thus this central mystery of Christianity, while it is also a mystery of faith, attests to itself as being a compelling act of acceptance possessing for man both desirability and intelligibility. This means for modern mankind that the promise of God made in the Scriptures is a continuation of His love for men, which was fulfilled (Lk. 1–2) and through this action the redemption was accomplished and we were made children of God through Christ (1 Jn. 3:2–3).

Thus, there was united in one Person two natures, the divine and human. This union is known as the hypostatic union. This assumption of a human nature by the Second Person of the Blessed Trinity is foretold in the promise of a redeemer, notably in the "Emmanuel prophecy" recorded in Isaiah (7:14): "The virgin shall be with child, and bear a son, and shall name him Immanuel." The accomplishment of this fact is stated in the Gospels (Mt. 1:23–25). St. John (1:14) states it simply and forcibly: "And the Word became flesh and made his dwelling among us." The purpose of the Incarnation is set forth by St. Paul (Rom. 1:16) who speaks of the Gospel as a "power of God leading everyone who believes it to salvation," for it was this "salvation" of men that was the mission of Christ on earth. St. Paul further declares (Ti. 3:4–8) that we have been saved through the Incarnation. The benefits of the Incarnation are God's goodness and grace, and these benefits are intended to be shared by all. This is declared by St. Paul (Ti. 2:11–15). (Cf. Redemption of Man; Salvation History.)

## Incense

Incense is made from the hardened resins of various plants or trees that give off an aromatic smoke when burned. Incense may be in the form of powder or small grains. Burned in the thurible, it is used in the liturgy of the Church to offer honor to the eucharistic God, symbolizing virtue and the ascent of prayer and man's good works to the throne of God. Also used in the liturgy are unburnt grains of incense, for example, grains are placed together with the relics in the sepulchers of altars and affixed, in the form of a cross, to the side of the paschal candle.

## Indefectability

The quality or condition of that thing which is free from failure, decay, or disintegration is known as indefectability. The broadest meaning of indefectability is freedom from defects. In its theological context it means the condition of the Church, which has not been nor can ever be other than that Church founded by Christ and through which His mission to the world will be carried on. By extension this also means that the People of God, the Mystical Body of Christ, cannot cease to exist while the world endures. Because of its unity, even though individuals or even communities may defect from the Church, the Church will survive. It will have permanence and indefectability as a Church because of: (1) the promise of Christ, "I for my part declare to you, you are 'Rock,' and on this rock I will build my church, and the jaws of death shall not prevail against it" (Mt. 16:18); (2) the apostolicity, through which the Church has a succession from the apostles and the sacramental, pastoral, and jurisdictional powers.

Over the years of history, change, disruption, wars, and social upheavals, the Church will endure until the parousia (1 Cor. 15:20–26). (See Marks of the Church.)

## Index of Forbidden Books

This official list, formerly published by the authority of the Holy Office, condemned books or writings judged by competent Church authority to be contrary to faith or morals, or discreditable to the Church. On June 14, 1966, the congregation for the Doctrine of the Faith directed that the Index and the penalties of excommunication no longer had the force of law in the Church. Thus, apart from the exercise of prudence, the formal Index is no longer a prohibitive listing. In the modern world of extensive publishing and translating it was an impossibility to monitor the printed matter. It is thought sufficient to have a precensorship of writings regarding the faith and morality of works prepared for members of the Church.

Legislation passed in 1975 by the Congregation for the Doctrine of the Faith directs that all books touching on religious matters, which are used in schools even as supplementary material, should have the "approval of competent ecclesiastical authority"; and that books not having the approval of competent ecclesiastical authority should not be displayed, sold, or distributed from churches. A member of the faithful is not to read a writing included in this list without permission of his ordinary. In certain cases, excommunication is involved.

The natural law alone forbids the reading of books that in prudent judgment are considered to be gravely dangerous to one's faith or morals. Thus it is not necessary that a book be listed in the Index to be forbidden. There are twelve classes of publications that are forbidden by general law (c. 1399). In brief, these are: (1) editions of the original text and the ancient Catholic versions of the Scriptures published by non-Catholics or translations of the Scriptures made or published by non-Catholics; (2) books that by argument defend heresy or schism or tend to undermine religion; (3) books containing attacks on religion, good morals, divine worship, and purity; (4) books by non-Catholics treating of religion or religious discipline unless approved by authority; (5) books presenting commentaries to or versions of Scripture, which are published without approbation; also works on visions and other supernatural phenomena published without approval; (6) books that attack Catholic dogma or the hierarchy or defend errors condemned by the Holy See; (7) books that teach or encourage sorcery, magic, or similar practices; (8) books defending forbidden acts, such as suicide, dueling, or divorce; (9) books treating of or narrating obscene things, or those that arouse the passions; (10) nonofficial editions of liturgical books; (11) books propagating false indulgences; (12) printed images of our Lord, the Blessed Virgin, the angels, saints, or other servants of God, which are not in keeping with the teachings of the Church.

## Indiction

This is a method of reckoning the years, based upon a cycle of 15 years, beginning with the year 313.

## Indifferentism

1. Denial of the worship of God, arising from a willful failure to recognize the duty of man in matters of religion.

2. The turning away from religious practices, patterned on the early Gnostics, out of the mistaken consideration that all religions are "relatively" true.

Indifference is one aspect of the attitude of the Christian to the world, which under the guise of freedom creates an unconcern for the will of God, for religion, and for the good that comes through religious adherence and service. It is the proper role of the Christian to be involved in the mission, history, and the eschatological purpose (or goal) of the Church, "to devote yourselves entirely to the Lord" as St. Paul says (1 Cor. 7:35).

## Individualism

A wide spectrum of divergent attitudes and views that have the singular characteristic of making one person stand out against the background of society, the community, or the collectivity of many persons is called individualism. No single philosophy embraces this form of "apartness" or "uniqueness," but rather the tendencies toward or adherence to other philosophical conceptions mark one as having individuality as a goal. Thus the individual forms his own norm of action and sets his own goal in contrast to the universal norms or goals. It thus marks an attitude to life and behavior. Not all aspects of individualism are unfavorable, such as pride, but rather some should be stressed, for example the search for privacy, a distinct personalism, and the antithesis of collectivity and the expression of creativity. In the modern world there should be greater emphasis upon individualism wherein the rights of the human person or man's reality in himself can be brought forth against the mind-control and enforced collectivity of social and ethical life. But it must be understood that individualism in its theological view cannot exist apart from Christianity since this is where man's genuine consciousness of self-hood and his relationship to God are attained and where the subjective effort to gain salvation can best take place through faith.

## Indulgence

The remission of the temporal punishment due for sins and hence, the satisfaction owed to God for one's sins is called an indulgence. The Church grants such indulgences after the guilt of sin and its eternal punishment have been remitted by sacramental absolution or by perfect contrition (c. 911). Indulgences are *plenary* or *partial:* plenary, when they remit all of the temporal punishment resulting from sin; partial, when a part of this punishment is remitted. Should one seek to gain a plenary indulgence but, because of some unforgiven venial sin, not all of the temporal punishment is taken away, that person gains at least a partial indulgence (c. 926).

As granted by the Church in terms of time (years, days, and quarantines), a partial indulgence remits as much of the temporal punishment as would be expiated by the performance of a canonical (imposed) penance in the early Church for that length of time or for the penances of a fasting season (quarantine). Indulgences granted by the Church may be gained for oneself or for the souls in purgatory, unless otherwise declared, but no one can gain an indulgence for another living person (c. 930).

The granting of indulgences is founded upon three doctrines of Catholic faith: the treasury of the merits of the communion of saints, Christ Himself, and the Blessed Virgin and the saints. Determination of the extent of an indulgence and the necessary terms for gaining it are given by the authority of the Church through the Sacred Apostolic Penitentiary. The conditions required for the gaining of an indulgence are: one must be baptized, a subject of the Church, free of excommunication, and in the state of grace and, if seeking it for oneself, one must have the intention of gaining it and perform the work for which the indulgence is granted. Plenary indulgences demand that one be free from every venial sin. Indulgences officially granted by the Church are published by the Sacred Apostolic Penitentiary and translated and published for use of the faithful by authorized publishers. Indulgences are strictly interpreted by the Church and governed by canon law (cc. 911-936).

## Indult

An indult is the grant of a special faculty, made by the Holy See to bishops or others in authority, to do something not otherwise permitted by the general law of the Church. It is similar to the issuance of a license to perform sacred functions over and above the ordinary rules. It differs from a dispensation. (Cf. Dispensation.)

### Indwelling of the Holy Spirit

The presence of God in the body and soul of a human person is attributed to the Holy Spirit in a singular manner, both in Sacred Scripture and the writings of the fathers. Although God, that is the three divine Persons, is present in all places by His power, a loving indwelling takes place in a special manner in those persons of grace and sanctity, in different degree, who accept this divine familiarity by their extent of love. Thus the indwelling is the more or less perfect extension of charity, or the love of God. As expressed by Christ: "Anyone who loves me will be true to my word, and my Father will love him; we will come to him and make our dwelling place with him" (Jn. 14:23). And the evangelist further explains: "If we love one another God dwells in us, and His love is brought to perfection in us. The way we know we remain in him and he in us is that he has given us of his Spirit." (1 Jn. 4:12–13). (Cf. Love of God.)

### Inerrancy

The fundamental freedom from error is called inerrancy. It may be applied to knowledge of a subject, primarily spiritual, or to the human person's knowledge of that subject. As a theological theme, apart from the consent given in faith ("But you have the anointing that comes from the Holy One, so that all knowledge is yours" 1 Jn. 2:20), there are the following instances of inerrancy:(1) God's omniscience, (2) the knowledge possessed by Adam in the primal state of grace before the commission of the original sin, (3) the knowledge that was Christ's, (4) Holy Scripture, (5) the Church's infallibility.

Other forms of inerrancy exist, for example, in the natural laws, in the mathematical and physical sciences when rightly demonstrated, and in the question of whether there can be an atheism without guilt and moral error. (See Revelation; Inspiration of Scritpure.)

### Infallibility

In its Catholic, doctrinal meaning, infallibility is the end result of divine assistance given the Church whereby she is preserved from the possibility and liability to error in teachings on matters of faith and morals. That infallibility was always present in the Church, even from apostolic times, is frequently affirmed by actions and declarations of the Apostles (Gal. 1:9) and spoken of by the fathers of the Church as the "charisma of truth" (St. Irenaeus). The doctrine of infallibility was defined by Vatican Council I (Sess. III, cap. 4) and promulgated on July 18, 1870, the day before war broke out between Germany and France, which led indirectly to formal suspension of the Council three months later. The doctrine defines that infallibility is: (1) in the pope personally and solely as the successor of St. Peter, (2) in an ecumenical council subject to confirmation by the pope, (3) in the bishops of the Universal Church teaching definitively in union with the pope (cf. Magisterium of the Church). As such, infallibility does not extend to pronouncements on discipline and Church policy and by no means includes impeccability of the pope or inerrancy in his private opinions. It is, briefly, the assured guarantee of the unfolding of the apostolic deposit of faith by authority of the Church whereby Christ's doctrine must and will be handed on by an infallible Church guided by the Holy Spirit. It is distinguished from both biblical inspiration and revelation. (Cf. Inspiration of Scripture; Revelation.)

Vatican II further teaches: "This is the infallibility which the Roman Pontiff, the head of the college of bishops, enjoys in virtue of his office, when, as the supreme shepherd and teacher of all the faithful, who confirms his brethren in their faith (cf. Lk. 22:32), he proclaims by a definitive act some doctrine of faith or morals. Therefore his definitions, of themselves, and not from the consent of the Church, are justly styled irreformable, for they are pronounced with the assistance of the Holy Spirit, an assistance promised to him in blessed Peter. Therefore they need no approval of others, nor do they allow an appeal to any other judgment" (LG 25).

And: "The Roman Pontiff is not pronouncing judgment as a private person. Rather as the supreme teacher of the universal Church, as one in whom the charism of the infallibility of the Church herself is individually present, he is expounding or defending a doctrine of Catholic faith" (LG 25).

And: "Although the individual bishops do not enjoy the prerogative of infallibility, they can nevertheless proclaim Christ's doctrine infallibly. This is so, even when they are dispersed around the world, provided that while maintaining the bond of unity among themselves and with Peter's successor, and while teaching authentically on a matter of faith or morals, they concur in a single viewpoint as the one which must be held conclusively" (LG 25).

And: "This infallibility with which the divine Redeemer willed His Church to be endowed in defining a doctrine of faith and morals extends as far as the deposit of divine revelation, which must be religiously guarded and faithfully expounded" (LG 25).

## Infamy

The serious loss of good name, infamy may be: (1) infamy of fact; as arising from a known and open crime, it is also canonically called "irregularity from crime" (c. 895); (2) infamy of law; this is brought about by a vindictive penalty imposed on one, or a condemnatory sentence imposed for certain crimes (cc. 2314, 2320, 2328, 2343, 2351, 2356, 2357). Infamy of law ceases only by dispensation of the Holy See since it arises from common law and is perpetual. Infamy of fact ceases when by good life and a probationary period of time the good name is restored; in canon law the ordinary may declare the time when this restoration has taken place (c. 2295).

## Infidel

An unbaptized person, or one not knowing or believing the divine origin of religion, was called an infidel.

## Infinite

Infinite is that which is without limits. In the negative sense, it is said of that which has no termination; in the positive, of a reality that extends without end. When referred to God, infinite is the attribute declaring that there is no limit to the perfection of God and that He has the complete fullness of every perfection, in Himself and through Himself, above all things existing or capable of existing by His creation. (See Immortality of the Soul.)

## Infulae

This Latin plural word is the term applied to the two lappets that hang down from the back of a mitre. They usually have fringed ends.

## Infused Virtues

These virtues are not acquired by the repetition of good acts prompted by grace but gained by a direct "pouring in" by God. Thus they are more accurately called supernatural virtues or principles of action placed by God into our souls as a special gift. They are higher than acquired moral virtues, and they grow with the increase and exercise of habitual grace. (Cf. Virtue.)

## Infusion

See Baptism, Sacrament of.

## Inquisition

1. Historically, a legal court of the Church, sometimes administered in cooperation with the civil authority, for the investigation and sentencing of persons professing or accused of formal heresy. As such, the inquisitions were first begun in 1233 by Pope Gregory IX, based on the "Inquisitorial plan" originated by Pope Lucius III. Between 1227 to 1299, French councils had already decreed that an "inquisition" or court consisting of one priest and two laymen should be set up in each parish to check and prevent heresy. Especially in view of the fact that barbarism was not entirely expelled by the Christian impact, this led to abuses that to some degree were in the structure itself and in the crude application of too zealous a form of justice. Some of these abuses were: refusal of legal advisers, acceptance of testimony of heretics and excommunicates, the use of torture, and the denial of natural rights to the accused.

Pope Gregory IX in a letter of Oct. 11, 1231 set up the initial procedure: "When you arrive in a city, summon the bishop, clergy, and people and preach a sermon on the Faith. Then select certain men of good reputation to help you in trying the heretics and suspects denounced before your tribunal. All who on examination are found guilty or suspected of heresy must promise to obey completely the commands of the Church. If they refuse, you must prosecute them according to the statutes which we have recently promulgated." From this we learn that the foremost action was a mere call to obedience. But given power among the ignorant, there were bound to be grave abuses especially when the Inquisitor himself was often ignorant or an aristocratic appointee.

2. Canonical inquisition is the inquiry made in accord with canon law prior to being summoned before an ecclesiastical court. (See Huguenots; Heresy.)

## Inquisition, Spanish

Established as a separate and distinct use of the tribunal inquiry, the Spanish Inquisition was set up by the Catholic sovereigns, King Ferdinand and Queen Isabella, by special authorization from the Holy See in 1476. Its purpose was primarily (1) to protect the *Conversos*, the Jewish converts, from retaliation of their fellowmen and from relapse; (2) to seek out the lapsed Jewish converts, the Maranos; (3) to prevent the relapse of the *Moriscos*, the Moorish converts and to keep them from forming harmful alliances with various heretical groups. Thus it became a semipolitical machine, a mixture of ecclesiastical and state effort to protect Christian Spain when the nation faced unusual conditions. It was, however, only six years after its institution that protest was made to Rome because of cruel and illegal practices, and Pope Sixtus IV issued a brief which threatened penalties for abuses of canonical procedures. Torquemada, appointed Grand Inquisitor in 1486, attempted to make the Inquisition effective and, while working under the commonly accepted criminal code and procedure of his day, introduced the law of 1492 whereby the Jews were given a choice of becoming Christians or exiles. This caused great hardships to Jews and led to open persecution and widespread abuses. It worked to the detriment of Spain and, although the number of its victims has been exaggerated historically, the Inquisition was a ruthless tool of both zealots and political self-seekers. The Inquisition was present on the North and South American continents where Spanish missions had become abusive, but there is no evidence that the Inquisition was ever in session in the continental United States. It continued, with vastly changed and controlled procedures, in Spain until the early nineteenth century.

**I.N.R.I.**

I.N.R.I. are the first letters of the Latin inscription which, by Pilate's order, was placed on the cross of Christ's crucifixion (Jn. 19:19). The words "Jesus of Nazareth, King of the Jews" were taken from Pilate's sentence. It was written in Latin, the language of administration in Judaea, and also in Hebrew (Aramaic) and Greek. Because of the irrevocability of a Roman sentence, this inscription stood as written, against the protest of the Jews who wished to disclaim Christ's kingship (Jn. 19:21). Thus it has become the lasting testimony of the kingship of Jesus.

**Inspiration of Scripture**

Foremost in the Catholic teaching concerning the Sacred Scriptures is this precept of inspiration by which is understood: that God is the author of the Sacred Books, that God used the agency of men to produce what He wished to be written, and that He placed in the Scriptures the contents that He wished men to have. First, we may state that the Jews accepted the fact of inspiration, as demonstrated by the record of King David when he declared: "The spirit of the Lord spoke through me; his word was on my tongue" (2 Sm. 23:2). Also, Moses is recorded as having written his canticle at the dictation of God (Dt. 31:19). St. Paul, speaking to the Jews at Rome (Acts 28:25–28), appeals to their acceptance of inspiration as an argument, stating, "The Holy Spirit stated it well when he said to your fathers through the prophet Isaiah: 'Go to the people and say: You may listen carefully yet you will never understand; you may look intently yet you will never see. The heart of this people has grown sluggish. They have scarcely used their ears to listen; their eyes they have closed, lest they should see with their eyes, hear with their ears, understand with their minds, and repent; and I should have to heal them.'"

Second, while inspiration is evident in Scripture, it is not necessary to depend upon this argument from Scripture itself to arrive at a conviction concerning inspiration. St. Clement of Rome, the fourth pope (d. 97), in an epistle to the Corinthians affirmed the inspiration of St. Paul who previously wrote to them (1 Clem. 47, 3). Likewise, St. Justin (d. 166) wrote of the prophets "being filled with the Holy Spirit."

Third, the Councils of Florence, Trent, and Vatican I declared the truth of inspiration.

Fourth, Pope Leo XIII defined inspiration "as a supernatural influence whereby God so moved and impelled the sacred writers to write, and so assisted them when writing, that the things He ordered, and those only, they first rightly understood, then willed faithfully to write down, and finally expressed in apt words and with infallible truth" (Prov. Deus. EB. 110). Vatican II affirms: "Since everything asserted by the inspired authors or sacred writers must be held to be asserted by the Holy Spirit, it follows that the books of Scripture must be acknowledged as teaching firmly, faithfully, and without error that truth which God wanted put into the sacred writings for the sake of our salvation" (DV 11). This sums up the affirmations of Catholic philosophers and theologians. (For the distinction between revelation and inspiration, see Revelation.)

## Installation

This is the canonical term for the procedure by which one can validly take possession of an ecclesiastical office or benefice (c. 147).

## Institute, Religious

As defined by canon law, a religious institute is a community of men or women who live in accord with special rules, practicing the observance of the vows, of poverty, chastity, and obedience, taken simply or solemnly (c. 487).

Vatican II declares: "In such communities the very nature of the religious life requires apostolic action and services, since a sacred ministry and a special work of charity have been consigned to them by the Church and must be discharged in her name. Hence the entire religious life of the members of these communities should be penetrated by an apostolic spirit, as their entire apostolic activity should be animated by a religious spirit" (PC 8).

## Institutes, Secular

Associations or societies of men or women, laity or priests, who while their members live in the world and carry on their professional life, dedicate themselves by vows or promises to follow the evangelical counsels and perform an apostolic work, are called Secular Institutes.

Each such institute develops along the lines of a special organization. First, it is a simple association of the faithful, called a pious union and having the approval of the local bishop. Second, having become established as a basically sound and ongoing group, the association, by grant of the bishop, becomes a recognized diocesan institute with the permission and norms of operation established by the Congregation for Religious and Secular Institutes. Third, this second stage is followed by a separate decree from this Congregation whereby it is raised from an institute of diocesan right to become an institute of pontifical right.

Secular Institutes arose in the late eighteenth century and were given full recognition by Pius XII, Feb. 2, 1947, in his apostolic constitution, *Provida Mater Ecclesiae.* In March of 1947 a special Vatican commission was established within the Congregation for Religious to regulate and meet the concerns of all institutes of secular status. The next year Pius XII in a motu proprio (March 12, 1948) commended Secular Institutes, and on March 19 of the same year a special instruction was issued concerning their role in the mission of the Church.

Vatican II recognizes Secular Institutes, declaring: "A life consecrated by a profession of the counsels is of surpassing value. Such a life has a necessary role to play in the circumstances of the present age. That this kind of life and its contemporary role may achieve greater good for the Church, this sacred Synod issues the following decrees. They concern only the general principles which must underlie an appropriate renewal of the life and rules of religious communities. These principles apply also to societies living a community life without the exercise of vows, and to secular institutes, though the special character of both groups is to be maintained. After the Council, the competent authority will be obliged to enact particular laws opportunely spelling out and applying what is legislated here" (PC 1).

And: "Secular institutes are not religious communities but they carry with them in the world a profession of the evangelical counsels which is genuine and complete, and recognized as such by the Church. This profession confers a consecration to men and women, laity and clergy, who reside in the world. For this reason they should chiefly strive for total self-dedication to God, one inspired by perfect charity. These institutes should preserve their proper and particular character, a secular one, so that they may everywhere measure up successfully to that apostolate which they were designed to exercise and which is both in the world and, in a sense, of the world" (PC 11).

Members of Secular Institutes do not take public vows and do not live in community life, but seek a special way of perfection in the everyday life of their work and apostolate.

## Institution, Church as

The entire complex makeup of the Church, the represented members, and the social, structural, united community, is included in the Church as an institution. St. Robert Bellarmine defined the Church as "the community of men who are united in the confession of the one Christian faith and the participation of the same sacraments and are governed by their lawful shepherds, especially by the one vicar of Christ on earth, the Pope of Rome."

In the exercise of its many functions the Church must be, in addition to the Mystical Body of Christ, a service entity, a "political" body, and a body having a human element giving external expression to what the Church teaches and exemplifies. Consequently, "the society furnished with hierarchical aspects and the Mystical Body of Christ are not to be considered as two realities, nor are the visible assembly and the spiritual community, nor the earthly Church and the Church enriched with heavenly things. Rather they form one interlocked reality which is comprised of a divine and a human element" (LG 8).

Thus when the institutional Church is spoken of, it extends to its spiritual and practical operations. It includes the necessary carrying out of the mission of Christ and the human action that makes the Church a viable entity in the society of men.

Vatican II spoke of the Church and her necessary institutions not as separate but as one. "In this Church of Christ the Roman Pontiff is the successor of Peter, to whom Christ entrusted the feeding of His sheep and lambs. Hence by divine institution he enjoys supreme, full, immediate, and universal authority over the care of souls" (CD 2).

And: "Until there is a new heaven and a new earth where justice dwells (cf. 2 Pt. 3:13), the pilgrim Church in her sacraments and institutions, which pertain to this present time, takes on the appearance of this passing world. She herself dwells among creatures who groan and travail in pain until now and await the revelation of the sons of God (cf. Rom. 8:19–22)" (LG 48).

And: "Catholics should try to cooperate with all men and women of good will to promote whatever is true and just, whatever is holy and worth loving (cf. Phil. 4:8). They should hold discussions with them, excelling them in prudence and courtesy, and initiate research on social and public practices which can be improved in the spirit of the gospel" (AA 14).

And: "In highly developed nations a body of social institutions dealing with insurance and security can, for its part, make the common purpose of earthly goods effective. Family and social services, especially those which provide for culture and education, should be further promoted. Still, care must be taken lest, as a result of all these provisions, the citizenry fall into a kind of sluggishness toward society, and reject the burdens of office and of public service" (GS 69). (See Church; Mystical Body of Christ.)

### Intellect

This is the highest faculty of the human soul, by which man knows not only individual objects but also things according to their general nature. In its more specific meaning the intellect is the mind itself, whereas intelligence is the refinement of the mind gained through trained reasoning abilities. The intellect may also be considered in a narrower sense as the totality of one's knowledge.

The intellect is both a power of the soul (by

which the human person lives and acts) and of the body. It thus depends upon and operates through the senses, physical applications, and the response to exterior stimuli. At the same time the intellect enables one to have abstract ideas, recognize immaterial realities, and arrive at a knowledge of unknown truths by reason. The intellect is also the source by which one is able to exercise the imagination, combine figures of abstract and real dimensions, and to speculate reasonably about things that are foreign to one's immediate knowledge. It is in the intellect that the human person comes to an apprehension of truth and can formulate opinions. Together with the will, the intellect makes choices and seeks them out, knows moral good and pursues it, and by the right exercise of conscience comes to act in accordance with the will of God, and strives for ultimate union with God.

It must be said that it is morally wrong to abuse the intellect through misuse or neglect, by use of drugs, alcohol, stimulants, or neglect from indolent habits that warp the training of the mind. (See Education.)

### Intention

1. The free prompting whereby the will chooses the end for which one acts and tends to use the means for undertaking the action.

2. Sacramental intention is the disposition and purpose necessary on the part of the administering person as well as on the part of the one receiving the sacrament. The one who seeks to administer a sacrament validly and with a right intention must be aware of the intention when the sacrament is given, that is, have an *actual intention,* but a virtual intention does not invalidate. This intention must concern the action required by the sacrament, to affect a specific person or definite matter through the sacrament. The intention necessary for the one who receives a sacrament should be at least an implicit habitual intention for valid reception; however, an explicit habitual intention is required for reception of ordination; and a virtual intention (that is, an intention placed consciously before the act even if at the moment of reception or during the ceremony one is distracted) is necessary for matrimony.

### Intercession

In general, intercession is one's praying or acting in behalf of another, usually at the request of the one to be benefited. The term is used in the Church in regard to the commendation of oneself to the saints. The Council of Trent declared in the decree to the bishops concerning instruction that they teach the faithful, "the saints, ruling together with Christ, offer their prayers for men to God, and that it is good and useful to invoke them suppliantly and to have recourse to their prayers and to their powerful help in obtaining benefits from God through Jesus Christ . . ." (Sess. 25, DB, 984).

The saints follow Christ in interceding for us with God the Father (Rom. 8:34; Heb. 7:25); also the act of *dulia* is performed not to obtain *from* the saints but *through* them (cf. Dulia). The saints, knowing of man's needs and that Christ as Mediator bestows all favors of grace through Mary, His Mother, unite theirs with the prayers of Mary, direct them to Christ, and aid us as intermediaries.

This is an instance wherein, through intercession, the union of the Church militant and the Church triumphant, through Christ, acts for the salvation of mankind as well as for the individual members.

## Intercommunion

The reception of the Eucharist in Catholic churches by members of other Christian churches is at present called intercommunion. On May 25, 1972, Pope Paul VI issued a Pastoral Instruction dealing with occasions of intercommunion. This instruction is entitled: "Instruction concerning Cases When Other Christians May Be Admitted to Eucharistic Communion in the Catholic Church." This followed an increasing number of requests from Protestants to receive Holy Communion in the Catholic Church together with the fact that many separated brethren, without asking, simply receive Holy Communion in the Catholic Church because they seek to receive the Body of Christ to satisfy their spiritual needs and do not have the opportunity to do so in their own churches for a variety of reasons.

The Instruction permits intercommunion under certain fundamental conditions that are outlined here: (1) The recipients must manifest a belief in the Real Presence of Christ in the Holy Eucharist in conformity with the belief of the Church, and they must express that belief; (2) they must experience a serious spiritual need for the Eucharistic sustenance; this need is to be understood as a need for an increase in the spiritual life and a need to be incorporated into Christ and united with His members; (3) they are unable, for some period of time, to have recourse to a minister of their own community; (4) they must ask to receive Holy Communion; this means that the desire to receive Holy Communion must be verbalized on their part; (5) they must have the proper dispositions and lead lives worthy of a Christian.

Exceptional circumstances whereby a properly disposed Christian may be admitted to Eucharistic Communion are: (1) danger of death (by interpretation of some bishops this includes a Protestant confined in a hospital or convalescent home), (2) imprisonment, (3) persecution, (4) serious spiritual necessity wherein no recourse to a minister of their own community or church is possible, (5) the displacement of large numbers of non-Catholic Christians into Catholic regions.

All of these exceptions, including the reception of Holy Communion at funeral Masses and weddings, are under the direct authority of the local bishop.

Catholics are forbidden to receive communion in the worship or ceremonies of other denominations, except in certain instances at Orthodox Liturgies, for which permission should be sought. The entire question of intercommunion centers around the ecumenical movement. (See Ecumenism.)

## Interdict

An interdict is a censure that deprives the faithful, either lay or cleric, of certain spiritual benefits but permits them to remain in the communion of the Church (c. 2268). An interdict may be either *personal* or *local*. The first affects a person immediately, whereas a local interdict may affect members of the faithful indirectly by being imposed upon a definite territory. It is said to be *general* when it includes the entire territory, and *particular* when it extends only to a part of the territory, for example, a church. A local interdict does not forbid the administration of the sacraments to the dying if regulations are observed, but it does forbid, with several exceptions, the celebration of any divine services in the territory. A personal interdict forbids one to take part in any divine service or attendance at them, with the exception of hearing sermons (c. 2275). The personal interdict is not as serious as excommunication but excludes the person from reception of the Sacraments, except the Sacrament of Penance, and from Church burial as long as the person persists in the activity for which he or she was interdicted. Anyone who causes a place to be put under interdict is personally interdicted (c. 2338). An interdict is imposed sometimes as a punishment on an entire parish for some scandal against religion or the clergy. (Cf. Censure.)

### Interim

Interim is the historical name given to three temporary settlements between Charles V of Germany and the Lutherans: Ratisbon in 1541, Augsburg in 1548, and Leipzig in 1548. Each was an attempt at restoration of religious unity. They are also referred to as "Interim Religion."

### Internal Forum

Forum means a place of judging, the one who judges, as well as the power of judging. In its canonical sense, the term is either *Internal forum* or *External forum*. The first is the tribunal or the power used in matters of sacramental confession or things committed to a confessor outside the sacrament. The second, External forum, refers to that jurisdiction exercised for the public or social good, for example, a dispensation granted privately and recorded in the diocesan archives or parish records. (See External Forum.)

### International Catholic Organizations

Those alliances of organizations or groups who wish to call themselves Catholic must abide by the guidelines set forth by the Council of the Laity of the Vatican. These are the regulations set forth in *Acta Apostolicae Sedis,* Dec. 23, 1971: (1) the leaders of such organizations will always be Catholics, and candidates for office will receive prior approval of the Secretariate of State of the Vatican. (2) The organization will manifest adherence to the Catholic Church, her teaching authority, and the teaching of the gospels. (3) There must be evidence that the organization is truly international in outlook and that it fulfills its particular mission through its management, meetings, and accomplishments. (4) Leaders of such organizations are cautioned concerning their personal engagement in political, trade union, or other public activities.

Vatican II has stated: "Now in view of the progress of social institutions and the fast-moving pace of modern society, the global nature of the Church's mission requires that apostolic enterprises of Catholics should increasingly develop organized forms at the international level. Catholic international organizations will more effectively achieve their purpose if the groups comprising them, as well as their members, are involved more closely and individually in these international organizations" (AA 19).

But: "No project, however, may claim the name 'Catholic' unless it has obtained the consent of the lawful Church authority" (AA 24).

All such organizations are able to seek collaboration with the "Conference of Catholic Organizations" organized in 1927 and established under the Vatican Secretariat of State in 1953. Its general Secretariat is located at 1, Route du Jura, Fribourg, Switzerland.

Recognized International Catholic Organizations to date are:

Ad Lucem, Work for the Third World
Apostleship of Prayer (cf. separate listing)
Apostolate of Independent Milieus (AIM), Evangelization of youth
Apostolatus Maris (Apostleship of the Sea)
Associationes Juventutis Salesianae (Associations of Salesian youth)
Blue Army of Our Lady of Fatima
Caritas Internationalis, Relief aid on an international level
Catholic Fraternity of the Sick and Infirm
Catholic International Education Office
Catholic International Federation for Physical and Sports Education
Catholic International Union for Social Service
"Focolarini," Focolare Movement
General Union of Pastoral Work for Youth
The Grail
International Association of Charities of St. Vincent de Paul
International Association of Children of Mary
International Catholic Auxiliaries
International Catholic Child Bureau
International Catholic Confederation of Hospitals
International Catholic Conference of Guiding
International Catholic Film Organization
International Catholic Girls' Society, welfare of girls living away from home
International Catholic Migration Commission
International Catholic Rural Association
International Catholic Scouters Conference
International Catholic Union of the Press
International Centre for Studies in Religious Education
International Christian Union of Business Executives
International Committee of Catholic Nurses
International Cooperation for Socio-Economic Development
International Council of Catholic Men
International Crusade for the Blind
International Federation of Catholic Parochial Youth Communities
International Federation of Catholic Medical Associations
International Federation of Catholic Pharmacists

International Federation of Catholic Rural
  Movements
International Federation of Catholic Universities
International Federation of Institutes for Social
  and Socio-Religious Research
International Military Apostolate
International Movement of Apostolate of Chil-
  dren
International Movement of Apostolate in "Inde-
  pendent Milieus"
International Movement of Catholic Agricul-
  tural and Rural Youth
International Young Catholic Students
International Young Christian Workers
Laity and Christian Community, universal
  brotherhood
Legion of Mary
Liga Catholica Internationalis Sobrietas, Inter-
  national Catholic League against Alcoholism
Medicus Mundi, medical service to the poor
Movement for a Better World
Our Lady's Teams (Equipes Notre-Dame), spiri-
  tual formation of couples
Pax Christi
Pax Romana
International Movement of Catholic Students
International Catholic Movement for Intellec-
  tual and Cultural Affairs
St. Joan's International Alliance
Salesian Cooperators, apostolate to youth
Serra International
Society of St. Vincent de Paul
Third Order of St. Dominic
Third Order of St. Francis
UNDA, International Catholic Association of
  Radio and Television
Unio Internationalis Laicorum in Servitio
  Ecclesiae
Union of Adorers of the Blessed Sacrament
World Catholic Federation for the Biblical
  Apostolate
World Federation of Catholic Youth
World Federation of Christian Life Com-
  munities
World Movement of Christian Workers
World Organization of Former Students of
  Catholic Schools
World Union of Catholic Teachers
World Union of Catholic Women's Organiza-
  tions

## International Committee for English in the Liturgy, Inc (ICEL)

This is an amalgam of eleven Episcopal Conferences of English speaking countries. The group of
representatives from the various countries, consisting of scholars, translators, and service people, is
supported by the several Bishops' Conferences and
by royalties gained through licensing of texts to
users. For this latter source, ICEL publishes a
"Schedule of Royalties" from time to time, stating
the policies of the group regarding publication in
the vernacular of translations. The groups in each
country operate under the Conference of Bishops
and in collaboration with the Committee on the
Liturgy established by each Conference of Bishops.
Meetings are held at least annually. The function
of the committee is to assure authenticity in the
vernacular use of liturgical publications.

## International Council of the Laity

This council, instituted by Pope Paul VI on Jan.
6, 1967, is intended to provide an assisting agency
offering counsel and serving in an advisory
capacity whereby the mind and intent of the lay
persons of the world may be fed into the hierarchical structure of the Church. Its functions are (1) to
serve as a means of promoting through cooperation all aspects of the lay apostolate, (2) to
coordinate all the apostolic works of the laity, and
(3) to serve as a documentation center for the
studies and enterprises of the laity.

The membership at this time is an appointed
group, drawn from all peoples of the world. Its
meetings are intended to be held annually or
semi-annually, but the effective action has been
more in the area of educational studies. It suffers
the problems of representation, which all such
groups face in a multi-society of cultural
backgrounds, and where the actions must be only
advisory in character as they should rightly be. The
personnel has been selective and will only have a
broader spectrum when more National Pastoral
Councils are established. (See Diocesan Pastoral
Council; National Pastoral Council.)

## Internuncio

A legate of the pope, a lesser representative than
a nuncio, his duty is to foster friendly relations
between a government and the Holy See or
transact certain dealings of a more personal
nature. He is also called "apostolic internuncio."

## Interpretation, Scriptural (Biblical)

Also called hermeneutics, this is the science or
study that determines the rules for finding and
explaining the true sense of Sacred Scripture.
There are two chief senses of Scripture: the *literal*
and the *spiritual* (also known as typological, mystical, or real). The literal sense is that concerned with

what is expressed directly by the words, that is, the meaning the writer intended to convey. The spiritual sense is the meaning expressed immediately through a person, an event, or a thing by means of words, or arising directly, not from the words but from what is signified by the words. In the spiritual sense, there are different kinds of expression: *metaphorical, allegorical,* or *anagogical.* A metaphorical example occurs in Psalm 117:22 in which the Israelites are described as the cornerstone; an allegorical meaning is Christ called the "Paschal Lamb"; an anagogical example occurs when St. Paul calls Jerusalem the heavenly city.

There are certain rules or principles under which interpretation proceeds. The *general* rules are those that examine the background (for example, the history and culture of the people of the Bible); the *writer;* the *book* or literary character; and the *vocabulary* or the meaning of the words as symbols of thought expressed. *Special* principles are those that consider inerrancy, the Church authority regarding Scripture, the faith as contained in the Bible and committed to the Church, and the harmony between the two Testaments, the Old and the New. (Cf. Exegesis; Inspiration of Scripture; Form Criticism.)

### Interracial Council, Catholic

See National Catholic Conference for Interracial Justice.

### Interregnum

1. That period of time between the death of a pope and the election of his successor is called an interregnum *(Sede vacante,* Latin, meaning the "See is vacant"). The rule of the Church, the election, and the exercise of jurisdiction over the city of Rome at this time are governed by norms set up by the Church, notably those proclaimed in the apostolic constitutions: *Vacantis Apostolicae Sedis* of Pius XII issued Dec. 8, 1945, and *Summi Pontificis Electione* issued by John XXIII, Sept. 5, 1962.

2. The Great Interregnum was that time in history when Frederick II, as head of the Holy Roman Empire, and one of the most dangerous enemies of the Papacy, attempted to control Italy and Sicily. He was excommunicated by Gregory IX in 1239. Frederick then attempted to establish an antipope in 1248 but died two years later. No one of the ruling heads would assume the responsibility of the empire and the interregnum lasted until 1273, until Gregory X attempted to provide a responsible ruler, but such damage had been done that recovery on the part of the German princes

was never to occur and the Church called for the fourteenth Ecumenical Council, the Second Council of Lyons.

### Interstices

Canon law determines the periods of time that must elapse between the reception of the orders before ordination to the priesthood. The interval is to be determined by the bishop. The legal time between is usually at least three months between deaconship and priesthood. Under certain conditions, these interstices can be lessened by the bishop (cc. 974 and 978). (Cf. Orders, Holy, Sacrament of.)

### Intinction

This is the term for a method of giving Holy Communion, now used by some Churches of the Byzantine and the Melkite rites. Before being given to the communicant, the consecrated bread is dipped into the consecrated wine. Since the Constitution on the Liturgy of Vatican II, there has been introduced into the Roman liturgy a widespread use of reception of Holy Communion by the method of intinction. However, this is governed by the regulations set down in each diocese by the local bishop. (See Eucharist, Celebration of; Communion.)

### Intoxication

See Gluttony.

### Introduction, Biblical

Biblical introduction is the formal study in courses of theology in which immediate preparation is given for the more advanced studies of the Scriptures. Under this title the general and special principles that govern the interpretation and defense of Scriptures are presented. It may be called biblical criticism or may be included under the broader course of study embraced by the term exegesis. (Cf. Criticism, Biblical; Exegesis; Interpretation, Scriptural.)

### Introit

The short passage of Scripture, usually from the Psalms or prophets, together with an antiphon, was formerly the introduction to the Roman rite Mass. Now replaced by the Entrance Ceremony, the Introit was read when the celebrant first went to the right side of the altar after he had said the prayers at the foot of the altar. The word is taken from the Latin word *introitus,* meaning an "entering" (cf. Mass). The Introit was added to the Mass in 1570 in a new missal published during the pontificate of Pius V. (See Eucharist, Celebration of.)

## Investiture

Investiture is the term given to the practice of the early Middle Ages that was an important feature of the feudal system. In this, it was the lord's or sovereign's right to make appointments to Church offices, thus subjecting churchmen, such as bishops, abbots, and priests, to the control of a lay person. It resulted in the historic evils of the succeeding years because no concern was paid to the qualifications necessary for assuming these responsible positions. Holy Orders were conferred on ignorant, unworthy people; ambitious men chose the clerical state to attain preferment and advancement, which sometimes led these Church opportunists to claim the right to marry. In turn, this gave rise to the custom known as "lay investiture," or the overlord conferring a ring and crosier on a prelate, as signs of the right to hold office and collect revenue. As the basic cause of many evils, lay investiture was cast aside in widespread reforms, beginning with the Concordat of Worms signed in 1122 between Henry V and Pope Callistus II.

## Invitatory, also Invitatorium

Formerly the invitatory was the opening prayer of the Divine Office recited before Matins on each day. It consisted of Psalm 94 and an antiphon that differed according to the day and season. It was omitted only on the feast of Epiphany and the last three days of Holy Week.

## Invocation of the Saints

See Saints, Intercession and Veneration of.

## Irenicism

Irenicism is the procedure whereby the leaders of the Church, clerical and secular, in seeking to form a better ecumenical association with other Christian groups capitulate or make conciliations that are beyond the normal procedures. In such efforts toward seeking "peace" through conciliatory means rather than through discussions and open dialogue, there is a resultant disruption of Christian unity and a disregard for the truths of faith as presented in the teachings of Christ.

Vatican II declared: "Nothing is so foreign to the spirit of ecumenism as a false conciliatory approach which harms the purity of Catholic doc-

trine and obscures its assured genuine meaning" (UR 11).

## Irregularity, Ecclesiastical

An irregularity may be defined as a perpetual impediment established by Church law, which forbids (1) the reception of the Sacrament of Holy Orders, and (2) the exercise of Holy Orders once they have been received (c. 968).

These irregularities arise from two classes: (1) those arising because of *defect* (hence they are not penalties because they may be incurred without culpability), such as: illegitimacy (can be dispensed); physical defect (some may be dispensed); mental defects; bigamy (in the canonical sense); judgment of a death sentence, given or received; public executioners and their assistants (c. 984); (2) those arising by *delict*, or by reason of certain specified personal, grievous, external (known) sins committed after baptism, such as apostasy, heresy, or schism; one baptized by a non-Catholic (except in a case of extreme necessity); those already married or in Holy Orders or with religious vows who attempt marriage; those who have committed voluntary homicide or procured an abortion; those who have mutilated themselves or other (notably) or attempted suicide; those clerics who practice medicine or surgery without permission, where death has resulted from such practice; those who, not being in Holy Orders, attempt to perform acts reserved to those in Holy Orders (c. 985).

## Irremovability of Pastors

This is the right granted by canon law whereby, in certain instances, the priest has stability in his assignment as pastor since he cannot be replaced without due process, voluntary retirement, or by personal request (cc. 2147-2156). (Cf. Parish Priest.)

## Isaac

Derived from the Hebrew, the name Isaac means "one who laughs" or "one who is merry," but it may be from a longer derivation that means "God laughs." In the genealogical tables of the Bible, Isaac is the solemnly promised son of Abraham and Sarah (Gn. 21:1-8). In the NT Isaac is called "our father" (Rom. 9:10), the "child of promise" (Gal. 4:28), and a hero of faith (Heb. 11:20).

## Isaiah, Book of

This prophetical book written in Hebrew is ascribed to the greatest of the prophets *(sic)*, Isaiah.

A script of the book was found among the Scrolls of the Dead Sea, along with other writings of the prophet. It is probably true that these writings were preserved by the Essenes because their way of life was patterned after Is. 40:3, which proclaimed: "In the desert prepare the way of the Lord! Make straight in the wasteland a highway for our God!" (Cf. Essenes; Scrolls of the Dead Sea.)

Isaiah was born about 760 B.C. His name in Hebrew means "Yahweh is Salvation." He was a citizen of the city of Jerusalem, the son of a family of rank, and a man of culture. When Isaiah was about 20 years of age, God revealed Himself to Isaiah in the Temple in a vision, seated on a throne and surrounded by angels who chanted: "Holy, holy, holy is the Lord of hosts!" (Is. 6:3). Isaiah was cleansed and sent by God (Is. 6:6–8), and he accepted his mission by wearing penitential clothes and walking barefoot for three years.

The work of Isaiah was multiple and enlightened. He spoke against entanglements with foreign nations so that the faith in the God of the Israelites might be firm (Is. 7:9). He recognized God's impatience with His chosen people, and that a spiritual remnant would return to God, the remnant of Jacob (Is. 10:20–22). It was through this remnant that God was to keep alive in the hearts of the Israelites the coming of the Messiah. And because Isaiah saw this as a vision bridging the hope of a Messiah with the coming peaceful kingdom of Christ, he has been called the "fifth" evangelist.

Isaiah described the future Messiah, the revelation of His divinity: "But a shoot shall sprout from the stump of Jesse, and from his roots a bud shall blossom. The spirit of the Lord shall rest upon him: a spirit of wisdom and of understanding, a spirit of counsel and of strength, a spirit of knowledge and of fear of the Lord, and his delight shall be the fear of the Lord" (Is. 11:1–2). And the prophet named the Redeemer: "Therefore the Lord himself will give you this sign: the virgin shall be with child, and bear a son, and shall name him Immanuel" (Is. 7:14).

The Book of Isaiah also speaks at length of the future suffering Servant, chapters 40 to 53. Isaiah saw that others were invited to a fellowship of suffering, and he also told of the coming of Christ and His suffering for mankind, describing how meekly and unassumingly the Messiah would come, bringing hope. And the Book concludes with the promise of faith and the mission of the Church: "I come to gather nations of every language; they shall come and see my glory" (Is. 66:18). (Cf. Jn. 14, 15.)

## Islam

The Arabic word meaning "submission to God" is also the name of the religion of which Mohammed was the prophet. In his preaching Mohammed called for submission to God, and a member of his religion is called a Moslem, meaning one who submits.

## Israel

The descendants of Abraham, with whom God made a covenant (Gn. 17:1–2), received their name as "the children of Israel" or Israelites, when God changed the name of Jacob to that of "Israel." Thus the name Israel is both that given by God to Jacob (Gn. 32:23–34), and the name of a nation of people. The blessing bestowed upon Jacob committed God to him and extended the covenant with His people. On this basis, by the covenant as renewed at Sichem, "Israel" came to designate the twelve tribes that issued from Jacob. By this title the descendants were to come into a stronger relationship with the promise of God (Ex. 19:3–4; Jos. 24). During the time that the ten northern tribes formed the Kingdom of Israel (931 to 721 B.C.), Israel became a political entity. After the exile the word regained its religious meaning and took on the expression of a messianic future in the fullness of time according to God's plan. This fullness of time was accomplished with the Incarnation of the Divine Son, Jesus Christ.

The Church founded by Christ became the *new* Israel, enjoying the promise, the glory, and the adoption as God's people (Rom. 9:3–18; 2 Cor. 3:18). The new Israel will come when the Jewish people rejoin the Gentiles in the Church (Rom. 11:25–29). Vatican II declares: "Israel according to the flesh, which wandered as an exile in the desert, was already called the Church of God (cf. Nm. 20:4). Likewise the new Israel which, while going forward in this present world, goes in search of a future and abiding city (cf. Heb. 13:14), is also called the Church of Christ (cf. Mt. 16:18). For He has bought it for Himself with His blood (cf. Acts 20:28), has filled it with His Spirit, and provided it with those means which befit it as a visible and social unity" (LG 9).

## Itala Vetus

Itala vetus is a name used in reference to the Latin version of the Bible before the fourth century. The translation of the Vulgate was largely made by St. Jerome (d. 420) from that old Latin version at the insistence of Pope Damasus I.

## Itinerary, also Itinerarium

The itinerary is a prayer consisting of the canticle Benedictus, an antiphon, the Our Father, versicles, and four collects. It has been provided as a "blessing" and prayer to be said by clerics when they are about to undertake a journey. Any prayer for a safe journey may be called an itinerarium, and many pilgrimages have begun with similar prayers for a safe and spiritually profitable journey.

I
J
K
L
M
N
O
P

## Jacist

Jacist is the name of a particular branch of the Jocist movement, the Young Christian Farmer (*Jeunesse Agricole Chretienne*). Its membership is made up of young farm workers, and it is dedicated to promote the spiritual welfare of its members through the ideal of Catholic Action (cf. Jocist).

## Jacob

The Hebrew name of the patriarch of the Jews is Jacob, the son of Isaac and Rebecca, from whom the twelve tribes of Israel sprang, that is, from his twelve sons: Ruben, Simeon, Levi, Juda, Issachar, Zabulon (sons of Leah), Joseph and Benjamin (sons of Rachel), Gad and Aser (sons of Zelpha), and Dan and Nepththali (sons of Bala).

It was through God's changing of Jacob's name that Israel takes its name and its people are called Israelites (cf. Gn. 32:27–29). Jacob is mentioned in the ancestry of Jesus (Lk. 3:34). St. Stephen gives a summary account of Jacob in Acts 7:8–16. The name Jacob also is a poetic synonym for the Israelites especially among the prophetic writings (cf. Is. 2:5–6; 8:17; Am. 3:13; Mi. 2:7; Ob. 17–18; Na. 2:3).

Jacob's Ladder refers to the dream recorded in Genesis (28:12), which records that of a stairway (ramp), one end of which rested on the ground and the top reached to the heavens, and up and down this stairway angels (God's messengers) were moving.

Jacob's Well is that place where Christ met the Samaritan woman (cf. Jn. 4:4–6).

Jacob's Oracles is a collective name for the curses and blessings that were the sayings of Jacob to his sons before his death (cf. Gn. 49:1–27).

## Jacobins

1. The name applied to members of a political group of the French Revolution. This group, founded in 1789 at Versailles, France, assumed a religious guise by accepting for membership persons from religious orders.

2. Name, more or less popular, applied to early French Dominicans. The name was derived from the first Dominican house in Paris on the Rue St. Jacques.

3. Name given to liberals or those holding radical views on matters of religion or politics. As such, it is derived from the French revolutionary group who later became radical extremists. When they seized control of the French government in 1793, they formed a dictatorial government, tried, and executed the members of their opposition and began what is known as the "Reign of Terror" (1793 to 1794). This ended with the execution of Robespierre in July of 1794, and the group lost its political effectiveness.

## Jacobite Church

A Monophysite church began in A.D. 543 by a Monophysite monk named Jacob Baradai, when he was consecrated bishop of Edessa. Those members of the true Church who had refused to accept the condemnation of the Monophysite heresy, that concerning the two natures in Christ, at the Council of Chalcedon joined the Jacobite church as a place of protest. However they were not as violently opposed as others of the heresy but were following a misunderstood idea advanced by St. Cyril of Alexandria. The Jacobite Church began as a church of protest and political and religious jealousy against the patriarch of Constantinople since this patriarchate was declared "first after Rome" by the Council of Chalcedon.

The Jacobites turned to the Arabs for support, welcoming their invasion of 636 as a deliverance from the yoke of the Byzantine Catholics.

It was not until the tenth century, when Syria was reconquered by the Byzantine forces, that the see of the patriarch moved into what is present-day Turkey. The current status is that, since 1500 when the Syrian Patriarchate was established, the Jacobite Church had lost its influence, and a movement was begun to obtain reunion with Rome, which continues to the present day.

Since 1959 the Jacobite patriarch resides in Damascus ruling over eleven dioceses; four in Syria, two in Iraq, two in Turkey, one in Lebanon, one in Jerusalem, one in Hackensack, New Jersey.

## James, St., Epistle of

This is the first of the "Catholic" epistles (the others are the letters of John, Peter, and Jude). The author calls himself "James, a servant of God and of the Lord Jesus Christ" (Jas. 1:1), and traditionally this was thought to be the Apostle James the Less. He was called "the Less" (cf. Mk. 15:40) not because of his position in the Church but probably because of his age or height in comparison with St. James the Greater, who was also an Apostle.

The authorship of the epistle bearing the name James is not known for certain. St. James the Less was one of the close relatives of Jesus, the Son of Mary the wife of Clopas (Mt. 27:56; Mk. 16:1; Jn. 19:25). He enjoyed particular importance in the early church, representing episcopal authority (Acts 12:17; 15:13–21; 21:18). He was martyred in the year A.D. 62, under the rule of Herod Agrippa I.

The importance of this letter and its teachings centers around two major facts: first, it is not really a letter in the usual sense but rather a gathering of sayings of a moral character, such as the abuse of riches and sins of rash speech. Second, it describes the action of the early Christians in conferring the Sacrament of Anointing of the Sick: "Is there anyone sick among you? He should ask for the presbyters of the church. They in turn are to pray over him, anointing him with oil in the Name of the Lord. This prayer uttered in faith will reclaim the one who is ill, and the Lord will restore him to health" (Jas. 5:14–15). (See Jerusalem, Council of.)

### James, St., the Greater

One of the twelve Apostles of Christ, James the Greater was the son of Zebedee. He was the brother of John and was called by Jesus from the trade of being a fisherman. Because of their personalities, James and John were called "sons of thunder"(*Boanerges*) by Jesus (Mk. 3:17). James the Greater was one of the three privileged to witness the Transfiguration, the raising of the daughter of Jairus, and the agony in the garden of Gethsemani. He was beheaded by Herod Agrippa I in A.D. 44.

### James, St., Liturgy of

This early form of the liturgy was developed in Jerusalem from the Antiochene liturgy and later supplanted by the liturgy of Constantinople. It now appears only in remnant form in the liturgies of some Eastern Churches. It influenced many of the liturgies that followed it, namely, the preparation and offering of the gifts, and the latitude allowed in the prayer forms that have only in modern times been widely used as in the various Prefaces of the Mass (See Liturgy.)

### Jansenism

This movement had its origin in the book, *Augustinus,* published in 1640, two years after the death of the author Cornelius Jansen, Bishop of Yprés. It developed a system whose principal teachings centered in the denial of man's ability to resist temptation and the rejection of the doctrine that Christ died for all men. These teachings were vigorously attacked by theologians, for they were contrary to the understanding of actual grace and the freedom of the individual. Also Jansenism stood for a Church of only predestined saints, opposed frequent reception of Holy Communion under its "unworthiness" teaching, and was against devotion to the humanity of Christ as presented in devotion to His Sacred Heart.

Later, in the seventeenth century, the followers of Jansenism practiced austerities and claimed that only persons with perfect contrition could receive the Sacraments of Penance and Holy Eucharist. It was a harsh, unyielding teaching that declared that men could not keep some of the commandments. Its influence was extensive for many years and led to a particularly unCatholic attitude toward moral issues, which is still evident in rigoristic moral teachings. Jansenism was condemned as early as 1654 by a decree of Pope Innocent X (d. 1655).

### Januarius, Miracle of St.

This name is applied to a famed liquefaction of a vial of solidified blood, said to be blood of the martyr St. Januarius (d. 305). The change of this blood from solid to liquid form takes place eighteen times during the year on major feast days. The vial is kept in the Cathedral of Naples. The action has never received thorough investigation, and although photographic evidence is available, there seems to be a considerable amount of speculation as to the purpose of the "miracle."

### Jefferson Bible

This printed work is the compilation of the third president of the United States, entitled: *The Life and Morals of Jesus of Nazareth, Extracted Textually from the Gospels in Greek, Latin, French and English.* It is called a "bible" but in reality is no more than a lengthy pamphlet that gathers together some of the religious teachings and principles upon which the writer of the Declaration of Independence based his personal philosophy of life. The manuscript of the original book is retained in the Smithsonian Institute in Washington, D.C. In his own writing, Jefferson referred to this collection as this "little book, which I call the philosophy of Jesus" (letter to Charles Thompson) and which he offered as a proof that he was genuinely Christian, which of course he was in spite of some accusations that he was an infidel. It most notably emphasizes the love of God and love of neighbor by repeating this teaching from each of the synoptic Gospels. The work also indicates that President Jefferson was a considerable scholar of languages, especially the classical languages, as well as French and his native English.

## Jehovah

Jehovah is a hybrid form of the Hebrew name of God, which is *Yahweh*. It is also called the Tetragrammaton, meaning "four letters," namely JHWH, read Yahweh.

## Jehovah's Witnesses

This religion was founded in the nineteenth century by a one-time Presbyterian, then Congregationalist, then non-believer, Charles Taze Russell. After what he claimed as a personal reclamation, he became a preacher of considerable energy and forcefulness, and this has influenced the convert-mission approach of the members who devote much of their time and efforts to recruiting new members.

The central approach of the Witnesses is a fundamentalist interpretation of the Bible, which they hold is the sole source of religious belief to the point that it assumes a rigorism of interpretation and practice. They also espouse a millennial view of the end of the world together with an imminent coming of the battle of Armageddon in which the Witnesses will survive and continue on into paradise.

When Russell died in 1916, Joseph F. Rutherford, a small town lawyer of Missouri, became his successor. He was addressed as "Judge" because he sometimes took over the bench of the regular judge. He assumed the leadership of the Watchtower Bible and Tract Society, becoming the official head of the Society, and he ruled with a group of directors. He and seven of the other directors were sentenced to Atlanta penitentiary for sedition. After serving nine months, he was released and made his headquarters in Brooklyn, N.Y., where he took up with special vigor the making of converts, using recorded sermonettes, books, pamphlets, a magazine *(The Watchtower)* and later *Awake!* and posters. His emphasis on the nearness of the end of the world, together with the pledged fervor of his followers, made considerable progress among the noneducated, especially through an inflexible stand on beliefs at variance

with theirs and attacks on the teachings of other Christian groups.

The basic teachings of the Witnesses (which are in conflict with many Christians) are: a denial of the Most Holy Trinity, a belief that Christ was once an angel and became a perfect man and a chief leader for God; a belief that the Holy Spirit is only an expression of the power of God and not a person. The Witnesses challenge the religious practices of others as a matter of course, basing these upon their own biblical interpretations and a complete denial of apostolic succession. Because of their beliefs they dissociate themselves from the secular community, oppose blood transfusions and blood donations, and they consider all baptized Witnesses ministers.

Although the Jehovah's witnesses have grown in numbers through widespread mission activities, they have been opposed to ecumenical response in any manner. Their leaders fail to recognize the derivative founding of their group and have instilled this into the followers. It is a religion of triumphalist arrogance and inflexibility.

## Jeremiah, Book of

A book of one of the major prophets, this is the writing of the prophet Jeremiah who was born about 650 B.C. of a priestly family at Anathoth, a village about five miles northeast of Jerusalem. He was called to his life as a prophet by God in the thirteenth year of his life, although he was chosen before his birth (1:5), and he performed his prophetic activity for 40 years at Jerusalem and finally in Egypt. His time of prophecy corresponds to the reigns of the last kings of Juda. In life Jeremiah had a particularly difficult time in God's service, not only because he vigorously warned the kings of the disaster approaching Jerusalem and the kingdom because of sin, but because he was intensely unhappy. Being sensitive and devout, Jeremiah was concerned with peace, but his last days were spent in exile in Egypt where he considered his life's work a failure. He never married (cf. 16:1–4) and was not able to enter into the social life of the community (cf. 16:5–9). His life, however, is characterized by a great love for his people, and he is remembered in the words of Onias who said of him: "This is God's prophet Jeremiah, who loves his brethren and fervently prays for his people and their holy city" (2 Mc. 15:14).

In content the Book of Jeremiah is difficult to catalogue because it is arranged in a disordered fashion. However, it breaks down into the lines of his preachments as follows: (1) pronouncements on Juda and Jerusalem; (2) the personal conflict of Jeremiah (cf. 11 to 17); (3) the prophecies against the pagan nations; (4) pronouncements on the salvation of Juda and Jerusalem, which includes the so-called "book of consolations" (cf. 30 and 31); (5) the passion or suffering of Jeremiah himself (cf. 36 to 45); (6) an appendix that gives the fulfillment of the prophecies of Jeremiah (cf. 52).

The principal themes of Jeremiah are: a concept of God that emphasizes the human's personal and intimate relationship to God; a preparation of the Jews for the "new" covenant especially among the remnant of the devoted Jews; an emphasis on the love of God and the preparation for the Christian way that is to come. In a special reference to the sadness over the slaughter of the innocents by Herod, Jeremiah foresaw this event and it was recalled by Matthew (2:17–18): "What was said through Jeremiah the prophet was then fulfilled: 'A cry was heard at Ramah, sobbing and loud lamentation: Rachel bewailing her children; no comfort for her, since they are no more'" (cf. Jer. 31:15).

### Jeronymites

Also called *Hieronymitae* or *Hieronymites*, these were several groups of religious hermits in Spain and Italy who followed the way of life of St. Jerome. They flourished for a time in the late fourteenth and early fifteenth centuries.

### Jerusalem

The principal city of Israel, once known as Jebus, is perhaps one of the oldest cities in the world; it is mentioned for the first time in a statement of "execration" in the Twelfth Dynasty of the Egyptian nation (1500 B.C.). Its name is taken from the Hebrew, meaning "city of peace." As early as 2000 B.C. in Egyptian texts Jerusalem was written of as a city under the name Ursalim. A strategic site midway between the northern and southern tribes of the Israelites, it was selected by King David (d. 972 B.C.) as his capital. His choice was made to establish the best site from a political, military, and religious point of view. It is the city in which the passion, death, and resurrection of Christ took place and is thus honored among Christians. The Jerusalem that Christ knew was destroyed in A.D. 70 by the Roman general, Titus. It is situated 15 miles west of the Jordan River on a range of mountains running north and south, lengthwise of Palestine, in a valley called by Josephus "the Tyropoeon Valley" (Valley of the

Cheesemakers). Jerusalem is celebrated as a symbol of the lot of the people of Israel, and it is borrowed as a symbol of reward or heaven (Rv. 21:2, 10–14).

Vatican II recognizes the use of the symbol of Jerusalem: "This edifice (the Church) is adorned by various names: the house of God (1 Tm. 3:15) in which dwells His family; the household of God in the Spirit (Eph. 2:19–22); the dwelling place of God among men (Rv. 21:3); and especially, the holy temple. This temple, symbolized by places of worship built out of stone, is praised by the holy Fathers and, not without reason, is compared in the liturgy to the Holy City, the New Jerusalem" (LG 6).

### Jerusalem, Council of

In about the year A.D. 49 the early Christians under the direction of the Apostles assembled at Jerusalem to discuss and clarify some of the problems facing the early Church. Those attending were Peter, James, Paul, Barnabas and the "presbyters." In particular, these problems concerned the regulations of the OT and ritual laws, especially since early Christian liturgy was derivative of Jewish ritual. These were practical problems that produced a definition between the relationship of the Old and New Testaments concerning the justification by faith or by law. The consensus was that there was no difference between Jew and Gentile in the Church in spite of the disagreement held by the Judaizers (Jewish converts to Christianity). Likewise there was a denial of the necessity of circumcision, and it is probable that there was some form of creed used as a profession of faith before baptism (cf. 2 Tm. 1:13–14; Acts 8:37).

From the actions of the Council recorded in Acts 15 and the fact that the decrees were sent to Church communities in Syria and Cilicia, it is evident that there came about a hierarchical organization of the Church, recognizing three descending grades: the bishops, the priests, and deacons. (See Council.)

### Jerusalem, Patriarchate of

Established in the administration of the Church, the see of Jerusalem became a patriarchate in 451 by declaration of the Council of Chalcedon. It was led into schism in 1453, partly because of political ill-feeling and continued resentment dating back to the time when Constantinople was given importance and recognition in the fifth and sixth centuries. It remains a unit of the Orthodox Eastern Church with its patriarch in authority.

## Jesse-Window

A Jesse-window is a stained-glass representation of the genealogy of Christ, in the form of a multi-branched tree. It takes its name from Jesse, the father of King David, who was the root of the line of descent (cf. 1 Sm. 16:18–22; Is. 11:1).

## Jesuats

This is a popular name applied to the members of the Congregation of the Apostolic Clerics of St. Jerome. They were suppressed in 1668 by Clement IX because of abuses of their rule. They are not to be confused with Jesuits.

## Jesuit Reductions

From the Spanish word meaning "settlement," the Jesuit Reductions were mission settlements founded by the Jesuits in South America, especially in Uruguay and Paraguay between 1607 and 1768. As a consequence of false accusations concerning the Jesuits' political ambition, these settlements were destroyed in the early eighteenth century.

## Jesuit Relations

Jesuit Relations are collections of letters written by Jesuit missioners from their missions, particularly those of North America. The Relations include personal letters, instructive letters to fellow religious, and most notably those documents intended for publication. They are a basic source of information on early life among the natives, topography and conditions such as weather and natural resources.

These reports, sent from Canada to France between the years 1632 and 1673, were notable for three reasons: they give great insight into the hardships of missionary work in North America; they supplied the French government with information that carried over even to the support given to the American colonial forces; and they told the supporters of the missionary activity about what was being accomplished. (See North American Martyrs.)

## Jesuit Rings

In the second half of the seventeenth century, the Jesuit missionaries used to award rings to converts in New York State territory. The rings were made of brass or bronze and showed religious representations.

## Jesuits

This is the name of members of the Society of Jesus. Originally this was a group of clerks regular, called the "Company of Jesus," founded by St. Ignatius of Loyola in 1534. The Jesuits engage in teaching, missionary and parish work, and conducting retreats.

The motto of the Society, *Ad majorem Dei gloriam* (For the greater glory of God), well explains the work of these dedicated members. As St. Ignatius envisioned a group of learned, efficiently organized, and disciplined men, they were to meet the requirements handed down by Pope Paul III in 1540 in their solemn recognition as an order of religious in the bull, *Regimini militantis ecclesiae,* "The Rule over the Church Militant." The Society is ruled by a Father General who is elected for life by the legislative body of the Society. Throughout the world there are provinces under the rule of the Father Provincial who is appointed by the Father General, and these provincials are divided into assistancies headed by a father assistant. These assistants serve as a group of advisors to the Father General.

Since devotion to the Church marks the Jesuits, they have suffered persecution and suppression from many governments: France, Spain, Portugal, Peru, and Venice. In modern times the Jesuits have been expelled or persecuted by the French, Mexicans, Spanish, Russians, and Chinese.

## Jesus

See Holy Name of Jesus; Christ.

## Jesus Christ

See Christ.

## Jesus Movement (Jesus Freaks)

The name Jesus Freaks is given to a group of dedicated youths, not entirely as opprobrium but as an identifying title. The members are fervid in their imitation of Jesus, particularly as He is shown in the Bible. Their work centers around a loose form of preaching, instruction, and pacifism. They have been criticized by their peers as simplistic in their approach to modern life, and some have been condemned by their elders because of a laxness regarding sexual morality and the use of drugs. Those who are sincere form quasi-pentecostal groups without Church affiliation, which are spread across the United States and Canada. Affiliation with a group may be terminated at will, and there are no binding vows or solemn pledges taken by the members.

### Jewish Canon of Scriptures

The listing of scriptural books accepted by the leaders of rabbinical schools was determined only in the late second century. The canon of the Hebrew Masoretic Texts is made up of 24 books: (1) Genesis, Exodus, Leviticus, Numbers, and Deuteronomy; these are considered not only for their historical content but primarily for their presentation of the Law. (2) The Prophetical writings listed are: Joshua, Judges, Samuel, Kings, Isaiah, Jeremiah, Ezekiel, and twelve contained in one book: Hosea, Joel, Amos, Obadiah, Jonah, Micah, Nahum, Habakkuk, Zephaniah, Haggai, Zechariah, and Malachi. Although some of these are listed as prophetical in nature, they are considered chiefly as historical by most scripture scholars, especially Samuel and Kings. (3) The other books listed as writings are: Psalms, Job, Proverbs, Ruth, Song of Songs, Ecclesiastes, Lamentations, Esther, Daniel, Ezra-Nehemiah (one book), and Chronicles (2 books in one).

While a simple comparison with the 73 books of the Catholic canon as finally defined by the Council of Trent in the dogmatic decree *De Canonicis Scripturis* (1546) would show the omission of many books, it is not as evident that certain portions of some books are missing, for example, parts of Esther and chapters 13 and 14 of the Book of Daniel. (Cf. Deuterocanonical Books; Protocanonical Books of Scripture.)

The canon of the OT followed by Protestant churches, arranged in 39 separate books, is the same as the Hebrew canon. Some Protestant groups do not accept the Epistle to the Hebrews, James, Jude, 2 Peter, 2 and 3 John and Revelation, but the Anglican and Calvinist Churches have retained these. The Greek and Russian Orthodox have the same New Testament as the Catholic canon, whereas some other Eastern rite Churches eliminate one or more of the previously listed books but consider them under investigation. (See Bible.)

### Jews

The name Jew is derived from the Hebrew for Judah, the name of one of the twelve Hebrew tribes and of one of the two kingdoms. The Jews are an ancient people whose ancestors were nomads and whose original home was Arabia from where they migrated to nearby regions. Their history as a nation begins with the call of Abraham to the worship of the one true God. From that time also dates the destiny of the Israelites as the Chosen People (Gn. 12:1–4). Their history comes up through the ages, with little unity achieved until King David (1012 to 972 B.C.) founded the first real monarchy. But after a revolt of the ten tribes, which was a divine punishment for Solomon's (d. 931 B.C.) worship of false gods, a division took place, resulting in the foundation of two kingdoms, Judah and Israel. With the last of the Macabees, Simon, in 134 B.C., the rule of Israel first passed on to the Hasmonean leaders and then to the Herodians in 40 B.C. Domination by the Romans followed and continued through the time of Christ. In the years A.D. 66 to 70, the Jews revolted but suffered bitter defeat resulting in the destruction of the temple in Jerusalem, that symbol of the religion identified with the Hebrew nation. This was the break between the new, rising Christianity and Judaism.

Then followed the *diaspora,* the scattering of communities of Jews throughout the world. From ancient time to the present, the Jews have suffered persecution, most frequently because of their refusal to accept the burden of responsibility as the chosen people or because of their religious and nationalistic feeling. The horrendous Nazi and Soviet persecutions of the twentieth century, and even the callous anti-Semitic feeling of the republican peoples, are types of this historic pattern. The Jewish religion, of external observance and deep interior piety, has maintained a singular nationalistic pattern, but in more recent times there has been a growing division in their formality of legal observances, namely, the distinction between the Orthodox and the Reformed. In many respects, the Jewish historians have been more fair in the treatment of their persecutors and the peoples among whom they reside than has been the record of history concerning them. After World War II, the Israeli nation, under the influence of widespread recognition and united effort, has again achieved a single land and center, though it is still a divided unit. Although this begins a new phase of Jewish history, it remains to be determined by future developments what this new nation will attain.

Vatican II states: "Those who have not received the gospel are related in various ways to the People of God. In the first place there is the people to whom the covenants and the promises were given and from whom Christ was born according to the flesh (cf. Rom. 9:4–5). On account of their fathers, this people remains most dear to God, for God does not repent of the gifts He makes nor of the calls He issues (cf. Rom. 11:28–29) (LG 16). (See Judaism.)

## Job, Book of

A wisdom book of the OT, this work is by an unknown author, probably a Palestinian Israelite, who wrote about the year 500 B.C. It consists of a prose prologue and epilogue but is otherwise a presentation in poetic dialogue. The theme of the book confronts the age-old belief of Israel that suffering is a punishment for sin. This concept was changing, for the justice of God in man's relationship to Him was changing, especially since the Jews could not explain the sufferings of the just in the light of a belief in life after death. The entire Book of Job goes beyond the traditional views on suffering; it treats the idea of suffering as a test of one's relationship with God and a purification as a prelude to more abundant blessings in the future. It emphasizes that God is an entirely free God, giving His blessings where He will, and is the very source of justice.

The account is narrated through the life and problems of a God-fearing man, Job, who lived in the land of Hus, which bordered Arabia. It teaches by giving a problem and its attendant solution, telling whether a man may be innocent and yet suffer the ills of nature and life. The answer is that this rests in the inscrutable will of God, His justice (31:3), and the duties of man toward his Creator. The book points out the fact that no man is innocent before God (4:17) but man will survive after death (14:15).

The entire book is considered one of the most beautiful and most difficult in the OT. This is partly because of its poetic style, which is filled with *hapax legomena,* wherein a thing or word is said only once.

## Jocist

The J.O.C. movement is taken from the French title *Jeunesse Ouvriere Chretienne* (Young Christian Workers). This was an organized movement of specialized Catholic Action founded in Belgium by Canon Joseph Cardinal Cardijn in the early 1920s. Its objectives are multiple but center on the union of effort by men to make, with the grace of God, all work and all pursuits an apostolate. It aims (1) to form the wage earner, the professional man, the farmer, and the student along the Christian pattern with Christ as the ideal; (2) to transform all these pursuits, the individuals, and their social life by Christlike ideals and by example to effect the spread of religion; (3) to form groups that will encourage and aid individuals along these ideals. Its pattern of effective method is to "observe, judge, and act," or size up a situation to see how best to apply Christian principles, and then take steps to change the situation along Christian lines. This Catholic Action movement was introduced into the United States at Manchester, N.H., in 1935, under the name "Young Christian Workers."

## Joel

This prophetic book of the OT is named after its author Joel (Jahweh is God), the son of Phatuel, who wrote about the year 400 B.C. The book tells of a plague and the penance of the people and the outpouring of the Spirit and salvation.

This minor prophet intended to call the entire nation to repent, warning of the coming Day of the Lord. He writes of ritual performance of penance and of the mercy of God (2:13). Its great significance is found in the prediction: "Then afterward I will pour out my spirit upon all mankind. . . ." (3:1–5), a prophecy that St. Peter includes in his first speech to the Apostles after the coming of the Holy Spirit on Pentecost (cf. Acts 2:14–21).

## Jogues, St. Isaac

See North American Martyrs.

## John the Baptist, St.

The son of the priest Zechariah and his wife Elizabeth, John was born a half year before Jesus Christ. His birth (Lk. 1:13–17) and the most important aspect of his life's work were foretold by the angel, Gabriel. His early life as a prophet was likewise foretold, and he spent his early years in a penitential manner in the Judean desert. By special grace John was chosen by God as a prophet; a special mission was given to him since he was the last of the Messianic prophets and one whose mission would have a single focal point, the person of Jesus. This is solemnly narrated by the evangelist Luke (3:1–22) who tells of the preaching and baptizing that John did and of his most solemn act of baptizing Christ.

John is called the bridge between the OT and the NT, because he was raised in the Jewish tradition, underwent the same ritual of Mosaic circumcision, and was especially called to announce that "the God of Israel has visited His people." He was the new Elijah (Sir. 48:1–10); he was the bearer of the news of preparation of the kingdom that Christ would bring in the plenitude of redemption and grace. He was a witness (cf. Jn. 1:6–15), and he was to be more than a prophet for he gave testimony with his blood—the death of martyrdom imposed upon him by Herod Antipas (cf. Mt. 14:1–12). John the Baptist is most familiarly called the "precursor" of Christ, and he is honored for this work in the liturgy with a solemnity recalling his birth (June 24) and a memorial of his death (Aug. 29).

### John de Brebeuf, St.
See North American Martyrs.

### John, Gospel of St.
The Fourth Gospel of the NT is not classed as synoptic but regarded as the culmination of the revelation of Christ. Traditionally, it is said to have been written by St. John, the evangelist and "beloved disciple," in about the year A.D. 100. It is regarded as a historical book of great dogmatic value, for the author, by recording certain events in the life of Christ and by special selections from His words, points out the revealed glory of Christ. In the words of St. John the book was written to record the special proofs of Christ's divinity: "But these have been recorded to help you believe that Jesus is the Messiah, the Son of God, so that through this faith you may have life in his name" (20:31). Its principal doctrines are: that Jesus of Nazareth is the Israelite Messiah and truly God, the Second Person of the Trinity (3:16–18); that Christ is the Savior; that the work of Christ continues through the Holy Spirit both for individuals and the Church (16:5–17); descriptions of the role of the Church, the interior working of grace, and the precept of charity.

It is the Gospel that singularly gives a testimony of faith; to the narration there is added a dimension that makes the facts recorded take on the vividness of love manifest. Because of this, the writing offers a firm unity of the Church and all Christians, through Christ and with one another.

### John, Epistles 1, 2 and 3
All of these letters were written by the Apostle John about the year A.D. 90. The entire content and purpose of the three are stated in the prologue of the first epistle: "This is what we proclaim to you: what was from the beginning, what we have heard, what we have seen with our eyes, what we have looked upon and our hands have touched— we speak of the word of life" (1 Jn. 1:1).

From these words we can understand two salient points of the letters of St. John: his eagerness to communicate the actual, real truth as he experienced it, and the love that he had for Jesus and that he seeks to convey to others.

In the first letter there is emphasis on the charity, which is the bond of unity between people and God, a charity that abides with God the Father who is love (1 Jn. 4:8), and that was secured for all through Christ.

The second letter, besides encouraging all Christians to perseverance, again emphasizes the charity that is manifest to all in "the truth that abides in us and will be with us forever" (2 Jn. 1:2).

The third letter, directed to Gaius in particular, repeats in a more personal way the perseverance mentioned in the second. It also gives insights into the early Church, the trials of some and the failings of others.

### John Lalande, St.
See North American Martyrs.

### John XXIII
See Vatican Council II.

### Jonah, Book of
This brief prophetical book of the OT was written by an unknown author in the fifth century before Christ. It takes its name from the hero of the account. It teaches the universality of salvation and prepares for the coming of Christianity through Jesus Christ. It thus protests against the particularism of the Jews following the exile in their claim to being the only persons to be saved. The writer points out the will of God to save all human persons, thus demonstrating the mercy and providence of God who is the divine ruler of the world and all things. Many regard the account of

Jonah as a parable, and the author really gives no historical detail to otherwise place the work, especially since it is paralleled by earlier writers (cf. Ez. 27).

### Jonah, Sign of

This is the answer given by Jesus to the Scribes and Pharisees who demanded a sign (proof) of his Messiahship. This sign may be interpreted as a direct acknowledgement of Christ's resurrection from the tomb. Jesus said: "An evil and unfaithful age is eager for a sign! No sign will be given it but that of the prophet Jonah. Just as Jonah spent three days and three nights in the belly of the whale, so will the Son of Man spend three days and three nights in the bowels of the earth" (Mt. 12:39–40). The three days and three nights are a more or less fixed expression for the beginning and ending time of the action. The sign is the confirmation by which God attests to the message of Christ, which will be brought to the world through the preaching of Christ and the Apostles (cf. Lk. 11:32).

### Joseph, St.

St. Joseph is the foster father of Jesus Christ, the betrothed (in Jewish law, the husband) of the Blessed Mother (Mt. 1:19). St. Joseph is characterized as a "just" man, and this is evidenced by his "just" treatment of Mary in not seeking publicity for her when she was known to be with child. It is through Joseph that Christ has "legal " descent from David. St. Joseph is honored in the church as her universal patron, and this patronage is celebrated on March 19. Another memorial is that of St. Joseph the Worker, celebrated on May 1.

Joseph is the link between Christ and the promise, and the "poor" man (cf. Lk. 4:22; Mt. 13:54–58). He is in tradition associated with the tools of a carpenter, the hammer and square, and is often symbolized with a flowering staff of lilies.

Besides being hailed as patron of the universal Church, Joseph is invoked in his litany as the patron of workmen, families, virgins, the sick, and the dying. He also has been recognized as the patron of prayer and the interior life, of the poor, those in authority, fathers, priests and religious, travelers, and all devotion to the Blessed Virgin Mary. In 1937, Pius XI named St. Joseph as the patron of the struggle against atheistic communism; in 1955 Pius XII proclaimed the feast of St. Joseph the Worker; and in 1961 John XXIII named St. Joseph the protector of the Second Vatican Council and in 1962 directed that the name of St. Joseph be placed in the canon of the Mass. (See Saint Joseph's Oratory.)

### Josephism, also Josephinism

The title Josephism is given to that movement arising under Joseph II, emperor of the Roman Empire (1765 to 1780), whose theory was to declare that the State was supreme in all matters concerning the internal and external affairs of the Church. He forbade all bishops to communicate with Rome, closed 700 religious houses as unnecessary, replaced religious schools with state institutions, organized a commission to regulate public worship, and limited to a maximum of 3,750 the number of religious permitted to live in Austria. In 1781 he issued the Edict of Toleration, which was both a toleration and a promotion of Protestantism; it indirectly endorsed Freemasonry. It created an atmosphere of religious unrest and brought about political changes. Like Febronianism, the movement reflected the Germanic dislike of Roman jurisdiction. Both systems were based on forms of Gallicanism, Erastianism, and Jansenism. Some of these actions were obstructive of the mission of the Church until the First Vatican Council.

### Joshua, Book of

Listed as a sixth book of the Bible following the Pentateuch, this work by an unknown author is historical in character. The Book of Joshua has many stories, both etiological and "hero," which contribute to its character and also point out that it was most likely written by several persons, probably in the Benjaminite era.

Joshua (Hebrew meaning: "God gives salvation"), around whom the book is structured, led the Chosen People under the inspiration of God. The book is also called a prophetical writing, and Joshua is listed as one of the early prophets.

The writing narrates the history of the Hebrews in their conquest of the land, listing the conquered kings, the union of the tribes (22:10–34), and the final renewal of the covenant at Shechem (24:16–28). The entire account reveals the religious and moral values of the Hebrews in the manner of God's leading of His people and ends with Joshua's plea of acknowledgement of God's fulfillment of His promises.

## Joy

The pleasure, delight, and satisfaction that are common to all human persons are singularly related to the Christian virtue of charity. It is thus both natural and supernatural in character. In its supernatural effects it is both the interior turning to the love of God in friendship and love as well as the resultant effect of holy and blessed response. It is the intersection or interaction of the senses and the spirit of the human person, resulting in pleasure and happiness. Joy is an integral part of the fulfilled promise of Christ's coming as foretold by Isaiah; thus it is raised to an eschatological height: "When you see this (the Lord's coming), your heart shall rejoice, and your bodies flourish like the grass; the Lord's power shall be known to his servants, but to his enemies, his wrath" (Is. 66:14) (cf. Rv. 19:7). The evangelist John speaks of the plenitude of joy that Jesus Himself communicated: "And this I tell you that my joy may be yours and your joy may be complete" (Jn. 15:11).

Pope Paul VI in an apostolic exhortation, *Gaudete in Domino* ("Rejoice in the Lord") released on May 9, 1975 and addressed to the bishops, clergy, and faithful, declared the need for joy in the hearts of all persons, and the special joy of the Christian.

He wrote: "In essence, Christian joy is the spiritual sharing in the unfathomable joy, both divine and human, which is in the heart of Jesus Christ glorified. As soon as God the Father begins to manifest in history the mystery of His Will, according to His purpose which He set forth in Christ as a plan for the fullness of time (cf. Eph. 1:9–10), this joy is mysteriously announced in the midst of the People of God, before its identity has been unveiled. . . .

"No one is excluded from the joy brought by the Lord. The great joy announced by the Angel on Christmas night is truly for all the people, both for the people of Israel then anxiously awaiting a Savior, and for the numberless people made up of all those who, in time to come, would receive its message and strive to live by it."

And in his conclusion: "Joy always springs from a certain outlook on man and on God. 'When your eye is sound, your whole body too is filled with

light.' We are touching here on the original and inalienable dimension of the human person; his vocation to happiness always passes through the channels of knowledge and love, of contemplation and action. May you attain this good quality which is in your brother's soul, and this divine presence so close to the human heart."

## Joyful Mysteries

See Mysteries of the Rosary.

## Joys of the Blessed Virgin Mary

See Crown, Franciscan.

## Jubilate Sunday

Jubilate Sunday is the name given to the third Sunday after Easter.

## Jubilee

1. In Church use, Jubilee is a time of prayer and penance, announced by the Holy Father. The Church proclaims special indulgences, notably a plenary indulgence, for the occasion. The word is probably derived from the Hebrew "Jabel," meaning "ram's horn used as a cornet." In Jewish history, the seventh year was the sabbatical year or a year of rest, and the fiftieth year was celebrated as a year of rest and restitution, particularly a fallow year; property reverted to former owners; slaves were emancipated; and debts were remitted or suspended (Lv. 25:1–55). Both events in Jewish Law were begun by the blowing of a ram's horn trumpet. In the Church, the first Jubilee was celebrated in 1300 by Pope Boniface VIII. Since 1470, the custom has been to announce an "Ordinary Jubilee" every 25 years. The pope may, however, proclaim an "Extraordinary Jubilee" in the event of any special centennial or unusual time, for example, a golden anniversary of a pope's ordination. Each jubilee proclamation is accompanied by a document that sets forth the requirements for gaining the indulgences and the special faculties granted to ordinaries and confessors.

2. The so-named "Book of Jubilees" is an apocryphal writing, narrating the OT and probably written in the late first or second century A.D.

## Judaism

From OT times, through the history of the Jewish people under the rule of the Sadducees, the hierarchical leaders up to the year A.D. 70, until the rabbinical schools that then followed, Judaism is the religion and practice of the Jewish people. The rabbinical leaders based their rule upon that of the Pharisees, following an acknowledgement of divine providence, freedom, resurrection of the dead, the existence of angels, and the last judgment.

However, Judaism must be considered as a phenomenon spanning religious, political, ethnic, social, and historical grounds. In history the broad understanding of Judaism goes back to the beginning of the twelve tribes, the establishment of the kingdom, the building of the Temple at Jerusalem, and its destruction in A.D. 70 by the Romans.

In its history and expression Judaism presents itself as that of a covenanted people, literally expressed by the Lord, "Therefore, if you hearken to my voice and keep my covenant, you shall be my special possession, dearer to me than all other people, though all the earth is mine. You shall be a kingdom of priests, a holy nation" (Ex. 19:5–6). And Judaism has been especially attached to the "land of Israel," which follows from the covenant made with God: "Keep all the commandments, then, which I enjoin on you today, that you may be strong enough to enter in and take possession of the land into which you are crossing, and that you may have long life on the land which the Lord swore to your fathers he would give to them and their descendants, a land flowing with milk and honey" (Dt. 11:8–9). And Judaism has continued a strong leaning toward the past; the once strong messianic expectation has never given way to the Messiah who accomplished Christian redemption.

Judaism was once called a "Mosaic religion," but it is basically a religion of law, a religion of reason. It is an ethical monotheism, which in its many features, Talmudic tradition, emancipation, Zionism, and the present return to the land of Israel, remains a system of practical conduct, religious ritual, the maintenance of tradition, and the hope of eschatological salvation because of acceptance of the yoke imposed by God through covenant and promise. (See Hebrew Feasts; Anti-Semitism.)

## Judaizers

Members of the early Church community (first century) who considered it necessary to observe the Mosaic law in order to fulfill the Christian faith were named Judaizers. The word meant "to live in the Jewish manner." Their opinion and thought were the first heretical reaction that the Church had to face. It was at the Council of Jerusalem in A.D. 49 that the Apostles and those called together by them (Acts 15) answered the Judaizers, and with this action also made clear the acceptance of the Gentiles into the Christian family. The influence of the Judaizers grew weak and eventually disap-

peared in the years following the destruction of Jerusalem in A.D. 70. (See Ebionites; Heresies.)

## Jude, Epistle of

The apostle Jude, whose name in Greek and Latin is the same as Judas, had the distinction of being referred to as "Judas, not Judas Iscariot" (Jn. 14:22) to distinguish him from the traitor. In Lk. 6:16 and Acts 1:13, he is referred to as "Judas, son of James." In the lists of Matthew (10:3) and Mark (3:18) he is called Thaddaeus.

Jude was a relative of Jesus (Mt. 13:55) and the author of the one epistle bearing his name, where he refers to himself as the brother of James (1:1). He addresses his letter "to those who have been called by God, who have found love in God the Father and have been guarded safely in Jesus Christ" (1:1). This letter was written about the year A.D. 70 especially to stimulate the Christians to stand up in defense of their faith against members of the community who would disrupt their unity. It is much like a written sermon, giving proof of God's love, speaking of the Christian's special calling and the assurance that Christ abides with them and guards them. The tenor of the exhortation is to stand fast in the faith (1:20–21), and it concludes with a doxology, a beautiful prayer: "Glory be to this only God our savior, through Jesus Christ our Lord. Majesty, too, be his, might and power from ages past, now and for ages to come. Amen" (1:25).

## Judges, Book of

The seventh book of the OT is so named because of the national heroes whose deeds form its main theme. The word "judge" here does not mean ruler but one who distributes justice to the people and maintains the rights of the down-trodden; thus, "judge" is used as the equivalent of "deliverer," and the book is named after the charismatic leaders of the Chosen People. As an historical book, Judges contains the religious history of Israel from the time of Joshua to Samuel. It covers a period of about 150 years (1200 to 1050 B.C.), and the time of the six great judges is arranged in chronological order. In particular, the book teaches the religious interpretation of the history of the chosen people, the wisdom of God, His justice and holiness, His mercy and His punishment of sin, especially grave sin, such as idolatry. God is declared faithful despite the backsliding of a rough people who entered into acts of idolatrous excess.

## Judges, Synodal

These judges of ecclesiastical courts are chosen in the diocesan synod; those selected outside a synod are called prosynodal. Such judges must be priests and should be skilled in canon law (c. 1574). (Cf. Synod.)

## Judgment, General

General Judgment is the act of God, sometimes called the "Day of Jahweh," prophesied to follow the end of the world as we know it, the cosmic ruin of the earth and its inhabitants (Jl. 3:1–5; Acts 2:17–21). It was to follow the second coming of Christ (1 Cor. 1:8). This time will be when the spiritual kingdom of God will be restored through the Second Coming, called the Parousia. It was foretold by Christ (Mk. 13:24). The event of the Parousia will be followed by the Judgment and the Renewal at the end. At this time, the former corporeal condition of man will be spiritualized; that is, men will arise in some transformation (1 Cor. 15:35–57). Then will all be judged, and their eternal reward or punishment fixed (Jn. 5:28–29).

Vatican II makes this meaningful to modern man: "Mindful of the Lord's saying: 'By this will all men know that you are my disciples, if you have love for one another' (Jn. 13:35), Christians cannot yearn for anything more ardently than to serve the men of the modern world even more generously and effectively. Therefore, holding faithfully to the gospel and benefiting from its resources, and united with every man who loves and practices, justice, Christians have shouldered a gigantic task demanding fulfillment in this world. Concerning this task they must give a reckoning to Him who will judge every man on the last day" (GS 93).

## Judgment of God

Judgment of God was an early method of trial practiced in the time before legal procedures were established, whereby it was contended that the innocence of a person would be established by the direct, perhaps even miraculous, intervention of God if the conditions were fair for such a conclusion. It was a superstitious practice.

## Judgment, Particular

Particular judgment is the judgment of the soul of one who has died, wherein the salvation or damnation of the person for all eternity is determined; it takes place immediately after death. This is not an intermediate step between the death of an individual and the final or general judgment of all mankind. It is the immediate satisfaction of hope for the individual in accord with his merit and degree of service and love as well as a judgment concerning guilt (Rom. 8:28–34). (Cf. Purgatory.)

## Judica Psalm

The name Judica Psalm is applied to Psalm 42. Preceded and followed by the versicle "I will go unto the altar of God," this Psalm was recited at the foot of the altar before all Masses except requiems and those said during Passiontide. Like the other preliminary prayers of the Tridentine Mass, it has been supplanted by the entrance ceremony in the New Order of the Mass.

## Judith, Book of

This historical book of the OT was most probably written in Hebrew by an unknown author, but undoubtedly later than the date of the events that it records, namely, the reign of Nebuchadnezzar (605 to 562 B.C.). Probably it was written in the second century B.C. Its doctrinal teaching is the merciful help of God and His justice.

This is recorded dramatic story, telling of God's aid to His Chosen People in their wars with their enemies. With the outcome a success, Judith is acclaimed as a national heroine: "You are the glory of Jerusalem, the surpassing joy of Israel; you are the splendid boast of our people" (Jdt. 15:9). In the liturgy of the Church, Judith has been likened to the Blessed Virgin Mary, for Mary also conquered the enemy of God through her acceptance of the Incarnation.

## Jurisdiction

This power belonging to the Church as a perfect society, whereby the Church effects a rule for the spiritual good of its members, has been defined as: "the public power granted by Christ or by His Church through canonical mission, of governing the baptized in matters referring to salvation." It is the right of a person or agency to pass or apply a given law in a specific situation. It thus refers to the power to make or pass laws and to enact and pass sentences and to punish. Jurisdiction is *ordinary* when it is attached to an office of the Church, for example, the power of diocesan bishops to govern in their dioceses. It is *delegated* when it is given by one having the right to another, for example, the faculty for hearing confession given to an assistant priest. Only the pope has universal jurisdiction, that is, it extends to all baptized persons everywhere, independently of any civil authority, in all that concerns the proper object of the Church's mission or the salvation of souls (c. 218).

The primatial power of jurisdiction, which is the

pope's as successor of St. Peter, is the "full and supreme power of jurisdiction over the whole Church, not only in matters that pertain to faith and morals, but also in matters that pertain to the discipline and government of the Church throughout the whole world" (Vat. I, DS 3064). The pope's ordinary jurisdictional power is an essential, constitutive power connected with the office itself; because it is not delegated by the episcopal body or the entire body of the faithful, there is no higher authority in the Church (cf. CD 2).

The bishops possess ordinary and immediate episcopal jurisdictional power. The bishops are "appointed by the Holy Spirit," or as the first Vatican Council declared "the bishops may be explicitly said to be the successors of the apostles and appointed by the Holy Spirit" (cf. Acts 20:28). They are thus "Vicars of Christ" and not "vicars of the pope." (See Collegiality.) The bishops exercise jurisdiction over their own faithful: "This power, which they personally exercise in Christ's name, is proper, ordinary and immediate. . . . In virtue of this power, bishops have the sacred right and the duty before the Lord to make laws for their subjects, to pass judgment on them, and to moderate everything pertaining to the ordering of worship and the apostolate" (LG 27).

The primatial power of the pope is limited by the "exclusively religious, supernatural end" of the Church; thus all actions must be directed to the universal good of the People of God. This jurisdiction of the Pope is also limited by the requirements of the natural law. The pope cannot ordain or legislate against the laws of nature. However, "insofar as these laws are connected with religious and moral life, and in the degree in which the teaching, interpretation, and application of these laws affects morality, the teaching Church can pronounce on them, delimit them, and define them more clearly" (Kloppenburg).

## Justice

1. The cardinal and moral virtue by which one, having regard for both law and duty, gives to everyone his due, that is, what is owed to him as a human being, be it in actual goods or intangibles that are his because of dignity. Therefore, justice extends to God, to one's neighbor, as well as to oneself. It is exercised in respect to the rights of others, while at the same time subjectively with charity, it governs man's relationship to others. It is the prime cardinal virtue and includes many subordinate virtues. As an imperative virtue, justice implies obedience, truthfulness, gratitude, and religion, as applied in regard to God, one's neighbor, or oneself. In the NT there is evident teaching concerning a higher justice that surpasses all others and is a gift of God (cf. Eph. 4:24; Phil. 1:11; Mt. 6:1). The Christian doing justice is that born of God (1 Jn. 2:29).

2. The state of *original justice* is that condition possessed by Adam and Eve before they sinned, or that condition under which they possessed everything that was their "due" as created by God for His glory.

3. *Social justice* is that which regards the rights of the common good or the relations of the individual to society. Vatican II states: "The demands of justice should be first satisfied, lest the giving of what is due in justice be represented as the offering of a charitable gift" (AA 8).

4. Justice may also take various subdivisions that in turn are only aspects of the application of the virtue. These may be for example: *commutative* justice, or the virtue regulating the actions or rights existing between single individuals; *distributive* justice, or that between superiors and subjects; *legal* justice, or that concerned with the individual and the society to which the person belongs.

## Justification

Primarily and simply justification is the possession of sanctifying grace in its Christian theological meaning. However, before this possession can be accomplished there must be baptism and this is preceded by faith and acceptance of the consequences of belief. Thus the Council of Trent (Sess. III, Ch. 8) declared "Faith is the beginning of man's salvation, the foundation and root of all justification; without which (that is, faith) it is impossible to please God and to obtain fellowship with his sons." Faith is man's assent to revealed truth (Council of Trent, Sess. III, Ch. 3). It is thus the basis of justification (Rom. 1:16–17). We are justified by Christ (cf. Is. 53:11) and by good works, as declared in the Epistle of James (2:24–26).

## Kamelaukion

The name derived from the Greek words for "camel" and "nape of the neck" is applied to the black, cylinder-shaped head-covering, with a flat brim at the top, worn commonly for liturgical functions by clerics of the Byzantine rite. Bishops and monks wear it with a veil that covers it and falls down to the shoulders. It was first made of

camelhair cloth; it is also spelled "Kalemaukion." It is thought that this form of head covering gave rise to the tiara worn by the pope. The kamelaukion is also worn by the Syrian Church clerics, both Catholic and Jacobite.

## Kamision

The kamision is the long, ungirdled vestment worn by clerics of the Byzantine rite. It is usually made of linen or silk, with wide sleeves, and may be white, red, or another suitable color, with embroidery on the hem, neck, and sleeves. It is also called the *sticharion*. A similar garment has been adapted to use in the Roman Rite by some clerics since Vatican II, but usually without any decoration. It is likened to the alb.

## Kanon

In the Byzantine Divine Office, or Breviary, a rhythmical composition of from two to nine odes that is divided into tropes, and corresponds to the canticles of Scripture, is called a kanon. In poetic form kanons are acrostics, with the first letters of the tropes forming a verse that has reference to the

feast of the day. A proper kanon is assigned to every feast and Sunday of the Church calendar of the rite.

## Kantism, also Kantianism

The title Kantism is given to the philosophy that evolved from the writings of Immanuel Kant (1724 to 1804). Kant's thought had especially far-reaching influence and came to be called "Kant's Copernican Revolution," derived from his major philosophical works, *Critique of Pure Reason* (1781) and *Critique of Practical Reason* (1788). As criticism, a first step in philosophy, Kantism is opposed to dogmatism on the one hand and scepticism on the other. Kantism results in a denial of everything that transcends experience.

Kant attempted to justify the certainty or even the necessity of a moral law, maintaining that man finds such a moral law in himself just as the human person finds the natural laws in his mind. This moral law he called the "categorical imperative."

This imperative is formulated in two propositions: (1) "Act only on that maxim through which you can at the same time will that it ought to become a universal law." Such a proposition, if carried out in the moral order would make a man sufficient to that which is willed and would destroy the possibility of a future remuneration of something beyond the person's ability to fulfill. (2) "So, act as to treat humanity, whether in your own person or that of another, always at the same time as an end, and never merely as a means." Thus Kantism makes the moral law not dependent on God, and hence theology is excluded from any ethical course of action since respect for the individual is missing completely. Kant declared: "You should, therefore you can," which makes man's freedom the only necessary condition of action in seeking a reward of happiness for doing what is right. This is contrary to faith in the promise of the redemptive act of Christ.

## Kathisma

The name Kathisma is given to any one of the twenty parts into which the Divine Office is divided in the Byzantine rite.

## Katholikon

The katholikon is the principal church of a monastery of the Byzantine rite; it is often likened to a cathedral. It is applied also to the Church of the Resurrection in Jerusalem as the Chief church of the Orthodox patriarch.

## Katholikos

The word, *katholikos,* meaning "universal" is the title of the bishops or primates of some Eastern rite churches, such as the Nestorian, Georgian, and Armenian churches. It was first applied like the term archbishop, especially when the bishop was not the metropolitan or primate, but now Katholikos and patriarch are indistinguishable, though the primacy of honor varies between the churches. The title of a prelate is delegated for a universality of causes; each Katholikos is elected by bishops of his own rite; he is approved by the pope and from him receives the pallium, symbolic of the office.

## Kenosis

This board term derived from the Greek word for "empty," is applied to the "kenotic theories" or certain heretical theories that have been advanced by Protestant theologians concerning the Incarnation. In one way or another they attempt to advance the idea that Christ "gave up" or "divested Himself" of certain divine attributes in becoming man, basing their idea on a mistaken interpretation of the passage of St. Paul's letter to the Philippians (2:6–9). Its proper meaning is not that Christ "emptied" Himself of a part or all of His divinity, but that he concealed or did not permit His divinity to be evident. (See Heresies.)

## Kergyma

This term, from the Greek word meaning "preaching" or "proclamation," is associated with the entire mission of the Church under "kerygmatic teaching." It means both the action and the message itself and is found in Scripture, particularly where the idea of salvation is joined essentially with the "word," and thus the word kerygma takes on the meaning of the "word of salvation."

The idea of mission of the Church upon examination takes on the concept of witness. The testimony given by the Apostles concerning Christ was more than a historical reality; it was a presupposition of faith, and it is also judicial in the sense that it was declared before a tribunal.

Apart from these manifestations of mission and witness, there is also the testimony found in the OT. This meant more than an "announcement" of a fact to be accomplished in the future. It is thus that Isaiah is called the "theologian of the mission" of God among all human persons (cf. Is. 41:8–16; 42:5–9; 43:8–12).

In the NT the missionary kerygma is found in the mission that Christ entrusted to his disciples, which they were to preach to all nations after His resurrection. From the very first it was evident that this was the activity of the Apostles and those who were sent forth by them, such as Stephen and Philip (cf. Lk. 10:1–9; Acts 1:8; 10:42; 13:2–6). And it is evident from Scripture that all members of the faithful are to participate in the mission of the Church (Acts 8:4).

Consequent to the act of witnessing is the "proclamation." This was to be more than missionary; it was to be joined to the Eucharist (cf. Lk. 14:23; 9:17), a sufficiency of food to bring all to salvation.

Thus there comes into the theology of kerygma the twofold approach, namely, the "preaching" and the "teaching" whereby all human persons are instructed in the truth of the "good news of our Lord, Jesus Christ." The faithful will see the kerygma in the life of the Church, in her carrying out in her liturgy the sacramental event, especially the celebration of the Eucharist within the framework of prayer, Scripture, and preaching. Through these especially there is to be attained a kerygmatical renewal whereby the truth of faith is presented as a unified whole. At its center is the Good News of redemption in Christ; the fruit of our sowing is the greater love of God.

It is because of these aspects of kerygma that we must have (1) an understanding of the faith brought about through catechesis; (2) a program of the catechetical apostolate; (3) an understanding of the instructive power of the liturgy; (4) an organic unity of the entire Christian message of salvation. All of these give emphasis to worship that is the very heart and fiber of Christian community life. (See Salvation History; Liturgy.)

## Key '73

The year 1973 was given over to a special effort of evangelization as an ecumenical enterprise. It failed in its major objectives but did have an interfaith impact upon certain world efforts of ecumenism. Its failure was probably as much a result of a miscalculation of the communications problems involved as it was from the general lassitude that such worldwide efforts meet when one or the other of the nations does not respond. (See Ecumenism; Evangelization.)

## Keys, Power of

See Power of the Keys.

## King James Version of the Bible

This translation of the Bible, known as the "Authorized Version," was undertaken in 1607 at the order of King James I of England. It is a revision of the earlier and faulty version, called the Bishop's Bible (1568). The King James Version became the official Bible of the Church of England, but it is now largely displaced by other versions although its language remains a beautiful example of classical English expression.

## Kingdom of Christ

This is the same as the Kingdom of God *(sic)*, yet it is within, that is, made up of all whom Christ has gained. It is declared in the gospels as eschatological and transcendent, a reward and eternal (cf. Mt. 25:34–46; Mk. 10:17–35).

Vatican II declares concerning this: "Since the kingdom of Christ is not of this world (cf. Jn. 18:36), the Church or People of God takes nothing away from the temporal welfare of any people by establishing this kingdom. Rather does she foster and take to herself insofar as they are good, the ability, resources, and customs of each people. Taking them to herself she purifies, strengthens, and ennobles them. The Church is mindful that she must harvest with that King to whom the nations were given for an inheritance (cf. Ps. 2:8) and into whose city they bring gifts and presents (cf. Pss. 71, 72: 10; Is. 60:4–7; Rv. 21:24) (LG 13).

## Kingdom of God

In the OT this was the governing of the people of Israel by God. Later, the Israelites came to look forward to a "new" kingdom. In the NT there are numerous references to the "kingdom of God" and parables that speak in a less direct manner of this kingdom which has come through Christ. Most emphatically the knowledge of this kingdom and the knowledge of the mystery of the Incarnation have been given to the disciples of Christ. It is a declaration of the divinity of Christ (Lk. 10:2–24), the knowledge of which the disciples will bring to others that they may attain to their salvation—participation in God's love in heaven.

Vatican II teaches: "The mystery of the holy Church is manifest in her very foundation, for the Lord Jesus inaugurated her by preaching the good news, that is, the coming of God's Kingdom, which, for centuries, had been promised in the Scriptures; 'This is the time of fulfillment. The reign of God is at hand' (Mk. 1:15; cf. Mt. 4:17). In Christ's word, in His works, and in His presence this kingdom reveals itself to men. The word of the Lord is like a seed sown in a field (Mk. 4:14). Those who hear the word with faith and become part of the little flock of Christ (Lk. 12:32) have received the

kingdom itself. Then, by its own power the seed sprouts and ripens until harvest time (cf. Mk. 4:26–29).

"The miracles of Jesus also confirm that the kingdom has already arrived on earth; 'But if it is by the Spirit of God that I expel demons, then the reign of God has overtaken you' (Lk. 11:20; cf. Mt. 12:28).

"Before all things, however, the kingdom is clearly visible in the very person of Christ, Son of God and Son of Man, who came 'to serve, and to give his life as a ransom for the many' (Mk. 10:45)" (LG 5).

## Kings, First and Second Books of

In many older editions of the Bible there were four books of Kings, the original number including the first and second books of Samuel. Thus in the modern listing of books what is now named the first and second books of Kings was originally the third and fourth books of Kings.

These historical writings were probably written by several now unknown authors in the ninth to sixth centuries before Christ. The books cover a span of history of some 400 years, recounting the last days of King David, the reign of Solomon, the division of the kingdoms, the building of the Temple at Jerusalem (2 Kgs. 3–11), the failure of the kings toward the people except the qualified approval of Hezekiah (2 Kgs. 18–20) and Josiah (2 Kgs. 22–23), and the destruction of the Temple by Nebuchadnezzar in 587 to 586 B.C. (2 Kgs. 25:9). The second book concludes with the plight of the Israelites in being carried into captivity in Babylon (2 Kgs. 25:1–21).

This is primarily a recording of God's plan for His Chosen People from the true worship of Yahweh in Solomon's Temple, through their disintegration, to the preparation of the pious remnant who would remain true to God's revealed truth up to the coming of the promised Redeemer. (See Bible.)

## Kingship of Christ

Based upon scriptural declarations (Lk. 1:33) and the traditional teaching of the Church, Christ is King by (1) birthright as the Son of God, divine filiation; (2) right as the Redeemer, the fulfillment of promises of everlasting life and final peace; (3) the power that is His as legislator, judge, and executor (Acts 10:42). In 1925, Pope Pius XI in his encyclical, *Quas Primas,* formally set forth the doctrine of the Kingship of Christ and declared the last Sunday in October the date for celebration of the liturgical feast of Christ the King, which is now a solemnity and the last Sunday in ordinary time (before the first Sunday of Advent).

Vatican II states: "By sacred ordination and by the mission they receive from their bishops, priests are promoted to the service of Christ, the Teacher, the Priest, and the King" (PO 1).

In biblical history the King was considered the "shepherd" of his people (2 Sm. 5:2), and he is called the "breath of life." When we consider Christ as the perfect King in these traditional contexts, we recognize Him as the ideal shepherd and the restorer to life everlasting (Lk. 15:1–7; Jn. 10:11; Is. 40:1–11; Ps. 2; 22; Rv. 7:13–17).

### Kiss, Liturgical Use of

The kiss as a mark of honor and reverence is frequently used in the liturgy of the Church, for example, kissing of the altar by the celebrant during Mass. As a more formal salute and a mark of brotherly affection of Christians, the *Pax* or "kiss of peace" was given at solemn Mass after the *Agnus Dei.* After kissing the altar, the celebrant placed his arms over the arms of the deacon and, while they bowed to each other, the celebrant said *Pax tecum* (Peace be to you) to which the deacon responded with *Et cum spiritu tuo* (And with your spirit). The Pax was then passed on similarly to other clerics present.

In the new Liturgy of the Eucharistic Celebration the Sign of Peace is spoken right after the doxology at the end of the Lord's prayer. The priest says: "Lord Jesus Christ, you said to your apostles: I leave you peace, my peace I give you, Look not on our sins, but on the faith of your Church, and grant us the peace and unity of your kingdom where you live for ever and ever." The people respond: "Amen." Then the celebrant says: "The peace of the Lord be with you always." And

the people respond: "And also with you." Following this, the deacon or celebrant may say: "Let us offer each other the sign of peace."

This, while not a kiss in the usual acceptance of the term (though some have considered this proper) is a return to the biblical "holy kiss" of greeting (Rom. 16:16; 1 Pt. 5:14). Thus the "peace" transfer is an act of communal acceptance exchanged between members present at the Eucharist and is usually done with a handshake and the words of greeting.

### Knights of Columbus

The Knights of Columbus is a fraternal organization of Catholic men founded in New Haven, Conn., in 1882, to develop and promote genuine Catholicity among its members. It is devoted to works for promotion of charity and education, furtherance of historical study, and provision of benefits to members and survivors in the families of deceased members. It is organized to function under an executive board, a supreme council and subcouncils that are either state or subordinate councils.

The organization has a wide-ranging program, including educational scholarships, social welfare activities, youth programs, and providing spiritual and physical aid in times of war or distress. The society's publication is the magazine *Columbia.*

### Knights, Orders of

The twelfth century saw the rise of several orders of knighthood that were actually religious orders although military in character. The knights took the three vows of poverty, chastity, and obedience, and shared the immunities of monks; they were directly under the Holy See. These orders were: Knights Hospitallers of St. John, founded in 1113; Knights Templars, organized in 1118; and the Teutonic Order of Knights, begun in 1190.

### Knights, Papal

Honorary titles are conferred by the papal court on laymen for outstanding services rendered to the welfare of society and to the Church and its welfare. In rank, the titles range from prince to baron, inclusive. According to their importance these are: (1) Supreme Order of Christ, (2) Order of Pius IX, (3) Order of St. Gregory the Great, (4) Order of St. Sylvester, (5) Order of the Golden Militia or Golden Spur, (6) Order of the Holy Sepulcher.

## Knock, Our Lady of

An apparition of the Blessed Virgin Mary, St. Joseph, and St. John the Evangelist occurred in the small village of Knock in County Mayo, Ireland, Aug. 21, 1879. St. John appeared as a bishop; his left hand held a book, and his right hand was raised as though blessing or preaching; St. Joseph appeared aged with grey beard and hair; the Virgin was in white garments and wearing a very brilliant crown, her hands were raised in the orante prayer position and her eyes turned toward heaven *(sic)*.

The significance of this apparition has been difficult to assess since no words were spoken, no message given, and no relationship to the village apparent. It is conjectured that, since there was an altar beside St. John on which there were a cross and a young lamb, this was to stimulate devotion to the Lamb of God, Christ.

The apparition was viewed by fifteen witnesses, with exact detail and conviction on the appearances. It was an apparition of comfort and solace to the faithful of Ireland. There have been thousands of cures, but only since 1936 has there been a Medical Bureau that attests to the genuine nature of those cures, which may be considered miraculous because the medical evidence is judged in an impartial manner. Our Lady of Knock has drawn a steady stream of pilgrims to the small village, a third of a million each year, and the celebration of the Eucharist there at the shrine is itself a mighty modern testimonial of devotion to Christ the Lamb of God.

## Knowledge

Knowledge is the intellectual virtue that is exercised by an act of knowledge; that is, that to utilize the virtue of knowledge one must strive for information and understanding. Epistemology investigates the conditions for our knowledge from the viewpoint of the concrete reality or content, that by which we know the object itself.

In a religious context, knowledge is a gift of the Holy Spirit by which we can judge the spiritual value and utility of created things. However, this is not infused knowledge independent of one's senses but a combination of sensible, perceptual, and experimental knowledge.

The human person must attempt to attain two kinds of knowledge that are essential to his salvation: that of God, and that of man's environment or his relationship to his neighbor. Concerning the first, Vatican II declares: "Through divine revelation, God chose to show forth and communicate Himself and the eternal decisions of His will regarding the salvation of men. That is to say, He chose 'to share those divine treasures which totally transcend the understanding of the human mind.'

"This sacred Synod affirms, 'God, the beginning and end of all things, can be known with certainty from created reality by the light of human reason' (cf. Rom. 1:20); but the Synod teaches that it is through His revelation 'that those religious truths which are by their nature accessible to human reason can be known by all men with ease, with solid certitude, and with no trace of error, even in the present state of the human race'" (DV 6).

And concerning man's knowledge in relationship to his environment, Vatican II states: "Within the individual person there too often develops an imbalance between an intellect which is modern in practical matters, and a theoretical system of thought which can neither master the sum total of its ideas, nor arrange them adequately into a synthesis" (GS 8).

## Know-Nothingism

This political movement began in 1852 in the United States as a outgrowth of the defunct Native American Party. Its object was to seize political power to carry out its program of marked hostility to foreigners and Catholics. The members of this secret society were all native-born Protestants who were bound by oath to answer all questions concerning their activities with the reply "I don't know." The movement gained enough power in several eastern states to put through several anti-Catholic statutes but, not being endorsed by either of the major political parties, it faded rapidly after 1857 and eventually disappeared entirely.

As a political party the Know-Nothings were committed to a Nativist program. They took advantage of the political unrest of the country, gained strength in thirty-five states, and passed anti-Catholic statutes in several state legislatures. In 1855 they could boast seventy-five members in Congress.

Abraham Lincoln aided the movement's demise when he wrote to Joshua Speed (Aug. 24, 1855), saying: "I am not a Know-Nothing, that is certain. How could I be? How can anyone who abhors the oppression of negroes be in favor of degrading classes of white people? Our progress in degeneracy appears to be pretty rapid. As a nation we began by declaring 'all men are equal.' We now practically read it 'All men are created equal, except negroes.' When the Know-Nothings get control it will read, 'All men are created equal except negroes, foreigners, and Catholics.' When it comes to this, I shall prefer emigrating to some country where they make no pretense at liberty."

### Knox Version

The translation of the Bible from the Vulgate, by Msgr. Ronald A. Knox is called the Knox version. Begun in 1939, it was published in 1949. The task was undertaken at the request of the hierarchy of England and Wales. This work is marked by a greater use of prose form and a choice of words that are based on the most recent research and thus are more compatible with modern spoken English. It has not been a popular version, but its literary qualities have given rise to many of the modern translations and adaptations.

### Koimesis

From the Greek word for "falling asleep," this is the name given to the feast of the Assumption of the Blessed Virgin Mary in the Byzantine rite.

### Koinonia

From the Greek, the word koinonia, meaning "fellowship" or "community," has come to be a collective word for the People of God, those ministered to through the mission of the Church (Acts 2:42–44; Heb. 13:16). (Cf. Community.)

### Kontakion

Kontakion is the name of a hymn that refers to the feast of the day in the liturgy of the Byzantine rite.

### Koran

The sacred book of the Moslems is called the Koran, a word derived from the Arabic word meaning "read." It is composed of the revelations, commands, and the believed eternal word of God delivered to the prophet Mohammed by the angel Gabriel. The first verse was said to be the inspired command of the angel declaring: "Read! read in the name of your Lord who created man."

Thus the word Koran was applied to each of the revelations announced by Mohammed and then to the entire book, including those compiled after his death by his secretary, Zaid Ibn Thabit at the command of the Caliph Abu Bekr. There are in the entire Koran 114 chapters, called *suras,* arranged by length rather than logically or chronologically. They are metrical in style, with strong cadences. The Koran urges submission to the one God Allah and the true faith that shows a

progression of revelation from Moses and Christ to the final prophet, Mohammed himself. Its aim is the guidance of the pious who believe in the mysteries of faith, say their prayers, give alms, and of course accept the Koran as beyond criticism. Because it is classic in language, it has become the standard of Moslem literature, science, social philosophy, morals, and worldly dealings. Together with all religious recognition, it has had a tremendous influence upon the entire Mohammedan world.

### Krishna

Certainly one of the most widely worshipped of the deities of the Hindu religion, Krishna is the greatest of the incarnations of Vishnu. In story and tradition Krishna is represented as hero, warrior, cowherd, lover, slayer of dragons, and he becomes in the *Bhagavad Gita, the* very god, even Brahman himself. It is through love, service, and devotion to him that salvation is possible for human persons regardless of their state in life of their caste.

### Ku-Klux-Klan

This variously formed organization was begun in the post–Civil War years at Pulaski, Tenn. It was a secret group organized against Catholics, Jews, Negroes, and the foreign-born. In Nashville, Tenn. in May, 1867, the Klan set up a multi-state organization, with the Grand Wizard of the Empire the highest ranking. Its history, with its various changes and reorganizations, is most ignoble. In 1928, its title was changed to "Knights of the Green Forest," and just prior to World War II it took on a Fascist-Nazi character. It is presumably defunct, local bad-boy antics notwithstanding, and has been rejected by all right-thinking people.

It had some revival in 1960, continuing anti-

Catholic, anti-black, and anti-alien activities, and worked against the election of John F. Kennedy. The Federal Bureau of Investigation, together with local leaders and members of the press, broke the structure, and although it still has twitchings of activity, it is ineffective as an organization.

## Kulturkampf

The German word literally translated "culture-war" is the name of the persecution of Catholics by Prussia, which began in 1873. The attempt to suppress religious differences in the confederated states of Germany begun by Bismarck brought on the *Kulturkampf.* His minister of worship, Adalbert Falk carried through the May Laws of 1873, which annulled papal jurisdiction over German Catholics, for 'all practical purposes; the Jesuits, Redemptorists, and other religious orders were abolished; those bishops who resisted were fined or imprisoned.

The Kulturkampf spread from Prussia to several other German states, but the Bavarian provinces of the Rhine and the areas of Prussian Poland formed an opposition party, led by Ludwig Windthorst. Known as the *Centrum,* it became politically powerful enough to pressure Bismarck into a new agreement with the Vatican in 1887.

The expression, Kulturkampf, has become by extension a term used to describe any position, political or general, which restricts religious freedom and the influence of the Catholic Church.

## Kummus

Kummus is a Coptic rite abbot; it is also a term of honor applied to distinguished priests of the Coptic rite.

## Kyr

From the Greek word for "lord" or "master," this is the title of a Byzantine bishop. It corresponded to the earlier Roman rite practice of referring to bishops as "Your Grace" or "Your Lordship," which has now been completely done away with.

## Kyriale

A book of chant, the kyriale contains the words and musical notation for the Ordinary of the Mass, that is, the Kyrie, Gloria, Credo, Sanctus, Agnus Dei, and the antiphons Asperges and Vidi Aquam. It is now used only in the chants of a Latin Mass, which is celebrated only with permission since the introduction of the New Order of the Mass and the finalizing of the Roman rite Sacramentary.

## Kyrie Eleison

The invocation of the Trinity was said in the Mass before the Gloria. It consists of: the invocation of God the Father by saying three times the Greek words Kyrie Eleison (Lord, have mercy!), the invocation of God the Son by reciting three times the words Christe Eleison (Christ, have mercy!), and the invocation of the Holy Spirit by repeating three times Kyrie Eleison. It is an optional part of the New Order of the Mass.

## Labarum

The military standard, first used by Constantine in 312 as a sign of his conversion to Christianity, consisted of a staff with a loosely fastened, short cross-arm from which the banner streamed. In the Church, it is sometimes seen in symbols, for example, a sheep holding the staff, or in banners heralding the resurrection.

## Labor

The activity of the human person whereby the necessities of life are satisfied and one's abilities are applied in accordance with his will and capabilities is called labor. Because of his physical and mental endowments the human person is given a place of pre-eminence in the world above all other created beings. This is the basis for the dignity of the human person, the place of trust and responsibility in his actions. In recognition of this and because of the dignity inherent in each person, the Church has always had a great concern for labor and has maintained a teaching program to enable the person to apply his abilities. The Church holds the belief that the purpose of human life, the honor of God, demands the conviction that one may serve his life in a manner consistent with his nature. Recognizing the principle of human dignity and destiny, the Church has taught that the individual has a sacred right to pursue those activities that will provide for the necessities to make life fruitful and fulfill the purpose of his creation, his salvation.

The human person is engaged in the work of a new creation. Through his acceptance of the dominion over things entrusted to him by God (Gn. 1:26; Ps. 8), he assumes by nature a dignity and the right to enjoy the fruits of his labor. He also assumes the obligation to extend this right to others and to help others less fortunate. Hence, involved here are rights and obligations, duties and responsibilities, fruits and distribution of them in justice (Rom. 15:27; 1 Tm. 6:18).

From apostolic times the Church has taught the dignity and rights of individuals. Because of this a. social doctrine has developed, with a constant fight against the exploitation of the worker, and a continuing effort to keep the rich and the State from doing anything to enjoin the right to private property.

Pope Leo XIII in an apostolic letter of March 19, 1902, wrote: "In the Catholic Church, Christianity is incarnate . . . Legitimate dispenser of the teaching of the Gospel, she does not reveal herself only as the consoler and redeemer of souls, but she is still more the internal source of justice and charity, and the propagator as well as the guardian of true liberty, and, no less of that equality which alone is possible here below. In applying the doctrine of her divine Founder, she maintains a wise equilibrium and marks the true limits between the rights and privileges of society. The equality which she proclaims does not destroy the distinction between the different social classes. She keeps them intact, as nature itself demands, in order to oppose the anarchy of reason emancipated from faith and abandoned to its own devices. The liberty which she gives in no wise conflicts with the rights of truth, because these rights are superior to the demands of liberty. Nor does she infringe upon the rights of justice, because these rights are superior to the claims of mere numbers or power. Nor does she assail the rights of God because they are superior to the rights of humanity."

Vatican II has this to declare: "Since economic activity is generally exercised through the combined labors of human beings, any way of organizing and directing that activity which would be detrimental to any worker would be wrong and inhuman. It too often happens, however, even in our day, that in one way or another workers are made slaves of their work. This situation can by no means be justified by so-called economic laws. The entire process of productive work, therefore, must be adapted to the needs of the person and to the requirements of his life, above all his domestic life. Such is especially the case with respect to mothers of families, but due consideration must be given to every person's sex and age.

"The opportunity should also be afforded to

workers to develop their own abilities and personalities through the work they perform. Though they should apply their time and energy to their employment with a due sense of responsibility, all workers should also enjoy sufficient rest and leisure to cultivate their family, cultural, social, and religious life. They should also have the opportunity to develop on their own the resources and potentialities to which, perhaps, their professional work gives but little scope" (GS 67).

And: "The distribution of goods should be directed toward providing employment and sufficient income for the people of today and of the future" (GS 70). (See Social Encyclicals.)

## Lady Chapel

Small chapels, dedicated to the Blessed Mother, are so named. They were often part of a cathedral, for example, the chapels at Canterbury, Winchester, and Ely. Also such chapels were places of private devotion in castles or homes of families with a special devotion to the Blessed Virgin Mary.

## Lady Day

This name is applied in some places to the Feast of the Assumption, Aug. 15.

## Laetare Medal

A gold medal is presented annually by the University of Notre Dame on Laetare Sunday. It is awarded to those persons of the United States who have served their country and their Church in a distinguished manner. A citation setting forth the reasons for the award accompanies the medal. (See Honors and Awards.)

## Laetare Sunday

The title of the fourth Sunday of Lent, taken from the first Latin word of the Introit, means "Rejoice." Although this part of the Latin Mass has been replaced by the New Order of Mass (see Latin Mass), the title of the Sunday continues by custom. This Sunday is distinguished in the liturgy as an occasion in the Roman rite when rose-colored vestments may be worn. It also is the day on which a traditional award of the Church, the Golden Rose, is blessed.

## Laic Laws

A sweeping series of laws were enacted in France between 1875 and 1907, culminating in the Law of Separation of 1905. Directed at the separation of the Church and state, these were named the Laic Laws. Their legal actions were effective in the secularization of French public life following the establishment of the Third Republic in 1870. The edicts restricted the role of the Catholic clergy in education and the direction of charitable asylums and institutions, and limited the right of the Church to possess property and hold services without the approbation of the secular authorities.

The attack by the ruling Republicans was launched because of their charge that the clergy were ignorant, not scientifically oriented, and that as representatives of the Church, they sought the downfall of the Republic. The effects of the Laic Laws were most seriously felt in the areas of education where all religious were removed from primary education, instruction in religion was prohibited, and the private schools were granted no financial support from the State.

Pope Leo XIII sought to reconcile the positions of the Republic and its avowed anticlericalism with the publication in 1884 of an encyclical *Nobillissima Gallorum gens* (Most Noble French People), and although some progress was made in relaxing the hostility to the Church, new troubles brewed following the clash between the conservatives and the radicals after the Dreyfus Affair.

A renewed attack on the Church, led by Justin Combes, brought forth a law declaring that "all religious associations must obtain special authorization to operate in France." This heralded a breaking off of diplomatic relations with the Holy See. The following year, 1905, saw passage of the Law of Separation that stopped all appropriations for public worship, the discontinuance of a traditionally recognized national faith, and the complete laicization of French secular life. The Church lost revenues and properties and any formal freedom of action in the political life of France. Although Roman Catholicism remains the predominant religion of the French people, it was not until 1920, following the first World War, that diplomatic relations became stable and the French embassy was reopened with the Vatican State.

## Laicism

Laicism is the erroneous concept that the administration of the Church can and should be in the hands of the laity. More recently, those advancing this idea of a break between Church and state, maintain that all affairs of human society, such as education, hospitals, government, and labor, should be conducted without regard to religion. These attempts are classed under the term secularism. Historically there have been many forerunners of laicism such as Gallicanism and

Febronianism. Laicism was condemned by Pope Pius IX, Dec. 8, 1864, in the encyclical *Quanta Cura,* called the "Syllabus of Errors." (Cf. Secularism.)

## Laicization

Laicization is the process of formal, voluntary appeal and action whereby one ordained to the diaconate, priesthood, or hierarchy is relieved of the Holy Orders, freed of the attendant obligations and all acts of ministry, and "officially" returned to the lay state. Such processes on the part of the diocesan clergy are filed with their ordinary who reviews them and forwards the petitions to the Apostolic Signatura of the Roman Curia. Upon review, the grant of an indult of laicization is given in accord with canon law.

The process is also applied to members of a religious order, congregation, or society whereby the applicant is relieved of the obligations of vows and membership in the religious institute. In such instances applications are filed with the proper religious superior and forwarded to the Congregation for Religious at the Vatican.

## Laity

The word laity is derived from the Greek word meaning "people." It is the general term used for all the members of the Mystical Body, of the Church universal, of the Catholic and other Christians who are not members of a professed religious order, society, or congregation, or are not ordained deacons, priests, or bishops. Sisters and brothers in religious life are considered members of the laity, except in canon law.

In this context the historic position of the Church regarding the laity must be examined, together with the role or mission of the laity apart from that of religious or cleric, and the present assessment of the laity since the *Decree on the Apostolate of the Laity* of Vatican II.

1. In history the Church has always considered that the laity are distinct and that they owe obedience to the hierarchy in their threefold episcopal function. This does not mean that the laity are passive or only a minor part of the active Church, although some have espoused this idea. On the contrary, there is a distinction only in the role and function of the laity as compared with those of the religious or clerical state. The laity are fully members of the Church, having received the faith and the Holy Spirit on their day of baptism. They are fit to become in their own right cooperators in the magisterium of the Church, because the Church is a fellowship *(koinonia)* wherein each seeking final perfection should tend to practice an ever more active charity, a more vibrant faith, and more extensive service to others of the community.

In scripture the laity look upon their pastors, bishops, and priests as ministers of Christ (Mt. 10:40; 18:18; Jn. 13:20; 2 Cor. 5:18–19). The laity lose access to salvation and their final award if they fall into error (1 Jn. 2:22–23; Heb. 13:8–9). Hence the lay person is a special witness particularly concerning relations between the Church and the world, even recognizing the opposition between these two (2 Pt. 3:1–3; Jn. 17:11).

Through baptism and confirmation the lay person becomes a member of the Church and is permitted to celebrate the Eucharist, offering with the bishop and the priests this spiritual sacrifice (1 Jn. 2:20–21; 1 Pt. 2:4–9; 1 Cor. 10:16–17; Rom. 12:1–2). It follows that the laity should assist the priests in Christianizing their community and world (Acts 18:2–3; Rom. 16:3; 1 Cor. 16:19). And the lay person, through a growth in sanctity will bring about a growth of the Mystical Body (1 Pt. 1:13–16; Eph. 4:15–20), and united together in charity, increase their union with Christ even as He is one with the Father (Rom. 12:10–21; Jn. 17:20–23). It is because of spiritual sacrifice that the lay person cannot be separated from the Eucharist, for it is by partaking of the Eucharistic offering that the faithful truly offer worship to God (Heb. 4:14–17; 7:19; 10:19–22) and become a "holy priesthood," a worshipping community (1 Pt. 2:9).

2. The mission of the laity is one and the same with the mission of the Church (Acts 8:4). And the necessary prerogatives are given to the lay person so that each may accomplish his or her mission (1 Pt. 2:9; Rom. 15:6–7). The Church, a new-covenanted people, exists in human society and is in the world though apart from it. It is in this temporal area that the lay person is especially emancipated to carry on those actions that are of the greatest service to the Church. The laity are not an isolated group, not a little island of obedient reaction, but truly a dynamic force working with the ordained ministers, by special mandate of the episcopacy, to achieve a society that is at once more holy and Christlike.

In the past it was thought that one way of attaining the broader cooperation of the laity was to give them special assignments through organizations and pious societies or to fulfill some directed form of Catholic Action. Although this was sufficient in its time, it left a vacuum since it did not challenge the individual as his or her special role in the mission of the Church required. There was to come a more basic involvement of, first, personal sanctification, and second, greater service to other members of the community. This came about with the drafting of the constitutions on the Church, especially *Lumen Gentium* (Dogmatic Constitution on the Church), *Sacrosanctum Concilium* (Constitution on the Sacred Liturgy), *Gaudium et Spes* (Pastoral Constitution on the Church in the Modern World), and *Apostolicam Actuositatem* (Decree on the Apostolate of the Laity).

3. While the people of God existed historically and scripturally and had achieved some form of organized fellowship, there was little recognition given to the "common priesthood" of each member of the faithful even though this had been formulated during the Reformation. The signs that the people of God were animated by the one Holy Spirit, that they have special charisms or gifts, that each is called to function in accord with his or her gifts and exercise services separate from but uniquely allied with those of the clergy were intended to achieve a distinct unity in the Church. This is coming to fruition even now through catechesis, the liturgy, and community sensitivity.

In Chapter 4 of *Lumen Gentium* (which formed the basis for the Decree on the Apostolate of the Laity), the special place of the laity in the Church was set forth.

We read: "The term laity is here understood to mean all the faithful except those in holy orders and those in a religious state sanctioned by the Church. These faithful are by baptism made one body with Christ and are established among the People of God. They are in their own way made sharers in the priestly, prophetic, and kingly functions of Christ. They carry out their own part in the mission of the whole Christian people with respect to the Church and the world.

"A secular quality is proper and special to laymen. It is true that those in holy orders can at times engage in secular activities, and even have a secular profession. But by reason of their particular vocation they are chiefly and professedly ordained to the sacred ministry. Similarly, by their state in life, religious give splendid and striking testimony that the world cannot be transfigured and offered to God without the spirit of the beatitudes.

"But the laity, by their very vocation, seek the kingdom of God by engaging in temporal affairs and by ordering them according to the plan of God. They live in the world, that is, in each and in all of the secular professions and occupations. They live in the ordinary circumstances of family

and social life, from which the very web of their existence is woven.

"They are called there by God so that by exercising their proper function and being led by the spirit of the gospel they can work for the sanctification of the world from within, in the manner of leaven. In this way they can make Christ known to others, especially by the testimony of a life resplendent in faith, hope, and charity. The layman is closely involved in temporal affairs of every sort. It is therefore his special task to illumine and organize these affairs in such a way that they may always start out, develop, and persist according to Christ's mind, to the praise of the Creator and the Redeemer" (LG 31).

And: "If therefore everyone in the Church does not proceed by the same path, nevertheless all are called to sanctity and have received an equal privilege of faith through the justice of God (cf. 2 Pt. 1:1). And if by the will of Christ some are made teachers, dispensers of mysteries, and shepherds on behalf of others, yet all share a true equality with regard to the dignity and to the activity common to all the faithful for the building up of the Body of Christ.

"For the distinction which the Lord made between sacred ministers and the rest of the People of God entails a unifying purpose, since pastors and the other faithful are bound to each other by a mutual need. Pastors of the Church, following the example of the Lord, should minister to one another and to the other faithful. The faithful in their turn should enthusiastically lend their cooperative assistance to their pastors and teachers. Thus in their diversity all bear witness to the admirable unity of the Body of Christ. This very diversity of graces, ministries, and works gathers the children of God into one, because 'it is one and the same Spirit who produces all these gifts' (1 Cor. 12:11).

"Therefore, by divine condescension the laity have Christ for their brother who, though He is the Lord of all, came not to be served but to serve (cf. Mt. 20:28). They also have for their brothers those in the sacred ministry who by teaching, by sanctifying, and by ruling with the authority of Christ so feed the family of God that the new commandment of charity may be fulfilled by all. St. Augustine puts this very beautifully when he says: 'What I am for you terrifies me; what I am with you consoles me. For you I am a bishop; but with you I am a Christian. The former is a title of duty; the latter, one of grace. The former is a danger; the latter, salvation' (LG 32).

It is therefore of the utmost importance in

understanding the laity and its role in the Church that we know the "full, conscious and active participation of the faithful" in the liturgy. Upon this, to a large extent, the unity of the people of God depends. Also it is important that the members of the laity recognize and execute their own mission in the Church in the "bond of peace." The laity and the clergy have a common end, salvation for all. Through these recognitions they will give witness to Christ in the world, testimony through faith, love, and hope, and fulfillment of their mission through service that is obedient to the hierarchy and supplemental to all their endeavors to fulfill the mandate of Christ to bring the world to Him. (See Apostolate; Liturgy; Stewardship.)

**Laity, Office of the**

An innovation following Vatican II was the establishing of Offices of the Laity to act as a secretariat working close to the chancery of dioceses. They variously are called Director of Lay Apostolate, Diocesan Lay Coordinator, or Council of (or for) the Laity. This office is a secretariat, staffed by lay personnel, which serves a variety of functions. It may be headed by a religious or member of the clergy, but in most instances these are less successful because of overlapping duties.

The Office of the Laity is maintained under the direction of the local ordinary to perform some or all of the following services: (1) coordinate all activities of national, diocesan, interparochial, and parochial organizations, which may be a hundred or more in some dioceses; (2) arrange and direct programs of instruction regarding diocesan parish councils, diocesan pastoral councils, or special activities groups; (3) maintain a calendar of events and where possible publish this in some newsletter form; (4) serve as a liaison person or public relations center for the diocese; (5) act as a service center for intergroup activities or intersocial programs; (6) act as a public relations representative for the media, newspapers, television, and radio; (7) act in cooperation with, either as a member or attendant, of State or Provincial Conferences.

This secretariat is neither a complaint center nor a policy-making branch of the clerical or religious of the diocese. Rather the role of this office is to be a diocesan ombudsman for the laity and to offer practical, balanced, projected, and efficient service to the wide spectrum of lay interests and activities within a diocese. It also is an exchange avenue for programs and activities of the lay apostolate of other dioceses in the regional, national, or international complex of organizations (Cf. Parish Council; Diocesan Pastoral Council; Priests' Councils.)

**Lalande, St. John**

See North American Martyrs.

**Lalemant, St. Gabriel**

See North American Martyrs.

**Lamb of God**

1. In Jewish sacrifices, especially at the Passover, a lamb was often the victim. Thus, in Scripture, the lamb prefigured the Messiah. As a title, it was applied directly to Christ by St. John the Baptist (Jn. 1:29–34) when he pointed his finger at Christ and declared "Behold the Lamb of God." In this sense, the lamb, a symbol of innocence, is Christ and He is designated as one sent by God to be offered up as God wishes. Further recognition of Christ as the Lamb of God was given at the Last Supper when Christ and his disciples gathered to eat the Pasch. The two sacrifices, the feast of the Pasch and of the New Law, instituted at the Last Supper, are paralleled (Lk. 22:7–23).

2. The lamb as a symbol in Christian art refers to Christ. It is often seen bearing a labarum, or as reclining on a book with seven seals as described by St. John (Rv. 5:1–6).

3. The title of a prayerful appeal, recited three times in the Mass.

**Lambeth Conferences**

The name of these conferences is taken from the Lambeth Palace, the episcopal home of the Archbishop of Canterbury, where these meetings are held every 10 years by the assemblage of Anglican bishops. The purpose of the conferences is to discuss matters of faith, doctrine, and in more recent years ecumenical dialogues. Sponsored by the Archbishop of Canterbury, the conferences began in 1865 at the urging of the Canadian bishops who sought a forum for the discussion of Church affairs. Because of some internal opposition the matter was referred to the Archbishop of

Canterbury, who thought this to be a good and practical proposal. He then sent invitations to all the bishops of the Anglican communion and the first assembly met in September, 1867. The conference issued a joint statement, "Address to the Faithful," and this established the pattern for the subsequent conferences, which are not juridical in nature but influential in the unification of the Anglican bodies.

The Conference of 1888 sought to establish a program for achieving unity with other Christian denominations. This was to be accomplished through a fourfold program proposed by the American Episcopalians two years previously. The articles of this ecumenical effort were: (1) that there be included essentially the Scriptures, as the Word of God; (2) that the Apostles' and Nicene Creeds be declared and accepted as a rule of faith; (3) that the Sacraments of Baptism and Holy Communion be one and uniform in all churches; (4) that the episcopacy be the central support of the governmental unity of the Church. While these four points were recognized as essential, it was also known that along these very lines there were difficulties because of the differences in these areas with other Protestant denominations.

From the Conferences there have arisen a sense of the international character of the Anglican Church, the drawing into unity of the missionary groups, especially of South Africa, China, and India, and the establishment and recognition of native episcopal bodies. In 1958 the Lambeth meeting had 310 bishops in attendance, presided over by Archbishop Geoffrey Fisher of Canterbury, and this was productive of a new Anglican concept of its total structure in relation to other Christian communions. It also was the small spark that brought into dialogue the Anglican Church and the Roman Catholic Church, which came about following Vatican II and still continues.

### Lamentations, Book of

This book of the OT, consisting of poetic elegies, has been attributed to the prophet Jeremiah, but is actually of unknown origin. It contains laments over the destruction of Jerusalem in 586 B.C. by the Neo-Babylonians and, since this and the accompanying sufferings followed upon frequent transgressions of God's law, there are also a number of confessions of guilt and appeals for mercy. The book emphasizes the power of God and the necessity to seek His mercy and records the description of the destruction of the Temple. Through this writing the confidence of the Israelites in God was urged and an attempt made to give a sense of responsibility to the individual Jew. The

Lamentations are recited in the Office of the Tenebrae during Holy Week.

### Lammas Day

This is an old and seldom used name for the feast of St. Peter-in-Chains, formerly celebrated Aug. 1.

### Lamps

First introduced into the Church out of necessity, lamps became later symbols of honor. In the early Middle Ages they were hung before reliquaries and the tabernacle. From the thirteenth century onward, the lamp has been used to honor continually the Divine Presence. It is now called the sanctuary lamp, and there is a requirement that at least one lamp should burn continually before the Blessed Sacrament. If more than one lamp is used, the number should be uneven. It also is required that this lamp burn olive oil, beeswax, or vegetable oils, and be suspended or rise at least 7 feet off the floor, or above eye level.

### Lance, Holy

1. The spear used to pierce the side of Christ during the crucifixion. Several portions are claimed as relics, but none are authenticated. One portion, allegedly found by St. Helena at Jerusalem, is preserved in St. Peter's in Rome.

2. A liturgical instrument called the *lance* is a small, usually golden, two-edged knife, used in Byzantine liturgies to cut portions of the bread to be consecrated.

3. A symbol in the form of a spear, of several saints, notably Sts. Matthew, Thomas, and Longinus.

### Languages, Biblical

The OT of the Bible was written in Hebrew and Aramaic, the NT in Greek. The original manuscripts of the Hebrew OT and the Greek gospels and epistles have disappeared. The copies made by hand have been lost or destroyed.

In 1947 the first of the Scrolls of the Dead Sea were discovered, and they revealed the entire writing of the Book of Isaiah, with the exception of two small portions. This parchment was found in a cave northwest of the Dead Sea and had been preserved in an earthenware jar, wrapped in yards of cloth and sealed with pitch. It had been written in the first century before Christ. There have been some manuscripts discovered through archaeological efforts since then, which are even older. (Cf. Scrolls of the Dead Sea.)

The oldest Greek manuscripts, which were

written in Greek because of the Hellenistic influence in the world at the time, are the Codex Sinaiticus, now in the British Museum, and the Codex Vaticanus, now retained in the Vatican. These Greek scripts were most likely written in the fourth century A.D. and contain nearly the entire Bible in the Greek script. There are some older fragments written in Greek on papyrus.

The Bible, or one of its testaments, has been translated into some 1200 languages of the world. The first translation into English was done by Wycliffe, Tyndale, Coverdale, and others who worked from the original languages. Wycliffe's Bible, published in 1383, was the first English Bible; it was written by hand. Tyndale's NT, issued in 1525, was the first printed English NT, while Coverdale's Bible, 1535, was the first printed Bible in English.

The first Bibles printed were in Latin, in Mainz, Germany, from type devised by Johann Guttenburg, from a manuscript of the Vulgate Bible. One copy of this first printing is owned by the Library of Congress, Washington, D.C., one of the three perfect copies printed on vellum.

In America the first Bible was printed in 1663 for the Indians of Massachusetts in their language; the translation was made by John Eliot. A German Bible printed by Christopher Saur in Germantown, Pa., in 1743 is the first in a modern language, and the first English Bible printed in America was done by Robert Aiken in Philadelphia, in 1782.

There were several translations into the Indian languages made by missionaries in Canada, the United States, and Mexico, in the Mohawk, Chippewa, Selish, and other languages; all were done from the sixteenth to the mid-nineteenth centuries. (See Bible.)

## Languages of the Church

In the Roman rite, Latin is the official language. Latin is also used for the official pronouncements, the definition of doctrine, the legal documents, and canon law of the Church. It is used for historical reasons and for accuracy from the standpoint of stability. By an apostolic indult of 1954, the Holy Office granted to the English-speaking Catholics of the United States and Canada the use of English in the ceremonies of matrimony, baptism, and extreme unction, with the exception of the words of the form and the exorcisms. This grant also permits the use of English in the giving of twenty-six blessings and the blessings for burial of adults and infants.

Since Vatican II the vernacular has been adopted throughout the world. The languages of the Eastern rite Churches are: Geez, Syriac, Greek,

Arabic, Slavonic, and other south European languages and dialects.

Vatican II teaches: "Within the limits set by the typical editions of the liturgical books, it shall be for the competent territorial ecclesiastical authority mentioned in Article 22, par. 2, to specify adaptations, especially in the case of the administration of the sacramentals, processions, liturgical language, sacred music, and the arts, but according to the fundamental norms laid down in this Constitution" (SC 39).

Although Latin is to be preserved in the Latin rite (SC 36), the vernacular has been introduced with the approval of Church authorities in all countries.

## Lappet

See Infulae.

## Lapsed

This term, from the Latin word *lapsi*, was applied from the third century to Christian converts who had abandoned the practice and faith of Catholics and returned to pagan practices and beliefs. There were three classifications: those who offered incense at pagan ceremonies, those who partook in pagan sacrifices, and those who obtained, false or true, legal documents saying they had conformed to pagan requirements. More recently, the term "lapsed Catholic" has been, not too accurately, applied to one who has become a heretic, apostate, schismatic, or who has failed to comply with the requirement of the Chruch's precept of receiving Holy Communion between the First Sunday of Lent and Trinity Sunday.

In the history of the Church there was a conflict during the third century between those who favored a merciful and charitable course for the *lapsi* and those who were for greater severity. The question was resolved with Church councils, especially the First Council of Nicaea (A.D. 325).

## LaSalette, Our Lady of

One of the three major apparitions of the Blessed Virgin Mary during the nineteenth century, which occurred on the slope of Mount Gargas rising above the village of La Salette in southeastern France is called Our Lady of La Salette. The apparition took place in the afternoon of Sept. 19, 1846, and as Pope Pius XII said at the centenary, it was a time "when the Madonna in Tears came to abjure her children to enter resolutely the path of conversion to her Divine Son, and of reparation for so many sins that offend the August and Eternal Majesty."

It is, however, in the message of the Virgin

Mother that these modern times find particular concern, for it is an essential part of the words spoken to the two children, Maximin Giraud and Melanie Mathieu. The core of the message was as Pope Pius IX declared: "Unless you do penance, you shall all perish." The prophetic words of the message were fulfilled: famine, suffering, war, and desolation. The Blessed Mother also gave a special message that was noted in the private message of Melanie, namely, infallibility of the Pope. Although the Church does not depend upon private messages or revelations, the dogma of papal infallibility was proclaimed in 1870.

Investigation of the apparition was carried on in a most meticulous manner, as were the cures that took place at the site. There is now a basilica built on the mountain's slope, and it is a place of universal pilgrimage.

### Las Hermanas

Literally, "The Sisters," this is the title of the organization of women religious of Spanish, Portuguese, or Latin American origin, which was formed in Houston, Texas, in 1971. Its objective was to be "actively present to the ever-changing needs of the Spanish-speaking people." It has a threefold program: (1) the promotion and direction of cultural awareness workshops whereby groups of women religious, civic, and governmental agencies are made more aware of the needs of the Spanish-speaking Catholics; (2) the Proyecto Mexico, which is an educational program for Mexican sisters who seek a greater interest in and involvement with parish ministries; (3) the offering of a nine-month pastoral, educational, and renewal institute for priests, religious, and lay persons who are engaged in the Spanish-speaking apostolate.

The organization has both sister and lay affiliates directed by a national board of coordination and is headquartered in San Antonio, Texas (P.O. Box 28185; 78228).

### Last Day

See Judgment, General; Parousia.

### Last Sacraments

The collective name Last Sacraments is given to the administration of the Sacraments of Penance, Annointing of the Sick, and Viaticum (Holy Communion) to a person before death. This is also called, particularly in secular journals, the "Last Rites," although this term has been eliminated from the recent liturgical language. (See separate listings of the sacraments.)

### Last Supper

At this momentous event of the gathering of the Apostles and Christ in the upper room for the eating of the Pasch, Christ instituted the Sacrament of the Holy Eucharist, the gift of Himself. This fact of the redeeming mission of Christ foreshadowed the sacrificial act that took place the following day: the crucifixion (Lk. 22:14–30). Christ's redeeming mission was to be repeated by the Apostles, and St. Paul (1 Cor. 11:24) recalls this 25 years later (cf. Eucharist, Sacrament of). It was also at the Last Supper that Christ spoke of His relationship to God the Father (Jn. 16:22–33) and the love of God that marks His followers (Jn. 14:23).

The Last Supper is the traditional name given to the Passover meal, which Christ ate with His Apostles in Jerusalem (Mk. 14:15; Lk. 22:12). The site is also known as the "Cenacle." It is certain that this meal was a Passover meal (Lk. 22:15), although some scholars think because of John's statement (13:1) that it was before the Feast of the Passover.

### Last Things

See Eschatology.

### Latae Sententiae

This expression refers to a penalty that is incurred by the very fact of transgression (*ipso facto*), that is, deliberate action. The wording of the law must indicate that the penalty, for example, excommunication is incurred by committing a forbidden act.

### Lateran Agreement

The final ratification of the concordat between the Italian Government and the State of Vatican City made on June 7, 1929 is called the Lateran Agreement. Through this agreement the pope was no longer confined to the limited papal lands, indemnification was made to Vatican City by the Italian Government for lands of the former Papal States seized by the Kingdom of Italy in 1870, and the Villa of Castel Gandolfo and its immediate surrounding lands as well as the Church of the Lateran in Rome were returned to Vatican State. This Lateran Agreement became Article 7 of the Italian Constitution on March 26, 1947. (See Lateran Treaty.)

### Lateran Church

Officially, the Church of our Most Holy Savior, called St. John Lateran, is the Cathedral of the bishop of Rome, the pope. It is considered the mother church of the Christian world. The basilica, part of a donation of the Laterani family, was presented to the Church in 311. It is the oldest of the Christian basilicas and from historic times was known as Constantine's basilica. Being one of four papal basilicas, the Lateran Church has a "holy" door, which is opened every twenty-fifth year to mark the beginning of celebration of a holy or jubilee year.

## Lateran Councils

Of those councils of the Church held at Rome, the first, in 313, decided against the Donatists; the second, in 649, condemned the false teaching of "one will" in Christ as advanced by the Monothelite heresy. The third, in 769, repudiated Iconoclasm; the fourth, in 1059, laid down the procedure for the election of popes; the fifth, called the First Lateran, was the ninth of the ecumenical councils and the first general council in the West, held in 1123 (cf. Ecumenical Councils). The sixth, called the Second Lateran, (tenth ecumenical), was convened in 1139 to settle the schism of the anti-pope, Anacletus; the seventh, called the Third Lateran (eleventh ecumenical), held in 1179, condemned the Albigenses and enacted clerical reforms. The eighth, called the "Great Council" (Fourth Lateran), met in 1215; presided over by Pope Innocent III, it established Easter Communion and set up the four years' truce of all Christian nations. The ninth, called the Fifth Lateran, of 1512, established a censorship of books among other actions. (Cf. Council.)

## Lateran Treaty

By this treaty between the Holy See and the Italian government, signed Feb. 11, 1929, Vatican City became an independent state; Catholicism was declared the official religion of Italy, and religion was made a part of public school courses; the Holy See renounced all claim to the historic Papal States; canon law of the Church was accepted as valid throughout the Italian countries. (Cf. Vatican State, City of.)

## Latin

Now called a "dead" language, Latin originated in Latium, the mid-province of Italy and became the dominant language of the Roman empire. It was the commonly spoken language of all peoples of the Western world, the legal language of Rome, and the means of transmitting the culture of Rome (cf. Languages of the Church). Because of its classical nature, the literature that developed with it, such as writings by Quintus Ennius (239 to 169 B.C.), Cato (234 to 149 B.C.), Cicero (106 to 43 B.C.), Vergil (70 to 19 B.C.), Horace (65 to 8 B.C.), and Livy (59 B.C. to A.D. 17), it was the finest expression of the writing of the fathers of the Church. For this reason, among others, Latin is recommended for studies by all who are deeply interested in the tradition of the Church (O.T. 13).

## Latin Mass

The Tridentine Order of the Mass was celebrated in Latin. The New Order of the Mass offers a revised version, contained in the Sacramentary, which in accord with the instruction issued by the Congregation for Divine Worship on June 1, 1971, may be celebrated in these instances: (1) bishops may permit the celebration of the Mass in Latin for mixed-language groups, that is, when the people present to participate would have no unifying vernacular language that all could understand; (2) priests may celebrate Mass in Latin in private, that is, when no people are present to participate; (3) the approved Order of the Mass as revised in Latin is to be used; (4) bishops may extend an exception to older or handicapped priests to use the Tridentine Order of the Mass in private celebration of the Eucharist. (See Order of the Mass, New; Eucharist, Celebration of.)

## Latin Rite

The Roman Church liturgy is called the Latin Rite. (Cf. Roman Rite; Liturgy.)

## Latria

Latria is that worship reserved to God alone. The word is derived from the Greek term for "to serve" and thus, by extension, has come to mean adoration. Distinctive of this form of worship, due to God because of His infinite excellence and the homage owed to Him by man as a created being, is sacrifice; the one and only sacrifice of the New Law is the most holy sacrifice of the Mass. (Cf. Cult; Dulia; Hyperdulia.)

This is called latreutic worship, since it is the ultimate service, the liturgy, whose sole purpose is to glorify God by giving Him honor as the Creator and final end of mankind. The liturgy is God-centered, God-directed, and offers adoration, thanksgiving, contrition, (or love), and petition. (See Liturgy.)

## Latrocinium

See Ephesus, Robber Synod of.

## Latten

See Brasses.

## Lauds

Literally "praises," this is the name given to the second hour of the Divine Office in the Latin Rite; it is also called the "morning" song since it was intended to be recited or sung at daybreak. It was composed of four psalms, a canticle together with antiphons, a little chapter, hymn and versicle, the Benedictus and orations, the collect of the day and commemorations. The traditional name has been retained but is structured differently in the new Liturgy of the Hours. (See Breviary; Liturgy of the Hours.)

### Laura

Literally translated from the Greek, this means "alley," and the term is applied to a series of streets or an area around which there are arranged small hermitages of monks, attached to or supported by a monastery. While the monks live a quasi-hermit life along or within the *laura,* they participate in some of the community life and in the religious duties of the monastery. The term now applies to any large monastery of the Byzantine Rite.

### Lavabo

Lavabo is the ceremony of purification during the celebration of the Mass. It takes place at the altar and consists of the physical washing of the hands by the celebrant. The title comes from the first word ("I will wash") of the portion of Psalm 25, which the celebrant recites while washing his thumbs and forefingers in the Tridentine Mass. The Lavabo follows the Offertory and is an act in preparation for the Consecration; it is an expression of the priest's desire for inward purification. Besides the evident use of the act, it is symbolic of the washing of the Apostles' feet by Christ which, in turn, was a symbolical act of spiritual cleanliness (Jn. 13:8–10).

### Law

Basically, law is a reasonable, intellectual rule that one who holds authority imposes upon many for the common good. Law can only be reasonable when the one in authority can see the consequences of what he imposes and knows and seeks the general good. Imposition of the law is by promulgation, that is, making it known to those it binds. It is applied to many rather than to one because it is to affect the group, that is, society. Law also is applied to a body or system of rules, for example, canon law.

Law may be divided into many cumulative groups of rules, such as common law or civil law. However, law as applied to human beings, called human law, is divided broadly into: *eternal, natural, positive.* Eternal law, also called *divine* law, is the divine wisdom that directs all created to their true end. A natural law is the eternal law as seen in all creation and by which all things are inclined to their natural acts and ends. Such natural laws may be *physical,* for example, the law of gravitation, or *metaphysical,* for example, the unchangeableness of the essence of a thing. A positive law is one that is

made known as the will of the lawgiver, for example, a moral law as "You shall not kill," or a jurisdictional law such as an article of the Bill of Rights. (Cf. Canon Law.)

Vatican II declares concerning divine law: "Christ, to be sure, gave His Church no proper mission in the political, economic, or social order. The purpose that He set before her is a religious one. But out of this religious mission itself comes a function, a light, and an energy which can serve to structure and consolidate the human community according to the divine law" (GS 42).

St. Paul in his epistle to the Romans says: "Christ is the end of the law. Through him, justice comes to everyone who believes" (10:4). This whole law of Christ can be summed up in the one commandment to love one another (Gal. 5:14), and this law does not rest like a burden, but is creative of a whole new relationship between Christians and their Lord, between mankind and God. It is thus basic to all other law.

### Law, Canon

See Canon Law.

### Law and Gospel

There is a distinction between law in regard to action and the Gospel, which is central to the Christian mission. A proper resolution of this distinction depends on the avoidance of two opposites, namely, Christianity and secularism. The Christian community is not a legalistic one, a religion based upon a rigoristic, ritualistic, conforming of teaching and practice. This Christ denounced.

Instead we speak here of that law written into the hearts of men (Rom. 2:15–16) and the direction of man's course in the history of salvation. It is not regulation for the sake of regulation, but that law which St. Paul called "spiritual," "good," and leading to the doing of what is right (Rom. 7:12–23). The Gospel as law is the response, freely made by the human person, whereby mankind gives a special obedience, for it is not the law itself we follow blindly, but the Christian's entire attitude toward the Person and the message of Christ. It is thus that Gospel is made more compelling than the law. It is a compulsion of love (Gal. 5:6). It is even more demanding because it is always beyond our reach, always challenging us to greater effort and response in faith, always propelling us beyond ourselves. Law in this context becomes for man the revealed word of God to be attained in seeking salvation. The law of the OT has yielded to the new covenant of redemption, to the new law of merit, and especially of grace. It is for everyone a reaching out to that time when law will be no more (Rv. 21:22–25). (See Salvation History.)

## Laxism

Laxism is a moral system whereby one who seeks a right or at least an informed conscience, is permitted to follow the opinion or evidence that favors or inclines toward liberty, that is, to evade the acceptance of an obligation even though the opinion is open to doubt and question. Laxism was condemned in 1679 by Pope Innocent XI because it leads to the judging of sinful practices as lawful.

## Lay Apostolate

See Apostolate; Laity.

## Lay Baptism

Lay Baptism is the administration of the Sacrament of Baptism by a lay person or one who is not designated as an ordinary minister. Lay persons may lawfully baptize only when there is danger of death and then only when no priest is present (c. 742). Also, should the one lawfully baptized by a lay person survive, those ceremonies omitted in the baptism must be supplemented in church as soon as possible (c. 759). (Cf. Baptism, Sacrament of.)

## Lay Brothers and Sisters

These men and women who are members of a religious order or community but are not in Holy Orders and are not choir monks or nuns, or brothers or sisters, devote themselves to the secular affairs of monasteries or convents. They do, however, participate in some prescribed religious duties, such as daily attendance at Mass and prayers.

Vatican II declared: "To strengthen the bond of brotherhood between members of a community, those who are called lay brothers, assistants, or some other name, should be brought into the heart of its life and activities" (PC 15).

## Lay Franciscans

See Tertiaries.

## Lay Investiture

See Investiture.

## Lay Organizations

See National Catholic Organizations.

## Lay Reader

This is the title of that layman who acts in certain Protestant churches in leading the people in prayer or readings, and sometimes preaching, in services where the minister needs help or is absent. Most frequently this is found in Anglican Churches, Christian Science bodies, and Mormon groups.

For the Anglican Church the role of the lay reader was described at the 1958 Lambeth Conference: "The work of the Reader should be described as that of an office, not of an order. The service is not deemed to possess any character of indelibility."

In the Catholic Church the duties or services of a lay reader are performed, in accord with prescribed operations, by the Lector or Commentator. This lesser ministry in the Roman Church was provided for by the *Constitution on the Sacred Liturgy* of Vatican II. (See Commentator; Ministries; Lector.)

## Laymen and Laywomen

In general, the laity, but these are also the men and women who are not members of a religious order or have not received Holy Orders. As members of the Church, lay persons form the greater portion of the faithful. They have certain duties, common to all members. The laity has also certain rights, for example, to receive the necessary spiritual goods from the clergy, in accord, of course, with Church discipline (c. 682). (See Laity.)

## Leadership

The free exercise of those qualities, both in secular and religious life, whereby a human person releases, inspires, stimulates, and evokes the greatest potential of individuals, whether of oneself or others.

The right to command, or the exercise of authority, is not the same as the ability or gift to influence the behavior of other persons. The dependence on authority, the threat of a consequence, is not the application or assumption of the leadership role. Rather, in the Church, the exercise of authority is in relation to the service one gives to the gospel mission, and it suffers when it has only this sense of office or position.

Leadership is that quality, not assumed but practiced, which brings out the best in others. It perhaps might be called the "orchestration" of actions rather than an act itself as it applies to the development of a genuine apostolate. It should lead to some exchange of ideas and thoughts, some resolve of difficulties, and some positive, constructive action beneficial to the greatest number. (See Authority; Parish Council.)

## Leadership Conference of Women Religious

This is an association of the major superiors of women religious communities in the United States.

Its purpose is broadly twofold: the promotion of the spiritual lives of their members, and the coordination, promotion, and expansion of their apostolic work for all members. It was organized in the late 1950s and approved by the Congregation for Religious and Secular Institutes, June 13, 1962. As an organization it has made great contributions to the professional roles, the intensification of the religious life among women, and the renewal of religious life in the face of large defections from all orders of women in the upheaval of understanding following Vatican II. The work of the Conference is to bring greater witness to the role and activity of women religious whereby they may exercise the special charisms that they have individually and in community.

The secretariat for the United States is head-quartered at 1325 Massachusetts Ave., N.W., Washington, D.C., 20005.

### Leaflet Missal

This is the title of the oldest of the so-called "missalettes," begun in the mid-thirties; it is the only continuous weekly printed missal offered to the American and Canadian Catholics. It has adapted to the new liturgy and now includes in weekly pamphlet form the order of the Mass for Sunday and the weekday liturgies, together with a selection of hymns that vary from time to time, together with some suitable meditative and prayer material. It is obtained by subscription or by parish adoption as the means of parochial participation.

### League of the Cross

League of the Cross is the name of the total abstinence society for English Catholics, which was founded in 1873 by Cardinal Manning (d. 1892).

### League for Religious and Civil Rights, Catholic

The Catholic League for Religious and Civil Rights was organized in Washington, D.C., in March, 1973, to obtain respect and equal rights for all Catholics. The League is a Catholic anti-defamation organization and civil rights union designed to protect the dignity and secure the rights due all Catholics. It is committed to speak out in defense of their religious and moral values and to express these values with the weight of coordinated opinion in order to provide Catholics with the same protection provided by other civil rights groups for other religious and ethnic peoples. It operates with elected officers and has a national board of directors.

In its formative process it announced: "While prejudice against Catholics and other religious minorities is not new or unique to this country, we are undertaking this action now because indications of increasing religious discrimination are beginning to surface in America. Furthermore, we are acting because we believe that tolerance of anti-Catholic prejudice has too long been the price of community good will in this country. Good will does not require acceptance of vilification of what Catholics or any other religious minority considers sacred or fundamental to their faith. Nor does good will, in its true sense, mandate docile acquiescence in massive social changes which threaten the home, life itself, or the rights of conscience in the professions, let alone the rights of churches to maintain their own institutions within their own lawful philosophic viewpoints. . . .

"Our major task, as we envision its evolvement, must largely be the rational and civil realignment of social thought in our time on the necessity of respect and decency due Catholics by those of other faiths or of no faith, by government as responsive to society, and particularly by the judiciary, which has been the source of the greatest discrimination against the rightful claims of the Catholic citizens of this country."

The League at present is headquartered at 714 North 26th Street, Milwaukee, Wisconsin, 53233.

### Lectern

A reading stand, movable or permanent, used in church is called a lectern. It is sometimes covered by a cloth corresponding in color to the liturgical color of the day. In modern churches, where the pulpit has been done away with, the lectern is frequently used to enshrine on its front panel the Lectionary or the Bible as a visible sign of the presence of the Word of God as a distinct part of the liturgy.

### Lection

See Lesson.

## Lectionary

A Lectionary is a book of readings but chiefly the one that contains the scriptural readings for the Sundays and feast days of the Church calendar; it is also a book containing the lessons for Matins.

The new lectionary containing all the readings from Scripture used in the Liturgy of the Eucharist is a "sign" of the liturgical action that takes place at this portion of the liturgy. As a sign, the lectionary is twofold: it reveals the hidden reality of the message of Christ, and it puts those who hear the message in greater contact with the reality of Christ who stands behind the sign. (See Readings, Cycle of.)

## Lector

Literally, a lector is a "reader."

1. The cleric who formerly received the second of the minor orders in the Roman rite (cf. Orders, Holy, Sacrament of).

2. The first scholastic theological degree conferred in Dominican schools of theology, for example, Lector of Sacred Theology, abbreviated S.T.L.

According to the revision of the minor orders after Vatican II, the modern ministerial role of *lector* or *reader* (sometimes called proclaimer) is a minor service performed by a lay member of the community of the parish. The assignment, training, and direction of the lectors are the responsibility of the pastor or his associate. The function of the lector is usually to carry the lectionary in the entrance procession, to read the first and second readings in the Liturgy of the Word, and to assist in other ways according to the practice and custom. There may be more than one lector assisting at a celebration of the Eucharist. The service of lector is not limited to laymen. (See Ministries; Readings, Cycle of.)

## Legate

A legate is an officially appointed representative of the pope. He is called a nuncio when assigned as a permanent representative before a civil government, or an apostolic delegate when representing the pope in the affairs of the Church. (Cf. Apostolic Delegate.)

Vatican II declared: "Since departments (of the Roman Curia) are established for the good of the universal Church, this Council wishes that their members, officials, and consultors, as well as legates of the Roman Pontiff, be drawn more widely from various geographical areas of the Church, insofar as it is possible. In such a way the offices and central agencies of the Catholic Church will exhibit a truly universal character" (CD 10).

Legates do not belong to conferences of bishops on the national or local levels (CD 38).

## Legate a Latere

This is the title of a special, confidential representative of the pope. Usually, he is entrusted with particular powers to enable him to carry out his mission. The legate may be a layman or laywoman.

## Legend, Golden

All legends are fictious stories about historical or imagined persons. During the Middle Ages, there were many such legends about saints and these became the supposed "lives" of such people. (See Lives of the Saints; Golden Legend.)

## Legion of Decency

Formerly a review group who assessed the morality of movies, the Legion of Decency has been replaced by the *Division for Film and Broadcasting* of the United States Conference of Catholic Bishops (USCC). (See Media and Communications.) The new group serves much the same purpose, rating movies for theaters. The classifications of films are made on a descending scale of categories: A-1, morally unobjectionable for general audiences; A-2, morally unobjectionable for adults and adolescents; A-3, morally unobjectionable for adults; A-4, morally unobjectionable for adults, with reservations; B, morally objectionable in part for all; C, condemned. There is also a classification of "no rating, not yet reviewed." Films made especially for television are not reviewed simply because national networks offer no opportunity for previous previewing.

The ratings are not meant to nor do they coincide with the ratings given by the motion picture industry, G, PG, R, and X. It should also be indicated that while such ratings are of value, they do not govern the individual in conscience for each person is obliged to form a morally right conscience concerning all visual entertainment. The reviewing of a movie, television program, radio broadcast by a trained critic is a valuable means of aiding one in forming a right conscience. (See Conscience.)

## Legitimation

A child is legitimate if conceived in or born of a valid marriage, unless the parents were under a solemn vow of chastity. A child, not legitimate because of some impediment or condition, is afforded legitimation by (1) the subsequent marriage of the parents, provided they could have validly married before the conception or birth of the child (if an impediment existed, it suffices that the impediment cease before the birth of the child); (2) dispensation when the dispensation is given by one who has ordinary power, or by a general indult.

## Lent

Lent is the period of six and one half weeks from Ash Wednesday to Easter Sunday. During Lent, for 40 days, excluding Sundays, fasting is recommended for all Catholics according to the laws of fast. This is reminiscent of the 40 days of our Lord's unbroken fast (Mt. 4:3–4). The entire period of Lent is also a time of spiritual preparation for the passion, death, and resurrection of Christ. It is observed as a time of penitence other than fasting, and as a time of prayer. The liturgy of the Church reflects the significance of this period of spiritual preparation: each day has a special Mass assigned to it; those Masses date back to the seventh and eighth centuries; there are no feasts observed on Sundays; purple vestments are the daily color (except Laetare Sunday); the organ is silent; the Gloria and Alleluia are omitted, and a special Preface of the season is said; the solemnization of marriage is forbidden. Special rules, regulations, and recommendations may be made by the ordinaries. (Cf. Abstinence; Fasting; Liturgy of Holy Week.)

Vatican II declares: "The Lenten season has a twofold character: (1) it recalls baptism or prepares for it; (2) it stresses a penitential spirit. By these means especially, Lent readies the faithful for celebrating the paschal mystery after a period of closer attention to the Word of God, and more ardent prayer. In the liturgy itself and in liturgy-centered instructions, these baptismal and penitential themes should be more pronounced" (SC 109).

Thus the spirit of Lent and the internal and individual actions are more related to the liturgy of the Church and are more a response of the members to the message and teachings of Christ. (See Liturgy.)

## Leopoldine Association

This historic mission-aid group was founded in Austria in 1829 to give help, both financial and spiritual, to the Catholic Church in America. It was named after Leopoldine, the daughter of Francis I of Austria, who was the empress of Brazil. Many churches and dioceses in the United States owe their early growth to the aid of this group. The reports of these mission activities were made in the Berichte papers, from 1831 to 1914, which became historic documents and also prompted the immigration of many Austrians as well as the arrival of many missionary priests from Austria and the southern German states.

## Leper Window

Some medieval churches had a low window in the chancel wall, usually with bars and shutters, through which lepers could observe and attend Mass and receive alms. It is more an architectural curiosity now than a window having use or purpose.

## Lepanto, Battle of

This was the last great naval battle fought in the Gulf of Corinth, Oct. 7, 1571, between the Ottoman Turks and the Christian forces gathered from the republics of Venice, Genoa, the Papal States, together with the forces supplied by King Philip of Spain. Also called the last battle of the Crusades, it is distinct as the last conflict fought by oared galleys.

The Christian forces were united in a Holy League under the command of Don Juan of Austria, the illegitimate brother of Philip II of Spain. Victory was finally achieved by the forces of Don Juan, but there were staggering losses considering the numbers engaged. The Christians lost 7,500, while the Turks suffered 20,000 to 30,000 dead or disabled. The battle attained no immediate results, but it marked the decline of the Turkish power in the Mediterranean Sea. One of those fighting in the Christian Forces was Miguel de Cervantes, author of *Don Quixote*.

The battle was written of by G. K. Chesterton in a poem of famous cadences, which have a clang of war. He called Don Juan the "last of the knights":

> Strong gongs groaning as the guns boom far,
> Don Juan of Austria is going to the war,
> Stiff flags straining in the night-blasts cold
> In the gloom black-purple, in the glint old-gold,
> Torchlight crimson on the copper kettle-drums,
> Then the tuckets, then the trumpets, then the cannon, and he comes. (Lines 24 through 28)

## Lesson

Lesson is the name of any passage of Scripture read during the celebration of Mass. In general, a lesson is a selection from the Scriptures, from the fathers of the Church, or other writers of the Church. These extracts are appointed to be read at religious ceremonies or as portions of the Divine Office. It may also be called a "lection." (Cf. Lectionary; Liturgy of the Hours.)

## Letters

See under the various headings of Epistles.

## Levirate

The term levirate, from the Latin, *levir,* "brother-in-law," is the biblical custom by which the widow remarried within the male membership of her former husband's family (Gn. 38; Lv. 22:13; Dt. 25:5–10). The intent of the levirate was to perpetuate the name of the dead person and to prevent the loss or alienation of the family possessions within the tribal structure. Although the custom was not an absolute duty, remarriage was possible and actually more frequent outside of the dead husband's family. The widow in the meantime returned to her father, but the father-in-law retained some authority and negotiating power. The widows, although poor both in symbol and reality, were protected by law. This metaphor of widowhood was carried over into other accounts of the Bible (Is. 1:17; Lam. 1:1; Is. 47:8–9; Rv. 18:7), and widowhood was a favored state as was virginity (1 Cor. 7:8; 1 Tm. 5:3–16; Jas. 1:27).

## Leviticus

Leviticus is title of the third book of the OT written by Moses, with revisions made by members of the priestly class sometime between 1200 and 400 B.C. This title is certainly pre-Christian in origin and appropriate since the book deals chiefly with the duties of the Levites (hereditary ministers) regarding sacrificial worship; it records the consecration of Aaron and his sons as the first priestly class of the Israelites. It was the liturgical book of the Israelites. The book also presents a number of moral teachings, notably the importance of liturgical service, the sanctity of priesthood, and the imitation of God's holiness.

## Liber Pontificalis

This is the title of a collection of the lives of the Popes, particularly one containing the biographies of the popes from St. Peter to Stephen V (d. 891). There is also a work that continues the lives of the popes, written shortly after their deaths, from Victor II (d. 1055) to Eugene IV (d. 1447). Such collections have no official status in the Church;

they are composed by various writers and in some instances are of doubtful historic value.

## Liber Usualis

Liber Usualis is the book containing the Proper of the Masses for all Sundays and for the feasts that supplant the Sunday, together with the hours of the Office except Matins and Lauds, and the accompanying chants. It is now obsolete. (See Sacramentary.)

## Liberalism

This system of philosophical thought found its origin in the eighteenth century period of Enlightenment and the French Revolution. It centered on the general but compressed idea that with the recognition of freedom, man had not only the task of attaining a free society, but also an unusual chance at self-determination apart from any God-centered message.

As a consequence, this movement of liberty gave rise to a variety of conflicts between the Church and the State, between authority and casual and rather rationalized autonomy of the individual. It also introduced a species of Christian liberalism wherein the individual was faced with the problem of reconciling self-justification with the theological concept of the mediatorship of Jesus Christ. Faith was confronted with a rationalized historical existence, stemming from many schools of religious history, as opposed to the scriptural truth and the orthodox history of salvation. (See Enlightenment.)

## Liberals, Catholic

Insofar as Catholics profess the views and principles of the "liberal," socialist or Communist parties, they may be classified as heretics. Thus, on degree of participation, for example, if one were to profess the liberal idea that the Church is subject to the state, he is a heretic. However, the term Catholic Liberals applies particularly to those Catholics who through their affiliation with liberalism sought to reject or limit the authority of the Holy See.

Liberalism as the political system opposed to absolutism is not condemned by the Church, but that aspect of it which seeks to obtain freedom or emancipation from moral restrictions is not to be accepted by Catholics and is condemned by the *Syllabus* of Pius IX. There must, of course, be a distinction made concerning the transposing of the words. Catholic Liberals are one group. They are not to be confused with "Liberal Catholics." The latter are not political in the broad sense of the word "liberalism." Rather they are individuals "qualified" by the term "liberal" and are variously engaged in promoting views that seek to inject Catholic thought into social and economic life in an effort to elevate the moral character of these activities. Although some of their views may be looked on as more "free" than is consistent with sound Catholic teaching, the "Liberal Catholic" is an individual rather than a party affiliate. (Cf. Modernism; Secularism.)

## Liberty

For the Christian, liberty means primarily a liberation from sin, and a freedom from the law under the OT and an obedience to the Law of the message of Christ. This latter is interiorized, for it makes us all realize the filiation we have with God (Gal. 4:4–7; Rom. 8:19–22). (See Freedom, Religious.)

## Licentiate

This academic degree is awarded for proficiency in theology, philosophy, canon law, and Scripture. It cannot be awarded in theology until the end of the fourth year of the theological course. The degree in theology is abbreviated S.T.L.

## Lie

A lie is any word, sign, or action through which one expresses the opposite as he knows or wills it. This is usually done with the motive of deceiving others. It is also a lie if one says what is true but believes it to be false. It is not a lie to say what is false if one believes what he says to be true. Actions that are habitual lies are classified as hypocrisy. Lies may be *malicious,* that is, injurious of another; *officious,* that is, those told for one's own or another's advantage; *jocose,* that is, a lie told for amusement. To lie is never permitted, because a lie is intrinsically evil. While in itself only venially sinful, a lie becomes mortally sinful as soon as it violates another virtue, for example, charity toward one's neighbor.

## Life

In the definition of life there are two factors that give the essential evidence and these are *spontaneity* (that by which an organism has self-motion or a principle of movement) and *immanent movement* (the capacity of self-perpetuation or the principle of its motion). Thus the human person in experiential life comes to realize that the meaning of life is self-evident, and his actions reveal this activity.

And from the human person's feelings, thoughts and self-propulsion, or movement, an awareness of movement by the person's own efforts shows the person to be his own agent. In this it is distinctly seen that the vital principle is separate from the matter and its chemical or physical properties. Biological life has several activities that are characteristic of life: response to stimuli (irritability), changes in position as creature parts (motion), the assimilation of food (nutrition), development from organism to a mature creature (growth), and the capability of producing new creatures of the same species (reproduction).

There are in modern times several definitions of life arising from the several disciplines of knowledge: science, philosophy, or religion. Each of these explain life in different ways. Our only concern here is the religious explanation that gives to lives a greater transcendence than that of mere biologic entities.

The highest form of life is God who not only moves Himself but all other creatures, and is not moved Himself; thus He is Pure Act and has no limits of life. God is the "living God"; He is the Life who makes us live. God is all-powerful and must be heard by man (Dt. 5:22–27). God is the source of life (Ps. 41) and man responds: "My soul yearns and pines for the courts of the Lord. My heart and my flesh cry out for the living God" (Ps. 84:3). God gives life: in His Trinitary life and in our own lives since we are able to become the Children of God. St. John says: "Indeed, just as the Father possesses life in Himself, so has He granted it to the Son to have life in Himself. The Father has given over to him power to pass judgment because he is the Son of Man; no need for you to be surprised at this, for an hour is coming in which all those in their tombs shall hear his voice and come forth. Those who have done right shall rise to live; the evildoers shall rise to be damned" (Jn. 5:26–29) (cf. 1 Jn. 1:1–3).

For the Christian then life takes on a movement to eternity, to the fulfillment of the salvific will of God who is Life itself. We have awaited the life of paradise since the fall of Adam. We seek the fulfillment of our salvation history culminating in union with God the Father, the source of life (cf. Jn. 15:1–6; Rv. 2:7; 22:1–2). It is while we live that we bear the fruit of the Spirit and have our life in hope (Gal. 5:5; Rom. 6:20–23).

Vatican II has spoken on the meaning of life, teaching us to seek throughout our lifetimes the salvation promised: "Nor are there lacking men who despair of any meaning to life and praise the boldness of those who think that human existence is devoid of any inherent significance and who strive to confer a total meaning on it by their own ingenuity alone.

"Nevertheless, in the face of the modern development of the world, an ever-increasing number of people are raising the most basic questions or recognizing them with a new sharpness: what is man? What is this sense of sorrow, of evil, of death, which continues to exist despite so much progress? What is the purpose of these victories, purchased at so high a cost? What can man offer to society, what can he expect from it? What follows this early life?

"The Church believes that Christ, who died and was raised up for all, can through His Spirit offer man the light and the strength to measure up to his supreme destiny. Nor has any other name under heaven been given to man by which it is fitting for him to be saved. She likewise holds that in her most benign Lord and Master can be found the key, the focal point, and the goal of all human history.

"The Church also maintains that beneath all changes there are many realities which do not change, and which have their ultimate foundation in Christ, who is the same yesterday and today, now and forever. Hence in the light of Christ, the image of the unseen God, the first born of every creature, the Council wishes to speak to all men in order to illuminate the mystery of man and to cooperate in finding the solution to the outstanding problems of our time" (GS 10).

It is the Christian, the entire People of God who must seek to express and may express the meaning of the "Living God" in their lives. They "are called to the fullness of the Christian life and to the perfection of charity" (LG 40). They have an apostolate in faith, love, and hope that will manifest through their lives the movement toward God for themselves and others through the welfare of the Church in all times. (See Salvation History.)

### Life, Spiritual

To become Christlike, to strive for perfection in imitation of the life of Christ, whether individually, in society, or in religious community, is the optimal objective of every Christian. Vatican II teaches: "There already exist many aids for lay persons devoted to the apostolate, namely, study sessions, congresses, periods of recollection, spiritual exercises, frequent meetings, conferences, books, and periodicals. All these are directed toward the acquisition of a deeper knowledge of sacred Scripture and Catholic doctrine, the nourishment of spiritual life, an appreciation of world condi-

tions, and the discovery and development of suitable methods" (AG 39).

Spiritual life flows from a deepening of one's knowledge of what God speaks to everyone in love. There are also the practical means that are helpful in attaining a spiritual life, which are: prayer, intensification of the sacramental life, the exercise of virtues according to one's state of life, and the willingness to become simple and humble. (See Imitation of Christ.)

### Ligamen

Ligamen is the bond of an existing valid marriage whereby both parties are forbidden to contract another marriage before the death of one of them.

### Lights

See Candle; Lamps.

### Lily

An often used symbol of chastity, the lily is used in regard to the Blessed Mother, St. Joseph, and other saints. (See Symbol.)

### Limbo

From the Latin word *limbus*, "fringe" or "edge," Limbo is considered to be "outside of heaven." There is a distinction as to the purpose:

1. "Limbo of the fathers" meant that state or reserve in which the souls of the just, such as Abraham, Isaac, and Jacob, were detained until the complete redemption by Christ through which heaven was opened to them. This was the "paradise" spoken of by Christ in addressing the good thief at the crucifixion (Lk. 23:39–43). It was the limbo of the just to which Christ's soul descended.

2. The "limbo of children" is that state wherein the souls of unbaptized children and adults, who die without committing grievous actual sin, enjoy perfect natural happiness. Here they are excluded from the supernatural excellence of heaven, namely, the vision of God, but they do know God and love Him with their perfected natural faculties. The Church has made no pronouncement concerning limbo, and persons should know that the divine love has made provision for such children beyond our comprehension.

Baptism alone confers the life of grace and the promise of salvation. No human person, simply by the fact of creation, has the natural right to the vision of God. This can only come through the supernatural life, which is gained through baptism, and for this reason the first consideration of the Church is for the human person to be given the benefit of the sacrament. (See Baptism, Sacrament of.)

### Linens, Altar
See Altar cloths.

### Linteum, also Lintheum
This ancient veil used to cover the chalice and paten in the early days of the Church today has been replaced with the chalice veil.

### Litany
The name is derived from the Greek word for "prayer." This is a prayer in the form of short invocations, said alternately or as petitions with responses. Originally litany was applied to any prayer of supplication repeated often; later it was introduced into the liturgy with the clergy leading and the people responding. The use of litanies was introduced into processions and certain ceremonies. We have an example, in shortened form, in the Prayer of the faithful of the Mass. Although there are many litanies, only five have been sanctioned for public devotions. These are: the Litany of Loreto (Litany of the Blessed Virgin), Litany of the Saints, Litany of the Holy Name, Litany of the Sacred Heart, and Litany of St. Joseph.

During the Easter Liturgy, within the liturgy of baptism, a litany of the saints is sung with the people responding.

### Literal Sense of Scripture
Literal sense of Scripture is the interpretation of the Sacred Scriptures, which seeks the actual meaning that the writer intended to convey. Frequently, a word has several meanings, but in context or its use with other words it is given but one meaning by the writer. There are distinguishing marks of literal sense. It may be *explicit,* that is, the actual statement conveyed by the words. *Implicit* sense may also be present, for the use of one word rather than another indicates that the writer wished to imply more than what the words actually mean. Every part of Scripture has, of course, a literal sense intended by the author. However, there may be texts that have several possible meanings. What is attempted by seeking the genuine literal sense is to determine whether a Scripture text may have more than one literal or inspired meaning. (Cf. Interpretation, Scriptural; Inspiration of Scripture; Form Criticism.)

### Literary Criticism, Biblical
See Form Criticism.

### Literary Qualities of the Bible
Like other great writings, but to a greater degree, the Bible possesses distinctive marks of great literary form. It contains poetry, historical writing, biography, prophecy, fiction (parables), stories of greatness, and sayings of wisdom. Often it is from the very literary form employed by the inspired writer that we derive our greatest enjoyment in reading the Bible, in addition to being aided in deeper understanding of the truth God wishes us to learn. Besides the literary forms, there are also all the marks of craftsmanship in the presentation, which make the writers outstanding as word artists.

In understanding all of these forms, we do not need a great appreciation of literature. But we should bring a realization of what the literary form adds to our reading and our learning of truth. It should be realized, for example, that biblical poetry was Jewish in character and differs from modern poetic forms. Thus it is not based upon a measured syllabic beat as found in English poetry but upon the symmetry, the balance, of clauses found in each verse. This balance is called *parallelism* and is perhaps best seen in the Psalms. (See Parallelism.)

In the NT we have three forms of literary presentation: the historical or documentary (the Gospels), the essay or teaching (the Epistles), and the prophetic (Revelation). In all history there is both chronological and logical order, which is true of the Gospels as well as the more didactic Epistles, but not of the prophetic writings. In these, the writer sweeps beyond the bounds of order to write more dramatically and symbolically. There are thus two major types of narrative employed in the NT: direct and indirect. The most prominent and frequently employed type, found in the discourses of our Lord as recorded in the Gospels, is the parable. (See Parable.)

### Little Office of the B.V.M.
In honor of the Blessed Mother, prayers containing the same elements as the Divine Office have been arranged in a shorter form. The "Little Office" introduced in the eleventh century has been attributed to St. Peter Damian. In content, it is made up of lessons, Psalms, the Lord's Prayer, canticles, hymns, antiphons, collects, commemorations, and the Ave Maria. It is the daily office

recited in common or privately by some groups of sisters and lay brothers and is obligatory for some tertiaries. The prayer as a devotion has grown in popularity with lay people and is often recommended to members of sodalities of the Blessed Mother. (See Liturgy of the Hours.)

## Liturgical Art

This collective name is given to a classification rather than a distinctive art form or style. It is embrasive of all the art used in the public worship of the Church. It applies to the structural art of architecture, to the decorative arts of painting, stained glass, mosaic, sculpture, as well as the graphic arts such as holy cards, pictures, liturgical books, hymnals, missals, and bulletins. This also applies to the art forms of music and ballet, as well as handicrafts such as banners, tapestry, macrame, batik, silk-screen, weaving, and other crafts. It is most essential that such arts should have a sacred content of both instruction and reverence in keeping with their intent and applied purposes.

Vatican II in its *Constitution on the Sacred Liturgy* states: "Very rightly the fine arts are considered to rank among the noblest expressions of human genius. This judgment applies especially to religious art and to its highest achievement, which is sacred art. By their very nature both of the latter are related to God's boundless beauty, for this is the reality which these human efforts are trying to express in some way. To the extent that these works aim exclusively at turning men's thoughts to God persuasively and devoutly, they are dedicated to God and to the cause of His greater honor and glory.

"Holy Mother Church has therefore always been the friend of the fine arts and has continuously sought their noble ministry, with the special aim that all things set apart for use in divine worship should be truly worthy, becoming, and beautiful, signs and symbols of heavenly realities. For this purpose, too, she has trained artists. In fact, the Church has, with good reason, always reserved to herself the right to pass judgment upon the arts, deciding which of the works of artists are in accordance with faith, piety, and cherished traditional laws, and thereby suited to sacred purposes.

"The Church has been particularly careful to see that sacred furnishings should worthily and beautifully serve the dignity of worship, and has welcomed those changes in materials, style, or ornamentation which the progress of the technical arts has brought with the passage of time.

"Therefore it has pleased the Fathers to issue the following decrees on these matters:

"The Church has not adopted any particular style of art as her very own; she has admitted fashions from every period according to the natural talents and circumstances of peoples, and the needs of the various rites. Thus, in the course of the centuries, she has brought into being a treasury of art which must be very carefully preserved. The art of our own days, coming from every race and region, shall also be given free scope in the Church, provided that it adorns the sacred buildings and holy rites with due honor and reverence. It will thereby be enabled to contribute its own voice to that wonderful chorus of praise in honor of the Catholic faith sung by great men in times gone by.

"Ordinaries, by the encouragement and favor they show to art which is truly sacred, should strive after noble beauty rather than mere extravagance. This principle is to apply also in the matter of sacred vestments and ornaments.

"Let bishops carefully exclude from the house of God and from other sacred places those works of artists which are repugnant to faith, morals, and Christian piety, and which offend true religious sense either by their distortion of forms or by lack of artistic worth, by mediocrity or by pretense.

"When churches are to be built, let great care be taken that they be suitable for the celebration of liturgical services and for the active participation of the faithful.

"The practice of placing sacred images in churches so that they may be venerated by the faithful is to be firmly maintained. Nevertheless, their number should be moderate and their relative location should reflect right order. Otherwise they may create confusion among the Christian people and promote a faulty sense of devotion.

"When passing judgment on works of art, local ordinaries shall give a hearing to the diocesan commission on sacred art and, if needed, also to others who are truly experts, and to the commissions referred to in Articles 44, 45, and 46.

"Ordinaries must be very careful to see that sacred furnishings and works of value are not disposed of or allowed to deteriorate; for they are the ornaments of the house of God.

"Bishops should take pains to instill artists with the spirit of sacred art and of the sacred liturgy. This they may do in person or through suitable priests who are gifted with a knowledge and love of art.

"For the training of artists it is also recommended that schools or academies of sacred art be founded in those parts of the world where they would be useful.

"All artists who, in view of their talents, desire to serve God's glory in holy Church should ever bear in mind that they are engaged in a kind of sacred imitation of God the Creator, and are concerned with works destined for use in Catholic worship for the edification, devotion, and religious instruction of the faithful" (SC 122-127).

## Liturgical Books

Liturgical books are official publications that govern the liturgical functions of the Church. In the Roman rite there are six major liturgical books: (1) the Roman Missal, official book of the Propers and Ordinaries of the Mass, arranged for the sequence of feasts throughout the liturgical year, together with the attendant ceremonies (See Sacramentary); (2) the Roman Breviary, containing the Divine Office (cf. Breviary); (3) the Roman Martyrology; (4) the Roman Ritual, containing the ceremonies of the sacraments and blessings for priests; (5) the Roman Pontifical; (6) the *Caeremoniale Episcoporum,* the book of sacraments, blessings, and ceremonies for bishops. In addition to these, but rather as abbreviations of the official six, there are: the *Memoriale Rituum,* containing the Holy Week ceremonies for small parish churches, replaced by the Order of the Mass for Holy Week; the *Clementine Instruction,* which governs the Forty Hours' Devotion; the *Officium Majoris Hebdomadae,* containing the music, psalms, and lessons for Holy Week; three singing books—the antiphonary, the *Graduale,* the *Kyriale.* Only the Holy See, through the Sacred Congregation for Divine Worship, can authorize changes in the liturgy. No bishop can authorize an essential change without an apostolic indult. The Sacred Congregation for Divine Worship publishes authentic decrees governing all liturgy. Translation is regulated by Church law. The printing of these books must be authorized, and the publishers must be approved.

## Liturgical Commission

In the National Conferences of Bishops and in each diocese Liturgical Commissions are established by regulation. It is the function of these groups, under the direction of the Conference or the local ordinary or both, to provide for, to convey, and to offer instruction toward the better exercise of rite and function in the celebration of the Eucharist, a better understanding of the Mass, the sacraments, and the prayer of the Church. Its purpose is directed to a fuller, more active and intelligent participation of the people of God in Catholic worship.

Each Liturgical Commission is headed by an appointed director with one or more clerical assistants. Serving on the Commission are priests, religious, and lay persons. It is also usual for the Commission to have a liaison person from the Priest's Council, the Diocesan Pastoral Council, the Office of the Laity, and the educational boards or offices of the diocese. Two committees are considered as standing committees of the Liturgical Commission in its very makeup, namely, the Committee on Education and on Art and Architecture. There may be additional committees formed for specific purposes, such as music, ministries, or communications, according to the need and action of the director and his assistants.

The Liturgical Commission is a center for the dissemination of information and the ongoing instruction or catechesis accompanying the celebration of the Eucharist, the Sacraments, sacramentals, and prayer. This work is carried on through news releases, seminars, conferences, and dialogue with the parochial liturgy structures. It extends the work of the Sacred Congregation for Worship and the liturgical apostolate.

Vatican II declares: "Regulation of the sacred liturgy depends solely on the authority of the Church, that is, on the Apostolic See and, as laws may determine, on the bishop.

"In virtue of power conceded by the law, the regulation of the liturgy within certain defined limits belongs also to various kinds of competent territorial bodies of bishops legitimately established.

"Therefore, absolutely no other person, not even a priest, may add, remove, or change anything in the liturgy on his own authority" (SC 22). (Cf. Liturgy; Priests' Councils.)

## Liturgical Life

In the liturgy the priestly office of Christ in His Church is exercised, and the Christian's response to this office and the message of Christ is the individual's continuing action and reaction in the salvation history of the present time. For each person, the liturgical life begins with birth into the people of God through baptism. It is renewed, carried on, and culminates in sanctification of one's days and the winning of salvation. It is both a personal and a communal commitment to the achieving of salvation and restoring all things in Christ.

Vatican II teaches: "The primitive Church

provided an example of community life when the multitude of believers were of one heart and one mind (cf. Acts 4:32), and found nourishment in the teaching of the gospel and in the sacred liturgy, especially the Eucharist. Let such a life continue in prayerfulness and a sharing of the same spirit (cf. Acts 2:42)" (PC 15).

And: "In areas or communities which are non-Christian, the gospel message draws men to faith and the sacraments of salvation. In the Christian community itself, especially among those who seem to understand or believe little of what they practice, the preaching of the Word is needed for the very administration of the sacraments. For these are sacraments of faith, and faith is born of the Word and nourished by it" (PO 4).

### Liturgical Ministry
See Ministries.

### Liturgical Movement
The basic intention of this movement is to put the liturgy into the life of moderns, more consciously and more effectively, and to teach them how to participate fully in the corporate worship of the Church. It is an effort to revitalize Catholicism and to encourage the members of the mystical body to realize the daily life of Christ through the Mass, the Divine Office, the sacraments, sacramentals, and attendant circumstances of art and practice. The modern movement began in 1840 under the urging of Dom Prosper Gueranger of Solesmes. However, the greatest impetus came in 1903 when Pope St. Pius X published his *Motu Proprio* and gave official approval to the movement.

### Liturgical Music
See Music, Church; Chant; Gregorian Music.

### Liturgical Year
See Calendar, Church.

### Liturgies, Experimental
This was a transitional term used during that time of adjustment and nonformulated rite between 1969 and the promulgation of the Sacramentary in the vernacular in 1974. Such provision had been permitted whereby new rites and adaptations could be introduced into the liturgy. In the *Third Instruction* issued by the Sacred Congregation for Divine Worship (Sept. 5, 1970) it was stated: "When liturgical experimentation is seen to be necessary or useful, permission is granted in writing by this sacred congregation alone; the experiments will be made according to clearly defined norms, under the responsibility of the competent local authority.

"With regard to the Mass, those faculties which were granted in view of the reform of the rite are no longer in force. With the publication of the new Roman Missal, the norms and the form of the eucharistic celebration are those given in the general instruction and the *Ordo Missae*."

And the Congregation for Divine Worship issued a statement of direction, Oct. 28, 1974, declaring in part: "Ordinaries, local and religious, should be vigilant so that, with the exception of non-Roman liturgical rites lawfully recognized by the Church and notwithstanding any pretext or custom, even immemorial custom, the Order of Mass of the new Roman Missal may be correctly accepted and that its content—a thesaurus of the inspired word and pastoral teaching—may be understood with greater zeal and reverence by all the priests and faithful of the Roman Rite." (See Sacramentary.)

### Liturgy
This word itself means public service or function done on behalf of the people. The sacred liturgy is the public worship that Christ, as divine Head of the Church, gives to God the Father, and that which the faithful of Christ give to Christ and through Him to God, the Father. It is thus the public worship by the mystical body. Its purpose is the greater glory of God and the sanctification of all people. The liturgical worship of the Church is made up of the sacrifice of the Mass, the sacraments, the Divine Office, and the sacramentals. The liturgy is defined as "the worship of God by His Church."

1. The eucharistic sacrifice of the Mass is the center of the religion of the Church established by Christ, for through this unbloody immolation, the

Church renews what Christ accomplished on the cross by offering Himself to God the Father. In Eastern Churches the Mass is called the "Holy Liturgy" or the "Offering." Private devotions that prompt the faithful to participate in liturgical functions, such as retreats, meditation, or the rosary, are paraliturgical. An analysis and understanding of the sacred liturgy were set forth in the encyclical *Mediator Dei* of Pope Pius XII, and more abundantly in the *Constitution on the Sacred Liturgy* of Vatican II.

2. The Divine Office is the official, universal prayer of the mystical body of Christ.

3. The sacraments and sacramentals are means of grace for the sanctification of members of the mystical body.

Although sometimes considered as a part of the liturgy, such adjuncts as music, church art, and vestments are only properly "liturgical appurtenances," which serve to make liturgy visible, effective, and pleasing. (Cf. Mass; Sacraments, Seven; Divine Office.)

Great thought has been given to the many facets of the liturgy in recent years. Clarification has come about not only through the developed teachings of Vatican II, but by the onward thinking and greater involvement of the faithful in liturgy. Because of this, we look more closely at the meaning and place of liturgy in the Church.

The German theologian, A. Verheul, defined liturgy as follows: "It is a personal meeting, under the veil of holy signs, of God with his Church and with the total person of each one of her members, in and through Christ and in the unity of the Holy Spirit."

*The Personal Meeting with God.* This encounter begins with Baptism and continues as a learning in the Liturgy of the Word in the New Order of the Mass. Here the modern person learns of the God of the Bible where God is revealed only by what He does. His plan of love and salvation was for all persons. God appeared in all His holiness—and only God is holy in Himself (Ex. 3:1–6; 19:6; Lv. 11:43–44; Dt. 26:18–19). It is God who saves and only God sanctifies His people in spite of their failures to honor Him. This we learn from the OT, and we can realize His greatness when we learn of how God, when He made His covenant with Abram, was awesome in His love and justice for "a trance fell upon Abram, and a deep, terrifying darkness enveloped him" (Gn. 15:12).

In the covenant of God in the NT we encounter God in "the holy Servant, Jesus" (Acts 4:27), and it is this One, Christ, who shows us not only the glory and majesty of God, but redeems us, teaches us how to be "like" God, and wins for us the unheard of grace whereby we can call God, "Father." And God not only accomplished our redemption, but He teaches us the marvels of His mercy and how we memorialize "Christ with us" and attain to that holiness whereby we are worthy of being called the children of God (cf. Rom. 12:1–2; 15:15–16; 1 Thes. 5:18–23).

It is in the liturgy that we realize and see the goodness of God: "Mighty and wonderful are your works, Lord God Almighty! Righteous and true are your ways, O King of the nations! Who would dare refuse you honor, or the glory due your name, O Lord? Since you alone are holy, all nations shall come and worship in your presence. Your mighty deeds are clearly seen" (Rv. 15:3–4).

In the celebration of the mysteries of the Eucharist we renew our knowledge of God and welcome the Divine Presence among us for our salvation. In the Encyclical *Mediator Dei*, Pope Pius XII stresses this in defining the liturgy: "The sacred liturgy then is the public worship . . . which the community of Christ's faithful pays . . . through Him to the Eternal Father" (Par. 20). And Vatican II follows this thought in the first chapter of its *Constitution on the Sacred Liturgy:* "Christ indeed always associates the Church with himself in this great work, wherein God is perfectly glorified and men are sanctified. The Church is his beloved Bride, who calls to her Lord, and through him offers worship to the Eternal Father" (SC 1). The liturgy is thus the highest expression of the life of the Church; it is an epiphany, a making visible of the Church; it is the power that activates the Church.

*The Sign Character of Liturgy.* Both in its sacramental and prayer aspect, we encounter the sign of the Liturgy. First, Christ is the preeminent sign—in His revealed body in the Liturgy of the Word in the Mass and also in His invisible presence in the Eucharist. As the Roman Martyrology declares: "He willed to sanctify the world through his gracious Advent." Christ and the Church become, united in sacrifice and prayer, a sign of and for the people of God.

As St. Peter wrote: "Praised be the God and Father of our Lord Jesus Christ, he who in his great mercy gave us new birth; a birth unto hope which draws its life from the resurrection of Jesus Christ from the dead; a birth to an imperishable inheritance, incapable of fading or defilement, which is kept in heaven for you who are guarded with God's power through faith; a birth to a salvation which stands ready to be revealed in the last days" (1 Pt. 1:3–5).

The liturgy is therefore a sign of hope for the people of God, again as St. Peter writes: "This is my beloved Son, on whom my favor rests. We ourselves heard this said from heaven while we were in his company on the holy mountain. Beside, we possess the prophetic message as something altogether reliable. Keep your attention closely fixed on it, as you would on a lamp shining in a dark place until the first streaks of dawn appear and the morning star rises in your hearts" (2 Pt. 1:17–19).

*Liturgy as Community and Mystery.* It was declared in *Mediator Dei* that "the whole public worship of the Mystical Body of Jesus Christ, Head and members" (par. 20) is for all, and this is realized only in the liturgy. It is the transference of holiness to everyone, which is accomplished by the entire worshipping community. As St. Paul writes: "And now, brothers, I beg you through the mercy of God to offer your bodies as a living sacrifice holy and acceptable to God, your spiritual worship" (Rom. 12:1; Eph. 4:12; 1 Cor. 16:15; 2 Cor. 8:1–7).

Liturgy is of the community; it is memorial but also a reactualization of becoming "like" Christ (Jn. 17:11) and acting "like" Him. In the community gatherings of the earliest Church the "breaking of the bread" was for all, done in a sacrificial manner (Acts 20:11; 1 Cor. 10:16). The priest performs a ministering function, but there is the priesthood of the universal Church community (cf. 1 Pt. 2:9–10). And this celebrating of the liturgy in Church community is a prophetic sign of the heavenly Church (Heb. 12:22). As Vatican II declares: "The Church, therefore, earnestly desires that those who have faith in Christ, when present at this mystery of faith, should not be there as strangers or silent spectators; on the contrary, through an adequate understanding of the rites and prayers they should take part in the sacred action conscious of what they are doing, with devotion and full collaboration. They should be instructed by God's word and be nourished at the table of the Lord's Body; they should give thanks to God; by offering the immaculate victim not only through the hands of the priest but also with him, they should learn to offer themselves; through Christ their Mediator, they should be drawn day by day into ever more perfect union with God and with each other, so that finally God may be all in all" (SC 48).

It is thus that through the liturgy we more intensely respond to and become more aware of the presence of the Holy Spirit in the Church and the intervention of the Spirit in our lives on our journey to holiness in God. (See Community; Paraliturgical Actions.)

## Liturgy, Children's

Unlike the formalism of the Tridentine Mass, the New Order of the Mass makes special provision for adaptation. Vatican II states: "Even in the liturgy, the Church has no wish to impose a rigid uniformity in matters which do not involve the faith or the good of the whole community" (SC 37).

One special area of adaptation has been that of liturgies geared especially to the understanding, interest, and spiritual development of children, notably those of pre-adolescent age, or those liturgies where the majority of participants are children. Here the language, the music, and the audiovisual aids are adapted to the child. This is in keeping with the entire idea of community, which means a group of persons united by something other than themselves. Here, the liturgy as a celebration of prayer, thanksgiving, and petition is made more understandable to the child. Such liturgies (like all others) should be planned, meaning that the processions, songs, Scripture readings be made more simple and in keeping with the vibrant response of children.

The New Order of the Mass devotes much to the Liturgy for children, declaring among other instructions: "The development of gestures, postures, and actions is very important for Masses with children in view of the nature of the liturgy as an activity of the entire man and in view of the psychology of children. This should be done in harmony with the age and local usage. (33) . . . Among the actions which are considered under this heading, processions deserve special mention as do other activities which involve physical participation (34) . . . The liturgy of the Mass contains many visual elements, and these should be given great prominence with children. This is especially true of the particular visual elements in the course of the liturgical year, for example, the veneration of the cross, the Easter candle, the lights on the feast of the Presentation of the Lord, and the variety of colors and liturgical ornaments.

"In addition to the visual elements that belong to the celebration and to the place of celebration, it is appropriate to introduce other elements which will permit children to perceive visually the great deeds of God in creation and redemption and thus support their prayer. The liturgy should never appear as something dry and merely intellectual.

"For the same reason the use of pictures prepared by the children themselves may be useful, for example, to illustrate a homily, to give a visual dimension to the intentions of the general intercessions, or to inspire reflection (36).

"Even in Masses with children 'silence should be

observed at the proper time as a part of the celebration' lest too great a role be given to external action. In their own way children are genuinely capable of reflection. They need, however, a kind of introduction so that they will learn how to reflect within themselves, meditate briefly, or praise God and pray to him in their hearts, for example after the homily or after communion (37).

"The general structure of the Mass, which 'in some sense consists of two parts, namely, the liturgy of the word and the liturgy of the Eucharist,' should always be maintained as should some rites to open and conclude the celebration. Within individual parts of the celebration the adaptations which follow seem necessary if children are truly to experience, in their own way and according to the psychological patterns of childhood, 'the mystery of faith . . . by means of rites and prayers' " (38).

There have been prepared, in addition to those Eucharistic prayers of the Sacramentary, new Eucharistic prayers especially for Masses celebrated with children. These include more simple language in the preface; they emphasize more participation by the entire congregation, with repetition of "Glory to God in the Highest" or "Hosanna in the Highest," and at four appropriate times this response is made: "We praise you, we bless you, we thank you." And there will be special Easter season variations and new emphasis placed upon the first Eucharistic prayer for Masses of reconciliation. (Cf. Liturgy.)

### Liturgy of the Eucharist
See Eucharist, Celebration of.

### Liturgy of Holy Week
See Holy Week, Liturgy of.

### Liturgy of the Hours
The general title given to the Roman Breviary in its revision (undertaken from 1965 to 1975), the Liturgy of the Hours is the book of daily prayer of the Roman Catholic Church. The modernized collection of prayers, contained in four volumes totaling about 8,000 pages, is arranged in a gathering of scripture passages, canticles, hymns, writings from the works of historic Church persons such as the Fathers, and prayers. The selections are arranged for special times of the day and are related to the calendar of the Church year.

The traditional terms of "hours," familiar in the daily breviary, namely, matins, lauds, terce, sext, none, vespers and compline, have been replaced with simpler terms under the headings: Office of readings, morning prayer, daytime prayers, evening prayer, and night prayer.

In the past the breviary was oriented to the monastic course of prayer with each succeeding hour of prayer progressing from the morning prayer (matins) to compline. Now, however, recognition is given to the prayer being the extension of the communal life of all the people of God. The clergy and religious, who were formerly under prescription to pray the breviary, are still most firmly compelled to pray the Liturgy of the Hours, but with a more adaptable arrangement. In addition, the special ministries of permanent deaconate and extraordinary ministries are encouraged to pray the Liturgy of the Hours. Moreoever, all members of the people of God in their community response are urged to participate daily or oftener, in the prayer life that is provided by the Church in this Liturgy of the Hours.

The modern Liturgy of the Hours has greater flexibility and more fluid forms and structures to make it a true part of the communitarian worship program. This public prayer of the Church, while it remains a basic personal and individual response or one's self-expression in prayer, is encouraged to become a community prayer. As yet there are no norms or guidelines that set up the community response, but the flexibility of the modern Liturgy of the Hours is intended to encourage this wherever possible. In addition, the daily prayer life of the Church is no longer a "limited obligation" meant only for the ordained, but individuals are enjoined to take up a prayer-response in keeping with their lives in the world. Truly the Eucharist is the center of the community worship. But second only to this most noble form, the daily prayer of the Church gives witness to the worship owed God as absolute. This then may be on the individual or family basis if the church-centered participation is not feasible. Thus Christian prayer should be made public through the media of words, gestures, actions, and periods of silent meditation whereby it is demonstrated that all are a faith-community, becoming a living prayer to God our Father. (Cf. Breviary; Liturgy; Prayer.)

### Liturgy of the Word
See Eucharist, Celebration of.

### Lives of the Saints
When we speak of lives of the saints, we refer to the collections of brief, informative biographies that give us the essential data regarding each saint. There were in the past great collections of such lives, notably the martyrologies. There also have

been several current listings that include saints canonized in more recent times: these are the multivolume collection of *Butler's Lives of the Saints; The Saints* by John Coulson; the *Dictionary of Catholic Biography* by John J. Delaney, James Edward Tobin, and other lesser gatherings in popular anthology-like collections. In addition many religious groups, such as the Franciscans, keep listings of saints who were members of their religious orders.

There are, however, hagiographical writings that treat of one, or at most a few, saints. These biographies take on a different intent, namely, besides giving the pertinent information, they probe more deeply into the personal life of the saint and try to ascertain what pathway of sanctity the individual saint followed. This form calls for more profound insight and enlightened evaluation. Its purpose is to give the reader information, promptings toward emulation, and the insights that may aid the reader in seeking his or her own course of salvation. The difficulties of such lives are that the writing is based mostly upon secondary research. The simple rule might be that the better the writer, the greater the ability to fulfill the task, and certainly the better and more profitable will be the writing for the reader. (See Hagiography.)

## Loaves of Proposition

In the worship of the Temple of Jerusalem, in the place before the Holy of Holies, in keeping with the law (Lv. 24:5–9), twelve loaves of bread, called the "loaves of proposition," or showbread, were placed as a symbolic recognition of the covenant of God with the twelve tribes of Israel. In accord with the priestly code it was prescribed that each week twelve loaves or cakes made of four-fifths of a peck of the finest flour, freshly baked on the Sabbath and placed in two piles of six cakes each be placed on the golden table "before Yahweh" and some grains of pure frankincense put on each pile. The loaves were eaten by the priests, those placed there on the previous Sabbath, before the fresh loaves were presented.

These loaves may have had their origin in pagan rituals, but the priestly class made these loaves a substitute for sacrifices, thus ensuring their continual memorial (Ex. 25:30), and Christ repeated the incident of the loaves to show that He was the New Temple (Mt. 12:1–7; 26:26).

## Loci Theologici

These "theological sources" were first introduced in a writing by Melchior Cano (d. 1560) and were listed as seven *prime* or proper bases of theological study and thought: Scripture, tradition, the magisterium of the Church, the councils, the decisions of the popes, the fathers of the Church, and theologians; and three *secondary* or improper basis: human reason, philosophy, and history.

## Loculi

Loculi is the Latin plural for "places." (See Catacombs.)

## Logic

Logic is the science or art that teaches the method of acquiring knowledge through the study and application of reason as a means of discovering the truth. It is introductory or preparatory to the study of philosophy. Logic is applied through inductive and deductive procedures; actually, sound reasoning.

There are four kinds of logic whereby orderly thinking is made less difficult and applicable: (1) poetic logic, such as applied in a work of literature, a drama, poem, or novel, which involves the emotions; (2) rhetorical logic, wherein the art of persuasion is applied to gain special effectiveness, such as in advertising, oratory or debate; (3) scientific logic, whereby the truth is sought without the interference of emotions; (4) demonstrative logic, which is applied in reaching a conclusion, for example, the angle of incidence is equal to the angle of reflection. All forms of logic are used in the service of truth through recognition of a problem, judgment of the problem, and reasoning to a right conclusion.

## Logos

Literally, "the Word," this term is exclusive with St. John (Jn. 1:1–18). Jesus, the Messiah, the divine Son of God is presented by St. John as the *Logos,* the second divine Person of the Blessed Trinity (cf. Trinity). In the Prologue of St. John's Gospel, the *Logos* is presented as eternal, distinct from God the Father, yet truly God who became man, the God-Man, Jesus of Nazareth. Perhaps the term was used by St. John because of his recognition of the term among Greek philosophers, but his choice was more one of inspiration. He chose a word that by its very force would satisfy the mind as does the "Word Incarnate." The term is interchangeable with the word "wisdom" as used by St. Paul (1 Cor. 1:24), thus the *Logos* is the wisdom of God made manifest in the Son. (Cf. Incarnation.)

## Lollards

This is the name of followers of the native heresy of medieval England, supported by John of Gaunt and the theologian John Wyclif. The movement, called Lollardy, was anticlerical and defied Church authority and, toward the end of the fourteenth century it sought, by individual interpretation, to emphasize the authority of the Bible. By the end of the fifteenth century, the movement had almost disappeared. (Cf. Heresy.)

## Longanimity

Longanimity is a virtue referred to hope, and one of the fruits of the Holy Spirit. It is both longsuffering and forbearance and teaches one to consider the future good, to wait with patience and constancy, that is, continuing over an extended period of time to practice virtues and seek sanctification.

## Lord

Translated from the Hebrew, Aramaic, or Greek, the word *Lord* means "master," a ruler, or a person in authority. In the OT Yahweh (God) is called Lord, and in the NT the word Lord is used to name God, for example, when Jesus Christ spoke of God the Father: "Lord of heaven and earth" (Mt. 11:25; Lk. 10:21; Acts 17:24). Jesus Himself was spoken of and addressed as Lord (Mk. 7:28). Jesus also referred to Himself as Lord (Jn. 13:13). And after the resurrection Christ was given the title of universal sovereignty (Jn. 20:28; 21:7). In Christ, the early Christians, like the Christians of today, speak of Christ as God and address Him as God in their prayer, for He gives light, grace, forgiveness, and healing (Acts 7:59–60; 9:10–15; 1 Cor. 1:2; 12:2–5; Rom. 5:1–2), and the Christians await the "coming again in glory" (1 Cor. 16:22; Rv. 22:20).

The uniqueness of Jesus Christ as the Second Person of the Blessed Trinity is repeated again and again in the scriptures of the NT, but especially because in Him salvation is realized (Jn. 10:11), and the "Sonship" of God is demonstrated by the mutual knowledge shared with the Father (Jn. 5:17–20; 10:14–15; 15:13–14). (See Christ; Trinity, the Most Holy.)

## Lord's Prayer

The *Pater Noster*, that is, the "Our Father" prayer, was taught by our Lord to the apostles (Mt. 6:9–13). Essentially, it consists of three prayers for the glory of God (hallowed be Thy name, Thy kingdom come, Thy will be done) and an expression of the extent of that glory (on earth as it is in heaven), followed by three requests (for food, forgiveness, and freedom from temptation) and a final plea for deliverance from evil, that is, moral evil.

In the new Order of the Mass the Lord's Prayer is given great prominence. It is said aloud by the celebrant and the faithful present, following the Eucharistic prayer and at the beginning of the Communion rite. The priest introduces the prayer, and with all standing, they recite:

> Our Father, who art in heaven
>   hallowed be thy name;
>   they kingdom come;
>   thy will be done
>   On earth as it is in heaven.
> Give us this day our daily bread;
>   and forgive us our trespasses
>   as we forgive those who trespass against us;
>   and lead us not into temptation,
>   but deliver us from evil.

The priest then continues: "Deliver us, Lord, from every evil, and grant us peace in our day. In your mercy keep us free from sin and protect us from all anxiety as we wait in joyful hope for the coming of our Savior, Jesus Christ."

A doxology is then acclaimed by the people:

> "For the Kingdom, the power and the glory are yours, now and forever."

## Lord's Supper

The Last Supper is sometimes referred to by this name. It is also a little used term for Holy Thursday.

## Loreto, Litany of

See Litany.

## L'Osservatore Romano

This is the title of the daily newspaper of the Holy See. Originating in July 1861 as an independent enterprise of four laymen, the publication was purchased by Pope Leo XIII in 1890. It has thus been referred to as the "official newspaper of the pope," but the only official news or announcements contained in its pages are under the heading "Nostre Informazioni." However, the newspaper does follow the teaching policies and the social and political attitudes of the Holy See. It is staffed locally, with reporters covering the news of Rome as well as many foreign correspondents who cover world affairs. An overall weekly edition in English was begun in 1968 and is obtainable by subscription. There are other weekly editions in Spanish, French, Portuguese, and German.

## Los-Von-Rom Movement

This German title literally means "away from Rome." This political and religious movement started in Germany in 1897; its leaders, by exploiting the racial feeling of Germans in Bohemia, sought to draw them away from allegiance with Catholic Austria and link them to Protestant Prussia.

## Lourdes, Apparitions of

A series of eighteen apparitions began Feb. 11 and ended on July 16, 1858. During this time, the Blessed Virgin Mary appeared to fourteen-year-old Bernadette Soubirous (canonized St. Bernadette on Dec. 8, 1933) in the rock cave of Massabielle along the river Gave near Lourdes in France. At the last apparition the Blessed Mother declared her identity, saying, "I am the Immaculate Conception." Four years previously (1854) the Church had defined as a dogma the truth of the Immaculate Conception of the Blessed Mother. After the apparitions at Lourdes, a flowing spring of water, with no unusual natural properties, has been the apparent means of effecting miraculous cures through the patronage of the Blessed Mother. Also there was constructed, in accord with the Virgin's request, a chapel that has become one of the great churches of southern France. People from all over the world go on pilgrimage to Lourdes in honor of the Blessed Virgin Mary. A feast in the Roman rite is celebrated in commemoration of these apparitions on Feb. 11.

Today there are medical bureaus and a hospital that examine each cure for its authenticity. The hospital has a worldwide organization of people who volunteer their time, on several days of each year, to serve as stretcher-bearers and wheelchair attendants, so that the sick, infirm, and crippled may approach the baths of water from the spring. As many as six million persons make pilgrimages to Lourdes each year. The account has been classically retold by the novelist Franz Werfel in his book *Bernadette*.

## Love Feast

This title is sometimes given to the celebration of the Eucharist. (See Agape.)

## Love of God

Love of God is the greatest of the virtues, both in practice and accomplishment. Embracing all other virtues, it is called the "essence of perfection." St. Thomas Aquinas declares this theological virtue of charity thus: "Essentially, the perfection of the Christian life consists in charity, first and foremost in the *love of God,* then in the love of neighbor." In the Church, this love is by *command,* by the direct *teaching of Christ,* and by tradition and teaching. We find this by *command* (Dt. 6:5), which is both the directive to adore God and give Him an absorbing love: "Thou shalt love Yahweh thy God with thy whole heart, and with thy whole soul, and with thy whole strength." As a religious precept, it is the center of the OT teaching and the center of the New Law that Christ established. Christ's teaching was direct and positive. He calls this the greatest commandment (Mk. 12:29–31) and demonstrates the manner of its practice: "Anyone who loves Me will be true to my word" (Jn. 14:23) assuring all that the Spirit of love will futher teach them (Jn. 15:26), and finally Christ declares the degree and extent of this love, using Himself as the example: "as I have loved you" (Jn. 15:12). The basic source of love of God is found in our dependence on God, for as St. Thomas Aquinas states, the love that God has for us "infuses and creates the goodness which is present in all things." God loves because He creates; we love because we are created. There is no brief statement that would serve to demonstrate how to practice this love of God, but it may be put as: giving one's self to God, avoiding sin, praying and meditating, practicing self-denial and conforming to the will of God. Since each is progressive and capable of extension, it is thus a continuous work of perfection of self. (Cf. Charity.)

## Love of Neighbor

The commandments of God are observed out of love for Him. In this there is the imitation of the divine morality, specifically in the practice of fraternal charity, that is, the love of one's neighbor. Neighbor does not necessarily mean one who lives nearby, but it is a collective term for the entire body of human persons. In order to fulfill this law, one must imitate Christ (Jn. 14:12–13; 15:7–8; 1 Jn. 4:20–21). In the fulfillment of the entire law, we find that charity is the "bond" of perfection (Col. 3:14).

This fraternal charity builds up the body of Christ and directs the charisms (1 Cor. 12–14). It is the Holy Spirit, dwelling in each of us, who is the source of charity: "And this hope will not leave us disappointed, because the love of God has been poured out in our hearts through the Holy Spirit who has been given to us" (Rom. 5:5) (cf. also Gal. 5:22). This charity also has its rising, its orison, in the Holy Eucharist, which constitutes the body of Christ.

The human person, faced with the hatred of the world about him, finds in fraternal love a sign of contradiction: "This, remember, is the message you heard from the beginning: we should love one another. We should not follow the example of Cain who belonged to the evil one and killed his brother. Why did he kill him? Because his own deeds were wicked while his brother's were just. No need, then, brothers, to be surprised if the world hates you. That we have passed from death to life we know because we love the brothers. The man who does not love is among the living dead. Anyone who hates his brother is a murderer, and you know that eternal life abides in no murderer's heart. The way we came to understand love was that he laid down his life for us; we too must lay down our lives for our brothers. I ask you, how can God's love survive in a man who has enough of this world's goods yet closes his heart to his brother when he sees him in need? Little children, let us love in deed and in truth and not merely talk about it. This is our way of knowing we are committed to the truth and are at peace before him no matter what our consciences may charge us with; for God is greater than our hearts and all is known to him" (1 Jn. 3:11–20) (cf. also Jn. 15:18–21; Jas. 2:1–4.)

It is then in Christ Himself that we must recognize our neighbor and in this recognition love Christ Himself (Mt. 25:31–46). It is thus that the social doctrine of the gospel (Lk. 12; 14:12–14; 16:19–31) and the social teaching of the Church result in a true expression, a unity of expression, in charity (Acts 2:42–44; 4:32–37; Gal. 3:28–29; Col. 3:11; Phlm. 16).

Finally there is an eschatological aspect of charity, namely, the ongoing activity of all who await in faith and anticipate in hope the new coming of Christ (Jn. 13:33–34; Gal. 6:10; Rom. 12:12–13), or as St. Peter states: "The consummation of all is close at hand" (1 Pt. 4:7–11). (See Social Action; Salvation History.)

## Low Sunday

Low Sunday is the first Sunday after Easter, also called "Sunday in white" *(Dominica in albis)*, or *Quasimodo* from the first word of the Introit of the Tridentine Latin Mass. It has been designated as "low" not because of degree of the feast, but simply because it follows the great feast of Easter.

## Ludwig Mission Association

Also, in German, the *Ludwig-missionsverein,* this association was founded in Bavaria in 1838 to aid the Catholic missionary activities in North America. Its founder was Frederic Rese (who also founded the Leopoldine Association), a German-born priest serving the missions of North America. Although the majority of its funds went to religious orders of men, by 1921 it had given almost $900,000 to the Catholic Church in the United States.

## Luke, Gospel of St.

The third of the synoptic Gospels was written by the Apostle, St. Luke, the physician, probably not before A.D. 70. In content this writing has been described as "the announcement of good tidings." It has six parts: (1) the narrative of the infancy of Christ; (2) the Messianic office of Christ; (3) the manifestation of this office in Galilee by Christ; (4) the preaching of Christ; (5) the Passion of Christ; (6) the culmination, the Resurrection, and Ascension of Christ. The Gospel is a genuine history of the origin of the Christian faith (its history of development is presented in Acts of the Apostles, also written by St. Luke). It is notable for its historic and literary qualities, its emphasis upon the joy of its author's message, its recognition of the necessity for prayer, and the place it gives to the Blessed Mother. It points to Jesus as the Son of God and the Son of Man, and the reign of God's will through the established Church of Christ. It proclaims the universal salvation of all human persons, which was accomplished by Christ through His death and resurrection.

Luke the Evangelist was probably a Greek from Antioch, a disciple of St. Paul, and his Gospel gives the tradition of St. Paul's teaching. St. Paul spoke of St. Luke as "the beloved physician," and he knew him as a Gentile convert and missioner. St. Luke wrote the Acts of the Apostles for Gentile converts in particular. (See Acts of the Apostles.)

## Lumen Gloriae

The Latin words mean "Light of Glory," an undefinable term, but known from scripture to be a singular "radiance" of God, Christ, angels, and those in heaven (Rv. 21:11; Mt. 17:2). By the literal understanding of this radiance it may be concluded that there is a luminosity of the person or spirit in heaven, which seems to be of the very person or spirit itself. However, this light does not in any manner indicate that there is otherwise darkness in heaven. Rather the light of glory is the quality of enthronement of Christ (Rv. 1:12–17; 5:1–14) and the enthronement of the new Covenant of salvation (Mt. 17:1–13).

## Luna, also Lunette

The luna is a small crescent-shaped clip or a circlet, made usually of gold, which holds the consecrated host. It is slid into the monstrance along a groove or track for exposition of the Blessed Sacrament.

Since the teachings on liturgy of Vatican II, the exposition of the Blessed Sacrament has been permitted without the use of the monstrance on simple occasions of adoration.

## Lust

The inordinate desire for or satisfaction of the appetite for sexual and carnal pleasure is lust. It does not include the natural and legitimate purposes of sex in which pleasure exists as a part of both the stimulus and the function. It is only inordinate when sought in a way not in keeping with the natural purpose of the appetite, or in the legitimate exercise of the appetite to an excessive degree. Lust is one of the capital or deadly sins. It may also be applied to the other human appetites, for example, tasting, but generally when these are inordinately exercised, they are classed as concupiscence. The virtues opposed to lust, which aid in its control, are: chastity and its subordinates, continence and modesty.

## Lutheran-Catholic Dialogue

Ecumenical thought has resulted in the conclusion among Lutherans, especially in America among both the amalgam of the American Lutheran Church and the Lutheran Church of the Missouri Synod (Concordia), that in the recognition of historical differences they still are closer to Catholics than they are to other Protestant groups. Hence, through the National Committee of the Lutheran World Federation, a series of discussions and conferences have been initiated, beginning in 1965 and still continuing, whereby special studies have been made of the doctrinal teachings of Vatican II, in particular the Dogmatic Constitution on the Church (*Lumen Gentium*). There is also exploration of the teachings of infallibility and the ministry of the Church universal. This has led to a joint statement of the National Lutheran-Catholic Dialogue (Mar. 4, 1974) entitled: *Papal Primacy— Converging Viewpoints*. There has also been an expression on the part of the Lutheran Federation for extended ecumenical studies and the establishment of suitable structures for reconciliation. (See Ecumenism.)

## Lutheranism

The religious belief practiced collectively by Lutherans had its rise in the teachings made up and taught by Martin Luther (d. 1546) in Erfurt and Wittenberg in Germany. As a teaching, it finds its center in a justification by faith alone, based on Luther's translation of Rom. 3:28. There is a confusion of original sin with concupiscence, since Luther held that original justice was connatural to Adam and Eve, and original sin so corrupted human nature that man could no longer do good, for his reason had degenerated and his free will had been taken from him. This resulted in man's domination by concupiscence, which in itself was looked on as evil. With man so fallen and so dominated, Christ's redemption was entirely done for us and, taking Christ's merits as one's own, there was no need for further effort on man's part, either in imitation of Christ or personal merit. Man could ignore or cover up sin. It follows that habitual grace is nonexistent; actual grace is God working in us, and therefore one needs only faith in or abandonment to God and His mercy. Thus Luther did away with the sacraments, keeping baptism, penance (as only a declaration followed automatically by remission), and a nonconsecrated eucharist wherein Christ is only present by faith of the believer. Thus there is no need for an established priesthood since truth comes from the Bible, which is freely interpreted. Luther also denied purgatory, indulgences, prayers for the dead, and the intercession of the saints.

## Lyons, Councils of

The first council convoked at Lyons, France, in 1245, by Pope Innocent IV was the thirteenth ecumenical council. The second, in 1274, convened by Pope Gregory X, was the fourteenth ecumenical council. Both councils were concerned with national and international affairs and moral reform. (Cf. Ecumenical Councils.)

The First excommunicated Frederick II and deposed him; a plea was presented for volunteers to free the Holy Land. There were also certain disciplinary regulations for Church figures and those who trafficked with the Saracens.

The Second declared that the Holy Spirit proceeds from the Father and Son in the Holy Trinity, mandated the use of unleavened bread in the Holy Eucharist, proclaimed that there is a true transubstantiation into the body and blood of Christ through consecration, and declared the supreme primacy of the Holy Roman Church over the entire Catholic Church. It also brought forward some disciplinary actions.

## Lyons, Rite of

Also called the Lyonnais Rite, until the universal promulgation of the New Order of the Mass following Vatican II, this was the liturgical peculiarity preserved and used in the archdiocese of Lyons, France. The Mass had different preparatory prayers from those of the Tridentine Mass, with different sequential prayers for Christmas, Epiphany, Ascension, and many other feasts, together with special prefaces for Advent, All Saints, and other feasts. The bread and wine were offered as one at the offertory, and there was a "little elevation" during the saying of the Lord's Prayer. There were also differences in the Breviary. The Lenten liturgical color was "ashen," that is, grey.

### Macedonianism

The heresy, begun in 360 by some Arian bishops and taking its name from one of them, Bishop Macedonius of Constantinople, taught that the Second Person of the Trinity was inferior to the First Person, and the Holy Spirit inferior to the First and Second. It was condemned at the second ecumenical council. (See Heresies.)

### Maccabees, First and Second Books of

These are two books of history, presenting the story of the successful resistance of the Jews to foreign dominance. Their authors are unknown, but the first book was written not later than 103 B.C. and the second possibly about 125 B.C. The title is derived from Maccabaeus, the assumed name of Judas, the third son of Mathathias, taken from the Hebrew name meaning "hammer," but some scholars consider the derivation of the word to be from the Hebrew word meaning "designated by Yahweh." Being books of history and accounts of action, their doctrinal content is slight, centered chiefly around survival after death, the resurrection of the body, and the eternal punishment of sin.

They treat in particular the struggle of the Jews against the influence of Hellenism, against what they considered the paganization of their land and people. The author's intent was not only to make an historical accounting but also to declare that there should be generosity in prayer and in one's gifts, and that there will be a manifestation of the Lord in glory (2 Mc. 15:34).

### Madonna

This name is applied to representations of the Blessed Mother in either painting or sculpture. Properly speaking, such representation is designated as a Madonna only when the central figure is that of the Virgin even when the Christ child or others are also depicted. The equivalent term in English would be "Our Lady." Various titles have been given to the Blessed Virgin Mary, which include the word "Madonna." This is also true of certain aspects of religion wherein Our Lady is prominent, for example, Madonna Window or Madonna Chapel.

In Church art the veneration of the Blessed Virgin Mary has been in the tradition of the Church since St. Epiphanius, who died in 403. Even before the fourth century there was a natural feeling of deep regard for Mary by all who believed in the divinity of her Son. The earliest art figures are on Christian sarcophagi, but in none of the sculptures or mosaics is the Virgin Mother shown alone; she is shown as part of a group as in a nativity scene.

It was after the Council of Ephesus (431) when the Nestorians who held there were two natures in Christ were refuted, that the Church teaching declared that Mary was indeed the Mother of God. Thereafter representations of the "Madonna and Child" became the approved expression in art of the Blessed Virgin Mary. Thus a "madonna," properly speaking and in keeping with tradition, is a representation in art (icon, mosaic, painting, sculpture, stained glass) of the Virgin Mother with the Christ-child.

However, because of great devotion to the Blessed Mother, not only because of her singular maternity role in salvation history, but because she is venerated as one having the feminine characteristics of purity, humility, fortitude, compassion, and faith, she has been depicted in great masterpieces throughout the history of art, as a woman of beauty and grace.

The first mention in history of any portrait or representation of the Virgin Mary, following Ephesus, was when the Empress Eudocia sent home from the Holy Land a picture of the Virgin holding the Child Jesus, which was placed in the Church in Constantinople. It was regarded as having been painted from life, but this was only a legend. In 1204 the painting was seized by the Venetians and has since been kept in the Church of St. Mark in Venice. In the following centuries, especially from the thirteenth through the seventeenth, there were masterpieces painted and sculptured by the greatest artists of those ages.

Many of these were commissioned by Church authorities or kingly patrons. The esteem and regard for the Blessed Virgin Mary continued to the present, in other arts, music, literature, poetry, all reflecting the words of Dante in his *Paradiso* (33, 4):

> Lady, thou art so great and hast
> such worth, that if there be who
> would have grace yet betaketh not himself to
>     thee,
> his longing seeketh to fly without wings.
> Thy kindliness not only succoureth whoso
> requesteth, but doth oftentimes freely
> forerun request.
> In thee is tenderness, in thee is pity,
> in thee munificence, in thee united
> whatever in created being is of excellence.

### Magdalen

This is a descriptive title conferred upon a penitent prostitute who has been placed or voluntarily seeks reform in a religious community. The name is derived from the place of residence of St. Mary Magdalen, Magdala.

### Magi

Originally the Magi, "wise men," were a priestly tribe of soothsayers of Media who served under their Persian conquerors. The name *magoi* was used by Matthew (2:1–12) to indicate "sages" who came to adore Christ. While they are declared to come from "the East," their homeland was most likely the land beyond the Jordan River and east of the Dead Sea. They probably visited Christ after the purification (Lk. 2:22–38), which took place 40 days after birth. The gifts they brought to the newborn Christ were products of their native land, Arabian in character, and were such as would be presented to a king. Although their names are not known, medieval legend calls them Gaspar, Melchior, and Balthasar.

In the account in the gospel of Matthew there are two special messages: (1) the contrast to the disbelief of the Jews; (2) that the salvation was universal, unlimited, and was the reward of a response to faith. This can also be derived from the grouping of nations around the king: "All kings shall pay him homage, all nations shall serve him" (Ps. 72:11). (Cf. also Is. 60:6; Lk. 1:32–33.)

### Magic

That form of superstition which claims to produce effects beyond the natural powers of man is called magic. The principles of the practice are: that a "cosmic" medium exists and interpenetrates,

influences, changes, or rules over the tangible world; that between the real and unseen world there is some analogy set up in the illusory world of sense; that this analogy can be discovered by the human person, controlled by one's will, and thus becomes the guide or master of the person and his or her fate.

There was a practice of the "magical arts" among the Israelites (Jer. 27:9; Mi. 5:11; Mal. 3:5), and since this carried over with the Jews of the NT, it also confronted the converts to the true faith. Once Christianity became their religion in the early Church, they foreswore forever the actions of magic (Acts 19:17–19). (cf. also Gal. 5:19–21.)

The Church teaches that the superstitious practices belittle God and make Him a cooperator in man's ignorance. As Coventry Patmore wrote: "The work of the Church in the world is not to teach the mysteries of life, so much as to persuade the soul to that arduous degree of purity at which God Himself becomes her teacher. The work of the Church ends when the knowledge of God begins." Thus the superstition of magic is contrary to the virtue of religion and the theological virtue of hope. Through magic we may not seek to harm another nor find a substitute for religion. (See Spiritism.)

### Magisterium of the Church

Magisterium of the Church is the power given by Christ to the Church together with infallibility by which the Church teaches authoritatively the revealed truth of the Scripture and holds forth the truth of tradition for salvation. This fact is contained in the nature and extent of the mission given to the Church (Mt. 28:19–20) and the recognized acceptance of that mission as recorded in the Acts of the Apostles. Thus the Church, taking the deposit of faith and gathering the orally transmitted and written truth (tradition), formally declares, through councils and infallible definitions, her magisterium. (Cf. Infallibility; Tradition; Apostolicity.)

The handing down of the teaching of Christ and the doctrine of the Apostles is on the one hand a part of tradition, and on the other the claim of the bishops of the Church that they, in Christ's name and assisted by the Holy Spirit, demand faith. In understanding that the Church is a community of faith in its Founder (1 Tm. 3:15) and that it cannot fail (Mt. 16:18), one acknowledges that the entire episcopate teaches with infallible authority in testimony to Christ and that this testimony should be accepted with an absolute assent of faith. It is through the magisterium of the Church that the concrete action of the Holy Spirit's guidance maintains the historical continuity with Christ, the Head of the Mystical Body. (See Collegiality; Authority.)

## Magnanimity

Magnanimity is that quality of soul which prompts a person to undertake great things for God and one's neighbor. It is the disposition to act selflessly with genuine motives. In this there is no feeling of ambition to direct or control others by wielding power over them, or any lesser motive such as money, recognition, glory. It is combined with unselfish thought, high ideals, or high-mindedness. It arises from a free practice of all virtues, notably charity and justice, in many diverse actions. Its opposite, actually a defect, is pusil-lanimimity, which causes one through a "smallness of soul" to refrain from acting for others out of fear of failure or out of a feeling that "there is not enough in it for me."

## Magnificat

This title has been given to the canticle spoken by the Blessed Mother on the occasion of her visit to her cousin, Elizabeth, as recorded in Luke (1:46–55). The Magnificat is an expression of genuine humility, which is drawn largely from OT thought, especially the Psalms (Ps. 22:8; 30:8; 33:4; 70:18). It acknowledges the goodness of God, that God is her Savior, and that God is to be served. The title comes from the first word of the Latin version. (Cf. Visitation of Mary.)

It reads: "My being proclaims the greatness of the Lord, my spirit finds joy in God my Savior. For he has looked upon his servant in her lowliness; all ages to come shall call me blessed. God who is mighty has done great things for me, holy is His name; His mercy is from age to age on those who fear him. He has shown might with his arm; he has confused the proud in their inmost thoughts. He has deposed the mighty from their thrones and raised the lowly to high places. The hungry he has given every good thing, while the rich he has sent empty away. He has upheld Israel his servant, ever mindful of his mercy; even as he promised our fathers, promised Abraham and his descendants forever."

## Major Orders

See Orders, Holy, Sacrament of; Ministries.

## Malabar Rite

Properly called the Syro-Malabar rite, this is the liturgy used by the Eastern Catholics of Malabar of southwest India, in the state of Kerala. The Syriac language and much of the Syriac liturgy are used, but many of the physical appurtenances of the Roman Church and even some of its prescribed ritual, for example, communion under one species, have been introduced. The calendar is the same as that of the Roman Church. In the late fifteenth century, the opposition established by the Portuguese almost threw this rite into heresy simply because the Portuguese suspected heresy. For a time schism broke out, but it was settled by the close of the nineteenth century. Still the Malabar Church has suffered because of the interference of Latin-minded Catholics of other countries.

## Malabar Rites

Not to be confused with the Malabar Rite, this is the name given to the series of Hindu and certain Brahmin observances that were introduced into or adapted to Christian custom. This produced a controversy that lasted until the suppression of the Jesuits in 1773. The practices were chiefly intro-duced with the permission of the Jesuit missioners, who were highly successful in their work, in the inland districts of Madura, Mysore, and the Carnatic regions. Some held these practices and observances to be superstitious, even idolatrous, but the Holy See was not entirely unfavorable although it insisted upon modification of the practices that might be considered at variance with the Christian liturgy.

## Malachi, Book of

This last book in the sequence of the OT writings of the prophets was written by an unknown author. Its title derives not from the Hebrew word meaning "messenger of Yahweh" as many have thought, but from the word of the first line of the book: "An oracle. The word of the Lord to Israel through Malachi" (Mal. 1:1), meaning, "my mes-senger." It was written about 445 B.C., probably at Jerusalem.

The book consists of six exhortations in dialogue form. It stresses the love of Yahweh for His people, reproaches the priests for abuses, rebukes the people for their divorces, gives the promise of Yahweh to send a messenger or come Himself, teaches that Yahweh is faithful even if the people are not, promises justice on the day of judgment (3:13–21), and concludes with the urging that the people observe the Law of Moses and the coming of Elijah, namely the one who is to come before the Messiah.

The book does give some historic information on the reforms brought about by Esdras, the externals of religious worship, and the laws of marriage and the workman's right to fair wages. But there is also an expression of the eschatological expectation, as understood at the time, concerning the Day of Judgment or the Day of the Lord.

The following quotation (Mal. 1:10–11) was declared by the Council of Trent to be a prefigurement of the offering of the Sacrifice of the Mass: "Oh, that one among you would shut the temple gates to keep you from kindling fire on my altar in vain! I have no pleasure in you, says the Lord of hosts; neither will I accept any sacrifice from your hands, for from the rising of the sun, even to its setting, my name is great among the nations; and everywhere they bring sacrifice to my name, a pure offering; for great is my name among the nations, says the Lord of hosts."

## Mammon

The word comes through the Latin from the Greek, from the original Aramaic word meaning "profit, wealth." As it is used in Matthew (6:24) and Luke (16:9–13), the adapted word is the personification of wealth as a power of the devil hostile to God. The word may also be interpreted as "wealth unjustly acquired."

## Man

Considered as a creation of God, of body and soul, and thus an eschatological creature, man must be examined from the philosophical anthropological aspect but more practically from the unity of the human person. This means that man must be considered in his epochal reality as known from scriptures, and also in the light of culture, environment, race, history, religion, ethics, aesthetics, as well as in the perspective of his biological, economic, social and political makeup.

Here we are concerned with man in his scriptural background (hermeneutical) and his development as a religiously oriented being. Man and woman God created them, not because man was first in the sequence, according to the act of creation (Gn. 2:7), but because God created the two human persons uniquely different (Gn. 2:23). This is also reasonable, for man and woman vary from each other not only in their uniqueness of creation, but also man from man and woman from woman because of their individual uniqueness since otherwise there would be identity and identity is a limitation of the creative act and cannot be said of the Creator.

Man was created in the image of God in all of his being but most particularly in his reason (intellect) perfected by grace (Gn. 1:26–27; 1 Cor. 11:7; Col. 3:10; Eph. 4:24; Rom. 8:29). And man as the unique creation of God was intended and is capable of being the one exercising dominion over all creation (Gn. 9:2–3; Ps. 8; Sir. 17:1–14). But this dominion is given to man so that man may learn to know God in creation, and knowing, will honor and serve Him (Rom. 1:19–28). And man awaits perfection that can only come about through faith, grace, merit and through Christ who gained these for man (Rom. 8:18–22; Phil. 3:17–21). Thence it is that the human person, created and sustained by God, will come to the "new creation" in the eschatological time (Rv. 21:4–5). (Cf. Salvation History.)

Man in his religious response ritualizes the marriage of God and His Church (Gn. 2:24; Eph. 5:22–33). The fidelity of man and woman, unique creatures of God, both coming from God and willed by God to return to Him, is the image of the fidelity of God (1 Cor. 6:15–20; 11:3–16; Mt. 19:3–9). In the Gospels kingdom and life were spoken of as synonymous (Mt. 5:20; 7:21; 18:8–9; 19:17–29; 25:34). All human persons are redeemed and by living without sin, or performing acts opposed to sin which is death of the body and soul (1 Jn. 3:14–15), come to life everlasting according to God's plan (Jn. 3:16–18; 6:37–50).

Vatican II teaches: "Christ instituted this new covenant, that is to say, the new testament, in His blood (cf. 1 Cor. 11:25), by calling together a people made up of Jew and Gentile, making them one, not according to the flesh but in the Spirit.

"This was to be the new People of God. For, those who believe in Christ, who are reborn not from a perishable but from an imperishable seed through the Word of the living God (cf. 1 Pt. 1:23), not from the flesh but from water and the Holy Spirit (cf. Jn. 3:5–6), are finally established as a 'chosen race, a royal priesthood, a holy nation, a purchased people . . . You who in times past were not a people, but are now the people of God! (1 Pt. 2:9–10)" (LG 9).

And: "All men are called to be part of this catholic unity of the People of God, a unity which is harbinger of the universal peace it promotes. And there belong to it or are related to it in various ways, the Catholic faithful as well as all who believe in Christ, and indeed the whole of mankind. For all men are called to salvation by the grace of God" (LG 13).

And: "Just as human activity proceeds from man, so it is ordered toward man. For when a man works, he not only alters things and society, he develops himself as well. He learns much, he cultivates his resources, he goes outside of himself and beyond himself.

"Rightly understood, this kind of growth is of greater value than any external riches which can be garnered. A man is more precious for what he is than for what he has" (GS 35).

## Mandatum

The title taken from the first Latin word of the first antiphon for the ceremony of Holy Thursday, when the celebrant washes the feet of men who have been chosen. It takes place immediately after the homily in the New Order of the liturgy for Holy Week. The ceremony commemorates the washing of the feet of the Apostles by Christ (Jn. 13:4–17).

## Mandyas

1. The short black cloak that is part of the habit worn by monks of the Byzantine Rite.

2. A long, full length mantle of blue or purple, fashioned as a cope, attaching by a clasp at the neck and at the front hem, which is ornamented with four squares of embroidery symbolizing the scriptures, and from which streamers of ribbon of red and white are attached, worn by a Bishop of the Byzantine Rite in choir or in a more plain fashion in black by an archimandrite.

## Manichaeism

This heresy was introduced in Persia by Mani, about 242. It taught a religious dualism, with a constant struggle going on in man's nature between two deities, God and Satan, or the good and the bad. The good principle (the Father of Majesty) lives in a place of light, while the bad (the King of Darkness) inhabits a place of darkness. From these came a series of emanations beginning with man, cut of the Father through the Mother of Life. A second emanation is the Spirit of Life who restores life in his rescue of the first man. This was not a Christian religion in any understanding of the word, and it gave rise to many allied heresies, such as Albigensianism and Catharism. (See Heresies.)

## Manifestation of Conscience

Manifestation of conscience is the disclosing of one's spiritual condition outside the Sacrament of Penance, usually done for the purpose of obtaining guidance. Religious superiors are forbidden (c. 530) to require a manifestation of conscience from their subjects.

## Maniple

This is a vestment formerly worn over the left forearm of the celebrant at Mass. Originally, it was merely a napkin of cloth that served a practical purpose; then, rather than being worn, it was carried in the left hand. After the twelfth century, this became more and more ornamental, until it is now but a reminder of the former "hand cloth" in the present-day vestigial maniple. This was of the same color as the vestments for the day, made of cloth, at least two feet in length, and loosely hung. This has been completely done away with in the New Order of the Mass. (See Vestments.)

## Manna

This food was continuously and miraculously supplied to the Israelites during the entire years of wandering in the desert as recorded in Exodus (16:1–36; Dt. 8:3–16; Neh. 9:20; Ps. 78:24). This bread from heaven was a true type of the Sacrament of the Eucharist, our spiritual food.

The description of this food is not too clear from the first recording of it in scripture: "It was like coriander seed, but white, and it tasted like wafers made with honey" (Ex. 16:31). A poetic description is given: "Instead of this, you nourished your people with food of angels and furnished them bread from heaven, ready to hand, untoiled-for, endowed with all delights and conforming to every taste" (Wis. 16:20). But it was a highly adaptable food, for the people could grind it and cook it in loaves (Nm. 11:8) and it could be boiled or baked (Ex. 16:23).

In the Messianic realization of the fulfillment of the promise of the NT, manna is compared to the heavenly food, which is prepared for those who have heeded the word of the Spirit (Rv. 2:17).

## Mantelletta

A mantelletta is an outer, sleeveless garment, which fastens at the neck, is open in front and reaches to the knees. It has slits through which the arms are put. The mantelletta, worn by cardinals, bishops, abbots and certain prelates, is red, purple, or black in accord with the dignitary who wears it. It is the outer garment of a bishop, other than the ordinary, on entering a church to pontificate.

## Mantum

Much like the cope, but with a short train, this garment is only worn by the pope. It is either white or red.

## Manuterge

The manuterge is a small linen towel used by the celebrant of Mass at the washing of hands after the offering of the gifts, to dry his fingers.

## Mappula

This name is infrequently used for the gremial veil.

## Marathonians

The followers of the Macedonian heresy were so named after their chief leader, a bishop of Nicomedia. (See Heresies.)

## Marburg, Colloquy of

The meeting that took place at Marburg, called by the German prince, Philip, Landgrave of Hesse, was intended to establish a solid political and social confederation between the dissident groups of Protestantism. It failed in its purpose, not because of nationalistic or political differences, but because of doctrinal differences that could not be resolved.

Present at the colloquy were Martin Luther (1483 to 1546), Huldreich Zwingli (1484 to 1531), and other prominent leaders of the Protestant churches. The two major opponents were Luther and Zwingli. The doctrinal disagreement was over the doctrine of the Real Presence of Christ in the Holy Eucharist. The controversy was over the literal meaning of the words of Christ: "This is My Body" (Mt. 26:26; Mk. 14:22; Lk. 22:19). Luther rejected the Catholic teaching of transubstantiation, proposing the idea that Christ is only consubstantially present, that is, present "together with" the bread. Zwingli, more drastically opposed to Catholic doctrine, maintained that Christ's presence could only be symbolically regarded as in the Eucharist. Because no one could resolve the two positions, the Marburg colloquy was a failure. It remains a modern stumbling block in the ecumenical efforts made since Vatican II.

## Marcionism

Begun in 144 by Marcion, this was the heresy that held that the God of the Jews was not the God of the Christians nor the Father of Christ. It imposed a rigoristic asceticism on its followers. It continued for about four centuries and was then condemned along with Manichaeism. (See Gnosticism.)

## Marialis Cultus

Marialis Cultus is the Latin title ("Devotion to Mary") of an apostolic letter of Pope Paul VI, promulgated Mar. 22, 1974. (Cf. Mariology.)

Besides giving the place of the Blessed Virgin Mary in the Liturgy and in devotions, there are clarifications and biblical and ecumenical guidelines for renewal of devotion to Mary, together with a distinction of the proper attitudes concerning devotion to the Blessed Mother. It states in part: "First, the Virgin Mary has always been proposed to the faithful by the Church as an example to be imitated not precisely in the type of life she led, and much less for the sociocultural background in which she lived and which today scarcely exists anywhere. She is held up as an example to the faithful rather for the way in which, in her own particular life, she fully and responsibly accepted the will of God (cf. Lk. 1:38), because she heard the word of God and acted on it and because charity and a spirit of service were the driving force of her actions. She is worthy of imitation because she was the first and most perfect of Christ's disciples. All of this has a permanent and universal exemplary value."

## Mariology

This is the study of the science, as a part of theology, which treats of the life, role, and virtues of the Blessed Mother of God. It demonstrates the prerogatives, the eminent fullness of grace that was hers, and her position as Co-Redemptrix and Mediatrix of all graces. (Cf. Mary, Virgin Mother of God; Mediatrix of all graces.)

It is through this study, derived from Scripture, that we have an understanding of the Motherhood of Mary. This was of the promise of a Messiah (Is. 7:14), where she is the one, a virgin, to bring salvation to all men. It was thus the blessing granted by God to those He loved, part of the promise made to Abraham. The maternity of Mary is the realization of this promise, in fact and her spiritual act of faith (Mt. 1:18–21). Mary is blessed because she listened to the word of God (Lk. 8:19–21; Eph. 1:3–10; Heb. 2:11–17), and so became the mother of all redeemed (Lk. 1:42). (See under separate listings.)

## Mark, Gospel of St.

The second of the synoptic Gospels was written by St. Mark in the period between A.D. 53 to 67. St. Mark was a close acquaintance of St. Peter, St. Paul, and Barnabas and wrote his Gospel chiefly to furnish the Christians of Rome with a record of doctrine, notably the preaching of St. Peter. It centers upon the ministry of Christ while on earth, with a strong affirmation of the divinity of Christ, declaring Christ the Incarnate Son of God.

This Gospel, derived chiefly from the preaching of St. Peter, strongly presents the truth that Christ was the Son of God incarnate. It places great stress on the spiritual mission of Christ, not as the Messiah by title, but on Christ as the Son of Man (Mk. 14:62). Christ is shown not as a temporal ruler but as one who has come to establish a spiritual kingdom (Mk. 10:35–45). That this Gospel was from the preaching of St. Peter, and probably others, is seen in the typical words of speech in the constructions used by story-tellers. It is also evident that this account was written not too far in time from the original catechesis of the Apostles, since it was colloquial in style and gives importance to dates (Cf. 1:13; 3:9; Acts 6:1).

## Marks of the Church

As declared by the Council of Trent (1545 to 1563), the marks of the Church are four: oneness, holiness, catholicity, and apostolicity. These are distinctive characteristics, evident in the oneness of doctrine; holiness, because it dispenses the means of sanctification; catholic, because of its extension to all through its mission to the world; and apostolic, because of its succession of ministry from St. Peter and the Apostles. (Cf. Apostolicity; Catholic; Holiness.)

Since Vatican II there has been an even more expanded concept of the mission of the Church in the world. Christ founded His Church and began His preaching with a declaration that the "reign of God is at hand" (Mk. 1:15; Mt. 4:17; see also LG 5). With Christ we learn that a new phase of history was initiated, "the final age of the world" (LG 48), and in Christ the kingdom of God began to take on a concrete form and message (LG 5). Christ began "to make ready the material of the celestial realm"

(GS 38). As a result through the Church "all the good fruits of our nature and enterprise, we will find . . . again, but freed of stain, burnished, and transfigured. This will be so when Christ hands over to the Father a kingdom eternal and universal; 'a kingdom of truth and life, of holiness and grace, of justice, love, and peace'" (GS 39). The Church, therefore, is the forming substance of the Kingdom of God, its earthly sacrament, and so "experiences the same earthly lot which the world does. She serves as a leaven and as a kind of soul for human society as it is to be renewed in Christ and transformed into God's family" (GS 40). See Vatican II, Documents of.)

## Maronites

This is the name of the members of the Eastern Catholic Church, Arabic-speaking Syrians, who inhabit Lebanon. The Maronites are in communion with Rome and have a college for the education of their clergy in Rome. In the year 1181, at the time of the Crusades, the entire body of the Maronite faithful, together with their bishops and Patriarch of Lebanon, made peace with Rome and became attached to the Holy See.

The liturgy of the Maronite Rite has five canons (Anaphoras), which vary with the mind of the celebrant. The most commonly used is called: "The Anaphora of the Holy Roman Catholic Church, the Mother of all Churches." Vestments of the Roman Rite are used; unleavened bread in the form of round hosts is used in the distribution of Holy Communion.

## Marriage Encounter

Marriage encounter is the not entirely euphonious title given to that form of retreat wherein husbands and wives, in a spiritual setting and context, reflect on the meaning and dignity of marriage and hold a dialogue among themselves on the spiritual growth factors of married life. It is thus the procedure within the usual context of a retreat, with its celebration of the Eucharist, its conferences, and private counseling, toward the intention that there will be a deepening of the married couples' spiritual lives. Such enrichment fulfills in a special manner the declaration of Vatican II: "By presenting certain key points of Church doctrine in a clearer light, this Council wishes to offer guidance and support to those Christians and other men who are trying to keep sacred and to foster the natural dignity of the married state and its superlative value" (GS 47).

Marriage encounters are usually held over a

weekend, beginning on Friday evening or Saturday morning and closing on Sunday afternoon. Such retreats are most fruitful when the joyful yet serious nature of married life is examined and shared. As such these retreats are by intent spiritual rather than psychiatric, aimed at prayerful reconciliation and building, rather than therapeutic treatment, although such a twofold purpose may be achieved.

### Marriage, Sacrament of

The Sacrament of Matrimony is the marriage contract between baptized persons, which was raised by Christ to the dignity of a sacrament (c. 1012). The marriage contract is that made by two persons of the opposite sex by which each acquires the exclusive and irrevocable right over their bodies, until the death of one of the parties, for the procreation and education of children. While this last is the primary end of marriage, there are secondary purposes, notably the mutual aid, both material and spiritual, and the overcoming of sexual concupiscence in a legitimate manner. Its essential properties are: *unity*, that is, one spouse; and *indissolubility*, that is, a contract for life. While the contract is that of the two parties, God is the author of marriage. The love of husband and wife, their mutual self-giving in a natural vocation for life, is called a gift (charisma) by St. Paul (1 Cor. 7:7). Marriage is symbolized in and modeled on the love of Christ for the Church, His bride (Rv. 19:7). (Cf. Impediments of Marriage.) Marriage is regulated by the divine law, church law (c. 1021-1141), and civil law.

Marriage in both society and religion has a special place in forming mankind into a social entity, and in providing the unit of the family. In its religious understanding the modern human person must find the unity and dignity, the sacredness of that bond that characterizes marriage. First, marriage is more related to the human

person's nature and existence in society, and in God's order is thus more determined and regulated by God's plan of salvation for mankind. Second, there is a uniqueness in the consecration of husband and wife over parenthood, the one being prime and the other secondary, yet both hold special graces in the sacrament. Third, the study of scripture presents an unfolding of greater meaning in the organization of both the family and the interpersonal relationship of the individuals. Fourth, the Church has developed with special care the singular significance of marriage and the family and the benefits for both the individual and society in general. This is particularly evident in the teachings of the documents and decrees of Vatican II.

In scripture we have several developing themes that provide us with the place of marriage in the salvation plan of God. "It is not good for the man to be alone" (Gn. 2:18), so a "suitable" partner was created for him. The love of God is the perfect example of the love of humans, and this "marriage" of God to the people and His uniting Himself with the Church to make it resplendent and holy is a major theme of scripture (1 Cor. 6:15–20; 11:3–16; Mt. 19:3–9; also, Ho. 1 and 2; Sg.; Ps. 45). The very "mystery" of marriage signifies one's initiation into the life of God (Eph. 5:31–32). As Vatican II declares among its many teachings concerning the Sacrament of Marriage, "Firmly established by the Lord, the unity of marriage will radiate from the equal personal dignity of wife and husband, a dignity acknowledged by mutual and total love.

"The steady fulfillment of the duties of this Christian vocation demands notable virtue. For this reason, strengthened by grace for holiness of life, the couple will painstakingly cultivate and pray for constancy of love, large-heartedness, and the spirit of sacrifice" (GS 49).

In virtue of the sacrament, in recognition of the mystery whereby a "fruitful love which exists between Christ and his church" (Eph. 5:32), and the very nature of the love-bond of the wedded couple, the Church has made the Sacrament of Marriage an adaptable liturgy. It states that there should be suitable and comprehensive instruction so that the married couple may reap the greater benefits of grace from the liturgy and from the celebration of the sacrament. The new rite of marriage states: "In the celebration of marriage (which normally should be within the Mass), certain elements should be stressed, especially the liturgy of the word, which shows the importance of Christian marriage in the history of salvation and the duties and responsibilities of the couple in caring for the holiness of their children. Also of supreme importance are the consent of the contracting parties, which the priest asks and receives; the special nuptial blessing for the bride and for the marriage covenant; and finally, the reception of holy communion by the groom and bride, and by all present by which their love is nourished and all are lifted up into communion with our Lord and with one another" (n. 6).

There is in the modern ritual great flexibility within the prescribed liturgy, which should encourage the couple in determining in their individual manner the depth of their mutual love. Thus, the selection of readings, the choice of songs, the decorations, and special prayers to be said may be by the selection and in accord with the couples' own views of their expression of their love-bond. Thus the sacrament becomes both an individual response on the part of the contracting couple, and the recognition of this as a community action wherein the bond of peace is extended to all who participate in the liturgy of the sacrament.

## Martyr

A martyr is one who suffers death for a cause. In the Christian tradition a martyr was one who, rather than apostasize, gave up his life (Heb. 10:26–31). There were martyrs of the OT, but, as St. Peter declares, they are only considered heroes of the faith in the Christian age (Heb. 10:39). St. Ignatius of Antioch urged the early Christians to make the sacrifice of their lives for Christ, and there is ample evidence that many did die during persecutions. The term has also been applied in the Church to those who died natural deaths, but whose lives were living testaments of the faith. In this latter sense, it is no longer recognized as a title; but it is in this sense, and because of her "living" sufferings that the Blessed Mother can be called the "Queen of Martyrs" as well as being their Queen in heaven.

Vatican II declares: "Since Jesus, the Son of God, manifested His charity by laying down His life for us, no one has greater love than he who lays down his life for Christ and his brothers (cf. 1 Jn. 3:16; Jn. 15:13). From the earliest times, then, some Christians have been called upon—and some will always be called upon—to give this supreme testimony of love to all men, but especially to persecutors. The Church, therefore, considers martyrdom as an exceptional gift and as the perfect proof of love.

"By martyrdom a disciple is transformed into an image of his Master, who freely accepted death on behalf of the world's salvation; he perfects that image even to the shedding of blood" (GS 42).

## Martyrology

1. A list of the early martyrs of the Church whose lives and holy deaths were witness to the faith, together with a brief note on the lives of many of them.

2. A listing by day throughout the year of the saints who are commemorated in the Church calendar. As Vatican II states: "The Church has included in the annual cycle days devoted to the memory of the martyrs and the other saints. Raised up to perfection by the manifold grace of God, and already in possession of eternal salvation, they sing God's perfect praise in heaven and offer prayers for us. By celebrating the passage of these saints from earth to heaven, the Church proclaims the paschal mystery as achieved in the saints who have suffered and been glorified with Christ; she proposes them to the faithful as examples who draw all to the Father through Christ, and through their merits she pleads for God's favors" (SC 104).

3. The Roman Martyrology, a liturgical book, is the listing with readings of the saints honored in the Church, and the names of newly canonized saints are added to it. It first was published in 1584, and now numbers more than five thousand entries.

4. The American Martyrology is a list of 136 martyrs and confessors of the Church (not all died a violent death) whose death occurred within the present territory of the United States.

## Martyrs' Shrine of Canada

This shrine located near Midland, Ontario, Canada, was founded in 1907. It is dedicated to the memory of and the devotion to the North American Martyrs who were canonized on June 29, 1930, and now stands near Fort Sainte Marie. The shrine began with a small chapel built on the ground where Brebeuf and Lallemant were killed, but it now stands on the place of the old fort where a fortress-like church was built with two tall spires that can be seen across the countryside. A restaurant and hotel have been added to accommodate some of the thousands of pilgrims who come to visit both the shrine, out of devotion, and also see the restoration of the fort and its museum out of a sense of history.

## Marxism

Marxism is the philosophical term used to describe the teachings of Karl Marx (1818 to 1883) together with the development of the communistic dialectic and the collectivism under its many formulations, which have come from his basic ideas. Thus the Marxism-Leninism has been a form associated with the Soviet Union; the Maoist-Marxism has been the ideology of the Chinese; the Hegelian-Kojer-Marxism is evident in France and grew under such proponents as Sartre, L. Goldman, and Merleau-Ponty; and the Gramsci-Marxism is the adaption in Italy.

Basically Marxism is an adaptation of Liberal Socialism, which had its scientific evolution from three leaders: Ferdinand Lassalle (1825 to 1864), Karl Marx, and Friedrich Engels (1820 to 1895). The new era was introduced with the publication in 1848 of the *Communist Manifesto* and the founding of the International Association of Working Men in 1864, followed by the publication of Marx's book *Das Kapital* in 1867. The notion of a real ideology, a natural philosophy that proposed opposition between idealism and materialism, has largely been abandoned under the developments of political and sociological thought fostered by followers of Marxism in the twentieth century.

The conflict of Marxism in its many forms with Christianity springs from the thesis of the German philosopher Feuerbach concerning the projection of human concepts on God, the humanistic-social ideology. In the modern world Marxism is too hypothetical to be a threat to Christianity, for religion does not wither and die because of methodology in the social order. Instead Christianity seeks to bring stability to the working classes through social teachings regarding wages, hours of work, natural and health benefits. As a prop of Communism, Marxism must suppress religion by force (Leninism) to be effective against it, and because of an imposed atheistic form of communism in such countries as Russia and China, the Church suffers.

## Mary, Feasts of

Certain days are set aside to worship God with special commemoration of events referring to Mary, the Mother of God. These are fourteen in number, but there are many other days when votive Masses of the Blessed Virgin are read and when commemorations of Mary are made during other Masses. In the order throughout the liturgical year the feasts of Mary are: Immaculate Conception of the Blessed Virgin Mary, Dec. 8; Solemnity of Mary, Mother of God, Jan. 1; Our Lady of Lourdes, Feb. 11; the Annunciation, Mar. 25; the Visitation, May 31; Immaculate Heart of Mary, the Saturday following the second Sunday after Pentecost; Our Lady of Mount Carmel, July 16; the Assumption, Aug. 15; the Queenship of

Mary, Aug. 22; the Birth of Mary, Sept. 8; Our Lady of Sorrows, Sept. 15; Our Lady of the Rosary, Oct. 7; Presentation of Mary, Nov. 21; and in dioceses of the United States of America, Our Lady of Guadalupe, Dec. 12.

## Mary, Saturday Office of

The New Liturgy of the Hours directs that: "For Saturdays in Ordinary Time on which optional memorials are permitted, one may celebrate a memorial of the Blessed Virgin Mary with its proper readings. The Office has the same format as any other memorial" (n. 240).

## Mary, Virgin Mother of God

The central point of the theology of Mary is that she is the Mother of God. It is because of the fact that Mary had been foreordained by God from the beginning to her divine motherhood and that she was conceived "full of grace" and thus placed in the singular position of being the most perfect human being that an omnipotent God could create. She was immaculately conceived; as God's Mother she cooperated in our redemption; she was our Lord's most intimate associate while He was on earth; and upon her death she was assumed bodily into heaven where she is queen, reigning over heaven and earth.

For our knowledge of Mary we depend upon the Scriptures and dogmatic tradition. From the Scriptures we attain our basic understanding of her as the Mother of God. In the OT, in a text called the *Protoevangelium* (Gn. 3:15), we find the first significant reference to Mary. There mention is made of the "Second Eve," through whom will be effected the redeemed restoration of all mankind. The seed is Christ (Gal. 3:16), and Mary, the Mother of Christ and the mother of all in the spiritual order (Rom. 9:7–8), is the woman who is designated to crush the dominion of the devil over men. Later, Isaiah (7:14–17) tells us of the Virgin who will conceive and bear a son and we find the fulfillment of this prophecy in the Gospel (Mt. 1:23). Another prophet, Micah, in speaking of the motherhood names the place (Bethlehem) where it will take place (Mic. 5:1–3). Also in the OT, we read of Mary as queen (Ps. 45) and the place on the right hand of the Messianic King—a place of recognized and reserved honor.

In the NT, the Gospels of Matthew and Mark narrate events concerning the life of the Blessed Mother, but in the Gospel of St. Luke we find the fullest treatment. He records the annunciation, and from his declaration of Mary as "full of grace" and other sources, the Church declared Mary's

Immaculate Conception (Papal bull, *Ineffabilis Deus,* Pius IX, 1854). St. Luke records the first miracle brought about by Mary: the sanctification of St. John the Baptist in the womb of Elizabeth at the Visitation. On that same occasion (Lk. 1:43), Elizabeth greets Mary as the "Mother of my Lord." From Mary, God the Son took His human nature, and He will forever remain the son of Mary and she will be forever the Mother of God. Finally we read of the place of Mary in heaven at the throne of God (Rv. 12), and we see her in glory as no other.

The Church, studying, searching, and interpreting both the Scriptures and tradition, has defined those doctrines concerning Mary about which the Scriptures are not specific. From extrascriptural sources we know Mary was the daughter of Joachim and Anne. These two saints are celebrated with a memorial (July 26) in the Church calendar. On Nov. 1, 1950, Pope Pius XII declared the doctrine of Our Lady's Assumption. Toward the close of the Marian Year (1954), on Dec. 8, the pope declared the doctrine of the Universal Queenship of Mary and established a feast, that of Mary, Queen, now celebrated as a memorial on Aug. 22.

From apostolic times, tradition, the Church, and the faithful have accorded to Mary, the Mother of God, the second highest degree of honor, hyperdulia. She has been celebrated in feasts throughout the year in the Divine Office, in devotions such as the rosary and litany, and by title she has been hailed the patroness of many countries, and has been honored in hymns, songs, poetry, sculpture, painting, and literature as no other creature. It is under her title of the Immaculate Conception that Mary was declared the Patroness of the United States, with the feast day celebrated on Dec. 8. The name of Mary, because she is the Mother of God, is honored with multiple titles: she is the Blessed Virgin Mary, the Co-Redemptrix, the Mediatrix of all Graces, the Blessed Mother. (Cf. Virgin Mary; Mariology.)

## Marymas

This name was used in medieval times to refer to any day on which the Blessed Mother was celebrated with a feast.

## Masonry, also Freemasonry

The Masonic brotherhood was begun in 1717 in London, England. It was originally a secret political society, but later, retaining its secrecy, it borrowed the naturalistic philosophy of French thinkers. It was condemned in April 28, 1738, by Pope Clement XII because of its philosophy, its secret plotting against the Church and some governments, and the danger to the faith of Catholics who might join it. Also many lodges, or branches, proved to be anticlerical, anti-Catholic, and anti-Christian. It was claimed, at the International Masonic Congress in Paris, 1899, that the organization had taken a leading part in all the revolutionary movements of the nineteenth century. Thus, according to canon law (c. 2335) anyone joining the Masons, or any group plotting against Church or state, is by the very fact *(ipso facto)* excommunicated, reserved simply to the Holy See. Before absolution, the penitent must sever all relations with the organization. This law and its application also holds for affiliated female societies. (Cf. Secret Societies.)

In a modern ruling, given in a letter of Sept. 18, 1974, the Congregation for the Doctrine of the Faith stated in part: "In considering particular cases, it must be remembered that penal law is always subject to strict interpretation. Therefore, one may safely teach and apply the opinion of those authors who hold that Canon 2335 refers only to those Catholics who join associations which plot against the Church."

The majority of Masonic lodges and others, such as the Eastern Star groups, were not considered this type. The same ruling, however, declared: "Clerics, religious and members of secular institutes are still forbidden in every case to join any Masonic association."

## Mass Before Vatican II

1. The Sacrifice of the Mass; the Sacrifice of the Most Holy Eucharist. Blessed Peter Canisius, S.J., in his *Catechism* defined the Mass as: "The Sacrifice of the Mass is really the holy and living representation and at the same time the unbloody and efficacious oblation of the Lord's Passion and that blood-stained sacrifice which was offered for us on the cross." We may establish that the Eucharist is a true sacrifice and a representation of our Lord's sacrifice. The real presence is affirmed by the words of Christ in instituting the Holy Eucharist, His supreme gift of Himself. He said: "This is My body" and "this is My Blood" (Lk. 22: 19–20) and asked that his act be repeated in "rememberance" of Him. This understanding was declared by St. Paul (1 Cor. 11:24–26), and the idea that this was a sacrifice is seen in his statement of the sacrifice being performed on the table (altar) (1 Cor. 10:21). This is again affirmed by St. Paul (Heb. 13:10).

The true nature of a sacrifice is realized in the Mass. By declaration of the Council of Trent,

Christ is recognized as the offering Priest, the Victim offered, and the immolation in the sacramental order. These essentials of the sacrifice are present in the three main actions of the Mass: the Offertory, the Consecration, and the Communion.

In apostolic times, the Mass was celebrated in the evening with the people partaking of a meal (1 Cor. 11:17–34) called "the charity" (cf. Agape). Thereafter the Eucharist was celebrated without a fast before Communion. However, toward the end of the first century the time shifted to the morning (cf. Catechumens). The name "Mass" is probably derived from the Latin word *Missio*, meaning a "dismissal," that is, the bidding of farewell to those who had gathered (usually at some home). The development of the liturgy, here meaning the sequence of parts and the prayers, was gradual over the first seven centuries; there was no essential change, but the adoption rather of symbolical associations, such as in the vestments used.

The parts of the Mass as we have it today are (those marked with an asterisk, change each day according to the feast): Introit,* Kyrie Eleison, Gloria (except when not permitted), Collects,* Epistle,* Gradual,* Gospel,* the Creed (except when not called for), Offertory,* Lavabo, Prayer to the Trinity, Secret,* Preface,* Sanctus; the Canon with the Consecration, the Our Father, the Breaking of the Host, Agnus Dei, and the preparatory prayers of the Communion; the Communion of the priest and faithful, the ablution, Communion,* Postcommunion,* the *Ite* or Dismissal, the Blessing, and a final Gospel. (Cf. Liturgy; Order of the Mass, New; Eucharist, Celebration of.)

There are four types of the Tridentine Mass, each being the same sacrifice, distinguished by its solemnity in the execution of the liturgy: pontifical Mass, solemn or high Mass, sung Mass *(Missa cantata)*, and low Mass. There are several other titles to distinguish a Mass, depending on where it is celebrated or on what occasion it is said: "conventual Mass" is celebrated daily in choir, in cathedral or chapter churches; a parochial Mass is said for the people of a parish; a votive Mass is said according to the wish of the celebrant, but not according to the feast of the calendar; the requiem Mass is said at a funeral or for a deceased person; *Missa recitata* is a Mass in which those attending respond to the prayers. (The parts of the Mass are explained under their separate entries.)

2. Sometimes the term "Mass" is used as designating the musical score to which the sung portions of the Mass are set, for example, a Bach Mass.

## Mass of the Catechumens

This name is given to the portion of the Mass from its beginning to the Offertory, at which catechumens were permitted to be present. It would correspond to the Entrance and the Liturgy of the Word in the New Order of the Mass. (Cf. Catechumens; Energumen; Discipline of the Secret.)

## Mass, Funeral

Properly the funeral Mass is that said prior to the burial of a deceased person. Provision for this is made in the new *Sacramentary* with the proper prayers and four Prefaces of Christian Death.

In the *Newsletter* of the Bishops' Liturgical Commission (U.S.A.), April, 1973, the proper terminology for the Rite of Funerals was given as follows:

"Since the publication of the new Rite of Funerals (1969) there has been considerable confusion concerning the terminology to be used in participation materials, liturgical calendars, and *ordos*. The term 'Mass of Resurrection,' used in death notices and in press releases, has caused part of the present difficulty. In order to clarify the issue and assist diocesan commissions and liturgical publishers, the terminology in reference to the Rite of Funerals should follow that of the rite itself and that found in the Roman Missal. Therefore, the following is offered:

"1. *Funeral Mass or Mass of Christian Burial* is the correct title for the Mass celebrated prior to interment (Mass of the Resurrection, although it emphasizes the festive tone of the resurrection, is inaccurate as it causes confusion with the celebration of Easter itself.)

"2. *Mass for the Dead,* formerly referred to as the Requiem Mass, is the correct title for any celebration of the Eucharist for the deceased. The preface used for this Mass is properly called the *Preface of Christian Death.*

"3. *Final Commendation and Farewell,* formerly known as the absolution, is to be regarded "as the last farewell with which the Christian community honors one of its members before the body is buried" (no. 10). This takes place immediately after the prayer after communion in the Mass or at the graveside."

The vestments for funerals are: black, white, purple, or another color where this has been granted for use by permission of the Conference of Bishops.

## Master of Ceremonies

In Church terminology, this is a male person, usually a senior acolyte or one in holy orders, who directs and assists at liturgical ceremonies, guiding the celebrant and assistants in the performance of the ritual. Now more a title of designation of duty than a special ministry. (See Ministries.)

## Master of Novices

In a religious community, the master or mistress of novices is the person chosen to direct the formation and spiritually guide the new, unprofessed members of the community. He or she should by custom be 35 years of age and professed for at least 10 years. The master should be eminently prudent and learned and has full authority over the novices, subject to the superiors (cc. 559-565).

## Master of the Sacred Palace

The Master of the Sacred Palace is the priest, usually an eminent theologian and canonist, who personally attends the pope. This office has always been awarded to a Dominican. His duties are to live in the Vatican, supervise the preaching before the Holy Father, and handle some secretarial affairs.

## Master of the Sentences

This title was awarded to Peter Lombard (d. 1160) for authorship. (Cf. Sentences, Book of.)

## Mater et Magistra

The Latin title (Christianity and Social Progress) is literally translated "Mother and Teacher"; this is the encyclical of Pope John XXIII issued in 1963. It is one of a long line of social teachings of the Church, which brings the Gospels and divine revelation together with the traditional teachings of the Church to focus directly on the questions of human rights, the poor, the underdeveloped countries, humane considerations, justice, and peace. It declares, speaking in general for all writings and teachings of the Church on related social doctrine: "What the Catholic Church teaches and declares regarding the social life and relationships of men is beyond question for all time valid.

"The cardinal point of this teaching is that individual men are necessarily the foundation, cause, and end of all social institutions . . . insofar as they are social by nature, and raised to an order of existence that transcends and subdues nature.

"Beginning with this very basic principle whereby the dignity of the human person is affirmed and defended, Holy Church—especially during the last century and with the assistance of learned priests and laymen, specialists in the field—has arrived at clear social teachings whereby the mutual relationships of men are ordered. Taking general norms into account, these principles are in accord with the nature of things and the changed conditions of man's social life, or with the special genius of our day. Moreover, these norms can be approved by all."

These and other teachings of the Church were expanded and clarified in the documents of Vatican II, especially in *The Pastoral Constitution on the Church in the Modern World (Gaudium et Spes)*. (See Social Encyclicals; Development of Peoples.)

## Materialism

Originally, this was the philosophy of Greek thinkers of Asia Minor of the sixth century B.C. who attempted to explain the beginning of the world in terms of matter, without reference to a creating, divine power. It gave rise to a development of materialistic monism, which declared that the real was the only substance (Spinoza), and then led to a form of idealism wherein the idea or the ego is the "forever becoming." More recently it has advanced the proposition that material goods, such as wealth or sensuous pleasures, are the only values for man (practical materialism).

Karl Marx developed a dialectic materialism, which maintains that material forces, economic and social, determine the development of society. This led to communism. The Church has opposed and condemned this philosophy of dialectics. Pope Leo XIII *(Rerum Novarum,* 1891) showed its evils, and Pius XI denounced communism in an encyclical ("On Atheistic Communism," 1937). The bishops of the United States declared that "Materialism excites greed" (Joint statement on Peace and War, November, 1939), and accused it as a false philosophy, of being the cause of economic depression (Statement on the Present Crisis, April 25, 1933). (Cf. Communism.)

Vatican II declared: "No doubt very many whose lives are infected with a practical materialism are blinded against any sharp insight into this kind of dramatic situation (discords in society). Or else, weighed down by wretchedness, they are prevented from giving the matter any thought.

"Thinking that they have found serenity in an interpretation of reality everywhere proposed these days, many look forward to a genuine and total emancipation of humanity wrought solely by human effort. They are convinced that the future rule of man over the earth will satisfy every desire of his heart" (GS 10). Thus where man seeks to place the material good above the spiritual, he creates a false idealism and personal unhappiness.

## Matins

Formerly matins was the name of the first and chief hour of the Divine Office. (Cf. Liturgy of the Hours.)

## Matrimonial Court

Chiefly, this is a diocesan tribunal whose duty it is to investigate and determine the validity of a marriage bond and handle appeals against the bond of marriage.

## Matrimony

See Marriage, Sacrament of.

## Matter, Sacramental

The term is applied to the outward sign in the administration of the sacraments, that is, to material that can be perceived by the senses or action that can be observed. This matter must be joined to the form (cf. Form) of the sacraments, and both must be valid. The matter of a sacrament may be (1) *remote,* which is the material used, for example, water in baptism; (2) *proximate,* which is the application of the remote matter, for example, the pouring of the water in baptism.

## Matthew, Gosepl of St.

The first of the synoptic Gospels was written by the Apostle, St. Matthew. It was the first of the Gospels; portions were originally written in the Aramaic language between A.D. 40 and 50 and later translated into the Greek sometime before A.D. 80. The characteristic of Matthew's writing was his orderly arrangement, with five major portions presenting narrative accounts followed by the same number of discourses, either sermons or inspirational judgments. The central theme is so phrased that the Gospel has been called the "Gospel of Fulfillment" or the "Gospel of the Kingdom," the latter name favored because of one particular verse on the kingdom found only in this account (21:43).

The purpose of Matthew's gospel is clear from its contents, namely, to show that Jesus is the promised Messiah. This is accomplished chiefly by drawing upon OT prophecies. This gospel best brings to light the new faith to which Christ called His people though based in the OT beginning of the salvation history of mankind; it shows what the new seed of Christ's covenant will bring forth from the old. And it expressly emphasizes the Kingdom, so it may be said that it is "rooted in eternity."

The Kingdom was that of the word of the Son of Man (Mt. 4:23; 9:35; 24:14); the Kingdom was also a society, the Church, made up of people (Mt. 16:18; 28:18; 20:1–16); and the Kingdom was to achieve its completeness in the future life (Mt. 8:11; 22:2–14; 25:1–13).

## Matthias, St.

St. Matthias is the shortened name of the Apostle, chosen after prayers and the drawing of lots (cf. Lv. 16:8), to replace Judas, the betrayer of Christ. He is thus the twelfth Apostle of the new Church (Acts 1:23–26), chosen between the time of Christ's Ascension and the descent of the Holy Spirit. There is little historic record of the life of Matthias as an apostle, though an apocryphal gospel was attributed to him and quoted once by St. Clement of Alexandria.

## Maundy Thursday

This name given to the Thursday of Holy Week is derived but corrupted from *Mandatum,* the first word of the rite of washing of feet. This act, retained in the liturgy of Holy Thursday, is one of humble example, for it was a lesson in humility that Christ performed this service (Jn. 13:1–17). It is also an act symbolizing purification. (See Holy Week, Liturgy of.)

## Maurists

Maurist is a popular name for members of the French Benedictines, founded by St. Maur in 1618 and disbanded during the time of the French Revolution.

## Meal

Meal is defined as the act or time of eating, including the food consumed. This term is frequently used in reference to the Eucharist, the sacrifice consumed in the Communion of the Mass. Although this seems to be a plebian word and too common a reference to something that is both sacred and a mystery, there is some biblical background for such a term. In the Hebrew language, there was no word meaning "meal" as we understand it. However, the Jews referred to the partaking of food in the daily routine of living as "to eat bread" *(ekol lehem),* which is now commonly translated, not always too appropriately, by the word "meal."

But it must be pointed out that to use the term "Eucharistic meal" simply as the act of eating is not entirely in keeping with the understanding of the apostolic teaching. The breaking of bread, as the early Church understood it, was indeed a religious meal rather than an ordinary one, and it was so mentioned among the religious actions together with preaching and prayer (Acts 2:42). Further, the very perseverance in the breaking of bread was declared to be an act of faithfulness to the command of Christ to repeat the act that He did and that took on genuine sacrificial significance (cf. Mt. 26:26; 1 Cor. 10:16; 11:24). It must then be understood that there is a difference between the "bread" of Christ, which is His teaching of truth and salvation (Lk. 22:18) and the bread of the Pharisees, the old Law (cf. Mt. 16:5–12). Further, it should be understood that the Eucharist is the "sacrament of unity, the bond of charity" (cf. Jn. 17; 1 Cor. 11:17–34). To equate the Eucharist with the mere consumption of nourishment is not to understand the truth and teaching of Christ.

### Medals, Religious

These are flat, mostly round, discs made of metal, wood, or plastic with a religious representation on one side or both, and an inscription, ejaculation, or both on the reverse side. Usually shaped like a coin, they can be retained on a person, pinned on, or worn about the neck by means of a connecting ring and chain or string. They are blessed and are sacramentals. Intended as "portable" miniatures, their use in the Church is very ancient, probably derived from the eastern icons. In the Middle Ages, medals were regarded as amulets; it was also customary to give them to pilgrims to demonstrate that they had gone on pilgrimage. The subjects depicted on medals may be of our Lord, the Blessed Mother, the saints, or as commemorative pieces of special religious events, for example, a year of jubilee. (See Miraculous Medal; Scapular.)

### Media and Communications

The Church has long been aware of the importance of communicating with people through the use of newspapers, magazines, cinema, radio, and television. All of this is part of the apostolate of the mission of Christ in the world. The use of television has led to development of the Catholic Television Network (CTN) in many dioceses in the United States, and the use of television as an educational aid for schools through diocesan programs. The visual arts, graphic and educational, are a part of the teaching apostolate of the Church.

The Church is also aware of the "control of lives," which the media promotes by the unscrupulous use of radio, cinema, and television in particular. Pope Paul VI, on April 28, 1975, before the celebration of World Communications Day (May 11), released a message that warned of "processes and techniques which, under the pretense of 'neutrality' and 'independence,' actually set themselves to manipulate the facts and thereby manipulate also the audiences to which they are presented." He noted five areas in which the mass media abuses its nobler purposes and flaunts the moral principles that must guide and direct mankind: (1) "A biased concentration on human degradation"; (2) "working on public opinion in such a way as to create an insatiable greed for an endless succession of consumer goods"; (3) "the presentation as desirable of manners of behavior that are immoral or at odds with what is actually found in real life"; (4) "suppression of facts, distortion of facts and selective presentation of facts in reporting important happenings, which arise in programs aimed at ideological conditioning"; (5) "the fashion of urging new difficulties, sowing new doubts, thus shaking the certainty of people on ethical matters which are beyond dispute."

The right of the Church to judge the media arises from the natural law. The right to seek regulatory actions that would benefit the peoples of the world and prevent the domination of their minds to the harm of their souls and their salvation is the Church's as the bearer of the mission of Christ to the world.

The United States Catholic Conference (USCC) has established a Division for Film and Broadcasting.

Vatican II teaches: "The Church's manifold apostolate regarding instruments of social communication calls for reinforced vigor. Under the guidance of its bishop, therefore, let every diocese of the world devote a day of each year to instructing the faithful in their duties on this subject. Let these faithful be urged to pray about the matter, and to make a contribution toward the sacred cause" (IM 18).

And: "Special duties bind those readers, viewers, or listeners who personally and freely choose to receive what these media have to communicate. For good choosing dictates that ample favor be shown to whatever fosters virtue, knowledge or art" (IM 9).

## Mediator

The role of a mediator, or one who serves "in the middle," is exercised by one person acting on behalf of others in human society. In the Church the mediatorship of Christ is unique, but He does not supplant or do away with the mediatorship of the Church in its spiritual ministry among mankind. Here we consider that only Christ is the mediator because: (1) He brought about the reconciliation of God and man; (2) He effected our salvation by reparation; (3) He made it possible for us, through Him, to act and share in the divine life and love and thus, through the cooperation with grace, merit our own salvation (Jn. 15:10–17). This work of Christ as Mediator is effective because He was sent by God, and at the same time is our representative: "God is one. One also is the mediator between God and men, the man, Christ Jesus" (1 Tm. 2:5).

Vatican II teaches: "Christ, the one Mediator, established and ceaselessly sustains here on earth His holy Church, the community of faith, hope, and charity, as a visible structure. Through her He communicates truth and grace to all" (LG 8).

And: "In order to establish peace or communion between sinful human beings and Himself, as well as to fashion them into a fraternal community, God determined to intervene in human history in a way both new and definitive. For He sent His Son, clothed in our flesh, in order that through this Son He might snatch men from the power of darkness and of Satan (cf. Col. 1:13; Acts 10:38) and that in this Son He might reconcile the world to Himself (cf. 2 Cor. 5:19). Through Him, God made all orders of existence. God further appointed Him heir of all things, so that in the Son He might restore them all (cf. Eph. 1:10)" (AG 3).

## Mediatrix of All Graces

The Blessed Virgin Mary, as mediatrix of all graces, depends completely on the merits of her Son, Jesus, as the Universal Mediator. The teaching of the Church is that all the same graces that are necessary for man and merited for all mankind by her Son through His redemption, are merited by Mary too, but *de congruo*, that is, founded on charity (love) and friendship with God. Mary pleads now in heaven for the application of graces and distributes them to us. The Church, by decree of Jan. 21, 1921, approved a proper Mass and Office of Mary, Mediatrix of all Graces.

Vatican II states: "By her maternal charity, Mary cares for the brethren of her Son who still journey on earth surrounded by dangers and difficulties, until they are led to their happy fatherland. Therefore the Blessed Virgin is invoked by the Church under the titles of Advocate, Auxiliatrix, Adjutrix, and Mediatrix. These, however, are to be so understood that they neither take away from nor add anything to the dignity and efficacy of Christ the one Mediator" (LG 62).

## Meditation

Composed of acts of the intellect and will, this "thought prayer" includes reasoning as to the purpose of one's prayer (direction), the analysis of concepts (picturing what one thinks about in relation to God), comparison (comparing one's thought with what is pictured in the mind), affections (the desire in the mind), resolution (the resolve to accept and follow the thought of God and His love), and culminates in a communion or inner joy with God and His saints. This prayer is mental discourse, the mind's "daydream" on some concept or proposition of God. Its object may be any mystery of our faith, the life of Christ, the history of the Church, the liturgy, or the saints. Its purpose is twofold: (1) to make one understand one's faith more deeply and apply its truths to oneself; (2) to love and hope in God and to will to do those things that serve God better. Meditation has several forms: thought and longing concerning the truths of faith, consideration and contemplation of the life of Christ, thoughtful reading of a spiritual text, and thoughtful colloquies or little "conversations" (discursive prayer) with Christ or the saints.

Mental prayer is defined as "a silent elevation and application of our mind and heart to God in order to offer Him our homage and to promote His glory by our advancement in virtue." Although considered the lowest or simplest form of mental prayer, it is one that everyone can exercise, become proficient in, and which alone can lead to higher forms of prayer. (Cf. Contemplation; Prayer.)

## Meekness

A virtue related to the virtue of temperance, meekness moderates anger by controlling the passion of anger and by not permitting one's anger to be aroused over trivial things. Meekness is not to be confused with indifference or spinelessness. As used in the Beatitudes (Mt. 5:5), it is the virtue of "manly resignation" to adversity.

## Meletian Schism

Headed by Meletius, bishop of Lycopolis in the year 306, this schismatic movement sought to supplant Peter (d. 311), the bishop of Alexandria. Its followers, after the censorship of Meletius by the first Council of Nicaea, turned to Arianism. The schism died out in the fifth century.

## Melkite Rite

The Melkite rite is a division of the Byzantine rite as used by the Melkites particularly those of the patriarchates of Alexandria, Antioch, and Jerusalem. It is in Arabic, but certain parts, for example, the lessons, are retained in Greek. The Melkites are Arabian-speaking Catholics of Syria, Palestine, and Egypt. There are a number in the United States whose clergy are subject to the ordinaries of the Roman rite.

## Membership, Church

Broadly, all of those persons who are baptized are members of the Church founded by Christ. Its more reserved interpretation includes all those who are baptized with the trinity baptism and are united to the Roman Catholic Church. In his encyclical, *On the Mystical Body of Christ* (1943), Pope Pius XII declared: "Actually, only those are to be included as members of the Church who have been baptized, and who profess the true faith, and who have not been so unfortunate as to separate themselves from the unity of the Body or have been excluded by legitimate authority for grave faults committed."

It is apparent from this statement that there are four requisite conditions: one ritual and sacramental (baptism); one of declaration or profession of faith in Christ; two by mandate of the gospel and unity with the Church, either by not separating themselves, or by not being legally excluded, that is, by excommunication, interdict, or other censure within the law of the Church. Sin does not exclude one from membership, except sin against faith or an action that would cause the Church authorities to declare the membership ended. But these (sin against faith and Church censure) may be done away with through repentance and the reception of the Sacrament of Penance (cf. Col. 1:18–20; 2:9–10; Eph. 1:19–22; 4:15; Rom. 1:17).

## Memento

A memento is a prayer for a specific intention. There were three mementos in the Canon of the Tridentine Mass. The first, the prayer for the living, beginning with the word *Memento* ("Be mindful"), was said right after the beginning of the Canon. This was followed by the second, the *Communicantes,* a commemoration of the Church triumphant. The third, the memento for the dead, was said as the second prayer after the consecration; it begins with the words *Memento etiam* ("Be mindful also").

The New Order of the Mass, as presented in the Sacramentary, has two commemorations, one for the living and one for the dead. There are also in the Eucharistic prayers mementos for the Church, the Pope, and bishop, and for all who hold and teach the Catholic faith.

## Memorare

This very popular prayer to the Blessed Virgin Mary was composed by St. Bernard of Clairvaux (1090 to 1153). Its title is the first word of the Latin version. The prayer was recalled and made popular through the efforts of a French priest, Claude Bernard, early in the seventeenth century. It is as follows: "Remember, O most gracious Virgin Mary, that never was it known that anyone who fled to thy protection, implored thy help or sought thy intercession, was left unaided. Inspired with this confidence, I fly unto thee, O Virgin of virgins and Mother; to thee do I come, before thee I stand, sinful and sorrowful; O Mother of the Word Incarnate, despise not my petitions, but in thy mercy hear and answer me. Amen."

## Memoria

1. Literally, a commemoration, the lowest ranking feast of the Benedictine and Dominican calendars.

2. Name of a reliquary; also a chapel built to enshrine the body of a saint.

## Memorial

See Feasts of the Church.

## Menaion

The name Menaion is applied to any one of a set of twelve liturgical books that contain the offices of the fixed feasts of the Byzantine rite, the liturgy (the Mass), and the Christmas Season office. It may be contained in fewer volumes in accord with modern practices of printing.

## Mendicant Orders

Mendicant orders include the "begging friars" or those who divested themselves of all earthly goods and supported themselves by appealing to the charity of alms. This development in the religious life of those who dedicated themselves to God in religious life was begun in the thirteenth century by two notable saints of the time: Giovanni Francesco Bernardone of Assisi, St. Francis of Assisi (1181 to 1226), and Dominic Guzman of old Castile, St. Dominic (1170 to 1221). It was to mark the beginning of revolutionary ideas in the area of socioreligious thinking. The two saints were the founders of the Order of Friars Minor (Franciscans) and the Order of Preaching Friars (Dominicans). When St. Francis encouraged the friars to seek alms, he would instruct them simply: "Go, because in these last days the Friars Minor have been given to the world for its benefit, so that the elect may behave toward them in such a way as to deserve the praise of the Judge on the day of judgment and hear the words, 'As often as you did it for one of my least brothers, here, you did it for me'" (Mt. 25:40).

This manner of seeking Christian perfection was an answer to the power that wealth brought and the rise of heresies that made men draw away from the Church, especially the Albigensian heresy. As a movement it found great appeal and led to the founding of two other mendicant orders: the Carmelites and the Hermits of St. Augustine. There was a response in vocations to such daring leadership, and at the third meeting of the Franciscans, ten years after their founding there were already 5000 members. The work of the mendicant orders has since spread around the world and led to the great objectives of Francis and Dominic, the knowledge and love of God by human persons.

### Mene, Tekel, and Peres

These three words appeared mysteriously on the wall at the last banquet of the Persian king Belshazzar (Dn. 5:5; 5:25). None of the wise men of the Babylonians could read or decipher them. Only Daniel, by the grace of God, could understand and tell what they meant. "This is the writing that was inscribed: *Mene, Tekel,* and *Peres.* These words mean: *Mene,* God has numbered your kingdom and put an end to it; *Tekel,* you have been weighed on the scales and found wanting; *Peres,* your kingdom has been divided and given to the Medes and Persians" (Dn. 5:25–28).

The words are the names of three Babylonian weights or measures: the *mina* (mene); the *tekel,* the sixtieth part of a mina; and the *peres,* a half mina. The arrangement of the letters may have been in a puzzling script, an acrostic, or an anagram. The words themselves as Daniel interpreted them were connected in some manner with the Aramaic root words "to weigh," "to divide," and "to number." No other "mystical" interpretation by witchcraft or other occult *(sic)* means can or should be sought. The importance of the message was God's imminent punishment of the Babylonians, according to His will; King Belshazzar died that same night, and the Medes and Persians did divide the land, as historic records of that time attest.

### Mennonites

See Anabaptism.

### Menology, also Menologion

1. A collection of lives of the saints, arranged in sequence according to their feast days, month by month.

2. A calendar of the liturgical feasts, with readings from the lessons of each feast, arranged for each day and listing the feasts of the saints on these days.

### Menorah

The name, from the Hebrew word meaning candlestick, given to two forms of candleholders: (1) the ceremonial seven-branched candelabrum, which is of the Jewish Temple and symbolizes the seven days of creation (cf. Ex. 37:17–24). This is called the lampstand in some translations of the Bible. (2) A nine-branched candelabrum used by Jews in the celebration of Hanukkah, which is also called the Feast of Lights and the Festival of Dedication. It is the piece of temple furnishing described by God to Moses (Ex. 25:17–37).

The Menorah has become in the Christian tradition a familiar symbol, representing Christ as the "Light of the World" (cf. Jn. 8:12). The symbol of the burning lamp is first noted in the history of salvation at the time of Abraham's vision (Gn. 15:12–17), and it is also symbolical of the "Pillar of

Fire" which lighted the way for the Chosen People into the Promised Land (Ex. 13:21).

Further the picture of the seven-branched candlestick refers to David, the anointed of the Spirit, who is the "lamp of Israel" (2 Sm. 21:17; cf. also 1 Kgs. 11:36; 2 Kgs. 8:19). But it is Christ the risen savior who shines forth as the fire of the sevenfold Spirit, fulfilling the divine promise: "I will place a lamp for my anointed" (Ps. 132:17; see also Rv. 21:23; Mt. 5:14–16; 25:1–13; 1 Thes. 5:4–5).

## Mensa

Literally, a table, in liturgical language, the mensa is: (1) the flat table-top of a fixed altar, (2) the altar stone of a portable altar. (Cf. Altar; Altar Stone.)

## Mensal Fund

A mensal fund is a fixed amount contributed from Church revenues to support a bishopric, usually that of a cathedral. It is also the amount subscribed each year for the support of a resident priest. The term is not commonly used. (See Cathedraticum.)

## Mental Reservation, or Mental Restriction

Mental reservation is the practice of putting into words a meaning that is different from that which the words ordinarily have. It is not to be considered merely an equivocation, nor is it dissembling. Mental reservation is either *strict*, that is, when the truth cannot be had from the words expressed; or *broad*, that is, when the truth can be readily determined from the words although it is not actually contained in them. Strict mental reservation (for example, the lie) is always forbidden. Broad mental reservation may be considered permissible if there is justifiable reason for it or on basis of the conviction that the questioner has no right to exact the truth. (Cf. Lie.)

## Mercy

Mercy is that moral virtue whereby one treats other human persons with compassion and offers spiritual and/or temporal aid according to the person's wants. It is the fulfillment of the command to love one's neighbor as one's self, so it goes beyond giving merely according to need or of one's surplus.

Mercy is one of the essential attributes of God (Dt. 7:9), and mercy itself was a proof of God's mercy (Lk. 6:36–37). In our attempts to be like God, aspects of the virtue of mercy should be developed: (1) We must be forgiving, even to the extent of "seventy times seven" or without limit or reservation (cf. Lk. 17:4; Mt. 18:21–22). Also the forgiveness of the Christian transforms itself into the pardon that one has received or as the Lord's prayer states "forgive us as we forgive" (Mt. 6:12–15; 18:23–35; Col. 3:13). (2) In mercy there is the fundamental of love: to love God on the one hand, and to love one's neighbor as oneself (cf. Lv. 19:18), making these "like one" in the exercise or application of Christian perfection (Mt. 22:34–40; Lk. 10:25–28; Mk. 12:28–31). This love is the giving in mercy, compassion, and understanding as God gave Himself for us (1 Jn. 3:14–17; 4:17–21; 5:1–4; Eph. 5:1–2). (3) Mercy, allied as it is with love, fulfills the "bond of perfection" (Col. 3:14) and fulfills the Law (1 Pt. 4:7–11). (4) Because of mercy we show hospitality to others even as Christ received us (Rom. 12:9–13: 15:5–7; 1 Tm. 3:2; Heb. 13:2). (5) We comfort others even as God in His infinite mercy comforts us (2 Cor. 1:3–7) and we are brothers in Christ (Gal. 3:28–29; Phlm. 16). And this love, as an expression of mercy and brotherly harmony, is expressed by Christians (Acts 2:42–44; 4:32–37).

The Christian's prayer of petition, the asking for something, be it forgiveness or a physical good, is an appeal to the mercy of God and a declaration in praise of God's mercy. And it is evident to each that what one has to give in mercy is not his own, so to speak, but what has already been received from God. It is this which in the conscience of the human person prompts him to show mercy to others and to the creatures of God. It is thus the virtue that best serves to combat violence or vindictiveness against others. (See Love of God.)

## Mercy Killing

See Euthanasia.

## Mercy, Spiritual and Corporal Work of

The spiritual and corporal works of mercy are acts of the virtue of charity done for the benefit of others. The corporal works of mercy are: feed the hungry, give drink to the thirsty, clothe the naked, shelter the homeless, visit the sick and imprisoned, ransom the captive, and bury the dead. The spiritual works of mercy are: instruct the ignorant, advise the doubtful, correct sinners, be patient with those in error or who do wrong, forgive offenses, comfort the afflicted, and pray for the living and the dead.

Vatican II states: "In various seasons of the year and according to her traditional discipline, the Church completes the formation of the faithful by means of pious practices for soul and body, by instruction, prayer, and works of penance and of mercy" (SC 105).

## Merit

1. Merit is a good work performed for another, which entitles one to a reward.

2. In the theology of the Church, merit is the effect or recompense of sanctifying or cooperative grace; it is the "fruit of grace." That there is a correspondence between merit and reward, that the merciful shall obtain mercy and the humble will be exalted is evident from the Sermon on the Mount (Lk. 6:27–39). In fact, Christ through the redemption has merited all for us. We ourselves, strictly speaking, cannot merit anything from God, for we can never repay adequately; we can do nothing to give profit to God who has all, and so God owes us no reward. God is not a debtor of us, but we are indebted to God. But, as St. Augustine says, our merits are "the gift of God" as they proceed from His grace, and in this sense we may merit for a good and supernatural work: first, in justice (de condigno) since we share, through the Church and sacraments, in the merits of Christ, and a reward has been promised; second, because of friendship (de congruo) and mercy; in the state of grace, we are deserving of a "friendly reward," and by the mercy of God we are assured of the possibility of reward (Rom. 8:28–30).

The teaching concerning merit is one that must be looked at in the entire complex of creation and grace, together with the fact that the human person must live an ethically balanced existence. This is the response cycle that mankind makes in gratitude to God. Vatican II speaks often of the end of mankind being such a response that the ultimate "merit" will be attained, an unworldly merit gained for everyone through Christ: "Its goal is the Kingdom of God, which has been begun by God Himself on earth, and which is to be further extended until it is brought to perfection by Him at the end of Time. Then Christ our life (cf. Col. 3:4) will appear, and 'the world itself will be freed from its slavery to corruption and share in the glorious freedom of the children of God' (Rom. 8:21)" (LG 9).

## Messiah (Messias)

The word Messiah, which is a Grecian form of the Aramaic word, means "the anointed one." It appears in translation only six times in the NT (Jn. 1:20, 25; 4:25, 29; Lk. 24:26, 46).

To understand Christ as the Messiah, one must survey the OT, learn what the Israelites expected, and then examine the NT to learn the many ways in which Christ fulfilled the role of the "promised one." The first prophecy in which messianism as such was found shows that the expectation was for a "royal" dynasty which in the history of Israel was related to the Yahwist history (2 Sm. 7:9–16; 1 Ch. 17:11–14). The future king as the Israelites saw in perspective would fulfill the universal ideal of their future (Ps. 2 and 72), and the royal Messiah would be at the continued service of the old covenant (2 Sm. 23:1–7). The sign of this new deified king would be a "star" (Nm. 24:17; cf. also Is. 14:12; Rv. 22:16).

In the OT this new king would stand in contrast to many of the former kings of Israel, and as such were Josiah and Ezechiah hailed. Then there came a gradual change in the thought of the Israelites, which took on the eschatological expectation of the kingdom of God, and this took precedence over the messianism as formerly held.

Christ, as prophesied in the OT, was to be someone entirely different from a king—He was to be a suffering Messiah (Is. 2) and different from the priestly Messiah presented in the Book of Sirach. He was to be born of a virgin and to be named Immanuel (Is. 7:14–23); he would be the ideal successor of David (Is. 9:1–6; 11:1–9), a "Prince of Peace" from the tree of Jesse. He was to be born in Bethlehem (Mi. 5:1–5), and He was to be an eternal priest (Ps. 110:4).

In the NT the gospels proclaim the fulfillment of the prophecies of the OT as pronounced by Christ Himself to the Apostles with whom He met at Emmaus: "'What little sense you have! How slow you are to believe all that the prophets have announced! Did not the Messiah have to undergo all this so as to enter into his glory?' Beginning, then, with Moses and all the prophets, he interpreted for them every passage of Scripture that referred to him" (Lk. 24:25–27). Then Christ would exercise His Messiahship by the sending of the Holy Spirit (Acts 2:32–35; Mt. 25:31). And He would be glorified with His Father (Rv. 5:1–14; Eph. 1:20–21; Phil. 2:9–11).

Also the NT records the fulfillment of the shepherd role that was to likewise proclaim the Messiah prefigured by David (1 Sm. 16:10–13; 2 Sm. 5:1–3) and fulfilled by Christ the Good Shepherd (Lk. 15:1–7; cf. also Jer. 23:4; Am. 3:12; Jn. 10:16). This pastor-role, Christ passed on to His Church (Jn. 21:15–17; 1 Pt. 5:1–4), and the bishops of the Church carry on this shepherding of the flock of Christ for they are, as Vatican II proclaimed: "Living instruments of Christ the eternal priest" (PO 12).

## Metanoia

From the Greek, this word means "conversion." In the modern thinking and teaching of the Church this term has come to mean the relationship of the Christian community within the Church as experienced by individuals. The first "conversion" is the fundamental gift that one receives in baptism; if this gift is lost through sin, another "conversion" (or return to the ecclesial community) is gained and makes the individual more vigorous in faith through the Sacrament of Penance. Thus *metanoia* means the exercise of the virtue of penance whereby the individual Christian completes the suffering of Christ, completing the unity of the Body of Christ and lives not for himself but for God in faith.

## Metaphysics

This part of the science of philosophy abstracts the nature of reality, or the essence or nature of things. It penetrates and analyzes being and the principles that are true of all beings. It is divided into: (1) general, called *ontology*, which treats of being, substances, and accidents; (2) special, which in turn is divided into (a) *cosmology*, the study of the world (from the universe to the atom as they exist in reality), (b) *psychology*, the study of the soul, (c) *theodicy*, the study of the reality of God.

A modern emphasis has been placed on existentialism, wherein there is a conflict seen between "thinking" knowledge and "comprehending" knowledge—thus the truth that man seeks would be imperfect or provisional knowledge. Such then would be religious faith, but in this area there is more than speculation for, apart from revealed truth, there is the entire origin and impulse of man as a thinking being over the ages.

## Metempsychosis

Metempsychosis is the theory of modern psychology, which pronounces that the souls of human persons after death pass from one body to that of another body, human or animal, for the purpose of purifying the soul of guilt. This theory denies the unique union of the human soul and body and, by a transferral-purification, takes away the teaching of the individual's moral responsibility. (See Merit; Grace; Purgatory; Being; Body, Relation of Soul and.)

## Methodism

The development of the Protestant aspect of Methodism followed from the Reformation as a movement within a reformed church body. It was founded by John Wesley (1703 to 1791). The name Methodist was given first as a term of reproach or ridicule because of the exactitude of their liturgical approach to religion. Later the so-called Holy Club, named because of the preaching of John and Charles Wesley (1707 to 1788) and their co-founder George Whitefield (1714 to 1770), became the general title of their followers, the Methodists.

The year 1738 marked the beginning of Methodism as a religion. It was then that the separation from the established Anglican Church became an evident and inevitable fact, and the official break took place in America in 1784 when the Methodist Episcopal Church was organized. In England it took place after the compromise measure of 1795, called the Plan of Pacification, and the services of the societies were accepted as a deviant but regulated policy. Although some groups wished to go their separate ways, steps were taken toward reunion, with British Methodism starting in 1932 and the Methodist Episcopal Church and several branches followed in 1939. In Canada the Methodist Church joined the Congregationalists, the Presbyterian Church, and the Union Churches to form the United Church of Canada.

In 1968 the British Methodist Conference authorized the experiment of the liturgical service of Wesley, called the Sunday Service. Although essentially Episcopalian in its makeup, its ministry is that of an "office" rather than an ordained person in holy orders. Recent developments have brought the liturgy, which was founded on prayer, preaching, and hymn singing, an expansion of the concept of service. As maintained by John Wesley "faith working by love" remains a loose or relaxed formulation. However, its liturgy in modern times has taken on a structure: (1) The morning service is (with various options) an invocation or prayer of adoration, confession, the Gloria or other hymn, the collect of the day, an OT reading and/or an epistle, the gospel reading of the day, sermon, intercessions, Lord's Prayer. (2) The Lord's Supper (which may follow the sermon of the morning service) has a prayer of peace, the Nicene Creed, an offertory with hymn, the thanksgiving, the breaking of bread, communion, final prayer, dismissal and/or blessing.

In the United States this liturgy would be called a "sacramental service," but the term was dropped in 1854 from general use. The ritual remains with several variations, but in 1966 several innovations were introduced toward a nonverbal or meditation-oriented form of worship.

## Metokhion

Metokhion is the Greek word that describes the domain or the cell of a monk of the Byzantine Rite.

## Metropolitan

This is the title of an archbishop who is the head of an ecclesiastical province or territory, in which one or more suffragan bishops may be ruling over dioceses or portions of the province. The metropolitan is always an archbishop and has the jurisdiction over his own diocese (usually that of the chief city of the territory) and has certain rights and duties regarding his suffragan bishops. (Cf. Bishop.)

## Mexican-American Cultural Center

This institute was founded Sept. 29, 1971, by the Texas Catholic Conference. The objectives of the cultural center are to provide research, education, publications, and a leadership program for the Spanish-speaking Americans, especially those of Mexican origin. Being fully Catholic oriented, the institute has the endorsement of the United States Catholic Conference. It also cooperates with two slightly more specialized groups: PADRES, an association of priests working in the field of Spanish-speaking Americans (called, "Padres Asociados para Derechos Religiosos, Educativos y Sociales"); and Las Hermanas, an association of women religious working in the apostolate of the Spanish-speaking.

The Cultural Center has a twofold purpose: cultural and spiritual development, with a wide range of community services, crafts, social programs, and the improvement of the development of rights and leadership among the Mexican-American people.

## Micah, Book of

Also called Michea, one of the lesser prophetical books of the OT, this writing was by a contemporary of the prophet Isaiah named Micah or Michea, meaning "who is like Yahweh?" The prophet lived in Juda in the eighth century before Christ. Because he lived far from Jerusalem, he was interested in the social problems and in the politics of the nation of the Israelites. He stressed both the wrath and the mercy of God. His writing touches most on ethical doctrine, thus placing religious worship as a value chiefly when combined with social justice reflected in both the individual and the community. For Micah the oppression of the poor was most condemnable, and he speaks simply but bluntly against this corruption.

The book concludes with a double prayer asking for signs from God (Mi. 7:14–17) and beseeching the compassion of God toward the guilty (Mi. 7:18–20).

## Middle Ages

Middle Ages includes the period of time from the end of the tenth to the end of the fifteenth centuries, which forms a "middle" period between ancient and modern times. Many historians hold that the time began much earlier, from the coronation of Charlemagne in 800. Because of this Catholic identity, this era is called "the age of faith," although this has caused many to speak against the Church, branding the thought and expression of faith it developed "medievalism." This of course is an unwarranted demeaning of both the Church and history itself.

Speaking only from the history of the Church, it was true that the Church held a unique position, but not one that was always enviable. It faced the inroads of barbarism, the clash of political authority between the Roman Empire as it was shattered and the establishment of the Holy Roman Empire as a measure to stem the tide of chaos. It was a time of monastic expansion, the mendicant orders, the missionary activity, and the struggle against heresies that were particularly virulent.

But it was also a time when there was great interest in and development of theological thought, a time of artistic expression in painting, sculpture, and architecture as in no period of modern development. Much of this was Church-related in every sense of the term. However, there were developments that did not spring from the aegis of the Church, such as economic progress and international commerce.

All of this, it must be conceded, led to a basic transition, with many adjustments and refinements that were evident as the world emerged into the Renaissance. Thus the period brought much as preparation for the time that was to follow, if not great and glorious enrichment, certainly a different and more culturally changed period of mankind's onward progress into history. (Cf. Salvation History.)

## Midrash

From the Hebrew word meaning "explanation," this is the title of an ancient rabbinical commentary and detailed explanation of the Hebrew Scriptures, their application to life, and practical conclusions of legal actions. Various copies and translations are available for scholars in collections such as the *Midrash Rabbah* (London, 1949) in ten parts.

## Migrant Ministries

Special emphasis has been placed on the ministry to the thousands of migrant workers who move from job to job, from one social environment to another. The majority of these people came from Mexico and were baptized Catholics, but because of the nature of their enterprises they have found it difficult to attend to their expression of religion. Family life has been difficult to maintain; the workers have been excluded from social and labor legislation; wages and security have been reduced to a below minimum level.

The ministry as a special apostolate has come about through the formation of associations to benefit the migrant workers (cf. Mexican-American Cultural Center.) Dioceses have assumed responsibilities toward these people and assigned priests and teachers to aid them. National organizations, such as the National Catholic Rural Life Conference, have initiated for these workers programs calling for the doing away with political inequities, better wage and working conditions, the encouragement to organize for their betterment through negotiated procedures, the overcoming of unfair competition, and the reestablishment of dignity and honor to the lives of the migrants through overcoming the problems that create migrancy. But most essentially, besides the social concerns of the Church, there is the more fundamental regard for the spiritual good of migrants through a ministry of understanding and catechetical education. (See Ministries.)

## Military Order

See Knights, Orders of.

## Military Ordinariate

Because men and women in the branches of military service are required to move often from base to base, within and outside the country, they do not have parish and diocesan affiliation. Therefore the Holy See canonically established, Nov. 24, 1917, a special diocesan arrangement called the Military Ordinariate for the servicemen and their families. Under the jurisdiction of the Military Ordinariate are: all military and Veterans Administration hospital chaplains; the servicemen and women and their children, as well as dependents who reside with them; the members of the Coast Guard, National Guard, Air National Guard, and Civil Air Patrol when on active duty, and all persons living on military installations as well as those attached to military offices or Veteran Affairs facilities.

This special operation has the Catholic chaplains as its personnel. They send the records of baptism, first communion, confirmation, and marriage to the office of the Military Ordinariate. (Cf. Status Animarum.) The chaplains do not thus keep parochial records as such, but these are kept in the office of the Ordinariate, and this office issues the various certificates for official records of the reception of these sacraments to the chaplains. The Ordinariate also keeps the statistical record of spiritual activities, society memberships, and instruction through the Confraternity of Christian Doctrine. Also the Ordinariate sends, upon request, testimonial letters for anyone in military service who wishes to enter the priesthood or religious life. Headquarters of the Ordinariate for the United States are located at 30 East 51 Street, New York, N.Y., 10022.

## Millenarianism

Millenarianism is that thought which stems from a too literal, incorrect, and faulty interpretation of Chapter 20 of the Book of Revelation. It is here that St. John, writing with the use of symbols, speaks of the triumph of Christ, the restraint of the devil, the arising of the martyrs who together with Christ will reign for a thousand years. Spiritual significance was given to these symbols, especially that of the use of the word "thousand." This can only be understood in a spiritual sense and in keeping with the teachings of St. Paul (Eph. 5:4–5; Col. 3:1) where the sharing in the resurrection of Christ can only come through faith, baptism, and grace.

As a movement, similar to and sometimes called chiliasm, the Millenarists had their beginning in Asia Minor, first offered as a teaching by Jewish converts and then taken up by non-Jewish Christians. There are a number of church groups that still adhere to this misinterpretation, notably the Jehovah Witnesses who believe that Christ will come soon after the battle between Gog and Magog, which in turn is based upon a too literal interpretation of Ezekiel (38, 39:1–6). While the Church rejects these erroneous beliefs, she teaches a true spiritual reign of Christ in the hearts of all on their journey to salvation.

## Millenium

There has been speculation from the early Jews to the present about this period. It was considered to be 1000 years of bliss when the just will reign. This was to be before the Second Coming of Christ (the general judgment) and also was heretically held to be a similar period after the final judgment. But according to interpretation of Rv.

20:1–10, millenium means an age of grace wherein the faithful are living, whether on earth or in heaven. (See Millenarianism.)

## Mina

This ancient weight was equivalent to a modern pound; the name comes from the Latin, and by derivation from the Aramaic and Greek. It was at periods of Israelite history divided into either 50 shekels (before the Babylonian captivity) or 60 shekels during and after the exile. It was thus a term of coinage as well as a weight of measure. It was variously used as a measure but is mentioned as the weight of gold (1 Kgs. 10:17) and in connection with silver (Ezr. 2:69; Neh. 7:71). In Luke (19:13–25) by interpretation the mina was a Greek coin of value approximating 100 drachmas.

## Minister

From the Latin word for "servant," in the ecclesiastical sense, a minister is (1) an ordained cleric or (2) one who has the authority to administer to others, for example, to confirm. Sometimes it is also a title of a superior of a religious community. It is more proper to say "celebrant" of the Mass rather than "minister," since there may be other clerics assisting the celebrant. (See Ministries.)

## Minister of the Word

The title was applied to those who were witnesses to the events in the life of Christ, namely the Apostles, and who in turn told them to St. Luke before his writing of his gospel (Lk. 1:2). The expression "ministry of the word" is found referring to those who were actively teaching the message of Christ, again meaning the Apostles (Acts 6:4). The word "ministry," that is, the teaching of the Christian message is found in several places in the scriptures, each connoting the special role in relating the word, the good news, to others (cf. Acts 1:7; 21:19; Rom. 11:13; 2 Cor. 4:1; 6:3; Col. 1:25; 4:17).

It is also clear that the use of "the word" meant "the word of God" (1 Thes. 1:6–8; Acts 6:2–6). Likewise this applied to the apostolate, and in more recent interpretations the term "minister of the word" has been applied to many who serve in the Church in communicating the scriptural message to the people of God. This implies that persons who take part in relaying the teaching of the word assume certain responsibilities toward God from whom the word comes, and that indifference in speaking and teaching the word or in any way corrupting it is to be avoided (2 Cor. 4:2–7). To witness to the word is to proclaim it in truth; to teach the message of Christ is to give witness in one's life to the truth of the message. (See Ministries; Lector.)

Vatican II teaches: "The Church knows that her message is in harmony with the most secret desires of the human heart when she champions the dignity of the human vocation, restoring hope to those who have already despaired of anything higher than their present lot. Far from diminishing man, her message brings to his development light, life, and freedom. Apart from this message nothing will avail to fill up the heart of man: 'Thou hast made us for Thyself, O Lord, and our hearts are restless till they rest in Thee'" (GS 21).

And: "Even against the intentions of their proponents, however, solutions proposed on one side or another may be easily confused by many people with the gospel message. Hence it is necessary for people to remember that no one is allowed in the aforementioned situations to appropriate the Church's authority for his opinion. They (laymen) should always try to enlighten one another through honest discussion, preserving mutual charity and caring above all for the common good" (GS 43).

And: "The apostolate of the Church and of all her members is primarily designed to manifest Christ's message by words and deeds and to communicate His grace to the world. This work is done mainly through the ministry of the Word and of the sacraments" (AA 6).

## Ministries

There is a great diversity of ministries in the Church. The voluntarily assumed role of minister has been emphasized greatly by Vatican II in its many documents and decrees. Thus here we present the variety and discoursiveness of the understanding of ministries from Vatican II teachings before we enter into the Church's reform in regard to tonsure, minor orders, and the subdiaconate, together with the ordained ministries, which in themselves constitute an expansion of thought and understanding concerning these areas of special service. We shall then follow with special ministries.

A. The teachings of Vatican II concerning ministries are extensive, covering many phases of life in the living Church, in the Christian community, and in the apostolate in general.

1. Christ is the first, the prime Minister to men: "He (Christ) is present in the sacrifice of the Mass, not only in the person of His minister, 'the same one now offering, through the ministry of priests,

who formerly offered himself on the cross,' but especially under the Eucharistic species" (SC 7).

And: "It was from Pentecost that the 'Acts of the Apostles' took their origin. In a similar way Christ was conceived when the Holy Spirit came upon the Virgin Mary. Thus too Christ was impelled to the work of His ministry when the same Holy Spirit descended upon Him at prayer" (AG 4).

2. In a special manner the bishops, as vicars of Christ, His representatives, have a singular ministry of caring for the people of God. "These pastors (the bishops), selected to shepherd the Lord's flock, are servants of Christ and stewards of the mysteries of God (cf. 1 Cor. 4:1)" (LG 21).

And: "In the bishops, therefore . . . our Lord Jesus Christ, the supreme High Priest, is present in the midst of those who believe" and through them teaches, sanctifies, directs, and guides the People of the New Covenant (LG 21).

3. Priests are ordained likewise to a singular ministry. "By the sacrament of orders priests are configured to Christ the Priest so that as ministers of the Head and coworkers of the episcopal order they can build up and establish His whole Body which is the Church" (PO 12).

And: "As ministers of sacred realities, especially in the Sacrifice of the Mass, priests represent the person of Christ in a special way—He gave Himself as a victim to make men holy. Hence priests are invited to imitate the realities they deal with. Since they celebrate the mystery of the Lord's death, they should see to it that every part of their being is dead to evil habits and desires" (PO 13).

And: "As cooperators with the pastor, assistant pastors make an outstanding and active contribution to the pastoral ministry under the authority of the pastor" (CD 30).

4. The members of the laity also are called upon to serve Christ and His Church, each according to his ability and the instruction and free acceptance of their place in service. "Some of them (laity) do all they can to provide sacred services when sacred ministers are lacking or are blocked by a persecuting regime. Many devote themselves entirely to apostolic work. But all ought to cooperate in the spreading and intensifying of the kingdom of Christ in the world" (LG 35).

And: "In the Church, there is diversity of service but unity of purpose" (AA 2). (Cf. Laity.)

B. Pope Paul VI in an apostolic letter (Aug. 15, 1972) established the norms that have changed the role of certain heretofore ministerial roles.

"Even in the most ancient times certain ministries were established by the Church for the purpose of suitably giving worship to God and for offering service to the people of God according to their needs. By these ministries, duties of a liturgical and charitable nature, deemed suitable to varying circumstances, were entrusted to the performance of the faithful. The conferring of these functions often took place by a special rite, in which, after God's blessing had been implored, a Christian was established in a special class or rank for the fulfillment of some ecclesiastical function . . .

"Nevertheless, since the minor orders have not always been the same and many tasks connected with them, as at present, have also been exercised by the laity, it seems fitting to re-examine this practice and to adapt it to contemporary needs, so that what is obsolete in these offices may be removed, what is useful retained, what is necessary defined, and at the same time what is required of candidates for holy orders may be determined. . . .

"Besides the offices common to the Latin Church, there is nothing to prevent episcopal conferences from requesting others of the Apostolic See, if they judge the establishment of such offices in their region to be necessary or very useful because of special reasons. To these belong, for example, the offices of porter, exorcist, and catechist, as well as other offices to be conferred upon those who are dedicated to works of charity, where this service has not been given to deacons. . . .

"Having weighed every aspect of the question well, having sought the opinion of experts, having consulted with the episcopal conferences and taken their views into account, and having taken counsel with our venerable brothers who are members of the Sacred Congregations competent in this matter, by our apostolic authority we enact the following norms, derogating—if and insofar as necessary—from provision of the Code of Canon Law now in force, and we promulgate them with this letter.

"1. First tonsure is no longer conferred; entrance into the clerical state is joined to the diaconate.

"2. What up to now were called minor orders are henceforth called 'ministries.'

"3. Ministries may be committed to lay Christians; hence they are no longer to be considered as reserved to candidates for the sacrament of order.

"4. Two ministries, adapted to present-day needs, are to be preserved in the whole of the Latin Church, namely those of *readers* and *acolytes*. The functions heretofore committed to the subdeacon are entrusted to the reader and the acolyte; consequently, the major order of subdiaconate no longer exists in the Latin Church. There is nothing, however, to prevent the acolyte being also called a subdeacon in some places, if the episcopal conference judges it opportune.

"5. The reader is appointed for a function proper to him, that of reading the word of God in the liturgical assembly. Accordingly, he is to read the lessons from sacred scripture, except for the gospel, in the Mass and other sacred celebrations; he is to recite the psalm between the readings when there is no psalmist; he is to present the intentions for the general intercessions in the absence of a deacon or cantor; he is to direct the singing and the participation by the faithful; he is to instruct the faithful for the worthy reception of the sacraments. He may also, insofar as necessary, take care of preparing other faithful who by a temporary appointment are to read the scriptures in liturgical celebrations. That he may more fittingly and perfectly fulfill these functions, let him meditate assiduously on sacred scripture. . . .

"6. The acolyte is appointed in order to aid the deacon and to minister to the priest. It is therefore his duty to attend the service of the altar and to assist the deacon and the priest in liturgical celebrations, especially in the celebration of Mass; he is also to distribute holy communion as an extraordinary minister when the ministers spoken of in canon 845 of the Code of Canon Law are not available or are prevented by ill health, age, or another pastoral ministry from performing this function, or when the number of those approaching the sacred table is so great that the celebration of Mass would be unduly prolonged.

"In the same extraordinary circumstances he may be entrusted with publicly exposing the Blessed Sacrament for adoration by the faithful and afterwards replacing it, but not with blessing the people. He may also, to the extent needed, take care of instructing other faithful who by temporary appointment assist the priest or deacon in liturgical celebrations by carrying the missal, cross, candles, etc., or by performing other such duties. He will perform these functions the more worthily if he participates in the holy eucharist with increasingly fervent piety, receives nourishment from it and deepens his knowledge of it.

"Destined as he is in a special way for the service of the altar, the acolyte should learn all matters concerning public divine worship and strive to grasp their inner spiritual meaning; in that way he will be able each day to offer himself entirely to God, be an example to all by his seriousness and reverence in the sacred building, and have a sincere love for the Mystical Body of Christ, the people of God, expecially the weak and the sick.

"7. In accordance with the venerable tradition of the Church, institution in the ministries of readers and acolytes is reserved to men.

"8. The following are requirements for admission to the ministries:

"(a) The presentation of the petition freely made out and signed by the aspirant to the ordinary (the bishop and, in clerical institutes of perfection, the major superior) who has the right to accept the petition.

"(b) A suitable age and special qualities to be determined by the episcopal conference.

"(c) A firm will to give faithful service to God and the Christian people.

"9. The ministries are conferred by the ordinary (the bishop and, in clerical institutes of perfection, the major superior) according to the liturgical rite *De Institutione Lectoris* and *De Institutione Acolythi* revised by the Apostolic See.

"10. Intervals, determined by the Holy See or the episcopal conferences, shall be observed between the conferring of the ministries of readers and acolytes whenever more than one ministry is conferred on the same person.

"11. Candidates for the diaconate and priesthood are to receive the ministries of reader and acolyte, unless they have already done so, and are to exercise them for a fitting time, in order to be better disposed for the future service of the word and of the altar. Dispensation from the reception of these ministries on the part of such candidates is reserved to the Holy See.

"12. The conferring of ministries does not imply the right to sustenance or salary from the Church.

"13. The rite of institution of readers and acolytes is to be published soon by the competent department of the Roman Curia.

"These norms shall come into effect on January 1, 1973."

C. Pope Paul VI, also on Aug. 15, 1972, issued another apostolic letter promulgating the norms for the Holy Order of Deacon. (See Orders, Holy, Sacrament of; Permanent Deacon.)

D. Other ministries of special note and some that are still evolving in the expansion of thought in regard to service by members of the faithful are truly diversified:

1. The catechist, the one who serves in an instructional role, giving care to the catechesis of adults, youths, and children. Thus it may apply to the office of teacher.

2. The extraordinary minister, that one who by appointment and free acceptance, assists in the

distribution of Holy Communion at Celebrations of the Eucharist.

3. The ministry of music, either the "psalmist" or the cantor who leads the assembly in singing hymns and responses, or the leader of songs and hymns, or the choir director or director of music, or the organist, may be a ministry to which more formal recognition in liturgical functions is given. (See Music, Church).

4. At the request of the American episcopal conference, there was granted in 1970, by the Congregation for the Discipline of the Sacraments, a special indult whereby women may fulfill the role of reader, and women have been chosen for fulfilling the role of extraordinary minister in the distribution of Holy Communion. The episcopal conference of bishops may permit women to proclaim the readings prior to the gospel.

5. While there is not intended that there be a wholesale proliferation of ministries, recognition may soon be given, in accordance with the rulings of the episcopal conferences, whereby others who serve may be duly recognized as giving ministerial service, for example, trustees of a parish, the members of a parish council, youth directors, educational coordinators, ushers, the designers or crafters who make banners or other Church decorations, and those who serve in some semiofficial capacity in chancery offices. (Cf. Orders, Holy, Sacrament of; Permanent Deacon; Apostolate.)

### Ministry, Team

See, Team Ministry.

### Minor Orders

See, Orders, Holy, Sacrament of; Ministries.

### Miracle

A miracle is a phenomenon in nature that can be seen by the senses and that is outside the ordinary law of nature and brought about by some power beyond nature, that is, by special activity of the First Cause, the source of all law, God. We have first to consider the miracles related in Scripture. Miracles were used to prove revelation. The Church, as set forth in the third chapter of the First Vatican Council, teaches: "In order that the service of our faith should be agreeable to reason, God has willed to join to the internal helps of the Holy Spirit some external proofs of His revelation, namely, divine deeds, especially miracles and prophecies, which, inasmuch as they plainly show forth the omnipotence and infinite knowledge of God, are most certain signs of revelation and are

suited to the intelligence of all. Wherefore, both Moses and the prophets, and above all Christ the Lord Himself, performed many and most manifest miracles and uttered prophecies; and we read of the apostles that 'they, going forth, preached everywhere, the Lord working withal and confirming the word with signs that followed.'" And from the same Council, we have the following canon of faith: "If anyone shall say that divine revelation cannot be made credible by external signs, but that men must be moved to believe solely by the internal experience or private inspiration of each one, let him be anathema."

In the process of canonization of a saint, the Church demands that proof of two miracles be presented and authenticated before beatification (except in a case of true martyrdom) and that two more miracles be proved to have taken place through the intercession of the beatified before the person is canonized and declared to be a saint (cc. 1999-2141). (Cf. Canonization.)

In the miracles that Christ performed, faith was always evident. He always chose to work those miracles that demonstrated the nature of the kingdom; they proved that the fullness of the time of salvation had come (Mt. 12:28; Lk. 11:20; Jn. 6:29–30). The miracles of Christ also made known three dominant truths: that He was the Messiah (Mt. 11:4–6; 12:28; Jn. 1:30–34); that He was the Savior (Mt. 9:2–8; Mk. 1:34; Lk. 4:34–37; Jn. 10:25–38); and that He was the suffering Servant (Mt. 8:16; cf. Is. 53:4). The miracles we read about in the gospels, like those of the OT, are signs more of what they reveal than we learn from the nature of their execution.

Vatican II declares: "The miracles of Jesus confirm that the kingdom has already arrived on earth: 'If I cast out devils by the finger of God, then the kingdom of God has come upon you' (Lk. 11:20; cf. Mt. 12:28)" (LG 5).

### Miracle of Grace

This name is given to the remarkable change in the soul whereby one is turned from a life of sin or converted to the faith. While it must be recognized that the "grace of God" is a free gift, St. Paul, the great writer on grace in all of his epistles, acknowledged a "prayer for grace" (cf. Phil. 1:2; 1:25). The fact that grace is "gratuitously" given, or free, means that whatever is given is not something "due" or something to which the person has a prior claim. The appropriateness of the term "grace" is recognition of the expansiveness of divine love. Prayer opens one to those graces to which one has no claim. (See Faith.)

## Miracle Plays, also Mystery or Morality Plays

This early form of drama began in the Middle Ages; it presented the lives of saints, a religious historic event, a Scripture story, or some teaching of the faith. Primarily, they were teaching aids, but later on action was introduced into these plays to serve the purpose of genuine drama. They were usually presented out-of-doors, frequently in the courtyard or square before a cathedral by touring troupes of players. Miracle plays preceded the mystery plays; the latter were distinguished by centering primarily on events of the OT or NT and lives of the saints. Many of them, following the pattern of the early Greek theater, introduced verse, which became the form of the drama for later centuries. The most famous morality play, which is still performed in theaters, is *Everyman,* an allegorical progression of man through life.

## Miraculous Medal

This medal was struck after the apparitions to St. Catherine Laboure in 1830. It shows on one side a representation of the Blessed Mother together with the words "O Mary conceived without sin, pray for us who have recourse to thee." On the opposite side it bears the letter *M* with a cross and twelve stars beneath, which are representations of the Sacred Heart and the Immaculate Heart of the Blessed Virgin.

## Mirari Vos

The Latin title, meaning "You Wonder" of the first encyclical of Pope Gregory XVI (1831 to 1846), issued on Aug. 15, 1832. The letter was considered an answer to a leader of the French liberal movement, Father Felicite de Lamennais (1782 to 1854), but it spoke out for Christian freedom, upheld the traditional rights of the papacy to ecclesial supremacy, condemned the thinking concerning the unrestricted liberty of conscience, indicated that too close an alliance of

the clergy with government was undesirable, and endorsed the separation of Church and State. It was a strong attack against indifferentism and the rise of rationalism in affairs of salvation. (Cf. Indifferentism; Rationalism, Theological.)

## Miserere

Miserere is the first word of its Latin version and title of Psalm 50. It is the fourth penitential Psalm and the most widely used Psalm of penance.

## Missa

The Latin word for Mass is Missa. (Cf. Mass.)

## Missal

The liturgical book of the Roman rite is the *Missale Romanum.* It contains the formulas and rites for the celebration of Mass together with the text of the Ordinary (portion said at every Mass) and the Proper (portion that changes with each feast) of the feasts throughout the year. It also contains the Masses for special occasions, prayers for the preparation before and thanksgiving after Mass, and various blessings. The missal began to take its present form under a law of 802 and its form was almost set as we now have it (except for the addition of new feasts, etc.) with the official publication ordered by Pope Pius V in 1570. It was not until the twentieth century, with the decrees of St. Pius X regarding frequent Communion, that the use of the missal by the laity assisting at Mass became widespread. (See Leaflet Missal; Sacramentary.)

## Missiology

The study of the Church's mission in the world together with its direct mission activity is called missiology. The role of the individual person in the mission of the Church is twofold: personal witness and extension of the teaching of the Church.

Vatican II teaches: "Since 'a common concern unites the captain of a ship with its passengers,' the whole Christian people should be taught that it is their duty to cooperate in one way or another, by constant prayer and other means at their disposal, so that the Church may always have the necessary number of priests to carry out her divine mission" (PO 11).

And: "'Mission' is the term usually given to those particular undertakings by which the heralds of the gospel are sent out by the Church and go forth into the whole world to carry out the task of preaching the gospel and planting the Church among peoples or groups who do not yet believe in Christ. These undertakings are brought to completion by missionary activity and are commonly exercised in certain territories recognized by the Holy See.

"The specific purpose of this missionary activity is evangelization and the planting of the Church among those peoples and groups where she has not yet taken root" (AG 6).

And: "But rather often men, deceived by the Evil One, have become caught up in futile reasoning and have exchanged the truth of God for a lie, serving the creature rather than the Creator (cf. Rom. 1:21–25). Or some there are who, living and dying in a world without God, are subject to utter hopelessness. Consequently, to promote the glory of God and procure the salvation of all such men, and mindful of the command of the Lord, 'Proclaim the good news to all creation' (Mk. 16:16), the Church painstakingly fosters her missionary work" (LG 16).

And: "Let priests train the faithful to pray for the missions" (AG 39). (See Evangelization.)

## Mission

This word has a variety of meanings as used by the Church, all of which stem from the apostolic commission given to the Apostles by Christ (Mk. 6:7–13), and are concerned with the teaching role of the Church in its mission to all men.

1. Mission is the smallest or simplest territorial organization of the Church. It may be attached to another parish and administered by the parish resident priest.

2. Mission is a title of ordination to Holy Orders (cc. 979-981).

3. A mission is a territory administered by a priest appointed by the Congregation of Propagation of the Faith. Some of these territories have been assigned to the administration of religious orders who appoint superiors over them. As soon as such a district develops, it is made into a prefecture apostolic.

4. Foreign missions are the work of the Church in pagan lands under the Sacred Congregation of the Propagation of the Faith.

5. So-called popular missions are series of instructions, sermons, and devotions conducted in a parish for the spiritual welfare of the people. They usually last for several days and may be conducted annually.

6. Mission Sunday is usually the second last Sunday in October. Those who make their confession, receive Holy Communion on that day and pray for the conversion of unbelievers gain a plenary indulgence (S.R.C. Apr. 14, 1926).

7. Divine Mission is the procession of one Divine

Person from another, proceeding by being sent, and producing a new effect in the one sent, for example, the Son from the Father. (Cf. Trinity, the Most Holy.)

The concept of mission for the individual is complementary to that of giving witness to Christ and His teaching (Acts 2:24–32; 3:15; 4:10). The Christian bearing the message of salvation is given special aids so that the mission may be accomplished (1 Pt. 2:9; Rom. 15:6–7; Gal. 4:14). Thus Christians have the understanding that theirs is a participation in the work of the Church in being sent and that this is expressed through: proclaiming the good news, service (cf. Stewardship), and acquiring a sense of community. (See Church.)

## Missionaries, also Missioners

All those persons who are actively engaged in the mission work of the Church are called missionaries. There are special callings to such service, in a variety of roles, but any individual who responds to the mission of the Church may be so named.

Vatican II teaches: "All missionaries—priests, brothers, sisters, and laymen—each according to his own state, need preparation and training if they are not to be found unequal to the demands of their future work. . . .

"It is above all necessary for the future missionary to devote himself to missiological studies: that is, to know the teachings and norms of the Church concerning missionary activity, the roads which the heralds of the gospel have traversed in the course of the centuries, the present condition of the missions, and the methods now considered especially effective. . . .

"Some should receive an especially thorough preparation in missiological institutes or in other faculties or universities. As a result they will be able to discharge special duties more effectively and to be a help, by their learning, to other missionaries in carrying on missionary work. In our time especially, this work presents very many difficulties and opportunities" (AG 26).

## Missions, Franciscan

See Franciscan Missions of California.

## Mitre

A mitre is a folding hat, made up of two equal, cone-shaped parts that rise to a divided peak at the top, the two parts being joined at the base by a cap of soft material to allow flat folding. Attached to the rim in the back are two lappets (*infulae*) that hang down and are usually fringed. The mitre is worn by cardinals, bishops, abbots, and certain dignitaries, such as prothonotaries apostolic, outside of Rome and on certain occasions. There are three types or grades of the mitre; the use of each is determined by the rubrics: (1) the *precious* mitre,

made of silk or cloth of gold, and highly ornamented with embroidery and gems; (2) the *gold* mitre, made of cloth of gold; (3) the *simple* mitre, made of white silk or linen with red-fringed lappets. The mitre has evolved to its present form, but its use as a headdress goes back to the Jewish priestly vestment (Ex. 39:26).

### Mixed Marriage

A marriage between a Catholic and a non-Catholic is forbidden by Church law, but a dispensation may be obtained. Such dispensation can only be obtained and the marriage made valid if promises *(cautiones)* are made. These are formal and serious promises made by both parties. The non-Catholic promises to cause no danger to the faith or to lead the Catholic into immoral practices. Both parties must promise to raise the children, present or prospective, in the Catholic faith alone. These promises should be made in writing. In the case of a mixed marriage, the banns are not announced, and there is no nuptial Mass; however, the ordinary may permit some ceremony. In those instances where the non-Catholic is baptized, it is called a marriage of *mixed religion*, and the marriage is unlawful but not invalid. Where the non-Catholic is not baptized, the dispensation is classified as one of Disparity of Worship and such a marriage is both unlawful and invalid. (Cf. Impediments of Marriage.)

### Modalism

The collective term for a number of condemned heresies of the early centuries of the Church, all of which asserted that the three Persons of the Most Holy Trinity are only modes, or determinations of

being, in the subsistence of the Father, Son, and Holy Spirit. These are thus each, according to their mode, self-manifestations of one and the same God. Under this heading we find the varieties of the heresy: Monarchianism, Patripassionism, and Sabellianism. (See Heresies.)

### Modernism

Called the "synthesis of all heresies," this was a result of subjectivist thinking that sprang up at the beginning of the twentieth century. Among others it took hold of the younger clergy, who found it impossible to reconcile teachings of the faith and the Church with the beliefs of modern science. Although encompassing a wide variety of teachings, all theories of modernism argued for bringing the doctrines of the Church into harmony with science by means of a radical innovation of reinterpretation. Modernism attacked the most fundamental teachings, such as revelation, faith, Scripture, and the authority of the Church. All its teachings also centered on Kant's philosophy of agnosticism and, with the destruction or refusal to accept even the scientific proofs for religion, the adherents set about to introduce a "spontaneous" religion. This took the form of establishing individual inner experience, "religious feeling," as the core of this religion, making it quite simply naturalistic. The Church, through Pope St. Pius X, issued two doctuments condemning modernism: the Decree of the Holy Office, *Lamentabili,* of July 3, 1907, and the encyclical, *Pascendi,* of Sept. 8, 1907. The decree lists sixty-five condemned propositions of modernism, and the encyclical offers an analysis of the propositions of modernism in the light of philosophy, theology, and the teaching of the Church. According to a declaration of the Holy Office of March 22, 1918, those confessors and preachers who make a profession of faith before receiving their faculties in accord with c. 1406 must take an oath against modernism.

Regarding the Church, not as a supernatural institution wherein human persons may attain salvation, modernism in its most current form makes the Church merely a social entity that advances civilization. But in its philosophical and ecclesial concepts, modernism is a repudiation of faith, for one does not progress from agnosticism in the "social" acceptance to faith in the order of religion. (Cf. Teilhardism.)

### Modesty

Modesty is the accompanying virtue of temperance, which enables one to moderate one's external manner, for example, in dress, deportment, and conversation. This virtue of modesty is an index of the restraint of thought that marks a person's actions. Its opposites are insolence, boorishness, and all unbecoming actions. It is not the same as chastity, though many confuse these. Modesty is positive in its psychological approach to actions; thus it requires both knowledge and motivation so that what is socially accepted is not confused with what is basically a moral action based upon fundamental principles of behavior.

## Mohammedanism

This is the name of the religion founded by Mohammed, called "The Praised One," who announced himself as the prophet of the one true God, Allah, and its adherents are called variously, Mohammedans, Moslems, Islamites, or Sunnites. It is a religion wherein the followers "surrender to the will of Allah."

Mohammed (also Muhammad or Mahomet) was born of a noble family of the Kareish tribe in the city of Mecca about the year A.D. 570. His father, Abdullah, died before his son's birth, and when Mohammed was about six years old his mother, Aminah, also died. The young Mohammed was raised by his grandfather and uncle who trained him during the caravan journeys. At age twenty-eight, he married a wealthy widow, Khadija, and in his journeys visited many countries including Palestine and Syria. It was thus that his thinking and the formulations of his religious system were influenced by Judaism, Christianity, and Hellenism. He was recognized as having considerable knowledge, wisdom, and honesty, and he gave succor to the oppressed. His religion owes less to Judaism than does Christianity, and it finally became a separate religious course toward salvation. Mohammed died in A.D. 632.

Mohammedanism as a religion is likewise a way of life. While its founder overcame the paganism and idolatry of his time by a passionate zeal for carrying out the mission of Allah, it was not at first accepted as a religion. In fact the people of his home city thought Mohammed demented, but he persevered, preaching that there is only one true God, Allah, and gave out a code of six pledges: (1) they will worship no one but the one God, (2) they will not steal, (3) they will not kill their children, (4) they will not commit adultery, (5) they will not slander anyone in any way, (6) they will obey the prophet in anything that is right.

The basic teachings of Mohammedanism rest upon scripture and the prophets, the main ones being the Pentateuch, the Psalms, the Gospel, and the Koran (cf. Koran). The followers are now divided into distinct groups, which adhere to much the same doctrinal content. There are the majority called *Sunnites,* who are the orthodox followers of Mohammed adhering strictly to the "Way," the *Sunna.* There are also the Shihites, a more liberal group of Islam, who look for a future savior or leader *(imam).* It is from the Shihites that a group arose who follow a mystical devotion called *Sufism,* and the messianic groups allied with the missionary group called *Bahaist.*

The doctrine of the Moslem faith rests on one God, who is addressed in prayer by 99 names. There are angels who serve as intermediaries, and there are good and evil spirits (jinn or genii). There are five requisite duties (called *din)* each Moslem must perform as ritualistic expressions of belief: (1) make a profession of faith daily reciting their creed; (2) pray five times each 24 hour period facing toward Mecca; (3) give alms, in particular for the poor; (4) fast every day from dawn to dusk during the month of Ramadan; (5) make a pilgrimage to Mecca once during one's lifetime. (See Islam.)

## Moicheia

The Greek word *Moicheia* means adultery but not only in the usually accepted sense of the term. It is a term of more broad implications, meaning a violation of the will of God and also a dishonoring of the human body by such actions as masturbation, lesbianism, and homosexuality since these involve sins against justice and religion because the human body is a temple of the Holy Spirit (Rom. 1:24–28).

Also in this connotation it is extensive; that is, it includes the very intent to commit adultery, and as such this is the broad understanding under which Christ spoke as recorded in Matthew (5:27–29). (Cf. also 2 Pt. 2:11–14; Heb. 13:1–4.)

## Moleben

From the Slavonic language, this term is used in the Greek and Slavonic rites for an occasional service of thanksgiving or petition. It is an optional service rather than a devotional activity.

## Molech, also Moloch

Molech was an ancient near-Eastern god who was venerated as the Canaanite "King" of the world of the dead. While this form of idolatry was widespread, in the seventh century before Christ, the worship of this "king-god" grew in Palestine as a result of the influence of the Assyrians (cf. 2 Kgs. 23:10; Jer. 32:35). The sacrifice of children, which was a pagan rite in the worship of Molech, was prohibited by the Mosaic Law (Lv. 18:21; 20:2–5), and the rite was foreign to the Israelites in any of their religious practices.

## Molinism

This theory was proposed by the Jesuit theologian Louis de Molina (d. 1600) on the relation between grace and free will. It was denounced by theologians of the Thomistic and Augustinian schools because Molina placed too much value on human cooperation at the cost of the efficacy of grace. It was thus the proposition of Molina that grace, either sufficient or efficacious, does not differ before we give our consent. Dominican scholars reject all forms of Molinism. (Cf. Grace.)

## Monarchianism

This heresy, which sprang from Adoptionism, was condemned at the councils of Antioch (A.D. 268). (See Modalism; Heresies.)

## Monastery

A monastery is the community residence of a group of religious who live in seclusion, lead a life of contemplation, and recite the Divine Office in common. This term is used of both male and female religious. The physical property of a monastery differs, but in general each is composed of a church, chapter house, cloister, refectory, work area, and individual cells, all usually forming a quadrangle. Over and above the requirements of the particular religious group, a monastery must be canonically erected; that is, permission in writing must have been obtained from the ordinary; and there must be sufficient means to support the community (c. 496).

Vatican II teaches: "While safeguarding the proper identity of each institution, let monasteries be renewed in their ancient and beneficial traditions, and so adapt them to the modern needs of souls that monasteries will be seedbeds of growth for the Christian people" (PC 9).

And: "If after consulting the appropriate Ordinaries the Holy See decides that certain communities or monasteries no longer offer any reasonable hope of flourishing, these should be forbidden thereafter to accept novices. If it can be done, they should be absorbed by a more vigorous community or monastery which approximates their own purpose and spirit" (PC 21).

## Monasticism

This mode of life developed very early in the history of the Church. It is basically characterized by asceticism and a life of self-denial that is followed by a group of religious who wish to live in common, under a specific rule, to perfect themselves in the love of God. It arose from the wish of some who sought to be hermits because of individual problems, and banded together for a specific purpose. As early as A.D. 451 at the Council of Chalcedon it was necessary, however, to place such groups under the authority of the bishops. The rule of St. Benedict of Nursia, drawn up in the sixth century, brought about the spread of monasticism in the west. Monasteries were the centers of education through the twelfth century but then were eclipsed by the universities and cathedral schools. The "golden age" of monasticism dates from the founding of the Abbey of Cluny in A.D. 910 through the thirteenth century. Their cultural contributions and their leadership in the physical and social sciences are well known.

Vatican II declares: "In the East and in the West, the venerable institution of monastic life should be faithfully preserved, and should grow ever increasingly radiant with its own authentic spirit. Through the long course of the centuries, this institution has proved its merits splendidly to the Church and to human society" (PC 9).

## Monasticism, Irish

The development of the monastic life in Ireland and Wales was indigenous. It owed little to the founders of monasticism in the early Church or to later establishment of a system by Sts. Augustine or Benedict. It was begun early in the fifth century and was devoted to a penitential way of life more closely associated with the early hermits. The recitation of the Divine Office was a lengthy program of prayer, sometimes seeming extreme in duration. But they introduced several individual practices that were historically significant: an educational system, the translation of the Latin works into the Celtic languages, the preservation of many texts, private confession, and the unusual practice of frequent reception of Holy Communion (with the bread being baked flat in the form of a cross and then cut into pieces that were then given to the monks according to their status, thus beginning at the bottom or foot of the cross, and the center portion—that of the crossing of the two arms of the cross—reserved for the celebrant). Early monasteries were: Clonard, Clonfert, Bangor, Lismore, as well as many others in Wales and Iona in Scotland. From these such missionary monks as St. Columban went to the mainland of Europe and opened monasteries, which began the great advent of such institutions in central Europe.

## Monism

From the Greek word meaning "alone" or "one," this is the philosophical term that is attached to the theory that there is only one basic or fundamental component that makes up every real thing. In a more restricted sense it may also be applied to those theories that declare that among the appearances of many there is only one that is real and the other visible things are only apparent.

The first form of monism presents the possibility of at least a dualism of matter and spirit in every real thing. The second is more directed to a spiritualist or idealist monism where only spirit exists, thus denying the material.

Spinoza (1632 to 1677) taught the second type of monism, positing a single, infinite, all-pervading spirit as the first principle, which constitutes a totality of being. This approximates the theory of Sophia, the world-soul, or world-spirit concept which opposes naturalist monism. This to some degree was the idea of overall immanence put forward by Teilhard de Chardin in a spiritualized concept of the cosmic-material where all are in the developing stage toward a single "one-ness" or a return to "God in existence" pattern, the "Unique Essential," the "Cosmic influence of Christ." (See Pantheism; Teilhardism.)

## Monita Secreta

This title is given to a spurious, fabricated code by a Polish Jesuit, Jerome Zahorowski, who was discharged from the Society in 1611. It alleged that the fifth general of the Jesuit order had given secret orders to expand the influence and power of the Society.

## Monk

Originally, the term referred to a hermit, or a member of a community of men who lived apart from the world under religious vows of poverty, chastity, and obedience in accord with a specific religious rule. More popularly, a monk is one who lives in a monastery, separated from the world in the company of other brethren, or one distinguished from other orders of clerks regular, congregations, or societies. Monks in the Roman Church now are: Benedictines, Cistercians, Trappists, Carthusians, Premonstratensians, and Camaldolese.

In the Bible there is a "mystique" of the desert or hermitage, for example, St. John the Baptist (Mt. 3:1; 11:7–10), the Rechabites (Jer. 35:5–10), and Christ Himself spent 40 days in the wilderness, apart from the world (Mt. 4:1–11).

Vatican II declares the tradition, adding, "The main task of monks is to render to the Divine Majesty a service at once simple and noble, within the monastic confines. This they do either by devoting themselves entirely to divine worship in a life that is hidden, or by lawfully taking up some apostolate or works of Christian charity" (PC 9).

## Monogamy

The union of one man and one woman is called monogamy. It thus means, to all religious intent, one marriage. It is the only form of marriage recognized by the Church founded by Christ. Only in this can there be an understanding of the "wedding" of Christ and His Church (Mt. 22:11–13; Rom. 6:2–13), which is brought about through the cross, and thus is the ultimate model of love of God, which can only be indissoluble.

Monogamy is the accepted form of union of two human persons, male and female, which prevails and is sanctioned in genuinely Christian societies. The exceptions would be in societies where there was a serious shortage of one or the other genders of persons. But for Christians, Christ gave the union of a man and woman a sacramental character. Man and woman are made for each other in faithfulness, under rewarding mutual conditions (cf. 1 Cor. 6:15–20; 11:3–16; Mt. 19:3–9). (See Marriage, Sacrament of.)

## Monophysism, also Monophysitism

This heresy was begun by Eutyches (d. 454) and condemned by the Council of Chalcedon in 451. It held that there was but one composite nature in Christ. (See Heresies.)

## Monotheism

The belief in one God or the belief in the unity of God is called monotheism. This unity of God is unique, a mystery, but one that can be learned from revelation to the extent that faith is attained and satisfied. This unity was revealed in a progression of revelations, from Abraham to whom the oneness of God was shown (Gn. 26:24; 28:13; 31:53), through Moses to whom it was shown that there could be no other gods (Ex. 3; 20:3–7; 34:14). Through the Incarnation it was revealed that God possessed such unity that He could be from Himself yet in God, that is, the Word made flesh, and all culminate in the divine unity of God's love, the Holy Spirit who fulfills the Church. Thus there is a trinity of Divine Persons but the one God.

In the Church this unity is again manifest, for Christ prayed that all might be one, that there would be unity in the whole body of the Church (Jn. 17:11–23). And it is through the Church that the entire universe is gathered up in Christ, or as St. Paul teaches: "By the might of his glory you will be endowed with the strength needed to stand fast, even to endure joyfully whatever may come, giving thanks to the Father for having made you worthy to share the lot of the saints in light. He rescued us from the power of darkness and brought us into the kingdom of his beloved Son. Through him we have redemption, the forgiveness of our sins. He is the image of the invisible God, the first-born of all creatures. In him everything in heaven and on earth was created, things visible and invisible, whether thrones or dominations, principalities or powers; all were created through him and for him. He is before all else that is. In him everything continues in being. It is he who is head of the body, the Church; he who is the beginning, the first-born of the dead, so that primacy may be his in everything. It pleased God to make absolute fullness reside in him and, by means of him, to reconcile everything in his person, both on earth and in the heavens, making peace through the blood of his cross" (Col. 1:11–20).

The opposite, the contradiction of monotheism is atheism. There are three forms of monotheism, two derived not from revelation but from theories of complex evolution of the god-concept. Thus, besides absolute monotheism as revealed, there is pantheism, which concludes that there is but one God but that every created or existent thing is in some manner a part of Him or that God is in all that is made. Then there is relative monotheism wherein there are a variety of gods, but only one of these is worthy of worship.

But the Christian acceptance of the unity of God attests to Christ being Himself the active presence of God in us (Gal. 2:20–21; Phil. 1:20–21; 2:12–13). Being "in Christ" has a mystical significance for the Christian, an ontological aspect, since through Christ all was gained for us (Rom. 6:4; 8:11; Gal. 2:20; Eph. 3:16; 2 Cor. 13:5). (Cf. Trinity, the Most Holy.)

## Monothelism, also Monothelitism

In the seventh century, when the emperor and the patriarch of Constantinople sought to bring the eastern factions together, the heretical teaching was advanced that Christ had only one will, both human and divine, thus denying the humanity of Christ. This heresy was condemned by the sixth ecumenical council of Constantinople in 680.

## Mons Pietatis

"Pawnshops for the poor," that is, funds to provide financial aid to the poor as loans or as

direct aid, were set up in the early sixteenth century through the Fifth Lateran Council (1511) and operated throughout Italy, France, Spain, and the Low Countries. They no longer operate as Church institutes, since they have been replaced by other charitable organizations on a diocesan or national basis.

## Monsignor

Monsignor is a title of honorary prelates of the pontifical household, both active and honorary, but who have no jurisdiction as prelates. There are various classes of honorary prelates ranging in degree of rank: (1) Apostolic Prothonotaries, (2) Honorary Prelates of His Holiness, and (3) Chaplains of His Holiness. Their title is Reverend Monsignor (abbreviated: Rev. Msgr.), and they are addressed either as Monsignor or Father. In dress they are permitted to wear violet, with the cassock and vesture varying according to the grade and the ceremonial function. (Cf. Rochet; Mantelletta.)

## Monstrance

Also called *ostensorium,* this is the special vessel for presenting the Eucharistic Host for adoration by the faithful. It is the portable shrine wherein the Blessed Sacrament is placed at the ceremony of exposition. The monstrance may be made of any metal, but mostly it is of gold or silver, solid or plated. Since the sixteenth century, when it came to be shaped like the sun, surrounded by rays, the monstrance has evolved to a degree that it may be of any suitable shape or size. However, by dignity it should be of high art in design and decoration. It is obligatory that there be a small cross on the top of the monstrance (S.R.C. 2957), and it is proper that it should not be ornamented with small statues or representations of saints. The lunette, bearing the host, is placed into the monstrance.

The monstrance is not required for exposition of the Blessed Sacrament except when there is to be a procession, extended exposition with devotional prayers or benediction. It is one of the sacred vessels and should not be ensconced simply as a decorative piece of church furnishings.

## Montana Case

Named because it was submitted to the Congregation of the Holy Office by the bishop of Helena, Montana, this marriage case concerned a nonbaptized man validly married to a woman baptized in the Anglican Church. After divorce, the man wished to become a Catholic, be baptized, and marry a Catholic. The decision of the pope through the Holy Office was to dissolve the previous nonsacramental marriage in favor of the faith, thus permitting a licit and valid marriage to the Catholic party. (Decision of Nov. 6, 1924.)

### Montanism

The heresy, begun by Montanus of Phrygia (circa 156) and flourishing for a short time, was based upon an unhappy and austere code of conduct; it denied the forgiveness of sins. Tertullian became an apostate by becoming a Montanist in 207. (See Heresies.) The Montanists expected a new kingdom of God to come about quickly and held that they should live apart from sinful mankind; thus they caused a social conflict by a denial of man and his works. Montanism also claimed a separate and superior revelation, and its own prophets assumed an authority over that of the bishops. Reaction against the heresy caused it to lose its appeal after the leaders were excommunicated.

### Montessori Method

The Montessori method is the system of teaching developed by Maria Montessori (1870 to 1952), the noted woman doctor who was both a psychiatrist and an authority on pedagogy. She first introduced a system of teaching feeble-minded, retarded, or less intelligent children in 1898 when she began the Orthophenic School, teaching according to the theories of the French physician, Eduard Seguin. In 1907 she opened her own school, the *Casa dei Bambini* (House of the Small Children) for underprivileged children. It was here that she, under opposition from more conventional systems of teaching, applied the methods of freedom of movement and practice, under a program of good order or sustained discipline.

In 1912 Dr. Montessori published her first book, *The Montessori Method,* which described her work and procedures for learning that she practiced among the slum children of Rome. As far as methodology is concerned, she merely sought to recognize and permit exploration of a child's periods of greatest sensitivity in the habits learned, which in turn might lead to great strides in the learning process. It was a success as a psychologically applied system, which has been recognized and adopted in many private and public schools throughout the world.

### Month's Mind

This is the nonofficial name for the anniversary requiem Mass said a month after the death or burial of a person. It is and has been a pious custom but is disappearing from practice because of both a strengthening of faith and the cost of stipends.

### Moral Rearmament

This is the name that has become the title of a system of moral reform begun by Dr. Frank N.D. Buchman (1878 to 1961). It thus also is known as Buchmanism.

Fundamentally its teaching is that of Protestant revivalism, but followers of Moral Rearmament (MRA) claim that it is not a religious movement but an ideological system. It claims that it can change people, friend and foe, strangers and the inhabitants of all nations. This is to take place through a broad borrowing of religious terminology, the most modern of communications systems and publicity, testimonials of notable persons, and an appeal to the higher classes of society. All summed up in the phrase "world changing through life changing," MRA seeks to propagate the message that everyone should be witness to "honesty, disinterestedness, purity and love." It is a system of moral resurrection without the cross.

In 1955 the Holy Office addressed a warning letter through the apostolic delegate in Canada, stating: "The Sacred Congregation is astonished to see Catholics and even priests seek certain moral and social objectives, however praiseworthy they may be, in the bosom of a movement which possesses neither the patrimony of doctrine or of spiritual life nor the supernatural means of grace which the Catholic Church has. It is even more astonishing to see that certain people have an exaggerated enthusiasm which apparently makes them believe that the methods and means developed by Moral Rearmament are more efficacious in this movement than in the Catholic Church itself. The danger of syncretism and of religious indifference, of which warnings have been given on Moral Rearmament, can no longer be ignored."

### Moral Theology

Properly, this is part rather than a division of the science of theology. In its more restricted sense, moral theology deals with God's laws, specifically with the determination whether acts are right or wrong in the light of God's laws. It provides the scientific exposition of human conduct as directed by reason and faith to the attainment of our supernatural end. It gives us the fundamental rules by which we must regulate our actions and discusses the application of these rules in an innumerable variety of circumstances, covering the whole of life. Moral theology is divided into three major parts: first principles, the commandments, and the sacraments (cf. Theology).

Greater emphasis upon making moral theology

serve life in a pluralist world for the Christian was stressed by Vatican II. "The institutions, laws, and modes of thinking and feeling as handed down from previous generations do not always seem to be well adapted to the contemporary state of affairs. Hence arises an upheaval in the manner and even the norms of behavior.

"Finally, these new conditions have their impact on religion. On the one hand a more critical ability to distinguish religion from a magical view of the world and from the superstitions which still circulate purifies religion and exacts day by day a more personal and explicit adherence to faith. As a result many persons are achieving a more vivid sense of God" (GS 7).

## Moral Virtues

The habits whereby the human will and sensual appetites are under the control of reason to thus enable the person to act accordingly are called moral virtues. Their object is goodness as opposed to the intellectual virtues whose object is truth, and so we may say that the moral virtues lead us to God, causing us to act "as it is written" or "as God wills." Simply, the human person has to be the master of his lusts (1 Cor. 6:12; 10:23).

There are several groupings of moral virtues, such as the basic four, the cardinal virtues of prudence, justice, fortitude, and temperance; the habitual virtues, which are acquired; and the infused virtues, which are produced supernaturally by God through grace. To these one must add those distinctions within the various virtue groups themselves, such as, the practical virtues or simply good habits; the social virtues of good manners and behavior; the political or expedient virtues, such as honesty in business and probity in political life. All the moral virtues are interrelated in some manner and are recognized by pagans and Christian as the means of practicing and living a good life. (See Cardinal Virtues; Basic Teachings for Catholic Religious Education.)

## Morality

In concept morality is the experience one has of the good. This has a dependence in life upon the basic structure of society, its *mores,* the environment, society, custom, and the community. When these areas of dependence are refined or understood in the light of education, faith, and the guides for a knowledge of the good, the human person becomes more free, for morality is not a juridical experience, that is, enforced law, but an experience of the consciousness of conduct.

1. The first means of this experience are prime,

namely, conscience by which one becomes aware of his own identity with the good. "Conscience is the most secret core and sanctuary of a man. There he is alone with God, whose voice echoes in his depths" (GS 16). By the formation of a right or informed conscience one is made aware of the good. As Vatican II goes on to teach: "Conscience frequently errs from invincible ignorance without losing its dignity. The same cannot be said of a man who cares but little for truth and goodness, or of a conscience which by degrees grows practically sightless as a result of habitual sin" (GS 16). (See Conscience.)

2. When one recognizes that conscience has a purity when it is attuned to faith, or when faith in Christ and the moral conscience are in harmony, then there is an abhorence for sin. One then acts to seek God with all one's heart and soul (2 Ch. 6:36–39), attaining a clear conscience, which places the Christian in direct relationship to Christ (Heb. 9:13–14; 10:19–23).

3. Morality for the Christian is not one of law but of response. It becomes faith acting through love. It attains a perception of action that attends to merit, that is, grace, or as St. Paul says: "Sin will no longer have power over you; you are now under grace, not under the law" (Rom. 6:14). The benefit is life in Christ (Rom. 14:23).

4. Realistically the Christian lives in an environment that is fallen, nonsympathetic to the life of faith or grace. It is here that the human person does not make compromise but works toward realizing the aspirations of all in a secularized society. Respect for conscience must be attained and the means of bringing the secular world to recognition of the good must be more widely used. Vatican II teaches: "The good news of Christ constantly renews the life and culture of fallen man. It combats and removes the errors and evils resulting from sinful allurements which are a perpetual threat. It never ceases to purify and elevate the morality of peoples" (GS 58).

## Morality Play

This term is applied to any religious drama that points out the struggle between virtue and vice, for example, *Everyman.* (Cf. Miracle Plays.)

## Moravian Church

This early heretical Christian Church followed the reform ideas of John Huss (d. 1415). It began as an evangelical movement in 1457 gathering church groups in Bohemia, Moravia, and Poland under the name *Unitas Fratrum* (Unity of the Brethren). They came to be known as Moravians in the eighteenth century. After the Catholic Reformation (1545 to 1563), the external organization of these churches was drastically changed and the *Unitas Fratrum* were absorbed into the Catholic, Lutheran, and other church bodies.

The modern history of the Moravians begins in 1722, when a group of those who had retained their tradition set up a colony, really a refuge, in Saxony on the estate of Count Nicholas Ludwig von Zinzendorf, their sponsor. It was at this estate, Herrnhut ("Lord's Watch"), that new members were added and a missionary effort was launched. And with centers established in England and America, the Moravians embarked on a missionary program that was the prototype of the modern Protestant missionary movement.

The teaching of the Moravians centers on the gospels; they practice infant baptism, celebrate a Communion service at least six times a year, and use a litany in Sunday morning service. While they have wide freedom in their forms of service, their hymnology is fully developed. Their beliefs are much in accord with other evangelical churches, maintaining the Headship of Christ over the church and the assertion that the church is His body.

The Moravian Church in America is divided into two provinces, south and north including Canada, and is ruled by a synod made up of clergy and laity forming a legislative assembly.

### Morganatic Marriage

A Morganatic marriage is a licit and valid marriage between a man of noble rank and a woman of inferior rank. It is usually subject to the condition that succession of the family title will not descend to the children. It does not differ in any way, insofar as Church law is concerned, from any other marriage and carries no special favors outside of the law.

### Mormons

The members of the Church of Jesus Christ of the Latter-day Saints are called Mormons. The name derives from a prophet who they maintain was the author of *The Book of Mormon*. It is not a church in the mainstream of Protestant thought. Mormonism arose in America after the claimed revelation to the founder, Joseph Smith (1805 to 1844) at Fayette, New York. Smith maintained that from 1820 to 1827 he received a number of visitations from heavenly beings, notably an angel named Moroni, who revealed to him that he was to found a new religion. To this end, Moroni told Smith of two golden plates, descended from two Jewish tribes who had come to the New World before the Christian era began. These plates were hidden in a hill somewhere between the towns of Manchester and Palmyra, New York. When these plates were located by Smith, he also found two miraculous stones called Urim and Thummim, which provided the means of translating the inscribed accounts on the golden plates. Upon completion of the translation, the plates disappeared and have never been seen since, although it is claimed they were taken up to heaven again by Moroni.

The translation of the plates by Smith led to the publication of *The Book of Mormon* (1830). It tells that the Western Hemisphere was settled by a Hebrew tribe called the Jaredites following the confusion brought about by God after the construction of the ziggurat, the Tower of Babel. It further records the emigration from Jerusalem of the tribe called the Nephrites who came to America in the year 600 B.C. Also it speaks of how Christ visited America after His resurrection and established His true church among these Nephrites who then died out in A.D. 420. The golden plates will be brought forth with a new tide of believers.

The Mormons have several branches namely, the original Mormons; then a group of separated brethren (1846) called the Reorganized Church of Jesus Christ of Latter-Day Saints, whose headquarters are in Independence, Missouri; and four smaller groups: the Temple Lot, the Bickertonites, the Cutlerites, and the Strangites.

The doctrine of the Mormons is liberal, with no set creed, but they accept in principle the teaching of the Apostles Creed. They believe in the Trinity, accept the Bible as fundamental, and hold that *The Book of Mormon* and the present revelation are issued as Doctrine and Covenants. They have an ordained priesthood (First Presidency, twelve Apostles, Seventy or seven quorums), High Priests, High Council Evangelists, bishops, elders, teachers, and deacons. They teach that God is immutable and that every person can approach God through spiritual gifts of confirmation, baptism by immersion, and healing (cf. Jas. 5:15).

### Morning Offering

Morning offering is a prayer recited each morning upon rising, which places the intention of offering all the works, prayers, sufferings, and joys of the day to God who sustains life and provides the food and means of making the day one in keeping with the will of God the Father. In the Liturgy of the Hours, the communal prayer of the Church, "the Morning prayer is designed to sanctify the beginning of the day. Many parts of the hour make that clear. Saint Basil the Great described very well the character of morning prayer: 'The Morning Prayer consecrates to God the first feelings and thoughts of our hearts; we should undertake no other care before we have been gladdened by the thought of God, for so it is written, *I was mindful of God and was gladdened,* nor should the body set itself to any task before we have done what is said here: *I pray to you, Lord, for at daybreak you listen for my voice; at dawn I hold myself in readiness for you. I watch for you'* (Ps. 5:4–5)." And the Liturgy of the Hours begins with the invitatory: "Lord, open my lips. And my mouth shall proclaim your praise" (followed by Ps. 95).

It is recommended for all the faithful that they unite their own activities of each day with the communal prayer of the Church, especially if they are not praying the Liturgy of the Hours. This can be a simple prayer, and it may be recalled often during the course of the day. As an example of such an offering, here is a Franciscan morning prayer:

> Jesus Lord, I offer you
> this new day because
> I believe in you, love you,
> hope all things in you
> and thank you for your
> blessings.
> I am sorry for having offended
> you and forgive everyone who
> has offended me.
> Lord, look on me and
> leave in me
> peace and courage
> and your humble wisdom
> that I may serve others
> with joy, and be
> pleasing to you all day.
>            *(Franciscan Herald Press)*

## Morning Star

Although the words morning star, plural and singular, appear in the Bible (Jb. 38:7; Is. 14:12) and have been translated as "Lucifer" or "Satan" in the Vulgate and more recent English versions, there is a wonderful recognition that Christ is the morning star. He is the One who is coming again, and so we await "until the first streaks of dawn appear and the morning star rises in your hearts" (2 Pt. 1:19). And Christ will give victory, that is, resurrection to those faithful (Rv. 2:28), and this means Christ will give Himself for He calls Himself the "Morning Star" (Rv. 22:16).

## Morse

The morse is the clasp that fastens and holds a cope about the shoulders. The morse may be of metal, consisting of a hook and eye or chain and hook arrangement, or it may be of cloth. Metal clasps are not used in Rome. The morse may be jeweled but only for copes of prelates.

## Mortal Sin

The transgression, with full knowledge and free consent of the will, of a divine law (every just law is derived from the divine law, either natural or positive) in a serious matter is a mortal sin. Sin is mortal because of: (1) Matter, which means when the nature of sin is such that it can never be venial (for example, unbelief, lewd actions) or when the matter is important compared to a light matter (for example, theft of a valuable as compared with stealing a trifle). (2) Full knowledge, which means the absolute consciousness that the act is mortally sinful. This clear awareness may be had when one makes up his mind to act and need not be a conscious advertence while performing the act. (3) Free consent of the will, which means that one freely wills an act even though he recognizes that the act is seriously sinful. (Cf. Sin.)

When the three essential conditions are present, the result of mortal sin is the loss of sanctifying grace, the loss of the gifts of the Holy Spirit, remorse, and the punitive effect of eternal separation from God. To avoid these consequences, the reception of the Sacrament of Penance is required to return to the love of God.

## Mortification

Mortification is any conscious form of self-denial. It is defined as: "The struggle against our evil inclinations in order to subject them to the will, and the will of God." Such ascetical practices are necessary to the perfection of the Christian: "Whoever wishes to be my follower must deny his very self" (Lk. 9:23). It is obvious that a closer union with God can only be attained by detaching oneself from love of material things (cf. Detachment). However, mortification should be effective; that is, it should be directed by a pure motive, for example, to give up sweets in order to lose weight is essentially different from mortifying one's love for sweets out of love of God. Although mortification involves the entire makeup of the pleasure urge of one's body, mind, and soul, it must be performed with discretion. At the same time, there is a broad basis for application, for example, all the senses may be subject to self-denial, thus custody of the eyes to avoid looking at or seeing pleasurable subjects may be practiced in many ways. (Cf. Asceticism.)

## Mosaic Law

Mosaic law, religious, moral, and civic, is contained in the first five books of the Bible. All law of the Hebrews had to be in keeping with the Law given by God to Moses on Mount Sinai (Ex. 20:1–24). This law was guarded by the priestly class and taught with joy to the people (Ps. 9:8–13).

There are five separate codes of law in the OT, and they can all be classed as Mosaic in nature if not in application: (1) the Decalogue or Ten Commandments (Ex. 20:1–17; Dt. 5:6–21); (2) the Law of the Covenant, which follows the Decalogue (Ex. 20:22 through 23:19); (3) the Code of Priests (Ex. 25 through 31; Lv. 1 through 16 and 23 through 27; Nm. 3 through 10; 17 through 19; 28 and 29); (4) the Law of Holiness (Lv. 17 through 22); (5) the Code of Behavior (deuteronomic) (Dt. 12 through 16).

The coming of Christ was the fulfillment of the Law (Lk. 16:16; Mt. 5:18), and when He died on the cross, the new covenant with mankind was sealed.

## Moses

Moses is the dominant figure of the Biblical persons recorded in the OT. Little is known about the interior thought of Moses, although his life is recorded in the Book of Exodus and he is mentioned 771 times in the OT.

The life of Moses was really his work. His mission, because he was spared by faith (Acts 7:35–44), was to lead the chosen people from Egyptian exile to the promised land. And in the mind of St. Stephen it was the vocation of Moses to prefigure the coming of the Son of God into the world. It was God who chose Moses to be His messenger, and he was a prelude to the sending of His Divine Son who in turn sent the Apostles (Mt. 10:19–20; Jn. 1:17). It was Moses who was favored by God but who sealed the covenant with blood, and Christ sealed the new covenant with His own precious blood (Mt. 26:28).

Moses was a lawgiver, presenting the Law given to him by God on Mount Sinai (Ex. 19:1–3; 20:1–24). And Christ was the lawgiver of His new law, but His law was born of the authority He had as God Incarnate (Mt. 5:43–45). Thus was Moses a prefigurement of Christ, but under the New Covenant the law is now a regimen of grace (Rom. 5:15). The Lawmaker, Christ, who rules over the hearts and minds of all human persons is now present in the paschal mystery, the Eucharistic memorial of His suffering and death and His continuing presence and love (1 Jn. 2:7–11).

## Moslems

Moslems are followers of Mohammedanism. Vatican II declares: "Upon the Moslems . . . the Church looks with esteem. They adore one God, living and enduring, merciful and all-powerful, Maker of heaven and earth and Speaker to men. They strive to submit whole-heartedly even to His inscrutable decrees, just as did Abraham, with whom the Islamic faith is pleased to associate itself. Though they do not acknowledge Jesus as God, they revere Him as a prophet. They also honor Mary, His virgin mother; at times they call on her, too, with devotion. In addition they await the day of judgment when God will give each man his due after raising him up. Consequently, they prize the moral life, and give worship to God especially through prayer, almsgiving, and fasting" (NA 3). (See Mohammedanism; Islam; Koran.)

## Mother of God

See Mary, Virgin Mother of God.

## Motive, Spiritual

Spiritual motive is the reason or purpose for action, which imparts an added moral goodness to a good act. (Cf. Love of God.)

## Motu Proprio

Literally, from the Latin, "by one's own accord," this term refers to papal documents, containing the words, *Motu proprio et certa scientia*. These documents are written on the personal initiative of the pope and are either administrative or confer personal favors of the pontiff.

## Movable Feasts

Because the Church calendar is determined upon a luni-solar cycle, there are some feasts that occur earlier or later in the civil calendar. The dates of these feasts are set by their place in regard to the feast of Easter. The feast of Easter is always the first Sunday following the first full moon after the vernal equinox, March 21. Easter, therefore, may come as early as March 22 or as late as April 25. The movable feasts, established in each year in relation to the date of Easter, are: Ascension Day, Pentecost, Trinity Sunday, and the feast of Corpus Christi. There are also other feasts that may be considered as movable from the standpoint that they do not fall on the same date but are determined by the calendar adjustment. (Cf. Calendar, Church; Feasts of the Church.)

## Mozarabic Rite

Also called the Rite of Toledo or the Visigothic or Isidorian rite, this was derived from the Gallican rite and used throughout Spain and what is now Portugal until the eleventh century. It is now used only in a chapel of the Cathedral of Toledo, chiefly as a memorial. The rite differs from the Roman in many aspects; for example, the bread and wine are prepared before the Entrance, the Gospel is sung, and it has multiple prefaces.

## Mozzetta

A nonliturgical vestment, the mozzetta is a short cape of silk or wool reaching to the elbows, open in front and only fastened at the throat although it has a row of buttons for fastening. To the collar in the back is affixed a small hood which, however, is not used but is rather a vestige of a vestment of earlier times. The mozzetta is worn over the rochet, is a mark of jurisdiction, and is permitted to be worn by cardinals, archbishops, and bishops in their own dioceses and by abbots in their abbeys.

## Mundatory

The linen towel used as a purificator in the Mass is sometimes referred to as the mundatory.

## Muratorian Fragment

This partial manuscript, written before A.D. 200 contains a list of books (canon of Scripture) that were recognized as authoritative at Rome at the end of the second century. The fragment was discovered by Muratori in the Ambrosian Library of Milan in 1740 and named after him. It includes the four Gospels, the Epistles of St. Paul (except the letter to the Hebrews), two Epistles of John and Jude, and the Book of Revelation.

## Music, Church

Music for the Church must be in accord with the spirit of the liturgy (c. 1264). Not recommended for general use in Church are Masses by Mozart, Haydn, Farmer, Lambilotte, Schubert, Wiegand, and also music based upon profane operas.

Music has always been a traditional part of the Eucharistic Celebration. The reform of the Liturgy brought about by Vatican II placed greater emphasis upon music as a communicating medium, a participation in the liturgy, and a renewal of forms and applications. There of course must be a gradualism in bringing about the change from traditional Church music (cf. *Motu Proprio* of Pope St. Pius X, Nov. 22, 1903) to the modern adaptations and instrumental uses that liturgical renewal envisions. A musical heritage is both traditional and developing in an ongoing process, but all music of the Church should be worthy of the worship of God in whatever celebration this takes place. Such a process must be carried on through a training in the priestly and deaconate candidacy, liturgical appreciation, and catechesis of all Church members.

That Church music has its place in fulfilling the mission of the Church was stated by the director of the Italian Association of Saint Cecilia (Sept. 26, 1974): "It is the wish of the Supreme Pontiff that public celebrations should not take place without some minimum of song, and that every Church should resound with music which elevates those present closer to God, satisfies their innermost aspirations, and strengthens their communion in faith and love."

Vatican II teaches: "The musical tradition of the universal Church is a treasure of immeasurable value, greater even than that of any other art. The main reason for this pre-eminence is that, as sacred melody united to words, it forms a necessary or integral part of the solemn liturgy.

"Holy Scripture, indeed, has bestowed praise upon sacred song (cf. Eph. 5:19; Col. 3:16), and the same may be said of the Fathers of the Church and of the Roman pontiffs who in recent times, led by St. Pius X, have explained more precisely the ministerial function rendered by sacred music in the service of the Lord.

"Therefore sacred music increases in holiness to the degree that it is intimately linked with liturgical action, winningly expresses prayerfulness, promotes solidarity, and enriches sacred rites with heightened solemnity. The Church indeed approves of all forms of true art, and admits them into divine worship when they show appropriate qualities.

"Accordingly, this sacred Council, keeping to the norms and precepts of ecclesiastical tradition and discipline, and having regard for the purpose of sacred music, which is the glory of God and the sanctification of the faithful, decrees as follows:

"Liturgical action is given a more noble form when sacred rites are solemnized in song, with the assistance of sacred ministers and the active participation of the people. . . .

"Great importance is to be attached to the teaching and practice of music in seminaries, in the novitiates and houses of study of religious of both sexes, and also in other Catholic institutions and schools. To impart this instruction, teachers are to be carefully trained and put in charge of the teaching of sacred music. . . .

"Religious singing by the people is to be skillfully

fostered, so that in devotions and sacred exercises, as also during liturgical services, the voices of the faithful may ring out according to the norms and requirements of the rubrics. . . .

"In the Latin Church the pipe organ is to be held in high esteem, for it is the traditional musical instrument, and one that adds a wonderful splendor to the Church's ceremonies and powerfully lifts up man's mind to God and to heavenly things.

"But other instruments also may be admitted for use in divine worship, with the knowledge and consent of the competent territorial authority. . . . This may be done, however, only on condition that the instruments are suitable for sacred use, or can be made so, that they accord with the dignity of the temple, and truly contribute to the edification of the faithful.

"Composers, filled with the Christian spirit, should feel that their vocation is to cultivate sacred music and increase its store of treasures.

"Let them produce compositions which have the qualities proper to genuine sacred music, not confining themselves to works which can be sung only by large choirs, but providing also for the needs of small choirs and for the active participation of the entire assembly of the faithful.

"The texts intended to be sung must always be in conformity with Catholic doctrine; indeed they should be drawn chiefly from holy Scripture and from liturgical sources" (SC 112-121).

The New Order of the Mass stresses the importance of singing in participation in the liturgy: "The faithful who gather to await the Lord's coming are urged by the Apostle Paul to sing psalms, hymns, and inspired songs (cf. Col. 3:16). Song is the sign of the heart's joy, and St. Augustine said: 'To sing belongs to lovers.' Even in antiquity it was proverbial to say: 'He prays twice who sings well.'

"Singing should be widely used at Mass, depending on the type of people and the capability of each congregation, but is is not always necessary to sing all the texts which were composed for singing.

"Preference should be given to more significant parts, especially those to be sung by the priest or ministers with the people responding or to those to be sung by the people together" (SC ch. VI).

In *The Ministry of Music* by W.A. Bauman (The Liturgical Conference) the setting of music in worship is given: "Music is ordered sound, reflective of thoughts and feelings of perhaps several artists: composer, arranger, performers. It is sound produced and ordered for listeners, with regularity and variation, with rhythm and tempo and pitch and intensity and timbre. It sings out and

sustains and varies precisely so that another person may hear it and grasp its message. It is communication; it is sharing; it can be true and beautiful; it can be at the heart of life and the focus of hope. It can be love. It can reach out to a whole community at once, sharing, enriching, serving. . . .

"The sound could be any sound—a drum, a horn, a harp, or a human voice. It is heard in a holy setting, a moment of prayer. It ought to be an honest sound, a true sound, a beautiful sound. It ought above all to be a servant sound to their prayer. This is a fundamental concept for the church musician—that music is the servant of prayer. There is no other reason for the musical utterance than to serve the prayer of the community. It is in this servant role that worship music gains its unique dignity, its precise value. If music becomes master rather than servant, it loses its reason for being. It becomes no more than entertaining communication. But in its servant role to prayer, music has a unique importance surpassing that of the other arts and more praiseworthy than any other use of music. . . .

"The servant role of music is by no means exhausted by its role in sung and heard texts. Service music performed with sensitivity to the actions and rhythms of worship continues to be a major opportunity for the musician. When the community reflects and meditates, when the gestures of prayer are unaccompanied by prayer texts (processions, preparation of bread and wine, cleansing of vessels, etc.) music serves the prayer. Every community benefits from a good prelude in the spirit of the day's prayer. Even choral music in which the word is not supreme can be used at such times for the human voice is the most versatile of all instruments. A reading is heard and the people are called to deeper reflection as a flute plays softly over plucked guitar strings.

"Music as servant to prayer thus has a threefold role in our worship: (1) To enrich the actual prayer texts of the people; (2) to better communicate texts the people listen to, be these texts God's word in scripture, calls to elicit prayer, or reflections upon word and prayer; (3) to accompany and embellish nonverbal prayers such as silent meditation and various gestures.

"In each and every case the music is clearly the servant of prayer. We are not praying at a musical performance. We are enriching the prayer of a community." (See Gregorian Music; Chant.)

### Music Coordinator

Music Coordinator is the title applied to the parish or diocesan director of music for

Church services. It is a distinct role of ministry and thus may be applied to a choir director, an organist, to one specially hired to teach and direct the musical arts, or to a special music teacher. When this role involves teaching, directing, and the playing of one or more instruments in a Church community setting, the person is salaried at professional wages. If the work of directing or playing the organ is done by several persons, the salaries are to be of the degree relative to the competence and service. It is not usual, when this person is so employed, that he or she share in stipends, stole-fees, or special offerings for services. Because this position is new in the Church, the standards are usually established by the diocesan Liturgical Commission.

## Music, Liturgical

See Music, Church.

## Myron

The Greek word meaning "sweet oil" is the name given to the Holy Chrism used in the Byzantine and Orthodox Rite Churches. It may be blessed only by Patriarchs or other Primatial heads of Churches. The oil is used in the administration of the Sacrament of Confirmation and thus is sometimes applied to the sacrament itself as a popular title.

## Mysteries of the Rosary

Mysteries of the Rosary are those events in the lives of Jesus and His Mother, Mary, upon which one is to meditate while reciting the prayers of the Rosary, either privately or publicly. There are fifteen mysteries, one for each of the fifteen decades of the Rosary. Each subject should be spoken or thought of before beginning a decade and, according to the practice of meditation, kept in mind during the reciting of the prayers. For convenience, and in sequence, the mysteries are divided into three groups of five. The *Joyful Mysteries* are: the Annunciation, Visitation, Nativity, the Presentation, and the Finding of the Child Jesus in the Temple. The *Sorrowful Mysteries* are: the Agony in the Garden, the Scourging, the Crowning with Thorns, the Carrying of the Cross, and the Crucifixion. The *Glorious Mysteries* are: the Resurrection, the Ascension, the Descent of the Holy Spirit, the Assumption of the Blessed Virgin into Heaven, and the Coronation of the Blessed Virgin as Queen of Heaven. It is also recommended that a cycle of these mysteries be observed when saying the Rosary daily, that is, a Rosary of

five decades. Thus, Monday the joyful mysteries are meditated on, Tuesday the sorrowful, and Wednesday the glorious. On Thursday, the cycle begins again. The Sunday cycle is this: during Advent and until Septuagesima Sunday, the joyful mysteries; from Septuagesima until Easter Sunday, the sorrowful mysteries; on Easter Sunday and continuing through to the first Sunday of Advent, the glorious mysteries are to be meditated upon. (Cf. Rosary.)

## Mysterium Fidei

See Transubstantiation.

## Mystery

1. The supernatural truths that the Church teaches and that cannot be known without revelation are not contrary to reason, but rather above reason. They are of such a profound nature that they cannot be understood by humans even after revelation and must, therefore, be accepted on faith in revelation and the authority of the Church. St. Paul speaks of the "mystery" as being that of the redemption, a composite of all the other mysteries: "No, what we utter is God's wisdom: a mysterious, a hidden wisdom. God planned it before all ages for our glory. None of the rulers of this age knew the mystery; if they had known it, they would never have crucified the Lord of glory. Of this wisdom it is written: 'Eye has not seen, ear has not heard, nor has it so much as dawned on man what God has prepared for those who love him.' Yet God has revealed this wisdom to us through the Spirit" (1 Cor. 2:7–10). To St. Paul, the greatest proof of God's love for us was our redemption in Christ (Eph. 1:7–12). Mysteries must be considered as ideas or works of God that are beyond the reach of natural human knowledge. Such mysteries, while they are innumerable in human experience, are part of belief in the Church, for example, the Redemption, the Incarnation, the Trinity, and the Eucharist.

Mystery is of kerygmatic importance, for it shows God as an infinite being (GS 19); it gives the human person the clarity to see the message of God even in his own personal experience and accept the reality of God's love; and it makes clear our relationship to the life of grace whereby we are fulfilled and ultimately come to glory and union with God.

2. From the Greek word meaning "something hidden," mystery is the ordinary word for a sacrament in the Eastern Churches. (See Mystery, Paschal.)

## Mystery of Christ

Although God is a "hidden God" and we come to Him only through following the message of Christ, Vatican II teaches: "To carry out the will of the Father, Christ inaugurated the kingdom of heaven on earth and revealed to us the mystery of the Father" (LG 3).

And: "Wherever God opens a door of speech for proclaiming the mystery of Christ (cf. Col. 4:3), there should be announced (cf. 1 Cor. 9:15; Rom. 10:14) to all men (cf. Mk. 28:19) with confidence and constancy (cf. Acts 4:13, 29, 31; 9:27–28; 13:46; 14:3; 19:8; 26:26; 28:31; 1 Thes. 2:2; 2 Cor. 3:12; 7:4; Phil. 1:20; Eph. 3:12; 6:19–20) the living God, and He whom He has sent for the salvation of all, Jesus Christ (cf. 1 Thes. 1:9–10; 1 Cor. 1:18–21; Acts 14:15–17; 17:22–31)" (AG 13).

## Mystery, Paschal

It is through the Church, founded by Christ, that the memorial of His death, resurrection, and promise of the kingdom is fulfilled. This is especially true of the Eucharist, which is celebrated by the priest and people in union with Christ. Vatican II declares: "This Church of Christ is truly present in all legitimate local congregations of the faithful which, united with their pastors, are themselves called churches in the New Testament. For in their own locality these are the New people called by God, in the Holy Spirit and in much fullness (cf. 1 Thes. 1:5). In them the faithful are gathered together by the preaching of the gospel of Christ, and the mystery of the Lord's Supper is celebrated, 'that by the flesh and blood of the Lord's body the whole brotherhood may be joined together'" (LG 26).

And: "By an apostolic tradition which took its origin from the very day of Christ's resurrection, the Church celebrates the paschal mystery every eighth day" (SC 106). (See Eucharist, Celebration of.)

## Mystery of Salvation

The pursuit of the unknowable by the human person is the salvific will of God directed toward the individual by grace. Vatican II teaches: "Wishing in His supreme goodness and wisdom to effect the redemption of the world, 'when the designated time had come, God sent forth His Son born of a woman, . . . that we might receive our status as adopted sons' (Gal. 4:4–5). 'He for us men, and for our salvation, came down from heaven, and was incarnate by the Holy Spirit from the Virgin Mary.' This divine mystery of salvation is revealed to us and continued in the Church, which the Lord established as His own body. In this Church, adhering to Christ the Head and having communion with all His saints, the faithful must also venerate the memory 'above all of the glorious and perpetual Virgin Mary, Mother of our God and Lord Jesus Christ'" (LG 52). (See Mystical Body of Christ.)

And: "By His death and His resurrection the Lord completed once for all in Himself the mysteries of our salvation and of the renewal of all things. He had received all power in heaven and on earth (cf. Mt. 28:18). Now, before He was taken up into heaven (cf. Acts 1:11), He founded His Church as the sacrament of salvation, and sent His apostles into all the world just as He Himself had been sent by His Father (cf. Jn. 20:21). He gave them this command: 'Go, therefore, and make disciples of all the nations. Baptize them in the name of the Father, and of the Son, and of the Holy Spirit. Teach them to carry out everything I have commanded you' (Mt. 28:19–20). 'Go into the whole world and proclaim the good news to all creation' (Mk. 16:15)" (LG 5). (See Salvation History.)

## Mystic

1. The human person who practices the extraordinary prayer of contemplation and union with God. In such prayer the mystic cannot do without symbol and image. It is prayer that has a rhythm and a heightened state of consciousness that is little understood but cannot be classed with "visions" or "voices" or other mystical phenomena.

2. Mystic prayer or extraordinary prayer is that prayer of union with God. The word mystic is used for "those supernatural acts or states which our own industry is powerless to produce, even in a low degree, even momentarily" (Poulain). This is what is called a mystic state and one to which only God can transport a person. St. Teresa of Avila, one of the greatest of mystics (along with St. John of the Cross, St. Catherine of Genoa, St. Gertrude, and St. Catherine of Siena) states in one of her letters to Father Rodrigo Alvarez: "Supernatural—so I call that which no skill or effort of ours, however much we labor, can attain to, though we should prepare ourselves for it, and that preparation must be of great service. . . ." Further she relates: "This is a thing supernatural, and which we cannot acquire with all the diligence we use." (Cf. Prayer.)

St. John of the Cross declares that this prayer is so far above the reality of humans as we know it and understand it that "the soul can never attain to the height of the divine union, so far as it is possible in this life, through the medium of any forms or figures." (That is by use of a formulated prayer practice, or a schema of prayer.) By this the saint meant that mystic prayer is of the *mind*, purely and simply, to that degree which God permits and for that purpose which God intends, and after the profoundest of preparation. Dionysius the Areopagite says: "The highest and most divine things which it is given us to see and to know are but the symbolic language of things subordinate to Him who Himself transcendeth them all: through which things His incomprehensible Presence is shown, walking on those heights of His Holy Places which are perceived by the mind" *(De mystica Theologia,* I, 3).

It is called "the Song of Love." For the Christian, the beginning of this prayer is "through Him, with Him, in Him," whereby each prepares in worship and service for the ultimate and when each will be able to see the bright supernatural glory of God. It is thus through the Eucharist that we escape from our separation from God and prepare for union with Him. Some human persons attain this gift of union on earth, this mystic prayer, as a direct gift of God, but even they, as St. Paul says, "see only darkly as in a mirror" (cf. Col. 1:25–27; 2:2–3). As stated in *Mysticism* by Evelyn Underhill: "All things are perceived in the light of charity, and hence under the aspect of beauty: for beauty is simply Reality [God] seen with the eyes of love." (See Mysticism; Prayer.)

## Mystical Body of Christ

The truth of faith, embracing the Scriptural teaching of Christ as the Head and the members of the Church as the "body" of Christ. Pope Pius XII in his encyclical, *Mystici Corporis Christi (The Mystical Body of Christ,* 1943) writes: "If we would define and describe this true Church of Jesus Christ—which is the One, Holy, Catholic, Apostolic, Roman Church—we shall find no expression more noble, more sublime or more divine than the phrase which calls it 'the Mystical Body of Jesus Christ.' This title is derived from and is, as it were, the fair flower of the repeated teaching of Sacred Scripture and the Holy Fathers." Pius XII then goes on to state who are members of the body: "Only those are really to be included as members of the Church who have been baptized and profess the true faith and who have not unhappily withdrawn from body-unity or for grave faults been excluded by legitimate authority." The term has been in use in the Church since the ninth century, but its basis in Scripture is most secure. St. Paul spoke of the "head of the Body" (Col. 1:18), and while the Head

is distinct from the body, it is united (Col. 1:24) with the body and is the cause of the supernatural growth of all the members. This is the teaching of the early Church, for all were "in Christ" and each was to grow into the likeness of Him, an image of the invisible God, and subserving the good of the whole, a unity based on charity.

Life "in Christ" begins with baptism (1 Cor. 10:1–2), and is continued through sanctifying grace and in the moral response that the human person makes to the commands and will of God (Gal. 1:15; Rom. 12:3–8; 1 Cor. 12:1–12), and this is extended to the community of the Church (Rom. 6:5; 8:29). Life "with Christ" will be participation in His kingdom and glory (Col. 3:4; Rv. 20:4). (See Church.)

## Mystical Sense of Scripture

Besides the literal sense (cf. Literal Sense of Scripture), there is another, the mystical sense of Scripture. It is also called spiritual or typological. Through this there is found a meaning authoritatively revealed by God to man, though not the exact meaning of the words. St. Thomas Aquinas states: "The things signified by the words (literal sense) may also signify other things (spiritual sense)." Thus the spiritual sense is founded upon the literal sense, with the spiritual sense brought out upon the solid findings of interpretation. There can be no exact limit on the ways in which the spiritual sense is derived, but there are certain guides: (1) We can make a derived understanding from the manner of expression, for example, if the literal sense is expressed in a metaphor, then the spiritual sense is in the metaphor, for example, Christ referring to Peter as the "rock," the spiritual sense being that in this person is the "foundation" stone of the Church. (2) We may gather, since the OT as a whole prefigures the NT, that there are types of the OT that prefigure the Church on earth, and this is the allegorical sense, which, like the anagogical, is a kind of spiritual sense (cf. Allegorical Interpretation, Biblical; Anagogical Sense, Biblical). The spiritual sense of Scripture, because of the difficulty in interpretation, should be used sparingly and founded upon sound exegesis. (Cf. Form Criticism.)

## Mystical Theology

More properly called ascetical theology, this portion of the science of theology is the furthest development of moral and ascetical theology. It considers not the ordinary ways of perfection but the extraordinary ways. As such it deals with infused contemplation, special supernatural gifts, and all supernatural experiences and phenomena related to contemplation. (Cf. Theology.)

## Mystici Corporis Christi

The Latin title of the encyclical of Pope Pius XII, issued on the silver jubilee of his ordination as a bishop, June 29, 1943, is translated *Of the Mystical Body of Christ*. It introduced a revival of the Pauline teaching of the Mystical Body and gave singular impetus to the liturgical movement that culminated in the documents and decrees of Vatican II. It also closed further discussion of this teaching. (See Mystical Body of Christ; Church.)

## Mysticism

The subject matter proper to ascetical theology is the study of the mystic states. In regard to the mystic, the word refers to those supernatural acts of states that our own industry is not able to produce, even in a low degree, or for a short, momentary time. St. Teresa of Avila reduces these to degrees of mystical contemplation, naming four: (1) the prayer of quiet, wherein the spirit rests without distraction; (2) full union, in which the presence of God is dominant; (3) ecstasy, in which the senses are not used; (4) transforming union, or the presence of God and the sharing of the divine life of Christ. This is one system, but there may be others in the sequence of perfection. Mysticism is the approach and investigation, and even participation, in the supernatural life.

It should be understood that mysticism is not restricted to a privileged few, for through response to the teaching of Christ and ascetical practice and prayer, the human soul attains mystic knowledge, which is fulfillment (cf. Jn. 10:10; Rom. 5:20; Eph. 1:8; 1 Tm. 1:14). There is a constant exchange whereby this mystic knowledge is gained: through prayer wherein we speak to God and through the revealed word (scripture) wherein God speaks to us. Thus there is for everyone, through the sacraments, especially the Eucharist, and through the reception and exercise of the mission of the Church, and in the self-communication of God in faith and love, the formation of a "mystical being." This leads to the salvation of one, the possession of uncreated grace through possession of the "font of grace" himself (cf. Mt. 11:28; Rv. 20:4).

## Mysticism, Eastern

Eastern mysticism is the formulation of practices of prayer, which in certain religions produce a control of the physical properties of the body through positions, mind control, and biological control as "yin and yang" and hatha yoga. However, it is admitted that posture and physical state have been a part of western mysticism. But in eastern mysticism this does not make it genuine, for the mystic can attain union with or contemplation of God only through asceticism and then after receiving this grace directly from God. (See Mystic.) Otherwise such practices lead to magic, diabolism, and the occult. (See Mysticism.)

## Myth

From the Greek word meaning "word" or "message," the term myth is probably based on an Indo-European word meaning "to think" or "to consider," and it also appears in the writings of Homer as "plan" or "purpose."

It can be said that myth, in its functional use, explains the origin of events or actions, and thus myths are the jumping-off point for things or events that humans cannot immediately grasp from their experiential knowledge.

Myths have appeared in all cultures and are used by the writers of scripture, for example, Sir. 20:19; 1 Tm. 1:4, and in accounts of creation, prophecies, and in the gospels. The romantic writers have used myths as a means of communicating realities that had some relation to the truth but were not really the same as the truth they wished to express, as in *Gulliver's Travels*.

## Nag Hammadi

This is the name of the Egyptian city, which has also become the name of a collection of thirteen books or ancient manuscripts found near there in 1946. Written in two dialects of the Coptic language upon parchment leaves and bound in codex form, these contain fifty-three writings of a Gnostic sect that existed from the first to the fourth centuries A.D. Among these are the "Gospel of Thomas," a collection of fourteen sayings of Christ, and mention of many other Gnostic writings that have long been lost. The colophon of the writing of Thomas appears at the end of the tract, in accord with the ancient practice of the scribes.

## Nahum, the Book of

The Book of Nahum is a prophetical book of the OT written by Nahum, whose name means "comfort." Little is known of the author except that he was an Elcosite of the tribe of Simeon, living in the town of Elcos. The book was probably written between 622 and 612 B.C. The writing is highly poetic, and the main theme is the fate of Nineveh, the oppressor of the people.

Its doctrinal content is evident in the emphasis on the judgment of God in the destruction of an evil city. For the Hebrews, this was a desired riddance of a hated capital city, and their joy over its destruction was an expression of their thankfulness to God for exercising His justice.

## Name, Christian

The Christian name is the name given to a child in baptism. It should be the name of a saint or a name abbreviated or derived from a saint's name. It is entered on the baptismal record. If the parents have not chosen a saint's name, the pastor supplies one, and this name together with that chosen by the parents is recorded on the baptismal certificate (c. 761).

It is also a practice, though not an obligation, to take the name of a saint at the time of receiving the Sacrament of Confirmation. Also when one enters a Third Order or becomes a professed religious, it is customary to choose a saint's name, and this saint in turn becomes one's patron or patroness in the spiritual life.

## Name Day

This is the day on which the feast of the saint whose name one bears is celebrated. In some countries the name day is observed rather than the birthday anniversary.

The customs vary, for example, Spanish-speaking people give the name "Jesus" to male offspring and some title of Our Blessed Mother to girls. However, this custom is weakening because of the duplication. The Irish often preface a name with the Gaelic "gil" meaning "servant," thus "Gilchrist" is translated "Servant of Christ."

## Name of God

Because a name is often the means of identifying a person or the name affirms one's ability to know someone (Gn. 29:32; 30:24; Ps. 9:11; Is. 52:5–6; Jgs. 13:6), it was for the Chosen People to name their God, the One Who had made a covenant with them. The name of God is *El* or *Elohim*, but the most personal name to the Chosen People was *Yahweh.* God has revealed His name to His faithful, but He reveals that His name is incommunicable—God's name is God Himself. Thus God revealed Himself: "God replied, 'I am who am.' Then he added, 'This is what you shall tell the Israelites: I AM sent me to you.' God spoke further to Moses, 'Thus shall you say to the Israelites: The Lord, the God of your fathers, the God of Abraham, the God of Isaac, the God of Jacob, has sent me to you. This is my name forever; this is my title for all generations'" (Ex. 3:14–15). Thus God was identified for the Israelites as the One who was revealed to them through the elders and the prophets. But this was not enough for them to fully understand, so they had to speak of Him through His attributes: His glory (Ex. 9:16; Jos. 7:9; 1 Sm. 12:22; Jer. 14:21); His omnipotence (Ex. 15:3; Ps. 106:7–12; Is. 52:13 through 53:12); the Most High *(El-Elyon)* (Gn. 14:17–24; Ps. 18:14); *God Sabaoth,* the heavenly ruler who ruled the worlds' powers, the Lord of Hosts (Is. 6:3; 9:18; 10:16). Christ, like Yahweh, is the Lord (Phil. 2:9; Heb. 1:4), and His name can also be invoked and believed in (Jn. 1:12).

In the NT the Christian finds God the Father revealed through Christ His Son (Jn. 12:28; 17:6). The name of God is hallowed (Mt. 6:9; Lk. 11:2). We pray to God the Father in the name of the Son (Jn. 14:10–16; cf. Mt. 18:19–20). And the Holy Spirit is the true witness (1 Jn. 5:5–10) whereby we too give witness to God together with and in Christ (Jn. 15:18–19; Acts 9:31; 13:52; 15:28–29; Rom. 15:4–5). (Cf. God; Yahweh.) Also the Christian, if he speaks against God, blasphemes the name of God (Rom. 2:24; Rv. 16:9) or that of the Lord (1 Tm. 6:1). It is the noble name that the Christian himself bears (Jas. 2:7).

## Name of Mary

The first mention of this name is made in Genesis. It was the given name of the sister of Moses. (Cf. Mary, Virgin Mother of God.)

## Names of Our Lord

Jesus Christ as the Second Person of the Blessed Trinity has been given a variety of names descriptive of His accomplishment of our redemption. Many of these are derived from the OT, from the descriptive names given to Christ by the Apostles, and many are names of honor given to our Lord by Christian writers or found in the liturgy. Examples from the OT are: Immanuel (Is. 7:14), Holy One and Prince of Peace (Is. 9:5); from the NT: Beginning and end (Rv. 1:8), Lamb of God (Jn. 1:29), Wisdom of God (1 Cor. 1:24). (Cf. Name of God.)

## Narcotics

See Gluttony.

## Nash Papyrus

A fragmentary piece of papyrus found in Egypt in 1902 by the archaeologist W. L. Nash, containing chiefly the Ten Commandments (Dt. 5:6–21), is the oldest surviving piece of the Hebrew OT at this time. It is thought to date from the second century before Christ and has the sixth and seventh commandments transposed followed by the Shema. (Cf. Shema.)

## National Assembly of Women Religious (NAWR)

For many years the disparate sisterhoods in the United States have felt a need for a more cohesive group to express their views and bring about concerted action. Thus in April, 1970, in a national convention the NAWR was formed with the intent of giving a "voice" to the sisters of the United States. The Assembly's objectives are: "to challenge women religious to communicate a valid concept of the role of the consecrated celibate women in the Church today, and to study, evaluate, establish priorities and make recommendations concerning areas in which women religious are critically needed."

With this lofty intent the sisters have been able to bring about changes in the localities where they have been called to give service and to formulate programs that would give an organized potential expression in local, national, and international affairs, especially where the liberation of oppressed peoples was concerned.

Membership in the NAWR may be held by individual sisters, sisters' councils, organizations of sisters, as well as clergy and lay associates. Headquarters are located at: 201 E. Ohio Street, Chicago, Illinois 60611.

## National Black Sisters' Conference (NBSC)

Organized in 1968, this Conference is unique to the United States and the offshore islands. It has for its prime purpose not the attainment of a division into nonintegrated bodies of sisters, but the achieving of an embrasive course of action along the priorities that will best serve the Black people. Thus the Conference has representation from many congregations of women religious and includes the Black sisters as members regardless of their affiliations in religious life.

The Conference has specific purposes: the "development of continuance of black vocations to religious life in the unique contemporary black life style"; the effective liberation of Black people; the setting up of a central supply center for information in religious life for Black sisters; the evaluation, extension, and personal apostolic fulfillment of Black sisters in religious life; aid to local programs and community services of organizations; better Black community schools and organizations and prison reform. The Conference publishes a quarterly, *Signs of Soul*. Its headquarters are at: 3508 Fifth Ave., Pittsburgh, Pennsylvania 15213.

## National Catholic Conference for Interracial Justice

The National Catholic Conference for Interracial Justice is the primary agency for formulating programs to foster better understanding among all races. The national body, with headquarters at 1307 S. Wabash Ave., Chicago, Illinois, 60605, serves Catholic human relations groups, urban groups, affairs groups, and sponsors educational programs on racial problems in city or rural communities.

The Church has from its foundation been opposed to any form of race discrimination or prejudice (cf. Acts 10:15, 25–28; Jn. 13:35; 17:22–23). The human person has a unique dignity, and each shares the Sonship of the Father through Christ. (See Anti-Semitism.)

## National Catholic Educational Association (NCEA)

Organized July, 1904, at St. Louis, Missouri, the Association has been and continues to be an agency for dispensing information and service to the parochial, diocesan, and national schools of the Church. In 1929 it assumed the title of National Catholic Educational Association. It serves teachers and entire school systems under these general aims: (1) to promote improved means of teaching, administration, and educational methods in Catholic schools in keeping with the principles and philosophy of Catholic education; (2) to give assistance and encourage scholarly research in the fields of education and school administration; (3) to serve as an agency for the exchange of information through news releases and publications concerning programs, curricula, texts, and general information for those engaged in teaching.

Being both an advisory group of experts and a participating body of experienced persons in the area of education, the Association has progressed in keeping with the newest developments in teaching aids, visual and audio, graphic and technical. It thus affords a means of improving the education of youth in parochial schools, high schools, colleges, universities, and seminaries as well as serving as a facility for spreading the necessary information among all participating teachers or agencies. It holds an annual national convention, usually the week following Easter, and its headquarters are located at: Suite 350, One Dupont Circle, Washington, D.C. 20036.

## National Catholic Organizations

Besides those listed especially because of their older, or in some instances newer, formation, the following are national groups whose activities cover a wide spectrum of service and association.

National Alliance of Czech Catholics
National Apostolate for Mentally Retarded
National Association of Catholic Chaplains
National Association of Church Personnel Administrators
National Association of Laity
National Association of Priest Pilots
National Association of Religious Brothers
National Catholic Bandmasters' Association
National Catholic Cemetery Conference
National Catholic Coalition for Responsible Investment
National Catholic Conference for Interracial Justice
National Catholic Development Conference

National Catholic Educational Association
National Catholic Forensic League
National Catholic Guidance Conference
National Catholic League for Religion and Civil Rights
National Catholic Music Educators' Association
National Catholic Office for Information
National Catholic Order of Foresters
National Catholic Pharmacists Guild
National Catholic Players of Catholic University
National Catholic Rural Life Conference
National Catholic Stewardship Conference (Cf. Stewardship.)
National Catholic War Veterans
National Catholic Women's Union
National Center for Church Vocations
National Christ Child Society
National Church Goods Association
National Clergy Conference on Alcoholism
National Coalition of American Nuns
National Conference of Catholic Charities
National Council of Catholic Laity (Cf. Laity.)
National Council of Catholic Men
National Council of Catholic Women
National Federation of Catholic Physicians Guilds
National Federation of Laymen
National Federation of Priests' Councils
National Office for Black Catholics
National Organization for the Education of Roman Catholic Clergy
National Sisters Vocation Conference
National Theatre Arts Conference
(See separate listings of national and United States' groups.)

## National Catholic Social Action Conference (NCSAC)

This association of organizations and individuals was formed in 1958 to serve as a guide and aid to laypeople engaged in social programs, to promote better organized approaches, and to further the application of sound social teachings of the Church to institutions and action groups throughout the United States. Besides being a clearing house through which pertinent information is channeled to members for uniform action, the Conference states its purposes as follows: (1) to give a sense of solidarity in the Mystical Body to all social actionists; (2) to increase the effectiveness of social action in those engaged in this apostolate; (3) to encourage the formation of other action groups in areas where they are needed; (4) to formulate the means of attaining a greater formative influence on national opinion; (5) to come to a total concept of the place and role of Catholic social action in our society in these times. (Cf. Social Action.)

## National Catholic Welfare Conference

As a successor to the National Catholic War Council (1918 to 1919), this national organization of the Catholic bishops of the United States was called into being on February 20, 1919. The first meeting of the National Catholic Welfare Conference (NCWC) was held September 24, 1919. The conference had advisory powers only, not jurisdictional, and as such was not looked upon as a formal council. Thus, when not in formal council, the bishops merely deliberated, suggested, and recommended to all bishops their resolutions for adoption throughout the United States. Yearly the conference prepared and publicized a joint statement expressive of the common viewpoint of the assembled bishops. The conference was organized to direct its attention to a wide variety of national problems concerning the Church and to procedures which, although friendly recommendations, bore the dignity of the teaching sphere of the Church.

In organization there was first an administrative board, which met annually in the spring at Washington, D.C. This board was headed by a chairman elected by the board members for a term of one year, and he was assisted by a vice-chairman, secretary, and treasurer. It was the work of this board to supervise through the heads of departments, as based upon the Papal Brief, *Communes*, of Pope Benedict XV, April 10, 1919. These departments were: the Executive Department, Department of Education, Legal Department, Press Department, Department of Catholic Action Study, Department of Lay Organizations, Department of Social Action (Social Work and Hospitals), and the Department of Youth. Besides these standing departments there were a number of episcopal committees, each concerned with a special work of current or permanent importance. Some of these committees were the American Board of Catholic Missions, Committee on the Propagation of the Faith, on the Confraternity of Christian Doctrine, on Seminaries, for Polish Relief, for the Spanish-speaking, on Motion Pictures, on War Emergency and Relief, for the Montezuma Seminary, to complete the Shrine of the Immaculate Conception, on the National Organization for Decent Literature, on the Mexican Seminary, for the North American College at Rome, and the Special Committee to Promote the Pope's Peace Plan. Their joint work, the annual statement of the assembly, and the periodic statements of the committees were a catalogue of Catholic Action in the United States.

This organization has been supplanted by the National Conference of Catholic Bishops (NCCB) and its sponsored body, the United States Catholic Conference (USCC). (See under separate entries.)

## National Conference of Catholic Bishops (NCCB)

The National Conference of Catholic Bishops is the national ecclesiastical body made up of the bishops of the United States through which the juridical authority of the Roman Catholic Church is exercised officially for the entire country. All bishops who have served or are now serving the Church in the United States and its territories and possessions are members and have voting rights.

The Conference was established by joint action of the United States hierarchy on November 14, 1966, and was set up with the approval of the Holy See in keeping with the directions of the *Decree on the Pastoral Office of the Bishops in the Church* (CD) of Vatican II. It was ratified during the November, 1967 meeting of the Conference of Bishops. It is a territorial conference, operating through an organizational structure, with elected officers (president, vice-president, treasurer, and general secretary), and it operates through a series of committees.

Administrative Committees are: the Executive Committee (officers); Committee on Budget and Finance; Committee on Personnel and Administrative Services; and the Committee on Research, Plans and Programs. These Bishop-Chairmen and other bishops form the Administrative Board.

The standing committees are: the American Board of Catholic Missions; Arbitration; Canon Law; Church in Latin America; Doctrine; Ecumenical and Interreligious Affairs; Lay Apostolate; Liaison with Priests, Religious and Laity; Liturgy; Men Religious; Missions; Nomination of Bishops; North American College, Louvain, Belgium; North American College, Rome, Italy (cf. separate listing); Pastoral Research and Practice; Permanent Diaconate; Priestly Formation; Priestly Life and Ministry; Vocations; Welfare Emergency Relief; and Women Religious.

Ad hoc committees, now numbering eleven, vary with the social and religious concerns of the nation and the participation of the priests, religious, and laity.

The NCCB, for meetings either quarterly or more often, and for the better operational procedures, has twelve geographic regions: (1) Maine,

Vermont, New Hampshire, Massachusetts, Rhode Island, Connecticut; (2) New York; (3) New Jersey, Pennsylvania; (4) Delaware, District of Columbia, Florida, Georgia, Maryland, North Carolina, South Carolina, Virgin Islands, Virginia, West Virginia; (5) Alabama, Kentucky, Louisiana, Mississippi, Tennessee; (6) Michigan, Ohio; (7) Illinois, Indiana, Wisconsin; (8) Minnesota, North Dakota, South Dakota, Wyoming, Colorado; (9) Iowa, Kansas, Missouri, Nebraska; (10) Arizona, Arkansas, New Mexico, Oklahoma, Texas; (11) California, Hawaii, Nevada, Utah, Caroline-Marshall Islands, Guam; (12) Idaho, Montana, Alaska, Washington, Oregon.

General headquarters are located at: 1312 Massachusetts Ave., N.W., Washington, D.C. 20005.

Vatican II taught much concerning the proper role, the ordinary, immediate, papal, national, and international place of the bishop in the Church of today. As Pope Paul VI said in speaking to the Italian Bishops (December 6, 1965), "To be a bishop today is a more demanding, difficult, and perhaps, humanly speaking, more thankless and dangerous task than ever before."

Concerning conferences of bishops, Vatican II teaches: "Nowadays especially, bishops are frequently unable to fulfill their office suitably and fruitfully unless they work more harmoniously and closely every day with other bishops. Episcopal conferences, already established in many nations, have furnished outstanding proofs of a more fruitful apostolate. Therefore, this most sacred Synod considers it supremely opportune everywhere that bishops belonging to the same nation or region form an association and meet together at fixed times. Thus, when the insights of prudence and experience have been shared and views exchanged, there will emerge a holy union of energies in the service of the common good of the churches.

"Wherefore, this sacred Synod issues the following decrees concerning episcopal conferences:

"1. An episcopal conference is a kind of council in which the bishops of a given nation or territory jointly exercise their pastoral office by way of promoting that greater good which the Church offers mankind, especially through forms and programs of the apostolate that are fittingly adapted to the circumstances of the age.

"2. Members of the episcopal conference are all local Ordinaries of every rite, coadjutors, auxiliaries, and other titular bishops who perform a special work entrusted to them by the Apostolic See or the episcopal conferences. Vicars general are not members. De jure membership belongs neither to other titular bishops nor, in view of their particular assignment in the area, to legates of the Roman Pontiff. . . .

"3. Each episcopal conference is to draft its own statutes, to be reviewed by the Apostolic See. In these statutes, among other agencies, offices should be established, which will aid in achieving the conference's purpose more efficaciously: for example, a permanent board of bishops, episcopal commissions, and a general secretariat.

"4. Decisions of the episcopal conference, provided they have been made lawfully and by the choice of at least two-thirds of the prelates who have a deliberative vote in the conference and have been reviewed by the Apostolic See, are to have juridically binding force in those cases and in those only which are prescribed by common law or determined by special mandate of the Apostolic See, given spontaneously or in response to a petition from the conference itself.

"5. Wherever special circumstances require and the Apostolic See approves, bishops of many nations can establish a single conference.

"Moreover, contacts between episcopal conferences of different nations should be encouraged in order to promote and safeguard their higher welfare.

"6. It is highly recommended that when prelates of the Oriental Churches promote in synod the discipline of their own churches and more efficaciously foster works for the good of religion, they take into account also the common good of the whole territory where many churches of different rites exist. They should exchange views on this point at interritual meetings held in accord with the norms to be given by the competent authority" (CD 37-38). (See United States Catholic Conference; Bishop; Jurisdiction.)

## National Council of Catholic Laity (NCCL)

As a coordinating organization the National Council of the Laity is a coalescence of two other Councils, namely, the National Council of Catholic Men and the National Council of Catholic Women. By bringing together the affiliated member-groups of these two large bodies of Catholics, along with other national lay groups, the NCCL represents some 15,000 organizations in the United States. Thus through clearing-house procedures and planned programs the Council makes it possible to offer services in leadership training, the publication called People, and diocesan and national programs. This is the prime national group of the

Catholic Laity with representation in all dioceses, in organizations, and indirectly in all state conferences, which are in contact with councils of the laity, from parishes to diocesan councils, through the offices of the laity in the dioceses. The NCCL operates with a national board of directors, elected officers, and an executive secretary. The national headquarters are located at 1312 Massachusetts Ave., N.W., Washington, D.C. 20005.

## National Council of Churches

In the United States this is the largest organization of ecumenical and cooperative church groups. It was established in 1950 and at present has three main program divisions working through five commissions. It is directed in its missions, educational, and communicational activities, its regional and local ecumenical works together with its relief services, by a governing Board of Directors of approximately 350 members. Its headquarters are at 475 Riverside Drive, New York, N.Y. 10027. (See World Council of Churches.)

## National Councils of Catholic Men and Women

These are organizations that comprise the United States Catholic Conference Department of Lay Organizations. They unify Catholic activity of more than three thousand national, state, diocesan, and local organizations of the laity. (See National Council of Catholic Laity.)

## National Federation of Priests' Councils (NFPC)

Organized in May, 1968, this Federation is composed of Priests' Councils, Priests' Senates, and diocesan Presbyteries of affiliated groups from the dioceses of the United States and its territories. There are also memberships of provinces of men religious and national priests' organizations. The Federation publishes a monthly entitled *Priests/ USA*. The headquarters are located at: 1307 S. Wabash Ave., Chicago, Illinois 60605.

Although the Federation is not an official group, it is constitutionally organized. Financially it is supported by the assessed dues of each member of a priests' council where the council is affiliated with the NFPC. Its purposes are: to give priests' councils a representative voice in matters of concern to the Church and with respect to problems facing the nation, including racism and poverty; to improve communications among priests throughout the country; to coordinate programs of research and make recommendations to priests, bishops, and others on specific matters; to cooperate with lay persons, religious, and bishops in better meeting the contemporary needs of the Church. (See Priests' Councils.)

## National Pastoral Council

A council that would serve the Conference of Bishops in an advisory role has been named a National Pastoral Council. It has been described generally as a "national-level body representing many segments of U. S. Catholicism and dealing with a broad range of issues of concern to the Church."

As a recommended national course of involvement made by Vatican II, this has been one of the slowest to develop and come to fruition. The problems are many and in larger countries seem to center on the type of representation such a council should have. Three possible solutions have been proposed: the membership shall be by appointment, or by general election, or by the designation of existing organizations supplying designated or elected representatives. The membership has been rather definitely fixed to be composed of lay men and women, religious and clergy.

The reasons that the concept of a national pastoral group have faltered in its organization are at present many and involved. Questions such as the following have been raised: Who will direct this group? Will it be liberal? Will it pick only those concerns that touch a few, or will it be more generally oriented? Will it confront the genuine and most vexing problems to face the country, or will it be provincial and divided? Many more questions could be presented. Fundamentally, in the years since the close of Vatican II this has been the area chosen to be the dupe of involvement, based on a false assumption that when one introduces democratic procedures, one must assure that all viewpoints are represented and have a voice.

The National Pastoral Council has been under consideration in the United States since 1970. No decisions have been reached on formation by the national steering committee, yet there is a claim that the Advisory Council of the USCC serves in such a capacity. Meanwhile, in other countries progress has been made, and internationally the Vatican Council on the Laity functions.

The lines are drawn quite sharply over whether a National Pastoral Council would have no authority, even shared, to set doctrinal matters or if such a Council would have limited competence in areas of collegial decisions of the body of bishops. The approach seems to be one of "wait and see." During the present delay in functioning the council is being utilized only for "pastoral consultation," which serves little purpose in keeping with the concept of a National Pastoral Council.

The Dutch Pastoral Council of the Netherlands has been cited as a too-liberal group for genuine communication in the Church. It is apparent that "dialogue" functions two ways: to join all in concerted action or to divide all into opposing units. The difficulty with National Pastoral Councils is present in these two lines of communication, and the result will be a slow determination of the use of such a national body in the structured society called the Church. (See Diocesan Pastoral Council; Parish Council.)

### National Synod

See Synod; United States Catholic Conference.

### Nationalism

Nationalism is a strong response on the part of individuals to their culture, traditions, history, language, and native institutions. Regard for one's country may develop a sense of exclusion from other nationalities; thus it takes on the coloring of racism or an antagonism to the people of other countries. It should not be confused with patriotism, which is the devotion and loyalty that all share as members of a national community.

Vatican II states: "The Christian faithful, gathered together in the Church out of all nations, 'are not marked off from the rest of men by their government, nor by their language, nor by their political institutions.' So they should live for God and Christ by following the honorable customs of their own nation. As good citizens, they should practice true and effective patriotism. At the same time, let them altogether avoid racial prejudice and bitter nationalism, fostering instead a universal love for man" (AG 15).

### Native American Party

See Know-Nothingism.

### Nativism

Following the cessation of the last state-church establishments, in Massachusetts in 1833, the civil actions restricting Catholics disappeared from all states except New Hampshire where Catholics were not allowed to hold public office until 1877 and the state constitution discriminated against Catholics as late as 1941. Clashes between Catholics and others continued, however, and the spirit, if not the direct intent, of the former Alien and Sedition Laws came out again in the form of "Nativism." This was an aggressive movement against Catholics and the Catholic Church, which according to the Nativists, was becoming too politically powerful and dominant through the immigration of peoples from predominantly Catholic countries of Europe. This had the direct result of frightening many from coming to

America. Riots, arson, and general hostility toward Catholics occurred in Philadelphia, New York City, and elsewhere. Congress was urged by the Nativists to lengthen the time for naturalization of immigrants, but this was defeated and the Native American Party disappeared by the late eighteen-forties only to give rise to Know-Nothingism in the ten years before the Civil War.

### Nativity of Christ

Vatican II teaches: "This union of the Mother with the Son in the work of salvation was manifested from the time of Christ's virginal conception up to His death. It is shown first of all when Mary, arising in haste to go to visit Elizabeth, was greeted by her as blessed because of her belief in the promise of salvation, while the precursor leaped with joy in the womb of his mother (cf. Lk. 1:41–45). This association was shown also at the birth of our Lord, who did not diminish His mother's virginal integrity but sanctified it, when the Mother of God joyfully showed her firstborn Son to the shepherds and Magi" (LG 57).

### Nativity of Mary

Although the exact date of the birth of the Blessed Mother is not known, her genealogy is given in Mt. 1:1–16, and a feast celebrated on September 8 commemorates the event. (See Immaculate Conception.)

### Natural Law

Considered apart from the "natural" laws that are present in the physical sciences and nature, we mean here the natural moral law. Broadly it includes the entire field of morality, those rules whereby the human creature is governed by the Creator in the development of all his human qualities. The human person is free to act under these rules, because he is responsive to reasoned order, human dignity, and to societal obligations.

In theological writing no distinction is made

between natural law in its wider sense of moral law and its stricter sense of the laws of nature, for both arise from the Creator. Both are also complied with out of necessity (natural laws) or out of acts of free will corresponding to or acting against the will of God. Natural law thus has its foundation in the acquisition of a knowledge of the world in which the human person lives, an understanding of man in his relationship with his fellowmen and his society, and the attainment of a knowledge of God whereby the human person may act freely out of love.

The human person responds to God the Creator and all created things and finds a relationship fundamental to the attainment of moral action. (Cf. Conscience.) Thereby the human person finds a relationship between being and obligation, between the creature and the incumbent demand of the Creator whose will must be served. These principles are embodied within the human being; they are not juridical in nature but flow from his existence in the creative plan of God.

Through knowledge one can penetrate to basic truths, and while one cannot acquire a perfect knowledge of his own place in the natural order, still he can know the principles. Further, beyond this basic knowledge, man can come to know the elevated stature of his own being, his relationship to salvation, and the attainment of his proper end through cooperating with the grace of God.

Although the Church has claimed the right to make authoritative statements concerning the natural law, there are laws of nature that the theologian must examine with regard to the goals of creation. In this light there is a continuing process whereby the human person learns more about natural laws as they are unfolded by scientific investigation and makes the adjustments within the reach of his knowledge and its application to his life.

It is readily accepted by the entire Christian community that the natural moral law is within man. The law is not man himself but is in the purposeful nature of man (cf. Rom. 2:14–16). It is within man, in the recognition of his purposes and goals, the development of himself as a person, that the changes take place, for through these, functioning through grace, man seeks and attains his true being in God (cf. Rom. 13:10; Col. 1:9–14).

## Natural Theology

Also called theodicy, or "philosophical theology," this is the highest branch of the study of philosophy, which investigates and demonstrates what human reason, unaided by revelation, can know about God. It is contrasted with "revealed theology." In Scholasticism natural theology is treated as a part of philosophy, considering as the chief objects of its study: God insofar as He can be known through His work, the human soul, the freedom of the soul, the immortality of the soul, and natural law. (Cf. Rom. 1:18–32.) In St. Paul this ability on the part of man to come to a knowledge of religious truth is declared to exist because God himself "made it so." This is more closely defined in the writings of Vatican I (De fide Cath.) where this knowledge is explained as coming from man's dependence upon God the Creator (cf. also Wis. 13:1–9). The natural knowledge of God is a previous preparation for the complete revelation of God through Christ, which in the history of salvation is carried on through the Church. This is the completion of God's revealing of Himself, which is attained through faith and love.

## Natural Virtue

See Virtue.

## Naturalism

Naturalism is a rationalistic system of philosophy and theology, which denies the supernatural and centers on nature alone. It has two main arguments: rejection of God through a pantheistic concept that deifies nature, and rejection of revelation. As applied in moral philosophy, naturalism is called humanism. (Cf. Humanism.)

## Nature

Considered only in its theological sense, rather than in its laws and order in the universe, we contrast nature with person, that is, we consider nature in its supernatural aspect, namely, as having grace. From biblical teachings we come to understand "the grace of God through Christ," which is the revelation of God to man by which man becomes a transcended being. We thus consider the Christ-centered character of the world (cf. 1 Cor. 15:24–28, 44–49; Rom. 8:19–30; Eph. 1:8–10; 3:10–11; Col. 1:15–20; 3:4; Phil. 3:21; Heb. 1:2–3; Jn. 1:3; 12:32).

In revealed truth we learn: (1) there is no other grace for us but the grace of Christ; (2) the grace of Christ extends to us even if we are sinful that we may have life in God through Christ (cf. Lk. 5:8); (3) freed from sin and justified in Christ, we are transformed by the Spirit of God who extends to us faith, a filial confidence and hope in God, and a love for our fellowmen; (4) the Holy Spirit, sent to us, assures the principle of resurrection and life eternal with God through sharing in the glory of Christ.

In the Church human nature is vivified and given the singular immanence of God Himself. Vatican II teaches "that the Church, 'one interlocked reality, which is comprised of a divine and a human element,' is, 'by an excellent analogy . . . compared to the mystery of the incarnate Word. Just as the assumed nature inseparably united to the divine Word serves Him as a living instrument of salvation, so, in a similar way, does the communal structure of the Church serve Christ's Spirit, who vivifies it by way of building up the body'" (LG 8). The point of comparison in 'this excellent analogy' is the close and inseparable union between the natural and supernatural elements in the service of God's saving action. As the Word manifests Himself in the human figure of Jesus, so the Spirit of Christ makes himself visible in the social structure of the Church. The Spirit 'vivifies, unifies, and moves the whole body. This He does in such a way that His work could be compared by the Holy Fathers with the function which the soul fulfills in the human body, whose principle of life the soul is' (LG 7)" (Kloppenburg).

Further: "All men are called to belong to the new People of God. Wherefore this People, while remaining one and unique, is to be spread throughout the whole and must exist in all ages, so that the purpose of God's will may be fulfilled. In the beginning God made human nature one. After His children were scattered, He decreed that they should at length be unified again (cf. Jn. 11:52)" (GS 13). (See Salvation History.)

## Nave

The main or central space of a church, comprised of the area between the entry and the sanctuary, is the nave. Formerly this included the transepts, if there were any, but now a distinction is made. It is in this area that the faithful are assembled. The term is said to be derived from the Latin word for "ship" *(navis)*; thus the area was symbolic of the Church as the "bark of Peter."

## Nazarene, also Nazorean

1. One living in the town of Nazareth in Israel.
2. The title applied to Christ because of His residence there during the years before His public life (cf. Mt. 21:11; Acts 10:37). Christ was also called "the Nazorean" (Jn. 18:7; Mt. 2:23). There are twelve scriptural references to the fact that Jesus lived in Nazareth.

3. The early Christians were given the title of "Nazoreans" in derision (Acts 24:5).

## Nazarites

The Nazarites were a sect of the Israelites whose name is derived from the Hebrew word meaning "consecrated," and who were especially dedicated to the service of God. They professed rigid rules, abstained from eating or drinking the fruit of the vine, let their hair grow without cutting, and avoided defilement that they might incur by being near or touching a dead body (cf. Nm. 6). It was a custom for many Jews during the Greco-Roman period to make similar vows as expressions of their dedication, as did St. Paul (cf. Acts 18:18).

## NC News Service

See United States Catholic Conference.

## Necedah, False Apparitions of

Necedah is the name of the small town in Central Wisconsin near which the apparitions of the Blessed Virgin Mary were said to have taken place. These falsely claimed apparitions were to Mrs. Fred Van Hoof, a farm lady, beginning in 1950, and according to this woman who maintains she sees and talks with the Blessed Mother, they are still occurring. These are false apparitions for the following reasons: (1) upon investigation there was found to be a background of spiritualism; (2) there were false claims of cures, which were neither documented nor verified; (3) there was on the part of the visionary a series of false statements in recorded and witnessed testimony, which are evidence of two proofs of falseness, namely, invention or falsification on the part of the seer and the introduction of political allegations *(The Graces of Interior Prayer,* R.P.A. Poulain, S. J.; Herder, pp. 340 ff); (4) the association of monetary benefit and possible real estate speculation based upon the disclosures, for example, claiming the only safe place in a future war would be in or near Necedah; (5) the refusal to obey Church authority, resulting in the personal interdiction of Mrs. Van Hoof and others associated with her, imposed by the Bishop of La Crosse, Wisconsin, May 1975. (Those who are under a personal interdict may not receive the sacraments and sacramentals [c. 2260] and are deprived of ecclesiastical burial according to canon 1240, par. 1).

The investigations conducted over a period of 25 years have confirmed the above, but submission to the rulings of the Church has not been given to this date.

## Necromancy

From the Greek words meaning "dead" and "divination," this is the practice of attempting to foretell the future by trying to communicate with the dead. It was practiced by the Egyptians (Is. 19:3) and was borrowed by some Israelites (Lv. 19:31; 1 Sm. 28:3–9). In modern times it is called spiritism or spiritualism and is a fraudulent practice, even though there may be unexplainable occurrences attributed to psychic phenomena; it is a superstition.

In the Bible the recourse to necromancy was contrary to the will of God and is recorded as the cause of the death of Saul (1 Chr. 10:13). Those who practiced this form of spiritism were punished by stoning (Lv. 20:27; 2 Kg. 23:24), and the practice was considered a defilement by God (Lv. 19:31).

## Nehemiah, Book of

This historical book of the OT was written by an unknown author, named Nehemiah, who scholars believe to be the same as the writer of the first and second Books of Chronicles. In some texts of the Bible the two books, that is, the Books of Ezra and Nehemiah, were considered as one recording, which included first, the religious reforms introduced in the postexilic period by Ezra, and second, the activities of Nehemiah in building up the ruins of Jerusalem in that same time, the fifth century before Christ (444 to 432 B.C.).

Nehemiah was the cup-bearer of the Persian king Artaxerxes, and he gained the king's favor to such an extent that he was granted permission to visit Palestine and arrived in Jerusalem on a journey to aid the people. While there he supervised them in rebuilding the walls of the city. When his grant of leave from the king expired, he returned to the Persian court but in 432 B.C. returned to Jerusalem and introduced regulatory laws and religious reforms, such as observance of the Sabbath and the denunciation of intermarriage of the Jews with others. This work of reform was carried on more intensely by Ezra who lived some few years later and came from the north to exert a change of heart among the people. (See Ezra, Book of.)

## Neighbor

In the Christian understanding one's neighbors are not only the persons living nearby but are considered in the total complex of the social and religious community. The concept of neighbor includes the sharing of activities, the friendship, regard for human dignity and the service through love whereby the mission of Christ is fulfilled in an embrasive and expansive measure toward all members of the human race. Christ gave the example and answer in the Samaritan parable (Lk. 10:29), but since this involved personal sacrifice, it has been refused and neglected by the unthinking.

However, the Christian teaching is that which St. Paul expressed when he declared the Creator-responsibility of God toward every human person and that "In him we live and move and have our being . . . for we too are his offspring" (Acts 17:28). For the Christian the very concept of neighborliness has been associated with the fellowship of man, the sonship of God the Father, the redemption and merit won for all men by Christ. Thus the idea of neighbor is not only in the love of one's neighbor as a command, but in the respect and recognized worth of man for men, nations for individuals, and races for mankind. It is an extension of grace, acquired through the practice of personal virtue, even as H. D. Thoreau wrote: "Through our own recovered innocence we discern the innocence of our neighbors." And thus as an extension of the virtue of charity in its reflective understanding, love redounds to love itself, even as we all must love God in our neighbor rather than through extending humanitarian aid alone. (See Charity.)

## Nemours, Edict of

Demanded by the Catholic League of France and signed by Henry III of France (d. 1589), this edict outlawed Calvinism in France.

## Neomeniae

The collective name for the first feasts celebrated by the Jewish people, which were patterned after pagan feasts to which they had been exposed. These were at first not pagan in the Jewish celebration but were made naturalistic by them, giving the feasts a ritual that was religious in character, for example, the feast of the new moon (Nm. 10:10; Neh. 10:33–34). The feasts were agricultural or nomadic or nature-oriented. In their history they were salutes to the design of God in creation and followed the seasonal pattern.

Later these feasts were condemned by God because they became attached to sacrifices that were unsuitable (Is. 1:10–14; Hos. 2:13; Am. 8:5). But the prophets sought to make these feasts spiritual, more directed to God (Is. 66:23). One feast, that of the seventh month, was to become the feast of trumpets (Nm. 29:1–6; Lv. 23:23–25), while that of the last month, the New Year, was to recall the creation, light, and judgment.

In the Christian teaching even these feasts were to become raised to a more profound understanding; the feast of trumpets became transformed into the celebration of the new creation and the judgment (1 Thes. 4:16–17; Rv. 8 and 9). (See Hebrew Feasts.)

### Neo-Scholasticism

This movement, also called Neo-Thomism, was begun in the late nineteenth century, notably at the University of Louvain, France. Neo-Scholasticism was effective in bringing Thomistic thought back into favor. Pope Leo XIII aided it by making Scholasticism official in the Roman colleges and universities and introduced it into all Catholic schools with the publication of his encyclical, *Aeterni Patris* (1879). The movement attained wide influence and transformed the intellectual position of Catholic philosophy throughout the world. It continues with widespread teaching and publication of numerous journals of philosophy and new translations of the works of St. Thomas Aquinas. One of its greatest proponents was the late Jacques Maritain (d. 1973).

### Nesteia

Fasting and/or abstaining from food as practiced in the Byzantine and other Eastern Rites is known as Nesteia.

### Nestorianism

A heresy begun by Nestorius, a priest of Antioch, after he became patriarch of Constantinople in 428. He declared that the Blessed Virgin was mother only of Christ's human nature and he banned the term "Theotokos" (Mother of God); he also taught that only Christ as man died on the cross. This heresy was condemned by the ecumenical council of Ephesus in 431, but persists to this day in an isolated group of Syria who have a Nestorian diocese in Malabar. (See Heresies.)

### New American Bible (NAB)

The New American Bible is the most recent authentic translation of the Bible, made directly into English from the original languages with the aid of the latest discoveries of texts found through archaeological studies. The work of translation was begun in 1944 and completed in 1970; it was sponsored by the Bishops' Committee of the Confraternity of Christian Doctrine. It is the second "Confraternity edition" but differs greatly from the first in its adaptation of language to the modern understanding of people.

The work of translation was undertaken by members of the Catholic Biblical Association of America, aided by scholars from other faiths.

There have been considerable objections to the texts as rendered in the NAB, especially where linguistics were stretched to the accommodation point of popular understanding. However, where readability is desirable in preference to neglect or indifference, it must be conceded that the NAB is straightforward and highly understandable. It also has arranged the poetic portions of the Bible into verse form, making for linear clarity besides giving proper emphasis. While portions may lack the fluidity of rich and semantically pure language, the NAB has a directness and a distinct tone. Thus it is readable in a wide acceptance by the majority of people. A concordance is being prepared, which will be an aid to further understanding. The New American Bible is not the required translation but is used in the liturgical books with few exceptions and is used texturally and by citation in this book. (See Bible.)

### New Moon

See Neomeniae.

### New Order of the Mass

See Order of the Mass, New.

### New Testament

See Bible.

### Newman Movement

See Campus Ministry.

### Nicaea (Nice), Councils of

The first ecumenical council was convoked at Nicaea by Constantine the Great in 325. It was called to settle the dispute over the relationship between the First and Second Persons of the Blessed Trinity, and it also condemned the heretical teaching of Arius (Arianism). The Second Council of Nicaea (Seventh Ecumenical Council) was held in 787 and defined the Catholic teaching regarding the veneration of images and condemned the heresy of adoptionism. (See Ecumenical Councils.)

### Nicene Creed

The formal and orderly presentation of the chief doctrines of the Catholic faith was formulated at the first ecumenical council of Nicaea (A.D. 325). It established, in an authoritative and true expression of belief, the divinity of the Second Person of the Trinity by pronouncing that the Son is "consubstantial with the Father." It was at the beginning of the eleventh century that this Nicene Creed, already incorporated in the liturgy of the Mass in some places, was officially made a part of the Roman rite of the Mass by Pope Benedict VIII, and it remains so today as a profession of faith said by the priest and the people.

In the New Order of the Mass the translation reads: "We believe in one God, the Father, the Almighty, maker of heaven and earth, of all that is seen and unseen. We believe in one Lord, Jesus Christ, the only Son of God, eternally begotten of the Father, God from God, Light from Light, true God from true God, begotten, not made, one in Being with the Father. Through him all things were made. For us men and for our salvation he came down from heaven: by the power of the Holy Spirit he was born of the Virgin Mary, and became man. For our sake he was crucified under Pontius Pilate; he suffered, died, and was buried. On the third day he rose again in fulfillment of the Scriptures; he ascended into heaven and is seated at the right hand of the Father. He will come again in glory to judge the living and the dead, and his Kingdom will have no end. We believe in the Holy Spirit, the Lord, the giver of life, who proceeds from the Father and the Son. With the Father and the Son he is worshiped and glorified. He has spoken through the Prophets. We believe in one holy catholic and apostolic Church. We acknowledge one baptism for the forgiveness of sins. We look for the resurrection of the dead, and the life of the world to come. Amen."

### Night, Dark, of the Soul

The term refers to a phase of the spiritual progress to perfection as outlined by St. John of the Cross in the first part of his writings. It is also called the "passive night of the senses" and as such is considered as a passive purification of the senses of the soul, which is to say it is concerned with internal trials positively willed by God or at least permitted by Him, as periods of aridity (a lack of will to pray), desolation, doubts in and temptations to despair of prayer, and other internal conflicts. St. John of the Cross teaches that souls are led into the passive night of the senses when God raises them from the state of beginners in contemplation to the more advanced state of proficients, that is, when they begin to partake of the first gifts of

infused contemplation. The dark night of the soul precedes the second purging, the passive night of the soul, which occurs before the soul is raised to the transforming union with God (insofar as this is possible in life) and which can only take place when the soul is purged of every least inclination to self-love. (See Mysticism; Contemplation.)

### Nihil Obstat

See Imprimatur.

### Nimbus

The nimbus is a radiance of light used in art, which may surround the head of a saint to depict sanctity. It differs from the halo in that it is less defined. (Cf. Aureole.)

### Nine Fridays

See First Friday.

### Ninety-five Theses

This is the collective name given to those statements against the Church's practice regarding indulgences, which were posted by Martin Luther on the main door of All Saints Church in Wittenberg, Germany, Oct. 31, 1517. The posting and subsequent circulation of these short statements were the fuse that set off the series of controversies of the Protestant Reformation. They gave rise not only to the discussion of the various practices but brought into perspective both abuses: financial manipulation and the national interests of countries that were caught up in the action and reaction to Luther's theses. (See Protestantism.)

### Noble Guards

Chosen from the Roman nobility, the members of the Noble Guards formed the highest rank in the corps of the papal military service. They appeared with the pope on state occasions of solemnity. Also called the Pontifical Noble Guard, the group was disbanded by Pope Paul VI, Sept. 14, 1970.

## Nocturn

1. Originally Nocturn was the title of the entire night office as said between midnight and 4 A.M., consisting of Matins and Lauds of the Divine Office.

2. In the Liturgy of the Hours, this is supplanted, except in a descriptive sense, by the Evening Prayer "which is celebrated when the day is drawing to a close so that 'we may give thanks for what has been given to us for the things we have done well during the day'." (See Liturgy of the Hours.)

## Nomocanon

The Nomocanon is a collection, in alphabetical arrangment, of Church and civil law in use in the Eastern Chruch.

## Non Expedit

The Latin words *non expedit* mean "it is not expedient." It is the title given to a decree issued Feb. 29, 1868, which forbade Catholics of Italy to take part in the voting of a civil election in order to counteract the threat of papal territory from being annexed by Italy. It is the usual title of any pronouncement where permission is refused or counseled against by papal authority; however it is seldom used today.

## Non-Believers, Secretariat for

See Secretariats.

## Non-Christians, Secretariat for

See Secretariats.

## None

Formerly None was the name of the ninth hour of the Divine Office. This part of the breviary was constructed like the other lesser hours. (Cf. Divine Office; Liturgy of the Hours.)

## North American College

Founded at Rome in 1859 by Pope Pius IX, the enrollment in this educational institution for the training of men for the priesthood is made up chiefly of students from the United States. Students study or take special courses at other colleges of Rome, such as the Gregorianum, the Angelicum, or other centers of special study in Rome or Vatican City.

## North American Martyrs

The North American martyrs are the Jesuit missionaries who were killed by the Indians of the North American continent and who are celebrated in two major shrines: in Canada (See Martyrs' Shrine of Canada) and in the United States at Martyrs' Shrine at Auriesville, New York. The martyrs are: St. Isaac Jogues, St. Rene Goupil, St. John Lalande, St. Charles Garnier, St. Gabriel Lalemant, and St. Jean de Brebeuf. All were canonized in 1930. Also celebrated with these martyrs at the shrine is the Lily of the Mohawks, Kateri Tekakwitha, who was canonized in 1980.

## Novatianism

A schism and heresy, organized by Novatian who established himself as the first anti-pope in 251, Novatianism taught among other things that those who had fallen away from the faith could never be reconciled with the Church. Novatian was condemned by Pope St. Cornelius and a Roman council. The schism lasted until about 350. (See Lapsed.)

## Novena

A novena is a cycle of prayers spanning nine days, usually of one day a week for nine consecutive weeks. It consists of prescribed prayers and devotions and usually includes the reception of the Sacrament of Penance and Holy Eucharist. A novena may be made in common in church or in private. The *Raccolta* lists 36 novenas that are indulgenced by the Church. The practice is commemorative of the "Novena of the Apostles," that is, the days spent in prayer by them in the Cenacle between the Ascension and Pentecost (Acts 1:13–14), and the only novena that should be observed in parochial churches is that preceding the feast of Pentecost.

## Novice

A novice is one who, having been confirmed in his or her religious vocation by a period of postulancy, enters a further time of preparation known as the novitiate. Usually the period of the novitiate is not less than one year, and at its conclusion, upon recommendation of the superiors, the novice is permitted to be professed as a religious. Reception into the novitiate is governed by canon law (cc. 542, 544).

## Novitiate

The period of training, and also the place of residence during such training, of those who are preparing to enter the religious life is known as the novitiate. After some period of probation or preliminary trial, namely the postulancy, the candidate is given the religious habit of the order, a series of instructions and spiritual directions, as well as a serious examination of the rule of the order or its constitution.

Vatican II teaches: "The suitable renewal of religious communities depends very largely on the training of their members. Therefore religious men other than clerics, and religious women as well, should not be assigned to apostolic works immediately after the novitiate. In suitable residences and in a fitting manner, let them continue their training in the religious life and the apostolate, in doctrine and technical matters, even to the extent of winning appropriate degrees" (PC 18).

## Numbers, Book of

The Book of Numbers is the title of the fourth book of the OT, written by scribes of the priestly school. It gives historical narratives and accounts on legislation, telling the history of the wanderings of the Israelites in the wilderness from the Sinaitic region to the plains of Moab, describing the ecclesiastical hierarchy of the Jewish priesthood and emphasizing the justice of God and the power of intercession. It covers a period of time from the tenth to the fifth centuries before Christ. The book is rich in types that prefigure the NT, for example compare Nm, 21:6–9 with Jn. 3:14–15 and Nm. 20:8 with 1 Cor. 10:4.

## Nun

A member of a religious congregation of women is called a nun. In canon law, nuns are classed as "moniales," that is, women religious in solemn vows.

Vatican II states: "The papal cloister for nuns totally dedicated to contemplation is to be retained. Still, it should be modified according to the conditions of time and place, and outdated customs done away with. In such matters, consideration should be given to the wishes of the monasteries themselves.

"Other nuns institutionally devoted to external works of the apostolate should be exempt from papal cloister so that they can better discharge the apostolic tasks assigned to them. They should, however, maintain the kind of cloister required by their constitutions" (PC 16).

## Nunc Dimittis

The title of the song of Simeon (Lk. 2:29–32), Nunc Dimittis is taken from the first words of the song's Latin version.

## Nuncio

Nuncio is the title of a representative of the Holy See. A nuncio serves in a permanent diplomatic capacity with the rank of ambassador. (Cf. Legate.)

## Nuptial Mass and Blessing

In the Roman rite there is a special Mass assigned to be read at a marriage. The blessing of the married couple is read by the priest immediately after the Lord's Prayer. The blessing, however, is never given without the Mass being celebrated. The solemn blessing with the Nuptial Mass is forbidden during Lent and on Easter Sunday, and during Advent and on Christmas Day. The ordinary may grant permission for the solemnity of marriage within this period. A simple marriage ceremony may take place at any time of the year.

## O Antiphons

So called because each begins with the letter O, these are the "great" antiphons recited in the Liturgy of the Hours, during Advent in particular.

## O Salutaris Hostia

These are the Latin words that open the last two stanzas of the Hymn Verbum Supernum ("Heavenly word"), which has become the accepted title of a hymn sung traditionally at the paraliturgical service of Benediction of the Blessed Sacrament. *Verbum Supernum* was one of five poems of praise and instruction on the Holy Eucharist written by St. Thomas Aquinas in about A.D. 1264 when the Feast of Corpus Christi was introduced by Pope Urban IV (1261 to 1264). There are many translations, some of which have been set to music, but not all of these musical hymns have been approved. In translation the O Salutaris reads:

O saving Victim, opening wide
The gate of heaven to man below,
Our foes press on from every side,
Thine aid supply, Thy strength bestow.

To thy great Name be endless praise,
Immortal Godhead, One in Three;
O grant us endless length of days
In our true native land with Thee.

## Oak, Synod of the

The synod held in A.D. 403 took its name from the place it was held, a suburb of the city of Chalcedon, called "the Oak." The purpose of the Synod was to depose St. John Chrysostom from his see of Constantinople; it was called together by the Exarch of Heraclea, Paul. After condemning St. John for a series of trumped-up charges, some too trivial even to be mentioned, the Empress of Arcadius (A.D. 395 to 408) accepted the judgment of the Synod and sent the Bishop into exile. The reaction of the people was riotious protest and coincidentally was accompanied by an earthquake, all of which frightened the Empress into recalling St. John, but the Great Greek Father of the Church died in exile in A.D. 407. It is an early example of Church-State relationships where the authority of the Church is falsely charged when it speaks out

against the abuses that the State imposes, and certain elements of the Church take up the false position held by the State authority.

## Oath

An oath is an invocation of God as witness to the truth of a statement or to the honesty and fidelity of a promise. It is thus made either as an assertion of the truth or as a promise to perform some action. For the oath to be valid and lawful, it is necessary that the one making the assertion is absolutely convinced of the truth, or that the one making the promise has firmly resolved to keep it. It also is necessary for validity that the oath be make according to a formula, direct or indirect, and that there·be an intention, at least virtual, to swear (cf. Perjury). We are advised against taking oaths lightly or using them too frequently by St. James in his Epistle, 5:12.

Some Christian church groups, for example, the Baptists, Mennonites, and Quakers, interpret the gospel passage of St. Matthew (5:33–37) as precluding any form of oath, but it is more accepted that this means that no oath should be taken lightly. Oaths are of two kinds: that of assertion, that is, referring to past or present actions; or promissory, which concern future actions. All oaths are held to be binding under consciousness of sin (cf. Rom. 1:9; 2 Cor. 1:23; 11:31; Gal. 1:20) and are so because of the calling upon God as witness.

## Oath Against Modernism

See Modernism.

## Oath of Succession

The Act of Supremacy made the King of England, Henry VIII, the supreme head of the Church of England. This act also required that every English subject take the Oath of Succession declaring and recognizing the validity of the marriage of Henry and Anne in defiance of the Pope. Most bishops, monks, and laity took the oath, but John Fischer, the Bishop of Rochester, and Thomas More, the ex-chancellor, refused and so were martyred (they were later canonized).

Once the religious had acquiesced to taking the Oath, Thomas Cromwell and his agents seized the Church properties, confiscated their possessions, and closed many of the monasteries and churches. This led to a rebellion in the north country of England, which was called a "Pilgrimage of Grace," but it was put down with further persecution. This in turn caused Pope Paul III, in 1535, to declare that the already excommunicated king should be deposed. However, for political reasons, the Catholic countries of Spain and France failed to support the Pope's request. Confiscation of Church property continued, and the rift between English authority and the Church widened into a different phase of the Protestant Reformation.

## Obadiah, Book of

Also called Abdia or Abdiah, this is a short book of prophesy, having only twenty-one verses, yet it is one of the most vigorous in its language and message. Written by the minor prophet Obadiah (in Hebrew, "Servant of Yahweh"), in the fifth century before Christ, the content is in three parts: the ruin of Edom because of abuses arising out of Jerusalem's misfortune; the declaration of the time when the Lord will pass judgment on all the nations—"The Day of the Lord"; and the restoration of Israel.

Although this shortest book in the OT has little theological significance, it declares two fundamental truths: that pride is the forerunner of sin and disillusion (v. 3) and that judgment will be given on everyone who lives or has lived (v. 15).

## Obedience

1. Obedience is the moral virtue by which one is enabled to submit to the will or law of one in authority or his representative. Through this virtue one is enabled to recognize the authority and follow the law without hesitancy. The application of this virtue may be called for by (a) a contract, (b) a vow, (c) piety, (d) the office of one in authority.

2. The counsel of obedience is the denial of self to combat pride and to submit one's independence of mind and will for a greater ideal (Lk. 9:23; Phil 2:8).

3. The vow taken by a religious obliges him to obey his superior in all things commanded in virtue of obedience. This is an explicit obligation when given "in virtue of obedience," whereas it may be only adherence to the counsel when some regulation is concerned.

4. Obedience in marriage: the wife has the obligation to obey the husband. This is not a formal vow but arises out of the effects of the marriage contract.

The word obedience is derived in Semitic languages from the word "to hear." It always implied two subsequent actions, namely to hear the command given, and to follow the will of the one giving the command or request. By interpretation there are two distinctions to be followed: the hearing of the will or mind of God means obeying

without condition or reservation; the response to the commands of men should be conditional, that is, authority must reside in the person requesting obedience, and the willingness to obey must be in accord with the respondent's free decision.

In the spiritual understanding of obedience, the response, through exercise of the virtue, is toward one in recognized authority, be this God or a human being (cf. Dt. 1–4; Eccl. 12:13; Is. 1:2; Jer. 2:4). The motive for obedience in the Christian response is: faith (cf. Rom. 1:5; 1 Cor. 9:21; 2 Cor. 9:13) and love (cf. Jn. 14:31; Mt. 6:9–13; Mk. 14:36). Insight into the meaning of obedience, the functions of authority, and the obligation imposed on the human person's freedom must all be explained and understood in religious and civic society. (See Freedom.)

## Obedience of Faith

In the unfolding of the revelation of God sin was always an act of disobedience. God placed certain demands upon the human person (Ex. 24:3–8; Dt. 6:20–25; Jer. 11:1–8). Original sin was presented in the Bible as an act of disobedience (Gn. 2:16–17); submission to the will of God was an act of obedience as exemplified in the Blessed Virgin Mary (Lk. 1:26–38) and in the perfect obedience of Christ to His heavenly Father (Mt. 26:36–44; Jn. 4:31–38; Phil. 2:5–11; Heb. 5:7–10). And the Christian prayer is submission to the will of God (the Lord's Prayer) (cf. Mt. 6:10; 26–34).

The theological virtues of faith, hope and love, bring life to the virtue of obedience. This is especially true of faith (Rom. 16:25–27; 2 Cor. 10:5–6). Thus Vatican II teaches that this obedience of faith "must be given to God who reveals, an obedience by which man entrusts his whole self freely to God, offering 'the full submission of intellect and will to God who reveals,' and freely assenting to the truth revealed by Him" (DV 5).

The Christian's first obedience is to God (Acts 4:18–21; 5:27–32), and the authority of the Church is linked with the obedience to Christ by and through its hierarchical superiors (Gal. 1:11–12; 1 Cor. 4:1–3). (See Faith.)

## Oblates

The name oblates is derived from the Latin word meaning "offered." It was first given to those children whose parents gave them at an early age to the care and upbringing of a monastery. It was the pious intent (and neglect of duty on the part of the parents) that the children would then become members of a religious order and be cared for in their youth and throughout their lives. This practice was halted by the Council of Toledo (A.D. 656) and ceased altogether.

Now the name oblates is assumed by: (1) those religious who have a special service to offer to the community of mankind, such as the Oblates of Mary Immaculate (missioners); (2) the persons who voluntarily, usually in their adult lives, even while married, serve a religious community. They take no vows, and the time and circumstances of their service may be limited.

## Oblation

Literally, an oblation is an offering. In the Mass, it is that act in which the celebrant places the unconsecrated bread on the paten and raises it up before the consecration, and then the wine in the chalice. This is part of the "preparation of the gifts," which precedes the Eucharistic prayer.

In the sacrifice of the Mass, the oblation is the Lamb of God, Jesus Christ (cf. Is. 53:6–8; Jn. 12:24–25; 11:47–54; Mt. 26:3–5; Heb. 9:5–14). The first Christians emphasized the sacrifice of the Last Supper each time they renewed "the breaking of the bread" (Acts. 2:42; 1 Cor. 10:16–17; 11:24; Acts 20:7–11), which was a common expression among the Jews for a "meal." And it is through this food, Christ's offered Body and Blood, that we have life (Jn. 5:21–26; 6:56–59; Col. 3:1–4).

We may therefore say that *what* we offer, both actually as in the fruits of bread and wine, and symbolically through our offertory giving, becomes our *spiritual food* and through this we have *life*. (See Eucharist, Celebration of.)

## Obligation, Days of

See Holy days.

## Obreption

In canon law, the term refers to a statement made in writing, which declares something as false in a petition or a rescript. (Cf. Subreption.)

## Obscenity

The word "obscene" is derived from the Latin word meaning "repulsive." In modern society obscenity is applied broadly to those activities of human conduct which are offensive or repulsive according to the moral standards and the consensus of consciences of human persons. These are applied most commonly to visual entertainments, oral or literary presentations, or to those actions which are repulsive in the course of demonstration. The standard of acceptance is not one of "majority" reaction but the conscience of the prudent person in witnessing such actions. Thus the standard is the rightly informed conscience acting in response to the virtues of chastity and modesty.

Modern standards, it is claimed, are more liberal and will accept what other generations rejected. This is not the condition of a true ethical or moral atmosphere, for this liberal attitude cannot be placed on the plane of tolerance as the norm of judgment. It is because of this that greater license has been claimed in those arts that are communal in nature, such as the dance, theatre, arts, and cinema, and those that are private in nature such as sexual relations, marriage, literature, speech, and photography.

There has been great emphasis upon liberal sex as the one area of obscenity. And while this clearly is predominant in the abuse of the virtues of chastity and modesty, there are other areas that may be judged obscene. These may be classed as those abuses of society that occur with regularity and that are equally repulsive. Among these are: racism, abuse of juridical power or authority, inhuman treatment of animals, and the disregard of natural rights and the good things of nature. For example, it is repulsive to see natural waterways polluted and food wasted. These come, of course, under the examination of other virtues, but they may be considered repulsive or obscene. (Cf. Natural Law; Virtues.)

## Obsession

This term of psychiatry refers to the mental state characterized by involuntary or unreasonable preoccupation with impulses or disturbing thoughts. It is a recognized compulsion neurosis, which is not well defined within the boundaries of clinical procedures. The obsession usually involves rumination and compulsion. Rumination, or mental "possession" of an individual, leads to compulsive thinking, such as scruples or superstitions. The obsessive-compulsive types of this condition are sometimes developments of the obsessive thinking, and the transition to action is easy, such as acts that are superstitious and have a ritualistic pattern like touching a rabbit's foot or wearing certain garments.

In the religious sphere obsession may be a simple preoccupation with some religiously oriented action or it may be nervous reaction to some religiously oriented prescription or admonition. When obsession is wholly unreasonable, it is sometimes thought to be diabolical in origin, the opposite of possession or a milder form of it. However, such obsessions may often be cleared by counseling or by clinical procedures. When a person develops a scruple about a religiously oriented subject or thing, it should be handled by counseling, except where it may have a basis in the physical area.

Superstitions should be avoided, for they are distractions from the love of God and His providence. While all obsessive actions are below the level of consciousness and may require some clinical treatment, superstitions often are only substitution techniques that are centered in the self rather than the reason. They may be mild obsessions and not spiritually harmful. (Cf. Possession, Demonic; Pastoral Counseling.)

### Occasion of Sin

This is not to be confused with the danger of sinning. An occasion of sin may be a person, place, or thing that offers one the opportunity, inducement, or enticement to sin. Occasion also involves the internal or subjective inclination to sin. The occasion may be proximate, that is, when it is such that it almost always results in sin. This proximate occasion may be (1) free, that is, easily avoidable, or (2) necessary, that is, avoidable only with difficulty, if at all.

It is always the "better part of valor" to avoid the occasions of sin, even when this means difficulty, for sin has not only a spiritually debilitating effect, but psychologically and physically it has a cumulative effect. Everyone of common sense knows that to repeatedly be imprudent through, say, the use of drugs, will cause one to become psychologically and physiologically harmed. (See Sin.)

### Occult Compensation

The taking, secretly or surreptitiously, of something that is lawfully yours or is justly owed to you is called occult compensation. It is a method of recovering debts. However, justice must be observed in one's actions even though both parties know that the object or valuable belongs to one by right of law. It is not just to use this in a manner of compensating one for that which one merely

claims to be his or hers by oversight or injustice on the part of the other person. For example, an employee, such as a clerk in a store, is stealing if he or she takes money or some object from the place of employment under the claim that the employer is not paying enough in wages and that the theft is justified. Likewise, the person cannot take, in justice, from another if that person cannot afford to have the object or money taken from him at that time.

In right ethical practice and moral judgment, all occult compensation is likely to be tainted with rationalization, which is false or selfish. Thus it is recognized that before resorting to compensating oneself, even when the obligation of the other party is acknowledged, it is best to arbitrate or discuss the method and means of compensation. Great abuse in this area results from one person "thinking" he is owed a just amount and thereby is justified in taking some course of action to compensate oneself. Such is the case of the laborer who thinks he is underpaid and therefore works only a part of the time he is on the job.

Occult compensation only seems to be an exception to the seventh commandment and is often disguised under the cloak of situation ethics. It must always remain within the confines of (1) the recognized debt by the one seeking compensation and (2) the recognition of the claim by the one from whom compensation is exacted.

### Occultism

The term occultism is derived from the Latin word meaning "concealed" and is applied to those theories, practices, and organized groups of rejected sciences that seek to reveal the future or to govern events that are to happen by an appeal to the preternatural. For some people these become elaborate systems, combining the parapsychological, the natural, the perverse, and the unnatural together with the preternatural. These may be controlled, uncontrolled, or contrived. Among those are the basically superstitious, the fraudulent, and the deceptive, such as, astrology, alchemy, palmistry, tarot cards, ouija-boards, witchcraft, voodoo, and satanism. Among the more elaborate forms of the occult are the systems developed with attendant mixed teachings, such as theosophism, illuminism, Rosicrusianism, and various forms of modern gnosticism.

The Church, while recognizing that there is a possibility of diabolical or preternatural action, condemns all occult practices and systems. This condemnation arises from the teaching that man is to seek from God the counsel and consolation of faith, for the wisdom of God has triumphed over human wisdom (Mt. 2:1–10; Acts 8:9–24; 13:6–11; 16:16–18).

### Occurrence

This is a term of accommodation that refers to an instance in the Church calendar when two feasts would fall on the same day, for example, the twenty-fifth of December being a Sunday. When this happens, the feast displaced by the greater is celebrated on the following day, or on the first free day thereafter.

### Octave

The eight days made up of a feast day and the seven following days are called an octave. The feasts of Christmas, Easter, and Pentecost, for example, have octaves. The name also applies to the last, the eighth, day of such Church feasts. (See Calendar, Church.)

### Octave Psalms

This name is applied to Psalms 6 and 11.

### Oecumenical

See Ecumenical Councils.

### Of Human Life

See Humane Vitae.

### Offerings

See Oblation; Offertory.

### Offertory

In the Mass, the Offertory is that essential action which follows the Prayer of the Faithful wherein the celebrant offers first the bread to be consecrated on the paten, then the chalice containing wine and water. In the law of the Israelites there were three kinds of offerings: thank-offerings or "sacrifices of praise" (Ps. 50:14), vow-offerings made in fulfillment of a vow (Ps. 61:9), and free-will offerings (Ps. 54:8). All are contained in the offering of the Mass. In the Sacrifice of the Mass, Christ offers Himself; bread and wine become the body and blood of Christ; Christ is the Priest and offers Himself for the whole world. Thus the Mass is a true, unbloody sacrifice. The Offertory follows the preparation of the gifts.

In the modern Church, by interpretation and by convenience, it is customary for the faithful to make a free, voluntary gift, usually in the form of money. This is inappropriately called the "collection," but it is a means whereby members of the worshiping community can further the mission of the Church, which is fulfilled by sacrifice and the teaching of Christ to the world. During the early days of the Church the community held goods or possessions in common (Acts 4:32) and directly supplied the substances of sacrifice, the bread and wine, but today this sharing in oblation and sacrifice is in keeping with the greater numbers in the community and the greater need of means to carry out the commands of Christ. (See Oblation.)

### Office

1. The Divine Office, the official prayer of the Church (cf. Breviary; Liturgy of the Hours).

2. Any portion of the Divine Office is often referred to simply as the "Office," for example, the Office of a particular feast.

3. The liturgy of the Church, including both the Divine Office for the day together with the Mass. (Cf. Liturgy.)

### Office of the Blessed Virgin Mary

See Little Office of the B.V.M.

### Office of the Dead

This is the title of the Divine Office as recited on November 2, All Souls' Day. The prayers are for the repose of the souls of the dead, and a form consisting of the morning prayer of the Liturgy of the Hours is often chanted before a funeral Mass.

### Official Catholic Directory of the United States

This annual publication is produced by P. J. Kennedy and Sons, 866 Third Ave., New York, N.Y. 10022. It is a complete listing of dioceses, bishops, diocesan officials, priests, ordinariates, vicariates, and religious, giving pertinent information as to place of residence, etc. The directory is a tool of many uses and serves especially to locate priests and to learn the service areas offered by each diocese. The first edition was published in 1817.

### Oil Stock

An oil stock is a cylindrical metal case, usually made with three separate compartments, one for each of the Holy Oils and marked with the initials of the oils. The method of keeping the oil in the stocks is to saturate a piece of cotton or wool. The oil stock is to be retained in a proper, safe place in the church. (Cf. Ambry.)

## Oils, Holy
See Holy Oils; Chrism.

## Old Believers
Those sects of the Russian Church which refused to accept the reforms of the Patriarch Nikon (d. 1681) of Moscow in the seventeenth century were called Old Believers, also Old Ritualists, "Raskolniki" that is, schismatics. They are now considered a part of the Orthodox Church, especially since the communist revolution.

## Old Catholics
Catholics who refused to accept the decree of papal infallibility as defined by the Vatican Council in 1870 were given this name.

## Old Testament
See Bible.

## Om, also Aum
Om is the sacred syllable of Hinduism used by all schools in their meditation system. It expresses the "world-soul" concept of Brahman. It is pronounced at the beginning of the recitation of the *mantras*. In practice, this concept is expressed in Hindu teaching as: "All humanity converging at the foot of that sacred place where is set the symbol that is no symbol, the name that is beyond all sound." In the system of practices that make up Hinduism, there is the possibility of introducing this concept through an intensified psychic response or through practices that are diabolic. Here there is real danger, for this concept permits one to enter into a simple, self-delusive attitude that misleads while at the same time acts to shut out all

other avenues of Christian response. Its danger is in the blandishment whereby a Universal Religion (the core of Karma or the at-onement of divine assumption of all into one) precludes sin since there is no one to sin against. Thus it has often been cryptically likened to the evolutionary religious concepts advanced by Teilhard de Chardin, namely, the *omega* concept: "The revealed Christ is identical with omega." This christology of Chardin, an evolutionary complex, is stated in like manner: "Man bears along with him the world of beings inferior to God." (Letter 8/7/23 in *Letters to Leontine Zanta*.) (See Omega Point; Teilhardism.)

## Ombrellino
From the Italian, literally, a "little umbrella," the ombrellino has a flat top made of white silk and ornamented with gold fringe; it is supported by a longer staff than the ordinary umbrella. The ombrellino is used as a canopy when the Blessed Sacrament is carried from one place to another in church, except in a solemn procession. (Cf. Baldachino.)

## Omega Point
The Omega point is the Christological interpretation given by Teilhard de Chardin, which he bases upon Pauline and Johannine texts. He states: "Christ is quite simply Omega. To demonstrate this fundamental proposition I need only refer to a long series of Johannine and especially Pauline texts where the physical supremacy of Christ over the universe is proclaimed in magnificent terms" *(Science and Christ,* p. 54). (Cf. Rom. 8; Col. 1:15–20.) It is a point beyond representation, beyond time and history.

In this cosmic outlook on Christian consciousness, there is an extension of the mystery of Redemption, as Chardin states: "Christ can no longer justify man except by that same act super-creating the entire Universe" *(Activation of Energy,* pp. 263-264). (See Om; Teilhardism.)

## Omnipotence
Omnipotence is an attribute of God, a recognition of the ability of the Creator to do all things that are possible. Knowledge (wisdom), will, and power are one in God. It is also the distinct mark of sovereignty, claimed by Christ in sending forth His disciples: "Full authority [i.e., power to accomplish all things] in heaven and on earth has been given to me" (Mt. 28:18). It is by this power that the worldwide kingdom, which the Resurrection inaugurated, will be established.

God was recognized by the Chosen People as

being omnipotent through creation (Gn. 2:7; Is. 29:15–16; Jer. 18:1–6; Rom. 9:19–24), and there was an association of the power of God with wisdom (Wis. 7:24–25; Jb. 37:14). The omnipotence of God is also manifest in His saving power (Ex. 4:1–5; Jer. 16:21; Is 50:2) and culminates in Christ (Mt. 8:1–27; Col. 1:10–12). The birth, miracles, and resurrection were all manifestations of the power of Christ (Lk. 1:35; Acts 2:22–24), and Christ was an expression, made manifest to all, of God's power to save mankind (1 Cor. 1:18–25). And power was shared by the Holy Spirit (1 Cor. 2:4–5; Eph. 3:16; Rom. 1:4; 15:13–19) and communicated to the Church through the apostolic gifts (Acts 1:8; Col. 1:28–29; 1 Thes. 1:5; 2 Tm. 1:7–8). In marvelous succession the omnipotence of God, His strength, is communicated to Christians through baptism (Eph. 6:10–13; Col. 2:12).

### Omniscience

This is God's attribute of knowing all things simply and absolutely. The doctrine of Providence implies omniscience, for God, in ruling and directing all things to His own glory, must know all things, even the most secret, and He must know them now rather than as a sequence. (Cf. Attributes of God.)

In the OT the prophets are the representatives of God's knowledge (cf. 1 Kgs. 20:35–38; 2 Kgs. 19:1–7), and they spoke out to reveal the salvific will of God (cf. Is. 14:26–27; 46:8–11; Bar. 3:15–38). God so wished men to know His wisdom that He sent His son, the Incarnate Word, to bring that knowledge to all men (cf. Col. 2:2–3; Jas. 3:13–18; Rom. 11:33–36; 1 Cor. 1:17–31; 2:6–16). And the wisdom of God is in opposition of the false wisdom of men (Rom. 16:25–27; 1 Cor. 1:24–25; Eph. 3:10), and it is given to men through the "foolishness of the Cross" (Rom. 1:19–25; 1 Cor. 1:21–25).

### Omophorion

A vestment worn by bishops of the Byzantine rite, the omophorion consists of a ten-inch wide band of silk or velvet, which is wrapped loosely around the neck so that one end hangs over the left shoulder in front and the other over the left shoulder to the back, the ends reaching almost to the ground. It corresponds to the pallium of the Roman rite.

### Only-begotten One

This title of truth given to Christ is unique (cf. Ps. 25:16; 22:21). It is reserved solely for the Son of God and indicates the relationship of obedience and mission that Christ had as the One chosen to be the Redeemer, revealed to man, and further revealing the Godhead. (Cf. Mk. 1:9–11; 14:61; Mt. 26:63; Lk. 22:67–71; Jn. 6:69.) Christ is the Word of God (Jn. 1:18), and the glory of Jesus is nothing less than the essential glory of God, His Father (Jn. 11:4–40; 17:4–8), for He is "begotten of God" (1 Jn. 5:18).

### Onomasticon

The onomasticon is an alphabetic list of the names of some 300 places, together with their location, which are mentioned in the Bible. It was compiled originally by Eusebius of Caesarea about A.D. 330 and translated from the Greek into Latin; various additions were made by St. Jerome. It is of value in studying the topography of the Holy Land.

### Ontologism

Ontologism was a philosophical system arising in France during the nineteenth century through such philosophers as V. Gioberti (1801 to 1852); it spread to Italy by the rationalizations of L. Brancherau in his writings of 1848. According to this philosophy human reason knows infinite being intuitively and this knowledge is present in the human mind. Thus human knowledge is a reflection in the mind of things as they are and things through which they exist. Hence the human mind intuitively knew creation and its origin.

In 1861 a set of seven "errors" of ontologism was condemned by the Holy Office and could not be held or taught. These were: (1) immediate knowledge of God is essential to human understanding; (2) the being is the divine since we know nothing without it; (3) all universals are identical with God; (4) we know implicitly all other beings in God; (5) all other ideas are only modifications of this concept; (6) created beings are outside of the indivisible God but are a part of Him; (7) God's creative act is the same act by which He knows and wills the creature.

Basically ontologism asserts that God Himself is the guarantee of the validity of human ideas, and thus it claims an impossibility of committing error. It is thus pantheistic and amoral at the same time. It is an error because it eliminates the supernatural character of intuitive vision.

### Ophites
See Heresies.

### Oplatki

A Polish word (ō-pwaf-kee) that refers to a family Christmas liturgical practice is again becoming popular in many parishes throughout the world. It consists of a wafer-thin piece of unleavened bread, usually baked in a form of host-iron with a picture of the Holy Family or a nativity scene incised on the iron and then transferred to the bread. The piece of bread is about three by four inches (10 by 15 cm.). The custom is that the breads are blessed, *not consecrated,* and given to families of the parish or by one family to another. The breads are then broken into smaller pieces and given to other members of the family or friends, or pieces are exchanged.

This symbolical practice has two deeper meanings: (1) that the body of Christ, which is everywhere symbolized by bread, becomes a part of each recipient and that Christ is welcomed into the lives of individuals by sharing in the Christ-life; (2) more broadly, this exchange of even a frail piece of bread symbolizes everyone's daily bread, the sustenance that comes from God the Father, and all the needed things that contribute to the health and well-being of each person. Its meaning is that through this simple sharing each person is ritually united with others, that each one is sharing in the need and blessing of a contemporary world even though the practice began over 1000 years ago among the Poles and Slovaks.

**Opus Dei**

The Latin words meaning "work of God."

1. Those associations of Catholics, who form and have membership in *Opus Dei* and practice privately and in groups a spiritual life, are composed of faithful having a diversity of professions and occupations. Members are under spiritual direction and strive to give special witness to Christ in the world, but live in their ordinary circumstances. No special solicitation of membership is made since all engage themselves voluntarily in the work for personal reasons or to carry on an apostolate. Recruitment of new members is usually made through older members or by those who are assigned as directors or spiritual leaders.

The movement called *Opus Dei* was founded originally in Spain by Msgr. Josemaria Escriva de Belaguer in 1928. It was approved by the Holy See in 1950. The present membership, made up of men and women, operates in all countries and directs itself to corporal works and educational activities. The headquarters in the United States are: 9 East 96th Street, New York, N.Y. 10028.

2. The term *Opus Dei* was a name given by the Benedictines to the Divine Office (Liturgy of the Hours) as an affirmation that prayer was their special duty as monks and their prime responsibility to God.

**Opus Operatum**

See Ex Opere Operato.

**Orange, Councils of**

The first of these councils, held in 441 at Orange (Aransio) in southern France, pronounced on the administration of the sacraments and ecclesiastical jurisdiction. The second was called in 529 and condemned semi-Pelagianism.

**Orante**

The *Orante* figure of early Christian art shows the classical attitude of prayer; raising the mind and soul to God is shown by lifting up the hands in an act of adoration and praise; the hands are opened to offer thanks and speak for the heart and also to receive divine gifts. In this position the priest stands upright, his arms raised to the side, palms facing forward, and the elbows slightly bent.

**Orarion**

The stole worn by the deacon in the Byzantine rite is called the orarion. It is made of a narrow band of silk, four yards long, and embroidered on it three times is the word "Holy" in Greek.

**Orate, Fratres**

From the Latin meaning "Pray, Brethren," the Orate Fratres was the formal invitation to prayer given by the celebrant to the assembly in the Latin Mass. This opening formula originated in Italy in the eleventh century. It was replaced by the word *Oremus,* "Let us Pray!" in most prayers of the Latin rite and is so used in the New Order of the Mass.

**Oratory**

An oratory is a place set aside for divine worship, but not primarily for the public; thus it differs from a church (cc. 1188-1196). There are three types of oratories: (1) public, that is, one erected for the use of a community, such as religious, but to which, for convenience or other reasons, the public has access for divine services; (2) semipublic, one that is intended for the use of some particular group (of some size), for example, a chapel in a seminary, to which the public does not have access; (3) private, that is, an oratory for the particular use of a family or person, usually within the house or manorial building. The establishment of such an oratory requires an apostolic indult.

## Oratory, St. Joseph's

See Saint Joseph's Oratory.

## Order

In its philosophical and theological meaning order is the unity of many elements in a given system. Thus we can speak of an economic order as that system of related balances, barters, and prices that acquire a stability insofar as they maintain the sequence of truth within the system; the order is placed in jeopardy when a political force, for example, enters the system and changes or destroys the elements, which thus effects the order.

Theologically, we speak of the *moral* order. Here the end of action is related to the affirmation of our salvation or our supernatural purpose. This is a transcendentally necessary end, for God has established this through His salvific will, has communicated the means through Christ, and makes it possible through His self-communication through grace.

Vatican II teaches: "The Council asserts that the primacy of the objective moral order demands absolute allegiance, for this order alone excels and rightly integrates all other fields of human concern, including art, however lofty their value" (IM 6).

And: "Since, in this age of ours, new problems are arising and extremely serious errors are gaining currency, which tend to undermine the foundations of religion, the moral order, and human society itself, this sacred Synod earnestly exhorts laymen, each according to his natural gifts and learning, to be more diligent in doing their part according to the mind of the Church,.to explain and defend Christian principles, and to apply them rightly to the problems of our era" (AA 6).

## Order of the Mass, New

The order of the Mass has been revised in accord with the Constitution on the Sacred Liturgy (*Sacrosanctam Concilium*) and approved by Pope Paul VI in the apostolic constitution *Missalis Romani*, dated April 3, 1967. It was officially promulgated by the Sacred Congregation of Rites, and its decrees took effect beginning Nov. 30, 1969, on the first Sunday of Advent.

The New Order of the Mass gives the structure, elements, and parts of the Mass as they are to be observed in the Roman Rite. (See Eucharist, Celebration of.)

Together with the promulgation of the New Order of the Mass there was published the *General Instruction on the Roman Missal*, which replaced the previous books of rubrics, the rite of celebration, the instruction on concelebration, and the publication of "current defects" in the celebration of Mass. In the United States this became effective on March 22, 1970.

"In the Order of Mass, the rites have been 'simplified, with due care to preserve their substance. Elements which, with the passage of time, came to be duplicated or were added with but little advantage' have been eliminated, especially in the offering of bread and wine, the breaking of the bread, and communion.

"Also, 'other elements which suffered injury through accidents of history' are restored 'to the earlier norm of the holy Fathers'; for example the homily, the general intercessions or prayer of the faithful, the penitential rite or act or reconciliation with God and the brethren at the beginning of Mass, where its proper significance is restored.

"According to the decree of the Second Vatican Council, that 'a more representative portion of the holy scriptures be read to the people over a set period of years,' the Sunday readings are arranged in a cycle of three years. In addition, on Sundays and feasts the Epistle and Gospel are preceded by an Old Testament reading or, at Easter, the Acts of the Apostles. This is to accentuate the dynamism of the mystery of salvation, shown in the words of divine revelation. These broadly selected biblical readings, which give the faithful on feastdays the most important part of sacred scripture, are complemented by the other parts of the Bible read on other days." (See Readings, Cycle of; Sacramentary.)

## Orders, Holy, Sacrament of

Holy Orders is the Sacrament of the New Law instituted by Christ, through which spiritual power is given together with the grace to exercise properly the respective office. The sacrament gives a permanent character, meaning that it cannot be repeated, and that it ordains one for all eternity.

"The liturgical rites by which admission of candidates for the diaconate and the presbyterate (priesthood) takes place and the ministries [acolyte and lector] are conferred should be performed by the ordinary of the aspirant (the bishop and, in clerical institutes of perfection, the major superior). . . . Before ordination candidates for the diaconate shall give to the ordinary (the bishop and in clerical institutes of perfection, the major superior) a declaration made out and signed by their own hand, by which they testify that they are about to receive the order freely and of their own accord. The special consecration of celibacy observed for the sake of the kingdom of heaven and its obligation for candidates to the priesthood and for unmarried candidates to the diaconate are linked with the diaconate. The public commitment to holy celibacy before God and the Church is to be celebrated in a particular rite, even by religious, and is to precede ordination to the diaconate. Celibacy taken on in this way is a diriment impediment to entering marriage" (cf. Laicization).

In accord with the directives of Vatican II the rite of ordination or the conferring of the Sacrament of Holy Orders was revised by Pope Paul VI in 1968. The essentials of the old rite remain, but emphasis is placed upon the "consent" of the assembled Church to the ordination, and on the fact that the Church is community, that all should participate in the liturgy, and that a man is ordained for the service of the entire Christian community to build up the Body of Christ. The ordaining bishop directs to each candidate a threefold exhortation concerning various aspects of his work in the community of the Church: (1) that he serve as a *teacher* as Christ Himself was and is; (2) that he serve like Christ the *priest*, since he unites the spiritual sacrifices of the faithful to the eucharistic sacrifice; (3) that he serve as Christ the *pastor*, to bring the faithful together in unity.

The new rite also specifies that under ordinary circumstances deacons and priests should be ordained in the local church or diocese where they will serve. And emphasis is given to the Church as a priestly people, each baptized person sharing in the threefold work of Christ as prophet, priest, and king—with the ordained priest at the center of this work forming all into the unity for which Christ prayed.

The procedure for the conferring of the Sacrament of Holy Orders follows these lines: (1) The choosing of the candidates—making official the assertion of the candidate himself, his free choice, the judgment of his directors or teachers who, after inquiry, can affirm the worthiness of the candidate. This is followed by the declared choice of the ordaining bishop, the call, so to speak, to the acceptance of the sacrament. (2) The consent of the people (the assembly), which is an active act of approbation for the candidate, affirmed by the entire priestly people. (3) The instruction of the candidates by the ordaining bishop as to the roles of teacher, priest, and pastor. (4) The examination

of the candidates whereby each affirms his willingness to celebrate the mysteries of Christ for God's eternal glory and the sanctification of Christians. (5) The candidates then make a promise of obedience to the bishop and his successors. (6) There follow the prostration of the candidates and the prayer of the Church (the Litany of the Saints), and the bishop invokes the Holy Spirit upon those to be ordained. (7) The impressive part of the ceremony is the laying on of hands, which is the actual conferring of the sacrament. First the bishop lays his hands on the head of each candidate, palms down. Then as a sign of the unity of the ordained priesthood, each priest present in turn lays his hands on the head of each candidate. (8) There ensues a prayer of consecration wherein the bishop asks that God may renew the spirit of holiness in each of the ordained men. (9) The investiture with the stole, a sign of priestly power in Christ, then takes place with the stole draped around the neck and hanging straight down. The chasuble is also placed on the newly ordained for the first time. (10) Next the palm of the hands of each new priest is anointed with holy chrism, and the bishop prays that each new priest may be kept worthy to offer the sacrifice of the Mass and that each will strive to make holy the Christian people. (11) The ceremony continues with the presentation of the paten (bread) and chalice (with wine and water) to each new priest while the bishop says: "Accept the gifts from the people to be offered to God. Be conscious of what you are doing, be as holy as the actions you perform, and model your life after the mystery of the Lord's cross." (12) The kiss of peace is then given to the newly ordained and to all priests present. The liturgy of the Eucharist follows and the newly ordained concelebrate their first Mass with the ordaining bishop.

Those who may receive the sacrament of Holy Orders are: deacons; presbyterate (priests); and bishops. The ordination of a bishop is the extension of the power of the priesthood to one who is "to govern the house of the living God" (LG 18). The bishop (who formerly was said to be "consecrated") is ordained to be the living, sensible, effective, and preeminent sign of Christ in His triple function of Teacher, Shepherd, and High Priest. (See Bishop.) He is thus identified with Christ and given the highest role in administering the sacraments (High Priest), in teaching, and in governing (Shepherding).

The Sacrament of Holy Orders as seen in scripture and the tradition of the Church is specific in that the laying on of hands is used, not only to give the Holy Spirit but to confer authority and spiritual powers (2 Tm. 1:6; Acts 6:6). The threefold role of the ordained: to teach, minister, and govern is also a part of the distinctive effect of the Sacrament (cf. Mt. 28:19–20). (See Deacon; Priest; Bishop; Ministries.)

## Orders of Knights

See Knights, Orders of.

## Orders, Minor

Minor orders is the collective term used up to the time of the promulgation and implementation of the documents of Vatican II, or until Jan. 1973 in the Latin Church, for the roles of reader (lector), acolyte, porter, and exorcist. These were considered preliminary steps to the reception of the Sacrament of Holy Orders, but not a part of the sacrament proper. They were always preceded by the reception of the tonsure.

Through the Apostolic Letter of Pope Paul VI, of Aug. 15, 1972, in *motu proprio* form and in force Jan. 1, 1973, the formerly established minor orders and tonsure were changed or eliminated. The rulings were: (1) Tonsure (that ceremony whereby a layman was said to enter into the life of a cleric) is no longer conferred. Entrance into the clerical state is joined to the diaconate. (2) The orders of exorcist and doorkeeper (Porter) are no longer ministries and are discontinued. (3) The major order of subdiaconate, which followed the reception of minor orders, no longer exists in the Latin Church. (4) Those minor orders, acolyte and lector (reader), are now called ministries. (5) These ministries, of acolyte and lector, may be committed to lay Christians. (6) In accordance with the tradition of the Church the ministries of acolyte and lector are reserved to men (exception may be granted through the episcopal conference). (7) The conferring of ministries shall henceforth be called "institution" and not ordination. (8) The ministries are no longer considered to be reserved for candidates for the Sacrament of Holy Orders. (9) All candidates for the permanent diaconate or transitional diaconate and the presbyterate (priesthood) are to be instituted into the ministries of acolyte and reader, and these are to be given at intervals of preparation and time established by the episcopal conferences. (See Deacon; Ministries; Permanent Deacon; Transitional Deacon.)

## Orders, Religious

Religious orders is a title loosely applied to all religious groups of men or women. According to canon law (c. 488), the following distinctions are made: (1) an order is a religious community, men or women, in which solemn vows are taken; (2) a congregation is one in which only simple vows are

made, and these may be temporary or perpetual; (3) exempt religious are those belonging to a religious institute that is withdrawn from the jurisdiction of the local ordinary; (4) a clerical community is one in which the majority of its members are priests; (5) a lay institute of religious is one wherein the majority are not ordained, for example, Christian Brothers.

## Ordinariate

An ordinariate is an ecclesiastical jurisdiction which for the benefit of the people and for special purposes is established by the Church, such as the Military Ordinariate.

## Ordinary

1. In Church law, this term designates one who exercises ordinary jurisdiction in the external forum (as well as in the internal forum), which is attached to an office by law. Thus it includes, besides the Roman pontiff, residential bishops (as of a diocese), abbots, prelates nullius, vicars-general, administrators apostolic, vicars and prefects apostolic and their successors in office, the administrator assigned to a vacant diocese, and the major superiors of exempt clerical communities (major superiors are: abbots, superior general, and provincial). Local ordinaries include all of those previously mentioned except the major superiors.

Vatican II states: "Members of the episcopal conference are all local Ordinaries of every rite, coadjutors, auxiliaries, and other titular bishops who perform a special work entrusted to them by the Apostolic See or the episcopal conferences" (CD 38). (See also Bishop.)

2. The Ordinary of the Mass is the constant (with slight exceptions) part of the prayers of the Mass (cf. Order of the Mass, New).

3. The ordinary is that portion of the Breviary which does not change, except for the Psalms.

## Ordination

"The use of the term ordination is limited to those ordination rites in which there is a distinct laying on of hands: diaconate, priesthood, and episcopacy—and only those so ordained are considered clerics.

"By their vocation and ordination, priests of the New Testament are indeed set apart in a certain sense within the midst of God's people. But this is so, not that they may be separated from this people or from any man, but that they may be totally dedicated to the work for which the Lord has raised them up" (PO 3).

And: "Established in the priestly order by ordination, all priests are united among themselves in an intimate sacramental brotherhood" (PO 8). (Cf. Rom. 1:9; Phil. 2:17.) (See Orders, Holy, Sacrament of.)

## Ordination of Women
See Women.

## Ordo
The Ordo is the usual title, which is also the first Latin word of the book "The Order for the Recitation of the Divine Office and the Celebration of Mass." The book contains, in sequence throughout the year, brief directions for the Mass and the Divine Office to be said every day of the Church calendar. Each diocese, religious order, and congregation has its own Ordo. It is a necessary book for the priest and is printed with a great number of abbreviations. The Ordo is also called an "ordinal," although this name may apply to the ritual book used by the bishop in conferring sacraments.

## Organizations, Catholic
See International Catholic Organizations; National Catholic Organizations.

## Oriental Churches, Sacred Congregation for the
This Roman Congregation of the Holy See exercises, according to canon law (c. 257), jurisdiction over the dioceses, bishops, clergy, religious, and faithful of the Oriental (Eastern) rites. The Orientals are bound by the Code of Canon Law, by all canons containing dogmatic definitions, and those dealing with faith and morals. In the United States, the "Catholic Near East Welfare Association," with headquarters in New York City, serves as an adjunct to this Sacred Congregation for the purpose of collecting alms for the faithful of the Oriental rites. (See Congregations.)

## Oriental Religions
See Hinduism; Brahmanism.

## Original Justice
See Justice.

## Original Sin
The consequence of the fall of our first parents, Adam and Eve (Gn. 3:1–24), who sinned against the all-loving God and thus lost divine grace, is called original sin or stain. The consequences of this first sin are death, concupiscence or the rebellion of man's lower appetites against reason and will, and a darkening of the intellect. By

Christ's redemption of man everyone was restored to the friendship of God and given the grace, beyond natural powers, to attain the everlasting love of God in heaven.

The nature of the sin committed by Adam and Eve is mixed and grave and affected all their descendants. It was a sin of pride in all its elements and also a sin of gravest disobedience and ingratitude. Its effects were overcome by the redemption, as St. Paul declares (Rom. 8:14–23). By baptism we receive the grace of incorporation in the body of Christ, and this life, guided by the Spirit and aided by the sacraments and the Church, leads to final triumph over concupiscence and death by bodily resurrection with Christ on the day of His final coming. St. Thomas declares: "Original sin is concupiscence, materially, but privation of original justice, formally" (I-II, qu. 82, Art. 3), and "original sin is called concupiscence rather than ignorance, although ignorance is comprised among the material defects of original sin" (Ibid.). (See Baptism, Sacrament of.)

## Orleans, Council of
Held at Orleans, in France, in 511, under the patronage of the Frankish King Clovis, this national council enacted important Church legislation.

## Orphrey
The name derived from the Latin *auriphygium*, meaning "gold embroidery," is the collective name given to the ornamental decoration of vestments. Such decorations may be embroidery, applique, dropped-stitch, or woven, and may be added to the vestment in a panel, the form of a cross, or other suitable design. Much latitude in such decorative detail has been allowed in more recent years, following the newer design of chasubles and stoles. Thus one finds panels of tie-dyed material, hand-

woven bands, and metalic threadwork used on vestments along with specially woven cloth. The current trend is toward simplicity and lightness of weight. (See Vestments.)

## Orthodox Church

The word "orthodox" was originally used to distinguish those Churches that accepted the Council of Chalcedon and its rulings from the heretics who rejected it. After the schism of 1054, which resulted from the age-old differences between the Greek Church and the Holy See, the term was used to distinguish those same Eastern Churches from Rome. The Orthodox Eastern Church was formed of a group of these Churches, united more or less under the patriarchate of Constantinople. (The Byzantine Greeks in Italy and the Maronites of Syria retained communion with Rome.) After the capture of Constantinople by the Turks, in 1453, the authority of the patriarch of that city was lessened. Thereafter the Orthodox Eastern Church broke up into the more or less autonomous national Churches of Cyprus, Georgia, Sinai, Russia, Greece, Bulgaria, Rumania, Yugoslavia, Albania, Czechoslovakia, Estonia, Finland, Poland, Latvia, Lithuania, and the previous patriarchates of Alexandria, Antioch, and Jerusalem. Some of their national status has largely been lost through the dominance of Russia over some of these countries. (Cf. Eastern Churches.)

## Orthodoxy, Feast of

Observed in the Byzantine rite on the first Sunday of Lent, this feast celebrates the restoration of the icons to the churches, the defeat of iconoclasm, and the triumph of orthodoxy (true doctrine).

## Osculatorium

The "Kiss of Peace" is also known by this Latin name.

## Osee, Book of

See Hosea, Book of.

## Ostensorium

See Monstrance.

## Ostiarius

Ostiarius is the Latin title for the lowest of the former Minor Orders. (Cf. Orders, Holy, Sacrament of.)

## Our Father

See Lord's Prayer.

## Our Lady

This familiar and endearing title of the Blessed Virgin Mary is a prefatory to many fuller titles given to the Blessed Mother for her favors to the Church, for example, Our Lady of Mount Carmel, Our Lady of Ransom, Our Lady of Hope, Our Lady of Fatima, Our Lady of Beauraing.

## Our Lady of Lourdes Shrine in Canada

This shrine is a memorial to the Blessed Virgin Mary. It is located near the city of Rigaud in the Province of Quebec on route 17, not far from the Ontario border. In 1874, Brother Ludger Pauze of the clerics of Saint Viator thought to spread the devotion to the Immaculate Conception of the Blessed Virgin Mary following the apparitions to the French girl, St. Bernadette. It is also under this title of the Immaculate Conception that the United States of America is dedicated to the Blessed Mother.

The Shrine is located on the rock face of Rigaud mountain in a natural amphitheater overlooking forests of pine and maple. From the first pilgrimage to the shrine in 1886 there has been a growth in the devotion; a domed, octagon-shaped, oratory was built on the highest point of the cliff a few years later. Each summer many travelers and pilgrims visit the shrine, and devotion is vigorous to both Our Lady and St. Bernadette.

## Oxford Movement

Initiated in 1833 by Dr. Keble of Oxford, this movement sought, with a considerable record of success, to return the Church of England to apostolic Christianity. In its wider scope it vindicated the supernatural character of Christianity. It was aided by such men as Cardinals Newman and Manning, and Hurrell Froude, F.A. Faber, W.G. Ward, and Isaac Williams. Its work was carried on through closely reasoned publications called "Tracts of the Times." Through the conversion of some of the leaders, notably Newman and Ward, and its work, the movement affected the entire Catholic Church of England.

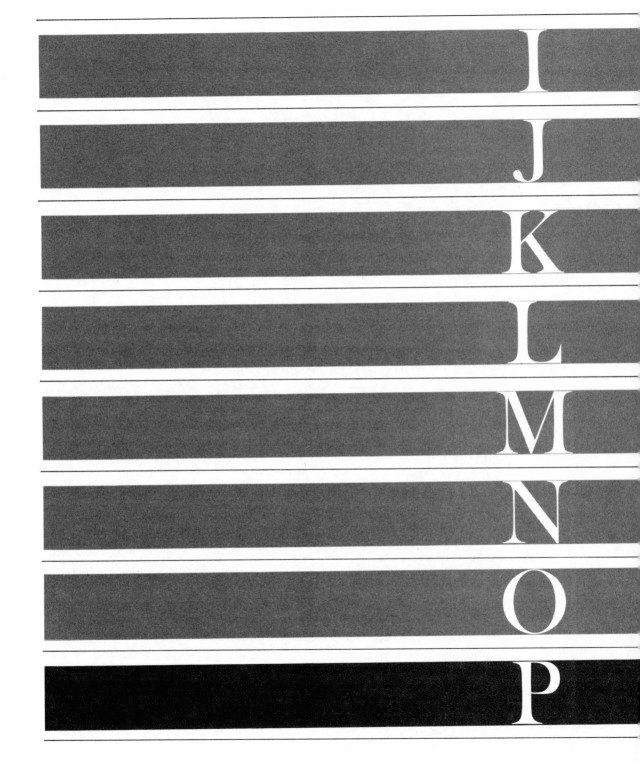

# Pp

## Pacem in Terris

*Pacem in Terris* is the Latin title *(Peace on Earth)* of the encyclical issued by Pope John XXIII in 1963. The prime purpose of this encyclical is to set forth the steps necessary for the human community of persons and nations to establish a sound basis for universal peace on earth, proclaiming the principles of justice, truth, charity, and liberty.

In its discussions of this objective the encyclical sets forth the following, together with the reasoning, scripture foundation, and human concerns: (1) the order existing and to be established between human persons; (2) the internal relations existing within a given State between the human persons and those making up the ruling authorities of the State; (3) the external relations existing between various nations—the international complex; (4) the internal and external relations existing between man, and those that are at present existing between the political communities and the world communities; and (5) the guidance and spiritual exhortation that involve the integration of faith and action.

This is the fourteenth encyclical of the twentieth century based on peace and its attainment. Repeatedly the popes of this century have called for this undertaking on a world scale. As Pope John XXIII declared: "There is an immense task incumbent on all men of good will, namely, the task of restoring the relations of the human family in truth, in justice, in love and in freedom—the relations between individual human beings; between citizens and their respective political communities; between political communities themselves; between individuals, families, intermediate associations and political communities on the one hand, and the world community on the other. This is the most exalted task, for it is the task of bringing about true peace in the order established by God."

This encyclical, in the great tradition of the Church in bringing the message of Christ home to the world, acknowledged that this hope of peace could not be accomplished simply by the instruments of men, but needed, as did all other efforts toward peace, prayer and the help of grace from God. As a statement of exalted principle, *Pacem in Terris* stands as one of the finest declarations

whereby the rights of man, under the recognized will and aegis of God, not only exist but may be brought to recognition and conclusion in our modern world. (See Social Encyclicals.)

## Pacifism

Pacifism is the teaching in modern times that war is (1) contrary to the teaching of the Gospels, especially the Sermon on the Mount (Mt. 5–9), and (2) against the humanitarian and Christian principles as interpreted in the modern world.

The Christian community is a part of the entire secular community and therefore submits to the enactments of the rightful authority in the exercise of force of arms when necessary. St. Thomas Aquinas set forth three conditions for entering into conflict, as for a "just war": (1) it must be on the authority of the sovereign ruler; (2) the cause must be just, that is, to overcome a real and present evil; (3) the belligerents should have the right intention of advancing the good and avoiding the evil. This was also treated in the Thirty-nine Articles of the Anglican Reformers (art. 37).

In modern times with the development and proliferation of military weapons and the fashioning of the atomic bomb, there has been added to all previous arguments the one of "proper means" *(debita modo)*. This means that the warfare must be carried on so that the means applied to the attainment of victory should be within the right moral order, should be morally directed, that is, not against civilian or noncombatant groups, and should not use inhuman devices, for example, nerve gases.

There arises the question of whether there can be a "just war" in our time. The arguments advanced by many that it is impossible because of a sophistication of armaments and the uncontrolled havoc that would result are germane. The other argument is that there is, because of the systems of governments that deny human freedoms, a necessity to seek a change of the political moral scene through recourse to arms.

For the Christian there remains first an adherence to the moral teachings of the Gospels and the Church. But for every Christian there is the constant, continual warfare of the spirit wherein the human person struggles against the forces of evil from without but especially from within. Thus when placed in the framework of personal attainment, yes there is a warfare; when within the area of national struggle, the attainment of peace is and must be one that is morally just and in keeping with the right conscience of individuals. (Cf. Eph. 6:10–17; 2 Cor. 10:1–6; 1 Pt. 5:8–11.)

### Pactum Callixtinum

Pactum Callixtinum is the Latin title of the Concordat of Worms. (See Concordat of Worms.)

### PADRES

Organized in Oct. 1969 by fifty-five Mexican-American priests, this is the abbreviated title of the Spanish name: *Padres Associados para Derechos Religiosos, Educatiovos y Sociales.* The prime purpose of the association is to aid the Church, its authorities, and organizations to better identify with and serve the religious, educational, and social needs of Spanish-speaking Americans.

The association has a national membership and is devoted especially to the leadership programs it has initiated for its members and Mexican-Americans. Its headquarters are located at 2518 W. Commerce St., San Antonio, Texas 78207. (See Las Hermanas.)

### Paganism

Paganism is a broad term, which today includes all religious beliefs, practices, and systems with the exception of Christianity, Judaism, and Mohammedanism. It is thus applied to all those that do not recognize a supreme being, the monotheistic or Trinitarian God-oriented religions that have developed from the revelations of God and are carried on through the fulfillment of the mission given by Christ to His Church.

It is a term derived from the Latin word meaning "countrymen," but it has departed from its bucolic and nationalistic leanings and assumed a controversial aspect, which threatens the beliefs of human persons in the true God, and which today includes antisocial and antireligious actions. In this latter sense it is applied to the countercultural manifestations that appear in morals and manners.

It would thus include the pornographic, amoral, and antimoral practices of modern society, as well as the superstitious practices of spiritism, witchcraft, and astrology.

### Pain Benit

The French term for "blessed bread" is pain benit. The ordinary bread blessed after the celebration of Sunday Mass and given to the people is a sacramental. It is not consecrated nor made like the unleavened bread used in the celebration of the Eucharist, but is a pious custom, recommended to be eaten for the good of body and soul. The practice dates back to the fourth century. (Cf. Antidoron; Oplaki.)

### Palatine

1. Persons having some lesser official standing at the Vatican.

2. Palatine library: the original name of the Vatican library, but now only used of a particular donation of books at the Vatican, made by Maximilian of Bavaria in 1622.

### Palimpsest

Those pieces of leather or parchment, usually from the skins of goats or sheep, cured and made thin, upon which writing was marked, are called palimpsests. The one condition that gives them this designation, more than their use as a writing material, is that a genuine palimpsest has had writing that was scraped off in an economic effort to erase it, and then was written upon a second or third time. In paleography such manuscripts become valuable because frequently in the attempt at erasure some or all of the first writing remained, at least sufficiently to make out the message. These first writings, being older, sometimes contained information that was substantive in learning earlier documents or verifying documents of a later writing. In the more valuable pieces the prescription postdates the original by several centuries, making them records of great worth in determining the original writing.

### Pall

1. Formerly, a piece of linen, about 5 or 6 inches square, folded two or three times and highly starched, which was placed on top of the chalice (over the paten when carrying it to the altar), and over which the chalice veil is draped. Today the practice is abandoned, giving way to the simple corporal. Pall also refers to the linen used to line baskets of altar breads or other containers used for

the purpose of carrying altar breads to the altar at the presentation of the gifts.

2. The funeral pall or the hearse-cloth, as it is sometimes called, is a black cloth of sufficient size, decorated simply, which is draped over the coffin during a funeral requiem Mass, or over the catafalque during a requiem when the body is not present.

### Pallium

The pallium is a narrow circular band made of white wool with two pendants about twelve inches long which hang down in front and back. It is ornamented with six small black crosses, one on each pendant and four on the quadrants of the circular portion. The pallium is worn around the neck and shoulders and over the chasuble by the pope and archbishops. Each metroplitan, within three months after his consecration or ordination, must petition the pope for the pallium. He wears it in solemn pontifical Mass, on certain days, and only within his province, and it is buried with him. Its use by archbishops dates back to the eighth century.

### Palm Sunday

Formerly the title of the Sunday feast before Easter, this day is now called Passion Sunday. On this Sunday palm leaves are blessed and carried in a procession that follows the blessing ceremony. The liturgy recalls the entry of Christ into Jerusalem, but the Mass recalls the Passion of Christ. The Gospel is the account of the Passion by Matthew, chapters 26 through 27. (See Holy Week.)

### Palms, Blessed

Leaves of the trees of the palm family are blessed on Palm Sunday and distributed to the people as sacramentals. They also may be the leaves and branches of the olive tree or of local trees or shrubs. This action is done to commemorate the triumphal entry of Jesus into Jerusalem when the people paved His path with olive branches as a sign of victory and of reverential honor (Mt. 21:8–10; Lk. 19:29–40).

### Panagia

From the Greek word meaning "all holy," panagia is a term of regard used in reference to the Blessed Virgin Mary in the Byzantine Church, much as we say "Our Lady." It is also sometimes applied in other Eastern Rites as a name for the enkolopian.

### Pannykhidia

From the Greek word meaning "the whole night," the pannykhidia is an office for the dead recited by monks and religious of Eastern Rites. (See Office of the Dead.)

### Pantheism

The affirmation whereby all things in the world are held to be in unity in being with God is called pantheism. This has appeared in all historic times and cultures and is the negation of an essential difference between God and created things. It eliminates the human person and places all things of the world into a value concept that destroys their intrinsic worth.

There are several forms of pantheism in the theoretical flow of modern scientism. One is that there is an overall cosmic perspective wherein God is absorbed into or manifested only through the unfolding multitude of created objects and things. Another theory holds that there is an evolutionary progression wherein man together with all created things is moving to ultimate oneness with God who is now only partially made manifest or is only revealed up to this time in our lives. It is called eventual-pantheism, meaning God is immanent in all things only partially, but will be wholly present in the final disclosure, and all will be in union with Him.

The only course that pantheism can take leads to atheism for in the Christian complex God is revealed to man, and all creation attests to this revelation as a substantiating factor not a denial. Likewise in the Christian's viewpoint there is the unity with God the creator attained in the Holy Spirit. It is thus for Christians an ongoing response through faith, hope, and love whereby the grace of God, given to mankind, has been won through redemption, and the sonship with Christ in God through baptism.

### Pantokrator

The name given in Eastern Rites to an image of Our Lord as the Ruler of Heaven and Earth is pantokrator. It is derived from the Greek word meaning "all mighty" and corresponds to the title "Christ the King" in the Roman Rite.

### Papabile

This popular, colloquial Italian term is applied to the one who, after the death of a pope, is considered most likely to be elected because of his record and other factors. It is also applied to those persons who might be chosen for a higher ecclesial rank.

### Papacy

1. A term that signifies: (a) the office of the supreme head of the Church as the Vicar of Christ and the successor of the apostle St. Peter; (b) the historic, political, and temporal power of the Church as it has been and is residing in Rome, and its influence on the national and international aspects of history in ages past and present.

2. The collective listing of the successive popes since St. Peter.

3. The length of reign of any one pope.

### Papal Blessings

The blessing bestowed by the Holy Father. The papal blessing may be given by bishops in their dioceses on Easter Sunday and on two other feasts they may choose. Its form is prescribed by the ritual. This blessing carries a plenary indulgence (A.A.S. 1942).

### Papal Chamberlain

See Monsignor.

### Papal Flag

The Papal flag is the official flag of the Vatican. It consists of two equal fields of yellow and white, divided vertically; on the white portion is the seal of the Vatican, which is formed of the tiara, the crossed keys, and the inscription in Italian "State of the City of the Vatican."

### Papal Letters

These are of six kinds, each having its specific use and each bearing some official pronouncement. They come either from the pope personally or through him from one of the official congregations or commissions of the Holy See. In the order of their importance, they are: bulls, briefs, autographs (written by the pope's own hand and comparatively rare), the *motu proprio,* encyclicals, and *epistolae* (ordinary letters signed by the Holy Father).

### Papal State

The independent state of Vatican city is comprised of approximately 104 acres of land entirely contained within the limits of the city of Rome (cf. Lateran Treaty). This Papal State is governed by a special commission with several functions performed by the Apostolic Signature. Before 1870, the papal states were the temporal land holdings of the papacy.

### Pappas

Pappas is the Greek word for "Father," such as it is used in addressing the Pope as "Holy Father." In the Greek-speaking Churches all priests are called *pappas.* It is also one of the official titles of the Orthodox Patriarch of Alexandria.

### Parable

A fictitious, verbal or written, but lifelike story, told to illustrate a fact or truth is called a parable (cf. Allegory). A great part of our Lord's teaching as presented in Scripture was told in parables, and He is the recognized master of this art of offering doctrine by means of happy illustrations from life. The word parable means "a placing of one thing beside another" for the purpose of comparison. It is a concrete method of teaching. There are more than thirty-two parables recorded in the Gospels, with a large proportion telling in indirect manner of the "reign of God" (Mt. 13:24–30; 22:1–14; Mk. 4:23–27). The power of the parables resides, over and above their exposition and their vividness, in the affinity that exists between the natural and the spiritual orders.

The parable was a manifested "sign" (Rom. 16:25–26; Eph. 3:8–12; Col. 2:2–3) through which the hidden things in the design of God, for example, the kingdom, were revealed (Mt. 13:34–35). Eventually there would no longer be need for parables, for the Holy Spirit would reveal all of God's design (Jn. 16:23–30). The "mystery of Christ" was actually the fulfillment of this design through the Incarnation and the Church (Eph. 1:9–10; 3:1–9; Col. 4:3).

## Paraclete

From the Greek meaning "advocate," the word is now used of the Holy Spirit, the Third Person of the Blessed Trinity. (Cf. Advocate; Holy Spirit.)

The Holy Spirit inspired the OT prophets to announce the promised Messiah, "The spirit lifted me up, and I heard behind me the noise of a loud rumbling as the glory of the Lord rose from its place: the noise made by the wings of the living creatures striking one another, and by the wheels alongside them, a loud rumbling" (Ez. 3:12–13).

The Holy Spirit was promised (Jn. 14:15–17) and was to confirm and strengthen (Acts 1:8; 2:32–33; 3:15), and it was this Holy Spirit who was the true witness (1 Jn. 5:5–10) and the Truth, even as Christ was the Truth incarnate. (Cf. Acts 9:31; Rom. 15:4–5; 1 Cor. 14:3.)

## Paradise

The word as used in Genesis (2:9) is derived through the Greek from its Persian origin, and means literally an "enclosed park." By adaptation, it has come to be a synonym for heaven. However, it is also used in Scripture for the state of bliss, lacking the vision of God, or limbo, as spoken by Christ to the penitent thief on the cross (Lk. 23:43).

There was a second "paradise" for God's Chosen People, the "land flowing with milk and honey," the promised land (Ex. 3:8; 13:5). This was the "heritage" which God promised, gave, and distrib-

uted (Ex. 6:2–9; Dt. 4:35–38; Ps. 105:10–11). When lost, this heritage was to be restored to the chosen people (Ez. 36:1–12; 47:13–22), and this heritage was promised to all peoples (Is. 19:24–25; 65:8–10) and fulfilled by Christ (Mt. 21:33–46; Heb. 1:1–4).

It is thus that paradise is likened to the "kingdom," the promised salvation gained for all by and through Christ. (Cf. Rom. 8:14–17; Gal. 4:1–11.)

## Paradosis

This is the technical word for "tradition," meaning especially the faithful handing on of the gospel in its vital integrity. As such it "includes everything which contributes to the holiness of life, and the increase of faith of the People of God" (DV 8).

Paradosis, meaning literally "beyond giving," is to be found as a living presence in the life and practice of the living Church (Dv 8). It originates with the Apostles and develops in the Church through the Holy Spirit, not as something added on but rather a growth in understanding of the reality and the very words themselves (Kloppenberg). Vatican II lists four factors in development which, with the aid of the Holy Spirit, help this growth: contemplation, study, the intimate understanding that the faithful receive of spiritual things, and the preaching of the successors of the Apostles. Thus, "the development of tradition is the work of the entire Church, of all the holy and prophetic people of God and not of the bishops alone (cf. LG 12)."

The bishops have a specific and exclusive function in regard to tradition, namely, the authentic interpreting of the word of God. Vatican II states: "In holding to, practicing, and professing the heritage of the faith, there results on the part of the bishops and faithful a remarkable common effort" (DV 10). (See Tradition.)

## Paralipomenon, 1 and 2

See Chronicles, Books of.

## Paraliturgical Actions

In the devotional and spiritual life of the Church, not a part of but closely joined to the sacramental life, are those actions that are not strictly a part of liturgy proper but associated with it to a greater or lesser degree. Among these are two grades: (1) those that are an extension of the administration of the sacraments, for example, exposition of the Blessed Sacrament (Eucharist); scriptural or prayer devotions joined to the administration of a sacrament, such as Penance; (2) those devotions that may be done privately or in a group, and among these would be classified the recitation of the rosary, the Stations of the Cross, retreats (in their various forms), and novenas.

Paraliturgical actions, which are always basically a worshipping action directed to God, are not strictly speaking acts of liturgy. They do not always need to involve the community of the faithful. However, in the history and tradition of the Church, these actions have promoted the spiritual lives of those who partake of them and have fulfilled in a singular manner the personal ministry of private and public devotion of the body of Christians who make up the Mystical Body of Christ. The singularity of the paraliturgical actions is found in the individual's response rather than in the fulfillment of a precepted action of the Church.

The liturgy of the Church, found in the Celebration of the Eucharist and the sacraments and in the Liturgy of the Hours, has precedence over paraliturgical actions in the religious order. They may thus be said to be secondary in importance, but in no way should they be discouraged or abandoned by those who seek a devotional life geared to their life style. (See Prayer.)

## Parallelism

A characteristic of the poetic form as found in the Scriptures, parallelism unites the lines by an equal distribution of thought in such a way that the individual lines correspond with each other. There are three kinds of parallelism: (1) *synonymous,* when the second line merely echoes the first, for example, "He who is throned in heaven laughs; the Lord derides them" (Ps. 2:4); (2) *antithetic,* when the second line is in direct contrast to the preceding, for example, "Though they bow down and fall, yet we stand erect and firm" (Ps. 20:9); (3) *progressive,* when the idea expressed in the first line is developed or completed in the following lines, for example, "The law of the Lord is perfect, refreshing the soul; the decree of the Lord is trustworthy, giving wisdom to the simple" (Ps. 19:8).

Parallelism as a poetic use is the union of lines, worked out by the balance of thought, which brings about the correspondence of the lines, achieving a balance by echoing the thought of one line to another, by contrasting the lines, or by having the following lines develop or complete what was expressed in the first line, for example,

"Happy the man who follows not the counsel of the wicked/Nor walks in the way of sinners, nor sits in the company of the insolent . . ." (Ps. 1:1). (Cf. Inspiration of Scripture.)

## Parapsychology

That branch of psychology which investigates extra sensory perception (ESP), psychokinesis (PK), thought transmission, and psychic phenomena in general is called parapsychology or psychical research.

There has been some clash of opinion over whether spiritism or spiritualism has not been classified as the dominant factor in investigations and experiments in parapsychology. Recent standards have evolved, however, which place the spiritist element entirely out of the mainstream of studies made in ESP. Even the evidence of mind control has been accepted as a legitimate area of study, as witnessed by the work of the British Center for Psychical Research.

There are two apparent divergent points of evidential study. One has to do with the techniques that have been developed. The other centers on the interpretation of the findings. Both meet general lack of acceptance because of the inability on the part of the practitioners and the public to arrive at any close type of accounting for the results in a context that can be understood.

The exploratory studies of ESP were first undertaken at Duke University (Durham, North Carolina) under Joseph B. Rhine. A formidable total of results of tests using ESP cards has now been compiled. (ESP cards are sets of 25, with five separate symbols on one side: the square, star, circle, equal armed cross, and wavy lines.) The evidence is indicative of the existence of unconscious, mental or spiritual-oriented phenomena. Further testing is necessary, especially for telepathic states where the bodily condition, such as health or illness, has an influence on the mental state.

There are of course conditions that exist in the spiritual awareness of many persons, which are quite inexplicable without laboratory controls. Among these are the alleged exudations of blood from the skin, the catatonic states that are induced and then claimed to be mystical in nature, and the multilingual transcription by someone in an apparent hypnotic condition. In spiritual circles substantial evidence is always required before a declaration of supernatural intervention is acknowledged. Studies are going forward in many centers, some under the close observation of Church authorities and scholars, to arrive at some analysis that has an accepted framework of recognition and spiritual benefit.

### Parasceve

Literally, a preparation, but as used by St. John (19:14), parasceve meant the preparation for the celebration of the Pasch. Thus it is used in the liturgical name of Good Friday: Sixth feria in parasceve.

It also may be used to refer to the preparation for the day of resurrection, and was thus often called "Preparation Day." (See Calendar, Church.)

### Parekklesia

From the Greek word meaning "beside-church," the parekklesia is any side chapel or apsidal addition to a church building in Eastern Rite Churches. It has many corresponding examples in the Roman Rite, such as "winter chapels."

### Parents, Duties of

Arising out of the office of parent and binding upon both, not by equal share but in fullness upon each (unless some physical reason prohibits), these duties are: to love the children and to show no preference between them, to provide for their upkeep and health, to set a good example, to protect them from occasions of sin, and to secure their education and instruction in Christian doctrine. The neglect of these duties is seriously sinful in the degree of responsibility.

Parenthood is one of the universal experiences that follows and embraces the purpose of marriage and the stability of all human society. In this regard the father and mother freely assume the broader responsibilities of society as a whole, that is, the cultural values to be transmitted, the continuity of the faith and the community.

Vatican II declares: "The family is a kind of school of deeper humanity. But if it is to achieve the full flowering of its life and mission, it needs the kindly communion of minds and the joint deliberation of spouses, as well as the painstaking cooperation of parents in the education of their children. The active presence of the father is highly beneficial to their formation. The children, especially the younger among them, need the care of their mother at home. This domestic role of hers must be safely preserved, though the legitimate social progress of women should not be underrated on that account" (GS 52).

And: "Since the family is a society in its own original right, it has the right freely to live its own domestic religious life under the guidance of parents. Parents, moreover, have the right to determine, in accordance with their own religious beliefs, the kind of religious education that their children are to receive" (DH 5).

### Parish

In general, a parish is a territorial division of a diocese. A quasi-parish is a division of a vicariate or prefecture apostolic. A parish is established as canonical when it has: (1) definite boundaries that have been determined by the local ordinary or by recognized custom; (2) a sufficient means of support from some source that need not be an endowment. This support, of course, means the financial means necessary to maintain the required buildings, at least in major part, and the assigned priest or priests; stole-fees may be a portion of the pastor's support; (3) a parish priest with the ordinary powers of that office. These are by virtue of the order of priesthood and official assignment of the bishop.

There are other qualified distinctions: (1) a *national* parish is one based primarily on the language spoken, but is only canonical in the above sense, even though it includes people who live in the territories of other parishes; (2) a *religious* parish is one authorized, with a priest of a religious community or order as habitual pastor. Such parishes are obliged to submit the same reports to the ordinary as those operated by diocesan clergy.

Vatican II declares: "The parish exists solely for the good of souls. Therefore, by way of enabling the bishop to provide more easily and effectively for pastorates, all rights whatsoever of presentation, nomination, reservation are to be suppressed" (CD 31).

And: "Because it is impossible for the bishop always and everywhere to preside over the whole flock in his church, he cannot do other than establish lesser groupings of the faithful. Among these, parishes set up locally under a pastor who takes the place of the bishop are the most important: for in a certain way they represent the visible Church as it is established throughout the world" (SC 42). (See Community; Status Animarum.)

### Parish Council

The parish council is a group of members of a parish, elected or appointed, who serve in an advisory capacity and give counsel and advice concerning the functions of the parish church and its affiliate properties, its liturgy, music, decoration, and sometimes its social activities. It is not intended to be decision-making, especially in doctrinal matters, or in the corporate structure of the parish where such is established, but rather it serves without being subservient. More broadly the parish council is a means of extending the total mission of the Church to all the nonordained ministers of the Church who are now called the laity or the faithful people of God. This is a parish-centered way of involving them in the aid and support of the members of the ordained ministry, the bishops, priests, and religious.

Vatican II laid the foundation for parish councils in many declarations, as: "In dioceses, as far as possible, there should be councils which assist the apostolic work of the Church either in the field of making the gospel known and men holy, or, else, in the charitable, social, or other spheres. To this end, the clergy and the religious should appropriately cooperate with the laity. While preserving the proper character and autonomy of each organization, these councils will be able to promote the mutual coordination of various lay associations and enterprises. Councils of this type should be established as far as possible also on the parochial, inter-parochial, and inter-diocesan level as well as in the national or international sphere" (AA 26).

A council is formed by mandate of the Bishop of a diocese or with the bishop's approval, or by the direct action of the pastor and parishioners. Each council has a constitution, which is usually approved or certified by Church authorities, and functions according to its constitution or bylaws.

The parish council as a group seeks to render many services to its parish community, to the pastors and associate pastors, and to the Church as a diocesan institution. It is a cooperative group extending service in several special areas: education, finance, maintenance, social action, ecumenism, and liturgy. It should initiate action where none is apparent, not depending upon the priest to point the way, and should emphasize the teachings of the Church on social justice. The council can broaden its own activities through additional committees or special studies. The prime objectives of the council are to serve, to seek a greater spiritual response among its own members and fellow parishoners, and to aid in the up-building of the Mystical Body of Christ in every way possible. It focuses on the parish as a Eucharistic, worshiping community.

For engagement in such opportunities there should be preparation—a catechesis of action. Leadership is a "learned" or acquired process for the majority of people; the mission of the Church is something that must be taught and implemented. Perhaps one day this service by individual parish members will become a special ministry of service, not with privilege but with grace.

Ideally the parish council unifies and coordinates all parish activities. It also leads to a broader involvement in religious concerns of the diocese, the national and universal Church. As an expression of the apostolate of the laity, a parish council is definitely encouraged: "In the Church there are many apostolic undertakings which are established by the free choice of the laity and regulated by their prudent judgment. The mission of the Church can be better accomplished in certain circumstances by undertakings of this kind" (AA 24). (See Diocesan Pastoral Council; National Pastoral Council; Laity.)

## Parish, Experimental

1. This descriptive designation was given more or less unofficially to certain parishes wherein a variety of innovations in the liturgy were permitted before the New Order of the Mass was introduced. The experimental parish role was often gratuitously assumed by some parishes, and some abuses arose from a too loose approach to the liturgy, especially the celebration of the Eucharist. The name is now meaningless.

2. The name experimental parish was also sometimes applied to those parishes that were without boundaries and that existed in a "floating" manner without a church building as such. Some of these still exist in the United States, but, judging from the national and some practical views they have not been successful in fulfilling the true concept of Church as community. (See Community.)

## Parish Priest

A parish priest is one who is designated (c. 451 ff), as the pastor of a parish. A parish priest has ordinary power and is not simply a delegate of the ordinary. As such he rules the parish in his own name but under the delegated authority of the bishop. Being fully qualified, the parish priest has a degree of stability in his office. As a pastor the parish priest may be *irremovable,* that is, given the pastorship of a parish so constituted, which cannot be changed without apostolic indult (c. 454). Or the parish priest may be *removable,* that is, the parish priest may be reassigned to another parish. Particular laws govern the assignment, transfer, and removal of parish priests. In the strict sense, no parish priest is considered irremovable since under the law the ordinary can transfer or reassign all priests for sufficient reason.

Besides rights, the parish priest has certain parochial duties. Before taking possession of the parish he must take the antimodernist oath and make the profession of faith. He also must not be absent from the parish without permission for any extended time; he must offer Mass for the people of the parish about 87 times a year (c. 466) on the proper days unless authorized by the bishop to say the Mass on another day. The sacraments must be given to the people upon reasonable request; he should know his parishioners by periodic visitation, train the young, bring back the lapsed, have care of the sick and dying, encourage works of charity in the parish, and augment faith and piety (through establishment of associations or otherwise). He must, of course, keep the parish books (finances) and make account of his personal effects. Broadly, these are the functions of administration; there are many other duties that arise out of pastoral cares.

Today the parish priest, be he the designated pastor or an associate pastor, is expected to extend his efforts to as broad a community as possible. He may thus be involved in civic and societal affairs, as well as being one who serves the day-in and day-out spiritual needs of those under his immediate care. Much emphasis is thus placed upon the counseling ministry of parish priests and upon their service in overcoming or meeting the ills of the society in which they carry out the pastorally oriented duties assigned to them. (See Pastoral Counseling.)

### Parish Report

See Status Animarum.

### Parishioner

A Catholic who by the fact of domicile or quasi-domicile lives within the territorial boundaries of a parish is called a parishioner. Thus one does not without the pastor's permission become a parishioner by paying pew rent or dues in another parish whose territory does not include his home. The parishioners are to be admonished to attend their own parish church; exceptions are those who belong to national parishes.

### Parochial Mass

1. The Masses that are prescribed by law to be said for the people of a parish by the pastor.
2. The principal Mass of the parish read on Sundays or holy days. Today the custom is to refer to all Masses celebrated in a parish church as parochial Masses, but this is more a description than a designation.

### Parochial School

The parochial school in its prime acceptance is a school of any grade, erected by the right of the Church to establish means of education, and built by the parishioners to serve the children of their parish. Catholic people should send their children, whenever possible to parochial schools or Catholic schools of higher learning. Parents need the permission of the ordinary to send their children to schools that are not Catholic, and even then it is mandatory to provide religious training for the children.

The educational role of the school is secondary to the responsibility of parents. The Church assumes a total educational role, which involves the entire community, adults, parents as cooperators in the religious education of their children, and extends this role to include the college and university students. (See Campus Ministry.)

There is a continuing catechesis that brings to the faithful the knowledge and understanding of the mission of the Church in the world.

### Parousia

Theologically, the parousia is the "second coming" of Christ, but in a more specific manner it is the transcendent act of Christ around which and in which the faith and hope of Christians are gathered. It is the fullness or completion of the salvation of man in the history of the world whereby the humanity of Christ the Savior and Messiah revealed in His glory and in His Church is now manifest and fulfilled in the revelation of Christ as God and Ruler of heaven (Mt. 24:36; 25:31–46; 1 Thes. 5:2; 2 Thes. 2:1–12; Rv. 20:11–15; 22:17–20).

The parousia is first the advent of Christ in the Church (Mt. 16:27–28) and His coming advent into glory (Mt. 24–25; Lk. 21:25–33; 1 Cor. 15:23; 2 Pt. 1:16; 1 Jn. 2:28).

For us it is the culmination of the economy of grace, the advent into eternal union with Christ in the Father (Rom. 15:17; 1 Cor. 1:30–31; 2 Cor. 10:17; Phil. 3:3; 1 Jn. 2:24). Life with Christ will then be a participation, each according to his uniqueness and merit, in the kingdom of Christ and in His glory. (See Judgment, General; Eschatology.)

### Participation in the Liturgy and Life of the Church

It is the modern interpretation, based upon research into the earliest practices of Christians that (1) all persons were given the mission of Christ (Jn. 8:38; Eph. 6:14–15); and (2) that having this mission the individual must take part in fulfilling this mission. "The Christian who does not take up the task of building the temporal order so as to make the world more human and just 'jeopardizes his eternal salvation' (GS 43), that is, he cannot enter into the kingdom of God" (Kloppenburg).

In the light of the teachings of Vatican II the Christian thus aspires "to be in Christ as the sacrament or sign and instrument of intimate union with God and of the unity of all mankind" (LG 1); "to be for the whole race a sure seed of unity, hope, and salvation" (LG 9); "to be an instrument of redemption for all" (LG 9); "to proclaim the kingdom of Christ and God, to establish it among all the nations, and to be the germ, beginning, and instrument of this kingdom" (LG 5); "to bring light to the whole world through the gospel message and to bring together in the one Spirit all men of all nations, races, and cultures" (GS 92).

For the laity Vatican Council II declares emphatically: "Hence the mission of the Church is not only to bring to men the message and grace of Christ, but also to penetrate and perfect the temporal sphere with the spirit of the gospel" (AA 5).

In the light of the above, the taking part in the liturgy of the Church is extended to its true dimension. Not only does the human person participate in the celebration of the Eucharist, sacraments, and prayer life of the Church, but goes beyond this "interior" order of expression to an "exterior" or societal, temporal, world-related order. (See, Liturgy; Community; Mission.)

Regarding taking part in the liturgy proper, Vatican II teaches: "The Church earnestly desires that Christ's faithful, when present at this mystery of faith, should not be there as strangers or silent spectators. On the contrary, through a proper appreciation of the rites and prayers they should participate knowingly, devoutly, and actively. They should be instructed by God's word and be refreshed at the table of the Lord's body; they should give thanks to God; by offering the Immaculate Victim, not only through the hands of the priest, but also with him, they should learn to offer themselves too. Through Christ the Mediator, they should be drawn day by day into ever closer union with God and with each other, so that finally God may be all in all" (SC 48). (See Community.)

## Pascendi Dominici Gregis

*Pascendi Dominici Gregis* is the Latin title ("Feeding the flock of the Lord") of the encyclical of Pope Pius X against the dangers of modernism. It was published Sept. 8, 1907.

This encyclical was a successor to that of Pius IX (d. 1878), which had condemned Modernism in his Syllabus of Errors (1864) and which in turn had been attached to the encyclical *Quanta Cura* ("How great the Care"). The Syllabus cited eighty errors that the liberal spirit of the times had produced, following the attacks upon faith by the rationalists and the emphasis upon the nonspiritual by the materialists. These liberal theories and movements were not only threatening the Church but were upsetting the political, scientific, and economic lives of great numbers of people.

In the *Pascendi* encyclical, the Holy Father set forth the teachings of the magisterium of the Church, the truth of revelation, and the substance of tradition. He attacked the modernist thought along three of its most erroneous lines: (1) the agnostic thinking that declared man could not attain any certain teaching concerning God; (2) the idea that man's belief in God arises from a necessity on the part of man to believe in a God; (3) and the evolutionary theories that held that the development of man had been concurrent with the development of doctrinal teachings and revelation.

The encyclical gave great impetus to overcoming these errors, especially where they were in direct conflict with Church teachings. As a present evil, Modernism does not threaten, for many Christians have recognized its errors. There exists today only a form of "social modernism" that poses as humanistic and is more politically oriented.

## Pasch

The feast of the Passover was originally the first great feast of the Jewish liturgical year, which later began with the month called Nisan (March-April). The feast commemorates the salvation of the Israelites when the avenging angel passed by their homes and struck down only the firstborn of the Egyptians (Ex. 11:1–10). The Pasch was celebrated at "eventide," that is, in the evening at sunset (Dt. 16:6) on the fifteenth of the month, the first day of the Azymes (agricultural feast of seven days), and consisted of the sacrificing of a lamb, roasting it, and eating it with bitter herbs and unleavened bread. The Pasch as a sacrifice was a type of the sacrifice of Christ on the cross and His eucharistic sacrifice.

## Paschal Candle

The Paschal Candle is the large candle blessed at the solemn service on Holy Saturday. Inserted into the candle, in the form of a cross, are five grains, or particles, of incense. The candle should be of beeswax for the greater part, about 75% or according to the percentage determined by the ordinary. The paschal candle is to be lighted at the solemn Mass or the parochial Mass and at vespers on Easter Sunday, Monday, and Tuesday; on Saturday after Easter and on all Sundays, until the Gospel of the Mass on Ascension Day. It may also be lighted on the major feasts of the Easter time. The paschal candle is used at the ceremony of blessing baptismal water when it, or part of it, is immersed in the water.

## Paschal Mystery

The words that designate the Christian redemption are alluded to frequently by Vatican II as the Paschal Mystery or *Mysterium Paschale.* By this is meant the Easter mystery, or Christ-event. Through this mystery of the passion, resurrection, and ascension of Christ fulfilling that promised in the OT (Passover), we have before us the conquest of death and the gift of eternal life (SC 5). Here we have the origin of the Church, of the sacraments, especially baptism and the Eucharist, and the continuing memorial sequence with the Christ-event that we celebrate in the Mass.

This mystery is the NT Passover, that time at which God the Father had determined that Jesus would fulfill the OT theme, would satisfy the promise of the Father. It is the fulfillment of the saving time of the Father in the salvation history of mankind. It is the time of the "Lamb," the sacrifice of change, the "hour" of Christ (cf. Jn. 2:4; 4:21; 5:25; 7:30; 8:20; 12:23). It is the Christian Passover, when the salvific event took place, when Christ the Sacrifice passes from death to life, and the Christian from death to the eternal life promised by God the Father. (Cf. 1 Cor. 5:7; Jn. 19:34–36; 1 Pt. 1:18; Heb. 3:7–13.)

Vatican II teaches concerning this mystery: "Since Christ died for all men, and since the ultimate vocation of man is in fact one, and divine, we ought to believe that the Holy Spirit in a manner known only to God offers to every man the possibility of being associated with the paschal mystery" (GS 22).

And: "The Church has never failed to come together to celebrate the paschal mystery: reading 'every passage of Scripture which referred to him' (Lk. 24:27), celebrating the Eucharist in which the 'victory and triumph of his death are again made present'" (SC 6).

And: "By celebrating the passage of these saints from earth to heaven the Church proclaims the paschal mystery as achieved in the saints who have suffered and been glorified with Christ" (SC 104).

And: "As the Church has always held and continues to hold, Christ in His boundless love freely underwent His passion and death because of the sins of all men, so that all might attain salvation. It is, therefore, the duty of the Church's preaching to proclaim the cross of Christ as the sign of God's all-embracing love and as the fountain from which every grace flows" (NA 4). (See Salvation History.)

## Paschal Precept

See Easter Duty.

## Passion of Christ

The Passion of Christ includes His suffering and sacrificial death on the cross, as it was foretold by Isaias (42:13–43;12) and recorded by all the evangelists (Mt. 26, 27; Mk. 14, 15; Lk. 22, 23; Jn. 18 through 20). The word "passion" alone usually refers to one of these Gospel accounts, read in the liturgy of Holy Week.

Vatican II declares: "The wonders wrought by God among the people of the Old Testament were but a prelude to the work of Christ the Lord in redeeming mankind and giving perfect glory to God. He achieved His task principally by the paschal mystery of His blessed passion, resurrection from the dead, and glorious ascension, whereby 'dying, he destroyed our death and, rising, he restored our life'" (SC 5).

And: "The liturgy of the sacraments and sacramentals sanctifies almost every event in their lives; they (the faithful) are given access to the stream of divine grace which flows from the paschal mystery of the passion, death, and resurrection of Christ, the fountain from which all sacraments and sacramentals draw their power. There is hardly any proper use of material things that cannot thus be directed toward the sanctification of men and the praise of God" (SC 61). (See Paschal Mystery.)

## Passion of the Martyrs

This is a name usually applied to the written account of the sufferings and death of a martyr.

## Passion Sunday

The Sunday of Lent one week (Palm Sunday) before Easter is so named because it begins the liturgical season of Passiontide. It is distinguished in that the attention of the liturgy is directed to the Passion of our Lord. (See Holy Week.)

## Passion Week

The week between Passion Sunday and Easter is known as Passion Week. (See Holy Week.)

## Passiontide

See Passion Sunday.

## Passover

This is the name of one of the three principal religious feasts of the Hebrew religion. The chief elements of the festival are given in chapters 11 and 12 of the Book of Exodus, which contain an account of the last of the plagues sent by God to free the Israelites from Egyptian slavery, namely, that of the slaughter of the firstborn.

The Jewish Passover as a commemorative religious festival is the combination of two different feasts, that of the Passover itself celebrated at home in the evening, and the feast of *mazzot*, the seven-day feast of unleavened bread. Historically both were of pre-Israelitic origin; the Passover was a rite of nomadic shepherds celebrated in the night of the full moon of the vernal equinox or on the occasion of going from their winter to their summer grazing grounds. The feast of *mazzot* had its origin with those living an agricultural life and was celebrated to commemorate the time between the old and new harvest by eating unleavened bread that contained no flour from the previous harvest. These two "nature" feasts were combined by the Israelites to memorialize the event of their liberation in the salvation history of the Chosen People of God.

Passover was a memorial celebration, as recorded in scripture: "This day shall be a memorial feast for you, which all your generations shall celebrate with pilgrimage to the Lord, as a perpetual institution" (Ex. 12:14). It was directed to God and was a sacrificial meal (cf. Dt. 16:1–8; 2 Kgs. 23:22–23). This symbolic reenactment, including the "night of watching" (Christian vigil), the possession of the promised land (the Christian redemption), the partaking of bread and wine (Jos. 5:10–12), and the "holy calling together" of the people (2 Chr. 30:25; Est. 9:20–26), prefigures the sign of the new covenant of Christ. There is likewise, not only a similarity between the OT Passover and the Eucharist of the NT, but there is also a prefigurement of the heavenly banquet prepared for all through the paschal death of Christ (Lk. 22:14–20), and a recalling of the moment when Christ "will come again" (1 Cor. 11:26). (See Paschal Mystery.)

## Pastor

See Parish Priest.

## Pastoral Councils

See Diocesan Pastoral Council; National Pastoral Council.

## Pastoral Counseling

Counseling is the communication process wherein priests, guidance counselors, and others seek to give another person an insight into himself or herself so that the subconscious can be stimulated to a greater output in the expression of truth and faith. For the priest-counselor this is a multifaceted role directed to the development and maintenance of a sense of community in the Church, extending to individual persons, marriage partners, and group counseling. It is also directed to the understanding of interpersonal relationships, the person-to-person encounter, and group dynamics.

This procedure is definitely not a part of the Sacrament of Penance, although some may take it upon themselves to extend the process in various areas.

The counseling role of the priest is a difficult one because his own span of information must be extensive, relating to marriage, alcoholism, the use of drugs, child abuse, youth, and old age. In these instances it is looked upon as a normal process of serving people. Where the priest-counselor becomes a true instrumentality to create a positive reaction, the counseling should result in: (1) further improvement in communication through sermons and other means of community direction; (2) interpersonal guidance and directional procedures whereby the person is led to a greater prayerful relationship to God.

In practice the priest-counselor should acquire the knowledge to recognize the abnormal behavior patterns of people's lives, especially the psychoneurological, and then serve as a referral aide to the person so that proper professional assistance can be obtained.

Pastoral counseling is a part of the educative role of the priest and the administrative and group activity relationships that the priest should acquire to establish true service-leadership between the souls in his care and God.

## Pastoral Counseling Centers

An established, ongoing program to instruct priests and others in the requisites of good pastoral counseling, especially in matters pertaining to marriage and the family, is becoming a part of the service complex of each diocese. In some instances this means a place designated for such programs to be taught along with the other means of communication on an interpersonal basis whereby the priest is trained in the necessary skills to serve the people under his care.

### Pastoral Epistles

The Epistles of St. Paul (1 and 2 Timothy and Titus) have been given this collective name since they were addressed to Timothy and Titus as individual pastors rather than to a church or a group.

### Pastoral Letters

Written by a bishop and addressed to all the faithful, both clergy and laity, under his care as members of his diocese, these are documents directed to the administration of the diocese. They may have emanated from the bishop directly or from a synod he has convened. The term has been applied incorrectly to the annual statement made by the bishops of the United States. (See United States Catholic Conference.)

### Pastoral Ministry

The words "pastoral ministry" are descriptive of the "care of souls," which is the direct charge of the bishops, priests, and deacons in providing the services that are to ensure the salvation of the souls entrusted to them.

However, the ministry of souls is also shared by religious and the laity, for to them has been given a prophetic and priestly role (PC 5 and LG 31). All are, to the degree of their capacities, called to bring the good news of Christ to the world in their work and living. Thus along with the bishops, priests, and deacons they also perform a "ministry of salvation" toward human persons (CD 35).

Pastoral ministry may be directed in a number of areas of endeavor, such as education, administration of the sacraments, and doing essential actions for obtaining the full functioning of the Church's mission. However, it should flow from three basic sources: (1) knowledge of the Church and its works, (2) personal spiritual commitment, (3) cooperation and communication with the community of the Church. Without these fundamental sources all ministry tends to function in a vacuum.

Vatican II teaches that liturgy and teaching are essential (SC 14 and CD 12) and stresses the means of social communication (IM 13) in all areas of pastoral ministry. It also gives the following basic

statements: "In this Church of Christ the Roman Pontiff is the successor of Peter, to whom Christ entrusted the feeding of His sheep and lambs. Hence by divine institution he enjoys supreme, full, immediate, and universal authority over the care of souls" (CD 2).

And: "As lawful successors of the apostles and as members of the episcopal college, bishops should always realize that they are linked one to the other, and should show concern for all the churches. For by divine institution and the requirement of their apostolic office, each one in concert with his fellow bishops is responsible for the Church" (CD 6).

And: "It is not only through the sacraments and Church ministries that the same Holy Spirit sanctifies and leads the People of God and enriches it with virtues. Allotting His gifts 'to each as he wills' (1 Cor. 12:11), He distributes special graces among the faithful of every rank. By these gifts He makes them fit and ready to undertake the various tasks or offices advantageous for the renewal and upbuilding of the Church, according to the words of the Apostle: 'To each person the manifestation of the Spirit is given for the common good' (1 Cor. 12:7)" (LG 12).

### Pastoral Ministry, Schools of

Those institutions of higher learning that offer courses in theology, scripture, Church law, pastoral procedures, music, liturgy, homiletics, sacramental care, and social concerns are called schools of Pastoral Ministry. They are actually postgraduate institutes of four years' duration, which were previously recognized as theologates.

The principal function of schools of Pastoral Ministry is to prepare candidates for the diaconate and the priesthood. To this end the graduate work in theology is combined with a spiritual life, a cultural life, and a recognition of the socioreligious role that the ordained ministers are to have in the modern world. Along with these, personal study programs are often introduced for individuals, which prepare them in specialized fields; these may be in social, spiritual, or physical sciences, in education or communications. (See Seminaries.)

### Pastoral Staff

See Crosier.

### Pastoral Team

See Team Ministry.

### Pastoral Theology

This branch of theology is not a distinct unit but rather a formal presentation of the application of other theological studies to the care of souls and the regulations concerning the administration of the sacraments on a practical as well as an ideal basis. Thus pastoral theology takes dogmatic teaching, moral theology, ascetical theology, and canon law and synthesizes them into the procedures of practical ministry. It directs the cleric in the knowledge of applying the office of teaching, ministering, and directing (governing), which is his by commission through the successors of the apostles. (Cf. Theology; Pastoral Ministry.)

It is a practical theology, which recognizes the fact that the essential mission of the Church must be carried on in contemporary society, using the means of the time and applying the various Church disciplines, sacramentally and corporally, to Christian life. As an extension of all the fundamental services of spiritual action, recognition is given to the socioreligious activities through which the Church is both a functioning entity and a structured organization serving and enlivening the society of Christian peoples.

The Church announces the gospel message of Christ for and through human society. It is thus a communicable mediation of teaching as well as a means of applying the material that such a theology should supply. Pastoral theology therefore sums up the needs of contemporary human society, analyzes them, and formulates the best means of bringing the truth into the evolutionary process whereby people find salvation. (Cf. Pastoral Counseling.)

**Paten**

One of the sacred vessels used in the celebration of the Mass, the paten is a shallow, concave, circular dish, slightly larger than the circumference of the top of the chalice, with thin edges. The paten should be made of suitable material, gold or silver plated with the inner or upper surface at least gold plated; it may be engraved on the lower or bottom side, but the top should be smooth. The paten is consecrated by a bishop or one authorized by him; it is used in the Mass to hold the host and to gather up particles of the broken host from the surface of the corporal (hence the thin edges). In modern usage the paten is usually a deeper dish to hold a larger number of hosts for consecration, and thus it may also serve as a container at the distribution of Holy Communion.

**Pater Noster**

These Latin words mean "Our Father." (See Lord's Prayer.)

**Patience**

An integral and potential part of the virtue of fortitude, patience moderates one's inclination to sadness or rebellion at the endurance of evils or sufferings. It is reasonable control, and in practice makes one withstand with reserve of soul all physical and moral sufferings, out of the motive of love of God and in union with Christ. Its opposite vices are impatience and insensibility but not indifference.

Of all the virtues this is said to be the one that brings to saints the greatest degree of real joy, for it is a prime means of acquiring perfection in the face of suffering and adversity.

**Patriarchs (Patriarchate)**

From the Greek word meaning "ruler of a family," a patriarch was one who held jurisdiction over primates and metropolitans. In the Roman Church, patriarch is largely an honorary title.

Today the extent of jurisdiction and the title are present in the patriarchates and attached to their patriarchs. These are: (1) Rome, the pope, by title Patriarch of the West, with actual jurisdiction over all of the Catholic Eastern Churches and the Church of the Roman rite; (2) the Coptic Patriarch of Alexandria; the Melkite, Syrian, and Maronite Patriarchs of Antioch; the Armenian Patriarch of Cilicia; and the Chaldean Patriarch of Babylon. These are patriarchs by title and have supreme jurisdiction, subject to that of the Supreme Pontiff of Rome.

Since the schism of the East and West, there are patriarchs of the non-Catholic Eastern churches who hold varying degrees of authority but each is supreme in his patriarchates. These are: (1) Orthodox: Constantinople, Alexandria, Antioch, Moscow, Serbia, Romania; (2) Coptic: Alexandria; (3) Syrian Jacobite: Antioch; (4) Nestorian: Iraq; (5) Armenian: the Armenians in the U.S.S.R., Constantinople, Sis, Jerusalem. These have no allegiance to Rome under jurisdiction.

## Patriarchs, Scriptural

The ancient heads of the tribes of the Israelites or the notable leaders of families who lived in Jerusalem (1 Chr. 8) are so named. In all there were nineteen patriarchs. Especially honored are Abraham, Isaac, and Jacob, and the period during which they reigned is known as the Age of the Patriarchs. The title patriarch as used concerning David (Acts 2:29) was one of honor.

## Patrimony

Referring to one of the conditions under which a cleric is permitted to receive Holy Orders, patrimony is actually defined as "sufficient means of his own" so that he need not depend upon others for his support (c. 979-981).

## Patriotism, Christian

As outlined by St. Paul (Ti. 3:1–3), the nation is derived from God. Faith in Christ, therefore, guarantees Christian patriotism, that is, that man fulfill his duties to society.

Vatican II declares: "Citizens should develop a generous and loyal devotion to their country, but without any narrowing of mind. In other words, they must always look simultaneously to the welfare of the whole human family, which is tied together by the manifold bonds linking races, peoples, and nations" (GS 75). (See Nationalism.)

## Patripassianism

An eastern form of the Sabellian heresy of the early third century was named Patripassianism because its adherents believed that God the Father suffered on the cross. (See Heresies.)

## Patrology

This branch of theology studies and investigates the life, writings and doctrines of the orthodox writers of Christian antiquity (cf. Fathers of the Church). Patrology concerns itself not with every writer on a Christian subject but only those who can be quoted with authority, whose writings have been approved by the Church, and, strictly speaking, whose lives have been deserving. The study may be limited to periods of time in the history of the Church or one or more ages. The period of patrology may, for example, be one or more of the following: (1) Christian antiquity, that is, the first eight centuries of the Church; (2) the Middle Ages, or shortly after the death of Charlemagne (d. 814) until about the Reformation; (3) the modern period from the Reformation to the present. Patrology gives a history of dogmatic teaching, a composite picture of the doctrines of the Church, a background of theological culture, and a source of apologetics and persuasive reasoning. This study is also sometimes called patristics. (See Tradition.)

## Patron

1. One who erects and provides the physical necessities of a benefice.

2. The saint, assigned by name, under whose intercessory protection a person, place, or thing is placed. Thus, a person's patron saint is the one after whom he or she is named. Since 1630 the patrons of cities, dioceses, countries, special work, religious orders, etc., must be approved by the Holy See (c. 1278). The titular saint of a parish church is selected by the bishop, and on the feast of the saint, parish priests must offer Mass "for the people" of the parish.

3. A saint who by popular devotion is selected as the patron, for veneration and intercessory affection, by groups, for example, St. Francis de Sales, patron of the Catholic press. A saint so selected may be confirmed by the Holy See as the official patron.

## Patron Saints

Those saints who are specially designated by the Church as intercessors for occupations, countries, and places are called Patron Saints. These are very numerous, since custom has elevated some to singular honor, while others have been more or less adopted by a popular response of the People. The Church officially designates very few patron saints but encourages the paraliturgical devotion to such saints as a means of bringing a greater spiritual depth to the association of veneration and occupation. (The dates included are those when the Church gave official recognition to the saint as a patron.)

*Special occupations:*

Accountants: St. Matthew
Actors: St. Genesius

Advertisers: St. Bernardine of Siena (May 20, 1960)

Alpinists: St. Bernard of Menthon (Aug. 20, 1923)

Altar boys: St. John Berchmans

Anesthetists: St. Rene Goupil

Archers: St. Sebastian

Architects: St. Thomas, Apostle

Armorers: St. Dunstan

Art: St. Catherine of Bologna

Artists: St. Luke, St. Catherine of Bologna

Astronomers: St. Dominic

Athletes: St. Sebastian

Authors: St. Francis de Sales

Aviators: Our Lady of Loreto (1920), St. Therese of Lisieux, St. Joseph of Cupertino

Bakers: St. Elizabeth of Hungary, St. Nicholas

Bankers: St. Matthew

Barbers: Sts. Cosmas and Damian, St. Louis

Barren women: St. Anthony of Padua, St. Felicity

Basket makers: St. Anthony, Abbot

Blacksmiths: St. Dunstan

Blind: St. Odilia, St. Raphael

Blood banks: St. Januarius

Bodily ills: Our Lady of Lourdes

Bookbinders: St. Peter Celestine

Bookkeepers: St. Matthew

Booksellers: St. John of God

Boy Scouts: St. George

Brewers: St. Augustine of Hippo, St. Luke, St. Nicholas of Myra

Bricklayers: St. Stephen

Brides: St. Nicholas of Myra

Brush makers: St. Anthony, Abbot

Builders: St. Vincent Ferrer

Butchers: St. Anthony, Abbot; St. Luke

Cab drivers: St. Fiacre

Cabinetmakers: St. Anne

Cancer patients: St. Peregrine

Canonists: St. Raymond of Penyafort

Carpenters: St. Joseph

Catechists: St. Viator, St. Charles Borromeo, St. Robert Bellarmine

Catholic Action: St. Francis of Assisi (1916)

Chandlers: St. Ambrose, St. Bernard of Clairvaux

Charitable societies: St. Vincent de Paul (May 12, 1885)

Children: St. Nicolas of Myra

Children of Mary: St. Agnes, St. Maria Goretti

Choir Boys: St. Dominic Savio (June 8, 1956), Holy Innocents

Church: St. Joseph (Dec. 8, 1870)

Clerics: St. Gabriel of the Sorrowful Mother

Comedians: St. Vitus

Communications personnel: St. Bernardine

Confessors: St. Alphonsus Liguori (Apr. 26, 1950), St. John Nepomucene

Convulsive children: St. Scholastica

Cooks: St. Lawrence, St. Martha

Coopers: St. Nicholas of Myra

Coppersmiths: St. Maurus

Dairy workers: St. Brigid

Deaf: St. Francis de Sales

Dentists: St. Apollonia

Desperate situations: St. Gregory of Neocaesarea, St. Jude Thaddeus

Dietitians (in hospitals): St. Martha

Dyers: Sts. Maurice and Lydia

Dying: St. Joseph

Ecologists: St. Francis of Assisi

Editors: St. John Bosco

Emigrants: St. Frances Xavier Cabrini (Sept. 8, 1950)

Engineers: St. Ferdinand III

Epilepsy: St. Vitus

Eucharistic congresses and societies: St. Paschal Baylon (Nov. 28, 1897)

Expectant mothers: St. Raymund Nonnatus, St. Gerard Majella

Eye diseases: St. Lucy

Falsely accused: St. Raymund Nonnatus

Farmers: St. George, St. Isidore

Farriers: St. John Baptist

Firemen: St. Florian

Fire Prevention: St. Catherine of Siena

First communicants: St. Tarcisius

Fishermen: St. Andrew

Florists: St. Therese of Lisieux

Forest workers: St. John Gualbert

Foundlings: Holy Innocents

Fullers: St. Anastasius the Fuller, St. James the Less

Funeral directors: St. Joseph of Arimathea, St. Dismas

Gardeners: St. Adelard, St. Tryphon, St. Fiacre, St. Phocas

Glassworkers: St. Luke

Goldsmiths: St. Dunstan, St. Anastasius

Gravediggers: St. Anthony, Abbot

Greetings: St. Valentine

Grocers: St. Michael

Hairdressers: St. Martin de Porres

Happy meetings: St. Raphael

Hatters: St. Severus of Ravenna, St. James the Less

Haymakers: Sts. Gervase and Protase

Headache sufferers: St. Teresa of Avila

Heart patients: St. John of God

Hospital administrators: St. Basil the Great, St. Frances X. Cabrini

Hospitals: St. Camillus de Lellis and St. John of God (June 22, 1886), St. Jude Thaddeus

Housewives: St. Anne

Hunters: St. Hubert, St. Eustachius

Infantrymen: St. Maurice

Innkeepers: St. Amand, St. Martha

Invalids: St. Roch

Jewelers: St. Eligius, St. Dunstan

Journalists: St. Francis de Sales (April 26, 1923)

Jurists: St. John Capistran

Laborers: St. Isidore, St. James, St. John Bosco

Lawyers: St. Ivo, St. Genesius, St. Thomas More

Learning: St. Ambrose

Librarians: St. Jerome

Lighthouse keepers: St. Venerius

Locksmiths: St. Dunstan

Maids: St. Zita

Marble workers: St. Clement I

Mariners: St. Michael, St. Nicholas of Tolentino

Medical record librarians: St. Raymond of Penyafort

Medical social workers: St. John Regis

Medical technicians: St. Albert the Great

Mentally ill: St. Dymphna

Merchants: St. Francis of Assisi, St. Nicholas of Myra

Messengers: St. Gabriel

Metal workers: St. Eligius

Millers: St. Arnulph, St. Victor

Missions, Foreign: St. Francis Xavier (Mar. 25, 1904), St. Therese of Lisieux (Dec. 14, 1927)

Missions, Negro: St. Peter Claver (1896, Leo XIII), St. Benedict the Black

Missions, Parish: St. Leonard of Port Maurice (March 17, 1923)

Mothers: St. Monica

Motorcyclists: Our Lady of Grace

Motorists: St. Christopher, St. Frances of Rome

Mountaineers: St. Bernard of Menthon

Musicians: St. Gregory the Great, St. Cecilia, St. Dunstan

Nail makers: St. Cloud

Notaries: St. Luke, St. Mark

Nurses: St. Camillus de Lellis, St. John of God (1930, Pius XI), St. Agatha, St. Raphael

Nursing and nursing service: St. Elizabeth of Hungary, St. Catherine of Siena

Orators: St. John Chrysostom (July 8, 1908)

Organ builders: St. Cecilia

Orphans: St. Jerome Emiliani

Painters: St. Luke

Paratroopers: St. Michael

Pawnbrokers: St. Nicholas

Pharmacists: Sts. Cosmas and Damian, St. James the Greater

Pharmacists (in hospitals): St. Gemma Galgani

Philosophers: St. Justin

Physicians: St. Pantaleon, Sts. Cosmas and Damian, St. Luke, St. Raphael

Pilgrims: St. James

Plasterers: St. Bartholomew

Poets: St. David, St. Cecilia

Poison sufferers: St. Benedict

Policemen: St. Michael

Poor: St. Lawrence, St. Anthony of Padua

Poor souls: St. Nicholas of Tolentino

Porters: St. Christopher

Possessed: St. Bruno, St. Denis

Postal employees: St. Gabriel

Priests: St. Jean-Baptiste Vianney (April 23, 1929)

Printers: St. John of God, St. Augustine of Hippo, St. Genesius

Prisoners: St. Dismas, St. Joseph Cafasso

Protector of crops: St. Ansovinus

Public relations: St. Bernardine of Siena (May 20, 1960)

Public relations (of hospitals): St. Paul Apostle

Radio workers: St. Gabriel

Radiologists: St. Michael (Jan. 15, 1941)

Retreats: St. Ignatius Loyola (July 25, 1922)

Rheumatism: St. James the Greater

Saddlers: Sts. Crispin and Crispinian

Sailors: St. Cuthbert, St. Brendan, St. Eulalia, St. Christopher, St. Peter Gonzales, St. Erasmus, St. Nicholas

Scholars: St. Brigid

Schools, Catholic: St. Thomas Aquinas (Aug. 4, 1880), St. Joseph Calasanz (Aug. 13, 1948)

Scientists: St. Albert (Aug. 13, 1948)

Sculptors: St. Claude

Seamen: St. Francis of Paola

Searchers for lost articles: St. Anthony of Padua

Secretaries: St. Genesius

Seminarians: St. Charles Borromeo

Servants: St. Martha, St. Zita

Shoemakers: Sts. Crispin and Crispinian

Sick: St. Michael, St. John of God, St. Camillus de Lellis (June 22, 1886)

Silversmiths: St. Andronicus

Singers: St. Gregory, St. Cecilia

Skaters: St. Lidwina

Skiers: St. Bernard

Social workers: St. Louise de Marillac (Feb. 12, 1960)

Soldiers: St. Hadrian, St. George, St. Ignatius, St. Sebastian, St. Martin of Tours, St. Joan of Arc

Speleologists: St. Benedict
Stenographers: St. Genesius, St. Cassian
Stonecutters: St. Clement
Stonemasons: St. Stephen
Students: St. Thomas Aquinas
Surgeons: Sts. Cosmas and Damian, St. Luke
Swordsmiths: St. Maurice
Tailors: St. Homobonus
Tanners: Sts. Crispin and Crispinian, St. Simon
Tax collectors: St. Matthew
Teachers: St. Gregory the Great, St. John Baptist de la Salle (May 15, 1950)
Telecommunications workers: St. Gabriel (Jan. 12, 1951)
Telegraph/telephone workers: St. Gabriel
Television: St. Clare of Assisi (Feb. 14, 1958)
Television workers: St. Gabriel
Tertiaries (Franciscan): St. Louis of France, St. Elizabeth of Hungary
Theologians: St. Augustine, St. Alphonsus Liguori
Throat sufferers: St. Blase
Travel hostesses: St. Bona (March 2, 1962)
Travelers: St. Anthony of Padua, St. Nicholas of Myra, St. Christopher, St. Raphael
Universities: Blessed Contardo Ferrini
Vocations: St. Alphonsus
Watchmen: St. Peter of Alcantara
Weavers: St. Paul the Hermit, St. Anastasius the Fuller, St. Anastasia
Wine merchants: St. Amand
Women in labor: St. Anne
Women's Army Corps: St. Genevieve
Workingmen: St. Joseph
Writers: St. Francis de Sales (April 26, 1923), St. Lucy
Yachtsmen: St. Adjutor
Young girls: St. Agnes
Youth: St. Aloysius Gonzaga (1729, Benedict XIII; 1926, Pius XI), St. John Berchmans, St. Gabriel of the Sorrowful Mother

### Patrons of Countries and Nations

Alsace: St. Odile
Americas: Our Lady of Guadalupe, St. Rose of Lima
Argentina: Our Lady of Lujan
Armenia: St. Gregory the Illuminator
Asia Minor: St. John, Evangelist
Australia: Our Lady Help of Christians
Belgium: St. Joseph
Bohemia: Sts. Wenceslaus and Ludmilla
Borneo: St. Francis Xavier
Brazil: Nossa Senhora de Aparecida, Immaculate Conception; St. Peter of Alcantara

Canada: St. Joseph, St. Anne
Ceylon (Sri Lanka): St. Lawrence
Chile: St. James, Our Lady of Mt. Carmel
China: St. Joseph
Colombia: St. Peter Claver, St. Louis Bertran
Corsica: Immaculate Conception
Czechoslovakia: St. Wenceslaus, St. John Nepomucene, St. Procopius
Denmark: St. Ansgar, St. Canute
Dominican Republic: Our Lady of High Grace, St. Dominic
East Indies: St. Thomas, Apostle
Ecuador: Sacred Heart
England: St. George
Europe: St. Benedict
Finland: St. Henry
France: Our Lady of the Assumption, St. Joan of Arc, St. Therese
Germany: Sts. Boniface and Michael
Greece: St. Nicholas, St. Andrew
Holland: St. Willibrord
Hungary: Blessed Virgin, Great Lady of Hungary; St. Stephen, King
India: Our Lady of the Assumption
Ireland: Sts. Patrick, Brigid, and Columba
Italy: St. Francis of Assisi, St. Catherine of Siena
Japan: St. Peter Baptist
Lesotho: Immaculate Heart of Mary
Lithuania: St. Casimir, Bl. Cunegunda
Malta: St. Paul, Our Lady of the Assumption
Mexico: Our Lady of Guadalupe
Monaco: St. Devota
Moravia: Sts. Cyril and Methodius
New Zealand: Our Lady Help of Christians
Norway: St. Olaf
Paraguay: Our Lady of Assumption
Peru: St. Joseph
Philippines: Sacred Heart of Mary
Poland: St. Casimir, Bl. Cunegunda, St. Stanislaus of Cracow, Our Lady of Czestochowa
Portugal: Immaculate Conception, St. Francis Borgia, St. Anthony of Padua, St. Vincent, St. George
Republic of South Africa: Our Lady of the Assumption
Russia: St. Andrew, St. Nicholas of Myra, St. Therese of Lisieux
Scandinavia: St. Ansgar
Scotland: St. Andrew, St. Columba
Silesia: St. Hedwig
Slovakia: Our Lady of Sorrows
South America: St. Rose of Lima
Spain: St. James, St. Teresa
Sweden: St. Bridget, St. Eric
United States: Immaculate Conception

Uruguay: Our Lady of Lujan
Wales: St. David
West Indies: St. Gertrude
(See Apostles of Places, Peoples.)

## Patroness of the United States

At the apparition of Guadalupe, the Blessed Virgin Mary declared herself the special Patroness of the Americas. It is under her title of the Immaculate Conception that she was declared, in 1846, by the concerted declaration of the Bishops of the United States to be the Patroness of the United States. In accord with this, the chief cathedral of the United States is called Immaculate Conception Cathedral. (See Guadalupe, Our Lady of; Immaculate Conception; Apostles of Places, Peoples.)

## Paul, St.

The Apostle Paul was the outstanding Apostle of the Church through his writings. His life, conversion, teaching, and missionary work make him singular among all the other Apostles and merit for him the title of "Apostle of the Gentiles."

Paul was born in Tarsus, about the year A.D. 5. His parents were Jews, devout and strict in their observance of the religious laws as members of the tribe of Benjamin (Rom. 11:1). This undoubtedly caused them to name their son Saul, after the first King of Israel. Although it is sometimes asserted that Paul changed his name from Saul when he began his missionary work among the Gentiles, it was not uncommon for Jewish youths to have two names, one Hebrew and the other Roman or Greek, because of the predominant influence of these nations on the lives of all at that time.

Paul's parents were Pharisees (Acts 26:4–5; Acts 23:6), and he was brought up in a religious manner (Phil. 3:5). His father and mother were, however, Roman citizens, which gave them a status unlike other Hebrews, for as the writer Cicero said: "If a Roman citizen is tied up, it is a misdeed; if he is struck, it is a crime; and if he is killed, it is as bad as murdering one's father." Thus Paul could not be scourged (Acts 16:35–40; 22:24–29); he could assume the protection of Roman authorities (Acts 23:27), and if brought before a court of law anywhere in the Roman Empire, he could appeal to the highest court in Rome (Acts 25:10–12).

Paul undoubtedly came to Jerusalem for his higher education, probably at about the age of 15. It is doubtful that he ever married but probably associated with and followed the life style of a community of Jews living near the Dead Sea, the Essenes, who considered celibacy an ideal. While in Jerusalem Paul had the advantage of being educated by one of the great teachers of the time, Gamaliel, a man of letters and great outlook, one who had a balanced attitude toward Christianity (Acts 5:33–39). There was undoubtedly some influence from the Greek community upon Paul's education (cf. Acts 21:37; 22:2), and since Greek was spoken everywhere, this was one of the languages in which he was well versed.

There is no mention in any of Paul's writings that he had met Jesus of Nazareth during his days in Jerusalem. But he was aware of Jesus certainly, as was his prime teacher Gamaliel (cf. Acts 5:38–39). And among the Greek-speaking Jews, those who showed great influence from the Greek or Hellenist culture were certainly Paul and Stephen (cf. Acts 6:8–15). It was at the death of Stephen that Paul realized a new force in the community of peoples about him, for he was present when Stephen preached (Acts 7:1–53) and witnessed his martyrdom (Acts 7:54–60).

Scripture tells us that Paul concurred in the death of Stephen and began to persecute the Church—and one may assume that such persecution was not an idle pastime but had to be a recognition of a new force of religion taking place, which would supplant Judaism (cf. Acts 8:1–3).

Paul's first encounter with Christ was on the road to Damascus where he went to arrest some followers of this new religion. It was here that God manifested his glory to Paul, as the Apostle wrote: "For God, who said 'let light shine out of darkness,' has shone in our hearts, that we in turn might make known the glory of God shining on the face of Christ" (2 Cor. 4:5–6). (Cf. also Acts 9:1–23; 22:1–21; 26:1–19.)

After his vision on the Damascus road, Paul went into the city and was baptized by Ananias (Acts 9:10–19), and it was in that city that the Apostle began his preaching. He went into Arabia (Gal. 1:17), and many have considered this a further preparation, like a retreat, for more apostolic work. At any account, Paul made a journey to Jerusalem and met St. Peter (Gal. 1:18–20; cf. Acts 9:26–30) and was accorded the recommendation of St. Barnabas (Acts 9:26–27).

The Apostle had a trade, that of a tent-maker (Acts 18:3), but he was not a tradesman in the usual sense. Rather, it was a competence that made it possible for him to work in various places and maintain himself (Acts 20:33–35). Because he was self-supporting, Paul could undertake his missionary work in lands where no Christian would come forward to give assistance to him until he had been effective among them. In all Paul made three extensive journeys about the eastern Mediterranean Sea, and his fourth took him to Rome where in the year A.D. 67 he was beheaded, the only form of capital punishment permitted for Roman citizens.

During his travels the Apostle Paul was a champion of champions. He took on all the fringe groups who were emerging in a world that was rapidly falling into moral collapse. He challenged the sceptics, the cynics who were the "wild ones" of the time, the Epicureans, the Stoics, and the Gnostics. In all his preaching, in the voluminous writings he sent out, the one constant message was freedom in Christ, declaring the eschatological certainty, the culmination of faith and hope: "For I am certain that neither death nor life, neither angels nor principalities, neither the present nor the future, nor powers, neither height nor depth, nor any other creature, will be able to separate us from the love of God that comes to us in Christ Jesus, our Lord" (Rom. 8:38–39).

The message Paul gives to the Church and to all Christians is a dynamic one (Rom. 1:4). He taught that the Christian life is coming to know the power of the resurrection of Christ (Phil. 3:10), that the material world is not the wisdom of salvation (1 Cor. 2:6–10), and that the spiritual is the right way to proceed. For Paul the spiritual man is one on whom God acts, one on whom Christ has a real and lasting influence. He declares: "The natural man does not accept what is taught by the Spirit of God. For him, that is absurdity. He cannot come to know such teaching because it must be appraised in a spiritual way. The spiritual man, on the other hand, can appraise everything, though he himself can be appraised by no one" (1 Cor. 2:14–15).

The importance of Paul to the world is twofold: he was chosen by Christ to be a special apostle; and he was a man of the utmost love because he had seen and could communicate the glory which he had seen. As Vatican II states: "Blessed Paul, the teacher of the Gentiles, who was 'set apart for the gospel of God' (Rom. 1:1), declares that he became all things to all men that he might save all" (PO 3). (See the Epistles under their several listings.)

## Pauline Privilege

This is not the dissolution of sacramental marriage, but applies only in the instance of the marriage of unbaptized persons. Those unbaptized cannot receive a sacrament, other than baptism itself. The Pauline Privilege is based upon the teaching of St. Paul presented in 1 Cor.

7:12–15, and is treated in canon law (c. 1120–1127). Its application is this: if in a valid marriage, contracted by two unbaptized persons, one of the parties later receives valid baptism and the unbaptized party refuses to live with the baptized spouse without causing the latter grave sin, the unbaptized person must be questioned as to whether he or she will be baptized or live in peace without causing sin to the baptized (called "giving interpellations"). These interpellations may be dispensed with for good reason. It follows then, that, if the answers are negative, the baptized party is free to contract marriage with a Catholic, provided he or she gave no cause of dissatisfaction to the unbaptized party after having been baptized. Thus, upon entry into the second marriage, the bond of the first is dissolved by force of the Pauline Privilege, which is given in accord to the will of Christ in favor of conversion to the Christian faith. (Cf. Marriage, Sacrament of; Montana Case.)

## Pax

Pax is the Latin word meaning *peace.*

1. The kiss of peace (cf. Sign of Peace).

2. *Pax dei,* the immunity from the consequences of private feuds granted to clerics and others and extended to some places as confirmed by Pope John XIX in 1030 (cf. Truce of God).

3. The Pax or *asculatorium,* a carved tablet or disc with a handle, used in medieval times to convey the kiss of peace from the celebrant to the people present. This is also called *pax-brede* in England.

4. *Pax Romana,* title of a confederation of Catholic University students whose objective is the promotion of international peace.

5. Peace be to you, the greeting which the bishop gives to those present at his Mass, instead of the "Lord be with you," after the *Gloria.*

## Pax Christi

This Latin title means "Peace of Christ." Established in 1948, Pax Christi is the name of an International Catholic movement for peace in the world. It supplants or augments to a large extent the work of *Pax Romana.* As a movement it was established in the United States in 1973, publishes the *Thirdly Publication* three times a year, and has its headquarters at 1335 N Street, N.W., Washington, D.C. 20005. It is not to be confused with the *Pax Christi* group, which forms a lay institute operating in the state of Mississippi.

## Peace

The concept of peace is used in many religious contexts. As it developed in the unfolding of the scriptural message, peace first meant simply happiness in all its many aspects. It was a possession of "good things." The biblical concept is essentially different from our modern idea and really more positive, especially as it was understood as *"shalom"* (Prv. 3:2), and to wish another person peace was in its true sense the giving of a sincere greeting.

The Israelites also understood peace in relation to the covenant God had made with them, the "covenant of peace" as Isaiah spoke of it (Is. 54:10; also Ez. 34:25–31). And this peace would be a gift of the Messiah (Is. 9:5–6), and as such would be one of justice (Is. 32:16–18; Zec. 9:9–10).

In the NT, under the new covenant, the term peace has taken on an even deeper meaning. First, it has lost the narrowness implied in its association with material things. Second, it embraced the very life of the Christian, bringing the good news of the kingdom (Lk. 1:28; 2:14; 19:38–40). St. Paul teaches that this peace is joined with grace (Rom. 1:1–7; 1 Cor. 1:1–3; Gal. 1:1–5), and peace is reconciliation with God (Phil. 4:4–9; Eph. 2:13–18; Rom. 5:1–2). For the Christian, then, the essential of peace is that of Christ Himself, by whom every Christian gives witness (2 Tm. 2:22–25; Jas. 3:14–18; Col. 3:12–15; Heb. 12:14; Rom. 14:19; Mt. 5:9).

In other contexts, peace is referred to as "the absence of conflict," or, philosophically, the "tranquility of order." It is the work of justice, and more basically the product of charity or the love of all in a new fellowship of understanding. Vatican II teaches: "As a body and individually, the laity must do their part to nourish the world with spiritual fruits (cf. Gal. 5:22), and to spread abroad in it that spirit by which are animated those poor, meek, and peacemaking men whom the Lord in the gospel calls blessed (cf. Mt. 5:3–9)" (LG 38).

And: "Peace is not merely the absence of war. Nor can it be reduced solely to the maintenance of a balance of power between enemies. Nor is it brought about by dictatorship. Instead, it is rightly and appropriately called 'an enterprise of justice' (Is. 32:7). Peace results from that harmony built into human society by its divine Founder, and actualized by men as they thirst after ever greater justice" . . .

"This peace cannot be obtained on earth unless personal values are safeguarded and men freely and trustingly share with one another the riches of their inner spirits and their talents" . . .

"Peace is likewise the fruit of love, which goes beyond what justice can provide" . . .

"A firm determination to respect other men and peoples and their dignity, as well as the studied practice of brotherhood, is absolutely necessary for the establishment of peace" (GS 78).

And: "Christians who take an active part in modern socioeconomic development and defend justice and charity should be convinced that they can make a great contribution to the prosperity of mankind and the peace of the world" (GS 72).

## Peace of God

See Truce of God.

## Peace, Sign of

In the Order of the Mass, in the Communion rite, following the Lord's Prayer and the doxology, the celebrant says the Sign of Peace, reading: "Lord Jesus Christ, you said to your apostles: I leave you peace, my peace I give you. Look not on our sins, but on the faith of your Church, and grant us the peace and unity of your kingdom, where you live for ever and ever." The people of the assembly answer: "Amen." The priest then adds: "The peace of the Lord be with you always," and the people answer: "And also with you."

Following this exchange, the priest or deacon may add: "Let us offer each other the sign of peace."

It is then that the people of the assembled community turn to their immediate neighbors and exchange a greeting, a shake of the hand, or other sign of peace and friendship. This need not be an elaborate exchange and there are no ritualistic words to be said, some preferring to say: "Peace be with you" or "The peace of Christ be with you" or "God bless you." The response may be equally simple.

This kiss of peace, both as a sign of recognition of fellowship, respect, or friendship, is essentially a sign of reconciliation, of expressing the mutual regard of Christian for Christian. As a sign of respect this had its beginning in Jewish history, meaning peace and material well-being (Jgs. 19:20; 2 Sm. 18:28; Mt. 10:12–14). It was also a ceremonial courtesy that was a preliminary ritual of eating a meal together, and as such should not be omitted (cf. Lk. 7:45). St. Paul recognized this sign of peace as an expression of Christian community (Rom. 16:16; 1 Cor. 16:20; 2 Cor. 13:12). And St. Peter considered this greeting a sign of union with Christ, or Christ-like togetherness (1 Pt. 5:14).

## Pectoral Cross

As an official ornament of office, this cross has come to be used only since the seventeenth century. It is worn on the breast, suspended from a chain or cord about the neck, by the pope, cardinals, abbots, abbesses, and certain other prelates. The pectoral cross should be made of gold and may be decorated with gems; that of a bishop usually contains relics of a martyr.

## Pelagianism

This is a heresy, begun shortly after A.D. 400 by a British monk, Pelagius. Its teaching rejected the doctrine of original sin, emphasized the natural over the supernatural to the extent that it was possible to attain salvation without grace. Its teaching was ably refuted by St. Augustine. Pelagianism was condemned by the Councils of Carthage (411) and Milevis (416). It died out after the condemnation given by the Council of Ephesus in 431. (Cf. Semi-Pelagianism.)

The position taken by the Pelagians was one that did away with the grace and freedom of the human person. Their chief error was in asserting that they could obtain salvation by themselves. (See Heresy.)

## Penalty, Ecclesiastical

See Censure.

## Penance

1. In essence penance is that virtue whereby the human person, through the grace of God, comes to know and recognize his own sin and sin in general. In turn penance turns toward contrition as an act directed to God, and it assumes the turning away from personal sin in the future.

2. Because of the acknowledgement of one's sin, there arises in the Christian a responsibility for personal sin and the desire to eradicate the effects of sin that are existential and cumulative. It is thus an act of courage or fortitude wherein one is willing to accept those acts of mortification,

prayers, and resolves to struggle against future sins, not out of a fear of God, but out of a love for God and a sense of humility.

## Penance, Sacrament of

An entirely new understanding of the Sacrament of Penance has taken place since the deliberations of Vatican II. A new name has been introduced; it may be called the *Order of Penance,* which is descriptive of the action in the sequential manner, or it may be called the *Rite of Reconciliation,* which is more accurate and descriptive of what the action accomplishes. But the simple title of Sacrament of Penance remains acceptable and official.

In the decree of the Sacred Congregation for Divine Worship, the basic background of thought for this change was set forth to teach and clarify what the sacrament intends. The *matter* of the sacrament: the sins committed after baptism and the necessary matter, the mortal sins that have not previously been forgiven, remain the same. Also, the *form* of the sacrament; the words of absolution together with the prayers, remains the same, although the formula may vary. (See Sacraments, Seven.)

The Decree states: "Reconciliation between God and men was brought about by our Lord Jesus Christ in the mystery of his death and resurrection (cf. Rom. 5:10). The Lord entrusted the ministry of reconciliation to the Church in the person of the Apostles (cf. 2 Cor. 5:18–21). The Church carries this ministry out by bringing the good news of salvation to men and by baptizing them in water and the Holy Spirit (cf. Mt. 28:19).

"But because of human weakness, Christians 'turn aside from [their] early love' (cf. Rv. 2:4) and even break off their friendship with God by sinning. The Lord, therefore, instituted a special sacrament of penance for the pardon of sins committed after baptism (cf. Jn. 20:21–23), and the Church has faithfully celebrated it throughout the centuries—in varying ways, but retaining its essential elements.

"The Second Vatican Council decreed that 'the rite and formulas of penance are to be revised in such a way that they may more clearly express the nature and effects of this sacrament.' In view of this the Congregation for Divine Worship has carefully prepared a new Rite of Penance so that the celebration of the sacrament may be more fully understood by the faithful.

"In this new rite, besides a *Rite for Reconciliation of Individual Penitents,* a *Rite for Reconciliation of Several Penitents* has been drawn up to emphasize the relation of the sacrament to the community.

This rite places individual confession and absolution in the context of a celebration of the word of God. Furthermore, for special occasions a *Rite for Reconciliation of Several Penitents with General Confession and Absolution* has been composed in accordance with the Pastoral Norms of General Sacramental Absolution, issued by the Congregation of the Faith on June 16, 1972.

"The Church is solicitous in calling the faithful to continual conversion and renewal. It desires that the baptized who have sinned should acknowledge their sins against God and their neighbor and have heartfelt repentance for them, and it tries to prepare them to celebrate the sacrament of penance. For this reason the Church urges the faithful to attend penitential celebrations from time to time. The Congregation has therefore made regulations for such celebrations and has proposed examples or specimens which episcopal conferences may adapt to the needs of their own regions."

In the early Church the Sacrament of Penance was referred to as a "second baptism," a baptism brought about through the tears of the penitent. In the new Rite of Penance it is said: "The Church possesses both water and tears; the water of baptism and the tears of penance" (n. 2). And it calls for an inner conversion, "This inner conversion of heart embraces sorrow for sin and the intent to lead a new life. It is expressed through confession made to the Church, due satisfaction, and amendment of life. God grants pardon for sin through the Church, which works by the ministry of priests" (n. 6).

And: "The sacrament of penance includes the confession of sins, which comes from the knowledge of self before God and from contrition for those sins. However, this inner examination of heart and the exterior accusation should be made in the light of God's mercy. Confession requires in the penitent the will to open his heart to the minister of God, and in the minister a spiritual judgment by which, acting in the person of Christ, he pronounces his decision of forgiveness or retention of sins in accord with the power of the keys" (n. 6b).

The people of God make up the Church and while the Church is holy as a mark of her divine institution, its members need purification and renewal (cf. Eph. 5:25–26). It is thus that penance in the life and liturgy of the Church and the seeking of perfection which Christ desires (cf. Mt. 5:48) continues repentance in many different ways. "In the sacrament of penance, the faithful 'obtain from the mercy of God pardon for their sins against him; at the same time they are reconciled with the Church which they wounded by their sins and which works for their conversion by charity, example, and prayer'" (LG 11) (n. 4).

The Sacrament of Penance is thus made up of the following essential parts: (1) contrition for sins (see Penance) including a heartfelt sorrow and the intention of sinning no more; (2) confession of sins, which is the acknowledgment of personal sin before God derived from a knowledge (examination of conscience) of one's sins; (3) the performing of an act of penance or satisfaction on the part of the penitent, which is in degree suited to the offense and which is intended to call attention to a renewal of life (cf. Phil. 3:13–16); (4) the sign of absolution, which is the action whereby the minister grants, through God, pardon to the penitent.

The celebration of the Sacrament of Penance may be in accord with the formulas established by the Church. It is celebrated in the "place and location prescribed by law." This may be a confessional, a counseling room, a room of reconciliation, or any suitable place. The sacrament may be celebrated at any time on any day. (Cf. Reconciliation Room.)

The sacrament may be celebrated in the following ways:

1. Through the rite for the reconciliation of individual penitents. This consists of: (a) prayer as a preparation and enlightenment; (b) the recall or reflection on the past, and examination of conscience; (c) a passage of scripture read or spoken by the priest; (d) the actual confession of sins, through a simple statement of the nature of the sin, keeping in mind *what* you did, *why* you did it, and *how* you can better yourself in the future, and giving the number of times a sin was committed if possible; (e) the saying of a prayer of sorrow (contrition) and the absolution of the priest; this is followed by a prayer in praise of God and the dismissal.

2. The Rite for Reconciliation of several penitents with individual confession and absolution. This is (a), (b), and (c) above with private confession by the individual.

3. The Rite for Reconciliation of penitents with general confession and absolution. "Those who receive pardon for grave sins by a common absolution should go to individual confession before they receive this kind of absolution again, unless they are impeded by a just reason" (n. 34).

4. Penitential celebrations, which "are gatherings of the people of God to hear the proclamation of God's word. This invites them to conversion and

renewal of life and announces the freedom from sin through the death and resurrection of Christ. The structure of these services is the same as that usually followed in celebrations of the word of God and is given in the *Rite for Reconciliation of General Penitents*" (n. 36). This is commonly called "communal celebration," but there is no statement of sins on the part of penitents. Rather this is a part of the catechesis of reconciliation, preparation, and renewal.

### Penitent

Penitent is the official name for the person who seeks reconciliation with God and with the community of the Church through the Sacrament of Penance. It is also more loosely used as designating one who seeks to perform individual acts of penance (mortification), either privately or publicly; or it may be applied to anyone who acknowledges sorrow for sins of the past.

### Penitential Psalms

Psalms 6, 31, 37, 50, 101, 129, and 142 have been given this collective name because of their expression of sorrow for sins and of repentance. (See Psalms, Book of.)

### Penitentiary, Sacred Apostolic

The first in rank of the tribunals of the Holy See, the Sacred Penitentiary exercises jurisdiction in the sacramental "internal forum," but only in the sense that it is an extension of the tribunal of penance. Its deliberations are most secret; it acts to grant absolution from reserved cases, to issue instructions to confessors, and it handles secret cases, such as dispensations from secret matrimonial impediments or private vows and has charge of the nondoctrinal aspects pertaining to indulgences. The Sacred Penitentiary came into existence as an aid, directly under the pope, during the pontificate of Pope St. Gregory (d. 604). Since 1917, the Sacred Penitentiary studies the dogmatic content of prayers and grants indulgences upon them after approval of the content.

### Pension

According to canon law, the local ordinary may impose upon a parish the obligation of a pension (fund for sustenance) for a pastor or priest who has resigned or been disabled. Such a pension continues only during the lifetime of the one pensioned (c. 1429, sec. 2).

### Pentateuch

From the Greek, literally, "five books," this is the collective name for the five OT books (the name

signifies a "book of five rolls") written by Moses. Consisting of Genesis, Exodus, Leviticus, Numbers, and Deuteronomy, the Pentateuch gives the religious history of mankind, particularly the Chosen People, from the creation of the world and the first man to the death of Moses. It also records the laws of the theocratic system of the Jews. The Pentateuch is referred to in the NT as "the book of the Law" (Gal. 3:10) and simply "the Law" (Rom. 3:21).

### Pentecost

Originally, this was the second feast in rank of the Jews, the celebration of thanksgiving for the harvest and the ending of Passover time (cf. Dt. 26:1–11). Later it was a celebration of the giving of the law to Moses at Sinai (cf. Ex. 20). In Christian recognition, Pentecost is the feast celebrated 50 days after Easter or ten days after the Feast of the Ascension. It commemorates the descent of the Holy Spirit on the Apostles (Acts 2:1–42), as foretold by Christ (Jn. 16:7). It marks the beginning of the active apostolic work and is hailed as the birthday of the Church, for it was through the coming of the Holy Spirit that the Church began to form the members of the new kingdom.

In carrying out the Christian tradition there was a transformation from the Jewish feast to the Christian feast, which is one of liberation. The new Pentecost was a step into the spiritual law of liberty or as St. Peter spoke on the first Pentecost of the new covenant: "You must reform and be baptized, each one of you, in the name of Jesus Christ, that your sins may be forgiven; then you will receive the gift of the Holy Spirit" (Acts 2:38). For the Christian there is the external law of God plus the internal law of the spirit, or the gift to obey this law (2 Cor. 3:1–3). It is the Spirit who makes effective the new law and by coming to each one, enables us to profit by and fulfill the acts necessary for salvation (1 Cor. 3:16; 6:9–20; Rom. 5:5; 8:26–27; 2 Thes. 2:13–14). Without the Spirit there is no fulfillment possible (Gal. 3:13–14; 4:3–7; 5:13–26; Rom. 7:6). Thus the feast of the harvest is transformed by the Spirit and made fruitful with the gifts of God through Christ (Rom. 8:1–7; Eph. 5:18).

## Pentecostal Churches

The Pentecostal movement began first in England in the eighteenth century and expanded and developed in the early twentieth century. It received its greatest impetus in Britain between the years 1925 and 1935 under the preaching of two Welshmen, Stephen and George Jeffreys and their nephew Edward Jeffreys. In America its greatest spread came about through the Assemblies of God denominations.

The Pentecostal belief is based fundamentally upon the teachings of John Wesley (1703 to 1791) as expressed in the Holiness churches. (See Methodism.) This belief is in a "second blessing," which is sanctification by the Holy Spirit wherein one feels exalted by the direct action of the Holy Spirit. This later developed into the teaching that the Holy Spirit acts not only in the emotional reaction but also in the outpouring of gifts, resembling those of the first Pentecost (Acts 2:4), namely, the speaking in tongues (glossolalia) and the gifts of prophecy and healing. These manifestations usually take place at revival meetings when a confession of sins is made and the preacher calls for the gifts of the Holy Spirit. Pentecostals further believe that all sickness is caused by sin and that all diseases can be cured by faith in Christ. All are fundamentalist in their biblical thinking.

In the United States and Canada there are a number of groups within the Pentecostal Fellowship of North America: Assemblies of God; Church of God; Church of God, Mountain Assembly; Congregational Holiness Church; Elim Missionary Assemblies; International Church of the Foursquare Gospel; International Pentecostal Assemblies; Open Bible Standard Churches; Pentecostal Assemblies of Canada; Pentecostal Holiness Church; Calvary Pentecostal Church; Pentecostal Church of God of America, Inc.; United Pentecostal Church, Inc.; Church of God, New York; Church of God in Prophecy; Church of God in Christ; Apostolic Overcoming Holy Church of God; and Pentecostal Assemblies of the World, Inc. (See Congregationalism.)

## Pentacostalism, Catholic

There has been much reported about a Catholic "revival" in the basic teaching of the action of the Holy Spirit in a direct manner. This has taken place in prayer groups, student activities, and conferences of activists of many localities. There is one predominant caution that must be emphasized: these persons must have and acknowledge an accountability to the episcopal authority as it rests in the Church. The Holy Father has offered three principles for judging what is truly of the Spirit: fidelity to authentic doctrine, discernment in striving for those gifts most useful to the community, and the presence of love. (See Charismatic Renewal, Catholic.)

## Pentecostarion

The Pentecostarion is the liturgical book containing the liturgical services from Easter Sunday to the Sunday of All Saints, the first Sunday after Pentecost, as used in the Byzantine Churches. It is one of the five principal liturgical books used in the Byzantine Rite.

## People of God

A biblical term that was brought to the fore by the documents of Vatican II, the people of God is a collective phrase. There is first a scriptural background for this term; secondly, its use is general in Church language. However, in neither instance should it be assumed that the term when used of the Church is all-inclusive of the attributes of the Church.

Thus Walter M. Abbott, S. J., wrote in comment on the *Dogmatic Constitution on the Church (Lumen Gentium)*: "Completing the study of the biblical images and designations in the second half of Chapter I, the Constitution devotes an entire chapter to the description of the Church as the 'new People of God.' This title, solidly founded in Scripture, met a profound desire of the Council to put greater emphasis on the human and communal side of the Church, rather than on the institutional and hierarchical aspects which have sometimes been overstressed in the past for polemical reasons. While everything said about the People of God as a whole is applicable to the laity, it should not be forgotten that the term 'People of God' refers to the total community of the Church, including the pastors as well as the other faithful" (Angelus edition, p. 24 f.).

1. *Scriptural background:* The essential difference between a "chosen people" and the "People of God" is that between two freedoms: the free choice of God in choosing a people, and the freedom of the individual in responding to God through faith.

From this follows a recognition between the two covenants of God with mankind (Gn. 17:1–14; Ex. 34:10–27; Ez. 16:1–5; Dt. 4:32–34; 7:7–9). The Israelites acknowledged the covenant God made with them, but it did not always move them and lacked the spirit (Is. 28:14–15; Jn. 8:31–47; Rom. 9:6–18). On the other hand God freely sought to bring a new "choosing," one that was realized through His divine Son and in His Church (Mt. 12:38–50; 15:21–28; Rom. 8 and 10). These new people of God's choices are not restricted "according to the flesh" nor are they limited by national designation but embrace all nations of the earth. We thus move from a restricted freedom lacking the spirit to a boundless freedom of mission and love through faith in Christ. (Cf. Mk. 14:24; Acts 3:25; Rom. 1:7; 1 Cor. 1:21; 2 Cor. 6:6; Gal. 3:7; Eph. 1:18; Heb. 2:16; 8:8–12; 1 Pt. 2:9; Rv. 1:6; 7:4–17).

2. *Church teaching:* There is an unlimited acceptance within the term "People of God." It is needless to speculate on the number comprising this group, for the salvific will of God extends not only to an individual person but also to all those who are in the unity of God's love and the love of their neighbor. This simply means that Christ died not for people as one or a group, but for *all*. Thus all are called and united in the Spirit of God, in faith, and the bond of freedom. To limit the number of the people of the new choice of God is totally undesirable elitism. If anything, the People of God are the sum total of all the justified, and this would include those who are not now fully incorporated into the Church.

"On all Christians is laid the splendid burden of working to make the divine message of salvation known and accepted by all men throughout the world.

"For the exercise of this apostolate, the Holy Spirit who sanctifies the People of God through the ministry and the sacraments gives to the faithful special gifts as well (cf. 1 Cor. 12:7), 'allotting to everyone according as he will' (1 Cor. 12:11)" (AA 3).

And: "The People of God has no lasting city here below, but looks forward to one which is to come" (LG 44).

From this we see the extension of God's choice, the response that the individual should give, and the fact that the People of God reach out to all who in any way belong to the Church in fact or potentially. (See Church; Salvation History.)

## Perfection

For Christians, the word perfection has always had a moral and religious sense. It was used by Christ (Mt. 5:48) to mean the fullness of the application of the new law and the attainment of the fullness of Christian life. Perfection is only relative as far as life here on earth is concerned, for

full perfection can only be attained after the resurrection of the body and the possession of the intuitive vision of God in heaven. Perfection is accomplished by the observance of the law, the practice of virtues, the use of sacraments, and the meriting of grace. In the Christian life perfection is judged primarily by the norm of charity, that is, according to the love of God and love of neighbor. It also is judged by the two other theological virtues, faith and hope. Union with God is one ultimate to the attainment of perfection. Even on earth such union is possible, first, through the Eucharist, second, through the various stages of prayer and contemplation. In this latter there are three groups of those seeking perfection: the beginners, those who live a spiritual life but have made no progress; the proficients, those who have tamed their passions and achieved a marked degree of fervor in prayer; the perfect, those who have attained stability in acting in a relatively perfect manner, or a total dominance of charity.

Man made in the image and likeness of God (Gn. 1:27) was understood to be more than a natural good—he possessed a supernatural "plenitude" whereby he was to become like God (Lv. 11:44). And for the Christian this is to be accomplished by the pouring out of the graces merited by Christ upon each individual, as St. Paul pointed out: ". . . the love of God has been poured out in our hearts through the Holy Spirit who has been given to us" (Rom. 5:5).

Vatican II teaches: "Thus He (the Word of God) entered the world's history as a perfect man, taking that history up into Himself and summarizing it. He Himself revealed to us that 'God is love' (1 Jn. 4:8). At the same time He taught us that the new command of love was the basic law of human perfection and hence of the world's transformation" (GS 38).

And: "Although the Catholic Church has been endowed with all divinely revealed truth and with all means of grace, her members fail to live by them with all the fervor they should. As a result, the radiance of the Church's face shines less brightly in the eyes of our separated brethren and of the world at large, and the growth of God's kingdom is retarded. Every Catholic must therefore aim at Christian perfection" (UR 4).

## Perfection, Counsels of

See Evangelical Counsels.

## Perfectionist Churches

As branches of the Pentecostal Churches, there are several church groups who are self-classified as

Perfectionist Churches. In the United States these are: the Church of the Nazarene, the Church of God (Anderson, Indiana), and the Pilgrim Holiness Church. (See Methodism; Pentecostal Churches.)

## Pericope

From the Greek word meaning "section," the Pericope is a passage of scripture that is appointed to be read during the eucharistic celebration in churches, especially the Anglican and Eastern Churches. (See Readings, Cycle of.)

## Periti

The Latin plural of the word *peritus,* meaning literally an "expert," was used to describe the staff of highly educated and knowledgeable consultants to the Fathers of the Second Vatican Council. However, the term is widely used where a constant staff of experts are engaged in some specialized work of the Church, for example, biblical studies or scriptural translation.

## Periodeutes

This word derived from the Greek word meaning "visitor" is a title of honor given to priests holding positions of responsibility, for example, in the diocesan offices and in the three Churches of the Antiochene Rite.

## Perjury

Lying or withholding truth under oath is called perjury. (Cf. Lie.)

## Permanent Deacon

During the extensive deliberations of Vatican II, two weeks were taken to discuss whether or not the Church at this time in history should restore the permanent diaconate. The discussion centered on the question of this particular role in today's Church, and it revolved around who would be ordained and the duties of this order. Thus, the deacon would be distinguished from a candidate for the order of priest who is ordained a deacon as the final step preceding his ordination as a priest. (This step is called the "transitional diaconate.")

On June 18, 1967, Pope Paul VI reestablished the permanent diaconate, allowing the individual Conferences of Bishops to work out the details. In the United States the National Conference of Bishops formally approved the concept and restoration in August, 1968, permitting the respective dioceses to make their own decisions within the limits and spirit of the guidelines.

These guidelines state the entire procedure for the selection, training, and role of the permanent deacon in the community of the Church. Each candidate is a voluntary male, not required to follow the celibate life (he may be married or become married); he must submit to instruction, come before the bishop to receive the order of diaconate, and express a willingness to accept the duties of the office and the desire to remain firm in the faith.

The Apostolic Letter of Pope Paul VI states: "It is most appropriate for permanent deacons to recite at least part of the Liturgy of the Hours each day as determined by the Conference of Bishops."

"The United States Bishops' committee on Permanent Diaconate recommends to all permanent deacons: (1) that the hour of vespers (or, at times, lauds) might be prayed in common with others—either the deacon's family or some community of people with whom he is working pastorally; (2) that the structures and expression of the deacon's prayer life be kept flexible, so that they bind more closely to his wife and children rather than separate from them; (3) that his personal, private prayer make use of the office of readings, so that consistent reading of the Bible will develop as a part of his prayer life."

The Guidelines present the deacon as one called and ordained as a servant to the People of God. Among other procedures and details they declare: "Catholic tradition has recognized the sacramental nature of diaconate as a sharing in the ministerial priesthood of Jesus Christ. But what distinguishes the deacon from lay people? In the past, the reservation of particular functions to the ordained deacon provided the most popular and practical means of distinguishing him from the Christian lay person. But the more penetrating view goes beyond those specific functions, which have varied according to different times and structures. Instead the deacon can be identified by his relationships to the Christian community that surrounds him.

"(a) Sacred Scripture describes the first deacons as men 'full of the Spirit.' The sacrament of holy orders is freely given at the initiative of the Holy Spirit. God calls and invites those whom He chooses, 'You have not chosen me but I have chosen you.' This is the active presence of the Holy Spirit, always at work in the Church and in her ministry. The vocation to diaconal service effects a new relationship to the Holy Spirit. The deacon's ministry becomes a visible response to the God who has called him.

"(b) The local church through the bishop by

means of sacramental ordination effects and witnesses to the call of the Spirit. Through the sacramental sign of holy orders, the Church gives public acknowledgement to the action of the Holy Spirit. Thus the call received and accepted in personal grace takes on a church-wide dimension. As is true of all sacraments, holy orders relates to the whole community of believers. The entire community is committed to the deacon and the deacon to the entire community. Through the bishop a new relationship to the entire Church becomes visible in the Christian who is ordained deacon.

"(c) The deacon enters into special fraternal relationship with all ordained priests of the universal Church. With them he is united in a fraternity of service and sacramental ministry. This sharing of the one sacrament in witness to the call of the Spirit makes them brothers in service and commitment to the People of God.

"(d) The vocation to ministry, whether priesthood or diaconate, implies a relationship of mutual trust and acceptance. The ministry of the Church calls for a bond of charity. The effectiveness of the deacon's service is very much conditioned by acceptance from those whom he would serve. Without this new relationship of trust, the deacon's service would be severely limited.

"(e) A final relationship is necessary in order that the diaconate be fully realized. The call of the Spirit and the imposition of hands by the bishop assume meaning and force only when the deacon fully and totally responds to and accepts the call with a responsible and permanent personal commitment. The commitment of the deacon is a dedication which accepts responsibility for communicating God's word and announcing His kingdom, with the special task of living and speaking and acting as one who shares the apostolic mission of Jesus. Thus the deacon becomes accountable in a new way for the task of building God's kingdom on earth. The deacon expresses his commitment in the way he lives out his relationship to the bishop, to the priests, and to the people whom he serves.

"The deacon, therefore, is more properly defined in terms of who he is rather than of what he does. He is a person with a special mission requiring special relationships within the community of God's people. With such a self-understanding, the deacon will realize that his roles, his duties, his functions of service are to be performed not only in response to the needs of the people but also in the light of all those relationships by which his office of deacon is verified. His functions will not be limited by historical precedent but will show a flexibility and a creativity that express his identity in any given place and milieu where the Holy Spirit invites his ministry. However much these functions may vary, the essential elements of diaconal identity remain: the invitation of the Spirit, the manifestation and realization of this call through sacramental ordination for the benefit of the universal Church, the special fraternal sharing of accountability for the kingdom with all ordained ministers, the acceptance by the community he is called to serve, and the complete personal commitment of self to serve in the name of Christ and His Church.

"Where the above elements are present, the deacon will be recognized, in whatever service he performs, as one who shares in a proper and distinct way in the priesthood of Christ, as one who is a special servant of Christ and His Church" (Permanent Deacons in the United States, U.S. Committee on the Permanent Diaconate, n. 13-15).

The members of permanent diaconate as a special ministry serve without compensation. They are not trained theologians, but are especially instructed in the duties of their roles in serving the Church. In their ministry they will give special assistance to parish priests, especially team ministries and minority ministries; they will give sacramental service especially to the sick and elderly and the confined; and they will aid by their personal lives in the encouragement of single young men to enter the seminary for training as priests. (See Deacon; Ministries.)

**Perpetual Adoration**
Perpetual adoration is the worship of God, especially at the altar where the Blessed Sacrament is exposed, continuously carried on by one or more persons, day and night. In several convents around the world perpetual adoration is established as an essential part of the religious life. This is also a practice in some designated parishes where the

people, together with a leader, practice this paraliturgical devotion.

## Persecution

Broadly, persecution is the enacting of law whereby it is demanded under penalty that one conform to a specific religious pattern. The Church has suffered a number of persecutions throughout the ages, ranging from those of the Romans to those of the twentieth century in Mexico and Russia and in places dominated by Russia. The objectives of persecution may be twofold: the supplanting of one religion with another or the attempt to destroy all religious belief.

Vatican II states: "Imitating Christ who was humble, they (the laity) have no obsession for empty honors (cf. Gal. 5:26) but seek to please God rather than men, ever ready to leave all things for Christ's sake (cf. Lk. 14:26) and to suffer persecution for justice's sake (cf. Mt. 5:10). For they remember the words of the Lord, 'If anyone wishes to come after me, he must deny his very self, take up his cross, and begin to follow in my footsteps' (Mt. 16:24)" (AA 4).

And: "This most sacred Synod heartily thanks God for continuing in our times to raise up lay persons of heroic fortitude in the midst of persecutions, and it embraces them with fatherly affection and gratitude" (AA 17).

And: "By martyrdom a disciple is transformed into an image of his Master, who freely accepted death on behalf of the world's salvation; he perfects that image even to the shedding of blood. Though few are presented with such an opportunity, nevertheless all must be prepared to confess Christ before men, and to follow Him along the way of the cross through the persecutions which the Church will never fail to suffer" (LG 42).

## Perseverance, Final

See Final Perseverance

## Person

The concept of person has been in the history of thought since Etruscan times. Person means "the actual unique reality of a spiritual being, an undivided whole existing independently and not interchangeable with any other" (Max Muller).

The person as a spiritual being is an individual. In Christian thought this is one who responds to the promise and the precept that God freely addressed to him or her, and whereby man becomes a partaker of the living reality of God. Thus man as person is understood only through the knowledge of and the response to God. The person thus freely, by his own decision, determines his final reality, that of union with God.

Man is finite, localized in space and in his body. He is complex, subject to the laws of his nature but capable of responding spiritually to the precepts by which his final reality is determined. Thus there is a conflict between man's finite nature and spiritual capacity.

Because of his nature man must be of the *world,* that is, related to nature, the setting in which he must act (Jn. 17:15). Also, because of his nature, he is one with his *community,* for man is not self-sufficient. He is thus a *social* being, for again, he is not "an island" but works through the social order to achieve those goods that will preserve the spiritual lives of all other persons.

In this perspective we see the Christian person as one with the hope of a collective salvation of all other persons. This is the salvation through Christ, which the death of the Lamb assured for the sheep whose lives were saved (Jn. 15:13–17). Because of Christ this salvation of all persons was made possible (Rom. 5:12–19; 1 Cor. 15:20–22). The works of the Christian will fulfill his own redemption (Mt. 25:31–46; Rom. 2:5–8; Acts 10:34–35), but because man is communal and social he is a part of the Church, a member of Christ, in faith and love of whom he will attain his full stature (Eph. 4:12–16; cf. also Rom. 12:4–5; Col. 1:18; Eph. 1:22–23).

## Peschitto

The word means "simple" and, as applied to a version of the Bible, refers to a simple text or one not marked with critical notations. It first appeared in the tenth century, when it was applied as a title to a Syriac version of the OT made from the Hebrew.

## Peter, Epistles of St.

Two epistles of the NT are attributed to St. Peter. However, modern scholars do not consider that St. Peter himself wrote either of these letters. The first was probably written by a disciple of the Apostle, believed to be named Silvanus, in spite of the fact that the first line declares the writer to be "Peter, an apostle of Jesus Christ" (1:1). The interpretation of this authorship is based on the critical examination of the text and the knowledge that it was composed in excellent Greek and could not have come from a man like St. Peter who lacked training in the Hellenist culture. It was written some time during the first century, probably at Rome. Its teaching is (1) to encourage the

Christians in the face of persecutions, and (2) to present the Church's earliest teaching on the sacrament of baptism (1:3 through 3:10), especially the description of the early Church's liturgy of baptism and the redemptive value of Christ's death.

The second Epistle was undoubtedly written by an unknown scholar toward the end of the first century. The book itself was not accepted as a part of the canon of scriptures until the fifth century. It assuredly contains the doctrine of St. Peter but was given literary form by either a disciple or one acting as a secretary. Its content urges the Christians to persevere in the faith (1:5–7), to await in hope the coming of Christ (3:3–7); it gives a doctrinal background to our supernatural knowledge of Christ and the promises He gave (1:16–19). It is in this second epistle that we read one of the truly great assurances for the human spirit (1:19).

### Peter's Chains, Feast of

Formerly celebrated in the Church liturgy on August 1, the feast commemorates the dedication of the basilica of St. Peter-in-Chains, recalling the captivity of St. Peter in A.D. 44 as recorded in Acts (12:1–25). It has not been placed in the new calendar as a feast.

### Peter's Chair, Feast of

Now called "Chair of Peter, Apostle," this feast commemorates the establishment of his episcopacy in Rome; it is celebrated on Feb. 12.

### Peter's Pence

Peter's Pence is the name of an annual collection, of a voluntary amount, taken up among all Catholics for the maintenance of the Holy See. It was begun in the eighth century and originally consisted of a tax of a penny on each household, hence the name. The amounts collected are now sent to Rome by the bishops and are sometimes a part of the annual appeal of a bishop in his diocese.

### Petrine Privilege

That portion of the Pauline Privilege that declares that a legitimate and consummated marriage of a baptized and an unbaptized person can be declared absolved by the Pope in virtue of the privilege of faith is also called the Petrine Privilege.

### Petrobrusians

The followers of Peter of Bruys, a rebellious priest, in the twelfth century were called Petrobrusians. (See Heresies.)

### Phantasiasm

This is the name given to aspects of the heresy of Docetism in which emphasis is placed upon the mere appearance of the divinity of Christ in His human nature. (See Docetism.)

### Pharisees

The Pharisees were a distinct religious group that arose in the Hebrew religious community in the second century B.C. Their objective was to practice the Mosaic Law in such a manner that there would be the strictest adherence to every minor detail, yet they themselves considered that they were somehow not always bound by the Law. They called themselves "comrades" in the Hebrew language, but they were known at the time of Christ by the Aramaic word meaning "those who separate themselves."

In history they were distinct from the priestly and aristocratic group known as the Sadducees. Their membership was almost entirely composed of laymen. Following the fall of Jerusalem in A.D. 70, they came to dominate the religious life of the Jews. They differed from the other religious groups such as the "zealots" and were politically more lenient toward the Romans. In contrast to the beliefs of Sadducees, the Pharisees affirmed the existence of angels and the resurrection of the dead. They also emphasized the tradition of the Israelite fathers but placed the Law more in the realm of the flesh, on pride and hypocrisy (Mt. 22:22–33; 23:2–39).

The word pharisaical now connotes the hypocritical way of the outwardly religious, self-righteous person. St. Paul, who was at one time a Pharisee, recognized the basic error in their way of life, that "good deeds" of themselves will gain salvation, and denied this vigorously (cf. Gal. 1:13–14; 2:16).

### Phelonion, also Phenolion

This is the topmost vestment worn by a priest of the Byzantine Rite. It corresponds to the chasuble in the Roman Rite, but it may also serve as a cope. It is a cloak-like garment of soft material, reaching nearly to the ground in the back and on the sides. In front it is cut away, slanting upward to the chest, with an opening for the head, and thus it is much like the bell-shaped chasuble.

### Philemon, Epistle of Paul to

The Epistle to Philemon is a very short letter (1 chapter, 25 verses), which was written by St. Paul about the year A.D. 63 at Rome, while the Apostle was in prison. Its main message is against slavery, and it teaches about the treatment of one's fellowman in keeping with the Christian context. It also reveals, in its brevity, something of the magnanimity of the Apostle and his respect for the friends he had met in the service of the Lord. The letter concludes with greetings from several of these companions and a blessing.

## Philippians, Epistle of Paul to the

This NT letter of the Apostle Paul was written about A.D. 57 while he was at Ephesus. The letter was to express Paul's gratitude for the financial aid sent him while he was in prison in Ephesus, but it was also intended to convey to Christians at Philippi that they should be united and seek humility as a way of obtaining unity among themselves. It further answered what had become a problem in the community, namely, that among them were those who were spreading false teachings based upon those of the Judaizers.

There was persecution at Philippi (1:28–30), and Paul gives the Philippians a strong exhortation to bear up against this out of harmony and love (2:1–18). He also shows his great love for the Christians at Philippi, urging them to seek peace and joy in Christ (4:4–9), and in finding the true road to Christian salvation.

## Philosophy

1. The science of natural reason that consists of the criticism and organization of all knowledge, whether drawn from empirical science, rational learning, experience, or other sources. Philosophy as a study includes logic, or the principles of thought and knowledge; metaphysics, or the reality of being and the order that exists among things; ethics, or the natural principles of good action; aesthetics, or the knowledge of beauty and its order. Philosophy, especially scholastic philosophy, must be studied for the gaining of a minimum of 15 to 18 credit hours by students for the priesthood (cc. 1365, 1366).

2. Philosophy of religion is a critical analysis of the reasonable nature and value of religion and its relation to revelation, ethics, and other topics. In this sense, it is general rather than applied to a particular religious belief. (Cf. Theology.)

## Pietism

A reform movement begun in the seventeenth century within the Lutheran Church based upon the preaching of a theologian by the name of Johann Arndt in the late sixteenth century is called pietism. The basic thought of Arndt was union with Christ, that "one must live in Christ and Christ in us." Although Arndt lost favor, his idea was

expanded by Philipp Jacob Spener who published a book in 1695 entitled, *Heartfelt Desires for a God-pleasing Reform of the True Evangelical Churches.* "Guilds of piety" (hence the name of the movement) were formed, which carried on a six point program: (1) a daily reading of the Bible in the home together with a "pious gathering"; (2) a concerted program of active conversion of one's neighbors; (3) the teaching that Christianity is a matter not of faith alone but of daily practice; (4) a seeking of a perfect union of all Christians through prayer, kindness and discussion; (5) a new approach to training for the ministry, with emphasis upon Bible reading and study; and (6) a greater emphasis upon content than upon the style of presentation in preaching. All of these seem quite basic, but they were coupled with a planned rigorism, which was emotionally disconcerting.

As a movement, pietism had more influence than actual members. The majority felt that they could not lead the rigorous life of constant prayer and Bible reading, nor could they follow the rigorous moral dictates. It had a reverse effect, causing people to turn away from religion especially because of the ban upon all amusements. It was learned from Pietism that a religion centered on emotion to the exclusion of intelligent response to religious experience could not stand against the agnostic trends of the eighteenth century, such as rationalism. (See Enlightenment, the Age of.)

## Piety

The virtue of the conscious sense of duty and the willingness to respond is called piety. It is a gift of the Holy Spirit through which the great virtue of charity is applied in a special manner, as a loving duty. Piety is not to be considered as the emotional response to things religious, nor is it to be an assumed attitude whereby the spirit is saddened by what might or ought to be done, often posed by cast-down eyes and folded hands.

Vatican II teaches: "To believers also the Church must ever preach faith and repentance. She must prepare them for the sacraments, teach them to observe all that Christ has commanded (cf. Mt. 28:20), and win them to all the works of charity, piety, and the apostolate. For all these activities make it clear that Christ's faithful, though not of this world, are the light of the world and give glory to the Father in the sight of men" (SC 9).

And: "The Christian is assuredly called to pray with his brethren, but he must also enter into his chamber to pray to the Father in secret (cf. Mt. 6:6); indeed, according to the teaching of the Apostle Paul, he should pray without ceasing (cf. 1

Thes. 5:17). We learn from the same Apostle that we must always carry about in our body the dying of Jesus, so that the life of Jesus too may be made manifest in our bodily frame (cf. 2 Cor. 4:10–11). This is why we ask the Lord in the Sacrifice of the Mass that, 'receiving the offering of the spiritual victim,' He may fashion us for Himself 'as an eternal gift'" (SC 12).

## Pilgrim

Pilgrim is the name given to one who goes on a pilgrimage, that is, who travels to a holy place, such as a shrine, with the intention of benefiting spiritually. The purpose may be to venerate, to do penance, to offer thanksgiving, or to plead for graces. It does not imply that the journey be made solely as a penitential undertaking with the attendant discomfort, real or contrived, as a necessary condition. The *Raccolta* (q.v.) lists the pilgrimages that have been indulgenced by the Church; for example, the faithful who visit the more important sanctuaries of the Holy City of Rome may gain a plenary indulgence on the day of their departure if they confess their sins, receive Holy Communion, and pray for the intentions of the pope (S.P. Ap., April 4, 1932).

## Pilgrimage

In its popular understanding a pilgrimage is a journey to a place of devotion to pray for grace or to petition for some favor. It may have other purposes such as fulfilling a vow or as an act of thanksgiving or penance. As such, pilgrimages have become a commonplace of travel-minded peoples. Some make such journeys to satisfy curiosity or for self-aggrandizement, but the intent of the journey is more serious if the pilgrimage is genuine. Pilgrimages have been celebrated in literature by poets such as Chaucer (1340 to 1400), who centered his attention on the travelers themselves, describing a monk as "fat as a whale, and walked as a swan." His *Canterbury Tales* pictures a motley group of pilgrims on a pilgrimage to Canterbury, but the poet sums up the proper attitude for making a pilgrimage:

"But Christ's lore and his Apostles twelve
He taught, but first he followed it himself."

There is scriptural foundation for the genuine pilgrimage, where they prayed "before God" (Jgs. 21:2; 1 Sm. 1:3). The Ark of the Covenant was taken on pilgrimage to Jerusalem by David and his men, with sacrifices made before the trip and dancing along the way (2 Sm. 6 and 7). This also was ritually followed by the procession of the ark to the Temple (1 Kgs. 8:1–10), and these pilgrimages were likened to the long trek made from Egypt to Sion (Ps. 68).

All this prefigured Christ's journey to Jerusalem (Lk. 2:22; 19:28–38), and Christ leads an eschatological procession for all human persons to the heavenly kingdom (Rv. 7:1–12; Heb. 11:8–16).

In our day the pilgrimage has lost some of its true religious characteristics. But there remains the fact that we all journey to God the Father through Christ.

## Pious Fund

Also called the Pious Fund of the Californias, this Fund includes the properties and monies that were originally gathered by the Jesuit missioners to finance their work in lower California. The Fund was begun by Fathers Eusebius Kino (1644 to 1711) and Juan Maria Salvatierra (1648 to 1717). Upon the expulsion of the Jesuits from the territory in 1767, the Spanish government confiscated the means and used them in part to aid the work of Franciscan and Dominican missionary efforts in both lower and upper California. In 1842 the Mexican government took over the Fund, and it fell into the hands of President Santa Anna. When the United States acquired upper California (1846), a claim was made by the bishop of California under international law and the Catholic Church was awarded almost a million dollars, to be paid annually. This was paid by Mexico until 1890. Thereafter a new judgment was made by the court and Mexico was to pay $1,420,682.61 in interest accumulated between 1869 and 1902 and then to pay $43,050, in perpetuity beginning in 1903. This was paid until and including the year 1913, but no further payments were made despite actions of the Department of State.

In 1967 the negotiations between Mexico and the United States resulted in a token settlement of $700,000 paid to the United States government by Mexico, and this sum was turned over to the Archdiocese of San Francisco.

## Pisa, Councils of

Properly, these were not councils, for both were convened without authority. The first, in 1409, was called by a group of cardinals to depose two popes, Gregory XII and Benedict XIII, but it only served to make a bad situation worse. The second, in 1411, was definitely schismatical and was denounced by the Fifth Lateran Council, which met the following year.

## Piscina, also Sacrarium

In churches, the basin with a pipe leading directly to the ground where the sacred water that remains after use at a ceremony is poured is called a *piscina* or sacrarium. This may be baptismal water, the water used for the first rinsing of corporals, or other water. The *piscina* is often built into the side wall of the sanctuary, on the epistle side of the altar, with a shelf that serves as a credence table. Today, the practice generally is to have the basin built into the sacristy wall.

## Pistoia, Synod of

This synod, an attempt by Grand Duke Leopold of Tuscany, and the Jansenist, Scipio Ricci, to gain control of religious affairs to dominate politically, was called without recognition by the Church in 1786. Ricci was condemned by Pope Pius VI and submitted to the judgment of the Church. Pius VI published on encyclical *Auctorem Fidei* ("The one responsible for Our Faith") in 1794, condemning the sixty-five propositions of Pistoia together with the errors of Jansenism. (See Febronianism.)

## Plain Chant

See Chant.

## Plan, Divine

See Salvation History.

## Planeta

This is the Latin name, rarely used, for the Roman chasuble.

## Plenary Councils

See Baltimore, Councils of.

## Plenary Indulgence

See Indulgence.

## Pleroma

This word coming from the Greek word meaning "plenitude" has been used in a twofold sense: (1) that Christ is preeminently this plenitude, since he is filled with all things as the divine Son of God; (2) that the members of the Mystical Body of Christ are filled with God, or with the benefits of the innumerable graces received from and through Christ. It thus means that pleroma is both the thing filled and that which fills it.

St. Paul used both senses of the word to give understanding to the Christians. He writes: "In Christ the fullness of deity resides in bodily form. Yours is a share of this fullness, in him who is the head of every principality and power" (Col.

2:9–10). He also teaches: "He has put all things under Christ's feet and has made him, thus exalted, head of the Church, which is his body: the fullness of him who fills the universe in all its parts" (Eph. 1:22–23).

Thus the charisms were so given or distributed to Christians that they might bring about the great growth of the Church. If each member, in his own way, and according to his graces, were to show that increase in himself, then the knowledge and faith in the Son of God would enter every part of the body and each would be perfected according to that plenitude which is Christ. As St. Paul teaches: "It is he who gave apostles, prophets, evangelists, pastors and teachers in roles of service for the faithful to build up the body of Christ, till we become one in faith and in knowledge of God's Son, and form that perfect man who is Christ come to full stature" (Eph. 4:11–13; cf. also Col. 2:7; 3:11).

## Plumbator

The duty of this lesser official in the apostolic chancery is to affix the lead seal of the Holy See to the documents of apostolic bulls.

## Pluviale

See Cope.

## Pneumatomachi

This was a group of the Macedonian heresy. Its members were so named because they were recognized as "enemies of the spirit." They were condemned at the second ecumenical council. (See Heresies.)

## Polanca

From the Spanish word meaning "lever," polanca is used by the members of the Cursillo movement to describe that a man can do something beyond his strength through prayer and sacrifice offered to God through an apostolate for the obtaining of grace. (See Cursillo.)

## Polyglot Bibles

Polyglot Bibles are editions of the Bible in which the text, translated into several languages, is printed in parallel columns. Such editions have a critical rather than practical value, for example, the Vatican edition of Sixtus V, published in Rome in 1587. (Cf. Hexapla.)

## Pontiff

See Pope.

## Pontifical Commissions
See Commissions, Ecclesiastical.

## Pontifical Institutes of Higher Learning
As listed in the *Annuario Pontifico*, those institutes that offer special studies in theology, canon law, philosophy, psychology, missiology, ecclesiology, social sciences, and Church history, as well as exceptional areas of research, are designated as Pontifical Institutes. Each is a specialized school for undergraduate and graduate studies. They are:

1. Pontifical Biblical Institute
2. Pontifical Institute of Oriental Studies
3. Pontifical Lateran University
4. Pontifical Urban University
5. Pontifical University of St. Thomas Aquinas, popularly called the *Angelicum*
6. Pontifical Athenaeum of St. Anselm
7. Pontifical Athenaeum Antonianum, affiliated with the School of Biblical Studies in Jerusalem
8. Pontifical Athenaeum Salesiannum
9. Pontifical Institute of Sacred Music
10. Pontifical Institute of Christian Archeology
11. Pontifical Theological Faculty—the "St. Bonaventure"
12. Pontifical Theological Faculty of Sts. Teresa of Jesus and John of the Cross, popularly called the *Teresianum*
13. Pontifical Theological Faculty, called the *Marianum*
14. Pontifical Institute of Arabic Studies
15. Pontifical Gregorian University

## Pontifical Mass
1. Solemn Mass celebrated by the pope.
2. The solemn Mass, celebrated by a bishop with the ceremonies as prescribed by the *Pontificale;* it is usually so called when a bishop celebrates Mass at the throne (from the opening prayer to the offertory) of his own cathedral. A bishop must have the permission of the local ordinary to pontificate outside of his own diocese.

## Pontifical Secrecy
In a press release of March 14, 1974, the Vatican gave out a new instruction on pontifical secrecy as a practical, operational procedure for handling confidential material. This does not refer to the Pope as the head of the Church in particular, but is the obligation, personal and real, of all those who make up the personnel of the Roman Curia, of the Ecclesiastical Commissions, and papal documents. The statement extended the rule of secrecy to cover all classified material, the persons bound by the rule, the nature of the obligation and sanctions for violations that include suspension and discharge from office. In part the release stated the reason for such secrecy under the most secure procedures as the "imperative requirement of the common good of the Church, as well as of dignity and personal honor." Since the Church is engaged in juridical processes and negotiations of the widest diplomatic nature and administrative concern, it is only reasonable that a security procedure be developed and stated clearly. In this manner it serves both as an assurance to those who seek the counsel of the Church and as a guarantee of moral probity.

## Pontificale
See Liturgical Books.

## Pontificals
In addition to the regular vestments, pontificals are the ceremonial vestments and adjuncts proper to a bishop, worn or used by him when celebrating a pontifical Mass; they consist of buskins, sandals, pectoral cross, tunicle, dalmatic, mitre, gloves, and ring. If the bishop pontificates in his own diocese, the crosier is included. Also considered pontificals are the gremial veil, the throne, the mozzetta, and the cappa magna; the last two are worn by the ordinary when entering the church.

Vatican II declared: "It is fitting that the use of pontificals be reserved to those ecclesiastical persons who have episcopal rank or some particular jurisdiction" (SC 130).

## Poor and Needy
The Church has declared itself to be a community that supports and affirms the rights of the poor. In its social teachings, in its worldwide campaigns, the Church has consistently asked that other more affluent groups and peoples "share our concern that the poor be enabled to participate in the decisions that vitally affect them."

Vatican II teaches: "The Fathers and Doctors of the Church held . . . that men are obliged to come to the relief of the poor, and to do so not merely out of their superfluous goods" (GS 69).

And: "Christians should collaborate willingly and wholeheartedly in establishing an international order involving genuine respect for all freedoms and amicable brotherhood between all men. This objective is all the more pressing since the greater part of the world is still suffering from so much poverty that it is as if Christ Himself were crying out in these poor to beg the charity of the disciples" (GS 88).

And: "In view of the immense hardships which still afflict the majority of men today, the Council regards it as most opportune that some agency of the universal Church be set up for the worldwide promotion of justice for the poor and of Christ's kind of love for them. The role of such an organization will be to stimulate the Catholic community to foster progress in needy regions, and social justice on the international scene" (GS 90). (See Campaign for Human Development.)

## Pope

The Pope is the Roman Pontiff who, by divine law, has supreme jurisdiction over the universal Church (c. 218-221). He is the supreme superior of all religious (c. 499). The pope may act alone or with a council in defining doctrine for the universal Church or in making laws (cf. Infallibility). He is addressed as His Holiness the Pope. By title and right he is: Bishop of Rome, Vicar of Jesus Christ, Successor of St. Peter, the Prince of the Apostles, Supreme Pontiff, Patriarch of the West, Primate of Italy, Archbishop and Metropolitan of the Roman province, and Sovereign of the State of Vatican City. (Cf. Apostolic Succession.)

Vatican II teaches: "This Church (of Christ) constituted and organized in the world as a society, subsists in the Catholic Church, which is governed by the successor of Peter and by the bishops in union with that Successor, although many elements of sanctification and of truth can be found outside of her visible structure. These elements, however, as gifts properly belonging to the Church of Christ, possess an inner dynamism toward Catholic unity" (LG 8).

And: "In exercising supreme, full, and immediate power over the universal Church, the Roman Pontiff makes use of the departments of the Roman Curia. These, therefore, perform their duties in his name and with his authority for the good of the Churches and in the service of the sacred pastors" (CD 9).

The Pope thus has (1) a genuine primacy of jurisdiction and not simply of honor, inspection, direction, or presidency (cf. Vat. I, Denzinger, 3064) and (2) an ordinary jurisdictional power, that is, a power connected with the primatial office itself as an essential, constitutive element. (Cf. Vat., I, Denzinger 3060.) (See Subsidiarity.)

## Popes, List of

The continuous series of reigning pontiffs since the first, or the visible heads of the Church since the ascension of Our Lord, is given, together with the dates of their pontificates, as supplied to this date by the official publication, the *Annuario Pontificio*. Pope John II was the first to change from his given name to a chosen one; with few exceptions this has been the practice since A.D. 1009.

1. St. Peter, who died in the year 64 or 67
2. St. Linus, 67 to 76
3. St. Cletus of Anacletus, 76 to 88
4. St. Clement 1, 88 to 97
5. St. Evaristus, 97 to 105
6. St. Alexander I, 105 to 115
7. St. Sixtus I, 115 to 125
8. St. Telesphorus, 125 to 136
9. St. Hyginus, 136 to 140
10. St. Pius I, 140 to 155
11. St. Anicetus, 155 to 166
12. St. Soter, 166 to 175
13. St. Eleutherius, 175 to 189
14. St. Victor I, 189 to 199
15. St. Zephyrinus, 199 to 217
16. St. Callistus I, 217 to 222 (St. Hyppolytus, 217 to 235)
17. St. Urban I, 222 to 230
18. St. Pontian, July 21, 230 to Sept. 28, 235
19. St. Anterus, Nov. 21, 235 to Jan. 3, 236
20. St. Favian, Jan. 10, 236 to Jan. 20, 250
21. St. Cornelius, March, 251 to June, 253 (Novatian, 251)
22. St. Lucius I, June 25, 253 to March 5, 254
23. St. Stephen I, May 12, 254 to Aug. 2, 257
24. St. Sixtus II, Aug. 30, 257 to Aug. 6, 258
25. St. Dionysius, July 22, 259 to Dec. 26, 268
26. St. Felix I, Jan. 5, 269 to Dec. 30, 274
27. St. Eutychian, Jan. 4, 275 to Dec. 7, 283
28. St. Caius, Dec. 17, 283 to April 22, 296
29. St. Marcellinus, June 30, 296 to Oct. 25, 304
30. St. Marcellus I, May 27, 308 to Jan. 16, 309
31. St. Eusebius, April 18, 309 to Aug. 17, 309
32. St. Miltiades, July 2, 311 to Jan. 11, 314
33. St. Sylvester, Jan. 31, 314 to Dec. 31, 335
34. St. Mark, Jan. 18, 336 to Oct. 7, 336
35. St. Julius I, Feb. 6, 337 to April 12, 352
36. Liberius, May 17, 352 to Sept. 24, 366 (Felix II, 355 to Nov. 22, 365)
37. St. Damasus, Oct. 1, 366 to Dec. 11, 384 (Ursinus, 366 to 367)
38. St. Siricius, Dec. 15, 22, or 29, 384 to Nov. 26, 399
39. St. Anastasius I, Nov. 27, 399 to Dec. 19, 401
40. St. Innocent I, Dec. 22, 401 to March 12, 417

41. St. Zosimus, March 18, 417 to Dec. 26, 418
42. St. Boniface I, Dec. 28 or 29, 418 to Sept. 4, 422 (Eulalius, Dec. 27 or 29, 418 to 419)
43. St. Celestine I, Sept. 10, 422 to July 27, 432
44. St. Sixtus III, July 31, 432 to Aug. 19, 440
45. St. Leo I, Sept. 29, 440 to Nov. 10, 461
46. St. Hilarus, Nov. 19, 461 to Feb. 29, 468
47. St. Simplicius, March 3, 468 to March 10, 483
48. St. Felix III (or II), March 13, 483 to March 1, 492
49. St. Gelasius I, March 1, 492 to Nov. 21, 496
50. Anastasius II, Nov. 24, 496 to Nov. 19, 498
51. St. Symmachus, Nov. 22, 498 to July 19, 514 (Lawrence, 498 to 505)
52. St. Hormisdas, July 20, 514 to Aug. 6, 523
53. St. John I, Aug. 13, 523 to May 18, 526
54. St. Felix IV (or III), July 12, 526 to Sept. 22, 530
55. Boniface II, Sept. 22, 530 to Oct. 17, 532 (Dioscorus, Sept. 22, 530 to Oct. 14, 530)
56. John II, Jan. 2, 533 to May 8, 535
57. St. Agapetus I, May 13, 535 to April 22, 536
58. St. Silverius, June 1, 536 to Nov. 11, 537
59. Vigilius, March 29, 537 to June 7, 555
60. Pelagius I, April 16, 556 to March 4, 561
61. John III, July 17, 561 to July 13, 574
62. Benedict I, June 2, 575 to July 30, 579
63. Pelagius II, Nov. 26, 579 to Feb. 7, 590
64. St. Gregory I, Sept. 3, 590 to March 12, 604
65. Sabinianus, Sept. 13, 604 to Feb. 22, 606
66. Boniface III, Feb. 19, 607 to Nov. 12, 607
67. St. Boniface IV, Aug. 25, 608 to May 8, 615
68. St. Adeodatus I (Deusdedit), Oct. 19, 615 to Nov. 8, 618
69. Boniface V, Dec. 23, 619 to Oct. 25, 625
70. Honorius I, Oct. 27, 625 to Oct. 12, 638
71. Severinus, May 28, 640 to Aug. 2, 640
72. John IV, Dec. 24, 640 to Oct. 12, 642
73. Theodore I, Nov. 24, 642 to May 14, 649
74. St. Martin I, July, 649 to Sept. 16, 655
75. St. Eugenius I, Aug. 10, 654 to June 2, 657
76. St. Vitalian, July 30, 657 to Jan. 27, 672
77. Adeodatus II, April 11, 672 to June 17, 676
78. Donus, Nov. 2, 676 to April 11, 678
79. St. Agatho, June 27, 678 to Jan. 10, 681
80. St. Leo II, Aug. 17, 682 to July 3, 683
81. St. Benedict II, June 26, 684 to May 685
82. John V, July 23, 685 to Aug. 2, 686
83. Conon, Oct. 21, 686 to Sept. 21, 687 (Theodore, 687) (Paschal, 687)
84. St. Sergius I, Dec. 15, 687 to Sept. 8, 701
85. John VI, Oct. 30, 701 to Jan. 11, 705
86. John VII, March 1, 705 to Oct. 18, 707

87. Sissinius, Jan. 15, 708 to Feb. 4, 708
88. Constantine, March 25, 708 to April 9, 715
89. St. Gregory II, May 19, 715 to Feb. 11, 731
90. St. Gregory III, March 18, 731 to Nov., 741
91. St. Zachary, Dec. 10, 741 to March 22, 752
92. Stephen II (or III), March 26, 752 to April 26, 757
93. St. Paul I, April 757 to June 28, 767 (Constantine, 767 to 769) (Philip, 768)
94. Stephen III (or IV), Aug. 1, 768 to Jan. 24, 772
95. Adrian I, Feb. 1, 772 to Dec. 25, 795
96. St. Leo III, Dec. 26, 795 to June 12, 816
97. Stephen IV (or V), June 22, 816 to Jan. 24, 817
98. St. Paschal I, Jan. 25, 817 to Feb. 11, 824
99. Eugenius II, Feb., 824 to Aug., 827
100. Valentine, Aug., 827 to Sept., 827
101. Gregory IV, 827 to Jan. 844 (John, Jan., 844)
102. Sergius II, Jan., 844 to Jan. 27, 847
103. St. Leo IV, Jan., 847 to July 17, 855
104. Benedict III, July, 855 to April 17, 858 (Anastasius, 855)
105. St. Nicholas I, April 24, 858 to Nov. 13, 867
106. Adrian II, Dec. 14, 867 to Dec. 14, 872
107. John VIII, Dec. 14, 872 to Dec. 16, 882
108. Marinus I, Dec. 16, 882 to May 15, 884
109. St. Adrian III, May 17, 884 to Sept., 885
110. Stephen V (or VI), Sept., 885 to Sept. 14, 891
111. Formosus, Oct. 6, 891 to April 4, 896
112. Boniface VI, April 896 to April 896
113. Stephen VI (or VII), May, 896 to Aug., 897
114. Romanus, Aug., 897 to Nov., 897
115. Theodore II, Dec., 897
116. John IX, Jan., 898 to Jan., 900
117. Benedict IV, Jan., 900 to July, 903
118. Leo V, July, 903 to Sept. 903. (Christopher, Sept., 903 to Jan. 904)
119. Sergius III, Jan. 29, 904 to April 14, 911
120. Anastasius III, April, 911 to June, 913
121. Lando, July, 913 to Feb., 914
122. John X, March, 914 to May, 928
123. Leo VI, May, 928 to Dec., 928
124. Stephen VII (or VIII), Dec., 928 to Feb., 931
125. John XI, Feb., 931 to Dec., 935
126. Leo VII, Jan. 3, 936 to July 13, 939
127. Stephen VIII (or IX), July 14, 939 to Oct., 942
128. Marinus II, Oct. 30, 942 to May, 946
129. Agapetus II, May 10, 946 to Dec., 955
130. John XII, Dec. 16, 955 to May 14, 964
131. Leo VIII, Dec. 4, 963 to March 1, 965

132. Benedict V, May 22, 964 to July 4, 966
133. John XIII, Oct. 1, 965 to Sept. 6, 972
134. Benedict VI, Jan. 19, 973 to June, 974
     (Boniface VII, 974; 984 to 985)
135. Benedict VII, Oct., 974 to July 10, 983
136. John XIV, Dec., 983 to Aug. 20, 984
137. John XV, Aug., 985 to March, 996
138. Gregory V, May 3, 996 to Feb. 18, 999
     ( John XVI, April, 997 to Feb., 998)
139. Sylvester II, April 2, 999 to May 12, 1003
140. John XVII, June, 1003 to Dec., 1003
141. John XVIII, Jan. 1004 to July, 1009
142. Sergius IV, July 31, 1009 to May 12, 1012
143. Benedict VIII, May 18, 1012 to April 9,
     1024 (Gregory, 1012)
144. John XIX, April, 1024 to 1032
145. Benedict IX, 1032 to 1044
146. Sylvester III, Jan. 20, 1045 to Feb. 10, 1045
     Benedict IX (for the second time), April 10,
     1045 to May 1, 1045
147. Gregory VI, May 5, 1045 to Feb., 1046
148. Clement II, Dec. 24, 1046 to Oct. 9, 1047
     Benedict IX (for the third time), Nov. 8,
     1047 to July 17, 1048
149. Damasus II, July 17, 1048 to Aug. 9, 1048
150. St. Leo IX, Feb. 12, 1049 to April 19, 1054
151. Victor II, April 16, 1055 to July 28, 1057
152. Stephen IX (or X), Aug. 3, 1057 to March
     29, 1058 (Benedict X, April 5, 1058 to Jan.
     24, 1059)
153. Nicholas II, Jan. 24, 1059 to July 27, 1061
154. Alexander II, Oct. 1, 1061 to April 21,
     1073 (Honorius II, Oct. 1061 to 1072)
155. St. Gregory VII, April 22, 1073 to May 25,
     1085 (Clement III, 1080 to 1100)
156. Blessed Victor III, May 24, 1086 to Sept.
     16, 1087
157. Blessed Urban II, March 12, 1088 to July
     29, 1099
158. Paschal II, Aug. 13, 1099 to Jan. 21, 1118
     (Theodoric, 1100) (Albert, 1102) (Sylvester
     IV, Nov. 18, 1105 to 1111)
159. Gelasius II, Jan. 24, 1118 to Jan. 28, 1119
     (Gregory VIII, 1118 to 1121)
160. Callistus II, Feb. 2, 1119 to Dec. 13, 1124
161. Honorius II, Dec. 21, 1124 to Feb. 13, 1130
     (Celestine II, 1124)
162. Innocent II, Feb. 14, 1130 to Sept. 24, 1143
     (Anacletus II, Feb. 1130 to Jan. 1138)
     (Victor IV, 1138)
163. Celestine II, Sept. 26, 1143 to March 8,
     1144
164. Lucius II, March 12, 1144 to Feb. 15, 1145
165. Blessed Eugenius III, Feb. 15, 1145 to July
     8, 1153

166. Anastasius IV, July 12, 1153 to Dec. 3, 1154
167. Adrian IV, Dec. 4, 1154 to Sept. 1, 1159
168. Alexander III, Sept. 7, 1159 to Aug. 30,
     1181 (Victor IV, 1159 to 1164) (Paschal III,
     1164 to 1168) (Callistus III, 1168 to 1178)
     (Innocent III, 1179 to 1180)
169. Lucius III, Sept. 1, 1181 to Sept. 25, 1185
170. Urban III, Nov. 25, 1185 to Oct. 20, 1187
171. Gregory VIII, Oct. 21, 1187 to Dec. 17,
     1187
172. Clement III, Dec. 19, 1187 to March, 1191
173. Celestine III, March 30, 1191 to Jan. 8,
     1198
174. Innocent III, Jan. 8, 1198 to July 16, 1216
175. Honorius III, July 18, 1216 to March 18,
     1227
176. Gregory IX, March 19, 1227 to Aug. 22,
     1241
177. Celestine IV, Oct. 25, 1241 to Nov. 10,
     1241
178. Innocent IV, June 25, 1243 to Dec. 7, 1254
179. Alexander IV, Dec. 12, 1254 to May 25,
     1261
180. Urban IV, Aug. 29, 1261 to Oct. 2, 1264
181. Clement IV, Feb. 5, 1265 to Nov. 29, 1268
182. Blessed Gregory X, Sept. 1, 1271 to Jan. 10,
     1276
183. Blessed Innocent V, Jan. 21, 1276 to June
     22, 1276
184. Adrian V, July 11, 1276 to Aug. 18, 1276
185. John XXI, Sept. 8, 1276 to May 20, 1277
186. Nicholas III, Nov. 25, 1277 to Aug. 22,
     1280
187. Martin IV, Feb. 2, 1281 to March 28, 1285
188. Honorius IV, April 2, 1285 to April 3, 1287
189. Nicholas IV, Feb. 22, 1288 to April 4, 1292
190. St. Celestine V, July 5, 1294 to Dec. 13,
     1294 (resigned)
191. Boniface VIII, Dec. 24, 1294 to Oct. 11,
     1303
192. Blessed Benedict XI, Oct. 22, 1303 to July
     7, 1304
193. Clement V, June 5, 1305 to April 20, 1314
194. John XXII, Aug. 7, 1316 to Dec. 4, 1334
     (Nicholas V, May 12, 1328 to Aug. 5, 1330)
195. Benedict XII, Dec. 20, 1334 to April 25,
     1342
196. Clement VI, May 7, 1342 to Dec. 6, 1352
197. Innocent VI, Dec. 18, 1352 to Sept. 12,
     1362
198. Blessed Urban V, Sept. 28, 1362 to Dec. 19,
     1370
199. Gregory XI, Dec. 30, 1370 to March 26,
     1378
200. Urban VI, April 8, 1378 to Oct. 15, 1389

201. Boniface IX, Nov. 2, 1389 to Oct. 1, 1404
202. Innocent VII, Oct. 17, 1404 to Nov. 6, 1406
203. Gregory XII, Nov. 30, 1406 to July 4, 1415 (Clement VII, Sept. 20, 1378 to Sept. 16, 1394) (Benedict XIII, Sept. 28, 1394 to May 23, 1423) (Alexander V, June 26, 1409 to May 3, 1410) (John XXIII, May 17, 1410 to May 29, 1415)
204. Martin V, Nov. 11, 1417 to Feb. 20, 1431
205. Eugenius IV, March 3, 1431 to Feb. 23, 1447 (Felix V, Nov. 5, 1439 to April 7, 1449)
206. Nicholas V, March 6, 1447 to March 24, 1455
207. Callistus III, April 8, 1455 to Aug. 6, 1458
208. Pius II, Aug. 19, 1458 to Aug. 15, 1464
209. Paul II, Aug. 30, 1464 to July 26, 1471
210. Sixtus IV, Aug. 9, 1471 to Aug. 12, 1484
211. Innocent VIII, Aug. 29, 1484 to July 25, 1492
212. Alexander VI, Aug. 11, 1492 to Aug. 18, 1503
213. Pius III, Sept. 22, 1503 to Oct. 18, 1503
214. Julius II, Oct. 31, 1503 to Feb. 21, 1513
215. Leo X, March 9, 1513 to Dec. 1, 1521
216. Adrian VI, Jan. 9, 1522 to Sept. 14, 1523
217. Clement VII, Nov. 19, 1523 to Sept. 25, 1534
218. Paul III, Oct. 13, 1534 to Nov. 10, 1549
219. Julius III, Feb. 7, 1550 to March 23, 1555
220. Marcellus II, April 9, 1555 to May 1, 1555
221. Paul IV, May 23, 1555 to Aug. 18, 1559
222. Pius IV, Dec. 25, 1559 to Dec. 9, 1565
223. St. Pius V, Jan. 7, 1566 to May 1, 1572
224. Gregory XIII, May 13, 1572 to April 10, 1585
225. Sixtus V, April 24, 1585 to Aug. 27, 1590
226. Urban VII, Sept. 15, 1590 to Sept. 27, 1590
227. Gregory XIV, Dec. 5, 1590 to Oct. 16, 1591
228. Innocent IX, Oct. 29, 1591 to Dec. 30, 1591
229. Clement VIII, Jan. 30, 1592 to March 3, 1605
230. Leo XI, April 1, 1605 to April 27, 1605
231. Paul V, May 16, 1605 to Jan. 28, 1621
232. Gregory XV, Feb. 9, 1621 to July 8, 1623
233. Urban VIII, Aug. 6, 1623 to July 29, 1644
234. Innocent X, Sept. 15, 1644 to Jan. 7, 1655
235. Alexander VII, April 7, 1655 to May 22, 1667
236. Clement IX, June 20, 1667 to Dec. 9, 1669
237. Clement X, April 29, 1670 to July 22, 1676
238. Blessed Innocent XI, Sept. 21, 1676 to Aug. 12, 1689
239. Alexander VIII, Oct. 6, 1689 to Feb. 1, 1691

240. Innocent XII, July 12, 1691 to Sept. 27, 1700
241. Clement XI, Nov. 23, 1700 to March 19, 1721
242. Innocent XIII, May 8, 1721 to March 7, 1724
243. Benedict XIII, May 29, 1724 to Feb. 21, 1730
244. Clement XII, July 12, 1730 to Feb. 6, 1740
245. Benedict XIV, Aug. 17, 1740 to May 8, 1758
246. Clement XIII, July 6, 1758 to Feb. 2, 1769
247. Clement XIV, May 19, 1769 to Sept. 22, 1774
248. Pius VI, Feb. 15, 1775 to Aug. 29, 1799
249. Pius VII, March 14, 1800 to Aug. 20, 1823
250. Leo XII, Sept. 28, 1823 to Feb. 10, 1829
251. Pius VIII, March 31, 1829 to Nov. 30, 1830
252. Gregory XVI, Feb. 2, 1831 to June 1, 1846
253. Pius IX, June 16, 1846 to Feb. 7, 1878
254. Leo XIII, Feb. 20, 1878 to July 20, 1903
255. St. Pius X, Aug. 4, 1903 to Aug. 20, 1914
256. Benedict XV, Sept. 3, 1914 to Jan. 22, 1922
257. Pius XI, Feb. 6, 1922 to Feb. 10, 1939
258. Pius XII, March 2, 1939 to Oct. 9, 1958
259. John XXIII, Oct. 28, 1958 to June 3, 1963
260. Paul VI, June 21, 1963 to Aug. 6, 1978
261. John Paul I, Aug. 26, 1978 to Sept. 28, 1978
262. John Paul II, Oct. 16, 1978

**Popish Plot**

This name was given to a fictitious deception begun by two Englishmen, Titus Oates and Israel Tonge. Following the death of Cromwell in 1658, the Catholics of England were put under pressure to conform to the Church of England. The King, Charles II (1665 to 1680) was inclined to be favorable to the Catholics, having married the Portugese princess, Catherine of Braganza, but he acceded to the wishes of the opponents of the Catholics. It was then that Oates and Tonge placed before the English parliament the false charges that the Catholics were plotting to assassinate King Charles and bring about a Jesuit-dominated monarchy headed by the Duke of York, the King's brother, James.

The two plotters were malcontents, passionately opposed to the Catholics, especially the Jesuits, and they took pleasure in using their scheme, padding it with forty-three charges, all of which were fabrications. It did increase persecution of the Catholics, however, and many were executed, among them Oliver Plunkett, the Archbishop of Armagh, Ireland, and five Jesuits. By the year 1684 a reaction set in and the plot was exposed for what it was.

## Populorum Progressio

Following the promulgation of the *Pastoral Constitution on the Church in the Modern World (Gaudium et Spes)* of Vatican II, Pope Paul VI published in 1967 his encyclical *Populorum Progressio* ("Development of Peoples"), which was a formulation of the social doctrine of that *Constitution*. It set forth boldly and clearly for the world the crucial issue of the exercise of social justice by both management and labor. It demonstrated that in the economic world of our time, good morality is not only good economics but is supportive of good society in general, and it stressed anew the dignity of the human person and his rights.

## Portable Altar

See Altar.

## Porter

See Doorkeeper; Ostiarius; Ministries; Orders, Holy, Sacrament of.

## Portiuncula

Literally, "little portion," this name is given to the small chapel within the basilica of St. Mary of the Angels, located near Assisi in Italy. More widely known is the *Portiuncula Indulgence,* originally attached to the chapel that was dedicated on August 2; thus the indulgence may be gained on that day. Since July 10, 1924, by decree of the Holy See, the Portiuncula Indulgence may be gained as a plenary indulgence *(toties quoties)* as often as the conditions are fulfilled. These conditions are: confession, reception of Holy Communion, and a visit to a church that enjoys the privilege, together with the recitation of the Our Father, Hail Mary, and Glory be to the Father six times each. The indulgence may be gained from midday of August 1 to August 2 (c. 923) and is applicable to the poor souls. Should the second of August occur on a weekday, the indulgence may be transferred to the following Sunday. It may be gained in all churches or public oratories of the Friars Minor, of the Capuchins, and of the Conventuals. Members of the Third Order Secular may gain it in any church or public oratory where the Third Order is canonically erected or, if none exists in the place, then in any church. Since May 1, 1939, any pastor may, with his bishop's permission, apply to the Sacred Penitentiary for the privilege of having the Portiuncula Indulgence in his parish.

## Positivism

The philosophical theory of positivism is not a distinct teaching but represents an attitude toward science and the theories of philosophy. Positivism was first derived from the ancient scepticism and the nominalism of the Middle Ages, especially concerning the question of universals. It was introduced by the English empiricists, Francis Bacon (1561 to 1621) and Thomas Hobbes (1588 to 1679), who sought to base all thought on experimental and inductive reasoning and rejected the metaphysical basis of law.

The first formulation of the theory of positivism was set forth by the French philosopher, Auguste Comte (1798 to 1857). The theory was to restrict all reliable knowledge to the findings of the positive sciences. Its basis was an empiricism that combines all the conclusions of the sciences into one world-view under the three headings of theology, metaphysics, and positive sciences. The synthesis of knowledge in this theory results in the ideas of man's dominance over nature and his independence from God; therefore, there is no need for God.

Positivism fails in theory and practice in that it restricts the method of inquiry and limits its dimensions by presuppositions and actual experience, which make *a priori* judgments unjustifiable.

Moral positivism has two further limitations: the idea that every obligation and the moral order itself are based on the absolute free will of God, and the assumption that the moral norms are discovered by man in his various methods of seeking social, political, and economic assurances in human society. In this sense it limits man in his self-realization in the community of peoples by making him self-determinative only in relation to his situation or his place in the social and moral structure. When morality is made relative, it becomes situational and thus results in amorality in application.

The danger of positivism is that an exactitude is demanded, which in reality denies a broadening of man's knowledge by narrowing the access to knowledge. In its moral tone, positivism reacts negatively to man's logical investigation of the revelations God has made to man, which are constantly unfolding in salvation history.

## Possession, Demonic

Demonic possession is the domination of a person's body by one or more evil spirits, that is, devils. The Church has always recognized this possibility (Christ drove out devils, Mk. 5:1–20) and also has recognized the power of Christ over the demons and His commission of this power to her. It must be remembered that the phenomenon of possession, as it is called, may be only the observation of a diabolic force as it exists in a given situation. Thus it cannot be equated with genuine mystical experience, since the diabolic tends to the destruction of the person (such as illness resulting from an aberrated conscience), while the mystical affects the spiritual nature of the person to that person's benefit. (See Exorcism.)

## Postcommunion

One of the presidential prayers, this final prayer of the Mass is a short prayer of thanksgiving and petition. The postcommunion is prayed before the concluding rite in the New Order of the Mass.

## Postulant

A person preparing to ask for admission to a religious novitiate is called a postulant. In religious communities where perpetual vows are to be taken, both men and women must spend at least six months as postulants (c. 539-541).

This period of time is a remote spiritual preparation for religious life (the proximate being the novitiate). Today when young people are sometimes entering the religious life for other reasons than the fulfilling of a desire to serve in a limited or special capacity, such as teaching or nursing, the time of the postulancy is very important. It gives the entrants a time to approach their participation in the spiritual life of a community, especially in regard to the type of service they seek, whether social service, missionary, or humane, while at the same time gauging their service within the concepts of a religious life. The postulancy should not be confused with "Sister formation" programs or the life of a Brother as a way of religious expression.

## Poverello, Il

Meaning "the little poor one," this is an Italian title of endearment for St. Francis of Assisi.

## Poverty

One of the three evangelical counsels, poverty is defined as the voluntary renunciation of the right of ownership and the reasonable use of material goods. The simple vow of poverty forbids the use of all things with a monetary value, without consent of one's superior; the solemn vow deprives the religious of all right of ownership and makes invalid all acts contrary to the vow. (Cf. Evangelical Counsels.)

The scriptural teachings on poverty in the OT begin to take on a more spiritual meaning. Thus it was not a person's material possessions or lack of them that made for poverty, but the interior spirit

of sacrifice (cf. 1 Kgs. 18:20–39; Is. 1:11–17). What a person possessed as wealth was mistrusted as a vanity (Sir. 5:1–8; Eccl. 5:9–19; Ps. 49). God was the creator of both the poor and the rich, but it was the role of the good person to help the poor (Jb. 29:11–17; Eccl. 4:1–10; Prv. 22:1–2).

The word *poor* took on the meaning of a spiritual awakening, and in the NT Jesus Christ was to be the "Poor One of Yahweh" (cf. Zec. 9:9; Mt. 21:1–10), or the One who rode only upon an ass as a recognition of poverty. (Cf. also Lk. 2:6–20; Mt. 8:18–20; Jn. 19:23.)

Further, the poor are themselves "blessed" (Lk. 6:20–26; Jas. 5:1–6; 1 Cor. 7:29–31; 2 Cor. 6:9–10). According to St. Luke, poverty will have special significance in the life of eternity (Lk. 12:13–21; 14:12–14; 16:1–13; 20:45–47). Christ will also be recognized in the poor, for He identified Himself with them (Mt. 25:31–46; Jn. 2:1–9). The human person may follow the example of Christ in giving assistance to the poor (Mt. 5:42; 2 Cor. 8:1–15). It is for the members of Christ's mystical body to practice poverty and detachment from material things (Acts 2:42–47; 1 Cor. 16:1–4; 2 Cor. 9:6–9), as St. Paul further says of his work among the Gentiles: "The only stipulation was that we should be mindful of the poor—the one thing that I was making every effort to do" (Gal. 2:10).

## Power

As a religously oriented concept, power is one of the primary attributes of God, His omnipotence. This is not power in the sense of brute force or energy derived from the generation of electricity. God manifests power in favor of His own people (Jos. 3:10–13); there is an association of the wisdom of God with His power (Wis. 7:25; 8:1; Jb. 37:14), and the power of God made manifest is an indication and proof of God's salvific power (Jer. 16:21; Is. 50:2; Ps. 44:4–9).

Salvation comes through the power of God, for it is considered in the terms of both forgiviness and conversion (Mi. 3:7–8; Wis. 11:21–23), even as faith in God's omnipotence is expressed by prayer and is acknowledged by the prayer of Christ to the Father (Jn. 17).

The good news of Christ is an expression of His power because Jesus shares in the power and knowledge of God. Christ disclosed that love is an essential feature of the power of God. "Jesus came forward and addressed them in these words: 'Full authority has been given to me both in heaven and on earth; go, therefore, and make disciples of all the nations' . . ." (Mt. 28:18). And this power is to be exercised for the establishment of an order centered on God (Rom. 13:1), although this is temporary (1 Cor. 7:29ff) and will be fully realized in heaven (Phil. 3:20).

Man as a subordinate being recognizes God's power. Through faith and perseverance, the human person returns to God who possesses all being and therefore all power in and of Himself. For the human person, power is exercised in self-sacrifice and in accepting the conditions of earthly life so that each may return to God as a child (Phil. 2:15–16; 1 Pt. 1:13–17) and by petitioning God through prayer (Mt. 7:7–11; 6:7–15). (See Omnipotence.)

### Power of the Keys

The grant of authority whereby Christ, through the metaphor of "keys," passed on to St. Peter and his successors the supreme jurisdiction over the Church on earth is known as the power of the keys. The fact, recorded in Matthew (16:18–20), is recognized as the transmission of authority and a definition of St. Peter's powers. These powers, consisting of a "binding" and a "loosing" in the spiritual order on earth, that is, all powers necessary to the well-being of the kingdom, were recognized by the apostles from the rabbinical terms for "binding," that is, of granting or forbidding, as contained in the Jewish law. (Cf. Authority.)

The key was a symbol of power for the Israelites (Is. 22:19–22), and Christ became the one who possessed the power to open the door of the Kingdom of Heaven (Lk. 11:51–52; Rv. 3:7–8). It was this possession on the part of Christ that made it possible for Him, through the Holy Spirit, to grant this power to the Apostles (cf. Mk. 9:37; Mt. 10:40).

### Powers

See Angel.

### Pragmatism

First formally presented by C.S. Peirce (1839 to 1914) and William James (1842 to 1910), this philosophical system judges truth by its useful results and interprets ideas in terms of their consequences. It states that the meaning of an intellectual conception should be considered in terms of the practical consequences that might result, and these consequences constitute the entire meaning of the conception. The assertion of any proposition must be tested in practice to see if it coincides with what is expected; a resultant judgment is true if it leads to a successful adaptation to the demands of the possible expectation. Knowledge is not an independent function in life but a service. Pragmatism arose toward the end of the nineteenth century and was largely worked out at Harvard University. This philosophy served to instill vague and uncertain thought as to the existence of God, the Freedom of the will, and immortality.

### Praises, Divine

See Divine Praises.

### Prayer

Prayer is the active expression of the virtue of religion, which can be practiced by all. It differs from sacrifice, which requires a minister. Prayer, by simple defintion, is the raising of the mind and soul to God. Classified by purpose, there are four types of prayer: adoration, praise, thanksgiving, and petition. Prayer is also distinguished by the manner of expression. *Vocal* prayer is the recitation of prayer according to a set form, for example, the Lord's Prayer or the Rosary. *Mental* prayer is the direction and control of thought toward God or a truth of religion (cf. Meditation). Prayer may be *private,* that is, said alone, or *public,* that is, said in a group or in the name of society together. Prayer is necessary for salvation, for it is seeking and expressing the "power of God unto salvation," the soul's communion with God. Christ Himself is the example of man in prayer. He prayed to the Father at all the moments of His life, and man prays in His name (Jn. 14:13–14). (Cf. Intercession; Mass; Liturgy.)

Vatican II speaks of prayer in almost all of its documents and decrees. It teaches: "In the house of prayer the most Holy Eucharist is celebrated and preserved. There the faithful gather, and find help and comfort through venerating the presence of the Son of God our Savior, offered for us on the sacrificial altar. This house must be well kept and suitable for prayer and sacred functions" (PO 5).

In thus speaking of the church as the place where the official public prayer of the Church is offered, we learn that the emphasis is on the presence of Christ in the Eucharist. To this must be added the public prayer of the Church, which is not centered in the church itself; "Because it is the public prayer of the Church, the divine Office is a source of piety and nourishment for personal prayer. Therefore priests and all others who take part in the divine Office are earnestly exhorted in the Lord to attune their minds to their voices when praying it. The better to achieve this ideal, let them take steps to improve their understanding of the liturgy and of the Bible, especially the psalms" (SC 90).

Pope Paul VI has said: "To live it is necessary to pray." At his general audience at the beginning of Lent, 1974, the Pope said: "The question of the presence of Christ in the exterior world of facts and institutions, and in the interior world of the hearts of men is at the center of our religion. . . . Let us limit ourselves to seeking his interior presence, in our minds, and thinking again of Mary, let us answer: Jesus is present, in the first place, through faith, within us. Some words of St. Paul say everything in this regard: 'may Christ dwell in your hearts through faith' (Eph. 3:17).

"The whole of the spiritual life of our religion is derived from this statement (which will be further integrated by another essential element, grace, and by another instrumental coefficient, the Church) . . . We know these things, of course, but we realize how alien they are to the modern outlook, so extrovert, so averse to knowledge through faith, so unsuited for meditation in the religious sanctuary of conscience, and so inexpert in the language of mental prayer.

"Well, we exhort you, on the contrary, to learn this language again. Without it, we cannot talk to God; we cannot even hear his voice, if he should deign to take part in this silent dialogue. But it is part of that spiritual renewal to which the Holy Year must lead us: to know how to pray, and in order to pray really, to know how to meditate. . . .

"We must dispose ourselves to talk to Christ, and through him to God, to that Christ-God who came such a long way to meet us; he came down from heaven. This conversation marks a new and extensive stage of Christian religious life. In short, we must learn to speak with the Lord, to speak to the Lord. A direct, sincere talk on our part with the Lord constitutes a kind of special prayer—personal prayer.

"The question arises: are we capable of personal prayer? We should certainly say yes, if by personal prayer we mean the recitation of some formulas of common prayers, which we all know and which, we like to think, give voice to our customary religious observance. Who does not recite an Our Father and a Hail Mary? And do not many of you recite some prayers at the beginning and end of every day? Moreover, many good persons say the Rosary every day, and other usual prayers which have become part of the day's program for the good Christian.

"So far, so good; very good. Let us preserve these elementary religious acts as a daily expression of our Christian character, of our faithfulness to the Christian concept of life; as a sign of our religious tribute to God, whereby we observe the first, most important and essential religious and moral commandment—that of love; as an invocation for divine help, without which our every speculative and practical virtue is insufficient; finally, as a solace for the daily toil in the accomplishment of our duties. It is a good thing, we repeat, to maintain scrupulously and earnestly the habit of reciting daily prayers, with childlike simplicity, so that this will serve as a hallmark and characteristic of every stage of our life."

The Holy Father then goes on to speak of spontaneous prayer, whereby the individual is orientated toward the quest for God. He then proceeds to speak of the prayer of praise and petition, saying, "Prayer is the first dialogue that man can desire to hold with God. Admitting the existence of a relationship with God, that is, a religion, the need rises spontaneously and becomes a duty to address a word to him. It springs—from more than sentiment, ignorance, or self-interest, as is often affirmed—from a fundamental act of intelligence, almost an instinctive, intuitive one. If God exists, if God is accessible to us, we owe him a word, an expression of ours; it is a spiritual and moral necessity (cf. *Summa theo.* IIa IIae, q. 83, a.2). Prayer is a normal and habitual attitude, deriving from the metaphysical relationship of our creaturehood in regard to him who is the supreme and necessary Principle, and this corresponds to the evangelical precept 'of praying always and not losing heart' (Lk. 18:1).

"Moreover, the two essential forms in which prayer is expressed justify this habitual need—at least potential—of prayer; praise and petition. God can be the object of our praise, of our 'elevation of the mind' toward him, an elevation which, in itself, should never be lacking, for it is part of our conception of life, of our consciousness of being a creature, of our awareness that we are always dependent on the omnipotent and gratuitous generating action of the First Cause. So God can be the object of our imploration, begging for the assisting action of Divine Providence." (See Liturgy of the Hours.)

### Prayer, Apostleship of
See Apostleship of Prayer.

### Prayer of the Faithful
In the Order of the Mass, after the Profession of Faith (the Creed), at the close of the Liturgy of the Word, there are offered by the assembly general intercessions. The celebrant invites the people to pray and make a particular response to the intercessions, such as "Lord, hear our prayer!" or "Lord, answer our need!"

As a rule the sequence of these intentions is: (1) for the needs of the Church, (2) for public authorities and the salvation of the world, (3) for those oppressed by any need, and (4) for the local community.

The intentions may vary in number and may be directed to other needs or problems, and they may be spontaneously offered by members of the assembly in accord with their spiritual disposition or according to a special occasion, for example a marriage ceremony.

### Prayer, Mystical
The highest form of prayer, called mystic prayer, must proceed through the four stages of ordinary prayer and attain the "reality through love." It is extraordinary prayer (cf. Mystic), which proceeds through methods: (1) *of the mind:* recollection, concentration, and meditation; (2) *of the will and imagination:* quiet, simplicity, and inward silence; (3) *of the heart:* contemplation and union.

These are the ordered progression, but few attain those gifts that are "of the heart," for these are only granted by God as the highest form of mystical prayer.

### Prayer Over the Gifts
See Order of the Mass, New.

### Preaching
The essential function of presenting knowledge of the Word of God, the message of Christ, is attained through orally instructing, explaining, and admonishing the people by means of preaching. The proper role of preaching involves the classical means of dialogue, discussion, persuasion, and clarification. The tools of classical oratory should also be utilized together with precise language. This means of course that there must be preparation on the part of the preacher so that in making clear the cyclic impact of the selected readings of the scriptures a greater understanding and appreciation of the message of Christ may be achieved. The purpose of the selected readings is to present a synthesis of the "heart" of the revelation of Christ through the Holy Spirit. Such a presentation need not be lengthy: better a single grain of truth than a mountain of sand that shifts with each added breath of the speaker. The custom of our time is to limit the homily or sermon to ten or fifteen minutes at the maximum. However, the solemnity of the occasion may require a sermon of greater length or a more oratorical presentation.

Vatican II taught much concerning the ministry of the Word, deriving its first inspiration from the preaching of Christ Himself and the entrustment of the Word of God by Him to His Church. It states: "Living in various circumstances during the course of time, the Church, too, has used in her preaching the discoveries of different cultures to spread and explain the message of Christ to all nations, to probe it and more deeply understand it, and to give it better expression in liturgical celebrations and in the life of the diversified community of the faithful" (GS 58).

And: "Just as Christ was sent by the Father, so also He sent the apostles, filled with the Holy Spirit. This He did so that, by preaching the gospel to every creature (cf. Mk. 16:15), they might proclaim that the Son of God, by His death and resurrection, had freed us from the power of Satan (cf. Acts 26:18) and from death, and brought us into the kingdom of His Father" (SC 6). (See Homiletics.)

### Pre-Cana Conferences
See Cana Conferences.

### Precentor
This is the title, only of honor, of the singer who intones the antiphons. It may also be applied to the person who prepares the music for divine services. Today this role is fulfilled by the ministry of the "music coordinator" or the cantor.

### Precepts of the Church
See Commandments of the Church.

### Precious Blood, Feast of the
This feast, commemorating the death of Christ, our redemption, and the Sacrifice of Calvary, has been dropped from the calendar of the Church in its revision.

## Preconization

This is the formal and public proclamation by the pope in the consistory of the appointment of a new bishop. The appointment may already have taken place, but preconization is necessary since precedence among bishops in protocol depends upon this announcement.

## Predella

Also called footpace, this is the platform on which the priest stands when saying Mass. It should be at least 3 feet 9 inches deep to permit genuflections to be made without difficulty. It is often inappropriately referred to as the top of the altar steps. In modern Church architecture the entire sacred space, that is, the area immediately surrounding the altar, is usually placed on a platform and the measurements for this vary accordingly. Where the altar is in the center of the Church for the purpose of enhancing the sense of community, the sacred space may be elevated entirely to give better visual contact between the celebrant and the members of the assembly.

## Predestination

Predestination means the determination, beforehand, of one's actions. The idea that God is selective, that He predetermines the eternal status of the soul of some individuals was an early heresy of the Church, which was condemned by the Council of Mainz in 848. In a wide sense, predestination may be taken as the divine providence of God whereby He rules the world, knowing by His infallible prescience the events of the future as they will occur in time. In its strict sense, it means God's supernatural providence and His promotion through grace of the eternal education of all rational creatures. It is thus that predestination means both the glory intended by God for all men and the means He has guaranteed for attaining that glory (1 Tm. 2:4–5, 2 Pt. 1:11–18).

However, the human person remains free under the divine influence, even while God moves the will to respond through grace (cf. Jn. 8:36). St. Augustine first discussed the problem of predestination, and although at first he was insistent on the sovereign independence of God, he came to the correct view, namely, the need for interior grace for the call to salvation and response to that call, which God gives to all human persons. Is it thus to be considered that in the supernatural order the human person can do nothing without grace, which like all other things comes from God. Through our lives we express our spiritual response by a dialogue, through worship and prayer, with a personal God.

St. Thomas Aquinas thus speaks of predestination: "If in predestination one considers the act of predetermining, the predestination of Christ is not the cause of our predestination. For God predestined him and us in one and the same act. But if one considers the end and object of predestination, the predestination of Christ is the cause of ours. For God has ordained from all eternity that our salvation should be brought about by Jesus Christ. For eternal predestination involves not merely that which is to come about in time, but also the manner and order according to which this is to take place in time" (Summa Theo., III, q. 24, a.4).

## Preface

Opening the Eucharistic prayer of the Mass, the preface is a solemn prayer offered by the priest in the name of all, opening with the dialogue prayer that exhorts all to lift up their minds to God in thanks. In the New Order of the Mass there are eighty-four prefaces, ranging in the order of their intent through the entire calendar year of the Church, and including the special solemnities as well as the prefaces prepared for special occasions, such as Thanksgiving, and the nuptial Masses or Masses for the dead. Each preface concludes with the acclamation of praise, sung or recited: "Holy, holy, holy Lord, God of power and might, heaven and earth are full of your glory. Hosanna in the highest. Blessed is he who comes in the name of the Lord. Hosanna in the highest."

## Prefect Apostolic, also Vicar Apostolic

These titles are conferred upon priests who by assignment and under the direct authority of the Holy See, whether they have episcopal consecration or not, govern a missionary district where the hierarchy has not been established. Their rights and faculties are governed by canon law (c. 293ff).

## Prelate

There are two groups of prelates: (1) ecclesiastics, having ordinary jurisdiction in the external forum, such as bishops, vicars general, prefects apostolic, and others; (2) honorary prelates, who have no jurisdiction in the external forum, for example, a titular bishop. Besides these two groups, there are minor prelates whose dignity and honor are conferred by title and rank. These are: Apostolic Prothonotaries, Honorary Prelates of His Holiness, and Chaplains of His Holiness. They are addressed as Reverend Monsignor, or less formally as simply, Monsignor. (Cf. Monsignor.)

## Presanctified, Mass of

Formerly the title of the Mass celebrated on Good Friday of Holy Week, when there is no consecration and the priest receives in Communion a host consecrated previously. It was not strictly speaking a Mass, but rather a Communion for the priest. (See Holy Week.)

## Presbyter

In the early days of the Church, a presbyter was a member of the group who served and advised the bishop. The group was more or less a governing body, and each presbyter could be commissioned by the bishop to perform certain official duties, for example, baptize and preach (1 Tm. 3:8–10).

## Presbyterian Church

Also called Presbyterianism, this form of Church polity derives its name from the system under which the Church is governed. Thus the chief officials of the Church are *Presbyters* or *Elders*. In this government there is a pyramidal structure of courts: the base is the *Consistery,* which is made up of the minister and the elders of a community church; the *Presbytery* consists of ministers and representatives of the elders of all churches within a given area; the *Synod* consists of members of one or more presbyteries within a larger area; and the highest court of appeal is the *General Assembly* composed of ministers and elders, usually of equal number, who are commissioned by the several presbyteries. All are representative, that is, elected popularly.

In teaching, Presbyterians hold strictly to a Calvinistic doctrine, with its main tenet being predestination as held by John Calvin (1509 to 1564) who taught that by the decree of God some men are destined to life everlasting while others are condemned to everlasting death. According to this doctrine there is no mitigation by grace but simply a selectivity based upon the *worth* of the individual apart from his or her own knowledge or aptitude for spiritual growth. Presbyterians also recognize two sacraments: baptism and the Lord's Supper; for them these are signs of "seals of the covenant of grace."

Among Presbyterianism there is one State-Church, that of Scotland; however, this is not a "mother" Church but maintains a spiritual independence. Worship is quite simple, divided into a "high" and a "low" form with the use of some liturgy or ritual, although some churches avoid portions of this to a degree. The concentration is on preaching, with a communion service, but Holy Communion as such is celebrated only infrequently.

In 1875 the *Alliance of Reformed Churches* was founded, which is a banding together throughout the world of those Churches that hold the Presbyterian system. The headquarters are in Geneva, Switzerland. Most of the English-speaking Churches belong to this Alliance. There has been some fragmentation among presbyterianism, and many church groups are now interested in ecumenical movements with the Northern Presbyterians interested in merging with the Episcopalians, the Methodists, and the United Church of Christ. (See under separate listings.)

## Presbyterium

See Priests' Councils.

## Presbytery

1. The governing council of a church in the early days of the Church. Of this group the bishop (*episcopos*) was a special presbyter, that is, one presiding (Acts 20:28; 1 Tm. 3:4–5).

2. The little-used name for the residence of a parish priest.

## Prescription

In canon law, as in civil law, this term is applied to the legal method by which one obtains title to goods or frees himself from certain obligations (c. 1508-1512).

## Presence of God

Vatican II teaches: "In the lives of those who shared in our humanity and yet were transformed into especially successful images of Christ (cf. 2 Cor. 3:18), God vividly manifests to men His presence and His Face" (LG 50).

And: "What does the most to reveal God's presence is the brotherly charity of the faithful who are united in spirit as they work together for the faith of the gospel and who prove themselves a sign of unity" (GS 21).

## Presence, Real

See Eucharist, Sacrament of.

## Presentation of the Blessed Virgin Mary

Celebrated on November 21, this memorial commemorates the presentation of the Blessed Mother as a child in the temple where she served and was trained. This fact is not mentioned in the Gospels but is spoken of in apocryphal writings, and the Church recognizes only the fact and not the details of narration.

## President

A modern, transliterated title given to the priest-celebrant of a Eucharistic celebration. The term is derived from the Latin verb, *"praecedo,"* in its transitive form, and is used in the sense of "preceding" others. However, its linguistic sense is "surpassing," as can be noted in the writings of Vergil, Livy, and Caesar.

As a title this is not popular but is accepted. The traditional "celebrant" now seems to be gaining in general acceptance as the title of the one who offers together with the members of the assembly the sacrifice of the Mass. (See Presidential Prayers.)

## Presidential Prayers

Those prayers that are recited from the Sacramentary by the celebrant of a Eucharistic celebration are called presidential prayers.

In the general instruction on the New Order of the Mass it is stated: "Among the parts assigned to the priest, the eucharistic prayer has precedence; it is the high point of the celebration. Next are the prayers: the opening prayer or collect, the prayer over the gifts, and the prayer after communion. The priest, presiding in the person of Christ, addresses the prayers to God in the name of the entire assembly and thus they are called presidential prayers.

"As president of the congregation, the priest gives instructions and words of introduction and conclusion indicated within the rite itself, proclaims the word of God, and gives the final blessing. He may also very briefly introduce the Mass of the day (before the celebration begins), the liturgy of the word (before the readings), and the eucharistic prayer (before the preface); he may give concluding comments before the dismissal.

"The presidential prayers should be spoken in a loud and clear voice so that everyone present can hear and pay attention. While the priest is speaking, there should be no other prayer or song, and the organ and other musical instruments should be silent.

"As president the priest prays in the name of the whole community. Besides this, he prays at times in his own name so that he may exercise his ministry. These prayers are said quietly with attention and devotion" (Gen. Ins. n. 10-13). (See President.)

## Press, Catholic

Catholic press is the collective name for the effective presentation of the current happenings within the Church as a religio-social body and the means of communicating the instructive messages that are for the general good and the good of each individual. The Catholic Press is exercised in every country of the world. It is the operation of a dialogue between the Church and the world. As such it includes all forms of the printed media, newspapers, newsletters, bulletins, magazines, books and pamphlets together with specialized material such as textbooks and catechetical material.

On June 3, 1971, the Pontifical Commission for Social Communications, in a Pastoral Instruction, stated: "In the Christian faith, the unity and brotherhood of man are the chief aims of all communications."

The excellence of journalism as a profession and craft, the competency of the staffs, and the satisfying of the instructional and informative needs of the People of God are foremost in the objectives of a good Catholic Press. Controversy, secularism, and the demeaning of the Christian polity is not to be a part of the Catholic Press. It is to persuade, to inform, to inspire—all lofty ideals that sometimes are not present in the daily covering of events, which is in the news of the modern day. (See Communications Foundation, Catholic.)

## Presumption

This sin is committed by one who either trusts too much in his own strength or who, in order to attain salvation, expects God to do something that He would not will to do. Thus, one who expects to attain salvation only by his own efforts or thinks he will attain it on account of the merits of Christ, without applying these merits or seeking them, sins by presumption. This sin is opposed to the theological virtue of hope.

## Prevenient Grace

That actual grace whereby the soul of a human person is granted the gift of the inspiration or illumination of the Holy Spirit preceding the free determination of the person's will is called prevenient grace. It is said thus to be the beginning of all activity leading to justification, which cannot be obtained without it, but its acceptance or rejection by a person is dependent upon free choice. The teaching about prevenient grace is based upon the scriptures (Ps. 59:10; Rom. 8:30; 2 Tm. 1:9) and the writings of Sts. Augustine and Thomas Aquinas.

## Pride

The chief of the capital sins, pride prompts and is partially present in all other sins. It is the inordinate desire for honor, recognition, and distinction. Pride arises from self-love. It is mortally sinful when it causes one to refuse to be subordinate even to God; it is less sinful if one, though submissive, still seeks inordinately for honor. Thus to be submissive to an inferior or to flatter one who does not deserve it for the sole purpose that he recognize you and esteem you, is sinful.

Fundamentally pride is a sin whereby man seeks to separate himself from God, refusing to acknowledge his dependence on God the Creator. It is unfaithfulness to the faithful God (cf. Gn. 3:1–9; Sir. 3:17–28] Jb. 21:14–16; also Lk. 5:30–32; 19:1–10).

In the books of Deuteronomy, the prophets, and the Psalms the sin of pride is shown to be capital both morally and religiously (Dt. 17:12–20; 18:20; Hos. 13:5–6; Is. 2:9–22; Jer. 13:9–11; Ez. 7:10–15). It was pride that was present in the heart of those who went from God (Sir. 10:12–13; Prv. 4:23; Jb. 21:14–16; Mt. 12:34). In the NT the Christian learns that the serving of one's neighbor is more satisfying to God, and that God will reward the meek through His mercy (Lk. 18:11; 2 Tm. 3:2; 1 Jn. 2:16). Those who would serve the Church must avoid the sin of pride (Rom. 3:27–28; Eph. 2:8–9; Gal. 6:14; Phil. 3:3) or as Paul further warns: "He should not be a new convert, lest he become conceited and thus incur the punishment once meted out to the devil" (1 Tm. 3:6). (See Humility.)

### Priest

A priest is one who is ordained or on whom the priesthood has been conferred, who offers sacrifice, and who has the threefold power of teaching, ministering, and governing. (Cf. Orders, Holy, Sacrament of.)

Vatican II teaches: "Though all the faithful can baptize, the priest alone can complete the building up of the Body in the Eucharistic Sacrifice. Thus are fulfilled the Words of God, spoken through His prophet: 'From the rising of the sun, even to its setting, my name is great among the nations; and everywhere they bring sacrifice to my name and a pure offering'" (Mal. 1:11) (LG 17).

And: "The divinely established ecclesiastical ministry is exercised on different levels by those who from antiquity have been called bishops, priests, and deacons. Although priests do not possess the highest degree of the priesthood, and although they are dependent on the bishops in the exercise of their power, they are nevertheless united with the bishops in sacerdotal dignity. By the power of the sacrament of orders, and in the image of Christ the eternal High Priest (Heb. 5:1–10; 7:24; 9:11–28), they are consecrated to preach the gospel, shepherd the faithful, and celebrate divine worship as true priests of the New Testament. Partakers of the function of Christ the sole Mediator (1 Tm. 2:5) on their level of ministry, they announce the divine word to all. They exercise this sacred function of Christ most of all in the Eucharistic liturgy or synaxis. There, acting in the person of Christ, and proclaiming His mystery, they join the offering of the faithful to the sacrifice of their Head. Until the coming of the Lord (cf. 1 Cor. 11:26), they represent and apply in the sacrifice of the Mass the one sacrifice of the New Testament, namely the sacrifice of Christ offering Himself once and for all to His Father as a spotless victim (cf. Heb. 9:11–28) . . .

"Priests, prudent cooperators with the episcopal order as well as its aids and instruments, are called to serve the People of God. They constitute one priesthood with their bishop, although that priesthood is comprised of different functions . . .

"All priests, both diocesan and religious, by reason of orders and ministry, are associated with this body of bishops, and serve the good of the whole Church according to their vocation and the grace given to them" (LG 28).

And: "The whole Christian people should be taught that it is their duty to cooperate in one way or another, by constant prayer and other means at their disposal, so that the Church may always have the necessary number of priests to carry out her divine mission" (PO 11). (See Vocation.)

### Priest, High

See High Priest.

### Priesthood

Priesthood is the name for the composite group of priests who, together with the bishops and deacons, serve the People of God. In modern times this has been looked upon as comprising a special professional group, a cadre of experts who share a common goal in their work. However, more than in other professions of the sciences or law, the priesthood calls for a special individual attention to a threefold form of life apart from the celibacy required of priests: (1) a program of ongoing training and learning, (2) a cultured competency that enables them to work in a variety of societal environments, (3) a personal spiritual life and exercise over and above the required praying of the Liturgy of the Hours.

Twentieth century life has placed great strain on life in the priesthood, on priests both as individuals and as a group. They have an enforced isolation; they have a life that is lonely according to the gregarious standards of our time; they have a demanding schedule that spans many disciplines but can be offset only by a dedication of special intensity.

The one-time renegade from Catholicism who later became a priest, Jean Baptiste Lacordaire (1802 to 1861), gave the classical description of the members of the priesthood:

"To live in the midst of the world without wishing its pleasures; to be a member of each family, yet belonging to none; to share all suffering; to penetrate all secrets; to heal all wounds; to go from men to God and offer Him their prayers, to return from God to men to bring pardon and hope; to have a heart of fire for charity and a heart of bronze for chastity; to teach and to pardon, console and bless always—what a glorious life! And it is yours, O Priest of Jesus Christ!"

Vatican II states: "Priests should remember that in performing their tasks they are never alone. Relying on the power of Almighty God and believing in Christ Who called them to share in His priesthood, they should devote themselves to their ministry with complete trust, knowing that God can intensify in them the ability to love.

"Let them be mindful too that they have as partners their brothers in the priesthood and indeed the faithful of the entire world. For all priests cooperate in carrying out the saving plan of God. This plan is the mystery of Christ, the sacrament hidden from the ages in God. It is brought to fulfillment only by degrees, through the collaboration of many ministries in the up-building of Christ's Body until the full measure of His manhood is achieved" (PO 22). (See Priest; Vocation.)

### Priesthood of the Faithful

The role of the People of God is a sacerdotal one because they are by vow of God to give worship of the holiness of God (1 Pt. 2:9; Ex. 19:5–6). As a redeemed people they are united to the Kingdom through the priesthood and the redemptive act of sacrifice offered by Christ for all (cf. Rv. 1:5–6; 5:9–10; 20:6). And it is through their moral lives, the integrity of their service, and their perseverance that they are each to offer sacrifice (cf. Rom. 12:1; Heb. 13:15–16; Phil. 2:17). Further each one in partaking of the Eucharist becomes aware of sacrifice and through the Eucharist offers sacrifice, memorializing not only the Sacrifice of Christ but union with Him the High Priest (Heb. 4:14–16; 7:19–21; 10:19–22).

### Priests' Associations

Groups of priests within a diocese or congregation of religious who form to exchange viewpoints and procedures are usually recognized as associations although they are not officially constituted. These are not dissident groups, but they are brought together by a singular purpose and consonance of thought. Membership is voluntary and fluctuates. The role served by these associations is spiritual, liturgical, or simply for a better base of communication in areas where information may be fragmentary or sparse. (See National Federation of Priests' Councils.)

### Priests' Councils

These councils are also variously called Priests' Senate or Diocesan Presbyterium. As an elected structure, the Priests' Council is an advisory aid to the ordinary of a diocese; it is made up of ordained priests, both religious and diocesan. The election of members follows a constituted pattern, and the body is directed by: (1) an executive board, and (2) a complement of officers who are elected by the Council members.

In its actions a Priests' Council functions independently of the Bishop but does not introduce doctrinal, disciplinary, or ordinary procedures. Each council has a number of standing committees, that is, regular and continuous, such as a personnel committee that advises on the placement of priests in certain positions of action or ministry. The councils also have a number of ad hoc committees that are appointed to carry out special programs of the diocese or to make special study of projects under consideration. It is usual for each priests' council to have liaison with other diocesan groups, such as the Liturgical Commission and the Educational Board of the Diocese.

The priests' council is more than an extended or organized democratization process. In reality the members are the helpers of the ordinary, organized for efficiency and consensus thinking in the bringing of ministerial and sacramental service to the faithful.

Vatican II declares: "By reason of the gift of the Holy Spirit which is given to priests in sacred ordination, bishops should regard them as necessary helpers and counselors in the ministry and in the task of teaching, sanctifying, and nourishing the People of God.

"Already in the ancient days of the Church we find liturgical texts proclaiming this relationship with insistence, as when they solemnly called upon God to pour out upon the candidate for priestly ordination 'the spirit of grace and counsel so that with a pure heart he may help and govern the People' [of God], just as in the desert the spirit of Moses was extended to the minds of seventy prudent men, 'and using them as helpers, he easily governed countless multitudes among the people.'

"Therefore, on account of this communion in the same priesthood and ministry, the bishop should regard priests as his brothers and friends. As far as in him lies, he should have at heart the material and especially spiritual welfare of his priests" (PO 7). (See Federation of Priests' Councils.)

### Primacy of the Pope

One of the historic purposes of Vatican II was to give a clear and final answer to the question of the primacy of the Pope in the Church. This was initiated in Vatican I (1869 to 1890). As Archbishop Melchers of Cologne stated: "We need a treatise on the bishops as successors of the apostles," and this was also announced by Pope John XXIII in convoking the Twenty-First Ecumenical Council. The issue was: "the harmonization of the relations which exist, can exist, and ought to exist between the primatial power of the Pope and the divinely given power of the bishops" (Kloppenburg).

The primatial power of the pope as the successor of St. Peter is: (1) a primacy of jurisdiction; (2) an ordinary jurisdictional power, that is, a power connected with the primatial office itself as an essential and constitutive element; (3) an immediate ordinary jurisdictional power, since this was given to him by Christ and because he can exercise it over all the faithful; (4) an immediate, ordinary jurisdictional power that is episcopal, that is, including the same pastoral functions as all bishops; (5) an ordinary, immediate, episcopal, jurisdictional power that is full, that is, no ecclesiastical power exists that is not included in the primacy; (6) an ordinary, immediate, episcopal, full, jurisdictional power that is universal, that is, without limit as to time, place, person, or subject; (7) an ordinary, immediate, episcopal, full, universal jurisdictional power that is supreme, that is, there is no higher authority in the Church, not even an ecumenical council (Documents of Vat. I and II). (See Authority; Collegiality.)

### Primate

Formerly, this was the title of a bishop who had jurisdiction over all bishops and metropolitans of a large area or nation, but was himself subject directly only to the Holy See. The title may now be honorary, for example, the Primate of All Ireland.

The position of primate is no longer recognized by canon law.

### Prime

Prime is the name of one of the hours of the Divine Office in its traditional divisions. However, this is now a part of the Morning Prayer. (See Liturgy of the Hours.)

### Principalities

See Angel.

### Prior

A superior of a monastic order who is an assistant of the abbot is known as a prior. In a monastery with no abbot, the prior is in full authority. The office is usually selective, and the one chosen serves only for a definite term. The title may be applied to the superior of a school founded and staffed by religious.

### Prioress

A prioress is the superior of a religious order of women. Her rank corresponds to that of a prior.

### Priory

An institution or monastery governed by a prior is called a priory.

### Priscillianism

A form of the Manichaean heresy, Priscillianism was introduced into Spain from Egypt in the fourth century. It was condemned at Bordeaux in 384 and died out after again being condemned at the Synod of Braga in 561. (See Heresies.)

### Private Mass

This term covers a variety of meanings. It may signify, according to its application: (1) a Mass said in a private place, (2) a Mass without a congregation, (3) a nonconventual Mass, (4) a Mass said in Latin, (5) a Mass said with less than the full liturgy of the day.

In the New Order of the Mass, recognition is given to a Mass without a congregation, and strictly speaking this is a private Mass. In form it varies in the following: The priest and minister (an acolyte) approach the altar and make the customary reverence and the sign of the cross. A greeting is given to the minister, a dialogue of exchange, followed by the making of their confession prayer together, with the priest saying the absolution; the priest then goes to the Sacramentary, which is on the left side of the altar and reads the entrance antiphon, followed by the three invocations prayed alternately with the minister. This is then followed with the speaking of the hymn of glory (when it is prescribed); then the opening prayer is spoken. The Liturgy of the Word is read, together with the psalm, the first and second readings by the minister or the priest. The gospel, or third reading, is read by the priest, and the profession of faith is made jointly, and the prayer of the faithful is read with the minister responding. The Liturgy of the Eucharist is then begun, and the responses are said by the minister. The communion and concluding rite are completed simply, and the priest and minister leave the sacred area together. (See Order of the Mass, New.)

### Privation

Also called *Privatio Officii*, this is the ecclesiastical penalty imposed upon a cleric, depriving him of his position or right without special procedure. The cause may arise out of the law or out of the actions of the cleric (c. 188).

### Privilege

In canon law, "a privilege is the concession of a special right made by the proper superior" (c. 63-79). It differs from a dispensation in the degree in which it is given, namely, a dispensation is a relaxing of a law, or subjectively, acting against a general law. Under a privilege the norm established is one of a valid type of action.

### Privileged Altar

A priest can gain a plenary indulgence for a departed soul for whom he celebrates Mass on an altar so designated (c. 916-918). The ordinary may designate one such altar in a cathedral, conventual, or parish church. However, there is usually one altar in most parishes. However, the privilege is usually extended during Forty Hours Devotion and on All Souls Day (Nov. 2) when the altar is considered privileged.

### Pro Maria Committee

The Pro Maria Committee is the title of a dedicated group whose sole purpose is to promote devotion to Our Lady of Beauraing. In the United States they are headquartered at 22nd Ave., Lowell, Mass. 01854. (See Beauraing, Our Lady of.)

### Probabiliorism

In this moral system, the lawfulness of a doubtful action is interpreted by maintaining that one is free to act against the law if the reasons for his opinion are more probable than those that favor the law.

### Probabilism

This system of moral interpretation, which is more commonly followed by Catholic moralists, declares that one may follow the opinion that favors liberty to act against the law as long as there is certainty that the opinion is well-founded, even though the contrary opinion may be more probable. This cannot be used in regard to the sacraments.

### Pro-Cathedral

A church is so called when it is being used by a bishop as a temporary cathedral.

### Process, Due

Due process is the service of the law established to protect the rights of individuals, not in a juridical sense, but through an action of recourse to arbitration and reconciliation. Among such procedural protections are, for example, the right to be informed of proposed actions that might prejudicially affect one's rights; the right to be heard in defense of one's rights; the right, which could result in the imposition of a penalty, to confront one's accusers and those who testify in support of the accusation; the right not to be judged by one's accusers.

The development of due process as a procedure of principle was introduced at the November, 1969 meeting of the National Conference of Catholic Bishops when the American episcopate accepted in substance a report on due process prepared by the Canon Law Society of America. This report strongly encouraged the establishment in each diocese of adequate and effective machinery for the settling of various disputes within the Church, particularly those regarding the alleged abuse of administrative authority. The report projected processes for reconciliation and arbitration, and specific guidelines for the structuring of administrative discretion for all ecclesiastical offices and services, and recommended that processes be adopted to the needs of the local Church.

It is not to be presumed that due process as a procedure in any way supplants, detracts from, or alters the singular prerogative of the ordinary of the diocese under the range of his jurisdiction to settle all disputes and conflicts that are outside the forums or ecclesial courts of the diocese. Provision for more expansive use of due process will be provided for in the projected revision of Canon Law. (Cf. Courts, Ecclesiastical.)

### Procession, Divine

In theological thought on the Most Holy Trinity,

the manner in which (1) God the Son (Jesus Christ) comes forth from God the Father, and (2) the Holy Spirit comes forth from God the Father and God the Son is called divine procession. The word is taken from the Latin *procedere,* meaning to "come forth."

In the scriptures these two processions are spoken of by Christ Himself: ". . . for I came forth from God, and am here. I did not come of my own will; it was he who sent me" (Jn. 8:42). Speaking further of the coming of the Advocate, which is also called *spiration,* Jesus said: "When the Paraclete comes, the Spirit of truth who comes from the Father—and whom I myself will send from the Father—he will bear witness on my behalf" (Jn. 15:26).

This procession of the person of the Son from the Father is one of generation, God the Father begetting the Son or fulfilling through the divine action the conditions necessary for such generation. The spiration of the Holy Spirit is the person which comes forth from the mutual love of God the Father and God the Son and which is true God because this love is one with the divine nature. The return of Christ to the Father (Jn. 16:28) is the reuniting of the Son with the Father in the peace of oneness in divine nature, a completion that is a mystery (Jn. 16:32). And it is through Christ, in the love of the Holy Spirit, that we follow Christ to the Father (Jn. 14:6–17). (See Trinity, the Most Holy.)

### Processions

Processions are parades by the clergy and the faithful, either within the church or from one place to another. They may be liturgical in nature, that is, part of the prescribed ceremony of a feast, or they may be simply devotional. They are undertaken as supplication, as a rejoicing, or as an act of piety. Liturgical processions are held on Candlemas day when candles are carried, on Palm Sunday when the newly blessed palms are carried, on Rogation days, and on the feast of Corpus Christi when the Blessed Sacrament is carried in the procession. The Roman Ritual prescribes the order to be followed and the attendant ceremony. In a procession of the Blessed Sacrament, the bishop or priest who carries the monstrance must walk. A plenary indulgence is gained by those who take part in a eucharistic procession, with confession, reception of Communion, and prayer for the intention of the pope (S.P., September 5, 1933).

In the New Order of the Mass there is permitted an entrance procession and a recessional procession, which are referred to more properly as the Entrance rite and the Concluding rite. Processional music has long been a part of the ritual of the Church and may vary from sung psalms, songs, litanies, to instrumental music.

### Proclaimer

See Lector.

### Procurator

Procurator is the title of the agent or representative acting in behalf of a religious group. A procurator may be assigned permanently. The most general office of procurator is that of one whose charge is to supply the material goods of an institution, such as food and clothing; in these matters he serves as an agent of management and purchase.

### Profanity

The disrespectful use of the name of God, either in anger or thoughtlessly, is venially sinful. Profanity is seriously sinful if the anger or thoughtless use is directed against God or if it has added seriousness such as scandal, denouncement of religion, or lack of charity. (See Blasphemy.)

### Profession of Faith

Profession of Faith (declaration of firmness of one's belief) may be demanded by divine law or Church law. By divine law, one is obliged to profess his faith publicly, if not doing so would imply or give the impression of denial, contempt for religion, insult to God, or scandal to those near. When the request arises from proper authority, one must profess his faith even at the risk of his life. By Church law, one is usually demanded to make a public profession of faith on occasion; examples are every adult about to be baptized and every convert from heresy before at least two witnesses. Church law also demands (c. 1406) that all administrators of vacant dioceses, diocesan consultors, vicars general, parish priests, rectors and professors of seminaries, censors of books, confessors, and preachers make the profession of faith found at the beginning of the Code of Canon Law. The usual form under which a profession of faith is made is the Creed of Pius IV with whatever additions are required.

In its most usual reference, Profession of Faith is the oral recitation of the Nicene Creed during the Liturgy of the Word in the New Order of the Mass. (See Nicene Creed.)

### Profession, Religious

This is the contract made by taking the public vows in a religious institute when one enters the religious state. It may be perpetual or temporary. It must be made according to the laws, for example, for valid profession one must be 16 years old before taking temporary profession, and 21 years old before perpetual profession (c. 572ff).

Vatican II teaches: "By her approval the Church not only raises the religious profession to the dignity of a canonical state. By the liturgical setting of that profession she also manifests that it is a state consecrated to God. The Church herself, by the authority given to her by God, accepts the vows of those professing them. By her public prayer she begs aid and grace from God for them. She commends them to God, imparts a spiritual blessing to them, and accompanies their self-offering with the Eucharistic sacrifice" (LG 45).

### Prohibition of Books

See Index of Forbidden Books.

### Promise of God

This term is not used in the Bible except in its understanding of a testament, that is, the will of the one who makes the promise, his inheritance. It is also used to express the "covenant" that God made first with Abraham, and the fulfillment of the promises made through Christ.

The promise of God was proclaimed as His inheritance for men (cf. Jer. 11:3–8; 29:31–34; 2 Mc. 2:17–18). When St. Paul spoke of the promises of God, he usually meant the messianic promises of the OT (2 Cor. 7:1; Gal. 3:16; Rom. 15:8).

For the Christian, through Christ and the fulfilling of the Law, the inheritance is part of the coming kingdom promised by Christ. The Christian comes into this final inheritance through identification with the Son of God and by keeping His commandments. Christ is the sole heir of the heritage that is the "glory of God" (cf. Mt. 21:33–46; Heb. 1:1–4; Gal. 3 and 4). Those who

were united with Christ by being "heirs with Him" and thus sons of the Father, would take part in the "right" to this heritage of glory (Acts 20:32; Rom. 8:17; Gal. 3:26–29; 4:1–11). In the attaining of the kingdom the "heirs" would come to share the life of the Father through the Son and in the Holy Spirit (Eph. 1:14; Heb. 9:15; 2 Cor. 1:22), or as St. Paul clearly stated: "By the might of his glory you will be endowed with the strength needed to stand fast, even to endure joyfully whatever may come, giving thanks to the Father for having made you worthy to share the lot of the saints in light. He rescued us from the power of darkness and brought us into the kingdom of his beloved son. Through him we have redemption, the forgiveness of our sins" (Col. 1:11–14). It is in this context that the promise of God is fulfilled. (See Salvation History.)

### Promoter of the Faith

The cleric who serves in a Church court or represents the side of the Church in a case is called Promoter of the Faith. His function is to examine and formulate objections as a defense of the Church's position. In cases of beatification and canonization of saints, the title is usually "Advocate of God" (cf. Canonization).

### Promoter of Justice

Usually trained in canon law, the Promoter of Justice is appointed in each diocese to serve in accord with canon law somewhat as a "district attorney" of the diocese. When serving in regard to marriage cases, he defends the "bond" of marriage and his role is governed by canon law, chiefly by canons 1791 through 1973.

### Propaganda, Congregation of

The Congregation of Propaganda is now called the Sacred Congregation of Evangelization of Peoples and Propagation of the Faith.

### Propagation of the Faith and Sacred Congregation of Evangelization of Peoples

The task of this branch of the governmental organization of the Church is to care for the administration and expansion of the mission fields in the world. It exercises jurisdiction over all missionary territory, that is, all parts of the world where the hierarchy has not been established. It appoints prefects and vicars apostolic, and supervises the clergy and faithful in these territories. It also maintains at Rome the Pontifical College of Propaganda Fide, known as the "Urban College"

from its founder Pope Urban VII, who established the school in 1627. (Cf. Congregation.)

## Propagation of the Faith, Society for

The Society for Propagation of the Faith is an international association, founded May 3, 1822, at Lyons, France, to aid the missionaries and missions of the Church throughout the world by prayers and alms. In the United States the headquarters are located at: 366 Fifth Avenue, New York, N.Y. 10001.

## Proper

1. The two major divisions of the Breviary: (a) the Proper of the season, that is, the liturgical passages appointed to be recited on days of the year that have a special Mass and office; (b) the Proper of Saints, that is, the liturgical passages appointed for feasts of saints throughout the year.

2. The Proper of the Mass is comprised of those parts of the prayers of the Mass which vary according to the feast being celebrated on each day. These are: entrance rite, presidential prayers, the readings of the scriptures in the Liturgy of the Word, and the concluding rite. There may also be a proper preface and sometimes a sequence. (See Order of the Mass, New.)

## Prophecy

A prophecy is a message of truth received from God and transmitted by a prophet who serves as the intermediary between God and the people (Jer. 1:9); it tells of future events that could not otherwise be known.

## Prophet

In biblical understanding a prophet is one "who speaks in God's name and under His inspiration." In this context the prophet brought forward the matters that pertained to the "conscience of Israel" and to the manifestation of God to all humans. In

Christ the prophetic history was fulfilled, even as St. John the Baptist was a prophet who attested to Christ the Messiah. In the OT there are 18 books

of prophesy, each developing an unfolding of the mind and will of God in the salvation of mankind. (See Salvation History.)

## Prophetical Literature of the Bible

Classed under this title are the writings of the four major and twelve minor prophets of the OT, together with the Books of Baruch and Lamentations, which are appendices of the Book of Jeremiah. The major prophets are Isaiah, Jeremiah, Ezekiel, Daniel; the minor are Hosea, Joel, Amos, Obadiah, Jonah, Micah, Nahum, Habakkuk, Zephaniah, Haggai, Zechariah, Malachi. (See under separate listings.)

## Prophetism

This is the process within the context of "revelation" whereby a message of God is proclaimed. Thus the prophet differs from the priest who is identified with worship and the conveying of a doctrinal message. Prophetism has been a part of all religious experience and history. In the biblical understanding this role has been recorded in various prophetical books. However, Christ is *the* prophet and His role is not only that of prophet (since He is the new Elias) but also of priest. Hence both His revelation and His teaching are the fulfillment of the Messianic era. He completed the work of all former prophets (Lk. 13:32–33; Mk. 6:4; Mt. 13:57–58; 17:12).

The content of the messages, particularly the source of the knowledge conveyed, must be examined. The prophecies of the OT and the NT are of divine disposition or from chosen messengers of God. In religions where divine origin cannot be established, the message cannot be considered a part of revelation, for Christ as prophet finalized the manifestation of God to all human persons. Thus where messages are declared through apparitions or mystical experiences, the content must coincide with the gospel teaching and the doctrines brought forward by the Church. Charisms therefore are of a different order, and the messages that are given, if the Church finds them doctrinally sound, are considered only as relevant in giving emphasis to what is genuine teaching and not in any way a part of revelation. The messages of private charisms are primarily exhortatory or encouraging to the individual rather than doctrinal. When made public, they must be examined by the Church.

## Propositions, Condemned

This is the title of the eighty propositions condemned by Pius IX in the syllabus attached to the papal bull, *Quanta Cura* (1864). They are under ten sections treating of Pantheism, Naturalism, Absolute Rationalism, Moderate Rationalism, Indifferentism, Latitudinarianism, Socialism, Bible Societies, Liberalism, and errors about the Church and her rights.

## Prose

Prose is the name for a passage that is not written in verse form.

## Proselyte

In current usage the term proselyte describes a convert or a catechumen; however the word has a biblical background. It is derived from the Greek, meaning a "newcomer" or a "foreigner." In Lv. 19:10 it is used to refer to an "alien," and such a person's station in life was like the poor and the widows'; that is, they were to be looked upon with compassion (cf. also Lv. 23:22; Dt. 24:14; 27:19). Later the word came to mean one who was converted to Judaism.

A feeling of undue pressure to make one a convert has entered into the language of today, as meaning "to be proselytized." Thus "to proselytize" has the derogatory sense of being unscrupulous in bringing one to another's viewpoint whether in religion or other areas.

## Proskomide

From the Greek word meaning "preparation," this is the name given to the preparatory part of the liturgy in the Byzantine Rite. It is during this period that the ministers of the celebration put on their vestments and prepare the wine and bread.

Prosphora

## Prosphora

This name is given to the altar-bread used in the Byzantine Rite. The word comes from the Greek meaning "offering." Unlike the hosts in the Roman Rite, the bread itself is a small loaf, sometimes shaped round, like a cake, which is ritually cut during the celebration of the Eucharist and the pieces are distributed at the communion.

## Prostitution

The use of one's body for the sexual satisfaction of another person for a sum of money or other payment is called prostitution. Vatican II declares: "Whatever is opposed to life itself, such as any type of murder, genocide, abortion, euthanasia, or willful self-destruction, whatever violates the integrity of the human person . . . whatever insults human dignity, such as subhuman living conditions, arbitrary imprisonment, deportation, slavery, prostitution . . . all these things and others of their like are infamies indeed" (LG 27).

## Protestant

Strictly speaking, the name is appled to any follower or adherent of a religious group or sect that separated from the Church at the time of the Protestant Reformation. It also includes those members who belong to one of the many offshoots of these original bodies. The term was first used when, after the Diet of Speyer in 1529, Frederick of Saxony and others "protested" against the Diet's degree permitting Catholic worship.

The modern interpretation of the word Protestant is "one who bears witness" and only in a very limited way does it refer to one who "protests." In our times it also has the understanding of "confession" or the meaning given by the earliest Protestants to the statements of their creeds, and thus "a solemn declaration or affirmation of religious belief."

The beliefs of all Protestants are affirmed as follows: (1) faith in Jesus Christ, the Lord and

Redeemer; (2) the Bible as the prime source of what is true and right; (3) the universal love of God for every human person; (4) the fellowship existing between God and each believer; (5) the forgiveness by God in response to one's faith and penitence; (6) the Church as the community of the followers of Christ; (7) the "priesthood of all believers," or each Christian's responsibility for his personal faith and life; (8) the duty of each Christian in learning and doing the will of God in his daily life; (9) the obligation resting on each Christian to advance the Kingdom of God in this world; (10) belief in the eternal life with God.

### Protestantism

Excluding traditional Christianity based upon Church authority, this religious system adheres broadly to three predominant principles: the supremacy of the Scriptures as the sole source and means of doctrine; the reasoning that justification is by faith alone; and the role of priesthood belonging to all believers. Among the various sects there are vast differences of interpretation of these principles with equally great innovations of dogmatic understanding. As a system, this new type of religion arose in the sixteenth century with the intervention of political forces, personal and administrative abuses within the Church, and the individualistic rebellion against the established form of Christianity. This was expressed by such leaders as Luther in Germany in 1521, by Zwingli in Switzerland a few years later, and in England by Henry VIII and Wolsey in 1527. The position of the Catholic Church was set forth in the twenty-five sessions of the Council of Trent (1545 to 1563), which supplies a definite statement of Catholic doctrines denied by Protestants.

There are approximately 418 different church groups in the United States. (This figure is constantly changing because of small segments breaking from established churches or new formations along some line of self-determination or nondefined cult). The major bodies of Protestants are: Baptists, Methodists, Lutherans, Presbyterians, Protestant Episcopals, United Church of Christ, the Christian Church (Disciples of Christ), the Holiness sects, Christian Scientists, Congregationalist, Disciples of Christ of the Latter-Day Saints, Episcopalians, Quakers, Jehovah's Witnesses, United Brethren, Churches of Christ. (See under separate listings.)

### Prothonotary Apostolic

See Monsignor.

### Protocanonical Books of Scripture

This title is applied to all books of the Scriptures that were found in the Hebrew Bible. The term protocanonical was first used by Sixtus of Siena in 1566 for denoting those books whose inspired character had always been accepted. (Cf. Deuterocanonical Books.)

### Protoevangelium

Literally the "first gospel," this is the title of that portion of the Book of Genesis (3:15) wherein God gives the prediction of the promise of redemption to fallen man.

### Protomartyr

Literally this means the first martyr. It is given primarily as a title of distinction to St. Stephen (Acts 7:60) who was the first of the Christians to be killed for faith in Jesus Christ. In the United States, as in all countries, the protomartyr is the first missioner killed by the inhabitants because of his missionary activities. Thus Father John de Padilla, O.F.M., who was killed in Kansas territory in 1542 is considered the protomartyr of the United States. In England it is held that St. Alban who was killed "on the 22nd day of June" was the protomartyr; he died sometime during the fourth century.

### Protopresbyter

Protopresbyter is title of the first in rank among presbyters. (Cf. Presbyter.)

### Proverbs, Book of

Called by the fathers of the Church the "Wisdom of Solomon," this book of the OT was written by several authors who are listed in the text, but the principal writer was Solomon, who supplied two collections of proverbs, numbering about 510. The subject matter of this book is the art of right living, with some points being more emphasized than others, for example, parents and children and the relations between God and men. Its central theme is wholesome teaching about true wisdom, taking special interest in the practical life that it aims to direct. The proverbs were written over many years, some as early as 800 B.C., while the last was probably added about 400 B.C.

## Providence of God

The Providence of God is the order and care of all things, both natural and supernatural, which God exercises to bring these to their prescribed end; it is manifested in the natural and positive divine laws and especially in the grace and help given to a person. Thus the Church is the provision made by God's goodness and mercy to work for the salvation of men through His providential care. The providence of God is not limited (Wis. 8:1); it extends to even the least (Mt. 6:24–30), and it frees man of anxiety. It does not mean that man is free from effort, but that he should calmly pursue his labor and God's provision will be evident. Likewise, it does not mean that man's life is free of difficulties because providence allows these that man may keep his thoughts occupied with the objective God prepared for him, eternal salvation.

Basically we may say that the Providence of God is the manifestation of God's will that nothing is allowed to fall outside His sovereignty, even while He permits this exercise of His power by other "secondary" causes. The biblical meaning of God's providence extends to nations as well as individuals (cf. Salvation History). But God so acted that never were the laws of nature abused, nor were these actions beyond the understanding of man. (Cf. Ps. 22; 77; 104; 105; Dt. 7:7–26; Jgs. 2:11–15; Is. 53; Rom. 3:25–26.)

## Providentissimus Deus

This is the Latin title ("Most Provident God") of the encyclical of Pope Leo XIII issued in 1893. This was and is considered one of the great documents to encourage the study, examination, reading, and interpretation of the scriptures. It dealt extensively with the nature of inspiration, inerrancy, and emphatically urged the more extensive study of the Bible in seminaries. One of its major teachings is expressed in these words: "Therefore it is not relevant to maintain that the Holy Spirit assumed men as instruments for writing in such a way that any falsehood could be attributed not indeed to the primary author but to the inspired writers. For he so aroused and moved them to write by a supernatural power, so assisted them as they wrote, that they should conceive with a right mind, will to write faithfully, and aptly

express with infallible truth, all those things which he ordered: otherwise he would not be the author of the whole scripture."

This teaching of inspiration was followed by a later encyclical of Pope Benedict XV (1920) called *Spiritus Paraclitus* ("The Paraclete and Spirit"). And this in turn was enlarged further by one written in 1943 by Pope Pius XII called *Divino Afflante Spiritu* ("Divine Inspiration of the Spirit"). All of these documents gave rise to the basic teachings formulated in the Constitution on Divine Revelation *(Dei Verbum)* of Vatican II. (See Form Criticism.)

## Province

1. Territory, consisting of two or more dioceses, over which an archbishop is head; the territory governed by a metropolitan in accord with canon 274. The archbishop is the ordinary of an archdiocese, but he has certain privileges and control over the other dioceses of his suffragan bishops according to law.

2. The extent of a religious community, that is, the district within which all properties and members comprise one unit, usually under the special management of a provincial.

## Provincial

The head of a province of a religious community, the provincial is either elected or appointed; his office is administrative, and he is subject to his superior general.

## Provision, Canonical

Canonical provision is the conferring and valid obtaining of an ecclesiastical office (c. 147).

## Provisors, Statute of

Issued by King Edward III (1327 to 1377) of England in 1351, this decree nullified papal appointments made without consent of the king. In his efforts to establish the Church of England as wholly separate from the papacy, Henry VIII (1509 to 1547) enforced the statute most strictly.

## Provost General

Provost General is title of the head of certain religious orders or congregations, for example, Jesuits, Discalced Carmelites, and others.

## Prudence

One of the four cardinal virtues, prudence enables one to judge rightly about an act of virtue and so is basic to the performance of all virtuous actions. Prudence is a virtue of practical reason and is directed particularly at the proper exercise of the moral virtues. All formal sin is opposed to the virtue of prudence.

In the natural order prudence is a virtue acquired and practiced through trial and experience. In the supernatural order prudence is infused at baptism and exercised through sanctifying grace. St Augustine said of prudence: "Love wisely discerns the means leading to the beloved amid obstacles which would bar the way." It can thus be interpreted in the natural order of man's love for others and in his pursuit of the means that will better enable him to fulfill his end in life, such as education, marriage, vocation, or family obligations. Likewise prudence is the seeing and recognizing of the will of God in all things that pertain to the individual's salvation, always with an awareness of the interdependence of all virtues in life.

## Psalmody

The art of singing the Psalms or portions of them in the liturgy is called psalmody. The liturgy here includes both the singing of psalms in responses and antiphons during the celebration of the Eucharist and the chanting of the Liturgy of the Hours. The usual form was a responsorial form with the leader singing the verse and the others singing a simple refrain or response. However, in the modern liturgy the participation of those at Mass or those singing in choir has expanded psalmody to a wider range, primarily direct psalmody where all sing. Likewise the music composition itself has been changing from simple plain chant to modern forms in singing and instrumental accompaniment. The singing form of psalmody follows the rhythm of the Hebrew poetry, as was introduced by the Jesuit, Father Joseph Gelineau and published in 1953.

In plain chant there are ten different psalm tones or melodies, eight being structured on the eight modes, while two follow no particular chant mode. With these it was possible to have a simple, easy psalmody that could be followed by many. Adaptations are occurring constantly as the Church develops and introduces modern musical forms and structures.

## Psalms, Book of

Also named the Psalter, this book of religious poems has been called "the inspired hymnal of the Old Testament." In the Catholic version of the Bible that follows the Vulgate and the Hebrew versions, there are 150 Psalms in a different numbering sequence than in the Protestant versions, and therefore there is a discrepancy in the numbered order. David, both a poet and musician,

was the author of many of the Psalms, certainly of numbers 2 and 15, 31, 68 and 109, because of references in the NT, attributing these to him. He was the recognized national poet of the Hebrews and the promoter of liturgical chant, but many of the Psalms were written before his reign (1012 to 972 B.C.). The dominant theme of the Psalms is the greatness of the one and only God, the Creator, Ruler, and King of Kings. Added to this are the themes of God's attributes, particularly His right to worship and His justice. Besides this theme, the Psalms record again the history from creation up to the Babylonian captivity.

In the new liturgy of the Church there is greater emphasis upon praying the Psalms, both in the antiphons of the Mass and in the Liturgy of the Hours. Thus, Vatican II declares: "Therefore priests and all others who take part in the divine Office are earnestly exhorted by the Lord to attune their minds to their voices when praying it. The better to achieve this ideal, let them take steps to improve their understanding of the liturgy and of the Bible, especially the psalms" (SC 90).

## Pseudo-Isidore

This term is applied to writings judged to be apocryphal and attributed to Isidore Mercator (d. 850).

## Psychoanalysis

The searching for and investigation of motives for action, which ordinarily are not in the consciousness. As based upon the approach developed by Sigmund Freud (1858 to 1939), this system is founded upon materialism, determinism, and hedonism, and it denies freedom and responsibility. However, he introduced the first workable methodology for the understanding of dreams and the possible interpretation as a part of therapy. Apart from this, the study of personality and the treatment of disorders have a place in the psychotherapeutic portion of medicine under the moral limits that protect the individual.

The person conducting the process of psychoanalysis is a psychiatrist who has received extra training in a psychoanalytic school. The use of psychoanalysis in the treatment of neuroses has expanded the work of the psychiatrist who formerly treated only psychoses. Recent studies by doctors, such as Hans Selye of Canada, have brought the study to a higher, more complicated plain, making research into mental stress and the relationship of biology and chemistry of the human body steps toward the treatment of many aspects of mental health.

## Psychology

This branch of philosophy, which studies the science of the mind, its functions, structure, and effects, is divided according to the type of problem studied, for example, abnormal, which treats of cases that depart from the "normal," and social psychology, which treats of group behavior and thought.

Although based upon the empirical sciences, psychology as a complete science is far from established, since it is dependent upon meta-psychological principles, and theories and hypotheses. This has led to a wide variety of trends that preclude the setting forth of the science in a complete form of principles, basic concepts as universals, and methods.

## Publican

One who collected taxes for the Roman Empire in any of its provinces was called a publican. He was usually a native of the country, and because he served a foreign government and worked against his own peoples' interests was considered despicable and rejected. In Palestine at the time of Christ publicans were considered sinners by the Pharisees, but St. John the Baptist baptized them (Lk. 3:12–13) and told them to be honest in what was expected of them. Christ did not shun them but counseled them (Mt. 9:9–13), praised their humility (Lk. 18:9–14), and called one of them, St. Matthew, to be one of the twelve Apostles (Lk. 5:27–32).

## Pulpit

This term is derived from the Latin word *pulpitum,* meaning a "stage" or "scaffold." Historically, it was first erected as a place from which one could address those in church and it replaced the *ambones,* which was erected on one side of the nave. No regulations are established for the construction of the pulpit from a liturgical standpoint, but it is assumed that it should be practical as well as decorative. Today with public address systems, the pulpit is generally simplified in structure since it is not necessary to consider acoustical advantages when placing it. It is simply a raised platform with a reading stand.

## Purgatory

The souls of those who have died in the state of grace suffer for a time a purging that prepares them to enter heaven and appear in the presence of the beatific vision. The purpose of purgatory is to cleanse one of imperfections, venial sins, and faults, and to remit or do away with the temporal punishment due to mortal sins that have been forgiven in the Sacrament of Penance. It is an intermediate state in which the departed souls can atone for unforgiven sins before receiving their final reward. (For an account of one making propitiation for the dead refer to 2 Mc. 12:39–46.) This state is not described in the teaching of the Church but its existence is a truth of faith defined by the Council of Trent (Sess. 25). Purgatory will last only until the general judgment. (Cf. Holy Souls.)

It must be understood that purgatory is an eschatological idea. Thus, its importance is its formal theological significance, and not its factual existence (cf. Lk. 16:19–31). The final testing of one's faith is not a "punishment" but one of response (1 Cor. 3:12–23). The center of the Church's teaching concerning purgatory as stated in the documents of the Council of Lyons is one of penance: "Because if they die truly repentant in charity before they have made satisfaction by worthy fruits of penance for (sins) committed and omitted, their souls are cleansed after death by purgatorical or purifying punishments . . ." (Denzinger, 464). To this is added the Christian teaching that such "purgatorical punishments" may be relieved by the offerings of the living faithful, such as Masses, prayers, alms, and other acts of piety and devotion. Such prayers are also considered to be prayers for the parousia (Rv. 22:17). (See Communion of Saints.)

## Purification of the Blessed Virgin Mary

In commemoration of the Blessed Mother having submitted to the Jewish law of ritual cleansing after childbirth (Lv. 12:1–8), a feast is celebrated in the new Church Calendar on Feb. 2, called the Presentation of the Lord. It retains its traditional name of Candlemas.

## Purificator

The purificator is a small linen cloth used during the Mass to dry and clean the chalice. It is usually from 12 to 18 inches long and from 9 to 10 inches wide and is ordinarily kept folded. It is also an adjunct to the bringing of Holy Communion to the sick, elderly, or to those confined or shut-in by circumstances.

## Purim

A minor but historical feast celebrated by the Jews, which occurs on the fourteenth day of Adar in the Jewish calendar. It commemorates the preservation of the Jews from massacre by the Persians (473 B.C.), as recorded in the Book of

Esther (9:26–32). It is both a national and secular holiday, with its important customs of giving to the poor and the mutual exchange of gifts between friends and relatives. The spirit of the celebration is one of joy, festivity, and merry-making.

## Puritanism

This term first came into the English language during the reign of Queen Elizabeth I of England, to describe the extremist group of English Protestants. These members were dissatisfied with the Elizabethan Settlement and sought even greater reforms in the "purification" of the Church. They rejected many religious practices, and when their clergy refused to wear vestments, their actions became the Vestiarian Controversy. They were at great odds with the Church of England and were not well received.

Puritanism had large support in Parliament, notably the House of Commons, and in 1572 the leaders published "An Admonition to Parliament," which was followed by a second admonition, both to gain legislative support for their cause. They failed in bringing about their reform. Some fled the country to seek religious liberty in Holland, while others in 1620 founded the Plymouth Colony in Massachusetts.

The term puritanism has come to mean any particularly rigid religious outlook or style and has been a word of derision against any person who has a moral sexual code.

## Putative Marriage

Invalid because of a diriment impediment or lack of consent, such a marriage, however, was contracted while at least one of the contracting parties was in good faith as to the validity. (Cf. Diriment Impediment.)

## Pyx

1. A small, round container, usually made of or coated with silver or gold, about 1½ to 2 inches in diameter and less than one inch deep, in which the Blessed Sacrament is carried to the sick. This is usually enclosed in a small silk-lined bag or pouch and suspended from the neck of the priest by a silk cord.

2. In the Middle Ages, a pyx was a form of tabernacle suspended above the altar from a chain. These were usually highly decorated.

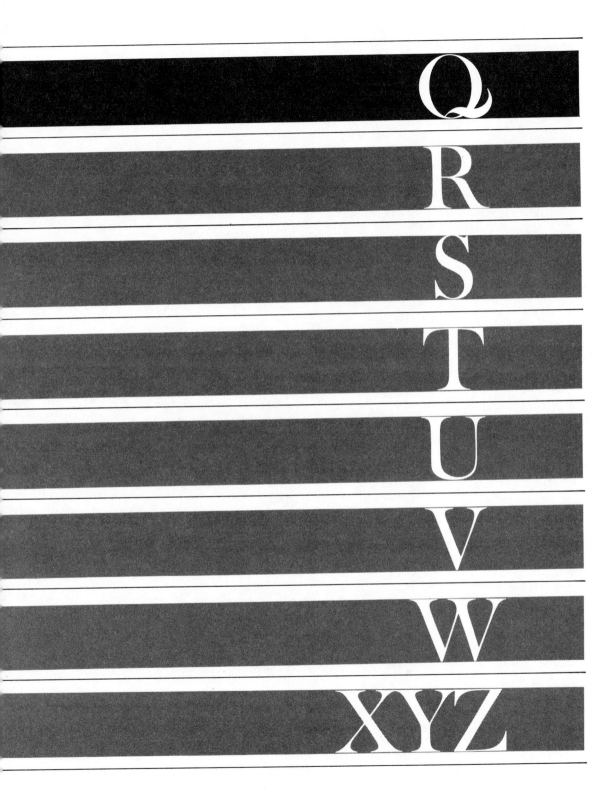

Q
R
S
T
U
V
W
XYZ

### Qoheleth

This Hebrew word is variously translated but has the meaning of "one who calls together an assembly." The term is translated in the Greek by the word *Ecclesiastes;* thus the book of the Bible called Ecclesiastes is sometimes referred to as the Book of Qoheleth. (See Ecclesiastes, Book of.)

### Quadragesima

From the Latin, meaning the "fortieth," the term has become the collective title for the entire period of Lent.

### Quadragesimo Anno

The Latin title ("Forty Years Afterwards") of an encyclical of Pope Pius XI, issued May 15, 1931. It was written to commemorate the fortieth anniversary of the issuance of the famous encyclical *Rerum Novarum* ("Of New Things") by Pope Leo XIII. (See *Reum Novarum.*)

Among the social documents of the Church, *Quadregesimo Anno* reemphasizes the social teaching of Pope Leo's document, and adds an examination of the evils that were arising in the world. It warned against the harmful results of free competition and administrative centralization, and the flawed concepts of socialism that are in direct contradiction to the Catholic teaching; it called for a reorganization of society, especially in the area of the rights of the working classes. Its thesis is the principle of subsidiarity.

Among its central thoughts are these extracts: "First, let it be made clear beyond all doubt that neither Leo XIII, nor those theologians who have taught under the guidance and direction of the Church, have ever denied or called in question the twofold aspect of ownership, which is individual or social accordingly as it regards individuals or concerns the common good. Their unanimous contention has always been that the right to own private property has been given to man by nature or rather by the Creator Himself, not only in order that individuals may be able to provide for their own needs and those of their families, but also that by means of it, the goods which the creator has destined for the human race may truly serve this purpose. Now, these ends cannot be secured unless some definite and stable order is maintained" (45).

And: "In the present state of human society, however, we deem it advisable that the wage contract should, when possible, be modified somewhat by a contract of partnership, as is already being tried in various ways to the not small gain both of the wage earners and of the employers. In this way workers and officials are made sharers in the ownership or the management, or in some way participate in the profits" (65).

And: "When We speak of the reform of institutions it is primarily the state We have in mind. Not, indeed, as if We were to look for all salvation from its intervention, but because on account of the evil of Individualism, as We call it, things have come to such a pass that the highly developed social life which once flourished in a variety of prosperous institutions, organically linked with one another, has been laid prostrate and all but ruined, leaving thus virtually only individuals and the state, with no little harm to the state itself. The latter, having lost its form of social regimen, and encumbered with all the burdens once borne by associations now rendered extinct, was in consequence submerged and overwhelmed by an infinity of affairs and duties" (78).

And: "Labor, indeed, as has been well said by Our predecessor in his Encyclical, is not a mere chattel, since the human dignity of the workingman must be recognized in it, and consequently it cannot be bought and sold like any piece of merchandise (R.N. 16). Nonetheless, under the prevailing conditions, the demand and supply of labor divide men on the labor market into two classes, as into two camps, and the contention between these parties transforms this labor market into an arena where the two armies are engaged in fierce combat. To this grave disorder which is leading society to ruin a remedy must evidently be applied as speedily as possible" (83).

### Quadrivium

This is the name for parts of the seven liberal arts studied in the Roman curriculum of studies and borrowed by ninth century teachers. The quadrivium consisted of arithmetic, geometry, astronomy, and music. The other three, called "Trivium," were grammar, rhetoric, and logic.

### Quaestor

This title was applied to one who went about preaching that alms might be collected.

## Quakers

This is the common or popular name for the members of a small group of Christians who are known as the Society of Friends. They were founded in 1648 by George Fox (1624 to 1691). It was the intention of Fox to return to a primitive Christianity, and he claimed that he became aware of an "inner light," which for some time was to take the place of any formal set of teachings. The followers were not well received and suffered persecution because they were "disruptive" of other religious services.

In America the most famous Quaker was William Penn (1644 to 1718), who had been converted to the Society of Friends in Ireland, was imprisoned for a time, and wrote a book on religion called *Cross and Crown*. It was when he obtained a grant from King Charles II of England in payment of a large sum of money owed to Penn's father, Sir William Penn of the admiralty, that young William Penn became the title-holder of a tract of land in the New World, which was called Pennsylvania or "Penn's Woods."

The Society of Friends places great emphasis upon education, basing their system upon religious training. Because of this they were able to carry on a wide missionary activity and effect social reform and promote programs for civic development and peace, yet they are opposed to swearing in courts of law and see sin in a simplistic manner. They place faith in the Christian religion as the source and means of obtaining peace.

## Quanta Cura

This is the Latin title ("What Great Care") of the encyclical of Pope Pius IX issued on Dec. 8, 1864. It was to this that the famous Syllabus condemning the doctrines of liberalism was attached. (See Syllabus.)

## Quarant 'Ore

Quarant 'Ore is French title of the Forty Hours Devotion; the words literally mean "forty hours." (See Paraliturgical Actions.)

## Quarantine

In the ancient Church, this was a period of 40 days of rigorous fasting, penance, and prayer. The quantity of indulgence guaranteed under the name quarantine is the amount of temporal punishment due to sin which would be remitted by this 40 day period of penance. (See Indulgence.)

## Quarter Tenses

See Ember Days.

## Queen Mary, Feast of the Blessed Mother

By proclamation of Pope Pius XII on November 1, 1954, this feast is to be celebrated yearly on May 31. In the new calendar of the Church this has been shifted to a memorial celebrated under the title "Queenship of Mary" on August 22. The queenship of Mary extends to the universal Church, for she is by divine prerogative Queen of heaven and earth. Her queenship is to be venerated "as something extraordinary, wondrous, eminently holy" *(Ineffabilis Deus)*. The queenship of Mary has been declared formally by Pope Pius XII, thus: "Mary is queen by grace, by divine relationship, by right of conquest and by singular election" (AAS, 38, 1946, 266).

## Quiet, Prayer of

St. Teresa of Avila gave this name (Life, Ch. 14) to that degree of contemplative prayer wherein the union of the soul is, by infused grace, characterized by a cessation of reason where contemplation is yet imperfect and where the intellect can still be distracted.

## Quietism

From the Latin word *quies,* meaning "repose," this is the error of those who limit their efforts toward perfection to as few as possible. Originating in the teaching of Miguel de Molinos (d. 1696), this system represented as the Christian spiritual ideal of perfection the complete passivity of the soul. Molinos' motto was: "Let God act." Thus the minimum of personal action on the part of the human person becomes the ideal of sanctity. His error was that a continuous act of love being made or attained does away with other acts of virtue, even with the resistance to temptations. Quietism was condemned as heretical by Pope Innocent XI in 1687.

## Quinisextum Council

The Synod held in Trullo in 692 is sometimes referred to by this name which literally means the "fifty-sixth" council. Its proceedings remained unsigned by the pope, Sergius I (d. 701).

## Quinquagesima

The first Sunday before Lent is called Quinquagesima. It refers to the period of time of "fifty" days before Easter, which in early times was the beginning of the prelenten abstinence. Occasionally the word is applied to the period of 50 days from Easter to Pentecost.

## Quire

This is a little used name for the place where choir singers stand in the church; more simply called the choir.

## Quirinal

Quirinal is the name of one of the seven hills of Rome, northeast of the Capitoline Hill. In the sixteenth century a papal palace was built there, which then became the residence of the kings of Italy from 1870 to 1946 and is now the home of the president of the Italian Republic.

## Qumran Movement

In the history of Judaism, this was a group headed by dissident priests who formed a separatist movement with an eschatological mentality. As a group they considered themselves the only genuine possessors of a religion consistent with the historical OT religion of the Israelites. After A.D. 70 they were considered an heretical sect and were excluded from the official body of Judaism because of their denial of the resurrection of the dead, the establishment of Yahweh over all Judaism in a rigid and exclusive pattern, and their rigorous interpretation of the books of the Torah. (See Essenes; Judaism.)

## Qumran Scrolls

See Scrolls of the Dead Sea.

## Qumranites

The name of members of a religious group called the Qumran Sect who were not directly associated with the Essenes in the first century B.C. and later, but were more likely joined in some religious and possibly political manner to the Zealots. Their contribution to the documents found on Massada were the so-called "Angelic Liturgies" or "Songs of the Sabbath Sacrifices," as determined by the dates and artifacts found in the Qumram ruins. The works of the Qumranites postdate the writings of the Scrolls of the Dead Sea. (See Essenes.)

## Quo Vadis

According to a legend first recorded in the apocryphal book called the "Acts of St. Peter" this was the portion of the question *"Domine quo vadis?"* (Lord, where do you go?). These words were allegedly spoken to St. Peter when he met Christ as he was supposedly fleeing from Rome along the Appian Way. St. Peter asked where he was going and the alleged reply was, "I am coming to be crucified again." This was understood by St. Peter to mean that He (Christ) was to be persecuted again in the person of His Apostle. So St. Peter returned to Rome and was martyred. There is a small church called Domine Quo Vadis, which was built in the seventeenth century on the Appian Way to commemorate this alleged happening.

The words became the title of a famous historical novel, *Quo Vadis,* by Henryk Sienkiewicz in 1895.

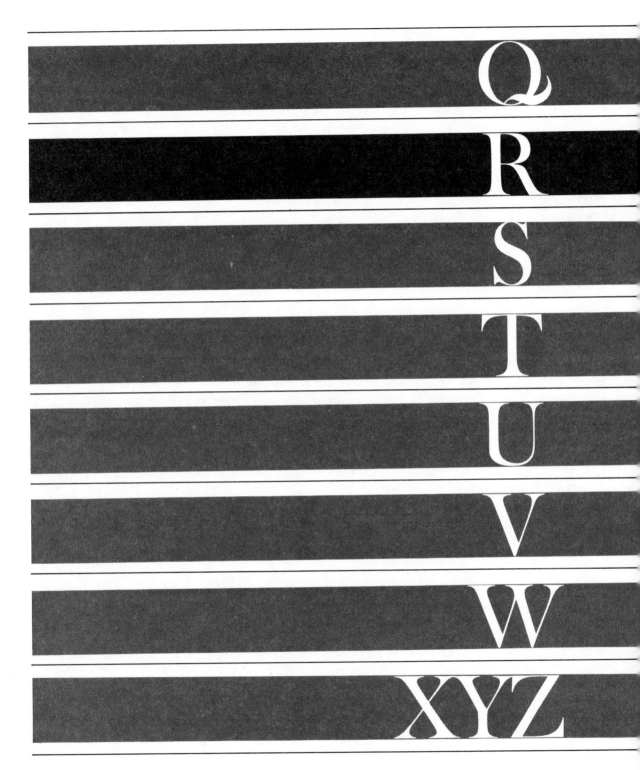

Q
R
S
T
U
V
W
XYZ

# R r

## Rabat

This French word is the name of a small piece of black, blue, or white cloth which is divided in the middle and which, attached to a rudimentary collar and resting upon the upper chest, is worn by some of the French clergy but is not generally in use. In white, it is worn by the Brothers of Christian Doctrine.

## Rabbi

1. The title, derived from the Hebrew word meaning "my master" or "my teacher" is one of respect and honor. It is given to those who graduate from one of the rabbinical schools or Jewish theological seminaries. We learn from the scriptures that this was formerly the title of respect given to scholars (Mt. 23:7). Christ was addressed as Rabbi (Jn. 1:38). In Jewish history Rabbi Judah (A.D. 135 to 217) is recognized as the paragon.

The distinction of rabbi in the Jewish tradition does not bestow a priestly status or degree upon the person. The rabbi bears this distinction because of his knowledge of the religious law and tradition of the Jews and because, in fulfilling his role, he is the one who educates others, supervises the dietary laws (the *kashruth*), marriages, and the religious life of the community.

Today the rabbi has had to assume the important task of preaching as a part of the Sabbath observance. He also extends his knowledge through lectures and service to the broader community. There are three classifications of the Rabbiniate: the Orthodox, Conservative, and the Reform. The distinctions are not in function but in the approach to the legal applications, for example, the Reform do not view the legal requirements of the Torah as binding upon their members. The traditional role remains the same.

2. Rabbi is the linguistically corrupted name for the stock or rabat as derived from the French *rabat*.

## Raccolta

Containing the prayers, devotions, and aspirations that the Church has enriched with indulgences, this book is periodically published in Latin under the title *Enchiridion Indulgentiarum* and its translation is permitted by authorization of the Holy See. It was first published in Rome in 1807 by Telesforo Galli. The conditions for gaining an indulgence and the amount of the indulgence as well as the date of grant made by the Sacred Congregation of the Penitentiary are listed with each prayer or devotion.

## Race

Arising from the biological characteristics, race is the group division of the human species. This division has no basis in singularity, for anthropological studies have shown that in spite of small distinctions there is no group of peoples that is completely homogeneous, no "pure" race. In accord with genetic studies there are six races of humans: early Europeans, European, African, Asiatic, American, and Australian.

In the religious sense Abraham was the founder of the People of Israel, the "father of nations" (Gn. 12:1–5). It was the beginning of the God-related people of the coming generations. Thus it was the reply of Christ to the Father and the new covenant that meant the faithful were to be the family of nations in the completion of the divine calling and gratuitous covenant made with Abraham that made possible the People of God. (Mt. 3:9; Jn. 8:39–40; Jas. 2:21–23; Lk. 19:7–10; Gal. 4:22–31.)

Vatican II has declared: "All peoples comprise a single community, and have a single origin, since God made the whole race of men to dwell over the entire face of the earth (cf. Acts 17:26). One also is their final goal: God. His providence, His manifestations of goodness, and His saving designs extend to all men (cf. Wis. 8:1; Acts 14:17; Rom. 2:6–7; 1 Tm. 2:4) against the day when the elect will be united in that Holy City ablaze with the splendor of God, where the nations will walk in His light (cf. Rv. 21:23–27)" (NA 1).

And: "There is in Christ and in the Church no inequality on the basis of race or nationality, social condition, or sex, because 'there is neither Jew nor Greek; there is neither slave nor freeman; there is neither male nor female. For you are all "one" in Christ Jesus' (Gal. 3:28, Greek text; cf. Col. 3:11)" (LG 32).

## Racism

The modern world faces a social problem which, for want of a more accurate term, is called racism. This is not a recognition of the dignity of the human person, but it is an "ingrowth," that is, a consideration by one group of people as superior to another group. It is a distinction arising out of ego factors rather than out of distinctions of small differences. It is attitudinal rather than reasoned;

it is emotional rather than intelligent. No group is free of racism regardless of their characteristics and will not be until the truth is recognized that in no group as group is there a superiority of intelligence, ability, or physical condition.

Vatican II teaches: "The Church, sent to all peoples of every time and place, is not bound exclusively and indissolubly to any race or nation, nor to any particular way of life or any customary pattern of living, ancient or recent" (GS 58).

And: "The Church admonishes her own sons, but also humanity as a whole, to overcome all strife between nations and races in this family spirit of God's children, and in the same way, to give internal strength to human associations which are just" (GS 42).

## Ransom

Christ is often referred to as the "Ransom." The development of this thought is that in salvation history there was a break in the relations of man as creature with God as Creator. The balance of this relationship was upset by man's actions, his sin. Man could not "ransom" or redeem himself, so it followed that a sacrificial system came into existence where the sacrifice was to be an appeasement of God as God willed. But this was inadequate and it was abused by those who followed the old covenant (cf. Lv. 4 and 5; Nm. 15:22–30), and even intercession would not suffice as was proved by the prophets. This balance then could only be restored by a just intercessor, a true and adequate sacrifice, and this was accomplished in time when God Himself offered the sacrifice, that of His Son, Jesus Christ. It was through Christ as the ransom that the human persons could offer to God a truly efficacious sacrifice, one of redemption (cf. Mt. 20:28; Jn. 10:17–18; Rom. 5:6–8; Gal. 3:13; Acts 2:32–36; 1 Pt. 2:19–25).

Man's response to this ransom can be seen in the fruits of holiness of life and the memorializing of the sacrifice of Christ, as St. Paul declares: "You have been purchased, and at a price. So glorify God in your body" (1 Cor. 6:20). (See Servant of Yahweh; Salvation History.)

## Rashness or Rash Judgment

Characteristic of rash judgment is the tendency to assent without sufficient reason or basis to the existence of a moral defect in another. It is a sin against justice and opposed to the virtue of prudence.

Rash judgment was condemned by Christ in the Sermon on the Mount: "If you want to avoid judgment, stop passing judgment. Your verdict on others will be the verdict passed on you. The measure with which you measure will be used to measure you" (Mt. 7:1–2). In the evaluation of another person in charity, there should be a recognition of the person's dignity as a human being, a knowledge of the person's circumstances, and a realization of the seriousness of the judgment given. It is thus rash to make statments about another person's character when one does not know enough to render a judgment, even when the judgment may be considered favorable to the other person (cf. 1 Cor. 13:4–5).

## Ratio Studiorum

Ratio Studiorium is the abbreviated and usual title of the system of pedagogy at first published by the Society of Jesus in 1599. The full title is *Ratio atque Institutio Studiorum Societatis Jesu*. In its broad scope and method, it set up the orderly system and subjects that would serve to train the minds of students while at the same time giving basic knowledge in the arts, particularly grammar, humanities, and rhetoric.

## Rationalism, Theological

This doctrine, originated in Germany by Christian Wulff (d. 1754), held that reason is the ultimate judge of truth. It made observance of the moral law the equivalent of religion, and it denied revelation. The term is also applied to the theory that the mind of man can and should assent only to those truths that are proved by reason, and it is developed in the Protestant principle of private judgment. As a repudiation of supernatural faith, rationalism is allied to deism, pantheism, and materialism and has been condemned by the Holy See. (Cf. Propositions, Condemned.)

Vatican II teaches: "Many, unduly transgressing the limits of the positive sciences, contend that everything can be explained by this kind of scientific reasoning alone, or, by contrast, they altogether disallow that there is any absolute truth" (GS 19).

And: "This sacred Synod, recalling the teaching of the first Vatican Council, declares that there are 'two orders of knowledge' which are distinct, namely, faith and reason" (GS 59).

## Reader

See Lector.

## Readings, Cycle of

Throughout the Church calendar there is assigned for every Sunday and Holyday three readings from the scriptures, which form the basic intent and sequence of the Liturgy of the Word in the Celebration of the Eucharist. These readings are usually made up of a selection from a book of the OT, a reading from an Epistle, and a portion of one of the Gospels.

These readings are gathered in a *Lectionary* and are divided into three cycles, named simply *A, B,* and *C* for Sundays and *I* and *II* for weekdays. The order of use for the cycle is as follows, beginning in 1975: *A* and *I;* 1976: *B* and *II;* 1977: *C* and *I,* and so on beginning over again with *A* and *II* and alternating. There are three lettered cycles for Sundays and Holy days and two Roman numeral cycles for weekdays, so the joining of the two cycles must· be adjusted in their alternation.

Through these many readings over a three-year cycle of Sundays it is the intent of the Church to bring to the people the interrelation of the continuity of teaching as contained in both the OT and the NT. It also provides a greater insight into the unfolding of the revelation of God and the sequential application to one's life in living out the teachings that God has provided and the Church teaches. (See Calendar, Church.)

### Reason, Age of

1. The presumptive age in Church law when one is able, through natural reason, to distinguish between moral right and wrong, is called the age of reason. This is seven years of age.

2.· The period of Enlightenment in the eighteenth century. (See Enlightenment, the Age of.)

### Rebaptism Controversy

See Donatism.

### Recension

In biblical studies the revision of a text based upon critical examination of the sources is called recension. This is not undertaken unless there is substantial foundation for acting, and never because of style changes in language. (See Form Criticism.)

### Rechabites

A fanatical group of reactionaries among the Israelites were called Rechabites, the name being derived from the ancient Semitic word meaning "to ride." They were desert nomads who were convinced that Yahweh could only be served in a materialistic manner in keeping with their nomadic ancestors' beliefs. They shunned the practice of drinking wine. The group was called "of the house of Rechab"(Jer. 35:6), and they were descended from Hammath and were called Kenites (1 Chr. 2:55). They were forced to remain in Jerusalem after the conquest by the Babylonian army under Nebuchadnezzar in 598 B.C., and their beliefs were tested by the prophet Jeremiah. Although he commended them for their obedience to their teachings, he did not approve of those teachings; they were, however, by their presence a connection between the Hebrews and the holy city of Jerusalem.

### Recidivist

One who, in spite of repeated confessions, relapses into the commission of the same sins with the result that little effort is made toward improvement, or the inclination to improve is lost, is called a recidivist. The degree of sincerity on the part of the penitent determines the pastoral care necessary so that the penitent can make spiritual progress.

### Recollection

In leading a spiritual life, recollection means the awareness of the presence of God in one's soul. Because of this awareness, excesses in actions and pleasures are curbed and distractions by the details of ordinary living are avoided. In practice, spiritual life is accompanied with a moderation in speech and the use of all senses (Eccl. 5:1–6).

### Reconciliation Room

This is a new adaptation of the place of confession of sins rather than a change in the Sacrament of Penance, and the reconciliation room offers an alternate to the confessional. It is set up so that (1) there is visible contact between the confessor and penitent; (2) the attitude is changed by the difference in surroundings or atmosphere; (3) it brings into focus the counseling aspects of the rite of the Sacrament of Penance; and (4) it provides an environment of relaxation, ease, simple comfort, and quiet dignity. In newer church construction there may be set aside one or more small rooms, sparsely furnished, well lighted, and expressive of the nature of the service in which penitents may choose to seek the Sacrament of Penance in privacy. The reconciliation room may be called a "counseling room" and may also be used for other purposes. (See Penance, Sacrament of; Pastoral Counseling.)

### Reconciliation, Sacrament of

See Penance, Sacrament of.

### Reconventio

This term is applied to the counter claim made by a defendant in an ecclesiastical court.

### Rector

1. A term synonymous with pastor (c. 216).
2. The head of a church that is neither a parish nor a capitular church, or one used by a religious community for divine services, for example, a church dedicated for worship by pilgrims.
3. The cleric who is in charge of a seminary or college chapel and by authority is the director of the institution; he is responsible for the buildings, the worship, and those in attendance.

### Recusants

Recusants is the name, from the Latin word *recusare* ("to refuse"), given to those Catholics who refused the mandate to accept the religion of the ruler or the state religion during the reign of Elizabeth I (1558 to 1603) of England. For the Catholics this would have meant a denial of faith and submission to restrictions of expressing their religious beliefs in practice. The name was used officially in a law promulgated in 1593 restricting all Catholics, although the term had been a popular one of derision for some time.

There were three classes of recusants: those who chose to remain in England and go against the authoritarian government, those who fled England and took up residence in other countries, and those who were forced by pressure tactics to leave the country and go into voluntary exile. Among the exiles were some religious orders who fled rather than have their membership dispersed. However, some religious orders were simply disbanded and their properties confiscated by Elizabeth, notably the Franciscans, Benedictines, Carmelites, Dominicans and Augustinians.

One result of the exodus of scholars and teachers from England was the expansion of the University of Louvain. Also an English college was established at Douai in France, founded by William Cardinal Allen. It was here, and at a similar College at Reims, France, that the translation of the Douai Bible was made and published in 1582. It become the standard Catholic English text for many years.

The exile of the recusants came to an end only with the passage of the Second Relief Act of 1791 in the reign of George II, which repealed many of the anti-Catholic laws and proscriptions.

### Red Mass

Red Mass was the name of a votive Mass to the Holy Spirit which was celebrated from the middle of the thirteenth century to mark the opening of the courts of law and to invoke the enlightenment of the Holy Spirit on the deliberations. It is called "red" because of the color of the vestments used in the celebration. It was likewise celebrated annually for the Roman Rota, the highest of the papal courts.

The Red Mass has become known as the Lawyers' Mass and was first celebrated in the United States for the Guild of Catholic Lawyers of New York City in 1928. Since that time many groups of Catholic attorneys have continued to celebrate the Red Mass as organizations, such as the St. Thomas More Society.

### Redditio of Creed

Redditio of Creed is literally the "giving back" of an acknowledgement of the faith through the saying of a creed; it is the name for the profession of faith made by the early Christians as a preliminary to reception of the Sacrament of Baptism after the catechumenate. In the present day liturgy of the rite of baptism, there is a questioning of the recipient, which recalls this early practice. The godparents respond to this in the name of the infant.

### Redemption of Man

This was the purpose for which Christ, the Second Person of the Blessed Trinity, came into the world as Man and God, that is, to save sinners (1 Tm. 1:15). In the OT we see the record of God the Father's merciful preparation and design to save the world, that is, man, through His Son. This was accomplished by the sacrifice of Christ who offered Himself on the cross to God as a victim and whose obedience ("to the death of the cross") was more meritorious than all of the sacrifices offered before by the Jews. Christ's act was prepared for and His arrival announced (Mt. 3:1–12). When He came, He declared: "This is the time of fulfillment. The reign of God is at hand! Reform your lives and believe in the gospel!" (Mk. 1:15). Through Christ's act of propitiation the kingdom (man's reinstatement in the friendship of God and in his right to heaven and the means of attainment, namely, the sacraments) was made known to the Apostles (Mt. 13:11) and it is given to all (Mt. 21:43) through love, the true source of all giving: the Father gives His Son (Jn. 3:16); the Son, Christ, gives Himself, His life (Mt. 20:28) on the cross and in the Eucharist (Mt. 26:26), and the Holy Ghost is given to confirm this opening of the kingdom by means of the Church and grace (Acts 2:38). The redemption of man accomplished by Jesus Christ is the regaining of the kingdom of heaven.

Vatican II teaches: "In the human nature which He united to Himself, the Son of God redeemed man and transformed him into a new creation (cf. Gal. 6:15; 2 Cor. 5:17) by overcoming death through His own death and resurrection" (LG 7).

And: "For this the Church was founded: that by spreading the kingdom of Christ everywhere for the glory of God the Father, she might bring all men to share in Christ's saving redemption" (AA 2).

And: "The Christian man, conformed to the likeness of that Son who is the firstborn of many brothers, receives 'the first-fruits of the Spirit' (Rom. 8:23) by which he becomes capable of discharging the new law of love. Through this Spirit, who is 'the pledge of our inheritance' (Eph. 1:14), the whole man is renewed from within, even to the achievement of 'the redemption of the body' (Rom. 8:23): 'If the Spirit of him who raised Jesus from the dead dwells in you, then he who raised Christ from the dead will bring your mortal bodies to life also, through his Spirit dwelling in you' (Rom. 8:11)" (GS 22).

And: "In the end, when He completed on the cross the work of redemption whereby He achieved salvation and true freedom for men, He also brought His revelation to completion" (DH 11).

## Reductions

See Jesuit Reductions.

## Reformation

The division of the Christian Churches that came about in the fifteenth and sixteenth centuries is called the Reformation. It was more than a religious movement, for in history it was a many-faceted event that involved humanism, poli-

tics, and economic factors. The trends at their center, however, were theological and religious. As launched by Luther, Calvin, and Zwingli there was a genuine search for and appeal to return to the ancient Christian truth that had suffered many deformations because of human failure, misinterpretation, and error. But the reform, which is parallel in some respects to the renewal of the Church in our times through the far-reaching elucidations of Vatican II, was looked upon by Catholic theologians of those centuries as an attack on, and rejection of, Christian truth. This resulted in many open and disguised attacks on the Church. (Cf. Protestantism.)

The Reformation in its impact upon the political, cultural, and ecclesiastical life was not able of itself to bring the Church to a complete insight into its role (cf. Jer. 1:10; Rom. 12:2; Gal. 6:15; Rv. 21:5). It could not for ages begin to unfold anew the revolution of truth that would result in a complete animadversion of the minds and hearts of men. Instead human forces began to shatter and disrupt the salvation-thrust that the world was to experience in the succeeding years. What had been hoped would accomplish a "return to the original form" of religion was side-tracked into areas where the truth was almost totally obscured.

Religion as contained in the message of Christ was to suffer division into denominations; one group of beliefs was set in opposition to others. The result, the error of many, was a fragmentation. It must be said nevertheless that the Reformation brought a certain awareness, an acute concentration upon the preaching of the truth of the scriptures, a simplification of structures, and an acknowledgement that the entire body of human persons who are believers are also of the "royal priesthood" and have an obligation to teach and effect the salvation of mankind through their faith and their living of the gospels.

Vatican II declares: "The first divisions occurred in the East, either because of disputes over the dogmatic pronouncements of the Councils of Ephesus and Chalcedon, or later by the breakdown of ecclesiastical communion between the Eastern Patriarchates and the Roman See.

"Still other divisions arose in the West more than four centuries afterward. These stemmed from a series of happenings commonly referred to as the Reformation. As a result, many Communions, national or denominational, were separated from the Roman See. Among those in which some Catholic traditions and institutions continue to exist, the Anglican Communion occupies a special place" (UR 13).

And: "The Churches and ecclesial communities which were separated from the Apostolic See of Rome during the very serious crisis that began in the West at the end of the Middle Ages, or during later times, are bound to the Catholic Church by a special affinity and close relationship in view of the long span of earlier centuries when the Christian people lived in ecclesiastical communion" (UR 19).

## Reformed Churches

See Calvinism.

## Refreshment Sunday

Laetare Sunday, that is, the fourth Sunday of Lent, is sometimes referred to by this name.

## Regimini Ecclesiae Universae

This is the Latin title ("Guides of the Universal Church") of a papal document published Aug. 18, 1967, under which the Roman Curia was to be reorganized over a four year period. (See Congregation; Curia, Roman.)

## Regina Coeli

Literally from the Latin "Queen of Heaven," this title is accorded the Blessed Virgin Mary; it is also the title of a poem composed in the twelfth century and the verse of a traditional hymn of the Easter season.

## Regions of Church Activities

In order to achieve a greater effective communication between the various commissions of dioceses and between bishops themselves, the United States has been divided into geographical territories. There are twelve such regions along state lines. (See National Conference of Catholic Bishops.)

## Reign of God

The central theme of the words and preaching of Christ, especially as recorded in the gospel of Matthew, is the message of the kingdom. The establishment of the kingdom of God and the salvation of all human persons through baptism and faith were to be accomplished *after* the redemption. A new kingdom that had been spoken of by the prophets (Is. 9:1–6; 11:1–9; 42:1–12; Ez. 17:22–24; 34:10–31; Jer. 30:8–10) was to come, and this was to be accomplished through Christ (Is. 2:12–21; 4:2–6; 30:19–33; Jer. 17:24–26). This new reign is the "good news" contained in the gospel (Is. 40:9–10; 52:7). Salvation is eschatological (Rom. 5:4–5; 8:22–25), and it becomes effective in the minds and hearts of the Christian believer by

his response (Rom. 1:16; Jas. 1:21; 1 Cor. 1:21; 15:2; Jn. 11:27).

As the evangelist Mark proclaims: "This is the time of fulfillment. The reign of God is at hand! Reform your lives and believe in the Gospel!" (1:15). (See Salvation History.)

## Relations

See Jesuit Relations.

## Relativism

Even the proponents of the philosophy of relativism find that they arrive at few identical conclusions. Thus we see that relativism denies the existence of absolute values.

In the religious sense, relativism is most evident in the area of moral theology, for here many deny the premises upon which moral law rests, whereas others consider only the existentiality of the momentary situation. Thus the expedient becomes the norm of good or evil. The denial of a standard of conduct is claimed under the assertion that one really cannot know which is the true one.

Relativism also extends to the nature and worth of knowledge. Thus for the relativist one cannot penetrate beyond the appearance of a thing or beyond what is a sense impression of reality. It therefore denies the mind of the human person, claiming that all is relative to what a thing is or why a thing exists. (See Ethics, Situation.)

## Relaxati

Literally, the "lax." (See Franciscan Controversy.)

## Relics, Sacred

Any part of the bodily remains of a saint is designated a sacred relic. Such relics if they are notable in size should not be kept in private homes without the bishop's permission. The relics of saints (martyrs generally) are enclosed in the sepulcher of an altar or altar stone (portable altar) (cf. Altar). It is forbidden to sell sacred relics. Sacred relics are to be authenticated, that is, declared by sworn statement to be genuine.

It is the common practice to classify lesser relics such as those items that have been intimately connected with the life of a saint, for example, pieces of clothing, as second class, and those objects that have been touched to the body of a saint, as third class. However, these are the distinctions borrowed from the practice rather than the recognition of the Church.

The cult of sacred relics (that is, the honor given to the remains of a saint or any part) is lawful, but these relics may not be exposed for public veneration without the approval of the ordinary. Relics that are considered sacred but are not portions of a saint's body are such objects as relics of the true cross. These must also be authenticated and are subject to the above rules. Other relics, not authenticated, but honored for ages may be retained, but the Church does not vouch for their genuineness.

## Relief Services, Catholic

The united agencies of Catholic overseas aid are incorporated separately in the overall organization of the United States Catholic Conference. Catholic Relief Services were founded in 1943 to bring aid to the civilian populace of European and North African nations where life was disrupted because of war and destruction. In the succeeding years they were expanded to include other nations of Asia, Africa, and Latin America. The range of these services is extensive, covering health, food, clothing, road building, homes, institutions, the establishing of small industries, and the encouragement of enterprise and agricultural pursuits. They are funded primarily through two annual collections from the people of parishes throughout the country. (See Campaign for Human Development.)

Vatican II declares: "Agencies of the international community should do their part to provide for the various necessities of men. In the field of social life this means food, health, education, and employment. In certain situations which can happen anywhere, it means the general need to promote the growth of developing nations, to attend to the hardships of refugees scattered throughout the world, or to assist migrants and their families" (GS 84).

## Religion

St. Thomas defines this as "a virtue by which men give due worship and reverence to God."

Although religion has various definitions, including the relationship between God and man without revelation, religion is, in the ultimate sense, the recognition by an intelligent creature of his origin and his ordered progress in coming to God. (Cf. Liturgy.)

Vatican II states: "Of its very nature, the exercise of religion consists before all else in those internal, voluntary, and free acts whereby man sets the course of his life directly toward God. No merely human power can either command or prohibit acts of this kind . . .

"Injury is done to the human person and to the very order established by God for human life, if the free exercise of religion is denied in society when the just requirements of public order do not so require" (DH 3).

Concerning non-Christian religions, Vatican II declares: "The Catholic Church rejects nothing which is true and holy in these religions. She looks with sincere respect upon those ways of conduct and of life, those rules and teachings which, though differing in many particulars from what she holds and sets forth, nevertheless often reflect a ray of that Truth which enlightens all men" (NA 2).

## Religious Freedom

The right of the human person to accept or reject or freely express himself on matters of religion is considered an inherent freedom. Thus religious freedom is a right for both the individual and for religious groups. As a fundamental right, prior to the positive law of the state or government, it follows from the nature of man as a free and rational being that he must have the freedom of religion.

As a right of man, it must be guaranteed by the State, and it is therefore looked upon as a governmental or constitutional right. But it has also been considered from the earliest days of the Church as a theological matter, involving the "liberty of mission" of the Church. However, the Church has been in conflict with many and has seemed to condemn religious freedom because it did not understand how this was to be reasonably obtained or guaranteed in the face of monarchial systems, and especially since theologians saw this as the foster father of indifferentism in religious matters. It was through the rational laws of nations then that the concept and clarification of religious freedom came about.

In the Church there was the theological recognition that the Church is the spiritual authority established by God, commissioned to preach the gospel to all mankind. Hence the Church claims two kinds of freedom: one personal, whereby humans can live in society and do so in accord with the tenets of their faith; the other social where the Church claims the right to freedom in every kind of organized power. In his encyclical on Human Liberty *(Libertas Humana)* Pope Leo XIII stated: "Of the various forms of government, the Church does not reject any that are fitted to procure the welfare of the subject; she wishes only—and this nature itself requires—that they should be constituted without involving wrong to any one, and especially without violating the rights of the Church" (n. 32).

One must, however, extend the freedom to others since it is an inherent right. To ensure the freedom of one Christian body at the expense of another by coercive actions against the other religion is to violate the concept of religious freedom (cf. 2 Cor. 11:26).

### Religious Life

Religious life is that life under a fixed mode with simple or solemn vows in which the ones who have chosen it keep the common precepts of Christian conduct and bind themselves to observance of the three public vows of poverty, chastity, and obedience. It is a life conducive to attaining a higher degree of perfection through the living of the counsels.

There are several distinctions that arise from the type of vow or condition under which the members live: (1) an *order* is a religious community wherein solemn vows are taken; (2) a *congregation* is one with simple vows, temporary or perpetual; (3) a *monastic congregation* is a union of independent monasteries under the same superior; (4) an *exempt religious institute* is one withdrawn from the jurisdiction of the ordinary; (5) a *clerical community* is one wherein most of the members are preists; (6) a *lay institute* is one whose members are not priests (cf. Nun; Sisters). The term *religious* is applied to

members of a religious institute, who are also called *regulars.*

In the mind of the Church the only concern for all members is sanctification through their lives. In regard to those in religious life, Vatican II states: "By their state in life, religious give splendid and striking testimony that the world cannot be transfigured and offered to God without the spirit of the beatitudes" (LG 31).

And: "Religious should carefully consider that through them, to believers and nonbelievers alike, the Church truly wishes to give an increasingly clearer revelation of Christ. Through them Christ should be shown contemplating on the mountain, announcing God's kingdom to the multitude, healing the sick and the maimed, turning sinners to wholesome fruit, blessing children, doing good to all, and always obeying the will of the Father who sent Him" (LG 46).

And: "The entire religious life of the members of communities should be penetrated by an apostolic spirit, as their entire apostolic activity should be animated by a religious spirit" (PC 8).

### Reliquary

A reliquary is a container in which a relic or relics are kept. In former times, the Latin term *theca* (plural, *thecae*) was sometimes used for reliquary.

In older times these receptacles were in many shapes and often richly ornamented, such as capsules, crosses, caskets, and rings. Among the most famous are the silver shrine of the Three Kings at Cologne, Germany, fashioned in the early thirteenth century, and H. Memling's reliquary of St. Ursula at Bruges, Belgium.

### Remnant

In scriptural studies the remnant is both a real and a symbolical expression of the mind of God. To Abraham God had promised uncounted descendants. When man set himself against the realization of this design of God, the remnant became the residue of a promise withdrawn and the "seed" of the new covenant. This seed of course is Christ, who brought about the fulfilling of God's design and was the Seed of the new people who are the Church that Christ instituted. Likewise, the Church will be the remnant till the end of time when she brings all together in Christ through whom they were saved.

As Isaiah prophesied: "On that day the remnant of Israel, the survivors of the house of Jacob, will no more lean upon him who struck them; but they will lean upon the Lord, the Holy One of Israel, in truth a remnant will return, the remnant of Jacob, to the mighty God. For though your people, O Israel, were like sand of the sea, only a remnant of them will return; their destruction is decreed as overwhelming justice demands" (Is. 10:20–22).

It was Christ who died alone (cf. Jn. 6:66; Mt. 26:56). When He alone was the last of the remnant, He prepared the People of God who were to constitute His Church (Mt. 26:28; Acts 2:41–47; 5:14), the adopted heirs of God through Christ (Heb. 1:1–4; Rom. 8:14–17; Gal. 4:1–11).

The remnant is symbolized by Elijah (1 Kgs. 19:10–18; Rom. 11:3–4). He was Christ's forerunner even as his mantle was to be that of John the Baptist (Mt. 3:4; Lk. 7:25–27). But Christ was the new Elijah, who came to establish a new reign of goodness through His suffering and death (Lk. 9:44–45; cf. also Jn. 1:21–25).

## Renaissance

Beginning in the fourteenth century in Italy and continuing at its height through the fifteenth and sixteenth centuries, the Renaissance was a period of radical changes in the intellectual, artistic, political, social, and even geographical structure of Christian civilization. It had its origin in a realization of the Greek culture and Greek scholarship, which succeeded the fall of Constantinople, and was centered on interest in classical culture. The Renaissance was augmented by the introduction and widespread use of the printing press. It marked the trend toward humanism and laid the groundwork for the Reformation.

## Renewal, Charismatic

During the twentieth century the Church has expressed an intent for renewal in general, especially through the teachings of Vatican II and later pronouncements of Pope Paul VI; however, a renewal has arisen, which does not have a structured means of gaining a true religious end. The purpose of renewal is unity, but this current form, sometimes referred to as Pentecostal, "renewal in the Spirit," charismatic, or "liturgy of the Holy Spirit" (cf. Acts 4:24–31; 1 Cor. 14) which has a prayer-meeting format, is an independent and sometimes divisive action in many instances. The charismatic renewal is not of itself divisive—only in its abuses and antiauthoritarian actions.

In all fairness we must point out many of the inherent problems that have come about through organized approaches or independent actions. These problems are: (1) The Christian should look upon charisms (gifts) as bringing about an upbuilding of the Church through love. This cannot be effective unless there is an increase of grace—and this means the recipient or participant should have or be in the state of sanctifying grace. Renewal for the individual, with the possible exception of penitential acts, cannot be accomplished by simply declaring or opting for the Holy Spirit apart from the sacramental channels of clear truth and knowledge afforded by the Church. (2) The renewal that many seek to express cannot be attained from a form of rebellion or disdain for competent ecclesial authority. (3) The Holy Spirit, through the communities of Christians, works only toward "the bond of unity in peace" which is the law of the Spirit (cf. 1 Cor. 3:16; 6:9–20: 15:28; Rom. 5:5; 8:26–27; 2 Thes. 2:13–14). (4) Those who participate or seek to have others participate in such a renewal should not be exclusive, saying they have the "light" and not all can share in this action of the Holy Spirit. (5) The practitioners of such renewal must be aware that they may experience interior joy, but they cannot expect or presume that this will free them from the opposite condition, the participation in the sufferings of Christ on the cross. (6) Participants should not look for "miracles" in the midst of noisy, sensible, external manifestations that place *feelings* above *spiritual* or interior benefits. (7) There should never be an approach to the sacred scriptures in a too literal, simplistic, or fundamental manner, for witness is given within the context of the Church's actions as guardian of the word of God. (8) Occurrences such as speaking in tongues or healing should not becloud one's approach to the Holy Spirit to the extent that such happenings become the whole of Christian life and holiness. (9) When one participates in a renewal, it should cause a change in grace, but essentially it should bring about the virtue of perseverance. (10) The terminology used by charismatics in seeking renewal should be precise and intend only what the Church teaches and not depart from scriptural exactitude. (See Semantics of Religion.) (11) The supplemental act of "laying on of hands" should never be considered a "sacramental" gesture, nor should "faith" healing be considered as an actual fact without evidence, especially in this day of psychosomatic medicine and illnesses that have a variety of sources and forms. (12) The renewal movement should never assume the role of teacher, introducing new doctrines or giving private witness. (Cf. Church.) (13) Charismatics must be aware, through study and teaching, that grace as a gift of God works through natural or secondary causes and not by direct action, for such would be a denial of cooperative grace. (14) The renewal movement should not assume or presume that it can make new interpretations of scripture and apply them in a limited or reserved manner, for the Word of God is universal and not the specialty of the few.

The ongoing investigation of renewal through the charismatic movement must be centered, not on exclusivism, nor on a multiplicity of scriptural interpretations, but on the fullness of the revelation of Christ, which is made through His Church. It should ever be predominant that the love of God and neighbor makes for charity through which the Holy Spirit works. The joy of renewal is only possible when it is present in the suffering endured for the salvation of all (Col. 1:24; 2:1; 2 Cor. 13:9; Jas. 1:2; Acts 5:41). (See Charismatic Renewal, Catholic.)

### Renunciation

1. The sacramental meaning of renunciation is found in the administration of the Sacrament of Baptism. Here the recipient (or godparent acting in the person's place) is asked to renounce the devil and his works. Thus to become a Christian, one is expected to forego all that is not in accord with the teachings and life of Christ. Embodiment with Christ means renouncing what is not of Christ.

2. In the spiritual sense renunciation is the sacrificing of something so that the human person may advance spiritually. It is through the exercise of free will that the person may relinquish rights to legitimate pleasures or to some other person or object that is valued. Also renunciation is the foregoing of those things that would distract one from God or make one less pleasing to God if not renounced (Mk. 8:30–34).

### Reparation

In the religious sense this is the repair of some spiritual damage done against a person. Thus in striving for forgiveness of past sins reparation is one of the four conditions of penance. Christ thus made reparation for the sins of mankind. One may pray as an act of reparation for past sins even

though these have been forgiven in the Sacrament of Penance. (See Restitution.)

### Repentance

Simply, the sorrow for sin is called repentance. However, in the dialectic of revelation this continues to be one of the themes of God's dealing with the Israelites and with all men: punishment, penitence, and forgiveness are for all men and all times. But in the OT and the NT repentance means a "conversion," a "change of heart," a "turning to God" or a "returning to Him" (Is. 31:6; Hos. 6:1–4; Jl. 2:12–17).

True repentance is the work of God's mercy (cf. Lk. 24:47; Jn. 20:21–23; see also Jas. 5:16–20). It is interior (Is 58:5–7; Rom. 2:29; Gal. 5:6, Col. 2:11), but it is also manifested by men through their acts of repentance that come with the granting of grace by God (Acts 3:19; Eph. 4:20–24; 1 Jn. 1:8–10). It is also because of man's response to the grace of God that there is joy in heaven, and if in heaven assuredly on earth (Lk. 15:1–10; Lv. 23:39–43).

### Requiem

A requiem was formerly a Mass for the dead. Now the Mass may be called Funeral Mass, Mass for the Dead, or Mass of Christian Burial. It is offered on All Souls' Day, on the day of death, on the day of burial, on the third, seventh, or thirtieth day after death, or on any day when the rubrics permit and the intention to pray for the dead is had by the celebrant. The Roman Missal or Sacramentary lists two Funeral Masses for outside of the Easter Season, one for during the Easter Season, and alternate prayers. It also lists anniversary Masses and alternate prayers for both outside the Easter Season and during the Easter Season, and various commemorations—for one or more deceased persons or for all the dead, together with various persons who have died. There is also included a Funeral Mass for a baptized child and a Mass for a child who died before baptism.

### Reredos

A reredos is a carved, decorated screen at the back of the altar and rising above it. It is sometimes built against the altar but should be entirely separate. Rules demand that it not interfere with the ciborium above the altar. It is any decorative panel above and behind the altar. In modern Churches this architectural detail is more usually omitted. It may be replaced by a hanging, stained glass, or a framed detail.

### Rerum Novarum

This is the Latin title of the encyclical "On the

Condition of Labor" by Pope Leo XIII, published May 15, 1891. It presents the Church's position on social morality and the principles of justice and charity that should regulate the relationship of capital and labor. On the fortieth anniversary of its publication, Pope Pius XI published the encyclical entitled *Quadragesimo Anno* (May 15, 1931), which treated of the same subject.

The Encyclical states: "First of all religion, whereof the Church is the interpreter and guardian, is exceedingly powerful in drawing rich and poor together, by reminding each class of its duties to the other, and especially of the duties of justice. Thus religion teaches the laboring man and the workman to carry out honestly and well all equitable agreements freely made, never to injure capital, nor to outrage the person of an employer; never to employ violence in representing his own cause, nor to engage in riot and disorder; and to have nothing to do with men of evil principles, who work upon the people with artful promises, and raise foolish hopes which usually end in disaster and in repentance when too late" (n. 16).

And: "The first duty, therefore, of the rulers of the State should be to make sure that the laws and institutions, the general character and administration of the commonwealth, shall be such as to produce of themselves public well-being and private prosperity" (n. 26).

## Rescript

The written reply of a religious superior to a request, report or question (c. 36-62) is called a rescript. In make-up, it repeats the request and its facts together with the reasons, and then offers the answer with the conditions. It is the usual form through which dispensations are granted or denied.

## Reservation of the Blessed Sacrament

This is the retaining of a consecrated host or hosts in the tabernacle, and also the removal of the Blessed Sacrament, reserved in the ciborium, from the main tabernacle on Holy Thursday to a place of proper reverence. This place may be an adjoining altar, called the "Repository Altar." This is the reservation of the Real Presence of Christ in the Eucharist, which in the past has given rise to paraliturgical devotions of great benefit for the individual's sanctification. (See Exposition of the Blessed Sacrament.)

Pope Pius XII brought the importance of this practice to the attention of all in his encyclical *Mediator Dei* ("Mediator of God"), which was issued in 1947: "The reservation of the Sacred Species for the sick and for all those who might come into danger of death, introduced the laudable custom of adoring this Heavenly Food as it was reserved in the churches. This cult of adoration indeed rests upon a valid and solid motive. For the Eucharist is both a Sacrifice and a Sacrament; and it differs from the other Sacraments because it not only produces grace, but it contains in a permanent way the very author of grace. When, therefore, the Church commands that we adore Christ hidden under the Eucharistic veils, and that we ask of Him the supernatural and earthly gifts of which we always have need, she manifests the living faith by which she believes her divine Spouse to be present under these veils, and she shows Him her gratitude and enjoys His familiar intimacy."

## Reserved Censure

See Censure.

## Residence

In canon law, this term applies to the rule that a parish priest may not be absent from his place of assignment for an extended time without permission of his ordinary (c. 143). (Cf. Domicile.)

## Responsorial Psalms

See Psalmody.

## Responsory

The responsory is a series of versicles and responses, sung or recited together with the *Glory be to the Father* after each lesson of the Divine Office. (See Liturgy of the Hours.)

## Restitution

1. The act of returning or replacing the goods that a person has found or stolen because of a violation of commutative justice. The obligation is grave in degree with the real or supposed value of the goods, and the obligation can arise out of wrongful possession or unjust damage, as to one's reputation.

2. The duty to compensate a person for his labor.

If one cooperates in doing damage to another person, he or she is also obliged to make restitution according to the extent of responsibility. Thus, gang vandalism is the sin not only of the instigator or leader but of everyone who takes part in the destruction. Likewise, in a negative manner, one incurs responsibility when he permits damage to be done which could be avoided, even though he does not take an active part in the action. The same principle is in force in divine law and positive law when the damage is to another's reputation, health, life, or chastity.

### Resurrection of the Body

That the body will be reanimated is a doctrine of revealed truth and an article of the Catholic faith. St. Paul, in speaking of the resurrection of the body (1 Cor. 15:1–58), bases his statement on (1) the Resurrection of Christ as the verification of the atoning power of Christ's Passion (1 Cor. 15:14); (2) the hope of Christians (1 Cor. 15:30); (3) the fact that it is not contrary to reason; (4) the parallels formed in nature (15:35–41). He concludes with a description of the excellence of the risen body (15:44–49). (Cf. Judgment, General.)

This idea of man's victory over death is biblical; the prophets of the OT spoke of it (Is. 26:19; Ez. 37), and the Chosen People foresaw the resurrection of the body (2 Mc. 7:9–26; 12:41–46; Dn. 12:2–3). It was associated with the resurrection of Christ (Jn. 11:1–44; Mt. 27:52–54; cf. also Rom. 6:1–11; 1 Thes. 4:13–17; Mk. 5:22–43). Through the resurrection of the body the life of the human person takes on a new mode of life (Mt. 22:27–33). It is an act of divine power (1 Cor. 6:14; 2 Cor. 13:4; Rom. 4:25; cf. also Acts 3:15; 4:10; 5:30). The soul and the physical body will reign "with Christ" (cf. Rv. 20:4), and this will be the fulfillment of the work of the Son of God, when God will be "all in all" (1 Cor. 15:28) (See Heaven.).

Vatican II declares: "When Christ shall appear and the glorious resurrection of the dead takes place, the splendor of God will brighten the heavenly city and the Lamb will be the lamp thereof (cf. Rv. 21:24) (LG 51).

### Resurrection of Christ

The physical rising from death by Christ on Easter as recorded in the Gospels (Mt. 28:1–20; Lk. 24:1–9; Jn. 20:1–18) was accomplished through the power that was His as the Son of God as He promised (Mt. 17:22–23). And through the subsequent coming of the Holy Spirit the certitude of

the Resurrection is brought home to the disciples (Jn. 16:13–16).

The recording of the Resurrection shows that it took place early in the morning and so was like the "awakening" of all mankind (2 Kgs. 4:31–37; Is. 26:19; Ps. 16:10; Jn. 20:1). In the Resurrection the fullness of God's salvific will was shown (Rom. 1:4; 1 Cor. 6:14; Eph. 1:19–20; Phil. 3:10; 2 Cor. 13:4).

Humans enjoy two forms of resurrection because of Christ: (1) the resurrection from sin through baptism (Rom. 6:1–11), (2) the resurrection from death gained and assured through Christ (Jn. 7:37–39; 10:14–17; 12:20–24). Thus the Resurrection of Christ is the center, the very heart of the fact, of the history of salvation. Knowledge of this event, historically, by teaching and from scriptures is both the object of faith itself and the divine self-communication that gives light and dynamism to that faith (cf. 1 Cor. 15:3–19; Gal. 2:1–10). Considered soteriologically, the Resurrection of Christ is the "exemplary cause" of the resurrection of every human person. (See Salvation History.)

### Retable

A retable is a modified reredos (q.v.). It is a low panel erected behind an altar, chiefly for decoration, but it may have a practical purpose, for example, to support lights.

### Retreat

1. Name of a period of time varying in length from several days to a month during which the faithful, cleric and lay, may undertake prayer, meditation, devotions, and spiritual exercises for the purpose of advancing in spiritual living or amendment of life.

2. Retreat is the name for the place, frequently called a "retreat house," which may be any suitable place of quiet, sometimes called a "poustinia."

There are several systems or set procedures for retreats, for example, the Spiritual Exercises of St. Ignatius. However, the basic requirements are solitude with the keeping of silence, a schedule of prayer, and a series of spiritual conferences or talks given by a priest-director who is usually titled "the retreat master."

In the modern interpretation several innovations have been added to the manner of procedure for a retreat; these of themselves do not change the concept of a retreat or its basic purpose, although they may arrive at a change of attitude in keeping with their intent. One of these is called an "encounter" where husbands and wives may make a retreat together for the purpose of better understanding their roles as parents. Another name "Search" is youth-oriented and seeks through dialogue and counselling to better understand prayer and the identity and dignity of the individual. The chief contribution of these innovations to the retreat concept has been the introduction of dialogue and the catechesis of the sacraments. (Cf. Cursillo.)

## Retribution

The reward of virtue and the punishment of sin are both included in the theological understanding of retribution. This is then the reward promised by God (Dt. 28:9–10), and the suffering that each endures, not as the punishment for sins committed as in penance, but for the love of God or that one may attain salvation (Jn. 16:21–22).

## Revelation

Revelation is the means by which man knows divine truths, the written font of truth such as the Scriptures and unwritten tradition, which have come down to us from practices and attendant arguments of history. In the Church which is, through Christ, the living teaching authority, there is a twofold revelation. As defined by the Council of Trent, this revelation is "contained in written books and in traditions without writing—traditions which were received from the mouth of Christ Himself and from the apostles under dictation of the Holy Spirit and have come down to us, delivered, as it were, from hand to hand" (Sess. IV, EB 46). Revelation as the Church possesses and exercises it is by the Holy Spirit, inspiring the Scripture and aiding the Church (1 Cor. 2:7–8). (Cf. Inspiration of Scripture.)

Vatican II devotes an entire Dogmatic Constitution to the subject of revelation (Dei Verbum) in which it essentially teaches: "In His goodness and wisdom, God chose to reveal Himself and to make known to us the hidden purpose of His will (cf. Eph. 1:9) by which through Christ, the word made flesh, man has access to the Father in the Holy Spirit and comes to share in the divine nature (cf. Eph. 2:18; 2 Pt. 1:4). Through this revelation, therefore, the invisible God (cf. Col. 1:15; 1 Tm. 1:17) out of the abundance of His love speaks to men as friends (cf. Ex. 33:11; Jn. 15:14–15) and lives among them (cf. Bar. 3:38), so that He may invite and take them into fellowship with Himself. This plan of revelation is realized by deeds and words having an inner unity: the deeds wrought by God in the history of salvation manifest and confirm the teaching and realities signified by the words, while the words proclaim the deeds and clarify the mystery contained in them. By this revelation then, the deepest truth about God and the salvation of man is made clear to us in Christ, who is the Mediator and at the same time the fullness of all revelation" (DV 2).

And: "To see Jesus is to see His Father (Jn. 14:9). For this reason Jesus perfected revelation by fulfilling it through His work of making Himself present and manifesting Himself: through His words and deeds, His signs and wonders, but especially through His death and glorious resurrection from the dead and final sending of the Spirit of truth. Moreover, He confirmed with divine testimony what revelation proclaimed: that God is with us to free us from the darkness of sin and death, and to raise us up to life eternal.

"The Christian dispensation, therefore, as the new and definitive covenant, will never pass away, and we now await no further new public revelation before the glorious manifestation of our Lord Jesus Christ (cf. 1 Tm. 6:14; Ti. 2:13)" (DV 4).

And: "In His gracious goodness, God has seen to it that what He had revealed for the salvation of all nations would abide perpetually in its full integrity and be handed on to all generations. Therefore Christ the Lord, in whom the full revelation of the supreme God is brought to completion (cf. 2 Cor. 1:20; 3:16; 4:6), commissioned the apostles to preach to all men that gospel which is the source of all saving truth and moral teaching, and thus to impart to them divine gifts. This gospel had been promised in former times through the prophets, and Christ Himself fulfilled it and promulgated it with His own lips. This commission was faithfully fulfilled by the apostles who, by their oral preaching, by example, and by ordinances, handed on what they had received from the lips of Christ, from living with Him, and from what He did, or what they had learned through the prompting of the Holy Spirit. The commission was fulfilled, too, by those apostles and apostolic men who under the inspiration of the same Holy Spirit committed the message of salvation to writing" (DV 7). (See Tradition.)

### Revelation, Book of

The Book of Revelation is the only prophetic book in the NT. Its name is derived from the Greek and means the "unveiling" of hidden things. The book was probably written during the reign of the Roman Emperor Domitian, or in about the year A.D. 95. Its authorship has been traditionally ascribed to St. John the Evangelist, the author of the Apostle John's Gospel. However, there is a difference in the writing styles of the two books, and this has led to a conjecture that the book was written by one or more of the disciples of St. John.

In its totality the Book of Revelation is a "rounding-out" of the development of the great, final eschatological events of the history of mankind. It tells of both the fulfillment of the promise given by Christ (cf. Jn. 16:13–33) and of the rightness of the Christian life in the outcome of the redemptive act of Christ. It affirms that Christ by his death, resurrection, and ascension has become the eschatological judge, for he is already standing at the door, prepared to fulfill his promise (Rv. 3:20–21).

The content of the book is difficult to understand because of its symbolism and oblique references. But in reality the book divides into a plan. Besides the prologue and epilogue, it has seven major sections, the first five containing seven items each and the next two giving an introduction to another series of seven. After the prologue (1:1–8) there follow seven letters to the seven churches of Asia: Ephesus, Smyrna, Pergamum, Thyatira, Sardis, Philadelphia, and Laodicea. Some are praised and others censured.

Thereafter it speaks of seven seals (5:1–14) that the Lamb alone has the right to open. The first six seals of the mysterious scroll signify war, strife, famine, persecution, and disturbances in the stars of the heavens, while the seventh seal introduces the vision of the just who are marked for blessedness and serves as an introduction to the next series of seven (8:1), the trumpets.

These are blown by seven angels; the first four cause cosmic disturbances on land, the oceans, rivers, and among the heavenly bodies (8:7–12); the last three trumpets sound the woes to come: the plague of demonical locusts (9:1–12), the invasion of diabolical horsemen (9:13–21), and the celestial worship (11:15–19); these trumpets also introduce the next series of seven, the Seven Signs.

These Signs are: the Woman (interpreted as the Church); the Beast of the Sea (interpreted as imperial power), which persecutes the just; the Beast of the Land (interpreted as the false prophet) who serves the other Beast (13:11–18); the Virgins (interpreted as the elect) who are companions of the Lamb (14:1–5); the three Angelic Heralds; the two Angelic Harvesters; and the Seven Angels who bear the last seven plagues (15:2–4) and the Seven Bowls from which the wrath of God is to be poured out.

These are all followed by the fall of Babylon, the consummation when Christ comes as the Divine Warrior (19:11–16); the triumph over Satan; the final Judgment; and the opening of the Heavenly Jerusalem (21:1–25). Then all is written of as confirmed truth of the eschatological events.

Much has been written of this book, borrowing erroneously from mythology and astrology. But the interpretation must be made in the light of Christian faith, for it emphasizes the place of Christ in the unfolding of history over which He rules in providence and loving protection of the Church he founded.

### Rheims-Douay Version

See Bible.

### Riddel

This is the medieval English term for curtains that were hung at either side of an altar.

### Rights of the Human Person

These rights are understood and recognized as the universal, inviolable, and inalienable rights possessed because the human person is a rational being endowed with free will. The human person possesses these by his nature as a person. They are safeguards of the dignity of the human person in a society which is often inimical (cf. Acts 4:19).

These rights were expressly set forth in the

Encyclical of Pope John XXIII *Pacem in Terris* ("Peace on Earth") as: (1) the right to life and a worthy standard of living, (2) rights pertaining to moral and cultural values, (3) the right to worship God according to one's conscience, (4) the right to choose freely one's state in life, (5) economic rights, (6) the right of meeting and association, (7) the right to emigrate and immigrate, and (8) political rights.

Vatican II states: "Human institutions, both private and public, must labor to minister to the dignity and purpose of man. At the same time let them put up a stubborn fight against any kind of slavery, whether social or political, and safeguard the basic rights of man under every political system" (GS 29).

And: "Theories which obstruct the necessary reforms in the name of a false liberty must be branded erroneous. The same is true of those theories which subordinate the basic rights of individual persons and groups to the collective organization of production" (GS 65).

## Rigorism

Rigorism is a condemned moral system. It declares that the law must be followed unless the contrary opinion is certain, which binds one at all times. (Cf. Probabilism.)

## Ring

A ring is a circular band of precious metal, sometimes bearing a precious gem. Rings used in the Church are: (1) the wedding ring; it is blessed at the marriage ceremony and worn on the fourth finger of the left hand as a sign of fidelity; (2) the pontifical ring of bishops, abbots, and prothonotaries; (3) the plain gold ring presented to nuns and sisters at their profession in religion to remind them of their espousal to Christ. Rules concerning the wearing of rings by clerics have been relaxed, but with the exception of married permanent deacons, the adornment of rings is looked upon as a "sign of commitment."

## Ring of the Fisherman

See Fisherman, Ring of the

## Rite

1. The collection or system of language, forms, ceremonies, and prayers, together with the accompanying rules, vestments, and other objects or implements, used in carrying out the public worship, the administration of sacraments and church functions of a church or group of churches. There are nine such rites in the Catholic Church: the Latin or Roman, Byzantine, Armenian, Chaldean, Coptic, Ethiopian, Malabar, Maronite, and Syrian. In this sense the word rite is often considered synonymous with "liturgy" (cf. Liturgy).

2. A single religious function with its prescribed form, such as the rite of baptism.

3. A group of ceremonies, forms and prayers that are joined in solemnity of an occasion or an event, for example, the rite of consecration and the rite of Holy Thursday.

4. A variation of ceremony permitted by Church law in which a particular group, because of custom, performs functions in accord with a special rule or ritual, for example, the Dominican rite, as a slight variant of the Roman.

Rites are historically local in origin. In ancient times they arose in a particular place, for example, Antioch, and slowly spread to other areas of adoption. They are likewise developments, with additions and changes being introduced. At the present time the rite is governed by law, with prescribed rules of execution carried out to the last detail. Also a member of a Church group becomes identified with the rite of that group, and under canon law it is forbidden for one belonging to the Roman rite to pass over to an Eastern rite, or vice versa, or to make a change back to the original rite, without permission of the Holy See (c. 98). Membership in a rite comes at birth, that is, children belong to the rite of the father; or membership can be by conversion into a particular rite. (See Eastern Churches; Order of the Mass, New.)

## Rites, Sacred Congregation of

The Sacred Congregation of Rites is now called the Sacred Congregation for Divine Worship. In the administrative bodies of the Holy See, this is the unit that regulates and controls liturgical worship, the veneration of relics, and the beatification and canonization of saints. It was not set up as an organized unit until 1588 when Pope Sixtus V consolidated previous recommendations and established the congregation. Today, according to canon 253, this congregaton has jurisdiction of rites and ceremonies of the Latin Church, that is, all rites recognized in the West. It also governs the ceremonies of the celebration of Mass, the administration of the sacraments, and other aspects of divine worship. (See Congregation.)

## Ritual

This liturgical book, the *Rituale Romanum,* contains the instructions, prayers, and ceremonies to be used in the administration of the sacraments, blessings, and devotions. An official, authorized publication of the Ritual is brought out from time to time with any changes authorized by the Holy See (cf. Liturgical Books). It is the official source of rubrics. There may be portions of this published for convenience, for example, that for music, Psalms and lessons of Holy Week, called the *Officium Majoris Hebdomadae.* (See Order of the Mass, New.)

## Robber Synod
See Ephesus, Robber Synod of.

## Rochet
The rochet is a shorter adaptation of the alb with tight-fitting sleeves. Worn by the pope, cardinals, bishops, abbots, prelates, and canons, the rochet is adorned with lace on the cuffs and lower edge, the length of the lace depending upon the dignity of the wearer.

## Rogation Days
The Monday, Tuesday, and Wednesday before the feast of Ascension are called Rogation Days and also the Lesser Litanies. They are marked by a procession to ask God's mercy and blessing upon mankind and His work. The Litany of the Saints is chanted during the procession. This is the Christian substitute for the ancient Roman feast called *robigalia,* which was marked by a procession on April 25 to obtain a good harvest. In the calendar reform that followed Vatican II (1969), the observance of rogation days is decided by the various national conferences of bishops.

## Rogito
The official documents, notarial attestations, reports, and other declarations that testify to the burial of a pope are called the Rogito.

## Roman Catholic
The designation of one as belonging to the Roman rite merely makes a distinction according to the rite followed. The name of the Church founded by Christ and of its members is Catholic. The term Roman Catholic has come to be the accepted designation of the one true Church and is recognized officially for legal documents and other purposes (cf. Catholic; Marks of the Church).

## Roman Catholic Church
See Church.

## Roman College
Usually, this name is applied to the Gregorian University in Rome. It may, however, be used as a collective title of all the schools and seminaries of Rome and the Vatican, thus of the College of Propaganda, Urban College, Gregorian University, the Angelicum, and the numerous national colleges.

## Roman Congregations
See Congregation.

## Roman Missal
See Sacramentary.

## Roman Rite
Also called Latin rite, this is the most widely used rite of the Catholic Church. It is the manner of celebrating Mass, administering the sacraments, and performing ecclesiastical functions as done in the diocese of Rome and governed by the Roman Ritual (cf. Rite).

## Romans, Epistle to the
This writing of St. Paul was probably done in the year A.D. 58 and sent from Corinth. It serves two purposes: it introduces Paul, a citizen of the Roman Empire, to the Christians in the city of Rome, Italy, and it gives assurances to the gentiles who were converts.

The content of the book is structured on a distinct plan of logic in theme. It begins with the usual greeting and then states its central theme of justification through faith in the first four chapters. In chapters five through eleven it then presents the assertion and certainty of salvation and the divine life that is for all. There is an exhortatory portion (12:1–15) and a conclusion.

It presents some unusual considerations, for example, the doxology wherein Paul bows before the mystery and wisdom of God (11:33–36), and the stress on the need of one to be humble in encountering the harmony in the exercise of spiritual charism (12:3–8) and the mutual love that must prevail among both the strong and weak People of God (12:9–21; 14:1–15). There is also the warning given (16:17–20), which may be addressed to any community of Christians of any time.

## Rome
The capital city of today's Italy, the seat of the government, and principal city of the ancient Roman Empire, was inhabited as early as the eighth century B.C. After having spent some time in Jerusalem and Antioch, St. Peter journeyed to Rome in A.D. 42 and established the Church, making numerous converts and enduring the

first-century persecutions. It is within the city of Rome, called the city of seven hills, that the entire area of Vatican State proper now is confined. By treaty with the Italian government certain other properties apart from the Vatican State are considered as territorial parts of the state of Vatican City. Since the founding of the Church there by St. Peter, the city of Rome has been the center of Christendom. The city itself is the diocese of the pope as bishop of Rome.

### Rood-Screen

The rood-screen was a more or less open screen of wood or stone, which separated the sanctuary transept from the nave in churches of the Middle Ages. It was usually as high as the middle of the arch and was extremely ornamental. The name is derived from the large crucifix (called "rood" in old English) that surmounted the screen, often with the figures of St. John and the Blessed Mother on either side of it.

### Rosary

This is the name of both a devotion and the chain of beads used for counting the prayers. As a devotion, the Rosary arose in the fifteenth century and became very popular. It was begun by a Dominican preacher, Alan de Rupe (d. 1475) in northern France and Flanders. Belief that the devotion was revealed to St. Dominic was based chiefly on a report of a vision of de Rupe. The devotion is directed to the Blessed Mother and has been highly indulged by the Church. The Rosary has three parts. It consists of an initial prayer, the Apostles' Creed, followed by the Our Father and three Hail Marys and a Glory be to the Father, which are said beginning on the crucifix and continue on the pendant portion of the chain of beads. There follow fifteen decades or groups of ten beads separated by a single bead. Each decade consists of the recitation of the Our Father, ten Hail Marys, and concludes with one Glory be to the Father. The devotion is for private or public use. While saying the prayers of each decade, the person praying is to meditate on the mysteries of the Rosary, fifteen in all (cf. Mysteries of the Rosary).

The implement, or the popularly called "beads," may be a chain with pendant and all fifteen decades, sometimes called a "full" rosary, or it may be only a pendant with five decades of beads, this latter being the more familiar. Blessed and with the permitted indulgences attached, the rosary implement is a sacramental.

A feast honoring the Blessed Mother and commemorating the Rosary is celebrated on October 7. One of the many indulgences attached to the devotion is that the faithful who recite the Rosary together in a family group, besides the partial indulgence of 10 years, are granted a plenary indulgence twice a month, if they perform this recitation daily for a month, go to confession, receive Holy Communion, and visit some church or public oratory. (S.P.M. March 18, 1932 and July 26, 1946.)

### Rose, Golden

See Golden Rose.

### Rose Window

A circular, stained glass window, with tracery radiating from the center is known as a rose window. Such windows are used frequently in churches of Gothic architecture and may be placed at the ends of transepts or in the facade of the nave.

### Rosh Hashanah

From the Hebrew meaning "head of the year," this Jewish feast is celebrated in the beginning of the seventh month (Tishri) as the New Year's Day. This term is not biblical but refers instead to the Day of the Blowing of the Trumpet (the Shofar), or the Day of Memorial or Remembrance.

It is also considered the Day of Judgment *(Yom Hadin)* when the fate of every individual will be inscribed in the Book of Life. It also begins the Ten Days of Penitence, which is the most solemn of the periods in the Jewish Calendar. The culmination is reached on the feast of the Day of Atonement *(Yom Kippur)*, which is considered the most sacred day of the Jewish year, the Sabbath of Sabbaths.

## Rota, Sacred Roman

The Sacred Roman Rota is the most renowned tribunal of the Holy See. It was founded as a court early in the thirteenth century. At present, fourteen judges serve the court. All cases handled by the Rota are decided by a panel of three judges, called *turnus,* all of whom must sign the verdict. As a rule all pleading before the Rota is in writing. The Rota has care of marriage cases, matters of ecclesiastical law, and handles cases after they have been presented before the first court and a court of appeal. Cases are handled gratuitously or with a minimum payment of expenses. There are two classes of lawyers, all versed in canon law and usually in civil law: consistorial lawyers, who are entitled to plead causes of beatification and canonization in consistories; and Procurators of the Sacred Apostolic Palaces, whose office permits them to plead before the Rota although their title is largely honorary. (See Curia, Roman.)

## Rubrics

Rubrics is the term for the rules of ceremony and form that govern a liturgical function or rite. (See Order of the Mass, New.)

## Rule, Religious

Regulating the order of life, the discipline, practice, and observance as laid down in the constitution of a religious order or congregation, the rule is usually directed to the particular work for which the order or congregation was founded. Many such are derived from the early formulation of rules laid down by Sts. Basil, Augustine, Benedict, Francis, and Dominic. The rule binds each member under obedience.

## Rural Deans

See Dean.

## Russian Church

This is for the most part the Byzantine Rite Church, which is made up of Russian Orthodox Christians. Following the Council of Florence (1438 to 1445) there were few Catholics under Russian rule until the partitioning of Poland. From 1795 on there were two groups of Catholic Christians, converts from the Starovery (the so-called Old Believers) and the Catholic Byzantines of Russia. In 1919 some of the Orthodox in eastern Poland returned to unity with Rome. In the present time the Catholics are among the expatriate groups of Russians residing in Paris, Lyons, Brussels, Berlin, and elsewhere, and they have an appointed episcopal visitor who resides at Louvain. These are Catholic Orthodox Christians of the Byzantine Rite using the Slavonic language. (See Orthodox Church.)

## Ruth, Book of

This historical book of the OT was probably written by a contemporary of King David, although it is looked upon as a post-exilic short story. It narrates the history of the age of judges and the ancestry of David. In content, the writing is deeply religious, mirrors divine Providence, justifies a more open attitude toward non-Jews, and forecasts the calling of the Gentiles.

## Ruthenian Catholics

Inhabitants of southwest Russia, these Catholics of the Byzantine rite, are now completely under the U.S.S.R. The Ruthenians have two bishops in the United States. (Cf. Eastern Churches.)

# Sabaoth

Meaning, literally, "of hosts" or "of armies," this has been attached as a title of majesty to the name of God, signifying His command over all earthly and heavenly forces (1 Sm. 17:45).

The term has also been applied to the heavenly "army," meaning the angels (Ps. 103:21), but as generally used by the prophets of the OT the term had a greater significance, namely, the dominion of God over·all powers of heaven and earth.

# Sabbatarianism

The erroneous teaching concerning the observance of Sunday, the Christian Sabbath, as a day of restrictions and "blue-law" thinking is called sabbatarianism. This was found early among the Protestant reformers and became quite severe with the publication of the book *The True Doctrine of the Sabbath* in 1595 by the Puritan, Nicholas Bownde. To allay the controversy, King James I of England issued a countering book in 1618 called *The Book of Sports,* and Charles I, in 1633, reissued this book when opposition became more pronounced for a rigid observance of Sunday. There was only a relaxation of the teaching when Parliament passed the "Lord's Day Observance Act" in 1781. Today Sabbatarians are still represented by the Lord's Day Observance Society and several other lesser groups of the English-speaking world.

# Sabbath

This is the seventh day of the week in Jewish religious law. Under Christian tradition it has been supplanted by Sunday, the Lord's Day. In Latin, *sabbatum* is the name of Saturday in liturgical writings.

The OT clearly indicates that there should be a day of rest observed weekly (Ex. 23:12; 34:21), which was both a day of going to the sanctuary of the Lord and a day of rejoicing. It meant resting from labor (Ex. 16:30; 31:17) and especially before the exile it was a joyous occasion (Hos. 2:13; Is. 1:13).

In the NT Christ made exception of the Sabbath as then interpreted (Mt. 12:10–14; Lk. 13:10–17; Jn. 5:8–18), and established the day as one on which one could serve his fellowman (Mk. 2:23–28;

Lk. 13:15). It was St. Paul who probably made the Christian celebration a Sunday observance (1 Cor. 16:2; Acts 20:7).

# Sabellianism

Sabellianism is another name for the Monarchian heresy as propounded by Sabellius (circa 220).

# Sacramental

Any object or action which the Church places within the reach of a person and by which a person receives certain spiritual favors from God through his own action is so designated. Sacramentals differ vastly from sacraments since they produce effects through the Church's prayer to God, and only certain sacramentals require a particular disposition on the part of the person using it, for example, blessed ashes on Ash Wednesday. The Holy See alone can constitute new sacramentals and abolish, change, or interpret those already in use. Examples of sacramentals are: Holy water, the sign of the cross, vestments, candles, rosary, and blessings.

Vatican II teaches: "Holy Mother Church has, moreover, instituted sacramentals. These are sacred signs which bear a resemblance to the sacraments: they signify effects, particularly of a spiritual kind, which are obtained through the Church's intercession. By them men are disposed to receive the chief effect of the sacraments, and various occasions in life are rendered holy" (SC 60).

# Sacramentarians

In the early sixteenth century, under the leadership of Huldreich Zwingli (1484 to 1531), Johannes Oecolapadius (1482 to 1531), and Andreas Bodenstein (1480 to 1541), there arose a group of Protestant reformers who denied the Real Presence of Christ in the Holy Eucharist. This group came to be called Sacramentarians and were opposed to the Catholic doctrine. They were at variance with Martin Luther (1483 to 1546) who maintained a literal sense of the words of Christ (Mt. 26:26–28; Lk. 22:17–20) and held the doctrine of impanation or companation or that Christ is in and with the elements of bread and wine.

The Sacramentarians taught that Christ was not physically present in the Eucharist but was present only in a metaphorical sense. In the nineteen fifties and sixties a similar short-lived proposal was made, notably among some Dutch theologians, who sought to supplant the word transubstantiation with the term transignification, or that the presence of Christ was to be considered as a spiritual or symbolic presence. (See Transubstantiation.)

**Sacramentary**

The current name for the Roman Missal is *Sacramentary*. It is the approved, revised edition of the former Missal called for by Vatican II and published with the authority of Pope Paul VI. It has been translated by the International Commission on English in the Liturgy for all English-speaking countries and, with the approval of the Conferences of Bishops, is used in all churches of the Roman Rite since February, 1974. Translations into the vernacular of other languages have also been accomplished.

The Roman Missal was formerly in Latin and was revised fifty-seven times; in the liturgical revision put forward by Vatican II the Sacramentary becomes the official book for use by the celebrant of the Eucharist. It is an altar book and a *sign* for the People of God. There is a multi-volume hand missal now available, but for the general use of the people, missalettes may be supplied or subscribed to since hymns are an essential part of the liturgy. (See Leaflet Missal.)

In content the Sacramentary has the following: (1) the Decree of the Sacred Congregation for Divine Worship and the Apostolic Constitution of Pope Paul VI, both declaring the officiality of the publication; (2) forward and general instructions; (3) a directory of Masses with Children present; (4) the Apostolic Letter of Paul VI concerning the Church Calendar, followed by the norms for the liturgical year, the general Roman Calendar, the proper of the country where it is used, and a table of moveable feasts; (5) the Proper of the Seasons; (6) the Order of the Mass, including the Prefaces and Eucharistic Prayers; solemn blessings; prayer over the people; and the Order of Mass without a congregation; (7) the Proper of the Saints by months; (8) the Commons; (9) Ritual Masses; (10) Masses and prayers for various needs and occasions; (11) Votive Masses; (12) Masses for the Dead (Masses of Christian Burial); (13) appendices, including preparation before Mass and thanksgiving after, the rites of blessing oils and consecrating chrism, music for the Order of Mass, and the Mass in Latin; (14) indices of celebrations and prefaces.

The Sacramentary is never a completely fixed book; there are changes and additions made as required by the times or situations. Introduced in 1975 were several liturgies for children and Eucharistic prayers but these are not yet incorporated into the bound volume of the Sacramentary. (See Order of the Mass, New.)

**Sacraments, Seven**

1. It is necessary to set forth the essential elements of a sacrament. These are: (a) a sensible sign instituted by God, which gives sanctifying grace; (b) both matter and form present with each sacrament; the matter is the material used, the form the accompanying words and action; and (c) a minister, someone authorized to give the sacrament with the intention of doing what the Church intends.

2 It is good to know that the sacraments produce grace. Since grace is a gift of God, the sacrament must come from and depend upon God. Sanctifying grace is given by reason of the rite itself *(ex opere operato)*, and grace is not given if the sacrament is not received with the necessary moral disposition. In addition, each sacrament confers a special grace, called sacramental grace. As defined by the Council of Trent, it is the teaching of the Catholic Church, that every one of the sacraments of the New Law was instituted by Christ. These are baptism (Mt. 28:18–20), Holy Eucharist (Mt. 26:26), penance (Jn. 20:21–23), matrimony (Mt. 19:3–9), anointing of the sick (Jas. 5:14–15), confirmation (Acts 2:42; 8:15; 19:6), and holy orders (Jn. 20:21–22). (See also entries under sacraments.)

Vatican II declares: "The purpose of the sacraments is to sanctify men, to build up the body of Christ, and finally, to give worship to God. Because they are signs they also instruct. They not only presuppose faith, but by words and objects they also nourish, strengthen, and express it; that is why they are called 'sacraments of faith.' They do indeed impart grace, but, in addition, the very act of celebrating them disposes the faithful most effectively to receive this grace in a fruitful manner, to worship God duly, and to practice charity.

"It is therefore of capital importance that the faithful easily understand the sacramental signs, and with great eagerness have frequent recourse to those sacraments which were instituted to nourish the Christian life" (SC 59).

## Sacred Art and Furnishings

It has ever been the mind of the Church that its art and furnishings should by their dignity and excellence promote the highest spiritual response upon the part of the observer. Such furnishings are not to be considered as ersatz, gaudy, overly decorative, but at the same time there should not be an excessive display of richness or luxury. The key word here is dignity, the suitableness of the object to the service and worship of God. Beauty and dignity have the essence of truth; together with the competence of the artist, these bring to the Church not lavishness but controlled beauty that inspires reverence.

The General Instructions on the Mass declare the following: "The buildings and requisites for worship, as signs and symbols of heavenly things, should be truly worthy and beautiful.

"At all times the Church needs the service of the arts and allows for popular and regional diversity of aesthetic expression. While preserving the art of former times, the Church also tries to adapt it to new needs and to promote the art of each age.

"High artistic standards should be followed when commissioning artists and choosing works of art for the church. These works of art should nourish faith and piety and be in harmony with the meaning and purpose for which they are intended" (n. 253, 254).

Vatican II declares: "Very rightly the fine arts are considered to rank among the noblest expressions of human genius. This judgment applies especially to religious art and to its highest achievement, which is sacred art. By their very nature both of the latter are related to God's boundless beauty, for this is the reality which these human efforts are trying to express in some way.

To the extent that these works aim exclusively at turning men's thoughts to God persuasively and devoutly, they are dedicated to God and to the cause of His greater honor and glory.

"Holy Mother Church has therefore always been the friend of the fine arts and has continuously sought their noble ministry, with the special aim that all things set apart for use in divine worship should be truly worthy, becoming, and beautiful, signs and symbols of heavenly realities" (SC 122).

## Sacred College of Cardinals

The members of the Sacred College are those cardinals who according to canon law (230) have a particular place in the Church: "The cardinals of the Holy Roman Church constitute the senate of the Roman Pontiff and aid him as chief counselors and collaborators in the government of the Church." Among many privileges granted to them is the very important function of electing a successor to a deceased or retired pope.

## Sacred Heart of Jesus

1. The Sacred Heart of Jesus is a devotion to Jesus Christ, consisting of worship of Him through His heart as representing His love shown in the Incarnation, His Passion and death, the institution of the Eucharist. The devotion is centered on reparation to Christ for man's ingratitude, manifested particularly by indifference to the Holy Eucharist. The worship is not directed to the Heart alone, but to the Person of Jesus Christ. The Church forbids public cult of the Heart separated from the rest of the body, but allows private veneration, as in the case of Sacred Heart badges. The devotion is based on the doctrine or dogma "God is love" as found in Scripture (1 Jn. 4:8).

2. A feast, requested by our Lord Himself, commemorates the unrequited love of the Sacred Heart in the Eucharist and is celebrated on the Friday after the feast of Corpus Christi.

3. Representation of the Sacred Heart of Jesus may be in picture, statue, medal, or the familiar "badge."

4. Enthronement of the Sacred Heart in the home is the acknowledgment of the sovereignty of Christ over the family. It is expressed through solemn installation by the head of the house of a representation of the Sacred Heart in a place of honor, together with an act of consecration, in the presence of the entire family. Another indulgenced practice for individuals or families is to spend an hour in reparation before the Blessed Sacrament or before an image of the Sacred Heart in the home between the hours of 9 P.M. and 6 A.M.

## Sacred Heart, Promises of

In the apparitions of Our Lord to St. Margaret Mary Alacoque (1647 to 1690) at the Visitation convent of Paray-le-Monial (France) beginning in 1673, twelve promises were given (within the octave of Corpus Christi in the year 1676) to increase devotion to the Sacred Heart of Jesus. They are: (1) I will give them all the graces necessary in their state of life. (2) I will establish peace in their homes. (3) I will comfort them in all their afflictions. (4) I will be their secure refuge during life and above all, in death. (5) I will bestow abundant blessings on all their undertakings. (6) Sinners shall find in my Heart the source and the infinite ocean of mercy. (7) By devotion to my Heart, lukewarm souls shall grow fervent. (8) Fervent souls shall rise quickly to high perfection. (9) I will bless every place where a picture of my Heart shall be set up and honored. (10) I will give to priests the gift of touching the most hardened hearts. (11) Those who promote this devotion shall have their names written in my Heart, never to be blotted out. (12) I will grant the grace of final penitence to those who communicate (receive Holy Communion) on the first Friday of nine consecutive months.

Based upon these promises the enthronement of the Sacred Heart has been promoted, wherein a painting, picture, or representation of the Sacred Heart of Jesus is displayed in homes. It also has led to the formation of First Friday Clubs whose members receive Holy Communion each First Friday of the month, as well as stimulating the devotion of the First Nine Fridays among the faithful.

## Sacred Host

See Host; Eucharist, Celebration of.

## Sacred Meal

Eating has long been a part of religious observance, whether ritual or cultic, and has been a part of sacrifical rites thereby called *theophagy* or *hierophagy*. In pagan ceremonies such meals were offered for the appeasement of gods but the offerer did not partake of the meal or food-offering, and hence it was called the "divine" meal"—or one consumed by a deity.

In the Christian development of this practice, reference is made to the Eucharist as "The Lord's Supper" (1 Cor. 11:20–34), thus a sacred meal. But it has, besides the sacramental reality, the idea of "fellowship" (cf. Koinonia). There is an identity in this sacred meal of the sacrifice and the recipient, in this "one bread" that is eaten and drunk as sacrifice (cf. 1 Cor. 10:16), as memorial, and most solemnly as the Body and Blood of Christ (cf. Acts 2:42–46; 20:7–11). The *agape*, which was historically a "fellowship" meal, was often joined to the celebration of the Eucharist but was not Eucharistic in itself.

The semantic understanding of "meal" in our modern society has a familial connotation, but it does not denote the sacrificial meal that is either Eucharistic or ritualistic. It would be more proper and correct in every instance to preface the word "meal," when used in the Catholic context, with the words "Eucharistic" or "Sacred" (cf. Jn. 6:55–56). (See Eucharist, Celebration of.)

## Sacred Music

See Music, Church.

## Sacred Roman Congregations

The Sacred Roman Congregations, employed by the supreme pontiff in the government of the Church, are administrative groups. "Each of the Congregations is in the charge of a Cardinal Prefect, or, if the Roman Pontiff himself is the Prefect, the Congregation is governed by a Cardinal Secretary" (c. 246). (See Congregation.)

## Sacred Scripture

See Bible.

## Sacred Vessels

These are the chalice, paten, ciborium, pyx, and lunette. They are used during the celebration of the Mass or as containers of the Blessed Sacrament. Less sacred are those closely associated with divine worship, the monstrance and the communion plate.

## Sacred Writers

In the documents of Vatican II special recognition is given to the Evangelists, Matthew, Mark, Luke, and John as the sacred writers. This is because they are the recognized communicators of the message of Christ to the world. It does not exclude in any way the contributions of the authors of the other books of scripture but rather gives them a lesser rank. Nor does this denigrate the writings of the Fathers of the Church who have carried forward the doctrinal tradition of the Church.

Vatican II declares: "The sacred authors wrote the four Gospels, selecting some things from the many which had been handed on by word of mouth or in writing, reducing some of them to a synthesis, explicating some things in view of the situation of their churches, and preserving the form of proclamation but always in such fashion that they told us the honest truth about Jesus" (DV 19).

And: "For their (the sacred writers') intention in writing was that either from their own memory and recollections, or from the witness of those who themselves 'from the beginning were eyewitnesses and ministers of the word' we might know 'the truth' concerning those matters about which we have been instructed (cf. Lk. 1:2–4)" (DV 19).

## Sacrifice

The supreme act of worship consists essentially in (1) an offering of a worthy victim to God, (2) the offering made by a proper person, as a priest, (3) the destruction of the victim, (4) offering for the purpose of obtaining pardon for sin or a favor (Lv. 8:1–36). In the Christian Law, the supreme sacrifice is that of the Mass, the unbloody repetition of the Sacrifice of Christ on Calvary. (See Eucharist, Celebration of.)

The sacrifice of Christ was first a perfect *inward* Sacrifice, the perfection of the One offered; it was also the one sacrifice that superceded all previous *ritual* or outward sacrifices (Heb. 10:5–7; Mt. 27:38; Lk. 18:9–14; Rom. 15:12). The Christian extends the spiritual and real sacrifice of Christ, and like Christ Himself, becomes the temple of spiritual sacrifice (1 Cor. 6:19) in poverty of spirit (Acts 2:42–47; 1 Cor. 16:1–4; 2 Cor. 9:6–9; Gal. 2:10) and in love through the Spirit (Acts 2:1–4; Mt. 3:11). (See Eucharist, Celebration of.)

## Sacrifice of the Mass

See Eucharist, Celebration of; Order of the Mass, New.

## Sacrilege

This term refers to the unbecoming treatment of a person, place, or thing that has been consecrated or dedicated to God. It is personal when directed against a person, for example, injury to a cleric; it is local when directed against a place, for example, murder done in a church; it is real when committed through the dishonoring of sacred things, for example, unworthy reception, administration, or profanation of a sacrament or sacred vessels. Thus, simony is also a sacrilege since it is irreverent misuse of a spiritual thing (cf. Simony).

## Sacristan

This title is given to the person assigned to care for the sacristy and its contents, to prepare for the celebration of Mass, that is, arranging the vest-

ments and other duties. He may be a priest, religious, or lay person.

## Sacristy

The sacristy is a room adjoining the sanctuary, with a door into the sanctuary and usually one connecting with the body of the church, where vestments, linens, and other articles used in divine service are kept. It is recommended that this room be not too small, be well lighted, and protected by barred windows because of the nature of the equipment retained there. St. Charles Borromeo (d. 1584) wrote extensive instructions for the fitting of the sacristy, many of which indicate the necessity for efficiency and convenience.

## Sadducees

One of the three chief religious parties operative in the pre-Christian period and in the time of Christ was called the Sadducees. (The other two were the Pharisees and Essenes.) The Greek name, derived from the Aramaic, means "to be just." The party arose in the second century B.C., and its members became "cooperators" during the Roman occupation of Palestine so that they could achieve a dominant place in the Sanhedrin.

They were denounced by St. John the Baptist (Mt. 3:7), and Jesus warned his disciples about both the Sadducees and the Pharisees (Mt. 16:6–11). Later the Sadducees were not only antagonistic to Christ but were the chief persecutors of the Apostles and Christians in Jerusalem (Acts 4:1).

## Saint Joseph's Oratory

Situated near the summit of Mont Royal in Montreal, Quebec, this shrine was founded July 20, 1896 by Brother André of the College of Notre Dame of Holy Cross and is the principal center of devotion to St. Joseph, the patron saint of Canada since March 19, 1624. The land was first acquired on its founding date, and Brother André began to collect funds for a small wooden chapel. It soon gained a reputation as a place of miracles, and crowds of pilgrims journeyed to the chapel. As a result the chapel was enlarged three times, each becoming crowded with the crutches and testimonials of favors of grace.

Some of these miracles were attributed to Brother André, whose lightsome ways belied the fasts and penances of his life, but he always remarked: "All this comes through Saint Joseph's prayers. I am only Saint Joseph's little dog."

The hope for a larger church began to be realized in 1918 when the crypt of Saint Joseph's Shrine was completed with its massive granite steps ascending the slope of the hill. Today the church is a magnificent temple, in classic Renaissance style, but the interior is modern. From great clusters of piers arises the dome that dominates the colorful, carefully kept gardens surrounding the shrine. The miracles and testimonials continue from the streams of faithful who make this probably the greatest shrine on the North American continent. It is a tribute to the Patron of the Church Universal, with a library containing every important book or document ever written about the foster father of Christ. The shrine's own radio station and color films, which carry the Saint's humble glory to millions of people, fulfill the dream of its founder to increase devotion to Saint Joseph.

### Saint Peter's Basilica

St. Peter's, the largest church in the world, adjoining the Vatican palace, the home of the pope, is built above the circus of Nero, where St. Peter, the first pope, suffered martyrdom. The building was first erected by Constantine, but the present structure dates from its completion in 1626. Many artists and craftsmen contributed to its singular beauty; the vast dome is the design of Michelangelo. Recent archaeological findings, excavated from beneath the church, attest to the history of the early Christian life and tradition. The church is kept in constant repair by skilled workmen, called *sampietrini*, and is served by a chapter of thirty canons. It is provided for by a Sacred Congregation whose members direct and govern the occasions and solemnity of celebrations, for example, jubilees, when the church is the place of ceremonies of worldwide importance.

### Sainte Anne-de-Micmacs, Shrine of

Also called Saint Anne of Ristigouche, this Canadian shrine is located in the village of Ristigouche, in the province of Quebec, on the Gaspé Peninsula on the north shore of the Bay of Chaleur. It was founded in 1745, although a mission to the Indians was begun there in 1600 by Franciscan Recollects who wished to colonize the Micmacs. The work of the Franciscans and Jesuits was successful; in 1610 the great chief, Membertou, was baptized and the entire tribe became members of the Church.

In the course of instruction, the Indians were told of Saint Anne and came to look upon her as their grandmother and named all of their churches after her. The mission church of Ristigouche was especially loved by the Indians, but when the last

sea battle between the French and English was fought at Ristigouche in 1760, the English were victorious and drove out the Recollects and the Jesuits. The mission suffered many years of hardship, and in 1894 the Capuchins were placed in charge of the mission. The present church dates from 1927, and this and the surroundings are for the Micmac Indians the center of their love and devotion to their heavenly "grandmother," Saint Anne.

### Sainte Benoit-du-Lac

This shrine (St. Benedict of the Lake) is near Magog, in the province of Quebec in Canada, and is considered one of the most beautiful and original monasteries in the world. It was founded in 1912 when a group of Benedictines chose a 600 acre site near Magog as the first foundation of their order in Canada. The community was successful, and soon its cheese, called Ermite cheese, was known all over North America.

The present monastery was the work of one of the world's outstanding architects, Dom Paul Bellot, a monk of the parent monastery of Solesmes in France. The work of Dom Bellot, such as the Quarr Abbey on the Isle of Wight which is considered his masterpiece, was recognized as outstanding and when he visited Canada from 1938 to 1939, his interest in and work on Sainte Benoit-du-Lac began. The five-sided building of Stanstead Vermont granite has a French chateau flavor, and the beauty of its setting makes this shrine, where a relic of St. Benedict is venerated, a place of delight to all pilgrims who seek it in spiritual aspiration and hope.

### Saints

The faithful may render veneration (*dulia*) and prayers of intercession to those members of the mystical body of Christ who have lived and died, whose lives were notable for holiness and virtues practiced, and who have been officially declared saints by the Church through the process of beatification and canonization. The saints are for the faithful, first, examples of the virtuous life, and second, as members of the Church triumphant, representatives of the living members of the mystical body and the suffering souls. There are several classifications of saints recognized by the Church, which are not based on their occupation in life but rather on the quality of their sanctity, for example, martyrs, virgins, confessors, doctors, and bishops.

Vatican II speaks of the saints as those "beholding 'clearly God Himself triune and one, as He is'" (LG 49). And also as those who are "finally . . . caught up in peace and utter happiness in that fatherland radiant with the splendor of the Lord" (LG 93); those who are "joined to Him in an endless sharing of a divine life beyond all corruption" and "have found true life with God" (GS 18); or those who "communicate in life and glory with Himself" (AG 2) and who "share in His happiness" (GS 21).

### Saints, Intercession and Veneration of

The Church has always recognized the intercessory power of saints. Arising from OT Jewish belief in the "merits of the fathers" (Jer. 15:1; Ez. 14:14), the Church recognized that all members unite in worship before the throne of God (Rv. 6:9–11). This uniting with the saints is not only through seeking their intercession, but also through the veneration that the Church gives to the saints, called *dulia,* which is adoration of God through the saints. That all the faithful have a close association with the saints is attested by St. Paul who addresses the living faithful as "fellow citizens of the saints and members of the household of God" (Eph. 2:19). (Cf. Intercession.)

Vatican II teaches: "This most sacred Synod accepts with great devotion the venerable faith of our ancestors regarding this vital fellowship with our brethren who are in heavenly glory or who are still being purified after death. It proposes again the decrees of the Second Council of Nicaea, the Council of Florence, and the Council of Trent. And at the same time, as part of its own pastoral solicitude, this Synod urges all concerned to work hard to prevent or correct any abuses, excesses, or defects which may have crept in here and there, and to restore all things to a more ample praise of Christ and of God.

"Let the faithful be taught, therefore, that the authentic cult of the saints consists not so much in the multiplying of external acts, but rather in the intensity of our active love. By such love, for our own greater good and that of the Church, we seek from the 'example in their way of life, fellowship in their communion, and aid by their intercession.' At the same time, let the people be instructed that our communion with those in heaven, provided that it is understood in the more adequate light of faith, in no way weakens, but conversely, more thoroughly enriches the supreme worship we give to God the Father, through Christ, in the Spirit" (LG 51). (Cf. Church Triumphant.)

### Salt, Liturgical Use of

1. As a symbol of wisdom and friendship with God (Mk. 9:50), a few grains of common salt, which have been exorcized and blessed, are placed on the tongue of the one being baptized.

2. Water to be blessed is mixed with a little salt. Following the ancient Hebrew thought (cf. Lv. 2:13), salt is also used by Christ as a symbolic representation of Christian wisdom (cf. Mt. 5:13).

### Salvation

Recognition of the salvific will of God that must be attained in faith is the mode of human existence and as such is recognized as the act of salvation. Man and woman are finite. They could not obtain for themselves the deliverance from sin and its effects. This could only be accomplished by God: as Isaiah declared: "He became their Savior" (63:8), and it is God who is "salvation" (Is. 12:2; 45:22). And Christ became the Redeemer, the divine Deliverer of mankind as He declared to Zacchaeus, "Today salvation has come to this house, for this is what it means to be a son of Abraham. The Son of Man has come to search out and save what was lost" (Lk. 19:9–10).

The entire content of the message of Jesus is one of the salvation of mankind. The Gospel is called the "message of salvation" (Acts 13:26) and the "way of salvation" (Acts. 16:17), and this salvation is brought about through the power of God (Rom. 1:16).

Salvation for the human person is a call to glory through Christ: ". . . you are the first fruits of those whom God has chosen for salvation, in holiness of spirit and fidelity to truth. He called you through our preaching of the good news so that you might achieve the glory of our Lord Jesus Christ" (2 Thes. 2:13–14). The Christian shares this salvation, or glory, already in the reception of the sacrament of baptism, but each human person awaits the fulfillment of the coming of Jesus in an eschatological climax in the Last Days (Heb. 9:28; Rom. 8:24; 13:11; Phil. 3:20; 1 Pt. 1:5).

Man and woman by and of themselves have no means of bringing about their own salvation. Not even faith (Rom. 10:9–13) or conversion (Acts 3:19; 5:31) or reception of baptism (Acts 22:16; 1 Pt. 3:21) or constancy throughout life (2 Thes. 2:10) can gain for one the right to salvation, though all of these are the forerunners of attainment through the efficacy of the redemptive sacrifice of Christ. (See Salvation History.)

### Salvation History

From the biblical history of origins (cf. Gn.

12:1–3) through the completion of the lives of human persons there is a constant admixture of the theological, interpretative, and traditional aspects of the history of mankind. It is not possible to gain insight into the purpose for which man and woman were created, their racial distinctions, and their knowledge and response to God from archaeology or the "readings" of natural signs when these are thought of only as scientific curios.

Salvation history is the entire God-relationship of the human race, from birth to glory in Christ, from the beginning of created time to the end of time. This begins with a formal creed or recognition of God's will to save man, not only from the moment of creation, but especially after man's fall and the idolatry of God's chosen people (Ex. 3:9–12; Dt. 4:32–40; 27:1–10). This was carried on by the grace of God, His fidelity, His gifts, through the covenant of the OT and the greater covenant of the New Law given by Christ, the Savior and Redeemer of all peoples. This entire sequence overrides time, generations, and nations. It is the one history that brings into the present understanding the realization of the end-time of the future in glory, which is the beginning of and culmination of everyone's life in God (cf. Mt. 5:11–12).

The OT was of itself a particular history of the self-revelation of God to man. It is a God-guided manifestation of a future, definite redemption (cf. 1 Cor. 10:1–6; Heb. 10:1). It was that period of history which came to fulfillment in the birth and death of Christ, a fulfillment from the very beginning of time which will culminate in the eschatological beginning of the kingdom of God.

In the NT this history takes on a new and fuller understanding. Here we have the time-period of Christ and His apostles, the formative and primitive realization of the Mystical Body. And we have the culmination in the time-period from the resurrection of Christ and the coming of the Holy Spirit to the second coming of Christ in glory, the parousia. When we look at these two NT time-periods of salvation history, we see two outstanding features: (1) in the first period Christ was present bodily, teaching and bringing His message to men and women fully and completely; (2) in the second period Christ remains present in His Spirit, and in the Eucharist, beginning His coming again in glory, and the fulfillment of the kingdom of God (cf. 1 Cor. 15:35–58; 15:28; 15:26).

The history of salvation is one of faith and hope by which the human person comes to a realization and understanding of his role in regard to God the Creator, God the Redeemer, and God as King and Ruler of all. It has thus a uniform continuity in the unchangeableness of God. It is present in the Church through her treasures administered for all (LG 48). (See Servant of Yahweh.)

**Salvation Outside the Church**

In the twentieth century, and stemming from the errors of the Jacobites (1442), there arose notable instances of triumphalism and pride that caused many to declare falsely that only as members of the Catholic Church could human persons obtain salvation. This false notion was never endorsed by Church authorities and was answered by Vatican II in several declarations.

The open admission was made: "Some, even very many, of the most significant elements or endowments which together go to build up and give life to the Church herself can exist outside the visible boundaries of the Catholic Church" (UR 3), and several sacred actions of the separated brethren "can truly engender a life of grace, and can be rightly described as capable of providing access to the community of salvation." (UR 3c). This indicates that the "mode of understanding" is the crucial approach to the salvation of those outside of the Church.

"Catholics must joyfully acknowledge and esteem the truly Christian endowments from our common heritage which are to be found among our separated brethren" (UR 4h). (See Ecumenism.)

**Salvation, Sacrament of**

This term is used to designate the Church founded by Christ, in the documents of Vatican II (cf. LG 5). (See Church.)

**Samuel, First and Second Books of**

Two historical books of the Bible, which in the Vulgate were called the first and second books of Kings, were originally one writing. The title is derived from the dominant figure in the first Book. Substantial portions of these books stem from the Deuteronomic (seventh century) tradition. The author is unknown, and it is probable that the books were written not long after David's death. It was Samuel who announced the new King of Israel, David, and so St. John the Baptist, is referred to as the new Samuel who announced the King of all, the Messiah, Christ the Lord (1 Sm. 9:14–17; 16:12–13; Lk. 1:7–15; 3:21–22).

The two Books of Samuel record the events that made up one of the most important periods in Hebrew history. Here the twelve tribes became a unit, instituted under the one kingship (1 Sm.

8:5–9). It was God who led David to the great heights of leadership and there was promised a lasting "kingdom" a "firm throne" (2 Sm. 7:16).

The basic religious idea of these books is that of "election," whereby God has chosen and made firm a people of His own and one in whom there would be carried out His salvific will toward the eventuality of a salvation of all individuals (cf. 2 Sm. 7). The beginning of the working out of God's plan of salvation for all mankind is recounted briefly in these books. (See Salvation History.)

## Sanctification

Sanctification is the entire process of obtaining holiness or making one holy. This is done through initiation into membership in the Mystical Body of Christ through baptism, the reception of the sacraments, the avoidance of sin, the practice of virtue, prayer, worship, and final perseverance, which are all means of acquiring sanctification. This ideal of holiness has been realized in the Church and the "new elect of God" (cf. Lk. 6:13–15; Acts 1:21–26; 1 Cor. 1:27–31; 1 Thes. 1:4; Jas. 2:5; Col. 3:12) are brought to share in God's holiness.

Vatican II declares: "Christ the Lord, Son of the living God, came that He might save His people from their sins and that all men might be made holy. Just as He Himself was sent by the Father, so He also sent His apostles. Therefore, He sanctified them, conferring on them the Holy Spirit, so that they too might glorify the Father upon earth and save men, 'for the building up of the body of Christ' (Eph. 4:12), which is the Church" (CD 1).

And: "The liturgy of the sacraments and sacramentals sanctifies almost every event in their lives; they (the faithful) are given access to the stream of divine grace which flows from the paschal mystery of the passion, death, and resurrection of Christ, the fountain from which all sacraments and sacramentals draw their power. There is hardly any proper use of material things which cannot thus be directed toward the sanctification of men and the praise of God" (SC 61).

## Sanctifying Grace

Infused into the very essence of the soul, sanctifying grace is a certain supernatural quality granted by God, without which we are not sanctified or assured justification and salvation. It is "God abiding in the soul" (Jn. 14:23), and the Council of Trent declared: "It is called our justice because by its inherence in us we are justified" (Denz. No. 809). Sanctifying grace is lost through mortal sin; it is increased through good acts done

for and through God, and particularly through the reception of the sacraments. It is also called habitual grace, but this is a broader term. (Cf. Grace.)

## Sanctity of the Church

See Marks of the Church.

## Sanctuary

In church buildings that portion of the church wherein the altar is located, extending to and including the communion stations, is called the sanctuary. Besides the altar it should be furnished with a seat for the celebrant, stools or benches for the ministers, a credence table, and a lectern. It also may have choir stalls, an episcopal throne, and an aumbry. In the modern church structures the sanctuary is called "sacred space" since this area about the altar is not an apsidal or enclosed area.

## Sanctus

Following the Preface of the Mass, this short prayer is a welcome and a hymn of praise heralding the opening of the Canon of the Mass. It recalls two events in the life of Christ, the welcome of the angels at the Nativity (Lk. 2:14) and the praise offered to Christ at His entry into Jerusalem (Mk. 11:1–10). It demonstrates in human terms the praise that the angels give before the throne of God in heaven (Rv. 4:11).

The words are: "Holy, Holy, Holy Lord, God of power and might, heaven and earth are full of your glory. Hosanna in the highest. Blessed is he who comes in the name of the Lord. Hosanna in the highest."

## Sandals

Sandals are low shoes, with leather soles and the upper part of silk or velvet, usually embroidered, worn by bishops when celebrating pontifical Mass. In color they correspond to that of the vestments worn. Sandals are not worn at requiem Masses or on Good Friday and may be omitted at will on other occasions.

## Sanhedrin

The highest court of justice in Jerusalem in NT times was called the Sanhedrin. The name is derived from the Greek word meaning "council," although it is also referred to as a "priests' council" presided over by a high priest (cf. Lk. 22:66; Acts 22:5). By tradition it was made up of seventy-one members (cf. Nm. 11:16), was priestly in character, but also had lay persons such as the Scribes and

Pharisees (cf. Mt. 26:57; Acts 24:1). Its primary function was to act concerning all religious matters of the Jews, to collect the taxes, and to act as a civil court for the city of Jerusalem (Mt. 26:3–5; Acts 4:5–6; 12:20–24). It ceased to function as a group after the destruction of Jerusalem in 70 A.D.

## Sapiental Books

The biblical books of Job, Psalms, Proverbs, Ecclesiastes, the Song of Songs, Wisdom, and the Book of Sirach are included in this collective title. (See Bible.)

## Sardica, Council of

Held in 343 at Sardica (now Sofia in Bulgaria), this meeting of Eastern and Western bishops was an attempt to settle the dispute over the approval or condemnation of Athanasius at various local councils.

## Sarum Use

This was a form of the Latin rite as formulated by St. Osmund (d. 1099). First used in the diocese of Salisbury, it was later introduced into Scotland and Ireland and replaced the ancient Celtic ritual. Until the Reformation, it was commonly used in England and Scotland. It resembles the Dominican rite as used today.

## Satan

Satan, also called Lucifer, the devil, is the chief tempter and head of the evil spirits. The name Satan first appears in Job (1:6) and means "the opponent" or "adversary."

Satan was the originator of the first sin and became the one having hostility to the posterities of all mankind (Gn. 3:15). When Christ came into the world, Satan was the "prince of this world" (Jn. 8:34–47; 14:30–31) and held the world in his power (Mt. 5:37; 1 Jn. 5:19; Acts 13:10).

It was through His cross that Christ redeemed us from the power of Satan (Col. 1:13–14; 2:14–15; Heb. 2:14–18). Although Satan remained the tempter, faith and prayer would deliver us from evil, and through a constant awareness and charity, and the seeking after justice and individual holiness one can defeat the devil (Lk. 22:31–34; 2 Cor. 11:14; Mt. 6:13; 1 Jn. 2:13–14; Acts 5:1–3; Eph. 6:10–17). The Holy Spirit, sent by God was to reveal to Christians that the "prince of this world" had been judged (Jn. 16:5–14), and Satan would be finally crushed forever (Rv. 9:11; 12:1–9; 17:1–6; 20:1–3).

## Satisfaction

1. The ancient legal meaning of this term was the compensation for a debt or offense. St. Anselm applied it to the redemptive act of Christ wherein the justification of man was established. Christ's death on the cross was the satisfaction for the sins of the whole human race.

2. Sacramental satisfaction is the voluntary acceptance on the part of a penitent of the sacrifice (penance, alms, or other means), which is necessary to expiate the temporal punishment due to sin. Like Christ, the Christian must die so that he may live in Christ (Gal. 2:19), walk in the Spirit (Gal. 5:25), and be a member of Christ (Gal. 2:20).

3. A term for the penance imposed by a superior in a religious institute.

## Saul

1. The first king of the Israelites, annointed about 1040 B.C. It was considered that an earthly ruler would be an affront to God, and this thinking prevailed until Samuel finally prayed to God for enlightenment and was answered (1 Sm. 8:6–18), and it was Samuel who poured oil upon Saul's head and declared him the ruler, saying, "The Lord anoints you commander over his heritage" (1 Sm. 10:1). Saul died in battle against the Philistines about the year 1000 B.C. (1 Sm. 31:1–6) and was succeeded by David. (See David.)

2. Saul is the name of St. Paul before he became an Apostle (Acts 8, 9). (See Paul, St.)

## Scala Sancta

Literally, "the holy stairs," this is a flight of twenty-eight steps leading to the papal chapel in the old Lateran palace. Although now covered with wood, the original stairs beneath were thought to be the steps leading up to the praetorium of Pilate. They were alleged to have been brought from Jerusalem by St. Helena about 326.

## Scamnum

This is the Latin name for the bench on the epistle side of the sanctuary where the celebrant and deacon, sit during parts of the high Mass. It is a bench without arms or back. It replaces the *sedilia* (q.v.). In practice this can refer to any moveable chair used about the altar, other than the episcopal throne.

## Scandal

Giving scandal means to provoke by words or conduct the occasion for the sin of another or to cause another's spiritual ruin. As such it may be direct or indirect: direct when the deliberate act leads to the sin of another, for example, seduction; indirect when the sin of another is foreseen as a result but is not intended to solicit the act of another, for example, selling harmful drugs to another (this is compounded by other more serious offences in most instances).

It is also possible that scandal may be given by someone when the action or words are not intended to give scandal or are not of themselves sinful, for example, a priest who is exceeding the speed laws.

Scandal may be taken without warrant by some people who have an insufficiently trained or informed conscience. In all such actions it must be remembered that the Christian acts first as a Christian and as one who seeks the salvation of all persons.

### Scapular

1. Basically a garment, a part of a religious habit, which consists of a piece of cloth, shoulder wide, which is placed over the head and hangs down, front and back to the prescribed length.

2. The scapular as a sacramental, in imitation of the larger form, is usually two small pieces of cloth, about two by three inches, which are joined by strings; it is worn around the neck, under the clothing, and hangs down front and back. There are about eighteen kinds of scapulars recognized by the Church, each being worn as a badge of some confraternity into which the wearer is enrolled. The most common are: the white (Trinitarians), red (Lazarists), brown (Carmelites), black (Servites), and blue (Theatines). The indulgences attached to the white, black, and brown scapulars can only be gained by having the names of those enrolled recorded and sent to a church where the confraternity is established.

3. The scapular medal, bearing on one side an image of the Sacred Heart and on the other a representation of the Blessed Mother, may be worn in substitution of the small scapular (see 2 above) only after one has been enrolled in the scapular of a confraternity. If it is worn in place of several kinds of scapular, the priest blessing it must make the sign of the cross over the medal—once for each scapular the medal substitutes for—and each new medal must be so blessed. Once enrolled, it is not necessary to be enrolled again and the small scapular, when replaced by a new one, may be worn without obtaining a blessing for the new one.

4. A garment resembling a scapular, called the *sanbenito,* was placed over the shoulders of persons condemned by the Inquisition. It had a red cross marked on the panels, front and back, and varied in color according to the crime as judged but was usually yellow. There was of course no religious value attached to such garments, and it was regarded as an opprobrious robe rather than a garment of penance.

### Schism

The action of one who voluntarily separates himself from the Church through refusal to submit to the authority of the Church or the pope and forms another sect is punished with excommunication incurred by the very fact of the action. Basically, schism is a breaking away from the Church, but it differs from apostasy and heresy. It means separated from ecclesiastical communion. Derived from the Greek, the word means "crack" or "flaw" or "tear." In this sense it was used by St. Paul as meaning one or several who because of their differences of opinion would "flaw" the unity of the Church (cf. 1 Cor. 1:10; 11:18; 12:25).

There was schism between the Jews and Gentiles, but this was righted by Christ who reconciled all (Eph. 2:11–22). It was Christ who intended that there should be unity in the Christian community, and so He prayed to the Father (Jn. 17:21; 10:16–30). And the eventual unity (fellowship) of all Christians is envisioned (cf. Rom. 11:11–15; Rv. 7:1–10). The Church also recognizes this eschatological hope of unity (cf. Heb. 12:22–23; Mt. 25:32; Jn. 11:52).

Vatican II states: "The Church recognizes that in many ways she is linked with those who, being baptized are honored with the name of Christian, though they do not profess the faith in its entirety or do not preserve unity of communion with the successor of Peter . . ." (LG 15).

### Schism, Eastern

After a series of minor breaks over iconoclasm and jurisdictional matters, the ecclesiastical leaders of the East and West split into two factions in the ninth century. One followed the pope of Rome, the other the patriarch of Constantinople. The immediate dispute was over the assumption of power by Photius (d. 897), with the confirmation of the Emperor Michael III. Photius was deposed in 896 by the new Emperor Leo VI. The breach had been accomplished by a series of political and religious actions that continued for the next 700 years. With the fall of Constantinople in 1453, the center of Oriental Christianity fell and, despite the efforts of the Council of Florence (1439), which had effected a brief reconciliation, the Orthodox Church became official under the Russian Empire.

## Schism, the Great

Also called the Western Schism, the dispute between allegiances to the claimants of the papacy, Urban VI (d. 1389) and Clement VII (d. 1394), divided the Church along lines of political and international rivalries; the Latin nations and France supported Clement, while the German and English rulers supported Urban. The Great Schism ended in 1417 with the election of Pope Martin V and the actions of the Council of Constance (1414 to 1418).

## Schoenstatt Movement

Basically an apostolic movement, this was founded at Schoenstatt, Germany, in 1914 by Father Joseph Kentenich, S.A.C. The purposes are twofold: to attain a high degree of spiritual development in keeping with Christian standards, and to overcome the materialism and secularism in the modern world by means of creating a community devoted to this ideal.

There are five secular institutes in the movement: one for laymen, two for women, and two for priests. The members seek through their work, in their own professional and special fields of endeavor, to achieve lay leadership and to maintain on the parish and community levels a program of religious education and apostolic work. (See Institutes, Secular.)

## Schola Cantorum

Literally, "choir schools" or "schools for singers," these are the means of carrying on the tradition of great music in the Church. The training is directed at not only singing, but also includes composition and instrumental training as a highly specialized education to aid the Church in maintaining this sacred tradition.

Vatican II states: "The treasure of sacred music is to be preserved and fostered with very great care. Choirs must be diligently promoted, especially in cathedral churches" (SC 114).

And: "Let them [composers] produce compositions which have the qualities proper to genuine sacred music, not confining themselves to works which can be sung only by large choirs, but providing also for the needs of small choirs and for the active participation of the entire assembly of the faithful" (SC 121).

## Scholastic

1. A student of scholastic philosophy.
2. A member of the Society of Jesus who has completed his novitiate and is studying in preparation for ordination.

## Scholasticism

Scholasticism is the name of a method and system of thought, which embraces all the intellectual, artistic, philosophical, and theological activities carried on in the universities of the Middle Ages. The name is derived from the term *doctores scholastici,* which was the ninth century term for a teacher of the arts. It was the system, taken from the Greek and adapted through recognition of revelation and tradition, which became the philosophy of a Christian society and which recognized the superiority of theology. As a method it was marked by emphasis upon logic, deduction, system, and the form of syllogistic argumentation, subordination to theology, and the disputation formula whereby a thesis or doctrine is defended by a syllogistic presentation against objections. (Cf. Neo-Scholasticism.)

## School, Parochial

See Parochial School.

## Schoolmen

The masters of scholasticism in the Middle Ages, such as St. Thomas Aquinas and St. Albert the Great, have been recognized by this name along with the Franciscans St. Bonaventure and Duns Scotus.

## Schools, Catholic

The role of education in the Church has endured from the earliest times. These schools include the present day parochial schools, but in general they are as diversified as the application of the educative principles to the process of learning and include everything from specialized schools, kindergartens, schools for the handicapped, adult study groups, and institutes of higher learning.

Vatican II recognized this role of the Church in many instances, among them: "The Church seeks to penetrate and ennoble with her own spirit those other means which belong to the common heritage of mankind, and which contribute mightily to the refinement of spirit and the molding of men. Among these are the media of social communication, many groups devoted to spiritual and physical development, youth associations, and especially schools" (GE 4).

And: "Schools, colleges, and other Catholic educational institutions also have the duty to develop a Catholic sense and apostolic activity in young people. If young people lack this information either because they do not attend these schools or because of any other reason, parents, pastors of souls, and apostolic organizations should attend to it all the more" (AA 30).

And: "This sacred Synod earnestly entreats pastors of the Church and all the faithful to spare no sacrifice in helping Catholic schools to achieve their purpose in an increasingly adequate way, and to show special concern for the needs of those who are poor in the goods of this world or who are deprived of the assistance and affection of a family or who are strangers to the gift of faith" (GE 9).

## Scotism

Developed by the famous Franciscan Schoolman, Duns Scotus (d. 1308), this system distinctly differs from Thomism. Primarily, it holds that immortality of the soul is beyond human reason; that these are two substantial forms in man; that will holds a certain superior position to intellect, and therefore ultimate happiness will be the act of loving God (will) rather than intellectual vision.

## Screen

See Rood-Screen.

## Scribes

In the OT the Hebrew term applied to an official of the court and was his title (cf. 2 Chr. 34:13), but it was also used to designate one of some accomplishment (Sir. 38:24–34).

In the NT it is chiefly the name given to Jewish scholars and lawyers, and members of the Sanhedrin (Mt. 2:4; 14:1); scribes were also members of the party of the Pharisees (Mt. 5:20; Mk. 2:16; Acts 23:9).

## Scripture

See Bible; Canon of the Scripture; Revelation; Tradition.

## Scrolls of the Dead Sea

Scroll is understood to mean any rolled piece of material upon which there have been inscribed words or symbols. Usually a scroll is made of parchment or animal skin.

The scrolls designated as those of the Dead Sea were discovered by two Bedouin shepherd youths in a cave near the Qumran area in the northwestern region of the Dead Sea in Palestine in 1947. The scrolls themselves were found stored in earthen jars, covered with a pitch or tar-like substance for preservation purposes. These decaying bundles of leather scrolls were found to comprise seven large scrolls and several fragments. They were all wrapped in linen. Written in Hebrew and Aramaic, the scrolls have proved to be of great significance and value to Biblical studies and the background of Christian development. The scrolls are now owned and retained by the Hebrew University where they are made available to qualified scholars for study.

Following the first discovery, natives and archaeologists made excavations leading to some 300 caves in the Dead Sea area, and twelve of these caves yielded additional material. Notable among the scrolls found were: *The Copper Scroll*, which gives clues to possible fabulous buried wealth; several scrolls of Biblical writings; twelve fragmentary scrolls of the Psalms; several manuscripts of the Book of Daniel; several Biblical commentaries; and some 40,000 fragments. The vast collection is of great linguistic and historic value and is now known variously as the "Dead Sea Scrolls," "Qumran Scrolls," and "Qumran Writings."

There was difficulty in placing a correct date on the scrolls, especially the date of their composition. The evidence and the consensus of scholars now place the time of the scrolls between the second and first centuries B.C.

It has also been determined that some of the scrolls contained original writings whereas others were copies of previous writings. For example, the original writings called the *Manual of Discipline* and the scroll of the *Thanksgiving Hymns* were original compositions of the practices of the groups of religious adherents called the Essenes. The evidence indicates that the scrolls were placed in the caves probably in the year A.D. 68 when the Roman legions passed through the area on their conquest to destroy Jerusalem, for no inhabitants were known to live in the area for many years after that date.

The scrolls were written in several Semitic languages, the majority in Hebrew, others in Aramaic, and some in a more ancient Hebrew, the Phoenician. There are only ten scrolls that are in a complete form. The Hebrew University has already published the scrolls in its possession. The other manuscripts and fragments are being examined textually and compared with the earliest known texts.

The first seven scrolls found in the first cave are: a complete scroll of the Book of Isaiah, written in Hebrew, 24 feet in length, and almost identical to the biblical text of Isaiah as we know it from the Hebrew bible; the *Manual of Discipline,* a manual of rules and regulations of a sect of the time, probably the Essenes; *Commentary on the Book of Habakkuk,* the first two chapters plus a commentary and interpretation; the *Genesis Apocryphon,* first called the *Lamech Scroll,* which contains apocryphal accounts of a few of the Patriarchs mentioned in the Book of Genesis notably Lamech, Enoch, Noah, and Abraham; an incomplete scroll of the Book of Isaiah, now called the *Hebrew University Isaiah Scroll;* the *War Scroll,* bearing the full title of "Scroll of the War of the Sons of Light Against the Sons of Darkness," which contains a survey of an eschatological war or a war of the members of the sect against their enemies; the *Scroll of Thanksgiving Hymns,* which contains about thirty hymns or poetic compositions similar to the Psalms.

Among the total of the other discovered manuscripts and fragments are copies of the books of the Hebrew Bible except the Book of Esther. Several are represented by more than one copy of a scriptural writing, for example, Isaiah, Deuteronomy, and some minor prophets.

The value of these finds, their study, and their time of writing have proved to be extensively encouraging to the understanding of the scriptures. They enable scholars to reconstruct the textual history of the OT. They demonstrate the general agreement and central substance of the essential ideas, which were well preserved in the Hebrew texts as we have known them. They also have been of value in the study of the development of the Bible and as insights into the background of Christian beginnings. (See Essenes.)

## Scruples

Because of confusion over the morality of actions, scruples arise when a troubled conscience, prompted by imaginary reasons, causes one to constantly dread sin where no sin exists or to hold a venially sinful action mortally sinful. A conscience with scruples is a conscience ruled by fear. The causes may be varied, such as disorder of health (physiological), predominance of sentiment over reason, or lack of judgment. Remedies are prayer and trust in God, restoration of health (if ill health is the cause), formation of a right conscience, and obedience to a counselor if one is required.

## Scrutiny

In the ecclesiastical sense, scrutiny is the examination of a person's spiritual fitness before awarding him an office in the Church. It also refers to the method of ecclesiastical election by secret ballot.

## Seal of Confession

The most grave obligation of keeping secret whatever has been revealed by a penitent in the Sacrament of Penance is always binding under mortal sin; no exception is made, not even in order to save one's life. The confessor is bound by the seal (c. 889), even if the confessor were a layman, masquerading. All sins confessed, even public sins, are subject to the seal. The obligation of the seal arises out of the role of judge in which the confessor acts, rather than from the act of absolving. It is founded upon the natural law, the positive divine law, and Church law.

## Search

See Retreat.

## Seasons of the Church

See Calendar, Church.

## Second Coming of Christ

See Judgment, General; Parousia.

## Secret, Discipline of the

See Discipline of the Secret.

## Secret of the Mass

This is the variable part of the Mass that immediately preceded the Preface in the Tridentine Mass and consisted of one or more prayers, said in a low voice by the priest as he bowed over the bread and wine. The prayers ask God to accept the offerings for the consecration, which will follow soon. Thus the Secrets are called *super oblata* prayers, that is, prayers over the oblations. (Cf. Mass Before Vatican II; Order of Mass, New.)

## Secret Societies

Membership in any such society is denied Catholics by law of the Church, but current interpretation permits it (*sic*). Besides the Freemasons (cf. Masonry), these societies are Good Templars, Odd Fellows, Sons of Temperance, Knights of Pythias, and any women's auxiliary group of these. These are forbidden under censure. Besides, the Church law states that those belonging to societies that are not necessarily secret but notoriously antisocial cannot receive ecclesiastical burial unless they repent (c. 1240), and members of any condemned society cannot be validly received into associations of the faithful (c. 693). Also the Holy Office (Nov. 5, 1920) warned against the dangers to the faith of the young by the activities of the Y.M.C.A. All societies that have religious rites or oaths of blind obedience fall under the general condemnation of the Church.

## Secretariats

In the Roman Curia there are three special Secretariats, which because of their special assignments are considered apart from the general administrative affairs. They are: (1) *Secretariat of Christian Unity.* This office, for the promotion of unity among Christians, oversees the work of ecumenism, sends representatives or observers to Christian gatherings, and invites or communicates with other Christian groups regarding Catholic affairs or meetings. It also has a special assignment concerning the Jews. The Secretariat operates out of two offices, one for the West and the other for the East, and the prefect-directors of the Congregation for Oriental Churches and of the Evangelization of People are ex-officio members of the Secretariat. (2) The *Secretariat of Non-Christians.* The special area of concern for this office is all the persons who neither are Christians nor profess any religious affiliation or belief. It is especially assigned to dialogue and promotion of relations with Moslems. Here the prefect-director of the Congregation for the Evangelization of Peoples is an ex-officio member. (3) The *Secretariat for Non-Believers.* In this office takes place the study of the philosophies and attitudinal approaches of all atheists and those who have no religious beliefs. (See Congregation.)

## Secular Clergy

See Diocesan Clergy.

## Secular Franciscans

See Tertiaries.

## Secular Institutes

See Institutes, Secular.

## Secularism

As defined in *Secularism,* the statement of the bishops of the United States on Nov. 14, 1947, this is "a view of life that limits itself not to the material in exclusion of the spiritual, but to the human here and now in exclusion of man's relation to God here and hereafter. Secularism, or the practical exclusion of God from human thinking and living, is at the root of the world's travail today." The bishops conclude: "The fact of God and the fact of the responsibility of men and nations to God for their actions are supreme realities, calling insistently for recognition in a truly realistic ordering of life in the individual, in the family, in the school, in economic activity, and in the international community." (Cf. Humanism.)

## Secularization

1. The civil action depriving the Church of use or possession of properties.

2. The act of separating a professed religious from his duties and obligations as a member of a religious congregation or order, through papal indult and in accord with canon law. (See Laicization.)

Secularization in the understanding of an anti-Christian movement became prominent between the two World Wars and was classed as a "religionless Christianity." This "living without God" or self sufficiency became popular in the "God is dead" movement. The newer attempts to place man in the world as master and yet as the creature who must live God's law are summed up in the freedom found in St. Paul's writing wherein he declares:

"Let there be no boasting about men. All things are yours, whether it be Paul, or Apollos, or Cephas, or the world, or life, or death, or the present, or the future: all these are yours, and you are Christ's and Christ is God's" (1 Cor. 3:21–23).

### Sede Vacante

Literally from the Latin, *sede vacante* means "the See is vacant." that is, the See of Rome. It is the expression for the period of time between the death of a pope and the election of a successor. It is also called "interregnum," meaning "between rules" but with less ecclesial accuracy. The procedures, norms of handling ecclesiastical affairs and filling the vacancy are set forth in two apostolic constitutions: *Vacantis Apostolicae Sedis* of Pius XII, Dec. 8, 1945, and *Summi Pontificis Electione,* of John XXIII, Sept. 5, 1962. (See Election, Papal.)

### Sedia Gestatoria

From the Italian, meaning "portable chair," the term is applied to the formal throne-like chair on which the pope sits and is borne on a platform during solemn processions of entry into St. Peter's and for other occasions. Those who carry the platform are dressed in crimson and are called *sediarii.*

### Sedilia

The sedilia is a throne-like bench, usually in three partitions and with a back, whereon the celebrant, deacon, or other ministers sit during parts of the Mass. Liturgically, it has been replaced by the *scamnum* in many churches.

### See, Episcopal

See Diocese.

### Semantics of Religion

In the communication of the message of Christ there are two broad essentials: (1) a knowledge of language (linguistics), and (2) a knowledge of the meaning of words (semantics).

In the present-day devolution of words—new words for old customs, newly created words—there is emphasis upon an exactitude of translation. However, in the same course of devolution there is reflected the "feelings" behind the words, the misconstruing of the right meaning of the word itself. Thus in the search for a contemporary religious idiom the language is too often dogged by a flatness of meaning. For example, somehow "so be it" will never supplant the simple and beautifully mindful "Amen."

The semantics of religion then require that what is sought is understandable communication, not simply "translation and interpretation." Semantics take into consideration the cultural and intellectual cooperation necessary to make effective our stores of knowledge and experience so that there may be ultimate mutual understanding among all peoples. In this sense language is social, and although it has a multitude of adaptations, for example cursing as opposed to saying, "God bless you!" that language remains the means of achieving what society and religion strive for.

For the Christian semantics are of the greatest importance—in teaching, preaching, administering, and obtaining a consensus of understanding. It is understood that the role of authority (leading others to Christ) is less effective when there are too many differences encountered in the understanding of essential truth. (Cf. Basic Teachings for Catholic Religious Education.) When, in conveying the message of Christ, there is no effort made to create true disciples, the result is only rote-acceptance of truth, which is lacking in understanding and consequently in application. Those who preach or teach without being creative in their presentations are likely to form a drab and unresponsive society of the People of God.

Semantics call for a creative, intense approach to the conveying of the message of Christ. As Dylan Thomas wrote: "Do not go gentle into that good night—Rage, rage against the dying of the light."

### Semi-Arianism

This heresy, promoted in the fourth century by Acacius, which taught that Christ the Son was only *like* God the Father, was condemned by the First Council of Constantinople (381). (See Heresies.)

### Semi-Pelagianism

This heresy arose in the fifth century. Propounded by a group of monks at the Abbey of St. Victor in Marseilles, it affirmed that grace is merited by man and is made efficacious by the human will. It was condemned by St. Augustine who wrote against it, and by the Second Council of Orange in 529. (See Heresies.)

## Seminarian

This is the name for one who attends an ecclesiastical seminary. Seminarians have certain obligations, arising out of the dignity of their purpose. Those who are incorrigible, seditious, wanting in disposition or health, or who are not able students are to be dismissed according to canon law.

Vatican II declares: "In seminaries and houses of religious, clerics are to be given a liturgical formation in their spiritual life. For this they will need proper direction, so that they can understand the sacred rites and take part in them wholeheartedly; and they will also need to celebrate the sacred mysteries personally, as well as popular devotions which are animated with the spirit of the liturgy. In addition they must learn how to observe liturgical laws. Thus life in seminaries and houses of religion will be thoroughly influenced by the spirit of the liturgy" (SC 17).

And: "Since doctrinal training ought not to aim at a mere communication of ideas, but at a genuine and deep formation of students, teaching methods should be revised as they apply to lectures, discussions, and seminars and with respect to the promotion of study among students, whether individually or in small groups" (OT 17).

## Seminary

A seminary is an ecclesiastical college of higher learning. Its sole purpose is to train young men for the reception of holy orders. It was customary to classify a preparatory school as a "minor seminary" and the more advanced schools as "major seminaries." The college school, however, had a six-year course of training, consisting of two years of philosophy (junior and senior years of college proper), and four years of theology. At present they are: secondary, college, and schools of ministry. Only those seminaries that are classified as having an apostolic faculty (c. 1378) can confer licentiate and doctoral degrees in theological subjects, canon law, or scripture. (See Pastoral Ministry, Schools of.)

## Semite

The name Semite is derived from Sem (Shem), whose Hebrew name means "name, fame," who is one of the five sons of Noah (Gn. 5:32). In the

Sethite genealogy this is the collective name for the descendants of Shem. The name Semite, however, was first used in 1781 by A.L. Schlozer to designate a group of related languages: Syriac, Aramaic, Hebrew, Arabic, and Phoenician. Later it was applied as a collective term for peoples who spoke these languages. But the list of Semites in the "Table of Nations" is based more on geographical locations than on a common language root, which is limited. The chief characteristic of the Semitic languages is that they all have a three-consonant formation of expressing basic concepts, thus differing from any inflected language.

In the question of race, there is no scientific basis that determines the Semite as distinct. Among those who speak the Semitic languages there has never been a single unification of nations, and the Semite cannot be identified except in the most broad terms of near eastern locality. People who speak Semitic languages are members of various races, certainly more so considering the highly nomadic life of most of these peoples dating back to 3000 B.C. (See Anti-Semitism.)

## Senses of Scripture

See Literal Sense of Scripture; Form Criticism; Inspiration of Scripture.

## Sentences, Book of

This compilation of theology in four volumes, by Peter Lombard (d. 1160), was the standard textbook of the time until replaced by the *Summa* of St. Thomas Aquinas.

## Separation

1. In marriage, this is the physical parting of man and wife (from bed and board) for due reason (cc. 1128-1132). Thus the innocent marriage partner may separate from the other in case of found adultery. Also, if one of the parties is a grave occasion of sin to the other, the innocent party may separate. This is not a divorce of the Church, though civil divorce may accompany the separation. The Catholic party to a valid marriage may not remarry after a separation until the other party dies. A Catholic should not seek a civil divorce without consulting the ordinary.

2. Separation of Church and state: in the United States the spheres of both religion and the state are established by constitutional law and definition. Thus "separation" can be understood as the guarantee of government that it will not set up an "official" church for the country, which would be favored by the government. The bishops of the

United States declared: "Authoritative Catholic teaching on the relations between Church and state, as set forth in papal encyclicals and in the treatises of recognized writers on ecclesiastical law, not only states clearly what these relations should normally be under ideal conditions, but also indicates to what extent the Catholic Church can adapt herself to the particular conditions that may take place in different countries." (Statement, *The Christian in Action,* Nov. 21, 1948.)

## Septuagesima

The third Sunday before Lent, the ninth Sunday before Easter, is known as Septuagesima Sunday. It begins the preparatory period for the penitential season of Lent.

## Septuagint

Translated from the Hebrew into Greek by seventy Jewish scholars and called the Alexandrian version, this Bible text was most widely used in the early Church. It is commonly referred to among scholars as LXX.

## Seraph

Seraph is the name of the angels of the angelic choir of Seraphim, which is one of the choirs who adore before God. The word comes from the Hebrew "fiery" (Is. 6:1–4).

## Sermon on the Mount

The sermon preached by Christ in the first few months of His ministry sounds the keynote of the new teaching He came to introduce. It is a declaration of the New Law, the guarantee that it will last, and it shows the new spirit in action. Love is to be the center, and love can ask more than fear (old law) can command (Mt. 5:1–7:29). (Cf. Beatitudes, the Eight.)

## Servant of Yahweh

In salvation history, God exerts His salvific action upon all men. He grants final representation among men by the Redeemer Christ, and through this "suffering servant," His divine Son, effects our salvation. The "songs of the Servant of Yahweh" are recorded in Isaiah (42:1–4; 50:4–11; 52:13; 53:12), telling of the one sent as teacher and lawgiver, who will expiate the sins of others. His redemptive action will touch all even to the ends of the earth. "Here is my servant whom I uphold, my chosen one with whom I am pleased, upon whom I have put my spirit; he shall bring forth justice to the nations" (Is. 42:1).

The Servant of Yahweh is the one who will appear as the great Representative of all the people, Christ the Savior. He is spoken of thus by the prophet Isaiah:

"He was spurned and avoided by men, a man of suffering, accustomed to infirmity, one of those from whom men hide their faces, spurned, and we held him in no esteem. Yet it was our infirmities that he bore, our sufferings that he endured, while we thought of him as stricken, as one smitten by God and afflicted. But he was pierced for our offenses, crushed for our sins, upon him was the chastisement that makes us whole, by his stripes we were healed. We had all gone astray like sheep, each following his own way; but the Lord laid upon him the guilt of us all. Though he was harshly treated, he submitted and opened not his mouth; like a lamb led to the slaughter or a sheep before the shearers, he was silent and opened not his mouth. Oppressed and condemned, he was taken away, and who would have thought any more of his destiny? When he was cut off from the land of the living, and smitten for the sin of his people, a grave was assigned him among the wicked and a burial place with evildoers, though he had done no wrong nor spoken any falsehood. But the Lord was pleased to crush him in infirmity. If he gives his life as an offering for sin, he shall see his descendants in a long life, and the will of the Lord shall be accomplished through him. Because of his affliction he shall see the light in fullness of days; through his suffering, my servant shall justify many, and their guilt he shall bear. Therefore I will give him his portion among the great, and he shall divide the spoils with the mighty, because he surrendered himself to death and was counted among the wicked; and he shall take away the sins of many, and win pardon for their offenses" (Is. 53:3–12).

All of this was in the design of God the Father for the salvation of the people He had created; this is the core of salvation history as it bridges the gap between the promise and the reality of the Church. As Vatican II states: "The Son came on a mission from His Father. It was in Him, before the foundation of the world, that the Father chose us and predestined us to become adopted sons, for in Him it has pleased the Father to re-establish all things (cf. Eph. 1:4–5; 10). The People of God believes that it is led by the Spirit of the Lord, who fills the earth. Motivated by this faith, it labors to decipher authentic signs of God's presence and purpose in the happenings, needs, and desires in which this People has a part along with other men of our age" (GS 11). (See Salvation History.)

## Server

See Acolyte; Ministries.

## Service

1. The common name often applied to any paraliturgical ceremony. It should not properly be used in referring to the celebration of the Eucharist.

2. Any social or religious work incorporating the corporal works of mercy is often called a service. (See Stewardship; Ministries.)

## Servile Work

Servile work is defined as any occupation performed by bodily action for material gain. Church law forbids all servile works, court sessions, and public markets, on Sundays and holy days of obligation.

Exception is made of the restriction against servile work when it is considered necessary for one's livelihood, the support of one's family, or for the common good of society, for example police and firemen.

## Seven Joys of the Blessed Virgin

These are events recorded in scripture together with two pronounced by the Church. They are: the Annunciation, the Visitation, the Nativity of Our Lord, the Adoration of the Magi, the Finding of the Child Jesus in the Temple, the Apparition of the Risen Christ to His Mother, the Assumption, and the Coronation of the Blessed Virgin. (See Crown, Franciscan.)

## Sex and Christianity

Sexual morality has always been considered in its Christian context as a part of the ethical and moral theological teaching. It is explained, not as merely antithetical to the positive virtue of chastity, but in its more positive aspects, including (1) the purpose of sexual morality, its moral significance in the interpersonal relationships of human persons; and (2) the effects of the individual's sexual nature and attendant behavior. Thus sexual morality is placed within the Christian moral teaching as a whole or human integral and not as only an isolated phenomenon of the human being, that is, not merely a biological process but a singular value in itself.

It thus appears that sexual activity must come under the right *order* of nature and the free *restraints* of the individual. Without this basic consideration sexual activity would only be a depersonalization and lead to anarchy in the body-spirit unity of the individual. This concept of sex recognizes the evaluative judgment whereby *sex* and *eros* have a distinct unity, the one biological and the other spiritual in expression. It places sexual energies, which admittedly have precise qualities outside of the interpersonal-love-begetting syndrome, in relation to the nature, dignity, and the spiritual significance of the human. Because of the qualities inherent in the sexual appetite, its continuous activity apart from procreation, its possibility of excess, and the need for continued enrichment of human life demanded by social living, the Christian must seek to be educated and directed by the revealed truths of faith.

In this context it is apparent that the Christian, responding to the universal command of love, must seek to acquire a content of fulfillment in the example of Christ's sacrificial love and the deeper understanding of *agape,* the love of Christian for Christian in the community. Even in the intimate person-to-person relationship of marriage, there must be the sharing, by indissoluble union, of the salvific fulfillment. In this light, human sexuality does not become a selfish expression but rather receives its value from the actions of the human will and the entire purpose of the whole of the human personality.

We can speak not of the "misuse" of sexuality, of its abuse or excess, but of that valueless approach to life that makes sex the ideological menace whereby the part is mistaken for the entire meaning and expression of life.

Because of the present day "sexual revolution" and our permissive society, there should be extensive education of the Christian—directed not at the expansion of sexual activity but at the true value of human sexuality in the light of God's truth. Thus Pope Paul VI authorized the prefect of the Doctrinal Congregation to declare:

"1. According to contemporary scientific research, the human person is so profoundly affected by sexuality that it must be considered as one of the factors which give to each individual's life the principal traits that distinguish it. In fact, it is from sex that the human person receives the characteristics which, on the biological, psychological and spiritual levels, make that person a man or a woman, and thereby largely condition his or her progress toward maturity and insertion into society. Hence sexual matters, as is obvious to everyone, today constitute a theme frequently and openly dealt with in books, reviews, magazines and other means of social communication.

"In the present period, the corruption of morals has increased, and one of the most serious indications of this corruption is the unbridled exaltation of sex. Moreover, through the means of social communication and through public entertainment this corruption has reached the point of invading the field of education and infecting the general mentality. . . .

"2. The Church cannot remain indifferent to this confusion of minds and relaxation of morals. It is a question, in fact, of a matter which is of the utmost importance both for the personal lives of Christians and for the social life of our times. . . .

"3. The people of our time are more and more convinced that the human person's dignity and vocation demand that they should discover, by the light of their own intelligence, the values innate in their nature, that they should ceaselessly develop these values and realize them in their lives, in order to achieve an ever greater development.

"In moral matters man cannot make value judgments according to his personal whim: 'In the depths of his conscience, man detects a law which he does not impose on himself, but which holds him to obedience . . . For man has in his heart a law written by God. To obey it is the very dignity of man; according to it he will be judged' (GS 16).

"Moreover, through His revelation God has made known to us Christians His plan of salvation, and He has held up to us Christ, the Savior and sanctifier, in His teaching and example, as the supreme and immutable law of life: 'I am the light of the world; anyone who follows me will not be walking in the dark, he will have the light of life' (Jn. 8:12)."

## Sexagesima

Sexagesima is the name of the second Sunday before Lent, the sixtieth day before Easter.

## Sext

The part appointed for the sixth hour of the Divine Office is called Sext. (Cf. Breviary; Divine Office; Liturgy of the Hours.)

## Shema

This is the title of the Jewish profession of faith which contains the words of the following passages of scripture: Dt. 6:4–9; 11:13–21; Nm. 15:37–41. Thus it begins: "Hear, O Israel! The Lord is our God, the Lord alone!" This creed is part of the most ancient synagogue ritual and has been used as a prayer recited by all orthodox Jews every morning and evening. A portion of the entire Shema is written on parchment and contained in the mezuzah.

## Shepherd, Good

Our Lord applied this title to Himself in the parable recorded in the Gospel of St. John (10:11). It is noted in other biblical references (Is. 40: Ez. 34); Christ, in attributing it to Himself, tells that He will offer Himself in immolation for men (Heb. 13:20).

The "shepherd" theme is one of the oldest in the Bible and has always symbolized the pursuit of God and renouncement of the world. The prophets announced that God would be the Shepherd (Am. 1:1; Jer. 22:21–22; Hos. 13:4–8) and that there would be a Messiah-Shepherd (Is. 11:2–6; Mi. 5:1–4; Jer. 3:15–17). This has been evident in other aspects of the Shepherd: His justice (Mt. 25:31–46; Rv. 12:5), His strength (1 Pt. 5:4), His sacrifice as Lamb (Jn. 10:11; Rv. 5:6). And the shepherding of the "little flock" was passed on by Christ to His Apostles and to His Church (Jn. 21:15–17; 1 Pt. 5:1–4).

## Shrine

Erected to encourage private devotion to a saint or Christian mystery, a shrine contains a picture, statue, or some central religious feature capable of inspiring devotion. The term has come to be used broadly to refer also to a special place of pilgrimage, such as Lourdes, where intense devotion or veneration is both a part of the religious motivation as well as a feature of the structure. Shrines may be set up in homes, churches, or outdoors. They should be considered as an aid to devotion rather than a curiosity or distraction.

## Shrines, Canadian

See Canadian Shrines.

## Shroud, Holy

The Holy Shroud is the winding sheet used in the burial of Christ in the tomb (Mt. 27:59–61). A famous relic, kept at Turin, usually referred to as the "Holy Shroud of Turin," is alleged to be that worn by Christ. Photographic evidence and chemical tests have demonstrated the image of a man who is claimed to be Christ. The Church has not pronounced upon this relic's authenticity. The figure is presented on the cloth in the manner current at the time of Christ's burial; that is, the sheet was placed lengthwise, the body laid upon it, and then the cloth was brought over the head and face and then again down the body's length on top before winding was wrapped around it and the body.

## Shrovetide

Shrovetide is the collective name of the few days immediately preceding Lent. It was customary to hold carnivals at this time in anticipation of the long fast of Lent. The feasting was climaxed on Shrove Tuesday, the day before Ash Wednesday, with a variously named festivity, such as Mardi Gras.

## Sign

An action performed or an object observed, which has a special religious significance, is called a *sign*. Thus the Sign of the Cross, the stole, the Sacramentary, the Crucifix, and the Lectionary are among some of the signs recognized by Catholics. The reason these are so designated is that they instill a spiritual response on the part of the one observing the object or the one performing the action. The Sacramentary on the altar is recognized as a sign because its presence is a communication of the sacred action that takes place through its use by the priest in celebrating the Eucharist.

## Sign of the Cross

The Sign of the Cross is the most frequently used sacramental of the Church. The sign is a repetition in motion of the symbol of our salvation, the cross on which Christ died. The sign of the cross is made during the Mass, at blessings, and generally at the opening and closing of prayer. The indulgenced sign is made by placing the left hand on the breast and with the right hand touching the forehead (saying: *In the name of the Father . . .*), and moving the right hand to the breast (saying: *and of the Son . . .*), then moving to touch the left shoulder (saying: *. . . and of the Holy . . .*) and then the right shoulder (saying: *. . . . Spirit. Amen . . .*). The faithful, as often as they devoutly sign themselves with the sign of the cross, are granted an indulgence of three years; whenever

they make the same holy sign with blessed water, they may gain an indulgence of seven years. (S.P. Feb. 10, 1935 and June 14, 1949).

## Sign of Peace

See Peace, Sign of; Kiss, Liturgical Use of.

## Signature

See Apostolic Signature.

## Simony

The term is derived from one Simon Magnus who tried to purchase the gift of the Holy Spirit from St. Peter (Acts 8). There are two kinds of simony:

1. Simony of divine right is the deliberate intent to buy or sell a spiritual thing, or a temporal thing connected with a spiritual thing for a price (c. 727). By spiritual things are meant graces, sacraments, prayers, etc.; a temporal thing connected with a spiritual thing is, for example, an indulgence. The price may be the money or any other consideration of value, even praise.

2. Simony of a Church right consists of the exchange of things as goods because of the irreverence to a spiritual thing connected with the exchange, for example, demanding compensation, in addition to the recognized stipend offering, for the expenses connected with divine service, such as candles, etc. The penalties are attached by canon law (c. 2392).

## Simple Feast

The lowest rank of feast celebrated in the Church is called a simple feast. (See Calendar, Church.)

## Sin

The free transgression of a divine law is a sin. Since every law is derived from the divine law, natural or positive, every transgression of a punitive law, that is, the law of legitimately constituted authority, is a sin. Sin may be *mortal* or *venial*. It is mortal when the transgression is of a divine law in a matter that is serious and when the consent to sin is made with the recognition of both the law and the serious matter. A sin is venial when it is committed out of imperfect knowledge and consent, when one transgresses a law that does not bind seriously, or when a sin is actually grave but, because of an invincibly erroneous conscience, the one committing it is ignorant of its gravity. Sin is also classified according to type: *internal sins* are those committed through use of the spiritual faculties, for example, imagination; *actual sin* is any sinful act or omission of a prescribed good act; *habitual sin* is the state of sin of one who has not repented. The sin is *formal* when it is deliberate against a law, even if the law is only supposed to exist; it is *material* when the transgression is against a law, but when knowledge of the transgression's sinfulness is lacking, there is actually no real sin because consent is lacking. (Cf. Commandments of God; Commandments of the Church.)

The Church has always taught that every sin, no matter how serious, can be forgiven (Mt. 16:19). Sin is present whenever man tries to separate himself from God and ceases, in degree, motive, matter, and circumstance to acknowledge his dependence upon God. Because of this, pride is considered the basic or fundamental sin, because it is an action that brings about a denial of the faithfulness of God (cf. 1 Cor. 10:10–13; also Jer. 14:7–9; Ps. 30:1–7).

God however pursues man with both His wrath and His love (Lv. 10:2; Nm. 11:1–3), for God's anger with humans was taken away "in Christ" (Is. 12:1–3; I Thes. 1:9–10; Rom. 5:8–10; 9:14–24), who is the infinite expression of the Father's love and His justice (1 Jn. 1:8–10; 2 Pt. 1:1–2).

Death is the result of sin, not only physical death but the spiritual death that separates the individual from God. Thus in the death of Christ and in His resurrection, our death, judgment, and resurrection are included (Jn. 5:13–19; 6:37–40). In Christ and through Him the spiritual death of man is done away with (Rom. 6:1–23; 8:1–18; 1 Cor. 5:5; 2 Cor. 1:9; Col. 3:3), and the human person will have life everlasting in the love of God (Rv. 21:2–5). Through mortification, which is our death to sin (Gal. 5:24; Rom. 8:13; Col. 2:3–5; 1 Cor. 15:31; 2 Cor. 1:5), and the physical death everyone suffers, we may all come to the fullness of life for those "who love God" (2 Cor. 5:6–8; Phil. 1:21–24).

Sin is thus seen as a disruption of the revelatory law and life given to the human person by God the Creator who wills that all be with Him in glory. Thus Vatican II teaches: "During its pilgrimage on earth, this People (of God), though still in its members liable to sin, is growing in Christ and is being gently guided by God, according to His hidden designs, until it happily arrives at the fullness of eternal glory in the heavenly Jerusalem" (UR 3).

And: "The good news of Christ constantly renews the life and culture of fallen man. It combats and removes the errors and evils resulting from sinful allurements which are a perpetual threat" (GS 58).

And: "Wherever God opens a door of speech for proclaiming the mystery of Christ (cf. Col. 4:3), there should be announced (cf. 1 Cor. 9:15; Rom. 10:14) to all men (cf. Mk. 16:15) with confidence and constancy (cf. Acts, 4:13, 29, 31; 9:27–28; 13:46; 14:3; 19:8; 26:26; 28:31; 1 Thes. 2:2; 2 Cor. 3:12; 7:4; Phil. 1:20; Eph. 3:12; 6:19–20) the living God, and He whom He has sent for the salvation of all, Jesus Christ (cf. 1 Thes. 1:9–10; 1 Cor. 1:18–21; Gal. 1:31; Acts 14:15–17; 17:22–31). Thus, when the Holy Spirit opens their heart (cf. Acts 16:14) non-Christians may believe and be freely converted to the Lord, and may sincerely cling to Him who, as 'the way, the truth, and the life' (Jn. 14:6), fulfills all their spiritual expectations, and even infinitely surpasses them" (AG 13). (See Penance, Sacrament of.)

### Singing

Following the most ancient customs and practices, the Church uses music and song in her liturgy. In the *Constitution on the Sacred Liturgy* of Vatican II (SC) there was a renewal of emphasis upon the singing by the People of God in community. "Religious singing by the people is to be skillfully fostered, so that in devotions and sacred exercises, as also during liturgical services, the voices of the faithful may ring out according to the norms and requirements of the rubrics" (SC 118).

And: "Holy Scripture, indeed, has bestowed praise upon sacred song (cf. Eph. 5:19; Col. 3:16), and the same may be said of the Fathers of the Church and of the Roman pontiffs who in recent times, led by St. Pius X, have explained more precisely the ministerial function rendered by sacred music in the service of the Lord" (SC 112).

And: "The texts intended to be sung must always be in conformity with Catholic doctrine; indeed they should be drawn chiefly from holy Scripture and from liturgical sources" (SC 121).

## Sins against the Holy Spirit

These sins, directed against the operations of the Holy Spirit in the soul, are: despair, presumption, envy, obstinacy in sin, final impenitence, and in particular the deliberate resistance to the known truth.

## Sirach, Book of

This is one of the books of wisdom of the Bible. In some translations it is called "Ecclesiasticus," which is derived from the Latin meaning "Book of the Church" *(Liber Ecclesiasticus)*. This book, in the Greek manuscripts of the Bible, is referred to as "The Wisdom of Jesus, Son of Sirach" or simply "The Wisdom of Sirach." It is included in the books of the Bible of the Catholic Church but is not recognized as canonical by the Jews and Protestants.

The authorship of this book is "Jesus, Son of Eleazar, son of Sirach" (50:27) and is along with Jeremiah one of the two books of the OT with a proclaimed author. It was written in the first half of the second century B.C.

In content the book is a typical compilation of Hebrew writings regarding the wisdom attained in life. It stresses good morals, a true philosophy of life, and the joys and sufferings one endures. Several quotations from the Book of Sirach are included among the sayings of rabbis in the Talmud. The text, not included in the Latin translation of Jerome, is from the older version made from the Greek. However, the existence of a Hebrew text and its verity in transmission have been made evident in the finding of the Scrolls of the Dead Sea.

The teaching of Sirach is that wisdom not only comes from God to humans but is an attribute of God Himself. It is also considered to be a preparation for the exercise of God's will in revealing Himself through the Eternal word, Christ (cf. Sir. 24).

## Sisters

Sisters is the name of the women members of a religious community or order. Usually there is this distinction: sisters are religious women with simple vows; nuns have taken solemn vows (c. 488). There are many groups of sisters who follow a particular order and whose lives are devoted to special works of charity. Among their manifold tasks are caring for the sick, teaching, perpetual adoration. (See Women.)

## Sistine Chapel

Called the "pope's chapel," this is the principal chapel of the Vatican palace. It is here that the consistory of cardinals meets to elect a new pope. The present chapel was begun in 1473 and completed only at the turn of the fifteenth century. It is most notable for its murals by the painters Michelangelo and Raphael, especially the ceiling frescoes by the former, which depict the creation and the religious aspirations of man.

## Sistine Choir

A group of twenty-four men and boys who are under expert direction and training and serve as the choir of the Sistine Chapel. The choir director is called *maestro di cappella,* and the group always sings without musical accompaniment, or *a cappella.* The choir was originally formed by Pope Hilary (d. 468) and was endowed by Pope Gregory the Great. It was one of the first choirs and has the longest continuous period of service in history, of the *schola cantorum,* which have served as training centers for leaders of liturgical singing. (See Singing; Music.)

## Situation Ethics

See Ethics, Situation.

## Skull-cap

See Zucchetto.

## Slander

The utterance, communication, and attribution of falsehoods about another person, which is sinful against charity and justice, is called slander. (See Calumny.)

## Sloth

See Capital Sins.

## Social Action

These words express the concept of "activity within a society," although this is not an entire explanation of the nature of what is involved.

Perhaps the best understanding can come through a declaration of what social action is not. It is not a panacea for the ills of society. It is not a familial, labor, rural, urban, professional, unskilled, youth or elderly attainment of privileges or concessions. It is not a welfare-oriented, racially focused, or nationalistic-minded program. It is not the individual activist nor the organization which is socially directed.

What then is social action? Perhaps the best way to come to an understanding of social action is to judge the *response* it elicits. Thus the employer who achieves a fair wage schedule, who bargains collectively, who accommodates the needs of his workers and adjusts accordingly, may be said to practice social action in accord with justice and charity. The employee who works fairly, does not defraud his employer, who acts in accord with justice and charity is also engaged in social action. The same may be said for those individuals or organizations engaged in the racial, rural, urban, welfare, medical, ethical, professional, and non-professional spheres. It is the gauging of the response that brings meaning to social action of whatever kind or intensity. For it is reasonable to see that if one shouts at or hits others over the head with a call to action and does not change the condition in the least degree, he or she has only been an activist, a do-gooder, or a theoretician.

When one analyses the response to a given instance of social action, one may find a more clear picture. And this brings us to a consideration of motivation for action. Why should one act for the good of society? Thus when one examines serious motive, one is immediately faced with the religious aspect of all action in behalf of society or one's fellowman. We arrive at the Christian concept of human society, at the right moral judgment that must make up the societal framework of man's enterprise. This is true and applicable to the many spheres of social action be it sociopolitical, socioreligious, socioeconomic, or sociojudicial.

The Christian concept of social action is one in which the participants, individuals, or organizations, the dispensers or the recipients have a conscious knowledge of, regard for, and application of the principles of justice and charity as known in natural and divine law. Without this, social action becomes activist-oriented, action for its own sake, and devoid of lasting response on the part of anyone.

Christian social doctrine has been clearly expressed and applies to all: the deprived, the racially distinct, the affluent, the skilled and professional, the trained and untrained, the physically unfortunate, and the physically strong. It is evident that when justice and charity are lacking the very organism perishes. Corruption sets in when those Christian teachings that made it viable cease to direct its actions. This is true of the family, business, government, or the courts.

Christianity has added a dimension to the entire social life of the community of human persons. Addressing himself to the domestic, civil, political, labor, and all other areas where salutary action would have effect, Pope Leo XIII stated in an apostolic letter of March 19, 1902, the social concept that springs from the font of Christianity. He declared in part: "Just as Christianity cannot penetrate the soul without making it better, so it cannot enter into public life without establishing order. With the idea of a God who governs all, who is infinitely wise, good, and just, the idea of duty at once seizes upon the consciences of men. It assuages sorrow, it calms hatred, it engenders heroes. If Christianity has transformed pagan society—and that transformation was a veritable resurrection, for barbarism disappeared in proportion as Christianity extended its sway—then, too, after the terrible shocks which unbelief has given to the world in our days, it will be able to set that world again on the true road, and bring back to their true order the states and peoples of modern times. But the return of Christianity will not be efficacious and complete if it does not restore the world to a sincere love of the one, holy, Catholic, and Apostolic Church.

"In the Catholic Church, Christianity is incarnate. She identifies herself with that perfect, spiritual, and, in its own order, sovereign society, which is the mystical body of Jesus Christ, and which has for its visible head the Roman Pontiff, successor of the Prince of the Apostles. She is the continuation of the mission of the Savior, the daughter of the heiress of His redemption. She has preached the Gospel, and has defended it at the price of her blood, and strong in the divine assistance and of that immortality which has been promised her, she makes no terms with error, but remains faithful to the commands which she has received to carry the doctrine of Jesus Christ to the uttermost limits of the world and to the end of time, and to protect it in its inviolable integrity. Legitimate dispenser of the teachings of the Gospel, she does not reveal herself only as the consoler and redeemer of souls, but she is still more the internal source of justice and charity, and the propagator as well as the guardian of true liberty, and, no less of the equality which alone is possible here below. In applying the doctrine of her divine Founder, she maintains a wise equilibrium and marks the true limits between the rights and privileges of society. The equality which she proclaims does not destroy the distinction between the different social classes, she keeps them intact, as nature itself demands, in order to oppose the anarchy of reason emancipated from faith, and abandoned to its own devices. The liberty which she gives in no wise conflicts with the rights of truth, because these rights are superior to the demands of liberty. Nor does she infringe upon the rights of justice, because these rights are superior to the claims of mere numbers or power. Nor does she assail the rights of God because they are superior to the rights of humanity."

Thus social action for the Christian takes on the fundamental role of spreading the gospel of Christ and bringing to everyone the beneficence of His teaching. Social action is Christian action applied in all the areas of human endeavor; it is the applied mission of everyone of faith. (Cf. Sociology; Society.)

## Social Encyclicals

The Church recognizes a society among men which, from the beginning, was guided by God (Ex. 19:3–6), and which was to be brought to salvation (Is. 53). No Christian is a person apart, but stands as an individual in the Church as a whole (1 Cor. 12:12–27; Rom. 12:4–5; Col. 1:18; Eph. 1:22–23). It is, however, in the community, the love of member for member, that each will find fulfillment in society (Eph. 4:12–16).

With the urgent demand of Christ, that all might be "one," the Church has been concerned for human society, the social status of the workingman, professional, or governmental leader, and for the common good through which the human person must strive to fulfill his or her role of membership in the Church and in society. To this end the Popes have spoken on many occasions regarding the nature of the society in which the individual may best fulfill this hope.

The collective term "social encyclicals" refers to the twelve encyclicals of Pope Leo XIII. Others of more recent times must be added to these because all contribute to the social doctrine of the Church.

The social encyclicals of Pope Leo XIII are: *Inscrutabili*, "On the Evils of Society"; *Quod Apostolici Muneris*, "On the Socialists"; *Arcanum*, "On Christian Marriage"; *Diuturnum*, "On Civil Government"; *Immortale Dei*, "On the Christian Constitution of States"; *In Plurimis*, "On the Abolition of African Slavery"; *Libertas Humana*, "On Human Liberty"; *Sapientiae Christianae*, "Chief Duties of Christian Citizens"; *Rerum Novarum*, "On the Condition of the Workingmen"; *Laetitiae Sanctae*, "The Rosary and the Social Question"; *Annum Sacrum*, "Consecration of Mankind to the Sacred Heart"; *Graves de Communi*, "On Christian Popular Action."

To these must be added the modern extensions of the social thinking of the Church: *Quadregesimo Anno*, "Fortieth Year," of Pius XI, commemorating the issuance of *Rerum Novarum; Mater et Magistra*, "Christianity and Social Progress" of Pope John XXIII; *Pacem in Terris*, "Peace on Earth" by Pope John XXIII and *Populorum Progressio*, "Development of Peoples" by Paul VI. (See under separate listings.)

## Socialism

The scientific phase of this movement, which sprung from the sources of liberalism, began with the leaders F. Lassalle (d. 1864), Karl Marx (d. 1883), and Frederick Engels (d. 1895). It was given impetus with the publication of the *Communist Manifesto* (1848) and the appearance of *Das Kapital* in 1867. Its basic purpose was to unite workers into a political party, to end private ownership of the means of production, and to exclude religion from education. It was opposed by the Church, notably by Pope Leo XIII. The American bishops declared in an extended statement for social reconstruction (Feb. 12, 1919): "Socialism would mean bureaucracy, political tyranny, the helplessness of the individual as a factor in the ordering of his own life, and in general social inefficiency and decadence."

In recent Church thought much has been written in twentieth century encyclicals concerning the "determining of a particular government" for peoples according to their "life style." Since this is a free choice in which the individual may participate only insofar as there is a clear exercise of freedom, some have assumed that the role of democracy is circumscribed by the political and economic factors over which the people have little or no control. It was this which brought John XXIII to state in his encyclical, *Mater et Magistra:* ". . . the course of events thus far makes it clear that there cannot be a prosperous and well-ordered society unless both private citizens and public authorities work together in economic affairs." To misconstrue the Church's social teaching as promoting a socializing process from an outside derived ideology is to misunderstand the position of the Church in society, for this is not a doctrine of social conformity in government but one of adapting the roles of Church and State to the best course for all individuals.

## Society

The interaction of individuals in the totality of relationships, whether a system of government, or a relationship based on language, custom, or unity of objective, is broadly called a society. It places responsibility and constitutes or recognizes authority. Only when society transcends itself is it able to seek fellowship, which gives the human persons the purpose and mutuality of means that enable them to attain goals satisfying to all.

In this light the Christian community, united under the bond with Christ in teaching and seeking salvation, comes to recognize its eschatological fulfillment (cf. Rom. 5:12–19; 1 Cor.

15:20–22; Acts 10:34–35). Through faith and love the individual acts in and serves the society of Christ's founding (cf. Eph. 4:11–16).

Vatican II teaches: "Thus she [the Church] shows the world that an authentic union, social and external, results from a union of minds and hearts, namely, from that faith and charity by which her own unity is unbreakably rooted in the Holy Spirit. For the force which the Church can inject into the modern society of man consists in that faith and charity put into vital practice, not in any external dominion exercised by merely human means" (GS 42).

And: "The common welfare of society consists in the entirety of those conditions of social life under which men enjoy the possibility of achieving their own perfection in a certain fullness of measure and also with some relative ease. Hence this welfare consists chiefly in the protection of the rights, and in the performance of the duties, of the human person. Therefore, the care of the right to religious freedom devolves upon the people as a whole, upon social groups, upon government, and upon the Church and other religious communities, in virtue of the duty of all the common welfare, and in the manner proper to each. . . .

"Government is to assume the safeguard of the religious freedom of all its citizens, in an effective manner, by just laws and by other appropriate means. Government is also to help create conditions favorable to the fostering of religious life, in order that the people may be truly enabled to exercise their religious rights and to fulfill their religious duties, and also in order that society itself may profit by the moral qualities of justice and peace which have their origin in man's faithfulness to God and to His holy will" (DH 6).

### Society, Religious

A religious society is a body of clerics, regular or secular, organized for performing an apostolic work.

### Socinianism

Developed by Socinus (d. 1604), this system of the Unitarian sect taught that Christ was only a lesser God who was given assignment by the Supreme God. Its followers were called "Socinians" or "Polish Brethren."

### Sociology

The name of this study of society and social relations is derived from a word first coined by Auguste Comte (d. 1857). As a science, its concept

of society is involved and its method is still developing in practice and study.

Sociology is the science of social activity wherein groups, institutions, and society itself function. It is an undeveloped science because of the difficulty of establishing norms for a wide variety of application, for example, political sociology, religious sociology, and industrial sociology. In both method and the arbitrary application of norms, sociology falls short of a true discipline in the scientific sense and comes closer to being an ideological exercise than an empirical technique.

### Sod-Church

This simple structure that made use of the material at hand was a singular phenomenon of the pioneer Church in North America. As Christians moved westward across the prairies, they could not obtain building materials. Consequently they used the sod of the countryside to build churches so that the worship of God could be continued while they were establishing themselves on the farmlands about them. Today only remnants of such churches exist in any degree of recognition, but there are some crude homes that were built at the same time (mid-1800s) and retain parts made of sod, especially in the sheep-grazing parts of the country.

### Sodality

A sodality is an association of the faithful for the promotion of piety, charity, and public worship. It may be either a pious union or a confraternity (c. 684ff).

### SODEPAX

This is the abbreviated title of The Joint Commission on Society, Development and Peace, which is an agency of the World Council of Churches (WCC) and the Pontifical Commission for Justice and Peace.

### Solea

Solea is the name given to the step or rise before the holy doors at which communion is given in Byzantine and Eastern Churches.

### Solesmes

This title has come to be addressed to both a musical method and the place where that method was first developed.

1. The place is the famous Benedictine monastery located in the area of Sarthe, France, dedicated to St. Peter. It was founded in 1010, but its

modern history begins with Dom Prosper Gueranger who settled there in 1833 with five other priests. In 1837 Gregory XVI, by constitution, declared this an abbey and the head of the French Benedictine congregation and named Gueranger its first abbot. Under the direction of its first abbot the monastery became the center of the liturgical movement in France and took a special place in the development of liturgical music. For a time (1901 to 1922) Solesmes was vacant because the monks had been expelled by the French government under a barrage of anticlerical legislation. Meanwhile the monks took up their work at Quarr Abbey on the Isle of Wight and returned to Solesmes in 1922.

2. Solesmes became the seat of the greatest resurgence, development, and culmination of the artistic expression of Gregorian chant, which became known throughout the world as the Solesmes Method. The basic principles of the method are: Gregorian rhythm is specifically of a musical nature and not the rhythm of human speech; the steps in the rhythmical synthesis are defined as the invisible primary beat, the elementary rhythms and binary and ternary compound beats, and composite rhythms; there is a complete independence of rhythm and stress; the rhythm is free from tonic stress in its movement; words are subordinate to the melody; and the traditional interpretation is followed in the expression of the music itself.

The Solesmes Method is recognized as achieving the highest spiritual expression of both the art of music and the sung prayer of the Church. It is the juncture at which liturgical participation and the divine worship of the Church meet and give guidance and inspiration to the present day expression of musical participation in the liturgy.

### Solemnity
See Feasts of the Church.

### Solitude
Individual solitude or separation from the world has always been considered a means of achieving a greater union with God. The prophets of old sought solitude to converse with God (Ex. 3:1–15; 1 Kgs. 19:9–18; 2 Kgs. 4:25), and Christ separated Himself from all as a preparation for His ministry to the world (Mt. 4:1–11). And early Christians lived in a spirit of separation from the world, thus giving an example for the much later times of monasticism (Acts 2:42–44; 4:32–37).

The hermits and anchorites of the early Church, the religious of the Cistercian and Carthusian Orders, and other groups of religious lived in solitude and many still do. This practice is also true of Oriental religions. In recent times it was practiced by such individuals as Henry David Thoreau in the nineteenth century and John Muir. Solitude is a basis for the retreats made by Christians and for other groups who seek some communication with God through prayer and meditation. (See Retreat.)

### Solomon
One of the dominant figures (d. about 933 B.C.) of the OT, Solomon was the first of the Kings of Israel to worship in a permanent Temple where the Ark of the Covenant was retained (cf. 1 Sm. 7:2–7; 1 Kgs. 8:1–13). As a king he ruled with justice but also followed the law (1 Kgs. 5:4–5; 1 Chr. 22:9; 1 Kgs. 3:16–28). It was Solomon who organized the country of Israel and through his wisdom, granted by God (1 Kgs. 3:4–15), became one who participated in governing the world as God wished; in this sense Solomon is a prefiguration of Christ. But Christ was greater because through Him the Holy Spirit was given to human persons to guide and direct them (Lk. 11:13, 31; 1 Cor. 2:6–16).

Solomon's reign was the high point of the ancient glory of Israel (cf. Mt. 6:29). His efforts at centralization of the government failed because the leaders of the twelve tribes were against such controls, and so after Solomon's death the kingdom was divided. Solomon's reign is remembered for the buildings he erected, especially the Temple. Hebrew writing attained its highest standards during his kingship, and it was probably because of this that there were many works of wisdom literature and poems attributed to him.

### Son of God
See Christ.

## Son of Man

This title is ascribed to Christ who alone is both God and man. As used by Christ in referring to Himself (Mt. 9:6), it means that Our Lord as a man among men claims to exercise the authority of God in heaven, and it is a declaration of the doctrine of the Incarnation.

## Song of Ascents

Song of Ascents is the collective name for the fifteen Psalms, 120 to 134 inclusive. The most probable reason for this title is that they form a collection of Pilgrim Psalms or songs that were sung by the pilgrims on their way up to the great Temple of Jerusalem for the annual celebration of the high feasts. (See Psalms, Book of.)

## Song of Songs

Also called the Canticle of Canticles, this book is listed as one of the wisdom writings of the OT. The title means that this song is one of exceptional excellence among the poetic writings of the Bible. It has been attributed to Solomon, but he is not considered the author since critical analysis of the language, with some words of Aramaic origin and some of Persian and Greek, indicates a time of composition about four and a half centuries B.C., although some passages are dated at possibly the eighth century B.C.

There are five poems in the Song of Songs. It has exotic dialogue, playing upon the boundless love of the figure of God (the lover) and His grace and Who reminds His bride of her faithlessness (His people) and recalls the former happiness and strength of their first love, together with a call for her to return. It is expressed in terms of physical love.

There are many opinions among scholars as to whether this is a dialogue "à deux," one between God and His People, or whether the words prefigure the future love of Christ for His Church. However, it cannot be said that this is a dialogue of physical love (Eros) or of spiritual love (caritas) or of the obligations of married joy and love. Most probably it is an allegorical expression of mutual love, first between Christ and His Church, as St. Bernard liked to declare, or between Christ and the individual of which Cardinal Newman was fond. That the Song of Songs uses lush language and that it utilizes marriage as a traditional biblical symbol (cf. Jn. 3:29; 2 Cor. 11:2; Eph. 5:23–32; Rv. 19:7–9) cannot be denied, but the reader may surely be inspired by the poetic expression of the time, which makes the Song of Songs a very beautiful writing of the OT.

## Sophonia, Book of

See Zephaniah, Book of.

## Sorrows of the Blessed Virgin Mary

Sometimes referred to as the Seven Dolors, they are: the prophecy of Simeon (Lk. 2:34), the flight into Egypt (Mt. 2:13), the loss of Christ on the visit to Jerusalem (Lk. 2:46), Christ on the way to Calvary, the crucifixion, the descent from the cross, and the entombment of Christ (Lk. 23:49–56). A memorial of Our Lady of Sorrows (Sept. 15) in the calendar of the Church commemorates these trials and sorrows of the Blessed Virgin Mary.

## Soteriology

In theology, this is the study of the central thesis of the Christian doctrine, that is, the salvation and sanctification accomplished by Christ (Rom. 3:23–25).

The word comes from the Greek meaning "salvation." It is in the theological sense that these dogmatic considerations form a systematic theology, that is, of understanding that salvation could not come about by man's work, but only through the freely given grace of God's communication of Himself and the efficacious grace that brings about man's response to God as revealed. (See Salvation; Salvation History.)

## Soul

The soul is the real spiritual substance created by God (Gn. 2:7) which, united to the body, constitutes a man. Man is of the "image of God" (Gn. 1:26–27); the soul is immortal (Mt. 10:28). The soul is declared by the Council of Vienne to be the immediate substantial form of the body. (Cf. Immortality of the Soul.)

The soul is the primary force of the subjective composite of consciousness, memory, decision, freedom, and the very principle of the human person's activity. It is of the very substance of the human being; thus it is what man makes of himself and what he can become. It is the principle of the human person's being.

To understand the soul, it is necessary to look at the person in relation to his capability for sin and redemption. Theologically it is through this recognition of human sinfulness that we arise from the plane of nature to that of grace. The Bible does not recognize the Greek dichotomy of body and soul. The spirit (soul) of the human person is the noblest part (cf. Rom. 8:14–16; 1 Cor. 2:10–13; Gal. 5:16), but in the OT the spirit is considered as life itself, that which God breathes into the person (Gn. 2:7; 6:17) and without this the body is dead (Nm.

16:22; Jb. 12:9–10; Lk. 12:16–20). Man by himself, a creature of flesh and blood, is a human entity without grace, incapable of achieving his own redemption. This could only come through being born again through Christ and the Holy Spirit (Mt. 16:17; 1 Cor. 15:50; Eph. 4:22–30; 6:10–13; Jn. 8).

## Soutane
See Cassock.

## Spanish Inquisition
See Inquisition, Spanish.

## Spanish Missions
See California Missions.

## Spiration
See Procession, Divine.

## Spirit, Holy
See Holy Spirit.

## Spiritism
Spiritism is the general term for the means and systems of trying to communicate with departed souls. This is attempted through often elaborately faked practices using seances, table-tapping, ouija boards, and aspects of witchcraft. The spiritualist sins against religion, and although the apparent manipulation of psychic phenomena may not be readily discerned, there is no proved or recorded instance of a spirit (psyche or soul) communicating with living individuals. (See Synteresis.)

## Spiritual Exercises of St. Ignatius
Written by St. Ignatius Loyola (d. 1556), the practical considerations and meditations contained in this book are directed to the amendment of one's life and the achievement of personal sanctification; they are psychologically penetrating. The first portion is devoted to the consequences of sin, the second to Christ as the exemplar, the third to amendment in imitation of Christ, and the fourth to the award of the good.

## Spiritual Works of Mercy
Seven in number, these are: to convert sinners, instruct the ignorant, counsel the wayward, comfort the sorrowing, bear adversities patiently, forgive offenses, and pray for the living and the dead.

## Spiritualism
See Spiritism.

## Spirituality
The presence of Christ in His Church makes possible the general and individual response to the gifts of God through the Holy Spirit. Through the special gift of the Holy Spirit, the faithful, individually and collectively, effect those manifestations "which are essential to a missionary activity which is still going on and growing, and indeed, which makes this activity possible" (E. Schweizer).

The People of God are given new and enriched means whereby there is a rebirth in the Spirit of truth and love (Jn. 3:3–5; 4:23–24; 6:63; 20:19–29). Through preaching and the sacraments, through devotion and prayer, the dynamic extension of the mystery of the Church is made possible. Thus the individual and the faithful can come to a realization of salvation. There is a unified society of human persons in the "bond of love" whereby an interior-exterior development will assure a renewal in the Spirit. This brings about the social effectiveness of the faith through its exercise, not simply in the action-encounter-with-God idea of Tielhardism.

Coming to the specifics of spirituality, we must begin with the individual. Without this a general resurgence is not possible wherein the spirituality of the Church militant can become effective. There must be a kerygma, a learning (Jn. 6:44–58), prayer and worship, on the part of individuals (Jn. 7:37) and in community (Jn. 8:27–29; cf. also Jn. 13:17; 15:4; Lk. 11:1–8; 22:17–20).

Vatican II teaches: "Neither family concerns nor other secular affairs should be excluded from their (the laity's) religious program of life. For as the Apostle states, 'Whatever you do, whether in speech or in action, do it in the name of the Lord Jesus. Give thanks to God the Father through him' (Col. 3:17). . . .

"The layman's religious program of life should take its special quality from his status as a married man and a family man, or as one who is unmarried or widowed, from his state of health, and from his professional and social activity. He should not cease to develop earnestly the qualities and talents bestowed on him in accord with these conditions of life, and he should make use of the gifts which he has received from the Holy Spirit" (AA 4).

## Sponsors
A sponsor is (1) the person who offers and speaks for one in baptism and assumes certain spiritual responsibilities; (2) the person who stands for one receiving the Sacrament of Confirmation. Church law requires that the sponsors for *baptism* (at least one and never more than two) should be

fourteen or more years of age, should be baptized, have the use of reason, and intend to undertake the responsibility. A sponsor may not be the father, mother, or spouse of the one baptized; he must be named by the parents or guardian; during the act of baptism he must touch the person baptized personally, or through a proxy. His responsibility is to watch over the religious education of the child. A sponsor contracts a spiritual relationship with the person baptized. In *Confirmation* the sponsor must be already confirmed, have the use of reason, and intend to act in this capacity. He must be a Catholic in good standing and may not be a parent or spouse of the one confirmed; he must be chosen by the parents or guardian, unless custom intervenes, and may during the ceremony touch the one confirmed personally or by proxy.

### Spoon, Liturgical

In the Easter Church Rites the spoon, usually of precious metal or gold or silver plated, is used for the giving of communion. In the Western Church, including the Roman Rite, the spoon has become an adjunct to the giving of wine in Holy Communion, especially to the sick who are unable to swallow with ease even a particle of bread.

### Staff

See Crosier.

### Stained Glass

Stained glass is a widely used art form that has been widely adapted to the decoration of church buildings or religiously oriented structures, and sometimes homes and other buildings. Chiefly, stained glass has become an expression of religion. Its best use is a perpetually decorative and silent proclamation of the story of God's love.

Stained glass is an art form in itself. Good stained glass becomes a part of the architectural whole; as a window it is a part of the wall.

Originated in the twelfth and thirteenth centuries, stained glass windows have become in many instances great art treasures, for example, the windows of the Cathedrals of Chartres and Mont St. Michele.

Unlike painting where color is placed on something, the color in stained glass is contained within the substance itself. Metallic ingredients such as gold, cobalt, chromium, and iron oxides are added to the glass while it is in a molten state. Some stains are painted on white glass to produce yellow tones, or a pigment of a reddish brown or black powdered oxide is added and made permanent by fusing with the surface of the glass at high temperatures.

Tiffany glass, used widely in America in the late nineteenth century, was developed by Louis Comfort Tiffany (1848 to 1933) after French experiments. The process achieved a soft brilliance by fusing powdered mother-of-pearl into the glass.

The antique methods of producing stained glass were of two kinds: (1) molten glass was poured onto a flat metal or stone surface, spread out thinly, and then cooled; (2) a fixed amount of molten glass was dropped on a flat surface, and it cooled into a flat circle with a raised center. Stained glass today comes in a variety of thicknesses and is made in sheets for the most part.

The art of stained glass is in the design, the use of color, the assembly of the colored pieces, and the fixing of them by strips of lead, and a final cementing and waterproofing. Some glass is stained and fired at a high temperature (1200° or more) and thus the features or delineated lines of the design are made permanent.

More recently the use of stained glass in faceted patterns has been introduced. In this process color is the predominant characteristic. Colored slab glass, up to an inch or more in thickness, is faceted by a process of shelling. This is done by striking the edge of the slab, or a measured part, with a metal hammer. This causes the glass to break away, leaving facets where the shelled piece is broken loose, and these facets give a jewel-like quality and sparkle to the glass. The glass slabs once faceted are embedded in an epoxy resin and while the epoxy appears cement-like, the faceted glass appears to be a decorative pattern of sparkling colors. (See Rose Window.)

### Stasidia

From the Greek meaning "standing places," this is the name given to the seats or benches behind the altar and in front of the iconostasis and extending around the walls of Byzantine

Churches. These are usually stood before rather than sat upon.

### State of Grace

The state of grace is the condition of the soul having habitual grace. (See Grace.)

### Stations of the Cross

Also called "The Way of the Cross," this devotion to the passion of Christ consists of prayers and meditations on fourteen occurrences experienced by Christ on His way to the crucifixion. The devotion is conducted either by the faithful personally, making the way from one station to another and saying the prayers, or by having the officiating priest move from cross to cross while the faithful make the responses. For the stations themselves there must be fourteen wooden crosses (pictures alone do not suffice), and they must be blessed by one with authority to erect stations. The devotion is heavily indulgenced.

### Stations, Roman

In early times, the Roman Stations were the churches of Rome and its environs to which the people and clergy went in procession. A church was designated for each day (eighty-four in all), and there the pope or his representative sang Mass. The days were those of Lent, Ember days, Sundays of Advent, and certain feasts.

### Status Animarum

From the Latin meaning "state" or "condition of souls" the *Status Animarum* is an annual report submitted to the ordinary of a diocese or ecclesial jurisdiction by pastors of parishes, administrators or heads of missions. It is submitted through the chancery office and is an official declaration of pertinent and essential information.

This report supplies the following information: (1) the names of the priests in residence, the outside assistants (visiting clergy or assigned priests), and the deacons who serve the parish; (2) the size of the parish, including the number of Catholics, children, their ages, together with attendance at Sunday Mass, the number of Black Catholics, American Indian Catholics, Spanish-speaking Catholics; (3) the number of envelope-holding (offering) members, the number of families in the parish, along with some substantiation of how the population figures were arrived at, such as the most recent parish census; (4) a statistical report including the number of baptisms, converts, and the administration of the sacraments; (5) the types of services provided, the schedule of Masses, the attendance figures, the confession schedule, devotions or other paraliturgical services, the visitation of the sick or confined, and a listing of the public and private institutions within the parish boundaries and served by the parish pastoral care; (6) a report on the school and the convent housing teachers together with the pertinent information concerning their apostolate; (7) a cemetery report for those parishes or institutes where a cemetery is a part of the parochial properties; (8) the organizational life of the parish, together with the names of officers, the parish council, and its makeup and accreditation; (9) a summary of the educational program offered by the parish, both the CCD program and adult religious education; (10) separate reports on all parish properties, their use and supervision; (11) the vocations to clerical or religious life, with detailed accounting; (12) the ecumenical activity of the parish; (13) the complete fiscal financial state of the parish; and (14) a parish profile, particularly including any extension of services. All reports are signed and dated.

In the modern parish greater emphasis is placed upon the types of service, the means of spreading the message of Christ, and an in-depth analysis of the makeup of the parish. This is in keeping with the greater involvement of people in the mission of the Church and the establishment of a sense of community within the parish, especially as it relates to the wider aspects of the Church in the diocese, the nation, and the world. Through this there is an applied means of keeping the parish from becoming "parochial" in its limiting sense and providing greater awareness of the various apostolates within the Church, which must reach out to Christians everywhere. (See Parish.)

### Sterilization

The operation performed upon male or female persons whereby they are made incapable of begetting children through the act of sexual intercourse is condemned by the Church, in particular in the encyclical *Casti Connubi* of Pius XII (Dec. 31, 1939). This practice is also condemned when it is directed at the mentally deficient, epileptics, and the handicapped, even though civil law has in many instances provided for this under the pragmatic reasoning of limiting children in the state or nation who might be genetically deficient.

### Stewardship

The concept of stewardship is derived from scripture. Its premise is the bounty given by God who is the Creator and the giver of all goods (Lv.

25:23; 1 Chr. 29:14; Ps. 24:1); the use of a thing is a practical step (Gn. 26:25) whereby one uses God's bounty wisely (Lk. 16:1–8; 6:38; Mt. 25:23; Gal. 6:2). Stewardship was the accepted Christian principle of applied good practice, even as a common purse was maintained for necessities and alms by the Apostles as they walked with Christ (Jn. 13:29), and it was derived from the thankfulness given to God (cf. Ps. 116:12). Likewise, Christians were given the urgent role to share and sustain each other (Acts 16:9; Phil. 4:15; 1 Cor. 4:2–7; 15:58; 2 Cor. 9:6; Jas. 1:17; 2 Tm. 2:5; Gal. 6:10). Stewardship today is the practical and shared methods whereby all respond to the mission of Christ to build up the Body of Christ in the world.

Stewardship as it applies to the modern Church is the ministry of the individual person who serves, together with a sharing of his benefits for the aid of others. It is sacrificial giving, which has been translated into a formula of the three *T's: time, talent,* and *treasure.* (Some add a fourth, *tenacity* or perseverance.) All form the methodology of the Christian's response to the fulfilling of the mission of the Church.

In application the first consideration is that of *time.* One takes the time to serve in some capacity: as one ordained, as a permanent deacon, as an extraordinary minister, as a minister, as a trustee, as a parish council member, and as an organization person. Each role wherein one serves the cause of "building up the Body of Christ" demands the giving of time.

The second is that of *talent.* As all are called to serve the building up of the Body of Christ (cf. 1 Cor. 3:1–23), which they should do because they have "knowledge" of a sacred and special nature (cf. 1 Cor. 8:10–12). The God-given talents or abilities of Christians are to be shared to the extent that they may be used by each person through grace to accomplish the work of God in the world. These talents need not be great skills but may be even the most simple open-hearted response to help others. Upon those who have great abilities the incumbent responsibility is greater.

The third is *treasure.* God has given to each something that can be shared with others. The financial burden of the exercise of religion is great in every age. Not to respond with alms for the Church and the People of God is to fail:

> Now thus says the Lord of hosts: Consider your ways! you have sown much, but have brought in little; you have eaten, but have not been satisfied;

> You have drunk, but have not been exhilarated; have clothed yourselves, but not been warmed;
> And he who earned wages earned them for a bag with holes in it (Hg. 1:5–6).

Through these three means the Church is called upon to exercise the gifts given to her to sustain and advance the light of human decency and to bring about personal human involvement whereby the mission of Christ is fulfilled in the world. This is the message given to all, men and women, young and old.

In the United States the impetus toward stewardship was given by such companies as Postal Church Service, Youngstown, Ohio and others. A National Catholic Stewardship Council has been established, whose headquarters are located at: 1234 Massachusetts Avenue, N.W., Washington, D.C. 20005.

### Stigmata

From the Greek, meaning "marks," this refers in Church use to the wounds, scars, or skin abrasions that appear on the flesh of individuals. They correspond to the wounds suffered by Christ in the crucifixion. Stigmata are accompanied by pain. Numerous instances are recorded of this charism having been bestowed on persons of unusual holiness, more than three hundred in all.

The majority of the stigmata are external, visible, and very painful. There are other marks of Our Lord's passion which are not visible, for example, those of St. Catherine of Sienna who requested that they not be evident. These are called invisible stigmata and are equally painful.

### Stikharion

In Eastern and Byzantine Churches, this is a priestly vestment that corresponds to the alb in the Roman Rite.

### Stipend

The voluntary offering now given to a priest is not meant as a monetary equivalent of the Mass but is representative of the bread and wine formerly given to the clergy by the faithful for use in the Mass. The amount of the stipend may vary in amount, but the minimum offering may be established by local law to avoid confusion. The acceptance of a stipend by a priest is a serious obligation to fulfill the intention, and the offering must be definite, for example, a priest may not say a Mass after a casual remark and then ask for a stipend from the person. Stipends are either *manual,* that is, given directly by the person out of devotion; or *quasi-manual,* that is, offerings from some fund established for that purpose. Stipends are governed by law of the Church (cc. 824-844).

## Stole

This vestment, a long, narrow strip of cloth the same color as the other vestments, is worn by the priest as a mark of his priestly office. The priest wears the stole about the neck, both ends hanging down in front, whereas the deacon wears it across his left shoulder and crossed at the oposite side beneath the arm. A purple stole is worn by a priest when administering the Sacrament of Penance, a white when giving Benediction of the Blessed Sacrament or the anointing of the sick, and a stole of the color of the feast (or white) when preaching.

## Stole-Fee

The sum given to the celebrant for performing parochial functions, for example, administering baptism or assisting at marriage, is called a stole-fee. The fee may be fixed as a definite amount by the local ordinary (cc. 1234-1237). However there are no stole-fees that may be demanded of the priest for the administering of services, for example, bringing the Holy Eucharist to a sick person or administering the anointing of the sick.

## Stylite

The term has been applied to a hermit who had his hermitage atop a pillar.

## Subdeacon

This order has been dropped as a part of the Sacrament of Holy Orders. (See Orders, Holy, Sacrament of.)

## Sub-Delegate

See Delegation.

## Subreption

In canon law subreption is the term for the suppression or distortion of truth in a petition for a favor by rescript.

## Suburbicarian Dioceses

These are the seven dioceses nearest to Rome: Albano, Frascati, Ostia, Palestina, Porto, Santa Rufina, and Velletri. Their bishops are designated cardinal-bishops, and each works in one or more of the Congregations or Commissions of the Vatican. (Cf. Cardinal.)

## Suffragan Bishop

A bishop of a diocese of a province other than the metropolitan is called a suffragen bishop. (Cf. Bishop.)

## Suffrages

Suffrages are additional prayers of the Divine Office for particular intentions, such as for the Church.

## Summa Theologica

This is the collective title of the chief dogmatic writings of St. Thomas Aquinas (1225 to 1274) who is recognized by the Church as a foremost theologian and scholar and has been given the title the "Angelic Doctor."

The *Summa* is a large work of three parts, consisting of treatises, questions, and articles. The first part *(Prima)* treats of God in Himself and as the Creator; the first part of the second part *(Prima Secundae)* studies God as the end of man, while its second part *(Secunda Secundae)* delves into man's return to God; and the third part *(Tertia)* studies Christ as man's way to God with the concluding sections dealing with the sacraments and eschatology. Portions of this last part were not completed by St. Thomas before his death but were finished by Reginald of Piperno working with related portions of other writings by St. Thomas. (See Scholasticism.)

## Sunday

The first day of the week, also called the "Lord's Day," is set aside for public worship. This was true in the early Church under the Apostles who recognized that the Christian mystery supplanted that of the Old Law, the Sabbath (Acts 20:7). On this day, called *Dominica* in the Latin, Catholics are obliged by law to assist at the sacrifice of the Mass.

By grant of the Congregation for the Clergy (Jan. 10, 1970), the faithful, where the bishop considers this a pastoral benefit, may satisfy the

Sunday precept of attending the Celebration of the Eucharist by participating in the Mass in the late afternoon or evening of the preceding Saturday. The same grant extends to the time before a holy day of obligation.

### Supererogation, Works of

In moral theology those acts that are not required by strict obligation but are simply good and meritorious in and of themselves are called supererogate. Into this classification fall the counsels of perfection and those works of a corporal or spiritual nature that arise out of one's charity or love as an expression of the love of God according to an interior motive.

### Suppedaneum

1. Another name for the predella of the altar.
2. The small footrest sometimes pictured beneath the feet of the figure on a crucifix.

### Suppressed

The term is applied to some action or devotion that is no longer promoted or endorsed by Church law. It is used, for example, of a feast dropped from the calendar, which thereby becomes a "suppressed feast." The word is really an interim term, which is a poor translation of the Latin verb *supprimo,* and should itself be "done away with."

### Surplice

Surplice, the name of the wide-sleeved garment of white linen that reaches to the knees, is derived from the Latin *superpelliciae,* meaning "above the fur clothing." It was used from the eleventh century to be put on above the practical, fur-lined tunics worn in the churches.

### Suspension

Suspension is a church censure, affecting only clerics. It forbids them to exercise certain powers of their office (cc. 2278-2285).

### Swedenborgianism

This is a mystical system developed by Emmanuel Swedenborg (1688 to 1772) wherein he became increasingly concerned with showing by scientific analysis that the universe has a basic spiritual structure. He claimed to have had a number of visions in 1745 wherein Christ instructed him in the spiritual sense of the scriptures and sent him out to teach this to others. His system was further developed through biological and physiological studies that were then interpreted as supportive of his original thesis.

The agency developed by Swedenborg was to lead to the New Church, which taught that his teaching supplanted Christianity. In this he refused to acknowledge a belief in the Trinity, original sin, the resurrection of Christ, and the sacraments except Baptism and the Eucharist. It is difficult to summarize what Swedenborg actually taught as his basic belief since it was a combination of pantheism and theosophic concepts, all of which were elaborated upon in a series of publications, principally an eight-volume exposition called *Arcana Coeléstia* (1756) and six other volumes that claimed to expose the new Christian religion. Remnants of this system are still to be found in the New Church groups and the Church of the New Jerusalem, whose name was taken from a 1758 book written by Swedenborg.

### Swiss Guards

The members of this small force are specially chosen young Catholic men from Switzerland who serve as personal guardians of the pope. They are guards of gates and doors of the Vatican State. Organized in 1505, they have two historic uniforms, one consisting of a blue tunic and breeches, the other, designed by Michelangelo, consists of a tunic, breeches, and stockings with alternate yellow, red, and blue vertical stripes. To this latter is added a helmet and breastplate of steel on state occasions. In all, the Swiss Guards number 110 men and six officers; they are now trained in modern arms but seldom carry anything other than a sword or halberd.

### Syllabus

The word, derived from the Greek, means a "collection." As a writing, emanating from the Holy See, a syllabus bears similarity to an encyclical but is a specific statement of the position of the Church. There are two famous such writings: (1) The Syllabus of Pius IX, published in 1846. Properly, this is the encyclical *Quanta Cura,* which condemned some eighty errors of the day. (2) The Syllabus of Pius X, *Lamentabili Sane Exitu,* published in 1907. It listed and condemned sixty-five propositions taken from the writings of the modernists, especially those that are heretical, such as denial of the divinity of Christ or divine origin of the sacraments. (Cf. Modernism.)

## Symbol

A symbol is an emblem of religious truth. In Church art, symbols arose as early as the third century and were used to represent persons and mysteries; for example, the cross is a symbol of Christ. The fish, also a symbol of Christ, is derived from the Greek letters for the word fish, which spell out the initials of the declaration, "Jesus Christ, Son of God, Savior." Symbols may be single and refer to one teaching or person, or mixed, referring to different doctrines, for example, grapes and wheat. Many of the symbols are multiple, taken from Scripture and language, and representative of a teaching, such as the symbol *Alpha* and *Omega*. (See Sign.)

## Symbolism

Symbolism is the signifying of something so that it may be more clearly understood. Thus, we have the symbols in scripture (Jer. 1:11–14). The Church also uses symbolism in its liturgy, such as the salt in baptism.

## Synagogue

1. The meeting place and a house of worship used by the Jews after the sixth century B.C. as a substitute for the Temple worship. It has remained a characteristic feature of Jewish religious affiliation to the present time. Each synagogue is like a church, and affiliation is reserved by a number of Jews. Historically the synagogue is a nonsacrificial place of worship, and its most important piece of furniture is the cabinet in which the sacred scrolls of the scriptures are kept. The gospels mention synagogues at Nazareth and Capernaum (Lk. 4:16; Mk. 1:21).

2. The Great Synagogue is that which was established in Jerusalem in the fifth century B.C. and consisted of a legislative body of 120 members. The latest mention of this was made in a Jewish writing *Pirqe Aboth* in the third century A.D..

## Synaxis

The Greek verb for "assembling" or "to assemble" has for its noun the word *synaxis,* which is Eucharist, Hence, its meaning in the first days of the Church was a "gathering together to celebrating the Eucharist." In the Byzantine rite, synaxis is the name of a feast where the people gather to honor the saints whose feast day preceded this celebration.

We learn from Vatican II that "they (priests) exercise this sacred (mediatorial) function of Christ most of all in the Eucharistic liturgy or synaxis. There, acting in the person of Christ, and proclaiming His mystery, they join the offering of the faithful to the sacrifice of their Head" (LG 28).

## Synod

This term is now applied to a periodic gathering of the clergy of a diocese, called at least every two years by the bishop to settle administrative matters. The bishop determines which members of the clergy will be present and might include all if the welfare of souls would not suffer. The bishop is the only legislator, and the clergy or religious act only in a consultative capacity. The subject matter is recommended by canon law (cc. 356-362).

## Synod of Bishops

The gathering of bishops on an international, national, territorial, or provincial basis to discuss and determine in a collegial manner the procedures most beneficial for the Church is called a Synod of Bishops. The name has been applied most specifically to the international Synod of Bishops held in Rome and opened by the reigning pontiff. Here bishops from all over the world, some representing national conferences of bishops, others present because of their leadership in a specific missionary territory, come to discuss matters pertaining to the Church universal.

Vatican II declared: "Bishops from various parts of the world, chosen through ways and procedures established or to be established by the Roman Pontiff, will render especially helpful assistance to the supreme pastor of the Church in a council to be known by the proper name of Synod of Bishops. Since it will be acting in the name of the entire Catholic episcopate, it will at the same time demonstrate that all the bishops in hierarchical communion share in the responsibility for the universal Church" (CD 5).

And: "From the very first centuries of the Church the bishops who were placed over individual churches were deeply influenced by the fellowship of fraternal charity and by zeal for the universal mission entrusted to the apostles. And so they pooled their resources and unified their plans for the common good and for that of the individual churches. Thus there were established synods, provincial councils, and plenary councils in which bishops legislated for various churches a common pattern to be followed in teaching the truths of faith and ordering ecclesiastical discipline.

"This sacred Ecumenical Synod earnestly desires that the venerable institution of synods and councils flourish with new vigor. Thus, faith will be spread and discipline preserved more fittingly and effectively in the various churches, as the circumstances of the times require" (CD 36).

And: "The responsibility to proclaim the gospel throughout the world falls primarily on the body of bishops. Now the Synod of Bishops is a 'stable council of bishops concerned with the entire Church.' Hence, among its affairs of general concern, it should give special consideration to missionary activity. For this is a supremely great and sacred task of the Church" (AG 29).

### Synoptic Gospels

The Gospels of Sts. Matthew, Mark, and Luke which, proceeding along similar lines of exposition, present a general view of Christ and His teaching and in so doing mutually support each other. Matthew, Mark, and Luke are thus called synoptists.

### Synteresis

In mystical life the point in time and spiritual attainment wherein the apex of union through the indwelling of the Spirit of God is fulfilled in a unique and conscious manner is called synteresis. In the spiritual development of the individual this is considered to be the apogee of union achieved only after the person has progressed through the four stages of the mystic union. St. Teresa of Avila described them in her last writing, *The Interior Castle* as: (1) the *incomplete mystic union,* or the prayer of quiet (from the Latin *quies,* repose, which expresses the impression experienced in this state); (2) the full or *semi-ecstatic union,* called by St. Teresa the prayer of union; (3) the *ecstatic union* or ecstasy; (4) the *transforming* or *deifying union,* or the spiritual marriage of the soul with God.

It is only after the intense prayer of meditation, contemplation and the charism of God that one attains to the fourth state, which is called synteresis. This is seldom attained without spiritual direction in one's prayer life.

### Syrian Rite

In the East the Syrian Rite is the same as the Chaldean rite; in the West this rite is the liturgy used by Catholic Syrians, Malankarese, and the Jacobites of Syria and Malabar. The liturgy is developed from that of Antioch of the fourth century; it is sometimes called the Liturgy of St. James. Distinctive features are: the words of the Consecration are sung aloud, Communion is under both species, the Divine Office has seven hours, baptism is by immersion and a "pouring on" of water. (Cf. Liturgy.)

# Tt

## Tabernacle

1. In the modern church the tabernacle is the place where the Blessed Sacrament is retained. According to canon law, "the most Holy Eucharist is to be preserved in an immovable tabernacle placed in the center of the altar" (c. 1269). This has been changed in accord with the liturgical developments of Vatican II. The tabernacle should be of durable material, skillfully constructed and safely locked, and should be humidity-proof. It likewise should be dignified and suitably ornamented. Before use, it must be blessed according to the Ritual. In the early days of the Church it was customary to have the Blessed Sacrament kept by lay people or clergy for security. By development, other means were used: a cupboard, a tower, or a suspended pyx. The name is derived from the word "tent."

2. In Scripture, the tabernacle was the center of the cult of the Jews. It is described in Exodus (26:1-37).

3. The Feast of Tabernacles is one of the most ancient of the Israelites and is agrarian, the "Feast of the Harvest" (cf. Ex. 23:16; 34:22; Dt. 16:13-15). In the new Covenant, Christ made His own body the offering of the feast (cf. Jn. 7:37-39; 1 Cor. 10:4; Heb. 9:2-15).

## Talitha Koum

The Aramaic spoken by Christ (Mk. 5:41) when He raised up or brought to life the dead daughter of Jairus, an official of the synagogue. The words mean "Little girl, get up!" It is in the original Aramaic a tender expression, *talitha* meaning "little lamb" followed by the feminine imperative singular *koum* as found in the Greek translations. It is one of the few recorded words of Christ retained in near original form in any of the gospels. It has been poetically expressed.

> Talitha koum—
> come now and live each day
> come now and truly learn of Me
> come now along the Way
> One who is Love, loves thee.
> Talitha koum
> come walk the wondrous Way
> come dance the flower years
> a lifetime is not a day
> the joy of life is not for tears
> Talitha koum.
>
> Robert C. Broderick

## Talmud

The name given to the collected body of Jewish civil and canonical law, made up of the text, *Mishnah,* and the commentary, *Gemara.* The name is derived from the Hebrew word meaning "study." It is much like an encyclopedia of Jewish tradition summarizing more than seven centuries of cultural growth and development, and includes not only the law but ethics, folklore, social institutions, history, and science.

The *Mishnah* is divided into six sections called *Sedarim* (orders) which are Zeraim, Moed, Nashim, Nezikim, Kadashim, and Taharot. These deal with, in order, agriculture; festivals; women, including divorce and family life; civil and criminal law; holy things and cultic details of Temple service; and ritual purity.

The *Gemara,* which is derived from the Hebrew meaning "a study of teachings," is an amplification of the previous six sections together with the necessary interpretation to meet the changes in Jewish society in keeping with the tradition of the people. (See Torah.)

## Tametsi

Tametsi is the opening word of the law, enacted by the Council of Trent (Sess. 24) on the solemn form of the marriage contract. The law stated that no marriage was valid unless contracted before the pastor or his delegate and two witnesses. The *Tametsi* law gave way to the *Ne Temere Decore* of April 19, 1908, which has been retained substantially in the Code of Canon Law under marriage legislation (cc. 1012-1141).

## Tantum Ergo

These Latin words have become the title of a Benediction hymn composed by St. Thomas Aquinas in 1264 at the request of Pope Urban IV. It is the last two stanzas of a longer hymn, the *Pange Lingua* (Sing, my tongue), and the Latin words *Tantum Ergo* mean literally "Therefore so great," but they have been variously translated to keep rhythm in the English version. In translation it reads:

> Down in adoration falling,
> Lo! the sacred Host we hail;
> Lo! o'er ancient forms departing,
> Newer rites of grace prevail;
> Faith for all defects supplying,
> Where the feeble senses fail.
>
> To the everlasting Father,
> And the Son who reigns on high,
> With the Holy Spirit proceeding
> Forth from Each eternally,
> Be salvation, honor, blessing,
> Might, and endless majesty.

The singing of this hymn, in any of its many musical compositions, is prescribed, along with the blessing of the people, as essential ritually for the Benediction of the Blessed Sacrament.

## Taoism

Taoism is both a philosophy of life and a religion put forth by its founder Lao-tzu (Laotsze) who was a contemporary of Confuscius in the fifth century B.C. Taoism is primarily an insight into the virtue of humility as the basis of greatness. The teachings were compiled in one volume entitled *Tao Teh Ching* ("The Way and Its Power"); it is quite brief, little more than 5000 words.

One of the features of Taoism is that of "passivity" or "nonassertiveness." It is composed of two approaches, first mental, then physical, wherein the person is not to make exertions that do not contribute to his direct or ultimate goals. Thus it is not action for action's sake, but stresses that by attaining a quietude of spirit everything essential will be granted to one. It follows that there can be no attachment to what one does or accomplishes. Philosophically it is expressed not in what one does but in what one is, and therein rests true happiness in this belief.

In the practice of Taoism, it is necessary to attain transcendency. This means one must endure or pass through certain disciplines, among which are "the fast of the mind" and "sitting and forgetting." To this must be added extensive periods of meditation, directing one's mind to concentrate on the "One." It is a practice of quietism.

Taoism is one of the three major religions of China. In recent years it has concentrated on a multiplicity of gods, superstitions, and magical formulas, though some of its more recent adherents have attempted to eliminate these magical aspects and accent its ethic of simplicity.

## Te Deum

The first words of the Latin version, and the title, of the most famous hymn in the Western Church. The words mean: "to You, God." It was written in the early fifth century by Nicetas, Bishop of Remesiana (d. 414). It is a prayer, a hymn of thanksgiving, a solemn invocation for a blessing, and a profession of faith. In translation it reads:

> We praise You, O God: we
> acknowledge You to be the Lord.
>
> You, the Eternal Father, all
> the earth does worship.
>
> To You all the Angels, to You
> the Heavens, and all the Powers therein:
>
> To You the Cherubim and Seraphim
> with unceasing voice cry aloud:
>
> Holy, Holy, Holy, Lord God
> of Sabaoth.
>
> The heavens and the earth are full
> of the majesty of Your glory.
>
> You, the glorious choir of the Apostles,
> You, the admirable company of the Prophets,
> You, the white-robed army of
> Martyrs does praise.
>
> You, the Holy Church throughout
> the world does confess.
>
> The Father of infinite majesty,
> Your adorable, true, and only Son,
> Also the Holy Spirit, the Comforter.
>
> You, O Christ, are the King of glory.
> You are the Everlasting Son of the Father.
>
> You did not abhor the Virgin's
> womb, when You took upon
> Yourself human nature to deliver man.
>
> When You had overcome the
> sting of death, You did open
> to believers the kingdom of heaven.
>
> You sit at the right hand of
> God, in the glory of the Father.

You, we believe, are the Judge to come.
We beseech You, therefore, help
Your servants whom You have
redeemed with Your Precious Blood.

Make them to be numbered with Your
Saints, in glory everlasting.

Save Your people, O Lord, and
bless Your inheritance.

And rule them, and exalt them forever.

Day by day, we bless You.
And we praise Your Name forever;
Yea, forever and ever.

Grant, O Lord, this day, to
keep us without sin.
Have mercy on us, O Lord; have mercy on us.

Let Your mercy, O Lord, be upon
us; even as we have hoped in You.

In You, O Lord, have I hoped:
let me not be confounded forever.

## Teaching Authority of the Church

See Magisterium of the Church.

## Team Ministry

The assignment made by the Ordinary of a
diocese whereby two or more priests are placed in a
territorial and canonically erected parish for the
care of souls is called Team Ministry. This form of
pastoral activity is an innovation that provides a
division of the spheres of responsibility; thus,
education may be handled by one priest, while
another may take care of liturgy and sacramental
concerns. The adjustment to harmonious work
must be made by the individuals to provide total
cooperation and at the same time provide complete
service to the People of God in that place and time.
In some instances this has led to a clash between
the place of social action in a given parish and the
sacramental concerns of the parish. Also, from the
business standpoint, one of those assigned must act
as a corporate officer in those dioceses that have a
multi-corporate structure, that is, with each parish
being a separate corporation in the overall diocesan plan of operation. This contrasts with the
"corporation-sole" where all properties, churches,
institutions are combined in one single corporate
structure.

Team ministries have in many instances led to
frequent changes in the personnel to avoid built-in
problems that work to the detriment of such

ministry, such as neglect of one activity in concentrating on another, or the polarization of parish
membership because of the preference given to
one program over another. Success is best obtained
when there is a genuine effort made to establish a
spiritual program that the members of the team
can apply and live with. (Cf. Parish.)

## Teilhardism

The system of propositions put forth by Pierre
Teilhard de Chardin (d. 1955), a Jesuit scientist
and anthropologist, are variously called *Teilhardism*
or *Chardinism*. It is his vision of reality, which is
contained basically in the term he introduced,
called "noosphere" (pronounced *new sphere)*, which
emanates from the mind of man. Chardin believes
in the fullness of the evolutionary process; he holds
that man is a product not only of heredity through
biological mechanisms but also of an ongoing
process of social, cultural, and religious development. It is a process-formula through which man
has a uniqueness in the entire universe, a destiny in
spiritual perfection, and a final humanity united
with God who draws all men unto Himself. For
Man to attain this ultimate, he must have knowledge of what his direction should be.

Chardin does not know what this "future"
cosmologic process will be or how it is to be
attained. The right toward which the will of man
must tend and man's ability to recognize that right
and move toward it are likewise not declared by
Chardin. His system is thus an ethic of science:
"We are now inclined to admit that at each further
degree of combination *something* which is irreduci-
ble to isolated elements *emerges* in a new order."
(*The Phenomenon of Man*, p. 268.) (See Om; Omega
Point.)

## Temperance

One of the four cardinal virtues, temperance
prompts moderation and self-control in actions
and thoughts, and particularly the pleasures of the
senses.

Man's mastery over his instincts is a prime
function of his intelligence and will. It is through
this measure of control that the human person
imposes his own reason on his passions. This
enables the person to create the proper spiritual
climate wherein he can respond to God and
progress toward salvation. Such controls were a
prescription of OT approaches to conduct (Sir.
31:12–31; 32:1–13; Prv. 20:1; 23:1–3; Is. 5:22).
Pride and lusts were to be overcome (Gn. 2:16; Dt.
8:6–14; Sir. 10:7–18; 15:14). In the NT temper-

ance was the means of becoming a successful Christian (1 Cor. 9:25; 1 Thes. 5:6–8; Eph. 5:18; 1 Pt. 1:13; 2 Tm. 2:22; Jas. 1:12; Rv. 2:10; 21:8). To obtain wisdom, a person should become temperate in the use of money and its inordinate love and should give alms (Cf. Ps. 49:7; Jer. 17:11; Mt. 19:21–26; Lk. 11:41; 12:33–34; Acts 9:36; 10:2).

## Templars

See Knights, Orders of.

## Temple

Three Temples were built in Jerusalem, each of which was called the "House of Yahweh" and directed to the worship of God for the sanctifying of His people. The first Temple was that of Solomon built about 960 B.C. which was a magnificent structure, composed of a vestibule called the "Holy" and an inner room called the "Holy of Holies" where the Ark of the Covenant stood (cf. Ex. 25:37; Nm. 12:8; Dt. 10:1–8; 1 Kgs. 8). Solomon's Temple was destroyed in 587 B.C.

The second Temple was built by Zorobabel, after the return from Babylonian exile, between the years 520 to 515 B.C. The precious utensils and vessels that had been taken into exile were returned to Jerusalem.

In the years 20 to 19 B.C. the Temple of Herod the Great was built to replace the second structure, which had fallen into ruin. This last Temple, which Christ knew in His time, was the spiritual center of the Israelite religion, its very symbol or sign. This third Temple was burned and razed by the Romans under Titus in A.D. 70.

But before the destruction of the Temple of Herod, the Christians had received and were prepared for the true Temple, Christ, in a true and lasting community of charity. When Christ was sacrificed on the cross, and the veil of the Temple of Herod was rent, the older Temple as symbol was violated and supplanted (Lk. 24:44–45). It was the Body of Christ that was to become the spiritual Temple and the source of grace for all human persons (Jn. 1:14; 7:37–39; also Mk. 13:1–26). And Christ remains the continuing dwelling place of the glory of God before men (Jn. 12:37–43). Through the sacrifice offered by Christians in union with and through Christ they in turn become the Temple of God's glory (1 Cor. 6:19; 1 Jn. 3:23; 4:13–16). Christ is and forever shall be the Temple of the heavenly Jerusalem for all who love Him (Rv. 7:15; 11:19; 15:5–8).

## Temporal Goods

Created material things are classed as temporal goods. This extends to creatures and possessions that are acquired, such as money, precious items, and pets.

Vatican II teaches: "God intended the earth and all that it contains for the use of every human being and people. Thus, as all men follow justice and unite in charity, created goods should abound for them on a reasonable basis. Whatever the forms of ownership may be, as adapted to the legitimate institutions of people according to diverse and changeable circumstances, attention must always be paid to the universal purpose for which created goods are meant" (GS 69).

And: "The Lord is 'the portion and the inheritance' (Nm. 18:20) of priests. Hence they should use temporal goods only for those purposes to which it is permissible to direct them according to the teaching of Christ the Lord and the regulations of the Church.

"With all possible help from experienced laymen, priests should manage those goods which are, strictly speaking, ecclesiastical as the norms of Church law and the nature of the goods require. They should always direct them toward the goals in pursuit of which it is lawful for the Church to possess temporal goods. Such are: the arrangement of divine worship, the procuring of an honest living for the clergy, and the exercise of works of the sacred apostolate or of charity, especially toward the needy" (PO 17).

## Temporal Power

1. The authority wielded by the Supreme Pontiff as a sovereign head of an independent state, the State of Vatican City, is the exercise of temporal power or authority.

2. It is the Church's role in society to point out and emphasize those conditions that promote the achieving of mankind's supernatural end and to encourage those relations that lead to a better communion among men. Thus the Christian has an obligation to submit to and act with the right decisions of the State. The Church's authority extends to all the realms of political life in its moral teaching and its direction of souls (cf. Mt. 22:15–22; Rom. 13:7; 1 Tm. 2:1–2; Ti. 3:1; Acts 4:19; 1 Pt. 2:13–17).

Vatican II teaches: "The apostolate of the social milieu, that is, the effort to infuse a Christian spirit into the mentality, customs, laws, and structures of the community in which a person lives, is so much the duty and responsibility of the laity that it can never be properly performed by others. In this area the laity can exercise the apostolate of like toward like. It is here that laymen add to the testimony of life the testimony of their speech; it is here in the arena of their labor, profession, studies, residence, leisure, and companionship that laymen have a special opportunity to help their brother.

"To fulfill the mission of the Church in the world, the laity have certain basic needs. They need a life in harmony with their faith, so they can become the light of the world. They need that undeviating honesty which can attract all men to the love of truth and goodness, and finally to the Church and to Christ. They need the kind of fraternal charity which will lead them to share in the living conditions, labors, sorrows, and hope of their brother men, and which will gradually and imperceptibly dispose the hearts of all around them for the saving work of grace. They need a full awareness of their role in building up society, an awareness which will keep them preoccupied with bringing Christian large-heartedness to the fulfillment of their duties, whether family, social, or professional. If laymen can meet all these needs, their behavior will have a penetrating impact, little by little, on the whole circle of their life and labors" (AA 13).

### Temptation

Literally this means, "putting to the test." Through original sin, human nature is subject to temptation and it is a truth of divine faith that the devil tempts men to evil (1 Pt. 5:8). Temptation is then the action upon the concupiscence, which may result in the commission of sin; it is an enticement to sin. By being watchful in mind and will, men can overcome temptation and gain merit by so doing.

Temptation always compels the person to practice those virtues needed to overcome it. Two immediate means are available in overcoming temptations that arise from outside sources. The first means is immediate and conscious and involves the avoidance of the occasions of sin whether they are persons or things (Eph. 5:15). The second is ongoing and always present, the formation of conscience, which is the acquisition of a balance in reasoned judgment between the satisfaction of instincts and their sublimation by self-control. Each person has the potential of overcoming temptation, but it must be exercised (1 Cor. 10:13).

### Tenebrae

This means, from the Latin, "darkness." The name was formerly applied to the public chanting of Matins and Lauds on the evenings of Wednesday, Thursday, and Friday of Holy Week, each

being the anticipated office of the following day. The lessons are chiefly from the Lamentations of the prophet Jeremiah and the Psalms, and the general intent is penitential. The ceremony is quite simple, consisting of the extinguishing of fourteen

candles on a multiple triangular candleholder, called the "hearse," and leaving a fifteenth white candle burning at the apex of the hearse. This final lighted candle is a symbol of the risen Savior. It is a paraliturgical devotion that may be considered biblical because of the readings, and as prayer since it petitions the coming of the Savior.

### Terce or Tierce

This is the third hour of the Divine Office. (Cf. Liturgy of the Hours.)

### Terna

Made up and presented to the Holy See by a chapter of canons, the *terna* was a list giving the three names of those whom the chapter had selected and approved for possible elevation to the episcopacy. Its use has been abolished by a decree of the Sacred Consistorial Congregation of July 25, 1916.

### Tertiaries

These are members of one of the three classes of associations of the laity recognized by the Code of Canon Law (c. 684 ff), namely Third Orders. The associations promote Catholic life and action. The members are not religious in the strict sense of the term, and although they may take private vows, they merely submit to following a daily practice of religion in their lives. They may be associated with the following religious orders: Franciscans, Dominicans, Premonstratensians, Carmelites, Benedictines, Augustinians, Servites, and Trinitarians.

## Testament

In its biblical sense, the word testament is derived from the translation of the word *testamentum,* which more properly should be translated from the Hebrew meaning "covenant." The major divisions of the Bible are the OT (Old Covenant) and the NT (New Covenant).

Vatican II teaches: "In carefully planning and preparing the salvation of the whole human race, the God of supreme love, by a special dispensation, chose for Himself a people to whom He might entrust His promises. First He entered into a covenant with Abraham (cf. Gn. 15:18) and, through Moses, with the people of Israel (cf. Ex. 24:8). To this people which He had acquired for Himself, He so manifested Himself through words and deeds as the one true and living God that Israel came to know by experience the ways of God with men, and with God Himself speaking to them through the mouth of the prophets, Israel daily gained a deeper and clearer understanding of His ways and made them more widely known among the nations (cf. Ps. 21:28–29; 95:1–3; Is. 2:1–4; Jer. 3:17). The plan of salvation, foretold by the sacred authors, recounted and explained by them, is found as the true word of God in the books of the Old Testament: these books, therefore written under divine inspiration, remain permanently valuable. 'Everything written before our time was written for our instruction, that we might derive hope from the lessons of patience and the words of encouragement in the Scriptures' (Rom. 15:4)" (DV 14).

And concerning the NT it states: "The word of God, which is the power of God for the salvation of all who believe (cf. Rom. 1:16), is set forth and shows its power in a most excellent way in the writings of the New Testament. For when the fullness of time arrived (cf. Gal. 4:4), the Word was made flesh and dwelt among us in the fullness of grace and truth (cf. Jn. 1:14). Christ established the Kingdom of God on earth, manifested His Father and Himself by deeds and words, and completed His work by His death, resurrection, and glorious ascension and by the sending of the Holy Spirit. Having been lifted up from the earth, He draws all men to Himself (cf. Jn. 12:32, Greek text), He who alone has the words of eternal life (cf. Jn. 6:68). This mystery had not been manifested to other generations as it was now revealed to His holy apostles and prophets in the Holy Spirit (cf. Eph. 3:4–6, Greek text), so that they might preach the gospel, stir up faith in Jesus, Christ and Lord, and gather the Church together. To these realities, the writings of the New Testament stand as a perpetual and divine witness" (DV 17). (See Bible.)

## Tetragrammaton

The technical name given to the four Hebrew letters (JHVH), which are translated as: "the Lord." The English equivalent would be Yahweh. (See Adonai.)

## Teutonic Knights

See Knights, Orders of.

## Thaumaturgus

From the Greek, meaning "wonder worker," this word is sometimes attached as a title to a saint who is noted for miracles, such as St. Vincent Ferrer.

## Thecae

See Reliquary.

## Theodicy

From its etymology, theodicy is that part of natural theology which concerns itself with the defense of the goodness and omnipotence of God. The term was first mentioned in a letter by G. W. von Leibniz (1697) and was intended to describe in philosophical and theological use a way "to justify the ways of God to man" (cf. Rom. 3:4–20; Ps. 51:6). It thus became a term that indicates the efforts of human persons to solve the problems of evil in the world. It later came to embrace the entire treatise on the philosophical knowledge of God. (See Omnipotence.)

## Theologian

1. One who is trained in the science of theology. This refers primarily to one who has not only studied theology in general but has made special scholarly studies in one or more of the branches of theology and has attained a doctorate or at least a licentiate degree.

2. A student aspiring to Holy Orders who is taking the last four years of study in a seminary. (Cf. Theology; Periti.)

## Theological Virtues

Faith, hope, and charity are the three theological virtues.

*Faith* is the supernatural virtue through which, aided by divine grace, one is enabled to believe firmly in the truth of the authority of God as He has revealed it. Because of God's revelation of this truth, one has the serious obligation to believe; from this evidence there also arises the duty to make an act of faith as soon as His revelation is recognized. It is further one's duty to make repeated acts of faith during one's life by practicing religion, such as attending Mass. And acts of prayerful faith should be made to effectively resist temptation (cf. Faith).

*Hope* is the supernatural, infused virtue through which one is enabled to rely on the omnipotence, goodness, and fidelity of God, and to look forward to eternal salvation to be attained through the means God has established. Acts of hope are necessary after one reaches the age of reason and is able to recognize his purpose in life. Acts of hope are also aids to overcome temptations, and expressions of faith. This is also explicitly done by the external practice of one's religion (cf. Hope).

*Charity* is the supernatural, infused virtue through which one loves God as the greatest good for God's own sake, and oneself and one's neighbors for the love of God. To make acts of love for God is a necessity, because they are the proper and essential means to attain salvation, for example, receiving the sacraments. It is of *precept,* upon reaching the age of reason, that one must make acts of loving God, such as avoiding mortal sin and avoiding temptation. (Cf. Charity; Love of God.)

## Theology

The term is derived from the etymology of the word itself. Theology is the science of God and the things that treat of God. It is the study of God in Himself and of His relations with creatures. As a science, theology is both methodical, that is, referring to the character of the knowledge, and systematic, that is, referring to the extent of knowledge and the integration of the various concepts into a unit. Like all science, it proceeds from certain definite prime or universal principles, which are evident in themselves. We thus come to a knowledge of God through reason and by revela-

tion. Theology, then, is the reasoned methodical and systematic exposition of revealed truths. (Cf. Revelation.)

Theology is a synthesis, a unit term embracing many divisions. Thus one does not become a theologian by studying one phase of theology or by reading one book of theology, but by gaining knowledge systematically, both in extent and application. The fruit of such study may be said to be the acquisition of the science of God.

The divisions of theology are many. As a method there is first *positive theology,* which is the recording and defending of revealed truth. This in turn is divided into *biblical* theology, that is the examination of truth as found in Scripture, and *historical* theology, that is, the examination of truths of God in both Scripture and Tradition, and the demonstration of the teaching of Christ and the Apostles as handed down through the Church. Second, *scholastic theology* is the explaining, illustrating, and deducing of new truths systematically. Third, the *positive scholastic* is the combination of the first two into effective presentation. As an applied system, theology embraces *dogmatic* and *moral* theology. Dogmatic theology is the demonstration of faith and reason, dealing with God's laws; this has two lesser branches called *ascetical* theology or the methods of perfection, and *mystical* theology or the extraordinary methods and gifts of perfection. Moral theology is the science of the laws that regulate the duties of man to God. There are also a series of the practical applications of theology, which are distinct studies for the trained theologian. These are: *liturgy,* or the manner of theology applied in worship; *apologetics,* or the reasoning of theology applied; *pastoral* theology, or the demonstration of theology applied. This third in turn comprises the study of canon law, the rules of the Church in applying theology; *homiletics,* the preaching of the truths of theology; *catechetics,* the teaching of the truths of theology; and *rubrics,* the ceremonial directions used in the application of the truths of theology. (See also entries under individual titles.)

Modern theology transcends the various branches in its application. As Pope John XXIII declared in his opening address to the Second Vatican Council: ". . . a doctrinal penetration and a formation of consciences in faithful and perfect conformity to the authentic doctrine which, however, should be studied and expounded through the methods of research and through the literary forms of modern thought. The substance of the ancient doctrine of the Deposit of Faith is one thing, and the way in which it is presented is another. And it is the latter that must be taken into great consideration, with patience if necessary, everything being measured in the forms and proportions of a magisterium which is predominantly pastoral in character."

### Theophany

The term, applied to the direct or hidden appearances of God in the Scriptures, is derived from the Greek, meaning literally "God in brightness." God appearing on Mt. Sinai (Ex. 19:1–25), in storm, in the cloud (Ex. 24:15–16), and at the transfiguration (Mt. 17:1–9) are examples. (Cf. Epiphany.)

The most ancient forms of God's appearances are in the forces of nature (Ex. 19:16–20; Ps. 18:12; Jb. 37:5), in fire (Ex. 3:1–6; 13:22), and in human "likenesses" (Gn. 18:32; Jgs. 6:11–23; Am. 9:1; Is. 6:1–8). In Christian times God is recognized by faith (Jn. 14:8–11), and the final theophany will be on the "Day of the Lord" (Is. 5:30; Mt. 24:26–36: Rv. 21, 22).

### Theotokos

Literally, "God-bearing," this title was given to the Blessed Mother in the fourth century and it signified the widespread devotion to the Blessed Virgin, which continues to the present day in both the Eastern and Western Churches. The term was disputed in the early fifth century when the Nestorian heresy denied the divine maternity of the Blessed Virgin. The doctrine was confirmed and the Nestorians were condemned by the third ecumenical council of Ephesus in 431.

### Thessalonians, First and Second Epistles of Paul to

The earliest letters of St. Paul written at Corinth in about the year A.D. 50 or 51 were addressed to the new Christians at the port city of Thessalonica. On Paul's second missionary journey, he had been forced to flee with two of his companions, Sylvanus and Timothy, from Thessalonica to Beroea, and thence to Athens (Acts 17:1–15).

The city of Thessalonica, named after the sister of Alexander the Great, was founded in 315 B.C. It became an important city in the Roman province of Macedonia, and although Grecian, it was a "free city." The inhabitants were made to suffer greatly because of the hostility of the Jews who had sought refuge there because of Roman oppression.

St. Paul had intended to return to the city to aid the Thessalonians but was frustrated in this effort, so he sent Timothy to strengthen their faith and to report to him. Learning of the problems there, which were not readily solved, Paul wrote two letters. In substance these are concerned with the second coming of Christ, the parousia, because the Thessalonians had been oppressed and were anxious for the return of Christ (an event that many early Christians thought would be imminent).

St. Paul explains the teaching of the resurrection from the dead: "We would have you be clear about those who sleep in death, brothers; otherwise you might yield to grief, like those who have no hope. For if we believe that Jesus died and rose, God will bring forth with him from the dead those also who have fallen asleep believing in him" (1 Thes. 4:13–14). And then Paul answers the question of when the parousia will take place, saying, "As regards specific times and moments, brothers, we do not need to write to you; you know very well that the day of the Lord is coming like a thief in the night. Just when people are saying, 'Peace and security, ruin will fall on them with the suddenness of pains overtaking a woman in labor, and there will be no escape" (1 Thes. 5:1–3).

In the second letter Paul also treats of the parousia, making more clear what undoubtedly the people misunderstood. At the same time the question arises of whether Paul was speaking in symbolic language (2 Thes. 2:5–7), but overall there is a clear teaching that the Church recognizes. (See Paul, St.)

### Third Orders

See Tertiaries.

### Thomism

Thomism is the system of scholastic thought developed by St. Thomas Aquinas (d. 1274). Basically, the work of St. Thomas was a systematic critique and elimination of Platonism in metaphysics, psychology, and epistomology, advancing along Aristotelian lines beyond St. Augustine. He developed a harmony of faith and reason, establishing man as an efficacious cause in the doctrine of creation, and presented this in his monumental work *Summa Theologica*. Thomism as a system is recognized and imposed by Church law (c. 1366). (See Scholasticism; Summa Theologica.)

### Throne

1. The platform with a canopy on which the monstrance is placed at Exposition of the Blessed Sacrament. A small throne is sometimes called a *thabor*. A throne is required for solemn Exposition; sometimes it is built into the tabernacle itself.

2. The name is applied to the episcopal throne, the *cathedra*, which is placed on the gospel side of a sanctuary. It is usually erected on three steps and is permanent in a cathedral.

## Thrones

See Angel.

## Thurible

See Censer.

## Thurifer

This is the title of the minister who is charged with the care and supply of the thurible.

## Tiara

The diadem that the pope wears at his coronation and at other solemn nonliturgical ceremonies is known as the tiara. This headpiece, consisting of a cloth-of-silver lining, rising about 15 inches, is circled by three ornamented crowns or coronets of gold, one set above the other. Pendants (infulae) are attached to the rim in the back, like those on the mitre. The origin of the tiara is not known, though it is fashioned after the Persian royal headpiece. Its symbolism is said to be representative of the threefold authority of the pope in the magisterium of the Church.

## Time

In history, time is a sequence of events progressing along a straight line from the past to the present and on into the future. This is chronographic time, which is measurable: a second, a minute, an hour, a day, etc. In the biblical understanding time takes on qualitative elements, such as "the heat of the day" or "the end of the day."

Time plays a great part in the biblical writings. In the OT God's time is shown to be eternity: He was *before* all created things and persons (Jer. 1:5; 2 Tm. 1:9; Ps. 89:2; 1 Cor 2:7), and He will be *after* all creatures (Rv. 21:6; 22:13). God is beyond all time as applied to creatures, and it is God who is the safeguard of the time of mankind for "Jesus Christ is the same yesterday, today, and forever" (Heb. 13:8). (Cf. also Rv. 1:4; Is. 43:8–12; 44:6–8; 2 Pt. 3:8.)

The *time* of the world is controlled by and directed by God toward that end when the fullness of the redemption will be accomplished, "the hour" of Jesus (Jn. 2:4; 4:21; 5:25; 7:30; 8:20; 12:23). It is thus that the Christian knows that time is linked inexorably to the fulfillment of the Kingdom, and this is recalled again and again in the liturgy of the Church (Col. 3:16; Eph. 5:14–19; 1 Tm. 3:16; Rv. 4:8).

It is from this examination that the Christian community knows the dawning of a new "age to come," the "acceptable time" (Rom. 13:11–12; 2 Cor. 6:1–2; Ti. 2:11–14). This is the "coming in

glory" or as St. Peter writes: "There is cause for rejoicing here. You may for a time have to suffer the distress of many trials; but this is so that your faith, which is more precious than the passing splendor of fire-tried gold, may by its genuineness lead to praise, glory, and honor when Jesus Christ appears" (1 Pt. 1:6–7).

Therefore we may conclude that for the Christian, time in its biblical sense means one's response in baptism and doing God's will, and acting in the liturgy, which exults in God's glory to come. These have meaning only in the light of the fulfillment of God's will in the salvation of all. This then is the sequence of the salvation history, rather than the events of one's birth-to-death time of existence. (See Salvation History.)

## Timothy, First and Second Epistles of Paul to

Timothy is a common Greek name meaning "honoring God." The Timothy to whom St. Paul addressed two epistles was one who might be referred to as Paul's man Friday, his co-worker, friend, traveling companion, and a favored and trusted disciple. The young Timothy was converted by St. Paul on the Apostle's first visit to Lyaconia, early during his second missionary journey. Entering into the Christian life along with Timothy were his mother, Eunice, and his grandmother, Lois (2 Tm. 1:5). When the Apostle retraced his journey, he found Timothy to have been a staunch Christian and welcomed him as his disciple (Rom. 16:21), and for the remainder of the second journey and the third (Acts 17:14–15; 19:22; 20:4) Timothy was Paul's "fellow-worker."

One might ask why St. Paul wrote to one who was so close to him. The answer rests in the fact that these two epistles, together with that addressed to Titus, are "pastoral epistles." They thus form a distinct type of writing in the NT because they present the pastoral duties and the extension of the Apostle's instructions on the care of souls, the actions and teachings against heresies, and the hierarchical structure of the Church. They are, one might say, more than instructions; they are official documents intended for the shepherds of souls and indirectly for the communities that Paul sought to instruct in a singular manner. When Paul went to Macedonia, he left Timothy in charge of the entire Ephesian church (1 Tm. 1:3) and bid him leave his post only to come to Rome where Paul was awaiting martyrdom (2 Tm. 4:21).

Both of the letters to Timothy were written early in the life of the Christian formation of peoples, the first perhaps as early as A.D. 48, and the second about ten or twelve years later, since they indicate the establishing of Christin communities rather than their more advanced development, and some consider these to be post-Pauline in their authorship. Timothy and Titus are both honored as bishops with a memorial on January 26.

## Tithes

This law of the Israelites (Lv. 27:30) required the offering of the tenth part of all produce, animals, and plants (cf. Mt. 23:23–24) for the support of religion. Today, canon law permits the law and custom of each locality to prevail in the support given to the Church.

## Tithing

The practice whereby a tenth of one's income or goods are given to the support of and extension of the Christian cause is called tithing. It is derived from the Old English word *teotha*, meaning "a tenth." This practice has been supported by Jewish law (cf. Dt. 14:22) and by NT interpretation (2 Cor. 8:2–6; Jas. 2:17).

Tithing however needs much understanding because of the varying economic standards, the distribution of goods, taxes, and the commitment to alms for social purposes apart from the needs of the Church in fulfilling its mission. It is evident that the message of Christ cannot become universal without the means of accomplishing this work. Nor can works of charity be extended without economic generosity. The Church teaches that each person, according to his or her means, is to give so that there will be an "upbuilding of the body of Christ." For some a tenth may be too small, for others impossible, for everyone too arbitrary. Hence, it is according to the conscience of each to do all he can. The motivation is not only self-respect and esteem, but the very feeling of accomplishment. (See Stewardship.)

## Titular Bishop

See Bishop.

## Titulus

The term is referred to the superscription placed on the cross on which Christ was crucified, declaring Him "Jesus of Nazareth, King of the Jews." (Cf. Crucifixion.)

## Titus, the Epistle of Paul to

Titus is the Roman first name of a Gentile who became a convert of St. Paul and was made the bishop of the island of Crete. He had accompanied St. Paul on his third missionary journey and was a native of Antioch (Gal. 2:1).

This letter addressed to Titus is one of the three pastoral epistles. (Cf. Timothy, the Epistles of Paul to.) It treats of the qualities desired in presbyters of the Church; the duties of various groups of society, such as old people, slaves, and the government. It concludes with a summary of the Christian virtues and warns against vain quarrels among the community members.

Titus, along with Timothy, is honored as a bishop in the Church's calendar with a memorial on January 26.

## Tobit, the Book of

Also, called Tobias, this is a storybook of the OT, classified as one of the historical books of the Bible. It was written by an unknown author in about 200 B.C. and relates the story of Tobit, a devout Jew who was forced to live in exile in the time of the Assyrian domination in the eighth century B.C. It is not factual history but a parable. Its lesson is edifying, recounting the heroic virtue of one man and giving the assurance that God will bless those who are faithful to Him in life and are charitable to their fellowmen. It is thus a story demonstrating the first two commandments.

The significant message of this book is the perseverance in faith that God expects and that He will reward. It also is an endearing story, one that was rejected by the Jews in their Bible and that Protestant versions have included only in recent translations. This book was written in both Hebrew and Aramaic, and fragments of the Scrolls of the Dead Sea bear portions of the story.

## Tonsure

This was formerly the introductory ceremony by which a layman became a cleric. It was not a part of the Sacrament of Holy Orders but was preliminary to its reception. In the ceremony, the bishop or his delegate cut or snipped small portions from the hair of the candidate, front, back, two sides, and crown, inviting the candidate to accept the Lord as "his portion." The candidate was then invested with the surplice. It is the practice in some religious orders to shave the top of the head in a circle, leaving but a "corona" of hair around the crown, as a permanent tonsure.

## Torah

1. The word Torah has two distinct meanings: (a) a law, precept, or divine revelation as included in Jewish literature; (b) the "Law of Moses" (Torah) contained in the Pentateuch. In its broadest sense it means the unending revelation of God through the Jewish tradition and understand-

ing. In its narrower sense it means the first five books of the Bible or the "five books of Moses."

2. The word Torah also refers to the scroll (rolled writings) upon which the five books are inscribed. One copy of the Torah is retained in the ark in every Jewish synagogue, and from this portions are read at religious services according to the Jewish calendar.

## Totalitarianism

The term totalitarianism is applied variously to systems of government such as Nazism, Fascism, and Communism. It basically describes any system of governmental dominance whereby the total life of the individual is controlled; thus the interaction of social conditions and the established form of government are out of balance.

As a system that usurps the private realm of the individual, restricts his creativity, and eliminates freedom, totalitarianism is rationalistic absolutism. It can exist only by some terroristic form of authoritarianism, either military or contrived, such as a secret or party police force. It thus alienates the person from the social and religious context of a society of free individuals. Surrender of freedoms to such a State brings about social disintegration. In the Christian context this is abhorent, for it obstructs the individual in his social mediation and equality under the rule of law. It is destructive of the freedom of determination in religious affairs.

## Totemism

The association of plants, animals, or nonliving things with a human person or a group is called totemism. The totem is not worshipped but plays a part in the religious rituals of the people because it is thought to be a beneficent representation and therefore must be held in high esteem.

## Toties Quoties

Literally, "so often as," this term is used in the granting of indulgences and declares that the indulgence may be gained as often as the action is required and the necessary conditions are fulfilled. (Cf. Portiuncula.)

## Tower of Babel

See Babel, Tower of; Ziggurat.

## Tract

1. The tract was a short penitential prayer that immediately followed the Gradual of the Mass and preceded the Gospel in the Latin Mass. It may be considered as a part of the Gradual with the Tract forming a Sequence or a second Gradual. When sung, it is chanted straight through without stop (cf. Mass).

2. The name given to a short writing or treatise, usually in the form of a leaflet, written about a religious subject.

## Tractarian Movement

See Oxford Movement

## Tradition

In a special sense, there is but one source of revealed truth and this source is divine Tradition. By this is meant the body of revealed truth handed down from the Apostles through the ages and contained in the doctrine, teaching, and practice of the Catholic Church. As defined by the Council of Trent (Sess. IV, EB 46), this includes both the Scriptures and the unwritten or oral traditions. It is the Church in her living magisterium, "the holder of Tradition," which gives life to Scripture. Tradition, as a distinct part of historic theology, also includes two main sources of teaching, namely, the writings of the fathers of the Church, and the archaeological, liturgical, and symbolical (tradition of the instruments) research that presents the historic proof of the practices of the Church as a continuing stream from its founding to the present (2 Tm. 2:1–2).

As B. Kloppenburg says: "Tradition is thus the gospel becoming real in the life of the Church; it is the faithful, integral, living, and vigorous handing on of the gospel. Development springs from the Church's native capacity to carry out its mission among the peoples of the world, to adapt and renew itself, to purify itself. Tradition is fidelity to the gospel (grace and truth) which must reach men in order to save them; development is fidelity to man who is to receive the gospel. By its nature the Church is tradition; by its mission the Church is development. If the Church abandoned tradition it would be unfaithful; if it abandoned development it would play the traitor. It would sin against tradition if it denied development; it would sin against development if it let tradition harden. Tradition is viable only when it envelops; development is possible only in tradition, in fidelity to gospel, Christ, and Church, in an identification with gospel, Christ, and Church. Like the teaching office which the bishops exercise, development (which, like tradition, is the work of the whole people of God, bishops and laity alike) must always be at the service of the word of God, never above it or separated from it. Development proceeds along two lines: one is the line of better understanding of and penetration into the revealed truths; the other is the line of constant adaptation of these truths and their practical implications to the varied historical, geographical, cultural, and religious situations of mankind. To help development along we need more than imagination, courage, and boldness; he alone is able to effect development who lives the gospel, tries to identify himself with it, and seeks to understand it in its richness, its divine life, its loving consecration to the Father, its faith in the active presence of the Lord, its confident self-surrender to the Holy Spirit."

Vatican II teaches: "Now what was handed on by the apostles includes everything which contributes to the holiness of life, and the increase in faith of the People of God; and so the Church, in her teaching, life, and worship, perpetuates and hands on to all generations all that she herself is, all that she believes.

"This tradition which comes from the apostles develops in the Church with the help of the Holy Spirit. For there is a growth in the understanding of the realities and the words which have been handed down. This happens through the contemplation and study made by believers, who treasure these things in their hearts (cf. Lk. 2:19, 51), through the intimate understanding of spiritual things they experience, and through the preaching of those who have received through episcopal succession the sure gift of truth" (DV 8).

And: It is clear that sacred tradition, sacred Scripture, and the teaching authority of the Church, in accord with God's most wise design, are so linked and joined together that one cannot stand without the others, and that all together and each in its own way under the action of the one Holy Spirit contribute effectively to the salvation of souls" (DV 10).

## Traditionalism

This philosophical system of the eighteenth and nineteenth centuries, which erroneously held that human reason without aid could not arrive at truth particularly in the moral and religious

orders, was condemned by the Church and today is generally rejected because of its gratuitous assumptions.

## Traditores

The Council of Arles (314) applied this term to those clerics who surrendered sacred vessels and writings into the hands of the persecuting authorities.

## Traducianism

This is the erroneous teaching of the fifth century that the soul of the offspring is originated and transmitted by the parents. It was condemned by Pope St. Anastasius II (d. 498).

## Transcendence

Transcendence is the nontemporal eternal event and actuality which is permanent in itself and therefore divine, and which is the beginning of all things. It is thus a progression from that which is given, to its essence, and thence to its supreme cause, or Being itself. It is because of the absolute transcendence of God that the world is turned by grace to that inmost principle whereby the creature himself has being. It can be said that the closer the independent being is to the Transcendent God, the closer the creature grows in the same proportion. This is the immanent fulfillment of the creature wherein the creature goes "from below" to a higher degree of being and thus rises above itself.

Finite man, therefore, cannot himself bring about his own fulfillment but can and must open himself to the recognition of God and the graces given. This is the very expectation of fulfillment, the "heartfelt expectation of the unknown Messiah" (M. Blondel) which for the Christian is the transcendence of grace elevating the human person to the plane where one can become with Christ an "heir of heaven." (See Salvation History.)

## Transcendental Meditation

This term, usually referred to simply as TM, is a system of basic meditation; it may be a preparation for religious meditation. Its purpose is to take a person out of his body consciousness. It thus "transcends" the natural and seeks to have the persons practicing TM remove themselves from immediate concerns and concentrate upon an aspect of their conscious being to bring this into a plane of keen observation and evaluation.

The method used is psychologically self-hypnotic. (1) Each person is given a "mantra," a sound to fit the person's personality. This sound becomes the personal key to enter into TM. Such sounds are not known to others, but are individualized, for example, the mantra assigned to a very dynamic person might be a strict contrast such as the susurrus of the wind or the rustle of a pine forest. (2) Concentration on the mantra for periods of 20 minutes or longer, gives the person better or refined concentration, a lowering of oxygen consumption, and decreased metabolic response. (3) The objective result is mental relaxation over muscle fatigue, a pervasive languor, and an ability to view the sources of fatigue and so conquer them or adjust the bodily function to actions that are more suitable to the person's makeup and stamina.

The practice of TM is considered to be a psychological exercise rather than a religious response. However, it may be both in that the inner insight gained may lead to a spiritual deepening or consciousness. TM has been introduced into athletics, research, and areas of monotonous human activity such as assembly-line work. It has its origin in the Indian and Asian countries and has become widespread in the modern world. (Cf. Ascetae.)

### Transfiguration

The divinity of our Lord was made manifest to Sts. Peter, James, and John by this event in the life of Christ (Mt. 17:1–8; Mk. 9:1–8). As the Scripture scholar Lagrange states, "the transfiguration serves as a sure pledge of Christ's future glory." A tradition, dating from the fourth century, identifies the mountain of transfiguration as that of Tabor in Galilee. St. Leo the Great explains the purpose of this event as the removal of the scandal of the cross from the hearts of the disciples. The transfiguration of Christ, together with the appearance of Moses and Elias, was a confirmation to the Apostles of what Christ had taught them concerning Himself as the Son of God and His relation to the Old Law. In the Church calendar a feast commemorates the transfiguration on Aug. 6.

The transfiguration prefigures the everlasting enthronement of Christ (Jn. 12:12–16; Mk. 1:9–11; Lk. 1:30–36; Heb. 1:5–14) and the beginning of His reign (Acts. 2:32–36; Phil. 2:6–11; Rv. 1:12–17; 5:1–14).

### Transitional Deacon

This new term distinguishes an ordained deacon who intends to proceed to the presbyterate (priesthood) as separate from the permanent deacons. When invested during the conferring of the sacrament, he is given the stole to be worn across one shoulder and across his body, with the ends fastened below the waist on the opposite side. (See Permanent Deacon; Orders, Holy, Sacrament of.)

### Transubstantiation

As defined by the Council of Trent, transubstantiation is "a singular and wondrous conversion of the total substance of bread into the body and of the total substance of wine into the blood of Christ, the external appearances only remaining unchanged." It is by this transubstantiation that the body and blood of Christ are present in the Holy Eucharist (Mk. 14:22–25).

### Tree of Jesse

This is basically a representation of the Blessed Mother of God. This symbol dates from the eleventh century and is based upon the prophecy of Isaias 11:1–5). (Cf. Jesse-Window.)

### Trent, Council of

The nineteenth ecumenical council of the Church, known as the Council of Trent, opened its first sessions in 1545, by action of Pope Paul III, and closed in 1547. It was reconvened in 1551 by Pope Julius III and adjourned the following year. Its third period, opened in 1562 under Pope Pius IV, closed finally after 25 sessions in December 1563. It drew up a platform of practical reform, defined doctrines, authenticated the Vulgate, enacted legislation on marriage (Tametsi), and formulated a revision of the Roman Breviary. Its work was so scholarly and extensive that for more than 300 years no other council was held.

### Trental

The Gregorian Masses are commonly so named in England.

### Tribunals, Roman

These are the courts of the Holy See, namely, the Sacred Apostolic Penitentiary, the Apostolic Signatura, and the Sacred Roman Rota. (See Curia, Roman)

### Tridion

In the Byzantine calendar, the Tridion is the title of the pre-Lenten season of preparation for the feast of Easter. It begins two days before Ash Wednesday as observed in the Roman rite calendar.

### Triduum

Triduum is the name of a three-day period of prayer. It is often held in preparation for a special feast.

### Trination

Trination is the name of the practice whereby it is permitted to celebrate the Eucharist three times in a twenty-four hour period. Ecclesiastical permission is required and is usually granted when there is a necessity to accommodate a large number of people.

### Trinity, the Most Holy

The most sublime mystery of the Christian faith is this: that "God is absolutely one in nature and essence, and relatively three in Persons (Father, Son, and Holy Spirit) who are really distinct from each other," but these Three are consubstantial, that is, identical with the divine substance. Christians know themselves to be the children of the living God, for under the New Law they have been raised to the state of sonship (1 Jn. 3:1–3). Christ the Son has revealed God the Father to those whom He has raised to sonship by the redemption and has taught them to pray "Our Father" (Mt. 6:9). At the same time, the Father reveals the Son: "This is my beloved Son. My favor rests on him" (Mt. 3:17). Thus, in the Son we see the Father and through Him we go to the Father (Jn. 1:18). And this mystery of the Father and the Son is confirmed by the Holy Spirit, the "Spirit of truth," whom the Son sends from the Father and the Father sends in the name of the Son (Jn. 15:26).

Through this revelation we have the Trinity which for us is a to-and-fro relationship of our possession of God and God's possession of us: "The grace of our Lord Jesus Christ, and the love of God, and the fellowship of the Holy Spirit be with you all (2 Cor. 13:13). Our life of sonship, our continuance in grace, through the Church, are functions of the Holy Spirit to whom is attributed the inspiration of Scriptures, the sanctification of Christ's mystical body, the distribution of the charismata, and the sanctification of the faithful. And Christians who receive the revelation of this tremendous Trinity through baptism and who, by being confirmed and benefited by grace, become "partakers of the divine nature," advance with faith assured, hope secure, and responding in love (2 Pt. 1:3–5).

### Triple Candle

The threefold candle once used in the liturgy of Holy Saturday represented the Blessed Trinity.

### Triptych

Threefold tablets joined by hinges are called triptychs.

### Trisagion

The Greek title of the thrice holy hymn: "Holy God, holy strong One, holy deathless One, have mercy on us" (cf. Is. 6:3). It is used in the Eastern rites and corresponds to a doxology in the Roman rite.

### Triumphalism

A concept, which arises out of an "assurance of having been saved," is called triumphalism. It derives from the idea that the merits of Christ are universal but are applied chiefly through the Church. Thus one is saved with little effort and tends to have a vaunting superiority, an established elitism. In the Christian this is a dangerous position for two reasons: (1) it leads to the presumption that one need not strive to become better through grace and response; (2) it tends to make salvation exclusive for some rather than others. This latter has been declared erroneous by the Church, which clearly teaches that there is salvation for peoples outside of the Church although the Church is the true sign of salvation, the "universal sacrament of salvation."

Vatican II teaches: "So it is that this Messianic people, although it does not actually include all men, and may more than once look like a small flock, is nonetheless a lasting and sure seed of unity, hope and salvation for the whole human race" (LG 9). (See Salvation.)

## Trivium
See Quadrivium.

## Truce of God
Accomplished by the Council of Elne (1027), the Truce of God prohibited armed hostilities from sundown on Saturday to Monday morning. Later it was extended from Wednesday night to the following Monday morning. The Synod of Clermont decreed the truce should be observed from Advent to the octave of Ephiphany and from Septuagesima to the octave of Pentecost.

## Trullo, Council in
The sixth ecumenical council, the Third of Constantinople, held in 680, is also referred to by this name.

## Truth Society, Catholic
See Catholic Truth Society.

## Tunic
Also called tunicle, this vestment is only a vestigial garment, worn at pontifical celebrations. It has an opening for the neck, with sleeves, and it is open at the sides and under the arms. It is less ornate than either the chasuble or dalmatic. (Cf. Dalmatic.)

## Turin, Shroud of
See, Shroud, Holy.

## Tutiorism
This is a moral system of interpretation of the law. As absolute tutiorism, it claims one must choose what is certain in every difference of opinion; as mitigated tutiorism, it claims one is free from an obligation if the opinion in favor of liberty is most probable.

## Twelfth Day
This is a little used name for the feast of Epiphany, 12 days after Christmas.

## Type
See Antitype; Mystical Sense of Scripture; Form Criticism.

## Typological Sense of Scripture
See Mystical Sense of Scripture; Form Criticism.

## Ubiquitarianism

This is the title given to a teaching held by many of the Protestant Reformers, notably, Martin Luther, that Christ is everywhere present in His human nature. Although this was defended for a time as an argument for the real presence of Christ in the Eucharist, it was later abandoned in its formal sense.

## Ultramontanism

This term came into use in the seventeenth century and stressed the movement within the Church that promoted papal authority over the episcopal jurisdictions. It was opposed to Gallicanism of the French Catholics who favored the establishment of national churches which would be independent of the Holy See.

The name derives from the expression *ultra montes,* meaning "beyond the mountains," that is, beyond the Alps. Thus the countries of Europe looked upon Rome as separate from secular governments and having the highest authority in the Church.

In the nineteenth century, this term was descriptive of the supporters of the definition of papal infallibility as set forth in the First Vatican Council. There were other issues that came under the efforts of the Ultramontanists, namely, the status of parish priests, the Roman liturgy, and the episcopal jurisdiction over clergy and religious orders. Many of the issues were more clearly defined in the teachings of Vatican II.

## Ultreya

From the Spanish word meaning "onward," this is the name given to the periodic or weekly meeting of cursillistas in a given area. It is called a "making visible" or manifest the Christian community attained through the Cursillo Movement. (See Cursillo.)

## Umbandism

Among the Umbanda natives of Brazil there is a representation idea whereby the image is transferred by magic to the man. It is an example of "initiative, symbolic sorcery," which is based on the occult law of "correspondence" wherein an image is substituted for the person, the effect is like the cause; by imitating the result desired, one brings the originating cause of that result into play.

This problem of Umbanda (a form of spiritism) is present in Brazil among some 12 million Brazilians who function in a state of complete and radical disorientation in the area of doctrine and religion. Here the introduction of native custom into Church response oversteps the bounds of the freedom to have a native cultism in the ceremony of the Church. Some think the problem will be solved by the establishment of a kind of Umbandist rite that will permit a certain degree of native adaptation in the ceremonies of the Church. There is an ongoing problem of how and to what degree the native or cultic ceremonies, be they dance or music, magic, or sorcery or other forms of spiritistic practices, may be allied with the traditional ritual of worship in the Church.

## Unam Sanctam

Published in 1302, the bull *Unam Sanctam* of Pope Boniface VIII declared the primacy of the Holy See.

## Unbaptized Infants

See Limbo.

## Unction

Used in connection with the administration of sacraments, the term refers to the anointing with holy oils.

Unction was a special sign very early in the Bible record. It was that ceremony wherein one was marked in a special manner for the service of Yahweh (1 Sm. 10:1–8; 16:1–13; 1 Kgs. 1:38–40). It was also the sign of the perfect one who was to be the future King, the Messiah (Ps. 2; 72; 110; Is. 45:1–8; 61:1–4). Jesus, "the Anointed One," was to be King, priest, and the One who was to be offered in the perfect service of sacrifice (Lk. 4:18–19; Acts 2:33; Heb. 1:3–9). It was through the anointing that Christ was given the threefold character: messianic, sacrificial, and filial (Lk. 3:22; 2:40). And this unction was to extend to all Christians as the messianic work to be done in establishing the Church through the Holy Spirit (cf. Mt. 3:16; Mk. 1:10; Heb. 1:1–12). (Cf. Extreme Unction.)

## Uniat (Uniate) Churches

Christians of the East who have been converted from the Orthodox Eastern Church and other older heresies are called Uniates. The Code of Canon Law designates them as *"Orientales"* (c. 1099). (Cf. Eastern Churches.)

## Uniformity, Acts of

The Acts of Uniformity were four pieces of legislation in England which enforced the use of the Common Book of Prayer, attendance at religious services, and the suppression of the Roman Rite Mass. The first was passed Jan. 21, 1549 in the reign of Edward VI; the second on April 14, 1552; the third in 1559 during the reign of Queen Elizabeth I; and the fourth was passed on May 19, 1662. The last, in an amended form, is still in force in England.

## Unigenitus

Literally, "one begotten," this is the first word and title of the bull of Pope Clement XI in which he condemned the Jansenistic teachings. It was published in 1713.

## Unitarianism

A form of Christian thought and religious observances which rejects the doctrine of the Most Holy Trinity and the divinity of Christ is called Unitarianism. It is thus a teaching of the unipersonality of God.

The Unitarians have no formal creed, and the development has taken on a rationalist form, with reason and conscience being the criteria of belief and practice. They believe in the omnigoodness of human nature and so implicitly deny the teachings of original sin, the atonement of Christ, and any further punishment for sins. The first Unitarian Church in America, King's Chapel, Boston, Massachusetts, opened in 1785. In more recent years Unitarianism has had an influence through the Divinity School of Harvard University.

## Union, Mystical

Mystical union is the highest state of the spiritual progression toward perfection, the culmination of the unitive way after the experience of the purgative and the illuminative stages. According to St. Teresa of Avila, in this full union (some call it "simple" union) God lays hold of all the powers of the soul and renders them fully passive so that the soul has no distraction and does not need to make an effort to maintain union. It is consciousness of the effects of sanctifying grace on the soul. (See Mysticism.)

## United Church of Christ

The merger of two Christian groups, the Congregational Christian Church and the Evangelical and Reformed Church, on June 25, 1957, brought into existence the American Protestant denomination known as the United Church of Christ. (Cf. Congregationalism.)

Negotiations that brought about the merger of these two church groups were begun in 1940, operating under a plan called the "Basis of Union." This was interpreted and refined in a drafting of the formula in 1947, and the leaders of the committees adopted the name United Church of Christ. Its beliefs recognize Christ as "our crucified and risen Lord," and teach a life after death and a judgment. Communion is celebrated weekly, and Christ is considered only spiritually present in the sacrament.

The United Church of Christ is governed by a system of associations and conferences held under a general synod, yet each church holds its own organization and autonomy.

## United Methodist Church

See Methodism.

## United States Catholic Conference (USCC)

This Conference is a civil corporation and secretariat in and through which the bishops of the United States serve together with other members of the Church on a broad basic program for the good of the Church and the society in which it functions. It is sponsored by the National Conference of Catholic Bishops. (See under separate listing.)

As a service agency for the National Conference, the USCC acts to carry out the civic and religious programs of the Roman Catholic Church in the United States. It is distinct from the National Conference in its purpose and function. Its general headquarters are located at: 1312 Massachusetts Ave. N.W., Washington, D.C. 20005.

On Jan. 1, 1967 the USCC took over the organization and operation of the former National Catholic Welfare Conference (see under separate listing). The USCC is to assist "the bishops in their service to the Church in this country by uniting the people of God where voluntary collective action on a broad interdiocesan level is needed." (Cf. Regions of Church Activities.)

The USCC acts through an Administrative Board with officers and committees. The programs are directed to major departments: Communications, Education, Social Development and World Peace. Each of these is directed by an equal number of episcopal and nonepiscopal members, priests, religious, and laity. Assisting the USCC is a National Advisory Council of bishops, priests, men and women religious, lay members whose function is to advise the Administrative Board concerning programs and enterprises.

The Committees, bureaus, and offices of the USCC are: (1) *Communications:* Communications development, National Catholic Office for Information, Film and Broadcasting, NC News Service, Creative Services; (2) *Education:* Elementary and Secondary Education, Higher Education, Religious Education, Family Life, Youth Activities; (3) *Social Development and World Peace:* Health Affairs, Chaplains' Services, Justice and Peace, Rural Life, Spanish-Speaking, Urban Affairs, Latin America, Migration and Refugee Services; (4) *Campaign for Human Development:* for anti-poverty programs (cf. separate listing); (5) *Related Organizations:* National Conference of Catholic Laity (cf. separate listing),National Catholic Community Service. (See National Pastoral Council.)

## United States Mission Council

See American Board of Catholic Missions.

## Unity

That which is characteristic and necessary to being is called unity. In theological terms this expresses the unity found in the Trinity wherein there is the unity of God in the plurality of Persons, the unity of the principle of being and the *one* being, the unity of substance, of action, the unity of substantial parts, etc.

In the revelation of God to mankind there was a progression in the manifestation of the mystery of His unity. At first there was only the cult of a single God. It was later in a progression of His manifestations that God revealed His transcendent nature over all pagan idols that had become the deities of mankind. God was the fullness of life from which it would be made evident that He is in Himself distinct from God yet in God. In this He came to reveal the Word made flesh and made more evident the depth of the mystery found in His unity (Jn. 5:16–24; 14:5–11; 17:10; 10:30 and especially Jn. 17:20–23).

The Son is witness of the Father (1 Cor. 15:24; 1 Jn. 47:17); the fatherhood which is communicated to mankind is the supernatural fatherhood (Jn. 6:46–47; Eph. 3:14–16). Although redeemed mankind has been made an heir of heaven, there is no communication of nature, yet we are truly sons, by adoption, of the Father (Jn. 3:3–7). Through the Holy Spirit, sent to mankind, who possesses the souls in faith (1 Jn. 4:8–21), all persons must come to live as God's children (Phil. 2:15–16; 1 Pt. 1:13–17) even as we have learned to petition Him as Father (Mt. 7:7–11; 6:7–15). Thus we must come

in the Christian progression, in the moral plan of God's will to save all, to "imitate" Christ in the relationship that exists in the unity of being between the Father and the Son in the life of Trinity through the Holy Spirit. This is stated by the Evangelist, John, in the narration of the prayer of Christ: "I am in the world no more, but these are in the world as I come to you. O Father most holy, protect them with your name which you have given me that they may be one, even as we are one" (Jn. 17:11).

It can be said that the unity of God is proved and reflected by the unity of Christians. As Vatican II declares: "By her relationship with Christ, the Church is a kind of sacrament or sign of intimate union with God, and of the unity of all mankind. She is also an instrument for the achievement of such union and unity. For this reason, following in the path laid out by its predecessors, this Council wishes to set forth more precisely to the faithful and to the entire world the nature and encompassing mission of the Church" (LG 1).

And: "The Lord Jesus, when He prayed to the Father, 'that all may be one . . . as we are one' (Jn. 17:21–22) opened up vistas closed to human reason. For He implied a certain likeness between the union of the Divine Persons, and the union of God's sons in truth and charity" (GS 24).

And: "The faithful are called upon to engage in the apostolate as individuals in the varying circumstances of their life. They should remember, nevertheless, that man is naturally social and that it has pleased God to unite those who believe in Christ in the People of God (cf. 1 Pt. 2:5–10) and into one body (cf. 1 Cor. 12:22)" (AA 18).

## Unity of the Church

See Marks of the Church; Unity.

## Universalism

1. The antinationalist teaching of some later Hebrew prophets (Isaiah and Jonah, for example) that God's plan of salvation included races other than the Jewish nation. It was in the refusal by Israel of the conditions of the messianic era that Christ, through the cross, was to bring about universal salvation (cf. Rom. 1, 2; Mt. 5:46–47), and He placed all under His domination (Col. 2:9–10; Eph. 1:10; 4:15), becoming the "King of all nations" (Rom. 9, 11; Rv. 15:3–4; 21:24–25).

2. The erroneous and heretical belief that hell is only a purgation and that it will eventually end and all persons will be saved at some time in the future. It is thus a contradiction by rationalization of the scriptural message.

## Upanishads

The commentaries and writings that form the basis for modern Hinduism are a collective work called Upanishads. (See Hinduism.)

## Urban College

See Roman College.

## Urbi et Orbi

From the Latin, meaning "to the city and to the world," this is the title applied to the solemn blessing given by the Holy Father immediately after his election at his coronation and during jubilee years. The faithful who with sentiments of piety and devotion receive this blessing given by the Supreme Pontiff, even by means of radio, may gain a plenary indulgence on the usual conditions.

## Urim and Thummim

Two Hebrew words used in the OT were designations for the means whereby the priests were able to give divinations of God's plan to the people (1 Sm. 14:41). There is no explanation of these terms, the word *urim* was used alone (Nm. 27:21; 1 Sm. 28:6), whereas *thummim* was not, and neither was used after the time of Solomon. The inclusion of Urim and Thummim in the breastplate of the High Priest in later times was probably a survival of the older tradition (cf. Ex. 28:30; Lv. 8:8;). The only clear understanding of these terms is in the marginal reference made in the Revised Version translation of the Bible wherein they are referred to as "the Lights and the Perfections."

## Usury

Usury is a sin against justice and requires restitution. It is committed when a lender demands a higher rate of interest on a loan of money than is established by law or custom.

## Utraquism

The teaching, first formulated by John Huss in 1414, that the laity like the clergy were to receive Holy Communion under both species of bread and wine. Although this is not a practice in the Roman Rite today, it is permitted according to the regulations of the Conferences of Bishops as set forth by the Vatican II document on the Liturgy.

## Vagi

Vagi is the canonical term for those who have no domicile or quasi-domicile. Such persons are bound by the laws of the place where they happen to stay. The ordinary of that place must be consulted when such a person wishes to marry (c. 91).

## Vaison, Councils of

These were two synods held by Church authorities at the city of Vaison in the southeastern part of France. They were primarily directed to matters of discipline. The first, which opened on Nov. 13, 442, formulated ten canons, including the ruling that priests were to receive the chrism at Easter from their own bishops, and the regulations for the adoption of children. The second, convened Nov. 5, 529, enacted five canons referring primarily to the liturgy, namely, that the Kyrie Eleison should be repeated three times in the Mass, that each Mass should have a prayer for the Pope, and that following the doxology of the "Glory be to the Father" there should be added the words: "as it was in the beginning, is now and ever shall be, world without end."

## Vakass

This is a tall, stiff collar worn around the neck by the celebrant in the Armenian Rite. This broad collar is distinctive of the Armenian priest's vesture for the liturgy.

## Valentinianism

This Gnostic heresy, formulated by Valentinus (d. 160), taught that mankind is divided into three classes: material men predestined to destruction, psychic men who may attain salvation through the redemption, and spiritual or perfect men who are destined to eternal life. The Valentinians, of course, considered themselves to be this third class. The heresy was refuted by St. Irenaeus. (Cf. Heresies.)

## Valid

Referring to the distinction between illicit and invalid, in canon law the term valid is interpreted:

when the law simply forbids an act, it is sinful and unlawful to violate it, but the act is valid in spite of the violation. However, when the law is worded so that nullity results from the violation, the act has no legal value and is called an invalid act (c. 11).

## Validation of Marriage

A marriage contract that is invalid because of one of these three essential conditions: presence of a diriment impediment, absence of true consent, or the lack of proper form, may be validated by dispensation or another correcting act. The procedure for validation is provided by canon law (cc. 1133-1137).

## Vandalism

The destructive action whereby one is deprived of what is good and useful is called vandalism. It is comparable to thievery and requires restitution on the part of the perpetrator. Widespread disregard for the rights of others through acts of vandalism is also criminal in its abuse of justice. Where such actions are directed against church property, they may also involve a sin against religion, especially where the desecration of church property takes place.

Psychologically vandalism is an expression of immaturity, the inability to cope with the world as it exists, and the personal lack of completeness in attaining more than a selfish attitude toward the values in life, resulting in retaliation. Violence is also associated with vandalism and indicates the frustration of, particularly, the spiritually unfilled person.

## Vartapet

In the Armenian Rite Churches the vartapet is a priest with the special function of being a preacher and teacher, but his rank is below that of the episcopacy. The Catholic Armenians (as distinguished from the dissident or Gregorian) have three degrees of the office of vartapet: the *masnavor* (minor), *zajrakouyn* (major), and the *aradchenord* (mitred). These would correspond to Reverend Monsignors in the Roman Rite.

## Vatican

1. The residence of the Supreme Pontiff in Vatican State.
2. The shortened term often applied to the state of Vatican City.
3. Descriptive term for the official position of the Roman Catholic Church on matters of religion and other issues.

4. Term sometimes applied, but not properly, to pronouncements of the Holy See on questions of doctrine or administration.

## Vatican Council I

The council convened in 1869 upon publication of the bull of assembly issued by Pope Pius IX in 1868. Its chief action was the definition of the doctrine of infallibility. In the debate over this, there were fourteen general sessions and sixty-four speeches were made. The dogma was promulgated in the council on July 18, 1870. In Sept. 1870, Pius IX suspended the council after the army of United Italy entered Rome. Vatican Council I was the twentieth ecumenical council, which although suspended indefinitely, could have been reconvened if necessary.

There were 700 bishops and other prelates in attendance, and 100 more came for the later sessions. The other significant teachings that came from the deliberations were: the Oneness of God, the Creator and Lord of all things visible and invisible; that God as Creator created both the material and spiritual worlds out of nothing; that all the books of the Scriptures are sacred, canonical, and inspired; the one true God can be known with certainty by human reason through observation and knowledge of created things; the revealed truths of God are believed because of the authority of God; miracles can be known and recognized with certainty, and the divine orgin of the Christian religion can be proved by miracles.

## Vatican Council II

The greatest religious event of the twentieth century, whose teachings and clarifications have yet to reach their full impact, was the twenty-first Ecumenical Council, called Vatican II or the Second Vatican Council.

The Council was opened by Pope John XXIII in St. Peter's Basilica, Rome, on Oct. 11, 1962. It was the first such council convened in the twentieth century, and only the second since the Protestant Reformation.

The announcement of the Council was made by Pope John on Jan. 25, 1959 after the celebration of a Mass for Christian unity. At the same time it was announced that there would be a diocesan synod held in Rome for the Diocese of the City and a complete revision of the Code of Canon Law.

Vatican II was the most widely attended, the most well prepared for council in Church history. It issued the most far-reaching statements of Church teaching since the beginning of Church history. As preparatory matter 119 booklets of

2060 pages were distributed, in which there were 67 schemata and the agenda for the meetings. These were prepared by thirteen commissions of experts in every field, all to be covered in the deliberations together with variant views to be considered. As the time drew near for the Council to begin, Pope John issued a motu proprio, *Appropinquante concilio* ("At the Approach of the Council") on Aug. 6, 1962, in which he provided for three kinds of meetings: (1) public, or solemn sessions with the Pope acting as president, for ceremonial purposes and for final voting on all constitutions; (2) general congregations or working sessions under the direction of the one to ten Cardinals of the Council of the Presidency, who would be named by the Pope personally, and in which sessions the debates, alternate position papers, and preliminary votes would be taken; (3) the commission meetings, which were to draft immediate changes and make any necessary additions.

The Council was held in the nave of St. Peter's Basilica, with arrangements to provide seating in two facing tiers of seats to accommodate the 2300 bishops and prelates. The papal throne was placed near the Confession of St. Peter, under the fore-arch of the dome. Provision was also made for representatives of the press, television, and radio, for the host of *periti* (experts) and for the governmental ambassadors and representatives of countries (a group excluded from Vatican I), and the official attendants from other Christian Churches. These groups were further expanded by the presence of 1000 superiors of religious congregations.

The first session of the Council opened solemnly in October, 1962, and closed Dec. 8, 1962. There were six schemata discussed in thirty-six general congregations. The second session was opened on Sept. 29, 1963, with seventy-nine schemata awaiting resolution, and it closed on Dec. 4, 1963. The third session began deliberations on Sept. 14, 1964, and only six days before its opening Pope Paul VI announced that for the first time in the history of the Church women would be admitted to the working sessions. This third session closed on Nov. 21, 1964. The fourth and final session convened on Sept. 14, 1965 and closed solemnly on Dec. 8, 1965.

Vatican Council II saw the death of its initiator; Pope John XXIII died on June 3, 1963, and Giovanni Cardinal Montini of Milan was elected the supreme Pontiff on June 21. He took the name of Paul VI, and the Council continued under the progressive position that Paul VI had expressed in support of the Council even before its beginning.

Sixteen documents of unusual insight, tremendous revision, and world-acclaimed contributions, came from the Council, as well as new disciplines in thought and action. It was to usher in "the beginning of a new era in Roman Catholic history." This Council was envisioned and stood in sharp contrast to all previous councils because, following the direction and guidance of the beloved Pope John XXIII, this was a "pastoral" council rather than one of dogmatic proclamations. It was to open to the modern world and to non-Catholic Christians neither a formula of condemnation nor a mold for a new status quo. Its every decree was to stimulate new developments, to loosen the restrictive and often rigid formulas of the past, and provide a far-reaching charter for the future. This can be seen especially in two basic shifts in the Church's outlook: first, there is a great renewal of biblical study and the consequent profound altering of the Church's devotional understanding and piety; second, the liturgical movement is the most revolutionary because of the great importance of worship in the lives of Catholics. It was in the *Constitution on the Sacred Liturgy* that the Council Fathers passed beyond the polemics of the Reformation period and established a new and incisive look into the man-God relationship of worship, of response and ministry, of participation and individual salvation consciousness.

Vatican Council II drew up and promulgated the following sixteen documents consisting of four Constitutions, nine Decrees, and three Declarations. These are presented here with a brief statement of their content, but they are not presented in the order of their adoption and promulgation.

1. *Dogmatic Constitution on the Church (Lumen Gentium):* this is a statement of the awareness of the role the Church has in the carrying out of the mandate of Christ, to make the light of the gospels shine in every person and in all nations.

2. *Dogmatic Constitution on Divine Revelation (Dei Verbum):* the assessment of the Church's role in fulfilling the words of St. John: "What we have seen and heard we proclaim in turn to you so that you may share life with us" (1 Jn. 1:3).

3. *Constitution on the Sacred Liturgy (Sacrosanctum Concilium):* wherein the entire liturgy of the Church is revamped and the emphasis placed on participation of all in the communal worship of the People of God.

4. *Pastoral Constitution on the Church in the Modern World (Gaudium et Spes):* this document in two main thrusts treats of "the Church and man's calling"

and "some problems of special urgency."

5. *Decree on the Instruments of Social Communication (Inter Mirifica):* although this is perhaps the weakest of the documents, due to a constant changing of the means, it still sets forth its intent to "unite the interior and the exterior life, contemplation and action, prayer and the active apostolate."

6. *Decree on Ecumenism (Unitatis Redintegrato):* this establishes a basis for Christian unity throughout the world.

7. *Decree on Eastern Catholic Churches (Orientalium Ecclesiarum):* this gives thrust and hope for a corporate reunion with those Eastern Churches not presently in union with the Church of Rome.

8. *Decree on the Bishops' Pastoral Office in the Church (Christus Dominus):* this reflects the comment of Pope Paul VI that a bishop must be "the image of the Father and the image of Christ."

9. *Decree on Priestly Formation (Optatum Totius):* this provides a theology of the presbyterate, joining the priestly office with that of the episcopacy.

10. *Decree on the Appropriate Renewal of the Religious Life (Perfectae Caritatis):* in an early statement of Pope Paul VI this sets forth "this state of life, distinctly characterized by the profession of the evangelical vows, is a perfect life according to the teaching and example of Jesus Christ" (1964, note 210).

11. *Decree on the Apostolate of the Laity (Apostolicam Actuositatem):* this reflects the existing divine plan for the human creature: "There is one Lord, one faith, one baptism; one God and Father of all, who is over all, and works through all, and is in all" (Eph. 4:5–6).

12. *Decree on the Ministry and Life of Priests (Presbyterorum Ordinis):* this points out that the priest "is the visible sign, the means and living instrument, of Christ the eternal Priest amid the community of believers."

13. *Decree on the Church's Missionary Activity (Ad Gentes):* this speaks on the mission of all men to the world, for as St. Benedict Joseph Labre said, "It is souls and not actions that are apostolic; the presence of a saint always sanctifies to some extent; and no intense life of the spirit is ever wasted as far as mankind is concerned."

14. *Declaration on Christian Education (Gravissimum Educationis):* this directs a dialogue with the modern world through the establishment of a pattern of human life in every aspect of living.

15. *Declaration on the Relationship of the Church to Non-Christian Religions (Nostra Aetate):* the emphasis here is placed on a single community of all peoples of faith.

16. *Declaration of Religious Freedom (Dignitatis Humanae):* here emphasis is placed on the dignity of the individual, human freedom, and the general welfare of society.

The study and meditation of each of the documents are most worthy for everyone, for Vatican II must be considered the start of a program that will progress through years to come with the ideals and ultimate results to be judged and reaped by future generations. As Pope Paul VI said to the Council Fathers at the closing: "From our long meditation on Christ and His Church, there should spring forth at this moment a first announcement of peace and salvation for the waiting multitudes. Before concluding, the Council wishes to fulfill this prophetic function and to translate into brief messages and in a language accessible to all men, the 'good news' which it has for the world and which some of its most respected spokesmen are now about to pronounce in your name for the whole of humanity."

## Vatican State, City of

The capital city of the Vatican State, which includes the principal territory of the surrounding city of Rome, was recognized as sovereign land of the Roman Catholic Church by the Lateran Treaty. It includes the Vatican palace, its gardens, the basilica and piazza of St. Peter's, and other official buildings on a plot of land about one square mile with approximately 1000 residents, all of whom are citizens. It is properly called the papal state and is governed by the pope as the sovereign ruler with executive, legislative, and judicial powers exercised through commissions or delegated groups. There are other properties fixed by the treaty not adjoining Vatican State yet under its sovereign dominion. These are the basilicas and buildings of St. John Lateran, St. Mary Major, St. Paul-outside-the-Walls, and the Holy Apostles, and the churches of Saint Andrea-della-Valle and San Carlo-ai-Catarini with their adjoining buildings, the palace of San Callisto and the papal summer residence, Castel Gandolfo. (Cf. Papacy.)

## Vaudois

This is the name of followers of Peter Valdo of Valdes, a merchant of Lyons, France, who preached repentance and the giving of all goods to the poor; hence they were called the "Poor Men of Lyons." (See Heresies.)

## Veil

There are six liturgical veils used in the Roman rite: the humeral veil, a vestment; the tabernacle veil; the chalice veil; the lenten veil, which is the purple covering placed over all crosses, statues, and pictures of our Lord and the saints from before Vespers of Passion Sunday until after the Gloria of the Mass on Holy Saturday; the gremial veil, a pontifical accessory; and the vimpa.

## Venerable

1. Title permitted by the Church to be prefixed to the name of a candidate for beatification. This does not authorize public veneration (cf. Blessed).

2. The title of address of some religious and superiors.

3. The title "Venerable Brother" is usually used by the pope in addressing a brother bishop in communion with Rome.

## Veneration of the Saints

Special worship, called *dulia,* is due to the saints and angels because they, as friends of God, participate in His excellence. It is permitted to venerate the saints anywhere, but those classed as "blessed" may be venerated only in those places where the Holy See permits and in the manner approved (c. 1277). Absolute veneration is that accorded to the saints or angels themselves; relative veneration is that given to images. Only genuine relics may be exposed publicly for veneration. (Cf. Relics, Sacred; Latria; Hyperdulia.)

According to the general instructions of the Roman Missal (Sacramentary) it is stated: "In accord with ancient tradition images of Christ, Mary, and the saints are venerated in churches. They should, however, be placed so as not to distract the faithful from the actual celebration. They should not be too numerous, there should not be more than one image of the same saint, and the correct order of saints should be observed. In general, the piety of the entire community should be considered in the decoration and arrangement of the church" (n. 278).

## Veni Creator Spiritus

This is the Latin title of a famous hymn, one that is most widely used as an invocation of the Holy Spirit. The author is probably Rabanus Maurus (776 to 856), although both St. Ambrose and St. Gregory the Great have been hailed as the writer of this devotional tribute to the Holy Spirit as Creator, that is, one of the Three Divine Persons who concurred in the Creation. The sevenfold gifts mentioned refer to the gifts of the Holy Spirit. (See under separate entry.)

The English translation is as follows:

Creator-Spirit, all-Divine,
Come, visit every soul of Thine,

And fill with Thy celestial flame
The hearts which Thou Thyself didst frame.

O gift of God, Thine is the sweet
Consoling name of Paraclete—
And spring of life and fire and love
And unction flowing from above.

The mystic sevenfold gifts are Thine,
Finger of God's right hand divine;
The Father's promise sent to teach
The tongue a rich and heavenly speech.

Kindle with fire brought from above
Each sense, and fill our hearts with love;
And grant our flesh, so weak and frail,
The strength of Thine which cannot fail.

Drive far away our deadly foe,
And grant us Thy true peace to know;
So we, led by Thy guidance still,
May safely pass through every ill.

To us, through Thee, the grace be shown
To know the Father and the Son;
And Spirit of Them both, may we
Forever rest our faith in Thee.

To Sire and Son be praises meet,
And to the Holy Paraclete;
And may Christ send us from above
That Holy Spirit's gift of love.

## Venial Sin
See Sin.

## Versicle
A versicle is a short part of the responses in the Divine Office. It is usually part of a Scripture verse.

## Versions of the Bible
See Bible.

## Vespers
The sixth of the canonical hours of the Divine Office, the evening hour, is usually composed of: five Psalms, their antiphons, a short lesson, versicle and response, a hymn, the Magnificat and antiphon, and the prayer of the day. As the evening service of churches, monastic and others, it is sung between 3 and 6 P.M. (See Liturgy of the Hours.)

## Vessels, Sacred
See Sacred Vessels.

## Vestments
Historically, these are the garments worn by priests and assistants in the celebration of Mass. They were not borrowed or adopted from those of pagan priests and priestesses, nor were they invented by the Church merely as decorative adjuncts. They were derived from the garments worn by priests and laymen during the early days of the Church, especially during the persecutions. They have been retained because of motives of reverence and as symbolic reminders of the early Church and the continuity of the Church down through the centuries. During the Middle Ages, after the number of vestments had been fixed, there were innovations of decoration and style, notably the Gothic, which modified their functional purposes, but retained the historic significance. In the Roman rite there are vestments of two kinds: the *outer* vestments of silk, the chasuble, dalmatic, tunicle, and stole; the *inner* vestments of linen, the amice, alb, and cincture. Canon and liturgical laws and Church tradition, together with the dictates of sacred art, prescribe the form and material of vestments.

The traditional colors are retained in the modern church, namely, white, red, green, violet, black, and rose (which may be used on the Third Sunday of Advent and on the Fourth Sunday of Lent).

Styles in wearing, color, design, function, and materials permit a wide adaptation to modern conditions.

## Viaticum
This is the name of Holy Communion when it is given in a public or private manner to someone in danger of death, during an illness, or to soldiers going into battle. It may thus be given without the Communion fast and may be repeated during an illness as often as required. When Anointing of the Sick is administered at the same time, viaticum precedes.

## Vicar
In general, vicar is the prefixed title of a cleric who takes the place of another according to canon law and exercises authority in an ecclesiastical office in his name in accord with the limitations laid down in the law. There are several designations: Vicar-Apostolic, who serves directly subordinate to the Holy See (cf. Prefect Apostolic); Vicar Capitular, elected by the cathedral chapter to govern a diocese during a vacancy; Vicar Forane, one presiding over a deanery; Vicar General, who is appointed within a diocese and who exercises the habitual powers granted to the bishop by indult; Vicar Parochial, who takes the place of a pastor.

## Vicar of Christ
This title signifies the supreme authority of the pope as the representative of Christ on earth and the visible head of the mystical body.

## Vice Chancellor

A vice chancellor is an assistant to a chancellor of a diocese; also appointed by the bishop.

## Vienne, Council of

The fifteenth ecumenical council was opened by Pope Clement V in 1311; it instituted many laws of reform and corrected the idea of Franciscan poverty as practiced. The edicts of the council, however, are only known from contemporaneous writings since the original records of the council have disappeared.

## Vigil

In Church use, the term is applied to the day preceding a feast, which is observed as a preparation for the feast by acts of penance or devotion, or both. (See Calendar, Church.)

## Vigil Light

Vigil light is the widely used term for a small votive candle usually burned before a shrine. These small candles, burned in cup-like glass containers, are symbolical of the light of prayer, but they are not blessed and are not required or liturgical.

## Vimpa

This is a seldom used veil, placed over the shoulders and hands and used by an attendant who holds the crosier at pontifical functions.

## Vincent de Paul, Society of St.

The members of this society are commonly referred to as Vincentians. It is an international society of Catholic laymen who serve as volunteers and perform works of charity for the poor. In particular, their objective is to relieve the physical needs of the poor and to counsel them so that they may overcome their wants and satisfy their spiritual needs. The society is under the regulation of the general council in Paris, and is established with national, central, diocesan councils, and particular councils. The society was begun in the United States in 1845, with the first branch in St. Louis, Missouri.

## Virgin Birth of Christ

This dogma of the Church declares that Christ, the Son of God, was born by external generation of only one parent, the Blessed Virgin Mary, and that she did not lose her virginity, either physical or spiritual. This doctrine is evident in the manner of expression, in the fact, and in the interpreted meaning of the Gospel record (Lk. 1:26–38). Mary was vowed to virginity; the angel in replying to Mary's question (Lk. 1:35) declares that God's design will not affect her vow, since the Child is to have no father but God, that is, be conceived of the Holy Spirit "Jesus is the Son of God not because of His temporal but because of His external generation."

## Virgin Mary

Accusation has been made by many rationalists and others attacking the perpetual virginity of Mary because of reference in the gospel to the "brethren" of our Lord. This reference denotes solely a group of cousins. It is clear from the gospels that Mary kept her resolve and had no other children after the virginal birth of Christ. Christ is named as the "only" child (Lk. 2:41–52) and was known in Nazareth as "the son of Mary" (Mk. 6:3). Further indication is given that Christ, in dying on the cross, gave his Mother to the care of St. John (Jn. 19:26–27). The doctrine of Mary's virginity as a perpetual state is also attested in the Church by the writings of Sts. Jerome, Ambrose, John Chrysostom, and Augustine. (Cf. Virgin Birth of Christ; Mary, Virgin Mother of God.)

## Virginity

The evangelical counsel of virginity is one that must be considered in the context of human sexual nature. This means that it can only be fully understood in terms of self-love, love of neighbor, and love of God. The person makes a free choice in the use of the sex faculty in the realization of his being as a person. This gives one the choice of the exercise of this faculty in the possibility of marriage or the decision to forego the use of the sex faculty.

Virginity is thus a form of chastity. There are options open to each person: to exercise the sex faculty; to forego the sex faculty; to sublimate the faculty; or to choose complete continence for a greater good.

Besides this *natural* approach there is also the eschatological sense or supernatural attitude toward sex as a faculty of the human person. Christ spoke of the eschatological sense in both its real and ideal applications when He said: "When people rise from the dead, they neither marry nor are given in marriage but live like angels in heaven" (Mt. 22:30; cf. also Mk. 12:25; Lk. 20:34–36; Rv. 14:4).

For the Christian there are the special considerations, for each Christian is motivated by and filled with a new life (cf. 1 Cor. 5, 6:12–19; Eph. 4:17–24; 5:20). In the exercise of the faculty of sex in marriage there is the obligation of subordinating this to the eschatological ideal (1 Cor. 7:29). In the foregoing of the use of the sex faculty, the human person exercises the choice of eschatological virginity for the higher ideal (cf. Mt. 19:10–12; Lk. 18:29–30).

In this regard, Vatican II declared: "The holiness of the Church is also fostered in a special way by the observance of the manifold counsels proposed in the gospel by our Lord to His disciples. Outstanding among them is that precious gift of divine grace which the Father gives to some men (cf. Mt. 19:11; 1 Cor. 7:7) so that by virginity, or celibacy, they can more easily devote their entire

selves to God alone with undivided heart (cf. 1 Cor. 7:32–34). This total continence embraced on behalf of the kingdom of heaven has always been held in particular honor by the Church as being a sign of charity and stimulus towards it, as well as a unique fountain of spiritual fertility in the world" (LG 42).

And: "For the counsels, voluntarily undertaken according to each one's personal vocation, contribute greatly to purification of heart and spiritual liberty. They continually kindle the fervor of charity. As the example of so many saintly founders shows, the counsels are especially able to pattern the Christian man after that manner of virginal and humble life which Christ the Lord elected for Himself, and which His Virgin Mother also chose" (LG 46).

## Virtue

A virtue is a habit that perfects the powers of the soul (intellect, will, and memory) and inclines one to do good. Virtues according to their source are either *natural*, those acquired by human activity, or *supernatural*, those infused by God. Virtues according to their object are either *divine* (theological) or *moral*: the former having God as their object, the latter, something created by God as their object, for example, one's fellowman.

In its widest sense and most perfect form of development, virtue is the highest expression of one's soul. It is thus primarily intellectual, the result of obtaining through education, family life, and example the greatest regard for values that affect the human person's life. Virtue in the more limited sense (that is, in its natural application) is the skill or ability to act rightly and with ease through acquiring and developing natural goodness.

The three highest virtues are the theological virtues, which are infused supernatural means whereby the human person's whole ethical, religious, and spiritual life is directed toward the possession of God. (See Salvation.)

## Virtues

This is the name for one of the choirs of angels. (Cf. Angel.)

## Visions

A revelation of the personal mystery of God to an individual is the free gift of God called a vision. Such visions are the fruit of contemplation and the reward of union with the majestic Being of God. St. Teresa of Avila speaks of these as having the following characteristics: that God "contains the will and even the understanding, as it seems to me, seeing that it makes no reflections, but is occupied in the fruition of God." St. Alfonsus Rodriguez wrote: "The bodily eyes see what is before them, not what is behind, but the eyes of the soul, which is a spirit, see not before only but also behind, to the right and left. Thus the soul is *enclosed in the midst of God,* possesses God, sees Him and knows Him from all sides by the aid of that bright light that God communicates to her for the purpose of seeing Him and tasting Him. But she does not understand Him, for He alone understands Himself."

## Visitatio Liminum Apostolorum

See Ad Limina.

## Visitation, Episcopal

The rule requires that bishops make a canonical visit throughout the whole of their dioceses once every five years.

## Visitation of Mary

The visit made by the Blessed Mother of Christ to her cousin, Elizabeth, while Mary was pregnant, is recorded in the Gospels (Lk. 1:39–45). The greeting given to Mary by Elizabeth, the mother of St. John the Baptist, namely, "Blessed art thou among women" is, in the Hebrew idiom: "More blessed art thou than all women." It was at this visit that the Blessed Virgin spoke her canticle, the Magnificat. (Cf. Magnificat.)

## Visitor, Apostolic

An apostolic visitor is a special legate of the Holy See. He is assigned the duty to visit and report on a diocese, an ecclesiastical territory, or the province of a religious order.

## Vladyka

From the Slovenian, meaning "ruler" or "master," this is the Slavic form for addressing a bishop.

## Vocation

In its ecclesiastical sense, vocation is the calling of one to a religious life, particularly the calling to the priesthood. There is an essential distinction to be made in this regard: first, the vocation must be considered from the standpoint of the person; thus if a man has the moral and intellectual fitness and a sincere supernatural motive (service of God through man), he may be considered to possess the disposition, at least, for aspiring to the priesthood. Second, from the standpoint of the need of the Church, that is, the direct call to serve given by the bishop after he has judged the candidate worthy and invited him to accept the Sacrament of Holy Orders. The fact of not receiving such a call or accepting it on the part of a person does not mean that the failure has been an instance of fault in the personal aspects of the aspirant. Both priests and laity should prudently encourage and instruct those who show an inclination to the priesthood or religious life (c. 1353).

Recent surveys have shown that there is a serious shortage of priests throughout the world. Some of the causes for this are the moral values of the modern world, the loneliness of the life of service, the defection of ordained priests and religious and the return to the lay state by many sisters and brothers, the absence of example, and the change in cultural values especially in the study and graduate work of students.

In the scriptures we have a further understanding of the idea of vocation. Each person is called, for God by calling each one to communion with His Son, invites us to peace, liberty, and sanctification (1 Cor. 1:9; Col. 3:15; Gal. 5:13; 1 Thes. 4; 7). The vocation of each Christian is the call to the heritage of everlasting life won for us by Christ (Heb. 9:15; Phil. 3:14; Mt. 22:1–14; Rv. 19:9; 1 Tm. 6:12; 2 Thes. 2:14). Further the Christian receives his vocation through the mediation of the Church, in the communal aspect of God's call to each one to seek salvation and perfection (cf. Rom. 9:7; 1 Cor. 12:1–11; Col. 3:15; Eph. 4:1–12).

Vatican II recognized this universal call of human persons: "In order for individual men to discharge with greater exactness the obligations of their conscience toward themselves and the various groups to which they belong, they must be carefully educated to a higher degree of culture through the use of the immense resources available today to the human race. Above all the education of youth from every social background has to be undertaken, so that there can be produced not only men and women of refined talents, but those great-souled persons who are so desperately required by our times.

"Now a man can scarcely arrive at the needed sense of responsibility unless his living conditions allow him to become conscious of his dignity, and to rise to his destiny by spending himself for God and for others" (GS 31).

And: "An outstanding cause of human dignity lies in man's call to communion with God" (GS 13).

## Vocationum, Opus

This is the title of a pious association whose main objective is the development and fostering of vocations to the priesthood. It may be canonically established in a diocese in order that a sufficient supply of priests be available; it may also provide the prayers, alms, and sacrifices upon which this supply often depends. Canonically established, this association is the Sodality for the Development of Priestly Vocations, under the patronage of Mary Immaculate Queen of the Clergy (A.S.S. 1922, 449).

## Voluntarism

Voluntarism is the teaching that holds that the will of the human person has precedence over reason. Theologically this leads to the idea of arbitrary determination of moral good by the will of God. Psychological voluntarism places the will as predominant in human life and consciousness. By will is meant desire, instinct, or action. However, this eliminates the psychophysical functions of the body that in no way depend on the will to function.

## Votive Mass

The name is given to a Mass said according to the intention or desire of the celebrant rather than according to the feast of the calendar. A votive Mass may also be said because it is directed by authority or because of circumstance. (Cf. Mass.)

## Votive Offerings

Such offerings are spiritual or material things, vowed, promised, or dedicated to God or one of the saints.

## Votive Office

A votive office is an office other than that which is proper for the day. The only votive office now permitted is that of the Blessed Mother, said on Saturdays when no other special feast occurs.

## Vow

A vow is a deliberate, voluntary promise made to God, binding under sin, by which one obliges oneself to do something that is pleasing to God and that does not hinder or prevent a higher good (c. 1307). A vow is public when it is made before a representative of the Church, for example, before one's parish priest; it is private when made without the intervention of any official person. Vows may be simple or solemn.

## Vulgate

See Bible.

QRSTUVWXYZ

## Wanderer Forum

The Wanderer Forum is a nonofficial, annual gathering of conservative-minded Catholics, sponsored by *The Wanderer,* a weekly conservative newspaper published in St. Paul, Minnesota. The forum meets in St. Paul and directs itself to a critical analysis of all Church-related pronouncements and actions. Although its membership is voluntary, it is directed by a relatively small number of conservatives who are not at ease with Vatican II changes. Its influence is regarded as minimal in the development of the liturgy and action of the Church in the United States.

## War, Morality of

According to Catholic teaching, both offensive and defensive war is lawful for a sufficiently just casue. This cause must be serious enough to justify the great evils associated with war. No one may take part in an evidently unjust war. In waging war it is not permitted to do any act or use any means forbidden by divine or international law. Although murder is forbidden by divine law, killing of the enemy is permissible in war on the ground of the lawfulness of defense against an unjust aggressor or to secure one's rights if no one in higher authority will protect them. (See Pacifism.)

## Washing of Feet

See Maundy Thursday.

## Water, Holy

See Holy Water.

## Way of the Cross

See Stations of the Cross.

## Week, Holy

See Holy Week, Liturgy of.

## Whitsunday

See Pentecost.

## Wine, Liturgical Use of

1. For the use in the Sacrifice of the Mass, the wine must be true, pure grape wine, that is, it must be properly fermented. It should not have less than 5% alcohol (with less it will spoil) and not more than 18%.

2. The pope after a solemn Mass, and newly ordained priests immediately after communion, receive a drink of consecrated wine.

3. A cask of wine is offered by a priest when he is consecrated a bishop.

4. Wine is used in the ceremonial washing of an altar before consecration; also wine is used in the consecration of the *antimension,* or portable altar, of the Byzantine rite.

## Wisdom

The goal of effort toward knowledge is wisdom: "wisdom is the truth beyond the effort of thought, which can still be attained without it, while truth is wisdom under the aspect of being arrived at."

Theologically, the "knowledge of truth" ran a parallel course with faith (1 Tm. 2:3–7; 2 Tm. 2:24–26; Ti. 1:1–3; 2 Jn. 1:1–3). And what transcends all knowledge is the mystery of God's love in Christ (Eph. 3:18–19; Col. 2:2–3; 1 Cor. 13:10–13).

## Wisdom, Book of

The title of this book of the OT in the Greek versions is "The Wisdom of Solomon." It is generally acknowledged that this book was written in the Greek language, which rules out Solomon as its author. It was written in the first half of the second century B.C. by an unknown author or authors. The style is that of an imaginative meditation on sacred history. It is broadly concerned with the rewards and punishments after death. The Book of Wisdom is deuterocanonical.

## Witness

The testimony of one's life, actions, and social responsibility is called the witness, which is the norm for the Christian.

Vatican II declared: "All the disciples of Christ, persevering in prayer and praising God (cf. Acts 2:42–47), should present themselves as living sacrifices, holy and pleasing to God (cf. Rom. 12:1). Everywhere on earth they must bear witness to Christ and give an answer to those who seek an account of that hope of eternal life which is in them (cf. 1 Pt. 3:15)" (LG 10).

## Women

The role of the woman in salvation is neither subservient nor entirely equal in the modern understanding of the term. In the OT women did not have a high social position but were considered as minors. (cf. Lv. 27:3–4; Nm. 27:1–10; Dt.

22:23–28). Yet woman was often considered as a model of virtue, a joy, and a favor of heaven (cf. 2 Sm. 11:1–5; Ez. 24:15–18; Sir. 36:23–27; Prv. 12:4–5).

The true understanding of women can be seen only in the position they have in the new covenant. Christ wished to free women of their former inferior position in society (Lk. 8:1–3; 10:38–42; Jn. 12). They are thus seen as man's equal, and they took an active part in the early Church; a woman was the first person to witness the resurrection (1 Cor. 7:3–5; Jn. 20:1–7; Rom. 16:1–2; Acts 5:12–16; 16:13–15; Phil. 4:2–3). In the assembly of the Church, by tradition and teaching, women are silent for the burden of proclaiming the word is the function of men (1 Cor. 14:34–35; 1 Tm. 2:11–12; cf. also Lk. 2:19).

In the modern Church it has been the consistent teaching that, while the part women are to take in the service of God is expanded to ministries, they are called to be "disciples and collaborators" but not ordained ministers, as Pope Paul VI has declared. They are called to seek greater leadership roles, expanded education, and collaborative work in the apostolate of all. (See Ministries; Apostolate.)

### World Council of Churches

This is an international organization which is described as a "fellowship of churches" all of which acknowledge Jesus Christ as Lord and Savior. It was established Aug. 23, 1948 in Amsterdam with the ratification of a constitution by 147 communions. Its work is social and doctrinal. In 1971 the International Missionary Council directed to World Mission and Evangelism was incorporated into the WCC. The Joint Commission on Society, Development and Peace (SODEPAX) and the Pontifical Commission for Justice and Peace of the Catholic Church are agencies of the WCC. Headquarters for the International Council are in Geneva, Switzerland.

### Worship

See Liturgy; Latria.

### Wreath, Advent

It is a custom, though nonliturgical, to suspend a circlet of boughs of cedar or pine, with four candles, as a symbol of the "Light of Christ" being born into the world.

### Wycliffites

See Lollards.

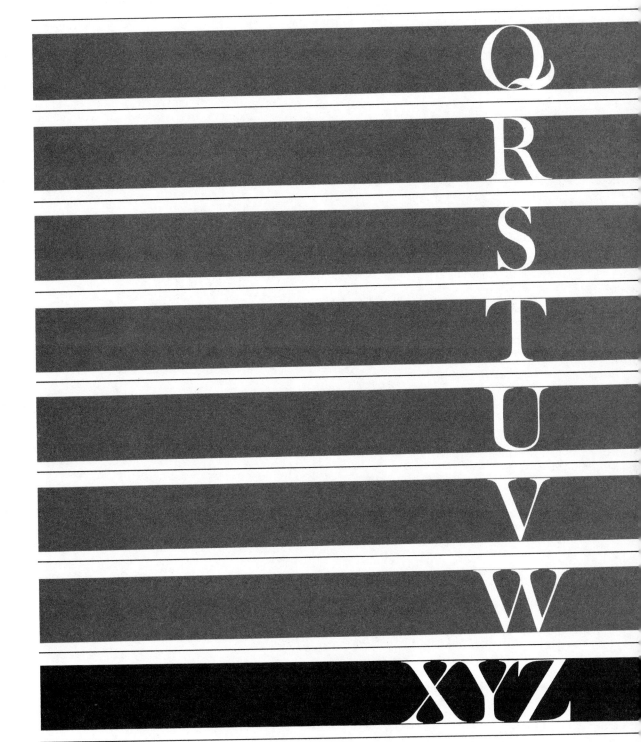

## Xerophagy

The fasting practiced by the members of the Montanist heresy, was given this name. It is also the fast of a more strict nature practiced by Eastern Churches. The word is derived from the Greek, meaning "dry food."

## Yahweh

In Hebrew, one of the proper names of God, often rendered in English as Jehovah, is Yahweh. The traditional explanation of the term is given in Ex. 3:14–17. (See Tetragrammaton.)

## Yoga

The meaning of this word from the Sanscrit is "to yoke." Today it has two meanings in India: (1) a system of discipline through which one attains to *moksha*, or salvation; (2) a system of philosophy, which is one of the six major schools of thought in India.

There are various kinds of Yoga: *Hatha-yoga* which is bodily in nature and is concerned with the physical preparation, the postures and the eight kinds of breathing exercises, all of which are preparatory to concentration. *Bhakti-yoga* is mystical and strives for union with the god Ishvara through devotion. *Raja-yoga* is concerned directly with concentration, by the exclusion of all outside distractions. *Jnana-yoga* is the highest form, and through this one attains the desired goal by means of knowledge. (See Hinduism.)

## Yom Kippur

See Hebrew Feasts.

## Youth, Impediment of

This term is sometimes used for "impediment of age." (Cf. Impediments of Marriage.)

## Youth Organization, Catholic

Abbreviated C.Y.O., this is an organization founded in Chicago, by Bishop Bernard J. Sheil, in 1930, to promote leadership, worthwhile occupation, and development in all phases of its members' lives. The organization may be established as autonomous in any diocese and is directed as an agency of the diocese.

## Zachary, Canticle of

See Benedictus.

## Zeal

Zeal is the motive of love and the resulting action that prompt one to serve God. It may be disturbed by a scrupulous attitude.

## Zechariah, Book of

The prophetical book of the OT, written by the Prophet Zechariah (the name in Hebrew means "God remembers") in the fifth century B.C., is one of the most difficult and enigmatic books of the Bible, but its central theme is Messianic, and in doctrine it refers to the eternal Jerusalem, heaven.

## Zephaniah, the Book of

Also called Sophonia, this prophetic book of the Bible whose author is a poet, Sophonia, was probably written in the seventh century B.C. It is concerned with four prophecies: the ills to befall Jerusalem (1:2; 1:15); against the nations (2:4–15); against the rulers of Jerusalem who were causing the city to fall (3:1–5) and consolation for the Gentiles (3:9–13). It closes with a joyful hymn.

The main theological significance of this book rests in the moral and eschatological areas, where pride is denounced and humility praised. It also emphasizes the sovereignty of God to whose holy will each one must submit to attain salvation.

## Zelanti

Literally, the Zealots; also called Spirituals. (See Franciscan Controversy.)

## Ziggurat

This ancient form of building was generally a square or rectangular pile of bricks, usually clay is composition; it rose to a height of approximately seven stories. A ramp or staircase wound around this tower on the outside leading from the ground to the top. The Book of Genesis (11:1–9) tells of such a tower, that of Babel, whereby man desired to reach equality with God. The Babylonians used ziggurats in their religious ceremonies as did the Sumerians who lived along the lower Euphrates valley. The ruins of the Ziggurat of Ur still stand, attesting to the strength of their somewhat pyramidal construction. (See Babel, Tower of.)

## Zimmarra

The zimarra is the black outer coat worn by bishops and other prelates. It has a cape, red buttons, and piping.

**Zucchetto**

The small, close-fitting skull-cap worn by bishops, abbots and other prelates is called the Zucchetto. It is usually made of a fine leather covered with silk. It is also called *pileolus*.

## Zwinglianism

The name of this teaching is derived from its advocate, the Swiss Protestant leader, Huldreich Zwingli (d. 1531). It advocated abolition of the Mass and the Sacrament of Penance. Zwingli would not accept any form of presence of Christ in the Eucharist; hence the term Zwinglianism is a characteristic attitude and teaching concerning the Eucharist. Zwingli accepted only a symbolic interpretation which he presented in his writing: *Commentarius de Vera and Falsa Religione,* published in 1525. It led to dissension among Protestant groups and made union among them impossible.